Other Outstanding CBS Books in For

Forensic Medicine

B. Umadethan

978-81-239-1908-9

Medicine
for the Police

B. Umadethan

Forewords by Jacob Punnoose and Justice K. T. Thomas

978-81-239-1905-8

Second Edition

Principles and Practice of Forensic Medicine

B Umadethan

CBS Publishers & Distributors Pvt Ltd

978-93-85915-37-6

Seventh Edition

Parikh's

Textbook of Medical Jurisprudence, Forensic Medicine and Toxicology

for Classrooms and Courtrooms

The original author of this book

Prof CK Parikh

was

Honorary Professor of Forensic Medicine and Toxicology
Seth GS Medical College and KEM Hospital (University of Mumbai)
Mumbai

Editor, *Journal of the Indian Medical Profession*, Mumbai

Visiting Professor
Forensic Science, Criminology, and Toxicology
University of Saugar, Sagar, India

Visiting Professor
Forensic Medicine and Toxicology
Universities of Zagreb, Yugoslavia, and Turku, Oulu, and
Helsinki, Finland

Editor's Note

The seventh edition of *Parikh's Medical Jurisprudence, Forensic Medicine and Toxicology* has been prepared adding new material without changing the style and pattern of the book as desired by the publishers. A thorough revision has been made keeping in mind the recent developments. New illustrations and photographs have also been added. This edition has been brought out in colour, using modern technology and coated paper to ensure high quality of reproduction of illustrations to match the currently published literature on the subject.

BV Subrahmanyam

Seventh Edition

Parikh's

Textbook of Medical Jurisprudence, Forensic Medicine and Toxicology

for Classrooms and Courtrooms

Editor

BV Subrahmanyam

MD DGL FAFM DYO MIAFM AAFS

Professor and Head,
Department of Forensic Medicine and Toxicology
Narayana Medical College and Hospital
Nellore 524002, AP, India

Former

Dean, Medical College, Bhavnagar, Gujarat
Add. Dean, Medical Colleges, Baroda, Surat, Gujarat
Medical Superintendent, New Civil Hospital, and Govt Medical College, Surat
Professor and Head, Medical Colleges, Baroda, Jamnagar, Surat, Imphal (Manipur)
Faculty Dean, South Gujarat University, Surat
Examiner, Indian and foreign Universities and PhD Guide
Reader, Institute of Medical Sciences, Banaras Hindu University
Assistant Professor, Osmania Medical College, Hyderabad
Tutor, SV Medical College, Thiruvattar

CBS Publishers & Distributors Pvt Ltd

New Delhi • Bengaluru • Chennai • Kochi • Kolkata • Mumbai
Hyderabad • Nagpur • Patna • Pune • Vijayawada

Seventh Edition

Parikh's

Textbook of Medical Jurisprudence, Forensic Medicine and Toxicology

for Classrooms and Courtrooms

Disclaimer

Science and technology are constantly changing fields. New research and experience broaden the scope of information and knowledge. The author and the editor have tried their best in giving information available to them while preparing the material for this book. Although all efforts have been made to ensure optimum accuracy of the material, yet it is quite possible some errors might have been left uncorrected. The publisher, the printer, the author and the editor will not be held responsible for any inadvertent errors, omissions or inaccuracies.

ISBN: 978-81-239-2646-9

Seventh Edition: 2016

Reprint: 2016, 2017

First Edition: 1970

Second Edition Under Indo-American Textbook Program: 1976

Third Edition: 1979

Revised Reprint: 1981

Reprinted: 1983

Fourth Edition: 1985

Reprinted: 1987, 1988, 1989

Fifth Edition: 1990

Reprinted: 1992, 1995, 1996, 1998

Sixth Edition: 1999

Reprinted: 2000, 2002, 2004, 2005, 2006, 2007, 2008, 2009

Revised reprint 2011

Reprinted 2012, 2013, 2014

Published by Satish Kumar Jain and produced by Varun Jain for

CBS Publishers & Distributors Pvt Ltd

4819/XI Prahlad Street, 24 Ansari Road, Daryaganj, New Delhi 110 002, India.

Ph: 23289259, 23266861, 23266867 Fax: 011-23243014 Website: www.cbspd.com

e-mail: delhi@cbspd.com; cbspubs@airtelmail.in.

Corporate Office: 204 FIE, Industrial Area, Patparganj, Delhi 110 092

Ph: 4934 4934 Fax: 4934 4935 e-mail: publishing@cbspd.com; publicity@cbspd.com

Branches

- **Bengaluru:** Seema House 2975, 17th Cross, K.R. Road, Banasankari 2nd Stage, Bengaluru 560 070, Karnataka
  Ph: +91-80-26771678/79 Fax: +91-80-26771680 e-mail: bangalore@cbspd.com
- **Chennai:** 7, Subbaraya Street, Shenoy Nagar, Chennai 600 030, Tamil Nadu
  Ph: +91-44-26680620, 26681266 Fax: +91-44-42032115 e-mail: chennai@cbspd.com
- **Kochi:** Ashana House, No. 39/1904, AM Thomas Road, Valanjambalam, Eranakulam 682 018, Kochi Kerala
  Ph: +91-484-4059061-65 Fax: +91-484-4059065 e-mail: kochi@cbspd.com
- **Kolkata:** 6/B, Ground Floor, Rameswar Shaw Road, Kolkata-700 014, West Bengal
  Ph: +91-33-22891126, 22891127, 22891128 e-mail: kolkata@cbspd.com
- **Mumbai:** 83-C, Dr E Moses Road, Worli, Mumbai-400018, Maharashtra
  Ph: +91-22-24902340/41 Fax: +91-22-24902342 e-mail: mumbai@cbspd.com

Representatives

- **Hyderabad** 0-9885175004
- **Nagpur** 0-9021734563
- **Patna** 0-9334159340
- **Pune** 0-9623451994
- **Vijayawada** 0-9000660880

Printed at: Nutech Print Services - India

Preface to the Seventh Edition

All efforts have been made to retain in this edition the original flavour of Parikh's book. Contents have been updated in all the areas to help the medical students and also the legal professionals. Latest material has been added at appropriate places, several old photographs replaced by better visuals, and many new photographs also added in the text.

Protection of children from Sexual Offences Act, recent changes in the criminal law in relation to rape, sexual deviations, penetrating sexual assault and acid attacks are incorporated. In the answers to the relevant questions, updated matter is incorporated. Body farming, virtual autopsy, narcoanalysis, hair dye poisoning, newer plant poisons like brasinolide, and khat abuse are added. Old photographs have been replaced with new and recent photographs with crisp captions in relation to decomposition, autopsy technique, various injuries, violent asphyxial deaths, snakes, scorpion, three-parent baby, and presumed consent in deceased organ donation also added.

Hope this book continues to enjoy its reputation in classrooms and courtrooms, besides among investigating officers and lawyers. Any new suggestions from the readers are welcome. The questions in the book are useful to the defence attorneys while questing the medical witness in cross-examination.

BV Subrahmanyam
Editor, 7th Edition

Foreword to Sixth Edition

Most modern textbooks of forensic pathology do not include discussions of those areas of civil and criminal law that interact with much frequency and importance on the medicolegal investigation of known, suspected, or alleged unnatural deaths. Forensic psychiatry and toxicology are two other major divisions of forensic medicine that are not usually included in such volumes. Similarly, one does not encounter many substantive references to pathology in books that are written for psychiatrists and toxicologists. Thus, it usually is necessary for medical students and practicing physicians to have access to several different texts while studying forensic medicine, or when confronted by actual clinical situations with medicolegal ramifications.

Dr CK Parikh has composed an outstanding single volume that combines a thorough review of the traditional topics in forensic pathology with the basic concepts of both psychiatry and toxicology as they relate to the courts and the legal system. Moreover, this noted academician and author has included broad coverage of matters that involve clinical situations with which the modern day forensic expert must be familiar, e.g. rape and sexual offenses, child and spousal abuse, paternity testing, and in vitro fertilization. These and many other highly complex and controversial subjects are issues that society will have to confront with increasing frequency in the foreseeable future.

Further enhancing the pedagogic value of this book is a large number of illustrations that depict many of the pathological entities discussed in the text. The reader can correlate the various entities quite easily in this fashion, and thereby gain a much better understanding and appreciation of what the author is describing.

Forensic medicine is a fascinating field of endeavor, arguably the most exciting, dynamic, and constantly challenging area of medical specialization. It is also one of the most complex and intellectually demanding of professional pursuits, combining as it does the vast and seemingly diverse bodies of knowledge that comprise two of the world's oldest and noblest professions, law and medicine. Without justice, law, and order, there can be no civilization. Without medicine and science, there can be no decent quality of life. Hence, the ethical and moral demands, as well as the mental achievement and emotional stability, of a truly knowledgeable medicolegal expert, are indeed quite substantial and formidable.

To teach and write about forensic medicine with clarity, accuracy, and perception is not an easy task. To compile a lengthy, detailed and authoritative textbook that covers the broad gamut of medicolegal subjects that span forensic pathology, toxicology, and psychiatry, as well as clinical forensic medicine and jurisprudence, is truly a remarkable accomplishment.

Parikh's Textbook of Medical Jurisprudence, Forensic Medicine, and Toxicology for Classrooms and Courtrooms is a very worthwhile and valuable addition to the medicolegal literature. The author, Dr CK Parikh, has once again demonstrated his great ability to share his wealth of knowledge, experience, and expertise with medical students and practitioners at all levels.

Cyril H. Wecht MD, JD

Past President, American Academy of Forensic Sciences; Past President, American College of Legal Medicine; Coroner, Allegheny County (Pittsburgh), Pennsylvania; Chief Pathologist, and Chairman, Department of Pathology, St. Francis Hospital, Pittsburgh, Pennsylvania, USA

Foreword to Sixth Edition

There is no shortage of books in the field of legal medicine. However, many are written by specialists for specialists, and are not particularly suited to those who are trying to learn, revised, or gain an ovrall insight into the subject. I know of no single book specially designed to meet the diverse requirements of persons working in the medicolegal field. Dr Parikh's book fills a vital gap in the literature on the subject. It covers forensic medicine, pathology, and biology, forensic psychiatry, clinical and forensic toxicology and medical jurisprudence.

It is seldom that one has an opportunity to see or review a book in the manuscript stage, as I had in this instance, and even more unusual to see one in which the concepts are simply and clearly explained. Knowledge is of little value while it remains confined within the heads of a few individuals, and it can only be uitlized when other understand the concepts involved. The vast majority of judges and jurors have not attended medical school, or studied a branch of science in depth, so it is incumbent upon those who possess large amounts of medical knowledge to express it in terms that most people can easily understand. Dr Parikh has rendered a service to the medical and legal professions by ensuring clarity, and by including a wide variety of material and concepts in a single volume.

In this basic book, the subject is developed step by step. Various advances, scattered throughout the literature, are included at appropriate places in the text. The question and answer format in relation to certain topics is a specially welcome feature. It provides a simple means of professional self-assessment, it will help encourage logical thinking, and it will most certainly help to prepare for examinations, and for courtroom appearances.

The text contains all that medical students and forensic nurses are expected to know. It will also assist postgraduate students in revision, because it compiles so much in a single volume, that it will save them from having to search through many unwieldy texts to locate necessary information. Likewise, medical practitioners, nurses working in sensitive areas, advanced providers of first aid, and law enforcement officers, will find in it answers to questions that will arise in the course of their work. It will help to develop a sense of emphasis and proportion towards the subject matter, and facilitate a grasp of the fundamentals, which may not so easily be acquired from larger textbooks.

This book also addresses material of interest to the newly qualified doctor working in an emergency setting, and will provide assistance whenever medical situations and/or questions arise. It will contribute to standards of forensic practice in the courts, especially in rural areas where there may be no local expert to call upon. Only when proper observations are made at the time, supported by appropriate photographs, X-rays, diagrams and documentation, will an expert be able to help when questions arise.

One of all fascinations of helping with such a text, is the amazing differences that exist between the various countries. Both Dr Parikh and I, routinely see things and encounter situations that are almost rarities to the other. Dr Parikh routinely encounters types of poisonings and violence that are not commonly seen in my part of the world. Likewise, I have seen many injuries from types of vehicles and weapons that are not quite familiar to him. As communications improve, and the world progresses to a global community, we all need to know more about the customs and behavior of other lands. **Our association has thus resulted in a text which is broader in scope, and which has hardly and geographical constraints.**

Unfortunately, dogmatic opinions dervied from outdated or unsound data, or drawn from texts that repeat previous dogmas, are all too common in the medicolegal field. **Times have changed and advances have been made. Accordingly, presentation of the current status of the subject is the need of the day, and this is a major point of this book.** For instance, an author may cite the details of tissue changes based on a study made in the period between about 1920 and 1940, and then try to use this data to make estimates of age or duration of injuries in the tissues of a victim kept alive by means of antibiotics, respirators, dialysis, and transfusions. Without modern techniques, the present subject would long since have been dead, and the two situations are certainly not comparable. Likewise, a book written in 1910s to 1930s may state from how far gunpowder grains are capable of marking the skin, but this data is no longer valid if newer shapes or sizes of grain, better capable of flying through the air, have since been introduced. Therefore, I have tried to make sure that my contributions are as accurate as possible, and I know Dr Parikh has done likewise.

This is, therefore, a book to be acquired for the amount of material it contains, for the sound tuition it gives, and for reference as a dependable aid to the practice of forensic medicine and everyday toxicology. The author has contributed a masterly work to the field of legal medicine.

Patrick E. Besant-Matthews MD

Consultant and Practicing Forensic Pathologist, Dallas, Texas, USA; Formerly, Deputy Chief Medical Examiner, South Western Institute of Forensic Sciences, Dallas, Texas, USA

Preface to the Sixth Edition

Modern forensic science is rapidly changing. This book is designed to meet the precise requirements of students, practitioners, and law enforcement authorities in the forensic field in the light of modern trends and recent knowledge. The various advances lying scattered in various specialised monographs are presented here at appropriate places in the text.

The subject matter follows a conventional pattern along with a practical approach. The language throughout is simple but scientifically accurate, style lucid, illustrations instructive, sequence of topics logical, and coverage comprehensive. The aim throughout has been to develop a sense of proportion toward the subject and a grasp of its fundamentals which one may not so easily acquire from larger books.

This book brings with it the expertise of several of my colleagues, both from India and abroad, and my experience both as a teacher and practitioner in the subject. Accordingly, while I have made reference to Indian laws and customs in some situations which are specific to Indian conditions, as for example dowry deaths, I have tried to keep the text as international as possible so that the principles outlined herein can be applied with advantage according to local circumstances elsewhere.

CK Parikh

Acknowledgements

I acknowledge the cooperation and help from many colleagues in the field, mention must be made of Dr SV Phanindra, Professor, Dr I Mohan Prasad, Dr K Rajesham, postgraduates Dr Manigandaraj G, Dr Aswani Kishore, Dr S Ganesh Kumar, Dr R Siva Kumar and Dr G Chandra Sekhar. The chapter on 'Asphyxia' has been revised by Dr SV Phanindra Professor, Narayana Medical College, Nellore.

My thanks are due to the CBS team, specially for all the cooperation. Thanks are due to Mrs A Karuna who took pains to do the cooperation patiently. To my better half Dr Saraswathi, Chief, Counselling Services, Narayana Superspeciality and General Hospital, who allowed lot many hours in isolation, during this heavy task of updating the popular textbook.

BV Subrahmanyam
Editor, 7th Edition

How to Use This Book

A proper method of study requires that a student glances through the type of questions which he will have to face in his respective subjects to pass his examinations on which his future depends. As such questions are not available in proper sequence, the present effort is made to fill such an important gap. The model answers with important points highlighted in bold and italic fonts will help many a student to prepare the subject systematically and thoroughly. It will also assist him to assess his preparation of the subject and to determine areas where further work on his part is necessary.

A practitioner/forensic expert facing a problem should refer to the index to get the desired information without loss of time. He will find the practical hints and procedures necessary for his specific purpose.

Law enforcement officers when faced with a problem should refer to the relevant chapter/topic and study it in full. They will find the possible questions, possible pitfalls, and necessary procedures to guide them in their work.

Lawyers will find ready made questions and correct answers to their problems even at a glance so as to question their witness in an appropriate manner.

CK Parikh

....

In a book of this length, there is always the problem of references, and in particular, how many should be included. Some authors prefer to cite hundreds of references, in fact, more than most people can read in a lifetime. In this book, I have limited the references to those I have personally examined, and found helpful. I believe, they are sufficient to meet with the day-to-day requirements of most users. Those few readers who desire more complete listings should request computer searches of the medical, legal, forensic and criminalistics literature, through the library of a major scientific institution or university, to meet with their specific requirements.

....

Why This Book

Every author must justify the addition of a new book to the existing ones in the market, I have more than ample justification for doing so.

1. Medical science is making such rapid strides that textbooks become dated unless revised at regular intervals, and a new edition published.
2. A new edition means substantial updating of old material, and addition of new material which has received the approval of most authorities in the field. A simple reprint with cosmetic changes here and there does not constitute a new edition.
3. There is a general complaint that textbooks are becoming voluminous day by day. While this has necessarily to be so, it is for the author to devise an approach to the subject that it can admirably meet the differing requirements of the various users.
4. A number of students are overwhelmed by the size of the various medical books. Time constraints make it difficult for them to go through all their textbooks from cover to cover.
5. Different types of users have distinctly different requirements:
   a. A student is interested to grasp the fundamentals of the subject, to assess his preparation for examination, and to determine areas where further work on his part is necessary.
   b. A doctor is interested to solve the practical problems encountered by him in his day-to-day practice. He wants to know how to prepare an age certificate or an injury report, when not to issue a death certificate, what precautions he should take to avoid an allegation of malpractice, etc. He wants a quick and definite answer to his problems.
   c. An expert is interested to know if the particular finding at autopsy is an antemortem injury or an artifact. He wants to know the precautions for autopsy on AIDS infected body. He wants to determine the absolute identity of a criminal by the special technique — DNA fingerprinting, and so on.
   d. A law enforcement officer wants to know the various aspects of the specific problem that he is handling at the time of inquest. As for example — a dead body with injuries is recovered from water — Is this a case of suicide, homicide, or accident?
   e. A forensic clinical nurse working in the trauma centre or emergency department must know what to do and what not to do to preserve and document evidence in victims of accident and violent crime.
   f. A lawyer, who generally does not have adequate medical background, wants to prepare pointed questions to ask the expert medical witness, in a court of law, at the time of cross examination.

   To meet these differing needs, one requires a monograph, sufficiently comprehensive and practical, to cover the diverse requirements of various users. And, for convenience of use, it should be in simple language. At the same time, it should be scientifically accurate, and in question-answer format. Such a format assures that a user can easily search and select a solution to his specific needs, and do proper justice to the job in hand.
6. And thus, such a monograph is the need of the day in the present circumstances. And **so, here it is,** fulfilling an important gap in the literature on the subject.

To ensure adequate and appropriate coverage, various experts have gone through most of the chapters with a critical eye. Their valuable suggestions have been carefully incorporated.

The style is lucid. Technical terms, when used, are defined. The text is in such simple but scientifically accurate language that a reader will find it a pleasure to go through it and study his requirements in proper perspective with ease of effort. For this purpose, the sequence of topics is logical, the description precise, and attention drawn to important points by headings and subheadings, and by the use of bold and italic fonts. Examples are given where necessary. Visual display, in the form of tables and illustrations, is utilised to explain difficult ideas or concepts. Repetition is used only when it would increase clarity. The index is comprehensive, thorough, and cross referenced.

Thus, this monograph is specially tailored to meet the diverse requirements of various users, and I have every confidence that it will serve its intended purpose in the most efficient manner and achieve the desired goal.

CK Parikh

Contents

• SECTION 3 •

PART 6: Forensic Pharmacology

• SECTION 11 •

PART 7: Appendix

• SECTION 12 •

PART 1: Medical Jurisprudence

Section 1

1

Introduction and Legal Procedure

Nowadays, the term **Legal Medicine** is being used synonymously with various other terms, namely, Forensic Medicine, Forensic Pathology, Medical Jurisprudence and State Medicine.

Q. 1.1. Explain the following terms giving examples: (i) Forensic medicine, (ii) Forensic pathology, (iii) Forensic nursing, (iv) Medical jurisprudence, (v) State medicine.

i. *Forensic medicine* (derived from FORUM) deals with the application of medical knowledge in the administration of justice by correlating such knowledge and applying it to purposes of law. The following are a few examples:

a. A person may die suddenly or unexpectedly, and therefrom a suspicion of foul play may arise. The dead body is submitted for autopsy to the medical officer to determine if death was due to natural causes or if there is any evidence of foul play, such as violence or poisoning.
b. A person may die of coronary thrombosis while walking on the road; his dead body may then be run over by a motor vehicle and the driver charged with manslaughter (culpable homicide not amounting to murder). Histochemical and biochemical studies of the injuries would establish that the injuries are sustained postmortem, and examination of the coronary arteries will reveal the presence of disease.
c. A person injured on the eye may feign blindness to bring the injury within the purview of grievous hurt. A careful medical examination would reveal the true condition.
d. A woman may complain that she has been raped and accuse a man. Medical examination will help to reveal, if she has been sexually assaulted or a false accusation has been made.
e. A person may be accused of being intoxicated while driving a motor vehicle. Medical examination would reveal, if he was so much under the influence of alcohol as to endanger public safety.

In all such cases, the doctor may be summoned to appear in a court of law as an *expert witness* and his evidence helps the court to assess the responsibility of the accused.

Thus, forensic medicine plays an important part in guarding the safety of each individual in the community, and also ensures that the accused is not unjustly condemned. Hence, forensic medicine is a subject which deals with all branches of medical knowledge, administered in a court of law for the purpose of administration of justice.

Forensic medicine is a vast subject. All branches of medicine are represented in it but the application of knowledge therefrom is viewed both from a medical as well as legal angle. As for example, when a surgeon sees a wound, he is interested to know, if it is infected or clean and how to treat it. It is of no great consequence to him about how and when it is caused. On the other hand, the Forensic expert is mainly interested to determine the kind of violence or weapon that has produced such an injury, whether the injury can be classified as simple or grievous, and the time when it was inflicted. This involves on his part, besides a basic and thorough medical knowledge, an understanding of certain provisions of the law of his country, e.g. Indian Penal Code (IPC), Criminal Procedure Code (CrPC), Indian Evidence Act (IEA), etc.

ii. ***Forensic pathology*** is a special field of pathology dealing with the medicolegal investigation of death. Accordingly, it is concerned with certain kinds of cases, such as sudden, unexplained, *suspicious, unnatural* and violent deaths. A full autopsy is required in most cases to determine the cause and manner of death. In fact, forensic autopsy is clinical autopsy plus the legal needs completed. Usually, pathology deals with the disease, whereas forensic pathology in addition deals with the cause of death, time since death, and the manner of death which are required for the purpose of investigation of crime.

iii. ***Forensic nursing*** is a speciality dealing with the scientific role of registered nurses in the medicolegal arena. It aims to provide a constructive response to the societal needs of the victims of domestic violence, sexual assault, drug and alcohol addiction, psychological abuse, trauma, and other death-related problems.

iv. ***Medical jurisprudence*** (*juris* = law; *prudentia* = knowledge) deals with the knowledge of law in relation to the practice of medicine. It deals with those relationships which are generally recognised as having legal consequences, e.g. (a) doctor–patient relationship, (b) doctor–doctor relationship, and (c) doctor–state relationship. In short, it deals with legal aspects of medical practice.

The following are a few examples:

a. ***Doctor–patient relationship:*** When a doctor accepts to treat any person, it constitutes an implied contract. Default on the part of the doctor to provide adequate standard of care may render him liable to have the damages assessed against such default, if it has resulted in either physical or mental injury or monetary loss to the other party, e.g. malpractice, wrong diagnosis and unnecessary surgery, criminal abortion, divulging professional secrets, etc.

b. ***Doctor–doctor relationship:*** A doctor criticising his colleagues or doing anything that means unfair competition is liable to face the consequences. As for example, a doctor making a derogatory remark about the practice or technique of another doctor may be guilty of such an offence. One example of such a remark is, "Oh, the other doctor has given you a bad X-ray burn".

c. ***Doctor–state relationship:*** A doctor is liable to face the consequences, if he does not (1) attend the court to give evidence in response to a subpoena or inform, the police if he comes across a case of homicidal poisoning or suspected homicidal injuries, such as stab or gunshot wounds, in his practice or the public-health authorities of a case of notifiable disease or of food poisoning from a hotel, restaurant or other eating establishment.

v. ***State medicine*** deals with the medical and health requirement of public, community and environmental health. It deals with the application of medical knowledge to prevent the spread of disease. It is the responsibility of the state to preserve the health of the public. Accordingly, a registered medical practitioner has certain statutory duties: He must inform the public health authorities of—(a) births, (b) deaths, (c) notifiable diseases, and (d) cases of food poisoning from a hotel, restaurant or other eating establishment so that appropriate medical statistics are maintained and spread of disease prevented by suitable measures—quarantine, preventive vaccination and inoculation, disinfection, control of vectors, etc. Forensic medicine is called as Legal medicine when it deals with legal issues, State medicine when it deals with the rules and regulations and other dos and dont's to be observed by the registered medical practitioners.

Q. 1.2. What is an inquest? Give some examples of its application in medicolegal work.

Inquest is an inquiry into the cause of death which is apparently not due to natural causes. Therefore, when a person dies, it is necessary to determine the cause of death, either natural or unnatural, to meet with the requirements of law. If death is due to any natural cause, such as coronary thrombosis, cancer or bronchopneumonia, no further investigation is necessary and the body can be disposed of according to religious/social customs. However, if it is due to any unnatural cause, such as violence or poisoning, an urgent investigation into the cause of death (inquest) is necessary to apprehend accused and punish the criminal. These deaths are unnatural or suspicious deaths and they must be reported to the authorities for investigation (Fig. 1.1). The following instances are examples of such deaths:

- Sudden unexpected death, the cause of which is unknown
- Suicide, homicide and infanticide
- Death from accident, poisoning, drug mishap or machinery
- Unexplained death or death under suspicious circumstances, like from burns, fall from height, etc.
- Death under anaesthesia or on the operating table

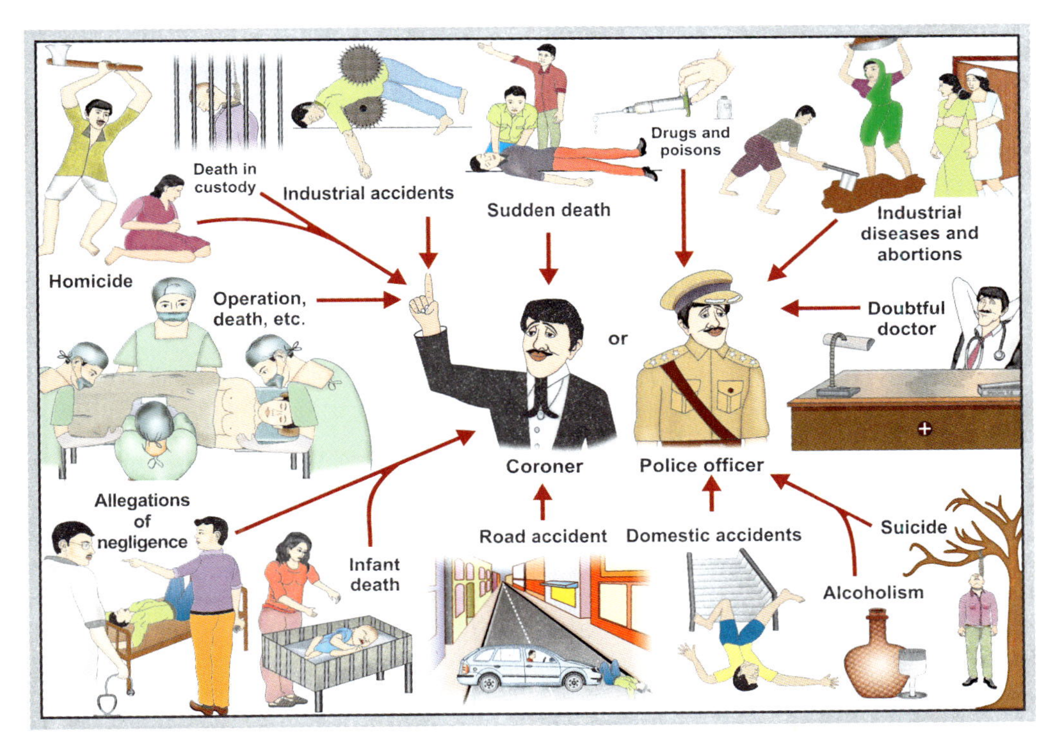

Fig. 1.1: Deaths that must be reported to a coroner or a police officer

- Death from postoperative shock or haemorrhage
- Death due to alleged medical negligence
- Death within 24 hours of admission in a hospital
- Death due to any industrial disease (not in India)
- Death of a prisoner
- Death of persons in police custody, mental hospital or correctional school (borstal school, certified school)
- Dowry deaths in India.

Q. 1.3. Name the different methods of judicial investigation adopted in India. Add a note on the Medical Examiner System prevalent in USA.

Methods of judicial investigation: There are two methods of judicial investigation (types of inquests) in India, *viz.* police inquest and magistrate's inquest. Coroner's inquest is abolished from the whole of India and does not exist now.

Medical examiner system: This system of inquest is prevalent in some States of America. The medical examiners are all board certified or board eligible forensic pathologists. They visit the primary scene of crime or accident, when necessary, to gather first-hand evidence and to interview people to obtain as much information as possible regarding the circumstances of death. They perform autopsy and correlate autopsy findings with this evidence and determine the cause and manner of death. The system, therefore, is superior to other systems where non-medical men/coroners conduct the inquest. The medical examiner submits his report to the district attorney for further action.

Q. 1.4. What is the significance of the term 'coroner'? What are his functions?

The office of the **coroner** is a very ancient office (about the year 1925) of the English Common Law, so-called, because he was the keeper of the pleas of the crown (corona curia regis or custodes placitorum coronae). One of the main sources of its income was the confiscation of property of felons and the appropriation to the treasury of all articles involved in unnatural deaths. The coroner then was obliged to investigate unnatural deaths, treasure trove, wrecks, fires, catches of royal fish, such as the sturgeon and so on, all of which had a mercenary aspect. Over the years, many of the responsibilities have been shed and the coroner of the present day is involved totally with the investigation of unnatural or uncertified deaths. Coroner's system does not exist in India now. Till recently in India, in Mumbai, a special officer known as the coroner was appointed by the government to inquire into causes of all unnatural or suspicious deaths. He is usually an advocate, attorney, pleader or first class magistrate with five years experience or a transferred metropolitan magistrate. He used to preside over the coroner's court and of the rank of first class judicial magistrate arid his territorial jurisdiction extended to the city limit only. He was governed by an Act known as the Coroner's Act (1871). Under this Act, his **functions** were as follows:

1. He was empowered to inquire into causes of all unnatural or suspicious deaths and also deaths occurring in jails within his jurisdiction. He used to commit any suspected person or accused to stand a trial before a magistrate.
2. He could view a dead body to decide whether or not an autopsy is required and, if necessary, hold an inquiry on it with the help of a jury.
3. He could order the exhumation of a body for identification or for medicolegal examination.
4. He was authorised to order any registered medical practitioner (usually the Police Surgeon) to hold a postmortem

examination and summon him as well as other persons as expert witnesses to give evidence in his court.

5. He could appoint a deputy coroner during his sickness or absence due to unavoidable circumstances.

Q. 1.5. Give a brief account of coroner's court and the procedure of coroner's inquest. (This is of historical interest for Indian readers.)

Coroner's court: This is only a court of inquiry into the causes of unnatural deaths. It is, therefore, not necessary that the suspected person or the accused be present. Its function ends when the inquiry is completed. It has no powers to impose a fine nor sentence the person concerned but such a person is committed to stand a trial before a judicial or metropolitan magistrate.

Coroner's inquest: This means an inquiry conducted by a coroner into the cause of any unnatural death within his territorial limits. He is assisted in such an inquiry by members of a *jury* in certain cases. He examines witnesses on oath, records their evidence and receives evidence on behalf of the accused. If necessary, he orders a medical officer to perform an autopsy, give evidence and be cross examined on it. When the evidence is completed, he finds a verdict as to the cause of death. The verdict embodies, such facts as the identity of the deceased, and the cause, time and place of death. If he finds a verdict of foul play against a suspected person, he issues a warrant for his arrest. Such person, along with his records, is sent to the metropolitan magistrate empowered to commit him for trial.

If the accused is not identified, the coroner returns an open verdict and the matter is kept in abeyance until further inquiry throws more light on the perpetration of the crime. *Open verdict* means an announcement of the commission of crime without naming the criminal. After the inquest, the coroner sends a copy of his report to the Commissioner of Police.

Q. 1.6. What is a police inquest? Briefly describe its procedure.

This means an inquiry by a police officer into the cause of any unnatural or suspicious death. In India, police officers, not below the rank of head constable, hold such inquests in all cases except where the magistrate has to conduct such an inquest. The police officer making the preliminary inquiry is known as the *investigating officer.* On receipt of informa-tion of any unnatural or suspicious death, the police officer informs about it to the nearest magistrate of the same area and proceeds to the scene of crime. Here, he holds an inquiry into the cause of such death in presence of two or more witnesses who are called *panchas.* He prepares a report about the probable cause of death as judged by him and the *panchas* from the appearance and surroundings of the body including the nature of injuries thereon. This report, known as *panchnama* (*Panch* = five; *nama* = document) used to be a document compiled by five respectable persons. *Inquest report* is then signed by him and the witnesses are presented. If no foul play is suspected, the dead body is released for disposal. In case of suspected foul play or doubt, the dead body is sent for autopsy to the nearest medical officer together with a requisition and a copy of the inquest report. If the autopsy report indicates that the death is due to any unnatural cause, further inquiry and trial of the case is conducted by the concerned magistrate to whom the entire case records are transferred by the investigating police officer.

Q. 1.7. Tabulate the differences between: (a) coroner's court and magistrate's court, (b) coroner's inquest and police inquest.

Tables 1.1 and 1.2 describe the differences between coroner's and magistrate's court and coroner's inquest and police inquest.

Table 1.1: Difference between coroner's and magistrate's court

Coroner's court	*Magistrate's court*
1. Court of inquiry	Court of trial
2. Accused need not be present	Accused should be present during trial
3. Cannot impose fine or punishment	Can impose fine and/ or punishment
4. Can punish those guilty of contempt of court when the offence is committed in the premises of his court	Can punish those guilty of contempt of his court when the offence is committed in or outside his court's premises

Table 1.2: Difference between coroner's and police inquest

Coroner's inquest	*Police inquest*
1. The coroner, because of his association with forensic work, is able to investigate on right lines and thus judge the cause and manner of death in proper perspective	For want of knowledge of forensic medicine, the police officers are likely to commit errors both in investigation and judging the cause and manner of death
2. Being able to judge the manner of death properly, e.g. suicide or homicide, he does not send dead bodies for autopsy indiscriminately. As for example, in a clear case of suicide, no action lies against any person and an autopsy is not necessary	Because of their inability to exercise such discretion, there is general tendency on the part of police officers to send dead bodies for autopsy indiscriminately, and thus increase the work load of the medical officer
3. In the coroner system, there are no *panchas*, and, therefore, there is no question about their reliability	The police officer may choose *panchas* at random without regard to their status and respectability, and such *panchas* may return any verdict to get rid of this unpleasant duty

Q. 1.8. What is meant by magistrate's inquest? Mention the type of cases in which it is held. Give the purpose behind such inquest.

Magistrate's inquest means an inquiry conducted by a magistrate to ascertain matters of fact. It is commonly held in the following cases:

1. Admission of a mentally ill person in a psychiatric hospital or a psychiatric nursing home under certain provisions of the Mental Health Act, 1987
2. Death of a convict in jail
3. Death of a person in police custody or during police interrogation
4. Death as a result of police shooting/ killing
5. Exhumation cases
6. Dowry deaths (Sec 176 CrPC)
7. Deaths on operation tables/anaesthetic deaths

Purpose: It is obvious that the ends of justice cannot be met by allowing a police officer to conduct an inquest in such cases. The main intention behind the inquest is to ensure that—(1) no person is unjustly deprived of his liberty and his rights as a citizen, (2) no person who is deprived of his liberty can die as a result of neglect or brutality by the people in whose charge he is, and (3) in case of a person who is already buried, if there is any doubt as regards identity, cause of death or manner of death, it will be settled by a judicial inquest and not a police inquest, (4) due to peculiar circumstances associated with dowry death, it should be investigated by a magistrate.

Q. 1.9. Name the criminal courts in India and their powers. Mention the sentences authorised by law.

The ***criminal courts*** in India in order of their power are as follows:

1. Supreme court
2. High courts
3. Sessions courts
4. Magistrate's courts, presided over by:
   a. Chief Judicial magistrate and in any metropolitan area, Chief Metropolitan magistrate
   b. Judicial magistrates of the first class and in any metropolitan area, metropolitan magistrates
   c. Judicial magistrates of the second class, and
   d. Executive magistrates

The Supreme Court, located in New Delhi, is the highest judicial tribunal in the country. Its function is supervisory and the interpretation of law as declared by it is binding on all the courts in India. It can pass any sentence.

The High Court, located usually in the capital of every state, is the highest judicial tribunal in the state. It is empowered to try any offence and pass any sentence authorised by law.

The Sessions Court is located usually at the district headquarters. It is, therefore, also known as District Sessions Court. It has jurisdiction over all kinds of criminal offenses but it can try only those **cases** which have been **committed** to it **by a magistrate**. It can pass any sentence authorised by law including a sentence of death which is subject to confirmation by the High Court. An **assistant sessions judge** may pass any sentence authorised by law except a sentence of death or of imprisonment for life or for a term exceeding **ten years.**

The magistrates' courts are presided over by magistrates. There are two kinds of magistrates, namely, judicial magistrates (including metropolitan magistrates in metropolitan areas) and executive magistrates. Judicial magistrates are divided into two classes, namely, first class and second class.

A judicial magistrate of the first class in charge of a district (not being a metropolitan area) is known as Chief Judicial Magistrate. A judicial magistrate in charge of a subdivision is known as Subdivisional Judicial Magistrate. The judicial magistrates in relation to metropolitan areas are known as Metropolitan Magistrates. The Chief Judicial Magistrate in relation to a metropolitan area is known as Chief Metropolitan Magistrate.

Executive magistrates are appointed by the state government. They are usually officers of revenue department, like district collector, subcollector or a tehsildar. They may be placed in charge of a district, subdivision or taluka and have all the powers of a district or subdivisional magistrate.

The *sentencing powers* of magistrates in order of their rank are as follows:

a. Courts of chief judicial magistrate and chief metropolitan magistrate	Imprisonment up to seven years; fine and without limit
b. Courts of judicial magistrate of the first class and metropolitan magistrate	Imprisonment up to three years; fine up to Rs. 10,000.00
c. Courts of judicial magistrate of the second class	Imprisonment up to one year; fine up to Rs. 5,000.00

Special magistrates, either metropolitan, judicial or executive, may be appointed by the Government for special purposes or when regular magistrates cannot cope up with the extra-load of work or the inquiry has to be completed within a certain time.

Juvenile magistrates, usually ladies, preside over juvenile courts and try juvenile offenders. *Juvenile offenders* are children (boys below 16 years and girls below 18 years of age) who are accused of having committed a crime. They are tried under the Children Act, 1960 (60 of 1960) which provides for treatment, training and rehabilitation of youthful offenders.

Sentences authorised by law: These are:

1. Death
2. Imprisonment for life
3. Imprisonment—rigorous, simple or solitary
4. Forfeiture of property
5. Fine
6. Treatment, training and rehabilitation of youthful offenders.

Q. 1.10. Write short notes on: (a) subpoena, (b) conduct money, (c) oath/solemn affirmation, (d) perjury.

Subpoena: A *subpoena* (sub = under; poena = penalty) or a *summons* is a document compelling the attendance of a witness, on a specified day and at a specified time, in a court of law under a penalty. It is issued by the court in writing, in duplicate, and signed by the presiding officer of the court. It is served on the witness by a police officer or officer of the court or other public servant. The witness retains one copy and returns the other one duly signed by him in acknow-ledgement of its receipt.

When a summons is served on a witness, he must attend the court punctually, give evidence, and produce such documents or other articles as required by the court. Failure to obey a summons without a just cause renders the witness liable to an action for damages in a civil case and fine, imprisonment or warrant of arrest and compulsory attendance in a criminal one.

Conduct money: In civil cases, a fee is tendered to cover the expenses to attend the court when the summons is served. This is known as **conduct money.** It is paid by the party that has called him as a witness. If the fee is not tendered, the doctor can ignore the summons. In case where a medical witness considers that the tender of fees is inadequate, he may inform the court accordingly and get it enhanced. In criminal cases, no such tender is made when the summons is served but a medical witness must always obey the summons, otherwise he will be charged with contempt of the court. An independent medical practitioner may claim a fee at the time of giving professional evidence before taking oath but should not insist on it if the presiding officer is not willing to grant it.

It may, however, be noted that provision is made by Government under section 312 CrPC for payment of reasonable expenses of an expert witness attending before any criminal court. Payment of reasonable expenses of an expert witness in magistrates' courts in summons cases is provided for under section 254 (3) and in warrant cases under section 243 (3) CrPC.

In general, criminal courts take precedence over civil courts and if a witness is called to attend two courts at the same time, one of which is civil and the other criminal, he must attend the criminal court and inform the civil court accordingly. If called upon to attend two courts of different status, such as magistrate's court and Sessions' court, higher courts get the preference. If, however, both the courts are of the same status, as for example, Principal Sessions Court and Additional Sessions Court, the witness should attend that court first from which he received the summons earlier, informing the other court of this fact or the time of appearance there may be adjusted by special arrangement.

Oath: Before giving evidence, a witness is required to swear by Almighty God that he will tell the truth, the whole truth and nothing but the truth. This is known as **oath** and it is the duty of the court to administer it. A Christian holds the Bible in his hand, a Hindu the Gita and a Mohammedan the Koran, and he is then sworn. If a witness is an atheist, he makes a **solemn affirmation** in the same terms, instead of swearing by God.

Perjury: A witness who after taking oath or making a solemn affirmation, wilfully makes a statement which he knows or believes to be false is guilty of the crime of **perjury** under section 193 IPC.

Q. 1.11. How is evidence recorded in a court of law? Describe the procedure.

Q. 1.12. Comment on: (1) leading question, (2) hostile witness, (3) cross-examination.

Having been sworn or affirmed in any court of law, the witness is first examined by the side which has called him. This is known as *examination-in-chief* (direct examination). This is followed by *cross-examination* by the opposing counsel, after which the witness may be *re-examined (re-direct examination)* by the first counsel.

Questions may be put *by the judge* or juror (coroner's court) to clear any doubtful points (Fig. 1.2).

Examination-in-chief: In private cases, this consists of questions put to the witness by the counsel (lawyer) for the side which has summoned him. In government prosecutions, the public prosecutor commences this examination. The *object* is to place before the court all the facts that bear on the case and if the witness be an expert, his interpretation of these facts. At this stage, no leading questions are allowed except in those cases in which the judge is satisfied that a witness is hostile.

A **leading question** is one that suggests its own answer. As for example, "Doctor, is this injury caused by a sharp weapon?" is a leading question. It should be worded as, "Doctor, what type of weapon would cause this injury?". A witness is expected to tell the truth but if he is influenced, intimidated or bribed, he may purposely conceal a part of the truth or give outright false evidence and is then liable to be found guilty of *perjury*. The court, in its discretion, may declare such a witness as a hostile witness. Thus, a **hostile witness** is one who purposely makes statements contrary to facts or to what he has already said in a lower court or in the same court on a previous occasion. When such a witness is being examined, leading questions may be asked in the examination-in-chief to elicit the facts. Generally medical witnesses are not declared hostile, as they are court-witnesses. In the Best Bakery case, the apex court on March 8, 2006 convicted the hostile witness for one year and a fine of Rs. 5000 as the witness frequently changed her statement in the court.

Cross-examination: During cross-examination, the counsel for the opposite side, that is counsel for the accused, seeks to extract from the witness, any facts that may appear to be favourable to his client and which he believes to be within the knowledge of the witness. Leading questions are, therefore, allowed. The *object* is to weaken the evidence of the witness by showing that his details are inaccurate, conflicting, contradictory or that his opinions are ill-founded and opposed to that of well-recognised authorities. The witness must, therefore, be prepared to face questions regarding his qualifications, experience and professional knowledge. The cross-examination need not be confined to the statements made by the witness in the examination-in-chief. When appropriate material is available, questions challenging even the character of the witness may be asked. The court can, however, forbid any question which may appear to be either insulting, annoying or needlessly offensive in form (section 152 IEA). There is no limit for cross-examination although the presiding officer can always overrule irrelevant questions.

Cross-examination may sometimes act as a double-edged weapon. If the opposing counsel is not familiar with the subject or does not put his questions with great caution, the answers brought out may be more adverse to his own case rather than those elicited in the examination-in-chief.

A medical officer was being cross-examined by the defence in a case of alleged medical negligence during a delivery.

Defence: Doctor, when did you conduct the last delivery?

Doctor: Some time in 1945 or 1946 when I was doing my midwifery term as a medical student and once thereafter some time in 1954 as an emergency when a neighbour delivered suddenly.

Defence: So, is it right to say now that it is 1979, that you conducted the last delivery about 25 years ago?

Doctor: Yes.

Defence: If as you say, you conducted the last delivery some time in 1954, how do you consider yourself competent to opine on a case of delivery in 1979 after a lapse of about 25 years?

Doctor: The process of birth has not changed since then.

RECORDING OF EVIDENCE

A case of death from penicillin injection – doctor as a witness:

EXAMINATION-IN-CHIEF

Q. **"Doctor, what precautions are necessary before injecting penicillin?"**

A. "A sensitivity test should be done."

CROSS-EXAMINATION

Q. **"Doctor, is it possible that an anaphylactic reaction may still occur even though the sensitivity test is negative?"**

A. "Yes".

RE-EXAMINATION

Q. **"Doctor, what would be the difference in the anaphylactic reaction in a case where the test was positive and another case in which it was negative?"**

A. "In the former case, it would be far more severe; in the latter case, it would be mild."

COURT QUESTION

Q. **"Doctor, is there no way by which one can be absolutely certain, if the patient is sensitive to penicillin or not?"**

A. "No."

Fig. 1.2: Recording of evidence

The charge was incest. The 14-year-old girl was trembling in the witness box. She was facing her father whom she was accusing of being the parent of her expected child. His lawyer was cross-examining.

Lawyer: Do you hate your father?

Girl: Yes

Lawyer: Do you want to see him go to prison?

Girl: I want to see him dead, every time I feel the kicking in my body.

It took the jury only five minutes to come in with a verdict of guilty.

Re-examination: After cross-examination, the witness may be re-examined by the counsel who called him. The *object* is (1) to clear up any doubts that may have arisen during cross-examination, and (2) to explain some matter (that may appear damaging his direct testimony) in proper perspective so that undue emphasis or possible misinterpretation can be avoided. (In one cross-examination, a lawyer had elicited an answer from the doctor to the effect that the injury was on the right arm and the blood spot seen on the shirt sleeve was attributable to the injury.)

On re-direct examination, it was brought out that the wound was just an abrasion, and the injury was simple in nature.

At re-examination, leading questions are not allowed, no new matter may be introduced without the permission of the judge and consent of the opposing counsel, and the opposing side has the right of cross-examination on the new points.

Court questions: The judge may ask any question to the witness at any stage of trial to clear any doubtful points.

The evidence thus recorded by the presiding judge or magistrate should be read by the witness, and signed by him after getting any corrections, if need be, done by the court under its initials. Subsequent to discharge, the witness is liable to be recalled, if his evidence needs further elucidation.

Q. 1.13. Discuss documentary evidence.

Q. 1.14. Write short notes on: (a) medical certificate, (b) medicolegal report, (c) dying declaration, (d) dying deposition.

Q. 1.15. What precautions will you take before issuing a death certificate?

Documentary evidence: This means and includes all documents produced for the information of the court. Such evidence may consist of: (1) medical certificates, e.g. sickness or death certificate (2) medicolegal reports, e.g. injury report, postmortem report, age certificate, dying declaration, etc. Documentary evidence is generally admissible in the court after cross-examination (oral-evidence) of its giver, save in a few circumstances.

Medical certificate: This is the simplest form of documentary evidence and may pertain to such facts as sickness, compensation, vaccination, death, etc. It is accepted by a court of law only when issued by a registered medical practitioner. The court may require the attendance of the certifying doctor to testify on oath the facts mentioned in the certificate and to be cross-examined on it, if necessary.

A number of doctors have landed into trouble on the matter of certification. The following points should be remembered:

1. Issuing of false certificates constitutes professional misconduct. The certificate must contain all relevant information. It should also contain two identification marks, signature or left thumb impression of the holder of the certificate for identification.
2. A certificate pertaining to illness should mention the exact nature of the illness. A certificate for compensation must state the exact disability arising from the accident or industrial disease, and if the disability is temporary or permanent. A vaccination certificate must mention the exact date of vaccination.

3. There are certain *specific requirements about death certificates.* If the doctor in attendance is convinced that death is due to any natural cause—(a) he must issue a death certificate, (b) he cannot charge any fees for the same, (c) he cannot delay it even if his own professional charges are not paid, and (d) the certificate must state the immediate cause of death like 'coronary thrombosis' instead of a vague term, such as heart failure or cardiac arrest and the underlying cause due to coronary artery disease.

   Before issuing a death certificate, the following *precautions* must be taken:

   The doctor must inspect the body to make sure that (a) the person is actually dead and/or not in a state of suspended animation, and (b) the cause of death is a natural one, and for this purpose, the body should be examined with specific reference to data mentioned in item 4 below.

A rural practitioner once visited an old man who was senile and apparently moribund. The next day, a Friday, relatives informed the doctor that the grandfather was dead and requested the issue of a death certificate. The doctor obliged. However, he was horrified to see the old man sitting in a deck chair on Monday. On inquiry from the rela-tions, he was told that the old man was expected to die and they did not want to be in a difficulty at the last moment especially a week-end when doctors are generally not available!

A general practitioner certified the death of an old man who complained of acute pain in the chest, as due to coronary thrombosis, without any examination. A neighbour, who complained to the police, alleged foul play, and the body was sent for autopsy where the cause of death was determined to be cardiac tamponade due to haemopericardium from a stab injury on the left side of the chest with an ice pick.

4. If death is due to any unnatural cause or there is any suspicion of foul play, such as violence or poisoning, the doctor must not issue a death certificate but must report this fact to the police at once for necessary investigation before the body is cremated, buried or embalmed. By granting a certificate in such a case, the doctor runs the risk of being accused as an accessory to a crime, should the death be found eventually due to foul play.

   To avoid issuing a certificate in a case of death from any unnatural cause: (a) the doctor should inspect the face for petechiae on the eyelids, conjunctivae and the lips; the mouth for injuries, foreign material or capsules; and the skin of the neck for bruises, ligature, ligature marks and signs of violence, (b) he should inspect the scalp and back of the head for obvious bumps, lacerations and wounds which may have been concealed by hair; the front and back of the chest for obvious traumatic lesions and abnormal colouration due to poisons; the upper and lower limbs to exclude obvious injuries; and (c) he should examine the body with special reference to temperature, postmortem lividity, and rigor mortis, to check whether these are consistent with the alleged time of death as stated by the relatives.

Medicolegal report: This is a report prepared by a doctor, usually in criminal cases, such as assault, rape, murder, poisoning, etc. in response to a requisition from a law enforcement authority. It is meant for the guidance of the investigating officer. It will be produced in court and is subject to cross-examination by the opposing counsel.

Examples of such report are: (a) injury report, (b) postmortem report, (c) age certificate, (d) dying declaration, (e) certificate of mental illness, (f) certificate in connection with sexual offenses, etc.

The report consists of two parts, viz:

1. The facts observed on examination, and
2. The opinion drawn from them. As far as possible, technical terms should be avoided and the opinion stated briefly and clearly.

The report must state the date, time and place of examination, and the names of the individuals, identifying the person or body examined or the means by which the body was identified. Two identification marks must be noted. In an injury case, the injuries must be described in detail. An opinion on their nature (simple, grievous, dangerous) and the class of weapon used in their production should also be given. If an opinion cannot be given immediately, the person should be kept under observation and necessary investigations carried out. In a postmortem report, the cause of death and the approximate time since death should be mentioned.

Dying declaration: This is a statement, verbal or written, made by a person since deceased narrating the cause of his condition or the circumstances leading to his impending death. If time permits, the attending doctor should arrange for a magistrate to record the dying declaration (deposition) of a person who is likely to die as a result of criminal violence. If the patient's condition is so grave (e.g. in bride burning cases, injury to vital organs, criminal abortion, etc.) that death or unconsciousness may supervene before the arrival of a magistrate, the doctor should record the statement himself bearing in mind the following points:

1. The doctor has to issue two certificates: (i) initially, he has to certify that the patient is in a sound mental condition *(compos mentis)* to make the declaration, and (ii) when the declaration is concluded, he should certify that it was made while the declarant was compos mentis, it was read over to him, and that he accepted it as having been correctly recorded.
2. The declaration may be made orally but the person receiving it should commit it to writing at that time.
3. It should be recorded in the vernacular of the declarant in the presence of two disinterested witnesses. The questions put to him and his answers to them must be written down in full details and in identical words.
4. Nothing should be suggested to the victim nor should any attempt be made to elicit information by leading questions.
5. In cases of extreme weakness or cut throat injuries where the victim is unable to speak but able to make signs in answer to questions, these should be recorded in the form of questions and signs.
6. The declaration, when concluded, should be read over to the victim who should affix his signature or left thumb impression to it. It should also be signed by the doctor recording it as well as by the witnesses. If the statement is written by the patient himself, it should be signed by him, the doctor and the witnesses.
7. If the declarant dies or becomes unconscious whilst the declaration is being recorded, the doctor should record as much information as he has obtained, and sign it himself.
8. The declaration should then be forwarded in a sealed cover to the appropriate magistrate.
9. The investigating police officer should not be allowed to remain present while the dying declaration is being recorded.

The **dying declaration** forms an important evidence in criminal trial in the event of the victim's death. If the victim survives, it ceases to have any legal value. This is made clear by the Apexcourt in Alladi Aruna case (SC 2010) wherein since the declarent Velu Durai did not die after making DD, his DD cannot be taken as the basis for conviction of Accused. The declarant must then come to the court to give oral evidence and be cross-examined for it. However, under section 157 IEA, the declaration may still be relied upon to corroborate the statement of the complainant at the time of oral examination.

Dying position: A **dying deposition** is a statement or oath made by a dying person to a magistrate in the presence of the accused and his lawyer who has the opportunity of cross-examining him (victim). Before the statement is made, the doctor should certify that the victim is compos mentis. A dying deposition *legally carries more weight* than a dying declaration because—(1) it is recorded by a magistrate, and (2) it is recorded in the presence of the accused and his lawyer who has the opportunity of cross-examining the declarant. In contrast to dying declaration, the dying deposition retains its full legal value even if the victim survives, hence, known as "bedside court".

Q. 1.16. Comment on: (1) oral evidence, (2) circumstantial evidence.

Oral evidence means and includes all statements which the court permits or requires to be made in relation to matters of fact under inquiry. They may be: (1) direct or (2) circumstantial.

According to section 60 IEA, oral evidence whenever possible must be *direct*. It must be the evidence of that person who has personal knowledge of facts in relation to the particular incident. Accordingly, if it refers to a fact which could be seen, heard or perceived in any other manner, it must be the evidence of that person who says, he saw, heard or so perceived it; if it refers to an opinion or the grounds on which that opinion is held, it must be the evidence of that person who holds that opinion on those grounds. If it refers to the existence or condition of any material thing, the court may require the production of such a thing for its inspection, viz. a blood-stained weapon, torn clothing or a broken portion of knife recovered from the body of a victim. *Hearsay* or *indirect* evidence is the evidence of a witness who has no personal knowledge of facts but repeats only what he has heard others say. As for example, if A has seen B hitting Mr. X with a stick and deposes that he has himself witnessed that incident, then it is direct evidence. On the contrary, if A has not himself seen it but deposes that Mr. Y told him so, then it becomes hearsay or indirect evidence. It is not permissible in law because the witness is unable to testify on oath as to its accuracy on cross-examination.

Circumstantial evidence is the evidence consisting of facts from which an inference may be drawn, such as the finding of blood on the clothes of the accused or a laboratory determination that a fatal bullet recovered from the body of a victim was fired from a revolver which was in possession of a suspect at the time of his arrest. The total yield from a crime detection laboratory qualifies as circumstantial evidence. And, in many cases, this is far more reliable than the evidence given by eye witnesses because they may turn hostile!

Q. 1.17. Mention the circumstances in which documentary evidence is admissible in a court of law without oral evidence.

Oral evidence is more important than documentary evidence because it allows cross-examination to determine its accuracy. If necessary, therefore, documentary evidence may be accepted by the court after oral testimony and cross-examination of the concerned person.

Admissibility of documentary evidence without oral evidence (exceptions to oral evidence): While it is desirable that oral evidence must always be direct and subject to crossexamination, there are circumstances when this is either not possible or strictly necessary. In these cases, the person who has actually witnessed a particular incident or heard or perceived a thing in any other manner, need not himself come and depose as to what he had seen, heard or perceived. His report, observation or statement is accepted as such. These **exceptions** are: (1) dying declaration,

(2) expert opinions expressed in a treatise, (3) deposition of a medical witness taken in a lower court, (4) report of certain government scientific experts, e.g. chemical examiner; chief inspector of explosives; director of finger print bureau; director of Haffkine Institute, Mumbai; Director, Deputy Director or Assistant Director of Central Forensic Science Laboratory or State Forensic Labo-ratory; and serologist to the government, (5) evidence given by a witness in a previous judicial proceeding, and (6) state-ments by persons who cannot be called as witnesses.

Dying declaration: Although this is hearsay or indirect evidence, this is accepted in court as legal evidence in the event of the victim's death. In fact, great sanctity is attached to it as it is legally presumed that a dying man will speak the truth during the last moments of his life (Sec 32 IEA).

Expert opinions expressed in a treatise: Expert opinions printed in books commonly offered for sale are generally accepted as evidence on the production of such treatise without oral evidence of the author (Sec 60 IEA).

Deposition of a medical witness taken in a lower court: This is accepted as evidence in a higher court when it has been recorded and attested by a magistrate in the presence of the accused who has had an opportunity to cross-examine the witness. However, the medical witness may be summoned, if his evidence is deficient in any respect or needs further elucidation (Sec 291 CrPC).

Report of certain government scientific experts: This is usually admitted as evidence without their oral examination (Sec 293(1) CrPC). The report is usually adequate and of a factual nature. However, the court is given discretionary power to summon and examine them if their report is found inadequate or requires further elucidation (Sec 293(2) CrPC).

Evidence given by a witness in a previous judicial proceeding: This is admitted as evidence in a subsequent judicial proceeding or in a later stage of the same proceeding when the witness is dead, untraceable or incapable of giving evidence or cannot be called without unreasonable delay or expense to the court (Sec 33 IEA).

Statements by persons who cannot be called as witnesses: These are admissible as evidence when the person who made them is either dead, untraceable or has become incapable of giving evidence or cannot be called without unreasonable delay or expense to the court (Sec 32 IEA).

With the concurrence of prosecution and defence, a presiding officer can dispense with calling of a witness, if parties accept the report.

Q. 1.18. What is meant by the term witness? Mention the kinds of witnesses and their functions.

A witness is a person who gives sworn testimony (evidence) in a court of law as regards facts and/or inferences that can be drawn therefrom. They are of two kinds, viz: (1) common or ordinary, and (2) expert or skilled.

Common witness: A common or ordinary witness is one who testifies as to facts, e.g. what he actually saw or heard. He cannot (1) draw any inference from observations made by him, (2) express any opinion on observations made by others, and (3) volunteer a statement.

Expert witness: An expert witness is a person especially skilled in foreign law, science, or art (Sec 45 IEA). His professional training or experience enables him to draw inference from or express an opinion on observations made by him or others. He can also volunteer a statement, if he feels that justice is likely to be miscarried owing to the court having failed to elicit an important point.

Examples of expert witnesses are: (a) handwriting expert, (b) fingerprint expert, (c) ballistic expert, (d) chemical examiner, forensic science lab asst., directors, etc. Medical personnel are skilled in special branches of medicine and are treated as skilled or expert witnesses.

A doctor is an ordinary as well as an expert witness. When he states that he found a wound on the body so many centimetres long and defines its position, he is acting as an ordinary witness. When he goes on to say that death was due to haemorrhage from a particular blood vessel and the injury was sufficient in the ordinary course of nature to cause death, he is acting as an expert witness.

Q. 1.19. Mention the principles to be remembered by a medical witness in giving evidence.

In giving evidence, the following principles should be remembered by a medical witness:

1. When the summons is served, he must attend the court punctually and produce such documents or other articles as required by the court. He should dress himself properly, consistent with his dignity as a doctor. As a rule, his evidence is taken at the appointed time as the court realises the importance of his time and duties. However, if delay occurs in taking up his evidence, he can politely inform the public prosecutor that he is waiting.
2. Before attending the court, he should *refresh his memory* about the facts of the case from his notes actually written at the time of examination and which should also be taken with him. Such notes may be inspected by the opposing counsel who may cross-examine him on the same. He should make careful study of recent literature on the subject and prepare himself for the questions that he is likely to be asked.
3. While in the premises of the court, he should avoid any indiscriminate talk or discussion of the case.
4. When he is called in and takes his stand in the witness box, oath is administered to him by the court clerk who also takes down his name, age, occupation and address. From then on, his evidence starts. While giving evidence, he should address the judge as "Sir" or "Your Honour". He should give evidence slowly and in a loud clear voice so as to enable the court clerk on one side to record his evidence (on the computer or typewriter) and the opposing counsel on the other side to hear what he is saying. Whenever practicable, he must restrict himself to simple words. For instance, it is better to describe an incised wound as a 'cut', a metacarpophalangeal joint as a 'knuckle', and a contusion of eye region as a 'black eye'. Technical terms should be kept to a necessary minimum and explained, if used. The answers should be brief and precise avoiding vague words, like 'about' or 'approximately' whenever possible. As for example, while describing wounds **which can be measured**, actual measurements should be given. A range or approximation may be given only when it is not possible to be accurate, e.g. while giving an opinion on 'age of a person, age of injury or time since death'.
5. There is a common misconception that the answers should be in the form of 'yes' or 'no'. Since the doctor must tell the truth and the whole truth, it is not always possible to do so if he restricts his answers to simple 'yes' or 'no'. He should qualify the answer or give an explanation when the answer is likely to mislead the court. Also, he should beware of going beyond facts which cannot be upheld. Doctor is allowed to volunteer and make statement in the interest of Justice.

6. Medicine is a vast subject and if the witness does not know the answer to any particular question, he should say so at once so that his credibility is maintained.
7. If a question is not clear or is ambiguous, he should ask for it to be repeated or clarified. If a quotation is read from a textbook which does not appear to him to be correct, he should ask for the book and not only read the context but also look at the date of publication before replying; medical science progresses rapidly and these advances are reflected in latest editions only.
8. A medical witness should remember that although called by one party, his evidence should be impartial and reflecting his scientific position. He should freely concede any points which may tell against the party calling him. He should also be prepared to admit any alternative explanation of the facts which is reasonable when put to him, even if he had not thought of it earlier. A special quality which brings respect and regard to a forensic expert is fairness to the other side.
9. When asked to express an opinion on observations made by another professional colleague, he should ensure that his views are in accord with the current scientific position and he should firmly and politely adhere to his conclusions. If the subject under discussion is open to different interpretations, he should say so and give reasons for his opinion.
10. He should not lose his temper but should keep cool and maintain dignity, even if questions of an irritable nature are put to him. Below are examples of some such questions:

Q. Doctor, do you agree that Dr. XYZ is an authority on this subject?

A. I am here to offer what I consider as a fair criticism on Dr. XYZ's opinion and not to praise him unconditionally (if Dr. XYZ's speciality is your speciality, say so).

Q. Doctor, are you infallible?

A. No (diffidently), but I believe, I am correct in this instance (confidently).

Q. Doctor, I put it to you that the entry in your record is false and was made for certain purposes.

A. I deny both (calmly and firmly).

Q. Doctor, is it not what you have told about the lapse of time between injuries and death a mere conjecture on your part?

A. Certainly not. It is my opinion based upon my findings and not a conjecture.

Q. Doctor, you are a friend of the plaintiff and you really want to see him win this case?

A. I am his friend and I want to see him win this case because I think he is right or else I would not be here.

11. There are some tricky questions. Here are four of them: (a) When a question is asked, "Doctor, is this all?" He should say, "That is all I remember at this moment." (b) "Doctor, are you getting paid to testify in this case?" The answer should be, "No, I am not getting paid to testify; I am only getting compensation for my time off work and the expenses (if any) incurred by me to be here." (c) "Doctor, have you talked or had consultation to anybody about this case?" The best thing is to say frankly that he has talked to whomsoever he has—attorney, witness, police, etc. and that he was just asked as to what the facts were. (d) "Doctor, how is it that in a certain journal, you stated something and today you are stating something different with respect to the same topic?" The answer should be, "I try to keep up-to-date with the latest advances" or "the context is different".
12. The medical witness should remember that the court has no special medical knowledge and his sole purpose is to aid the court to arrive at a just decision by describing and explaining the medical aspects of the case and the conclusions

which can be drawn therefrom. Hence, while an ordinary witness cannot *volunteer a statement,* a medical witness can do so, if he feels that justice is likely to be miscarried owing to the court having failed to elicit an important point.

13. The doctor must remember that if a judge directs him to do so, he must answer any question. In India, professional secrecy is not recognised by a court of criminal law. Nevertheless, he should not volunteer these secrets, but should divulge them under protest, to show his sense of moral duty, when pressed upon to do so. The information can be written and handed over to the judge. Medical witness does not have any legal immunity.

When the evidence is concluded, this record, known as his deposition, should be read and signed by him after getting any corrections if need be, done by the court under his initials.

The medical witness should not leave the court until permission to do so is granted. If he so desires, the court will issue him a certificate of attendance to enable him to claim travelling expenses. Subsequent to discharge, the witness is liable to be called again, if his evidence is found deficient in any respect or needs further elucidation.

Write short note on pretrial conference. Pretrial conference is held by the medical witness with the public prosecutor to get acquainted with the case and its likely context. This helps both the doctor and the lawyer to know the way of questioning and answering within the permissible limits of science and dispels any doubts to be clarified. In India, this practice is still not there.

2 Law and Medicine

LAW IN RELATION TO THE MEDICAL PROFESSION

In India, the general control of the medical profession is vested with the medical councils. They are created under the Medical Act.

The *Indian Medical Degrees Act,* 1916, is the principal All India Statute which regulates the grant of titles implying qualifications in Western medical science. It also penalises persons who voluntarily and falsely assume any medical title or use any imitation of such titles.

The *Indian Medical Council Act,* 1933, whereby the Indian Medical Council was created is now replaced by the Indian Medical Council Act, 1956, and the Indian Medical Council (Amendment) Act, 1964, which extend to the whole of India.

Several state governments have created the state medical vouncils by passing the **State Medical Council Act.**

Q. 2.1. Describe in brief the functions of (a) Indian Medical Council, (b) State Medical Council.

Q. 2.2. What is meant by registration? Outline the procedure of inquiry into professional misconduct of a registered medical practitioner and state the action that can follow from such an inquiry.

Q. 2.3. What is meant by infamous conduct in a professional respect? Illustrate your answer with suitable examples.

The Indian Medical Council (MCI)

The Indian Medical Council consists of a certain number of members of the profession elected from each state, each university and some nominated by the Central Government. They hold office for a term of five years. A president and a vice-president are elected from amongst the members.

The Council carries out the purposes of the Indian Medical Council Act through an executive committee and through such other committees as the Council may deem necessary. These committees are constituted from amongst its members.

The main functions of the Council relate to: (1) Undergraduate and postgraduate medical education, (2) medical qualifications, (3) register of medical practitioners, (4) advising the Central Health Ministry on appeals against disciplinary actions taken by the state medical council, (5) issuing of warning notices, (6) issuing certificates of good conduct and character to doctors going abroad, (7) sponsoring and organising continuing medical education (CME) programmes, and (8) prescribing a code of medical ethics.

Medical education: The Council maintains the standards of undergraduate medical education and lays down the requirements, e.g. accommodation, equipment, teaching staff and their qualifications, and other facilities. It appoints inspectors to inspect these requirements and standard of examinations held by the medical institutions or universities in India for the purpose of recommending recognition of the medical qualifications awarded by them to the Central Government. Such an inspection is held for every medical qualification when it is introduced and every five years thereafter. If the requirements are not met with or found unsatisfactory, it can make a representation to the Central Government to withdraw recognition of any medical qualification of such medical institution or university. It prescribes standards for postgraduate medical education for the guidance of universities. It also lays down criteria for transfer of students from one medical college to another.

Medical qualifications: It recognises the Medical Act under three schedules of qualifications: the first schedule includes recognised medical qualifications granted by medical institutions or universities in India; the second one includes recognised medical qualifications granted by medical institutions outside India; part I of the third schedule includes recognised medical qualifications granted by medical institutions in India not included in the first schedule, and part II includes recognised medical qualifications granted by medical institutions outside India not included in the second schedule.

The Council has authority to enter into negotiations for the setting up of schemes for the reciprocal recognition of medical qualifications with the authority in any state or country outside India, which is entrusted by its constitution with the maintenance of a register of medical practitioners. A special provision is made in certain cases for recognition of medical qualifications granted by medical institutions in countries with which there is no scheme of reciprocity.

Medical register: It maintains in the prescribed manner a register of medical practitioners known as the Indian Medical Register containing the names of all persons who are enrolled any state medical council and registered after recognised medical qualifications.

To ensure that doctors update their skills continuously, the Delhi Medical Council has decided that doctors practising in Delhi have to apply for fresh registration every five years. It is just a matter of time before other states adopt such a measure. In developed countries, doctors have to apply for a fresh registration every five years. In the United States, for instance, doctors have to fulfill certain requirements of "continuing medical education" before they are registered again. CME credit hours are now insisted in many states of India.

Advice on disciplinary actions: It advises the Central Health Ministry when an appeal is made by a registered medical practitioner against the decision of the state medical council on disciplinary matters.

Warning notices: It may issue warning notices in relation to certain unethical practices which are regarded as falling within the meaning of the term infamous conduct in a professional respect.

Certificates: It is empowered to issue certificates of good conduct and character to medical students or doctors going abroad for higher studies or service.

CME programmes: It sponsors and organises continuing medical education programmes for medical practitioners to help update their knowledge.

Code of ethics: It follows the Declaration of Geneva as modified by the World Medical Association.

The Council appoints a **Registrar** for its day-to-day work which includes the maintenance of the Indian Medical Register and to update it periodically by erasing the names of those practitioners who have died or who have been convicted by a criminal court or who have been found guilty of infamous conduct in a professional respect, and by restoring the names of those practitioners whose period of temporary erasure expires.

The State Medical Councils

The State Medical Council consists of members elected by the registered medical practitioners and those nominated by the state government. The president and vice-president of the Council are elected by the members from amongst themselves. The main functions of the state medical councils relate to: (1) maintaining a register (2) medical etiquette and ethics (3) disciplinary control, and (4) warning notices.

State Medical Register

The Registrar or Secretary of the Council maintains a Register in the prescribed manner to provide for registration of medical practitioners within its jurisdiction. Any doctor possessing requisite medical qualifications as prescribed by the Indian Medical Council is eligible for registration on payment of the prescribed fee. A provisional registration is granted to a doctor who has passed the qualifying examination but has to undergo a certain period of training in an approved institution before such qualification is conferred on him. It is the duty of the Registrar to inform the Indian Medical Council, from time to time, about the additions and deletions from the State Medical Register.

As long as a doctor is a registered medical practitioner, he enjoys the following **privileges:** (a) He is entitled to set up medical practice anywhere in India and to prescribe medicines listed in the Dangerous Drugs Act, (b) he can hold official and semi-official appointments, (c) he can sign statutory medical certificates, such as birth, death, mental illness, etc., (d) he can perform medicolegal autopsies, (e) he can give evidence as an expert, (f) he is exempted from serving on a jury and at an inquest, and (g) he can sue for his fees in a court of law unless he is prevented from doing so by the institution whose qualifications he holds.

Medical Etiquette and Medical Ethics

The terms medical etiquette and medical ethics are understood by convention as follows:

Medical etiquette is the subject concerned with the conventional laws and customs of courtesy which are generally followed between members of the same profession. Accordingly, a doctor should behave with his colleagues as he would like to have them behave with him. He should treat the colleague as his brother and, therefore, not charge him or members of his family for professional service. Regrettably, this is not so now.

Medical ethics is the subject concerned with moral principles for the members of the medical profession in their dealings with each other, their patients and the state. The aim is to honour and maintain the noble traditions of the medical profession. To give a few examples, a medical practitioner should not take charge of a patient who is under the care of another practitioner. He should not refuse to give professional service on religious grounds. He must remember his duty to the State in relation to notifiable diseases, and to the public to give emergency care on humanitarian grounds.

Declaration of Geneva

The oldest code of medical ethics is the Hippocratic Oath. It is now restated in modern style by the World Association, and known as the Declaration of Geneva. **It is followed by the Medical Council of**

India as the Code of Ethics. Accordingly, every applicant, at the time of registration shall submit the following, written and signed, declaration to the concerned Registrar attested by the Registrar himself or a registered medical practitioner. Any deviation therefrom is treated as unethical practice.

1. I solemnly pledge myself to consecrate my life to the service of humanity.
2. I will give to my teachers the respect and gratitude which is their due.
3. I will practise my profession with conscience and dignity.
4. The health of my patients will be my first consideration.
5. I will respect the secrets confided in me.
6. I will maintain by all means, in my power, the honour and the noble traditions of the medical profession.
7. My colleagues will be my brothers.
8. I will not permit consideration of religion, nationality, race, party-politics or social standing to intervene between my duty and my patient.
9. I will maintain the utmost respect for human life from the time of conception.
10. Even under threat, I will not use my medical knowledge contrary to the laws of humanity.

Disciplinary Control

The state medical councils exercise disciplinary control over their members by reprimanding or erasing temporarily or permanently from the Register the name of the practitioner found guilty of infamous conduct in any professional respect, also known as professional misconduct. They also have the power to direct the restoration of any name so removed.

Infamous conduct or professional misconduct is defined as conduct on the part of a medical practitioner during the practise of his profession which would be reasonably regarded as disgraceful or dishonourable by his professional colleagues of good repute and competence.

The state medical councils take cognisance of any offence of misconduct committed by a registered medical practitioner only: (1) when a written complaint in this respect is received by them or (2) when a medical practitioner is convicted by a court of law.

After hearing the complainant as well as the medical practitioner, either in person or through his lawyer, the Council decides whether any disciplinary action is necessary. Depending on the gravity of the offence, the action may be in the nature of (1) a warning or (2) erasure of the name from the Register either for a temporary period or permanently. Such erasure is known as *penal erasure* and when it is permanent, it is known as *professional death sentence.* It deprives the practitioner of all the privileges of a registered medical practitioner.

A medical practitioner is entitled to appeal to the Central Health Ministry against the decision of the state medical councils, and the ministry in consultation with the Indian Medical Council may modify the same.

The **following list** gives some examples of instances of unethical practices which constitute what is termed as **professional misconduct.** The Council is not precluded from considering any other form of professional misconduct which is not covered under this list:

a. ***Association with unqualified persons:*** This includes:

1. Employment of unqualified or unregistered assistants
2. Assisting an unqualified person as by giving an anaesthetic for some procedure
3. Having relations with uncertified persons which enable them to practise midwifery or issuing certificates which enable such practices to occur (covering of unqualified persons).

b. ***Advertising:*** Direct advertising includes:

1. An unusually big name plate
2. Inserting name in a telephone directory in a special place or in bold type
3. A prescription paper containing anything other than his name, qualifications, speciality, address, telephone number and service timings
4. Notification in the lay press of his address or telephone number or consulting hours unless he has—(i) started practice afresh, (ii) changed his office, (iii) resumed practice after temporary absence or (iv) changed the type of his practice, in which case such an announcement may appear not more than twice.

Indirect advertising includes:

1. Other than contributing articles to lay press on public health and allied matters
2. Appearances on broadcasting or television which may have the effect of advertising
3. Allowing the use of his name on the price list of publicity materials.

Canvassing would ordinarily mean using of touts or agents for procuring patients.

c. *Adultery:* A doctor should not abuse his position to seduce a female patient or some other member of the family.

d. *Abortion:* This includes procuring, assisting or attempting to procure an illegal abortion. (Four As)

e. *Disregard of personal responsibilities to patients by:*

1. Use of unsterile instruments.
2. Not furnishing patients with proper information about drugs or diet.
3. Giving positively wrong information, e.g. that a benign tumour is cancer and performing unnecessary operations.
4. Ordering unnecessary laboratory tests.
5. Not attending a patient who is already under his treatment.
6. Attending a patient while under the influence of drink or drugs.
7. Suddenly terminating service to a patient.
8. Arranging for a substitute without prior intimation to the patient.
9. Experimenting on a patient without his valid consent, etc.

f. *Avoiding consultations* in certain situations, e.g. in a case of poisoning, when diagnosis is in doubt, when a case has taken a serious turn, when an operation is to be performed in a case in which there has been a criminal assault, in operations of a mutilating or destructive nature on an unborn child, when desired by the patient or his representatives, etc.

g. *Attending a patient who is under the care of another practitioner* or taking charge of such patient.

h. *Refusing* to give **professional service on religious grounds.**

i. Contravening the provisions of the Drugs Act and regulations made thereunder, e.g. by selling schedule poisons to the public under cover of his own qualifications except to his patients.

j. Writing **prescriptions in a secret formula** known to some particular pharmacy only.

k. Commercialisation of a **secret remedy.**

l. *Running an open shop* for the sale of medicines, for dispensing prescriptions of other doctors or for the sale of medical or surgical appliances.

m. Improper association with **drug manufacturing firms.**

n. *Receiving or giving commission* or other benefits from or to a professional colleague, a manufacturer, trader, chemist, etc. Giving of a commission by one doctor to another for referring, recommending or procuring any patient for medical, surgical or other treatment is known as *dichotomy* or fee-sharing or fee-splitting.

o. *Issuing false certificates* in respect of birth, cause of death, illness, injury, vaccination, mental illness, etc.

p. *Talking disparagingly* about other colleagues or doing anything that means unfair competition.

q. *Conviction* by a court of law for offenses involving moral turpitude.

Q. 2.4. Briefly discuss the compulsory and voluntary duties of a medical practitioner towards the State and the patient. Mention the circumstances under which a medical practitioner should seek a consultation.

Q. 2.5. Comment on doctor-patient relationship.

Q. 2.6. Discuss the obligations of a medical practitioner in respect of professional secrecy.

Q. 2.7. What is a privileged communication? Giving examples, discuss the position of a medical practitioner with respect to such communication.

Compulsory Duties of a Medical Practitioner

These relate to: (1) compulsory notification, and (2) responsibilities to the state.

1. *Compulsory notification:* Births, deaths, infectious diseases, and food poisoning from a restaurant. In some states, industrial diseases are also notifiable.

2. *Responsibilities to the state:* (a) Responding to emergency military service, (b) reporting cases of homicidal poisoning or suspected homicidal injuries, such as stab or gunshot wounds, (c) reporting certain cases coming under category of privileged communication, especially as regards moral and social duties, and responsibility in criminal matters, (d) reporting unnatural deaths, and (e) reporting suspected abuse of children, spouse or elderly in some countries.

Voluntary Duties of a Medical Practitioner

These relate to: (1) responsibility to patients, (2) medical examinations, (3) operations, (4) issuing of certificates, (5) prisons and reformatories, (6) medicolegal examination and certificates, (7) postmortem examination, (8) sending pathological material by post, and (9) attending to accidents.

1. *Responsibility to patients:* Implied contract (a) to continue to treat, (b) reasonable care, (c) reasonable skill, (d) keep professional secrets inviolate except under privileged circumstances, (e) not undertaking procedures beyond skill, (f) special precautions to be taken in case of children and adults not capable of taking care of themselves, e.g. when applying hot water bottles, (g) special precautions in respect of dangerous drugs and poisons, (h) consultation with another colleague under certain circumstances, (i) keeping abreast of recent advances in the field.

2. *Medical examinations:* (a) Consent taken, (b) results kept secret, (c) laboratory aids utilised when necessary, (d) X-rays taken in all cases of accident unless trivial.

3. *Operations:* (a) Consent taken, (b) nature, extent and risks explained, (c) precautions taken not to operate on wrong patient or wrong part, (d) precautions taken for the safety of the patient by ensuring fitness for anaesthesia, check of count as regards sponges, needles, and instruments, and postoperative care, (e) no experimentation.

4. *Issuing of certificates:* Illness; vaccination; death; and for insurance, compensation, cremation, etc. The data mentioned in the certificate must be true to the best of doctor's knowledge and belief.

5. *Prisons and reformatories:*

a. Certifying to facts regarding pregnancy
b. Checking diet
c. Inspection of lavatories.

6. *Medicolegal examination and certificates:* (a) Proper authorisation, (b) identification, (c) verification of facts, e.g. in mental illness certificates, (d) material preserved when necessary, e.g. in cases of poisoning, drunkenness, (e) laboratory aids utilised, e.g. X-ray, microscopy, histopathology, antibody testing, (f) certificates issued promptly, (g) all details given, (h) copy preserved.

7. *Postmortem examination:* (a) For scientific purposes and only after obtaining consent, (b) not to be undertaken in medicolegal cases without proper authorisation.

8. *Sending pathological material by post:* Precautions to be taken to prevent spread of disease.

9. *Attending to accidents:* A physician has an absolute right to select his patients. The physician who responds in an emergency, such as a traffic accident is expected to exercise a reasonably prudent physician's standard of care and to offer that much help that is possible under the circumstances. Normally, first aid is rendered and the victim referred to his physician or hospital.

10. *Examination of accused under arrest:* Consent not necessary.

Practitioner and Patient

While a doctor cannot be forced to treat any person, he has certain responsibilities for those whom he accepts. It is an implied contract. An **implied contract** is a contract which is not written, but nonetheless, it is legally effective because of the circumstances surrounding the transaction. Default on the part of either party renders that party liable to have the damages assessed against it, if the default has resulted in injury to the other party. *This contract requires that the doctor must continue to treat a patient, whom he has accepted, with reasonable care and reasonable skill, and to keep inviolate his secrets. He should not undertake any procedure beyond his skill.* A doctor is not free from legal obligations as regards these requirements even when rendering a voluntary service without fees.

A doctor–patient relationship (implied contract) is **not established** when (1) the doctor renders first aid in an emergency, (2) he makes a pre-employment medical examination for a prospective employer, (3) he performs an examination for life insurance purposes, (4) he is appointed by the trial court to examine the accused for any reason, and (5) when he makes an examination at the request of an attorney for law suit purposes.

The various requirements of the doctor–patient relationship can be briefly discussed as follows:

Continue to Treat

Responsibility towards a patient is undertaken as soon as a doctor agrees to examine the case. He must not then abandon his treatment except under the following circumstances, viz.:

1. The patient is well.
2. The patient is under some other responsible caregiver.
3. The doctor has given due notice for discontinuing treatment.
4. The patient has signified his intention of changing the doctor.
5. The patient does not co-operate and follow the doctor's instructions.
6. The patient does not pay the doctor's fees.
7. The patient consults another doctor without the knowledge of the attending doctor.
8. The doctor is convinced that the illness is a feigned one.

Reasonable Care

A doctor must use proper and clean instruments and appliances, and furnish his patients with proper and suitable medicines, if he has a dispensary. If he has no dispensary, he should legibly write prescriptions, using well-accepted abbreviations and mention full instructions for the pharmacist. He should give in simple language full directions to his patients as regards administration of drugs, and other remedial measures, including diet. He must suggest consultation with a specialist in difficult cases or when in doubt. He is liable under the doctrine of 'negligent choice' for referring his patient to an incompetent or inappropriate doctor.

Consultations: These are specially necessary in the following circumstances:

1. When the case is obscure and difficult, the diagnosis is in doubt, the patient is not responding to treatment or has taken a serious turn.
2. When the question arises whether it is necessary to perform an operation which may be dangerous to life.
3. When an operation is to be performed on a case in which there has been a criminal assault.
4. When an operation is to be performed which may vitally affect the intellectual or reproductive functions of a patient.
5. When it is a question whether pregnancy of over 12 weeks duration should be terminated under the Medical Termination of Pregnancy Act.
6. In case of pregnancy in which criminal interference has already taken place.
7. In operations of a mutilating or destructive nature on an unborn child.
8. In cases when there is a suspicion of poisoning or other criminal act.
9. When desired by the patient or his representatives or whenever it appears that the quality of medical service may be enhanced thereby.
10. When, in an apprehensive or neurotic patient, full disclosure is not possible and there is no relation from whom informed consent can be obtained.
11. When a do-not-resuscitate (DNR) order is to be issued.
12. In medicolegal postmortems in case of 'dowry deaths' (in India).

The doctor's duty to care also includes warning the patient, spouse, family, employer, or authorities, in appropriate circumstances, when he discovers a medical condition (e.g. epilepsy, narcolepsy, kleptomania, schizophrenia, hepatitis B, hepatitis C, AIDS, etc.) that may impair the patient's functioning and safety to himself and/or to others.

Reasonable Skill

The degree of skill that a practitioner undertakes to bring to the treatment of his patient is the average degree of skill possessed by his professional colleagues of the same standing as himself. The doctor is not responsible for an error in judgement but he must bring to the discharge of his duty reasonable care, skill and knowledge. He has full liberty to adopt any theory of medicine or surgery in which he honestly believes but no new form of treatment in the nature of an experiment could be practiced without the consent of the patient or his guardian. A specialist is bound to bring to the discharge of his duty that special degree of skill and knowledge possessed by specialists in the light of their standing in the profession and current knowledge.

Professional Secrets and Privileged Communication

A professional secret is one which a doctor comes to know in his professional capacity. He should not divulge anything which he has thus learnt. This is an ethical and legal obligation (implied contract) and a practitioner is liable to damages for its neglect.

Dr Playfair, a well-known gynaeco-logist, was called in to examine Mrs. Kitson, his sister-in-law. He removed something which he diagnosed as a product of conception. As Mr Kitson was abroad, Mrs Kitson was receiving an allowance of Pounds 500 per year from her husband's brother. Dr Playfair, regarding the preg-nancy as illegitimate, communicated the circumstances to the brother-in-law, with the result that her allowance was stopped. Mrs Kitson brought an action for slander against Dr Playfair and was awarded Pounds 12,000 damages.

In certain circumstances, a doctor is justified in disclosing information about his patient and the communication is regarded as privileged. A **privileged communication** may be defined, in a general manner, as a communication made by a doctor to a proper authority who has corresponding legal, social and moral duties to protect the public. Such a privilege can be claimed, and disclosure of professional secrets justified, in the following circumstances: (1) when as a witness in a court of law, the doctor is directed by the judge to do so, (2) when the doctor has a moral or social duty to perform, (3) when it is to safeguard the doctor's own interests, (4) when the doctor's duty as a citizen to assist in the apprehension of a person who has committed a serious crime outweighs his obligation to his patients, and (5) in certain other cases.

In a court of law: A doctor must disclose, when a judge so rules, any secret information about his patients which he may have obtained in the course of his professional relationship. Failure to do so may be treated as contempt of the court. In such a situation, the information can be written and handed over to the judge.

Moral or social duty: This arises under circumstances, such as:

1. A bar-maid who develops a chancre or open tuberculosis is not a fit person for serving drinks to the public nor a typhoid carrier as a hotel waiter.
2. A bus driver who has pronounced hypertension or brittle diabetes is unsafe to be in charge of a public vehicle.
3. An engine driver who is colour blind or epileptic is not fit for this job.
4. A person suffering from a communicable disease should be prohibited from entering a swimming pool or contracting a marriage till cured.
5. Doctors have ethical as well as legal responsibility to warn partners of patients with the AIDS virus, since AIDS is fatal.
6. Doctors also have ethical as well as legal responsibility to report all cases of suspected child abuse—physical, sexual, or emotional—and to protect the child from further harm.
7. Doctors have ethical as well as legal responsibility to warn parents or guardians if they find in their patients a tendency to any violent act, e.g. suicide or homicide.

The facts are written and sent in a sealed cover marked "privileged communication" to the proper authority.

In the doctor's own interest: A medical practitioner cannot withhold professional secrets in those cases where he has a statutory duty to the public health authorities or the state. He must notify births, deaths, communicable diseases as well as those cases which pose a danger to the public, e.g. cases of food poisoning from a restaurant or eating house or contamination of public drinking water. He must also notify, to the police, cases of homicidal poisoning coming under his observation.

Responsibility in criminal matters: If a practitioner is called to treat a patient who he believes to be a victim or accused of a serious crime, e.g. murder, robbery, jail breaking, etc., he should inform the proper authorities (Sec 39 CrPC). A man might come with a wound, e.g. a firearm injury or a stab injury, which might be supposed to have been inflicted in the course of a deadly scuffle. The doctor would be wrong in hiding evidence of such crime. He is not legally bound to inform the authorities in cases of attempted suicide unless the person dies (Sec 202 IPC). His responsibility in case of criminal abortion and poisoning is discussed at appropriate place in the text.

Other cases: The following examples in relation to professional secrecy and privileged communication serve to illustrate certain important situations of everyday life.

When **a servant is sent by a master** for medical examination, the master naturally wants to know the result of the examination as the condition of the servant may affect his capacity for work. The communication is supposed to be privileged, if made only to the employer and only in cases where the employer has an interest in knowing. Such reports should, however, be confined to those matters only which have an immediate bearing on the question at issue, viz. fitness for service, necessity for leave, extent of disability, etc. The same position applies in cases where a medical officer is called upon to report on the health of employees or when a worker claims compensation.

In connection with **insurance reports,** a doctor can report anything found on examination, as for example, high blood pressure, and no action can be taken by the proposer as such reports are privileged. However, there are cases where a proposer has previously consulted the doctor and the doctor has some knowledge about the disease for which the proposer has been treated by him. There may be no signs of the disease at the time of examination. Under such circumstances, the doctor cannot report the disease from previous knowledge as it would amount to breach of professional secrecy. In such cases, it is better to refuse examination on account of previous knowledge.

In connection with **inquiries,** a doctor should not answer queries addressed to him by an insurance company, solicitor or anyone else, in respect of a person who might have consulted him, without the patient's consent. Even parents and relatives are not entitled to know the results of examination of adult family members unless the patient consents. Similarly, any inquiry about the cause of death of a deceased person should not be answered without the consent of the nearest surviving relative.

Q. 2.8. Discuss briefly medical examination and consent.

The term consent means voluntary agreement, compliance or permission. Section 13 of the Indian Contract Act lays down that two or more persons are said to consent when they agree upon the same thing in the same sense (meeting of the minds).

The consent may either be implied or express. An *implied consent* is a consent which is not written, that is, its existence is not expressly asserted, but nonetheless, it is legally effective. It is provided by the demeanour of the patient and is by far the most common variety of consent in both general and hospital practices. It implies consent to medical examination in a general sense but not to procedures more complex than inspection, palpation, percussion and auscultation. An *express consent* is one the terms of which are stated in distinct and explicit language. It may be oral or written. For the majority of relatively minor examinations or therapeutic procedures, oral consent is employed but this should preferably be obtained in the presence of a disinterested party. Oral consent, where properly witnessed, is as valid as written consent, but the latter has the advantage of easy proof and permanent form.

To be legally valid, the consent that is given, must be informed and intelligent, that is, the consent must be given after understanding what it is given for and of the risks involved. It is, therefore, imperative for the doctor to give reasonable information to his patient about the (a) diagnosis, (b) nature of treatment or procedure, (c) risks involved, (d) prospects of success, (e) prognosis if the procedure is not performed, and (f) alternative methods of treatment. Thus, what the law requires is that (1) the patient be fully informed of every risk and factual material for the making of a proper consent and (2) the consent itself based upon such material disclosure. However, all informed consent rules recognise the so-called *therapeutic exceptions,* e.g. the apprehensive or neurotic patients who may be harmed by such full disclosure (either in discarding a needed procedure with minimal risk or else in suffering psychological harm from such disclosure and thus becoming an increased surgical risk). In such instances, it is advisable for the doctor to obtain informed consent from a responsible relation or in his absence, to obtain medical consultation and chart the intentional omission and the therapeutic exception-basis in regard thereto.

In regard to what is safe to tell the patient, the following guidelines are helpful:

"If the risk of untoward result is statistically high, the patient should be informed regardless of the effect on his morale. If the risk is statistically low, but the consequences of a rare untoward occurrence may be severe, the patient should likewise be informed. On the other hand, if the statistical risk is low or the severity of the risk is not great, the physician may safely tailor his warning so as not to excite the patient's fears."

The consent given may be invalid because (a) the act consented to is unlawful, e.g. a criminal abortion, (b) the consent was given by one who had no legal capacity to give it, e.g. a minor or mentally ill, (c) it is not an informed consent (vide supra), and (d) it was obtained by misrepresentation or fraud.

The concept of written, witnessed or express consent in hospitals has assumed considerable importance in recent years for two reasons: (1) It is not possible to cover by implied method of consent the greatly increased number of diagnostic and therapeutic measures which are being routinely carried out. Sophisticated radiological investigations, cardiac catheterisation and numerous other procedures are sufficiently risky to require express consent, and (2) the consent is valid only for a specific procedure, when the general nature of that procedure has been explained to the patient who can assess the risks and decline the procedure, if he so wishes *(informed refusal).*

In view of the above legal position, the usual blanket consent forms utilised by most hospitals and surgeons in which the patient in effect authorises the attending physician or surgeon to do whatever he thinks best for him under the circumstances (sometimes even including a postmortem) may later turn out to be of no value in court particularly as it does not refer to any specific procedure or operation that was originally contemplated and consented to, or that the patient was not given sufficient information to make an informed consent.

A medical practitioner must remember the following **principles in respect of consent** in relation to examination or treatment:

1. Ordinarily, when a patient calls on the doctor with his complaints, his consent for necessary medical examination is implied. However, if the patient is unconscious and any delay in obtaining the consent would be dangerous, the doctor may examine and treat without consent such a gravely ill person who needs immediate treatment or surgery. Save this exception, a doctor should not examine or treat any patient without his consent. Even in such cases, care should be taken that the surgical procedures do not go beyond the minimum required to save life, and whenever possible, amputation of limbs, etc., is postponed till such time that proper informed consent can be obtained.

A minor was taken to a surgeon by his two adult sisters for tonsillectomy. The child died under anaesthesia. The court ruled that there was no emergency to justify the surgeon to operate without parental consent, and the father could recover damages.

A minor's leg was crushed under a truck. The leg was amputated immediately. The court ruled that parental consent was implied by the prevailing emergency.

2. It should also be remembered that a visit paid to a practitioner by a patient implies consent to a certain amount of examination only. Operative and certain other procedures, such as blood transfusion, require a special written consent. A written consent is also necessary in special situations, e.g. (1) while examining the private parts of a person, (2) to determine age, potency or virginity, and (3) examination of cases of alleged sexual offence, etc.
3. It must be remembered that examination of a patient without his consent legally amounts to a trespass or an assault even an indecent assault in appropriate circumstances. This is equally true in the examination of medicolegal cases, as the *person* (not the *patient*) has not come voluntarily to the doctor but brought by the police and thus implied consent cannot be taken for granted. This is, however, subject to the exception laid down in section 53(1) CrPC.
4. The consent must not be obtained by fraud, undue pressure or duress. It must be free and voluntary, and given after a full explanation of the reasons for which it is required *(informed consent).*
5. In any case where there could possibly be any doubt, written consent should be obtained.
6. The consent should be broad enough to cover everything contemplated as likely to be required but the so-called blanket consent forms should be avoided. It is also usual to point out that the procedure need not be carried out by any particular doctor as this aspect has given rise to court proceedings in some cases.
7. Consent should be obtained from the parent or guardian where a person is incapable, through age or through lack of understanding, of giving a valid consent. In India, a person of and above 12 years of age can give consent for medical examination or treatment.
8. When consent has been obtained, the examination should, whenever possible, be made in the presence of a third person, preferably a female nurse, especially while a male doctor is examining a female patient and vice versa.
9. In any procedure affecting the rights of a spouse, e.g. sterilisation, hysterectomy, artificial insemination, etc., informed consent from such spouse should also be obtained.
10. Under section 53(1) of Criminal Procedure Code, an accused can be examined by a medical practitioner at the request of the police, even without his consent, and by use of force, if there is reasonable ground to believe that such examination will afford evidence, as to the commission of an offence. The examination may include taking of fluids in cases of intoxication, etc. Section 53(2) lays down that whenever a female is to be examined, the examination shall be made only by or under the supervision of a female registered medical practitioner. Under section 54 CrPC, an arrested person may be examined by a doctor at his request to detect evidence in his favour.

Illustrative Cases

Case 1: **Necessity of consent for examination:** The necessity of obtaining consent is stressed in an Indian case in which the question was whether a particular lady was the daughter of one of the defendants to the suit. The trial court directed that the defendant should be sent to a doctor for medical examination to ascertain whether any issue had been born to her. The order was challenged and the appellate court held that in as much as the medical examination of a lady, if not voluntarily consented to by her, would amount to assault and battery, the order of the lower court directing a medical examination was invalid.

Case 2: **Consent and emergency treatment:** A patient who had been bitten by a poisonous snake was not warned by his physician of the possible hazards in receiving snakebite serum. He suffered ill effects. He was not, however, allowed damages because of emergency nature of the situation.

Case 3: **Treatment without consent:** A surgeon flatly denied to the patient that he was going to remove her breast. When she awoke from surgery, she discovered that her breast was removed. She was allowed to recover damages from the surgeon on the ground that the defendant had performed a completely unauthorised operation and this amounted to "assault and battery".

Case 4: **Non-validity of blanket consent:** A female patient entered the hospital for an appendectomy. The surgeon removed the appendix and then, while she was under general anaesthesia and without her prior consent, performed a total hysterectomy, the surgeon noticing fibroid uterus. In holding the surgeon liable for damages despite the blanket consent form signed by the patient, the court observed that the so-called authorisation is so ambiguous as to be almost worthless, and certainly so, since it fails to designate the nature of the operation authorised and for which consent was given. It was pointed out that though it may be convenient for a surgeon to correct unrelated conditions discovered during the course of the operation, in the absence of an emergency threatening the life of a patient, the surgeon should not attempt to extend surgery beyond the scope of the patient's consent.

Case 5: **Necessity of informed consent for diagnostic procedures:** The patient had injured his neck in a fall. Several months later he re-injured his neck while in his automobile. His physician recommended that he undergo a diagnostic procedure known as a myelogram. The patient claimed that the physician told him the procedure was merely exploratory and that he had nothing to worry about. He further claimed that he suffered a herniated disc during the procedure which caused a "foot drop". He contended that the physician failed to inform him of this risk. The question, the court said, is not whether the reasonable medical practitioner would have disclosed the risk of foot drop. The question is whether or not the physician disclosed sufficient information to enable the patient to intelligently decide whether to undergo the myelogram. If he did not, the court ruled, he would be liable for all injuries sustained by the patient as a result of the procedure.

Case 6: **Consent by fraud:** A patient's legs and ankles were badly burned and ulcerated as a result of X-ray treatment for eczema. He alleged that if the defendant physician had made known to him that there was great danger that X-ray treatment might result in burns and ulcers, he would not have permitted the treatment and the injuries complained of would not have occurred. He further alleged that the defendant physician misled him not only by failing to warn him of the danger but also by affirmatively assuring him that X-ray treatment would cure his eczema within 8 weeks. The defendant physician was held liable.

Case 7: **Duty of disclosure and its extent:** A 19-year-old man was experiencing severe pain between his shoulder blades. A myelogram revealed a filling defect in the region of the fourth thoracic vertebra. A neurosurgeon recommended that the man undergo a laminectomy. Prior to the operation, the neurosurgeon did not inform the man or his mother that the laminectomy involved the risk of paralysis. The patient sued the neurosurgeon for damages. Regarding paralysis as risk of laminectomy, the neurosurgeon testified that there was only a very slight possibility. Paralysis can be expected somewhere in the nature of 1% of all cases. He further testified that it was not good medical practice to inform patients of the risk of paralysis. The disclosure of this risk might deter patients from undergoing the laminectomy that they needed or that it might cause an adverse psychological reaction that could decrease the possible success of the operation. The neurosurgeon was held liable. The court ruled that in all uncommon treatment or procedures, the doctor has a legal duty to inform the patient of the risk of death or serious bodily injury.

Case 8: **Duty of disclosure and its extent:** A patient who was given a pint of blood in connection with dilatation and curettage developed serum hepatitis. She alleged that the defendant hospital was negligent in failing to warn her of the risk of contracting serum hepatitis. The court said, "Considering the frequency of the use of transfusions, the nature and extent of the risk involved in comparison with the alternative risk, the possible detrimental effect of advising the patient of the risk, and the general practice in the local medical profession not to so advise patients, the court feels impelled to conclude that the defendant did not have a legal duty to the plaintiff to advise her in advance that serum hepatitis might be communicated".

Case 9: **Alternative treatment:** Without advising a patient with prostatic disorder that the recommended surgery would inevitably sterilise him or that there was another method of curing the disorder, the surgeon operated. In upholding the jury's award of damages to the patient, the appeals court held that in the absence of an emergency, the patient should have been advised of all alternatives by the defendant surgeon. He had a right to be given a chance to make up his own mind as to the alternative he preferred.

Case 10: **Consent for treatment by a particular doctor:** A patient was operated upon for hernia by a house surgeon instead of an experienced and senior surgeon. The patient alleged that he had been shocked that an apprentice had operated upon him without obtaining his consent when he had engaged a skilled craftsman. It was, however, admitted on the patient's behalf that the operation had been performed in an entirely competent manner. It was held that the house surgeon had operated without the plaintiff's consent and that for an unauthorised person to do so, was a highly technical form of trespass. Although, the house surgeon had behaved in accordance with the traditions of his profession, as there had been technical trespass, the patient was awarded nominal damages amounting to twenty shillings.

Case 11: **What constitutes informed consent:** A patient underwent electroshock and insulin subcoma therapy for severe depression and anxiety complicated by alcoholism. He consented orally to the treatment before hand; there was no question of mental incompetence. The treatment, which was not immediately necessary to save his life, was carried out by qualified medical staff competently and without negligence. In the course of the treatment, the plaintiff suffered fractured vertebrae during a convulsion though all reasonable precautions had been taken to prevent this. Medical evidence was given that shock therapy carried a high risk of fracture. One doctor assessed it at 18%. The plaintiff did not complain that the treatment was not recommended by good medical practice or that it was not competent nor did he deny that he had given consent. He brought an action on the ground that he had not been informed of inherent risks and dangers and that the doctors had been negligent in not giving him this information. He said that he would not have consented had he known of the hazards. The court considered the following facts: (i) the risks of fracture were matters of fact and not speculation, (ii) the risks were high, (iii) the incidental hazard of fracture was not a danger which the ordinary patient would know about without special information, (iv) there was no emergency, (v) the patient was not mentally incompetent and could understand explanations, and (vi) there is reason to believe that the plaintiff would not have consented to the treatment had he known of the dangers. It was held that a prima facie cause for action in negligence was established.

Duties of a Patient

When a patient employs a medical practitioner for the treatment of his ailment, he has the following duties:

1. He must divulge all information that may be necessary for the proper diagnosis and treatment of the case.

   A patient died from ruptured ectopic pregnancy. She told the physician that she had no intercourse since her last child was born, he made a diagnosis of ovarian abscess. The relatives of the deceased did not succeed in getting compensation from the doctor.
2. He must co-operate with the practitioner in regard to recommended laboratory aids, viz. X-rays, cardiogram, etc. that may be necessary for the diagnosis or as a guide to treatment.

3. He must carry out all instructions as regards drugs, diet, exercise and report to the practitioner as often as advised.
4. He must pay the practitioner for his service unless it is understood to be free.

While a registered medical practitioner may sue in a court of law for the recovery of fees due to him, failure on the part of the patient in connection with the other duties would free the practitioner of any responsibility for the result of his treatment.

Q.2.9. Discuss professional negligence in detail. Make a brief reference to the Consumer Protection Act.

Q.2.10. Discuss civil negligence giving examples.

Q.2.11. Discuss criminal negligence giving examples.

Professional Negligence

With a professional person, the word 'negligence' has a special meaning. It is defined as the omission to do something **(act of omission)** which a reasonable person would do or doing something **(act of commission)** which a reasonable person would not do. The consequences of negligence, product liability, etc. are covered in India under **The Consumer Protection Act.** (Refer to Precautions Against Negligence).

Professional negligence, **malpraxis** or **malpractice** is defined as lack of reasonable care and skill or wilful negligence on the part of a medical practitioner in the treatment of a patient whereby the health or life of a patient is endangered. It is not mere neglect or carelessness; it is neglect or carelessness where there is a legal duty to take care and failure in that duty causes damage/injury. Any want of proper skill or care that causes the patient's death, diminishes his chances of recovery, prolongs his illness or increases his suffering constitutes injury in a legal sense. However, negligent a doctor may be, the patient is not entitled to any compensation, if no damage has occurred.

It is not possible to lay down any fixed standards for medical care but the degree of skill that a practitioner should bring to the treatment of his patient is the average degree of skill possessed by his professional colleagues of the same standing as himself. An error in diagnosis or treatment is not negligence provided proper care and skill has been exercised. A specialist who is expected to possess specialised knowledge and skill might be held negligent in respect of treatment which when given by a general practitioner could be regarded as satisfactory.

The term **damage** in an action for negligence also has a special meaning. It must be distinguished from damages. Damage to the patient may be physical, mental or financial and includes such rather nebulous concepts as 'pain and suffering' which often clear up remarkably quickly once the case is settled. **Damages** are assessed by the court under a number of different headings, viz. loss of present and future earning power of the damaged person; actual medical and surgical care costs; and the reduction in quality of life which may be caused by lameness, deafness, blindness, and so on.

In order to achieve success in an action for negligence, a plaintiff (a patient or his representative) must be able to establish to the satisfaction of the court that—(1) the defendant (doctor) owed him a duty to conform to a particular standard of conduct, (2) the defendant was derelict and breached that duty, (3) the plaintiff suffered actual damage, and (4) the defendant's conduct was the direct or proximate cause of the incurred damage. If he can prove this, he is entitled to damages in terms of money.

Generally speaking, it is for the patient in an action for negligence to establish the guilt of the doctor, whose innocence is otherwise assumed. There are certain comparatively uncommon circumstances in which the doctrine of **res ipsa loquitur** (it speaks for itself) can be invoked. The three essential conditions considered necessary are: (1) the nature of injury suggests by common knowledge or expert evidence that without negligence, it does not occur, (2) the plaintiff must not contribute to his own injury, and (3) the defendant must be in exclusive control of the instrumentalities. In such cases, the error is so self-evident that if the case comes to trial, the doctor has to establish his innocence, rather than the patient having to prove the doctor's guilt. An example is afforded by the case of Cassidy *vs* Ministry of Health (1951, 2 KB 343), in which the plaintiff had undergone an operation in 1948 for the relief of Dupuytren's contracture affecting two fingers of one hand by an experienced full time surgeon of the hospital. The hand was splinted for some fourteen days but when the splint was removed, it was found that the two previously affected fingers were still bent and stiff and two other fingers were also affected. The maxim of res ipsa loquitur was successfully pleaded in this case. Lord Justice Denning said the patient went to the hospital to be cured of two stiff fingers but has come out with four stiff fingers and his hand is useless. That should not have happened, if due care had been taken. The doctrine of res ipsa loquitur has been held applicable in medical professional liability actions chiefly in cases of foreign bodies and slipping instruments in surgical procedures, burns from heating modalities, injury to a portion of the patient's body outside the field of treatment and gross prescription errors of toxic drugs.

An action for negligence in such cases may be brought against a medical practitioner in a civil or criminal court as the case may be. And, the negligence is accordingly known as civil or criminal negligence. It can also form the subject of inquiry by the Medical Council and even action under The Consumer Protection Act.

Civil Negligence (Malpractice)

This question arises: (1) when a patient or, in the event of his death, his relatives, sue a doctor in a civil court for compensation for the injury or death of the patient as the case may be, due to negligence of the doctor or (2) when the doctor brings a civil suit for realisation of his professional fees from the patient or his relatives who refuse to pay the same on the ground of mal-practice.

Failure in regard to the contractual obligations by a doctor when he agreed to treat a person constitutes civil malpractice. The burden of proving negligence and damage resulting therefrom lies with the patient, save the exception already mentioned. The question is whether there has been a want of competent care and competent skill to such an extent as to lead to bad results. The following are some examples.

Diagnosis: It is difficult to justify failure to X-ray a case of injury to bones or joints in which there is a doubt about diagnosis, and such a failure is frequently the basis of a successful plea in an action for negligence.

With the increasing use of the ophthalmoscope in diagnosis of conditions which are not essentially ocular, failure to use an ophthalmoscope or refer the patient to a specialist may be regarded as negligence.

The Medical Defence Union had a case in which a doctor failed to diagnose a chronic subdural haematoma with fatal result. The practitioner did not look for evidence of raised intracranial pressure with an ophthalmoscope and this fact weighed heavily with the council in deciding to settle the case. Though it is doubtful, if the doctor could have made the diagnosis of raised intracranial pressure had he looked but, there can be no doubt that, in view of the presenting symptoms and signs, he should have known that such an investigation should be undertaken by some competent person.

Failure to suggest consultation with a specialist under certain circumstances may be regarded as negligence.

Treatment: Some general guidelines must be remembered. As for example, every care should be exercised while using dangerous drugs, and excessive exposure of the patient to radiation should be avoided.

Following a course of chloramphenicol for cystitis with a total dose of 45 gm, the patient developed aplastic anaemia. In view of the dosage and the circumstances in which it was given, the claim by the widow and her children was settled for Pounds 7564 (MDU 1964).

A boy sustained an injury by a pellet from an air gun. During an operation to remove it from his arm, an unsuccessful attempt was made to locate the slug by repeated X-ray screening. Five days later, there was erythema of the skin of his arm which was followed by a large chronic ulcer requiring prolonged treatment and plastic surgery. He was left with permanent scarring and limitation of movement of his arm. The case was settled for Pounds 3000 (MDU 1962).

Duty to warn: The practitioner must warn the patient of any known or probable side-effects of a drug or device. Failure to do so renders the practitioner liable for the harm suffered by the patient and the injuries caused to third parties (e.g. while driving under the effect of a narcotic analgesic or while operating machinery).

Certificates: It is necessary that the certificate should be true to the best of doctor's knowledge and belief. He should fully satisfy himself about the accuracy of the statement contained therein and especially so if the certificate is based on the statement made by others, as for example, in mental illness.

Workmen's Compensation Act: Under the Act, provision is made for disabilities suffered as a result of industrial accidents or occupational disease, while in service, provided the worker himself was not responsible for the injury or was negligent. Medical practitioners who may be called to deal with such workmen should have a clear understanding of the provisions relating to this Act:

1. They are required to certify relating to fitness or unfitness for work.
2. They have to give an opinion and evidence upon which depends the decision as to whether an injury that a workman is suffering from, is the result of accident while at work.
3. They are required to certify the extent of disability of workmen arising from accidents or industrial diseases. The payment of compensation to the injured workmen is largely determined from such certificates.

The certifying of such a case is not as easy as the usual injury certificate. The worker may malinger and make false claims or he might have developed a neurosis after the accident. While a doctor should not approach any case with a suspicious mind, a very thorough examination is essential, keeping the worker under observation, if necessary, to assess the degree of disablement.

Criminal Negligence

This question arises in case of death or serious injury to a patient attributable to criminal negligence or undue interference by the doctor in the treatment of a patient. In case of death, a doctor may be prosecuted by the police and charged in a criminal court with having caused the death of his patient by a rash and negligent act amounting to culpable homicide under section 304-A IPC, if death was the result of gross ignorance, gross carelessness, gross negligence, or undue interference by him in his professional duties. Such cases are generally due to drunkenness or impaired efficiency from use of drugs by the doctor. In case of serious injury, the doctor may be charged under sections 336, 337 or 338 IPC. The degree of negligence must be so grave as to go beyond a matter of compensation. The following are *some examples:*

1. Gross carelessness during treatment, anaesthesia, operation or postoperative period.

2. Not doing sensitivity testing when indicated.
3. Injecting basal anaesthetics in a fatal dosage or in the wrong tissues.
4. Amputation of the wrong finger, operation on the wrong limb, removal of the wrong organ or errors in ligation of ducts.
5. Operation on the wrong patient.
6. Leaving instruments or sponges in the abdomen or any other part of the body.
7. Leaving tourniquets too long.
8. Giving wrong or infected blood.
9. Gangrene after too tight plastering or paralysis after splints.
10. Dressing with corrosives instead of bland liquids.
11. Performing a criminal abortion or criminal operation.
12. Mismanagement of delivery under the influence of alcohol/drugs.

In the case of Bateman, the death of a woman in child birth was ascribed to gross negligence on the part of the doctor. The case was that of a difficult labour requiring the application of forceps, version of the child, and manual removal of the placenta. A dead child was eventually delivered, but at the conclusion, the patient was ill and in poor condition. The doctor did not decide to send her to hospital until the fifth day. She died two days later. At autopsy, it was found that a part of uterus had been torn, urinary bladder ruptured, and large intestine crushed against the spine. Dr. Bateman was prosecuted for manslaughter (culpable homicide) and found guilty (R *vs* Bateman, 1925).

Indian position at present is to follow supreme court guidelines. Before filing a gross (304-A) negligence case, police should get opinion from medical board authorised for the purpose. A doctor should not be arrested or harassed before the said opinion is obtained. In a living will, a person can direct his physician regarding future action in a state wherein he cannot by himself decide the action, e.g. using the organs for donation, withdrawing CPR, etc.

Resuscitate or Not

There are occasions during treatment of a patient when no treatment options are available that would be medically beneficial to the patient. These conditions include chronic progressive disorders, such as malignancies, some neurologic diseases, extensive trauma to vital organs, advanced renal failure, etc. when there is a substantial chance of multiple complications from cardiopulmonary (GPR) resuscitation. In situations of this sort, a physician is justified in issuing a do-not-resuscitate (DNR) order. There is no legal duty to continue treatment once it has become futile in the opinion of qualified medical personnel. However, the decision that any treatment would be futile should be based on prevailing medical standards before a DNR order is unilaterally issued. Legally, the physician who provides futile treatment to a patient may be liable to the patient, the patient's family and the patient's insurer/s for the costs incurred. The leading cases of Commonwealth *vs* Edelin and Barber *vs* Superior Court clearly state that 'so long as the physician is not flagrantly mistaken about futile treatment and the patient's survival, the physician will not be subject to criminal liability'. Any civil liability would most likely arise only if the physician is negligent in diagnosing the patient's condition or even though the diagnosis is correct, if the physician incorrectly determines that the patient fits one of the DNR profiles. Despite this legal position, it is desirable to inform the patient and his family and also obtain a second opinion before a DNR order is issued. Choice to withdraw CPR can be left to the patients immediate relative, if no living will exists.

Q. 2.12. Mention the duties of a doctor with regard to administration of anaesthesia. Outline the procedure to investigate anaesthetic deaths.

Complaints of malpractice connected with anaesthesia may arise from death or illness caused by the anaesthetic used, burns, explosions or injuries caused to the patient while he is unconscious. Modern anaesthesia is complex and by no means free from danger. The following precautions are necessary:

1. As far as possible, an anaesthetist should be a specialist. He should not be under the effect of drink or drugs while on duty, and must possess the requisite experience for the procedure.

A child aged two years was administered general anaesthesia to permit an operation for the repair of a hernia. A critical situation arose during the operation when the child's heart stopped beating. This was corrected but the child re-mained unconscious until its death a month later. At autopsy, it was found that death was due to cerebral softening probably due to lack of oxygen (anoxia) during the operation. There had been a failure to change from an empty to a full cylinder of oxygen due to the incapacity of the anaesthetist who was a drug addict. The anaesthetist was charged with manslaughter on the ground that his condition and the manner in which he administered the anaesthetic showed an utter disregard for the patient's safety, and was found guilty (R. *vs* Gray, 1959).

2. Barring emergencies, the same practitioner should not administer anaesthesia and also perform the operation.
3. If he is employed by the surgeon, he must put down in writing the surgeon's instructions as regards anaesthesia or the anaesthetic solutions to be used and the procedure for the same. If he is employed by the hospital, he must use only those procedures which are authorised by the hospital. If he is a specialist, he must select that anaesthetic and procedure which he considers to be in the best interest of the patient.
4. Before administering the anaesthesia, he must properly identify the patient, obtain his informed consent save in emergency, examine him for physical fitness with special reference to disease, infection, allergy or any specific condition contraindicating the procedure or calling for special precautions. One person was to be operated on deflected septum in ENT OT. Another person was to be in surgical OT for a testicular biopsy. When the person was called and a testicular specimen was removed, the patient was annoyed, as there was a faux pass. Both the patients have similar name and one entered while the other was called (NCHS Surat).
5. He should position the patient carefully and check the drugs to be given including bottles and cylinders.
6. He should satisfy himself that the apparatus through which anaesthesia is to be administered is correctly set up and such faults as can be observed are duly corrected. He should also take precautions to prevent static electric spark and burns.
7. He should make sure that the proper drug is administered in the right manner, right site, right quantity and at the right time taking adequate precautions to avoid any mishap during the procedure.
8. He should satisfy himself that adequate first-aid equipment is ready for use at a moment's notice and the help of another person preferably a doctor or trained nurse is available in the case of emergency.
9. It is his duty to see that the patient is safeguarded till he recovers enough from the effects of anaesthesia to be left safely to the care of the nursing staff or relations. This aspect of care is too often neglected.
10. During anaesthesia on a female patient, a nurse or a female relation should invariably be present, unless the doctor happens to be a female doctor.
11. All deaths under anaesthesia must be reported to the authorities.

Investigation of Anaesthetic Deaths

The so-called anaesthetic deaths can be classified in two groups, viz. (1) deaths due to anaesthesia, and (2) deaths associated with anaesthesia and surgical procedure.

Deaths due to anaesthesia: It is the responsibility of the anaesthetist to maintain adequate anaesthesia, adequate respiratory function and proper functioning of the anaesthetic apparatus. Deaths that can be attributed to anaesthesia may be due to—(1) the anaesthetic agent, (2) the technique, (3) the apparatus, and (4) some functional problems.

Anaesthetic agent: The direct action of the anaesthetic agent may sometimes result in cardiac arrhythmia and cardiac arrest. Such an occurrence is possible with halothane especially in those cases where it has been administered earlier, even years before. The muscle relaxant, especially succinylcholine, may give rise to malignant hyperthermia, resulting in death. In as much as malignant hyperthermia and other forms of sensitivity are genetically controlled, the importance of taking a good preoperative history cannot be overemphasised.

Technique: Hypoxia due to obstruction of the airways or faulty gas connection commonly results from carelessness, lack of experience or unfamiliarity with the equipment. This is the most common but avoidable cause of fatality and medical malpractice. It is not commonly realised that an apparently satisfactory induction of anaesthesia may be due not so much to the presence of the anaesthetic as to the absence of adequate oxygen, and unless this is corrected, the patient may suffer from the immediate or long-term effects of hypoxia.

Equipment: Unfamiliarity with equipment commonly leads to mechanical problems, such as, kinked pipes, cross-tubes, overdosage, malfunction of the apparatus and explosion. These are potent causes of avoidable fatality.

Functional problems: The common problems relate to vagal inhibition; obstruction of the glottis due to spasm, tube or vomit; cardiac arrhythmia; and hypotension. The unconscious patient poses a special problem in regard to anaesthesia as he is unable to take corrective reflex action against inhalation of foreign material.

Deaths associated with anaesthesia: These are deaths which cannot be directly attributed to the anaesthetic agent. They may be due to—(1) injury, (2) condition of the patient, (3) postoperative events, (4) surgical mishaps, and (5) unforeseen problems.

Injury: With increasing complexities of life where disputes are settled in a violent manner, the injuries themselves may be such as to result in death, with anaesthesia and surgery playing no part. The surgical procedure is usually undertaken in the hope that some miracle may occur and the patient's life may be saved.

Condition of the patient: Sometimes, the physical condition of the patient, e.g. old age, diabetes, high blood pressure, etc. does not justify the risk of the procedure but the operation is undertaken as an emergency, as for example, in a case of a strangulated hernia.

Postoperative events: Fatalities due to phlebothrombosis, pulmonary embolism, hypostatic pneumonia, etc. which may follow are neither related to the anaesthetic procedure nor to surgery.

Surgical mishaps: Inadvertent tearing or cutting of a major blood vessel may result in death. In one case, in Bombay Hospital, Mumbai, India, while resecting a cervical rib, the subclavian artery was cut resulting in uncontrolled bleeding, leading to brainstem death in ten days time, the patient remaining unconscious throughout, despite several blood transfusions.

Unforeseen problems: Sufferers from haemoglobinopathies, especially sickle cell anaemia, are unduly susceptible to low oxygen tension in blood and this may pose a hazard to the unwary surgeon or anaesthetist. Coronary thrombosis may supervene in a patient operated upon for injuries. Transfusion hepatitis is not unknown. AIDS infection through transfusion is a distinct possibility. Delirium tremens may supervene operative management of fracture of the leg in a patient addicted to alcohol. Emergency coronary artery bypass graft surgery following a myocardial infarct or an operation for relief of bile duct obstruction in a jaundiced patient may prove fatal due to the disease process itself, even with or without surgical intervention. In all such cases, the risk is either unforeseen or undertaken on account of the urgency of the situation.

Investigation of the so-called anaesthetic deaths is by no means easy. The dividing line of responsibility between the surgeon and the anaesthetist cannot be well defined. While the surgeon is responsible for his decision to operate, the extent of operation, and whether to complete or abort it in the event of a problem, he is to be guided by the anaesthetist as to the patient's preoperative state and his condition during the operation. To maintain the patient's physical state by intravenous fluid replacement therapy is a function of the anaesthetist during operation, and of the surgical team, thereafter.

The presence of the surgeon, anaesthetist and forensic pathologist is essential so that agreement can be reached on what was actually found at autopsy. There should be a free and full discussion between them as regards the events leading to death as functional problems, like vagal inhibition, spasm of the glottis, cardiac arrhythmia, and hypotension leave no trace at autopsy. The pathological evidence is mainly intended: (1) to discover natural disease, (2) to exclude mechanical blockage, and (3) to demonstrate morphological changes in the brain due to hypoxia and these include diffuse severe leucoencephalopathy of the cerebral hemispheres, demyelination and obliteration of axons, and infarction of the basal ganglia. The following guidelines should be kept in mind:

1. It is essential that the surgical and anaesthetic devices, e.g. indwelling needles, intravascular canulae, self-retaining catheters, endotracheal tubes, monitoring electrodes, etc. that may have been introduced into the patient should not be removed before autopsy as their proper placement and patency may need to be checked.
2. In case of suspected malposition of an endotracheal tube, a pre-autopsy X-ray in AP and lateral views is necessary.
3. In case of failure of any equipment, expert examination is essential.
4. The pathologist may find significant pre-existing disease, e.g. lung disease, ischaemic heart disease, hypertension or diabetes. It is then necessary to determine, if it was noted or not, and if not, whether it should have been noted before the operation.
4. Care must be taken to detect any surgical emphysema, pneumothorax or air embolism. Where infusion or transfusion mishap is suspected, the possibility of air embolism should be considered.
5. Toxicological analysis may indicate overdosage of the anaesthetic or other therapeutic agent. Preoperative blood or fluid samples, if available, are helpful to check blood group in transfusion mishaps, and to assess any biochemical or enzymatic abnormalities, e.g. creatine phosphokinase in malignant hyperthermia, that may be responsible for death.

Q. 2.13. Write short notes on: (a) novus actus interveniens, (b) therapeutic misadventure, (c) product liability, (d) precautions against negligence, (e) contributory negligence, (f) vicarious liability, (g) euthanasia, (h) malingering, (i) Medical indemnity insurance.

Novus Actus Interveniens

The assailant is responsible for all the consequences of his assault—the immediate and remote—which link the injury to death. Sometimes, such a continuity of events is broken by an entirely new and unexpected happening which cannot reasonably be said to be a foreseeable complication. When this happens, novus interveniens (unrelated intervening action) is said to have occurred and the legal proceedings stand to be modified, as shown in the following examples:

A man bleeding from a punctured abdominal wound was brought to a hospital. The house surgeon examined the wound under an anaesthetic and during return to consciousness, the patient vomited and chocked. The anaesthetic would not have proved a danger to his life, if he had not misinformed the anaesthetist about the time of his last meal. It was the dead man's own mistake for which the assailant could not be held fully responsible, and the major charge failed.

An injured man was being taken in an ambulance to the hospital, with good chances of recovery, for suture of a limb artery which was cut during a stab injury. The ambulance overturned in a ditch with fatal result. The assailant could not be held fully responsible for the resulting death, and the major charge failed.

Similarly, the assailant cannot be held fully responsible for the death of the victim, if death could be attributed to leaving an instrument or sponge in the abdomen during surgery or accidental substitution of a poisonous drug in place of an innocuous one.

Therapeutic Hazards/Therapeutic Misadventure

It is common knowledge that many drugs (cytotoxic drugs, antihypertensives, steroids, etc.) have dangerous side effects and many therapeutic procedures (angiography, myelography, transfusion of blood or fluids, anaesthesia, surgery, etc.) carry inherent risks. By therapeutic misadventure is meant an injury or death of an individual due to some inadvertent or unintentional act by a doctor or his agent or hospital. Such mishap does not provide ground for negligence unless the doctor has failed to draw the patient's attention to such potential risks and also failed to take the possible steps to avoid such mishaps.

Product Liability

The manufacturers of drugs and medical equipment have a legal duty to protect the public against un-reasonable risks of injury associated with their products.

Injury or death due to drug reaction may result from negligence to use care in research and development of the drug and failure to provide proper instructions for its use. Injury or death of the patient may result from failure to exercise due care in design, manufacture, assembly, packaging, inspection or testing of the equipment.

The implantation of heart assist devices, artificial heart valves, permanent pacemakers, defibrillators and other prosthetic devices continue to be fraught with the usual legal problems inherent in any device implantation procedure or use.

To succeed in a claim for damages in general or under the Consumer Protection Act, the plaintiff must prove that—(1) the product was defective when it was sold (2) it did not conform to implied warranty because of the defect, and (3) the defect was the proximate cause of injury.

Precautions Against Negligence

While the principles to be followed in various situations have been dealt with at appropriate places, the following general guidelines should be remembered to avoid a charge of negligence, and action under the Consumer Protection Act:

1. The health care professional should keep abreast of the latest advances.
2. The diagnosis where possible should be confirmed by laboratory tests including biopsy. Every precaution should be taken to establish early diagnosis in cases of suspected cancer.

3. X-rays should be routinely advised in case of injury to bones or joints or where diagnosis is doubtful.
4. Consultation with a specialist should be suggested in obscure cases.
5. Immunisation/prophylactic antibiotic cover should be considered a necessity where there is danger of infection.
6. Sensitivity tests should be done before injecting preparations likely to cause anaphylactic shock.
7. The drugs to be administered by injection or otherwise should be verified.
8. No procedure should be undertaken beyond one's skill.
9. No experimental methods should be adopted without prior consent.
10. The instruments to be used for any procedure should be properly sterilised, safe and in proper working condition.

Contributory Negligence

This is defined as a concurrent negligence by the patient and doctor resulting in delayed recovery or harm to the patient. The negligence of both parties has contributed to this harm.

In suits of malpractice, if such conduct on the part of the patient is proved, the patient loses his right in whole or in part to claim damages against the doctor for any harm that ensued. However, the doctor is expected to foresee that the patient may harm himself and to warn him accordingly. Without giving such a warning, a doctor cannot plead contributory negligence. *Contributory negligence is a good defence for the physician in civil cases but not in criminal cases.* The burden of proving such negligence rests entirely on the doctor. The usual defence is that the patient did not give correct history or failed to give the doctor an opportunity to examine the case properly or did not follow the doctor's instructions regarding laboratory tests, drugs or diet, and in such circumstances, the medical practitioner cannot be blamed and the patient has to blame himself for his condition.

A doctor was injecting a person using a thin hypodermic needle. He had warned the patient to keep his arm steady lest the needle might break. The patient suddenly moved the arm. The needle broke and had to be removed surgically. The patient did not succeed in getting damages from the doctor.

A gynaecologist diagnosed the ailment of a woman as a fibroid tumour of the uterus. In answer to a specific question whether she was married, she had said 'no' and suppressed the fact that she had had an intercourse. The gynaecologist did not perform any tests for pregnancy although she was within the child bearing age group. At operation, she was found to be pregnant. Surgery was immediately terminated. The patient had a spontaneous abortion sometime later. She was not successful in recovering damages on charge of wrong diagnosis and unnecessary surgery.

A woman asked her six-year-old son to give bath to his two-year-old sister when she was busy cooking. The bath tub was not draining properly, the drain pipe having partly choked. The two-year-old child died of drowning. While it was held that the mother should not have entrusted the bathing of her two-year-old daughter to her six-year-old son, contributory negligence of the landlord who did not care to get the drain pipe repaired in time, was successfully pleaded in this case.

Vicarious Responsibility

Vicarious responsibility means that the liability exists in spite of the absence of blameworthy conduct on the part of the master. In law, a master is responsible for the negligent acts of his servants within the scope of his employment but is not so liable where he has employed an independent person to do something for him. Accordingly, hospital and nursing homes are liable for the negligent acts and omissions of their non-medical staff and full time junior medical staff. The honorary medical and other senior medical staffs are, however, in a different position because, between them and the managers of the hospital, there is no true relationship of master and servant. In addition, doctors being registered medical practitioners are responsible for their own actions. To summarise:

1. The hospital management is responsible for the negligent acts of resident physicians and interns in training who are considered employees when performing their normal duties.
2. The hospital management is not responsible for the negligent acts of senior medical staff, if it can be shown that the management exercised due care in selecting properly qualified and experienced staff.
3. A physician is responsible for the acts of residents and interns carried out under his immediate direction and control.
4. Physicians and surgeons are not responsible for acts of qualified nurses unless such acts are carried out under their immediate supervision and control.
5. A physician is responsible under the doctrine of 'negligent choice', if he refers his patient to an incompetent or inappropriate doctor. He is not so responsible otherwise.

In the case of Darling *vs* Charleston Community Memorial Hospital (211 NE 2d 253, 111 1965), the hospital was held liable for the negligent act of its staff physician. The physician had attended a patient whose leg had been broken in a football game. Eventually, the leg had to be amputa-ted. The hospital was held liable for failing to require the physician to hold consultations with the specialists in the orthopaedic field.

In the case of Peterson *vs* Dumouchel (431 P 2d 1963, 1967), the hospital was held liable for the negligent act of its staff surgeon. In that decision, a staff surgeon, called into see a child with a fractured jaw, left the hospital when surgery was being performed by a dentist. The child suffered brain damage from the negligent administration of the anaesthetic.

In Joiner *vs* Mitchell County Hospital (186 SE 2d 307, 1971), the patient's wife took him to the hospital for severe chest pain. The emergency room physician gave him a prescription and sent him home. His condition worsened and he died of heart attack on the way back to the hospital. The court found that the widow stated a good cause of action against the hospital and the doctor.

In case of Dickenson *vs* Mailliard (175 NW 2d 588, Iowa, 1970), the court held that the hospital was not liable for the negligence of a physician when the physician is an independent contractor and not an employee in the true sense or when the negligence relates to a matter of professional judgement since the hospital does not and cannot exercise any control over the judgement. The patient in that case had been involved in a wreck. The physician in that case did not diagnose fractured dislocations of the fifth and sixth cervical vertebrae.

Euthanasia

Euthanasia literally means mercy killing or putting a person to painless death especially in case of incurable suffering or when life becomes purposeless as a result of mental or physical handicap (eu = good; Thanatos = death).

This question arises on three occasions, viz. (1) at the beginning of life (at birth), (2) at the end of natural life (terminal stage), and (3) when a person is severely impaired as a result of brain damage (unforeseen mishap). The author offers his views on the problem with special reference to the purpose of life and duty of the doctor.

The main purpose of life is to be happy, to make others happy, if possible, to grow old gracefully, and to die with dignity. The main duty of the doctor is to relieve pain and suffering, even if the measures he takes may incidentally shorten life.

At birth: The problem arises in the case of a physically or mentally handicapped infant. Since the infant is not able to make his own decision, the matter rests with the parents or doctors, aided or confused by the law of the land. The decision should be based on the quality of life the child can expect and its consequent impact on the parents, society and the resources of the state. The blessings of early painless death can be balanced against the purposeless life, the probable suffering of the child, and its consequent impacts. In addition, the care of the child after death of parents also needs consideration.

Terminal stage: The conscious dying patient can make his own decision. The refusal to consent to any treatment whatsoever always rests with the patient. There is no moral obligation on the doctor to preserve life at any cost and if, in the course of good terminal care, the use of drugs actually hastens death, it would not amount to crime or malpractice because the ensuing death would be the result of natural causes.

Unforeseen mishap: In the case of a person who is severely impaired as a result of brain damage, it is now possible to sustain life, but in a state of animation, by artificial means. The brain damage may be due to violence, poisoning or natural causes but in all these cases, the brain suffers hypoxic damage from which it cannot recover, irrespective of the treatment given. When medical treatment has nothing to offer, the patient can be allowed to die in comfort and with dignity. In such cases, one wonders if treatment is prolonging death or life. In the former event, for all practical purposes, the patient is dead and the decision to continue or terminate artificial means of support to life should depend upon the subsequent use of the body for transplant purposes, if possible. Such a step would also save the resources of the State for more rational uses.

A Michigan prosecutor has charged euthanasia guru Jack Kevorkian with first-degree premeditated murder over his videotaped mercy-killing of a terminally ill patient. So far, he was well known for his assisted suicide crusade for which he has been acquitted each time by the Court. He has now taken a step further, and practised euthanasia.

Oakland county prosecutor David Gorcyca told a press conference on Wednesday that Dr Kevorkian was also being charged with criminal assistance to a suicide and delivery of a controlled substance in connection with the mercy-killing of Thomas Youk by lethal injection. The 52-year-old suburban Detroit man, who was afflicted with Lou Gehrig's disease, died on September 17, 1998, after giving his consent.

Part of the videotape was aired on national television on Sunday by CBS network along with an interview in which Dr Kevorkian said his action was meant as a direct challenge to authorities to charge him or leave alone to end the long stalemate over his assisted suicide crusade.

CBS, whose decision to air the tape sparked outrage around the country, turned over the videotape to Michigan prosecutors after being issued a subpoena. Dr Kevorkian was sentenced for his act of assisted suicide (euthanasia). Recently discharged after completion of prison term.

Malingering

Malingering means a deliberate attempt on the part of the patient to deceive the doctor. The person generally feigns a disease. This may be resorted to for several purposes. Personnel in army, navy and air force who are not allowed to leave their jobs feign insanity; business people also feign insanity to avoid the consequences of a business transaction; a worker may feign certain industrial disease to get compensation; an assaulted person may exaggerate the effects of injury to bring it within the purview of grievous hurt; and a prisoner may feign a disease to avoid hard work.

It is very difficult for a person to live continually in a state of suspense; prolonged and careful observation is normally sufficient to detect malingering. Lack of medical knowledge prevents a malingerer from conforming to any known type of disease and if the malingerer and his relatives or associates are interviewed separately, their history about the ailment may be so different that malingering can be easily detected. The detection of malingering, however, is not always easy. Mistakes have been made by the inexperienced, e.g. when psychological impotence following trauma to spine or genitals and retrograde amnesia following concussion have been attributed to malingering. In the former case, the impotence may be construed as an attempt to get more compensation while in the latter case, the prosecution or defence may suggest that this selective loss of memory is merely a pretence to escape answering inconvenient questions. In such cases, consultation with an expert is necessary.

Medical Indemnity Insurance

A medical practitioner in his daily work constantly faces the risk of being involved in proceedings against him on grounds of negligence, misconduct, etc. The obvious precaution is to insure as far as possible against such risks with some medical defence society. Such societies undertake not only to conduct the defence but also to pay such damages as may be awarded against the doctor.

If any suggestion of negligence or malpractice is made against a doctor who is thus insured, he should refer the matter at once to his medical defence society. He should not even express regret that the treatment has not turned out to be as successful as was hoped, since this may easily be converted into an implicit admission of liability by him. The freedom from worry and anxiety as well as from expense which such societies ensure, makes it absolutely essential for every practicing doctor to join one in his own interest.

Medical indemnity insurance in India is available through Oriental Insurance, National Insurance and others.

Q. 2.14. What are the guidelines for medical research?

The guidelines are prescribed by the ICMR (Indian Council of Medical Research). Any research proposal must be approved by the Institutional Ethics Committee. An agreement is made between the researchers, sponsors and the Institutional authority. Informed consent is a prerequisite for accepting any volunteer, patient for examination and investigation under the research project.

Q. 2.15. What is IEC? How is it formed? What are its functions?

IEC is constituted by the Institutes undertaking research. It shall contain odd members 9, 11, etc. of member. The chairman is from outside institute. One lawyer, one lady member, one social worker must be included. Functions—To review the work from time to time and check whether the work is progressing as per procedure.

PRACTICE OF LEGAL MEDICINE

It will be apparent from the discussion of the various topics in this book that medicolegal procedures and interpretation of medicolegal reports, e.g.: (i) autopsy examination and interpretation of pathological changes as well as (ii) interpretation of injury reports and laboratory reports, are not simple procedures. They involve an understanding of—(1) time sequences, (2) physical data related to the direction of traumatic forces, and (3) the role of poison and diseases, if any, suspected to have played a part in terminating the life of the assaulted/deceased. Therefore, if justice is to be done, there must be a proper interpretation and explanation of the findings related to the scene and circumstances of assault/death. While in most instances, the autopsy report, injury report and laboratory reports are self-explanatory, the observations and opinions in such reports reflect special interpretation of scene and circumstances of assault/death which may be subject to doubt or better alternative explanation when reviewed by another expert. This is not to say that the medical officer who examined the assaulted victim or performed the autopsy, is biased in his approach or medical testimony. It only means that an alternative explanation may explain the findings in an equally satisfactory or sometimes even better manner.

Since the medical officer, who examines the injured victim or performs the autopsy, appears as a prosecution witness, his testimony is brought out as a result of questions from the public prosecutor (District Attorney). Unless, therefore, the other party is also knowledgeable on such matters and appreciates the intricacies of an injury report, postmortem report and laboratory reports, it cannot provide the best possible defence for its client. This problem is all the more acute in those places where (a) cold storage facilities to preserve dead bodies are not available, (b) laboratory facilities are conspicuous by their glaring inadequacy, (c) autopsies are done by medical officers who have hardly had any training or experience in this field, (d) health care practitioners are neither specially trained to collect and preserve evidence from live victims or perpetrators of crime nor are they trained to testify in court regarding their examination, and (e) senior experts are not available for assistance in the correct interpretation of unusual findings, including postmortem artifacts.

It is amazing that many insurance companies employ attorneys to write policies and contracts, actuaries and statisticians to calculate the odds against life, physicians to tell them which diseases are bad, and investigators to inquire into what happened and yet continue to pay huge amounts of money (even thousands of dollars) on the basis of poorly conducted autopsies and poorly worded reports, but seldom consult anyone who has the necessary experience in the forensic field.

With the complexities of life, forensic medicine is broadening in its scope and forensic expertise is expected in cases pertaining to therapeutic misadventures, charges of police brutality, drug overdosage, human rights abuses, occupational and environmental hazards, auto and blunt injury evaluation, sexual assaults, and child abuse, which come before the court. It is obvious that if the forensic aspects of such cases are not interpreted in proper perspective, an innocent person may be convicted, a convicted person may undergo higher sentence than he deserves or a criminal may be acquitted. If, therefore, justice is to be done, the defence must also take advantage of the services of a practicing forensic expert who can interpret autopsy findings or medicolegal reports in proper perspective. The medical expertise of such an expert is associated with a thorough understanding of the related legal issues. He is the proper person to advise on any possible inconsistencies between apparent injury/death scene and actual scientific findings, so crucial in many civil and criminal cases. He is cognizant of the true significance of artifacts and the serious misinterpretations to which they are subject.

At the present moment, in some countries, there is practically very little scientific opposition to the prosecution's presentation of evidence and interpretation of laboratory reports. This too often means that contrary opinions and alternative possibilities are not presented in court in a comparatively expert manner. And this is not fair as it may create the perception that justice is not being done in a discipline dedicated to the discovery and appreciation of truth. This pitfall needs to be avoided by provision for the services of a medicolegal expert to assist the defence also.

On a number of occasions, such assistance is indeed essential to interpret photographs and reports of pathologists and laboratory scientists or else, the one sided interpretation of data, if unchallenged, could lead to serious miscarriage of justice. *In fact, well-informed opposition is the need of the day. It can also improve medical standards.*

INTRODUCTION TO FORENSIC NURSING: A NEW PERSPECTIVE IN HEALTH CARE

Virginia Lynch, MSN, RN Fellow, American Academy of Forensic Sciences President, International Association of Forensic Nurses, USA

As the practice of medicine becomes more sophisticated, it becomes necessary for hospital administrators, physicians and nurses to realise that medical practice can no longer be restricted to treatment only. Emergency department physicians and trauma care centres handle a number of cases which involve legal problems also. The proper and complete management of such patients requires that the legal facets of their case are handled with as much care as is exercised in treatment. While the various medical specialists do a fine job as far as treatment is concerned, a serious gap exists in attending to the legal facets in an equally satisfactory manner. This is an area where forensic nurse specialists can play a vital role. Their nursing background combined with medicolegal education is ideally suited for this purpose.

The management of a victim of violence involves team work where nurses form an integral part. Physicians are normally tuned to treat patients. Most of them do not have specific awareness of forensic requirements. Vital forensic evidence is frequently not collected, lost or mishandled, resulting in miscarriage of justice. Health care providers, who treat victims of violence, have a responsibility to protect the patient's legal rights also. The service of forensic nurses and other professionals with forensic knowledge would unquestionably go a long way to fulfil this need.

Marching by the times, some Institutions now provide facilities for the study and practice of forensic nursing through various programmes, such as (a) internship in the medical examiner's office, (b) critical care programmes integrating forensic applications, and (c) elective studies in some universities. The basic aim is to utilise the untapped potential of nurses in the overall management, both medical and legal, of the diverse situations affecting various patients, which is the need of the day.

While the various areas where the expertise of the forensic nurse can be utilised with advantage would be delineated gradually, it is apparent that they are well suited to handle certain situations, such as victims of: (1) trauma, (2) domestic violence, (3) sexual assault, (4) drug abuse, and (5) handling certain cases of death investigation.

The advantages of utilising the expertise of forensic nurse specialists are many: As the forensic nurse will collect and preserve evidence in the emergency department and other situations, it will leave the physician free to attend to his and her medical duties without the anxiety of having to spend time in court. It will also ensure proper justice to the victim, the medicolegal evidence having been well cared for by the forensically trained nurse.

About half to two-thirds of the medical Examiner's case load constitute natural deaths which do not need high investigative profile. It can be handled by the forensic nurse with impunity, thus enabling the medical examiner to devote more attention to other cases where it is necessary. The Canadian experience indicates that: (1) the service of forensic nurse investigators suits the next-of-kin, hospitals, doctors, and medical examiner system, (2) supplements the role of police investigators, (3) meets with most problems of survivors on account of personal contact of the nurse investigator, and (4) significantly reduces the resentment and stigmata of death investigation. This model of inquiry in sudden death cases is being adapted in progressive death investigation systems in some countries.

Investigation of Trauma

Emergency department nurses are routinely involved in the management of patients who are admitted for trauma care. The injuries may be crime-related or self-inflicted. These cases require that the nurse is specifically aware of the manner in which (1) evidence should be collected and preserved, and (2) injury documented.

Evidence: It is important to recognise and preserve trace evidence through careful handling of the patient's clothing and personal property. Clothing worn at the time of the incident may contain trace evidence (hair, fibres, paint chips, broken glass) and stains (blood, semen) that may link the assailant with the victim or crime scene.

Careful observation of defects in clothes can be compared to the victim's wounds. This may provide a hint as to the type of assault weapon. Some self-inflicted wounds may be confirmed by non-alignment of the clothing damage with the injuries.

In cases involving hit and run accidents, tearing of the clothes, grease marks, road dirt, glass particles, metal particles, paint fragments, etc. may all assist in reconstructing the event and even identifying the type of vehicle involved.

In firearm deaths, gunshot residues on the clothing may provide vital evidence about the range of discharge and identity of the ammunition. Bullets found in clothing or bandages or removed from the body need to be carefully handled. They may show markings which may help to identify the firearm from which it was fired. It is important to wrap the bullet with cotton to prevent rattling and place each bullet in a separate container, preferably a clear plastic one so that it is visible from outside, and the container sealed and labelled with the following information, viz. (1) victim's name, (2) medical identification number, (3) date and time of recovery, (4) site of recovery, (5) signature of the medical officer who removed the bullet and/or the nurse who packed it, and (6) other information in relation to chain of custody.

Clothing should never be discarded or thrown on the floor, as this can result in cross-contamination of trace evidence with debris from the treatment environment. If a victim can remove clothes, it should be done with the victim standing on a clean large sheet of paper. This will catch any trace evidence that may be dislodged.

In medicolegal cases, there should be a written order in the chart with instructions, such as: (a) hold clothing for medical examiner/coroner, (b) save clothing for the police, (c) chain of custody for clothing, (d) air dry clothing and hold as evidence.

Evidence may be obscured by emergency trauma care. The original characteristics of the wounds may change due to surgical extension, excision or natural healing process. It is then not possible to reconstruct the original injury pattern. The only way to preserve this potential valuable evidence is to: (1) sketch the wound on body diagram or preferably photograph it prior to alteration, (2) record its location and measurements, and (3) document the alterations due to therapy. This is helpful to reconstruct the original injury pattern in subsequent investigation or at autopsy.

If a bullet hole is cored during treatment, the initial appearance of the wound should be recorded and the cored tissue saved for gunshot residue analysis. The injury should be sketched or photographed prior to alteration. Any hair that may be shaved during treatment must be preserved.

Rules of evidence require a chain of custody for each item recovered from the patient. This includes physical and trace evidence, laboratory specimens of blood/body fluids, clothing and personal articles.

Every unexpected death has actual or potential medicolegal aspects that must be recognised. While the best specimen for hospital use is the most recent one, the best for forensic purpose is usually the first or the initial one. After hours or days of intensive therapy, it will be impossible to determine what the concentration of alcohol, carboxyhaemoglobin or drug was at the time of injury. Hence, although the hospital may not make use of a specimen drawn at the scene of injury, there is an obligation to retain it for the FSL or public prosecutor. Availability of proper specimens to decipher objective data is necessary for the administration of justice.

Where criminal activity or accidental death is suspected, special forensic care is necessary to handle even the dead body. It should be left in the same condition as it was prior to death, with tubings, catheters and appliances in place, till a forensic assessment is made. Thus, injuries can be distinguished from therapeutic alterations. Therapeutic needle punctures can be marked by a pen to distinguish them from others which are not so. Cleaning of the body and packing of body orifices should not be done. If the victim died of gunshot injury or sexual assault, the hands should be enclosed in paper bags to protect any evidence, such as gunshot residues or fragments of skin or hair beneath the finger nails.

Documentation: Injuries should be described with special reference to anatomical landmarks. One should be familiar with the appropriate terminology required to describe them.

The injuries are primarily categorised as (This subject is dealt with in detail in the Chapter 16 on 'Mechanical Injuries':

Sharp force injuries: These include stab wounds and incised wounds.

Blunt force injuries: These usually result from assaults, abuse, accidents or resuscitative intervention. Abrasions, bruises, lacerations and fractures are blunt force injuries resulting from impact of a blunt object against the body.

Fast force injuries: These are usually gunshot injuries. Their understanding requires some knowledge of wound ballistics so as to recognise any particular pattern. In documenting these injuries, it is necessary to understand certain terms commonly used in their description, such as entrance wound, exit wound, shored exit wound, gunshot residue, stippling, abrasion ring, etc. (These and other vital facts necessary to document gunshot injuries are addressed in the Chapter 17 on 'Firearms and Firearm Injuries'.)

Dicing injuries: These usually result from motor vehicle accidents. They are characteristic right-angled or V-shaped cuts caused by the diced or cubical fragments of tempered glass of a broken side or rear window being struck by or striking the victim. (This subject is dealt with in detail in the Chapter 21 on 'Transportation Injuries'.)

Bite mark injuries: Human bite marks are usually indicative of abuse and are generally associated with sexual assault. Animal bite marks are usually accidental but the owner may be liable, if the animal is neglected, tortured or trained into causing an injury or if a dangerous animal, e.g. a tiger escapes captivity by negligence or other illegal action. (Please see the topic 'Forensic Odontology' in the Chapter 4 on "Identification in Mass Disasters".)

Patterned injuries: These are injuries the pattern of which reflects the identity or the nature of the wounding object. (Also, please see the topic 'Injury Patterns' in the Chapter 16 on "Mechanical Injuries".)

Defense wounds: These usually indicate the posture of a victim against an attack. While they are most often found on the hands and arms, they may be located on any part of the body used to shield. They may be either sharp or blunt depending on the weapon used. (For further information, see the topic 'Defence Wounds' in the Chapter 16 on "Mechanical Injuries".)

Hesitation wounds: These are usually sharp force superficial wounds made just prior to the fatal injury or wounds that may be in the form of old, superficial, parallel scars, on the wrists and neck, which are indicative of previous attempts at suicide. (For further information, please refer to the topic 'Hesitation Cuts' in the Chapter 16 on "Mechanical Injuries".)

Domestic Violence

Abuse involving children, elderly patients and battered women is a universal problem that varies only in quantity for any given society. Many victims of physical and emotional abuse or neglect do not even realise that they are victims. Often, it is the emergency department nurse who is the first to identify the victim as a victim. Forensic nursing emphasises awareness of these crimes.

Nursing assessment in this area calls for attention to characteristic battering patterns of injuries to the face, neck, breast(s), abdomen, back and genitalia. Also suspicious is any set of multiple injuries to various parts of the body as well as injury during pregnancy. Adequate documentation is crucial in all such cases. (For further information, please refer to the Chapter 23 on 'Violence in the Home'.)

Sexual Assault (SANE/SART)

Forensically trained nurses are being utilised in the United States for examination of victims of sexual assault. The primary responsibility of the sexual assault nurse examiner (SANE) is to identify signs of physical and emotional trauma and to collect evidence. The nurse examiner performs a general physical and pelvic examination paying particular attention to signs of minor trauma, abrasions, contusions and lacerations. The pelvic examination serves to document common findings, such as introital tears, perineal erythema and perineal ecchymoses. Swabs and slides are made as required. The help of medical staff is utilised for treatment of concomitant injuries. Following the examination, the nurse examiner discusses prevention of possible pregnancy and sexually transmitted disease. Where necessary, follow-up appointments and consultation or referral for crisis intervention or other agencies, such as child protection, social service, etc., are arranged for the victim and her family. Based on the findings of examination, evidence collected, laboratory data and their interpretation, the nurse examiner testifies in court as an expert witness, and assists the administra-tion of justice. The special organisation which coordinates these services is known as the Sexual Assault Resource Team (SART).

Implementation of this approach:

1. Decreases the workload on the emergency physician.
2. Provides prosecutors with greater accuracy of evidence.
3. Reduces emotional trauma of the victim and her family.
4. Provides law enforcement officials with a liaison who is knowledgeable of medicolegal issues.
5. Ensures justice to the victim.

For detailed information, reference may be made to the topic 'Rape' in the Chapter 27 on "Natural Sexual Offenses".

Conclusion

Forensically educated and trained nurse can be a critical component in the recognition and proper collection of forensic evidence in many situations with medico-legal implications. With the emerging application of DNA profiling, virtually any scrape of genetic evidence, such as blood, semen or tissue, may provide the crucial answer to the identification and apprehension of the perpetrator of crime.

The emergency department nurse can significantly aid law enforcement efforts by retaining evidence, maintaining chain of custody, preventing changes in the physical condition of evidence, and assuring significant testimony in court, as she/he is the first to see the patient and relatives, first to handle property, first to collect and deal with laboratory specimens, and first to contact potential sources or obtain data necessary to determine the cause and manner of death. While the physicians will provide necessary medical care, the forensic nurse will assume the responsibility of legal care, thus filling a gap in the total care of the patient.

PART 2: Forensic Medicine and Pathology

Section 2

3

Personal Identification

Q. 3.1. What is identity? When does the question of identity arise?

By identity, we mean establishment of the individuality of a person.

Identification of a person or dead body means the recognition of that person or dead body. It is based on certain physical characteristics unique to that individual. It may be complete or partial. Complete identification means the absolute fixation of the individuality of a person. Partial identification means ascertainment of only some facts (e.g. race, sex, age, stature, etc.) about the identity while the others remain still unknown.

In the living, in civil courts, identification is required in cases, such as insurance, pension, and inheritance claims; marriage, disputed sex; and missing persons. In criminal courts, it is required in cases, such as absconding soldiers and criminals; persons accused of assault, rape, murder, etc.; impersonation; and interchange of newborn babies in maternity hospitals.

In the dead, identification is required: (1) in cases of fire, explosion and accidents, (2) when an unknown dead body is found on the road, in the fields, railway compartment or in water, and (3) in cases of decomposed bodies, mutilated bodies or skeletal remains. Accurate identification is mandatory for establishment of the corpus delicti after homicide since unclaimed bodies, portions of dead body or bones, are sometimes brought forward to support a false charge. The term *corpus delicti* means the body of the offence (essence of crime and not the physical body of the victim) and in a case of homicide, it includes: (1) positive identification of the body, and (2) proof of its death by a criminal act of the accused. Once the identity is established, a trial for murder can take place on circumstantial evidence, even in the absence of recovery of the dead body.

Visual identification is not reliable in a majority of cases. Therefore, two important marks of identification must be noted and described in detail in all certificates relating to the living or the dead. The description of the identification mark, e.g. a mole, should include all relevant particulars, such as its situation with reference to an anatomical landmark, size, colour and other specific characteristics, such as raised or flat, fixed to the skin or free, and hairy or non-hairy. Where no distinct mark is available, a left thumb impression may be taken.

The **points to be considered** for the establishment of identity are: (1) race, (2) religion, (3) sex, (4) age, (5) general development, (6) congenital features, viz. personal appearance; anthropometric measurements; fingerprints or dactylography including poroscopy (Locard's method); footprints; and congenital malformations, viz. birth marks or moles, etc.,

(7) acquired peculiarities, viz. occupational marks; tattoo marks; scars; and acquired malformations (deformities), (8) miscellaneous data, and (9) obliteration of identity. The information is considered in Combination. It is not of much value when considered individually.

Race

It can be determined from: (1) clothes, (2) complexion, (3) hair, (4) eyes, and (5) lips. The skeletal factors which can help in determination of race are discussed in the next chapter.

Clothes: Traditional Indian dress (*dhoti* and *sari*) is different from traditional Western dress (suit and skirt).

Complexion: The skin is dark in Negroes (in USA, the term used is black), brown in Indians, and fair in Europeans. Decomposition readily produces changes in external appearance. This is, therefore, of limited value.

Hair: The hair of Indians are black, long and fine; of Chinese and Japanese black and thick; of blacks wooly, short, curly (and arranged in tight spirals); and of Europeans fair, light brown, reddish or blonde, and of any length.

Eyes: Indians have a dark or brown iris. Europeans have a blue or grey iris. Variation in colour, however, is common.

Lips: Negros have thick lips which are slightly everted.

Religion

Hindus and Mohammedans form the largest proportion of the population of India. Traditionally speaking, certain externals of dress and religious markings may serve to distinguish them.

Hindu males are normally not circumcised. The sacred thread, necklace of wooden beads and religious marks on the forehead, if present, are helpful. The dress is of help sometimes. Hindu females generally put on saris and paint vermillion on their head. They may have a nose-ring in the left ala of nose, fewer openings on the helix for ear-rings and tattoo marks.

Mohammedan males are normally circumcised. They may have corns and callosities on lateral aspects of knees and feet due to their attitude during prayer. Mohammedan females normally put on trousers and have no vermillion mark on their head. They have a nose-ring in the septum, several openings on the helix for ear-rings and usually no tattoo marks (Fig. 3.1).

Q. 3.2. Describe the evidence on which sex is determined in normal cases and in doubtful cases. Give its medicolegal aspects.

Q. 3.3. Write short notes on nuclear sexing with special reference to the Barr body and the Davidson body.

Sex

The evidence of sex is divided into: (1) the most certain, (2) the highly probable, and (3) the presumptive.

In **normal cases,** in the living, the most *certain evidence* of sex depends on the possession of ovaries in the female and testes in the male. The *highly probable evidence* of sex includes the possession of sexual structures, e.g. developed breasts, female distribution of hair, appropriate physical development and distribution of subcutaneous fat, and the vagina in the female; and the absence of breast tissue, male distribution of hair, appropriate physical development, and a penis in the male. The *presumptive evidence* of sex includes the outward appearance of the individual, the features and general contours of the face, the presence or distribution of hair upon it or evidence of shaving, the length of head hair, the clothes, the figure, the habits, the inclinations, the voice, etc.

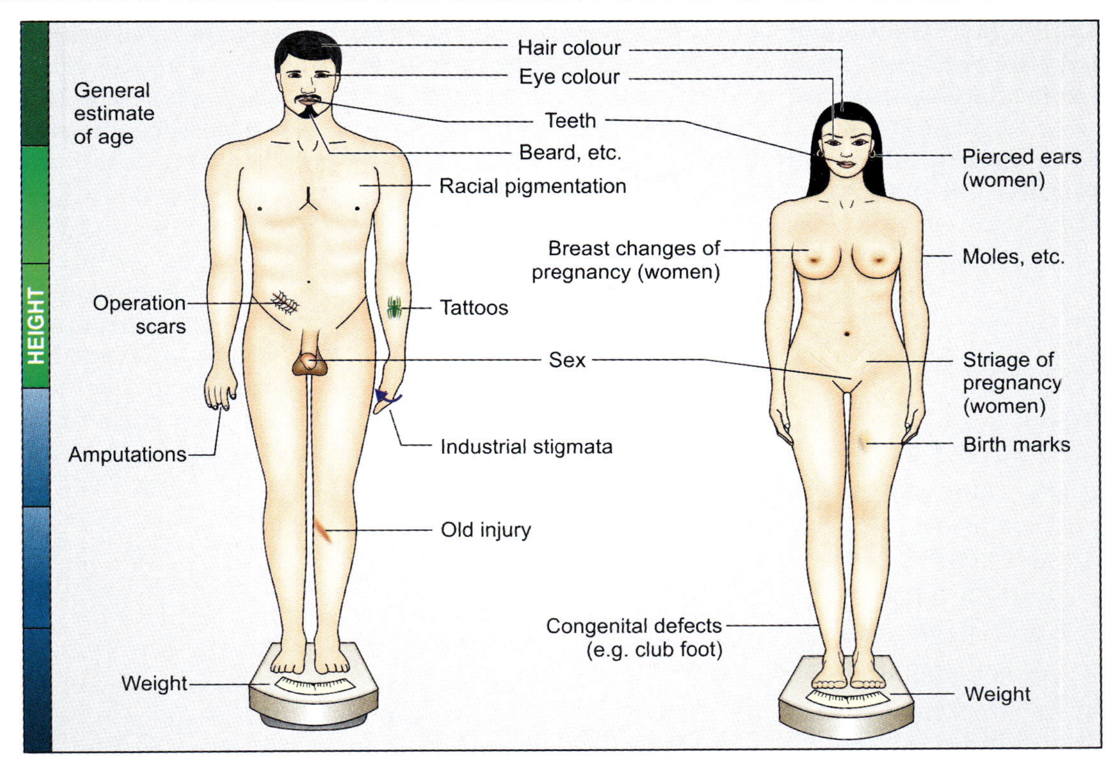

Fig. 3.1: External features useful for establishing identity

In **doubtful cases,** the true sex of a person can be determined from a—(1) thorough external examination, (2) thorough internal examination, (3) gonadal biopsy, (4) nuclear sexing, and (5) study of sex *chromosomes*.

Nuclear sexing, a method of sexing cells, may be of help in determining sex in doubtful cases, decomposed bodies, mutilated bodies, and fragmentary remains. A small planoconvex mass of chromatin, known as the *Barr body,* is present close to the nuclear membrane. In the buccal smear, the percentage of cells showing the presence of such Barr bodies varies from about 20 to 80 in the females (chromatin positive) and 0 to 4 in the males (chromatin negative). Females also show a thin drumstick-like projection on the polymorph nucleus—a *'Davidson body'* in about 6 per cent of cells.

The *study of sex chromosomes* involves demonstration of sex chromosomes (XX or XY) in the cells that are dividing, e.g. blood stains, cartilage, bone marrow, teeth pulp and hair. The Y chromosome in the male is fluorescent to quinacrine. Root sheath cells of hair are of special interest, they resist putrefaction and both Barr body and Y chromosome can be demonstrated in them.

Medicolegal aspects: Sex determination is important as regards identification, inheritance, marriage, divorce, liability for military service, sexual offenses, participation in Olympic games, etc.

Q. 3.4. Write briefly about variations from normal sex.

Q. 3.5. Comment on: (1) intersex states (2) concealed sex.

Variations from Normal Sex

Variations from normal sex are due to defective development of the single mass of cells from which the sex organs of both sexes are derived. This may result in—(1) the presence of certain male and female structures in the same individual (intersex states) or (2) imperfect differentiation of external genitalia, viz. (a) small penis resembling a clitoris, (b) enlarged clitoris resembling a penis, (c) bifid scrotum resembling labia majora or (d) fused labia majora resembling a scrotum.

Intersex States

These are conditions in which male and female characters, e.g. gonads, physical form and sexual behaviour co-exist in varying proportions in the same individual. They are classified into four groups, viz:

1. Gonadal agenesis,
2. Gonadal dysgenesis,
3. True hermaphro-ditism, and
4. Pseudohermaphroditism.

Gonadal agenesis: In this condition, the sexual organs (testes or ovaries) have never developed. This abnormality is determined very early in foetal life. These cases are chromatin negative.

Gonadal dysgenesis: In this condition, the external sexual structures are present but the testes or ovaries fail to develop at puberty. The most important examples of such conditions are: (1) the Klinefelter syndrome in the male, and (2) Turner syndrome in the female.

In the *Klinefelter syndrome,* the boy grows and develops normally initially but puberty is delayed. On examination, one or more of the three classical features become apparent: the testicles are small and firm in consistency; gynaecomastia may develop; and there may be signs of eunuchoidism, such as long arms and legs, scanty pubic and axillary hair, and poor or no beard growth. Nuclear sexing indicates that he is chromatin positive, like a female, and that his sex chromosome pattern is XXY (47 chromosomes). He is naturally sterile and cannot procreate.

The Turner syndrome is characterised by three principal features, viz. sexual infantilism, short stature and congenital anomalies, e.g. webbing of neck, cubitus valgus, coarctation of aorta, red green colour blindness, renal abnormalities and osteoporosis. Sexual infantilism is manifested by primary amenorrhoea and consequent sterility; lack of breast development with widely spaced nipples, and hypoplastic areolae; scanty pubic hair; infantile external genitalia, uterus, and fallopian tubes; and streak ovaries containing no ovarian follicles but fibrous tissue. Nuclear sexing indicates that she is chromatin negative, like a male, and her sex chromosome pattern is XO (45 chromosomes). She is naturally sterile and cannot bear a child.

True hermaphroditism: In this rare condition, also known as double sex, the external genitalia may be of both sexes and the internal genitalia may consist of both ovaries and testes or ovotestes. The nuclear sex is usually female but may be male. Hypospadias, cryptorchidism, and inguinal herniae are frequent findings in such cases.

Pseudohermaphroditism: In this condition, there is lack of clear-cut differentiation of the external genitalia while the internal genitalia are of only one sex. They are classified as male or female according to the presence of testes (nuclear sex XY) or ovaries (nuclear sex XX), independent of anomalies of external genitalia which may be the reverse of normal.

The *medicolegal complications* created by hermaphroditism pertain chiefly to marriage, inheritance and civil rights.

Concealed Sex

Criminals sometimes attempt to conceal their sex by a change of dress or other methods to avoid detection. This can be detected by physical examination.

Q. 3.6. How is age determined for medicolegal purposes?

Q. 3.7. Write a short essay on temporary teeth and permanent teeth.

Q. 3.8. Comment on ossification of bones from a medicolegal standpoint to determine age.

Q. 3.9. By an examination of a complete skeleton, how will you opine that the bones belong to a female aged above 18 years and below 25 years?

Age

The age of an individual, *up to about 25 years,* can be determined, within a range of one to two years, from a combination of data provided by—(1) teeth, (2) ossification of bones, (3) height and weight, and (4) miscellaneous particulars which include: (a) birth record, (b) changes occurring at puberty, and (c) changes due to old age. The information, when considered individually, is not of much value. The skeletal features to determine age are discussed in the next chapter.

Teeth

For age estimation from teeth, it is necessary to know—(1) the difference between the two sets of teeth, (2) the time of their eruption, and (3) the period when their root calcification is complete, and this can be ascertained on X-ray examination (Fig. 3.2).

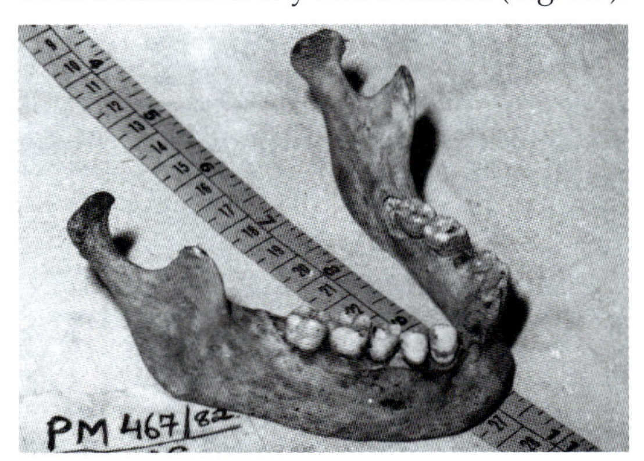

Fig. 3.2: Age estimation from teeth. There is no eruption of third molar but there is a space for third molar (*Courtesy*: Dr AA Qureshi)

The two sets of teeth are: (1) temporary, deciduous or milk teeth and (2) permanent teeth. Temporary teeth are 20 in number, viz. four incisors, two canines, and four molars in each jaw. Permanent teeth are 32 in number, viz. four incisors, two canines or cuspids, four premolars or bicuspids, and six molars or tricuspids in each jaw.

The time of eruption of teeth gives a good indication of age up to 18 to 25 years but there are variations depending upon dietetic, geographic and other factors.

In general, as compared to permanent teeth, the temporary teeth are smaller except the molars, whiter, more constricted at the neck (junction of the crown with the root), and have serrated edges. The difference between the two sets of teeth, and the approximate period of their eruption and root calcification are tabulated in Tables 3.1 and 3.2.

Generally, temporary dentition begins about the sixth month and is completed by about 2½ years. The average child should have eight teeth at 1 year, 16 teeth at 1½ years, and 20 teeth at 2–2½ years. The temporary teeth begin to shed from the six

Table 3.1: Difference between temporary and permanent teeth

Temporary teeth	*Permanent teeth*
1. Small, narrow, light and delicate	Big, broad, heavy and strong
2. Crowns China-white in colour	Crowns ivory-white in colour
3. Junction of the crown with the fang	Junction of the crown with the fang not often marked by a ridge
4. Neck more constricted	Neck less constricted
5. Edges serrated	Edges not serrated
6. Anterior teeth vertical	Anterior teeth usually inclined somewhat forward
7. Molars are usually larger. Their crowns are flat, and their roots are smaller and more divergent	Bicuspids which replace the temporary molars are usually smaller, their crowns have cusps which sharply differentiate them. Their roots are bigger and relatively straight

Table 3.2: Approximate time period for eruption and complete root calcification of temporary and permanent teeth

Temporary teeth	*Eruption time*	*Complete root calcification*
Central incisors (lower)	6–8 months	1½–2 years
Central incisors (upper)	7–9 months	1½–2 years
Lateral incisors (upper)	7–9 months	1½–2 years
Lateral incisors (lower)	10–12 months	1½–2 years
First molars	12–14 months	2–2½ years
Canines	17–18 months	2–2½ years
Second molars	20–30 months	3 years
Permanent teeth	*Eruption time*	*Complete root calcification*
First molars	6–7 years	9–10 years
Central incisors	6–8 years	10 years
Lateral incisors	8–9 years	11 years
First bicuspid	9–11 years	12–13 years
Second bicuspid	10–12 years	13–14 years
Canines	11–12 years	13–15 years
Second molars	12–14 years	14–16 years
Third molars ('wisdom')	17–21 years	18–25 years

to the seventh year, after the eruption of the first molar behind the second temporary molar tooth. The period of mixed dentition persists till about 12 to 13 years.

The permanent teeth appear first in lower jaw and then in upper jaw. The bicuspids are most irregular and are of little value in fixing the age. The first molars appear about the sixth year, and the second molars about the twelfth year. The eruption of the third molar (wisdom tooth) is very irregular. Due to evolutionary reduction in the length of the jaw bone, the third molar may remain impacted (wedged between the second molar and jaw bone). Therefore, after 12 years, the lengthening of the ramus of the lower jaw behind the second molar, known as 'space for the last molar' should be looked for.

The presence of one wisdom tooth usually means that the subject has passed the age of 17 years. If there are two—about 19 yrs, three about 21 yrs and all the four 22 yrs or above. If the wisdom teeth are errupted, an X-ray should be taken to ascertain if their roots are calcified; if they are not, there is a strong presumption that the age is *below 25 years*. Normally, complete calcification of the roots of the teeth takes place within three or four years of the date of eruption. The extent and degree of calcification can also thus help in the estimation of age. If there is a wide gap from birth, it is called "Diastema". Sometimes the teeth on the first look, appear to be all present filling the upper and lower jaw. On counting, less number may be seen. Congenital absence of teeth can be seen in about 4–6% of cases (Grays Anatomy mentions it). It is verified by Dr Subrahmanyam, present editor, in his 1977 study at BHU Varanasi, India. Overriding teeth supernumerory teeth, persistent temporary teeth all become accessory dental identification tools.

Gustafson's method of age estimation consists of microscopic examination of the longitudinal section of the central part of the tooth to assess the changes in teeth as a result of wear and tear with advancing age. These changes are graded into six types, viz. attrition or gradual wearing out of teeth; periodontosis or loosening of teeth; secondary dentition formation or infilling of the normal root cavity; cement apposition or increase in the tissue holding the root in place; root resorption; and root transparency. Such an examination is somewhat helpful to estimate the age between 25 and 60 years.

Boyde has devised a **method** for accurate age estimation by means of incremental lines. These lines can be seen on histological section of the teeth. They appear as cross-striations on the enamel and represent daily increments of growth. An exceptionally well-marked line, known as the neonatal line, is formed at birth. The number of cross-striations from birth (neonatal line) until death are counted and this provides the most accurate estimation of age.

Ossification of Bones

The bones of the human skeleton develop from separate ossification centres. From these centres, ossification progresses till the bone is completely formed. These changes can be studied by means of X-rays. It is, therefore, possible to determine the approximate age of an individual by radiological examination of bones till ossification is complete.

While the time of ossification gives a good indication of age, it should be remembered that—(1) there are variations due to dietetic, geographic, hereditary and other factors, (2) union of epiphysis in cartilaginous bones takes place earlier in the female by about two years than in the male except in case of skull sutures where obliteration sets in a little later and proceeds more slowly in the female than in the male, and (3) under tropical conditions, ossification is observed earlier than in temperate areas.

The following chronology of ossification data provides the principal points for determination of age. The **data are for males** unless where specifically stated otherwise:

1. At birth, the lower end of femur shows a centre of ossification about ½ cm in diameter. A centre of ossification will be present in talus and calcaneum, and may be present in cuboid, upper end of tibia, and head of the humerus.
2. By about 1½–2 years, the anterior fontanelle should be closed. The metopic suture also closes.
3. By the end of 2 years, the condylar portions of the occipital bone fuse with the squama.
4. Between 2 and 6 years, the number of carpal bones present on X-ray represents the approximate age in years, as for example, four carpal bones—4 years.
5. By 4 years in females and 6 years in males, a centre of ossification appears in the medial epicondyle of the humerus.
6. By about 6 years, the condylar portions of the occipital bone fuse with the basiocciput.
7. Between 7 and 8 years, the rami of pubis and ischium unite. Sacral vertebrae are separated by cartilage.
8. Between 8 and 10 years, a centre of ossification appears in the olecranon.
9. Between 10 and 12 years, the pisiform ossifies.
10. Between 13 and 14 years, the lateral epicondyle of the humerus unites with the trochlea and capitulum.
11. Between 15 and 16 years, the epiphysis of os calcis (calcaneum) joins the bone; the tri-radiate cartilage of acetabulum fuses; the coracoid process should be united to the scapula; olecranon should be united to the ulna; the heads and ends of metacarpals unite with their respective shafts.
12. Between 16 and 18 years, all the epiphyses at the elbow (except the medial epicondyle), head of the femur, and lower end of the tibia join the respective shafts. In the females, the epiphyses at the elbow join their respective shafts by 13–14 years.
13. Between 18 and 20 years, all the epiphyses at the wrist, knee, crest of ilium, and lateral end of the clavicle should be united. The acromion process should be united to the scapula.
14. Soon after the 20th year, the articular facets of the ribs should be united. By 21–22 years, the ischial tuberosity should be fused in the females.
15. By 22 years, the inner (secondary) epiphysis of the clavicle fuses.
16. Between 18 and 22 years, the basiocciput should be fused with the basisphenoid.
17. By 23 years, sacral vertebrae should be united with one another from below upwards.

18. The four middle pieces of the sternum fuse with one another from below upwards between 14 and 25 years of ages.

If all the epiphyses are united, the person is above 25 years of age. From these data, it is seen that the probable age can be determined within a year or so before puberty, and within a range of two years thereafter until the consolidation of the skeleton at 22 to 25 years.

The areas which are routinely X-rayed to determine the age of a person are: (1) wrist and hand in children (Figs 3.3 and 3.4), (2) elbow, shoulder, pelvis and knee in adults (Figs 3.5 to 3.7) and (3) skull, vertebrae, and sternum in old people (Fig. 3.8).

In clinical forensic medicine, most cases which come before the medicolegal expert for age determination pertain to age of consent, and attainment of majority. The author's usual practice is to make a radiological examination of the wrist, elbow and shoulder joints, and when necessary, hip bone and clavicle. The indication of age is based on the union of epiphyses, as per the following data, with a range of six months on either side. In some cases, one or more wisdom teeth may not erupt at all.

Region	*Girls*	*Boys*
Elbow	13–14	15–17
Wrist	16–17	18–19
Shoulder	17–18	19–20
Crest of ilium	18–19	20–21
Ischial tuberosity	21–22	23–24
Inner end of clavicle	21–22	23–24

After 25 years, some indication of age may be obtained from the following data. These changes indicate that the body is that of an elderly person. Age can, therefore, be estimated in decades only:

1. The xiphoid process unites with the body of the sternum at about 40 years and the manubrium unites with the body in old age, at about 60 years.
2. The absence of closure of any suture of the skull indicates that the age does not exceed 30 years. An exception to this general rule is the basilar suture; the fusion between basiocciput and basisphenoid is complete by 18–22 years. Generally, evidence of commencing union of sutures is first seen on the inner and then the outer surface, the inner surface closing several years before the outer. The closure starts with the sagittal (30–35 years), coronal (35–40 years), and lambdoid sutures (45–50 years) (variable), followed by parietomastoid and squamous sutures (55–60 years), and the sphenoparietal suture which closes by about 70 years. The palate suture closes at 45–50 years.
3. The lipping of lumbar vertebrae occurs after the age of 40 years. The osteophytic outgrowths from the anterior and lateral margins of the intervertebral discs rarely become prominent before 40 years. The disc undergoes atrophic changes by about 40–45 years.
4. The greater cornu of the hyoid unites with its body between 40 and 60 years.
5. In old age, laryngeal and costal cartilages ossify. General rarefaction of bones also occurs.

Height and Weight

A full-term child at birth is about 45–50 cm in length. It is generally 60 cm at the end of six months, 68 cm at the end of one year, and roughly double its length at birth at the end of the fourth year, i.e. 90–100 cm. The average weight at birth is from 2½ to 3 kg and this increases at the rate of approximately 0.5 kg per month for the first year so that a normally growing child is roughly double its birth weight in the first six months and three times its birth weight at the end of the first year. Tables of average heights and weights indicate in a general way the rate of growth but the individual variations are so great that they are of little value from medicolegal point of view for fixing the age.

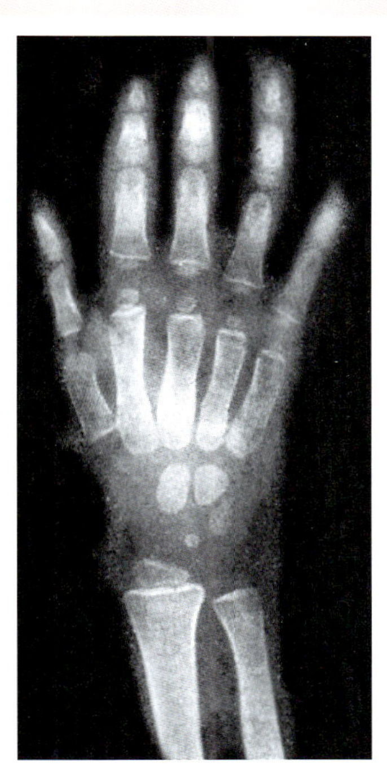

Fig. 3.3: Age estimation from bones (children). X-ray of carpal bones. Four carpal bones are seen. Age four years

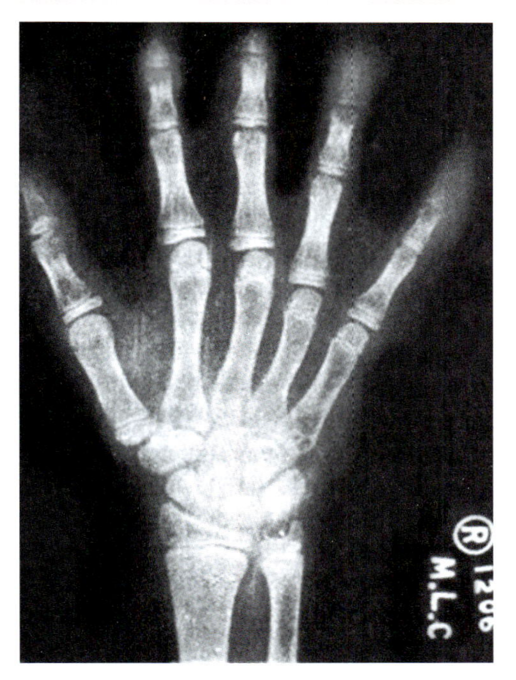

Fig. 3.4: Age estimation from bones. X-ray of wrist and hand of a girl. Age 12–15 years. Pisiform ossified (10–12). Heads of metacarpals and phalanges not fused (fuse at 15–16). Lower ends of radius and ulna not fused (fuse at 16–17) (*Courtesy*: Dr PE Prabhakar)

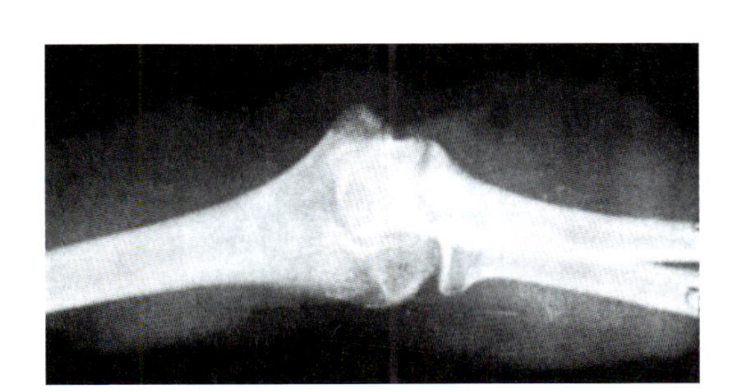

Fig. 3.5: Age estimation from bones. X-ray of elbow joint of a girl. Age about 14 years. Epiphyses at lower end of humerus fusing with shaft (13–14). Olecranon uniting with ulna (13–14) (*Courtesy*: Dr PE Prabhakar)

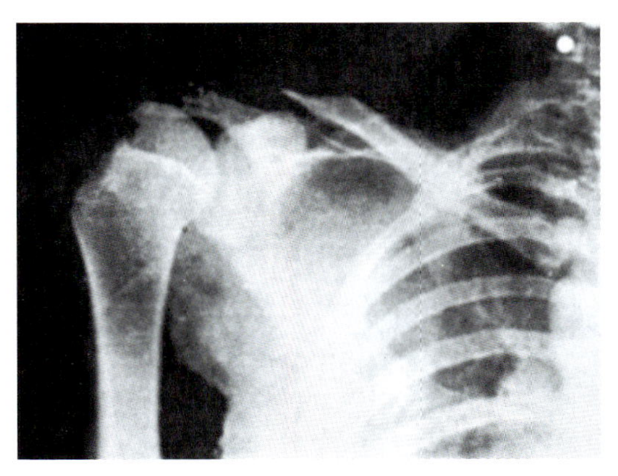

Fig. 3.6: Age estimation from bones. X-ray of shoulder joint of a girl. Age about 6–17 years. Coracoid process fused (fuses at 15–16). Inner end of clavicle not appeared (appears at 16–18). Acromion appeared but not fused (appears at 17–18). Upper end of humerus is partially fused (fuses at 17–18) (*Courtesy*: Dr PE Prabhakar)

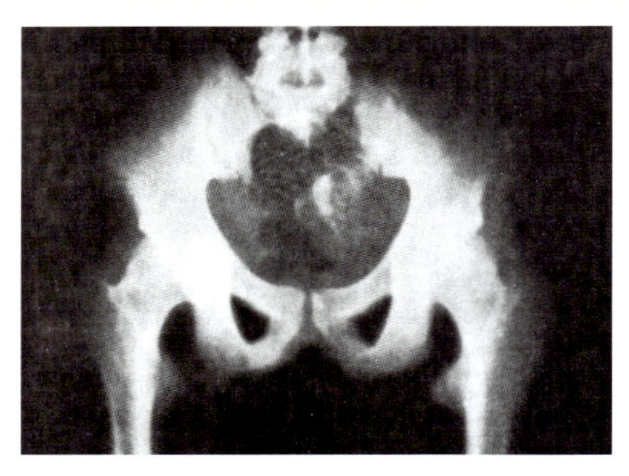

Fig. 3.7: Age estimation from bones. X-ray of pelvis of a girl. Age above 21 years. Tri-radiate cartilage fused (15–16). Head, greater and lesser trochanters of femur fused (17–18). Ischial tuberosity fused (21–22) (*Courtesy*: Dr PF Prabhakar)

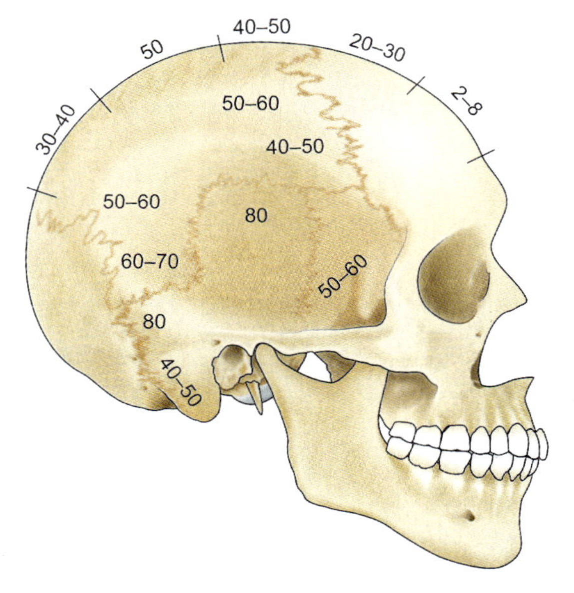

Fig. 3.8: Age estimation from bones (old persons). Diagram showing approximate age of closure of sutures of cranial vault. The process is always slightly more advanced internally

Miscellaneous Particulars

The particulars generally considered under this head are: (1) birth record, (2) changes occurring at puberty, and (3) changes due to old age.

Birth record provides legal proof of identity, age, nationality, parentage and civil status of the individual.

Changes occurring at puberty are of some use. Hair appear first on the pubis and then in the axilla.

In the male, fine downy hair begin to appear on the pubis by about 14 years, on the axilla by about 15 years, and on the chin and upper lip between 16 and 18 years. In about a year or two, the fine hair become thick and the colour darker. The voice becomes deeper and "Adam's apple" more prominent by about 16 to 18 years.

In the females, breasts begin to develop by about 13 years and fine downy hair appear on the mons veneris. By about 14 years, menstruation starts, fine pubic hair become thick and dark, and fine hair appear in the axilla becoming darker in about a year.

Changes due to old age: General retro-gressive changes, like wrinkles on the face, appear after 40 years. *Arcus senilis,* a ring of opacity in the peripheral part of the cornea, may also appear after 40 years but is seldom complete before 60. Hair in the auditory meatus rarely begin to appear before 50 years. Greying of hair starts on the scalp at about 40 years first at the temples, followed later by the beard and moustache, and still later the chest. As age advances, scalp hair become less dense in the male and there is loss of axillary hair in the female. Cataract appears in old age when teeth also begin to fall out.

Q. 3.10. Mention the circumstances in which the question of age may form the basis of medicolegal investigation.

Q. 3.11. Explain the medicolegal importance of age 14,16 and 18. Add a note on age certificate.

Evidence as to age may be demanded in the following circumstances, viz. (1) criminal responsibility, (2) judicial punishment

(3) kidnapping, (4) rape, (5) marriage, (6) attainment of majority, (7) employment, (8) infanticide, (9) criminal abortion, (10) impotence and sterility, (11) competency as a witness, and (12) identification.

Criminal responsibility: In law, responsibility means liability to punishment. Under section 82 IPC, a child under the age of seven is incapable of committing an offence. This is so because action alone does not amount to guilt unless it is accom-panied by a guilty mind. And a child of that tender age cannot have a guilty mind or criminal intention with which the act is done. This presumption, however, is only confined to offenses under the IPC but not to other Acts, e.g. the Railway Act.

Under section 83 IPC, a child above seven and under twelve years of age is presumed to be capable of committing an offence, if he has obtained sufficient maturity to understand and judge the nature and consequences of his conduct on that occasion. The law presumes such maturity in a child of that age unless the contrary is proved by the defence.

Under section 89 IPC, a child under 12 years of age cannot give valid consent to suffer any harm which can occur from an act done in good faith and for its benefit, e.g. a consent for an operation. Only, a guardian can give such consent.

Under section 87 IPC, a person under 18 years of age cannot give valid consent, whether express or implied, to suffer any harm which may result from an act not intended or not known to cause death or grievous hurt, e.g. consent for a wrestling contest.

Judicial punishment: Juvenile offenders, that is children (boys below 16 years and girls below 18 years of age), who have committed a crime, are tried by the Juvenile court and, on conviction, are entrusted to parents or guardians for special care or sent to a Correctional school, with facilities for education, vocational training and rehabilitation. They are not detained there beyond the age of 18 years in case of boys and 20 years in case of girls. Delinquent juveniles are neither sentenced to death nor sent to jail. Women magistrates try these cases.

Kidnapping: This means carrying away a person from lawful guardianship by illegal means. It is an offence — (a) to kidnap or abduct a child with the intention of taking dishonestly any moveable property from its person, if the age of such a child is under 10 years (Sec 369 IPC), (b) to kidnap or abduct a minor from lawful guardianship, if the age of a boy is under 16 and that of a girl under 18 years (Sec 361 IPC), (c) to procure a girl for illicit intercourse or to sell or buy a girl for purposes of prostitution, if her age is under 18 years (Sec 366A IPC), and (d) to import into India from a foreign country, a girl for illicit intercourse, if her age is less than 21 years (Sec 366B IPC).

Rape: Under section 375 IPC, sexual intercourse by a man with a girl under 15 years of age, even if she be his wife or any other girl under 16 years of age, even with her consent, constitutes the offence of rape.

Marriage: The Child Marriage Restraint (Amendment) Act (Act XLI of 1949) lays down that a girl under 18 years of age and a boy under 21 years of age cannot contract a valid marriage.

Attainment of majority: Under Indian Majority Act (Act IX of 1875), persons domiciled in India attain majority on completion of 18 years, except when under a guardian appointed by a court or under a court of Wards, when the individual attains majority on completion of 21 years. Persons under this age are minors. A minor cannot make a valid will, sell his property or serve on a jury.

Employment: Under the Factories Act 1984 (Act LXIII of 1948), a child below 14 years of age cannot be employed in any factory or mine or hazardous occupation. A person who has completed 15 years of age, is allowed to work as an adult on a certificate of fitness granted by a certifying surgeon to the effect that he is fit for a full day's work. Under the Bombay Shop and Establishment Act 1948, children under 12 years of age cannot be employed.

Infanticide: A charge of infanticide can be sustained only if it can be proved that the foetus had attained the age of viability, that is 210th day of intrauterine life, and in exceptional circumstances 180th day.

Criminal abortion: It is necessary to recognise the stage of development of the products of conception in view of the enhanced punishment for the crime after the pregnancy has advanced beyond the stage of quickening. It is also necessary to find out if the woman has passed the child-bearing period, lest it might be a false charge.

Impotence and sterility: A boy is sterile though not impotent before puberty. There is no upper limit regarding potency or sterility of men. Women become sterile after menopause.

Competency as a witness: Under section 118 IEA, no age limit is laid down for this purpose. Every person is competent to testify provided he is able to understand the questions put to him by the court.

Identification: The determination of age may be required for the identification of an individual, either living or dead. When a person suddenly appears after many years and claims to be the missing person or when a dead body is produced as that of the missing person, the approximate age is an important link in any chain of identity data.

Age Certificate

As it is not possible to be accurate while giving an opinion about age, the certificate should give a range and be worded as "From the general physical, dental and radiological examination of_____________, bearing the following identification marks, I am of the opinion that the individual is aged between ______ and ______ years" (lower and upper range to be given).

Identification marks:

1. __________
2. __________

Place Date Medical Officer
Degrees and designation

General Development

By this, we mean the recognition of a person by his height, weight and general muscular development, when considered along with other facts. It is important to record the height and if possible, the weight of all persons to be examined or bodies to be autopsied.

Congenital Features

These include personal appearance, anthropometric measurements, fingerprints or dactylography including poroscopy, footprints and malformations, e.g. birth marks, mole, etc.

Personal appearance: By this, we mean the way we recognise individuals by their complexion, facial characteristics, etc. This method is not error-free. For example, the same individual may appear different by modification in the trimming of his moustache or beard or by shaving. On the other hand, it frequently happens that different individuals bear a striking resemblance to each other. Therefore, *a doctor when requested by the court, while giving evidence, to identify the person examined by him earlier, should verify the identification marks recorded by him,* before answering.

Anthropometry (Bertillon system): This system is based on the principle that the measurements of various parts of the human body do not alter after adult age (21 years) and that no two persons show the same measurements in all respects. The system involves registration of the characteristics under three heads, viz.—(1) *descriptive data,* such as colour of hair and iris; complexion; and shape of nose, ears, chin, etc.; (2) *bodily marks,* such as moles, scars, tattoo marks, etc.; and (3) *body measurements,* eleven in number, pertaining to certain body parts. The photographs of the full face and right profile are also taken. This system has many drawbacks. It is now replaced by fingerprint system and the only measurements still made as a routine are height and weight. Iris is used now for identity in airports, corporates, etc.

Q. 3.12. Discuss the use of fingerprints in medicolegal work illustrating your answer with suitable examples.

Fingerprints (Dactylography, Dermatoglyphics, Galton System)

A fingerprint means an impression made by the ball of a finger. The fingerprint system is based on the principle that the skin of the balls of the fingers and thumbs is covered with ridges and grooves, the pattern of which varies between individuals and makes absolute identification possible. The important features of the ridges are—(1) they are present from birth, both on the epidermis and dermis, (2) they remain constant for the life of the individual and cannot be altered except by destruction of the true skin, and (3) they form patterns that are absolutely individual. They are not entirely alike, even identical twins.

These patterns are classified on the basis of arrangement of ridges into four main types, viz. loops, whorls, arches and composites or compounds, the loop being the commonest of all (Figs 3.9 to 3.12).

It is accepted that the chances of two fingerprints matching sixteen ridge characteristics are infinitely small. In the world's crime records, no two identical fingerprint patterns have been reported. While in the case of criminals, impressions of all the digits of both hands are taken and preserved by the police for future identification, it is customary in India to take usually the left thumb impression of illiterate persons in lieu of a signature on many legal and other documents.

The advantages of this system are:

1. It is applicable to persons of all ages
2. Prints can often be obtained even from putrefied bodies
3. Absolute identification is possible
4. No special training or expensive instruments are necessary
5. The system lends itself to easy classification
6. The actual print is always available to check any suspected error, and
7. The print can be transmitted from one place to another as a coded or digitalised message. The development of computerised automated fingerprint identification system (AFIS) now permits rapid entry, comparison and identification in minutes to hours as opposed to weeks to months using conventional manual search methods.

The ridge impressions are due to moistening of the skin by sweat and sebum from the skin glands. At the scene of crime, they are found on door knobs, furniture, weapons and various other articles, unless the criminal has worn gloves. Fingers soiled with blood or grease also leave appropriate impressions. If the impressions are faint, the fingerprint expert can make them visible by special techniques, for example, by the use of dusting powder. In a dead body, if the fingerprints are dried up, the prints can be taken after soaking the fingers in an alkaline solution for some time. If the skin has peeled off as a result of burns, putrefaction or drowning, the prints can still be recorded either from the dermis or from the peeled off skin hardened by formalin.

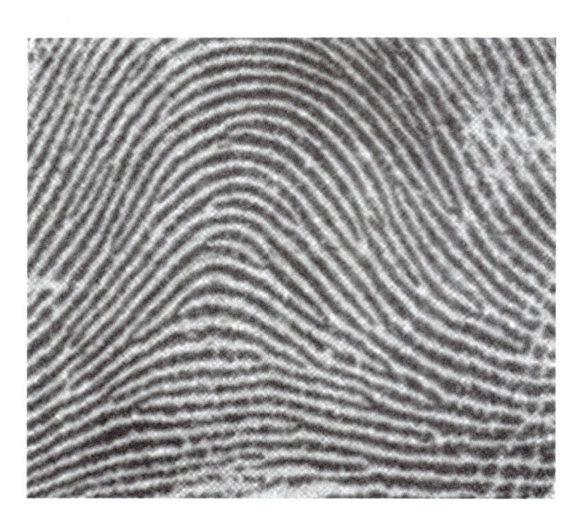

Fig. 3.9: *Fingerprint pattern of arch.* The ridges run from one side of the print to the other and, as the name implies, in an arch-like fashion. The ridges terminate at the sides of the print approximately equidistant to each other and do not make a backward turn. (From: Cherill—The Finger Print System at Scotland Yard. By courtesy of Publishers: HMSO, London)

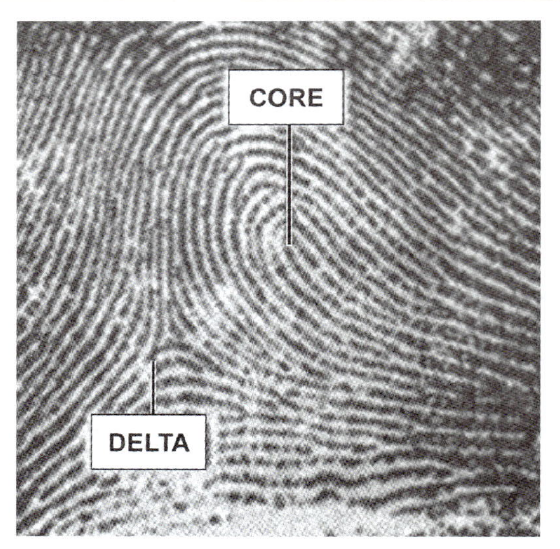

Fig. 3.10: *Fingerprint pattern of loop.* The ridges about the centre of the print arrange themselves somewhat in the form of a hairpin, the ends of which point more or less in a downward slanting direction. A varying number or ridges group themselves around the centre loop formation. There are two fixed points in all prints of the loop type, viz. the delta and the core. They are important because they are used for classification purposes. (From: Cherill—The Finger Print System at Scotland Yard. By courtesy of Publishers: HMSO, London)

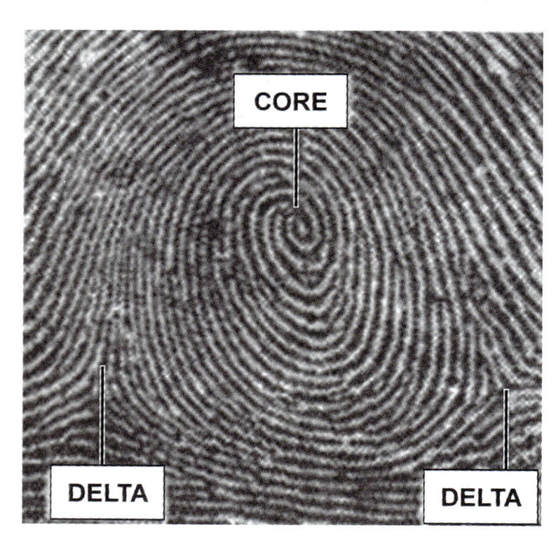

Fig. 3.11: *Fingerprint pattern of whorl.* The ridges form a more intricate pattern than in arches and loops. The circular design of the ridge groupings is conspicuous. The ridges may take a clockwise or anti-clockwise turn. There are two deltas both of which are utilised for classification. The core is indicated for reference purposes but is not used in the Henry system. (From: Cherill—The Finger Print System at Scotland Yard by courtesy of Publishers: HMSO, London)

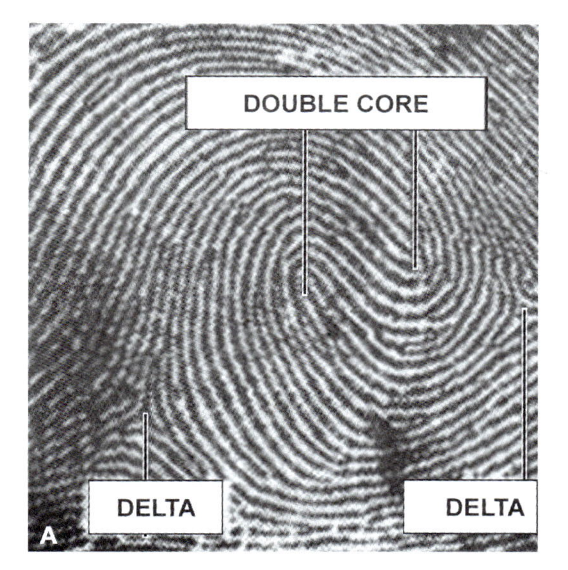

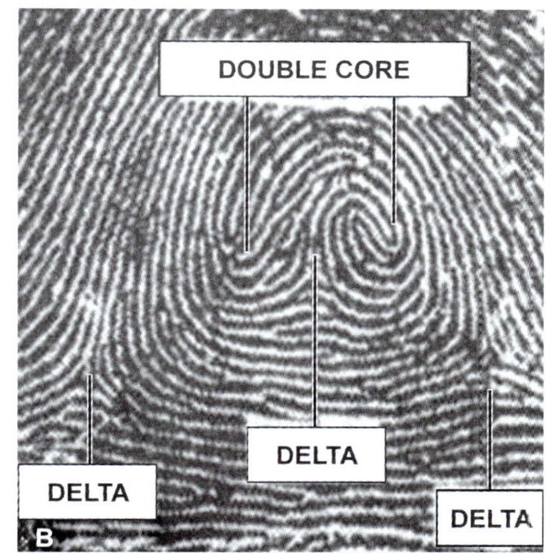

Fig. 3.12: Fingerprint pattern. As the name implies, this pattern consists of two or more of the preceding patterns. There are always two deltas (A), but sometimes there are three (B), and sometimes even four are observed. (From: Cherill—The Finger Print System at Scotland Yard. By courtesy of publishers: HMSO, London)

The practical applications of this method include: (1) recognition of chance impressions left at a scene of crime, (2) identification of the weapon used for committing suicide or homicide, e.g. firearm, (3) identification of habitual criminals, suicides, deserters, persons suffering from loss of memory or those dead or unconscious after being involved in an accident, (4) identification of decomposing or mummified bodies of unknown persons, (5) prevention of impersonation, and (6) as an extra precaution on cheques, bank notes and other legal documents which may bear a fingerprint in addition to manual signature.

The ridges of the fingers and hands are studded with minute pores which are the mouths of ducts of sweat glands situated below the epidermis. The pores are permanent and differ in number, size, shape and arrangement for a given area in each individual. This method of identification by examining the pores is known as **poroscopy** or **Locard's method.** It is very useful when only a part of the fingerprint or a fragmentary print is available for examination and identification.

Dr Subrahmanyam's 'Namaste' Technique

In one case partly decomposed and crushed hand up to the wrist level was brought for examination. There was a question whether this hand belonged to a person admitted in orthopaedic ward and amputated at upper arm. Dr Subrahmanyam got an idea. When we keep both hands in 'NAMASTE' position, turn them to right and left and observe in normal person both hands fit in. On X-ray also, the bones tally and fit in. In this case, the decomposed hand was kept on the hand of the patient in orthopaedic ward and X-ray taken in the flat side, Namaste position. Similarly, as controls decomposed hand was kept on hands of four of the colleagues and X-rays taken on the same lines, the decomposed hand and the patient's hand tallied as evidenced by apt alignment. The hands of controls did not tally, so a positive opinion could be given and the accused were promptly arrested.

Footprints (Podogram)

A footprint means an impression left by the sole of a foot. The skin pattern of toes and heels is distinctive and the impression is, therefore, helpful for—(1) identification in relation to chance footprints found at the scene of crime, and (2) to prevent deliberate or accidental substitution of babies in maternity hospitals. Footprint records are maintained for all air force flying personnel in most countries since feet often resist destruction by aircraft accidents, fires, etc.

While comparing the footprint of the suspect with the original, peculiarities, such as flat foot, supernumerary toes, etc. should be specially looked for and, if present, are helpful for identification. In the case of boot mark, the pattern and arrangement of nails may be useful.

Since footprints are made when a person is standing, walking slow or fast, running or jumping, create a difference, the evidential value of footprints in criminology is obviously less than that of fingerprints. It acts mainly as a corroborative evidence.

Congenital Malformations

Congenital malformations, such as supernumerary or webbed fingers or toes, harelip, cleft palate, dental peculiarities, undescended testes, birth marks, moles, etc. may help to establish identity. Such deformities are hereditary in many cases. While noting **birth marks and moles** as identification marks, a full description as to their situation with reference to an anatomical landmark, size, colour and other characteristics, such as raised or flat, fixed to the skin or free, and hairy or non-hairy, should invariably be given.

Acquired Peculiarities

These consist of occupational marks, tattoo marks, scars, acquired malformations (deformities) and miscellaneous features.

Occupational Marks

Occupational marks are characteristics which result from adaptation to work. Materials, like flour, paint, grease and nature of stains on the clothing or body of a person, indicate respectively that he is a baker, painter, mechanic or a dye worker. Callosities, scars, tattooing and stains of specific distribution may be found in persons working as dental mechanics, blacksmiths, miners and photographers. Rough skin on the outer side of terminal phalanx of the left index finger caused by constant needle pricks is seen in tailors. Smooth hands are indicative of one not used to hard manual labour. The occupational marks may thus indicate the identity and social position of the living or the dead.

Q. 3.13. Discuss briefly the medicolegal significance of tattoo marks.

Tattoo Marks

Tattoo marks are designs affected by multiple small puncture wounds made through the skin with needles or similar penetrating tools dipped in dye.

The permanency of the tattoo marks depends upon the type of dye used, the depth of its penetration, and the part of the body tattooed. Black, blue and red dyes are more durable, almost permanent, and therefore, commonly employed. The optimum depth of penetration is up to the superficial layers of the dermis.

To reveal latent tattoo marks, the use of high-contrast photography, computer image enhancement, ultraviolet lamp or infrared photography is helpful. Tattoo marks on unidentified putrefied bodies may be photographed with sharp definition, if the loose epidermis is first removed and the design on the dermis recorded. This method is of special value in the case of bodies recovered from water. A tattoo mark described by relatives which is absent at autopsy may lead to a mistaken identification unless it is remembered that lymph nodes in the neighbourhood of a tattoo mark always show a deposit of the pigment used.

A tattoo design may be altered or eliminated or a second one superimposed in an attempt to conceal identity. Various artificial means have been devised for elimination, and these include: (a) dermabrasion, (b) application of caustic substances or carbon dioxide snow, (c) electrolysis, (d) surgery, and (e) exposure to laser beams. While the first three methods will leave a visible scar, surgical removal with skin grafting would leave a less obvious scar. Exposure to the laser beams destroys pigmented cells and evaporates the dye from the tattooed areas without any pain, damage or alteration of skin structure. Chronic eczema may cause the tattoo designs to disappear and confluent small-pox would obliterate them in children.

While *describing* a tattoo mark, special note should be made of its anatomical situation, size, colour and design. A photograph or sketch is of value. The possibility of the same emblem in the same situation in more than one person due to the same tattooist executing the design must be kept in mind.

The important complications from tattoo marks mainly relate to sepsis and transmission of diseases, like syphilis, leprosy, tuberculosis, hepatitis and AIDS.

The **medicolegal importance** of the tattoo marks is as follows: They may indicate—(1) the identity of a person—special design; one's own name; name of spouse, close relation or friend; date of birth, marriage, service, etc., (2) race—extensive tattooing of the chest and limbs is common amongst the Japanese, (3) religion—design of Hanuman, Lord Krishna, Cross or Christ, (4) profession/occupation—some criminal gangs have certain specific emblems of tattoo marks. Some occupations, e.g. coal-miner's leave visible tattoo marks on the hands and face from the material handled by the workers, (5) behavioural characteristics—erotic tattoos of the sexual fanatic, blue bird design on the extensor surface of the web of the thumb of the homosexual, number 13 inside the lower lip of drug pushers, addict type of tattoo marks to conceal injection sites, etc., (6) social status—tattoos are generally practiced in India by the lower class of society, (7) political convictions, e.g. cow and calf, sword and sickle, etc., and (8) as a fashion among glamour seekers, e.g. models, sports persons, etc. Nowadays, tattoing all over body or on genitalia like on shaft of the penis appears to have bocome a craze among the elite, drug users, film-stars, sports-persons, sports fans, etc. Excessive sex-oriented tottoos suggest sexually deviant orientation (Fig. 3.13).

Q. 3.13. What is a scar? Give the time required for scar formation.

Scars

A scar is a permanent cicatricial mark which results from healing of a wound. A superficial injury involving only the epidermis, e.g. an abrasion, does not result in a scar; if the dermis is involved, a scar is produced. A scar is devoid of hair follicles, sweat glands, pigment and elastic tissue, and is covered by a few layers of simple epithelium.

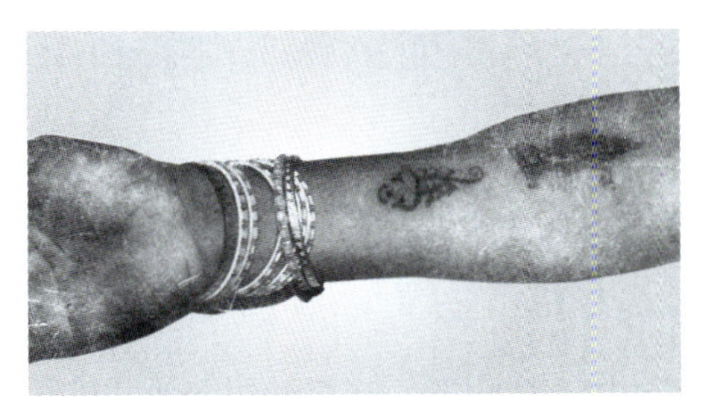

Fig. 3.13: Tattoo mark (in a hijra) (*Courtesy*: Dr BV Subrahmanyam)

Time Required for Scar Formation

This varies according to the nature, size and method of wound healing; presence or absence of sepsis; vascularity of the part; and the age and general health of the person.

A clean, incised, surgical wound normally heals in about a week and a definite scar appears in about two weeks. A scar forms earlier in smaller wounds than in bigger ones. It forms quickly, if healing is by primary (first) intention and is delayed in the presence of sepsis. Scar formation is earlier in a vascular area as compared to an avascular one. It forms earlier in the young and healthy as compared to the old and undernourished.

Q. 3.15. Write short notes on: (1) scar and causative agent, (2) age of scars, (3) growth and disappearance of scars,(4) examination of scars, (5) medicolegal significance of scars.

Scar and Causative Agent

An incised wound produces a linear scar; a gaping wound a wide scar; a stab wound an elliptical scar; a punctured wound a puckered scar; a lacerated wound an irregular scar; and a bullet wound a circular, ovoid or elongated depressed scar. Burns, scalds and corrosives, produce irregular scars with a tendency to keloid formation, and scars from scalds and corrosives often show some evidence of splashing about the main injury. Surgical operations leave a linear scar with stitch/suture marks at regular intervals along the length of the scar, and, such scars are seen in definite anatomical situations. Linear needle track scars are seen in intravenous drug abusers and depressed scars in skin poppers.

Smallpox vaccination scars, one to three in number, are circular or oval, slightly pitted, and found on the outer side of the arm or thigh. Syphilitic scars are thin, tissue-paper-like, and are seen on the genitals. Many skin diseases, like smallpox, leave characteristic multiple scars.

Age of Scars

The approximate age of a scar can be estimated from its ageing process, viz. vascular to avascular (2 weeks to 2 months), tender to non-tender (2 to 6 months), and soft to tough (more than 6 months).

1. Depending upon vascularity, a recently formed scar may appear reddish or bluish. It is tender and soft. The age of such a scar is up to two weeks.
2. As the vascularity diminishes, the scar becomes pale and white but is still tender and soft. Its age is up to two months.
3. With age, the scar contracts. It becomes smaller and whiter but it is still a little tender and soft. The age is between two and six months.
4. As the scar further contracts, it becomes tough, white and glistening. The age is probably not less than six months to an indefinite number of years.

Growth and Disappearance of Scars

Scars produced in childhood grow in size with the natural development of the individual, especially if situated on the chest and limbs. A well-developed scar never disappears but scars from minor wounds may become very difficult to detect.

Examination of Scars

Good lighting is essential. The record should include the number, site, size (being accurately measured), shape, colour, consistency, the level it bears to the body surface, relationship to deeper tissues whether fixed or free, tenderness if any, and the presence or absence of glistening. The condition of the ends whether tapering or otherwise and the probable direction of the original wound should also be determined. Irregular scars should be sketched or preferably photographed.

Faint scars may be rendered visible by exposure to ultraviolet light or by massaging the area to increase the blood supply when the avascular scar stands out in contrast to the hyperaemic skin. Suspected scars in the dead can be examined microscopically. In fragmentary remains, a scar may be confused with lineae albicantes (striae of old pregnancy on the anterior abdominal wall). A scar contains no elastic tissue. Linea albicantes formed by stretching of the skin contains elastic tissue.

Medicolegal Significance of Scars

The forensic importance of scars is as follows:

1. Scars help in identification.
2. The shape of the scar generally corresponds to the type of wound sustained, e.g. a linear scar of incised wound. It is, therefore, possible to infer the instrument causing it.
3. The age of the scar corresponds to the time of occurrence of the event (crime). This is especially important in pleas of self-defence in cases of murder.
4. The old scars on wrist or throat indicate previous attempts at suicide. Many scars on the front of the lower legs indicate repeated falls of a chronic alcoholic.
5. If as a result of an accident, the injured person be disfigured, he cannot be compelled to submit to plastic surgery to lessen the defendant's responsi-bility. Nor may the defence attempt to mitigate the damages by references to possible benefits which the plaintiff might obtain from plastic surgery.
6. Sometimes, wounds may be delibera-tely kept infected or rarely covered with irritants, like copper sulphate to promote slow healing and to obtain unsightly big scars, to bring the injury within the purview of grievous hurt.
7. The accused may attribute scars of wounds to diseases or therapeutic procedures.
8. Linea albicantes may indicate certain diseased conditions, like ascites or previous pregnancy in a female. Scars from rupture of the posterior commissure of the vagina or tears in the external os uteri are usually indicative of previous labour.
9. Linear needle track scars indicate an intravenous drug abuser and depressed scars a skin popper.

Acquired Malformations

Acquired malformations, such as malunited fractures, dental extractions and fillings, poliomyelitis, deformities, etc. help in the establishment of identity to a certain extent.

Miscellaneous Data

Clothing found at the scene of crime provides valuable clues: (1) name—laundry mark, (2) age—size of clothing, (3) sex—male and female dress, (4) occupation—uniforms of school children, mechanics or persons in army, navy and air force (5) evidence of crime, especially struggle and nature of assault: (a) disarranged, torn clothes, missing buttons, mud stains and presence of foreign hair suggesting struggle, and (b) cuts, holes, burns and blackening from firearm; odour of kerosene, petrol, etc.; stains due to poisons, vomit, faecal matter, blood, saliva, semen, corrosives, etc., suggesting nature of assault.

Features, such as artificial teeth, handwriting, habits and other personal effects such as visiting cards, diary, keys and eye glasses found at the scene of crime provide an indication of personal identity and social status in the living or the dead to a certain extent. If any disease is found in a dead body, such as cerebral cortical scars, biliary or renal calculi, uterine fibroid, etc. or there is evidence of an operation, e.g. an appendectomy scar, reference to medical records may be very helpful.

The voice is normally not relied upon for the purpose of identity since it may be altered intentionally or by disease.

Artificial light, moon light and flash light have their own limitations for recognising a person, and so also identification by persons with defective vision even in daylight. It is, therefore, important to make a proper observation regarding the condition of the eyes with special reference to the cornea and the lens in all cases, and especially those involving vehicular accidents.

Q. 3.16. Discuss the ways in which the identity of a dead person may either be effaced or obliterated.

The identity of a dead person may be effaced or obliterated by the following methods:

1. Removal of identifying features, such as fingerprints, tattoo marks, scars, hair, teeth, etc. and other articles including clothing belonging to the missing person.
2. Animals, e.g. rats, dogs, jackals and hyenas, and birds, such as vultures, which may attack the dead body, may mutilate it in a very short time when the body is lying exposed in the open.
3. Burning the body.
4. Advanced putrefaction.
5. Dismemberment and extensive mutilation by any means including bomb explosions.
6. Throwing different parts of the body in different places.

Dr Raju's case: In this case, an army doctor dismembered the remains of his Mrs whom he killed and put them in different newspaper covered bundles, threw them into Hussain Sagar. A dog brought the remains out and onlookers informed the police. The way the dismembering is done as if by a man with the knowledge of anatomy, the dental data identified by a dentist in Chandigarh and the superimposition technique used to identify the skull, all put together the identity of the lady was established and when confronted with the impending truth, the accused jumped from the building and died.

7. Intermingling of parts from different bodies or animals.
8. Throwing of the body into the sea, lake, well, canal or river.
9. Dissolving the body in corrosive acid.
10. Putting the dead body on a railway track so that gross mutilation is brought about, the body being reduced to a shapeless pulp at times.

Some of the above methods are used or resorted to by criminals to make homicide appear as suicide or accident.

4

Identification in Mass Disasters

Q. 4.1. Define mass disaster. Mention the objectives of forensic investigation. Enumerate the specific points on which the identity can be established in mass disasters (fragmentary remains).

Mass disaster generally means the death of more than 12 victims in a single event. However, it is more logical to define it as the number of deaths which exceeds the capacity of the local death investigation system can handle.

The *objectives* of forensic investigation are:

1. To find the cause of the disaster, such as bomb or detonator fragments that may be embedded in the bodies of the victims.
2. To obtain samples for toxicological analysis (especially alcohol and carbon monoxide) where appropriate.
3. To determine the cause and manner of death of each individual.

In mass disasters, such as air or train accident, an entire body may not be available, and examination may have to be carried out from the available fragmentary remains.

Identification from remains begins at the scene of death. It should proceed in an orderly manner and be documented by photographs and diagrams. It is achieved by building up a description for each person as regards: (1) appearance, (2) clothing, pocket contents and other personal effects, (3) deformities, birth marks (moles), occupation marks, scars, and tattoos, (4) race, (5) sex, (6) age, (7) stature, (8) fingerprints, (9) footprints in military personnel and newly born children in some hospitals, (10) dental status, (11) miscellaneous data and (12) data from specialised techniques.

Q. 4.2. Comment on: (1) photographs, (2) faked photographs, (3) superimposition photography, (4) facial reconstruction.

Photographs

Photographs are helpful in medicolegal work as they provide accurate documentation. Photographs, preferably with a scale in the plane of interest, serve various useful purposes:

1. They help to identify the body.
2. They provide an accurate picture of the scene of crime, e.g. evidence of struggle, if any; position of the body; presence of injuries; amount of blood lost; crime weapon, etc.
3. They may help the witness to refresh his memory about the findings.
4. They help the court to understand the testimony in its proper perspective.
5. Relevant photographs enhance the credibility of evidence especially with regard to those observations and interpretations which are supported by them, e.g. tailing of an incised wound indicates its direction.

Faked Photographs

The possibility of faked photographs should be considered on some occasions. The important deciding points are—(1) shadow inconsistencies, (2) grain distribution, (3) indication of grafting, (4) inconsistencies of body proportions, (5) retouching, (6) environmental profile, and (7) other data. All these factors can be easily understood from a brief discussion of the photographs of Lee Harvey Oswald (armed with gun), the alleged assassin of US President John F Kennedy, where the authenticity of photographs produced before the investigation commission became a matter of dispute. The photographic experts suspected that the head of Oswald was superimposed on a photograph of someone else and there were a number of other inconsistencies and problems also, such as height to rifle length ratio, and visual retouching of the chin area.

***Shadow inconsistencies*:** The shadow on Oswald's face cast by his nose and eyebrows showed that the sun is directly overhead while the long shadows on the ground showed that the sun was in the late afternoon.

The body shadows did not relate to other shadows in the picture. The gun could be seen at an angle to the body which did not relate to the angle of the shadow.

Grain distribution: The grain distribution may not be uniform. In composited photographs, the grain distribution may be noticeably different.

Indication of grafting: There was a line running directly across Oswald's chin as evidence of compositing. No unnatural line could be discerned on the original negative when inspected using magnifying and microscopic equipment, varying density exposures and digital image processing.

The pictures of Oswald's backyard were visually inspected with stereoscopic techniques that permit the prints to be viewed in three dimensions. This analytic technique is useful to detect fakery because photographs of prints, when viewed in a stereo, will not project a three-dimensional image unless made from different view points along one axis. Any retouching of an original photograph of a scene can be detected because when two photographs of a scene are viewed in stereo, the retouched item will appear to lie either in front or behind the plane in which it should be lying. It is virtually impossible to retouch one or both images of a stereo pair with enough skill to escape detection when viewed stereoscopically.

Inconsistencies of body proportions: This can be studied photogrammatically. Photogrammetry is the science of ascertaining the positions and dimensions of objects from measurements of photographs of these objects. This method was given particular emphasis in studying critical shadow areas in Oswald's case. It was also found that the height to rifle length ratio did not match.

From a study of Oswald's photographs, it was apparent that Oswald's face did not precisely fit the neck and body in each picture. Furthermore, the facial portrait of Oswald was exactly the same in each photograph, whereas the posture and distance of the body from the camera differed. In addition to that, using the length of his face as a standard of measurement, it was found that one of the bodies in one picture was clearly taller than the corresponding body in another picture.

Oswald had a rounded chin while the photograph showed a square chin. Thompson, a British forensic photographic expert, said. "It is apparent that from the upper lip to the top of the head is Oswald and one can only conclude from the photograph that Oswald's head has been stuck on to a chin, not being Oswald's chin."

Retouching: The visual areas of retouching should be carefully observed. The retouching was very obvious in certain parts of Oswald's photograph. There was retouching in the chin area indicating that the face was added on to the chin.

Environmental profile: The photographs of Oswald's backyard were supposedly made in February or early March when there is no grass on the ground and there are no leaves on the trees in Texas. However, the photographs showed an amount of foliage on the grass, the bushes and the trees; a phenomenon observed usually in late April. It would imply that the shadows were added by transparent retouching. The date of taking the photographs had, therefore, to be shifted to signify their genuineness. Digital image manipulation is now possible.

Other data: (a) The photographs may contradict each other, (b) they may not corroborate other evidence, such as X-rays, (c) they may be of poor quality, (d) they may not be of first generation, (e) scaler references may be lacking or when present may be positioned in such a manner as to make it difficult or impossible to obtain accurate measurements of critical features, such as wounds from anatomical landmarks, (f) identifying features of the victim, such as name, autopsy case number, date, place of examination, etc. may not have been included. Rarely, one area in the photograph may be out of focus to the camera while the rest of the picture both foreground and background may be in perfect focus, thus obtaining a photographic impossibility. Almost all these features were seen in the Kennedy autopsy photographs that were presented before the House Select Committee investigating his assassination, when their authenticity was questioned.

Superimposition Photography

If the skull of the deceased is recovered from the fragmentary remains, it is X-rayed. The photographs of the front and side view of the head of the deceased taken while he was alive are enlarged to the same size as that of the X-ray photo of the skull. These positive portraits and the negatives of the skull are photographically superimposed to determine, if they tally in contours of the face and skull. The technique can provide corroborative or sometimes conclusive evidence. The method is of greater value negatively to exclude a certain person. Alternatively, superimposition may be carried out by two video cameras, one looking at the skull and another at the photograph, and then superimposing the two signals.

Facial Reconstruction

Forensic sculptors working with skeletal remains and modelling clay can reconstruct facial features often sufficiently close to permit identification. Computer programmes are available to simulate aging as well as reconstruction of appearance, so that if the interval between disappearance and death or discovery is long, a more accurate depiction of facial features is possible.

Q. 4.2. Describe the evidence on which race can be determined from the remains consisting mainly of bones.

It may be possible to determine the race from examination of the skull, mandible and teeth, and relative measurements of limb bones. However, individual variations as well as variations within races often preclude a precise opinion. Genetic blood typing factors may help.

Skull: Certain differences exist between the Negroid (black), Caucasoid (Europeans) and Mongoloid (native Americans, Koreans, Japanese, Chinese, South-east Asians) skulls. They can be determined by the cephalic index (CI) also known as breadth index, the height index (HI) and the nasal index (NI). The cephalic index is obtained by multiplying the maximum transverse breadth by 100 and dividing it by the maximum anteroposterior length. The breadth is the greatest diameter across the skull above the mastoid process. The length is measured between the glabella and the external occipital protuberance. The measurements should be done by calipers and not measuring tape.

A skull is dolichocephalic or long-headed when the index is between 70 and 74.9, mesaticephalic or medium long-headed between 75 and 79.9, and brachycephalic or round-headed when the index is 80 or above. The skull of Aryans, aborigines and blacks is dolichocephalic, that of Europeans and Chinese mesaticephalic, and that of the Mongolian race brachycephalic.

The *height index* (HI) is obtained by multiplying the height of the skull (tip of the mastoid process to the bregma) by 100 and dividing it by the length of the skull.

The *nasal index* (NI) is obtained by multiplying the width of nasal aperture by 100 and dividing it by the height of the nasal aperture.

The following table represents the data in relation to race based on these indices:

	Blacks	*Europeans*	*Mongols*
CI	70–74.9	75–79.9	80 and above
HI	72	71	75
NI	55	46	50

The cheek bones or zygomatic arches, which determine face width, are specially prominent in Mongols. In these persons, unlike other groups, the face width generally exceeds the head width.

The other differences in the skull in the different races are as follows:

	Blacks	*Europeans*	*Mongols*
Orbits	Square	Triangular	Rounded
Nasal opening	Broad	Narrow and elongated	Rounded
Palate	Rectangular	Triangular	Rounded or horseshoe-shaped

Mandible and teeth: The lower jaw is strongly prognathic and a star-shaped configuration is often seen on the occlusal surface of the molars, and the third molar is bigger than the first two molars in the blacks but not in other races. The upper incisor teeth of Mongols are frequently shovel-shaped.

Limb bones: The greater length of radius and tibia in the blacks gives the following indices:

	Europeans	*Blacks*
Radiohumeral index	Below 75	Above 80
Tibiofemoral index	Below 83	Above 83

Q. 4.3. What are the main skeletal differences to be noted in determining the sex of a skeleton sent for examination? Give details particularly of pelvis and skull.

Sex cannot be determined from a skeleton with a full amount of certainty in individuals who have not reached puberty as the sexual characteristics do not begin to manifest by then. Table 4.1 shows the principal points of differentiation thereafter.

Table 4.1: Principal points of differentiation from a skeleton between males and females after puberty

Males	*Females*
General	
1. Skeleton comparatively bigger and stouter, weight approximately 4.5 kg	Skeleton comparatively smaller and slender, weight approximately 3.00 kg
2. Muscular ridges, depressions and processes more prominent	Muscular ridges, depressions and processes less prominent
3. Shaft of long bones relatively rough and the articular surfaces and ends larger	Shaft of long bones relatively smooth and the articular surfaces and ends smaller
Pelvis	
1. Bony framework massive	Bony framework less massive
2. Inlet: deep and narrow	Inlet: shallow and wide
3. Ilium less expanded and hence, walls are not splayed	Ilium more expanded and hence, walls are splayed
4. Anterior superior iliac spines not widely separated	Anterior superior iliac spines widely separated

(*contd.*)

Table 4.1: Principal points of differentiation from a skeleton between males and females after puberty (*contd.*)

Males	*Females*
5. Suprapubic arch narrow, V-shaped, angle not more than about 70° and hence, less distance between ischia	Suprapubic arch wide, U-shaped, angle more than a right angle and hence, more distance between ischia
6. Ischial tuberosities—inverted	Ischial tuberosities—everted
7. Obturator foramina—ovoid	Obturator foramina—triangular
8. Greater sciatic notch narrow, deep and less than a right angle	Greater sciatic notch wide, shallow and almost a right angle or even more
9. Preauricular sulcus narrow, shallow and without marked edges	Preauricular sulcus broad and deep in parous women
10. Acetabula wider and deeper	Acetabula narrower and shallower
11. Sacrum long and narrow, has five or more segments and well-marked promontory	Sacrum wide and short, has five segments, and promontory less marked
12. The curve of the sacrum is more or less equal over the entire length	Sacrum practically straight in the first three segments, the curve being confined to a point below the centre of 3rd sacral vertebra
13. Articular surface of sacrum extends to 2½ to 3 vertebral bodies	Articular surface of sacrum extends to 2 to 2½ vertebral bodies
Femur	
1. Acetabula are wider and deeper, head of femur is larger and articular surface forms more than two-thirds of a sphere	Acetabula are narrower and shallower, the head of femur is smaller and the articular surface forms less than two-thirds of a sphere
2. The pelvis being narrow, the neck femur forms an obtuse angle with shaft	The pelvis being wide, the neck of femur forms a right angle with the shaft
Skull	
1. Bigger, heavier and more rugged	Smaller, lighter and less rugged
2. Cranial capacity almost 10% more	Cranial capacity almost 10% less
3. Frontal sinuses more developed	Frontal sinuses less developed
4. Frontonasal angulation distinct	Frontonasal angulation not well marked
5. Glabella, supraorbital ridges, zygomatic arch, mastoid process, occipital protuberance, occipital condyles and muscle attachments are more pronounced	Glabella, supraorbital ridges, zygomatic arch, mastoid processes, occipital protuberance, occipital condyles and muscle attachments are less pronounced
6. Orbital opening comparatively big and rectangular	Orbital opening comparatively small and rounded
7. Facial bones more massive and not delicate in texture	Facial bones less massive and delicate in texture
Spinal Column	
1. Mean breadth of first cervical vertebra 83 mm	Mean breadth of first cervical vertebra 72 mm
2. Lumbar lordosis less marked	Lumbar lordosis more marked
Mandible	
1. Lower jaw more massive	Lower jaw less massive
2. Chin (symphysis menti)—square	Chin (symphysis menti)—pointed or rounded
3. Symphyseal height—more	Symphyseal height—less
4. Ramus—more broad	Ramus—less broad
5. Angle region—everted	Angle region—not everted
Thorax	
1. Thoracic cage—longer and narrower	Thoracic cage—shorter and wider
2. The ribs have a less pronounced curvature and are less oblique	The ribs have a more pronounced curvature and are more oblique
3. The body of the sternum is bigger and generally more than twice the length of the manubrium	The body of the sternum is shorter and generally less than twice the length of the manubrium
4. The upper border of sternum is generally on level with lower part of the body of second thoracic vertebra	The upper border of sternum is generally on level with lower part of the body of third thoracic vertebra

Except the difference in the frontal sinus and frontonasal angulation, most of the other differences can only be assessed by a skilled anatomist.

Mathematical measurements of the skeletal parts, such as length of femur and humerus, have some significance for sexing but cannot be used per se because of the considerable overlap in size between the two sexes in at least 10% of cases. However, the following measurements are found more useful than the length of the long bones.

Scapula: The dividing line between male and female glenoid height is 36 mm.

Femur: When the vertical diameter of the femoral head is more than 47 mm, it is male; and when less than 45 mm, it is female. When the bicondylar width is more than 78 mm, it is almost certainly male; and when less than 74 mm, it is almost certainly female.

Humerus: When the vertical diameter of the humeral head is more than 45.5 mm, it is male; and when less than 41.5 mm, it is female.

Sacrum: The *sacral index* (SI), calculated by multiplying the breadth of the base of sacrum by 100 and dividing it by its anterior length, gives a figure of 116 for females and 112 for males.

Pubis: The *ischiopubic index* (IPI), calculated by multiplying the pubic length in mm, the length being measured from the point where they meet in the acetabulum, will determine sex in 90% of skeletons provided that the material follows the same racial pattern. The IPI for males is 73–94 and females 91–115.

A method for sexing the bones by the use of **medullary index** has also been described. The humerus, radius, ulna and tibia are the most reliable bones for this purpose.

According to **Krogman,** the estimated degree of accuracy in sexing adult skeletal remains is as follows:

Entire skeleton	—	100%
Pelvis and skull	—	98%
Pelvis alone	—	95%
Skull alone	—	90%
Long bones alone	—	80%

Q. 4.4. Mention the data to determine the age of a person from an examination of (a) mandible, (b) spinal column, (c) hip bone, and (d) sacrum.

Mandible: The mandible helps in a very general way to estimate the age of a person. *In infancy,* the ramus is short and makes an obtuse angle with the body, the condyloid process is nearly in line with the body, the coronoid process projects above the condyle, and the mental foramen opens near the lower border of the body. *In adult life,* the ramus makes nearly a right angle with the body, the condyloid process is elongated and projects above the coronoid process, and the mental foramen opens midway between the upper and lower borders of the body. *In old age,* the ramus again makes an obtuse angle with the body which is reduced in width due to absorption of the alveolar margin after loss of teeth from their sockets. Therefore, the mental foramen looks apparently nearer to the upper border of the body of the mandible (Figs 4.1 and 4.2).

Spinal column: In youth, the upper and lower surfaces of the bodies of the vertebrae bear radial markings which are pronounced at about the age of 10 years. Thereafter, they begin to fade and disappear by the age

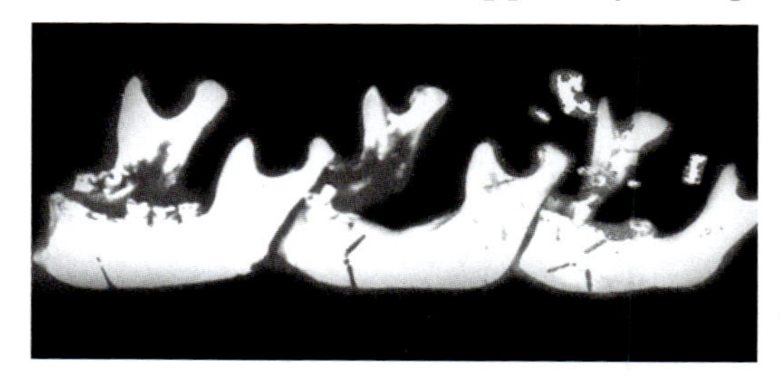

Fig. 4.1: Different presentations of mandible

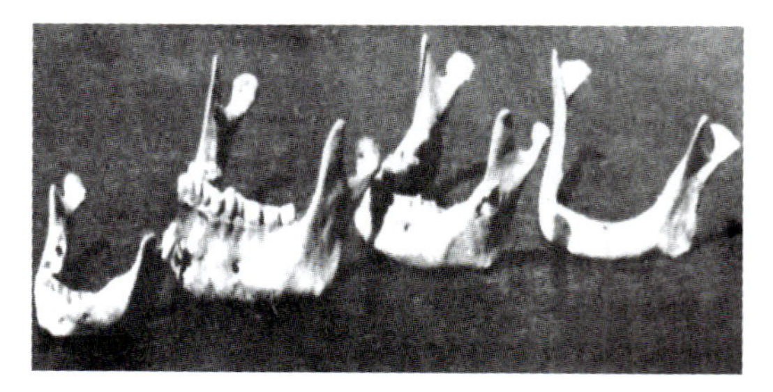

Fig. 4.2: Age changes in mandible. From left to right—mandible of a child, an adult, a middle-aged, and an old person. Note the changing angle, upgoing position of the mental foramen, and absorption of alveolar margin

of 30 years. The lipping of the bones occurs after the age of 40 years and is generally seen in lumbar vertebrae and joints of extremities. The osteophyte outgrowths from the anterior and lateral margins of the intervertebral discs rarely become prominent before 40 years. The disc itself undergoes atrophic changes by about 40–45 years.

Hip bone (Fig. 4.3): The symphyseal surface of the pubic bone undergoes a number of changes between the ages of 16–50 years. It has a layer of compact bone near its surface before 20 years. At about 20 years, it is very irregular with transverse ridges across the articular surface. By the age of 30, the irregularity is much less obvious, and at 50 or over, the ridges disappear, being replaced by a surface having a granular or eroded appearance.

When these changes are graded according to the symphyseal formula technique, it is found that the age estimates based on this single event are more dependable than similar age estimates from other bones.

Sacrum (Fig. 4.3): The several elements that comprise the sacrum begin to fuse from below, then upwards, and along the sides.

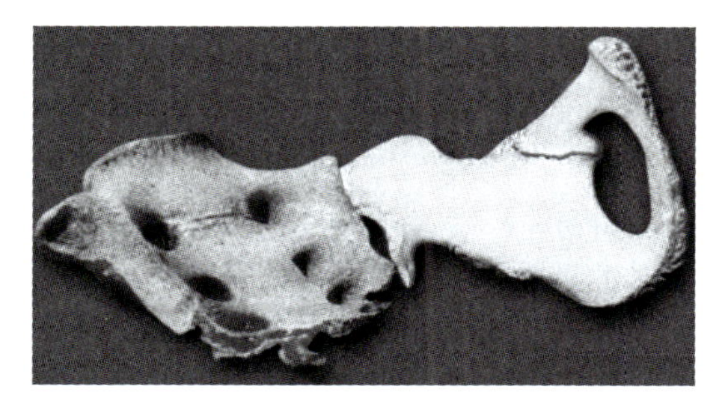

Fig. 4.3: Age determination from sacrum and hip bone. On left, the sacrum shows non-union between the first and second sacral vertebrae. By 23 years, usually all the pieces cf sacrum are united but non-union between the first and second pieces may persist up to 32 years of age (Krogman). On right, the ileum has not united with the pubis. The age is, therefore, less than 25 years. The symphyseal surface of the pubis shows wavy ridges of the type found usually around 20 years

By 23 years, ossification is complete except between first and second pieces where a gap may persist up to 32 years of age.

Q. 4.5. How will you determine stature in unknown human remains?

If a complete skeleton is available, stature is determined by the length of the skeleton plus 2.5 cm for thickness of soft parts. The height given by the relatives is usually misleading as it commonly includes the height of the shoes and hair. It should also be remembered that the corpse length is approximately 2 cm more than the living stature but can be less, if the corpse is in a state of rigor.

If the body is mutilated, its approximate stature is determined from the following data:

1. The stature of an individual is equal to the length measured from the tip of the middle finger to the tip of the opposite middle finger when arms are fully extended.
2. The symphysis pubis normally forms the centre of the body from 20th or 25th year onward. Accordingly, stature is twice the length from the vertex (top of the head) or heel to the top of symphysis pubis.
3. The height can be ascertained from one arm by multiplying its length by two and adding 30 cm for the two clavicles and 4 cm for the sternum.
4. The length of forearm measured from the tip of the olecranon process to the tip of the middle finger is equal to 5/19 of stature; the length from the sternal notch to pubic symphysis is 1/3 of stature; the vertical distance from top of the head to the tip of the chin is about 1/7 of stature; and the length of the skull is approximately 1/8 of stature of the person.

Mathematical formulae, such as those of Dupertius and Hadden, and Trotter and Glesser for Americans; Breitinger for

Germans; Telkka for Finns; and multiplication factors devised by Indian workers for Indians, can be applied to the length of long bones. The principle is to measure the length of a long bone, multiply it by a given factor, and then adding a fixed factor. Weight bearing bones give better appreciation of stature. The measurement of long bones requires a special but simple apparatus known as an *osteometric board*. While applying the various formulae, due account needs to be taken of the sex and race of the deceased by reference to appropriate tables.

In general, the humerus represents 20%, tibia 22%, femur 27%, and spinal column 35% of the stature.

Q. 4.6. Give a brief account of forensic odontology with special reference to its role in identification.

Forensic Odontology

Forensic odontology is a specialisation in dentistry, especially examination of teeth, as it relates to law. The subject normally concerns: (1) the identification of persons from data of their teeth pattern, and (2) the investigation of criminal cases where **bite marks** are involved and the identity of the biter sought. The teeth also provide evidence as to the age of the individual, his general facial characteristics, his economic status from the condition of his teeth and type of dental repair, and sometimes his occupation. Loss of teeth due to assault constitutes grievous hurt.

Teeth help in establishing identity because—(1) each adult has 32 teeth with five surfaces, each with their own characteristics of shape, size, position and spacing, with the result that no two sets of teeth are exactly alike, (2) teeth extracted after death leave a completely different socket from those removed during life, (3) when a tooth is removed or dental work of any sort carried out, the teeth pattern is changed and its record may exist with the dentist, (4) in natural decomposition, teeth are practically indestructible, (5) they are not easily destroyed by fire, (6) being sheltered in the oral cavity, they are generally not damaged, and (7) teeth as well as dentures made of acrylic resin are generally resistant to the action of corrosive acids.

The identification from data of authenticated teeth depends entirely upon the accuracy and completeness of authenticated records made during life. The record should include:

1. Number and situation of teeth present.
2. Number and situation of teeth lost including evidence of how long lost (note teeth lost postmortem).
3. Arrangement, irregularities, erosion, caries and fillings.
4. Bridge, crown work and dentures (artificial teeth).
5. Exact shape of edentulous jaws. A dental radiograph, when available, constitutes one of the most valuable pieces of evidence for identification purposes. Panorex X-ray technique provides excellent pictorial dental record easily understood by the layman. The Computer-Assisted Postmortem Identification (CAPMI) System compares dental records of victims of mass disasters and enables rapid identification of air crash, flood and explosion victims.

Some of the common identifying features of teeth pertain to: (1) faulty development, (2) faulty alignment, (3) presence of stains, (4) localised wear on certain teeth, and (5) missing teeth.

Faulty development: Teeth may be undersized (small), oversized, notched or may present some other irregularity as a result of faulty development and malformation. Hutchinson's teeth constitute a classical example of malformation of the incisors in congenital syphilis. The changes are most conspicuous in the central incisors which are usually small, widely spaced, notched and less broad at the cutting edge than at the gum margin giving them the appearance of the tip of a screw driver.

Faulty alignment: The defect in the alignment may be—(1) in the space between the teeth, e.g. widely spaced teeth, overriding teeth, (2) between the teeth of the upper and lower jaw. When there is protrusion of upper incisors resulting in overlap of the lower incisors, the bite pattern is known as overbite. The reverse pattern is known as cross-bite.

Stains: Pan (betel leaf, tobacco) chewing habit stains the teeth with dark, brown or black deposit. Yellowish or dark brown stains on the back of incisor teeth are common in cigarette smokers. Chalky white or yellowish brown areas of discolouration, striations and mottling on enamel, are found in fluorosis (excessive fluoride intake). Metal poisoning may cause pigmentation of the gums and thereby suggest a cause of death. Copper causes a green, and mercury and lead a blue-black line on the gums. Gum hyperplasia induced by phenytoin (dilantin) may aid in identification and also suggest epileptic seizure as a cause of death.

Localised attrition: A pipe smoker may have localised wear of teeth, either on incisors or at the angles of the mouth due to position of the pipe. Notched incisors from holding thread, pins or nails between teeth on a day-to-day basis may suggest that a female was a tailor or hair-dresser or a male was a cobbler.

Missing teeth: In decomposed bodies or skeletal remains, the teeth commonly loosen from their bony sockets and are found in the surrounding soil. Such displaced teeth should be saved, labelled as to body and/or location at site, and later secured into the intraoral position using adhesive cement with the help of a dentist, if necessary.

Most open alveoli are generally the result of postmortem tooth loss. The possibility of traumatic loss of tooth or extraction of teeth before death should, however, be remembered. The following points should be borne in mind while examining such cases:

1. The antemortem loss of teeth due to trauma at or near the time of death is frequently associated with fracture of the thin bony plate surrounding the alveolus. In a loose tooth which has fallen out, this is not so. This should be remembered as false and malicious reports are sometimes made about the loss of a tooth in order to charge an 'enemy' with grievous hurt.
2. Extraction or tooth loss in a living person is followed by bleeding from its socket which stops in about 24 hours or sometimes two to three days when the clot forms in the raw socket. By about 14 days, the clot is obliterated by fibrous tissue and the alveolar rim smoothened by resorption of bone. By about five to six months, gradual new bone formation fills the socket but its outline is still visible on X-ray examination. By about six months to one year, remodelling of new bone completely obliterates the socket leaving a slight depression and the socket outline is no longer visible on X-ray examination.
3. In recently recovered remains, postmortem tooth loss discloses a clean socket devoid of blood clot. In skeletons in which postmortem loss of teeth is common, the bony rim of the alveolus is sharp and feathered.

Bite marks can permit precise identification because the alignment of teeth is peculiar to each individual. The mark may be on the articles of food found at the scene of crime or on human beings involved in sexual crimes, and may be found on the skin of neck, breast, shoulder or buttock. It is important to realise that a bite on human flesh can leave a mark not necessarily due to a break in the continuity of the skin but due to a small subdermal or thin deep haemorrhage.

Bite marks are always contaminated by saliva and, therefore, contain amylase, ptyalin and blood groups which can be determined, if the biter is a secretor. The identity of the biter can also be determined, if the cast of the suspect's mouth is made and a transparency of his bite compared with that of the unknown bite. It should be remembered that bite marks on skin are apt to be modified by its elasticity when the teeth are withdrawn. Generally, it is easier to exclude a certain person than to identify one conclusively from the bite mark. However, the pattern of teeth marks with the arrangement of teeth within a dental arch provides a valid and simple method of demonstrating points of similarity and dissimilarity to a court. On a number of occasions, abnormalities of tooth position or arrangement within a dental arch of a suspect confirm or completely eliminate the accused as a perpetrator of a bite mark.

Q. 4.7. Outline briefly the special techniques for identification in mass disasters. Discuss the use of X-rays in detail. Describe briefly the importance of radiography.

These include: (1) X-rays, (2) ultraviolet rays, (3) postmortem serology, and (4) DNA profiling.

X-rays

All bodies which are found under suspicious circumstances and which are rendered unrecognisable due to prolonged immersion in water, burning by fire or acid, or by any other destructive means, such as explosion, should be routinely X-rayed. Radiography can provide information in relation to: (1) age, (2) sex and race, (3) occupation, (4) diagnosis of certain conditions, (5) identification, and (6) cause of death.

Age: The use of X-rays to establish age by radiography of bones and teeth (for root calcification) is already discussed. Calcification of costal cartilages and osteoarthritic changes in large joints and the spine also help.

Sex and race: Sex may be deduced from the shape of the pelvis, angle of neck of the femur, sinus outlines and from measurements of other bones. Racial characteristics in the skull (orbits and nasal aperture) and occasionally in the hands and feet (radiohumeral and tibiofemoral index) of negroid races can be deduced in some cases.

Occupation: This can sometimes be deduced from X-rays. The whole range of pulmonary occupational diseases, such as silicosis, asbestosis and other pneumoconioses may show specific radiographic findings. The radial artery in labourers using pneumatic drills may show calcification. Coal carriers and professional wrestlers are liable to calcified lesions of the ligamentum nuchae. Football players may show calcified haematomas of the thigh muscles.

Diagnosis: The presence of a foetus may be diagnosed as early as the middle of the fourth month of pregnancy. *Spaulding's sign* (overriding of skull bones in a foetus) is indicative of the death of the foetus and its consequent maceration in utero.

Radiography of the *battered baby* can detect the presence of fractures of different ages and in different stages of healing, their number, type (green stick, nobbing), position and, at least in some cases, indicate how they were caused, and show contributing factors (treated or untreated) causing their final appearance. *Nobbing fractures* are due to the assailant holding the child with both hands and shaking it violently, thus fracturing ribs on both sides close to the spine, giving a nobbing appearance, when the ribs begin to heal. An excessively large amount of callus formation is seen in untreated fractures.

The X-rays are widely used to diagnose *fractures* and their age. An X-ray is important to demonstrate a fracture of thyroid cartilage or hyoid bone in cases of strangulation. X-ray films provide a permanent record of osseous disease and injury. In addition, soft tissue injuries, e.g. pneumothorax, pneumomediastinum, interstitial emphysema and pulmonary emboli can be easily demonstrated. X-rays are most valuable especially in the diagnosis and interpretation of extremity long bone injuries which are not commonly subjected to autopsy dissection.

X-rays are also used to locate the presence of radio-opaque foreign bodies, such as pins, needles, glass particles, broken knives and bullets. In case of bullets, metallic fragments may indicate the path taken by them. Radiography is invaluable particularly in those cases where bullets or bullet fragments are carried in the arterial or venous system as emboli. Fragments of bomb casings or contents may be easily missed and thereby very important evidential information may be lost without an X-ray.

Angiography of the coronary arteries has been used for the diagnosis of the severity of *coronary artery disease.* Postmortem injection of radio-opaque material to diagnose *traumatic basal subarachnoid haemorrhage* is now an accepted investigative method.

X-ray examination also helps in the diagnosis of poisoning by metals. A film of the abdomen will reveal radio-opaque shadows in acute arsenic poisoning; opaque particles in the intestine are seen, if paint or other lead products have been ingested recently. X-ray evidence of transverse bands of increased density at the growing end of bones in children is seen in chronic poisoning by arsenic, lead or iron. Multiple bands represent repeated episodes of poisoning.

Failure to X-ray 'in vivo' a case of injury to bones or joints in which there is doubt about diagnosis is prima facie evidence of negligence (malpractice).

Identification: Radiographs taken after death can, if compared with similar views of the same part X-rayed in life, provide positive identification of an otherwise unrecognisable corpse. Skull features suitable for comparison include frontal sinus outline, mastoid air cells, pituitary fossa profile, arterial and venous markings and suture patterns. Superimposition photography can provide corroborative or sometimes conclusive evidence of identity.

Cause of death: Fracture of bones as seen on X-ray may indicate their antemortem origin, and these include depressed fracture of skull, fracture of hyoid, fracture dislocation of cervical vertebrae, severe injury to bones by a cutting instrument or fracture of several ribs which are incompatible with life. Foreign bodies in the upper respiratory tract provide valuable clues. Bullets found in the body and broken parts of a weapon (e.g. knife) serve the same purpose. Foreign bodies, such as abortion sticks, in the female genital tract provide evidence of criminal abortion. Evidence of poisoning by heavy metals, and signs of disease, such as malignant growths, may be apparent.

Ultraviolet Rays

An ultraviolet lamp can be used to locate and define tattoo marks and scars on burned and decomposed remains, to interpret illegible ink markings on clothes, and to segregate bones in case of a mix-up. When examined by ultraviolet light, washed blood stains are readily seen, and seminal stains show a bluish white fluorescence.

Postmortem Serology

A known postmortem blood grouping of an individual serves to narrow the range of possible identities. The inability to obtain whole blood postmortem does not eliminate the use of this method as fragments of congested tissues, such as lung, liver or skeletal muscle can be utilised for blood group determination. Even in putrefied bodies, blood group antigens may be detectable for serologic studies. The bone marrow in skeletal remains may still retain serologically detectable antigens.

DNA Profiling

This is useful, if suitable tissue (blood, semen stored in bank) is available. If no such tissue is available, the DNA profile of autopsy derived tissue should be compared by single probe analysis with that of parents, children, siblings, and if necessary other relatives. This is now used worldwide in aircraft and other major accidents. (For further details, please refer to the Chapter 34 on 'Forensic Examination of Biological Fluids, Stains and Other Materials'.)

Certain legal issues: National Research Council of the USA (an authority in DNA testing) states that it would not be scientifically justifiable to speak of a match as proof of identity without mentioning how much rare are the matching characteristics. In Premjibhai Bachubhai Khasiyor in state of Gujarat 2009 (4) RCR (criminal) 186, the Gujarat High Court observed that the science of DNA is at a developing state. If the random occurrence ratio is not provided in the test result report and it only mentions that DNA profile of accused matches with the fetus, this alone cannot be taken as conclusive proof. If it is a solitary piece of evidence with a negative result, then it conclusively excludes the accused involvement. The Supreme Court of India in Smt. Kamti Devi *vs* Poshi Ram, 2001 (cs) Sec. 311: AIR 2001 Sec. 2266, made the observation that only a genuine DNA test is scientifically accurate. Wherever and whenever the samples match, the probability of identity of an individual depends upon a strong database. As of now CDFD (Centre for DNA Printing and Diagnostics) has not published any data bases of Indian population. The DNA report that does not show statistical probabilities is not likely to be accepted by the court as an infallible evidence.

5

Medicolegal Autopsy

Autopsy (autos = self; opis = view) literally means to see for oneself. A medicolegal autopsy (necropsy) or postmortem examination (necros = dead; opis = view; post = after; mortem = death) is a special type of scientific examination of a dead body carried out under the laws of the State mainly for the protection of its citizens and to assist the identification and prosecution of the guilty in cases of unnatural deaths. As such, it requires State permission and must meet with certain essential requirements.

Q. 5.1. What are the objectives of a medicolegal postmortem examination? What are its essential requirements?

The *objectives* of a medicolegal autopsy are:

1. To determine the identity of the person.
2. To determine:
   a. The cause of death, whether natural or unnatural
   b. If unnatural, whether suicide, homicide or accident
   c. In all cases but more important in homicide, to collect and document trace evidence, if any, left by the accused on the victim
   d. To identify the weapon, person or poison responsible for death
   e. In case of fatal wounding, to determine the volitional activity possible after such trauma.
3. To estimate the approximate time since death.
4. In case of newly born infants, to determine the question of live birth and viability of the child.
5. In case of mutilated, fragmented or skeletal remains, to determine if they are human; and if human, the probable cause of death and approximate time since death.
6. To restore the body to the best possible cosmetic appearance before it is released to the relatives.

The *essential requirements* of a medicolegal autopsy are:

a. It should be performed by a registered (licensed) medical practitioner having special training or experience in forensic medicine (forensic pathology).
b. The examination should be meticulous and complete; and one should routinely record all positive findings and important negative ones, e.g. absence of skull fracture in a case of head injury; absence of defence injuries in a case of struggle; or condition of coronary arteries in a case of sudden natural death.
c. All information must be preserved by written records including relevant photographs, radiographs, sketches on body diagrams, measurements and weights.
d. Trace evidential material when recovered should be properly documented and preserved.

e. From the data so obtained, the medical officer should provide a factual and objective medical report for the law enforcement agencies keeping in mind that he may have to explain his findings and opinions at the time of cross-examination in a court of law.

It is *necessary* that those who undertake medicolegal autopsies are familiar with the appearance of healthy and diseased organs. It is important to remember that colour changes are frequently found in the liver, kidney, stomach, duodenum, etc., due to the colouring matter of bile and food permeating the tissues, and these may be mistaken for signs of inflammation or putrefaction. Visceral hypostasis may also mislead an inexperienced medical officer.

Q. 5.2. Mention the precautions you will take while conducting a medicolegal autopsy. What are the differences between a clinical (pathological) autopsy and a medicolegal autopsy?

The following precautions are necessary: (1) authorisation, (2) identification, (3) visit to the scene of crime, (4) history of the case, (5) examination, (6) verification of injuries noted at the inquest (by the police), (7) preservation of viscera and other tissues, (8) notes, (9) list of articles, and (10) chain of evidence.

Authorisation: Authorisation for a medicolegal autopsy is given by the coroner, police or magistrate. When a dead body is sent for autopsy, it is always accompanied by a dead body challan, an inquest report or panchnama, and the "first information" report.

A *dead body challan* is a requisition submitted by the investigating police officer to a medical officer while handing over the body for postmortem examination. It contains the name, age, sex and religion of the deceased as well as suspected cause of death and the purpose for which the body is sent for autopsy. It also gives the place and distance from where the body has come, names of persons accompanying the body for protection and identification, identification marks, time of despatch from the village, and details of the articles and clothing accompanying the body. The medical officer should fill in the columns indicating the time of arrival of the body in mortuary and time of postmortem examination.

An inquest report or *panchnama* is a report which contains: (1) the available history of the case, (2) circumstances under which the body was found, and (3) opinion of witnesses and the police officer regarding injuries, manner of their causation, cause of death, and any indication of suspected foul play.

In case of death from injuries, either homicidal, suicidal or traffic accident, a copy of the accident register filled in by the medical officer from the hospital where the deceased was first taken for treatment and also the case-sheet from the hospital where the deceased was an in-patient, are also forwarded. In case of traffic accidents, the sketch of the accident is also provided.

In most accidental deaths, ideally an autopsy is required to rule out any foul play. As for example, a person who is under the influence of alcohol may be pushed down from a terrace and the subsequent death misinterpreted/misreported as an accidental death.

Identification: The body of the deceased should be identified by the police constable who brought it and by the relatives in presence of the medical officer who should make a note of the names and addresses of such persons.

In all cases, and especially in the case of unknown bodies, it is necessary to note all particulars, such as race, religion, sex, age, social status, height, weight, dental formula, etc. A wide variety of internal peculiarities, e.g. ingredients of the last meal, presence of disease in an organ, evidence of a previous fracture, absence of appendix, etc. may help to establish or exclude a given identification. In the case of unknown bodies, the police usually take a photograph before forwarding the body, and the medical officer should take fingerprint impressions, both plain and rilled, for examination by the fingerprint expert. Identification forms an important link in the chain of evidence. It may have to be proved before a charge can be made.

Visit to the scene of crime: A crime scene visit is worth undertaking, when the scene exists.

Noguchi records an instance in which insulin was injected in the intravenous drip tube to a victim undergoing treatment in a hospital. The scene was kept intact and the foul play detected by correlating autopsy findings and meticulous examination of the scene.

Knight records the instance of a husband who placed the body of his strangled wife in his car and secretly pushed it over the edge of a mountain road; unfortunately for him, he had left the ignition key in the off position.

If due to pressure of work, hour of day, distance, etc. the medical officer is not able to visit the crime scene, a written report of crime scene evaluation by a forensically trained investigator is very helpful. In a number of cases, crime can be excluded in favour of natural causes, suicide or accident. **When such is the case, a costly murder investigation, autopsy and laboratory procedures can be spared.**

The medical officer should proceed with the examination only after the scene has been documented by photograph, diagram or sketch, and the search for physical and trace evidence is concluded. The position of the body when found, its relationship to surrounding objects, the presence and position of weapons, blood stains, and marks of struggle, should be noted. If any poison/drug or remains thereof are found in a cup or in a bottle, they should be carefully preserved. Any possible inconsistencies between the apparent death scene and actual scientific findings (e.g. postmortem lividity not found on dependent parts of the body) should be recorded. The method of body handling, keeping together of clothing and personal effects, prevention of loose bullets and other items from dropping out of the clothing, and prevention of body contamination during removal, are all working decisions of the medical officer.

While removing the body from crime scene to mortuary, the head and each hand should be enclosed in a paper bag secured by a tape. In case of suspected rape murder or abortion, the vulva should be covered by an absorbent pad to prevent the loss of any discharge.

Some **disadvantages** in not visiting the crime scene are:

1. In the process of removal of the body to mortuary, fresh abrasions may be produced.
2. Clothing will be disarranged; blood stains may form on parts of the garments originally free from them.
3. Rough handling of the dead body by mortuary assistants may result in fresh tears in clothes and even fracture of ribs or bones of the extremities especially in the elderly or the debilitated.
4. Existing rigor mortis may be broken down at least partially.
5. Body temperature will change. All these may mislead the medical officer.

Even a delayed visit can be of help at times. In one case, Dr Subrahmanyam could track and hand over to police two live bullets found under a pile of wood.

History of the case: The medical officer should obtain all available details of the case so that:

1. He can take special care to examine a particular body part, e.g. neck in a case of asphyxial death or uterus and fallopian tubes in case of abortion, needle marks in case of injection of poison.

2. He may use special equipment, e.g. sexual assault kit.
3. He can preserve finger nail scrapings and clippings for trace evidence (hair, blood or skin of the assailant). The opinion of even the most eminent medical officer may be of decreased value, if he is ill-informed of the history and crime scene information.

In a case of a sudden death of a woman, the only finding at autopsy was a ruptured spleen. Only on inquiry, a history of 'kick on the abdomen' was given. At re-examination, the abdominal skin revealed faint abrasions in the region of the kick. The subtle mark was missed at the first examination.

In the case of a homicidal death from a plastic bag placed over the head of an intoxicated person, there was hardly any indication of the cause of death as the bag was removed prior to examination. The cause and mode of death could be arrived at only from a tactfully obtained history.

A customarily sedentary 50-year-old man dropped dead after running one mile in an attempt at physical conditioning. The autopsy disclosed atheroma in his coronary arteries with no focus of more than 60% stenosis, a normal weight heart, moderate obesity, and no other abnormality. Toxicological studies and histopathological study of the heart including the conduction system were not contributory. It was only from the history of unaccustomed physical exertion vis-a-vis his cardiac condition that helped to determine the cause and manner of death.

Examination: When a medicolegal autopsy is being performed, those not officially concerned with the investigation of the case should not be allowed. If the deceased had been under medical care, his physician should be encouraged to be present so as to obtain appropriate information regarding medical history and administered therapy. The accused or the relatives of the deceased should be informed of the place and time of autopsy so that they may be represented by a lawyer or doctor. This is to be preferred to a second autopsy.

The autopsy should be performed without undue delay after receiving the requisition. The medicolegal autopsy is performed on all the days of the week inclusive of public holidays to avoid any delay in the process of crime investigation. The examination should be done in day light. Unless adequate artificial light is provided, jaundice, characteristic post-mortem stains in certain cases of poisoning, and colour changes in bruises, may otherwise be difficult to appreciate. In peripheral places where cold storage facilities are not available, even if the body is brought by the police at any time of night, an external examination should be carried out immediately with special reference to body temperature, postmortem lividity, rigor mortis, external injuries, etc. so as to obviate the effects from advanced post-mortem changes, when autopsy is done the next day. The examination should be as thorough and complete as circumstances permit because (1) the obvious cause of death may not be the real cause of death, (2) coincident diseases contributory to the cause of death may be found in more than one organ. As for example, the finding, early in autopsy, of arteriosclerotic heart disease does not warrant concluding that the subject was immune to cerebral aneurysms or choking and is, therefore, not an acceptable reason to omit the examination of head and neck. *Special care should be taken, if the body is believed to be (1) hepatitis B positive, (2) HIV-infected (male homosexual, intravenous drug abuser, haemophiliac treated with repeated blood transfusions, female prostitute, and victim of sex abuse) or (3) there is suspicion of poisoning from cyanides or organophosphorus compounds.*

After autopsy, also visit to the scene going may be of help.

Verification of injuries: The injuries recorded in the inquest report should be verified. Postmortem changes/injuries may have been misinterpreted as antemortem injuries. As for example, postmortem lividity may be mistaken for bruises, putrefactive blisters under the skin for burns, postmortem ant-bite marks for antemortem abrasions, and postmortem injuries by rodents and animals for antemortem violence.

Points likely to be misinterpreted should be carefully clarified. *It is not commonly realised that skin and most body soft tissues tend to darken as they dry.* Thus, a 1/4 inch diameter circular abrasion on a child may be mistaken for a cigarette burn. If small petechial haemorrhages are observed on the skin adjacent to a gunshot entry wound, then a note that they do not represent grains of gun powder or impact from them is mandatory.

In the event of major discrepancy in the description of injuries as given by the police and as observed by the medical officer, it is advisable to ask for a second panchnama (inquest) to be held, preferably by a magistrate.

Preservation of viscera and other tissues: These are preserved for chemical analysis under the following circumstances:

1. When the investigating officer so requests.
2. When the medical officer suspects the presence of poison by its smell or some other evidence while conducting autopsy on injury cases.
3. To exclude poisoning in instances where the cause of death could not be arrived at after a full autopsy and there is no natural disease or injury.
4. In decomposed bodies.
5. In alcoholics. Any tissue which is likely to provide evidence should be preserved in 10% formalin for histopathological examination. In most cases, preservation of blood, urine, bile and vitreous is all that is required. When blood or other fluid is found within a body cavity, the quantity should be measured and recorded.

Where drug overdosage/abuse is suspected, toxicological analysis can provide valuable information about the life style, and mental and physical health of an unidentified person. Analysis of blood or tissue revealing anticonvulsants point to epilepsy; antidepressants to clinical depression and suicidal circumstances; and cocaine, amphetamines, and opioids to drug abuse.

Notes: While one is working with both hands, a small pocket tape recorder may be found very valuable for recording notes. In absence of photographic facilities, a diagram or sketch of all injuries is essential (Fig. 5.25). The notes form the basis of the written report and can be referred to when giving evidence. Nothing should be erased from the notes and all alterations should be initialised.

List of articles: A list should be made of all the articles removed from the body, e.g. clothes, jewellery, bullets, etc. They should be labelled, sealed, mentioned in the report and handed over to the police officer in exchange for a signed and dated receipt.

Chain of evidence: It is absolutely essential to preserve the chain of evidence by identifying the body and maintaining absolute control of the specimens removed at autopsy. The defence attorney has a right to ask how a specimen was taken, identified, preserved and despatched to the appropriate laboratory to ensure that no mistake in reporting has occurred.

Below is an excellent example where most of the standard requirements at autopsy were not observed and precautions

- Y-shaped incision from Acromian process on both sides along the lower part of breast to the xiphisternum in midline and downward up to symphysis-pubis skipping round the navel.
- Midline incision from symphysis menti to symphysis pubis skirting round the navel are well known incisions at autopsy. These leave visible stitch marks.

  Visible incision marks even though stitched are likely to be less appreciated if there is a way of keeping them away from front position. Amarjyoti Patowari has deviced a technique on those lines. This is presented in the form of illustration with due acknowledgements to the author and the publisher. (Am J Forensic Med Pathol 2010 31:1, pp 37–41).

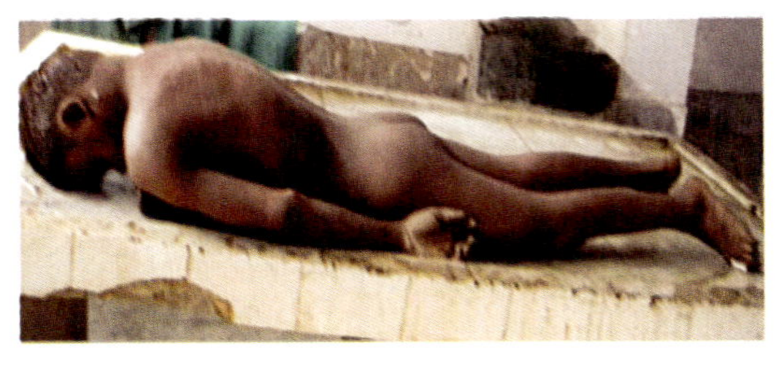

Fig. 5.1: Body in position

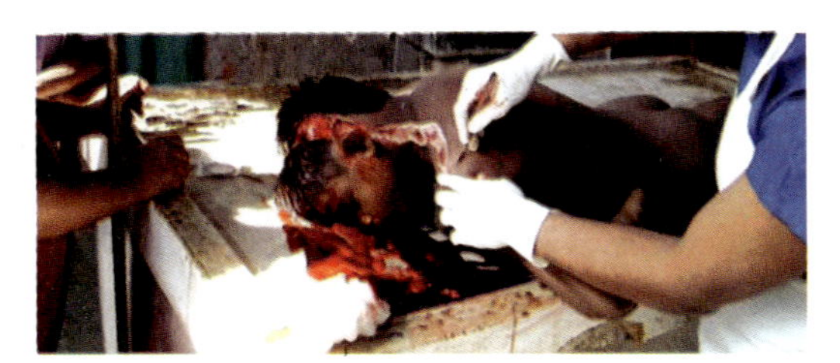

Fig. 5.2: Scalp incision extending to acromion process

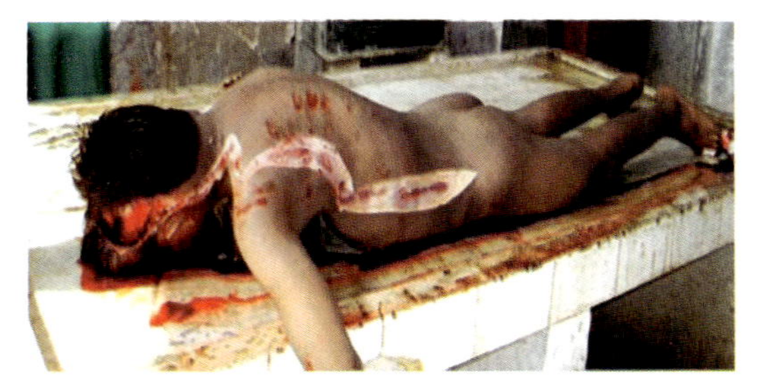

Fig. 5.3: Side view of back incision

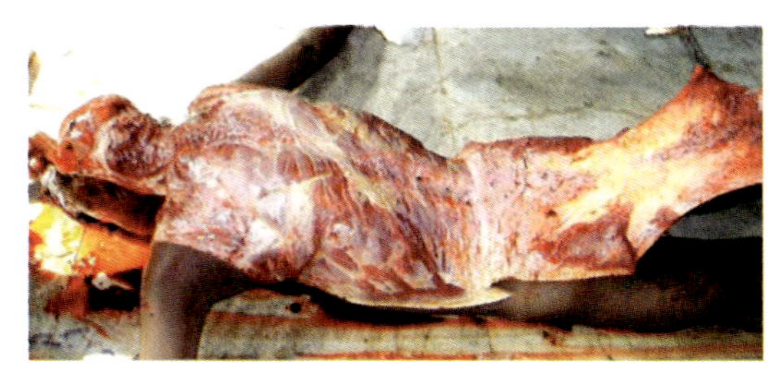

Fig. 5.4: Back flap lifted up to gluteal region

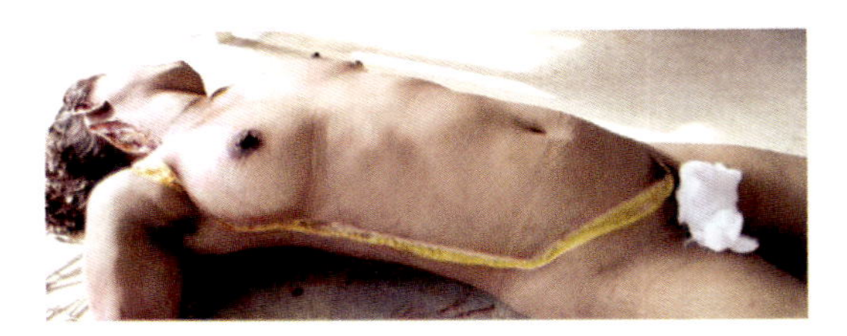

Fig. 5.5: Front view of incision

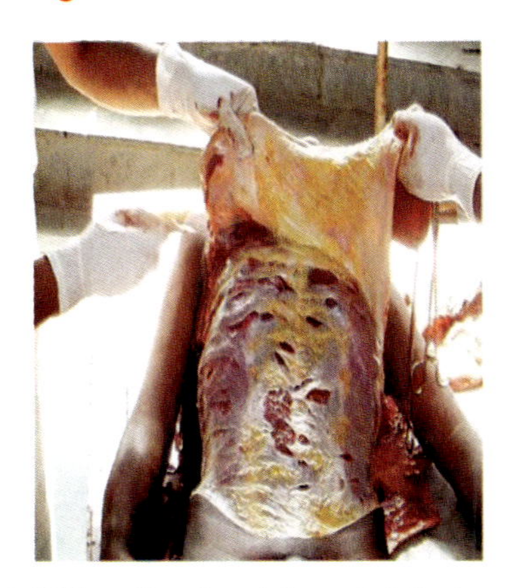

Fig. 5.6: Lifting the front flap (while inspecting wounds)

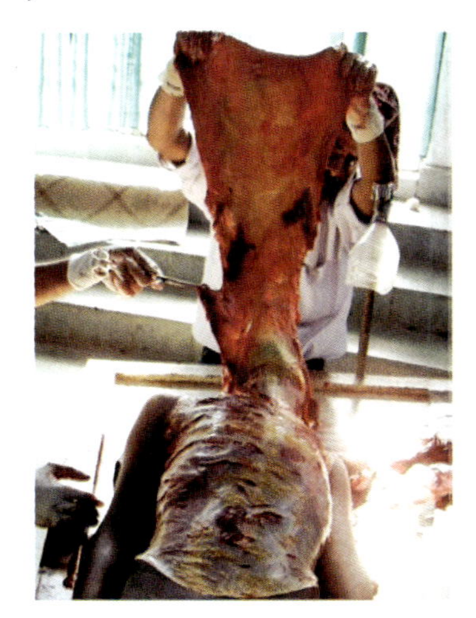

Fig. 5.7: Total flap held

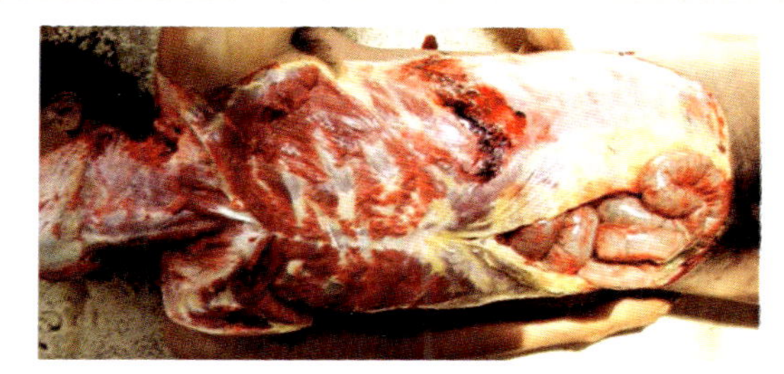

Fig. 5.8: Rectus abdominus opened paramedian incision

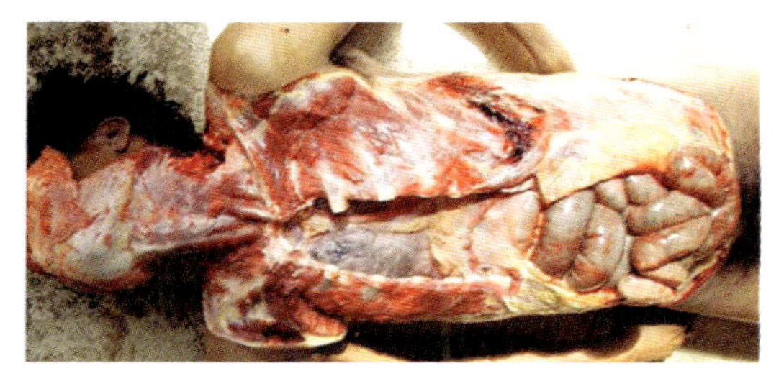

Fig. 5.9: Removing breast bone (sternum)

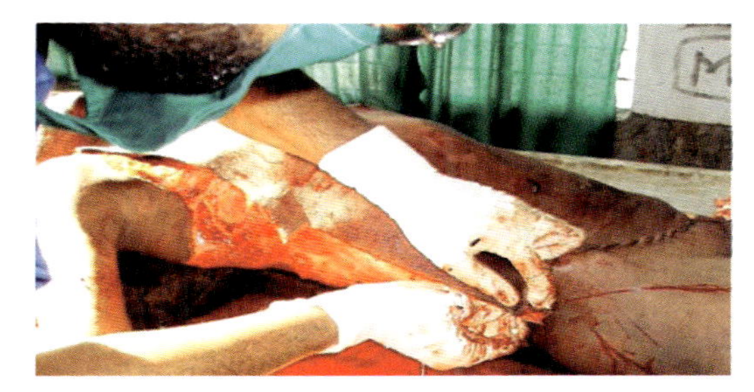

Fig. 5.10: Stitching front and back flaps

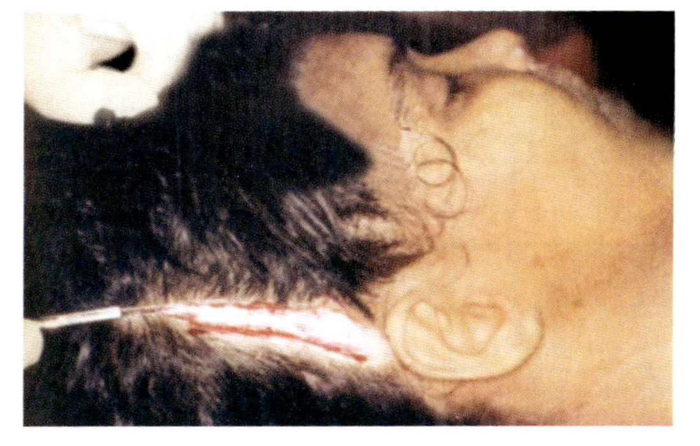

Fig. 5.11: Coronal plane scalp incision

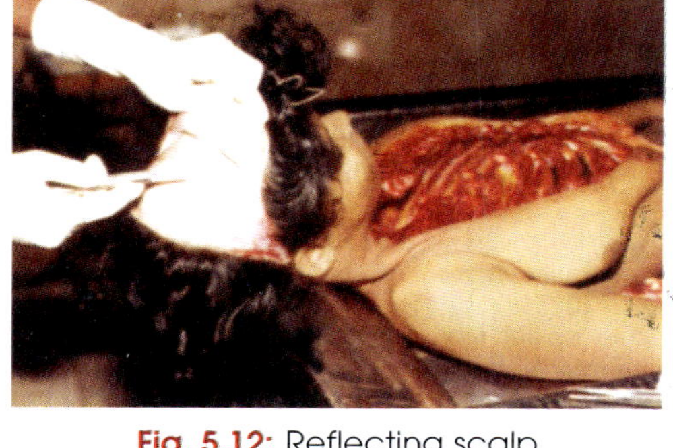

Fig. 5.12: Reflecting scalp

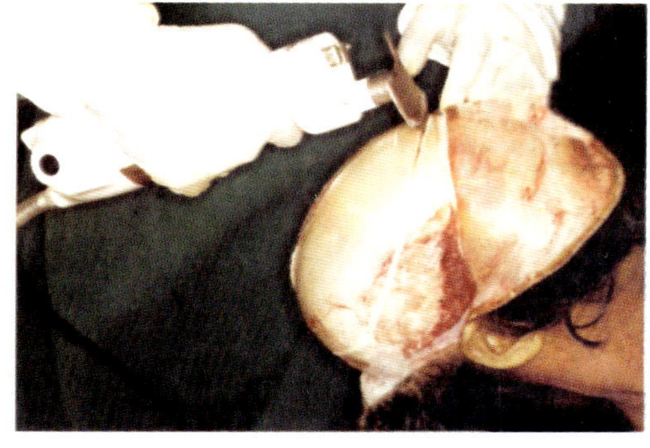

Fig. 5.13: Opening skull by styker autopsy saw

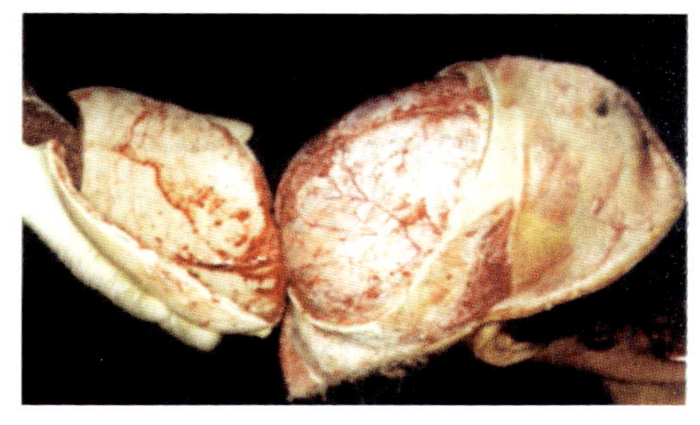

Fig. 5.14: Calvarium lifted. Meninges exposed

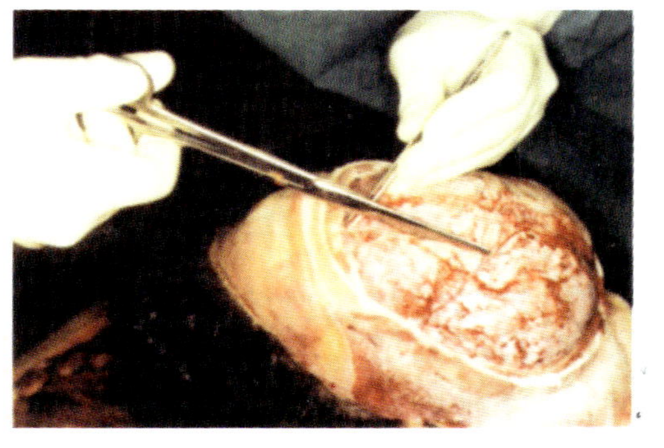

Fig. 5.15: Slitting dura mater

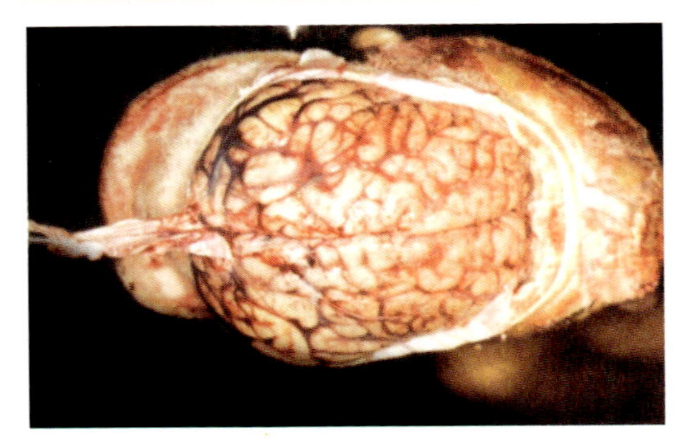

Fig. 5.16: Exposing brain

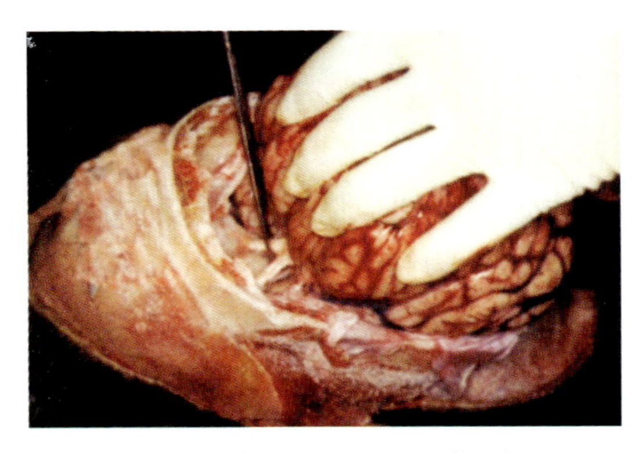

Fig. 5.17: Optic nerve sectioning

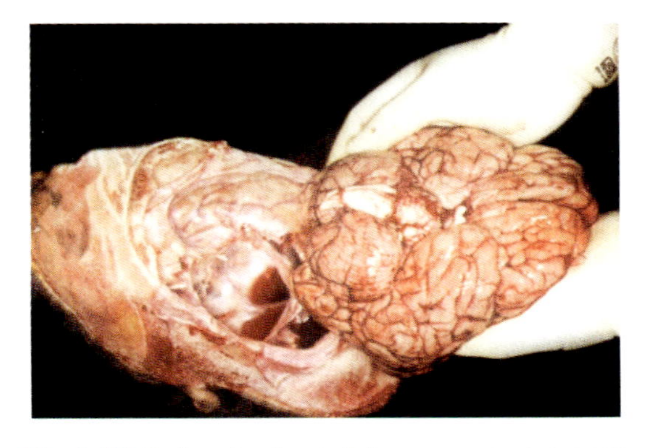

Fig. 5.18: Delivering brain into prosector's hands

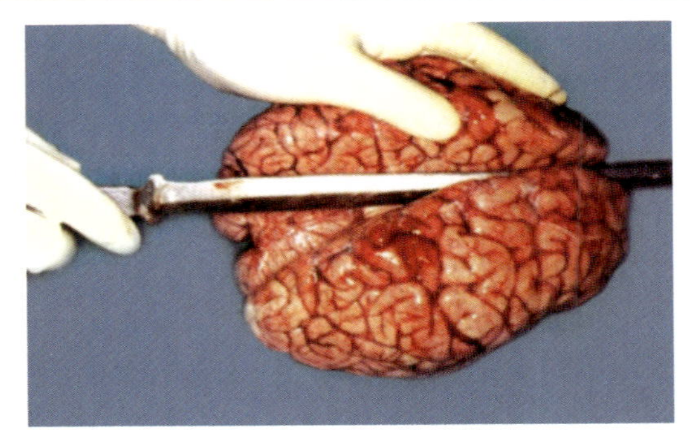

Fig. 5.19: Separation of cerebral hemispheres in middle

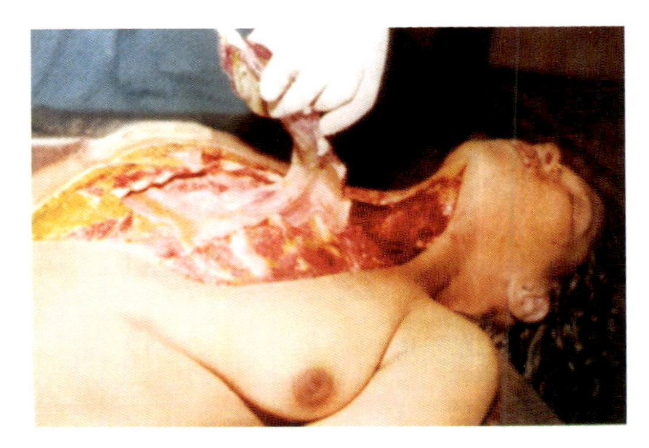

Fig. 5.20: Opening thorax, lifting breast bone

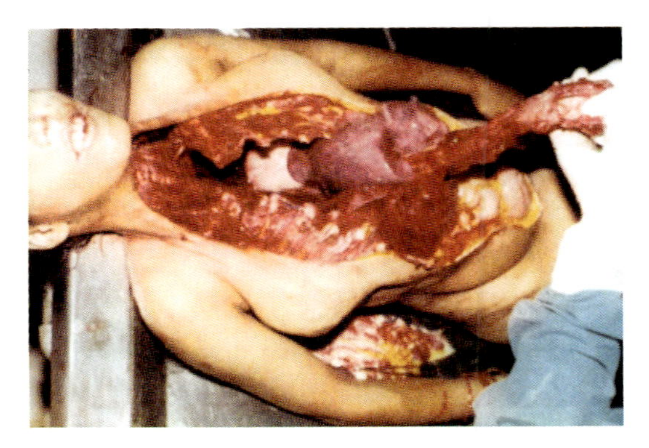

Fig. 5.21: En masse dissection of organs

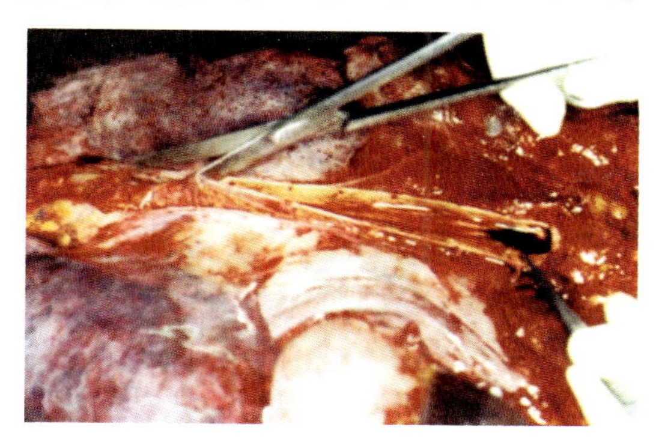

Fig. 5.22: Aorta slit open

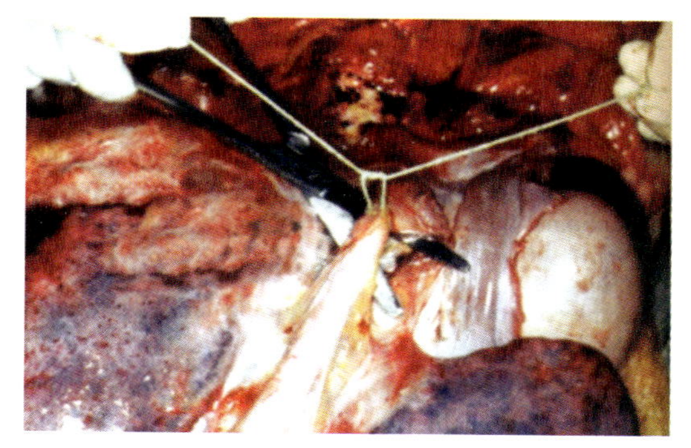

Fig. 5.23: Cardiac end of stomach esophageal ligating

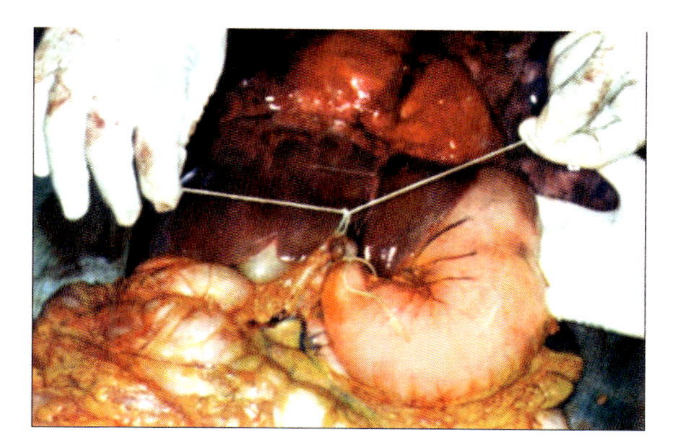

Fig. 5.24: Applying ligature at duodenal end

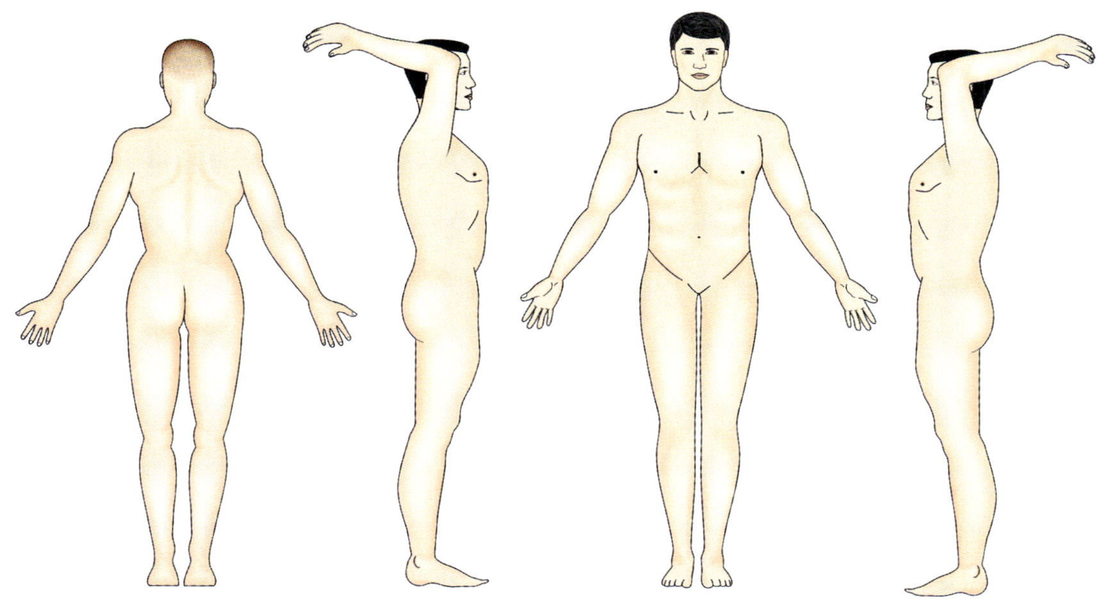

Fig. 5.25: (*Contd.*)

(*contd.*)

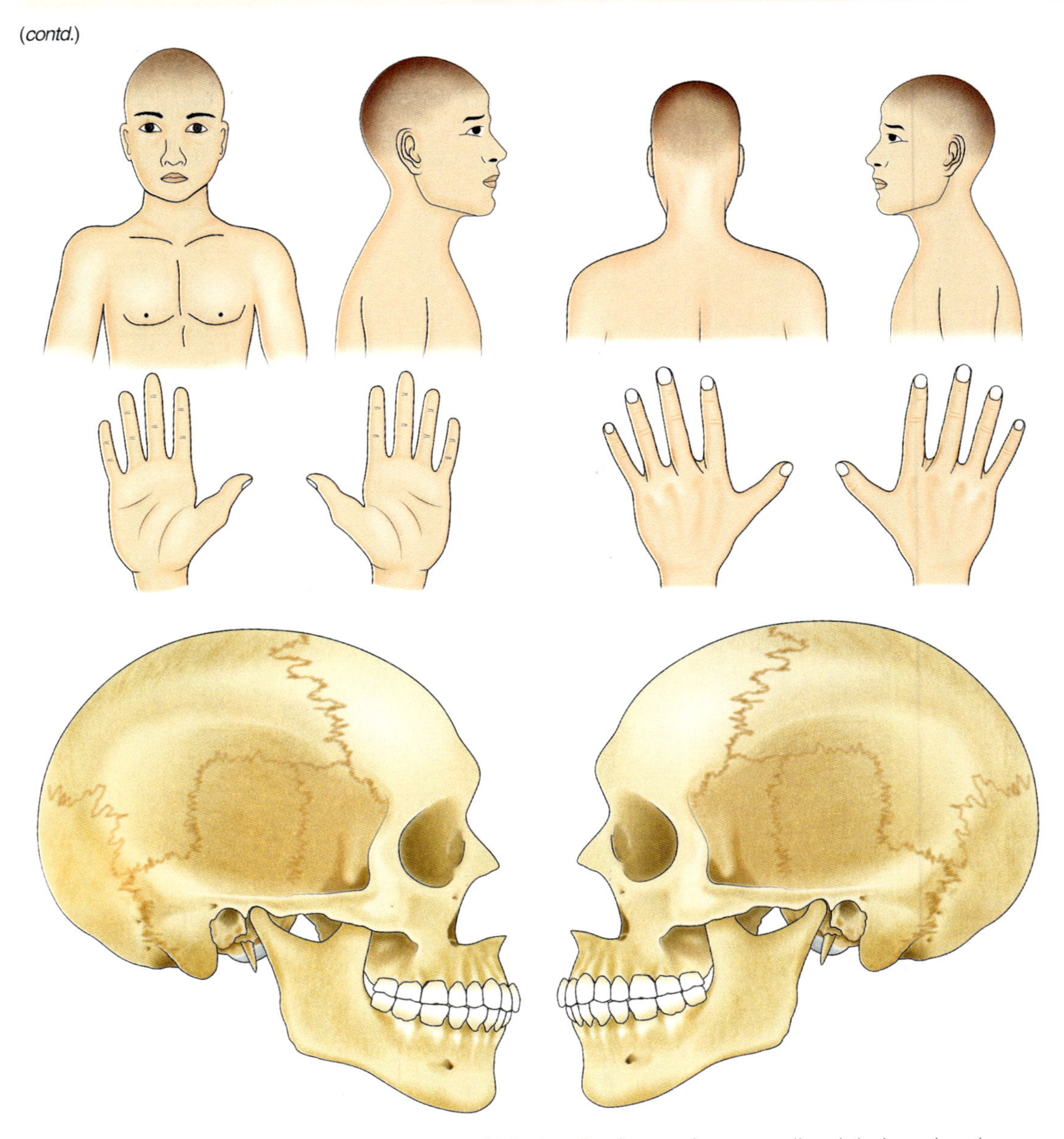

Fig. 5.25: Diagrammatic representation of injuries. Proforma for recording injuries at autopsy

not implemented, with the result that the autopsy report created considerable controversy which could not be satisfactorily resolved, even by a special investigation committee.

In 1979, the US House Select Committee on Assassinations investigated the records of the postmortem examination of John F. Kennedy, Former President of the United States, and reported it to be fraught with the following procedural errors:

1. The President's body was taken out of the hands of those who by law were responsible for investigation of death and autopsy in Dallas County, Texas.
2. Those performing the autopsy had insufficient training and/or experience to evaluate a death from gunshot wounds.

3. Physicians who treated the President at the Parkland Memorial Hospital in Dallas, Texas, were many hundreds of miles away from those who were performing the autopsy. This hindered communication so that there was some confusion between the features of injury and the therapeutic alteration of wounds.
4. Circumstances at the time of autopsy were not sufficiently controlled by the pathologists conducting the examination. A number of command military officers were present and they issued orders about autopsy procedure. One officer reportedly gave orders not to dissect or explore the gunshot wound of the neck.
5. Many allegations were made concerning the number and adequacy of photographs, which could have been eliminated by making copies available for examination.
6. The President's clothing was not examined appropriately—a classic error.
7. The autopsy procedure was incomplete because (a) external examination did not accurately locate the head wound and other wounds, (b) the bullet tracks were not dissected to determine their course through the body, (c) the angles of the bullet tracks through the body were not measured relative to the body axis, so as to permit easy reconstruction of trajectories, and (d) the brain was not properly examined.
8. The autopsy report was prepared without proper reference to photographs and radiographs. It was organised and worded in a way such that it led to comments and criticism.

Table 5.1: Differences between clinical/pathological autopsy and medicolegal autopsy

Clinical/pathological autopsy	*Medicolegal autopsy*
To find out cause of death	To find out cause of death and manner of death
Consent from relatives next of kin required	Not required
Requisition from clinician	Requisition from police/ magistrate
Autopsy report given to clinician	Given to police/magistrate
Necessary laboratory tests done in the concerned laboratory	Material to be sent to forensic science laboratory
Complete autopsy or partial autopsy sometimes, depending on consent	Always complete autopsy

Q. 5.3. Briefly describe the procedure for external and internal examination at autopsy. Outline the salient features.

External Examination

Those observations which pertain to the objectives of a medicolegal autopsy are specially looked for and these include: (1) data for identification, (2) detailed examination of clothing and whole body pointing directly or indirectly to the cause of death, (3) photographs or sketches of evidential value, and (4) data indicative of time since death.

1. ***Data for identification:*** A brief general description of the body should be given as regards sex, age, hair on various parts of the body with their length and colour, colour of the iris, tattoos, scars, deformities, etc. for the purpose of identification. The general condition of the body whether stout, emaciated or decomposed, should be mentioned. When poisoning is suspected, the body weight must be recorded to determine, if the quantity of poison detected could have caused a fatal outcome. The height is important in cases of assault where the relative size of the assailant and victim would matter. It is a good general rule to measure the height and weight of the body accurately in every case.

2. ***Detailed examination:*** The points relating to the probable cause of death must include everything that is indicative of the mode of death. In forensic work, the common causes of unnatural death are violence and poisoning.

The clothing should be described as regards its nature and condition, noting any tears, loss of buttons or disarrangement (indicating possible struggle). Cuts, holes, burns or blackening from firearm discharges should be described. The odour, if any, should be noted. Stains on clothes due to poisons, vomit or faecal matter, should be kept for analysis.

The condition of natural orifices, viz. nose, mouth, ears, urethra, vagina and anus, should be observed and any change from the normal noted. Irritants, e.g. cocaine, severely ulcerate nasal mucous membrane any smell, e.g. of alcohol, insecticides, etc., should not escape attention nor the presence of a foreign body. The mouth may reveal foreign bodies, drugs, damaged teeth, injured gums and lips (ruptured frenum of child abuse), and the bitten tongue of epilepsy. Any abnormal position of the tongue in relation to the teeth should be noted. The ears are examined for leakage of blood or CSF. Samples of discharges from urethra, vagina and anus should be taken on swabs (or smears prepared on slides).

The whole surface of the body should then be carefully examined, before and after washing from head to foot, and back and front, and the details noted. Multiple tattoos on the upper extremity to hide needle tracks are seen in drug abusers. Bile marks on tongue, lips or cheeks, may suggest terminal seizures from an overdose of cocaine or amphetamines. The presence of surgical emphysema, skin disease and other signs, such as oedema of the legs, icterus or eruptions of fevers should be recorded. A note should be made of the presence of signs of hypodermic injection and stains on skin from blood, mud, vomit, faeces, corrosive or other poisons or gun powder residues. A precise or detailed description with a scaled photograph or sketch of stains and injuries should be made. External injuries, such as abrasions, bruises, lacerations, fractures, cuts and stab wounds, burns, scalds and singeing of the hair, should be recorded systematically with full descriptive details and measurements where possible. Scalp injuries may be covered by hair and may be missed; scalp hair should be shaved, if necessary, and if shaved, they should be preserved for comparison in blunt injury cases, and gunshot residue tests in a case of firearm injury. Deep or penetrating wounds should not be probed until the body is opened. The limbs and other parts of the body should be examined for fractures and dislocations (by suitable movement and palpation), and for any condition that would suggest, if the deceased was right or left handed. A radiological examination is desirable in cases of firearm injury, decomposed bodies, bodies exposed to fire or explosions, child abuse, occult neck injury and suspected cases of air embolism.

Certain parts of the body should receive special attention (Fig. 5.26). In case a cord or ligature is found round the neck, the method of tying should be photographed and described before removal. The knot should be preserved by cutting the body of the loop. Binding the cut ends with thread prevents their fraying and opening out. The arrangement of the loop can then be reconstructed, if necessary if the cut ends are somehow marked to reveal the back, front, right and left. The ligature mark, if present externally, is studied as regards its position, width, character and extent of injuries. The hands should be examined for cuts about the fingers or abrasions over the knuckles, and if clenched, to ascertain, if anything is grasped in them. The finger nails should be examined for damage, presence of tags of epithelium, blood, dust,

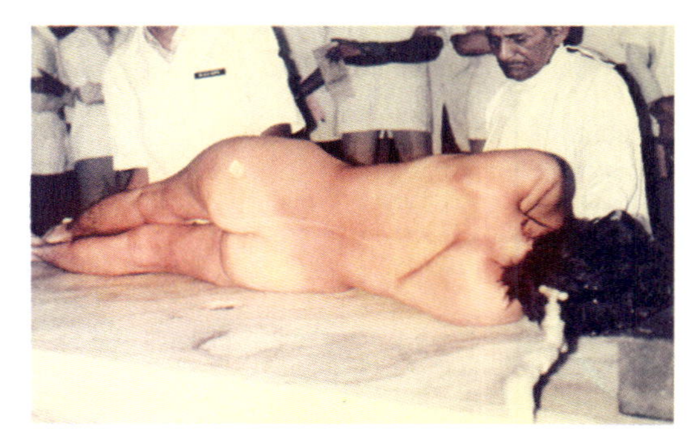

Fig. 5.26: Areas of contact flattening on the gluteal region

hair or any other foreign matter, indicating a struggle. In males, the testes should be palpated and later examined during the internal examination, as deaths due to squeezing of testes are reported. The eyes should be examined for corneal opacities, cataract, absence of eyes and artificial eyes. In vehicular accidents, such conditions may have contributed materially to the accident. In other cases, when the crime has occurred at night, this observation is important to verify the correctness of dying declarations made by such persons. In suspected asphyxial deaths, the eyes should be examined for subconjunctival petechiae. The condition of pupils, whether dilated or contracted, should be noted.

If a *cardiac pacemaker* is present, it should be removed lest the heating of the mercury batteries result in an explosion in the crematorium or cause environmental pollution, in due course, when buried. It is also necessary to check, if the pacemaker was still functioning properly (electrical performance) especially if death was sudden and apparently due to cardiac malfunction (as opposed to pneumonia!).

In the case of a body of a newly born infant where the question of live birth and viability is to be determined, it is necessary (a) to examine the umbilical cord, (b) to note the shape of the chest, and (c) to look for certain ossific centres. The umbilical cord is examined for its total length when possible, how it is severed, and the nature of any ligature thereon; and its condition, whether dry, healing or separated. The chest is examined for its shape, whether arched or flat. The ossific centres in the following bones are looked for: (1) calcaneum (20th week), (2) talus (28th week), and (3) lower end of femur (36th week).

3. ***Photograph/sketches of evidential value:*** A certain minimum number of photographs with a scale in position is essential. At least, one photograph should be taken of the scene for a permanent record and another to identify the body. Further photographs are necessary to document stains, and injuries, and to correlate external and internal injuries. Pathologic processes other than those of traumatic origin may also be photographed. In absence of photographic facilities, sketches may be made on body diagrams.

4. ***Data indicative of time since death:*** The data to estimate the approximate time since death from external examination include: (a) rectal or nasal and environmental temperature, (b) presence and extent or absence of rigor mortis, (c) incidence, extent, colour and degree of fixation of postmortem lividity, and (d) presence, character and extent of putrefaction.

Internal Examination

Incisions must be adapted to suit the circumstances of the case. All three major cavities of the body, viz. skull, thorax and abdomen, should be opened and examined as a routine (Fig. 5.27). The spinal cord need not be examined except in cases of: (1) local injuries, (2) sudden death following trauma without apparent local injury, (3) death from convulsions, (4) battered babies, and (5) when such an examination is specially requested by the investigating officer.

If the naked eye examination fails to reveal the cause of death, the medical officer should take appropriate specimens for histology and culture.

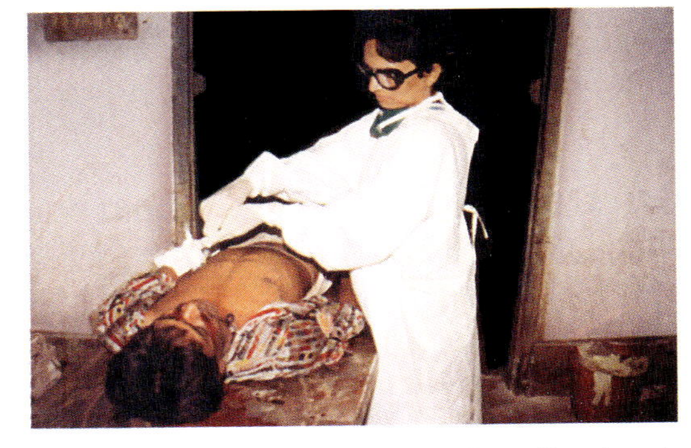

Fig. 5.27: Mortician dissecting the body (*Courtesy:* Dr BV Subrahmanyam, Dr PK Patel)

Any one of the following three methods may be followed: In the first method, a midline incision is made from just above the thyroid cartilage to the pubic symphysis avoiding the umbilicus and any injuries in the line of incision (I-shaped incision). This method is mainly followed as a routine on account of its simplicity and convenience. In the second method, two incisions are made. They commence on either side of the neck from the angle of the jaw to meet at manubrium sterni and then continue as a single incision down to pubic symphysis (Y-shaped incision). This method is specially suited when a detailed study of neck organs is required, e.g. in cases of asphyxial deaths due to compression of neck. In the third method, the two incisions commence on either side of the chest from anterior axillary fold, curve under the breasts to meet at xiphisternum, and continue as a single vertical incision down to pubic symphysis (modified Y-shaped incision). This method is desirable in those cases (especially females) where it is customary to keep a dressed body on view for some time after death.

The choice of opening the skull or body cavities first is governed by circumstances. In cases of head injury, it is a common practice to open the skull first and then the thorax and abdomen. In asphyxial deaths due to compression of neck, it is desirable to open the trunk first and then the skull. The draining out of blood from neck vessels via the trunk and skull then provides a relatively clean field for study of neck structures.

Q. 5.4. Describe briefly how would you make postmortem examination of the skull and its contents?

a. The body lies flat on its back with a wooden block underneath the shoulders and the head resting firmly on a head rest. The scalp is incised from mastoid to mastoid over the vertex taking care not to cut large masses of hair. This is done by inserting the scalpel at the right mastoid with the cutting edge facing the dissector and cutting the full thickness of the scalp from beneath outward over a coronal line curving over the vertex to the opposite mastoid. The scalp flaps are reflected forwards and backwards and a note is made of any injury or oedema. Any depressed fracture, if present, is recorded with its dimensions and contour.
b. The temporalis muscle is incised about its middle on each side. The skull cap is sawn and removed, the line of severance following a point just above the superciliary ridges in front and through the occiput behind, and preferably making an angle of 120° between the anterior and posterior cuts. This ensures that the skull cap will not shift on reconstruction of the body. The removal of skull cap is facilitated by gently inserting and twisting a chisel at various places through the cut taking care not to produce any postmortem fractures or extend the existing ones, and to avoid any damage to the meninges and brain.
c. The dura is examined from the outside for extradural haemorrhage, and the superior sagittal sinus for antemortem thrombus. The weight and/or volume of extradural haemorrhage, if present, is recorded. An antemortem thrombus in the superior sagittal sinus can lead to back pressure in the bridging veins crossing the subdural space resulting in subdural haemorrhage. In old persons, the meninges over the vertex are often white and thickened with small calcified patches (arachnoid granulations).
d. The dura is cut along the line of severed skull cap and pulled gently from front to back while cutting the falx cerebri. A note is made of subdural and subarachnoid haemorrhages, if any. The weight and volume of subdural haemorrhage,

if present, is recorded, and its effect on the brain—flattening, asymmetry, etc. assessed.

e. If the injury is recent (hours) and blood is not preserved at or near the time of injury, the extradural and subdural haematoma can be preserved for toxicological analysis, especially alcohol and drugs.

f. Four fingers of left hand are inserted between the frontal lobes and skull and the frontal lobes drawn backward. The nerves and vessels as they emerge from the skull are cut with right hand. A CSF sample is obtained by aspiration with a Pasteur pipette from the base. The tentorium is cut along the superior border of the petrous bone. The cervical cord, first cervical nerves and vertebral arteries, are cut as far below as possible, and the brain along with cerebellum removed. During the procedure, the brain is supported throughout with left hand. It is weighed and transferred to a clean dish for subsequent examination.

g. The remaining venous sinuses are examined for antemortem thrombi.

h. The pituitary is removed by chiselling away the posterior clinoid processes and incising the diaphragm of sella turcica around its periphery. Incising the diaphragm alone is sufficient in many cases. The gland is examined, if necessary, after fixation in 10% formal saline, for tumour, infarct, atrophy or any other pathological condition.

i. The dura is pulled out to examine the base of the skull and the rest of the cranial cavity for any fracture. If this is not done, even a big fracture may be overlooked.

j. A wedge-shaped portion of petrous temporal bone is removed to examine the mastoid for any collection of pus, haemorrhage or fluid in the middle ear (some drowning victims show haemorrhage in the middle and inner ear). The orbits and air sinuses are examined, if necessary.

k. The skull cap is inspected for fracture by holding it against light or tapping it to elicit a cracked sound.

l. The brain is examined for any swelling, shrinkage or herniation; its upper and lateral surfaces for asymmetry or flattening of convolutions; circle of Willis for aneurysm; and smaller cerebral arteries for embolism.

m. The cerebellum is separated at the pons transversely just below the cerebral peduncles.

n. The brain is cut in serial coronal sections about 1 cm apart (or cut obliquely at intracerebral fissure) exposing the basal ganglia, lateral ventricles and white matter. It is examined for thickness of grey matter, haemorrhage or other abnormality. Shrinkage of cerebral cortex (grey matter) is common in chronic alcoholics. Cerebral fat emboli which have completely obstructed the small vessels of brain may be visible to naked eye as punctate haemorrhages in the white matter. Petechial haemorrhages in white matter are commonly found in death from anaphylactic shock. In head injury, oedema is seen in white matter around or deep to contusions, lacerations or ischaemic lesions. If there are wounds of the brain, successive sections parallel to the wounded surfaces are made till the whole depth of the wound is revealed.

o. The cerebellum is cut vertically through the vermis to expose the fourth ventricle. An oblique cut is made through each hemisphere to expose the dentate nucleus. Any disease, injury or haemorrhage, if present, is noted.

Q. 5.5. Describe briefly how would you make postmortem examination of the spinal column and spinal cord?

Either an anterior or posterior approach can be used. The examination of thoracic spinal column is facilitated by the anterior approach. High cervical injuries are best demonstrated by the posterior approach, which is in common use:

a. The body is turned over on to the face with a block beneath the thorax. A routine midline incision is made from the base of skull to sacrum. The paraspinal muscles and fasciae are scraped off from the spinous processes and laminae. A laminectomy is performed on each vertebra by sawing through the entire length of spine on each side of the spinous processes. The laminae of first cervical vertebra are not severed or else the head will move too freely on the spine. The spinous processes and attached laminae are removed en masse. The spinal cord can also be removed from the front after the trunk is eviscerated.

b. The dura is examined for any pathological condition, such as inflammation, haemorrhage, suppuration or tumour. It is cut in midline. The spinal nerves are cut from below upwards as they pass through the spinal foramina. The cord is separated at the foramen magnum, carefully lifted from the vertebral column and placed on the table.

c. After some fixation usually of several days duration, the cord is cut transversely at several places and examined for any pathological condition, such as softening, crushing, haemorrhage, infarction, inflammation or intramedullary tumour, and some tissue is retained for histological examination.

d. The vertebral column is examined for fracture (especially of the odontoid process and cervical vertebrae), disc protrusion, tumour, dislocation and vertebral collapse. Bruising under the prevertebral fascia should be taken as indication of whiplash injury or fracture of the cervical vertebrae which should be specially looked for.

Q. 5.6. Describe in detail the dissection and examination of the heart and coronary arteries.

The pericardial sac is inspected for its contents and any abnormality. Normally, the pericardial cavity contains about 10 ml of fluid. If haemorrhage is present, its site of origin (ruptured ventricle or aorta) is determined, and the volume of any blood that is present is measured. The pericardial sac is opened by an anterior midline cut with scissors. The coronary vessels are inspected for segmentation and the right side of the heart observed for its size and palpated for crepitation as evidence of air embolism. The pericardium is cut over the diaphragm.

The heart is held at the apex and lifted upwards. It is isolated by cutting the vessels entering and leaving it (inferior and superior vena cava, pulmonary vessels and ascending aorta) as far away as possible from its base. The isolated heart is then studied as regards its size and weight (after sectioning). At this stage, it is important to note the amount of epicardial fat. The weight alone, without a comment on the epicardial fat, can make a borderline weight almost impossible to interpret. Ventricles should be separated and weighed, if accurate weight of each ventricle is required.

The heart is frequently cut along the direction of blood flow—right atrium, right ventricle, pulmonary arteries, pulmonary veins, left atrium, left ventricle and aorta. The right atrium is cut between the openings of superior and inferior vena cava. One blade of scissors is passed through the inferior vena cava, and the right atrium is cut till the blade emerges out of the superior vena cava. An additional cut opens the right auricle. The tricuspid opening is inspected. It should normally admit three fingers. The knife is then directed through the tricuspid valve to cut the right ventricle along its lateral border up to its apex. The incision is then carried along one cm lateral to the ventricular septum on the right side, passes through the pulmonary valve at the junction of its anterior cusps, and enters the pulmonary trunk and pulmonary arteries. The left atrium is opened by cutting between the openings of pulmonary veins. An additional cut opens the left auricle. The mitral opening is inspected. It should normally admit two fingers. The knife is then directed through the mitral valve to cut the left ventricle along its lateral border up to its apex. The incision is then carried along one cm lateral to the ventricular septum on the left side, passes through the aortic valve ring in the region of the commissure between anterior and left posterior valve cusps, and enters the aorta. If stenosis or incompetence of valves is an issue, the diameter of the valve rings is measured.

The auricular appendages are examined for thrombi. The state of the myocardium, size of heart chambers, state of endocardium (subendocardial haemorrhage in left ventricle in sudden hypotension, e.g. shock, postpartum haemorrhage, ruptured viscus, and poisoning by arsenic, oleander, etc.), valvular lesions, and condition of aorta as regards any aneurysm, atherosclerosis or syphilitic aortitis (tree bark appearance) are described. The state of aorta is examined around orifices of coronary arteries.

The heart can also be studied after fixation by cutting in a series of rings not more than 5 mm thickness. This provides a good opportunity for overall study of state of valves, endocardium, myocardium, and coronary arteries.

The sinuses of Valsalva are examined to detect congenital hypoplasia and obstruction of the coronary ostia. This examination is too often neglected. The coronary arteries (particularly the left coronary artery) are examined by making serial incisions down the course of vessels about 2–3 mm apart, to demonstrate any narrowing or antemortem thrombus, the common site being about one cm away from the origin of left coronary artery. A longitudinal cut with fine scissors provides a better measure of the extent of atherosclerotic disease. If coronary artery disease is suspected, it is a sound practice to examine them before the heart is opened.

Q. 5.7. Comment on pulmonary thrombi and pulmonary emboli at autopsy.

Before cutting the pulmonary artery; while isolating the heart from other thoracic organs, it should be palpated for any evidence of **thrombi**. The thrombi, if present, can be pulled out by making a longitudinal incision in the pulmonary artery and probing the artery with a pair of forceps. A thrombus may be coiled upon itself. Sometimes, the pulmonary artery and its branches contain clots which form in stagnant blood after death and fit these vessels as a perfect cast. It is essential to be able to differentiate these postmortem clots from antemortem thrombi. An antemortem thrombus is firm and dry, may be adherent to the lining endothelium, and has a transversely ridged surface because it is formed in layers in flowing blood. A postmortem clot is weakly adherent to the lining endothelium, wet looking, and generally forms after its blood settles down with the result that it appears either yellow (chicken fat) or soft and red (current-jelly).

In all cases of pulmonary embolism, the legs, thighs, and pelvic veins, must be examined for the presence of thrombi by making transverse cuts through popliteal and mid-calf regions, the cut ends of veins being examined for thrombus or by making vertical incisions along the course of veins in the calf muscles, back of knee, and inner side of thigh.

If fat or air embolism in the pulmonary artery is suspected, e.g. in a case of suspected abortion or open wound of neck, the following procedure is recommended: To demonstrate **fat embolism** in the pulmonary artery, it is opened under water with a pair of scissors before the lungs or heart are dissected. Fat droplets can occasionally be seen to escape. Microscopic examination of frozen sections of lungs stained for fat, with Sudan III or osmic acid, is confirmatory. In pulmonary **air embolism,** death is due to mechanical obstruction to outflow of blood from right ventricle. If possible, a regional X-ray may be taken with the beam projected horizontally. To demonstrate air emboli, the pericardial sac is cut anteriorly, filled with water, and the edges grasped with haemostats on each side. The right side of heart is then punctured when bubbles of air and frothy blood will be seen to emerge. It is possible to trace the path of air bubbles. To do this, the right border of heart is cut through right atrium between the two vena cavae. The incision is continued along the septal wall of right ventricle into pulmonary trunk and its main branches.

Q. 5.8. Write short notes on: (a) tests for pneumothorax, (b) dissection and examination of lungs.

Pneumothorax is suspected by bulging of chest wall. It can be confirmed by the following tests:

1. A 16 gauge needle attached to a 25 ml syringe filled with water is inserted through an intercostal space into pleural cavity; air bubbles will appear in the syringe, if air is under pressure.
2. The rib cage can be opened in an appropriate manner, and an intercostal muscle punctured under a pool of water supported by the reflected skin flap, when bubbles of air will be seen to escape.
3. Where facilities permit, an X-ray may be taken with the beam horizontal.

Dissection of the lungs: The hilar vessels are cut, first the left, and then the right, and the lungs removed (from the thoracic cavity) for examination. They are weighed before cutting as appreciable oedema fluid can run out during dissection. The lungs are cut laterally through the hilum, first the left and then the right. The cut surface can be opened like a book and examined for oedema, consolidation, emphysema, atelectasis, congestion, infarction, and petechiae. The bronchi and their ramifications are inspected for mucosal thickening, infection, and blockage. The smaller pulmonary vessels are inspected for thrombi and emboli that are not visible in the larger vessels.

In some medicolegal cases where an industrial disease, e.g. pneumoconiosis or asbestosis is suspected, the lungs should be inflated with formalin before cutting. This preserves the shape of the lungs and provides excellent specimen for histology.

Q. 5.9. Briefly describe the procedure for the dissection and examination of the following viscera at autopsy: (a) stomach, (b) bowels, (c) kidneys, (d) prostate, (e) testes, (f) female genitalia.

a. *Stomach:* When the oesophagus is cut while removing thoracic viscera en masse, a ligature is tied at the lower end of oesophagus. This ligature near the cardiac end of the stomach includes the lower 5 cm of oesophagus. A double ligature is tied at the pyloric end and the stomach divided between these ligatures. It is placed in a clean enamel tray and cut along the greater curvature to examine the mucous membrane, contents, **state** of digestion of food, smell, colour, and presence of foreign or suspicious matter. When poisoning is suspected, a detailed study of stomach and its contents is required.

b. *Bowels:* The small intestine is separated from the mesentery by using a long autopsy knife like a saw. The caecum and colon are mobilised by cutting their lateral and posterior attachments. The rectal contents are milked upwards. The freed bowel is cut between double ligatures from jejunum to sigmoid in the female and to rectum in the male and kept aside for further dissection and examination.

The small intestine is opened with an enterotome along the line of mesenteric attachment to examine its contents and mucous membrane. The appendix is examined for any pathological condition. The large intestine is cut with an enterotome along the anterior taenia and examined for congestion, ulceration or any other abnormality of its mucous membrane and its contents.

A quick method to examine the intestines is to irrigate them in a sink with tap water through one end, to allow the contents to pass through a sieve at the other end so as to retain worms, worm segments, and any other material that cannot pass, and then to open with an enterotome to examine the mucous membrane.

The possibility of traumatic perforation of intestine should be borne in mind in cases with a history of violence. In all such cases, it is essential to exclude ulceration or disease of the intestine.

c. *Kidneys:* The kidneys are removed after removal of the suprarenals, first left and then right, by incising the peritoneal fat just outside their lateral margins. They are measured and weighed. The kidney is held firmly between the thumb and fingers or between layers of gauze or sponge to prevent it from slipping. It is then cut horizontally through the convex border to the hilum and opened like two halves of a book. The capsule is stripped from the cut halves by a toothed forceps. The capsule strips with difficulty in chronic nephritis, hypertensive nephrosclerosis, and pyelonephritis. In these conditions, the kidneys are small in size and the cut surface appears granular. The cut surface is examined for the width of the cortex (about 1 cm in a healthy subject), granularity of the surface, clarity of the corticomedullary junctions, size of the renal pelvis, and any pathological process, such as inflammation and degenerative changes. The renal pelvis is examined for calculi and evidence of inflammation. A block is taken from the kidney in such a way as to include the mucosa of the renal pelvis and all other layers.

d. *Prostate:* When the urinary bladder is drawn backwards from symphysis pubis, the prostate is palpated, urethra divided distal to it, and prostate removed along with the urinary bladder. The prostate is then examined for enlargement or malignancy. Vertical sections are made through lateral and median lobes.

e. *Testes:* The deep aspects of the inguinal canal from beneath the reflected skin are cut. Spermatic cords are identified at the inguinal ring. The testes are removed from the scrotum by separating them from the inside of scrotal sac by gentle blunt dissection. The testes and epididymis are cut longitudinally and examined for evidence of any disease or injury especially ecchymosis. Local bruising can be demonstrated in the tunica albuginea or the body of the testis.

f. *Female genitalia:* In cases of abortion death, the entire genital tract is removed in one block as follows and then examined.

The legs are widely abducted, and an incision made outside the labia up to the symphysis pubis above and including the anus below. Another incision is made round the level of the pelvic brim and continued downwards to the pelvic outlet till it reaches the vaginal incision. The entire genital tract together with urinary bladder and rectum can then be removed. In other cases, the ovaries and fallopian tubes are freed from pelvis, the vagina cut at the upper third, and the whole block removed from the pelvis. Each organ, e.g. ovary, fallopian tubes, and uterus, is separated. The uterus is then examined for its size, shape, weight and any abnormality. It is cut longitudinally to expose the endometrium, thickness of the uterine walls, and contents, if any—fluid, foreign body or foetus. If a foetus is present, its intrauterine age is assessed. The ovaries are cut longitudinally and examined for corpora lutea. The fallopian tubes are cut across at intervals to examine patency. The vagina is examined for marks of injury, presence of foreign body, condition of its mucous membrane, presence of rugae, and the condition and type of hymen. Any fluid, if present, in the vaginal canal is aspirated for determination of acid phosphatase or creatine phosphokinase, blood group substances, and spermatozoa. The condition of the cervix and any marks of instrumental injury are noted.

If any foreign body is found in the genital tract, it is preserved along with such portion or whole of the genital tract as deemed necessary.

Disposal

Organs not required are replaced into the body cavities. The body is stitched, washed, and restored to the best possible cosmetic appearance, and handed over to the police, under a receipt, for further disposal.

Preserve, Pack and Label

(a) Specimens for toxicological analysis and histological examination where necessary, (b) Blood from leg (femoral vein) or arm (subclavian vein) for grouping, alcohol estimation, and toxicological analysis, (c) Any tissue providing material evidence. Commonly, in most cases, blood, bile, urine, vitreous, and stomach contents provide the necessary information.

Q. 5.10. Mention the viscera routinely preserved for chemical analysis in case of suspected poisoning.

If the *patient is alive,* the following material should be preserved, preferably in the quantity mentioned:

1. Vomit	300 ml	If less available, the whole quantity
2. Stomach washout	500 ml	If less available, the whole quantity
3. Blood and urine	As below	

Since many poisons are ingested, and after absorption pass through the liver, and are excreted via the kidneys in the urine, the following materials should be routinely preserved in the dead, irrespective of the nature of the poison (Table 5.2).

Table 5.2: Materials' quantity preserved in the dead, irrespective of the nature of the poison

Material	*Quantity*
1. Stomach	Whole
2. Stomach contents	300 ml. If less available, whole quantity
3. Small intestine	100 cm in adults, 200 cm in children, and whole in infants, preferably tied at short lengths
4. Small intestine contents	
5. Liver, preferably the portion containing gallbladder and its contents*	100 ml. If less available, the whole quantity
6. Spleen+	500 gm or 5 cm thick slice of liver in adults, and whole in children and infants
7. Kidneys	Half in adults, and whole in children
8. Urine	Half from each kidney in adults and both kidneys in children 100–200 ml. If less available, the whole quantity
9. Blood	10 ml, preferably more, 100 ml
10. Vitreous	As much as can be withdrawn

*The gallbladder and bile should be routinely preserved because examination of bile or, if the gallbladder was empty at postmortem, the gallbladder itself will show the presence of a large number of drugs including morphine (free and conjugated), cocaine, methadone and its metabolites, and major tranquillisers or their metabolites.

+If septicaemia is suspected and the cause of it is not obvious, the spleen should be cultured. It may reveal an unsuspected terminal infection.

Q. 5.11. Give some examples of those cases of poisoning which require additional viscera, tissues, and materials for chemical and/or microscopic examination.

Additional viscera and materials may be required in the following circumstances (Table 5.3).

Table 5.3: Additional viscera and materials required for chemical and/or microscopic examination in cases of special circumstances

Nature of poison	*Material to be preserved*
1. Alcohol	About 10 ml blood from a peripheral vein and as much vitreous as can be withdrawn
2. Barbiturates	10 ml blood
3. Carbon monoxide	About 10 ml blood
4. Chloroform	About 10 ml blood
5. Corrosive poison	Skin at least 2.5 cm square from the affected area and similar portion from the opposite area as control
6. Heavy metals (chronic poisoning by arsenic, antimony, etc.)	About 10 cm of shaft of long bone, about 5 gm of plucked scalp hair, all finger or toe nails, skin of back, and a wedge of quadriceps muscle before opening the abdomen to avoid contamination
7. Hydrocyanic acid and cyanides	About 20 ml blood
8. Inhalation or solvent and volatile substances	Tie off trachea. Collect entire lung and place in air tight container
9. Injected poisons	Skin, subcutaneous tissue and muscle forming the injection track, and similar material from opposite side as control
10. Nux vomica and strychnine	Spinal cord, heart, and one-half of brain
11. Opium	10 ml blood, gallbladder and its contents
12. Pesticides	Fatty tissue from abdominal wall or perinephric region and myoneural junction, if possible
Special circumstances	*Material to be preserved*
1. Criminal abortion	Vagina, uterus, fallopian tubes, ovaries, urinary bladder, rectum, and abortion stick or foreign body in the genital tract
2. Decomposed bodies	Insect eggs, maggots, and pupa
3. Embalmed bodies	Embalming fluid, bone marrow
4. Exhumed bodies	Soil samples from above, beneath, and sides of the coffin, and control samples from some distance away from the coffin. Any fluid found in the coffin
5. Extensive trauma in drunken individuals	Vitreous fluid for estimation of alcohol
6. Firearm injuries	Skin around the entrance and exit wounds
7. Hydrophobia (rabies)	Brain for negri bodies (for pathologist)
8. Stained clothes	Stained as well as surrounding unstained portion as control

(*contd.*)

Q. 5.12. Comment on collection and preservation of (1) blood, (2) CSF, (3) bone, (4) bone marrow, (5) hair, (6) maggots, (7) muscle, (8) nails, (9) skin, (10) urine, (11) vitreous.

Blood: At least 10 ml should be collected in a bottle, preferably from a peripheral site, such as vessels of the neck, arm or leg. The common practice is to collect it from subclavian vessels when the neck is being opened or by milking the femoral artery from thigh to abdomen. For alcohol estimation, blood should not be collected from heart, pleural or abdominal cavities as it may give a higher value due to proximity of stomach from which there may be seepage. If it is required only for grouping, no preservative is necessary. It may alternatively be absorbed on to a white filter paper or clean sterile cloth or gauge-piece and dried.

CSF: As much as can be withdrawn. CSF is obtained by—(a) cisternal puncture, (b) aspiration with Pasteur pipette from the base of brain after reflecting the frontal lobes, or (c) puncture of the lateral ventricles. Normally, it takes about 30 minutes for any drug injected in a living person to enter CSF. If a drug is injected even intravenously after death, it does not enter CSF.

Bone: About 200 gm should be collected. It is convenient to remove about 10–15 cm of the shaft of the femur.

Bone marrow: The required quantity is obtained from sternum, femur or vertebrae.

Hair: An adequate sample (10 gm and if less available, the whole quantity) of head and pubic hair should be removed by plucking out, complete with roots, and not by cutting, and preserved in separate containers. An artery forceps is helpful for plucking.

Maggots: These are dropped alive into boiling absolute alcohol or 10% hot formalin which kills them in an extended condition. This is necessary to disclose the internal structure of the larvae. If time of death is an issue, some larvae/maggots should be preserved alive for examination by an entomologist. Maggots may reveal the presence of drugs in decomposed bodies or skeletonised remains.

Muscle: A wedge of thigh muscle (quadriceps) is suitable. It should be removed before abdomen is opened to avoid contamination.

Nails: All the nails (fingers and/or toes) should be removed from their bed, and collected in separate envelopes.

Skin: A piece of at least 2.5 cm square from the affected area in case of corrosive poisoning and from thigh or back in case of suspected heavy metal (such as arsenic) poisoning is taken. If there is needle puncture, the whole needle track and surrounding tissue should be excised. Control specimens should be taken from some other area on the opposite side of the body and preserved in a separate container. In firearm injury cases, a skin portion of suitable size around the entrance and exit wounds should be excised.

Urine: A specimen should be obtained by suprapubic puncture or when the urinary bladder is opened.

Vitreous: A fine hypodermic needle attached to a 5 ml syringe is inserted into the outer canthus of the globe after pulling the eyelids aside. The needle is positioned in the centre of the globe and as much vitreous as possible slowly drawn from both eyes.

Preservation and Despatch of Viscera

The stomach, stomach contents, small intestine, and small intestine contents should be preserved in one wide mouthed glass bottle; pieces of liver, spleen and kidney, in another bottle; and urine in the third bottle. When additional material is required to be sent, it should be despatched in separate bottles, viz. brain in one bottle, and vomitor stomach washout in another bottle. Blood should be sent in a vial or vials. The bottles and vials required for preservation are normally supplied by the office of the Director, Forensic Science Laboratory (FSL)/Government Medical Stores, in India.

The transportation of the viscera to the forensic science laboratory and their examination at that end would naturally take some time. In order that putrefaction may not set in and render chemical analysis difficult, certain preservatives should be used, as shown below:

1. In all cases of poisoning, inclusive of carbolic acid but exclusive of other acids, saturated solution of common salt should be used.
2. In cases where poisoning by acids is suspected, except carbolic acid, rectified spirit should be used.

3. Whenever blood is preserved, the anatomical location from where it has been drawn should be stated. The preservative for liquid blood when taken for grouping is an equal quantity of 5% w/v solution of sodium citrate in water containing 0.25% v/v formalin. About 2–3 ml blood is sufficient. In suspected cases of poisoning including alcohol but excluding oxalic acid, ethylene glycol, fluoride, and carbon monoxide, the preservative for 10 ml of blood is a mixture of 30 mg potassium oxalate (anticoagulant) and 10 ml sodium fluoride (enzyme inhibitor). In case of poisoning by oxalic acid and ethylene glycol, 30 mg sodium citrate should be used in place of potassium oxalate; and in case of poisoning by fluoride, 10 gm sodium nitrite should be used in place of sodium fluoride. Heparin and EDTA should not be used as anticoagulants since they interfere with detection of methanol. In case of poisoning by carbon monoxide, a layer of 1–2 cm liquid paraffin should be added immediately over the collected blood sample to avoid exposure to atmospheric oxygen.
4. Urine is preserved by adding an equal quantity of saturated solution of common salt or rectified spirit or some fine grains of thymol. Other preservatives that can be used are: one gm of sodium benzoate or 5 ml concentrated hydrochloric acid for about 200–500 ml of urine.
5. Ten per cent formalin is used as a preservative for tissues meant for histopathologic examination.

The stomach and intestines are opened before they are preserved. The liver and kidneys are cut into small pieces to ensure penetration of the preservative. The bottle should not be completely filled with the preservative; however, it is necessary that the quantity of preservative should be such as to completely immerse the viscera after the contents are well shaken. As an additional precaution, 2–50 gm of common salt or a column of 2 cm of rectified spirit as the case may be, should be added. If the material is not completely submerged in the solution, decomposition will take place with the result that gases may form and either undo the lid spilling the contents or even break the bottle.

The stoppers of the bottles should be well fitting, covered with a piece of cloth and tied by tape or string and the ends sealed using a departmental seal. Each bottle should be suitably labelled, the label containing the autopsy number, name of the deceased, name of the organ, date, time and place of autopsy, followed by signature of the doctor who performed the autopsy. A sample of the preservative used, either 100 ml of rectified spirit or 25 gm of sodium chloride is separately preserved and sent for analysis to rule out any poison being present as a contaminant. The sealed bottles are then put in a viscera box which is locked and the lock sealed. The viscera box is a wooden box and is supplied by the office of the Director, FSL or the government medical stores, in India. It has well-padded compartments into which the bottles snugly fit. Different boxes should be used for sending viscera belonging to different persons. The key of the box and a specimen of the seal used is put in a separate envelope, and the envelope is also sealed. All these precautions are necessary to ensure that no tampering with the contents of the viscera box occurs during its transit to the FSL, and the chain of evidence is maintained.

The sealed box and the envelope containing the key is then handed over to the police constable in return for a receipt. He delivers it personally to the office of the FSL after obtaining a receipt for the same. Along with the viscera box, the following documents are also sent: (1) a copy of the *panchnama*, if available; brief facts of the case, and the case sheet, (2) a copy of autopsy report, and (3) a letter requesting him to examine the viscera and inform the medical officer of his findings. The viscera box is transported by the constable authorised to do so; similarly, authority from a magistrate for the FSL to examine the viscera is necessary in some states. Therefore, in such cases, the medical officer should also address a letter to the concerned magistrate requesting him to authorise the FSL to examine the viscera and other articles and to depute a police constable to transport the viscera box to the FSL.

Unless the viscera and other articles are sent to FSL, they are to be preserved for a period of six months and then destroyed after obtaining the magistrate's assent or when the investigating officer informs the laboratory that the case is closed.

Q. 5.13. How will you report the cause and manner of death after a postmortem examination? Add a note on negative or obscure autopsy.

When the autopsy is completed, the medical officer must form an opinion as to the cause and manner of death and probable time since death. The abstract of this opinion should be given to the police constable accompanying the dead body for communication to the investigating officer. The information must include account of the decedent's history, description of the fatal environment, and circumstances surrounding death. The following are illustrative examples:

1. From the history of the case and autopsy findings, I am of the opinion that this 50-year-old man died due to haemorrhage from ruptured spleen as a result of a blow on the abdomen by the assailant.
2. This 45-year-old man died as a result of perforating gunshot wound of the head. Internal examination also disclosed heart disease of the kind occasioned by a progressive narrowing of the coronary arteries. Information available at the time of examination combined with the finding of entry wound with visible powder residues on the roof of the mouth support the conclusion that the manner of death was suicide.
3. This 50-year-old woman died of coronary thrombosis. The automobile crash in which she was involved is believed to have been the result of her death at the wheel. Laboratory examination of blood and tissues does not reveal alcohol or other drugs.
4. This 50-year-old woman collapsed and died after her handbag was seized and stolen. Autopsy discloses arteriosclerotic heart disease. The cause of death is arteriosclerotic heart disease with a contributory cause of emotional stress. (The manner of death is homicide).

The report should state the authority ordering the autopsy; name, age, and sex of the deceased; date, place, and time of examination; and the means by which the body was identified. A complete description of external examination including detailed description of the injuries, their age, etc. is then given. Information about treatment is included when necessary. This is followed by a complete description of internal examination. This part of the report contains details of positive findings, important negative findings, and general condition of other viscera. For instance, absence of airway obstruction, condition of the coronary arteries and heart valves, absence of pulmonary emboli, surgical absence of the appendix, and the contents of stomach, gallbladder and urinary bladder, all merit inclusion. This is followed by conclusion as to the cause and manner of death, and approximate time elapsed since death, based as far as possible on postmortem findings. Photographs, radiographs, sketches, weights, measurements, and laboratory reports provide an objective record and enhance the value of the autopsy report.

The opinion regarding the cause of death is given in the form of a certificate filling up all its columns. This is followed by the signature, qualifications, and the designation of the medical officer.

The certificate about the cause of death is issued within 24 hours after conducting the autopsy. In cases of poisoning, decomposed bodies, and/or when the cause of death requires further examination, e.g. chemical or microscopic, the opinion as to the cause of death is given when the result of such examination is known.

a. *Cause of death:* It is defined as a disease or injury or a combination of both that brought about cessation of life. When there is delay between the onset of a disease process or infliction of injury and the ultimate death of an individual, the proximate and immediate cause of death must be distinguished. The proximate cause of death is the disease or injury that initiated a series of events that led directly to the immediate cause of death. Suppose a person dies of peritonitis two weeks after a stab in the abdomen. The immediate cause of death is peritonitis. The proximate cause of death is a stab wound of the abdomen. The physiopathological or biochemical disturbance, e.g. shock, sepsis, metabolic acidosis, ventricular fibrillation, respiratory arrest, etc. produced by the cause of death constitutes the **mechanism of death.**

b. *Manner of death:* This is an expressed opinion based upon all available information of a particular case. This includes autopsy findings, laboratory reports, scene of death, medical history, etc. It can be classified as—(1) natural, (2) suicide, (3) homicide, (4) accident, and (5) undetermined (presumed natural).

Illustrative examples of cause and manner of death:

1. *Cause of death*: Ischaemic heart disease; manner of death—natural.
2. *Cause of death*: Incised wound of the wrist, self-inflicted; manner of death—suicide.
3. *Cause of death*: Asphyxia by throttling (manual strangulation); manner of death— homicide.
4. *Cause of death*: Shock and haemorrhage due to multiple fractures, run over by a truck; manner of death—accident.
5. *Cause of death*: Unknown or unascertainable—no disease, no injury, no poisoning; manner of death—undetermined, presumed natural.

When there is no grossly discernible cause of death, histological examination should include at least six sections of the heart to exclude myocarditis.

Sometimes, in a case of poisoning, the FSL reports that no poison has been detected. Under such circumstances, it is possible that the poison has been vomited out, excreted, neutralized, metabolised or detoxified, or it is so obscure or present in such small quantity that it cannot be detected by the existing methods of chemical analysis.

In some cases, in spite of a thorough postmortem examination, chemical analysis and microscopic examination, the cause of death cannot be arrived at. In most cases, such a death represents functional failure of a vital tissue or an organ, without recognisable structural abnormality, and such an autopsy is termed as **a negative or obscure autopsy.** Such cases include deaths precipitated by—(a) functional inhibition of the vagus or excessive sympathetic discharge, (b) endocrine disturbances, e.g. diabetes and adrenal insufficiency, (c) iatrogenic disorders, like sudden withdrawal of steroids or beta blockers, (d) trauma, such as concussion, self-reduced neck injury, concealed puncture wounds which escaped detection at autopsy and (e) other conditions like idiopathic epilepsy, chronic asthma, convalescence from recent infection especially in athletes, SIDS, and probably some obscure poison. In these circumstances, the medical officer should frankly admit that the cause of death cannot be determined. The investigating officer may still proceed with the case, if he so desires, depending on circumstantial evidence.

Q. 5.14. Discuss the data on which the approximate time since death may be determined in medicolegal cases. Mention the factors that influence such an estimation.

Reference should be made to the Chapter 11 on "Medicolegal Aspects of Death Investigation" for details of the various points discussed here.

For investigation of crime, it is very important to determine time since death, also known as *postmortem interval* (interval between death and the time of postmortem examination). It provides a clue to the investigating officer to institute suitable inquiries to apprehend the persons likely to be responsible for the crime, to check on the movements of suspected persons, and to eliminate others from suspicion.

The points to estimate the approximate time since death include (Fig. 5.29): (1) cooling of the body, (2) postmortem lividity, (3) rigor mortis, (4) decomposition changes, (5) con-tents of the stomach and bowels, (6) contents of the urinary bladder, (7) biochemical changes, and (8) circumstantial evidence.

Cooling of the body: A progressive fall in temperature is one of the most prominent early signs of death, the amount of cooling indicating the approximate time since death. The rate of cooling is not uniform but is related to the difference in temperature between the body and its surroundings. In a tropical country like India, the average heat loss is roughly 0.5–0.7°C per hour and the body attains environmental temperature in about 16–20 hours after death. However, if the environmental temperature is high, e.g. 40°C, the body temperature will go up (refer postmortem caloricity).

Postmortem lividity: The incidence, extent and degree of fixation of postmortem lividity is important. It commences within an hour after death. In an average case of sudden death, it presents as a series of mottled patches over the dependent parts in about 1–3 hours. These patches coalesce in about 3–6 hours. The lividity is fully developed and fixed in about 6–8 hours. However, this is somewhat variable. Lividity will not be seen—(1) if the body is constantly altering its position, e.g. in drowning, (2) if the skin is dark, and (3) if much blood is lost, e.g. in massive haemorrhage.

Rigor mortis: The presence and extent or absence of rigor mortis should be noted. In India, it usually commences in about 2–3 hours after death, takes about 12 hours to develop from head to foot, persists for another 12 hours, and takes 12 hours to pass off, in the same order in which it occurred. These timings are, however, subject to variation.

Decomposition changes: The presence, character and extent of putrefaction is very valuable indeed. In India, a greenish patch over the caecum and flanks appears in about 12–24 hours. It spreads over the whole of abdomen and the rest of the body within the next 24 hours.

Vascular marbling commences after 24 hours. Putrefactive odour is noticed at about the same time. By 36–48 hours, marbling is prominent.

In 12–18 hours, gases collect in the intestines and distend the abdomen. From 18 to 36 or 48 hours, gas formation is abundant. Gases collect in the tissues and hollow viscera, and cause false rigidity and pressure effects. In about 36 hours after death in summer, the female genitals appear pendulous. In about 48–72 hours, the rectum and uterus protrude.

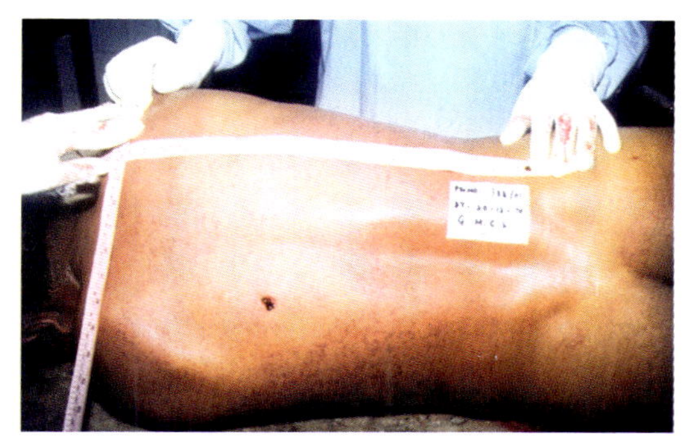

Fig. 5.28: Hypostasis demonstration

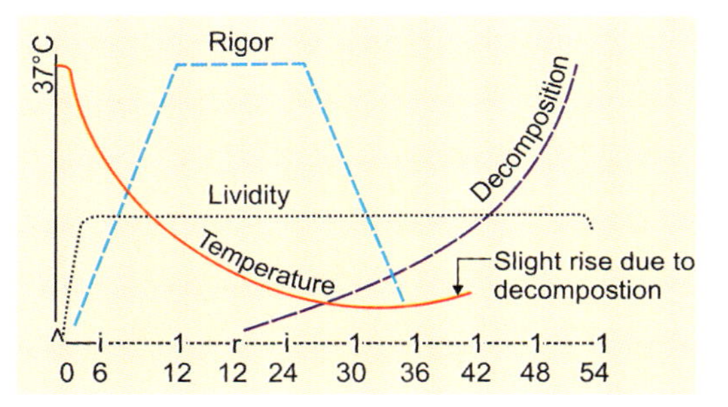

Fig. 5.29: Graph showing some factors helpful in estimation of **time since death**. This graph shows the approximate rate of cooling of the body after death; the approximate time of onset and progress of postmortem lividity; the approximate time of onset, duration, and offset of rigor mortis; and the approximate time of onset and progress of putrefactive changes. All these times are approximations because all these factors are subject to a number of variations. However, gross inaccuracies can be avoided by attention to these factors taken into consideration collectively

By about 18–36 hours, flies lay their eggs. The eggs hatch into maggots or larvae in about 24 hours. In the course of 4–5 days, maggots develop into pupae and in another 4–5 days, pupae into adult flies. It should be remembered that eggs can be laid even before death, if the victim is debilitated or unconscious, the common sites being the wounds, and moist areas, such as the eyelids, lips, nostrils, genitalia, and anus.

In 3–7 days, teeth and sutures of skull in children and young adults become loose. In 5–12 days, soft tissues liquefy and break down. Only the more resistant viscera which putrefy in 2–3 weeks are discernible. In 1–3 months, the body is skeletonised.

The process of decomposition may be modified into adipocere formation or mummification. The time required for adipocere formation in our country is 5–15 days, the shortest recorded period being 3 days and 22 hours. The time required for complete mummification of a body varies from 3–12 months or longer.

Contents of the stomach and bowels: The site and state of digestion of the contents of the stomach and bowels may be of some value in fixing the hour of death in relation to the last meal. Sometimes, the stomach contents can be matched with a particular meal known to have been consumed.

The length of time required to empty the stomach after a meal is very variable, and depends on the type of meal ingested, stomach tone, pyloric function, and the psychological state of the individual. Fear and anxiety, for example, may cause great delay in the emptying rate, and power of digestion may remain suspended for a long time in conditions of shock and coma. Food has been seen in the stomach remaining undigested in persons who received severe head injuries soon after their meal and died within 12–24 hours.

In general, milk leaves the stomach rapidly but *the large vegetable meals consumed in India do not usually leave the stomach for at least 4 hours. Chapattis (bread) digest to a pulp fairly quickly,* within about 2 hours, but do not leave the stomach quickly when other foods are present with them. Dals (pulses, lentils, beans) of all kinds retain their form up to 2 hours, and rice grains up to 3 hours. If meat has been eaten along with vegetable foods, it is seldom distinguishable as such after 3 hours, and after 4 hours both the green vegetables and roots are indistinguishable. *In general, if at autopsy, one finds that the stomach is full, it would suggest that the victim died within 2 hours of taking the last meal, if food was distinguishable, and 4 hours, if it was indistinguishable.*

Fluids, such as milk, tea, coffee, reach the upper small bowel in 15–20 minutes. Commonly, the bulk of the meal leaves the stomach within 2 hours, and the stomach is emptied in 4–6 hours. The residue of the meal reaches the hepatic flexure in about 6 hours, splenic flexure in 9–12 hours, and pelvic colon in 12–18 hours.

It must be remembered that the process of digestion may not cease at death; the enzymes released may autodigest the stomach wall resulting in perforation. Such an event, when found, makes the state of food in the stomach an unreliable indicator of time since death, even if the time and nature of the last meal are known.

The presence or absence of faeces in the large intestine may be of some value. With most persons, it is customary to evacuate the bowels in the morning. If, therefore, the large intestine contains faeces, one may presume that death may have occurred sometime in the night, and if empty, sometime after evacuation in the morning.

Contents of the urinary bladder: The amount of urine in the bladder may give some indication of the time since last micturition.

Biochemical changes: Chemical constituents of CSF, such as lactic acid, non-protein nitrogen (NPN), and amino acid content increase in the first 15 hours after death but the rate is not uniform and is influenced by cooling of the body. The potassium content of vitreous humour of the eye steadily rises after death. The range is, however, too wide. A progressive increase in levels of lactic acid, non-protein nitrogen, and certain enzymes, has also been observed after death, and this can be plotted graphically.

Circumstantial evidence: This includes:

a. Growth of hair on face
b. Presence of lice on hair
c. State of dress
d. Personal effects, and
e. Other data.

Males generally shave the chin every day. Beard hair grows at the rate of 0.4 mm per day. From this, a rough estimate may be made of the time since the last shave. Hair does not grow after death. The presence of lice is generally found on long hair of the head and infrequently even on short hair on other parts of the body. Lice generally die within 3–6 days of death of the individual. The state of dress, e.g. office dress or night dress may indicate the time of day that death has occurred. Personal effects, e.g. wrist watch, letters, diary, food, etc. all provide valuable data. If the body is in a room and lights are burning, it indicates that death occurred at night. If the body is lying on green grass (shrubs and plants), the grass becomes pale due to non-exposure to sun's rays for about 5 days. Therefore, if pale grass is found under the body, it would suggest that death occurred more than 5 days ago.

A **summary** of important points in assessing time since death is appended in Table 5.4. It must be remembered that these

Table 5.4: Summary of important points in assessing time since death, according to condition of body

Time since death	*Condition of the body*
Less than 1 hour	Body warm
3 hours	Patchy postmortem lividity
6–8 hours	Lividity fully developed and fixed
12 hours	Rigor present all over. Green patch showing over the caecum
24–36 hours	Body cold. Rigor receding absent. Green discolouration over whole abdomen and spreading to chest. Abdomen distended with gases. Ova of flies seen
48 hours	Trunk bloated. Face dis-coloured and swollen Blisters present. Moving maggots seen
72 hours	Whole body grossly swollen and disfigured. Hair and nails loose. Tissues soft and discoloured
One week	Soft viscera putrefied
Two weeks	Only the more resistant viscera distinguishable Soft tissues largely gone
1–3 months	Body skeletonised

times are average times in average circumstances and based on evaluation of general and individual variations; they apply to tropical climate; in cold weather, they may be doubled or trebled; and in the hills, they are quite inapplicable. It should also be remembered that these times refer to undisturbed and unmutilated body. Insects, birds and wild animals, can skeletonise the body surprisingly quickly.

The difference between the body temperature at the time of death of the person and the atmospheric temperature at that instant is quite reasonable. For temperate countries. Marshal and Hore formula is applicable with reasonable satisfaction. The ideal conditions for the use of this formula are as follows:

a. The atmospheric temperature should be around 60°F (15.5°C)
b. The body should ideally be uncovered
c. The limbs should be outstretched
d. The formula gives different rates of fall of body temperature, for subjects of different body built, as follows:

In tropical countries, measurement of the body temperature is not a good criterion for the purpose of determination of the time of death, because, the difference between the body temperature during death and the atmospheric temperature is not very high. This formula is not applicable for India except in hilly regions. The rate of fall of the body temperature is taken on an average to be about 0.4°C or 0.7°F per hour in summer in the non hilly parts.

Q. 5.15. What is the difference between cold climates and hot climates, in relation to time since death?

In hot climates, all the above changes occur earlier and in cold climates, much later (Table 5.5).

Table 5.5

Time passed after death	*Thinly built subjects*	*Average built subjects*	*Fatty built subjects (thick)*
Up to 3 hrs	@ 1⅓ rd°F	@ 1°F	@ ⅚°F
3 + to 6 hrs	@ 1⅓ rd°F	@ 2°F	@ 1⅔ rd°F
6 + to 9 hrs	@ 2⅓ rd°F	@ 2°F	@ 1⅔ rd°F
9 + to 12 hrs	@ 1⅓ rd°F	@ 1½°F	@ 1⅓ rd°F
12 + to 15 hrs	@ 1⅓ rd°F	@ 1⅓ rd°F	@ 1⅓ rd°F

6 Autopsy on Decomposed Bodies, Mutilated Bodies, Fragmentary Remains, and Bones

DECOMPOSED BODIES

Q. 6.1. What is meant by a decomposed body? Discuss the medicolegal value of autopsy on such a body.

Decomposed bodies are bodies which show putrefactive changes in varying degree depending upon the time elapsed since death. In most such cases, evidence of trauma, e.g. haemorrhage and fractures, can be recognised and even evaluated by an expert. The following information is specially looked for:

1. Identification,
2. Cause of death, and
3. Time since death.

Decomposed bodies sometimes have earth and clothes stuck to them and/or are infested with maggots. Under such circumstances, the body may be immersed in a tank of weak carbolic acid (lysol) to soften the earth and get the clothing away without disintegration. A day or two of weak carbolic bath kills the maggots, and greatly facilitates the examination of the body and its subsequent dissection. Samples of insect eggs or maggots, if required for laboratory examination, should be obtained prior to immersing the body in lysol.

Identification: Remnants of genital organs, bones, hair, and teeth which resist putrefaction help to determine the sex and age of a person. The peeled off skin of the fingers can be used for fingerprints. Hair, its colour and dyeing (when present), are useful in identity. The teeth, their number and characteristics, and acquired peculiarities, such as tattoo marks and malunited fractures are of help. Personal properties, such as clothing, rings, bangles, bracelets, watch, belt, etc., also provide valuable data. Selected X-rays, dental X-rays, and/or total body X-rays are helpful, if antemortem X-rays are available for comparison.

Decomposed bodies are so much distorted by gas that they are rendered unrecognisable. They should, therefore, be looked at again after autopsy when gas has escaped and fluids have drained when the original shape is possibly more recognisable.

Cause of death: Fracture of bones may indicate their antemortem nature. Depressed fracture of skull, fracture of hyoid, rib fractures, and knife scratches on cervical vertebrae should be specially looked for. Clothes tied round the neck, hand, and feet, or foreign bodies in the upper respiratory tract provide valuable clues. Bullets found in the body and broken parts of a weapon (e.g. knife) when present serve the same purpose. The uterus is one of the last organs to decompose and its condition may reveal attempts at criminal abortion; foreign bodies, such as abortion sticks, may be present in the genital tract. The presence of solid faeces in the rectum negates cholera as the alleged cause of death.

Appropriate viscera should be preserved for chemical analysis for evidence of suspected poisoning. Poisons which resist putrefaction include amongst others: carbon monoxide, cyanides, fluoride, barbiturates, organophosphorus compounds, endrine, dhatura, hyoscine, strychnine, yellow oleander, nicotine, etc. and metallic poisons, such as arsenic, antimony, mercury, lead, thallium, etc. Maggots may reveal the presence of drugs.

Time since death: This may be inferred from progressive changes in the body after death, described elsewhere in this book. Samples of insect eggs, maggots or pupae, should be retained for laboratory examination. They provide data about time elapsed since death.

MUTILATED BODIES AND FRAGMENTARY REMAINS

Q. 6.2. What is meant by (1) a mutilated body, and (2) fragmentary remains? A dead body without head has been forwarded to you for autopsy. Describe the procedure of examination.

Q. 6.3. A human arm, roughly sawn through above elbow, is found in a field. What investigations would you carry out to determine the age, sex, stature, occupation, and identity of the individual to whom it belonged?

While solving these questions, frequent and liberal reference should be made to the earlier chapters on identification.

A **mutilated body** is one which is disfigured, deprived of a limb or a part of the body. In this condition, the soft tissues, muscles and skin are still attached to the bones (Figs 6.1 and 6.2). **Fragmentary remains** include only fragments of the body, such as head, trunk or limb.

A number of questions can be answered with ascending degree of completeness depending upon the type and condition of the material received for examination. The following information is specially looked for:

1. Source, whether human or animal
2. If parts belong to the same individual

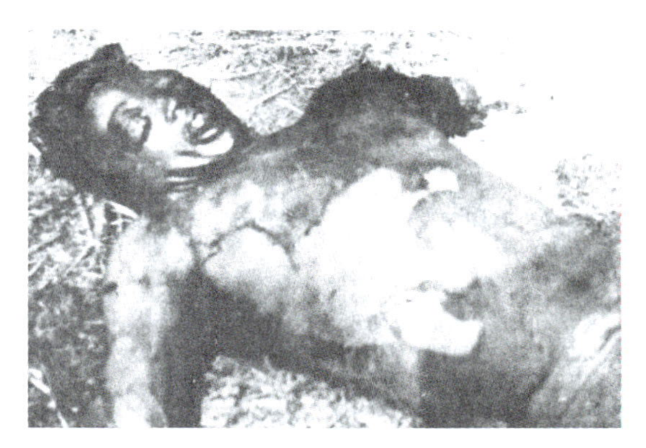

Fig. 6.1: Highly decomposed body mutilated by animals. Body of a male aged 30 lying on the outskirts of a village discovered 9 days after death. In figure, left forearm is not present. Pointed end of the humerus devoid of soft tissues is seen. It suggests postmortem injury by animals, which may be mistaken for defence injury (*Courtesy*: Dr V David Edward)

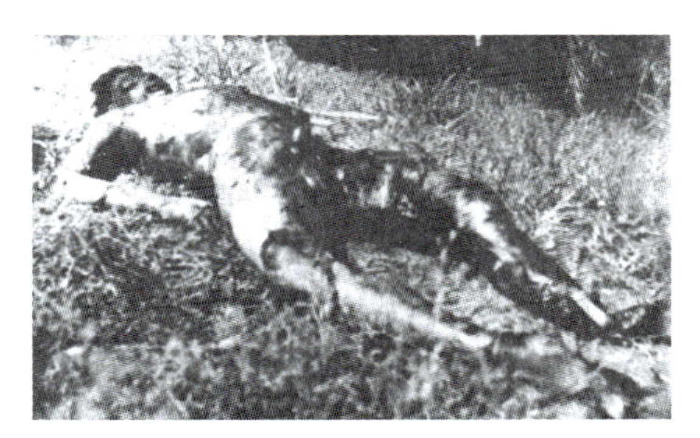

Fig. 6.2: Highly decomposed body mutilated by animals. The left forearm is absent. Punched out areas are seen on the front and inside of the thighs. Bones of the foot and leg are exposed. These are postmortem injuries caused by animals. In addition, abdomen is bloated and discoloured due to generation of decomposition gases. The skin shows postmortem blebs and peeling of the cuticle. The eyes and the tongue are protruded from the same cause. Maggots were present. (*Courtesy*: Dr V David Edward)

3. Age
4. Sex
5. Stature
6. Race
7. Identity
8. Special features
9. Cause of death
10. Time since death

Source: This can be determined from the knowledge of anatomy. In case of doubt, a part of the soft tissues, provided decomposition is not too far advanced, is sent in a dry condition and without adding any preservative to the forensic science laboratory for a precipitin test. The antiglobulin inhibition test is more sensitive than the precipitin test but requires more expertise.

In places situated near the medical colleges and anatomy dissection halls, parts of human bodies, improperly disposed of, may be brought for examination. It is easy to determine their source from the dark colour, formalin odour, and the presence of red lead in the blood vessels and nutrient canals of bone.

If parts belong to the same individual: A mix-up of parts may occur in mass disasters. The parts belong to the same individual, if they can be fitted together and there is no disparity or duplication. Testing for similarity of blood group and DNA from different parts is more conclusive (Fig. 6.3).

Age: This can be determined from the state of epiphyses; state of teeth and lower jaw; calcification of laryngeal and sternal cartilages and hyoid bone; changes in the sacrum; closure of the cranial sutures; condition of the symphyseal surface of the pubic bone; changes in the joints; and colour of hair on the scalp, beard, moustache, and pubis. Histomorphometric methods based on correlation of the number of osteons per unit area of bone samples and age as established by researchers are helpful.

Sex: The prostate and non-pregnant uterus resist putrefaction for a long period. Gross and microscopic examination of internal genitals, if available, is confirmatory. In their absence, the nature and characters of the soft parts and configuration of pelvis

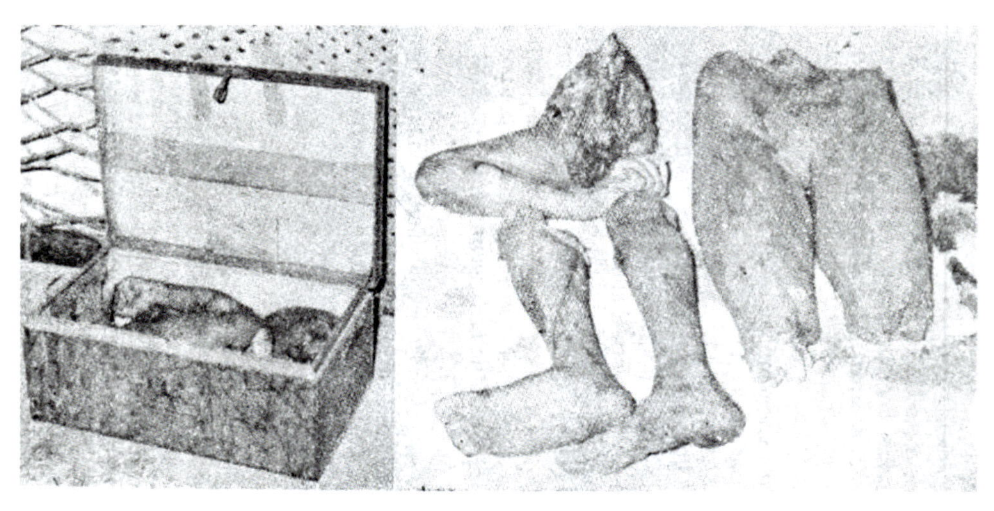

Fig. 6.3: *Alignment of dismembered part to determine if they belong to the same individual.* The husband strangled his wife and when she became unconscious, he decapitated her and dismembered the body for surreptious disposal. While the parts were being put in a trunk, he was discovered by his brother. Identity was established by alignment of the various parts. (Sessions case no. 465 of 1973 . State vs. Jehangir Abdul Rehman Shaikh under section 302 IPC. The accused was sentenced to death). (*Courtesy*: Dr PP Phatnani)

are helpful. If only the head is received, sex can be surmised from the presence or absence of beard. Sex can also be determined by nuclear sexing or sexing root sheath cells of head hair.

Stature: This is already discussed in the Chapter 4 on 'Identification in Mass Disasters'.

Race: This can be determined from hair and skin, if available, and from nasal bridge height, nasal aperture shape, facial prognathism, palate shape, incisors, the skull (cephalic index), pelvis, etc.

Identity: This can be determined from fingerprints, dental status and personal property or articles in close proximity to the body. Also helpful are the congenital features, like moles and acquired peculiarities, like tattoo marks, condition of the palms, scars, deformities, and amputation marks. Evidence of any disease, e.g. gallstones, uterine fibroids, and appendectomy scar when present, is corroborative. Determination of blood group antigens A, B and H from teeth pulp might help to establish identity, if the blood group is known. Selected X-rays, dental X-rays, and/or total body X-rays are helpful, if antemor-tem X-rays are available for comparison.

Special features: Mutilation may be the work of—(1) persons with anatomical knowledge, (2) other without such knowledge, (3) animals, or (4) may result from decomposition changes. Each has its own characteristics and, therefore, the manner in which the parts are mutilated, is quite important.

Persons with anatomical knowledge destroy identifying features, as in the well-known Ruxton case. Others without such knowledge disfigure the body haphazardly, as for example, by use of saw, axe or any heavy weapon. Animals generally attack the exposed parts and produce ghastly wounds resembling haphazard mutilation; however, careful examination will reveal, if the bones are gnawed through by animals or cut by sharp weapons. In addition, animals generally eat away the medulla of long bones and spicules of cortical bone are found depressed in the medullary cavity. A separation of body parts is brought about by decomposition also. The natural sequence is: soft parts, articular cartilages and ligaments. Separation of joints of the hyoid as a result of decomposition may be mistaken for fracture. Captain Raju's case: Dogs brought fragmentry remains over a couple of days from the Tank bund area of Hyderabad. The remains were examined and were like the work of a skilled person. The woman's remains were identified from the dental record tracked to Chandigarh. Finally, captain Raju was confronted with details of his wife's killing. He jumped from the Central Crime Station building and died.

Cause of death: An opinion as to the cause of death is possible when there is some evidence of antemortem violence, such as injury to some large blood vessel or some vital organ or the recovery of a bullet. It must, however, be remembered that mutilated fragments of the body decompose quickly and antemortem changes disappear or become indistinguishable from postmortem ones. Sometimes, there may be some clues, such as a depressed fracture of the skull, fracture of hyoid, fracture-dislocation of cervical vertebra, severe injury to bones by a cutting instrument or fractures of several ribs. Sometimes, chemical examination of the available material for evidence of poisoning may also help. Obvious signs of disease, such as a malignant growth of soft tissues, bones, etc., should be looked for.

Time since death: The probable time since death can be ascertained from the condition of the soft parts in relation to the process of putrefaction.

BONES

Q. 6.4. A bundle of bones has been forwarded to you. Describe the procedure for examination.

Q. 6.5. A collection of skeletal remains in an alleged murder case is sent to you for examination. Discuss briefly the possible inferences which can be drawn from your examination.

A complete list of bones received for examination is prepared preferably along with the photograph of each bone. The bones are cleaned, if necessary, then arranged in the normal anatomical manner, and the reconstructed skeleton photographed.

The scheme for the examination of bones is similar to that for mutilated bodies. An anatomist, dentist, anthropologist, and radiologist with medicolegal experience should be consulted. An opinion can be given on the following aspects (Figs 6.4a and b): (1) source, whether human or animal, (2) belong to one or more individuals, (3) age, (4) sex, (5) stature, (6) race, (7) identity, (8) special features, (9) cause of death, and (10) time since death.

Source: This can be determined from:

1. Gross anatomical characteristics of human and animal bones

(a)

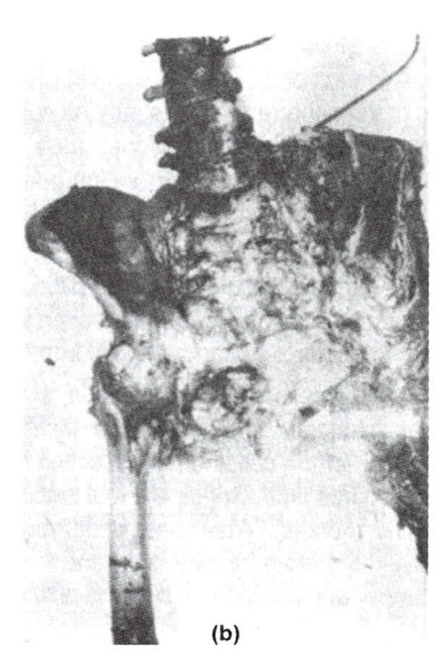

(b)

Fig. 6.4a and b: *Decomposing partly skeletonised body.* Head and trunk recovered from two different places. Cervical vertebrae 2 to 6 were recovered later, but could be articulated with good alignment with 1st and 7th cervical vertebrae. The following expert opinion was given: The bones are human and belong to the same individual; the skeleton is incomplete; the skull and trunk also belong to the same person (after articulation with the cervical vertebrae received later); the sex of the person is male (from bones and penile muscles shown by arrow); the caste is a Hindu (waist thread); the age is between 30 and 40 years (skull and other bones); the height is about 168 cm (from examination of bones); and there is no evidence of any antemortem injuries. The body was subsequently identified as that of a male aged 35 years. Hindu, and with a height about the same as mentioned. He was murdered by his wife and paramour. The dead body was buried in the house for 18 days and subsequently, part of it was thrown in the tank. The decomposing partly skeletonised parts were recovered from two different places viz. the house and the tank and sent for examination, and later the missing cervical vertebrae were also found and sent. (*Courtesy*: Dr V David Edward).

2. Microscopic characteristics
3. Chemical analysis of bone ash. In case of doubt, a precipitin test may settle the issue.

One or more individuals: This can be determined from the number of bones received for examination, noting the side to which they belong, and checking for their fitting, duplication, and morphological similarities. For example, if a skull belongs to a female aged about 18 years, other parts should also be of a female about that age. Similarly, there can be only one right humerus. However, supernumerary ribs, toes and fingers must be borne in mind. If a mix-up of bones is suspected, they can be subjected to short wave ultraviolet lamp to separate them by the difference in colour emission.

Age: This can be determined from state of epiphyses; state of teeth, and lower jaw; calcification of laryngeal and sternal cartilages and hyoid bone; changes in sacrum; closure of cranial sutures; condition of symphyseal surface of pubic bone; changes in joints; histological examination of teeth; and cross-section of mid-shaft area of femur, tibia or fibula.

Stature: This can be calculated, if a long bone, such as femur, tibia, humerus or radius, is available in its entirety, using the formulae of Dupertius and Hadden and Trotter and Glesser for Americans; Breitinger for Germans; Telkka for Finns; and multiplication factors devised by Indian workers for Indians. While applying the various formulae, due account needs to be taken of the sex and race of the deceased by reference to appropriate tables. However, the following data provide simple means to estimate the stature of a person. In general, humerus represents 20%, tibia 22%, femur 27%, and the spine 34% of the stature.

Race: An expert can determine this in a high proportion of cases from an examina-tion of skull, mandible and teeth, pelvis, and limb bones.

Identity: Malunited fractures, healing fractures or deformities of bone, when present, are helpful. When the skull is available, superimposition photography and facial reconstruction may be attempted. An X-ray of any bone taken during life may be compared with an X-ray of the same bone. Determination of blood group antigens A, B and H from teeth pulp might also help in establishing identity, if the blood group is known. DNA profiling also helps. It may be possible to obtain material for blood grouping and DNA profiling from cancellous bone.

Special features: By a meticulous examination of the ends of long bones, one can determine if the bones are cut by a sharp instrument or sawn through or whether they are gnawed through by animals and medulla eaten away. In bones that are gnawed through, spicules of cortical bone will be found depressed into the medullary cavity.

Cause of death: This is difficult to determine unless there are some clues. Fractures, especially of skull, hyoid, ribs, and other bones, should be looked for; knife scratches on cervical vertebral bodies and other bone or joint surfaces, if found, are informative. An opinion on these features, however, is difficult since the antemortem evidence disappears rapidly after death. A foreign body, such as a bullet when present in a bone, is helpful. Bones or their charred remains may be subjected to chemical analysis for the detection of metallic poisons, such as arsenic, as these are not destroyed by heat. Neutron activation analysis technique helps to detect certain metallic poisons in quantities far below the limits of conventional analysis. Maggots may reveal the presence of drugs.

Time since death: This is also difficult to estimate. Bodies exposed on the ground may be skeletonised even in a day if attacked by animals. However, an inference can be drawn from the following:

In the process of skeletonisation, soft tissues disappear first, then articular cartilage and finally the ligaments. In case of a fracture, examination of the callus after dissecting it longitudinally may give some clue as regards time. Bones are foul smelling and humid in recent cases (about 1–3 months). When they undergo putrefaction, they lose organic matter and, therefore, become light and fragile. Old bones tend to be dry, light, fragile, and the marrow cavity is also dry, and free of fat.

7

Handling HIV-Infected and Hepatitis B Positive Bodies

Q. 7.1. Briefly discuss the precautions necessary while handling HIV-infected and hepatitis B positive bodies.

HIV infection should be suspected if the body is of—(1) a male homosexual, (2) an intravenous drug abuser, (3) a haemophiliac who has received repeated blood transfusions, (4) a female prostitute, and (5) a victim of sex abuse. The staff should be vaccinated against hepatitis B and re-vaccinated at intervals when the antibody titre falls below protective level. At every stage, care should be taken to avoid direct contact of skin and mucous membranes with body fluids and tissues. Hands should be washed thoroughly with soap and water after each activity, even if gloves are worn.

Special precautions are necessary at each stage, viz.—(1) at the scene, (2) in the autopsy room, (3) in the laboratory, and (4) in the court, in addition to (5) general precautions.

At the Scene

1. Disposable shoe protection by persons at the scene is necessary.
2. Food or smoking should not be allowed at the scene.
3. Blood-contaminated clothing or other material should be handled carefully. Dried blood or wet blood material that is not to be stored as evidence should be decontaminated and properly disposed off by incineration.
4. Non-disposable material used during the investigation and collection of evidence at the scene should be decontaminated by usual hypochlorite solution.

In the Autopsy Room

1. ***Admission:*** No unauthorised person should be admitted to the autopsy and body preparation rooms.

2. ***Clothing:*** Protection includes complete covering of the body by wearing double gloves, gowns, waterproof aprons, caps, masks, goggles, if eye glasses are not worn, and shoe covers.

3. ***Instruments:*** Minimum instruments as required should be kept. At the start of the autopsy, a knife, scalpel, scissors and forceps are kept to start with. Scissors with slightly blunted points should be routinely used and the small sharp ones only when needed. Special care is necessary to handle sharp items, such as needles and scalpels to prevent accidental pricks and cuts.

4. ***Disposal requirements:*** Instruments, working surfaces used in the procedure, associated gloves, protective clothing, and waste materials must be disinfected, sterilised or incinerated as appropriate.

5. ***Handling specimens for laboratory examination:*** Gloves should be worn at all times by laboratory as well as autopsy room and mortuary personnel when handling specimens from suspected cases.

6. *Clean up procedure:* New intact disposable gloves should be worn. Small spatters and spills of blood and other body fluids can be wiped up with disposable tissues or towels which are discarded in special biohazard bags and properly disposed off, and the area then covered with a disinfectant and wiped clean.

7. *Disinfection:* A 1:10 dilution of household bleach or a freshly prepared sodium hypochlorite solution, the active ingredient in the bleach, in equivalent concentration of 5000 ppm, is recommended.

8. *Accidental injury and prophylaxis:* In the event of an accidental injury, contaminated or not with bloody and body fluids, either at autopsy or in the laboratory, the wound should be disinfected and the incident reported to the proper authority. Blood sample should be taken from the source of exposure and tested for HIV and hepatitis B. Blood sample should be taken from the injured person for immediate testing and for comparison during the follow-up period. The test should be repeated at 6 weeks, 3 months, 6 months and 1 year after the episode. Any person who is accidentally exposed to HIVshould have a prophylactic course of zidovudine, 500 mg twice a day, for 6 weeks. Any person exposed to hepatitis B and who is not vaccinated should have prophylactic hepatitis B immunoglobulin within 72 hours of the incident, followed by active vaccination.

In the Laboratory

1. Disposable gloves should be worn and counter top covers used in areas where biological material is examined. This should be disposed off in an authorised manner.
2. Food or smoking should not be allowed in the work area.
3. All biological specimens should be considered contaminated and treated accordingly.
4. Mouth pipetting of biological material should no be allowed.
5. If possible, specimens to be destroyed should be burnt or chemically decontaminated.
6. Hands should be washed before leaving the work area.

In the Court

1. Whenever possible, biologically contaminated evidence should be referred by photographic or other means rather than presenting it in court.
2. When necessary, bullets, clothing, etc. should be handled using disposable gloves and over paper, or the (dry not wet/moist) evidence should be enclosed in a sealed, clear, plastic bag.
3. The hands should be washed after handling the evidence.

General Precautions

The best key to control the dissemination of HIV or hepatitis B is prevention—prevention of unnecessary contamination of the work area and of injuries. Prevention requires strict attention to details, carrying out the required autopsy and body preparation procedures with care, neatly and cleanly, avoiding spattering and confining any flow of body fluids within limited bounds of the work area.

The major danger to all personnel would be any action that produces an aerosol of biologic material, such as that produced by a saw during autopsy or by a blender in toxicology studies. The most common known methods of accidental exposure include being pricked with a used needle or other contaminated material, and the contamination of an area or surface, which would not be expected to be so, by the thoughtless techniques of a careless fellow employee. Washing hands and cleaning floors, doors, door knobs, and telephone with a disinfectant capable of killing viruses will protect the employees.

8

Autopsy on Bodies Contaminated with Radioactive Compounds

Q. 8.1. Give the salient features of autopsy procedure on bodies contaminated with radioactive compounds.

All the soft tissues, organs and mainly the bones show the presence of radioactive material. Special precautions must, therefore, be taken in the disposal of radioactive corpses by everyone concerned. The following is a brief account of the points which must receive attention.

The body and the accompanying clinical chart should be tagged in such a way as to make it clear immediately that the patient has been treated with radioactive material. The tag should give the date of the last treatment, amount and identity of the isotope given, and also the date when precautionary measures are no longer necessary. It is desirable to have a Geiger counter available in the autopsy room so that the prosector in a pertinent case may know beforehand the amount of radiation to which he will be exposed during a specific time. There is no danger in dealing with bodies that have received a large dose of external radiation, or only tracer doses of any isotope for diagnostic purposes.

The beta radiations that are normally absorbed by the superficial tissues can reach the hands of the prosector as he dissects the organs. This radiation is very intense but falls off rapidly with increasing distance from the radioactivity and is readily absorbed by material interposed between the source and the hands. It is, therefore, necessary to use long handle instruments and wear extra-thick rubber gloves for protection. Any delay between death and autopsy reduces the radiation levels by the natural decay of radioactive material. Temporary implants, if any, should be removed from the body, before autopsy is commenced. If the amount of radioactivity is less than 5 millicuries, no extra precautions are necessary beyond the wearing of rubber gloves. When a body is likely to contain more than 5 millicuries of radioactive material, it is advisable to consult a radiation safety officer to prescribe the working time for the examiner at various distances from the body. If the safety officer is not available and the body contains less than 30 millicuries of radioactive material, a Geiger counter showing in advance the radiation exposure must be employed.

Two thick pairs of gloves should be worn to reduce the amount of radiation reaching the skin and to prevent any chance of skin contamination through leakage. Plastic aprons and plastic shoe covers should be worn to reduce contamination of the wearing apparel. Spectacles will prevent contamination of the eyes. Instruments with long handles should be used, especially knives with extra-long handles and oversized forceps.

Organs that are most radioactive are removed first and placed in a glass jar, properly labelled, and preserved in a fixative or in the refrigerator for later examination when the radioactivity has fallen to a safe level. Fluids from the cavity should be removed by means of a trocar and cannula and stored, if necessary. A syringe is less suitable for removal of fluids because it is to be held in hand. The cavity should then be irrigated with saline or water and the fluid disposed of directly into the sewer. Blood and clots may be disposed of without special precautions. Spillage of blood, urine and other fluids during autopsy must be avoided.

Detailed dissection of any organ, must be done away from the body. Finer dissections of organs showing radioactivity above the permissible level may be done after a period of cold storage or fixation to permit radioactive decay.

If the body contains more than 30 millicuries of radioactivity, the presence of radiation safety officer is essential. If the radiation level is very high, the use of a team to complete removal of organs or fluids may be necessary, to minimise the exposure.

In case of accidental injury during autopsy, the procedure must stop forthwith and the gloves removed. The autopsy may be continued by another pathologist. The wound must be washed with copious amounts of running water and the safety officer notified so that he may determine the presence of residual contamination.

Autopsy on bodies containing more than 30 millicuries of radioactivity should be completed as speedily and cleanly as possible. Gloves should be washed thoroughly before being removed from the hands. Contaminated wearing apparel and instruments should be cleaned thoroughly with soap and water. If towels and gowns contain radioactivity above the permissible level, they should be stored for decay of the radioactive material before being sent to the laundry. It is important to avoid contamination of the floor of the autopsy room which should be washed thoroughly with water and detergent, if necessary. The safety officer should monitor the room, tables, instruments, shoes and clothes to check that there is no residual radioactivity. The pathologist encountering radioactive specimens should equip himself with a monitor and be properly instructed in its use. When the body contains more than 30 millicuries of radioactivity after autopsy, it should be embalmed in the hospital morgue, and/or disposed off in accordance with the regulations to prevent radiation hazards.

9

Postmortem Artifacts

Q. 9.1. Discuss artifacts.

For medicolegal purposes, an artifact may be defined as a change in the natural state of the body that is likely to be misinterpreted at autopsy. Such artifacts may be introduced before death due to therapy, about the time of death or after death, and are accordingly known as—(1) therapeutic artifacts, (2) agonal artifacts, and (3) postmortem artifacts.

A medicolegal autopsy is not a simple procedure. Some unusual lesions cannot be identified with certainty. In such circumstances, these lesions should be photographed and reference made to senior experts for assistance in the correct interpretation of such findings. While the various artifacts are already dealt within the text at appropriate places, some of the important ones are briefly reviewed below.

Therapeutic Artifacts

If a victim of lethal violence survives long enough for surgical and other therapeutic effects to be instituted, the task of the pathologist performing autopsy becomes somewhat complicated. These effects may simulate antemortem injuries and can lead to serious misinterpretation, if he is not cognisant of their origin and significance. Before commencing an autopsy, therefore, the pathologist should procure and study all records of antemortem treatment and should contact attending medical personnel directly to know the antemortem state of the body. The following are a few examples:

1. The importance of recognising the traumatic effects of resuscitation cannot be overestimated. In intracardiac injection, the heart may show focal contusion and blood may collect in the pericardium giving the impression that death was due to cardiac tamponade as a result of blunt injury. Vigorous external cardiac massage which may result in sternal and multiple rib fractures, occasionally accompanied by laceration of the liver and upper abdominal organs, can create an erroneous impression of crushing force applied to the chest, e.g. a homicidal attack or accidental injuries resulting from impact on the steering wheel. The latter impression is reinforced, if a ring-like bruise caused by the defibrillator is also present. Incised wound made on the chest for purpose of performing cardiac massage may be misinterpreted as a stab wound. Careful documentation of all resuscitative measures is required to obviate such errors. In fact, it is a sound practice, once the overall appearance of the body has been described, to proceed to a heading of "Evidence of Treatment" and briefly list the features present.
2. Shape and size of unusual injuries may be altered by surgical intervention. Stab

wounds may be enlarged and incorporated into surgical incisions to facilitate exploration and repair.

3. The appearance of entrance and exit gunshot wounds may be altered by washing and their dimensions changed by suturing or excision. Bullets may be lost in the emergency room when they drop out unnoticed during removal of the victim's clothes. They may be displaced, misplaced or lost in the operating room by persons unfamiliar with their evidentiary value.
4. With the passage of time, injuries heal, become septic or otherwise change; alcohol and other toxic substances are metabolised or excreted; and anatomic artifacts are frequently introduced by therapeutic measures.

Agonal Artifacts

Agonal period is the time between cardio-respiratory arrest and brain dysfunction or death. Froth and stomach contents may be seen issuing from the nose and mouth during this period. It could be due to handling of the body, resuscitation or convulsive movements preceding death in some cases. In case of doubt, a study of lung tissue by histopathological examination is of help; if food particles are found beyond the secondary bronchioles, it indicates that the inhaled food particles are antemortem in origin.

Absence of gross bleeding does not necessarily indicate postmortem injury nor does the presence of extravasated blood in the tissues always indicate antemortem injury.

During the terminal moments of life, if the victim goes rapidly into vascular collapse or shock, e.g. in repeated stabbing where the blood pressure falls to low levels before the assailant ceases his assault, haemorrhage may be minimal.

Postmortem blunt injuries occur when an individual may have collapsed and died in the street of natural causes but is subsequently run over by a vehicle. This may lead to accumulation of large amounts of blood in the body cavities and even some degree of haemorrhagic infiltration of tissues at the site of gross traumatic lesions.

Since stab wounds and lacerations which bleed internally, it is not possible to determine their antemortem or postmortem nature unless the wound was sustained at least 20 minutes or more before death when microscopic signs of inflammation appear.

Despite such possibilities, most antemortem injuries can be distinguished from postmortem ones on the basis of data outlined under antemortem and postmortem wounds. It may be remembered here that **certain events cannot happen after death:** (a) pavementation and exudation of white blood cells (white blood cells which are due to haemorrhagic extravasation should not be confused with those due to leucotoxic effects of trauma), (b) proliferation of fixed tissue cells, (c) formation of significant amounts of carboxyhaemoglobin, (d) formation of laminated thrombi, (e) migration of emboli, and (f) significant propulsion of food along the gastrointestinal tract.

Postmortem Artifacts

These may be due to—(1) improper handling of the dead body, (2) improper autopsy procedures, (3) embalming (4) anthropophagy, and (5) postmortem changes.

Improper handling of the body: In the process of removal of the body from the crime scene to mortuary, fresh abrasions may be produced; blood stains may form on parts of the garments originally free from them; fresh tears in clothes may result from rough handling. Rough handling of the dead body by mortuary assistants may also result in fracture of ribs or bones of the extremities, especially in the elderly or the debilitated, who have been in bed for a long time and have developed osteoporosis with consequent increased fragility of bones. Such fractures are commonly sustained during attempts to straighten the extremities bent as a result of severe joint disease or contracted in a state of rigor mortis. In exhumation, fractures may be produced during the process of digging. Careful observation at the time of dissection will not reveal any evidence of ecchymosis or bleeding at fracture site in all such cases.

Improper autopsy procedures: These may result in artefactual fractures, haemorrhages and emboli.

As a routine, the skull cap is sawn and removed by gently inserting and twisting the chisel at various places through the cut. This should be done carefully lest the existing fractures may extend or linear fractures extending into the middle cranial fossa may be produced. Bodies dropped on hard surfaces may also sustain skull fractures. Therefore, *if there is possibility that death may have resulted from skull injury, the chisel should not be used to remove the skull cap.*

Improper removal of neck organs may fracture the hyoid and thyroid cartilages, especially in the elderly. Extreme care should, therefore, be exercised in removing the neck organs. It should be remembered that bony union between the segments of the hyoid may be unilateral. *Spring action or recoil test:* By holding the greater cornu between thumb and index, and adducting gently, gives a recoil, if hyoid is intact. In the absence of recoil, a dissection or X-ray exam clarifies the status.

Fisher records an instance in which a man was found guilty of killing his wife by throttling (manual strangulation) in which the principal evidence was the report by an inexperienced pathologist that the hyoid bone was fractured not realising that what appeared to be a fracture at first sight was unilateral non-union between the segments of the hyoid.

When head injury is suspected, the skull should be opened only after the cardiovascular system has been decompressed by opening or removing the heart. If blood is not drained from a passively congested head, damage to dura and major venous sinuses during removal of the skull cap by sawing can lead to escape of blood in the subdural space. This is likely to be confused with antemortem subdural effusion and in the event, an antemortem scalp contusion is accidentally present, an erroneous diagnosis of death from head injury may be made.

During removal of the sternum, damage to the heart or internal mammary vessels may lead to seepage of blood in the pleural or pericardial cavities, and such haemorrhage may be attributed to antemortem injury.

Fragmentation of the bloodstream in the meningeal arteries produced by pulling the dura in the sagittal plane may be confused with systemic or arterial air embolism. Likewise, air in coronary vessels, due to handling the lung and the heart after internal mammary vessels are cut, may simulate air embolism.

Embalming: The embalming process consists of making incisions in the axillary or supraclavicular area through which arteries are entered. Trocars are then inserted and embalming fluid is pumped under pressure via the arterial system until it returns on the venous side. Incisions may then be made in the area of the trunk to clear excess embalming fluid. Trocar wounds may be mistaken for stab wounds or bullet wounds. Some blood may be forced out of injured or disrupted blood vessels and may accumulate in the tissues with appearance of antemortem haemorrhage. Skin bruises may be markedly accentuated due to increased transparency of overlying skin resulting from the embalming process.

Anthropophagy: Ants and insects mostly attack the exposed parts and moist areas of the body, such as face, arms, genitals, groins and axilla. Rats, cats and dogs attack exposed parts and destroy soft tissues of the face, head and hands, with little or no damage to clothed areas. Although rats attack any dead body, cats and dogs do not attack their masters unless they are starving. Marine animals mostly attack exposed areas and projecting body parts, such as lips, nose, ears, fingers, scrotum, etc. All these injuries are without a vital reaction and their edges appear nibbled. A careful look for the tracks of these invaders may explain peculiar lesions on body surfaces.

Animals, such as dogs, jackals, hyenas, which attack the exposed parts, produce ghastly wounds resembling haphazard mutilation with bone involvement. A careful examination will reveal, if bones are gnawed through by animals or cut by sharp weapons. In addition, animals generally eat away the medulla of long bones, and spicules of cortical bone are found depressed in the medullary cavity. Animals commonly select for their activities those areas where skin is broken; the antemortem wounds are thus enlarged to a great degree by postmortem invaders.

Postmortem changes: These artifacts are due to—(1) rigor mortis, (2) postmortem lividity, (3) autolysis, (4) putrefaction, and (5) heat.

Rigor mortis: The time of onset and duration of rigor mortis vary depending on the age and condition of the body, mode of death, and the season. Existing rigor mortis may be broken down at least partially while removing the body from the crime scene to mortuary, and all these may cause errors in interpretation of time since death.

Postmortem lividity: Isolated patches of postmortem lividity may be mistaken for bruises. Such patches on the front and sides of the neck may be mistaken for bruising due to throttling (manual strangulation). Lividity of the internal organs may be mistaken for congestion due to disease. Postmortem staining in the heart can simulate effects of coronary occlusion; in the lungs—pneumonia; and in the gastrointestinal tract—irritation due to poisoning. Certain conditions, such as carbon monoxide poisoning, cold, etc., impart a distinctive colour to postmortem lividity.

Autolysis: When tissues die, as in cardiac infarction, there is a rise in certain enzyme levels. Likewise, after death, enzymes are released from tissue cells. An aseptic chemical process known as autolysis thus commences and continues steadily for two or three days, sometimes longer, when body tissues are autolysed. The process is characterised by a spectrum of changes ranging from delicate alteration of individual cells to loss of complete architecture. Autolysis of endothelial cells leads to their separation from one another with resultant escape of haemolysed blood into the surrounding tissues. This leads to discolouration of skin and viscera. Such changes are promptly visible in gallbladder, pancreas, liver, kidney, gastrointestinal mucosa, and brain, where they may simulate injury or disease. As for example, the pancreatic parenchyma presents generalised or multifocal areas of reddish-brown discolouration suggestive of acute inflammation. Perforation of the stomach due to autolysis may have to be distinguished from that due to corrosive acid or peptic ulceration.

Absence of cellular response in discoloured areas establishes the postmortem origin of these changes. Inflammatory exudate, if found in association with autolysed cells, must have been present before death.

Putrefaction: Pathologists with little experience of autopsy on decomposed bodies are easily mislead by putrefactive artifacts.

The blood becomes darker in putrefaction with the result that the brain, heart and lungs appear congested, and a mistaken diagnosis of asphyxia may be made.

In India, the decomposed bodies commonly received for autopsy present a swollen neck and exaggerated skin folds. In addition, the beaded threads and ornaments worn round the neck produce depressed marks which look like ligature marks. Unless, dissection of the neck reveals antemortem evidence of violence in the underlying tissues, no importance can be attached to these findings. Sometimes, the simple observation that the jewellery or ornaments are more than big enough to fit a normal size neck (not swollen due to putrefaction gases) is sufficient to make the distinction.

The bulging of eyes, protrusion of tongue, and discharge of red-stained froth from mouth and nose may be mistaken for signs of throttling (manual strangulation). Added to this, softening of 'synchondrosis' between the body and greater cornuae of the hyoid bone producing abnormal mobility may be further confused as a fracture.

Owing to pressure effects of putrefactive gases, postmortem stains may be displaced in any direction and may simulate antemortem bruises. Likewise, internal lividity may resemble haemorrhage particularly in the meninges, kidneys and retroperitoneal tissues leading to serious misinterpretation.

Putrefactive blisters may be confused with blisters from burns and contact with petroleum products. The skin from the hand may peel like a glove as in burns.

Froth and stomach contents (gastric juice) which issue from the nose and mouth tan the facial skin and may simulate antemortem burning. Such a change is sometimes observed on exposure to gasoline and may be mistaken for fire in an automobile accident or plane crashing.

The skin splits from putrefaction, and may give a false impression of antemortem lacerations, incised wounds or thermal injuries.

The female genitals appear pendulous and may be mistaken by the novice as a sign of sexual assault.

In bodies interred for sometime and exhumed later on, fungus growth is common on some parts of the body. When it is removed, the part appears as if it is bruised.

Heat effects: When skin is exposed to heat, it becomes tense, leathery, hard, and frequently shows splits which may be mistaken for wounds. These splits may be distinguished from the effects of violence—(1) by the presence of nerves, blood vessels, and connective tissue, running across the split from side to side, (2) there is no clotted blood in these fissures and no extravasation of blood in the surrounding tissues since heat coagulates the blood in the vessels, and (3) there is no bruising or any other sign of vital reaction in the margins of heat rupture.

Heat applied to the skin of a dead body may loosen the epidermis from dermis and produce a postmortem blister. It can be easily differentiated from an antemortem one. A postmortem blister is limited in size, contains air, or if it contains fluid, it is practically non-albuminous and without chlorides and blood corpuscles, there is no line of hyperaemia round the blister, and its base is not injected.

When the head has been exposed to intense heat, the scalp may show fissures. The skull cap may present fissured fractures and these may be mistaken for fractures due to violence. The fractures due to heat are usually located on either side of the skull above the temples. Characteristically, they consist of several lines which radiate from a common centre and may cross a suture line. Outward bursting of the bone flaps and protrusion of brain tissue through the defect may occur as a result of steam pressure within the skull. Curiously, heat fractures do not generally involve the sutures of the skull even in young individuals with open sutures. When fractures are present at the base of the skull, one can assume that these are not produced as a result of steaming of the brain. Such fractures, of course, could have resulted from falling structures, during attempt to escape from a burning house.

The brain may be congested and oedematous or shrunken and extradural haemorrhage (*heat haematoma*) may be found. The haematoma is due to rupture of blood vessels caused by heat with subsequent coagulation of blood and has certain characteristics. It is a soft, friable clot of light chocolate colour, and may be pink, if blood contains carbon monoxide. The clot is not uniformly solid but is spongy and is not related to the site of heat fracture. This is in contrast to traumatic fractures where the intracranial haematoma is closely related to the position of the fracture or is contre coup to the fracture site.

Fat droplets may be found in the pulmonary vessels and a mistaken diagnosis of pulmonary fat embolism may be made.

A tight collar on the neck may spare an area of skin from burning. And, the appearance of a groove thus produced may be mistaken for a ligature strangulation.

Q. 9.2. What is virtopsy or virtual autopsy?

Virtual autopsy is to look into the organs without actually cutting and dissecting them. We can look at all organs and in different planes and angles using modern scanning methods, like modified MRI, CT and others. In this way, it is possible to know about the health or disease status of organs and we can preserve the record for presenting evidence in the court of law also. It is possible to study the status of cranial and cardiac vasculature also. This can avoid cutting the tissues and organs and avoid disfiguration and distortion due to autopsy. For taking various tissues for histopathology, we have to do 'biopsies' as per the need as soon as death is declared or at the virtual autopsy setting. In the same way, other materials like blood, saliva, urine, etc. also may be collected and sent for required analysis.

Advantages: (1) No mutilation, (2) evidence preserved for court, (3) in cultures where conventional autopsy is not allowed, virtopsy is useful.

10 Exhumation

Q. 10.1. What is exhumation? Mention the precautions that you will take and briefly describe the procedure for autopsy on an exhumed body.

Exhumation is defined as the lawful disinterment or digging out of a buried body from the grave. It becomes necessary: (1) for purposes of identification, and (2) to determine the cause of death, when foul play is suspected. As the Hindus who form a majority of the population cremate their dead within a few hours, exhumation in North India is quite rare or an officer authorized for the purpose. In South India, exhumations for second autopsy are more common. South Indians by and large bury the dead bodies. In India, no time limit is fixed for exhumation. Only a magistrate can order it.

The procedure can be divided into: (1) general precautions, (2) identification of the grave, opening it, and collections of samples of earth, (3) identification of the coffin and collection of samples, (4) identification of the body and its viewing by magistrate or coroner, and (5) autopsy, if necessary.

General precautions: Exhumation is carried out under the supervision of the medical officer and in the presence of a police officer. The police officer provides witnesses to identify the grave, the coffin and the dead body. It is necessary to carry out exhumation in the early morning so that the whole process of digging, and autopsy, if required, can be completed during the day.

Identification and opening the grave: The grave is formally identified by the warden of the cemetery from the records, and the exact site by friends and relations who have been present at the time of burial. The sexton and caretaker may confirm this identification procedure. A (tarpaulin) screen is erected around the grave which is then dug up carefully to avoid damage to the coffin and its contents. In a suspected case of poisoning, samples of earth in a quantity of about 500 gm are collected from above, below and sides of the coffin, and control samples at some distance from it, in separate clean, dry, glass bottles for chemical analysis. It is advisable to be congnisant of the nature of geological layout of the cemetery and direction of any water drainage. If the grave is water logged, samples of water should also be taken. Where the soil contains arsenic and arsenic poisoning is suspected, the concentration of arsenic in various organs should be more than that in the earth.

Identification of the coffin: The coffin top should be cleaned up and the plate exposed. This should be identified by the original undertaker who made it, and a photograph of it is of value. The coffin can then be raised to the surface, and before examining the contents, the lid is lifted to allow escape of gases. To avoid inhaling offensive gases, one should stand on the windward side. Samples of earth from above, below and sides of the body are collected in the usual manner. If the coffin contains water, it should be drained off, the total volume with sludge measured, and a sample collected for analysis. Further, samples are collected from coffin wood and burial clothes to exclude any possibility of contamination from external sources.

Baden records the case of a London based husband whose numerous rich wives died one after the other of suspected poisoning. Scotland Yard exhumed their bodies and found arsenic. The husband went to the gallows proclaiming his innocence, and years later, a curious student of toxicology tested the soil where the wives were buried, and found that it was full of natural arsenic. The poison could well have seeped into the coffins. The student wondered if the wives were really poisoned. However, it was too late, to surmise or to prosecute.

Identification of the body: An attempt is then made to identify the body by any person who was present when the body was placed in the coffin. The magistrate or coroner views the body and orders a reburial or an autopsy.

Autopsy: Strict and meticulous attention to the health and safety of the participants in the exhumation should be ensured. Special care should be taken that the gloves worn are in a perfect condition. A full autopsy must be carried out in the usual manner preferably in the mortuary when possible or near the graveyard, and the autopsy report duly prepared.

The doctor should have a complete history of the case so that his attention is properly directed to important points. The body should be photographed and if necessary, X-ray examination should be undertaken. The injuries, if any, should be described in detail. Since soft tissue injuries may disappear due to decomposition, fractures of bones, such as the skull, hyoid and ribs, should be specially looked for. The possibility of such fractures having been produced during the process of digging should be kept in mind. It should be remembered that ununited pieces of sternum, costal cartilages and epiphyses of long bones may also be mistaken for fractures in children.

Any organ or part that may appear to offer any evidence should be removed for further examination and/or chemical analysis by the forensic science laboratory. If organs are not distinguishable, masses obtained from areas of these organs should be preserved. If viscera are not present, hair, nails, teeth, bones and skin should be collected. The whole procedure of examination and autopsy is better videographed. In southern parts of India, bail is more common and hence exhumation too.

Before leaving the place, the medical officer should make sure that he has taken all specimens that may be required for later examination as it will not be possible to re-examine the remains, once reburial has been affected.

Section 3

11 Medicolegal Aspects of Death Investigation

The medicolegal study of death falls within the unit of forensic thanatology (*thanatos* = death; *logos* = science).

Q. 11.1. Define death. What are the differences between cerebral death and brainstem death? How will you diagnose and certify brainstem death?

Diagnosis of death: Traditional death definition is irreversible and permanent cessation of life as evidenced by stoppage of brain function, respiratory activity and cardiac function. Since organ retrieval and scavenging for transplantation has come into vogue, brainstem death is legally synonymous with death.

Differences between cerebral death and brainstem death: Due to severe brain damages patient breaths spontaneously, opens and closes eyes, swallows and shows facial grimaces. In cerebral death, a person is in a persistent vegetative state. If this state continues to persist, it is called permanent vegetative state. In brainstem death pupils are fixed in diameter, light reflex, corneal reflex, oculocephalic reflex, heat and cold response, vestibulo-occular reflex are lost/absent. Gag reflex is absent. Respiratory movements are absent on withdrawal of machanical respirator. Death is declared once it is confirmed. As per the Organ Transplantation Act in India, brainstem death is legal death.

Death occurs in two stages, viz: (1) somatic, systemic or clinical, and (2) cellular or molecular. The term 'death' as commonly employed means somatic death. It is due to complete and irreversible cessation of vital functions of the brain, followed by cessation of the functions of the heart and lungs. Formerly, cessation of heart beat and respiration were used as the criteria of death but now that cardiac transplantation is possible, emphasis has shifted to irreversible cessation of brain function.

After somatic death, tissues and cells survive for a varying period depending upon their oxygen requirements. When these individual tissues and cells die, it is termed as cellular or molecular death. It occurs piecemeal, e.g. nervous tissue dies rapidly, say within five minutes, while muscles survive up to about three to four hours. Molecular death is accompanied by cooling of the body, and changes in the eye, skin, muscles, etc. It is generally complete within three to four hours of somatic death.

Diagnosis of somatic or clinical death is not always easy in the following conditions:

1. Soon after death when the body is likely to be warm.
2. Suspended animation.
3. Coma following excessive doses of sedatives or hypnotics especially barbiturates.
4. Hypothermia, particularly in the elderly.
5. Electrocution and lightning accidents.
6. Drowning particularly in cold water.

The distinction between somatic and molecular death is important for two reasons, viz.:

a. disposal of the body, and
b. transplantation.

a. *Disposal of the body:* In the rare instances, when the body is cremated soon after somatic death, spontaneous movements of the hands and feet may occur on the funeral pyre. This may give rise to doubt that the person was not actually dead but was prematurely disposed off.

b. *Transplantation:* The viability of transplantable organs falls sharply after somatic death—a liver must be taken within 15 minutes, a kidney within 45 minutes, and a heart within an hour.

A person whose brain may have been injured irreversibly can now be kept alive by maintaining circulation of oxygenated blood to the brainstem by artificial means. Such a patient, after appropriate brainstem reflex testing, can now be declared dead legally, and organs required for transplantation can be removed even though the circulation and respiration have not ceased due to artificial maintenance under the Organ Transplantation Act in India.

Q. 11.2. Mention the various modes of death and give in brief the autopsy findings in each.

There are three modes of death irrespective of what the remote cause of death may be. These modes are: (1) coma, (2) syncope and (3) asphyxia. This is also called Bichot's classification of death.

Coma: This is death from failure of the function of the brain and irreversible damage to its vital centres. It is due to:

1. Raised intracranial pressure from diseases of the brain or its membranes, and injuries to the brain.
2. Poisons, such as opioids and alcohol.
3. Metabolic disorders, like uraemia. The autopsy will reveal the specific cause except in cases of poisoning or metabolic disorders when oedema or congestion of the brain and its covering membranes is commonly found.

Syncope: This is death from failure of function of the heart resulting in hypoperfusion and hypoxia of the brain. It is due to—(1) heart disease, (2) haemorrhage, (3) pathological states of blood, (4) exhausting diseases, or (5) poisoning due to digitalis, potassium, aconite or oleander. At autopsy, the heart appears contracted. It contains very little blood, if death is due to haemorrhage. The viscera appear pale and the capillaries congested.

A syncopal type of death may also result from reflex cardiac arrest due to:

1. Vagal stimulation, commonly known as *vasovagal shock, vagal inhibition or neurogenic shock.*
2. Rarely ventricular fibrillation due to cardiac problems or spontaneous sympathetic nervous discharge.

Vagal inhibition is important in certain cases of accidental hanging; throttling (manual strangulation); blow to the epigastrium; abortion; emotional tension; sudden immersion of the body in cold water; insertion of an instrument into the uterus, bladder, rectum or any other body cavity; and light anaesthesia. In these conditions, as the trauma may be very trivial, the injury is not visible. Therefore, there are no characteristic postmortem appearances and the cause of death is inferred from the history and negative findings, viz. no natural disease, injury or poisoning, to account for the cause of death.

An instance is recorded of a man who attempted to molest a girl. He tried to prevent her from shouting by putting his hands on her mouth. She suddenly went limp and her dead body was in his hands. (An example of death due to vagal inhibition).

Petty records an excellent example of emotional trauma causing instantaneous physiologic death. A 17-year-old white girl, shop-lifted a small, pocket-sized, snapshot album. The theft was noticed, and a security guard followed her outside the store, then stopped her, and asked that she remove the album from her purse. She handed her babe in arms to her accompanying mother and turned to the guard. The security guard stated, "she was looking directly at me and the pupils of her eyes became very large, and she dropped to the ground." Mouth-to-mouth artificial respiration administered by the guard was of no avail; resuscitation in the ambulance and at the hospital also failed. No disease process was discovered at autopsy; all organs and viscera appeared normal. Toxicological examination failed to find any toxic substances in the body tissues and fluids. The mother of the deceased substantiated the statement of the security guard. The brother of the deceased maintained that the guard had "scared her to death."

Asphyxia: This is death from failure of respiratory function. It occurs in pathological conditions of the respiratory system, such as in pneumonia, paralysis of respiratory centre as in opioid poisoning, occlusion of air passages, breathing of irres-pirable gases, and in traumatic asphyxia. In all these conditions, respiratory function ceases before that of the heart. The autopsy appearances are indeed characteristic and comprise cyanosis, pronounced lividity, petechial haemorrhages, visceral congestion, and sometimes cardiac dilatation, in addition to special changes dependent upon the type of death, e.g. local injuries to neck in hanging, strangulation, and throttling, and colour of blood in acute carbon monoxide poisoning.

While certifying the mode of death, e.g. coma, syncope or asphyxia, it is necessary to mention the precipitating cause, e.g. coma due to meningitis, syncope due to haemorrhage or asphyxia due to hanging. *Without the cause, the diagnosis is too non-specific.*

Q. 11.3. Define sudden death. What is its medicolegal significance? Mention its various causes.

The name sudden death is given to those deaths which are not preceded or are only preceded for a short period, say about a day or two, by morbid symptoms. They are important from a medicolegal standpoint as they may raise a suspicion of foul play.

It is quite possible for a person to be in apparently perfect health but at the same time suffering from a serious disease of which he may not be aware. When a person of normal health dies, within twenty-four hours of onset of the symptoms and signs of terminal illness, it is called as sudden natural death. Sudden unnatural deaths are due to accidental, suicidal or homicidal causes.

A male aged 30 was found dead near a cinema theatre. Autopsy revealed haemopericardium with about 300 ml fluid blood and blood clots in the pericardial cavity, and haemothorax. Aneurysmal dilatation of the ascending aorta was found with a rupture in the aneurysm close to the heart.

It happens sometimes that a sudden death in connection with which there appears to be no reason for suspicion proves on examination to be one of murder or suicide.

An old man was thought, after inspec-tion of the body, to have died from heart failure, but was subsequently found to have shot himself in the mouth with a revolver. There was no external evidence of the cause of death; no alteration of features; no effusion of blood; and no weapon was found until some days after the event.

Thus, in cases of sudden death, it is usually not possible to certify the cause of death from an external examination of the body. In all such cases, an autopsy is necessary to obviate the possibility of unnatural death escaping investigation. A doctor who issues a death certificate in such a case, runs the risk of being accused as an accessory to a crime and obstructing the course of justice, should the death be found eventually due to foul play. If a doctor has not attended the patient within two weeks prior to the death, it is advisable not to issue a death certificate.

Causes of Sudden Natural Death

The **causes** of sudden natural deaths are classified as follows: (1) cardiovascular, (2) respiratory, (3) CNS, (4) abdominal, (5) endocrinal, (6) iatrogenic, (7) miscellaneous, (8) special causes in children, and (9) indeterminate.

1. *Cardiovascular:*

a. *Coronary artery disease:* (i) atherosclerosis, (ii) thrombosis, (iii) syphilitic infection producing narrowing of the coronary ostia.

b. *Congenital heart disease*, e.g. ASD, VSD, PDA.

c. *Valvular heart disease:* (i) rheumatic, (ii) syphilitic, (iii) other types.

d. *Hypertensive heart disease.*

e. *Infection:* (i) pericarditis, (ii) myocarditis, (iii) endocarditis.

f. *Cardiac tamponade:* (i) ruptured myocardial infarct, (ii) trauma. Other conditions:

 i. Fiedler's myocarditis,

 ii. Cardiomyopathies.

h. *Rupture of aortic aneurysm:* (i) atherosclerotic, (ii) dissecting, (iii) other, e.g. syphilitic.

2. *Respiratory:*

a. Pulmonary thromboembolism

b. Massive haemoptysis from tuberculosis or malignant disease

c. Severe infections, such as fulminating viral pneumonia

d. Bronchial asthma

e. Airway obstruction from any cause

3. *CNS:*

a. Intracerebral haemorrhage associated with cerebral atheroma and infarction or hypertension

b. Subarachnoid haemorrhage from a ruptured aneurysm

c. Cerebral thrombosis and subsequent infarction

d. Cerebral embolism

e. Infection of the meninges

f. Tumour of the brain producing pressure or sudden haemorrhage in a tumour

g. Epilepsy

h. Functional inhibition of the vagus

4. *Abdominal:*

a. Massive haemorrhage into the alimentary tract from a bleeding gastric or duodenal ulcer or colon in ulcerative colitis or diverticulitis

b. Rupture of abdominal aneurysm

c. Haemorrhage in relation to female generative organs, such as in abortion or ruptured ectopic gestation

d. Ruptured diseased viscus, e.g. perforated peptic ulcer, ulcerative colitis

e. Infarcted intestine from mesenteric thrombosis or embolism

f. Fulminant hepatic failure

g. Acute haemorrhagic pancreatitis.

5. *Endocrinal:*

a. Adrenal insufficiency or haemorrhage

b. Diabetic coma

c. Myxoedemic crisis

d. Parathyroid crisis

e. Pituitary infarction (Sheehan's syndrome).

6. *Iatrogenic:*

a. Abuse of drugs

b. Sudden withdrawal of steroids or beta-blockers

c. Anaesthetic mishaps

d. Mismatched blood transfusion.

7. *Miscellaneous:*

a. Anaphylaxis

b. Bacteraemic shock

c. Malaria

d. Sickle cell crisis

8. *Special causes in children:*

a. Cot deaths or SIDS

b. Congenital cardiac or cerebral abnormalities

9. *Indeterminate:* This conclusion should be reached only in a fresh body after exhaustive histological and toxicological examination. In decomposed bodies, this is a more frequent diagnosis.

Signs of Death

The signs of death are sub-divided into three groups, viz. immediate, early and late. Immediate signs constitute somatic or clinical death. Early signs follow within about 12–24 hours after death and denote molecular or cellular death. Late signs follow after about 24 hours after death and represent decomposition or decay or a modification of this process by adipocere formation and/or mummification.

Signs of Somatic or Clinical Death (Immediate Signs)

These include: (1) insensibility and loss of EEG rhythm, (2) cessation of circulation, that is loss of ECG rhythm, and (3) cessation of respiration.

Insensibility and loss of EEG rhythm: Insensibility means loss of sensation, viz. perception of touch, pain and temperature, and loss of the voluntary power to move. The reflexes are also lost. These signs are not conclusive of death as they are found in conditions, such as fainting attacks, vagal inhibition, epilepsy, drowning and electrocution, where some of the victims recover entirely. They can be taken as conclusive only when associated with loss of EEG rhythm for a continuous period of five minutes.

Cessation of circulation: The stethoscope is placed over the region of the heart apex (left fifth intercostal space). If on careful auscultation, the heart sounds are not heard for a continuous period of five minutes, it is acceptable as evidence of death. It may be difficult to hear the heart sounds—(1) if they are feeble, (2) if the chest wall is thick, and (3) in emphysema. In case of doubt, an ECG will settle the issue. It will record the electrical activity of the heart, however, feeble it may be. A flat ECG for a continuous period of five minutes is acceptable as evidence of death.

Life is compatible with a temporary suspension of heart beat and respiration. Such a state is known as **suspended animation.** It is a condition in which the vital functions of the body (heart beat and respiration) are at such a low pitch (as in hibernating animals) that they cannot be detected by routine methods of clinical examination. This state is also called **apparent death,** as the person is not really dead. It may persist from a few seconds to several minutes after which a person can be revived. Involuntary suspended animation may occur in the apparently drowned; in the newborn; after anaesthesia; in cerebral concussion; electrocution; heat stroke; mesmeric trance; in prolonged illness, such as typhoid fever; overdose by barbiturates or opiates; and in deep shock. These patients can be revived by resuscitative techniques. In such cases, a death certificate should not be issued without an EEG and an ECG record, if necessary. Some persons, like yogis can go into suspended animation voluntarily and remain so for a long time.

Cessation of respiration: Respiration may cease for a very short period without death ensuing: (1) as a purely voluntary act, (2) in Cheyne-Stokes breathing, (3) in the drowned, and (4) in the newborn infants. The stethoscope is applied to the upper part of the lungs in front or to the larynx itself where the faintest breath sounds can be heard. Complete absence of breath sounds for a continuous period of five minutes constitutes proof of death.

Signs of Molecular or Cellular Death (Early Signs)

The signs of molecular or cellular death follow within 12–24 hours after death, and include: (1) cooling of the body, (2) changes in the eye, (3) changes in the skin, (4) postmortem lividity, and (5) changes in the muscles.

Q. 11.4. Comment on the following changes in the body after death: (1) cooling of the body, (2) changes in the eye, (3) changes in the skin.

Cooling of the Body

This is also known as *algor mortis* (algor = coldness; mortis = of death). During life, there is a balance between heat production and heat loss. After death, heat production stops, and the body loses heat by conduction, convection and radiation, till it is in equilibrium with the temperature of its surroundings. The progressive fall in temperature is one of the most prominent early signs of death, the amount of cooling indicating the approximate time elapsed since death. (Environmental or ambient temperature must be lower than body temperature).

The temperature of the dead body is recorded by a **chemical** (not clinical) **thermometer (thanatometer),** 25 cm long, with a range from 0–50°C, and graduated in subdivisions of single degrees. It is inserted about 8–10 cm in the rectum after ensuring that there is no local injury or homosexual activity, and swabs are taken before insertion. It is left there for two or three minutes. In cases involving homosexual activity, the **thermometer or thermocouple probe** can be inserted in the **auditory meatus or nostril** as deeply as possible. The temperature can also be recorded by making a small slit in the abdomen and inserting the thermocouple under the liver. This wound must be recorded so as not to confuse it with antemortem injury. The environmental temperature is also recorded and the time noted. Records are made at intervals to determine the rate of fall of temperature.

Normally, the body begins to cool shortly after death except in serious illness when the hands and legs begin to cool before death due to failure of circulation. This coolness gradually extends to the trunk. During life, the normal body temperature may be higher (fever) or lower (collapse, exposure to cold). This must be taken into consideration while calculating the time since death from postmortem cooling.

As heat loss occurs only in the body surface and as heat from the interior can reach the body surface by conduction, the fall of internal body temperature must await the establishment of a temperature gradient towards the surface. It thus remains unchanged for a short period. Accordingly, when the body temperature is normal at the time of death, there is no fall in the rectal temperature for about 45 minutes, this phase being known as the *isothermic phase.* Thereafter, the rate of cooling is not uniform but is related to the difference in temperature between the body and its surroundings. In the first two hours, the average rate of fall of temperature is roughly half the difference between the temperature of the body and its surroundings. In the next two hours, the temperature falls at half this rate, and in the subsequent two hours, at quarter this rate. Thereafter, it falls much slowly till the body is in equilibrium with the temperature of its surroundings.

In a tropical country, like India, the average heat loss is roughly 0.5–0.7°C per hour, and the body attains environmental temperature in about 16–20 hours after death. A rough estimate about the time in hours since death is obtained by using the formula: normal body temperature (37.2°C) minus the rectal temperature, divided by the average rate of fall of temperature per hour (0.6°C). The temperature estimates apply mainly to countries with cold or temperate climate. *There are very few reliable records of the temperature changes of the cadaver in tropical conditions and it is, therefore, not justifiable to base any far reaching conclusions on this observation.*

In certain parts of India, notably in Punjab, the room temperature is frequently much higher than body temperature during hot weather. Under such circumstances, the body does not cool. There are certain conditions in which heat may be retained or even be increased in the first two hours after death. Such conditions include:

1. Sunstroke and pontine haemorrhage, when before death, the mechanism of heat regulation is profoundly disturbed.
2. Tetanus and strychnine poisoning, when there has been a great increase in heat production in the muscles due to convulsions.
3. Acute bacterial or viral infections, such as lobar pneumonia, typhoid fever, encephalitis, and encephalomyelitis, when there has been pronounced bacterial or viral activity. This phenomenon is known as **postmortem caloricity** (post = after; mortem = death; calor = heat). After the initial rise of temperature, the body begins to cool as usual.

The **rate of cooling of the body** is modified by the following conditions: (1) age and condition of the body, (2) mode of death, (3) surroundings, and (4) environmental temperature.

Age and condition of the body: Children and adults of small stature cool rapidly owing to their large body surface as compared to their weight. Lean bodies cool rapidly, and fat bodies slowly, since fat is a bad conductor of heat. As women are comparatively fat, their bodies cool less rapidly than those of men.

Mode of death: In case of sudden death in a healthy individual, the body tends to cool slowly, whereas after a long and wasting illness, the body cools rapidly, and the temperature may commence falling even before death takes place. The body keeps warm longer in deaths from asphyxia, lightning and carbon monoxide poisoning.

Surroundings: Movement of atmospheric air accelerates cooling by convection. Therefore, a body lying in a well-ventilated room cools more rapidly than a body lying in a closed room. Similarly, a body cools more quickly in water than on land because of loss of heat by conduction. Cooling is delayed when the temperature of water or atmospheric air is high. Clothing is a bad conductor of heat, and a body covered with clothes and lying in bed or in a cess pool or dung-heap, cools less rapidly than a naked body lying in open air.

Environmental temperature: The body cools rapidly when the difference in environmental temperature and body is great. The rate of cooling under such circumstances is already discussed.

Changes in the Eye

1. The clear glistening appearance of the *cornea* is lost. The cornea becomes dry, cloudy and opaque due to the failure of production of tears. The corneal reflex is lost but as it is also lost in cases of brain-stem death, it is not a reliable sign. The light reflex is abolished.
2. The intraocular tension falls. The *eyeballs* become flaccid and tend to sink into the orbits; this flaccidity can be appreciated by palpation.
3. The bloodstream in the *retinal vessels* rapidly becomes dotted first and then segmented ("cattle trucking"), and the optic disc becomes pale.

4. As the *pupils* usually dilate at the time of death and later become constricted through the development of rigor mortis, their state after death is no indication of their antemortem appearance. The early state of the pupil, however, can have some practical significance in suspected narcotic poisoning; pupils may be unequal.
5. *Taches noires* appear on sclera within three hours of death, if the eyes remain open. These are areas of brownish-black discolouration, on the exposed sclera between the eyelids, due to the formation of cellular debris and dust settling thereon. The potassium content of *vitreous humour* rises steadily.

Changes in the Skin

The skin assumes a pale, ashy white appearance, more noticeable in fair skinned persons. It loses its elasticity so that postmortem incised wounds may not gape to the same extent as antemortem wounds. The lips tend to darken due to drying.

Q. 11.5. Discuss in detail postmortem lividity with special reference to its usefulness in medicolegal work.

Postmortem lividity (postmortem staining, hypostasis) means discolouration of the skin and organs after death due to accumulation of fluid blood in the toneless capillaries and small veins of the dependent parts of the body. Being the result of stasis of blood due to gravitational forces, the staining is of the same colour as that of the blood.

The process commences within an hour after death and, in the case of a person dying slowly from circulatory failure, it may be pronounced shortly after death. In most cases of sudden death, it presents itself first as a series of mottled patches on the dependent parts within about 1–3 hours; these patches gradually increase in size and coalesce in about 3–6 hours; and the lividity is fully developed and fixed, i.e. becomes unchangeable in about 6–8 hours. *Contrary to popular belief, fixation of lividity is due to packing and complete stagnation of blood in the distended toneless capillaries and small veins, and is not due to coagulation of blood.* After the development of lividity, but before it becomes fixed, if the position of the body is changed, these patches will disappear and fresh ones will develop in the new dependent areas, but lividity to a slight degree will remain in the original area due to staining of the tissues by haemolysis. However, if the position of the body is changed after lividity is fixed, the pattern of lividity is not altered significantly under normal circumstances because—(1) the blood cannot flow away easily from the distended toneless capillaries, and (2) the tissues are already stained by diffusion of haemoglobin from haemolysed red cells.

Generally, it can be said that if the pressure of the thumb blanches the area, the lividity is not fixed and the time since death is less than 8 hours; if the pressure of thumb does not blanch the area, the lividity is fixed and the time since death is more than 6 hours. From the distribution and fixation of lividity, therefore, it may be possible to determine the position in which the body has lain after death and to form some estimate with regard to the time since death.

The **site of distribution and pattern** of lividity depend upon the position of the body after death. In hanging, the lividity is observed circumferentially over the dependent lower limbs, external genitalia, and lower parts of forearms and hands. In drowning, as the body usually floats face downward with hands extended, the lividity is observed in the head and upper parts of the body which are heavier and, therefore, dependent. If a body is constantly changing its position, e.g. in a case of drowning in moving water, lividity may not develop at all. According to Bonte, the lividity is sharply limited to a horizontal line corresponding to the water level, if electrocution occurs in water (usually a bath tub).

As the discolouration is due to filling of blood vessels, it is not developed over areas of *contact flattening,* that is, in those areas of the body which are in actual contact with the surface on which the body is lying because the toneless capillaries are compressed and occluded by the weight and pressure of the body. Thus, in a person lying on his back, while the lividity is observed on the back portion of his body, viz. posterior aspects of head, trunk and extremities, it is not seen on the back of shoulder blades, buttocks and back of calves, as these are areas of contact flattening in this case (Fig. 11.1). Misinterpretation of areas of such contact flattening can result in serious errors. As for example, the white band on the neck produced by a tight collar, beaded threads or ornaments may be mistaken as a mark of ligature strangulation; the parallel marks on the neck of a body whose head is turned to one side may be mistaken as pressure marks of the fingers (manual strangulation); and the alternate dark and light strips on the back of a body lying on a crumpled blanket may be mistaken as bruises due to assault.

While lividity is commonly observed only on the dependent parts, Gordon and Shapiro point out that isolated areas of lividity may be observed over the front and sides of the neck in a person lying on his back. These areas of lividity result from incomplete emptying of the tributaries of the superficial veins of the neck, e.g. external jugular and common facial veins. Such artifacts should not be mistaken for bruises, due to throttling, particularly in putrefied bodies.

The **colour and intensity** of lividity depend on the colour of blood and mode of death (Fig. 11.2). Normally, the staining is at first bluish-pink, and afterwards bluish-purple. In severe anaemia and death from haemorrhage, the staining is very faint. In death from asphyxia, where the blood is deoxygenated and may not readily coagulate, the lividity is intensely developed and purple in colour. In conditions where blood coagulates quickly, e.g. in lobar pneumonia, lividity is less obvious. The colour of lividity is better appreciated in fair skinned persons than in dark skinned ones in whom it may be easily missed unless the colour of nails and palms is carefully examined. Certain poisons impart a distinct colour to lividity, e.g. carbon monoxide—bright cherry red, cyanide—pink, chlorates—chocolate brown, phosphorus—

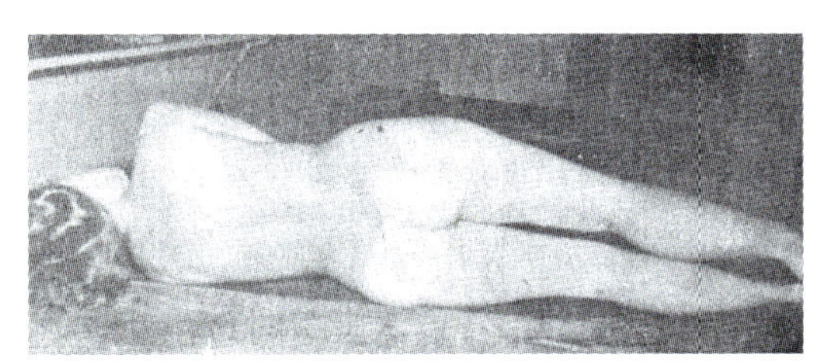

Fig. 11.1: Postmortem hypostasis (livor mortis) and areas of contact flattening at the buttocks and shoulder blades indicative of the **position of the body at the time of death.** Lividity is fully developed and fixed in this case. It is, therefore, possible to form some estimate with regard to the **time since death**

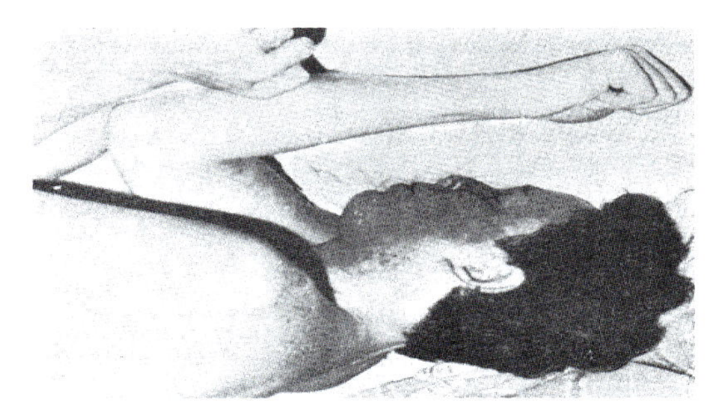

Fig. 11.2: Appearance of the face and postmortem lividity in a case of opium poisoning. The face is deeply cyanosed, almost black. The intensity of lividity depends on the colour of blood. This person was a fair skinned person and it was, therefore, possible to appreciate these changes with ease. (*Courtesy*: Dr PP Phatnanai)

dark brown, nitrites—red brown, hydrogen sulphide—bluish green, and opiates—almost black. Cherry red staining is also found in death due to burning, and exposure to cold. Grayish brown staining is often found in death from septic abortion caused by *Clostridium perfringens*.

In certain cases, isolated patches of lividity remain separate from large areas of lividity and may resemble bruises caused by violence during life. The principal **differences between lividity and bruises** are given in Table 11.1, but in any case where there is doubt or where the bruise is on a dependent part, it is advisable to cut into the suspect area and to remove a portion of it or microscopic examination.

Lividity of internal organs develops in the same way as that on the skin. The site of distribution depends upon the position of the body. When a person is lying in the supine position, lividity is seen on the posterior aspects of ventricles of the heart; dorsal portions of the lungs; dorsal portions of the liver, kidneys, and the lowermost coils of the intestine. It is important to differentiate such livid staining from congestion due to disease. As for example, postmortem staining in the heart can simulate effects of coronary occlusion, in the lungs — pneumonia, and in the gastrointestinal tract — irritation due to poisoning or ischaemia. The differentiating features between postmortem lividity and congestion are given in Table 11.2.

Table 11.1: Principal differences between postmortem lividity and bruise

Postmortem lividity	*Bruise*
1. Due to engorged vessels showing through the skin	Due to ruptured vessels either superficial or deep
2. On dependent parts, and front and sides of the neck in supine position (not uncommon)	Situated anywhere (at site of blunt force trauma)
3. Margins clearly defined, usually horizontal	Margins irregular, not horizontal
4. Uniform in colour	May be variegated in colour
5. No swelling	Swelling (possibly)
6. No superimposed abrasion	Superimposed abrasion may be present
7. Incision shows a few oozing points at the site of severed capillaries. This blood can be easily washed away	Incision shows extravasated blood staining the surrounding tissues which cannot be easily washed away
8. Microscopically, blood elements are found within the blood vessels and there is no evidence of inflammation	Microscopically, blood elements are found outside the blood vessels and there may be evidence of acute inflammation

Table 11.2: Differential features of postmortem lividity and congestion due to diseases

Postmortem lividity	*Congestion due to disease*
1. Irregular and on dependent parts of the organ only	Involves the whole organ diffusely
2. Normal appearance of the non-dependent part of the organ	Pathological change in the organ is evident
3. Hollow viscera, such as stomach and intestine, when stretched show alternate stained and unstained areas	Hollow viscera, such as stomach and intestine, when stretched show uniform staining
4. Cut surface shows variegated appearance with distinction between livid area and other areas	Cut surface oozes blood (and fluid) throughout

A suspicion that a man who had died suddenly had been poisoned by his wife with arsenic was aroused owing to the failure to interpret livid reddening of the intestines as due to simple postmortem staining.

Areas of lividity undergo changes when putrefaction sets in. There is haemolysis of blood, and owing to the pressure of gases developed in the blood vessels, the position of postmortem staining is altered. It may extend to the upper parts of the body, viz. head and neck. And here, it may be mistaken for violence to the head or smothering. As the process advances, lividity undergoes a series of changes in colour, viz. dusky, brown and green, before finally disappearing with destruction of blood. In mummification, lividity turns from brown to black with desiccation of the body.

The **medicolegal importance** of post-mortem lividity is as follows:

1. It is a reliable sign of death.
2. It may give information about the position of the body at the time of death and if it has since been altered (as may happen in a case of murder).
3. It helps to estimate the time since death.
4. Its colour may suggest the cause of death.
5. Its distribution may sometimes suggest the circumstances or position of the body at the time of death, e.g. hanging, drowning, electrocution.

Q. 11.6. Describe the changes which occur in muscles after death. How are these changes brought about and how are they useful medicolegally?

Q. 11.7. What is rigor mortis? Discuss the circumstances which modify its onset and duration. Briefly describe the conditions which simulate it.

Except where cadaveric spasm becomes immediately established, usually in a small group of muscles and this is rare, the muscular tissues of the body, after death, pass through three stages, viz: (1) primary relaxation or flaccidity, (2) rigor mortis or cadaveric rigidity, and (3) secondary relaxation.

Primary Relaxation

Immediately after death, in ordinary circumstances, there is relaxation of general muscular tone with the result that the lower jaw droops, pupils dilate, muscles become soft and flabby, joints are flexible, and the sphincters relax and this may result in incontinence of urine and faeces. However, as molecular death does not occur for about 3–4 hours after somatic death, the muscles still react to external stimuli, viz. mechanical, chemical or electrical, and the tissues are still alkaline.

Rigor Mortis

Rigor mortis (rigor = rigidity; mortis = of death) is a condition characterised by stiffening and shortening of the muscles which follow the period of primary relaxation. It is due to chemical changes involving the structural proteins of the muscle fibres and indicates the molecular death of its cells.

The contractile element of the muscle consists of protein filaments of two types, viz. myosin and actin, which are arranged and organised in interdigitating manner. In the relaxed state, the actin filaments interdigitate with myosin filaments only to a small extent but when the muscle contracts, they interdigitate to a great extent due to the presence of ATP (adenosine triphosphate). The production and utilisation of ATP are constantly balanced in life. After death, ATP is resynthesised for a short time depending upon the glycogen available locally, but after this glycogen is used up, ATP cannot be resynthesised. This leads to the fusion of myosin and actin filaments into a dehydrated stiff gel resulting in the condition known as rigor mortis. During rigor mortis, the reaction of muscle changes from slightly alkaline to distinctly acid owing to the local formation of lactic acid. Rigor mortis persists until autolysis of myosin and actin filaments occurs as a part of putrefaction. When autolysis occurs, the muscles soften and secondary relaxation sets in.

Rigor mortis can also be broken by mechanical force. Thus, if a limb, which is stiff due to rigor, is flexed forcibly at a joint, the limb becomes flaccid and will remain so thereafter. This is known as *breaking of rigor mortis.* Existing rigor mortis is broken down at least partially in the process of removal of the body from the crime scene to mortuary, and this may mislead the doctor in estimation of time since death. It is, therefore, essential to make a note of its stage of development while visiting the crime scene.

All muscles of the body, voluntary and involuntary, are affected by rigor. It first appears in involuntary and then in voluntary muscles. It is not dependent on the nerve supply as it also develops in the paralysed limbs. It is *tested* by—(1) attempting to lift the eyelids, (2) depressing the jaw, and (3) gently bending the neck and various joints of the body.

In the involuntary muscles, rigor mortis appears in the heart within an hour after death. The left chambers being thicker appear more affected than the right.

In the voluntary muscles, the *sequence* is as follows: Rigor mortis first appears as a rule in the muscles of the eyelids in about 3–4 hours, and then in the muscles of the face (4–5 hours), neck and trunk (5–7 hours), followed by the muscles of the upper extremities (7–9 hours), and then of the legs (9–11 hours). The last to be affected are the small muscles of the fingers and toes (11–12 hours). When rigor mortis is thus established, the jaw, neck and extremities become fixed in position with the arms bent at the elbows and the legs at the knees and hips, and movements at the joint are possible only within a very limited range. The rigidity generally passes off, in the same order in which it occurred, due to autolysis of muscle proteins.

When the erector pilae muscles of the skin are affected by rigor mortis, the skin presents a granular puckered appearance known as goose skin or cutis anserina (cutis = skin; anser = goose). The extremities are mainly affected. The skin papillae stand out prominently with hair standing on end. Such a condition is also found when the body is exposed to cold water, e.g. in drowning, and is due to spasm of the erector pilae muscles.

In India, rigor mortis commences in 2–3 hours, takes about 12 hours to develop from head to foot, persists for another 12 hours, and takes about 12 hours to pass off. Thus, the presence and extent or absence of rigor mortis helps to provide a rough estimate of the time since death (Fig. 11.3). As for example, if rigor mortis has not set in, the time since death would be within 2 hours and if it has affected the whole body, the time since death would be within about 12–24 hours (Fig. 11.4).

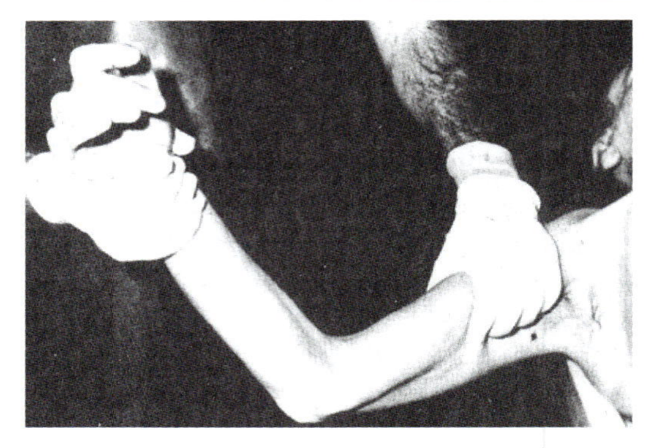

Fig. 11.3: The presence and extent or absence of **rigor mortis is tested by** gently bending the various joints of the body. If rigor mortis is present, the flexed limbs should be consistent with the posture of the body at the time it is found in a rigid state

Below is an excellent example of the valuable information that can be obtained from cooling of the body and rigor mortis.

The body of a woman stabbed to death was found at daybreak one morning in a public park. She was last been seen about 9 pm the previous night in the company of a young man. A slipper which was proved to be the property of this man was found not far from the body. The man was charged with murder. He admitted having

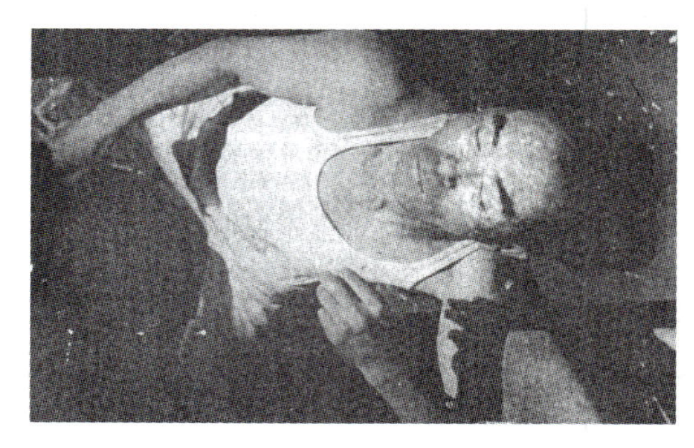

Fig. 11.4: Rigor mortis. Peculiar stiffening of the hands and feet which are held without any support. Time about 12–24 hours after death. (*Courtesy*: Dr NK Mohanty)

accompanied the woman to the park and the ownership of the slipper but stated that he had left the woman in the park and had gone home. Several witnesses testified to his having been at home from 11 pm onwards. The body when examined at 7 am was still quite warm to touch; rigor mortis was present in the eyelids and jaw, but the limbs were quite flaccid. Medical evidence was to the effect that the woman had not been dead more than about three hours. The murder could not, therefore, have been committed by the accused, who was then acquitted.

The **medicolegal importance** of rigor mortis is as follows: (1) It is a sign of death, (2) It helps to estimate the time since death, (3) It may give information about the position of the body at the time of death and if it has been altered after rigor has set in. As for example, if a person dies with the hands and legs supported against a brick wall and the position of the body has been changed after rigor set in, the hands and legs would remain raised in an unnatural position (without support).

The **factors which influence** rigor mortis are: (1) age and condition of the body, (2) mode of death, and (3) surroundings.

Age and condition of the body: In children and old people, rigor develops earlier than in the adults. The onset of rigor is later and the duration longer in the strong muscular person. The more feeble or poorly developed the muscles, the more rapid is the time of onset, and the shorter the duration.

Mode of death: In chronic diseases and convulsive disorders, rigor appears early and passes off quickly due to depletion of glycogen stores. In strychnine poisoning, rigor sets in almost immediately and passes off early. In cases of sudden death, in healthy adults, a late onset and a long duration is usual. In death from drowning, rigor appears early due to muscular exhaustion but lasts longer due to coldness of water. As a general rule, the longer it takes to appear, the longer it lasts, and vice versa. Rigor is frequently absent in septicaemic conditions. As for example, if one lower limb is the seat of purulent inflammation, rigor will not appear in that limb. This is important to remember owing to the marked contrast between rigidity in the corresponding opposite limb and flaccidity in the septicaemic limb.

Surroundings: Being a chemical process, rigor is delayed by cold and accelerated by heat. There may, therefore, be considerable seasonal variation in the time of onset and duration of rigor.

Conditions Simulating Rigor Mortis

There are three other conditions in which the body stiffens after death, viz. freezing, heat coagulation, and putrefaction, and there is one more condition, viz. cadaveric spasm, which simulates rigor mortis. Their differentiating features are as follows:

Freezing or cold stiffening: When a body is exposed to freezing temperature, the tissues become frozen and stiff. On thawing out, the stiffening rapidly disappears and the body will go into a state of rigor, which comes on rapidly, lasts less time, and is of less intensity than rigor seen under ordinary circumstances. Cold stiffening can occur in India in the higher regions of the Himalayas, North Bihar, UP and Kashmir. Bodies preserved in a cold chamber of a modern mortuary at freezing temperature (4°C) undergo cold stiffening due to solidification of body fat.

Heat coagulation or heat stiffening: This condition is found in bodies which have been subjected to heat, over 70°C, as in death from burning, high voltage electrocution or falling into vats of hot liquid. The heat coagulates the proteins of the muscles, and causes stiffening and contraction to a greater degree than that seen in rigor mortis. The body assumes an attitude called the *pugilistic* (pugilist = boxer) *attitude* with the lower limbs and arms semi-flexed and the hands clenched. Normal rigor mortis does not develop in these cases and the stiffening persists until the coagulated albumin liquefies in the process of decomposition.

Putrefaction: The stiffening is due to accumulation of putrefactive gases in the tissues which cause false rigidity resulting in stiff limbs which can be held up without any support.

Cadaveric spasm: This is a condition characterised by stiffening of the muscles immediately after death without being preceded by the stage of primary relaxation. It is, therefore, often called *instantaneous rigor.* The phenomenon is quite rare. The conditions necessary for its development are: (1) somatic death must occur with extreme rapidity, (2) the person must be in a state of great emotional tension, and (3) the muscles must be in physical activity at that time.

The spasm is primarily a vital phenomenon in that it is originated by normal stimulation of the muscles but for some obscure reason, it persists after death while other muscles are undergoing primary relaxation. It commonly involves particular groups of muscles only, such as the muscles of the forearm and hands, but in some cases, when there has been extreme nervous tension, the whole body is affected. When some object of light weight is held in the hand of a person at the time of death, e.g. a knife in suicidal cut-throat, grass or weeds in drowning or hair in a homicidal scuffle, the development of cadaveric spasm may result in this object remaining firmly grasped after death. This is conclusive proof that the object was gripped at or about the moment of death. An object cannot be grasped in this manner during development of rigor mortis. It is impossible to simulate cadaveric spasm. The contraction of the muscles involved in cadaveric spasm is more pronounced than in the case of rigor mortis. Whereas in rigor mortis, only a moderate degree of force is required to break the rigor, in cadaveric spasm, very great force is necessary. Cadaveric spasm passes off only when putrefactive changes in the muscle groups involved break the contraction.

The principal points of differentiation between cadaveric spasm and rigor mortis are described in Table 11.3.

The **medicolegal importance** of cadaveric spasm is as follows:

1. It indicates sudden death associated with great emotional tension.
2. It indicates the muscles in physical activity at the time of death.
3. It may indicate the nature of death, viz. suicide, homicide or accident. Cadaveric spasm is seen in a small proportion of suicidal deaths when a weapon of light weight, such as a razor in cases of cut

Table 11.3: Principal points to differentiate cadaveric spasm from rigor mortis

Cadaveric spasm	*Rigor mortis*
1. This is the continuation after death of the state of contraction in which muscles were at the instant of death stage of primary relaxation; the stiffening is, therefore, instantaneous at the time of death	This is due to changes in muscles after the mole cular death of their cells and is preceded by general relaxation of the muscles. A 2–3 hours lapse is absent, therefore, necessary before stiffening occurs
2. Certain preconditions are necessary	It occurs in all deaths, for its onset
3. Generally, only certain groups of voluntary muscles are affected	All muscles, both voluntary and involuntary, are affected in a specific sequence
4. The muscle contraction is quite marked and considerable force is required to break it	The muscle contraction is less marked and only moderate force is required to break it
5. It sometimes helps to indicate the circumstances of death, whether suicide, homicide or accident	It offers some evidence to indicate the time since death
6. Mechanism not known	Mechanism known

throat or a pistol in case of firearm injury, is found tightly clenched in the hand of a deceased person; in certain cases of drowning when grass, weeds or other objects in the fluid medium are clutched by the deceased; in certain cases of homicide when some portion of clothing or hair belonging to the assailant is found in the deceased's hands; in soldiers killed in action; and in certain cases of accidents, such as mountain fatalities, when branches of shrubs or trees are seized by the deceased.

4. In the event of homicide, when some portion of clothing or hair belonging to the assailant is found in the deceased's hands, it helps to identify the murderer.

Secondary Relaxation

With the disappearance of rigor mortis, the muscles become soft and flaccid once again but do not respond to mechanical or electrical stimuli. Their reaction again becomes alkaline. This stage is synchronous with the onset of putrefaction.

Late Signs

These are changes that take place in a dead body after about 24 hours since death. They represent decomposition and decay or a modification of this process. These signs include: (1) putrefaction, (2) adipocere formation or saponification, and (3) mummification. Sometimes, the process of putrefaction becomes arrested at some stage and the fatty tissues of the body may become converted into fatty acids, a change known as adipocere formation or the body tissues may become dehydrated as in mummification or occasionally, both changes may occur in the same body, some parts showing adipocere formation and others mummification.

Q. 11.8. What is putrefaction? How is it brought about? Describe in sequence the changes that occur in a dead body undergoing putrefaction in a warm climate.

Putrefaction

Putrefaction or decomposition is the last stage in the resolution of the body from the organic to the inorganic state and is a certain sign of death. It is brought about mainly by two processes, viz: (1) autolysis, and (2) bacterial action. Aerobic fungi, insect larvae, protozoa, and adult insects also take part.

Autolysis: When tissues die, as in cardiac infarction, there is a local rise in lytic enzyme levels. Likewise, after death, enzymes are released from tissue cells. They soften and liquefy the tissues of the body. This process, known as autolysis (auto = self; lysis = destruction), commences three or four hours after death and continues steadily for two to three days, sometimes longer.

Bacterial action: Bacteria produce a large variety of enzymes which act on carbohydrates, fats and proteins. Therefore, those conditions, such as warmth, moisture, or air, which favour bacterial growth accelerate the onset and progress of putrefaction. The microorganisms responsible for putrefaction are both anaerobic and aerobic, chief amongst which are *Clostridium welchii*, streptococci, *Esch. coli*, and *B. proteus*. The worst offender is *Clostridium welchii*. It produces lecithinase which hydrolyses the lecithin present in all cell membranes including blood cells, and thus is responsible for bringing about not only haemolysis of blood but also initiating the process of putrefaction. During life, these microorganisms are found in large numbers mainly in the large intestine but within a short time after death, they enter the blood vessels and spread rapidly throughout the body. Organs receiving the greatest blood supply, and those nearest the source of bacteria are the earliest to be invaded by bacteria and putrefy first.

The following account represents the **sequence of putrefactive changes** in warm climates. In cold climates, all these changes are considerably retarded. The changes can be described under: (1) colour changes, (2) development of foul smelling gases, (3) pressure effects of putrefactive gases, (4) appearance of maggots, and (5) other sequelae.

Colour Changes

The first external sign of putrefaction is usually a greenish discolouration of skin over the caecum and flanks, and internally on the under surface of the liver because it is here that the contents of the bowel are more fluid and full of bacteria. The discolouration varies from green to black and is due to the formation of sulphmethaemoglobin. As a result of bacterial action, blood is haemolysed. The liberated haemoglobin is converted to sulphmethaemoglobin by the action of hydrogen sulphide which is formed by the microorganisms in large intestine. The sulphmethaemoglobin thus formed diffuses into the surrounding tissues.

The *greenish discolouration* over the caecum and flanks makes its appearance in 12–24 hours after death, though it may appear as early as 6 hours in summer and may be delayed for more than 24 hours in winter. This discolouration spreads over the front of the abdomen and to the external genitals. Patches also appear successively on the chest, neck, face, arms and legs. These patches coalesce and the whole body is discoloured within about the next 24 hours.

Shortly after the discolouration of skin has commenced, the veins converging on the root of neck, over the shoulder, and running into the groins become visible as bluish or greenish lines due to the pigments from decomposing blood staining the vessel walls. The course of these veins is thus visible as a bluish network. The condition, owing to its mosaic appearance or arborescent pattern, is known as *marbling* (Fig. 11.5). Incision shows gas bubbles and haemolysing blood in these veins. Marbling commences after about 24 hours and is seen prominently in 36–48 hours.

Gases of Putrefaction

Simultaneously with the colour changes on the abdomen, the body begins to emit a foul nauseating odour due to the gradual development of gases of decomposition, such as hydrogen sulphide, ammonia, phosphorated hydrogen, and methane.

These gases form below the skin, in hollow viscera, and eventually in solid viscera. In 12–18 hours in summer, gases collect in the intestines and distend the abdomen. From 18–36 or 48 hours, gas formation is abundant and gases collect in the tissues and hollow viscera. They cause false rigidity, exert considerable pressure, and produce effects that are of some medicolegal importance. When sufficient gases accumulate, the cadaver becomes light and floats in water in cases of drowning (Fig. 11.6).

Pressure Effects of Putrefactive Gases

The rise in pressure of gases displaces the diaphragm upwards compressing the lungs and heart. Gases also escape into the body cavities and into liquefied tissues causing a frothy or emphysematous appearance. The following pressure effects are seen: (1) bloating of features, (2) shifting of areas of postmortem lividity, (3) changes in the skin, hair and wounds, (4) extrusion of fluid from the nose and mouth, (5) emptying of the heart, and (6) changes in the appearance of genitals.

Bloating of features: In about 36–48 hours, the face becomes so swollen and altered in colour that visual identification becomes impossible. Even the likeness to a human being is sometimes difficult to recognise since lips, nose, eyelids and cheeks are distended into a bulbous green mass. The eyes bulge from their sockets and the tongue becomes blackened and thrust in between the teeth. The protrusion of tongue and reddish discharge from the nose and mouth may be mistaken for strangulation.

The cellular tissues are also gas filled throughout. The breasts in the female are enormously swollen. When thus bloated, it is quite safe to conclude that the body has been dead for more than 36 hours. In about 48–72 hours, the rectum also protrudes, and the pressure of gases is such that if the abdomen is opened, the gases escape with a loud hissing noise.

Expansion of the body surface may be sufficient to split the skin and/or impress pressure marks from previously well fitting clothes. Such a mark on the neck from a collar may be mistaken for strangulation.

Shifting areas of postmortem lividity: Due to decomposition, blood clots are liquefied, and the blood is haemolysed. Owing to the pressure of gases, postmortem lividity may be displaced in any direction. Therefore, when putrefaction has commenced in a dead body, inference about the position of corpse since death based on postmortem lividity is markedly weakened. If the lividity extends to the head, it may be mistaken for violence to the neck or smothering.

Changes in the skin, hair and wounds: Putrefactive blisters (blebs, bullae) appear under the skin in about 36–48 hours (Figs 11.7 and 11.8). They should not be confused with blisters caused by burns. A putrefactive blister contains mainly gas and a little reddish-coloured fluid. When it is punctured, gas escapes and the blister being a postmortem phenomenon, there is no evidence of a vital reaction. However, when a putrefactive blister breaks, patches of raw skin simulating fresh scalds may be seen. The cuticle is denuded and the bruises and abrasions, therefore, become unrecognisable.

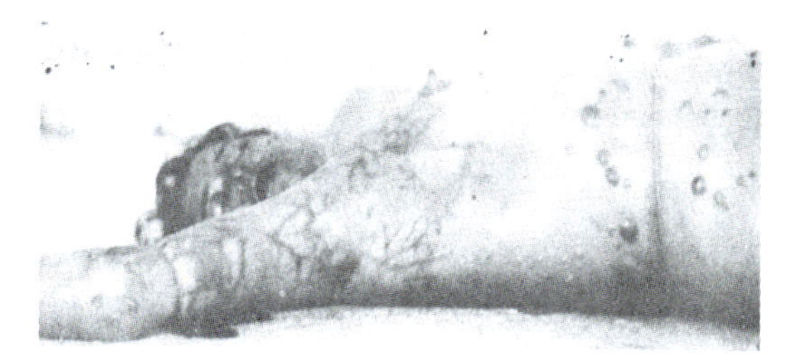

Fig. 11.5: **Marbling of skin** as seen 36 hours after death. The veins look prominent due to diffusion and staining of their walls by the altered haemoglobin. (*Courtesy*: Dr NK Mohanty)

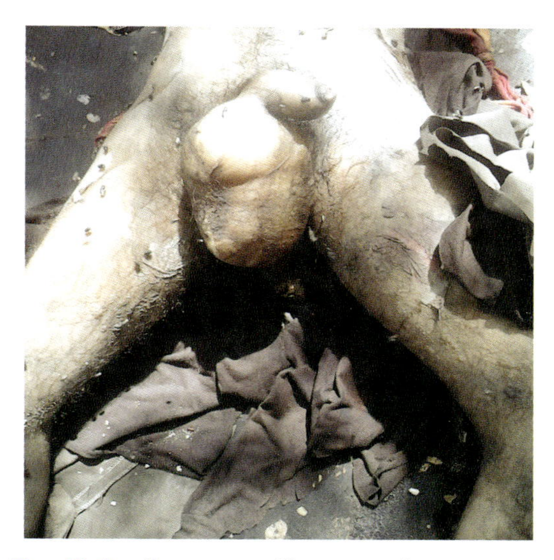

Fig. 11.6a: Decomposition—swollen scrotum and penis due to accumulation of gas in tissues. Postmortem skin peeling and presence of flies on the body (*Courtesy*: Dr R Sivakumar)

Fig. 11.6b: Presence of maggots in decomposed body (*Courtesy*: Dr R Sivakumar)

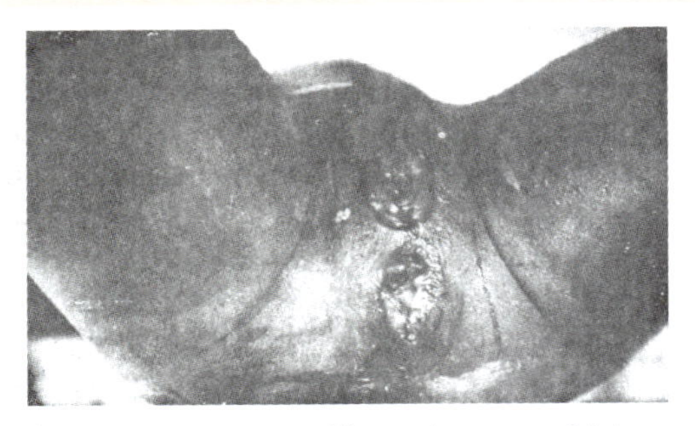

Fig. 11.7: Decomposition changes 36 hours after death in summer. The appearance of the female genitals and anus is due to decomposition changes. These may be mistaken by the novice as a sign of sexual assault

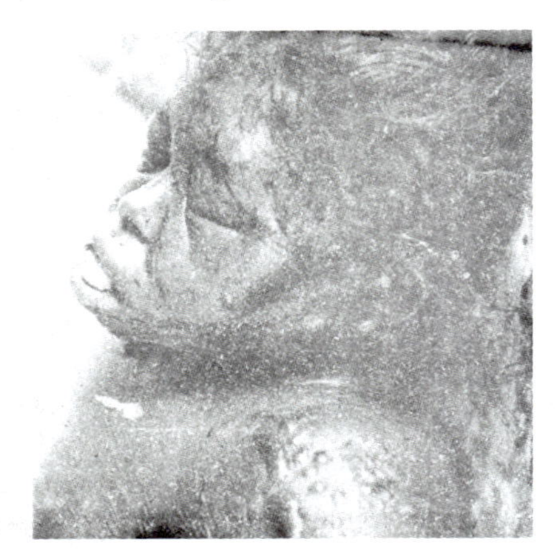

Fig. 11.8: Decomposition changes 36–48 hours after death in summer. Blister formation. Tongue is protruding due to pressure of gases and this may be mistaken as a sign of death due to violent asphyxia

The skin from hand or foot may peel off like a *glove/stocking* in 48–72 hours. The nails stay with the skin. Such peeling off is also observed in severely burned bodies and in cases of drowning when the dead body remains in water for two days or more. *The glove can often yield a full set of finger prints and should be retained until identification is certain. The hair also become loose and can be pulled out easily.*

Wounds caused before or after death begin to ooze blood (postmortem bleeding) and become so altered in appearance that it is difficult to form an opinion as to whether they were caused before or after death.

Extrusion of fluid from the nose and mouth: Due to pressure of gases in the abdomen, the diaphragm is forced upwards compressing the lungs and heart. Blood-stained froth exudes from the nose and mouth. Contents of the stomach may be forced out and find their way into the larynx. The finding of such substances below the larynx, is likely to have happened in life, terminally during the agonal period. A study of lung tissue by histopathological examination is of help; if food particles are found beyond the secondary brochioles, it indicates that the inhaled food particles are antemortem in origin.

Emptying of the heart: The heart is commonly found empty and similarly the vascular tree. It may be difficult to obtain a sufficient volume of blood from any part of circulation when analysis appears desirable.

Changes in the appearance of genitals: In about 36 hours after death in summer, the penis and scrotum are enormously swollen. The female genitals appear swollen and may leak blood-tinged fluid. These changes may be mistaken as showing features of a sexual assault. In about 48–72 hours, the cervix of the uterus protrudes. In cases where a woman is pregnant, the foetus may be expelled from the uterus (postmortem delivery).

Appearance of Maggots

Flies are attracted to the putrefying body (or even a debilitated live body, neglected child) and lay their eggs especially in open wounds and in exposed moist and sheltered natural orifices, such as the nose, mouth, vagina, and anus, by about 18–36 hours. The eggs hatch into maggots or larvae in about 24 hours. These crawl into the interior of the body and help to destroy the soft tissues. In the course of about 4–5 days, maggots develop into pupae, and in another 4–5 days, pupae into adult flies. A study of the insects that infest a dead body is known as **forensic entomology** and can be of some importance in estimating the time since death. Maggots may also reveal the presence of drugs.

A gang of robbers attacked the hut of a villager, and a scuffle ensued during which one robber was wounded in the abdomen. The police were unable to trace the where-abouts of the wounded robber until about a week later when they visited a village about 10 miles away, where a man had died six days before, the cause of his death having been reported as cholera by the village headman. The body was exhumed and the medical officer who performed the postmortem reported that there was a stab wound on the left side of the abdomen, the wound and the abdominal cavity were full of maggots, and the stomach contained a partially digested meal of rice. The headman's explanation of the presence of wound on the abdomen was that it was made by the police to get him into trouble. He was convicted of knowingly harbouring a robber. It was obvious that the deceased had not died of cholera as his stomach contained a meal of rice. The time that had elapsed between exhumation and postmortem was not sufficient to allow the appearance of maggots in the wound and the abdominal cavity, if the body had been stabbed after exhumation; the wound was, therefore, present before burial.

Other Sequelae

As the process of putrefaction goes on, in about 3 to 7 days, teeth may become loose in their sockets and may fall out. They may appear pink due to diffusion of haemoglobin into the dental canaliculi. The sutures of the skull in children and young persons may become loose and opened out, and liquified brain substance may run out. In about 5 to 12 days, colliquative (colliquative = liquefaction) putrefaction begins. The various tissues become soft and loose and are converted into a semi-fluid black mass. They ultimately liquefy and break down. Only the more resistant viscera which putrefy in 2 to 3 weeks are distinguishable. Cavities burst open. The abdomen bursts and the stomach and intestines protrude. In children, the thorax also bursts and the diaphragm is pushed upwards. The process is not distinguishable by stages.

If putrefaction still continues, the liquefied, disintegrated soft tissues, separate from bones and fall off. The bones are consequently exposed and orbits are empty. The body is thus *skeletonised* in about 1 to 3 months (Fig. 11.9). The cartilages and ligaments are similarly softened and ultimately the bones are destroyed. The time taken up by these changes varies widely depending on the manner of burial, the temperature, and the medium in which the body lies, and therefore, it is generally not possible to express any definite opinion on the time since death from these changes. In India, bones begin to decompose in about a year in uncoffined bodies, and in about 3–10 years in bodies laid in coffins. Decomposing bones lose weight and become fragile from loss of organic matter, and may be totally destroyed in about 10–25 years or more. In a cold climate, the time sequence of all these changes is considerably retarded.

It must be remembered that bodies lying exposed on the ground, on outskirts of villages, are usually attacked by animals, such as jackals, lizards, crows, coyotes, and rodents. They nibble and destroy the soft tissues in a very short time, and skeletonise the body sometimes in even less than **24** hours. They do not spare even the bones.

Internally, the process of decomposition generally keeps pace with the conditions seen externally. The various organs putrefy at different rates depending on their difference in structure, vascularity, and access to air and bacteria. Attention may be drawn to the appearance of certain organs, such as the stomach, liver, and brain as a result of putrefactive changes.

Stomach: The stomach will show dark-red irregular patches first on the posterior wall and then on the anterior wall, followed possibly by perforation as a result of autolysis. The dark-red patches on the walls of stomach may be mistaken for effects of irritant poisons. The effects of irritant poisoning are observed generally on the mucous membranes only; decomposition involves the whole thickness of the stomach wall. *Perforation* of stomach as a result of autolysis may have to be differentiated from perforation due to corrosive acid ingestion or peptic ulcer. In autolysis, perforation consists of an area of discoloured sloughing, mainly the fundus, and is devoid of vital reaction. In corrosive acid perforation, there is corrosion of mucous membrane, softening of stomach wall, and ragged irregular margins of perforation showing evidence of sloughing. In chronic ulcer perforation, the margins of the ulcer are visible and are indurated, regular, and punched out; and scarring and adhesions to the surrounding structures may be present. Microscopy is often diagnostic.

Liver: The liver becomes softened and flabby. Owing to the evolution of gases in its substance, it becomes spongy and present a honey-combed appearance (foamy or Swiss cheese liver). The patch of greenish discolouration appears early and gradually extends to the whole organ which ultimately becomes black (Fig. 11.10).

Brain: Soft cysts that appear in the brain may mimic encephalomalacia but the Swiss cheese pattern of their cavities easily indicates their postmortem character.

Table 11.4 represents organs which decompose early and those which decompose late. The organs in the first group putrefy in about 24–48 hours while those in the second group in 2 to 3 weeks.

Table 11.4: Organs decompose early and late

Early putrefaction	*Late putrefaction*
• Larynx and trachea	• Heart
• Brain of infants	• Lungs
• Stomach	• Kidneys
• Intestines	• Bladder
• Spleen	• Oesophagus
• Omentum and mesentery	• Pancreas
• Liver	• Diaphragm
• Adult brain	• Blood vessels
	• Prostate, testis
	• Non-gravid uterus, ovaries

Thus, the importance of autopsy even in states of advanced decomposition is plain, for organs, like kidneys, prostate or uterus,

Fig. 11.9: This is an exhumed body showing skeletonisation. The body was exhumed after about a month. The soft tissues have separated from the bones and fallen off. The bones are exposed and the orbits are empty. Till the stage of skeletonisation, as the cartilages and ligaments are not destroyed, most of the joints are intact as seen here. (*Courtesy*: Dr CA Franklin)

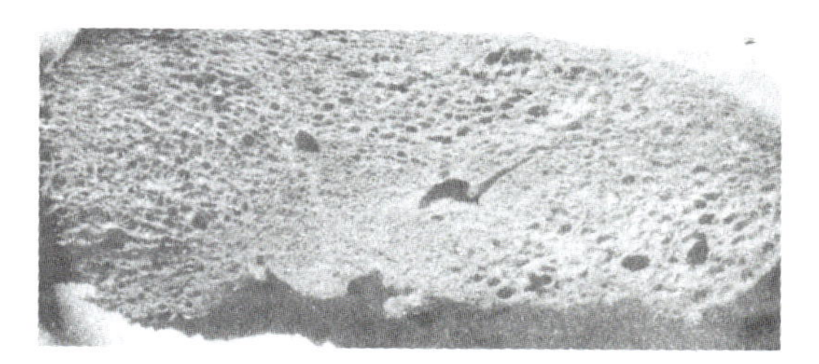

Fig. 11.10: *Foamy liver.* Postmortem decomposition changes in the liver giving an appearance like that of a sponge. This is due to evolution of gases in its substance due to the action of gas forming organisms

and blood vessels, may still remain, and provide vital information. Vascular walls resist decomposition and evidence of coronary insufficiency can often be observed.

Q. 11.9. Comment on 'putrefaction in water'.

Certain factors influencing decomposition are peculiar to immersion. They are as follows:

As the head is heavier, it tends to lie lower than the rest of the body in water. Therefore, blood tends to gravitate into it and colour changes of congestion and decomposition may give it the appearance of asphyxiation. Sometimes, the head of a drowned person is so much discoloured from putrefaction, and the rest of the body so little affected, that a suspicion of foul play may arise. When the neck swells, a collar band may appear and a suggestion of ligature strangling may be raised (Fig. 11.11).

Within 2–4 days of immersion, the skin of the hands and feet become loose and peel off like a glove or stocking; the nails also finally become loose (Figs 11.12 and 11.13).

The order of superficial appearance of colour changes is usually altered when a body is immersed in water, as shown in the following table. Internally, the brain putrefies before the abdominal viscera.

Decomposition in water	Decomposition in air
Face and neck, thorax, shoulder, arms,	Abdomen, chest, face and neck, legs, abdomen, legs shoulder, arms

A body lying completely submerged in water putrefies slowly because of:

1. Exclusion of air,
2. Protection from clothes, and
3. Low temperature of water as compared to atmospheric temperature. On removal from water, such bodies putrefy rapidly as the tissues have imbibed much fluid.

Still or running water, polluted water or sea water, all have their own influence on the process of decomposition depending on

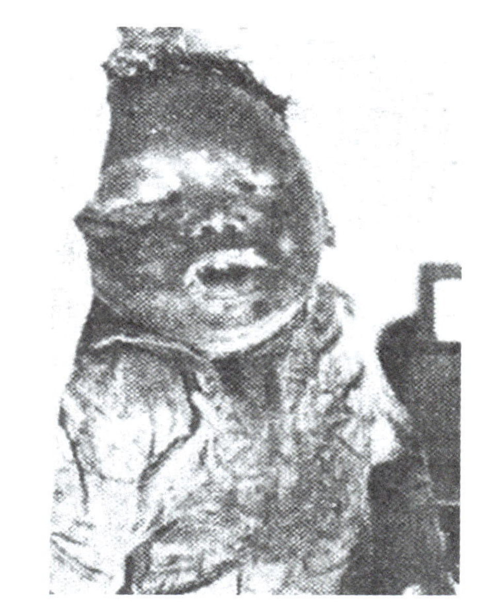

Fig. 11.11: Putrefaction in water. Bloating and discolouration of face in a case of drowning. The rest of the body was not much affected. (*Courtesy*: Dr J Chandra)

Fig. 11.12: Putrefaction in water. A case of drowning showing formation of blisters on the forearm. The skin of the hands was wrinkled, bleached and sodden like that of a washer-woman. (*Courtesy*: Dr J Chandra)

Fig. 11.13: Hands of a body recovered from water after one week. Corrugation and peeling of the skin are distinctly seen. The skin glove can often yield a full set of finger prints for identification. (*Courtesy*: Dr NK Mohanty)

their bacterial and animal content. Water animals, such as fish, crabs, crocodiles, and insects, when present, destroy soft parts and expose the bones in a very short time. Clothing protects the soft tissues from their ravages. In warm water, a thick covering of algae may form over the exposed parts of the body and also seal up body orifices. This offers some protection to the body against small animals, and the sealed orifices, especially the vagina in the female, would offer a good opportunity to examine its contents—of great forensic value in cases of rape-murder.

Unless the body is entangled in the weeds, or otherwise secured, or weighed down, *floatation of the body* occurs when sufficient putrefactive gases accumulate in it. When the body floats, the abdomen is above and the spine below because of the lightness of the abdomen from presence of gases in the intestine and heaviness of the spine. Floatation occurs in about 24 hours in summer and 2–3 days in winter.

Hehin records a case in which floatation of a body weighing about 50 kg occurred in about 30 hours although it was tied to a stone weighing about 40 kg and thrown in a well with a water level of about 3–4 metres. This shows the tremendous capacity of putrefactive gases to make a body float and the rapidity with which they are generated.

The **time required for floatation** depends upon various factors, such as: (1) age, (2) sex, (3) condition of the body, (4) season, and (5) quality of water.

Age: The bodies of newly born mature infants take less time to float as compared to those of stillborn or immature ones.

Sex: On account of higher fat content—fat being lighter than water—bodies of females float sooner than those of males.

Condition of the body: Clothed bodies and obese bodies come to the surface earlier than non-clothed or lean and thin ones. Bodies covered in loose clothes, like a *dhoti* or *pyjama,* may float soon after death due to buoyancy caused by air getting trapped under the loose wet clothes.

Season: Bodies float quicker in summer than in winter, the moist warm air in summer being favourable to the process of putrefaction.

Quality of water: Bodies float more rapidly in sea water than in fresh water on account of the higher specific gravity of the former. Likewise, bodies immersed in ponds float more rapidly than those immersed in deep water of a running stream on account of the warming effect of the sun's rays on pond water and a consequent favourable action on the process of putrefaction.

Q. 11.10. Briefly describe the principal external and internal factors modifying the process of putrefaction.

The principal external factors modifying the process of putrefaction are: (1) warmth and clothing, (2) moisture, (3) air, and (4) manner of burial. The principal internal factors are—(1) age and condition of the body, (2) sex, and (3) cause of death.

External Factors

Warmth and clothing: Putrefaction begins at about 10°C and occurs rapidly at about 37°C, the *ideal temperature.* At freezing point, bacterial growth is inhibited and putrefaction will not occur. A dead body may thus be preserved indefinitely in cold storage, snow, or ice. A case in point is the 4–5,000-year-old body found near the Swiss-Italian border a few years ago. The process is also retarded by temperature above the ideal since fluids are dried up and mummification may occur.

The **clothing** initially hastens putrefaction by maintaining the body temperature at which putrefactive organisms multiply for a longer period. At a later stage, they delay decomposition by protecting the body against the ravages of flies and insects.

Moisture: For putrefaction, moisture is necessary. It helps the rapid multiplication of organisms. Therefore, after death from oedematous conditions, putrefaction is very rapid, and bodies recovered from water, if left in air, decompose with remarkable rapidity. Organs with a high moisture content putrefy more rapidly than dry ones. Thus, the brain with its high moisture and fat content will putrefy early in contrast to dry structures, like nail, hair, teeth, and bones. Muscular organs, such as the heart resist putrefaction and decompose late.

Air: The presence of air promotes decomposition and its absence retards it. Bodies lying in water putrefy more slowly owing to the exclusion of air and lowering of temperature.

Manner of burial: In airtight coffins, the body remains with very little change for long periods, while bodies buried without coffins putrefy at once. Similarly, bodies in deep graves putrefy much more slowly than those in shallow ones because of exclusion of air. When a body is buried in lime (Mrs Dobkin murder case), decomposition is retarded and soft tissues are largely preserved. Formation of adipocere is encouraged in clayey, water logged soils, whereas sandy and porous soils in general are conducive to mummification.

Internal Factors

Age and condition of the body: The bodies of newborn or stillborn infants are mostly sterile. Therefore, putrefaction can only occur from invasion of the body by external organisms in contrast to adult bodies where putrefaction commences from within outward. Even then, as the body of a newborn cools rapidly, the putrefactive process is considerably slowed.

Fat and flabby bodies of children contain plenty of moisture and putrefy rapidly whereas the lean and dry tissues of old age tend to do so slowly. Those parts of the body which are the seat of bruises, wounds, or fractures, or which have been mutilated, decompose very early. Gravid and postpartum uterus will putrefy early.

Sex: This has but little influence except in case of bodies of women dying after child birth, especially when death has been caused by septicaemia. In such cases, putrefaction is rapid.

Cause of death: When a person dies of septicaemia, e.g. intestinal obstruction, peritonitis, and pyelonephritis, the organisms required to initiate putrefaction are already present in abundance. Putrefaction is, therefore, rapid. Contrary to popular belief, putrefaction is accelerated in alcoholic subjects as most of them are fat and flabby.

Putrefaction is retarded in wasting diseases, such as anaemia and malnutrition owing to the reduced quantity of blood, and the dryness of the tissues. Bodies of persons dying suddenly and in apparently good health decompose slowly.

Poisoning by substances which preserve the tissues and destroy bacteria delays putrefaction. These include chronic poisoning by arsenic, antimony, and other heavy metals.

Q. 11.11. Discuss briefly the role of putrefaction in toxicological analysis, giving examples.

Putrefaction complicates the problems of toxicological analysis and leads to difficulties in the interpretation of results as shown by the following examples:

1. Some substances that might be present in the tissues may undergo chemical changes and may no longer be identifiable, e.g. nitrite. In the case of hydrolytic chemical changes, the breakdown product instead of/in addition to the original poison may be detected, as in the case of aconite, parathion, carbaryl, etc.
2. Putrefaction of normal tissue components may produce substances which yield chemical reactions similar to those obtained from basic toxic compounds, such as neurine, beta-phenylethylamine, tyramine, and other amines. Though these can create considerable interference problems, methods to overcome the same are available.
3. Volatile substances may be lost as a result of putrefaction.
4. Ethyl alcohol may be produced from normal tissue components in putrefaction.

Despite these limitations, most toxic substances are still identifiable, and these include amongst others: carbon monoxide, cyanides, fluoride, barbiturates, organophosphorus compounds, endrine, dhatura, hyoscine, strychnine, yellow oleander, nicotine, etc., and metallic poisons, such as arsenic, antimony, mercury, lead, and thallium, etc.

Q. 11.12. Write a note on body farming.

Body Farming

Body farming can be defined as a study of the dead bodies for the purpose of gaining a better understanding of decomposition process, for evolving better methods for estimation of time since death and also to infer circumstances of death. This is first started by Dr William W Bass (1981) in USA.

It can be done by isolating a prepared body-farm, which receives the donated bodies and allows them to decompose by exposing in different ways. A detailed record of observations are made in regard to the onset and development of changes after death including onset, spread, progressive events in a body undergoing degesition. Also careful record of entamology of on the dead body and suroundings is made.

This is useful to the investigating officers and doctors undergoing training besides for the purposes of court of law in arriving at time since death and other useful information, this is also useful to do forensic osteology research regarding demineralisation and also ageing, as well as in offering opinions regarding human parts and skeletal remains for purpose of crime investigation.

Q. 11.13. Comment on the process and the medicolegal significance of: (a) adipocere, (b) mummification.

Adipocere: Adipocere formation or **saponification** is a modification of the process of putrefaction. It derives its name from its properties which are intermediate between those of fat and wax (adipos = soft fat; cera = wax). It results from conversion of unsaturated liquid fats (oleic acid) to saturated solid fats (hydroxystearic acid and oxystearic acid) by bacterial fat splitting enzymes, particularly the Clostridia, from the intestine and the environment. Moisture, warm temperature, and relative diminution of air are further facilitating factors. Therefore, a body upon which moisture has been constantly acting, whether it is immersed in water or in damp soil, may undergo this change.

Adipocere is a yellowish white, greasy, wax-like substance with a rancid smell. As its specific gravity is less than that of water, it floats. It cuts easily and burns with a faint yellow flame giving an offensive odour due to ammonia and traces of sulphur compounds. Fresh adipocere is soft and moist but old samples are dry and brittle.

Since the process involves hydrogenation and hydrolysis of body fats, it forms in any site where fatty tissue is present. The moisture required for hydrolysis is derived from the body tissues which, therefore, become dry and dehydrated. In a body immersed in water, e.g. in a case of drowning, the environment provides the moisture and the body tissues are, therefore, not dehydrated. Adipocere is usually first seen in the subcutaneous fatty depots of cheeks, breasts, buttocks, and abdomen. The limbs, chest wall, or other parts of the body, may be affected (Fig. 11.14). Rarely in infants and infrequently in obese persons, the process may involve the whole body. In wide-spread adipocere, the soft tissues are markedly dry unless there has been prolonged immersion in water. The gross features of the organs may be appreciated even though the cells are lacking.

When adipocere develops in the face, the features are well preserved. When the entire body is involved, the features are well retained and injuries are also recognised, and therefore, it may be possible to determine the cause of death.

The time required for formation of adipocere varies greatly. In summer, the shortest time for its formation to an appreciable extent is about 3 weeks. It takes about 3–6 weeks for an adult limb and about 12 months for the whole body to be converted into adipocere. In the tropics, the process may develop in a much shorter

Fig. 11.14: Hand showing **partial adipocere formation.** The features are well preserved. (*Courtesy*: Dr NK Mohanty)

Fig. 11.15: Mummified body. The body is shrivelled and black in colour. The hard, dry, leathery skin closely adheres to the shrunken body. The features are well preserved. (*Courtesy*: Dr AA Qureshi)

time in bodies that are immersed in fluid media. In India, it has been observed to occur in 5–15 days, the shortest recorded period being 3 days and 22 hours.

The formation of adipocere provides the following information for **medicolegal** purposes:

1. It helps to establish the identity of a person when external features are well preserved.
2. It gives an indication of the cause of death when injuries are recognisable.
3. It gives some indication of the time elapsed since death.
4. It indicates the place—water or moist ground—from which the body has been recovered.

Mummification: Mummification is a modification of the process of putrefaction. Sometimes, the process of putrefaction, may become arrested at some stage and the body tissues may undergo mummification. It is characterised by dehydration or desiccation of the body tissues and viscera after death. The body desiccates by losing its moisture from evaporation. The ideal conditions for its formation are—a high atmospheric temperature devoid of moisture with a free circulation of air around the body—conditions exactly opposite to those required for the formation of adipocere (Fig. 11.15).

Mummification is not a common condition in adults but is seen occasionally in bodies that have been buried in dry soil, e.g. in desert sand. The tissues of infants are usually free from organisms at birth and they do not develop normal putrefactive changes. Therefore, mummification is commonly seen in infants who have been exposed to warm and dry atmospheric conditions shortly after death, e.g. when kept perched up on trees, roof rafters, or concealed in trunks. Chronic arsenic or antimony poisoning is said to favour the process of mummification in dry, warm climates. Slight adipocere formation is common in mummification since utilisation of body water to hydrolyse fat in turn helps to dehydrate the tissues.

The exposed parts of the body, such as the lips, and tips of nose, fingers and toes, mummify first. The process then extends to the rest of the body. A mummified body is shrivelled, practically odourless, and often very dark almost black in colour. It has lost weight. The skin is hard, dry, leathery, and adheres closely to the shrunken body. Viscera are shrunken, dark-brown; or black, and blend together and may not be visible. A striking result of the process is the preservation of the anatomical features of the deceased for many years unless attacked by animals or insects. Injuries may also be easily recognised.

The time required for complete mummification of a body varies greatly from a period of three months to a year or longer depending on the size of the body and temperature of the atmosphere. The process is more rapid in bodies of infants on account of the greater surface area as compared to weight from which evaporation can take place.

The formation of mummification provides the following information for **medicolegal** purposes:

1. It helps to establish the identity of a person since the features are well preserved.
2. It gives an indication of the cause of death since injuries are recognisable.
3. It gives some indication of the time elapsed since death.
4. It indicates the place—hot, dry area—from which the body has been recovered.

A body may be mummified artificially for the purpose of its preservation by a process known as *embalming*. The process consists of injecting embalming fluid containing formaldehyde, or solutions of lead sulphide, and potassium carbonate, into the femoral artery, the aorta and/or the carotids. The procedure is commonly resorted to: (1) in the US and other Western countries, (2) in the medical institutions to preserve dead bodies for anatomical dissection, and (3) when dead bodies have to be transported from one country to another for burial or cremation and the time taken in transit is such as would ordinarily lead to putrefaction.

Embalming preserves the body from destruction by microorganisms also. However, as the body tissues are hardened by embalming, detection of certain poisons is rendered difficult. Therefore, removal of specimens for investigation from such bodies should be completed before embalming.

The *conditions which preserve the body after death* can be briefly summarised as:

1. Natural—adipocere formation and mummification.
2. Artificial—embalming and cold storage, or refrigeration.

Q. 11.14. Write short notes on: (a) presumption of death, (b) presumption of survivorship.

Presumption of Death

The presumption of death may need to be considered in certain circumstances when death has not been witnessed and the body has not been found, e.g. in insurance claims, inheritance of property, resolution of partnerships, person serving in armed forces who are reported to be missing, or when a particular person has gone atkoad and has not been heard of for a considerable time and is alleged to have died. Sections 107 and 108 of the Indian Evidence Act lay down that if a person is proved to have been alive within 30 years, the legal presumption is that he is still alive, unless it is proved that he has not been heard of for seven years by those who would normally have heard of him, if he had been alive, in which case, the law presumes that he is dead. The law, however, presumes nothing as to the time of his death which, if material, must be proved by evidence.

Presumption of Survivorship

This interesting question arises when two or more persons, natural heir of each other, die almost simultaneously in circumstances, such as shipwreck, air-crash, earthquake, motor accidents, battle, etc., which render it uncertain which of them survived the other or others. This consideration is important because, if Mr X in a 'will' leaves his property to Mr Y, and both of them die in a common catastrophe, the heirs of Mr Y will inherit the property only if Mr Y survived Mr X. If Mr Y dies earlier, legally he has died before acquiring the property. The property naturally passes to other heirs of Mr X. In such situations, as eye witness evidence is generally not available, the case is to be decided on presumption and hence it is known as presumption of survivorship. Section 21 of Hindu Succession Act, 1956, on Presumption in Case of Simultaneous Death states that the younger will be presumed to survive the elder, unless the contrary is proved. The underlying guiding principle in such a presumption is that the stronger survives the weaker. A careful consideration is, therefore, given to the following factors: (1) postmortem changes, (2) nature of injuries, (3) age, (4) sex, (5) constitution, and (6) mode of death.

Postmortem changes: The several changes, viz. cooling of the body, postmortem lividity, rigor mortis, decomposition, etc., which the body undergoes after death, as well as the inferences regarding time since death to be based thereon, have already been discussed.

Nature of injuries: Injuries even small on vital parts or main blood vessels are obviously more serious and cause death earlier as compared to injuries which, though extensive, are on non-vital parts of the body.

Age: The young and the old usually succumb earlier than the adults who have greater power of resistance.

Sex: Males being stronger survive longer than females except when physical endurance is involved where females survive longer than males.

Constitution: The weak, the debilitated, the diseased, and the addicts, succumb earlier than the strong robust ones.

Mode of death: *Mother and child during parturition*—Except death from haemorrhage, the mother is presumed to survive longer than the child. Proof of live birth of a child is necessary in case of survivorship of child.

Asphyxia: A person who is doing muscular effort requires more oxygen and would, therefore, live less than the one who is not doing so in such an atmosphere. In suffocation due to debris from house fall or earthquake, survival will depend on the injuries sustained and the depth to which one is buried. One with least injuries or injuries on non-vital parts of the body and not buried deep under the debris is presumed to have lived longer. In drowning, a swimmer is presumed to survive longer than a non-swimmer. Injuries in such cases also help to determine survival to a certain extent.

Starvation: Fat people usually survive longer than the thin and lean. Females usually have more fat in them, and accordingly survive longer than males. One who is deprived only of food lives longer than the one who is deprived of both food and water.

Cold: As opposed to heat, children and old people are unable to withstand cold to the same extent as adults and, therefore, succumb earlier. Owing to greater deposit of subcutaneous fat, females are likely to endure cold longer than males.

Heat: Children and old people are "unable to withstand heat as compared to adults and accordingly succumb earlier when exposed to such a danger.

Burns: Infants, young children, and the elderly succumb much more readily than adults not only from the initial shock but also from the subsequent complications. Burns on the head, trunk, and genitals, are said to be more dangerous than in other parts of the body. Extent of part of the body affected is of much greater importance than the depth and severity.

12

Deaths from Asphyxia

The use of the term asphyxia (Greek meaning pulselessness) in the forensic field is restricted to those forms of oxygen lack (anoxia, hypoxia) which result from mechanical interference with the process of respiration, that is, anoxic anoxia. The fact that these conditions are associated with violence provides a sound basis to use this term in such a restricted sense.

The term asphyxia is often misused to describe other anoxic states, such as, those due to impaired circulation of blood, deficiency of haemoglobin, or poisoning, e.g. cyanide, when the uptake of oxygen by the tissues is impaired. These types of anoxias are known as stagnant, anaemic, and histotoxic, respectively.

Q. 12.1. Briefiy describe the traditionally accepted signs of asphyxia on the basis of their pathogenesis.

Q. 12.2. Comment on petechial haemorrhages (Tardieu spots).

The traditionally accepted signs of asphyxia are due to pathological changes resulting from anoxia. The effect of anoxia on tissues is mainly twofold, viz. non-specific and specific. As a result of non-specific effects, body tissues undergo parenchymatous degeneration. As a result of specific effects, the following systemic changes are seen: (1) cyanosis, (2) increased capillary permeability, and (3) petechial haemorrhages (Tardieu spots). These signs develop when mechanical obstruction to breathing is maintained for about 30 seconds and a close look in a good light is necessary to notice cyanosis and Tardieu spots.

Cyanosis: This is due to a diminished oxygen tension in the blood and an increase in reduced haemoglobin. It becomes apparent when at least 5 gm of reduced haemoglobin is present. Blood appears purple or dark in colour. This colour change is reflected in the skin especially where livid stains develop, in the lips, and in those organs where the venous and capillary bed is abundant, e.g. the lungs, meninges, liver, spleen, and kidneys.

Diminished oxygen tension leads to capillary dilatation and this leads to stasis and pooling of blood. Venous return to heart is thus diminished. Pulmonary flow is eventually both slowed and reduced in volume, resulting in deficient oxygenation, making the condition worse. A vicious circle is thus established: Asphyxia → capillary dilatation → stasis → reduced venous return to heart → reduced pulmonary blood flow → deficient oxygenation further asphyxia.

Increased capillary permeability: This results from, anoxia and stasis. The pores between the endothelial cells are enlarged and blood (plasma and cells) transudes into tissues and tissue spaces. This may result in—(1) gelatinous moistening of the organs,

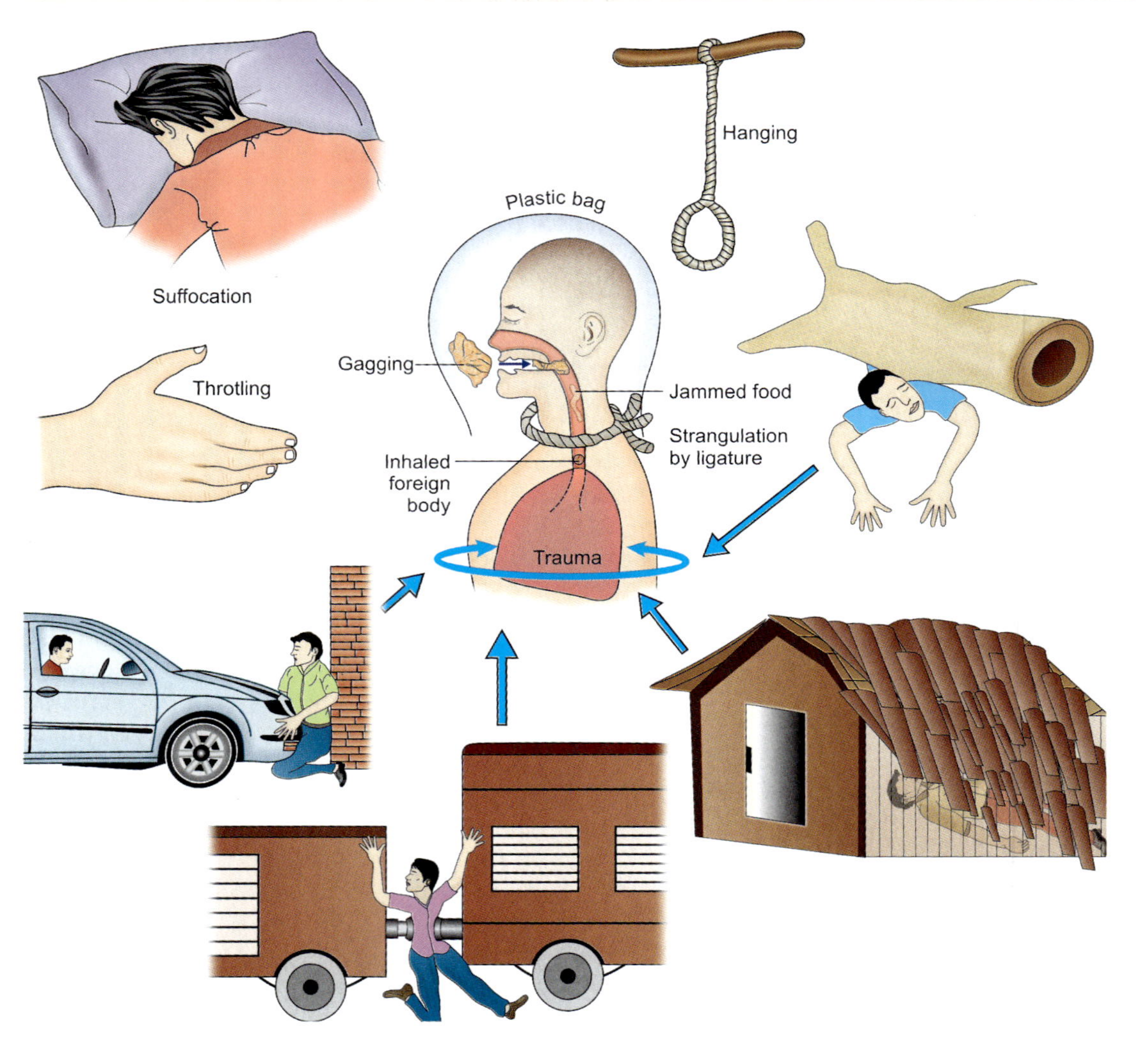

Fig. 12.1: Diagrammatic representation of the mechanism of some violent asphyxial deaths of common occurrence

e.g. the brain and myocardium, (2) development of excess fluid in serous sacs, e.g. pleura and pericardium, and (3) oedema of some tissues, e.g. mediastinal tissues and lungs. Pulmonary oedema may rapidly develop in such conditions.

Petechial haemorrhages: These are often referred to as **Tardieu spots,** after the French Police Surgeon who described them in 1866. They are due to anoxia, stasis, increased capillary permeability, and rise of intracapillary pressure.

The spots are usually round, dark-red, well defined, and about the size of a pin-head but may occasionally be larger. They are generally found in those parts where capillaries are least supported, e.g. face, conjunctivae, epiglottis, serous surfaces of heart and lungs, meninges, and thymus. They tend to be more pronounced in those areas where intracapillary pressure rises rapidly, e.g. above the level of constriction of neck in strangling, and chest in traumatic asphyxia, and their distribution may thus be diagnostic. They are better made out in fair-skinned persons, readily visible in fresh bodies, and tend to disappear as putrefaction sets in.

It is important to remember that *post-mortem petechial haemorrhages* (sometimes erroneously described as Tardieu spots) on the skin of hand and legs (but not on the serous surfaces of heart and lungs) can occur, if a dead body is suspended for some time. They are due to gravitation of blood to the dependent parts where capillaries rupture from over-distension. They are usually large and less circumscribed.

Petechial haemorrhages are often seen in the reflected scalp, especially if it is congested. These haemorrhages are due to tearing of small blood vessels and do not signify asphyxiation. While it may be difficult to see petechiae in intensely congested skin, petechiae in the skin behind the ears are more readily seen after blood has drained out from the tissues. It is, therefore, advisable to examine the skin again after completion of autopsy.

Though Tardieu spots are one of the classical features of many fully developed asphyxial deaths, they are not pathognomonic of asphyxiation, as they are found in other forms of death also, e.g. in those associated with bleeding disorders, such as scurvy and leukaemia; sometimes in coronary thrombosis; electrocution; poisoning; in persons on anticoagulants, and in blood dyscrasias (thrombocytopenia). However, in these conditions, their distribution is more generalised in contrast to deaths from violent asphyxia. It should, however, be remembered that absence of Tardieu spots does not exclude death from asphyxia—Tardieu spots are rarely prominent in drowning.

Since asphyxial signs are common to a number of other conditions besides those in which mechanical interference with respiration takes place, it is necessary to furnish such evidence while attributing death to asphyxia by violence. Such evidence may be furnished by:

a. Signs of compression of upper airways by pressure on the neck as in hanging, and ligature or manual strangulation.
b. Occlusive blocking of mouth and nose by gags as in smothering.
c. Obstruction by a foreign body as in choking.
d. Flooding of air passages as in drowning.
e. Blunt force trauma and pressure on to the chest as in traumatic asphyxia.

Q. 12.3. Describe the autopsy procedure in a case of death (from asphyxia) where a detailed study of neck organs is required.

A V-shaped incision and a careful dissection of neck, layer by layer, are essential. It is desirable to eviscerate cranial, thoracic and abdominal viscera so that the body is drained of blood. Such draining provides a clean field for study of neck organs and prevents any artefactual seepage of blood in soft tissues of the neck. Where facilities permit each step of dissection should be photographed.

The skin flap including subcutaneous tissue and platysma is reflected as one layer above the thyroid cartilage up to the lower border of lower jaw, and inspected. The investing layer of deep cervical fascia is incised and reflected from the ventral surfaces of anterior cervical muscles and submandibular salivary glands. The sternomastoid muscle is inspected, freed from its clavicular and sternal attachments, separated from underlying fascia, and reflected. The same procedure is adopted for the other sternomastoid muscle. It is necessary to dissect the neck muscles on both sides simultaneously to compare and evaluate any haemorrhagic foci. This is followed by exposure, inspection, and reflection of the delicate omohyoid muscle, followed by the strap muscles, viz. sternohyoid, sternothyroid (medial and lateral), and thyrohyoid. These layers are easy to dissect along fascial planes. The thyroid gland and carotid vessels are also freed by blunt dissection from their investing connective tissue. The larynx, trachea, and oesophagus are mobilised by blunt dissection and reflected upwards from the precervical fascia. At this point, the tongue and all the neck structures between the carotid arteries are removed en bloc for detailed examination. The cervical spine is inspected and palpated. It is then possible to study systematically in detail the various structures that are important from a medicolegal point of view. Carotid artery damage must be sought with care because the process of opening the vessel may destroy the torn area. A radiological study of the excised hyoid–larynx complex should be carried out, if there is any suspicion or suggestion of mechanical injury.

Q. 12.4. Comment on: (1) autopsy findings in case of asphyxial deaths, (2) presence of stomach contents in the air passages.

Postmortem findings in deaths from asphyxia are characterized by (1) intense venous congestion and cyanosis with pronounced lividity, (2) petechial haemorrhages (Tardieu spots), and (3) right-sided dilatation of heart.

The following description represents a brief account of the *signs common to all forms of asphyxial deaths*. These features vary according to the mechanism of asphyxia in each case but their presence is essential to diagnose death from asphyxia. Sometimes, when sufficient asphyxial features are not found, the cause of death is expressed as *'consistent with asphyxia'*.

Externally, if there is no obstruction to venous drainage, as in some cases of hanging, the face is usually pale and placid but in most cases of violent asphyxial death, e.g. strangulation and suffocation, there is obstruction to venous return. In such cases, the face is cyanosed, marked with petechial haemorrhages, and may be swollen. The eyeballs appear prominent due to congestion, the conjunctivae are injected, subconjunctival haemorrhages present, and the pupils are dilated. The lips, ears, and finger nails are deeply cyanosed, and the neck veins appear prominent. Blood-stained froth oozes from the mouth and nostrils. The tongue is swollen, and sometimes bruised and bitten. Hands may be clenched. Semen may have been voided. Sphincters may have been relaxed and there may have been incontinence of urine and faeces. Postmortem lividity is well developed and purple in colour. The body temperature usually rises by 2° to 3°C in deaths associated with intense asphyxial signs due to convulsions and muscular action, and this should be taken in consideration when estimating time since death.

Internally, blood is dark in colour due to diminution of oxygen tension and an increase in reduced haemoglobin. It is more fluid and coagulates slowly on account of increased fibrinolysin activity. Engorgement of the right side of the heart is a non-specific finding, common in all types of congestive deaths, and is useless as a diagnostic sign of an asphyxial process. The large veins are full of blood. The lungs are engorged and deeply congested. Pulmonary oedema may be present. On cut section, the lungs exude copious frothy fluid, often blood-stained. The bronchi and trachea also contain blood-stained froth and their mucosa is congested. Numerous subserous petechiae may be found on the surface of the lungs and heart. The abdominal viscera are congested and so also the brain and meninges, and petechial haemorrhages may be found in the brain. The cranial sinuses are usually filled with dark blood.

Terminal vomiting, due to medullary hypoxia, is common. As a result, the air passages may be filled at the end of asphyxial event by inhaled vomit, the subject being already unconscious. It is important, especially in infants, that this finding is not automatically assumed to be the cause of asphyxia; it is more likely to be the consequence.

Doctors not familiar with medicolegal matters often find the **presence of stomach contents in upper airways** at autopsy a very confusing observation. It may be due to:

1. Inhaled vomit as a terminal event in asphyxial deaths.
2. Movement of the body after death when it is in a relaxed state, thereby mechanically redistributing fluids and the gastric contents.
3. Disorganised and uncoordinated muscle movements during terminal moments of life which often result in regurgitation of stomach contents.
4. Intoxication and unconsciousness as a result of alcohol/drugs.
5. An after-effect of head injury. Vomit inhalation is, therefore, usually an incidental finding or a final common event in such cases and more often than not does not constitute the cause of death which is properly defined as the injury, illness, or combination of the two, however, brief or prolonged, which initiates a series of events ending in death. The only sure way to diagnose inhalation or aspiration of gastric contents is by copious lung histology when products of digestion are found beyond the secondary bronchioles.

It must be remembered that asphyxial signs are very striking in fresh bodies only. They progressively disappear with lapse of time, and many of the signs disappear as a result of putrefaction.

13 Violent Asphyxial Deaths

Violent deaths of common occurrence which may be classed as asphyxial deaths are: hanging, ligature strangulation, throttling (manual strangulation), suffocation (smothering, choking, traumatic asphyxia), and drowning.

HANGING

Q. 13.1. Define hanging. Give the symptoms, cause of death, fatal period, and postmortem appearances.

Q. 13.2. Discuss in detail the ligature mark in hanging.

Hanging is defined as a form of violent asphyxia as a result of suspension of the body by a ligature round the neck, the constricting force being the weight of the body. The ligature constricts the neurovascular bundles in the neck and/or the upper airways. When the feet do not touch the ground and the weight of the whole body acts as a constricting force, it is called complete hanging. When the weight of only the head, and not the whole body, acts as a constricting force, it is called partial hanging. The weight of the head is sufficient to produce a fatal result.

Symptoms follow rapidly — flashes of light before the eyes, ringing in ears, followed by *sudden loss of consciousness* and death.

Cause of death: Death may occur from:

1. Cerebral ischaemia and anoxia from obstruction of arterial blood flow to the brain by pressure on the carotid arteries.
2. Cerebral congestion, due to compression of the jugular veins.
3. Blockage of the air passages by direct compression or because the root of the tongue is pulled upwards by the ligature.
4. Vagal inhibition from pressure on vagus nerves or carotid sinus.
5. Injury to spinal column or cord, especially in judicial hanging.
6. A combination of any of the above.

Contrary to popular belief, the more common cause of death by hanging in most instances is compression of neurovascular bundles in the neck and not asphyxia by airway obstruction. Supporting evidence for this includes: (a) cases of suicidal hanging by persons with tracheostomy below the level of the noose, and (b) finding of vomitus in the bronchi of hanging victims below the level of neck constriction. Carotid arteries are occluded by a tension of 3.5 kg, jugular veins by 2 kg, while trachea by 15 kg and vertebral artery by 16.6 kg.

An American performer was in the habit of making public exhibitions of hanging. On one occasion, it proved fatal. It is possible that slight shifting of the ligature from under the jaw caused compression of the carotid arteries resulting in rapid loss of consciousness and death. No attempt was made to save him until it was too late, the spectators being under the impression that he was prolonging the experiment for their entertainment. He was allowed to hang for 13 minutes!

Fatal period: If the hanging is associated with a drop of many feet as in judicial hanging, death may be instantaneous from a fracture of cervical vertebrae and associated injury to the spinal cord although the heart may continue to beat for 15 to 20 minutes thereafter. If there is no injury to spinal cord and blockage of air passage is not complete, five to eight minutes are the common fatal period.

Postmortem Appearances

These vary according to the mode of dying. They are discussed under: (1) external appearances, (2) ligature mark, (3) internal appearances. *In an asphyxial death, the appearances would be as follows:*

External appearances: The asphyxial features already described will be present. The other features are as follows:

The neck is stretched due to upward pull of the ligature and the head is always inclined to the side opposite the knot due to gravitational forces. The face is usually pale but in some cases where there is obstruction to venous drainage, it may be congested and swollen with profuse petechiae in the head and neck. The hands and nail beds are cyanosed. Eyeballs appear prominent due to congestion. The tongue, turgid due to congestion, may protrude due to pressure by the ligature at its base and the exposed part may become dark brown or almost black as a result of drying. In some cases, saliva may be found dribbling from corner of the mouth opposite to the side of the knot. It is due to pressure on salivary glands by the ligature. Postmortem lividity is observed circumferentially on the skin of the dependent arms and legs, and skin of the face and neck above the ligature.

All the above appearances will be found in a body even when it is suspended postmortem. Petechiae, known as postmortem petechial haemorrhages, may also be found but only on the skin of arms and legs. These are due to gravitation of blood to the dependent parts where capillaries rupture from overdistension (petechiae cannot be produced postmortem on the serous surfaces of heart and lungs). Therefore, all these signs do not indicate that death was due to hanging, as they will be found when the person is suspended before or after death. The important external sign is the ligature mark, which, however, can also be reproduced, if the body is suspended during the two hours succeeding death (Fig. 13.1).

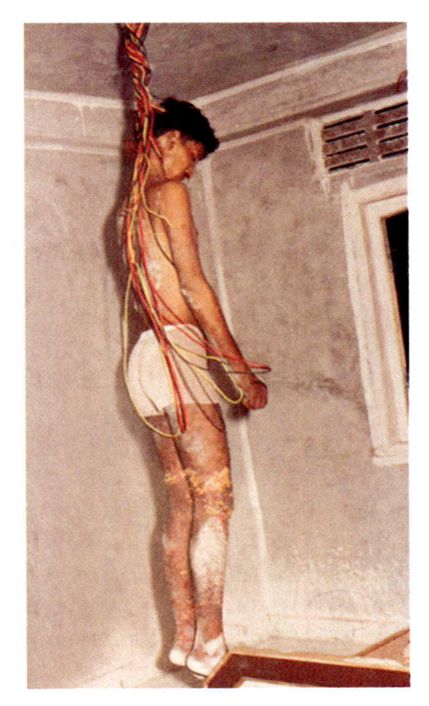

Fig. 13. 1: Hanging with electrical wire bunch (*Courtesy*: Dr BV Subrahmanyam)

Ligature mark: This is a pressure mark on the neck at the site of the ligature. It appears as a groove. In the early period after death, it looks pale. Later, it becomes yellowish brown, dry, hard, and parchment like. Abrasions and bruises of skin may be seen at the site of the knot and in the bed of the groove. The abrasions may show relative upward motion of the ligature in respect to neck with small skin tags (observable by a hand lens) indicating the direction. Along the edges, there may be areas of hyperaemia and occasionally a few ecchymoses. Fibres from the ligature may be found adhering to the skin.

In complete hanging, the ligature mark is *situated* above the level of thyroid cartilage between the larynx and chin. It is directed obliquely upward along the line of the mandible and reaches the mastoid processes behind the ears. It is sometimes absent at the back where the two limbs of the noose stretch upward toward the knot. The mark is better seen on the front and sides of the neck than on the nape where firm muscular tissue and scalp hair intervene. In cases of partial hanging, the ligature mark may be situated at a lower level (Fig. 13.2).

The ligature and the knot may form a fixed noose or a running noose. A fixed noose is one in which the rope is knotted. A running noose is one in which one end of the rope is passed through the loop made from the other end. In case of a fixed noose, two limbs of the noose near the knot will be pulled upward assuming the shape of an inverted V. The ligature mark will, therefore, have a corresponding *course* often with a zone of unmarked skin at the apex of the V caused by the head falling away from the knot. In case of a ruinning noose, the body weight will cause the noose to tighten mainly in a horizontal position. The ligature mark will, therefore, also be mainly horizontal but there may be an additional vertical mark caused by the suspending ligature. At autopsy, the method in which the noose was tied should be photographed and described before its removal and the knot preserved by cutting the body of the noose. Binding the cut ends of the noose with thread prevents their fraying and opening out. The ligature may be marked right, left, front, and back, to facilitate its reconstruction, when the question arises in the court (Fig. 13.3).

The *character* of the ligature mark depends upon the nature of the ligature, body weight, length of time the body has remained suspended, and number of turns of the ligature round the neck. If a thin rope is used, the ligature mark is deep and narrow and its pattern may be imprinted on the skin as a pressure abrasion (mirror image phenomenon) or bruise. When a broad fold or soft piece of cloth, such as a sari is used, the mark is wide and shallow and in some cases it may even be difficult to define. The head is always inclined to the side opposite to the knot, and therefore, the mark is deep and well defined, at this site. The impression of the knot on the skin close to it may or may not be visible. The ligature mark is well defined, if the body is heavy and time of suspension long. If the ligature has gone round the neck more than once, corresponding number of marks, one above the other and close to each other, are seen. In such cases, there may be evidence of skin pinching and bruising, if it is caught between the turns of the ligature or blanching of the skin in between the folds (Fig. 13.4).

Internal appearances: A careful dissection of the neck, layer by layer, is essential. In case of hanging with a significant drop, e.g. judicial hanging, much local injury may be found. In case of hanging without a significant drop, local injury is not common. The fibres of platysma and sternomastoid are sometimes torn and the posterior horns of thyroid cartilage may be fractured from pressure on the thyrohyoid ligament but the hyoid is rarely injured, except in persons over 40 years of age due to increased calcification and brittleness of the bone. Such fracture involves the greater cornuae at the

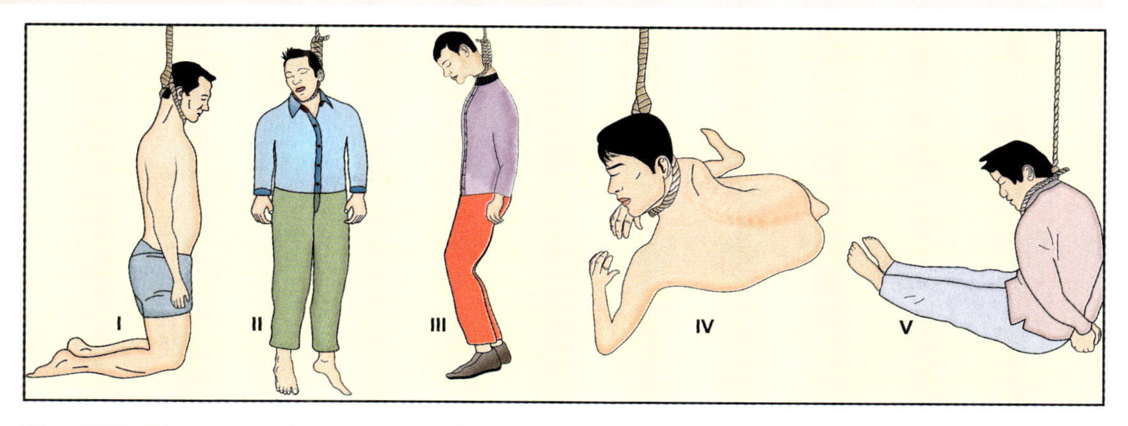

Fig. 13.2: Diagrammatic representation to show how hanging can occur in any position, (I) Partial hanging with feet resting on the ground, (II) Complete hanging with feet above the ground, (III) Hanging with feet just touching the ground, (IV) (Accidental) hanging from belt tied to a shower curtain rod, (V) Hanging in a reclining position

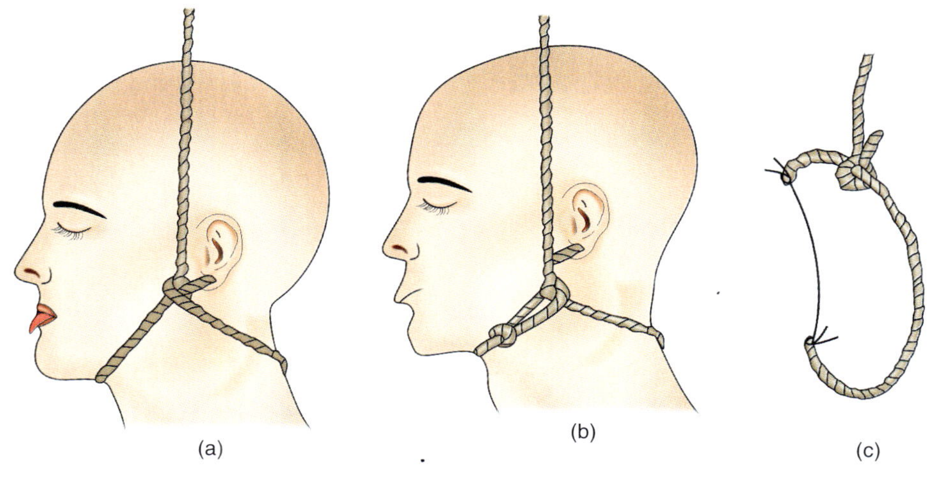

Fig. 13.3: Fixed noose (a); Running noose (b); Method of cutting the noose and preserving the cut ends and the knot (c)

junction of the inner two-thirds and outer one-third, the broken fragments being displaced outward. The periosteum is torn only on the inner side of the bone. Therefore, the broken fragments can be easily moved outward, but inward movement is limited to the normal position only.

If suspension has taken place when the victim was alive: (1) there is usually hyperaernia of the trachea and epiglottis, (2) the lymph nodes above and below the ligature mark show evidence of congestion and haemorrhage, (3) there are frictional intimal tears of carotid arteries with sub-intimal haemorrhage, and (4) dissection of neck under the ligature mark reveals a dry and compressed white band of subcuta-neous tissue perhaps with a few petechial haemorrhages into or around its substance, and occasionally a few ecchymoses. These findings are *never seen in postmortem hanging.*

The other internal appearances reveal findings of asphyxia, as already described, though in some cases, even these may be slight or absent, if death is sudden and due to vagal inhibition.

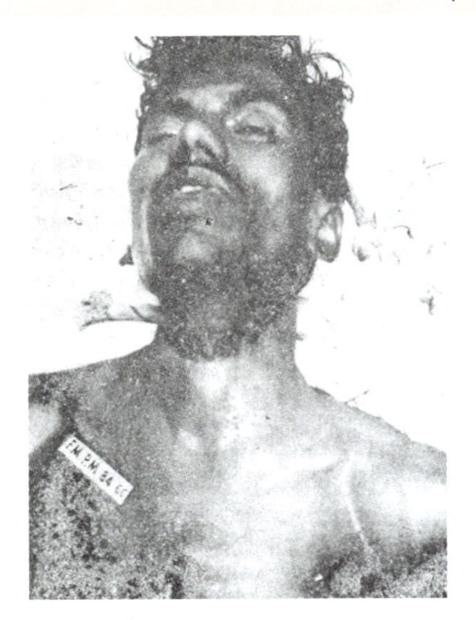

Fig 13.4: Ligature mark, this is a case of suicidal hanging. Readily available material has been used as the ligature. The waist thread has been twisted round the long sleeve of the shirt to make it into a rope and used as a ligature. The situation and typical characteristics of the ligature mark are clearly seen

Q. 13.3. Discuss the medicolegal questions likely to arise in a case of hanging.

Q. 13.4. Write short notes on: (1) judicial hanging, (2) synching, (3) sexual asphyxia.

The medicolegal questions likely to arise in a case of hanging are: (1) whether death was due to hanging, and (2) whether it was suicidal, homicidal, or accidental.

Whether death was due to hanging: It is not uncommon in India and possibly elsewhere also to kill a victim and then suspend his body (postmortem hanging) from a tree or rafter to mislead the relatives and the police. In such a case, a ligature mark is usually found. Therefore, when a person is found dead and his body suspended, no opinion can be given from the ligature mark alone. Death could be attributed to hanging only on a prospective evaluation of the following findings:

1. A ligature mark with petechial haemorrhages and ecchymoses into or around its substance (intravital signs).
2. A tear of the intima of carotid arteries with extravasation of blood within their walls.
3. Congestion and haemorrhage in lymph nodes above and below the ligature mark.
4. Fracture or fracture dislocation of cervical vertebrae.
5. Absence of other fatal injuries and poisoning (to be established only after a full autopsy). The doctor should also note: (i) if the ligature is strong enough to-bear the weight and jerk of the body, and (ii) if the ligature mark is consistent with the ligature material.

Suicide, homicide, or accident: Hanging is a common method of suicide among men in some countries. A typical account of suicidal hanging is as follows:

The suicide finds some secluded place where he is unlikely to be disturbed. He chooses readily available material, such as dhoti, sari, shirt, or rope, as the ligature and ties one end to a beam, roof, fan hook, or branch of a tree. He stands on a stool or climbs the tree and adjusts the noose round his neck, and then kicks off the stool or jumps off the tree. This results in complete hanging, the feet being above the ground. In the process of climbing and/or jumping, bruising and abrasions may be sustained and cause confusion. Though the suicide may arrange things so that he hangs with his feet above the ground, this is by no means necessary to achieve a fatal result. As mentioned earlier, a tension of as little as 3.5 kg can block carotid arteries and this can be easily achieved even by partial suspension, as seen in numerous cases where suicides have been found with their knees on the floor or heads reclining against a door or a bed post to which a noose has been tied (Fig. 13.5).

It must be remembered that, in suicide, the body must be in a position compatible with self-suspension and, so also, the position of ligature with reference to knot and the manner in which it is attached to the support. A suicide may give himself a drop, and may even tie his hands and feet together to make more certain of the result. Sometimes, hanging is adopted as a last resort after other forms of suicide, e.g. ingestion of poison or cutting of throat, have failed. Signs of struggle are not found in a suicidal hanging. A farewell (suicide) note may be left (about 25% cases) or the deceased will have made several arrangements to ensure that others would not be distressed by his death. A history of despondency, mental depression or a psychiatric disorder may be available on specific questioning *(psychological autopsy).*

Homicidal hanging is rare. Except in cases of weakness from senility or some other cause or under unusual circumstances, such as under the influence of drink or drugs, the act cannot readily be perpetrated by one assailant. Homicidal hanging may be suspected in a victim when: (a) the knot is tied on the back of neck, (b) mouth is gagged, (c) limbs are tied, (d) injuries are found on the body which could not have been self-inflicted, and (e) signs of struggle with some other individual are present (the presence of crescentic abrasions close to the ligature's impression should arouse suspicion as they may represent throttling attempts or attempts to remove the ligature by the deceased).

Homicidal hanging occurs in cases of judicial hanging (justifiable homicide) and lynching (non-justifiable) where the circumstances are obvious.

Judicial hanging is one of the official methods of execution of the death sentence. The face of the condemned person is covered with a dark mask. He is made to stand on a platform above trap doors which open downward through the mechanism of a lever. A rope is looped round the neck with the knot under the angle of the jaw and with a sufficient length of rope to allow a drop of five to seven feet or more according to weight, age, and build of the person, so as to cause fracture of cervical column but not decapitation. When the lever is brought into action, the person drops to the length of the rope. The sudden stoppage of the moving body associated with the position of the knot causes fracture dislocation of the cervical column at the level of second and third, or third and fourth cervical vertebrae. The upper cervical spinal cord is stretched or torn. Extensive laceration of neck structures sometimes occurs. Muscular tears in the sternomastoid are often seen. A transverse tear of the intima of carotid artery with extravasation of blood within its wall may be observed. The pons and medulla may be injured. Death is instantaneous due to damage to spinal cord or brainstem though the heart may continue to beat for 15 to 20 minutes and muscle jerking may occur for quite some time.

Fig. 13.5: Partial hanging (suicidal)

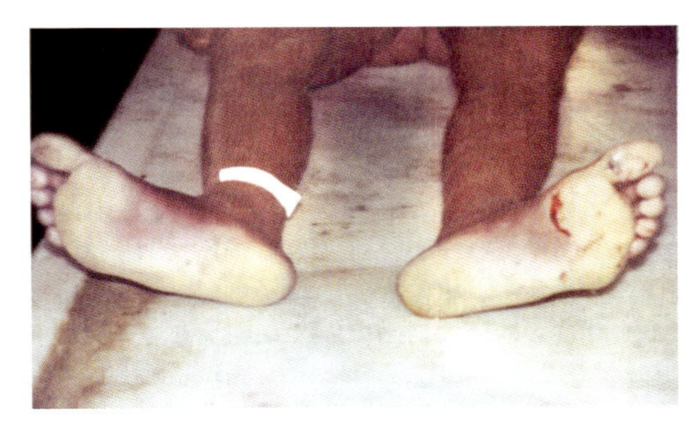

Fig. 13.6: Hypostasis in feet

Lynching is a condition where several persons acting jointly and illegally overpower an individual and hang him by means of a rope to a tree or some similar object.

Accidental hanging sometimes occurs and the circumstances are usually obvious. It takes place in little children who get caught in the cords of window blinds while at play or in toddlers by slippage of restraining straps. Though by definition, a ligature is used for suspension, on rare occasions, hanging can occur without ligature, e.g. when a person slips down a ladder and gets suspended by one of its rungs holding up his chin. It occurs in children when they lose their grip during tree climbing and the head gets caught between the branches of the tree. Accidental hanging may also occur in sexually deviant individuals during their masochistic exercises, the condition being known as sexual asphyxia.

Sexual asphyxia (autoerotic hanging) is a peculiar type of hanging where the victims are usually young males with some form of abnormal sexual behaviour, usually masochism and transvestism. Sexual pleasure can be enhanced by partial reduction of blood supply to the brain. This is usually achieved by compressing the blood vessels of the neck with a padding under the constricting noose. Since there is a fine line between the compression necessary to produce sexual pleasure and that which produces unconsciousness, the victim may place himself in a position of accidental black out and unexpected death. The presence of padding under the noose, nakedness or semi-nakedness of the victim, feminine attire, exposed genitalia, and pornographic literature are the hallmarks of these deaths. At the scene, a search should be made to find evidence that this was a repetitive practice (self-taken photographs, numerous rope marks on the beam or tree, etc.). Toxicological analysis may reveal the presence of 'recreational drugs', such as alcohol, cocaine, or narcotics, or some inhalant, which may also be found at the scene. It is necessary to recognise the true accidental nature of these deaths to avoid a costly homicide investigation and a false suicide verdict which can have financial implications in respect of life insurance.

Q. 13.5. Discuss the difficulties in diagnosis of death from hanging.

It is easy to diagnose death from hanging when one finds the classical features already described. However, all the features are seldom present together. Besides, there may be injuries on the body. A proper assessment of various factors is, therefore, necessary under such circumstances.

Ligature mark: Instead of an obliquely directed ligature mark, this may be circular, if the material is tied round the neck. Sometimes, there may be two ligature marks. This may be due to slippage of the ligature or ligature strangulation followed by hanging. If a ligature is tied two or three times round the neck and then goes up to the knot, in addition to encircling marks, there is an inverted V-shaped mark. This is confusing to those not familiar with the combination of such marks who may associate the lower (horizontal) marks with ligature strangulation and the upper one with hanging. There may be nail marks on the neck in addition to the ligature mark (Fig. 13.7). This could be due to throttling (manual strangulation) or attempts to free oneself from an assault to the neck and may thus be self-inflicted. The ligature mark may be faint, if a soft material is used or if the ligature is cut immediately after hanging. Ligature mark due to hanging resists putrefaction (due to avascularity of the area which retards access of bacteria) and has been seen in bodies exhumed six days after death. Therefore, in absence of a ligature mark, it is hazardous to diagnose hanging on history alone. Ecchymosis on dissection of a ligature mark is a vital sign but is rare, as compared to deaths from ligature strangulation. Sometimes, therefore, a diagnosis may have to be made on the presence of a ligature mark, evidence of asphyxial signs, and absence of any other cause of death.

Injuries: Several possibilities exist for their causation. They might be suicidal, such as cut throat, cuts of wrist, etc. They could also be homicidal, the individual having been beaten to death and then subsequently hanged to make it appear as a case of hanging. The nature of injuries will help in many cases. As for example, fractures of multiple ribs, several contusions all over the body, and rupture of viscera, can only be homicidal. It should be remembered that accidental injuries may occasionally be sustained due to convulsions which may precede death when the body of the person may strike the nearby wall or furniture. Postmortem injuries, such as fractured limbs or ribs, may occur when the ligature is cut and the body falls from a height or during attempts at resuscitation. If the rope is cut and the body falls, impact of the head against the floor can give rise to a laceration that can be mistaken for one due to a blow on the head.

LIGATURE STRANGULATION

Q.13.6. Define strangulation. Give its symptoms, cause of death, and postmortem appearances.

In some countries, the term strangulation is used to mean ligature strangulation while the term throttling is used to mean manual strangulation. Strangulation is **defined** as a form of violent asphyxia caused by constricting the neck by some means other than body weight. The means used may be a ligature, the hand (throttling), the elbow (mugging or choke-hold), or some hard object, such as a stick (bansdola).

Symptoms: Sudden and violent compression of the windpipe often renders a person powerless and may cause almost immediate insensibility and death. If the windpipe is not completely occluded, the face becomes cyanosed; bleeding occurs from the mouth and nose, due to congestion and rupture of the various venous plexuses; the hands are clenched; and convulsions precede death. As in hanging, loss of consciousness is quite rapid.

Cause of death: Where a ligature is used, death usually results from asphyxia and compression of cervical vasculature but it may also result from various other causes as described under hanging.

Postmortem Appearances

These may be divided into: (1) external appearances, (2) injuries on neck, and (3) internal appearances.

External appearances: The external signs of asphyxia, already described, will be apparent. The extent and character of these signs will depend in large measure upon the cause of death and on the pace and course of asphyxial process as shown in Table 13.1.

Table 13.1: External signs of cause of death of asphyxia

Cause of death	*Signs*
1. Vagal inhibition	Death instantaneous. No asphyxial signs
2. Slight vagal effect and some venous constriction	Slight asphyxial signs: cyanosed face with occasional petechiae, suffused eyes, dilated pupils
3. Moderate venous constriction and some respiratory obstruction	Moderate asphyxial signs: cyanosed face, bulging eyes, ecchymosed conjunctivae, and few petechiae
4. Pronounced venous and respiratory obstruction	Well-marked asphyxial signs: deeply cyanosed face, blood shot eyes, bruised bitten tongue, and many petechiae in eyelids, conjunctivae, and face

Thus, when death supervenes from vagal inhibition, asphyxial signs are absent. However, as is usual, when the airway and vascular constricting force has been considerable, the signs are well marked. In addition to usual asphyxial signs, the following signs are also seen: The tongue may be swollen, bruised, bitten by teeth, and protruded. Petechial haemorrhages are common into the skin of the eyelids, face, forehead, behind the ears, and scalp. The body temperature may rise by 2° or 3°C due to convulsions and muscular activity, and this should be taken into consideration while estimating time since death. There may be injuries on face, chest, etc. indicating a struggle.

Injuries on the neck: These vary according to the means used for strangulation. They may be — (1) ligature, (2) stick, or (3) foot.

When a **ligature** is used, a ligature mark is seen round the neck as a depression (groove). In the early period after death, it looks pale. Later, it becomes dry, yellowish brown, hard, and parchment-like. Along the edges of depression, abrasions and ecchymoses are often seen indicating that the mark was made during life. The ligature mark is situated at the level of thyroid cartilage or below, is almost horizontal, and encircles the neck completely or nearly so. It may be absent at the back due to interposition of hair or clothing. It may be oblique as in hanging, if the victim has been dragged by the ligature or strangled in a recumbent position. Portable articles, e.g. electric cord, laundry wire, etc., which can be easily concealed are commonly used as ligatures. The character of the mark depends upon the nature of ligature but is also affected by the number of turns round the neck and length of time it remains applied. The pattern of the ligature may be imprinted on neck as a pressure abrasion (mirror image phenomenon) or bruise. If the ligature has gone round the skin more than once, corresponding number of marks, one above the other and close to each other are seen. In such cases, there may be evidence of skin bruising, if it is caught between the rounds of ligature. There is always some damage to skin underneath the ligature. A careful search of the neck may reveal minute fibres or any other material from the ligature. The ligature should be examined for presence of blood, hair, or suspicious substances.

In case where one **stick** is used, there is a bruise in front of the neck in the centre and when two sticks are used, one in front and the other behind the neck as in bansdola, there will be a corresponding mark on the nape of neck also.

Where a **foot** is used, there is irregular widespread bruising with local injuries to neck depending on the force applied. A foot with a boot on, will cause more abrasions than when a bare foot is used, which will cause contusions.

Internal appearances: A V-shaped incision and a careful dissection of neck, layer by layer, is essential. It is desirable to eviscerate cranial, thoracic, and abdominal viscera so that the body is drained of blood and a comparatively cleaner field is available for the study of neck organs. The extent and character of the signs will depend in large measure upon the cause of death and the pace and course of asphyxial process as mentioned above. There is usually severe congestion and haemorrhage into the tissues in and about the area of compression.

In ligature strangulation, injuries to deeper tissues of neck are more common than in hanging, as a result of considerable force which is used. The subcutaneous connective tissue under the ligature mark is usually ecchymosed. The neck muscles, laryngeal cartilages, tracheal rings and carotid arteries may be injured. The superior horns of the thyroid cartilage are commonly fractured but the hyoid is rarely injured, due to the level of constriction being below this bone, unless considerable violence is applied to neck. Hyoid fracture may occur in persons over 40 years of age. In characteristics, it is similar to that in hanging, with the broken fragments commonly displaced outward.

When a stick or foot is applied to compress the neck, extreme injury to internal cervical structures is common. Similar injury is caused by a karate blow to the neck.

Q. 13.7. Discuss the medicolegal questions likely to arise in a case of strangulation.

The medicolegal questions likely to arise in a case of strangulation are: (1) whether death was due to strangulation, and (2) whether it was suicidal, homicidal or accidental.

Whether death was due to strangulation: Usually, no inference can be drawn from the presence or absence of a ligature mark alone. Decomposed bodies commonly received for autopsy present a swollen neck and exaggerated folds of skin. Besides, any beaded threads and ornaments worn round the neck may produce depressed marks. Creases may be seen on the necks of elderly people who have lesser amount of fat beneath their skin, in those dying in bed with their head propped up, and also when a body is placed in a mortuary refrigerator with the head propped on a block. In children, dribbling on to a skin crease followed by refrigeration with the head raised on an adult size block can also cause confusion; also, in very young children, the fat appears to have different characteristics upon refrigeration, and this may lead to the most alarming looking folds and creases on the neck. All these look like ligature marks and are quite misleading, especially to those who lack experience in the field. Unless therefore, dissection of neck reveals antemortem evidence of violence in the underlying tissues, no importance should be attached to the mere finding of the above appearances which could only represent postmortem decomposition changes. It is also necessary to exclude possibility of other causes of asphyxial death.

Suicide, homicide, or accident: *Suicidal* strangulation is not common although instances have been known. To effect suicide by ligature requires the employment of some means (e.g. a tourniquet) whereby the ligature is kept tight independently of any muscular effort on the part of the suicide. In suicide, the ligature should be found in situ and the body should be free from other signs of violence or marks of struggle. The knot is usually in front.

Homicidal strangulation is a common form of murder. In fact, strangling should be assumed to be homicidal until the contrary is proven to be more likely under the circumstances. A suspicion of homicide should arise when:

a. Knot is tied on the back of neck
b. Mouth is gagged
c. Limbs are tied
d. Other injuries are found on the body
e. Signs of struggle are present
f. In case of a female, if she is sexually assaulted; and in such a case, material that is readily available at hand, e.g. a nylon stocking, pantyhose, or the scarf of the victim, is used as a ligature. Tearing of clothes may be seen.

The unusual pattern of injuries on Mrs Levin's neck indicated that she was strangled by twisting of her own blouse while facing her assailant. This evidence and the fact that the constriction of the neck would have to be maintained for some time to cause brain death by oxygen deprivation led to the realisation that death was neither unintentional nor unexpected and to Chamber's conviction.

Extensive injuries to the neck are far more common as the murderer generally employs more force than is necessary to cause death.

Infanticide by strangulation may be caused by passing the umbilical cord round the neck. In such a case, examination of umbilical cord may show that it has been roughly handled and Wharton's jelly is damaged. Other signs of violence may be present on the body.

Homicidal strangulation may be committed with such silence that even persons in close vicinity may not be aware of the act since sudden and violent compression of windpipe renders a person powerless to raise an alarm or call for assistance.

An aged woman was strangled in her shop by an apprentice in so short a time and with such ease that her husband who was separated from her only by a slight partition heard no noise or disturbance during the murder but came to know of it only after the assailant had escaped.

Accidental strangling is rare. It may occur in the newborn when umbilical cord at the time of birth is tightly twisted round the neck. It may occur in children restrained in their cots by a harness. It may arise in the course of one's occupation when a necktie or scarf is caught in moving machinery. It may occur when a string or strap, normally attached on the head and used for suspending a weight on the back, slips from across the forehead and compresses the neck. In all such cases, the circumstances sufficiently indicate the accidental nature of the occurrence.

Q. 13.8. Describe the methods in common use, other than ligature strangulation, to perpetrate homicidal strangulation.

Apart from ligature strangulation, the methods in common use to perpetrate homicidal strangulation are: (1) throttling (manual strangulation-vide infra), (2) mugging (choke-hold), (3) garrotting, and (4) bansdola.

Mugging (choke-hold): When strangulation is effected by compressing victim's neck against the forearm, it is known as mugging (choke-hold). It may leave no external or internal mark of injury. This hold is not permitted in wrestling because of its danger.

Garrotting: When a victim is attacked from back without warning, and strangled by throwing a ligature over the neck and tightening it quickly, it is known as garrotting. It can overpower and kill even a healthy robust male without any struggle. Loss of consciousness is so rapid that the assailant is able, single handed, to tie the ligature with one or more turns. Garrotting, as a **mode of execution,** was practised in Spain, Portugal, and Turkey.

Bansdola: This is a form of strangulation practised in Northern India. In this, the neck is compressed between two sticks or hard objects, usually bamboos, one being placed across the throat in front and another behind. These are strongly fastened at one end and a rope is passed at the other end to bring the two bamboos together. And, the unfortunate victim is thus strangled to death. Sometimes, the throat is pressed by means of a bamboo or lathi placed across the front of the neck, the murderer standing with a foot on each end of the bamboo or lathi, thus squeezing the victim.

Q. 13.9. Tabulate the differences between hanging and strangulation.

Differences between hanging and strangulation are described in Table 13.2.

Table 13.2: Differences between hanging and strangulation

Hanging	*Strangulation*
1. Suicidal usually	Homicidal usually
2. No signs of struggle	Signs of struggle
3. Ligature found in position, above thyroid cartilage, mark incomplete, directed obliquely upward with a gap indicating position of the knot with no damage to the skin in the gap	Ligature may not be with the body but when found, usually completely encircles the neck horizontally below thyroid cartilage. There may be more than one turn of ligature and there is always some damage to skin underneath

(*contd.*)

Table 13.2: Differences between hanging and strangulation (*contd.*)

Hanging	*Strangulation*
4. Abrasions and bruises around ligature mark rare	Abrasions and bruises around ligature mark common
5. Dissection of ligature mark reveals a dry and glistening white band of subcutaneous tissue	Dissection of ligature mark reveals ecchymosed subcutaneous tissue
6. Neck usually stretched	Neck not stretched
7. Fracture of hyoid rare	Fracture of hyoid not rare in throttling cases (in the aged)
8. Fracture of laryngeal cartilages and tracheal rings rare	Fracture of laryngeal cartilages and tracheal rings common
9. Injury to carotid arteries in cases with a long drop	Injury to carotid arteries common
10. Injury to muscles of neck rare	Injury to muscles of neck common
11. Fracture dislocation of cervical vertebrae common in judicial hanging	Fracture dislocation of cervical vertebrae rare
12. Saliva running out of the angle of the mouth vertically down along the neck and front of chest and abdomen	Saliva may not have escaped from mouth but if so, usually blood tinged and may not be vertically down
13. External signs of asphyxia may not be well marked when death is due to any cause other than asphyxia	External signs of asphyxia usually well marked because of considerable violence that is commonly employed
14. Face usually pale	Face congested and with pronounced petechiae
15. Bleeding from nose and mouth very rare	Bleeding from nose and mouth common

THROTTLING (MANUAL STRANGULATION)

Q. 13.10. Define throttling. Describe the autopsy appearances.

Throttling is defined as a form of strangulation effected by hand, and is, therefore, often referred to as manual strangulation.

Autopsy Appearances

These may be divided into: (1) external appearances, (2) injuries on the neck, and (3) internal appearances.

External appearances: External signs of asphyxia, already described, will be present. The extent and character of these signs will depend in large measure upon the pace and course of the asphyxial process. Signs of asphyxia may be very slight, if death has supervened quickly from cardiac inhibition due to pressure on carotid sinus or vagus nerve. When the constricting force has been considerable, the signs are well marked. In addition, the following signs are also seen: The tongue may be bruised, bitten by teeth, and protruding. There may be injuries on the face, chest, etc., indicating a struggle. The face and eyes may show multiple petechial haemorrhages. The body temperature at death may be raised.

Injuries on the neck: The situation and extent of bruised area on neck will depend upon the relative position of the assailant and victim, manner of grasping the neck, and amount of pressure exercised on the throat. The bruises (ecchymoses) are often found on the front or sides of the neck, chiefly about the larynx, and above it. The conformation of neck injuries indicate the way in which the hands have been applied to the neck.

When only one hand is used to throttle, there may be a single bruise on one side due to pressure of the thumb and obliquely directed multiple bruises, one below the other, on the opposite side, due to pressure of finger pads or finger tips. Their shape may be oval or round depending upon the size of the finger tips but continued bleeding into the contused area usually increases the size, merging the bruises together. When both hands are used, the bruising pattern depends upon the relative position of thumbs and fingers, and the degree of pressure applied to the throat. The bruising caused by the thumb is generally broader than that caused by the fingers. In addition to bruises, curved impressions, or crescentic abrasions, caused by finger nails, are also seen. The scratch caused by the thumb nail is deeper and wider as compared to that from finger nails. The distribution of various marks (bruises and finger nail scratches) may be regular as mentioned above but is more often irregular due to renewed attempts at grasping the neck when the victim struggles to escape or to loosen the hand holding the throat. It is, therefore, important to examine the nails of the victim. Skin fragments or blood under the nails may provide blood group or DNA characteristics that can be matched to the alleged assailant. Other valuable trace evidence, such as hairs and fibres, may be trapped in a torn finger nail. The finger nail scrapings of the alleged assailant, when possible, may be taken, especially if the victim has neck abrasions, so that they can be compared with the tissue types of the victim. The back of neck should not be overlooked for the hands may have been clapped on the neck from behind. In such cases, bruising is occasionally noted on the sides of neck and across the shoulders due to pressure of assailant's forearms. It is necessary to remember that abrasions on skin of the neck may become visible only after the skin has begun to dry and may not be visible soon after death. There are instances in which persons have been immersed in water after throttling and abrasions have not been visible until the skin began to dry after removal of body from water (Figs 13.7 and 13.8).

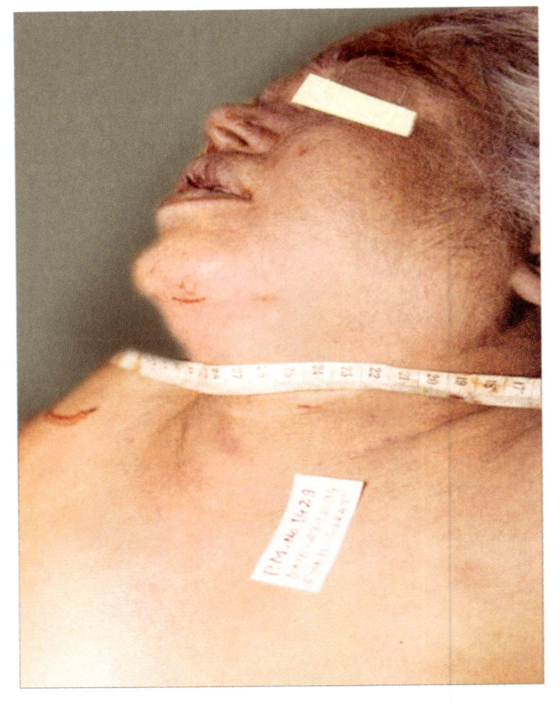

Fig. 13.7: Nail marks

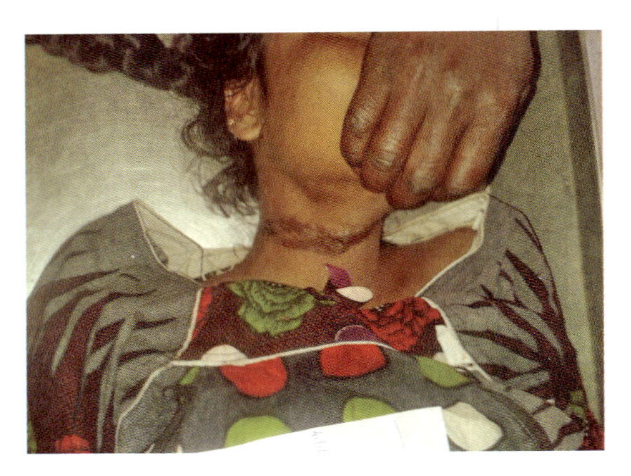

Fig. 13.8: Ligature mark in hanging. (*Courtesy*: Dr Manigandaraj)

Internal appearances: A V-shaped incision and a careful dissection of neck, layer by layer, are essential. The extent and character of the signs will depend in large measure upon the cause of death and the pace and course of asphyxial process.

In the usual case where the constricting force has been considerable and signs of asphyxia well marked, the soft tissues of the neck are compressed and forced upward and backward against the cervical vertebrae, and the subcutaneous tissues of the neck show extravasation of blood beneath the injured areas. Haemorrhage in subcutaneous tissues and in muscles underlying nail marks is usually scanty as compared to external injuries (Fig. 13.9). Conversely, absence of externally visible neck injury does not preclude possibility of underlying trauma. The superior horns of thyroid

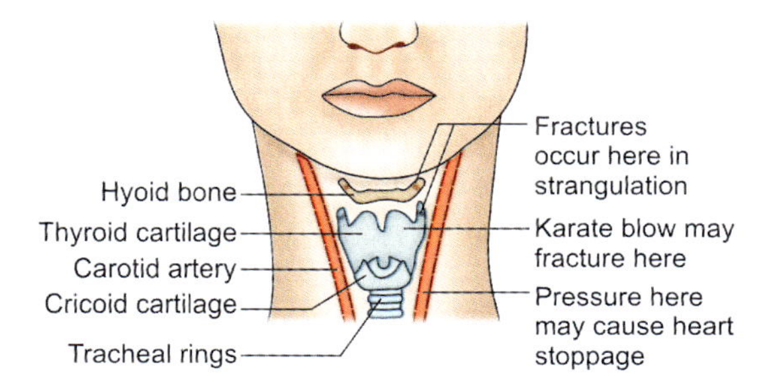

Fig. 13.9: Diagrammatic representation of the structures of the neck with special reference to throttling (manual strangulation)

cartilage are more commonly fractured than the hyoid due to local pressure. Occasionally, there are no fractures but only submucosal haemorrhages of larynx, and well-marked bruising of muscles surrounding the larynx. A fracture of laryngeal cartilages and hyoid are common in persons above 40 years of age. When found, the hyoid fracture is in the region of greater cornuae which are generally squeezed violently during the process, the broken fragments being commonly displaced inward. The periosteum is torn only on the outer side of the bone. Therefore, the broken fragment can be easily moved inward, but outward movement is limited to the normal position only. A blow from the front of the neck may also result in a similar fracture. The fracture should not be diagnosed as antemortem in the absence of haemorrhage at the fracture site. Bruising (haemorrhage) at the base of tongue may sometimes be the only evidence of throttling.

Q. 3.11. Discuss the medicolegal questions likely to arise in a case of throttling.

The medicolegal questions likely to arise in a case of throttling are: (1) whether death was due to throttling, and (2) whether it was suicidal, homicidal, or accidental.

Whether death was due to throttling: Evidence of violent compression of neck during life is obtained from:

1. Nail marks on and bruising of neck due to thumb and fingers.
2. Swelling of tissues at and above the level of compression.
3. Bruising of larynx, trachea, and surrounding muscles and vessels.
4. Fracture of cornuae of laryngeal and occasionally the hyoid.
5. General signs of asphyxia.

Suicide, homicide, or accident: Self-throttling is impossible because as soon as unconsciousness supervenes, the hand will relax and the grip will be released.

Homicidal throttling is a common form of murder, especially when the physical size and strength of the assailant exceeds that of the victim. The victims, therefore, are usually infants, children, and women. In an adult, signs of struggle are usually present, but if the throat is seized and firmly compressed, the victim cannot struggle.

A woman may be sexually assaulted and then throttled or throttled and sexually assaulted. Often, the victim is gripped by the throat or throttled during intercourse to stop her from shouting. Adults may be throttled when under the influence of drink or drugs, or taken unawares. Though 15–20 seconds of a strong suffocating grip can dispose off a healthy adult and give rise to pronounced congestive signs, in most cases, the grip is maintained for several minutes. The time factor is of great importance here. When the gripping time is just a few seconds (before the congestive signs appear), the court may reasonably believe that the intention to kill may have been absent. If a healthy adult male is found dead from manual strangulation, one should look for some form of diminished ability to resist either from alcohol intoxication or use of drugs. It is not commonly appreciated that an intoxicated person can be throttled with so little force applied to neck that there may be no external or internal evidence of injury, although the force is sufficient to occlude blood vessels of the neck. DiMaio records two such cases in which intoxicated women were raped and then throttled in this manner.

Accidental cases are rare. They are due to vagal inhibition following sudden seizing of the throat, or grasping the neck with both hands, either as a measure of affection or threat.

A man laid his hand on the neck of his wife who had annoyed him by treading on his toes. She just went limp and he failed to rouse her. The cause of death was vagal inhibition and the manner of death—accident.

Q. 13.11(a) Write short note on hyoid bone.

Hyoid bone is mobile and suspended from styloid process at the base of the brain by stylohyoid ligament. It has a body, a greater cornu and a lasser cornu. The joint between greater cornu and the body is a synovial joint. There are two types of hyoid bone fracture. Abduction fracture or outward compression fracture and adduction fracture or inward compression fracture. In throttling, adduction fracture occurs. In hanging, though rarely, abduction fracture occurs. In old age, the joint is calcified. In case of doubt, if there is no fracture, the horns recoil back when held and lightly pressed in between thumbs and fore fingers. If there is fracture, no recoil is seen.

SUFFOCATION

This is a form of asphyxia caused by a mechanical obstruction to the passage of air into the respiratory tract by means other than constriction of neck or drowning. It includes: (1) smothering (obstruction to air passages from outside), (2) choking (obstruction to air passages from inside), and (3) traumatic asphyxia (obstruction to respiratory movements).

SMOTHERING

Q. 13.12. Define smothering. Describe the autopsy appearances. Add a note on medicolegal aspects.

Smothering is a form of asphyxia caused by mechanical occlusion of external air passages, viz. the nose and mouth by a hand, cloth, plastic bag, or any other material.

Autopsy Appearances

A visit by the pathologist or a photograph to document the crime scene is essential. If necessary, the V-shaped incision of neck is continued behind ear-lobes to allow a full access to enable the pathologist to examine the face, inside of the mouth, tongue, and lips. The orbits can be examined by cutting the optic nerves and orbital muscles, the eye globes remaining supported by the eyelids.

In homicidal smothering, abrasions and bruises are generally found in the region of nose and mouth. However, these may be absent, if the face has been pressed against soft material, such as a pillow or bed clothes. In such cases, particular attention should be paid to the sides of head and neck for any possible signs of violence. Injuries on the inside of lips from pressure against the teeth, bruising of gums, or sometimes superficial splits in delicate tissues, such as frenulum of the lip or tongue, may be found. They may be missed at autopsy unless specially looked for. These injuries are usually produced as a result of struggling and may, therefore, be absent in infants, young children, the aged, intoxicated, and debilitated persons.

On microscopy, the findings are usually entirely non-specific but mild acute emphysema, oedema of the lungs, scattered areas of petechiae and congestion may be found. The air passages often contain eosinophilic fluid with red blood cells and varying amounts of desquamated respiratory epithelium.

Obstruction to breathing by *plastic bag* exemplifies suicidal or accidental smothering, especially in cases of solvent abuse (glue sniffing). The solvent of the glue, usually xylene, induces drowsiness and confusion, which in turn results in rebreathing of the contents of the bag. The moisture accumulating in the plastic bag containing the glue contributes to the adherence of the plastic bag to the skin and cuts off access of outside air to respiratory passages. Death may be due to lack of oxygen or more often cardiac arrhythmia following inhalation of halogenated hydrocarbons contained in the solvent. The plastic bag, lungs, liver, and blood should be preserved for laboratory examination. Whenever the presence of a solvent or other foreign chemical is suspected, the bag should be preserved in an air-tight container, such as a clean can or similarly sealed preferably glass utensil, to permit subsequent laboratory examination and analysis. The presence of solvent in the lungs indicates that glue has been inhaled while its presence in liver or blood indicates systemic absorption. In cases of homicidal or suicidal deaths from plastic bags placed over the head, there may be little or nothing to see at the time of autopsy, if the bag has been removed prior to examination. This is one of the most difficult situations to deal with and there are many classic cases in which diagnosis has been completely missed, either through lack of circumstantial information or more frequently, insufficient experience to realise that *circumstances surrounding death may be sometimes more important than the autopsy itself.*

Medicolegal Aspects

Smothering is mostly **accidental.** It may occur in alcoholics who roll over and bury their face in the pillow while in bed; or in epileptics who fall on to a bed, or in bins of flour, or such other material, and fail to revert to a favourable posture. This is known as *postural* or *positional asphyxia.* At birth, an infant may die of smothering, if it is born with placental membranes adhering the nose and mouth. Infants may be smothered by the weight of the bed clothes when they cover the face. Children may die while playing with plastic bags, some of which are large enough to hold an entire body. Sexually perverted individuals may envelope the head in a plastic bag during their autoerotic experiments.

Overlaying is accidental smothering of a child due to its mother or other person sharing the same bed, rolling over the baby during sleep, and thereby asphyxiating it. Overlaying is not common and some of these deaths are likely to be cases of SIDS.

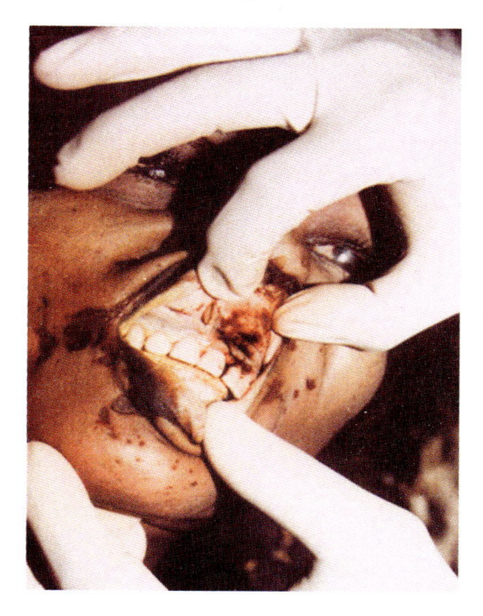

Fig. 13.10: Lip bruising and ulceration

Homicidal smothering may be committed by closing the mouth and nostrils with a hand, clothing, or a pillow. It is a common method of infanticide. Homicidal smothering of adults is difficult unless they are weak, or stupefied by drugs, or drink, as for example in burking, or are overpowered by a number of persons.

Burking is a form of asphyxia arising as a result of a procedure used by the murderers Burke and Hare, to kill their victims and to sell their bodies for dissection to the Edinburgh Medical students. Burke used to sit on the chest of his inebriated victim covering with one hand the mouth and nostrils and pushing up the jaw with the other hand while Hare used to pull him round the room by the feet. The method provides a mixed example of smothering and traumatic asphyxia.

Suicidal smothering by one's own hand is impossible but suicide by closing the respiratory passages by a plastic bag is becoming common among the elderly. Awareness of this method of suicide raised in the media may lead to 'copy cat' types of death. It is the method advocated by euthanasia societies.

CHOKING

Q.13.13. Define choking. Describe the autopsy appearances. Give the medicolegal significance. Add a note on cafe coronary.

Choking is a form of asphyxia caused by mechanical occlusion of the lumina of the air passages by a solid object. Generally, the object excites violent coughing to expel the object but if this fails, choking results. The size of the object is not of much importance. Even an object smaller in size than the lumen of respiratory passages may bring about reflex spasm of air passages with fatal consequences. Death may ensue from (1) asphyxia, (2) vagal inhibition, (3) laryngeal spasm, and (4) bronchospasm.

Gagging is a means to effect choking by prevention of air entering through mouth or nose. The gag is commonly composed of a handkerchief, sari, or dhoti. It is usually stuffed tightly into position. It thus not only fills the mouth but also obstructs breathing through the back of throat. Where a gag is so packed, choking may occur as soon as saliva, mucus, vomit or other fluid moisten the material and obstruct the cloth pores producing an airtight occlusion.

Autopsy appearances: The tongue should be specially examined for its position, and presence or absence of bruising or bite marks. In post-epileptic choking, a history of epilepsy, bite marks on tip and side of the tongue, and an empty urinary bladder are important.

In choking due to a foreign body, in addition to asphyxial signs, the object responsible for choking should be found in respiratory passages. The possibility that a foreign body was removed or dislodged during resuscitation attempts must be remembered. Even when the mechanical obstruction is removed in time, the aged and the very young succumb due to their inability to clear the bronchi of accumulated secretions. Life may be saved, if the condition is recognised in time and air passages cleared by suction.

In gagging, the gag is sometimes found in position with injuries in the characteristic situation.

In cafe coronary (vide infra), toxicological examination for alcohol and drugs is essential. To avoid missing this condition, all persons who die in likely situations, e.g. kitchens, rest houses, bars, and restaurants should be autopsied, regardless of history of pre-existing disease.

Medicolegal aspects: Death from choking is usually accidental. It arises from:

1. Impaction of food, fish bone, denture, or other foreign bodies in air passages.
2. Inhalation of vomited material by a person under the influence of alcohol, anaesthetic agents, during an epileptic fit, or in coma.
3. Regurgitation of food in infants. Impaction of objects, like a marble, coin or pea, may occur in children while playing.

Cafe coronary is a condition of accidental choking which occurs when a bolus of food produces complete obstruction of the larynx. It is so-called because it occurs in a cafe or a pubic house and, its suddenness and associated collapse mimic a coronary heart attack, especially in older persons. The condition occurs commonly when gag reflex is suppressed, e.g. in intoxicated individuals and following large doses of tranquillisers in mental institutions. Death is due to asphyxia from inability to breathe or reflex cardiac arrest consequent upon stimulation of laryngeal nerve endings. Autopsy reveals a bolus of unchewed food impacted in larynx (Fig. 3.11). Cyanosis may be marked. The diagnosis is important from a medicolegal standpoint because additional insurance benefits may be due to surviving relatives when death is accidental as opposed to natural. A litmus paper test of the bolus to determine acidity will ascertain whether it originated from the mouth or consisted of vomitus. Timely treatment sometimes helps. A blow on the back, on the sternum, or application of pressure on the abdomen (Heimlich manoeuvre) may cause coughing and expel the foreign body. The foreign body can occasionally be removed by the middle and index fingers provided it is in the hypopharynx.

Homicidal choking is usually confined to cases of infanticide where all sorts of foreign articles may be introduced and impacted into infant's air passages.

Bleeding into respiratory passages in cut throat injuries may lead to choking. It may also occur after a tonsillectomy operation or tooth extraction and lead to an allegation of *criminal negligence*. It is important to remember that concussed victims of accidents may inhale blood from an injured nose, lips, or jaws. Life may be saved, if air passages are cleared in time.

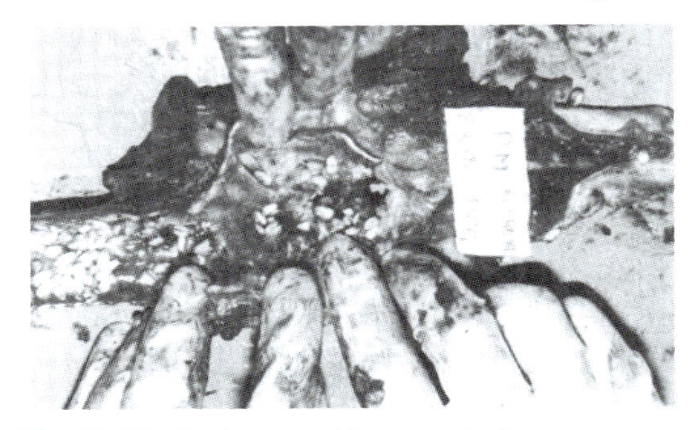

Fig. 13.11: Grains blocking respiratory pessage (*Courtesy*: Dr BD Gupta)

Gagging is mostly homicidal, the victim generally being an infant or a child. An adult may be gagged to prevent him from raising an alarm but death may not be intended. Instances are recorded when a woman is gagged and raped. A man may be gagged, his hands tied behind his back so that he may not remove the gag, his legs tied so that he may not run for help, during a burglary, and death may ensue due to asphyxia, after the burglars leave.

Suicidal choking is rare, except in mental patients or prisoners, who thrust a foreign body into the throat.

TRAUMATIC ASPHYXIA

Q. 13.14. Define traumatic asphyxia. Describe the autopsy appearances. Add a note on the medicolegal aspects.

Traumatic asphyxia or crush asphyxia, as the name suggests, is a form of asphyxia resulting from trauma to the chest or external pressure on the chest, abdomen, or back which prevents normal respiratory movements.

It may be due to: (1) pressure on the chest from unconcerted movements of persons in a crowd, e.g. in a stampede, and (2) non-penetrating trauma from: (a) being pinned down by a car in motor car mechanics, (b) loss of space within a vehicle when it is compressed or collapsed in a road accident, and (c) house collapse. The commonest form of accidental death from traumatic asphyxia in farm workers is the overturn of a tractor, and in trench workers the fall of earth from ill-prepared trenches, with sufficient force to prevent effective breathing movements. Restraint of suspects by *hogtying* practised in some States in USA by the police has occasionally resulted in sudden death due to *positional asphyxia*. The victim is handcuffed with the hands behind his back with or without binding the ankles to the handcuff. The restraint inhibits breathing especially as the subject lies on his stomach.

Autopsy appearances: In addition to signs of asphyxia, and mud or other foreign material on clothing as the case may be, there are three characteristic features, viz. (a) deep cyanosis of face, (b) numerous petechiae, and (c) a demarcation line. The mechanism is as follows: Compression of chest displaces blood from the superior vena cava and subclavian veins into the veins and capillaries of the head and neck. No valves are present in superior vena cava because back pressure is normally not present in the venous system above the level of heart. Valves in subclavian veins prevent spread of the hydrostatic force set up in the blood column to the veins of upper limbs. The valveless veins and capillaries of the head and neck are, therefore, considerably engorged and the hydrostatic pressure in them rises so rapidly as to burst their walls. Therefore, the face and neck of the victim are deeply cyanosed—almost black, the eyes blood-shot, and *numerous petechiae* are found over scalp, face, neck, and shoulders. The level of compression is indicated by a well-defined demarcating line between the discoloured upper portion of body and the lower normally coloured part (Fig. 13.12).

In mild cases of traumatic asphyxia, injury to the lungs may be in the form of traumatic emphysema wherein the air in the lungs is forcibly redistributed producing small bullae along the edges of the lung. Depending on the mechanism of trauma, other injuries may be found in various other parts of the body. In severe cases, injuries to the chest include: (a) fracture of the ribs, which are usually bilateral, multiple, and at their angles, with occasional damage to the diaphragm, and (b) injuries to lungs and heart.

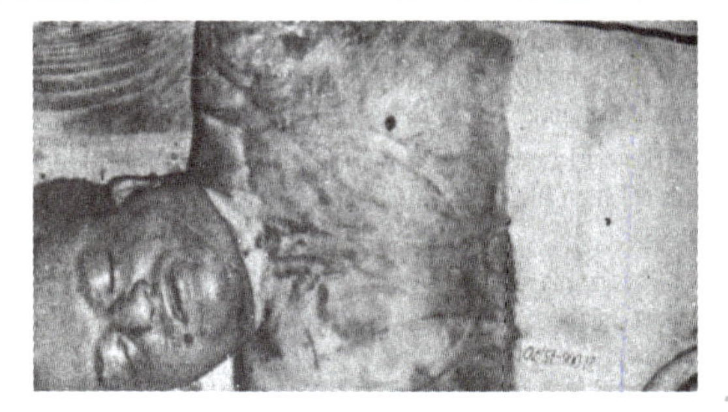

Fig. 13.12: Traumatic asphyxia sustained by being run-over in a road accident. The level of compression is indicated by a well-defined **demarcating line** between the discoloured upper portion of the body and the lower normally coloured part. **The face is deeply cyanosed**

Medicolegal aspects: This is mainly accidental but can be homicidal as in burking, or bansdola, which is rare. Rarely, an obese mother, sharing the same bed, may roll over a child in sleep and cause death of the child from traumatic asphyxia.

Bansdola is homicidal compression of the chest by means of a bamboo or bamboos. It is not common nowadays (*bans* = bamboo).

DROWNING: IMMERSION

Drowning is a form of asphyxial death in which access of air to the lungs is prevented by submersion of the body in water or other fluid medium. Complete submersion is not necessary, sufficient fluid to cover the nostrils and mouth being all that is required.

Classification

Drowning is classified as: (1) typical, and (2) atypical. The term typical drowning indicates obstruction of air passages and lungs by inhalation of fluid and is known as wet drowning. Typical signs of drowning are found at autopsy. The term atypical drowning indicates conditions in which there is very little or no inhalation of water in the air passages, and includes—(a) dry drowning, (b) immersion syndrome (vagal inhibition), and (c) submersion of the unconscious. None of the typical signs of drowning found at autopsy. There is one more category of drowning, viz. (d) near-drowning, a term that is used synonymously with secondary drowning syndrome.

Q. 13.15. Discuss (a) typical drowning, (b) atypical drowning.

Typical Drowning

Wet drowning: Water is inhaled and the victim gets severe chest pain. The entry of water into the lungs reduces the chances of survival. Fresh and salt water when inhaled cause different physiopathological changes. However, in most cases, this differentiation is not possible.

In *fresh water drowning,* large quantities of water cross the alveolar membrane into circulation and produce hypervolaemia. The red cells swell or burst and haemolysis ensues with liberation of potassium. The circulation may suffer 50% dilution within 2–3 minutes. The heart is, therefore, submitted to the insult of anoxia, hypervolaemia, potassium excess, and sodium deficit. Anoxia and potassium excess lead to ventricular fibrillation and death in about 4–5 minutes.

In *salt water drowning,* the marked hypertonicity of inhaled water causes loss of fluid from circulation into the lungs giving rise to fulminating pulmonary oedema with progressive hypovolaemia, circulatory shock, and eventually cardiac standstill or asystole, the process taking 8-12 minutes.

Atypical Drowning

a. ***Dry drowning:*** About 20% of all submersion casualties are cases of dry drowning. When water enters the nasopharynx or larynx, it triggers sustained laryngeal spasm. Little or no water therefore enters the air passages or lungs and death may result from asphyxia. This is the best type of case for successful resuscitation.

b. ***Immersion syndrome (vagal inhibition):*** Death results from cardiac arrest due to vagal inhibition as a result of—(1) sudden impact with very cold water, (2) falling or diving into water with feet first or duck diving by the inexperienced, and (3) horizontal entry into water with a consequent impact on the epigastrium.

c. ***Submersion of the unconscious:*** This is possible, if the victim is an epileptic, or suffers from heart disease, especially myocardial ischaemia, or dizziness due to hypertension, or is drunk, or sustains a head injury (concussion) during the fall into water. The rupture of a cerebral aneurysm or onset of cerebral haemorrhage may also cause abrupt collapse. As a rule, in such cases, a complete picture of death by drowning is not found. Ballooning of the lungs may be absent and formation of froth may be negligible.

d. ***Near-drowning or secondary drowning syndrome:*** If a person survives from drowning the event is referred to as near-drowning, and the complications as near-drowning syndrome. It is due to hypoxic encephalopathy and secondary changes in the lungs, known as fibrosing alveolitis, as a result of infection from contaminants in inhaled water. It is characterised by rigid stiff lungs which though heavy do not appear oedematous. Microscopically, the brain shows typical ischaemic red neurons and the lungs show the characteristic features of the *adult respiratory distress syndrome (ARDS),* viz. swelling and proliferation of the alveolar lining cells, albuminous fluid in the alveoli, thickening of alveolar septa, and formation of hyaline membrane. Death occurs some hours or even days after resuscitation from the combined effects of cerebral hypoxia, pulmonary oedema, aspiration pneumonitis, electrolyte disturbances, and metabolic acidosis.

Mechanism of Drowning

When a non-swimmer falls into water, he sinks, partly owing to the force of the fall and partly owing to the weight of his body. He rises to the surface owing to natural buoyancy of his body. This is assisted by air trapped between the body and clothes and struggling movements of his limbs in order to save himself. On coming to the surface, violent attempts to breathe and shout are first made; while some air is inhaled into the lungs, water also passes into the mouth, and some of this may be aspirated into the air passages and some swallowed into stomach. The water that is aspirated into the air passages causes violent coughing and increased panic. A certain amount of air is expelled from the lungs and its place taken up by water which is drawn into the lungs. The specific gravity of body is thereby raised and the body will sink below the surface once again. Irregular movements of the limbs may once again bring it to the surface. It may again sink due to inhalation of more water. This happens several times during which air is lost from the clothing, energy reserves are exhausted, and finally the body sinks to the bottom. Convulsive movements then occur, followed by coma or suspended animation and death. During the course of drowning, respiratory efforts continue and result in filling of the air passages and lungs with water. Water into the respiratory passages acts as an irritant and stimulates secretion of mucus. Water, respiratory mucus, and air are intimately churned up due to violent respiratory efforts and produce a fine froth which blocks the alveoli.

In a few cases, a localised muscle group spasm is occasionally found in muscles of the hand and continues without undergoing the stage of primary relaxation just after death (cadaveric spasm). In such a spasm, the hand may close on weeds, mud, or sand, and if death occurs in the course of such a spasm, these substances will be retained in the tightly clenched hand, thus providing absolute proof of the person being alive prior to immersion.

Q. 13.16. Comment on the symptoms, cause of death, and fatal period in a case of drowning.

Symptoms: The subjective symptoms felt by a drowning person are auditory and visual hallucinations and possibly return to memory of past events. In some cases, there is mental confusion.

Cause of death:

1. Asphyxia is the most common cause of death and results from:
   a. Obstruction to the air passages by inhalation of fluid.
   b. Laryngeal spasm due to entry of water in nasopharynx or larynx.
2. In fresh water drowning, death results from ventricular fibrillation while in salt water drowning it is due to cardiac standstill from fulminant pulmonary oedema and associated changes.
3. Death may result from other causes, such as:
   a. Vagal inhibition due to impact with water.
   b. Hypothermia, that is, chilling by immersion.

In some cases, death may result from other conditions, such as (a) concussion or injury to any vital organ received during falling, (b) development of unconsciousness from any cause, as for example, an epileptic attack or rupture of cerebral aneurysm, (c) cardiac failure due to an old heart lesion especially myocardial ischaemia, or from exhaustion, and (d) from secondary drowning syndrome.

Therefore, in order to determine, if drowning is the sole cause of death, a complete examination of all organs is essential to rule out any disease process which may have caused or contributed to death. As for example, incapacitating or fatal trauma to the head and neck may occur without externally visible injury. Impact of the forehead on floor of the pool may cause hyperextension of the neck, loss of consciousness, and subsequent inhalation of some water. In such cases, the autopsy findings would consist of internal head injuries and haemorrhages in deep neck muscles with or without cervical vertebral fractures.

Fatal period: Death occurs in about five minutes of complete submersion. Death takes place more quickly in fresh water, about four to five minutes, as compared with eight to twelve minutes in salt water.

Q. 13.17. Describe the postmortem signs that will prove beyond doubt that death was due to drowning in a body recently recovered from water.

Q. 13.18. Write short notes on: (1) cutis anserina, (2) washer-woman's hands, (3) Gettler's test, (4) diatoms.

Q. 13.19. Give reasons: (a) froth at the nose and mouth of a victim of drowning is fine, white, lathery, and lasting, (b) in death by drowning in a well, the postmortem staining is on the head, neck, and front of the chest.

These are signs of asphyxia unless death occurred from shock, syncope, or concussion supervening immediately upon submersion. The typical appearances are seen only in recent cases; when putrefaction advances, signs of drowning are masked or entirely obliterated. The following external and internal appearances are seen in bodies examined in a fresh condition.

External appearances: If the body is recently removed from water, the clothes are wet and may be soiled by mud, sand, or weeds. The skin is wet, cold, clammy, and pale due to contraction of its blood vessels. The face may or may not be cyanotic. The eyes are half open or closed, conjunctivae congested, and pupils dilated. The postmortem hypostasis may be absent, if the body is in constant motion. When present, it is confined to head, neck, and front of the chest, lower arms, feet, and the calves, the most dependent parts, when body is immersed in water. Rigor mortis appears early due to muscular exhaustion.

Two important signs may be present, viz. (a) fine froth at the nose and mouth, and (b) rarely, the presence of weeds, mud, etc., in the tightly clenched hand. The fine froth at mouth and nose is pathognomonic of drowning. It is white or rarely blood stained, lather-like, abundant, and increases in amount with compression of the chest; even if wiped away, it gradually reappears, especially if pressure is applied to the chest (Fig. 3.13). Froth in the nose and mouth means an oedematous condition of the lungs. Such a condition is also obtained in certain poisonings, such as opioids, cocaine, barbiturates, and organophosphorus compounds. However, in these cases, froth is neither so fine nor so copious and persistent, and none of the typical signs of drowning are present. Froth is not seen when death results from laryngeal spasm. The presence of weeds, mud, sand, etc. in the tightly clenched hand, when present, is indicative of death from drowning as it indicates the victim's struggle for his life.

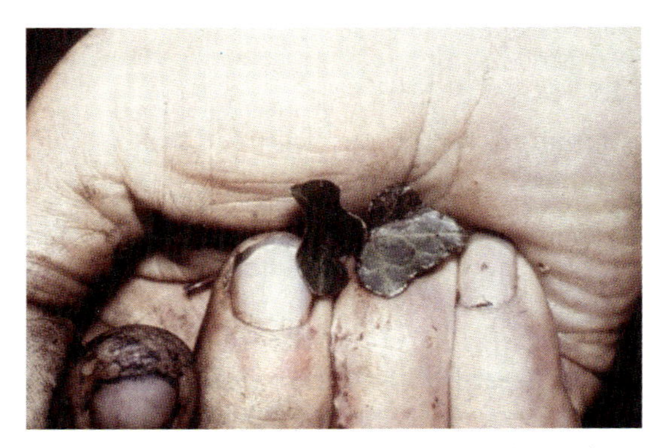

Fig. 13.13: Cadaveric spasm in drowning. (*Courtesy*: Dr SV Phanindra)

Cutis anserina or **goose skin** has **no value** as a diagnostic sign of death from drowning. It is produced by spasm of the erector pilae muscles and is due to exposure to cold water at the time of death. This sign is rarely seen in India, water being usually warm. It may be found in winter when water is cold. The skin appears granular and puckered, with hair standing on end. Extremities are mainly affected. This sign is also produced by rigor mortis of the erector pilae muscles. Likewise, retraction of the penis and scrotum also have no value as a diagnostic sign.

The skin of the finger, palms, and later the soles of the feet may be wrinkled, bleached, and sodden. It is due to osmotic action of water, on thickened epidermis. It is not a sign of death from drowning but may give some indication of the time that the body has been in water. The immersion changes in the skin became known as **hands and feet of a washer-woman** as such changes were seen on the hands and feet of women who did laundry for a living and had to keep their hands and feet in soapy water for prolonged periods. In the Western countries where machines are used for washing, the condition is seldom seen in the living and the term may no longer be understood but in parts of the world where laundry is still done manually, the name and appearance are still familiar.

Internal appearances: Asphyxial changes are seen in the body. Special attention should be devoted to:

1. Changes in the respiratory tract.
2. Biochemical changes in blood.
3. Presence and character of water in stomach and intestine.
4. Presence of diatoms in tissues.
5. Other signs or evidence indicative of death from drowning. These features are found in death from typical drowning only.

Changes in the respiratory tract: The over-all picture is described as ballooning of the lungs or *emphysema aquosum.* They are water-logged, voluminous, may completely cover the heart, and bulge out of the chest when the sternum is removed. They retain their shape and often show impressions of ribs upon them. Their surface is pale and they pit on pressure. On section, blood-stained frothy fluid streams away from cut surfaces. Tardieu spots are seldom seen, the vascular bed being compressed by water-filled alveoli. The respiratory passages usually contain fine white froth, occasionally blood-stained, and also some foreign material, such as algae, weeds, mud, sand, depending on the medium of drowning. Regurgitated particles of food may be found. As soon as putrefaction ensues, the fluid transudes from the lung into pleura, and this important sign of drowning is lost.

Due to inhalation of water and resultant obstruction to pulmonary circulation, the right heart and large veins are distended with dark blood.

The typical appearances of lungs are not found in all cases of wet drowning. The lungs in salt water drowning are heavy and more markedly water-logged. After the body has been in water for a few hours, these changes gradually disappear, and the difference in appearance of the lung in salt water drowning and fresh water drowning becomes far less clear. The degree of ballooning is less in case of pleural adhesions and pulmonary fibrosis. The lungs are relatively dry and distended, if circulation has continued for a short time after removal of the victim from water or if resuscitative measures are carried out when most of the water will be absorbed in blood.

***Biochemical changes in blood*:** Numerous laboratory criteria to diagnose drowning have been reported and accepted for a short time till experience showed their questionable value. *Gettler's test* to estimate the chloride content of blood from both sides of the heart is found to be of little value in practice. Now that modern resuscitation mixes the blood, it is of no use.

Water in stomach and intestine: The stomach often contains water which has been swallowed during the struggle for life. This may be salty or fresh, clean or dirty, and may even contain algae, weeds, mud or sand, varying according to the medium in which drowning has taken place. This is of value provided the deceased did not drink this water immediately before submersion and the body is not putrefied. This water, by peristaltic movement, may enter the small intestine and provide absolute proof of death from drowning, subject to the limitations mentioned above. In dead bodies thrown in water, it is not possible for water to get beyond the cardiac sphincter and into the stomach and intestine. However, when putrefaction sets in, cardiac and pyloric sphincters may relax and allow water with its contaminants, like algae, weeds, and sand to get into stomach and small intestine. This observation, therefore, has no significance in a putrefied body.

Diatoms: Most natural waters contain diatoms, a class of microscopic, unicellular algae, suspended in water. They have a silicaceous cell wall which resists acid digestion, heat, and putrefaction. Most species occupy a size between 10 and 80 microns. They live free or unite to form colonies drifting either in plankton or attached to mud, sand, or any other solid substrate. Only a live body with a circulation can transport diatoms from the lungs to the brain or bone marrow from where they, may be detected microscopically after suitable treatment. The value of this test is disputed by various authorities.

The current technique for isolation of diatoms involve acid digestion of tissue—commonly bone marrow, lung, blood, or kidneys—with subsequent centrifugation and washing. The final residue is examined by phase contrast microscopy (Fig. 13.14). Water taken from the presumed site of the fatality and suitable laboratory controls are also examined.

(a)

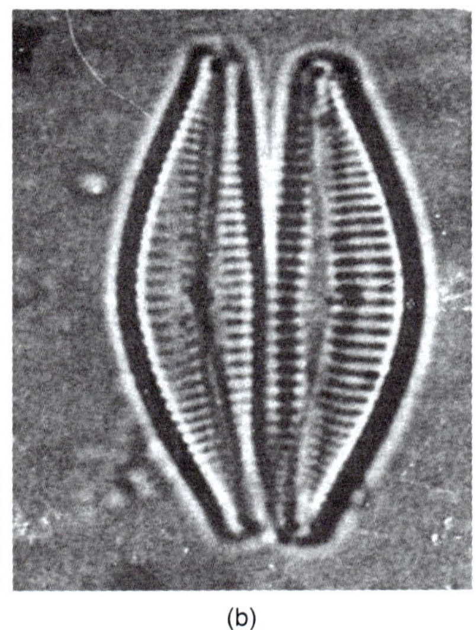

(b)

Fig. 13.14: Phase contrast photomicrograph of diatoms. (a) A diatom from a sample of water **showing chromatophobes before acid digestion.** (b) **Pair of diatoms** from a water sample after acid digestion

The diatom test is valid only if it can be shown that:

1. The deceased did not drink this water immediately before submersion.
2. The species recovered from the specimen are all present in the sample from the site of drowning.
3. The various species are present (if sufficient are found) in the same order of dominance for the admissible size range and in approximately the same proportions.

Since diatoms resist putrefaction, diatom test may have some value in examination of decomposed bodies. The test is negative in dead bodies thrown in water and in dry drowning.

Other signs: The temporal bones may be examined; some drowning victims will show haemorrhage in the middle and inner ear cavities. However, no great pathological significance should be attached to it as such haemorrhage is not peculiar to drowning alone.

In order to determine, if drowning is the sole cause of death, as mentioned earlier, it is essential to rule out any disease process that may have caused or contributed to death. As for example, a sailor, who is working on a boat, may have a myocardial infarct, lose his balance, and fall into water. Only careful dissection of coronary arteries can reveal the true condition. Incapacitating fatal trauma to head and neck may occur without externally visible signs of injury. Such a case would require careful examination of cervical vertebrae for fracture.

Toxicological studies should include estimation of blood alcohol, sedatives, and anti-epileptic drugs. The presence of therapeutic quantities of phenobarbitone and phenytoin may be the only clue to suggest that the deceased was suffering from epilepsy; absence or very low level of these drugs in a known epileptic may help to explain drowning. The haemodilution in fresh water drowning must be borne in mind while interpreting the results.

Q. 13.20. Discuss the medicolegal aspects of death due to drowning.

The medicolegal questions likely to arise in a case of drowning are:

1. Whether death was due to drowning or the body was thrown into the water after death
2. Whether drowning was suicidal, homicidal, or accidental.
3. The length of time the body was in water.

Whether death was due to drowning: In certain parts of India, and perhaps the world, it is common to throttle or kill a person or poison him and then throw his body in water to avoid detection of crime. It is essential to remember that abrasions of throttling may only become visible after the skin has begun to dry. In a typical case where death has occurred from drowning, the following signs are found:

1. Persistent, profuse, fine foamy, lathery froth at the mouth and nose.
2. Material grasped in hand which could only have been obtained from water.
3. Fine typical froth in the air passages.
4. Increased volume and oedematous condition of the lungs.
5. Findings of diatoms in tissues, especially the brain and bone marrow. The typical signs of drowning are seen only if the body is examined within a few hours after death. They are considerably modified by putrefaction. Therefore, in doubtful cases, where a definite opinion cannot be given, viscera and body fluids should be preserved for chemical analysis. Sometimes, the cause of death may have to be given as 'consistent with drowning'.

Suicide, homicide, or accident: The appearances of drowning are the same whether the deceased jumped in, was thrown in, or fell into water; the circumstances of the case will have to decide this question.

Suicide by drowning is fairly common in India especially among women, mostly on account of the problem of dowry, and more especially in sea towns, or where there are rivers or canals. Women usually make sure to tie up their clothes in such a manner that their private parts are not exposed after death. Sometimes, a woman takes her child with her. A determined suicide may tie his hands and legs together or attach weights to his body before immersion. These findings are, therefore, compatible with suicide unless it can be shown that the deceased could not have tied himself in the manner in which he was found. Likewise, a determined suicide may take poison, cut his throat, and jump into the well. However, the body in such cases should be free from marks of any injury indicating an assault or struggle. While the body is under water, it is subject to injury by fishes, frogs, crabs, and water animals, or by passing boats and such injuries may arouse suspicion of homicide. The usual signs of vital reaction, in such injuries, are absent.

Homicidal drowning is not uncommon because (1) the victim's body remains concealed for some time, (2) it is carried by water currents to a different location, and (3) by the time it is discovered, identity may be difficult due to postmortem decay and injuries from predators and passing boats. An adult may be intoxicated, drugged, or over-powered and then thrown into water.

Some miscreants attacked a person and robbed him. They then tied his hands and legs, and a heavy stone to his body, and threw it into the well to hide the crime.

While injuries may be found in a case of homicide, it is very easy to drown a person without leaving any suspicious mark behind, especially if the person is already in water, either taking bath or swimming.

George Joseph Smith was convicted of serially drowning his three wives in the bath tub and was hanged. The courtroom demonstration of the case to show the ease with which a person could be so drowned almost produced another victim—the police woman who acted as a 'bride in the bath' required resuscitation following immersion.

Accidental drownings quite common and seen in drowning of children, bathers, fishermen, dock workers, and intoxicated and epileptic subjects. Women may fall accidentally in a well while drawing water. Injuries may be sustained during such accidental falls and it may be difficult to distinguish such injuries from assault. Accidental drowning may also occur in precipitate labour, when the baby may fall into a bath tub or lavatory pan, and die.

Q. 13.21. A dead body has been recovered from water. State how you will proceed to establish the time since death.

The time since death in bodies recovered from water cannot be fixed within very close limits. However, a close approximation can be arrived at by attention to the following points:

1. If the deceased had worn a non-waterproof wrist watch, it may stop and indicate the time. Some wrist watches show the date also.
2. Temperature of the body falls rapidly. Cooling rate is approximately twice as rapid as compared to air.
3. Rigor mortis sets in early due to muscular activity prior to drowning and death.
4. Wrinkling of skin begins to appear shortly after immersion, bleaching of cuticle in about 4–8 hours, and sodden appearance of epidermis in about 18–24 hours.
5. Floating of the body due to accumulation of putrefactive gases occurs in about 18–24 hours in summer and 24–36 hours in winter in India.

6. Fleas are drowned in about 24–27 hours. If any of these insects are found on the body, they should be placed onto a watch glass and observed. If they have been immersed for a few hours, they may partially recover in about 4 hours. The majority of lice die within 12 hours but a few may live under water for 48 hours.
7. Putrefaction first begins in the upper parts of the body. It is retarded as long as the body is under water. But once the body is brought out, it sets in rapidly, in hours, especially during summer.
8. The skin of the hands and feet becomes loose and peels like a glove or stocking in about 2–4 days.
9. Adipocere formation may take place in India in about 5 to 15 days, the shortest recorded period being 3 days and 22 hours.

Q. 13.22. Discuss the difficulties in diagnosis of death from drowning.

Difficulties in diagnosis of death from drowning in a body recovered from water arise in three distinct sets of circumstances, viz.—(1) when signs of drowning are absent, (2) when injuries are present, and (3) when the body is decomposed.

Absence of signs: The signs of drowning are absent in bodies that are recovered from water or liquid medium (1) if the person died of shock or laryngeal spasm, (2) if the person was killed and then thrown into water, and (3) if the body is decomposed. (4) Minimal signs are found in submersion of the unconscious.

Injuries: Injuries found on bodies recovered from water naturally arouse suspicion. They could be suicidal cuts, homicidal wounds, or accidental while falling, as a result of striking some hard object, such as a stone or a machine fixed inside an irrigation well. However, it should be remembered that injuries sustained before or during drowning, although antemortem in nature, do not show bleeding prominently because they are being continuously washed by the surrounding water. A microscopic examination of the doubtful sites is, therefore, necessary.

The most common injuries are those caused after drowning by fishes, frogs, crabs, and water animals, or by passing boats. Animals attack the projecting parts of the body, such as eyelids, nose, ear lobules, fingers, and scrotum. Such injuries may mimic homicidal injuries and thus lead to a mistaken diagnosis, if this is not remembered. The distribution of injuries, their postmortem nature, and nibbled irregular margins help to clear the doubt in such cases.

Decomposed bodies: When putrefaction sets in, signs of drowning are masked or entirely obliterated. Fine froth is replaced by postmortem froth. The lungs undergo softening and blood-stained fluid accumulates in the pleural cavities. The stomach is usually empty; the contents usually transude out or have been forced out.

In the early stages, diagnosis of drowning is possible in some cases. Although fine froth may not be present at the nostrils, it may be found in the trachea, if it is opened *in situ* without handling. Even aquatic material may be seen there. Also, pleural cavities may contain several pints of watery fluid, often blood-tinged, as a result of transudation from voluminous lungs.

In an advanced stage of decomposition, it is not justifiable to diagnose drowning on the presence only of aquatic material in upper respiratory tract suggestive of drowning but where all other signs have disappeared. In such cases, viscera should be sent for chemical analysis. Diatoms resist putrefaction. Their presence especially in the brain and bone marrow may provide valuable evidence of death from drowning. Besides, chemical evidence of viscera may provide evidence of poisoning, if any. In the event of a negative report from chemical examination and a negative diatom test, the cause of death cannot be given. The postmortem and chemical examinations have helped to exclude fatal injuries and poisoning respectively. It could still be a case of drowning where all signs have disappeared (consistent with drowning on the basis of circumstantial evidence).

Q. 13.22a. What are the positive signs of drowning?

Positive signs of antemortem wet drowning are:

- Froth—fine, foamy, copious, lathery.
- Positive diatoms test.
- Weeds or grass in cadaveric spasm of hands, if present.
- Emphysema aqosum or hydremia of lung.
- Ribmarkings on the lungs.

14

Deaths from Starvation, Cold, and Heat

DEATHS FROM STARVATION

Q. 14.1. Discuss starvation, its symptoms and signs, cause of death and fatal period.

Starvation (protein-calorie deficiency) may result from total deprivation of food, partial deprivation of food, and from use of unsuitable food, e.g. lacking in proteins and vitamins. It may be acute or chronic. Acute starvation occurs when food has been suddenly and completely withheld, e.g. in entombment in pits, mines, or landslides; wilful withholding of food; or wilful refusal to take food. Chronic starvation occurs when there is gradual deficient supply of food, e.g. in concentration camp conditions, and famines. The number of calories required by a person depends upon his ideal weight (not current weight), his normal work, and daily activities. If a person has a desk job and lazy week ends, he will require only about 30–35 calories for every kilo of body weight. For an ideal weight of 60 kg, for example, the caloric requirement would be about 1800–2100 calories per day. If one does heavy physical work and is active at week ends, his caloric requirement would be much higher. Manifestations of starvation appear when the diet does not meet minimum caloric requirements of the body.

Symptoms and signs: In acute starvation, hunger pain is felt in the stomach, for about two days, and it is relieved by pressure. The feeling of hunger is lost thereafter but thirst becomes intense. Apathy is pronounced and fatigue comes on easily. There is progressive loss of body weight. Emaciation, due to loss of subcutaneous fat, begins to take place and bones stand out. The victim soon appears pale due to nutritional anaemia; the skin is thin, dry, wrinkled, pigmented, sometimes fissured and ulcerated due to superadded infection, and drawn tight, like parchment, over the bony prominences; the lips are dry and cracked; cheeks hollow; eyes sunken and glistening; abdomen concave; and legs and arms like broomsticks. The hair becomes dry, lustreless, and brittle; and nails brittle and ridged. The tongue is dry and doated with thick fur, and the saliva thick and scanty. The voice becomes feeble, almost a whisper. Muscular weakness progresses day by day. The body emits an offensive odour. The temperature may be subnormal, the pulse feeble, and blood pressure low due to cardiac atrophy. Oedema resulting from hypoproteinaemia usually occurs. Urine is scanty and deeply coloured, and acetone may be present. Though the bowels are constipated in the beginning, a terminal non-infective diarrhoea is common. The mind is usually clear but sometimes just before death, delirium and coma may take place. In the chronic form, the symptoms are the same as in the acute form but more drawn out and the emaciation is, therefore, much greater.

Cause of death: In acute starvation, death occurs from inanition and circulatory failure. In partial/chronic starvation, the vitality of the individual is reduced and he may die from intercurrent disease.

Fatal period: In cases of starvation, the length of time a person can survive depends upon the age, sex, environment, and the state of health of the individual. The loss of 40% of the body weight ordinarily ends in death. As a rough average, an adult may survive for about a 7–10 days without food and water, and about 50–60 days, if water is supplied. The very young and the aged suffer most from starvation. Females can withstand starvation better than males on account of more fat in their bodies. If the weather is cold and the victim exposed, death will supervene from starvation more rapidly. Healthy persons can withstand starvation better than the sick, and the obese better than the lean.

Q. 14.2. Describe the postmortem appearances in a case of death due to starvation. Mention the medicolegal implications.

The postmortem appearances vary with the length of time which elapses before death occurs. If the fatal period is a prolonged one, there may be great emaciation, and if short, the emaciation may be comparatively slight.

External appearances: The findings confirm the features already described. In addition, the muscles are flabby, and much reduced in size. The muscle fibres lose their striations and undergo granular degeneration. As the vitality of the tissues is reduced, rigor mortis comes on early and lasts a short time. Decomposition sets in early (Fig. 14.1).

Internal appearances: There is a general reduction in size and weight of all organs except the brain. It is, therefore, important to weigh them to compare with standard tables for sex and age. The organs are frequently pale, and the heart, liver, kidney, and spleen, atrophied. The lungs are pale, small, and exude very little blood when cut. Blood volume is reduced and there is marked anaemia. The omental and mesenteric fat is lost. The digestive tract is atrophic. The stomach is empty and may be no wider than the ordinary colon. The small intestine may be so thin as to be almost transparent. This appearance of the intestine is considered as **typical** of death from starvation. The large bowel may contain faecoliths and it may be affected by non-specific ulceration. In contrast to all these appearances, the gallbladder is full and distended, there having been no call for bile from the intestine. Gallstones may be present and the urinary bladder may be practically empty. The bones are demineralised and areas of rarefaction seen on X-ray. In children, the skeleton shows spinal curvature, rickets, and dental defects. In adults, progressive osteomalacia is common. Stress fractures may occur.

In criminal cases, the victims are usually females and children. It is a common phenomenon that they are given food when they are beyond survival. In such a case, food will be found in the stomach, the remains of a grim last meal given in the hope of averting suspicion.

The **medicolegal questions** likely to arise in a case of starvation are: (1) whether death was caused by starvation, and (2) whether it was suicidal, homicidal or accidental.

Whether death was caused by starvation: The characteristic postmortem appearances of starvation are: the almost complete disappearance of body fat which is not seen in any of the wasting diseases; disuse atrophy of the digestive tract, the small intestine appearing almost transparent; and the distension of the gallbladder due to accumulation of bile from lack of stimulation. **Before certifying** starvation as the cause of death, the medical officer must exclude mental or physical disease as the contributory or even sole cause for such changes and evidence should, therefore, be sought for mental disease or any other condition, such as tuberculosis, cancer, pernicious anaemia, stricture or malignancy of oesophagus, Addison's disease, diabetes, or chronic diarrhoea.

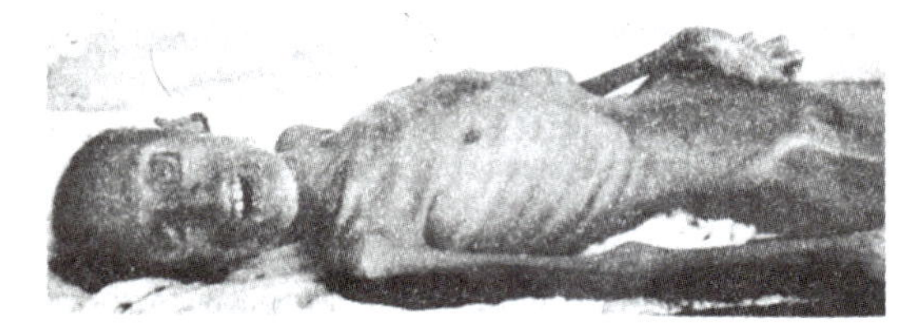

Fig. 14.1: Starvation death. This case shows typical features. The body was emaciated, the eyes were sunken and glistening, the abdomen was scaphoid, the hands and legs appeared like broomsticks, and the bony prominences were well marked. The skin was thin and dry, and the lips were cracked

Suicide, homicide or accident: Suicide as a result of complete-starvation is rare, for the person cannot usually resist the intolerable thirst or the desire for food when they are placed within his reach. However, it may occur in the mentally ill or in prisoners who may go on hunger strike. **Forcible feeding** in such cases is not an assault but quite lawful because the prisoners are under the care of the State which must take adequate steps to prevent a prisoner from injuring himself or taking his own life. The two definite *criteria for* a medical officer to advise forced feeding are loss of weight and acidosis. Repeated examinations are necessary before this decision can be arrived at. However, the Council of the World Medical Association which met in Tokyo in October 1975 views the matter rather differently. It has laid down that forcible feeding in the case of a prisoner whose capacity for rational judgement is unimpaired is not only to be deplored but is also not permissible. Occasionally, a person may decide to starve himself to death for a certain cause, in the name of public interest.

Homicidal starvation is met with in cases of illegitimate children who are done to death by depriving them of proper food and at the same time exposing them to cold. Rarely, a mother-in-law may starve her little daughter-in-law to death. Some cases occur in the old and helpless persons or in young children. The Bombay Children Act, 1948 (Bombay Act No. LXXI of 1948) provides special enactments to discourage the neglect of children. It states that whoever having the actual charge of, or control over, a child wilfully assaults, ill-treats, neglects, abandons or exposes him or causes or procures him to be assaulted, ill-treated, neglected, abandoned or exposed, or negligently fails to provide adequate food, clothes or medical aid, or lodging, for a child in a manner likely to cause such child unnecessary mental and physical suffering shall, on conviction, be punished with imprisonment of either description for a term not exceeding two years or with fine which may extend to one thousand rupees or with both. For the purpose of this Act, a child means a boy or girl who has not attained the age of 16 years. According to section 88 IPC, the infliction of reasonable punishment on a child for proper reason, presumably by way of a correction, shall not be deemed to be an offence. In most cases of criminal neglect and starvation, there is no absolute deprivation of food, and the victim lingers on for much longer periods, the fatal issue being precipitated by some intercurrent disease.

Bimla Devi was married to Om Prakash in October 1951. The relations between them were strained in 1953 and she went to her brother's place where she stayed for a year. On an assurance of no ill-treatment, she went to her husband's house, where she was chronically starved and ill-treated. On many occasions, she was denied food for days together being given only gram-husk with water at intervals of five to six days. On 5 June 1956, she managed to escape from the house and went to the Civil Hospital, Ludhiana. The lady doctor and Bimla Devi's brother informed the police about Bimla Devi's serious condition and the magistrate recorded her statement. Om Prakash was convicted under section 307 IPC for an attempt to commit murder. In judgement, it was stated that the act towards commission of murder need not be a penultimate act: the course of conduct adopted by the accused in regularly starving his wife in order to accelerate her end constitutes an attempt to commit murder. (State of Punjab vs Om Prakash 1961 (2) Crim L. Jnl. 1961, 63, 848; Supreme Court, AIR, 1961, 1982).

In cases of accident, the circumstances are self-explanatory, such as famine, shipwreck, entombment in mines, or some disease, such as stricture of the oesophagus. These cases have little medicolegal significance.

DEATHS FROM COLD

Q. 14.3. Give a brief account of the effects of cold on the human body, and the postmortem appearances of a case of death from cold.

The effect of cold upon the human body may be local or general, and the severity of such effects depends mainly on the intensity of the cold and duration of exposure. The other factors are the age, sex, health, habits, and clothing of the individual. A moist cold atmosphere is more damaging than a dry cold one. The human body can withstand considerable cold, if it is well nourished and suitably clothed. Fatigue, indulgence in alcohol, hunger, lack of sleep and anything that causes mental depression increase the danger. Adults withstand cold better than children and old persons. Owing to a greater deposit of subcutaneous fat, women are likely to endure cold longer and better than men. In India, death from cold occurs in the higher regions of the Himalayas, north Bihar, UP and Kashmir almost every year. Exposure to cold is a common method of infanticide in temperate climates, death occurring rapidly.

Symptoms and signs: As cold grips the body, metabolism is lowered. The respiratory rate is slowed, the heart rate is slowed, and there is a marked fall in peripheral circulation in order to maintain core body temperature by minimising heat loss. The surface of the body, therefore, becomes pale (vasospasm). Oxygen does not readily dissociate with the result that anoxic changes occur in the tissues and transudation of fluid may take place due to capillary endothelial damage. Muscles become gradually stiff and contract with difficulty. On prolonged exposure, the vasomotor control is paralysed, the capillaries dilate, and the exposed parts of the body appear red. The body temperature falls to a level which cannot be registered on a clinical thermometer. A standard clinical thermometer does not register temperature below 35°C. At 21°C, vital processes cannot function and death ensues.

Dilatation of capillaries results in stasis of blood and thrombosis. The blood vessels are thereby blocked and this leads to tissue necrosis. The exposed parts, such as the tip of the nose, ear, fingers and toes are the worst to be affected. Continued exposure to low temperature without adequate protection may lead to hypothermia (a condition in which the body temperature is less than 35°C). Death is preceded by a sense of fatigue and drowsiness (due to cerebral anaemia). Sometimes, convulsions and delirium precede death.

The type of cold injury that results from exposure to different climatic conditions include: (1) frost bite, (2) trench foot, (3) immersion foot, and (4) hypothermia.

Frost bite: This refers to tissue necrosis from vascular spasm or thrombosis. It is the result of local effect of cold on exposed parts of the body, such as the tip of the nose, ears, fingers and toes. The skin on exposed parts is patchy-red with a general pallor elsewhere.

Trench foot: This refers to a form of cold injury to the foot occurring after sustained exposure to cold under moist conditions, as typically experienced by soldiers during winter warfare, especially in trenches.

Immersion foot: This refers to a form of cold injury to the foot occurring after prolonged exposure to cold water, as typically experienced in Arctic areas and in warfare.

Hypothermia: This is a condition resulting from continued exposure to a low-temperature environment, without adequate precautions. The body temperature is less than 35°C. The diagnostic findings are: icy cold skin, generalised muscular stiffness, slow pulse, low blood pressure, and depressed reflexes. In extreme cases, suspended animation may occur. Since the chilly environment markedly reduces oxygen requirements of vital centres, successful resuscitation is possible after periods that would have proved fatal much sooner under ordinary circumstances.

Cause of death: The blood parts with its oxygen less rapidly at low temperatures. Metabolism is, therefore, lowered. When the body reaches a temperature of 21°C, vital processes cease to function. Death may also occur from pulmonary oedema.

Treatment: The gradual restoration of warmth to the patient, attention to pH and electrolyte balance, and treatment of inflammatory conditions (if they arise after reaction has set in), are the main aims of therapy.

Postmortem appearances: These are not very characteristic either externally or internally. The skin of exposed parts often acquires a red florid colour in patches, and generalised pallor is seen elsewhere. The patches are commonly seen over the large joints, e.g. elbows, hips, and knees. Localised changes, like frost bite or immersion foot, may be seen. The internal vessels are engorged with blood which tends to be pink in appearance. There may be pulmonary oedema.

In prolonged hypothermia, the vitality of tissues may so deteriorate that gastric or intestinal erosions, pancreatic or hepatic necroses, may develop from small vessel coagulopathy. A variable degree of pancreatic fat necrosis is a constant finding. The body may be completely stiff from freezing and it is only after thawing that normal rigor mortis occurs. Postmortem lividity is bright red in colour due to non-dissociation of oxygen. These are the only postmortem appearances and they may all be absent. A diagnosis will have to be made from the lack of any other cause of death and from the actual circumstances of the case.

Medicolegal aspects: Suicide need hardly be taken into account. Cases of homicide occur by exposure of little children, the aged or the mentally ill to inclement weather. The newborns, especially those born clandestinely, are particularly susceptible. Death from cold is usually accidental, as in the cases of drunkards falling asleep in the snow or people lost in snow-drifts.

Q. 14.3a. What is paradoxical undressing?

The scientific medical literature includes references to a condition commonly known as **paradoxical undressing.** It appears that a small number persons who have been exposed to prolonged cold experience a feeling of intense warmth or heat when the tightly constricted subcutaneous vessels dilate and relax in the minutes immediately prior to death. The terminal vasodilation is supposed to be due to the blood vessels giving up their attempt to maintain the core body temperature by constriction any longer. Due to the resulting vasodilation and consequent feeling of sudden warmth, the individual may remove all or part of the clothing. The body temperature falls still more and death results. Thus, the victim of exposure may be found undressed in the cold. And, if the victim is a female, it may give rise to a false suspicion of sexual assault.

DEATHS FROM HEAT

Q.14.4. Describe the manifestations of exposure of a human body to high temperature. Write a brief note on postmortem appearances from heat stroke, and its medicolegal implications.

Exposure to high temperature causes three clinical conditions, viz.; (1) heat cramps, (2) heat exhaustion, and (3) heat stroke. Soidiers on the march, furnace men, stokers, miners, workers in bakeries, laundries, sugar refineries, and in general those working in confined spaces with hot and humid atmosphere may be affected in one way or another. Alcoholism, fatigue, hunger, lack of sleep, lack of adequate fluid intake, and anything that causes mental depression are important predisposing factors.

Heat cramps: These are painful spasms of voluntary muscles which follow strenuous work in a hot atmosphere, as for instance in a furnace man, stoker or miner. These cramps are caused by loss of water and salt from profuse perspiration. The mortality rate in this syndrome is low.

Heat exhaustion (heat collapse, heat syncope, heat prostration): This is a condition of collapse without any elevation of body temperature, which follows exposure to hot and humid atmosphere. The syndrome is characterised by prostration accompanied by evidence of peripheral vascular collapse, such as poor venous return, facial pallor, and hypotension. It occurs in those persons who are susceptible to heat. Thus, travelling standing in an overcrowded smoking carriage may prove more than a person can deal with. There may be a preliminary circulatory stimulation, as evidenced by subjective sensation of heat, flushed face, throbbing temples, and scanty perspiration, followed by collapse. As a general rule, the patient recovers and death is unusual from uncomplicated heat exhaustion.

Heat stroke (hyperpyrexia, sunstroke, systemic hyperthermia, thermic fever): This is attributed to an impaired functioning of the heat regulating mechanism caused by failure of cutaneous circulation and sweating. It is due to prolonged exposure to the sun's infrared rays, and/or to hot atmosphere. A temperature of 32°C with 100% humidity may lead to heat stroke. The onset may be sudden but usually there are prodromal symptoms, viz. headache, nausea, vomiting, dizziness, weakness in the legs, and excessive desire to micturate. Sudden unconsciousness supervenes and the victim falls and hence the condition is known as heat stroke. Suspended animation may occur. The face is flushed, and the skin is hot and dry, as if sweat cooling has failed. The pulse is full and rapid, respirations are stertorous, pupils contracted, and the temperature rises as high as 43°C or over, and hence the condition is called hyperpyrexia. Delirium and convulsions may precede death. The mortality rate in this condition is relatively high, death resulting from paralysis of the medullary heat regulating centre. The fatal period varies from a few minutes to three days.

Treatment: Heat cramps can be prevented by giving saline water to drink. Sedatives may be necessary to relieve the pain due to cramps. In heat exhaustion, the patient usually recovers, if he receives supportive treatment, such as glucose, saline and sodium bicarbonate, in a cool place, and is actively cooled down. Prevention of heat stroke is achieved by regulating temperature and humidity of the atmosphere in work-place, and avoidance of overburdening of clothes. Treatment aims at reducing the temperature by every means available, such as cool or ice water sponging, till the body temperature *drops to 38°C,* when energetic cooling may stop. Temperature measurements must continue at appropriate intervals for several hours to guard against secondary hyperpyrexia, until the regulatory mechanism regains control.

Postmortem appearances: When death occurs from heat stroke, there are no characteristic necropsy findings. The temperature remains high after death or may rise further (postmortem caloricity). Dead bodies with eyes open will show such changes as drying of the cornea, and pitting and sinking of the eyeballs within a few hours after death, giving sometimes an appearance of avulsion of the eyes. Rigor mortis sets in early and disappears early. Putrefaction is rapid. Lividity is marked. Degeneration of neurons in the cerebral cortex, cerebellum, and basal ganglia, is common. Visceral congestion is usually well marked and petechial haemorrhages are found in the skin, viscera, and in the walls of the third and the fourth ventricles and the aqueduct. Pulmonary oedema is sometimes found.

Since intemperate indulgence in alcohol often precipitates a fatal attack during the heat wave, blood should be preserved for alcohol estimation.

Medicolegal aspects: There is no medicolegal importance attached to deaths from heat stroke except in those cases when a worker dies at his work place where adequate facilities for temperature regulation are not provided, adequate fluid intake somehow impeded, and compensation is being claimed. The condition is accidental and diagnosed by the circumstances of the case, e.g. the prevailing temperature, occupation, symptoms of the attack, and the absence of any other cause of death.

The most frightening **new findings about sun exposure** link it to rapid and unexpected increases in the incidence of skin cancer and one sun burn may be enough to bring it on.

15

Anaphylactic Deaths

Q. 15.1. Define anaphylaxis. Describe the autopsy appearance of a case of death due to anaphylactic shock.

Anaphylactic shock is defined as a fatal condition occurring rapidly after exposure to an antigen and producing clinical features of profound generalised shock, acute respiratory distress, asphyxia, severe hypotension, and death. While occurring most frequently with intravenous or intramuscular administration in highly sensitive persons, it can also occur after ingestion or inhalation of the antigenic substance. The common offending agents are bee or wasp stings; serum or drug therapy in previously sensitised persons; injection of penicillin or local anaesthetics, and desensitisation injections with pollen extracts.

If death is suspected to be due to anaphylactic shock, a detailed history should be obtained as regards the possible cause and history of allergy to any known pollens, etc. Autopsy should be done as soon as possible as laryngeal oedema recedes after death and may not be observed otherwise. Many of the following features will be seen. These may be grouped under: (1) external examination, (2) internal examination, and (3) microscopic findings.

External Examination

The site of injection or sting must be sought, photographed, and excised with a 5 cm margin of skin and underlying tissue for laboratory examination of antigen. There is usually local swelling of the involved tissues.

There may be oedema of face, eyelids, conjunctivae, and lips. Asphyxial changes include subconjunctival haemorrhages and froth in the mouth and nostrils. Generalised petechial haemorrhages in the skin are usually present due to vasodilatory and increased permeability effects of histamine and other vasoactive amines.

Internal Examination

There may be oedema of the glottis and epiglottis spreading to the vocal cords and causing laryngeal obstruction. This oedema recedes soon after death. The rima glottidis together with epiglottis should be photographed from above for a permanent record.

The tracheobronchial tree contains frothy fluid and mucus. The lungs are heavier than usual, greatly distended, and show alternating areas of pink emphysema and plum-coloured collapse. The visceral pleura often shows scattered petechial haemorrhages. On cut section, the lung exudes copious frothy haemorrhagic fluid. Features of bronchospasm are often found: The bronchi may appear constricted, their lumen narrow, and filled with frothy, blood-tinged fluid.

Petechial haemorrhages may be found on the visceral pericardium and the pericardial sac may contain a moderate amount of straw-coloured transudate. The right heart is dilated due to acute pulmonary failure. A specimen of blood should be retained for immunological studies (antibody titre) and for drug levels.

There is acute congestion of abdominal viscera. Oedema or haemorrhage is sometimes found around one or both renal pelves. The lymph nodes at the porta hepatis and in the mesentery may be enlarged and hyperaemic.

The brain shows diffuse congestion often with petechial haemorrhages in the white matter.

Dr Rita Vij, 27 years of age, was working as a gynaecology registrar at the JJ Hospital, Bombay. She died of anaphylactic shock in about 5 minutes after a long-acting penicillin (Penidure) injection was given intramuscularly. She had been suffering from rheumatic heart disease and had undergone surgery to replace her mitral valve in July 1988. Since then she was being treated regularly with injection of longacting penicillin intramuscularly. When this injection was given on 10 December 1988 at the OPD, she started to gasp for breath (bronchial constriction—histamine effect) and began sweating profusely. She could not be saved despite resuscitative measures which included mouth to mouth respiration, oxygen, cardiac massage, adrenaline and steroid injections, etc. At postmortem, submucous haemorrhages in the respiratory tract; distended, heavy lungs; and petechial haemorrhages in the pericardium and white matter of the brain were found.

Microscopic Findings

When autopsy is not carried out quickly, laryngeal oedema recedes; however, submucosal laryngeal oedema and eosinophilic infiltration can still be seen on microscopic examination.

Histology of the lungs confirms diffuse or focal pulmonary distension (acute emphysema) alternating with collapse and bronchiolar constriction (histamine effect). Pulmonary arterioles and capillaries show marked dilatation.

Hyperaemia and occasional haemorrhages may be seen in the Peyer's patches of the small intestine, lymph nodes of the porta hepatis, and lymph nodes of the mesentery. The spleen shows eosinophilic leucocytes in red pulp.

Q. 15.2. Describe sudden death in bronchial asthma.

Bronchial asthma: Chronic bronchial asthma is associated with sudden death in a small percentage (~5%) of all cases of chronic asthma.

- Sudden death can occur without a prolonged attack (acute asthmatic paroxysm).
- The frequency of sudden death in these cases appears to be increased at night or in the early morning.
- The known triggers of asthmatic attacks are — allergens, both air-borne and food (house dust, mites, peanuts)
- Infections (viral or bacterial)
- Occupational exposure to allergens
- Certain drugs (e.g. aspirin)
- Certain gases (e.g. sulphur dioxide, ozone).
- Psychological stress
- Exertion/exercise
- Cold air
- Death results due to reduction of flow with ventilation perfusion mismatches which lead to decreased oxygenation of the blood, an elevation in the pCO_2, and right ventricular overload.
- Decreased airflow occurs as a result of allergic release of histamine and other vasoactive compounds from inflammatory cells (eosinophils and mast cells), which in turn cause bronchial smooth muscle contraction, and intrabronchial mucous secretion.

- In non-resuscitated individuals, autopsy usually shows hyperexpanded, puffy, pale lungs, with abundant mucous plugging of the bronchi (central and peripheral). In cases where CPR is done typical picture may not be seen.
- Microscopic examination: The lungs show characteristic changes of chronic asthma, with increased numbers of eosinophils present in the bronchial mucosa, submucosa, and/or peribronchiolar tissue. Representative section should be taken from all areas of the bron-chial tree (central, mid, and peripheral), for histopathology at autopsy.

Section 4

16 Mechanical Injuries—General Aspects

For convenience, injuries are discussed under the headings: (1) mechanical injuries, (2) firearm injuries, (3) transportation injuries, and (4) thermal injuries including chemical injuries, and injuries due to electricity, lightning, and explosions.

An injury or a wound means a solution or disruption of the anatomical continuity of any of the tissues of the body. Under section 44 IPC, an injury, is defined as any harm whatever illegally caused to any person in body, mind, reputation, or property. Injuries caused by application of physical violence to the body are known as mechanical injuries.

MECHANISM OF INJURY

The main factors responsible for a mechanical injury are: (1) force, (2) area over which it acts, (3) specific effect of the force, and (4) time taken over which the kinetic energy is transferred.

1. According to the laws of physics, force $= 1/2\, mv^2$, where m is the mass and v the velocity, the damage from the latter being much greater on account of its being squared. It means that a brick gently pressed against the scalp will cause no injury but the same brick falling from a height on to the head may smash the skull.
2. The area over which the force acts is also important; the damage to the tissues is much greater, if the narrow edge of a plank is used to strike the skin rather than the flat surface. The resulting damage depends on—(i) the effect of the force, e.g. compression, traction, torsion, tearing, etc., (ii) the nature of the tissue involved, e.g. skin, muscle, lung, liver, brain, bone, etc., and (iii) the movement as a whole of the part that is struck. As for example, the skin when struck with a blunt weapon often escapes injury though the underlying tissues may be seriously damaged.
3. Blast effect (compression) from explosion may do little harm to the muscle but may rupture the tympanic membrane, lung, or intestine. A blow to the chest may bend the ribs without fracture but may damage the thoracic viscera. A torsion force may leave the thigh fat unaffected but cause a spiral fracture of the femur.
4. In firearm injuries, if a bullet exits, it means that it has not transferred all its energy to produce the wounding effect. The dum-dum bullets and the explosive tipped bullets which expand on striking the target and do not exit from the body transfer all their energy and produce greater wounding effect. The function of seat belts in motor vehicles is to lessen the effect of an impact in the event of a collision. This is achieved by stretching of the belt fabric which slows down the impact and spreads its effect over a wider area.

Classification

Depending on how they are caused, e.g. by blunt force, sharp weapon, or firearm, they are classified as follows. Simple names which are used in evidence are shown in parenthesis:

1. Abrasions (scratches, grazes, imprint or pressure marks)
2. Bruises (contusions)
3. Lacerations (splits, tears)
4. Fractures
5. Incised wounds (cuts)
6. Stab wounds
7. Firearm injuries (gunshot)

In medicolegal work, the following three technical terms based on interpretation of the nature of injuries are commonly used irrespective of the weapon causing them. Their description is, therefore, included in this chapter for convenience.

a. Defence wounds
b. Self-inflicted wounds
c. Injury patterns

Firearm injuries form a class by themselves and are, therefore, discussed separately. Fractures are discussed under Chapter 20 'Regional Injuries'.

From a purely medical as well as medico-legal standpoint, the ability to distinguish between various types of injuries is of paramount importance. As for example, a doctor may be confronted by a semi-conscious young female patient, arrived as an emergency, lying on a stretcher, with a linear injury to her forehead. If this injury is due to a sharp instrument, such as a razor, there is little to be done except some suturing. If the linear injury was due to her being struck forcefully by the edge of a sheet of plywood blown from a building by the gust of wind, the problem is quite different and obviously involves wound contamination, blunt force injury, potential for skull fracture and neck injury, plus the need to consider possible brain injury with or without subdural bleeding. The conclusion is obvious: you are not in a position to treat the patient appropriately until you are able to distinguish a linear sharp injury from a linear blunt injury and, to make matters worse the place, they are most frequently found and mistaken for one another, is in surface areas which have bone beneath.

ABRASIONS

Q. 16.1. Define an abrasion. Give the classification mentioning the significance in relation to its various types.

An abrasion is a injury involving only the superficial layers of the skin. It is caused by friction and/or pressure between the skin and some rough object or surface. It bleeds very slightly, heals rapidly in a few days, and leaves no scar. Depending upon the manner in which they are caused, abrasions are classified as: (1) scratches, (2) grazes, and (3) imprint, pressure, or contact abrasions.

A **scratch** is a linear injury produced by a sharp object, such as a pin, thorn, or finger nail, running across the skin. The object causing the scratch carries the torn epithelium in front of it. The direction of injury is, therefore, indicated by a sharp edge initially and heaped up epithelium at the end.

A **graze** is an injury which is produced when a broad surface of skin slides or scraps against a rough surface. It is also known as *brush or friction burn* because it is caused by the frictional force of rubbing against a surface and resembles a burn, after drying. It is commonly found in traffic accidents, especially when the body has been dragged. The direction of injury is indicated by the serrated border initially and heaped up epithelium at the end. Such abrasions are usually contaminated with grit. Abrasions caused by a fall on the ground are also contaminated with grit but are generally found over bony prominences of elbows, front of knees, and hands (Fig. 16.1).

An **imprint, pressure** or **contact abrasion,** is an injury which is produced as a result of direct impact or pressure of or contact with some object which, crushing the cuticle, stamps a reproduction of its shape and surface marking upon the skin. It is, therefore, also known as a *patterned abrasion.* It is usually associated with a bruise of the surrounding area. Examples are: ligature

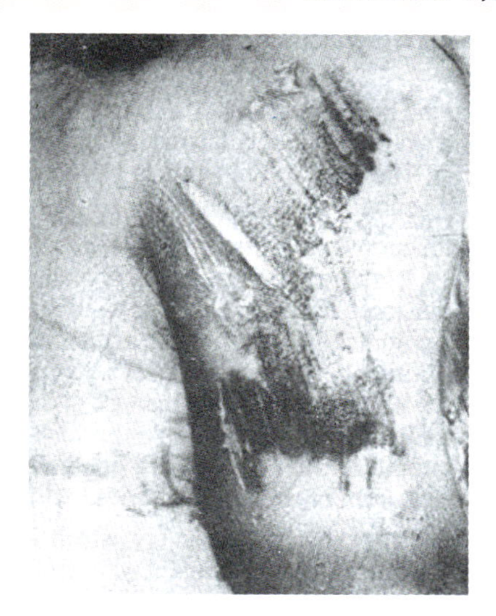

Fig. 16.1: Abrasions (grazes). This 35-year-old man was involved in a vehicular accident. Graze type abrasions over the right shoulder and arm are seen indicating that the body was dragged

mark in hanging and strangulation; nail and thumb marks in throttling (manual strangulation); teeth marks in biting; whip marks in beating; radiator, grill, or tyre marks in vehicular accidents; and muzzle marks in gunshot injuries (Fig. 16.2).

SN tyre tread marks are caused by tyre passing over that part of the body. Generally on the back or front of abdomen. They are a replica of the passing tyre and so the design helps in identifying the type of tyre. It is an abrasion and contusion and is often associated with internal lacerations and fractures.

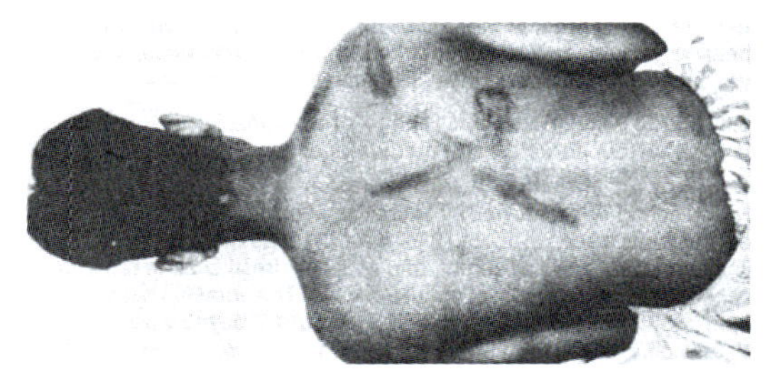

Fig. 16.2: Multiple linear **imprint abrasions.** These injuries are inflicted with a cane. Note the two parallel haemorrhages (contusions) for each impact. These abrasions follow the contours of the body and, therefore, provide information about the nature of the weapon (flexible linear object) causing the injury in this case. (*Courtesy*: Dr NK Patoria)

Q. 16.2. Write short notes on: (1) age of an abrasion, (2) antemortem and postmortem abrasions, (3) medicolegal significance of abrasions.

Age of an abrasion: A fresh abrasion is bright red in colour. An abrasion during life is followed by exudation of blood, serum or lymph which dries and forms a scab in about 12–24 hours. A scab is a collection of injured epithelium, dried blood or serum, and lymph. A fresh scab is red in colour but becomes reddish brown in about 2–3 days. The abrasion heals from the periphery by new growth of epithelium in about 4–7 days by which time the scab falls off. Healing is complete by about 10 days depending on the size of the abrasion and the area involved.

Antemortem and postmortem abrasions: Abrasions in the living may readily *escape notice,* if the victim is examined in poor light, or if they are only slight, or *if the skin is wet.* There are classic instances in which individuals have been immersed in water after throttling (manual strangulation) and abrasions have not been visible until skin began to dry after removal from water. An antemortem abrasion appears reddish brown and its margins are blurred due to vital reaction. A postmortem abrasion may appear dark brown or even black, and parchment-like, as a result of the drying of the moist exposed surface, when it may be mistaken for burns. However, its margins may be sharply defined due to absence of vital reaction. In case of doubt, histological examination for evidence of a vital reaction may help.

Abrasions should also be **distinguished from:** (1) postmortem injuries caused by ants or insects and marine animals in drowned persons, (2) excoriation of skin caused by excreta, and (3) pressure sores.

Ants or insects attack the exposed parts and mostly moist areas of the body, such as face, arms, axilla, genitals, and groin. Marine animals mostly attack the exposed areas and projecting parts of the body, such as lips, nose, ears, fingers, scrotum, etc. All these injuries are without a vital reaction and their edges appear nibbled. Excoriation of skin by excreta is generally seen in infants (nappy rash) and its distribution is self-explanatory. The distribution of pressure sores is also self-explanatory.

Medicolegal aspects: Important points to consider in evaluation of abrasions include:

1. Site of impact and possibility of internal injury
2. Identification of the object causing the injury
3. Cause of injury
4. Direction of injury
5. Time of injury
6. Possibility of infection, and
7. Confusion with burns.

Site of impact: The presence of an abrasion suggests the site of external impact. In some cases, it may be the only external sign of a serious internal injury, e.g. rupture of viscera due to a kick on the abdomen, or runover injuries.

Identification of the object: A patterned abrasion permits the identification of the object causing the injury, e.g. ligature mark in hanging, tyre marks in vehicular accidents, and teeth marks in biting.

Cause of injury: The site of an abrasion helps to determine the cause of an injury. Abrasions are found on the neck in throttling (manual strangulation), around the nose and mouth in smothering, around the face, thighs and genitals in rape, around the anus in sodomy, and on the bony processes in a fall.

Direction of injury: This may be surmised on examination with a hand lens to show the sharp edge or serrated border initially and heaped up epithelium at the end.

Time of injury: This can be surmised from the estimated age of the abrasion.

Possibility of infection: In surviving individuals, the abrasion may act as an entry site for infection. The type of contamination, viz, grease, mud, etc., may indicate the crime scene.

Confusion with burns: Abrasions tend to dry and darken after death, when they may be confused with burns.

BRUISES (CONTUSIONS)

Q. 16.3. Define a bruise. Give its classification and special characteristics. Discuss the factors modifying the appearance of a bruise.

A bruise can be defined as blunt force machanical trauma causing disruption of vessels and collection of blood in tissues or organs with the surface intact, i.e. skin, mucus membrane, etc.

A bruise (contusion) signifies haemorrhage into the skin, the subcutaneous tissues, or deeper tissues. It is due to an infiltration or extravasation (extra = outside; vasa = vessel) of blood into the tissues, following rupture of small vessels, as a result of application of blunt force, e.g. stick, stone, kick, or fist. Usually, there is no loss of continuity of the skin. Depending upon its location, it is classified as: (1) intradermal, (2) subcutaneous and (3) deep.

Intradermal bruise: When a bruise is made by impact with a patterned object, the haemorrhage may lie in the immediate subepidermal layer and its pattern may correspond to the form of the object or the weapon causing it, e.g. whips, canes, bicycle chain, motor tyre, etc.

Subcutaneous bruise: The usual bruise from a blunt impact is situated in the subcutaneous tissues. It is somewhat blurred at the edges and raised above the skin surface due to infiltration of blood in the subcutaneous tissues. It usually appears soon after injury and may vary in size from a small pin-head bleeding to a large localised collection of blood known as a *haematoma.*

Deep bruise: This signifies bleeding deeper to the subcutaneous tissues and some swelling may be apparent when the opposite limb or part of the body is compared with the injured area. It may take hours or one or two days to appear at the surface. Therefore, *living persons who have been assaulted should be examined again after an interval of one or two days* when they may show bruising which may be initially suspected by tenderness on pressure or slight swelling. Infrared photography may demonstrate such bruises in early stages and provide useful evidence for production in court.

Some deep bruises may not appear externally at all. Though the terms bruise and contusion are used synonymously, the term bruise implies that the lesion is visible through the skin and the term contusion implies that bleeding can be anywhere in the body. Therefore, when bleeding occurs in viscera, such as spleen, liver, mesentery, and tissues, such as muscles, and it is not visible nor does it appear externally at all, it should appropriately be called a contusion, rather than a deep bruise.

An extensive haemorrhage in the tissues *may fail to show* at the surface especially in plump persons and battered babies; it can be revealed by incision of the suspicious areas of the body at autopsy, e.g. sacral and iliac prominences, spine, and shoulder blades. Bruises and abrasions or lacerations are often found together since all of them are caused by blunt objects, though in the case of laceration, the skin is split.

Characteristics: It must be remembered that *a bruise may not always be present at the site of impact as is the case with an abrasion* since blood may gravitate and appear at an entirely different area and such a bruise is called **ectopic bruise**. However, if an abrasion is present at the site of impact, it will signify the exact position of the application of force. As a general rule, the greater the force or violence used, the more extensive is the bruise. However, as the bruise spreads due to continued extravasation and consequently occupies a wider area, it is not possible to assess the area of impact and severity of violence in such cases.

Though the extent of bruising is generally related to the causative agent and amount of violence, bruising should be *interpreted with caution* as certain factors will modify the effect.

Factors modifying the appearance of a bruise: These are—(1) site of injury, (2) vascularity of the part, (3) age, (4) sex, (5) colour of skin, (6) natural disease, and (7) gravitational shifting of blood.

Site of injury: The important points to be considered here are—(a) sites over bones, and (b) looseness of tissues.

Bruising is more marked in sites overlying bones without intervention of fibrous tissue, e.g. over tibia. Since the abdominal wall is not supported by bones, it is rare to find bruising of the abdominal wall and its absence gives no indication of the possible injury to viscera.

It is easier for blood to escape in loose tissues and fat. Therefore, bruising is more common in lax tissues around the eyes, face, and genitalia, and rarely found on the scalp, sole of the foot, and palm of the hand. A boxer or an athlete with his good muscle tone can sustain, without bruising, blows which would leave an alcoholic extensively bruised.

Vascularity of the part: The greater the vascularity of the injured part, the greater is the bruising and vice versa.

Age: Children and old people tend to bruise easily. In the former, it is due to looseness and delicacy of the skin; while in the latter, it is due to loss of elasticity of skin and blood vessels. This means that the severity of injury in these cases is not always proportional to the extent of bruising.

Sex: Women tend to bruise easily because of the delicacy of tissues and more subcutaneous fat.

Colour of skin: Bruising is more evident in fair skinned persons than in dark skinned ones.

Natural disease: Bruising may be caused by slight injuries in persons suffering from nutritional deficiencies, e.g. scurvy, blood disorders, such as leukaemia, and in the aged with atherosclerosis. The obese, alcoholics, and those in poor physical condition, are prone to bruise easily.

Gravitational shifting of blood: The fascial planes at the point of impact may prevent blood from torn vessels reaching the surface. This may result in a bruise appearing in a place remote from the point of injury. For instance, a bruise round the tissues of the eye and eyelids *(spectacle haematoma, black eye)* may result from—(a) a blow to the orbit, (b) fractured orbital roof, (c) a blow to the forehead, or (d) a fall on the vertex. A bruise behind the ear (Battle's sign) may result from fall on the vertex or fracture of the base of the skull rather than a direct blow behind the ear. A fractured femur may cause a bruise on the outer side of the lower thigh. A blow to outer part of the thigh may cause bruising round the knee. A blow to the calf muscles of the leg may cause a bruise round the ankle.

Q. 16.4. Write short notes on: (1) colour changes in a bruise, (2) age of a bruise, (3) antemortem and postmortem bruising, (4) bruise and postmortem lividity, (5) medicolegal significance of bruises including comments on artificial bruising.

Colour changes in a bruise: After a bruise has appeared, it tends to get smaller from periphery to centre and passes through a series of colour changes. These are due to disintegration of red blood corpuscles by haemolysis and breakdown of haemoglobin into the pigments haemosiderin, haematoidin, and bilirubin, by the action of tissue enzymes and histiocytes. Haemosiderin is an iron containing pigment and is dark blue or brown in colour. Haematoidin is an iron-free pigment and is greenish in colour. Bilirubin is yellow in colour.

A fresh bruise is red at first. This colour changes from red (haemoglobin) to blue (deoxygenated haemoglobin) in a day, bluish black to brown (haemosiderin) in about two to four days, green (haematoidin) in about five to seven days, and yellow (bilirubin) in about seven to ten days. The yellow colour slowly fades and the skin regains its normal colour in about 14 to 15 days, when the pigments are removed by phagocytes. The time sequence is very variable.

Red to blue—one day

Bluish-black to brown—two to four days

5–7 days 7–10 days 14–15 days
↑ ↑ ↑
Green ⟶ yellow ⟶ normal skin colour

Subconjunctival haemorrhage *(black eye)* does not show similar colour changes owing to haemoglobin being kept oxygenated by air. It is red at first, then becomes yellow, and finally disappears.

An approximate **age of a bruise** may be determined either from the colour changes or occasionally by histology. The colour changes reflect the natural healing process and depend not only on the size and situation of a bruise but also the age and physique of the person and presence or absence of disease. Since these factors are very variable, one often finds the presence of several colours in a bruised area on a number of occasions. Any opinion about the age of bruise from colour changes should, therefore, be given with great caution unless the bruise is obviously very recent or fresh. For histological examination, a number of sections should be taken so as to have a truly average and representative sampling of tissue.

Antemortem and postmortem bruising: As there is no internal pressure in the small vessels that have to be ruptured, the size of the postmortem bruise is small in relation to the degree of force used. It can be differentiated from antemortem bruise by its sharp well-defined margins in contrast to antemortem bruise whose margins are indistinct and which is elevated. Blanching test is positive in lividity. In bruise, the test is negative.

The signs indicative of antemortem production of bruising are: (1) swelling of tissues, (2) discolouration of skin with blurred margins, and (3) extravasation of blood into the true skin and subcutaneous tissues with infiltration. In a doubtful case, microscopic examination should be made to verify the presence of infiltrated blood. A bruise is likely to be disfigured by putrefaction and then it is difficult to differentiate between a bruise caused during life and that caused immediately after death.

Bruise and postmortem lividity: In certain cases, isolated patches of lividity remain separate from large areas of lividity and may resemble antemortem bruises. The principal differences between bruise and lividity are already tabulated in an earlier chapter. Lividity may be blanched till about six hours after death by continuously applied pressure which forces the blood out of surface vessels. The antemortem bruise cannot be blanched by this test. In any case, where there is doubt, or where the bruise is on a dependent part, it is advisable to remove a portion for microscopic examination.

Medicolegal aspects: Bruises provide information in regard to:

1. Identification of the object causing the injury in some cases
2. Degree of violence
3. Cause of injury
4. Time of injury, and
5. Possibility of infection.

They are of less value than abrasions because:

a. They may not appear at the site of injury due to gravitational shifting of blood.
b. A deep bruise may take hours or one or two days to appear, or may not appear externally at all.
c. Its size may not correspond to the severity of violence due to continued extravasation.
d. They do not indicate the direction of force.

Identification of the object: In some cases, the external pattern of a bruise may be relatively precise and correspond in form to the object or weapon causing the injury, e.g. whips, canes, chains, etc. In such cases, the two parallel marks enable one to determine the nature of the object. In addition, bruising from flexible objects, like cycle chains, follows the contours of the body (Fig. 16.3).

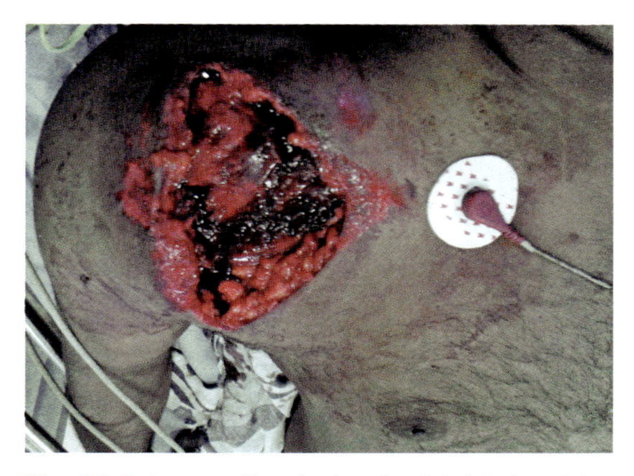

Fig. 16.3: Laceration in front of right shoulder (*Courtesy*: Dr R Sivakumar)

Degree of violence: Though a bruise is usually a simple injury, it may prove fatal when it involves an important internal organ, such as heart or lung even without visible injury to the chest wall. Multiple bruises, though individually trivial, may result in death due to shock and internal haemorrhage.

Cause of injury: The distribution of bruises may provide information about the cause of injury, e.g. around the neck in throttling (manual strangulation), around the nose and mouth in smothering, around the arms or legs in restraint; around the thighs and genitals in rape, around the anus in sodomy, and on the arms and face during a struggle.

Time of injury: The colour changes in a bruise may be of help to determine the age of injury.

Possibility of infection: The effused blood may serve as a nidus for bacterial infection.

Self-inflicted, homicidal, and accidental bruises: Self-inflicted bruises are rare. To substantiate a false charge of assault, **artificial bruises or pseudo-bruises** are sometimes caused by the application of irritant substances, like marking nut juice, calotropis, root of plumbago on parts within easy reach. These can be differentiated from true bruises by the presence of vesicles and inflammation. The irritant substance may be discovered on laboratory examination. Homicidal bruising is common. Their shape and size may indicate the object used for violence. Accidental bruises are common. Their position, arrangement, and circumstances surrounding the case normally clear up the matter.

LACERATIONS

Q. 16.5. What is a laceration? Give the classification mentioning the significance of its various types. Briefly discuss the characteristics of lacerations.

A laceration is a wound in which the skin, mucosa, or underlying tissues are torn as a result of application of blunt force. If the underlying tissue is a rigid structure, e.g. skull beneath the scalp, laceration occurs readily and may simulate an incised wound; when underlying tissue is flexible, e.g. cheek, soft parts of limbs, and abdomen, laceration occurs less readily and is often jagged and irregular. Thus, while a blow over the cheek bone may cause a laceration, an identical blow on the cheek itself may cause only a bruise. When the blunt force exceeds the tensile strength and elasticity of an internal organ, e.g. liver, internal laceration may result without any external tear on the surface.

Depending upon the manner of their production, they are **classified** into:

1. Split laceration (due to blunt perpendicular impact)
2. Stretch laceration (tangential impact)
3. Avulsion (horizontal impact)
4. Tears (irregularly directed impact)
5. Internal laceration (impact exceeding the tensile strength and elasticity of an internal tissue or organ)

Split' laceration (incised-like or incised-looking wound): Split lacerations are usually found in parts overlying bones without much tissue in between. They are, therefore, commonly seen on scalp, face, hands, and lower legs. They are caused by a blunt and almost perpendicular impact. The injury is due to crushing of the skin between two hard objects, viz. underlying bone and the object responsible for injury. The result is a linear split in the skin and the injury may simulate an incised wound (Fig. 16.4). However, on close examination with a magnifying lens, the injury shows all the characteristics of a lacerated wound. When such a wound is on the scalp, hair round about the injury must be shaved to ensure proper examination.

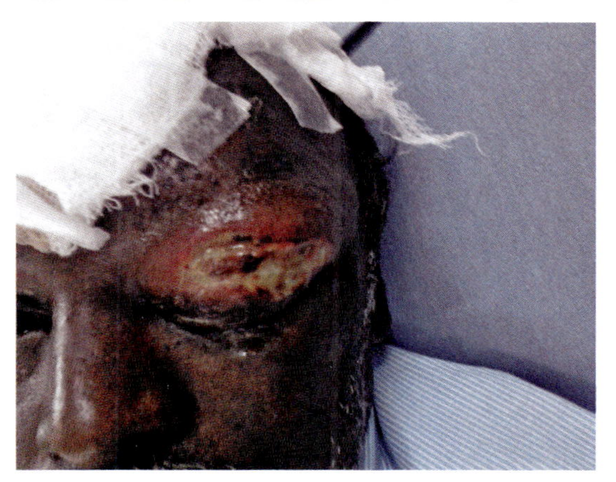

Fig. 16.4: Infected wound in left eyelid. (*Courtesy*: Dr R Sivakumar)

Stretch laceration: This is due to over-stretching of the skin till it splits and produces a flap, the flap indicating the direction of the force. Such an injury is commonly produced by a blunt tangential impact, e.g. laceration of the scalp when the head strikes a motor car wind screen, or by run-over motor vehicle injuries. It is also produced when sudden deformity of a bone occurs after a fracture. Small stretch lacerations may occur from glancing kicks with a boot.

Avulsion: This is due to grinding compression of tissues to such an extent as to separate the skin from deeper structures (degloving of the skin) and crush the muscles underneath. The injury results from a more or less horizontal crushing impact as is commonly produced by a lorry wheel passing over a limb (refer Chapter 21 on Transportation Injuries) or by machinery (Fig. 16.5).

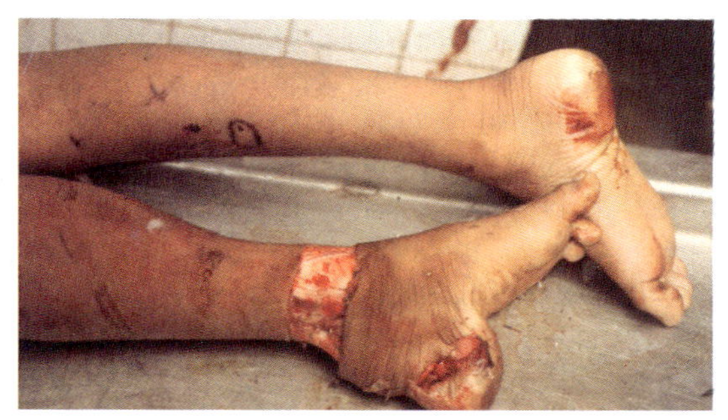

Fig. 16.5: Lacerated wound—avulsion

Tears: These are due to impact against irregular or sharp objects, e.g. motor car door handles, blows from broken bottles, or falls on earthen-ware pots. The injury results from irregular tearing of the skin and tissues. When there is doubt regarding the cause of a tear, a search for foreign material in the wound depth may give the clue.

Internal laceration: When the blunt force exceeds the tensile strength and elasticity of an internal organ or tissue, laceration may result in such organ without any surface tear; in such a case, there may or may not be an abrasion or bruise at the impact site.

The **characteristics** of lacerations are as follows: the edges are ragged, irregular, *and frequently bruised;* the margins are commonly abraded and the abraded area corresponds to that of the impacting surface; the deeper tissues are unevenly divided with the result that strands of tissues are seen to be crossing the deeper parts of the lacerations (tissue bridging); hair follicles, if present, are seen to have been crushed; blood vessels are usually crushed so that external haemorrhage is not pronounced; and foreign material is usually found in the wound.

In most cases, the lacerated surface appears depressed with the convexity pointing in the direction of the force. A hammer produces a crescentic laceration, a blunt pointed metal rod produces a stellate laceration, and a stick produces a linear laceration with a split end resembling Y. The healing of a lacerated wound is followed by a conspicuous scar.

Lacerations from linear objects, such as sticks are sometimes confused with those from falls but can be differentiated from shelving, e.g. one margin over-riding the other as a result of angulation or glancing. Such lacerations are also associated with linear parallel abrasions along the margin or margins of the wound. The direction of shelving of the margins indicates the direction of the blow.

Lacerated wounds produced by blows from stones, bricks, bottles, or earthen-ware pots, and falls on rock frequently contain foreign material and this is of great value in investigation.

A victim sustained a clean cut knife injury during a quarrel. The injury was attributed by defence to a fall on some crockery that was lying nearby. This allegation was inconsistent with the clean and even appearance of the wound margins. The assailant in whose possession the knife was found was convicted.

Wounds caused by marine animals, like fish, frogs, turtles, crabs, etc., in bodies recovered from water should cause no difficulty in identification. Besides being postmortem injuries, they are mainly restricted to projecting parts of the body, such as fingers, lips, nose, ears, scrotum, etc., and their edges appear nibbled. Antemortem lacerations, when the survival in water is long enough, are characterised by vital reaction, bruising, eversion of edges, and gaping of margins (Fig. 16.6).

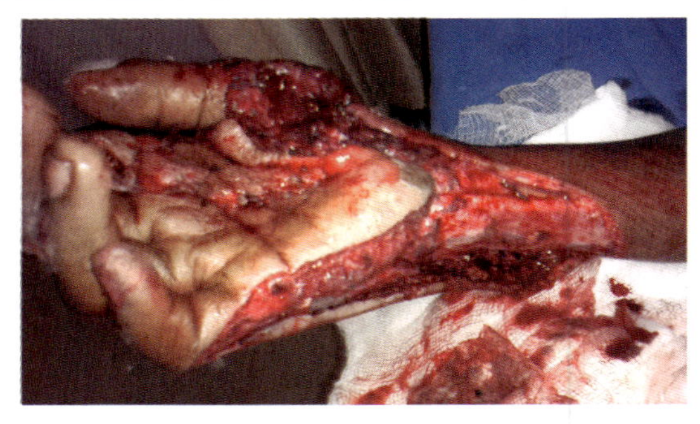

Fig. 16.6: Avulsion laceration. (*Courtesy*: Dr R Sivakumar)

Q. 16.6. Discuss the medicolegal factors that you will keep in mind in the examination of a victim of lacerated injuries.

In the examination of a victim who is alleged to have received blunt (lacerated) injuries, the following essentials should be kept in mind:

1. However, severe a blunt impact may be, external evidence of injury may be frequently minimal or absent even though massive internal injuries may be present. As for example, a kick or punch on the upper abdomen may injure the duodenum or pancreas and cause death within a few days from resultant peritonitis. Injury to abdominal wall is seldom visible in such cases. A forceful impact to the precordial region may cause sudden cessation of effective heart beat sometimes without demonstrable injury to the chest wall.
2. Tissues which are crushed will bleed less and may give rise to infection, if the victim survives.
3. Inspection into the depth of a lacerated wound may reveal foreign material or trace evidence, such as pieces of paint, grease, grit, etc., indicating the agent or surface responsible for injury.
4. If possible, a search of the scene may help to find an object that is blood-stained or some evidence of contact with the tissue, i.e. blood, hair or tissue fragments.
5. It should be remembered that bedsores may sometimes be confused with lacerations. Their typical location and the circumstances in which they are found are self-explanatory.
6. Suicidal lacerations are rare because they cause much pain during their infliction. However, a mental patient may occasionally inflict such injuries on himself, during the active phase of illness.

7. Homicidal lacerations are produced by a wide range of objects. The usual site is the head. A careful assessment is necessary. Sometimes, the pattern of injury may suggest the shape of the blunt weapon.

Dr Barowcliff records a case of a woman who was attacked with a car jack on the head and the car then driven into a tree to simulate an accident. Three medical practitioners who saw the deceased accepted that the injuries were due to a road traffic accident. Postmortem examination, however, revealed a pattern and severity of injury *not consistent with* the minor damage to the vehicle.

8. Commonly, lacerations are accidental and involve the exposed parts of one side of the body and their severity is *consistent with* the circumstances of the case.

INCISED WOUNDS

Q. 16.7. Define an incised wound. What are its characteristics? Briefly discuss its medicolegal significance. Include a note on: (1) hesitation cuts, (2) chop wounds.

An incised wound is an injury caused by a weapon with a sharp cutting edge when it is drawn across the skin. Such weapons include knives or objects, such as jagged portions of metal or pieces of broken glass and the like. The injury varies in sharpness according to the character of the weapon and the nature of stroke made.

The length of an incised wound is greater than its depth. The margins are clean-cut and may be straight or jagged depending on the shape of the cutting instrument but there is no bruising of the wound edges. All tissues are clean and the blood vessels are cut across and not torn, bleeding profuse, and not confined as in a bruise. Sometimes, the underlying bones show superficial cuts (Fig. 16.7). Observation of subcutaneous tissues may sometimes give a better indication of the true nature of the wound than the skin margins alone (refer to lacerated wounds—page 218).

The incised wound is normally straight but may be irregular, if inflicted over an area of lax tissue, like scrotum. It is then known as a wrinkled wound. The term *wrinkled wound* is generally used to describe a situation wherein a single sweeping cut or motion of a sharp instrument contacts the skin in more than one or several locations in sequence as it passes by. This may occur, if the skin is in folds or is deeply creased, if the individual is obese, or if clothing intervenes. Under such circumstances, the number of cuts, slashes or thrusts reported by a witness may not match the findings. A closely similar situation is seen when the arm is bent at the elbow and a cut sustained. The two cuts, one on the arm and other on forearm, appear unrelated and separate when the arm is by the side during treat-ment or at autopsy.

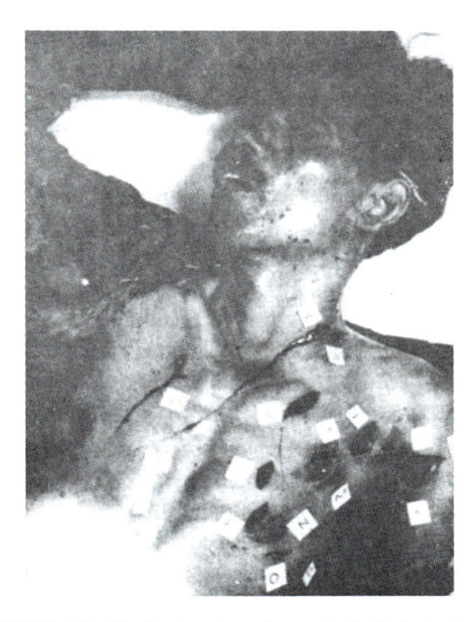

Fig. 16.7: Multiple incised and stab injuries. At the commencement of incised injuries, the tissues are divided more deeply than at the termination where the incision tails off to a superficial wound. The tailing thus signifies the direction of the wound. The stab wounds show elliptical appearances and clean cut margins indicating that the weapon was double edged and sharp. (*Courtesy*: Dr V David Edward)

Incised wounds tend to gape owing to retraction of the skin and there is eversion of margins, especially if the wound lies across the axis of a limb. As a result of gaping, the width of the wound is greater than the width of the blade of the weapon causing it and the wound appears spindle-shaped. Deep incised wounds of limbs may produce permanent paralysis and wasting of muscles due to severed nerves.

At the commencement of a cut, the tissues are divided more deeply than at its termination, where, as a rule, the incision tails off to a superficial skin wound. **Tailing** of the wound signifies the direction.

If the blade of a cutting instrument enters obliquely, the margins are bevelled, and a flap is raised, if the blade enters horizontally. In a homicidal assault, this may help to indicate the relative position of the assailant and victim. Cuts in clothes do not always coincide with the wound, especially if the clothing is loose since it may be drawn forward by the weapon and cut at quite a different level, or folded and then cut.

In incised wounds made by curved weapons, such as a sickle, the pointed end of instrument may make a stab or puncture and the blade a cut wound, sometimes with intact skin in between. If the blade has a dull serrated edge instead of a cutting edge, it would cause a laceration. Wounds from jagged portion of metal or pieces of broken glass have the appearance of incised wounds but are usually irregular and their edges are generally bruised.

If the edges of an uncomplicated incised wound are approximated surgically, it usually heals by primary union with linear scar formation. If the wound does not extend into a body cavity or involve an internal organ, traumatic shock is not common.

Hesitation cuts derive their name from the hesitation with which these incisions are inflicted by a person intending to commit suicide by a cutting instrument. He usually makes preliminary cuts before gathering sufficient courage to make a final deeper incision. He is in effect trying to find out how painful it would be to make a deeper and fatal cut. The preliminary cuts, also known as *tentative cuts,* are generally small, multiple, superficial, somewhat parallel, and usually skin deep. They are seen near and at the commencement of the incised wound and may merge with the main incision. Such incisions are commonly found in suicidal cut throat and in suicidal cuts on wrists. A right-handed person will hold the razor in his right hand and will start incising from left to right. The tailing of the wound is, therefore, seen on the right side. Hesitation cuts are not found in homicidal assaults.

Medicolegal significance: Incised wound may be homicidal, suicidal, or more rarely accidental, the identification being based upon situation, character, and circumstances. Generally, the presence of incised wound indicates *intent* and they should, therefore, be described very carefully.

Incised wounds with hesitation cuts indicate suicide. They are generally seen at sites of election, viz. wrists, elbows, groins, and throat. They are nearly always multiple, superimposed, and with varying depth. The doctor treating such a case should bear in mind the possibility of prior suicidal attempts or gestures and consider the need for psychiatric help to avert the possibility of future attempts.

Homicidal incised wounds are without hesitation cuts. They are often multiple and involve face, neck, and genitals. They are usually associated with *defence injuries.* Incised wounds of neck may cause death either from massive haemorrhage due to cut carotid artery or from air embolism due to partial severance of jugular vein.

Incised wounds may be caused accidentally by falls on broken tumblers or glass bottles and the like. They may then appear irregular in shape but close examination with a hand lens will reveal that they are clean cut and their edges are everted. In traffic injuries, accidental incised wounds that are caused by pieces of broken glass are seen on exposed body parts. Fragments of glass may be found in such wounds. Such fragments provide valuable evidence.

Incised wounds on palm indicate defence injuries. Multiple superficial incised wounds on accessible parts of the body indicate fabricated injuries.

Chop wounds (chop lacerations) are caused by a blow with a moderately sharp splitting edge of a fairly heavy weapon, like hatchet, an axe, a sabre, or a cleaver, striking at a body part overlying bone (Fig. 16.8). The dimensions of such wounds correspond with the cross-section of the penetrating blade. The margins are moderately sharp and the edges may show abrasions and bruising with marked destruction of underlying tissues and organs. If the edge of the weapon is blunt, margins are irregular.

Chop wounds are commonly seen on exposed and easily accessible parts of the body, such as head, face, neck, shoulders, and extremities, and are accompanied by injuries to underlying bone also. The majority of such injuries are homicidal, few are accidental due to machinery, and very rarely they could be suicidal. Sometimes, chop wounds are found on bodies recovered from water. They could be due to propellers of passing boats or homicidal. If the soft tissues show haemorrhagic infiltration, one can be sure that it is an antemortem injury. Absence of bleeding does not indicate that the injury is postmortem because the injury is being continuously washed by surrounding water and may not show ecchymosis. Microscopic examination in such cases is usually of help.

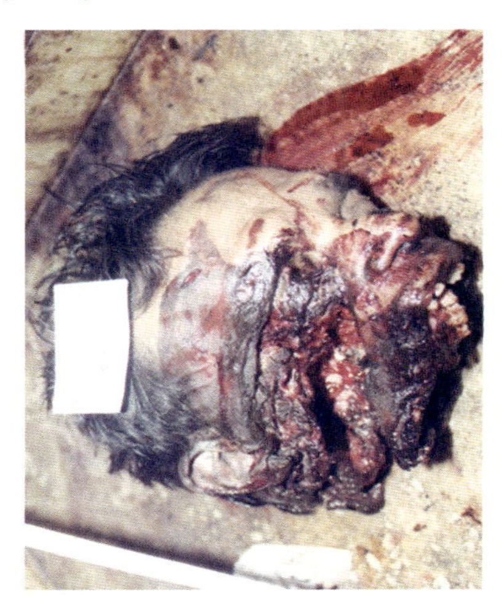

Fig. 16.8: Multiple chop wounds

STAB WOUNDS

Q. 16.8. Define a stab wound. How will you describe it? Mention its medicolegal importance at appropriate places. By way of example, briefly describe an imaginary stab wound of thorax or abdomen.

A stab wound *(punctured wound)* is an injury caused by a more or less pointed weapon when it is driven in through the skin and its depth is the greatest dimension. Such weapons include a knife, dagger, needle, spear, arrow, scissors, bitchva, ice pick, etc. When the weapon enters a body cavity, such as the thorax or abdomen, the injury is termed a *penetrating wound.* When the weapon, after penetrating the body tissues, comes out from the other side making an exit wound, the injury is termed a *perforating wound* (transfixing wound).

The **description** of a stab wound should include: (1) wound of entry—shape, size, margins, and presence of foreign bodies, if any, (2) depth and direction, and (3) wound of exit, if present (Figs 16.9 to 16.12).

Wound of entry: The wound of entry is generally bigger than the wound of exit because the stabbing weapon so often has a tapering tip. Clothes may be pushed into the wound of entry.

The *shape* may correspond to the blade of the weapon used. Thus, a knife with one sharp cutting edge and other blunt edge may produce a wedge-shaped injury or injury with one end pointed and other end blunt or with a small tear; a double-edged knife may produce an elliptical injury; a round pointed weapon a circular injury; and a pointed square-shaped weapon may produce a cruciate injury. The occurrence of stab wounds in a paired pattern suggests the use of a two-pronged sharp weapon, such as a fork, pair of scissors, etc. It is important to keep this in mind as the number of wounds observed will exceed the number of reported blows or thrusts.

During stabbing, there is often considerable relative movement between the assailant and victim. The shape of the entry wound may, therefore, not correspond to the weapon used. It may have an atypical appearance, e.g. triangular or cruciate, if the knife is twisted during withdrawal from the tissues. Such atypical appearance may also result when the injury is caused by a relatively blunt-edged weapon, such as a bayonet, due to simultaneous cutting and tearing of the skin during the process of stabbing. Repetition of a stab wound without complete withdrawal may "double" the entry wound. Scrimmage enlargement is a term occasionally used to imply extension of a wound due to motion of the weapon or body against the cutting edge.

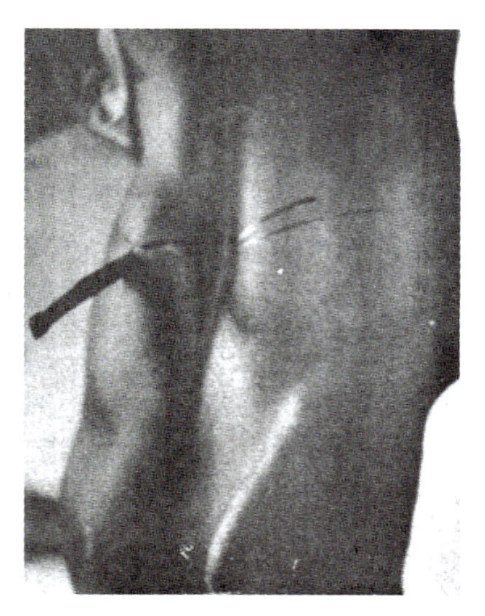

Fig. 16.9: Stab wound—left flank. The weapon is seen intact. Spleen injured. Splenectomy done. Patient survived. In a case like this, it is obvious that the shape of the wound would correspond to the weapon used for stabbing. Scratch abrasion are seen on the right flank. (*Courtesy*: Dr MN Ganapathy)

Fig. 16.10: Stab wound—lung. The shape of wound in case of injuries to internal viscera generally corresponds to the type of penetrating weapon causing the injury. (*Courtesy*: Dr MN Ganapathy)

Wounds of internal viscera correspond to the type of penetrating weapon used but their shape in many cases is modified by the muscular and elastic fibres in the capsule and framework of the organ.

To indicate the general character of the instrument responsible for the stab wound, the terms incised or lacerated should be used preferably in the description of such wounds, e.g. punctured-incised, punctured-lacerated, penetrating-incised, penetrating-lacerated, and perforating-incised or perforating-lacerated.

The size does not necessarily correspond to the breadth or length of the blade. Generally, the skin aperture is little smaller than the breadth of the weapon due to elasticity of the skin. However, a homicidal stab wound is rarely inflicted without some cutting taking place at the same time. The knife may be pulled upwards or downwards during insertion or withdrawal, thereby causing an injury which is broader than the widest part of the blade. An opinion about the size of the blade should, therefore, be given with great care. The least twisted or split entry wound is a guide to the maximum breadth of the blade, provided the wound edges are apposed.

The margins of the entry wound are clean cut and the edges inverted. Some abrading and/or bruising of the edges may be seen due to the thrusting force or if the weapon is not quite sharp, or if the weapon is tapering and then becomes larger in cross-section.

When a weapon, such as a knife or dagger, is thrust into the tissues with considerable force, the skin surrounding the wound may be abraded or bruised by the hilt (guard) of the weapon. Such a condition suggests that the blade has been completely inserted. It is imperative in such cases that the suspected knife, if available, be examined by the medical officer performing the autopsy to decide the compatibility of the shape of the abrasion or bruise around the stab wound with the hilt of the weapon in question.

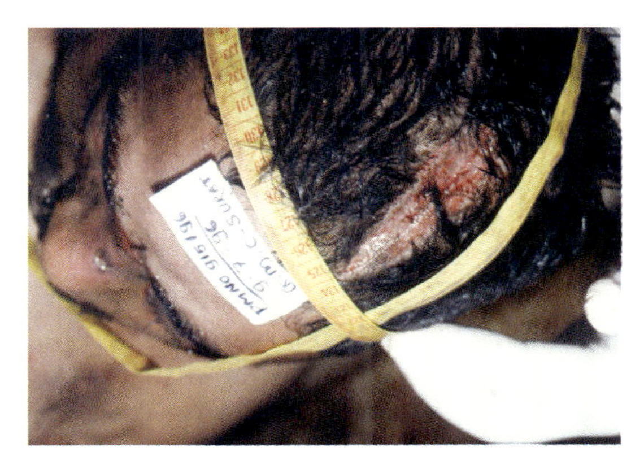

Fig. 16.11: Stitched scalp wound

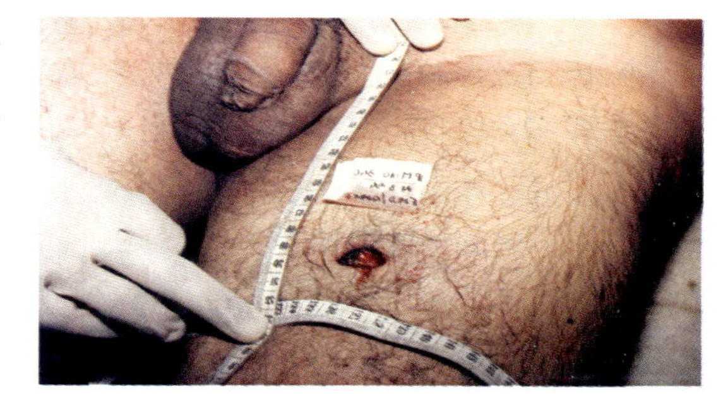

Fig. 16.12: Stab wound—thigh

When a punctured wound is produced by a fall on some sharp object, such as a glass pot or sharp stone, the wound will have bruised edges and a part of the *foreign body* may be found broken off in the wound.

Punctured wounds made by pins and needles, especially on concealed parts of the body, may not be obvious. They are, therefore, sometimes known as *concealed puncture wounds* and are commonly found in such parts of the body as fontanelle, inner canthus of the eye, up the nostrils, down the throat, nape of the neck, axilla, vagina, rectum, etc. They should be carefully looked for especially in cases of infanticide where no other cause of death is obvious. Death may result in an infant, if a pin or needle is pushed into the brain through the fontanelle, or inner canthus of the eye, or into the medulla through the nape of the neck. Pointed instruments may enter the peritoneal cavity through the vagina during attempts at abortion and may cause death.

Depth and direction: The external examination of a stab wound gives no indication of its depth, direction, or internal injuries. The most vital injury may lie beneath a trivial looking entry wound.

In a quarrel between a son and his aged father, the son threw an ice pick at the father which penetrated his left chest. There was hardly any external bleeding from the trivial looking entry wound. The old man complained of distress in the chest and died before the doctor arrived. The cause of death was cardiac tamponade.

The *depth* of a stab wound is greater than its length and breadth. It does not depend on the length of the blade alone but is also dependent on the thrusting force. It may correspond to the length of the blade but is greater, if the injury is caused on the part of the body that yields, such as the abdomen. It is generally not possible to measure the depth accurately due to the presence of blood clots or injury to internal viscera. It is not advisable to probe a stab wound in the living or to pull out a knife from a stab wound, if located in the chest or near a large blood vessel, lest it may dislodge a blood clot and cause fresh bleeding. If the weapon is broken in the depth of a wound, especially when it encounters a bone or cartilage, the broken part may be found in the wound and provide valuable evidence either for the prosecution, or to prove the cause of accidental injury. It is, therefore, desirable to X-ray all stab wounds in search for a possible broken part of a weapon or foreign body. At autopsy, when the stab wound is seen to go through cartilage or bone, the cut surface must be saved in formalin for possible tool mark comparison with a suspect weapon.

The *direction* of a stab wound can be ascertained by drawing a line joining the wound of entry and wound of exit. If the weapon enters obliquely, it will bevel the side from which it enters and produce a wound with an overhanging margin, and thus indicate the direction. This is helpful to determine the relative position of the victim and assailant.

A single track is usually found in relation to a single entry wound of stabbing but in certain cases where the weapon is partially withdrawn and then inserted in another direction, two or more tracks may be found in relation to a single external opening.

The depth and direction can be determined accurately only at autopsy by meticulous dissection, in layers. However, it is not easy in fully clothed (like woolen suit) or when wound is on front abdomen.

Stab wounds and cuts will either gape or remain slit-shaped depending on their location with reference to *cleavage lines of Langer*. These are lines of tension determined by the direction of the elastic and collagenous fibres in the dermis of the skin. A cut which is inflicted across the natural lines of tension will tend to gape while one which is inflicted parallel to these lines will remain slit-shaped and relatively undistorted. Therefore, in case of a gaping stab wound, it is necessary to approximate the edges manually to record the dimensions. Restoration of a stab wound to its actual size usually shows the resulting slit to be considerably longer than the oval-shaped wound present on the body. This is of great importance to counter a possible later claim that the knife in question could not have produced a stab wound of such small dimensions. *Such reconstruction should be a normal routine in the examination of every stab wound.*

Wound of exit: This is smaller, if a tapering weapon is used and its edges are everted.

Example: Stab wound of thorax

The entry wound is a punctured-incised wound, elliptical in shape. It is located in the left upper thorax above and lateral to the nipple, 15 inches below the top of the head, and 7 inches to the left of the midline. It is 1 inch long (1.25 inches when the edges are apposed) and 1/4 inch wide at the skin surface. It is horizontally oriented. The lateral corner is blunted and the medial corner acutely angulated. There is no abrasion or bruising at the wound margin.

The track is 5 inches deep, evenly cut, directed from left to right, front to back, and angulated slightly downward. No tissue bridging is noted. The track perforates the chest wall through the third intercostal space, perforates the lingula of the upper lobe of the left lung, the pericardial sac, and penetrates the heart perforating the left ventricular wall. (Detailed description of wounds may be included here). The entire wound track is infiltrated with blood and 1000 ml of liquid and clotted blood is found in the left chest cavity. There is no exit wound.

Example: Stab wound of abdomen

The entry wound is a punctured-incised wound, elliptical in shape. It is located in the right upper quadrant of abdomen, 26 inches below the top of the head, and 3 inches to the right of the midline. It is 1 inch long (1.3 inches when the edges are apposed) and 1/3 inch wide at the skin surface. It is vertically oriented. The superior corner is blunt and the inferior corner acutely angulated. There is no abrasion or bruising at the wound margin.

The track is 3 inches deep, evenly cut, directed from front to back, slightly left to right, and slightly downward. No tissue bridging is noted. The track perforates the abdominal wall and penetrates the liver. (Detailed description of wounds may be included here). The entire wound track is infiltrated with blood and 1000 ml of liquid and clotted blood is found in the peritoneal cavity. There is no exit wound. So it is called as penetrating stab wound.

Q. 16.9. What factors will you keep in mind in the examination of a victim of a stab injury, from a medicolegal standpoint? And what inferences are possible therefrom?

In the examination of a victim of a stab wound, the following essentials should be kept in mind:

1. The effects of stabbing will vary with the direction and depth of penetration of structures involved. Considerable volitional activity may be possible before collapsing from a potentially fatal wound. There are cases on record where a victim with a penetrating wound of the heart or great vessel has continued his fight with the assailant, chased him, or has gone to bring a weapon to retaliate, before succumbing from fatal blood loss.
2. The position of the wounds in relation to the defects in the clothes may give some indication about the position of the victim at the time of injury. If the arm was raised in defence at the time of attack, a hole in clothing at the back will be at a higher level. It will appear to lie at a much lower level when the arm is lying by the side of the body after death. Similarly, a skin wound may not correspond with the underlying injuries. If the arm was raised in defence, as in the above instance, the wound track would spare the scapula which would have otherwise sustained an injury, if the arm was by the side. The track of blood stains may also indicate, if the victim was standing or lying prone. Hence the clothing forms an integral part of the evaluation and should be saved in suspicious or criminal cases.
3. In assessing the depth of penetration, it is essential to remember that organs of the victim lying on an operation table or in a cadaver lying supine on a mortuary table are not in the same position as that in an upright living person.
4. Multiple stab wounds in a male victim suggest a homosexual assault when associated with sexual mutilation.
5. Homicidal stab wounds are frequently associated with defence wounds unless the victim is taken unawares or his powers of resistance impaired by drink, drugs, debility or very old age.
6. If the victim is admitted to a hospital after a stab injury, there is every possibility of the stab injury being surgically altered or an additional therapeutic stab injury instituted by way of a drainage tube, thus confusing autopsy interpretation, unless the medical officer performing the autopsy consults the treating surgeon and/or reviews the victim's chart.

It is interesting to know that in a majority of homicidal stabbings, the assailant says that the victim ran over a knife and sustained a fatal injury. In such an event, the appearance and site of wounds on the body and clothes may help to determine the position of the victim at the time of attack. The track of the wound may not match. A wound caused by running over a knife is more or less horizontal. And, the presence or absence of defence injuries may give out the real picture.

Stab wounds may be suicidal, homicidal, or accidental. Suicidal stab wounds of the thorax are situated almost exclusively over the heart area. *Hara-kiri* is an unusual form of suicide where the abdomen is boldly punctured by a short sword in a sitting position resulting in one large fatal wound, causing sudden evisceration of internal organs resulting in sudden fall of intra-abdominal pressure, followed by collapse, and death. Stab wounds over the abdomen, trunk, and limbs, other than over the heart, are suggestive of homicide. Stab wounds on the back are almost always homicidal. Punctured wounds may be caused accidentally from falls while a person is in the act of running with a pointed instrument in his hand or pocket. Such wounds may also be caused by running over a knife, or falling upon sharp pointed objects, such as broken pieces of glass. The absence of defence wounds and the circumstances of accident clarify the situation.

From a careful examination of a stab wound, it may be possible to determine:

1. The nature of the weapon, single-edged, double-edged, paired, round, pointed stone, or broken glass
2. The approximate dimensions of the weapon
3. The thrusting force from the depth of the wound
4. The position of the assailant and victim from the direction of the wound
5. The identity of the weapon, if a broken piece is found in the wound
6. Volitional activity
7. The nature of injury, e.g. homicide, accident, or suicide
8. A stab wound is a converging wound and a fire arm injury is a diverging one.

Q. 16.10. Tabulate the salient features of lacerated wounds, incised wounds, and stab wounds.

Salient features of lacerated, incised and stab wounds are given in Table 16.1.

Table 16.1: Salient features of lacerated, incised and stab wounds

	Lacerations	*Incised wounds*	*Stab wounds*
1. Production	Blunt force	Sharp cutting force	More or less pointed objects
2. Site	Usually over bony prominences	Anywhere	Anywhere but usually chest, abdomen, or neck
3. Shape	Usually irregular	Linear or spindle-shaped	Depends on the weapon
4. Margins	Irregular	Clean cut and everted	According to nature of the weapon
5. Dimensions	Variable	Longer than deep but often gaping	Depth greater than length
6. Hair and blood vessels	Crushed	Clean cut	Variable
7. Haemorrhage	Not pronounced. Exception: scalp	Usually profuse	Varies – may be concealed internally
8. Surrounding	Abrasion and bruising usually present	Abrasion and bruising not present	Abraded or bruised due to thrusting force or if the weapon is blunt
9 Foreign bodies	Frequently present	Normally free from foreign bodies	Foreign bodies may or may not be present

Q. 16.11. Comment on: (1) defence wounds, (2) self-inflicted wounds, (3) injury patterns.

Defence Wounds

These are injuries sustained by a person while warding off an attack. The nature of injuries will vary depending upon the kind of weapon used. When the weapon is sharp, defence cuts or stabs will be produced.

The person may either try to grasp the weapon or raise the upper limb to ward off the attack, and may sustain injury to those body parts which are used for defence. Thus, defence wounds are usually found on the grasping surfaces of hands, ulnar borders of forearms, or raised upper limb, and the dorsum of palm when used to cover the head or face.

Defence injuries are not necessarily confined to upper limbs. In case a person happens to fall down, he may even use his legs to defend himself and thereby receive injuries to his lower limbs. If he ducks in, he may injure his back. Thus, any body part may be injured depending upon the method of defence. Defence injuries on lower limbs are more common, if the victim is a female and they suggest a sexual assault (Fig. 16.13).

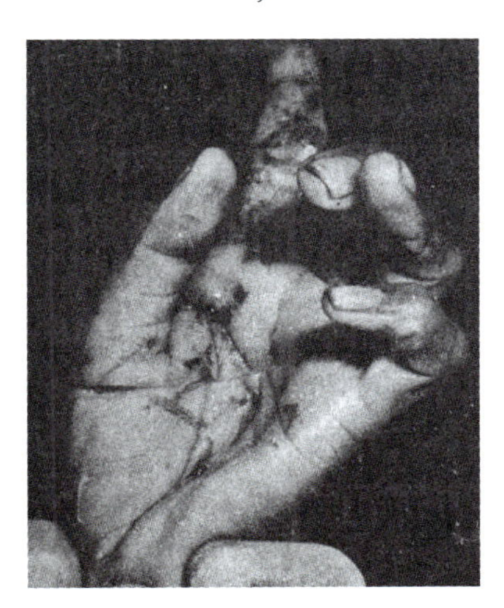

Fig. 16.13: Defence wounds on the left palm in characteristic position. The victim was assaulted by an aruval (sharp-edged sickle) from which she tried to protect herself by grasping it. During the process, she received defence injuries on the left hand and shoulder. (*Courtesy*: Dr PG Paul)

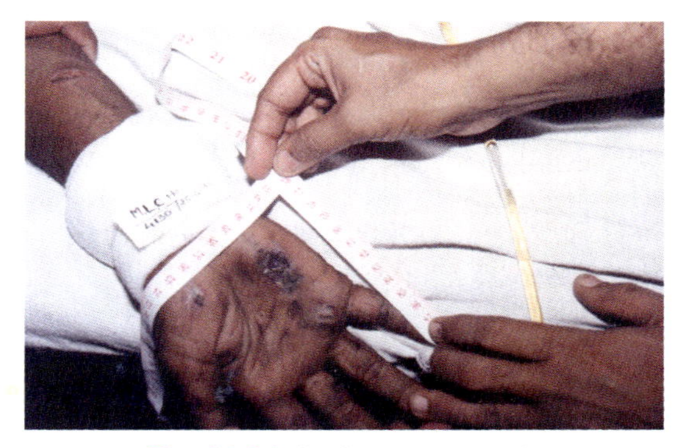

Fig. 16.14: Defence wounds

Defence injuries indicate a homicidal attack. When present, they help to assess the victim's awareness, consciousness, ability to resist, nature of attack, and the type of weapon. They are not seen, if a person is attacked when he is unaware, unconscious, or unable to defend himself, e.g. when his arms are held or hands tied. The postmortem examination in such cases should include incision in the arms and wrists to reveal bruises caused by the restraint (Fig. 16.14).

It is necessary to remember that defence injuries on hands and especially palms may not be obvious at autopsy, if the hands and arms are placed by the side of the body and become fixed by rigor mortis with fingers in flexion.

Self-inflicted Wounds (Fig. 16.15)

Also known as *factitious injuries, forged or fabricated wounds,* or *invented injuries,* these are injuries produced by a person on his body (self-inflicted) or caused by another acting in agreement with him. The object is: (1) to support a false charge against another person with an ulterior motive, or (2) to avert suspicion from oneself.

To support a false charge with ulterior motive: Fabricated injuries may be inflicted with a view:

1. To charge an enemy with assault or attempted murder

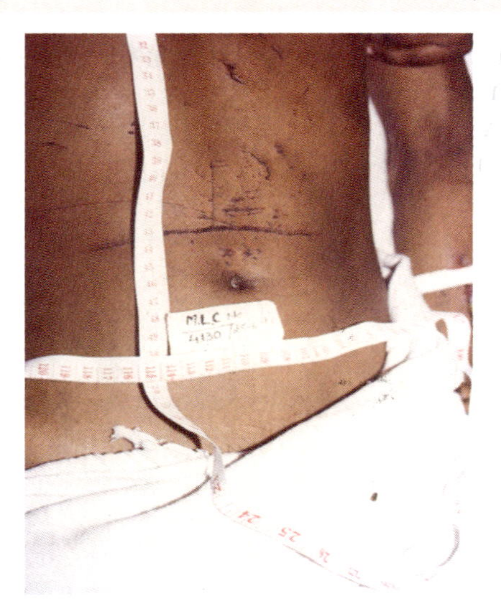

Fig. 16.15: Self-inflected wounds

2. To convert simple injury into a grievous one
3. To bring a charge of beating or ill-treatment by officers during detention of persons in prisons or police custody, or on occasions, such injuries may be inflicted by
4. Girls to bring a charge of rape, or
5. By conscripts or new recruits to escape military service, usually by instilling an irritant in the eye and thus producing conjunctivitis.

To avert suspicion: Fabricated injuries may be inflicted:

1. To destroy evidence of a certain injury which might connect a person with crime
2. By an assailant to show that he was acting in self-defence, or
3. By policemen and watchmen acting in collusion with robbers to show that they received injuries while defending property, or by employees in cases of theft, or messengers carrying money, for the same reasons.

Fabricated wounds are often cut wounds, occasionally stab wounds, and sometimes bruises. The use of marking nut juice to produce artificial bruise is not uncommon in India. Contused or lacerated wounds are rarely fabricated on account of the pain they cause and the force required to produce them. Still rarer are firearm injuries and burns.

Fabricated injuries are commonly seen over those body parts that are easily accessible, such as top of the head, forehead, neck, outer side of left arm, front of left forearm, front and outer side of thighs, and front of abdomen and chest, so as to simulate defence injuries, strangulation, rape, etc.

The fabricator usually produces only that much injury as he thinks necessary to confirm his story. He is careful to avoid any serious harm to himself. The injuries are, therefore, usually multiple, superficial, and not situated on vital body parts.

The **diagnosis** of fabricated injury can be arrived at from a careful examination of clothes, characteristics of injuries, and the explanation of complainant in respect thereto.

Since the fabricator rarely injures himself through his clothes, an examination of his clothes is very valuable when such suspicion exists. Even when the clothes are damaged, they are damaged in a way incompatible with the number, length, direction, and nature of wounds.

When examining a case of suspected fabricated injuries, one should look for not only recent injuries but old scars also. A provisional diagnosis of fabricated injury is made when one discovers recent injuries which are multiple, superficial, half-hearted, and not on vital body parts. Multiple scars of different ages when present, on various body parts for which there is no satisfactory explanation, add to the evidence. Besides this, *characteristic defence wounds are absent* despite the history of an assault.

When the fabricator is closely questioned about evidence of the alleged assault with reference to the identity of the weapon, number of blows, method of their infliction, and the way he tried to defend himself, his explanation will be found so inconsistent with observed facts that it will confirm the diagnosis.

Injury Patterns

In evaluating cases of traumatic injuries, the individual injuries are examined in detail vis-a-vis their distribution over the entire body, both external and internal, to recognise an injury pattern. It may help to categorise the injury, as for example, suicide—multiple superficial incised wounds over the wrist/neck; battered child syndrome—injuries of different ages and in different stages of healing; overkill murder victim—homosexual tendencies; gunshot wound residue pattern suggesting range of firing; motor vehicle accident victim—driver, passenger, pedestrian, etc. The occurrence of stab wounds in a paired pattern suggests the use of a two-pronged sharp weapon, such as a fork, pair of scissors, etc. Body diagrams are very useful to interpret injury patterns and while giving evidence in court. The injury pattern, e.g. only on one side of the body (accidental lacerations), or on bony prominences (fall), or not consistent with the scene in context with all available information may indicate a sequence of events leading to a proper conclusion regarding the cause and manner of death (Dr Barrowcliff's case).

17

Firearms and Firearm Injuries

PART 1: FIREARMS AND BALLISTICS

Q. 4.12. Explain the following terms in relation to firearms: (1) action, (2) ballistics, (3) bore, (4) buckshot, (5) bullet, (6) calibre, (7) cartridge, (8) cocking, (9) musket, (10) primer, (11) tattooing, (12) yaw.

Action means the assembly of the firing mechanism of the gun. It closes the breech end of the barrel. It consists of a breech block, hammer, and trigger. Its key functions are cocking and releasing the hammer by trigger pull.

Ballistics is the science of the motion of a projectile. *Exterior ballistics* is the study of motion of a projectile after it leaves the barrel of a firearm. *Interior ballistics* is the study of physicochemical phenomena within the firearm from the moment of detonation of primer to the time the projectile leaves the barrel. *Terminal ballistics* is the study of the effect of impact of a projectile on the target (resulting in wound formation—*wound ballistics).*

Bore *(gauge, calibre)* means the diameter of the interior of the barrel of a firearm and is expressed in inches or in millimetres e.g. 0.22″, 0.32″, 0.38″, 0.410″, 0.45″; or 6.35 mm, 7.62 mm, 7.65 mm, or 9.00 mm, etc.; or the number of lead balls of size almost fitting the barrel of a shotgun which can be made from one pound of lead, e.g. 12, 16, or 20, etc.

Buckshot means a larger shot (as compared to the bird shot) used in shotgun cartridges. Generally, its diameter is in the range of 0.20″–0.36″.

Bullet means the projectile of a rifled firearm. A *dum-dum bullet* is a jacketed bullet with its nose cut off to expose the core. The modern version is a *soft point* or *hollow point* bullet for expansion and higher incapacitation index on the target, usually large game. *Tandem bullets* are bullets ejected one after the other, when the first bullet, having been struck in the barrel, fails to leave the barrel, and is ejected by the subsequently fired bullet. This is in contradistinction to *Duplex* rounds which contain two projectiles by design. They enter the target at different points.

Calibre technically means the diameter of the inside of the bore (land to land) in 1/100th of an inch, and the term (as nominal calibre) is often used to designate the firearm or the cartridge. Thus, calibre 22 means 22/100 inch = 0.22″.

Cartridge means one unit of ammunition. It consists of (1) a cartridge case with a percussion cap containing the primer at the base, (2) the propellant charge, (3) the projectile, and (4) the wads, if any.

Cocking refers to the readying of the firing mechanism of the gun. It may be accomplished by pulling the hammer or slide or, in the case of hammerless guns, by closing the firearm.

Musket is a smooth-bored shoulder firearm firing a round, like 0.410 shot, sometimes used by the police in India.

Primer means a small metal cap, at the base of the cartridge, holding a sensitive mixture that is detonated by a blow either from a hammer or firing pin.

Tattooing consists of powder particles which are embedded in and under the skin through the force of their impact. It is seen only when the weapon is near enough for the powder grains to strike with force. When the range increases to the point that the powder particles do not embed themselves but still leave a visible mark, it is called *stippling*. It is necessary to examine critically the shape and size of the skin markings as they reflect the shape and size of the powder grains of which they are made.

Yaw means the deviation between the long axis of the bullet and the axis of the path of the bullet. It can cause a key hole entry wound, if the bullet is unstable or destabilised by contact with something. A bullet that rotates end-on-end during its path is known as a **tumbling bullet.**

Q. 17.1. Define a firearm. Describe in general its different parts and give a brief account of the operating principle.

A firearm is a specialized **device** designed to propel a projectile (shot/bullet/missile) by the expansive force of gases generated as a result of combustion of the propellant (powder) at its base in a closed space. This combustion results in building up of optimum pressure which forces the missile out of the muzzle (mouth of a firearm) with sufficient velocity resulting in firearm injury.

In general, a firearm **consists of:** (1) a barrel, (2) action, and (3) a grip or butt stock, as the case may be.

Barrel: This consists of a steel tube. It is long in rifles and shotguns, and short in revolvers and pistols. Its proximal end is called the *breech end* and the distal end, which is always open, is called the *muzzle.* The breech end may have a *chamber* to accommodate the cartridge and may carry an extractor to help remove the cartridge case after firing.

Action: This consists of (a) breech block or bolt, (b) firing pin or striker mechanism (or hammer), and (c) trigger(s).

The *breech block* is a metal block which seals the breech end of the chamber (barrel) when the firearm is closed. It can be opened to insert a fresh cartridge. It is generally pierced in its centre to accommodate the firing pin. The *trigger* is a lever, normally situated below the block. It is operated by finger pressure.

Grip or butt stock: This is that part which is normally gripped in the hand. In long-barrelled weapons, such as the shotgun and rifle, the butt stock is elongated and shaped to fit against the shoulder. In handguns, this part is gripped in the hand. A *magazine* is a spring-loaded container carrying a number of cartridges. It is attached to the forestock of rifle, carried as a tubular magazine in a repeating shotgun, and lodged in the grip of a pistol.

The operating principle is essentially the same for most firearms. A firearm is: (1) loaded, (2) cocked, and (3) fired, when the trigger is pulled. This releases a firing pin which strikes the percussion cap and detonates the sensitive composition in the primer. The detonation of the primer ignites the main propellant charge (through the flash hole(s) inside the cartridge base) and results in rapid formation of expanding hot gases at very high pressure. The pressure of these gases builds up to an optimum value and forces the missile out of the barrel with substantial velocity; at the same time, the base of the cartridge case is forced backward against the breech block. As a result, microscopic details on the breech block may get imprinted on the base of the cartridge resulting in breech face marks.

The velocity of the missile as it emerges from the muzzle end is known as the *muzzle velocity*. It depends upon many factors which include the amount of powder, bullet weight, the accuracy with which the projectile or the wad obturates (seals) the barrel, and the efficiency of combustion of the powder. The velocity diminishes as the missile travels ahead to strike at the target. The latter is called *striking velocity*. The release of the projectile is accompanied by a variable amount of flame, hot gases, soot, discharge of burnt, burning and unburnt grains of powder, fine lead fragments (in the case of lead bullets), grease, and wadding (when present in the cartridge). The *fired cartridge case* or *empty* (sometimes referred to as the *fired shell)* is left after the firing of the cartridge and this may have to be removed manually or is automatically ejected.

Q. 17.2. Describe in general the various parts of a cartridge.

In general, a cartridge consists of: (1) a cartridge case with a percussion cap containing the primer at the base, (2) the propellant charge, (3) the projectile, and (4) wads (if present) (shotgun cartridges).

Cartridge case: This is the outer shell or covering of the cartridge. It keeps the various components of the cartridge in place, provides a water-proof cover for the contents, and helps proper preservation. Generally, it is made of brass. The shotgun cartridge case is, however, made of cardboard or plastic with a rimmed brass base. *Caseless cartridges* are also in use now. The whole cartridge is combustible and hence no cartridge case remains for identification.

The *percussion cap* at the base contains a small amount of sensitive detonating composition known as the *primer*. A misfire (non-firing) or hangfire (delayed firing) can result from defective primer. The priming composition may contain potassium chlorate, antimony sulphide, lead styphnate, barium nitrate, mercury fulminate, etc. The primer residues around the gunshot wound or shot hole on victim's clothing can yield important clues in respect of identifying an entrance wound, and firing distance.

Propellant charge: This is so-called, because it propels the missile forwards. It is composed of black powder or smokeless powder in the form of grains, pellets, thin cylindrical cords, or flakes. It lies between the primer and the projectile. Its ignition results in rapid formation of expanding hot gases under pressure, and when optimum pressure is built up (which is different for different firearms), the projectile is driven forward in the barrel giving it the necessary muzzle velocity and striking energy.

The *black powder or gun powder* consists of charcoal (15%), sulphur (10%), and potassium nitrate (75%). When ignited, it produces a lot of smoke and some of the powder is partly burnt or not burnt at all. Consequently, a good amount of blackening and tattooing is observed around the injury when the weapon using black powder is fired from a close range. Generally, black powder is used in muzzle loaders, blank cartridges, refilled cartridges, and country made cartridges. *Smokeless powder* contains nitrocellulose (single base) or sometimes nitroglycerine in addition (double base). It is more effective than black powder as it burns more efficiently and produces much less smoke. Consequently, less blackening and tattooing are observed around the injury when the weapon using smokeless powder is fired from a close range. Smokeless powder is used in all modern cartridges, such as those of shotgun, pistol, revolver, rifle, etc.

A black powder substitute, *Pyrodex*, is recently manufactured for use in old firearms. It contains potassium nitrate, charcoal, and sulphur but is different from ratios in black powder. In addition, it contains potassium perchlorate, sodium benzoate, and dicyandiamide along with small amounts of dextrine, wax, and graphite, which permit differentiation of Pyrodex residues from those of black powder.

Projectile: This means an object propelled by the force of rapidly burning gases or other means. Those fired from rifled weapons, such as a rifle, revolver, or pistol, are bullets. Those fired from smooth-bored weapons, like shotguns, are lead (or recently steel) shots and pellets. Other projectiles met with in medicolegal work are pellets and slugs in air guns; and metal scrap, nails, stones, etc. in muzzle loading guns.

A bullet is made of lead which has higher sectional density (mass/diam^2) so essential for a steady flight. Since lead is a soft material and easily deformable, the bullet is jacketed either fully or partly with cupro-nickel, copper, or other harder casing. The tip of the bullet is known as the nose. The bullet is cylindrical from the base onwards and conical towards the tip (nose). This ensures least resistance to its passage in air. The striking energy of a fired bullet is proportional to its mass (m) and the square of its velocity (v) (energy $= 0.5 \times m \times v^2$). Modern military science, therefore, designs missiles of a smaller mass and high velocity. The smaller mass enables transportation of a large amount of ammunition; the high velocity causes sufficient tissue damage.

To ensure maximum damage, some bullets are specially designed to slow down or stop within the body to utilise maximum striking energy in wound production. Such a bullet was used in the assassination attempt on President Reagan. Soft-nosed bullets flatten on impact and some are designed to fragment. The dum-dum bullet with its tip cut off and the military missile with an air cavity at its tip mushroom on impact and thus cause more damage by spending maximum striking energy in wound production. Weapons intended to **combat hijacking** are designed to be non-ricochet and to stop within the body to avoid puncture of the pressurised aircraft. A round of this ammunition, known as **'short-stop** or **short-range ammunition'** consists of a 0.38 special/0.357 calibre cartridge enclosed in a plastic cap housing fine lead shot. On striking the body, the shell of the projectile ruptures and the pellets are scattered along the wound track. The projectile does not exit the body regardless of the range of fire unless it grazes or encounters little resistance. Accuracy is reasonably good up to about 15 to 25 feet. At ranges up to 10 feet, it causes fatal wounding. Under 6 feet, it will perforate the aircraft's wall, if it misses the intended target.

A rifle bullet is elongated with a pointed nose. The revolver and pistol bullets are shorter with a rounded nose. Although round or spherical bullets (except shotgun pellets) are obsolete, these are still used in 0.410″ muskets in India.

Lead (or recently steel) pellets are generally used as projectiles in case of shot-guns. Their size may vary from single spherical ball (diameter 0.65″), a rifled slug, to a buck shot, viz. LG (diameter 0.36″), SG (diameter 0.33″), etc. to shot size 2,4,6 (diameter 0.134″, 0.12″, 0.10″ respectively), which is generally indicated on the top wad or the side of the cartridge case.

Wad: This means a circular disc of various thicknesses used to adjust the contents of a shotgun cartridge. One or more wads may be present. The wad—(1) separates the projectiles from the propellant, (2) seals or obturates the bore effectively, (3) prevents expanding gases from escaping, and (4) allows optimum pressure to develop. The wad may be made of felt, cardboard and stout paper (air cushion), or plastic (such as power piston type which holds the shot inside a polythene cup). The felt wad is impregnated with grease and this lubricates the bore (Fig. 17.1).

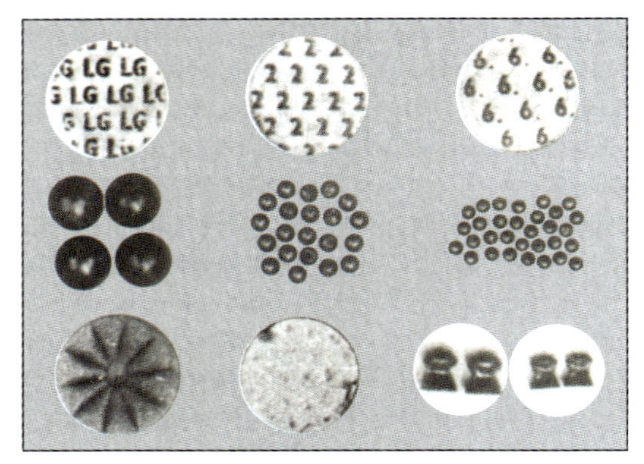

Fig. 17.1: Shot and wads. *First row* (from left to right): 12 bore top wads, LG: No. 2; No. 6. *Second row:* Shots: LG: No. 2; No. 6. *Third row:* 12 bore air cushion wad; 12 bore under shot wad; 0.22 air gun pellets; 0.177 air gun pellets

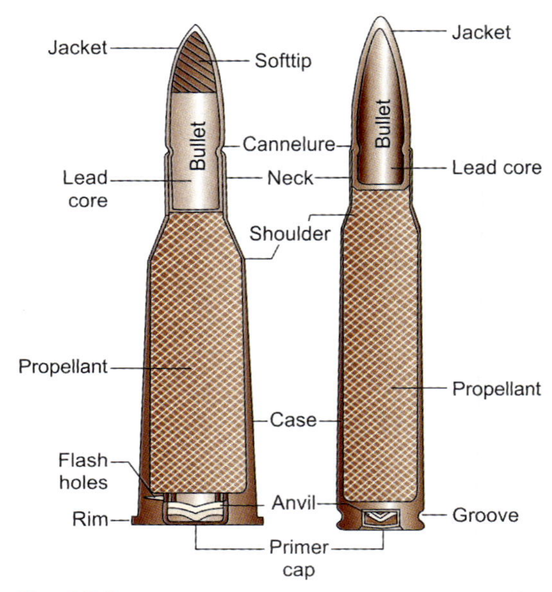

Fig. 17.2: Rimmed and rimless (grooved) rifle cartridge with jacketed bullets

Q. 17.3. Describe the various components of the cartridge in (1) rifled firearms, (2) shotguns, (3) country made guns.

Cartridge of rifled firearms: This has a metal case which may be cylindrical, tapered, or bottle necked. It contains a primer at the base in the percussion cap, propellant charge, and the bullet. The bullet may have a groove or grooves known as *cannelures* near to its base to retain its position or for lubrication (Fig. 17.2). The other details have already been described.

Cartridge of shotgun: This is cylindrical in shape, its length being generally 6–8 cm (2½″–3″), and its diameter varying with size (12 bore cartridge—outer diameter 0.790″). It consists of a crimped cardboard or plastic case with a rimmed brass base containing a percussion cap in the centre, the propellant charge, a felt (or equivalent) wad with cardboard discs lying in front and behind it, the lead shots, and again a disc of cardboard known as the overshot (top) wad on which the size of the shot may be indicated. The overshot cardboard wad is meant to keep the shot in place. The shot charge in a 12 bore shotgun is usually 1–1½ ounce (Fig. 17.3). **Some** modern cartridges have brightly coloured plastic granules as a filler between the shot. The other details have already been described.

Country made cartridge: This is generally an iron rimmed tube with necessary

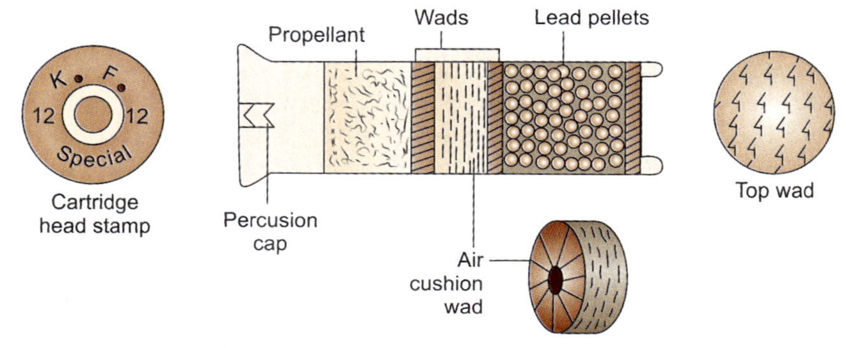

Fig. 17.3: 12 bore shotgun cartridge

provision for percussion cap or device. The propellant is black powder, and the wads may be of cloth or paper. The projectiles in these cartridges may be home made shots of lead, stout nails and metal scrap, stone pieces, etc. followed by an appropriate top wadding, if necessary. Refilled cartridges using fired cartridge cases are also used.

Q. 17.4. Comment on: (1) blank cartridge, (2) baton round.

Blank cartridge: This is a cartridge with primer, gunpowder, and wadding but without a bullet. It is used in starter pistols in sporting events, stage performances, and army manoeuvres. It may be sealed with a paper disc or may have a crimped neck. It cannot inflict injuries at a distance as there is no bullet but can be very dangerous in contact or close range firing up to a few inches.

In a stage accident in London, a hero fired at a villain with a 12 bore shotgun using a blank cartridge. The villain was killed on the spot. At autopsy, three felt wads were found to have penetrated his heart.

Baton round: This is *a device, utilising rubber and plastic bullets, for riot control.* The bullet is meant to be fired at a range of 25 to 50 yards so as to keep the crowd beyond stone throwing distance. When it hits, its impact on the body is felt like a hard punch or kick and may result in a painful bruise. The disadvantage of the missile is its inaccuracy. Much depends on the part of the body that is struck. The rubber baton round is now superseded by a shorter round made of *Teflon.* It can be fired with greater accuracy and thus more effectively. Many serious injuries and some deaths have been reported from plastic bullets.

Q. 17.5. Classify firearms. Give a detailed account of smooth-bored firearms.

The principal types of firearms are the: (1) smooth-bored firearms and (2) rifled firearms. Smooth-bored firearms may be breech loading (shotguns) or muzzle loading (country made guns). In the breech loading guns, the cartridge is loaded at the breech end, and the gun closed. It is then ready for firing. While these are the usual weapons causing serious injuries, there are others, like air pistols, and air (or gas) and spring guns, which are also capable of producing grave injuries. The smooth-bored weapons fire non-spinning missiles of variable dimensions. The rifled weapons fire missiles spinning on their longer axis. Firearms with long barrels, like the shotgun and rifle, are fired from the shoulder while those with short barrels, like revolvers and pistols, are fired from the hand.

Smooth-bored firearms: These include (sporting) shotguns, muzzle loaders, and muskets, the shotgun being more common. In these weapons, the bore (inside of the barrel) is perfectly smooth.

The barrel length of the shotgun usually varies from 24 to 30 inches. The *bore* (sometimes called *gauge)* is measured by the internal diameter in inches (e.g. 0.410″) or by the number of lead balls of size almost fitting the barrel, which can be made from one pound of lead. *The most common bore is a 12 bore (diameter 0.729″).* Thus, the 12 bore gun is one whose bore diameter is that of a ball of lead of such a size that 12 balls can be made from one pound of lead. It is obvious that the greater the bore number, the smaller the size of the lead shot, and vice versa. The cartridge is loaded in the chamber which is larger than the actual bore and is connected to the bore by a taper. The weapon is made to 'break' (open) on a hinge for loading a cartridge or extraction of the fired cartridge case.

The shotgun cartridge has as its projectile lead or steel pellets or shot which vary in size from single spherical ball to a number of small pellets depending upon the type of cartridge employed. The shot charge is generally 1–1½ oz for a 12 bore gun. When the weapon is fired, the pellets disperse soon after their exit from the

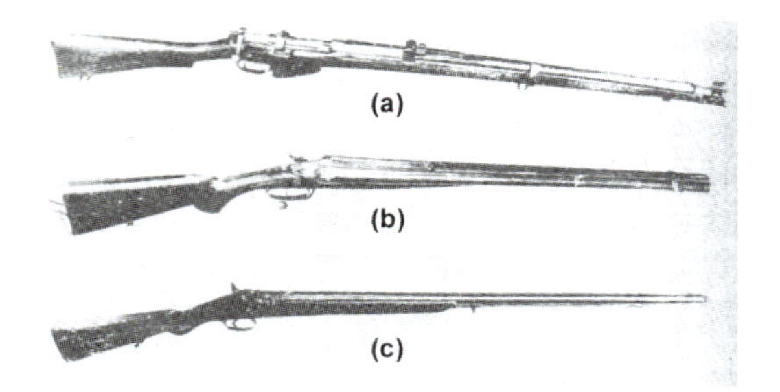

Fig. 17.4: (a) 0.303 **rifle;** (b) 12 bore DBBL **shotgun;** (c) **muzzle loading gun**

muzzle and this dispersion increases with the range. The degree of dispersion can be controlled to some extent by a relatively small but significant reduction near the muzzle end commonly amounting to no more than 1 mm. This is called *choke.* It imparts compactness to the shot so as to keep the main charge closer together for a greater effective distance. Some modern weapons are designed to convert a cylinder barrel to a choke barrel.

Muzzle loading guns are now becoming obsolete. They require filling of the propellant (gun powder) through the muzzle, followed by wadding material (cloth, fibre-coir, paper), the shot charge, and the top wadding. They are fired by detonation of a percussion cap placed on the nipple attached to the base of the barrel at its rear end (Fig. 17.4).

Amongst the smooth-bored weapons, mention may be made of 0.410 **muskets,** used by the constabulary in India for riot control, or by the railway protection force. These fire a single lead ball of mass about 6.2 gm, at a velocity of 1700 plus minus 100 ft/sec. The muzzle velocity of 0.410 shot fired from these guns varies a great deal ranging from about 1150 to 1950 ft/sec.

Q. 17.6. Give a detailed account of rifled firearms.

These include service and sporting rifles, revolvers, pistols, etc. The rifle is an example of a high velocity weapon, pistol a medium velocity one, and the revolver a relatively low velocity one. In these weapons, the inside of the bore is rifled, that is, cut longitudinally with a number of spiral grooves (4 to 7 generally) which run parallel to each other, but are twisted spirally from chamber end to muzzle end. This is called *rifling*. The magnitude of the *twist* (distance required for one complete turn of rifling) varies from model to model but generally causes a bullet to rotate about its longitudinal axis only once in about 25–35 cm of forward motion. The raised portions on the bore are called *lands* and the lowered ones the *grooves* (Fig. 17.5). Rifling varies in number, direction (left or right handed), depth, and width, and these variations are reflected on the fired bullets.

Recently, *polygonal rifling* has been introduced. In these weapons, a smooth transition occurs between the lands and the grooves with the result that the markings they impart on the fired bullets are very fine, making identification of bullets fired from such guns quite difficult.

The rifled weapons are generally designed to fire a succession of single bullets. A bullet while passing through a rifled barrel rotates or spins on its longer axis. The *spin* (1) imparts gyroscopic stability (like that of a spinning top) to the bullet, (2) in view of its stability, it increases the accuracy with which a target can be hit,

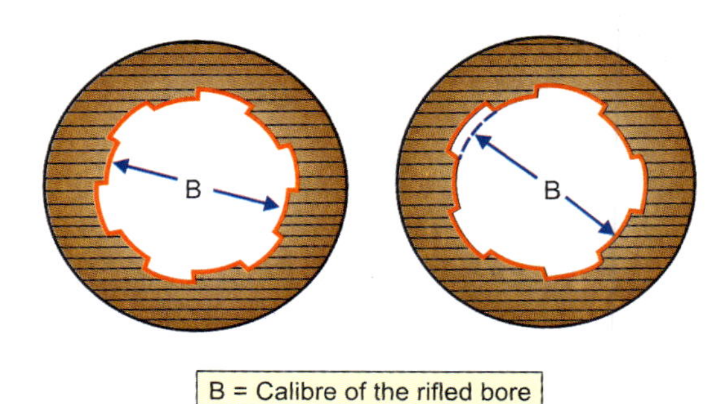

Fig. 17.5: Section of a **rifled bore,** showing lands and grooves

and (3) prevents the bullet from wobbling as it travels in the air. The gauge or (nominal) calibre indicates the *land to land* width of the barrel and is expressed both in 1/100th of an inch or millimetres i.e. 0.22, 0.32, 0.38, 0.410, 0.45, etc., in inches; and 6.35, 7.62, 7.65, 9.0, etc., in millimetres.

Bullets fired from **rifles** have a high velocity. A 0.30 calibre rifle fires a bullet with a muzzle velocity of around 2500 ft/sec. A rifle with a twist of 10 inches in rifling and a bullet velocity of 2500 ft/sec would give a spin of 3,000 revolutions per second. A 0.30 calibre rifle bullet is effective at an extremely long range, well over a mile, with an accuracy range of the order of about 600 yards.

A **revolver** is a rifled handweapon, with an overall length of 10 inches, with a rotating drum or cylinder behind the barrel. The drum has chambers for loading generally five or more rimmed cartridges. Each time the revolver is cocked, the cylinder rotates (hence the name revolver) to bring a fresh cartridge in line with the barrel and firing mechanism. The cartridge of a revolver has a projecting rim at the base and the empty cartridge case requires to be removed by hand (Fig. 17.6). Revolver bullets have relatively lower muzzle velocities of the order of 600–800 ft/sec. Their accuracy range is about 100 yards.

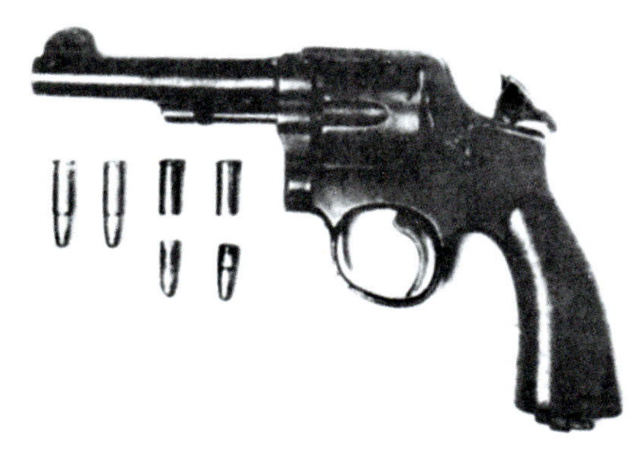

Fig. 17.6: Photograph of a **revolver** with cartridges, fired empties and bullets

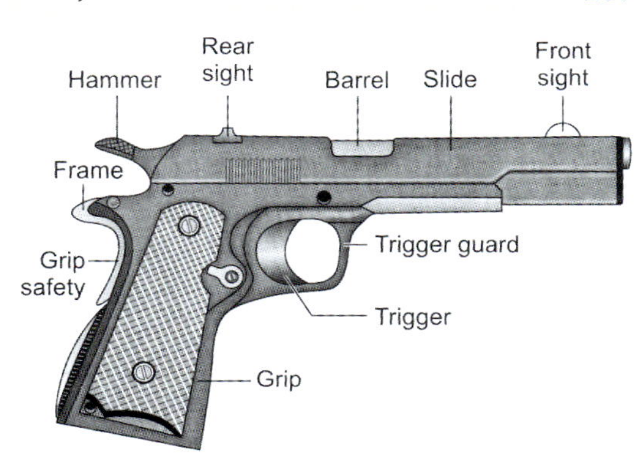

Fig. 17.7: Drawing of a self-loading pistol showing the various parts

A **pistol** (Fig. 17.7) is a hand weapon with a rifled short barrel, generally not over 10 inches in length. It differs from a revolver in respect of direct loading of the cartridge into the chamber as against that into the cylinder in the case of a revolver. The rimless grooved cartridges, commonly about 5–10 in number, are contained in a vertical magazine which is usually housed in the grip of the pistol. The fired cartridge case is automatically ejected and usually remains at the scene of a crime. The pistol bullets usually have muzzle velocities of the order of 1200 ft/sec. Their accuracy range is about 100 yards. These are generally of a self-loading, semi-automatic type.

Q. 17.7. Write short notes on: (1) paradox guns, (2) stud guns, (3) air pistols and air guns.

Paradox guns: These have the initial part of the barrel smooth but last few inches at the muzzle end rifled. Paradox shotguns have two shallow grooves at the muzzle end. A special projectile, paradox slug/bullet, needs to be fired through this gun to achieve better aim and range.

Stud guns: These are industrial tools capable of firing metal nails or studs into wood, concrete, or even steel. Calibres usually range from 0.22 to 0.38. Due to their marked penetration power, they can cause severe injuries. Accidents can occur while

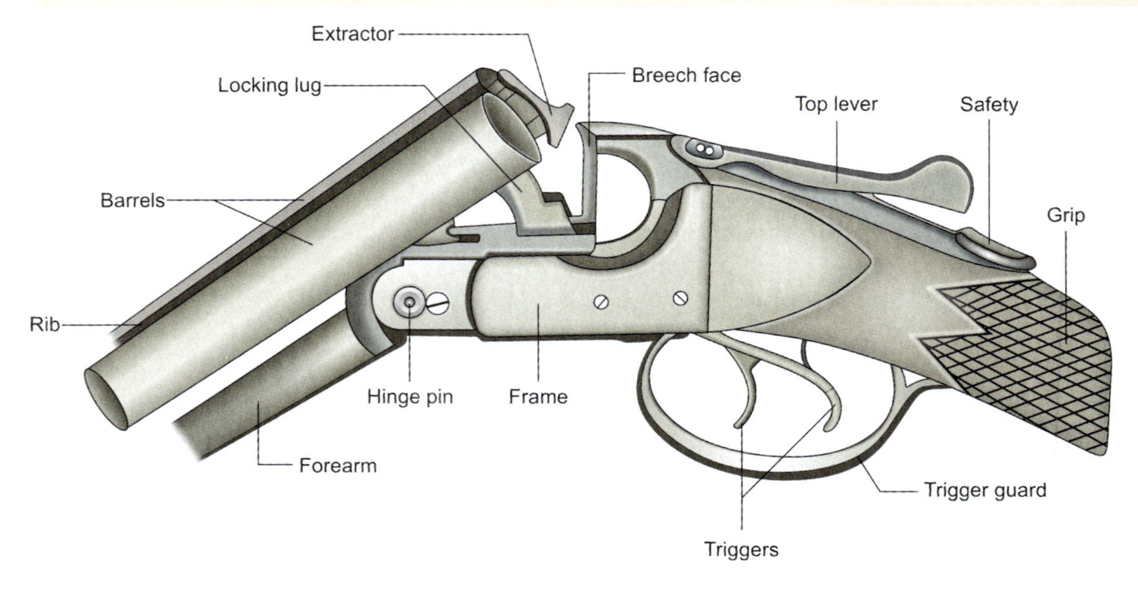

Fig. 17.8: Drawing of a **hammerless shotgun**

operating the stud guns. Likewise, these can be and have been used for suicidal purpose.

Air pistols and air guns: These release lead shots or pellets (skirted) which are propelled by air/gas compressed in a cylinder. Their range for killing squirrels, rats, etc, is about 30 yards. The muzzle velocities of air gun pellets are in the range of 400–700 ft/sec. Injuries sustained due to air gun pellets (usually No. 1–0.177" and No. 2–0.22") are not uncommon. Some air guns, air pistols, and gas operated guns, can impart effective velocities to shots or pellets to cause penetration into the human body including thin bone. A 0.17 air gun pellet causing fatal injury by penetration into the skull of an 11-year-old girl and 5 mm (0.2") air gun pellet killing a 5-year-old boy have been described.

Q. 17.8. Discuss in detail the salient points of medicolegal importance for the determination of the identity of a suspected firearm with the fired cartridge.

The ballistic expert (firearms examiner), given the suspect firearm, an empty (fired cartridge case), or bullet from crime scene/ recovered from the victim, can often prove the identity of the crime weapon. He also finds helpful evidence from examination of the firearm, victim's clothing, and other observations.

The firearm: When found at the scene of the crime, a note should be made of its position either in the premises, or victim's hand (suicide), or if it has been planted to appear so. The manner in which the trigger was operated (forefinger, or toe in the case of a long firearm, or indirectly) also requires attention. The firearm should be lifted carefully for fingerprint examination. If it is loaded, the position of the cartridge/s noted, and the cartridge/s removed. It is checked to determine, if it has been used (soot, barrel fouling, etc.), and if so, if it has been recently fired in which case smell of burnt powder may have persisted.

The crime gun is sent to forensic science laboratory (FSL) to determine: (1) if it is in working order, (2) if it is prone to accidental fire, and (3) if it has been fired prior to its despatch to the FSL as shown by analysis of barrel washings, etc. It is also required for test firing of bullets and cartridge cases to ascertain, if the crime bullet or cartridge case was fired from the suspect gun. Restoration of erased serial number, manufacturer's identification marks, bore/calibre and proof marks, may be necessary.

When the firearm is not recovered, the nature of the weapon may be deduced from: (1) the nature of injuries/shot holes on the clothing, etc., (2) the missile or part thereof recovered from the victim/seen by radiography, or that recovered from crime scene, or (3) a fired cartridge case, if recovered at the scene of crime. Typical shotgun injuries are readily differentiated from injuries due to other firearms. A shot hole due to a large calibre bullet will differ from that due to a smaller one. Bullets, bullet or jacket fragments, shots or pellets, and wads, if any, recovered at the scene of crime or from the victim, throw light on the type and calibre of the firearm.

Cartridge case: Examination of the fired cartridge case helps to reveal the nature of the weapon used from—(1) the material of the casing, viz. brass, cardboard, or plastic, (2) the presence of a rim/groove at the base, and (3) the markings stamped on the base. A shotgun cartridge has cardboard/plastic tube, and a rimmed metallic base. Revolver cartridges and some rifle cartridges also have a rimmed base. The cartridges for rifles, pistols, and revolvers have brass tubes. The cartridges for pistol and some type of rifles are rimless but have an extractor groove at the base for automatic ejection. Such automatically ejected empties are likely to be found at the scene of crime. The marking on the base of a cartridge is called its *head stamp*. It indicates the bore (gauge/calibre) of the weapon with which it can be fired, and also reveals the manufacturer. The caseless cartridges, now in use, would not leave any empty for examination. The cartridge case found at the crime scene is designated as *crime/exhibit cartridge case*. Similar terminology is used for bullets recovered at the scene of crime or from the victim's body. To identify the crime weapon by the examination of the fired empty, it is necessary to compare it with test fired empties.

Test fired cartridge cases or test empties and bullets are collected in the laboratory by firing into cotton wool, water, or other appropriate media. The fired cartridge case may be *labelled* or marked on its side for ready identification in court.

An individual firearm imparts the fired cartridge case its specific markings. The crime cartridge case can thus be linked to the weapon in question through the various characteristic details, like firing pin or striker impression; breech face markings; ejector, extractor, or chamber marks; firing pin scrape; and breech scrape. The identification of a crime cartridge case is possible by comparing it with a test fired cartridge case by microscopic examination individually or under a comparison microscope.

Fired bullet: Examination of a bullet recovered from the body of a victim or at the scene of crime will provide valuable evidence about the weapon used, its calibre, and the number, width, and twist of the lands and grooves. This will corroborate the type of weapon used. Its surface details, on careful microscopic examination, can identify the crime weapon. Lead bullets are commonly used in revolvers while semi-automatic pistols and most rifles fire jacketed lead bullets, i.e. cased in cupro-nickel, copper, or other harder casing. The bullet, during its passage through the barrel, receives on its surface certain characteristic marks and, these are utilised to determine whether a particular bullet was fired from a particular weapon. The comparison microscope is used for this purpose.

In identifying bullets, an expert reaches an opinion generally from two types of characteristics, viz.: (1) class characteristics, and (2) individual or microscopic characteristics by which the bullet can literally be *fingerprinted*.

The *class characteristics* include calibre, chambering (cartridge type), number of grooves and lands, the degree of twist, the spacing, the direction, etc. These vary with different guns so that an expert, having a bullet on which the marks of the grooves and lands are visible, can usually arrive at the make of the weapon (or narrow it down to a relatively few) from which the bullet was fired. It is sometimes very easy to exclude a particular weapon, e.g. a bullet bearing a land and groove impression with a left hand twist could not have been fired from a barrel made with a right hand twist rifling.

The *individual* or *microscopic characteristics* represent the individual scratches on the bullet which are caused by blemishes, tool marks, etc., in the individual barrel of the weapon from which the bullet was fired, and these are visible under the microscope.

Where the bullet has not been too badly defaced or distorted, it is possible by the use of a comparison microscope to conclude with certainty, if the crime bullet has been fired from the same firearm as the test bullet. The identification of the crime firearm may be possible even from the examination of a deformed/brushed or a mutilated bullet as long as sufficient characteristic features are available. *It is imperative that the medical officer who extracts a bullet from a live person or during an autopsy takes care that he does not add any new markings or obliterate those that are present. For this purpose, the bullet should be removed with bare fingers or rubber-tipped forceps and not toothed forceps.*

The **comparison microscope** has a common eyepiece, in which, by means of prisms, a section of one bullet appears side by side with the other having a sharp dividing line. The bullets are mounted on little spindles which can be rotated by means of a micrometer stage. The expert rotates the bullets till he reaches a point when the land and groove impressions together with individual striations on the test bullet match with those of the crime bullet or till he is convinced that there is no point at which the striations coincide. He thus reaches a decision whether the crime bullet was fired from the same firearm or not.

Unlike the bullets, the lead shot or pellets fired from smooth bored weapons cannot be matched to the gun except in rare cases. It has been found helpful to compare the trace elemental composition of crime lead shot with the lead shot that may be found with the accused. Case to case variation of trace elemental pattern (TEP) illustrates the high evidential value of such matching.

Other contents of the cartridge: The identification of other contents of the cartridge, viz. primer, propellant, and wads, etc. also provides useful evidence. The gunshot (primer) residues, commonly denoted as GSRs, are detectable by hypersensitive instrumental analysis. These residues generally comprise of antimony, barium, copper, lead, etc. Their identification may throw light on the type of the cartridge used.

Residues of fired propellant, i.e. powder residues, may be present on the clothes, skin, etc. in case of close distance firing. These comprise of burnt, partially burnt, or unburnt, powder particles. Their microscopic and chemical examination would reveal—(1) whether black powder, Pyrodex, or smokeless powder has been used, and (2) the nature of the propellant, and therefrom the type of cartridge. Microchemical (TLC) analysis for propellant additives is also helpful for this purpose.

The wad, if any, may be found at the crime scene or embedded in the wound. Its examination throws light on the weapon used and its type as also the range of firing. In muzzle loading weapons or refilled/ home-made cartridges, the wad may consist of paper, fibre-coir, cloth, etc. The shotgun wads are distinctive, as already described.

An interesting case of a paper wad matching in a case of homicide (New York 1948) by firing a refilled shotgun cartridge is described. The wad had lodged in the brain. The paper wad inclusive of printing thereon was perfectly matched with the remnant of torn newspaper found in the house of the accused.

Q. 17.9. Comment on: (1) dermal nitrate test, (2) modern body armour.

The dermal nitrate test (paraffin test): This was in vogue earlier to determine, if a suspect had discharged a firearm. The blow back powder residues deposited on the back of the palm and web of the alleged accused hand were collected on paraffin cast and tested for nitrate using diphenylamine reagent Lunge's reagent. This test is now obsolete as it is given by common oxidising substances and non-incriminating materials, like fertilisers, cigarettes, urine, etc. Better chemical tests for nitrate and GSRs (antimony, barium, copper, lead, etc.) are now used to examine hand swabs washings. The modern instrumental methods used for this purpose are neutron activation analysis, atomic absorption spectrophotometry, scanning electron microscopy with X-ray analyser, etc.

Modern body armour: The traditional heavy metal armours to protect vulnerable portions of the body from gun fire have been replaced by lighter synthetic materials. The modern helmets for relatively low velocity bullets/fragments are made up of fibre glass. These are effective for projectiles up to, say, 0.38 pistol shot. Likewise, the body armour vests worn presently even by the sophisticated criminals comprise of around a dozen or so layers of synthetic heavy fabric (polyamide like Kevlar 29) which would require a total vest mass in the range of 1 to 4 kg. A 0.7 kg body armour worn on the back by a Mumbai criminal extortionist targeting the rich (builders, doctors, film actors and allied personnel) was found to stop bullets up to 9 mm pistol shots. The medical aspects of the projectile stoppage by such body armour include, however, the danger of internal injury due to blunt trauma effect. For this purpose, at least, a nine layer vest of nearly 1 kg mass has been provided to law enforcement officers in USA.

PART 2: SOME MEDICAL ASPECTS OF FIREARM INJURIES

Firearm injuries are wounds caused to the body tissues due to impact, entry, and passage of a missile discharged from a firearm. They generally simulate contused wounds. When a missile passes tangentially, the wound may simulate an abrasion, or a gutter. Slit-like exit wounds are occasionally encountered. They are due to the bullet exiting on its broad side or due to exit of a fragmented bone. Such injuries may simulate incised wounds or stab wounds.

Table 17.1 summarises in general the effects of a firearm discharge at various ranges.

Table 17.1: Observation of effects of firearm discharge at various ranges

Range	*What is observed*
1. Long/distant	Bullet
2. Medium	Bullet and powder
3. Short/close	Bullet, powder, and soot
4. Contact: near/close	Bullet, powder, soot, with or without' gas tearing, and burn
5 Contact: actual contact	Bullet, powder, soot, with or without barrel marks, gas tearing, and burn

Q. 17.10. Describe in detail the characteristics of shotgun injuries at varying ranges.

These are due to: (1) multiplicity of the projectiles including shots and wads, (2) shot dispersion with distance, and (3) unusual projectiles in refilled cartridges or in muzzle loaders. Here, the criteria given below are of very little use. Local knowledge and experience is necessary to interpret these wounds.

When a shotgun is fired, the projectiles travel in a compact mass. As the range increases, the individual pellets spread out and collectively travel in a cone-like manner. Their velocity decreases with distance. A rough estimate of the rate of spread is about one inch per yard from the muzzle of a *full choke gun*. For example, the diameter of the pattern or group of average size bird shot hitting the target at 10 yards would be about 10 inches. The target area covered by the shot thus increases with the distance travelled. Meanwhile, the pene-trating power of each pellet decreases.

As a general rule, it may be said that the shot enters as a single mass up to about a yard. Up to 2–3 yards, the shot produces an entrance hole with individual pellet holes round the periphery. As the range of fire increases, the charge of shot begins to spread in the manner discussed above (Figs 17.9 and 17.10). The following generalisations can now be made.

When a shotgun is fired in **contact** or **near-contact** with the body, it is likely to show the following features:

a. The shot enters as a mass, and the consequent wound is single, circular, and about the size of muzzle diameter (called balling of shot).
b. If the muzzle is pressed firmly, soiling or burning is absent; muzzle impression may be found.
c. If the muzzle is not pressed firmly or is loosened by recoil, flame, gas and soot may escape sideways and soil the adjoining skin.
d. If clothing interposes between the muzzle and skin, soot will be found on the clothing as well as skin. The clothing may be singed and there may be burning around the skin wound.
e. The gases will cause laceration of deeper tissues and even fragmentation of bone. The wad is often found in the wound and this may prove an important clue to the type of cartridge used. The wound track and adjacent tissues appear pink due to absorption of carbon monoxide. This appearance is sometimes helpful to

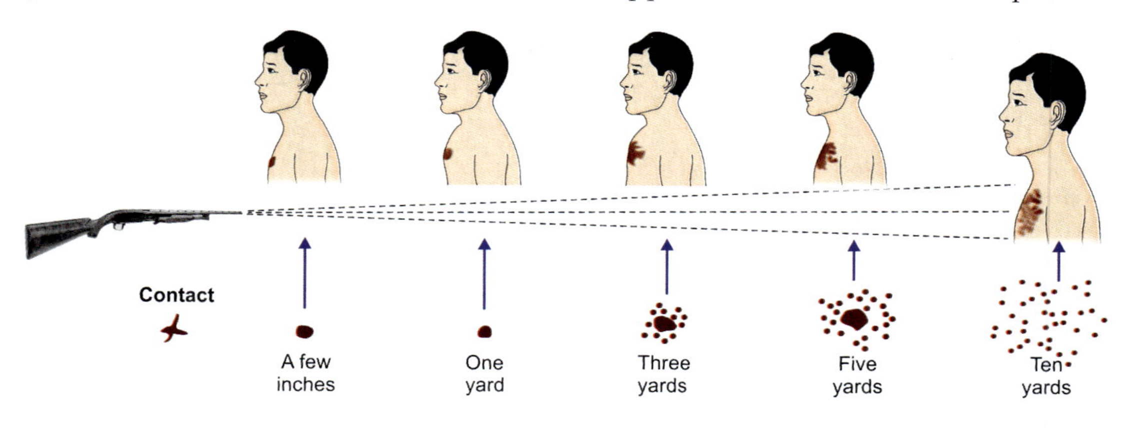

Contact	A few inches	One yard	Three yards	Five yards	Ten yards
Ragged tear. Burning, blackening and tattooing (in the wound track). Carbon monoxide. Wads	Single (irregular) hole. Burning, blackening and tattooing. Carbon monoxide. Wads.	Single hole. Singeing. Blackening? Tattooing. Wads.	Irregular wound. Satellite pellet pattern. Wads.	Irregular wound. Satellite pellet pattern of diameter 5"	Pellet pattern of diameter 10"

Fig. 17.9: Characteristics of shotgun injuries at varying ranges

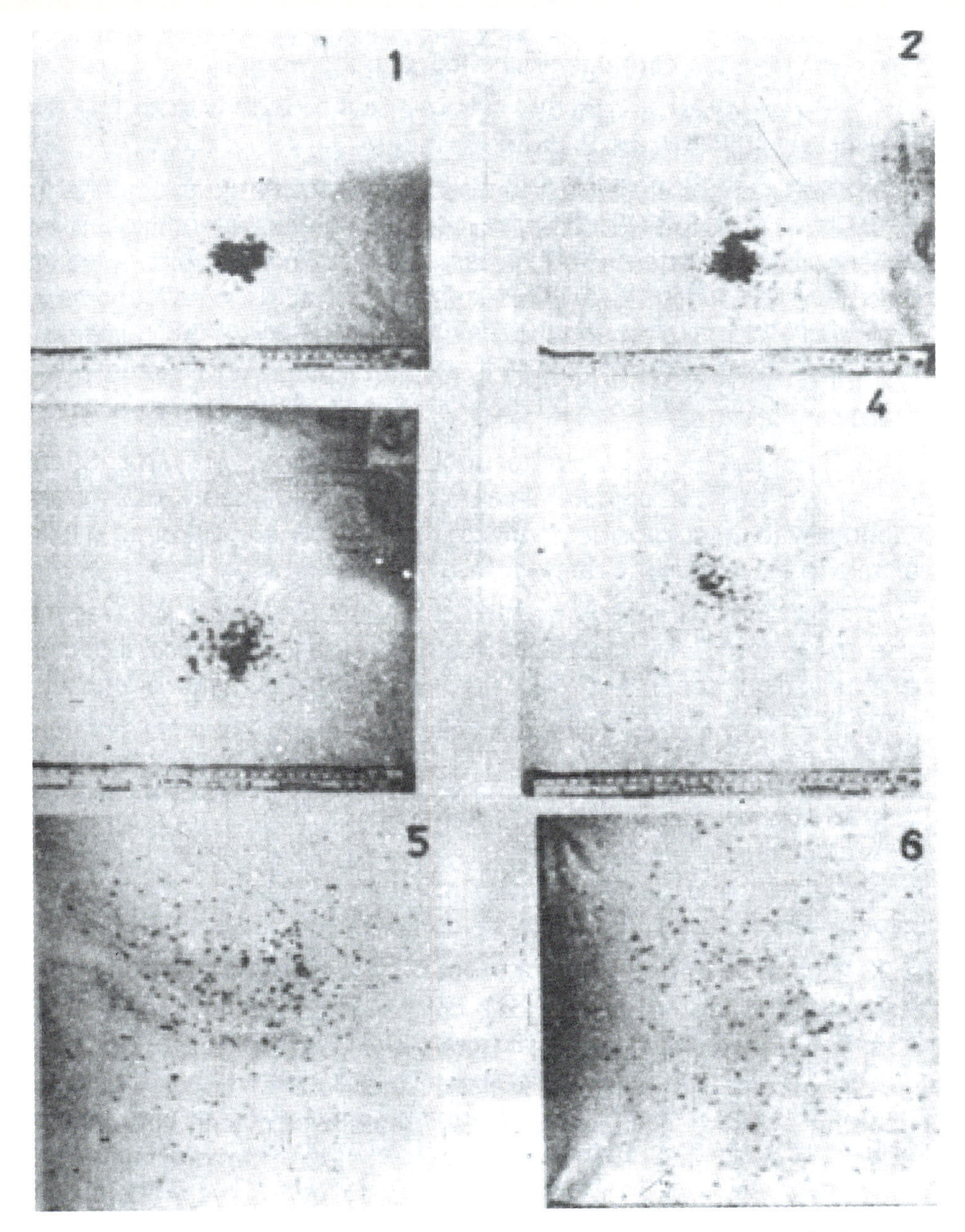

Fig. 17.10: Patterns from a standard shotgun: (1) 8 ft, (2) 10 ft, (3) 15 ft, (4) 25 ft, (5) 30 ft, (6) 40 ft

distinguish entry wound from exit in decomposed bodies. Wad imprint abrasion is some times seen.

f. Contact shotgun injuries differ in their appearance, depending upon the site, whether it is the head or the relatively non-resistant parts, e.g. chest or abdomen. In the former case, as the gases have restricted space for expansion, extensive mutilation is common. In the latter case, in spite of grave internal damage, there is generally no exit wound with small shots. Big shots, however, 0.3–0.36" may do so.

g. Usually, shotgun projectiles do not move out of the body unless: (1) the shot size is sufficiently large or large calibre buckshots or rifled slugs are used, (2) the firing has taken place from a sufficiently near distance, (3) the part of the body hit is not massive, e.g. extremities or neck (4) the victim is a child or lean adult, or (5) the gun is discharged suicidally in the mouth.

A close discharge, that is between actual contact and about six inches, is likely to show the following features:

a. Where clothing is present, it will trap most of the soot and powder grains, and may reduce the flame effect.
b. Scorching of skin, singeing of hair, and blackening and tattooing (far less with smokeless powder) of skin are generally seen.
c. Depending on the angle of firing, the wound is circular or elliptical, and the edge may be smooth or crenated depending on the size of the pellets. There are no separate pellet holes.
d. The wound track and adjacent tissues appear pink due to absorption of carbon monoxide. Any felt or cardboard overshot wads or plastic cups from the cartridge will be found in the wound.

A mid-range discharge, that is from about six inches to six feet (two yards), is likely to show the following features.

The findings are similar to the close range discharge except that: (a) soot soiling is less and will disappear at over 8 to 16 inches, and (b) with increasing distance:

i. The edge of the wound will be abraded and crenated (rat hole) especially with larger shot
ii. The pellet holes will progressively increase around the main wound.

A long-range discharge, that is beyond two yards, is likely to show the following features:

a. There will be no burning or soot beyond about two yards. Sparse tattooing may be seen on careful search up to about three yards. Infrared photography to detect powder marks particularly on dark-coloured clothing is of help to estimation the range.
b. Wadding injury may be seen up to about five yards. The wad may cause an independent impact abrasion. The plastic cup device, if present, opens us in flight and, may produce a characteristic abrasion or bruise.
c. The charge of shot progressively spreads so that small apertures due to separate pellets appear round the main wound. With further increase in range, this is followed by more even distribution of pellet injuries with disappearance of the central aperture. At far longer ranges, the shot, depending upon its size and velocity, may not lodge in the body. 0.33" and 0.36" buckshots are extremely dangerous even at 100 yards.

Q. 17.11. Describe in detail the characteristics of rifled firearm injuries at varying ranges.

Rifled weapons may produce two wounds, one of entry and one of exit. Their dimensions generally vary with the calibre of the weapon. The power of penetration of the tissues is generally greater with rifle and pistol bullets than with revolver bullets. When there is only one wound of entrance, it means that the bullet is still in the body

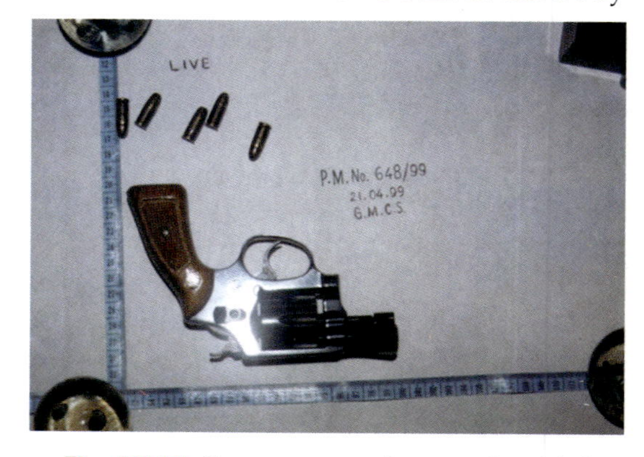

Fig. 17.11: Firearm country made pistol

or, in very exceptional circumstances, it has been coughed out, or lost in the vomit or faeces. When a bullet makes entry into the human body, it first indents and stretches the skin and, subsequently depending upon the energy, effects penetration into the soft tissues and/or bones, and lodges either in the body or comes out causing an exit wound. After entry of the bullet, the skin partially returns to its original position. The size of entry wound may, therefore, be smaller than the size of the bullet, especially at lower velocity.

When a bullet *traverses the skull* and emerges, an examination of the entrance wound will show that the aperture in the bone differs in relation to the outer and inner tables; the defect is larger in the direction in which the bullet travels. At the entrance, there is a clean cut hole on the outer table and bevelled opening on the inner table. The converse is found at the site of the exit wound. This difference in size and appearance is useful to *distinguish* a bullet wound *from* a surgical burr hole in a skeletonised skull received for examination. The bullet track can also be established by alignment of skull bone fragments to inspect the direction of bevelling. Pieces of bone from the entrance wound are often driven into the cranial cavity and may establish the bullet track. Thus the entry firearm projectile causes clean cut opening on outer table of skull. The exiting projectile causes clean cut opening on inner table.

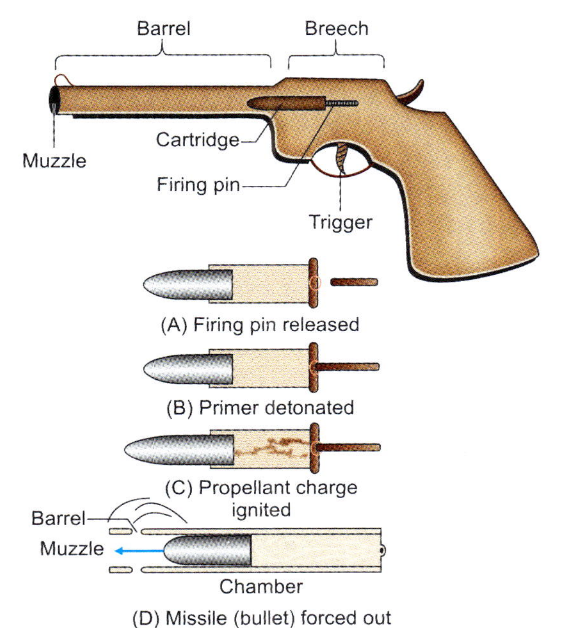

Fig. 17.12: (*Above*) Diagrammatic representation of a firearm and (*below*) the sequence of events which take place when a firearm is discharged. (A) The pulling of the trigger releases a pin or hammer whose tip strikes the percussion cap containing the sensitive primer at the base of the cartridge. (B) The primer is detonated. (C) The detonation of the primer ignites the main propellant charge. (D) The ignition of the main propellant charge results in an explosive formation of hot gases at very high pressure. The pressure of the expanding gases builds up to an optimum value and it forces the missile out of the barrel

Firearm wounds should be photographed with an attached scale, and the body X-rayed in both anteroposterior and lateral views for the location of bullets (if not exited) or any fragments thereof.

Entry wound: Entry wounds are classified in relation to the distance of the muzzle of a firearm from the body. When a weapon is discharged, the projectile leaves the muzzle at its maximum velocity and is accompanied by a flame, hot gases under considerable pressure, soot, discharge of burnt, burning and unburnt particles from the propellant charge and metallic particles. At close ranges, all these will cause injury to the body giving entry wound many special characteristics which the exit wound will lack. The appearance of the entry wound and its extent are also influenced by the type of weapon and its calibre, the nature of the projectile and powder used, the site of body hit, and the striking velocity as a result of loss of velocity of the projectile before hitting the body.

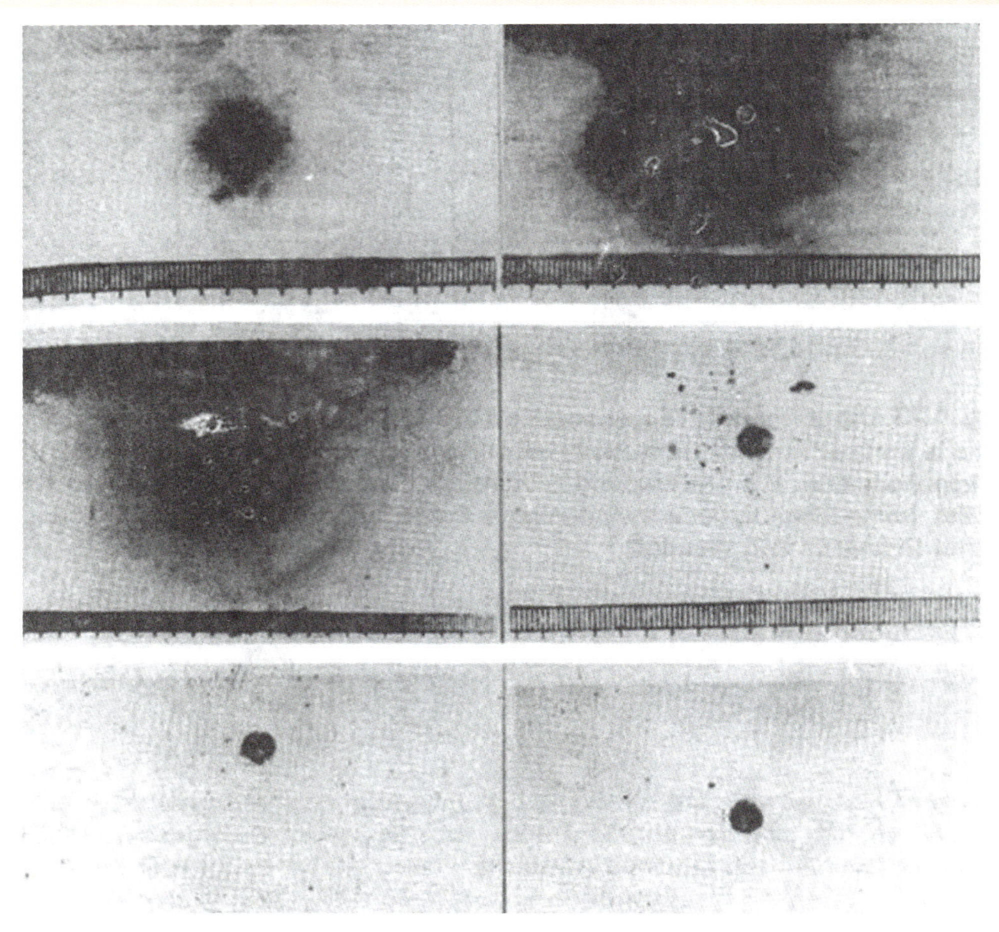

Fig. 17.13: Patterns from a 0.22 rifle: (1) Contact, (2) 1″, (3) 6″, (4) 12″, (5) 24″, (6)

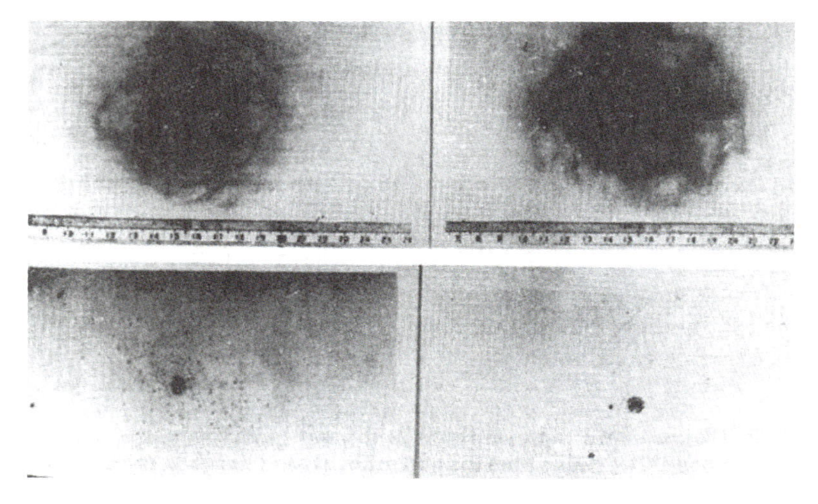

Fig. 17.14: Patterns from a 0.32 revolver: (1) 3″, (2) 6″, (3) 12″, (4) 18″

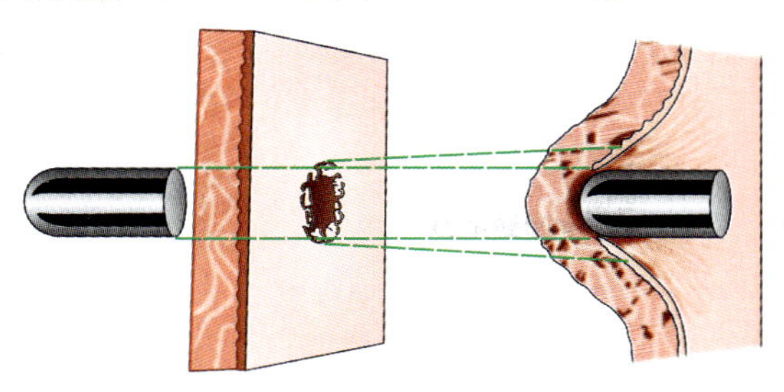

Fig. 17.15: Diagrammatic representation of a bullet penetrating the skin. The skin is pressed inwards, stretched and perforated. It then partially returns to its original position. The entry wound is, therefore, smaller than the diameter of the bullet. Immediately around the opening is the abraded collar or confusion ring. (After Svensson and Wendel)

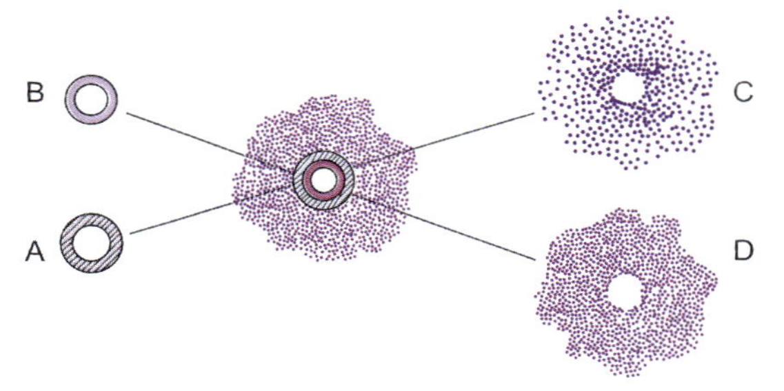

Fig. 17.16: Diagrammatic representation of the **marks which may be found around the entry wound of a bullet in a close shot.** (A) Abraded collar or contusion ring, (B) grease/dirt collar, (C) powder distribution (tattoo marks), (D) deposit of smoke (blackening). (After Svensson and Wendel)

In a **contact range shot** (Fig. 17.17), the discharge from the muzzle, consisting of flame, powder grains, metallic particles, and hot gases under pressure, may be blown into the track taken by the bullet through the body. Consequently, there may be no burning, no soot, and no tattooing, around the entrance wound. However, the physical *imprint of the muzzle* may occasionally be found on the skin surrounding the entrance wound. The muscles around the track of the bullet may be bright pink owing to formation of carboxyhaemoglobin. The entrance wound itself may be small and regular or large and

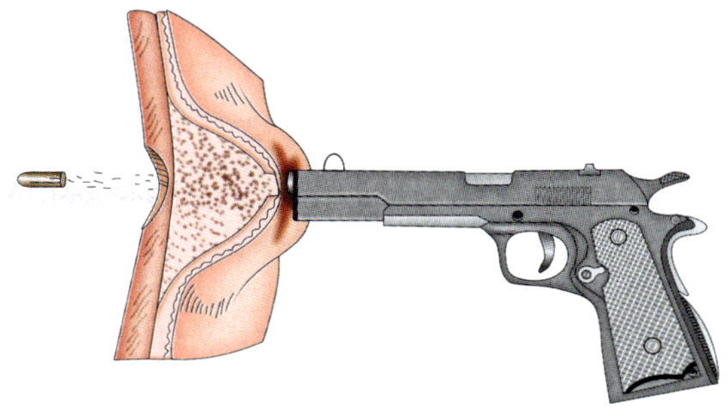

Fig. 17.17: Diagrammatic representation of a **hand gun discharge.** Contact shot on the head. The gases from the explosion expand between the scalp and skull resulting in a bursting effect and a ragged entrance wound. (After Svensson and Wendel)

irregular, depending upon the underlying structures. As for example, the skin wound is large and irregular in head wounds where the gases may expand between the scalp and skull resulting in undermined, ragged, *cruciform* opening with everted margins. Thus, there may be a semi-explosive tearing type of soft tissue injury and may be associated with 'bursting fractures' of the skull. Soot is frequently deposited on the bone underlying a contact gunshot wound.

In a **close range shot** (Fig. 17.18), that is, within the range of flame, soot, and powder blast, so to say, within a few inches from

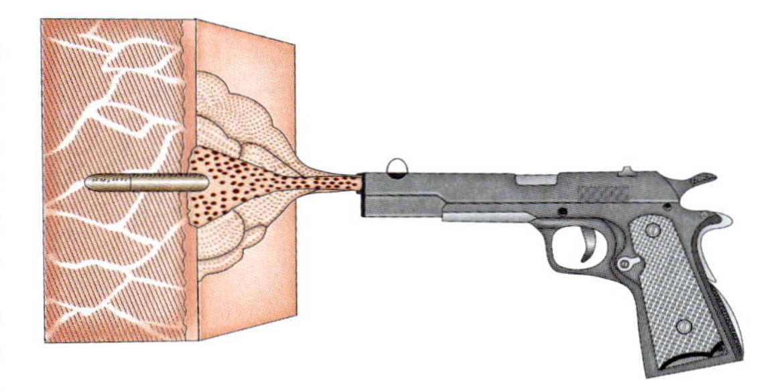

Fig. 17.18: Diagrammatic representation of **a hand gun discharge. Close shot.** Both incompletely burnt powder grains (tattooing) and smoke deposits (blackening) are seen. The powder grains are concentrated immediately around the entrance wound. (After Svensson and Wendel)

the muzzle, the entrance wound is circular, singed by flame (not with smokeless powder), surrounded by soot, if black powder is used (comparatively less blackening with smokeless powder), and shows tattooing. Blackening and tattooing may be absent on the body, if the injury is on a clothed part or on the head with dense hair. The soot or blackening is due to fine carbon particles around the shot hole and can be readily wiped off the skin. Infrared photography to detect carbon particles particularly on dark-coloured clothing is helpful. The tattooing is due to coarse particles of unburnt and partly burnt powder being driven into the skin and, therefore, cannot be wiped off. Hair are burnt and shrivelled, and singeing is generally absent, if the body is covered with the clothing. The usual *abraded collar* or *contact ring* is present in which the superficial skin layers are abraded. It results from the bullet's initial attempt at perforating the skin. As there is some contusion also associated with it, it is also known as *contusion collar*. The skin in the region of this ring dries quickly and becomes dark. In addition to the abraded collar, there may be a *smudge ring* (lead ring, grease collar) or *dirt collar* on the entrance wound. This is due to the wipe of the soft metal of the bullet, or dirt present on it, or grease carried from the barrel and is deposited round the entrance wound internal to the abraded collar. The smudge ring may, therefore, be absent when the jacketed bullet has passed through clothing. The smudging in case of lead shot or unjacketed bullets can be detected microchemically on the target (skin/cloth). It should not be confused with blackening which is due to soot and represents a near range of discharge while smudging may be present even in distance ranges. The forensic value of bullet wipe is to establish a hole as a bullet hole, to determine the entry site, and on occasion the sequence of shots or bullet's passage through multiple objects. Smudging is due to dirt or grease and blackening is due to soot and can be wiped with a wisp of cotton that thenceforth turns black.

In a **near range shot** (Fig. 17.19), that is, within the range of powder blast but outside the range of flame, so to say, within about 1–2 feet in case of hand guns and more in case of other weapons, the deposit of soot and tattooing is spread out over a larger area but there is no singeing of hair or charring of the skin and the entry wound (opening) has the appearance of a distant shot.

As the **range increases,** tattooing from the powder becomes more sparse until no trace of powder marks can be found and this is normally beyond a yard. Infrared photography may be helpful to detect this 'halo' of soot and tattoo marks when it is difficult to do so otherwise.

In a **distant range shot,** there is no burning, no soot, no tattooing. The wound is circular with inverted margins and may be of the same size or even smaller than the bullet owing to the initial stretching of the skin. The edges may be slightly contused. The adjacent skin may be abraded and soiled, and accordingly shows two zones—(1) an outer abraded zone, dark-red or red in colour when fresh, and known as the abrasion collar, and (2) an

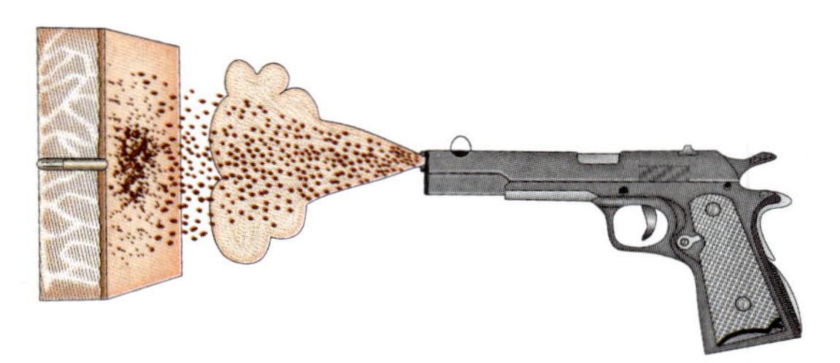

Fig. 17.19: Diagrammatic representation of a hand gun discharge. **Near shot but from greater distance**. The deposit of unburnt powder grains (tattooing) is seen but there is no smoke deposit (blackening) around the entrance wound. (After Svensson and Wendel)

inner zone soiled by grease and known as the grease collar or dirt collar. The fibres of the clothes may be turned in at the entrance.

Exit wound: This is free from signs of burning, blackening, or tattooing, and usual collars of entrance wound. It will show an atypical abrasion when the skin is supported at the exit by a belt, tight clothing, or wall **(shored exit wound).** The atypical abrasion is irregular at the edges, lopsided, and too large as compared to the abrasion collar of an entry wound. The fibres of the clothes may or may not be turned out. An uncomplicated exit wound is usually split from within outward. It has everted irregular edges. It is often slightly bigger than the missile. Usually, there is more bleeding at the exit wound than at the entrance. Where the energy of the bullet is reduced, as for example, at the end of its course or after striking a bone, there may be no exit wound. The bullet may take a very erratic course when it meets with resistance, such as hitting a bone, while passing through the body. Its path through the body can be located by means of X-rays, if any bullet fragments are present in the track, or on a careful postmortem examination for the internal damage.

Q. 17.12. Comment on: (1) the relationship between entry and exit wounds, (2) multiple entrance wounds, (3) multiple exit wounds, (4) multiple entrance and exit wounds.

Relationship between entry and exit wounds: The wound edges may be inverted at the entry and everted at the exit. The abrasion ring will help to distinguish entry from exit. In case of difficulty, microscopic examination and X-ray examination of the skin or clothing may be undertaken. Evidence of carbonisation, swelling, homogenisation of dermal collagen, presence of lead ring if any, and carboxyhaemoglobin at the entry wound, will distinguish it from the exit wound.

The entry wound may be smaller than the exit under the following circumstances:

1. In a distant range shot, the entry wound may be slightly smaller than or of the same size as the exit wound.
2. When the bullet exists sideways or carries bone splinter with it.

The entry wound may be larger than the exit under the following circumstances:

1. In a contact range shot, when the soft tissues at the entry are torn by in-rushing gases.
2. When a bullet is yawing as it enters perhaps because of ricochet.
3. When an entire bullet enters and breaks up with only a small portion exiting.
4. Tangential entry wounds with focal avulsion of tissue and bone.
5. Bullets entering through creased or folded skin but exiting through a less complicated surface.

It is, therefore, necessary to emphasise that size alone is not a reliable indicator of entry or exit wound. Therefore, it is essential that these wounds are sketched or photographed, and their edges and other characteristics carefully defined, to enable the expert to interpret the findings at a later date, in case of doubt.

Multiple entrance wounds: A single soft-nosed bullet hitting a victim after ricochet can produce a number of entrance wounds. Duplex or tandem cartridge can result in two entrance wounds in a single fire.

Multiple exit wounds: A single entrance injury may result in more than one exit wound—(1) if a soft-nosed unjacketed bullet splits into large fragments, (2) when a high velocity bullet resulting in a comminuted fracture imparts sufficient energy to the fractured parts *(secondary missiles)* to cause corresponding exit wounds, and (3) in cases of tandem bullets, following different trajectories in the body and giving rise to separate exit wounds. When the first bullet fails to leave the barrel and is ejected by the subsequently fired bullet, the bullets are ejected one after another and are known as *tandem bullets.*

Multiple entrance and exit wounds: There may be multiple wounds of entrance and exit depending upon the posture of the victim when he was hit. A bullet may perforate an arm and pass through the chest so that four wounds result. A bullet, traversing the chest, thigh, and lower leg of a man bending on his haunches, can produce six wounds. When the entrance wounds are odd in number and more and exits are even and less in number, the pestibility is that at least one bullet is inside the body. If the exit holes are more and the entry holes are less, the projectles might have split and made exit. If the entry wounds are more and exit wounds are less, we must do careful search for the projectile in the body, if necessary guided by imaging technology. This is called odd and even rule, which is thumb rule for autopsy surgeon.

Q. 17.13. Tabulate the differences between the wound of entry and wound of exit caused by a bullet.

Differences between the wound of entry and wound of exit caused by a bullet are described in Table 17.2.

Table 17.2: Differences between entry wound and exit wound caused by a bullet

Exit wound	*Entry wound*
1. The wound is smaller in size (except at contact range when the skin may be torn by blast or rarely when the bullet ricochets, or loses its gyroscopic stability)	The missile tears out the tissues and has sharply defined outwardly split edges
2. In flat bone, especially the skull, the entry wound is clean cut on the outer surface and chipped inward	In flat bone, especially the skull, the exit wound is bevelled and everted
3. Edges are inverted because the missile penetrates from outside. In fat persons, they may be everted due to protrusion of fat	Edges are everted because the missile forces its way out
4. Abrasion collar is present; grease collar may or may not be present	Abrasion collar is absent except in shored exit wounds when irregular abrasion will be seen. Grease collar is never seen
5. Burning, blackening, singeing, and tattooing may be seen at appropriate distances	Burning, blackening, singeing, and tattooing cannot be there except from another overlapping wound with its own pattern
6. Clothing may be turned in and carried into the wound	Clothing may or may not be turned out
7. Track near the entry wound may be bright pink due to carboxy-haemoglobin in the case of near discharge	Not usually so but very exceptionally gas can be blown along a wound track
8. Lead ring may be seen on radiological or micro-chemical examination	Lead ring absent

Q. 17.14. Discuss the conditions which affect the appearance of firearm wounds.

Q. 17.15. In case of firearm injury to a person, how will you decide the distance and direction from which the weapon was fired. Add a note on ricochetting of a bullet.

The firearm wounds should always be photographed with an attached scale. Some of the conditions which may affect the appearance of these wounds are: (1) the weapon firing the projectile, (2) nature of the projectile, (3) velocity and stability of the missile at the moment of impact, (4) ricocheting of the bullet, (5) distance of the firearm, (6) angle at which the firearm struck the part of the body, and (7) the time elapsed since the discharge.

1. *Weapon:* This may be a smooth-bored one or a rifled one. In addition, there are air pistols and air guns. All these are already described. The nature of entry and exit wounds from the shotguns and the rifled weapons is also already discussed.

2. *Projectile:* The projectile fired may be shots, pellets, or slugs, as in shotguns and air guns. Air guns are considered least hostile to humans. The editor (Dr Subrahmanyam) has seen a case of air gun killing the owner of the weapon who ordered his servant to clean the barrel and was peeping through the muzzle end. The servant triggered and air-gun-pellet hit the lower orbit front passed through the venous sinus and got lodged near pituitary fossa. So, one should be always be alert to such possibility (Subrahmanyam. BV and Chandulal. R, For. Sci 1971, Vol. 1). Large bullets cause greater damage to the body structures than small ones and round bullets produce larger wounds than cylindroconical ones. Lead bullets are easily deformed, if they strike a resistant object but bullets partly enclosed in cupronickel or steel jackets are likely to mushroom. A *dum-dum bullet* is a soft point or hollow point expanding bullet or a full jacketed bullet with its nose cut off. As it slows down and mushrooms on hitting a target, it is more destructive than ordinary bullets. Fragments of military shell are also destructive and cause extensive wounds.

3. *Velocity:* A bullet at high velocity (and stabilised) frequently passes through the body and if no resistance to its passage is encountered, the size and shape of the entrance and exit wounds may be similar except for some abrasion and possibly inversion of the edges in the former and sharpness and possibly eversion of the edges in the latter (Fig. 17.21).

When a projectile passes through the body, it crushes the tissue it strikes and stretches the surrounding tissue in a radial manner along its path. Tissue crush causes permanent *cavity*. Tissue stretch causes temporary cavity and can tear tissues centrifugally alongside the missile path and also cause distant vascular damage. The degree of cavitation depends on the specific

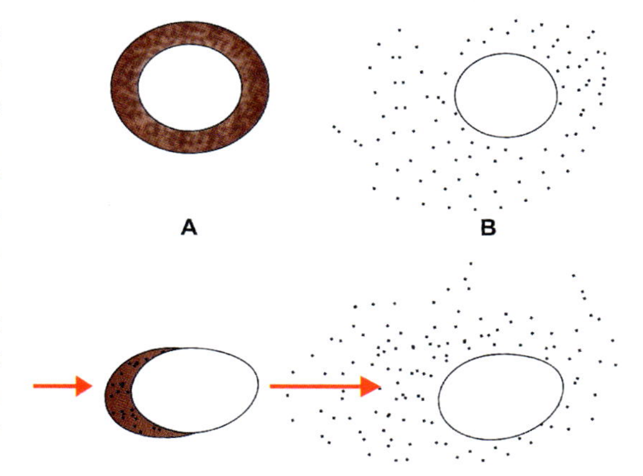

Fig. 17.20: Illustrative sketches showing—(A) **abraded collar,** and (B) **powder distribution** (tattoo marks) in a **perpendicular hit** (above), and an **oblique hit** (below). The abraded collar is of uniform width in a perpendicular hit (above) but is wider on one side in an oblique hit (below). The wider side indicates the direction from which the bullet entered and it thus helps to determine the direction of fire

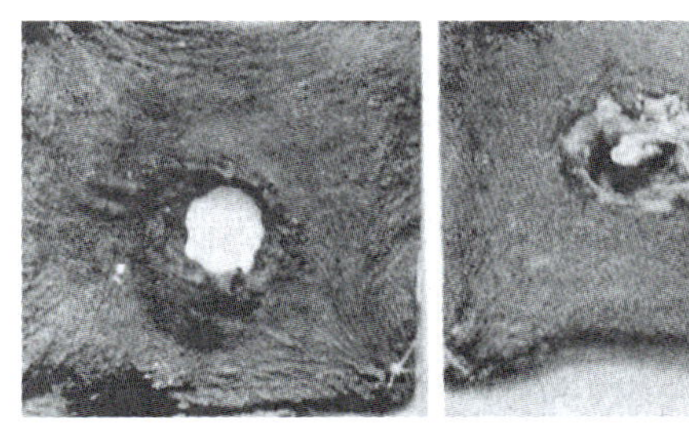

Fig. 17.21: Typical entrance wound on the left showing oblique hit characterised by abraded collar and inverted edges, and typical exit wound on the right showing everted and lacerated edges. (*Courtesy*: Dr R Chandulal)

properties of the tissue involved. Lung tissue being largely air is not greatly affected. Life may be endangered, if solid organs, e.g. brain or liver, are so traumatised.

The effect of high velocity projectiles shows many variations. If a bone is hit, the bone may fragment and the pieces will cause still further destruction (secondary missiles). At medium velocity ranges, the bullet tends to pass cleanly through the tissues and cuts a clean hole through the bones (single entry and exit wound). A low velocity bullet can easily be deflected, when it strikes a hard object such as bone, and often lodges in the body (entry wound but no exit wound).

4. *Ricochet*: A ricocheted bullet is one which is deviated (deflected) from its course by striking an intermediary object. This results in deformity, loss of velocity, and loss of stability. The following phenomena may be observed.

a. The bullet which strikes the body after ricochet may abrade or bruise the body surface or produce a gutter and then fall to the ground without entering the body.
b. The bullet may enter the body. The entrance wound assumes a bizarre shape due to deformity. It may enter on its broad side and produce a *keyhole entrance wound.*
c. Extensive focal lacerations of tissues may be found, if the bullet ricochets after entering the body and hits a bone. It may fracture the bone. It may somersault so that its nose may face the entrance wound.
d. The path of a bullet which has ricocheted inside the body is less predictable and unusual deviations may be found.

The author has seen a case in which a bullet entering through the umbilicus hit the spine, ricocheted along the ribs, and exited with a piece of ruptured liver. The entry wound in the umbilicus was hardly noticeable giving an impression that the bullet was still in the body. Dr J Gargi records a case in which a bullet entered the cranial cavity and after hitting the interior of skull vault ricocheted into the spinal column in the lumbar region. Whole body radiographs were necessary before it could be located.

It is not practicable to make a bullet ricochet intentionally (even on the surface of water) with a view to inflict injury on a particular person. Therefore, if there is reason to suspect that a bullet has ricocheted before it struck the body, the bullet should be examined for typical sliding, graze-like, so-called brush marks, and particles of foreign matter that may have struck in the flaws of the bullet from the intermediary object. Such a bullet should be handled with great care lest the foreign body particles should fall off and valuable evidence thus lost. The characteristics of ricochet marks on targets of different nature help to reconstruct the event. Frangible bullets do not ricochet as they disintegrate on striking.

5. *Distance:* The characteristic features of the wounds in the case of shotgun and rifled weapons both at close and distant ranges have already been discussed.

6. *Angle:* When a firearm is discharged, the bullet travels with considerable velocity and it generally traverses through the body tissues in a straight trajectory or a slightly curved path. Therefore, when wounds of entry and exit are present, a line joining them, or a line approximately joining the wound of entry and the site where the missile is lodged, when extended, would indicate the direction of fire, barring instances where the bullet (shot) has been deflected within the body. While interpreting the direction of fire, the posture of the victim when he was hit at should be kept in mind. If a bullet is found to have deviated after striking a bone, one should record the direction it followed until it deviated.

If a bullet (with black powder) is fired within a few inches of the skin, a burn is produced round the wound. If it fired at right angle to the body, the burn covers an area circular in shape with uniform abraded collar and blackening and tattooing.

If the burnt area is oval in shape, the indication is that the barrel of the weapon is inclined, the broad end indicating the point of initial contact of the bullet. The direction of the inclined bullet is from the wide to the narrow side. In oblique and close fire, marks of burning, abraded collar, blackening and tattooing, are more intense on the side nearest to the point of fire. At this point where the bullet made entry, the edge is bevelled, the other edge being overhanging. As the obliquity of the fire is increased, the wound becomes elongated in shape, and if the skin is struck at a tangent, penetration may fail to occur and only a slight linear furrowing of skin may be produced.

When the *projectile traverses the skull,* the angle struck is ascertained from the way the track has opened up. An entrance bullet hole bevels inward and, therefore, the entrance is usually clean cut and the defect on the inner surface of the bone is larger than that on the outer surface. An exit hole on the skull is bevelled outward. It is larger on the outer than on the inner surface of the bone.

In unusual circumstances, a small bullet (22 type) striking the skull at an angle may be deflected in such a way that it may produce a continuous wound track under the scalp without penetrating the skull. In the same-manner, a bullet striking the rib at an angle sometimes passes under the skin and partly encircles the chest without penetrating the pleural cavities *(rat-hole injury).*

7. *Time of discharge:* The development of a reaction to injury is the same in all types of wounds. Clothing and microorganisms may be carried into the body and set up infection as in any other type of wound. The various changes may help to determine the time of discharge.

Q. 17.16. Outline the differentiating features of suicide, homicide and accident by firearm.

Differentiating features of suicide, homicide and accident by firearm are described in Table 17.3.

Q. 17.17. Comment on 'physical activity after fatal firearm injury'.

This depends upon the site of injury and the organ involved. Unless there is gross destruction of brain, cardiovascular system, or pulmonary system, some physical activity is possible in many cases. However, it is shorter in firearm victims than in victims of stabbing. In a pistol shot through the right temple perforating the brain and exiting on the left temple, the victim was in a position to sit and answer questions nine hours after the shooting, though he succumbed to the injuries then. A man who got shot in his heart by a pistol bullet could

Table 17.3: Differentiating features of suicide, homicide and accident by firearm

	Suicide	*Homicide/accident*
1. Victim	Generally adult male	Any
2. Site	Side of temple, centre of forehead, roof of mouth, under the chin, front and left side of chest, occasionally the epigastrium	Any part of the body
3. Distance	Contact or very close shot	Usually distant shot but occasionally medium or close shot
4. Direction	Consistent with self-firing	Any
5. Number of shots	Generally one but may be more hesitation shots may have been fired at random	Any number of shots
6. Cadaveric spasm	Rarely, a weapon may be firmly grasped by cadaveric spasm, difficult to simulate by a murderer to give an impression of suicide	Weapon may be missing, or may not be found. No cadaveric spasm
7. Scene of crime	No evidence of disorder generally	Evidence of disorder and struggle may be there

walk half a mile before he collapsed. A victim of 0.32 calibre bullet, which penetrated his heart, lung, and liver, fell to the ground, pulled out his gun, and shot the assailant in the chest. He died 20 minutes later. Death is instantaneous, if there is a gaping wound of the heart or the medulla is involved. An apparently less hit person may die faster than an extensively bleeding person. In a direct deep medullar or upper spinal hit, instant death without evidence of much bleed may be seen.

In addition to routine precautions, the following points require special consideration while conducting an autopsy on a victim of firearm injury: (1) Crime scene, (2) clothing, (3) firearm injuries, (4) cause of death, and (5) chemical analysis.

1. *Crime scene:* If possible, the medical officer should visit the scene of crime. A concise description of crime scene, e.g. the place where the body is found, signs of struggle, etc., with appropriate photographs and sketches is essential. It is important to locate fired cartridge cases and wads, if any, since their position may determine the location of the firer.

2. *Clothing:* This should be removed with care keeping in mind the possibility of finding bullets/pellets in them. They should not be cut through bullet holes. Other observations, such as blood stains, powder marks, bullet holes and their relation to body injuries, may be made. Due to the presence of creases in the garment, several holes may result from a single bullet. It should be noted, if the fibres of the clothes are turned inward or outward (this is not always a reliable indication of direction). All these observations may have great significance to determine the position of the deceased at the time he was shot, the range from which he was shot, and if death was suicide or homicide, and if homicide whether it is consistent with self-defence. Pertinent positive and negative findings (e.g. absence of visible residues) should be recorded. If any residues are found, one should document the character, distribution, and size of the areas involved in relation to the point at which the bullet entered. Photography is very helpful and so also good description. The clothing should be carefully handled, folded, air-dried, if necessary and packed for subsequent examination by the forensic science laboratory (FSL).

3. *Firearm injuries:* The wounds should be assigned a number and described fully with special reference to anatomical landmarks, and recorded in the report under the heading "evidence of injury". A photograph with attached scale is desirable. A body sketch giving your impression of the wound profile is helpful. The description should include the characteristic features that distinguish it as an entry or exit wound; its shape, e.g. stellate, round, slit-like, or jagged, the width of the marginal abrasion, particularly if it is oval, the diameter of the powder residue deposits, and the track. If presence of gunpowder inside the wound is suspected, the wound should be excised for microscopic examination.

Hairy areas, such as the scalp, may be shaved for proper documentation on a photograph. One of the gravest errors made during the autopsy of President Kennedy was the fact that the head was never shaved. Hair as well as a skin portion of suitable size around the entrance and exit wounds may be preserved for examination by the FSL. It may reveal the presence of fine granules of burnt and unburnt gun powder indicating a medium, close, or contact shot. Careful examination of the markings on the skin may help to determine the shape of the powder grains that were involved. Chemical examination for the presence of carboxyhaemoglobin is useful when the range of fire is close.

The bullet path should be traced by careful dissection, and not by indiscriminate probing. It should be described in anatomical order. It is best documented by following the track of haemorrhage through the organs before their removal from the body. It may be straight from entrance to exit or deflected. An X-ray examination before dissection is of great help to visualise any metallic fragments along the path and makes bullet recovery easier.

Occasionally, an entrance and exit wound on the scalp are located within an inch or two of each other, and on autopsy, one finds that a subcutaneous track connects the two injuries. This is due to separation of a fragment of metal from the bullet, the metal particles proceeding under the scalp while the major part of the bullet enters the skull and may or may not exit in a different location.

It is also helpful to trace a bullet which has not exited. It is often surprising to find it palpable under the skin opposite the entrance wound. Occasionally, a bullet penetrates a hollow viscus and its position is considerably altered. As for example, a bullet in the stomach may pass in the intestines due to peristalsis, and one in the aorta to anywhere in the large arteries of the body due to circulation. The latter is known as *bullet embolism*. While looking for the bullet, it is necessary to feel through large blood clots, and as many fragments as possible should be recovered. In a case of hunting rifle injury at the right knee, a bullet splinter eventually made its way into the large vein system, then into the right heart, and thence into the pulmonary arteries, and finally got stuck there for over a whole year *(souvenir bullet)*.

The crime bullet recovered may be intact and in good condition, or mutilated, brushed, or deformed (Fig. 17.22). It is imperative that the medical officer who extracts a bullet from a live person or during an autopsy takes care that he does not add any new markings or obliterate

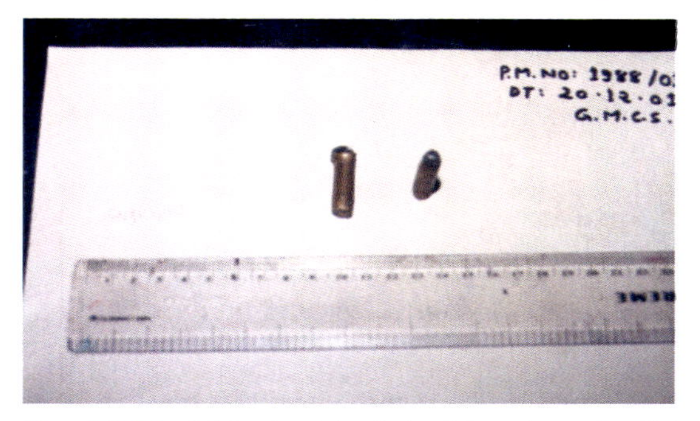

Fig. 17.22: Distorted bullets (*Courtesy*: Dr BV Subrahmanyam)

those that are present. The following **precautions** are essential:

a. The bullet should not be mishandled but removed with bare fingers or rubber-tipped forceps, and not with toothed metal forceps.
b. The recovered bullet should be dried and not washed as it wound remove any powder residues and blood sticking to it.
c. A note may be made of its size, the kind of metal it is made of, presence or absence of striations, and the deformity, if any. A deformed nose, for example, suggests that a bullet has hit against a hard surface. These details, besides providing useful information, help to identify the bullet. In addition, for purpose of ready identification, the bullet may be marked on any area that is free from any impressions, such as the lands or grooves, or marks, such as powder or loading.
d. Other relevant particulars may be noted, e.g. pattern of weave of clothing on the nose of the bullet, which is sometimes found when a bullet hits a clothed part of the body.
e. The bullet should be dried, wrapped in paper, and preserved in a container.

Particular care must be exercised in removing a bullet from bone. Excision of a segment of bone containing the bullet followed by manual bending and prying of the specimen usually releases the missile without even handling it, or else the bony portion containing the bullet may be sent directly to the FSL.

Medical officers extracting a bullet from a live person or during an autopsy face a danger from *exploding ammunition* now being used in USA and elsewhere. The bullets have a hollow tip with a container in which there is a detonator and charge with a tiny anvil and a single lead pellet. Such bullets may not explode on impact but may do so during extraction. However, their injury potential is low (eyes need protection).

4. *Cause of death:* Haemorrhage and injury to vital organs leading to shock are the common causes of death. In abdominal wounds, infection is another common immediate cause of death. Complications, like peritonitis develop due to leakage of contents from the gastrointestinal tract and lead to death in due course. Pneumonia develops frequently in head injuries with prolonged unconsciousness. Hypostatic pneumonia develops in elderly patients who are bed-ridden even for a few days.

5. *Chemical analysis:* This includes determination of blood group, and blood (or urine) alcohol content of the victim. The former generally furnishes circumstantial evidence in relation to blood stains found at the crime scene, or on the shot/wad.

Q. 17.18. What is a Souvenir bullet?

A Souvenir bullet is one which is found lodged generally stuck to or in a bone or vertebral area in a prior and past firing. It can be X-rayed and preserved. It might have been left unattended or left out during surgical intervention for reasons of safety. It is enveloped by fibrous coat consequent to foreign body response of the hosts body.

18 Injuries—Medicolegal Aspects

Q. 18.1. Explain the following terms: (1) assault, (2) cognisable offence, (3) homicide, (4) suicide.

Assault: An assault is an offer of threat or attempt to apply force to the body of another in a hostile manner. The actual blow, even though it may be plucking at the coat in an angry manner, is termed *battery*. Thus, battery is actual application of force to the body; it is the assault brought to completion. In Indian law, the term assault is taken to cover assault and battery.

Cognisable offence means an offence for which a police officer may arrest the offender without warrant, e.g. kidnapping, rape, and murder.

Homicide: In general, this means killing of one human being as a result of conduct of the other. It may be lawful or unlawful.

Lawful homicide may be: (1) justifiable, or (2) excusable. These terms are understood as follows:

Justifiable homicide is the term applied to homicide which is justified by circumstances, e.g. (1) judicial execution, (2) in suppressing riots or effecting arrest, (3) in self-defence or defence of another person against a dangerous assault, and (4) in preventing some forcible and atrocious act, such as, rape, murder, or burglarious entry into a dwelling house.

Excusable homicide is the term applied to homicide which occurs under certain circumstances, such as—(1) in self-defence or a sudden quarrel, (2) in defence of one's home or family, (3) when there is no other way to escape, (4) when it follows from some misadventure beyond control of the accused, as following upon an operation of a lawful character, (5) from lawful and moderate punishment, and (6) in a sport, such as, boxing.

Persons with XYY chromosome pattern have a natural tendency to violence. Whether such violence is excusable or not is for the courts to decide. Wilber records the case of an young Australian who was acquitted of a murder charge because the defence claimed that the accused had an XYY chromosome complement and that this imbalance had predisposed him to criminal behaviour.

Unlawful homicide implies both the fact of death and an accompanying state of mind, known as 'malice aforethought' on the part of the killer'. Without such a state of mind, the act is known as culpable homicide not amounting to murder.

Murder {culpable homicide – Sec. 300 Indian Penal Code (IPC)} means killing of a person with malice aforethought, express or implied. In the crime of murder, the accused must accept the risk of state of health, age, and sex of the deceased when the injury was inflicted. The criteria for a charge of murder are: (1) intention to kill, (2) preparation for the act, (3) malice aforethought, and (4) preparation of alibi.

Culpable homicide not amounting to murder (manslaughter – Sec. 299, IPC) arises (1) when the accused has intentionally attacked the deceased without the necessary intention to kill, e.g. when there is gross provocation, (2) when there is no intention to kill but death results from unlawful conduct by the persons responsible, e.g. culpable omission to perform a duty, such as, failure to take necessary precautions in the administration of anaesthesia, and (3) when doing a lawful act recklessly, e.g. driving a car (Sec. 304-A, IPC).

Suicide means self-murder. Attempted suicide is an unlawful act and the person is held responsible for the immediate consequences of the act in India.

Q. 18.2. How will you proceed to examine a case of injury? Outline the procedure of entering wounds in an accident register.

In the examination of wounds, whether the victim be alive or dead, great care should be exercised. If no opinion can be given immediately, the person should be kept under observation and this fact reported to the police. In cases which are likely to die from the effect of criminal violence, during clinical examination, a dying declaration should be recorded. In every case, all observations should be entered in the accident register with appropriate sketches or diagrams. If possible, the photograph of the site of crime should be taken before anything is touched, and photographs with an attached scale taken of the various wounds.

An **accident register** is a register maintained by doctors/hospitals in which the details of examination of the injured person are recorded by the medical officer. The particulars to be entered are: (1) serial number, (2) date, time and place of examination, (3) name including father's name and surname, (4) age, (5) sex, (6) occupation, (7) address both of residence and office with telephone number, if any, (8) brought by whom, (9) two identification marks, (10) dying declaration, if necessary, (11) consent for examination, (12) brief history of the case as alleged—beaten by whom, with what, when, and where, (13) detailed description of injury, (14) opinion on the nature of injuries—simple/grievous/likely to prove fatal, (15) remarks, and (16) signature of the medical officer. Points 8, 11, 12, and 15 need some elaboration.

Brought by whom: A medicolegal case is generally brought by a police constable and occasionally by relations, friends, or passers-by. If the case is brought by a police constable, his name, number, and the police station to which he belongs should be recorded. If brought by relations, friends, or passers-by, their names and addresses, with telephone numbers, if any, should be recorded, and intimated to the police station. The purpose of maintaining this in the entry of hospital register is to keep record of these cases and as and when needed and deemed fit certificates can be issued based on the record. It is a very important record of evidence useful for inrestigators and the courts of law. It is fundamental as an FIR of police.

Consent for examination: In India, a person of and above the age of 12 years can give valid conse nt for medical examination and treatment. It should preferably be written, witnessed, and bear the signature or left thumb impression of the patient. In case of persons below the age of 12 years, or the mentally defective, consent from a parent or guardian is necessary. The consent should be obtained after a full explanation of the reasons for which it is required (informed consent).

Brief history of the case as alleged: The injured person may or may not give a correct version of the kind of weapon and mode of assault. The medical officer should satisfy himself, if the injuries could have been caused by that kind of weapon and in the manner as alleged.

Remarks: This may include any information that is considered essential by the medical officer, such as general description of the victim, e.g. size, weight, stature, etc.; his general condition, e.g. in shock or coma, bleeding from the nose, mouth, etc; injuries and stains on his clothing; age of injury; or if he was admitted to hospital; if special investigations, e.g. X-ray, ECG, are necessary; or if the injuries are self-inflicted, etc.

All the above particulars are entered by the medical officer in his own handwriting. They are also recorded in the injury certificate or injury report.

Q. 18.3. What is an injury certificate? Give a specimen of injury certificate with fictitious name.

An injury certificate is a document containing the details of injury as recorded by the medical officer. When a wounded person is sent by the police for medical examination, the medical officer is served with a requisition containing the patient's statement in vernacular, and a printed form known as 'injury certificate' in duplicate, the columns of which he is required to fill in after examination of the injured person. One copy of the injury certificate is despatched to the investigating police officer, in a sealed cover, and the other retained as office copy for future reference. A injury certificate with fictitious name as given herein shows how the various columns are filled.

Injury Certificate

To,

THE SUB-INSPECTOR OF POLICE, BURLA POLIC STATION

Sir,

I forward herewith the result of my examination of Mathura Prasad, son of Hari Prasad, resident of Buria, Dist: Sambalapur.

Name of injury, i.e. whether a cut, bruise or burn, etc., etc.	Size of each injury in cm, i.e. length, breadth and depth	On what part of the body inflicted	Whether "simple" or "grievous"	By what kind of weapon inflicted	Remarks
(1)	(2)	(3)	(4)	(5)	(6)
1. Lacerated wound	3 × 1 cm bone deep	On forehead 3 cm above the middle ofleft eye-brow	Opinion reserved, X-ray of skull required	These injuries might have been caused by any hard blunt object	Age of injuries is within 24 hrs.
2. Contusion (livid red colour)	3 × 3 cm	On left malar prominence	Simple		
3. Abrasion	5 × 3 cm	On outer aspect of left forearm in the middle	Simple		
Identification marks: 1.			2.		

I certify that the said Mathura Prasad was asked the question(s) noted below and gave the answer(s) recorded:

Q: Are you willing to be examined by me? **A:** Yes

Signature or thumb impression of the person ....

Identified by Constable No. ....

Name .... P.S ....

Yours faithfully
Signature of the doctor
(designation)

Q. 18.4. Comment on: (1) nature of injury, (2) simple, grievous, or dangerous injury.

Nature of Injury

While describing the injuries in columns 1, 2 and 3 of the injury report, the whole body should be examined in good light and where necessary, a magnifying lens may be used. The description should follow the anatomical pattern, e.g. injuries on the head, trunk, extremities, etc. The nature (abrasion, bruise, laceration, fracture, incised wound, or stab wound, etc.), exact position with reference to anatomical landmarks, shape, margins, edges, direction, and dimensions of every injury found should be described. Even a trivial injury needs adequate description. As for example, a faint abrasion around the nose and mouth may indicate attempted smothering. The presence of any extraneous material in the wound should be carefully noted. If the patient complains of pain in some region of the body, it must be recorded even if there is no apparent injury, and the patient kept under observation, if necessary.

Simple, Grievous, or Dangerous Injury

A **simple injury** is one which is neither extensive nor serious, and which would heal rapidly without leaving any permanent deformity or disfiguration and which does not fall under grievous injury.

A **grievous injury** is one: (1) which is extensive or serious, (2) which does not heal rapidly, and (3) which leaves a permanent deformity or disfiguration. Section 320 IPC defines following injuries as grievous:

1. Emasculation (cutting of off the penis, castration, or causing loss of power of erection due to spinal injury).
2. Permanent privation of the sight of either eye.
3. Permanent privation of the hearing of either ear.
4. Privation of any member (part, organ, limb) or joint.
5. Destruction or permanent impairing of powers of any member or joint.
6. Permanent disfiguration of head or face.
7. Fracture or dislocation of a bone or a tooth.
8. Any hurt which endangers life, or which causes the sufferer to be, during the space of 20 days, in severe bodily pain, or unable to follow his daily routine. Section 319 IPC defines hurt as bodily pain, disease, or infirmity, caused to any person.

Contrary to popular belief, a simple stay in hospital for 20 days does not constitute grievous injury. During this period, the injured person must be in severe bodily pain or unable to follow his ordinary pursuits. If the healing of a simple hurt is deliberately delayed by the patient for 20 days, it does not amount to grievous hurt. Sometimes, a simple injury may be made to appear grievous by the injured person feigning a serious disorder. As for example, a person injured on the eye may feign blindness. A careful examination in all such cases provides valuable information.

In India, it is not uncommon to make a false report about the loss of a tooth in order to charge an enemy with grievous hurt. Sometimes, a loose tooth has fallen off or has been pulled out or some other tooth is produced as the fractured or dislocated tooth. When such suspicion exists, the medical officer should make a note of: (1) number of teeth present in each jaw and other details, such as, whether temporary or permanent, and whether they are firm, loose, or diseased, (2) condition of the socket to determine, if there is any bleeding, laceration, or fracture of the thin bony plate surrounding the alveolus, or presence of stump of the fractured tooth, and (3) condition of gums or lips for evidence of injury. The tooth should also be examined to determine, if it corresponds to the missing tooth, and its fangs examined to determine if the tooth has been fractured or dislocated. In false complaints, there are generally no signs of injury to lips, gums, or adjacent teeth, although the alleged weapon is a stick or a stone. The cavity is old and contracted and the tooth usually unbroken, old and dry, or diseased.

A **dangerous injury** is a variety of grievous injury. It is an injury which endangers, i.e. poses an immediate danger to life. It is either extensive or serious in relation to the organ or part wounded. The injury is fatal in the absence of surgical aid. Common examples of such injuries are: gun shot wounds, compound fractures of the skull, trauma to a large or important blood vessel, and rupture of some internal organ, e.g. spleen. This is generally caused by a shooting, stabbing or cutting implement.

Q. 18.5. What is meant by a dangerous weapon? Mention the common weapons of offence and state the external characteristics of injuries produced by them which will help you to infer the type of weapon used for offence.

Sections 324 and 326 IPC define a *dangerous weapon* as any instrument used for shooting, stabbing, or cutting, or any instrument which, if used as a weapon of offence, is likely to cause death.

The *common weapons of offence* can be grouped into: (1) hard blunt objects, e.g. stick, stone, fist, (2) light weapon with a sharp cutting edge, e.g. knife, scalpel, razor, (3) heavy weapons with a sharp splitting edge, e.g. hatchet, axe, saber, (4) pointed weapons, e.g. knife, dagger, needle, arrow, ice pick, and (5) firearms, e.g. smooth-bored (shotgun) and rifled (rifle, revolver, and pistol).

It is usually possible to infer the type or kind of weapon from an examination of wounds and clothes.

Blunt objects can cause abrasions, contusions, lacerations, and fractures, either singly or in combination, depending on the nature of the object, severity of the blow, and part of the body struck. The injuries having combined features are described as contused abrasions, contused lacerated wounds (CLWs), etc. The surface of a weapon coming in contact with the body may sometimes bear some pattern and give a clue to the weapon used, e.g. canes, chains, hammer, etc. Lacerations over bone may simulate incised wounds but examination with a hand lens would reveal their true nature.

Light weapons with a sharp cutting edge produce incised wounds. Their characteristics are already discussed. Wounds from jagged portions of metal or pieces of broken glass may simulate incised wounds but they are generally irregular in shape and their edges are generally bruised. Sometimes, the foreign body responsible for the wound may be found broken off in the wound.

Heavy cutting weapons with a sharp splitting edge cause chop wounds. The dimensions of such wounds correspond with the cross-section of the penetrating blade. The margins are sharp and edges may show abrasions and bruising with marked destruction of underlying tissues and organs. If the edge of the weapon is blunt, the margins are irregular. The majority of such injuries are homicidal, and a few are accidental due to machinery.

Pointed weapons cause stab wounds (punctured wounds). Their characteristics are already described. To indicate the general nature of the weapon responsible for such wounds, the terms punctured-incised, punctured-lacerated, penetrating-incised, penetrating-lacerated, and perforating-incised or perforating-lacerated, are used. When a punctured wound is produced by a fall on some sharp object, such as a glass pot or sharp stone, a part of foreign body responsible for the wound may be found broken off in the wound and easily detected with a magnifying lens.

Firearm wounds have their own characteristics which are already described.

The weapon may be brought by the police along with the injured person or later during the course of investigation. The medical officer should ascertain, if the injuries could have been caused by that kind of weapon and in the manner as alleged. The kind of weapon used in inflicting the wound can be judged from an examination of the weapon for its appearance, weight, dimensions, tip, etc., with special reference to the nature of wound, e.g. size, shape, margins, edges, direction, etc. The weapon must also be examined for the presence of blood stains, hairs, fibres, etc., sticking to it. A foreign body found in the wound, e.g. glass piece, stone, sand, mud, grease, broken tip of knife, projectile, wadding, etc., may sometimes give a clue. The clothes are also examined for cuts, tears, stains, burns, blackening, etc., and for their correlation with bodily injuries.

If the medical officer is convinced that the injuries are such as could not have been caused by the kind of weapon and in the manner suggested by the police or injured person, he should specifically record it so as to avoid unnecessary cross-examination while giving evidence in court.

The weapon should be described and labelled in such manner that its identification later on in court is not difficult. It should be returned to the police in a cover with a private seal, taking the signature of constable receiving it.

Q. 18.6. Give the data necessary to determine the age of injuries, without any special examination.

The age of injuries can be obtained from the following data of its healing process which itself is dependent on several factors such as: (a) vitality of the injured person, (b) extent of damage, (c) vascularity of the part, (d) infection, (e) mobility of the part, (f) nutrition, (g) diabetes, and (h) other factors that interfere with healing. It is therefore possible to give only the approximate age of injury without special examinations.

A fresh **abrasion** is bright red. The exudation of serum dries and forms a red scab in about 12–24 hours. The scab becomes reddish brown in 2–3 days. The abrasion heals from the periphery by new growth of epithelium in about 4–7 days by which time the scab falls off. Healing is complete by about 10 days.

A fresh **bruise** is red at first. The colour changes from red to blue in a day, bluish black or brown in about 2–4 days, green in about 5–7 days, and yellow in about 7–10 days. The yellow colour slowly fades, the skin regaining its normal colour in about 14–15 days. This time sequence is very variable and one frequently sees various colours simultaneously.

In **clean aseptic wounds** whose edges are in apposition, healing occurs without formation of granulation tissue. The edges are red and swollen after about 12 hours after infliction of wound. A small wound may show scab formation by about 24 hours. Epithelium begins to grow at the edges after 36 hours, and epithelialization of small clean wounds may be complete in 4 to 7 days depending on the vascularity of the part. Scar tissue is formed in 1–2 weeks. Factors which influence scar formation are: (a) the nature, size, and method of wound healing, (b) presence or absence of sepsis, (c) vascularity of the part, and (d) age and general health of the patient. A clean, incised, surgical wound normally heals in about a week and a definite scar appears in about two weeks. A scar forms earlier in smaller wounds than in bigger ones. It forms quickly, if the healing is by primary (first) intention and is delayed in the presence of sepsis. Scar formation is earlier in a vascular area as compared to an avascular one. And, it forms earlier in the young and healthy as compared to the old and undernourished.

The approximate age of a scar can be estimated from its ageing process, viz. vascular to avascular (2 weeks to 2 months), tender to non-tender (2 to 6 months), and soft to tough (more than 6 months).

1. Depending upon vascularity, a recently formed scar may appear reddish or bluish. It is tender and soft. The age of such a scar is up to two weeks.
2. As the vascularity diminishes, the scar becomes pale and white but is still tender and soft. Its age is up to two months.
3. With age, the scar contracts. It becomes smaller and whiter but it is still a little tender and soft. The age is between two to six months.
4. As the scar further contracts, it becomes tough, white, and glistening. The age is probably not less than six months to an indefinite number of years.

Scars produced in childhood grow in size with the natural development of the individual, especially if situated on the chest and limbs. A well-developed scar never disappears but scars from minor wounds may become very difficult to detect.

A **wound** which is **not** thoroughly **aseptic** or is **gaping** due to loss of tissue heals by formation of granulation tissue. Signs of inflammation, such as redness, swelling, and exudation of lymph, are seen in about 12–24 hours. Pus may be seen after a period of about 36 hours. Granulation tissue of appreciable extent will rarely be seen within a week. The stage of granulation lasts for a variable period depending on a number of factors and, therefore, it is not possible in such cases to determine the age of the wound with any degree of accuracy.

In **fractured bones,** the reparative process helps to fix the approximate age of fracture. A histological and X-ray examination of fractured part is desirable. Histologically, signs of clot organisation are seen in about 48 hours, the formation of osteoid matrix in about 3 days, and its transformation into soft callus by about a week. The *soft callus* is due to osteogenic granulation tissue between fractured ends. If the fracture is not adequately immobilised, the granulation tissue will be damaged and result in delayed union or malunion, and a charge of negligence against the doctor. Callus formation is well advanced in about 10 to 12 days but it is not visible on X-ray examination till about 3 weeks. The gap between the fractured ends is filled up by callus in about a month and, in about six weeks to two months, this callus is transformed into bone *(hard callus)* and bony union takes place. Remodelling and reabsorption of excess callus takes about six months. At this stage, an approximate estimation of age can be made from the extent of remodelling, smoothness of edges, and the form of trabeculae passing through the line of fracture. If the fracture is a recent one, two or three X-rays should be taken at intervals of a week to ascertain the rate of change at the fracture site.

In the repair of **fractures of skull,** healing occurs without formation of a visible callus because the injured periosteal vessels impede the formation of an external callus. The edges of a fissured fracture stick together in about a week. Calcification of inner table and rounding of sharp edges of fracture are seen in about two weeks. Bands of osseous tissue are seen running across the fissure in three to four weeks. In comminuted fractures where edges are not in apposition, bone formation does not occur. The gap is filled up by fibrous tissue any time between one to three months depending on the size of the gap, the fracture lines remaining permanently visible on X-ray.

In the **dislocation of a joint,** in recent cases, the colour changes in the bruise accompanying it, and in older cases, the amount of new fibrous tissue, may give some indication.

When a **tooth** has been knocked out, bleeding from its socket stops in about one to two days and a clot is formed. The clot is obliterated by fibrous tissue in about 14 days. The socket is completely filled with gradual new bone in about a year, as seen on X-ray examination.

In some cases, it may be necessary to determine the age of wounds by *microscopic examination* and *enzyme histochemistry* (refer page 278 antemortem and postmortem wounds).

Q. 18.7. Comment on: (1) necessarily fatal injury, (2) injury likely to cause death, (3) injury sufficient in the ordinary course of nature to cause death.

A **necessarily fatal injury,** as the phrase implies, ends in death as a direct result of injury, irrespective of any medical aid. Such injuries include extensive damage to vital organs, i.e. brain, heart, lungs, and abdominal viscera; massive intracranial haemorrhage; extensive burns; and the like.

An **injury likely to cause death** is one in which death is merely not possible but is likely. It is an injury which poses a danger to the life of the victim due to its severity or the structures involved. *In legal language, it is an injury wherefrom death as a consequence is not surprising.*

An **injury sufficient in the ordinary course of nature to cause death** is one that can in virtue of its own direct effects bring about a fatal result. The fact that in exceptional cases death may not ensue or that medical aid might have saved a person's life is not material. The injuries which prove fatal by intercurrent disease, e.g. tetanus, pneumonia, septicaemia, etc., are not included in this category. A scratch may become infected with spores of tetanus and cause death or an old man confined to bed on account of wound on the leg may die of hypostatic pneumonia. In both these cases, death is due to intercurrent disease resulting from injury but this fact does not make the original injury sufficient in the ordinary course of nature to cause death.

The assailant is charged with culpable homicide not amounting to murder (Sec. 299 IPC), if the injury is likely to cause death. The offence is murder (Sec. 300 IPC), if the injury is sufficient in the ordinary course of nature to cause death. An example will make this distinction clear. A stick blow on head is likely to cause death (culpable homicide). An axe blow on head is sufficient in the ordinary course of nature to cause death (murder).

Generally speaking, the following injuries may be considered sufficient in the ordinary course of nature to cause death. *In legal language, these are injuries wherefrom recovery as a consequence will be surprising.*

1. Injuries to brain and spinal cord especially if situated high up in the cervical region.
2. Injuries to heart and large blood vessels.
3. Serious injuries to the respiratory apparatus.
4. Injuries to highly vascular organs, e.g. liver and spleen.
5. Penetrating wounds of the alimentary canal.
6. Extensive burns and scalds even of slight severity. Burns involving about one-third of total body surface are sufficient to cause death.
7. A number of injuries, none of which is sufficient to cause death, may together by their cumulative effect be sufficient to do so.
8. Rapid loss of one-third of blood from the body.

Q. 18.8. Enumerate the causes of death in wounds of varied nature and comment on the medicolegal implications.

The ***causes of death*** *are: (1) immediate or direct, and (2) remote or indirect. And, the assailant is responsible for the death of his victim from any of these causes.*

Sometimes, the terms 'proximate' and 'immediate' are used in the description of the cause of death, as in the autopsy report. As already stated, the proximate cause of death is the disease or injury or a combina-

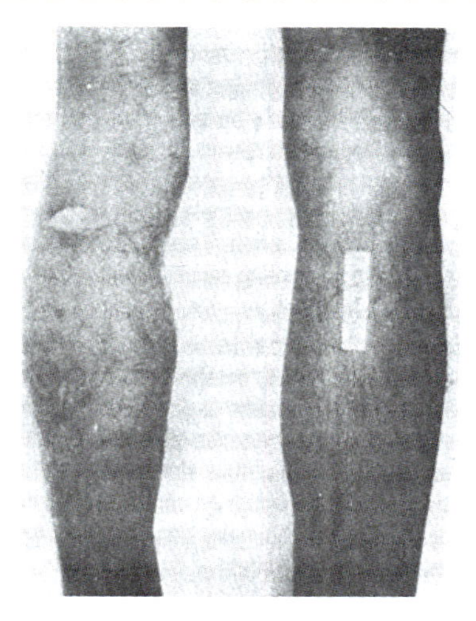

Fig. 18.1: Death due to multiple homicidal injuries on legs, none of which is fatal by itself. A male aged **38** was beaten by several people in Kollur on **14** August **1966** at about **10.00** am, with a barisa, an axe, and sticks. He expired at the General Hospital, Guntur, at **6.55** pm, the same day. Postmortem revealed multiple lacerated wounds, incised wounds, contusions, and fractures, confined only to both legs which were diffusely swollen and deformed. He **died** of shock and haemorrhage **from the cumulative effect of these injuries** on the legs—a common method of homicide in the districts of Guntur and Krishna of Andhra; in India

tion of both that initiated a series of events that led directly to the immediate cause of death (Fig. 18.1). As for example, a person dies of peritonitis two weeks after a stab in the abdomen. The immediate cause of death is peritonitis. The proximate or initiating cause of death is a stab wound of the abdomen.

Medicolegal implications: Under section 300 IPC, to substantiate a charge of murder, it is necessary to determine that—(1) the injury inflicted on the deceased was actually the cause of death, and (2) it was sufficient in the ordinary course of nature to cause death. A thorough and careful postmortem examination is, therefore, necessary: an assailant is not responsible for the death of his victim, if it can be proved that—(a) the victim died of natural disease, or (b) the injury was in no way responsible either as the direct or indirect cause of death.

If death is attributed to injuries and there are several of them, it is necessary to determine the actual one causing death, since all the injuries may not have been inflicted by the same assailant or even at the same time, or with the same weapon, as happens in gang feuds. This can be done by examining the injuries individually and noting those which involve a vital organ, or major blood vessel, or led to complications. If no such injury is found, the possibility of death from the cumulative effect of various injuries may be considered.

Under section 299 IPC, a person can be convicted of culpable homicide, if (1) he caused bodily injury that was likely to cause death, or (2) he caused injury to a person who is labouring under a disorder, disease, or bodily infirmity, and thereby hastens his death, e.g. assault resulting in rupture of an enlarged spleen, perforation of chronic intestinal ulcer, rupture of aortic aneurysm, etc. To substantiate a charge under this section, it is necessary to establish from postmortem examination the existence of disease that caused death and its relationship to injury that hastened it by showing that—(1) neither the disease nor the injury was the sole cause of death, and (2) death occurred at that time due to the combined effects of the presence of disease and infliction of injury.

Q. 18.9. Discuss the immediate causes of death from wounds.

The **immediate causes of death** are: (a) haemorrhage, (b) injury to a vital organ, (c) neurogenic shock, and (d) a combination of any of these.

HAEMORRHAGE

Haemorrhage may be external or internal and may lead to death from shock. If it is due to trauma, it is called traumatic haemorrhage in contrast to spontaneous haemorrhage which occurs in the absence of obvious trauma. The bleeding may be in the form of minute haemorrhagic spots (petechiae), blotchy areas of extravasated blood (ecchymoses), localised collection (haematoma), or a large effusion (apoplexy—the term being commonly used for cerebral haemorrhage).

As a rule, the more rapid the loss of blood, the more likely is death to occur. Children and old people are more severely affected by haemorrhage than young adults, and men resist haemorrhage better than women, although the latter can sustain enormous loss of blood during childbirth without fatal results. The state of health of the victim is also important. A minor injury may produce death in persons with haemophilia or haemorrhagic diathesis. The blood volume in a normal healthy adult is 8–8.5% of body weight or 80–85 ml/kg. Generally, a rapid loss of two litres of blood (one-third of blood from the body) is sufficient to cause death from haemorrhage. *A person suffering from haemorrhagic shock is usually conscious till the end though the sensorium is slightly blunted.*

Death from haemorrhage is diagnosed by extreme pallor of the skin and mucous membranes; poor development of lividity; pale bloodless appearance of internal organs, e.g. spleen; and collapsed and virtually empty sinusoids. The heart may show subendocardial haemorrhages.

In **external haemorrhage,** an approximate idea of blood loss may be obtained from, saturation of the clothing and ground about the victim and the relative anaemio state of viscera. As a rough estimate, one square foot of blood on the surface and clothing equals 100 ml of blood loss.

In **internal haemorrhage,** the amount of blood loss can often be judged fairly accurately, and can often be measured at autopsy. However, the effects of such blood loss are only partially dependent on the amount of blood lost. Even a small amount of blood may cause death by interfering with the vital functions of the body depending on the site of haemorrhage, as shown below:

Site of haemorrhage	*Cause of death*
1. Extradural, subdural, or subarachnoid	Cerebral compression
2. Medulla	Failure of vital functions
3. Pericardial sac	Cardiac tamponade
4. Pleural cavity	Collapse of lung and displacement of mediastinum
5. Respiratory passages, e.g. in cut throat injury, or tonsillectomy	Asphyxia

Injury to a Vital Organ

Extensive damage to vital organs, i.e. brain, heart, and lungs, is usually fatal. In such cases, the cause of death is clearly manifest but death is not necessarily instantaneous and considerable volitional power may be present for some time after receipt of such injuries. It must be remembered that extensive damage to abdominal viscera may be present without visible marks of injury.

Neurogenic Shock

This is also known as primary shock or vagal inhibition. It is characterised by sudden stoppage of heart and respiration as a result of reflex stimulation of the vagus nerve and consequent paralysis of cardiac and respiratory centres.

It occurs as a result of sudden stimulation of trigger areas or receptive spots in the body. As for example, holding the throat in an excited person may result in his collapse and instantaneous death. Other examples are: a blow on the epigastrium, sudden joy, fear, pain, etc. The person collapses and drops dead.

The cause of death is arrived at from negative findings: the history should be typical, viz. a blow on receptor area which may not have left a mark; instantaneous death; absence of fatal wounds; absence of poisoning; and no natural disease.

Q. 18.10. Discuss the remote causes of death from wounds.

Q. 18.11. Comment on: (1) thrombosis, (2) fat embolism, and (3) air embolism, as remote causes of death.

The **remote causes of death** are: infection; renal failure, formerly known as crush syndrome; thrombosis; embolism; secondary shock; consumptive (disseminated intravascular) coagulopathy, and other indirect results of injury. Death may also result from previous disease accelerated by injury; supervention of new disease; consequences of operative procedure; or to neglect of treatment on the victim's part.

Infection

All wounds may become infected and the type of infection varies from country to country. The infection may result in (a) local sepsis or septicaemia and pyaemia, (b) infective processes in internal organs, (c) necrosis or sloughing of parts, and (d) tetanus and anthrax in some countries. It is forensically important to prove a chain of causation due to the original injury.

Sepsis: In abrasions, infection may result in local sepsis or a spreading cellulitis. In septic complications, such as septicaemia and pyaemia, the spread of infection from injury must be traced. It should be remembered that bruising without breaking the surface skin can also lead to infection.

Infective processes in internal organs: With penetrating wounds of abdomen, there is always risk of peritonitis due to introduction of an organism or puncture of the bowel. In injuries to the thorax, an empyema may result. Bladder infection is a common sequel of any accident to an old person and may lead to pyelonephritis. In head injuries, a suppurative meningitis may ensue, especially if a fracture communicates with one of the sinuses, the common organisms being *Streptococcus pyogenes*, *Staphylococcus pyogenes*, and the pneumococci.

Necrosis or sloughing: This is the result of loss of blood supply, i.e. ischaemia. Necrosis of cervical vertebra has been seen in a cut throat injury by glass in a motor car accident.

Tetanus: In all wounds, and particularly in torn (lacerated) wounds and deep stab wounds, there is always the possibility of clostridial infection, especially tetanus. In order to associate the disease with the injury, it is necessary to show that the onset of disease is consistent with its incubation period, that is to say that the microorganism was implanted at the time of and as a result of injury. In India, symptoms of tetanus usually manifest within three to ten days after injury; sometimes, they may be delayed for about two to three weeks.

Renal Failure (*Crush Syndrome*)

This is a common sequel to extensive muscle damage, burns, and some poisons. Recent work suggests that it is due to damage to juxtaglomerular apparatus, renin-angiotensin system, and the effect on the glomeruli of disseminated intravascular coagulation, rather than acute tubular necrosis. The effects are similar to those associated with incompatible blood transfusion. Crush injuries may be complicated by fat or other emboli.

Thrombosis

A mass formed from constituents of blood within the vessels or the heart during life is called a thrombus and the process of its formation is known as thrombosis.

A frequent delayed complication of trauma is the formation of thrombi in veins giving rise to emboli. In almost all cases, the source will be found in the vessels draining into the femoral veins, though pelvic vessels are rarely involved in relation to pregnancy and abortion. Traumatic lesions of lower limbs, e.g. fractures of long bones, commonly result in the formation of thrombi. They take about 1–3 weeks to develop. A variety of changes may then take place. They may be detached in part or whole and result in emboli that are carried to pulmonary arteries. Occasionally, thrombi are formed in dural venous sinuses or subclavian and axillary veins after trauma. Trauma is also responsible occasionally for arterial thrombosis and embolism, e.g. thrombosis of carotid arteries after stab wounds of the neck and embolism of the middle cerebral arteries after bullet wounds of head. Apart from obvious association of thrombi with trauma, anybody who is confined to bed by an accident may develop phlebothrombosis particularly in the leg veins. In such cases, phlebothrombotic material may become detached in part or in whole and result in emboli that are carried to pulmonary arteries.

While about 80% of the victims of embolism have predisposing history of injury, surgical operation, or immobility in bed, the remaining 20% have no such history; they are ambulant and healthy. In the latter cases, the cause effect relationship after trauma is difficult to prove except by histological aging of the thrombus. Since it is the junction between the thrombus and the vein wall that provides most information about the maturity of the thrombus, the vein containing the thrombus and the adjacent muscle should be taken out for examination.

Embolism

Embolism means partial or complete obstruction of some part of the vascular system by any mass carried in circulation. The transported material is called an embolus. Emboli are classified as solid (detached thrombi), liquid (fat globules), and gaseous (air). They may be bland or septic, and venous, arterial, or lymphatic. Solid emboli are already discussed above.

Fat Embolism

This may be due to intrinsic fat (body fat) released as a result of trauma or rarely natural disease, or extrinsic fat introduced in body from outside.

Intrinsic fat embolism may result from:

1. Injury to adipose tissues which forces liquid fat into blood vessels
2. Multiple contusions in fatty areas
3. Crush injuries
4. Fractures of long bones, especially femur
5. Complications of manipulative surgery especially during operation on joints fixed by adhesions, incision of abdominal wall, amputation of breast, etc.
6. Burns
7. Occasionally transport of the injured person
8. Occasionally natural disease without trauma as in sickle cell anaemia.

As a result of trauma, especially crush injury, two things happen: (1) fat is set free from fat cells due to injury to adipose tissue, and (2) blood vessels are ruptured resulting in haemorrhage. The local rise of pressure from haemorrhage or inflammatory reaction and movement of the injured part may force the released fat in the ruptured veins, thus leading to fat embolism. **Other types of emboli,** such as bone marrow embolism, amniotic embolism, and occasionally tissue embolism, such as liver, may follow crush injuries. In case of fracture of long bones, marrow fat may enter the veins of Haversian canals.

Extrinsic fat embolism may result from: (1) injection of fatty substances as a therapy when fat may enter a vein, and (2) injection of fatty substances (usually soapy fluid) into the uterine cavity as an abortifacient, when fat may enter the circulation.

Fat embolism is of two types, viz: (1) pulmonary fat embolism, and (2) systemic or arterial fat embolism.

Pulmonary fat embolism: This is the result of fat emboli in pulmonary capillaries impeding the flow of blood through the lungs. Death occurs in about 10 hours from asphyxia due to impairment of gaseous exchange in the lungs. At autopsy, the lungs show congestion, oedema, and slight hypostatic pneumonia. The pulmonary vessels, arterioles, and capillaries are filled with globular fat emboli. Tardieu spots are also seen. To *demonstrate* fat emboli, pulmonary artery must be opened under water with a pair of scissors before the heart and lungs are dissected. Fat droplets can then be seen to escape. Diagnosis can be confirmed by squeezed out fluid from the lungs or microscopic examination of frozen sections of the lungs stained for fat, with Sudan III or osmic acid.

Systemic or arterial fat embolism: This is the result of fat emboli passing from pulmonary capillaries to the left side of heart and entering the systemic circulation from where they can reach any organ of the body. These emboli are arrested in the capillaries of various organs where they may give rise to perivascular haemorrhages. Serious consequences follow when the target organ is the brain. Clinically, cerebral fat emboli present in two ways: (1) immediate coma frequently misdiagnosed as due to head injury, or (2) by loss of consciousness after a lapse of 24 to 48 hours after injury. The incidence is due to shifting of globules of fat into smaller vessels of the brain causing complete obstruction. At autopsy, they may be visible to the naked eye as punctate haemorrhages in the white matter of the brain. Diagnosis can be confirmed by microscopic examination of the frozen sections of tissues stained for fat. Externally, fat embolism may be suspected from the presence of punctate haemorrhages into the skin, looking like flea bites.

With the exception of burns where fat can be melted from tissues in the agonal period, any injury inflicted after death cannot transmit fat or marrow to the pulmonary capillary bed in absence of effective cardiac function. This is helpful to differentiate antemortem from postmortem fractures.

Air Embolism

This results when air is introduced into circulation during life. The bubbles of air act as emboli and block the capillaries. About 10–20 ml of air may cause death, if it infarcts a vital portion of brain or causes coronary obstruction. Normally, about 100 ml of air is necessary to produce air lock in the heart or major blood vessels. Usually, death ensues in one or two minutes or it may be delayed for 20 minutes or more. Simpson found that even two hours may elapse before death occurs following introduction of air in the uterine cavity.

Air embolism is of two types, viz: (1) pulmonary or venous air embolism, and (2) systemic or arterial air embolism.

Pulmonary or venous air embolism: This results when air gains entry into systemic veins from where it is carried to the right side of the heart.

Here, it is churned into a frothy mixture which is driven into the branches of pulmonary artery and lung capillaries, causing mechanical obstruction to the outflow of blood from the right ventricle.

Pulmonary air embolism may result from:

1. Faulty technique of giving intravenous injection, such as saline drip
2. Cut throat or incised wounds of neck involving jugular or subclavian veins when air is sucked into them as a result of negative pressure
3. Injury to the superior sagittal sinus

4. Injection of air or fluid mixed with air into the uterus as an abortifacient
5. As a complication of therapeutic procedures such as pneumoperitoneum or air encephalography
6. Crush injuries of the chest resulting in penetration of the lung. Contrary to popular belief, pulmonary air embolism does not follow insufflation of fallopian tubes to test their patency.

At autopsy, the significant findings are: distension of right ventricle with air under pressure and bright red frothy blood on the right side of heart, inferior vena cava, pulmonary arteries and coronary veins. It may be possible to trace air bubbles back to the site of entry. The right ventricle and inferior vena cava should be punctured under water when air bubbles will be seen coming out from them. An X-ray prior to beginning of autopsy is an excellent means to demonstrate venous air embolism and to determine the site of its entry, provided the X-ray beam is projected horizontally.

Systemic or arterial air embolism: Systemic air embolism results when air enters a pulmonary vein. It may result from—(1) penetrating wound of the chest, (2) crush injuries of the thorax, and (3) surgical procedures on the chest. The air is carried to the left side of heart from where it may reach the different organs especially the cerebral and coronary vessels with serious consequences.

At autopsy, cerebral and coronary arteries appear segmented (beaded) due to the presence of air. The presence of air bubbles in these vessels should, however, be interpreted with *caution.* Air in cerebral vessels may be an artefact produced by removing the skull and in the coronary vessels due to moving the heart and lungs within the chest cavity after internal mammary vessels are cut when the chest plate is removed. The best method to detect air embolism, when it is present in significant amount, is to X-ray the body before it is autopsied, provided death is not due to gas forming organisms and the body is not putrefied.

Secondary Shock

This is a constitutional disturbance which may develop insidiously. It results from reduction of total circulating blood volume. It may be due to loss of fluid at the site of injury, increased capillary permeability, hypotension, etc. Other factors, such as infection, exposure to cold, etc., may contribute to it.

Consumptive Coagulopathy

Also known as disseminated intravascular coagulopathy (DIC), the condition is due to a series of insults, such as crush injuries, sepsis, and other acute events. It triggers the coagulation mechanism of the body, consumes and precipitates fibrin in vessels leading to both vascular and obstructive effects, uses up all the available coagulation components, and thus results in massive bleeding, since the normal blood clotting process cannot now occur. The medical officer may be at a loss to know the cause of bleeding, unless such a possibility is considered. Microvascular obstruction leading to reduced function, infarction, and bleeding are the major dangers.

Indirect Effects

The onset of delirium tremens after fracture of the leg in a person addicted to alcohol, or the onset of pneumonia in elderly people confined to bed, may be considered indirect results of injury. Transfusion hepatitis may result from accidental introduction of virus from the blood or serum used to treat shock.

Acceleration of Pre-existing Disease

If the injury hastens or precipitates death, responsibility of the consequences rests on the assailant under section 299 IPC. A disease process such as tuberculosis of the lungs or quiescent septic infection may be disturbed by the injury and thereby enabled to spread. A person suffering from arteriosclerosis, or fatty degeneration of the heart may die from cerebral haemorrhage or heart failure due to increased blood pressure as a result of violence. Peptic ulcer might perforate due to violence and cause death. Similarly, an aortic aneurysm or an enlarged spleen may rupture from little violence.

Supervention of New Disease

If symptoms of disease appear within a reasonable time in a previously healthy person, there is a presumption that the injury is a causal factor and the attacker is responsible for the consequences of his violent act. Meningitis may supervene after violence to the head with or without physical damage. A dissecting aneurysm of aorta may result from blunt injury to the chest in a person with atherosclerotic aorta. A wound of the abdomen may, after healing, be followed by strangulated hernia. An injury affecting spinal column or cord may cause paraplegia and end fatally in due course from septic cystitis, bed sores, and general exhaustion. Ewing's postulates are accepted as reasonable foundation for new growth appearing after injury (refer Chapter 19 on Trauma, Work Stress, and Disease).

Operative Treatment

If death follows anaesthesia or surgical operation, the assailant is responsible for the result, if the wound was such as would have proved dangerous without such interference. The liability of the assailant is not lessened even if life is saved by such skilful procedure. However, the assailant is not responsible, if the injury was simple and death followed by some unusual remedy adopted by the patient.

Neglect of Treatment

It is not obligatory for the assaulted person to submit himself for treatment. Even if death occurs from this omission or through disobedience of the physician's instructions by the victim, the assailant is responsible for his act and its consequence and he can not take any such plea.

VOLITIONAL ACTS AFTER INJURY

Unless it can be shown that a particular injury would be immediately incompatible with life, it is seldom possible to state that a deceased person could not have performed some activity before death in instances such as a cut throat, fracture of the skull with laceration of brain, bruising of heart, and rupture of internal viscera, such as intestine, spleen, liver, etc.

A Finnish man who committed suicide made a home'movie of himself firing a pistol into his brain. There was immediate collapse but, just at the end of the four minutes film, the victim opened his eyes and raised his head, finally dying after some uncertain time after the film ran out.

Q. 18.12. Comment on the medicolegal significance of antemortem and postmortem wounds. Describe the naked eye appearance of such wounds.

The distinction between antemortem and postmortem injuries and their proper timing is one of the cardinal problems of forensic medicine. It helps not only the conviction of the guilty but also the acquittal of the suspected but, in fact, not guilty. As for example, a person, may after natural death, be run over by a car. If the medical officer does not recognise that the car injuries are postmortem in nature, an innocent person may be arrested or even found guilty. On the other hand, erroneous observation or interpretation may lead to acquittal of the guilty. As for example, the body of a murdered person may be placed on a railway track in order to simulate suicide or accident. If the medical officer does not recognise that the rail injuries are postmortem in nature, the guilty person would escape the rigors of law. It is, therefore, necessary for the medical officer to make detailed observations in such cases on the following lines:

a. Naked eye appearance of wounds
b. Histological timing of wounds
c. Histochemical timing of wounds
d. Biochemical timing of wounds if the facilities exist.

Naked Eye Appearance of Wounds

Sometimes, it is possible to determine the nature of a wound, either antemortem or postmortem, on the basis of its naked eye appearance. Wounds incurred during life bleed freely; extensive infiltration of deeper tissues occurs; the edges of the wound may be gaping, are everted, become somewhat swollen; and firmly coagulated blood will be found in and about the wound. Arterial spurting marks may be seen. In a postmortem wound, bleeding is slight from cut veins and there is no infiltration of tissues. The edges of the wound do not gape nor are they swollen, and little or no coagulated blood will be found in and about the wound.

If life has lasted for some time after wounding, the distinction between antemortem and postmortem wounds is simple; signs of vital reaction such as inflammation and repair will be present in antemortem wounds. However, this is not always so and in cases of doubt, it is necessary to distinguish an antemortem wound from a postmortem one by additional methods of examination, such as histological, histochemical, and biochemical.

Q. 18.13. Give in brief the histological, histochemical and biochemical method of timing of wounds.

Histological Timing of Wounds

The histological estimation of the age of injuries is based on the morphology of various stages of wound healing. The series of events in response to initial injury generally follow a definite order. The following schema summarises chronologically the various histological findings in traumatised tissues. It must, however, be emphasised that the various timings listed therein are only approximations based on the experience of competent authorities.

1. ***Survival period less than 4 hours after injury:***
   a. No distinct histological signs of inflammation.
   b. Histological distinction between antemortem and postmortem wounds is not possible during this period (Fig. 18.2).
2. ***Survival period 4 to 16 hours:***
   a. At 4 hours, some neutrophil granulocytes appear perivascularly.
   b. At 8–12 hours, polymorphonuclears, macrophages, and activated fibroblasts from a distinct peripheral wound zone.
   c. At 12–16 hours, granulocytes dominate macrophages in the ratio of 5:1.
   d. Imminent necrosis in the central wound zone.
3. ***Survival period 16 to 48 hours:***
   a. At 16–24 hours, the relative number of macrophages increases, the ratio of polymorphonuclears to macrophages falling to 0.4.

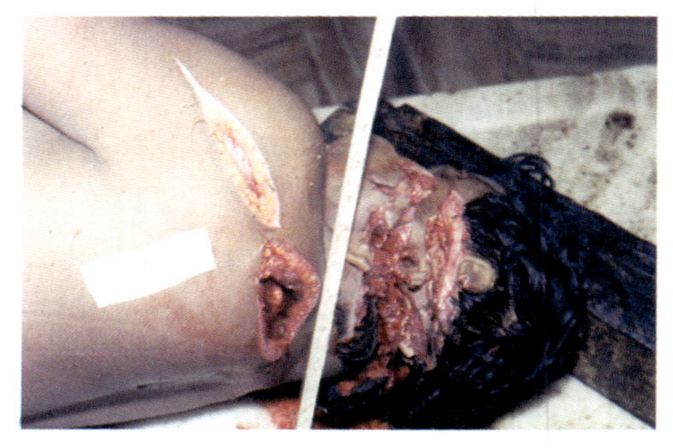

Fig. 18.2: Postmortem incised wound and antemortem injury

b. After 16 hours, "older" fibrin stains red with Martius scarlet blue, whereas before 16 hours "newer" fibrin stains yellow.
c. At 24 hours, the number of granulocytes and the amount of fibrin increase to maximum (they remain at this level until 2–3 days).
d. At 24–48 hours, the epidermis grows from the incised edge toward the centre of the wound.
e. At 32 hours and thereafter, necrosis is apparent in the central wound zone.
f. At 48 hours, macrophages reach their maximum concentration in the peripheral zone.

4. *Survival period 2 to 4 days:*
   a. At 2–4 days, fibroblasts migrate from the nearby connective tissue to the wound periphery.
   b. At 4–5 days, epithelialization of small wounds and abrasions is complete. Thereafter, the regenerated epidermis becomes highly stratified find thicker than the normal surrounding epidermis.
   c. At 3–4 days, capillary buds appear.
5. *Survival period 4 to 8 days:*
   a. At 4 days, the first new collagen fibres are seen.
   b. At 4–5 days, there is profuse ingrowth of new capillaries. The capillaries continue to proliferate until the eighth day.
   c. At 5–7 days, epidermal thickness decreases to nearly normal in the epithelialised small wounds.
   d. At 6 days, lymphocytes reach their maximum concentration in the wound periphery.
6. *Survival period 8 to 12 days:* At 8–12 days, there is decrease in the number of leucocytes, fibroblasts, and capillaries. There is increase in the number and size of collagen fibres.
7. *Survival period over 12 days:*
   a. Over 12 days, there is definite regression of cellular activity in both epidermis and dermis. The vascularity of dermis diminishes. Collagen fibres are restored. Epithelium shows a stainable basement membrane.
   b. At 14 days, fibroplasia reaches its peak. Thereafter, there occurs a gradual shrinkage and maturation of connective tissue in the wound.

Histochemical Timing of Wounds

Histological investigation greatly contributes to the estimation of age of injuries and thus it is an essential part of timing of wounds. There is, however, the disadvantage that no definite leucocytic zone is visible until 8–12 hours after injury. This latent phase is far too long since in most cases of forensic interest the survival time is shorter than 8–12 hours after wounding. It is, therefore, necessary that histological investigation should be complemented by enzyme histochemical examination of the wound when required.

The histochemical method involves the study of enzymes in the wound region. The enzymes studied are adenosine triphosphatase, aminopeptidase, acid phosphatase, and alkaline phosphatase. In antemortem wounds, two distinct zones of enzyme activity are seen. The 100–300 μm deep peripheral wound zone shows increase in enzyme activity, beginning as little as one to eight hours after injury—probably indicating repair. Such increase in the peripheral wound zone is called **positive vital reaction.** In the most immediate vicinity of the wound edge, the 200–500 μm deep central zone exhibits a progressive loss of enzyme activities, probably indicating imminent necrosis. This regressive phenomena is called **negative vital reaction.** It is demonstrable as a **diminishing stainability** and becomes visible 1–4 hours after wounding.

The activity of adenosine triphosphatase, and esterase in peripheral wound zone increases as early as about one hour after injury, that of aminopeptidase at two hours, of acid phosphatase at four hours, and of alkaline phosphatase eight hours. The consecutive appearance of enzymes, demonstrable by various methods of enzyme histochemistry, allows the construction of a biological time table which is useful in the approximate timing of antemortem wounds and to distinguish between antemortem and postmortem wounds.

The following case illustrates the practical use of the enzyme histochemical time table in forensic practice.

A jealous man believed that he had killed his fiancee when he hit her head with a stone. He carried the body to a fenced railway track to simulate suicide. Two hours later, a train arrived and caused fatal injuries. A medicolegal autopsy was performed and the wounds examined histochemically and histologically. In a laceration on the head the activity of the enzymes, adenosine triphosphatase, esterase, and aminopeptidase, was increased. By contrast, there was no increase in the activity of acid and alkaline phosphatase. The results indicated that the laceration on the head was produced at least two hours before the final fatal wounds caused by the train. The girl had obviously been unconscious after the initial head injury. When the police confronted the man with these facts a confession of the sequence of events was forthcoming. The man was convicted.

A man died of heart attack while walking on the road. His dead body was subsequently run over by a car. The course of events was reconstructed by histochemical and biological studies of the injuries and it was established that the injuries were postmortem in nature. The driver was exonerated from the charge of manslaughter.

It is important in practice that the histochemical vital reactions are recognisable several (up to five) days after death. There is no increase in enzyme activity in the periphery of postmortem wounds.

There are certain exceptions in the biological time table when it is applied to human autopsy material. Conditions, such as far advanced senility, cachexia, and very severe and multiple injuries, may impair the local reaction of wounded skin. The enzymatic response to injury is quantitatively influenced by such factors as severe blood loss and coldness. However, the increase in the activity of various enzymes

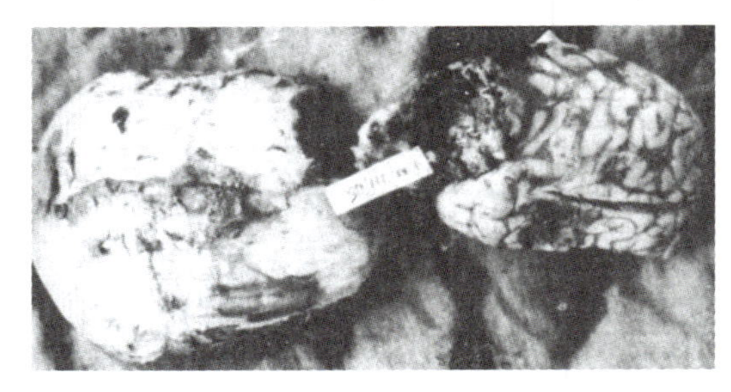

Fig. 18.3: Brain injury not immediately fatal. A male aged 60 was alleged to have been beaten with an axe on the left frontal region. At operation, there was a depressed fracture of the skull in the left frontoparietal region. Broken fragments of the skull and blood clots were removed from the brain. The liquified portion of the brain was evacuated and irrigated. A large cavity is seen in the frontoparietal region. The patient expired 11 days after the injury

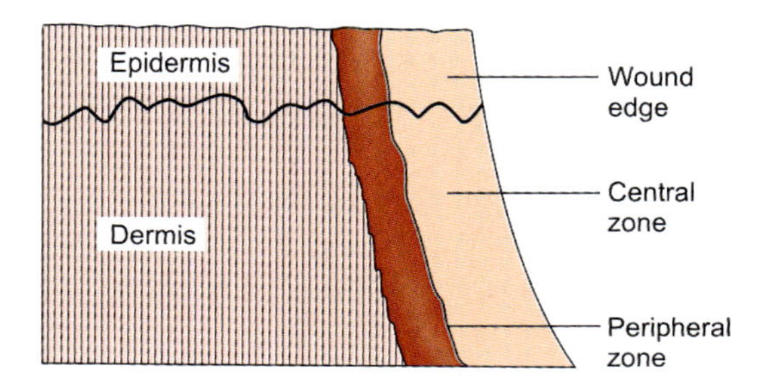

Fig. 18.4: Schematic diagram showing **the zones demonstrable by enzyme histochemistry of an antemortem wound.** Two distinct zones of enzyme activity are seen. In the immediate vicinity of a wound edge, a central or superficial zone, 200–500 μ deep shows decreasing enzyme activity surrounding the central area, a peripheral zone 100–300 μ deep exhibits an increase in enzyme activity. These changes are demonstrable as early as one hour after wounding in antemortem injuries only

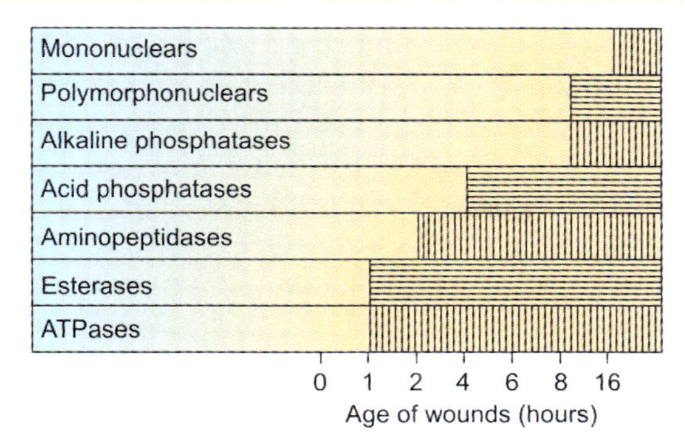

Fig. 18.5: Schematic diagram showing the **histochemical estimation of the age of antemortem skin wounds.** (*Courtesy*: Dr J Raekallio)

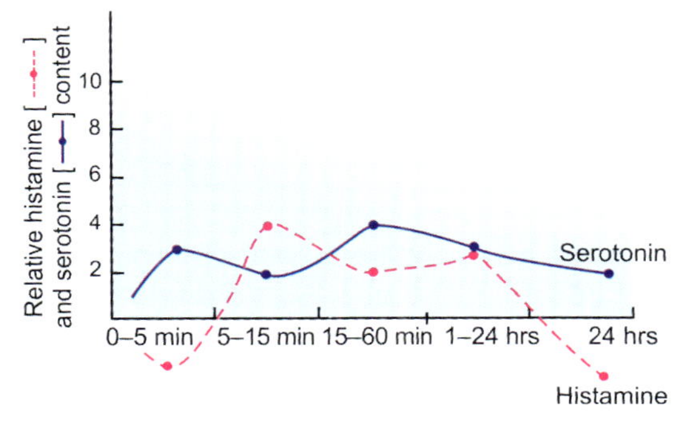

Fig. 18.6: Comparison of the relative serotonin —•— and histamine - - -•- - - contents in wounds inflicted at different points of time before death

appear according to the general biological time table in spite of the presence of these endogenous and exogenous factors.

The methods of enzyme histochemistry permit the recognition of tissue reaction to injury at an earlier phase than is possible by the standard techniques of classical histology. In practice, the methods of enzyme histochemistry act as a guide to the approximate age of wounds, especially those inflicted 1–8 hours before death. Histochemical methods are thus useful as supplements to the histological study which is still indispensable to evaluate the timing of wounds for forensic purposes.

Biochemical Timing of Wounds

Although enzyme histochemistry has shortened the "latent" period to about one hour, it still leaves that very last hour before death as a challenge for further study.

As we know, in the first period of inflammation, the vascular response is dominated by vasoactive substances, including histamine and serotonin. The biochemical timing of wounds depends upon the measurement of histamine and serotonin contents of the injured skin. These are compared to the histamine and serotonin contents of a control sample, removed from the neighbouring intact skin of the same person. This is necessary as there are great individual and regional differences in the contents of these amines.

On the basis of extensive autopsy studies, the increase in serotonin content of the injured tissue must be at least two-fold and that in the histamine content 1.5-fold or more (as compared to the respective contents of control samples) to indicate that the wound was inflicted before death. There is no increase in the serotonin and histamine contents in wounds inflicted after death.

The results of biochemical serotonin and histamine determinations have been compared with each other. In wounds inflicted immediately before death, there is usually a great increase in the serotonin content and often even a slight decrease in the free histamine content. In wounds inflicted 5–15 minutes before death, there is relatively a higher increase in histamine than in serotonin while in wounds inflicted 15–60 minutes before death, the reverse is true.

Several cases of road accidents have been encountered where it has been possible to show that the driver was dead before the crash. In these cases, there have been signs of coronary artery disease and the cause of death had been, obviously, natural. There were no changes in the relative serotonin and histamine content of the—often severe—wounds caused by the crash. This is under-standable as the wounds were caused after death.

The following case illustrates the practical use of the enzyme histochemical timetable in forensic practice.

The naked body of a young woman was found in a storage cellar. No signs of vio-lence were visible on external examination. Sperms were found in her vagina. At autopsy, the organs were cyanotic and congested. The blood in the heart was dark and fluid. Small haemorrhages were found in the lungs, pericardium, pleura, and larynx. In addition to these signs of asphyxia, there were no visible marks on skin and no injuries to deeper structures of neck. Skin samples were excised from the front of the neck. The serotonin content was twofold and the histamine content about 1.5-fold as compared to those of the control samples taken from the subclavicular skin. There were thus *biochemical signs of violence* in the front part of the neck. In view of the general signs of asphyxia found at autopsy, a suspicion of throttling (manual strangulation) was confirmed. The police confronted the owner of the cellar with an accusation that he had raped and throttled the woman. The man broke down and confessed that he had, indeed, compelled the woman, by threats of killing her, to have intercourse with him, and to prevent her from screaming he had pressed his hand on the front of her neck and she suddenly ceased to breathe.

To conclude, a more accurate timing of wounds is now applicable. The distinction between antemortem and postmortem injuries is possible by using biochemical serotonin and histamine methods, after a survival time of as little as a few seconds or minutes. The methods of enzyme histochemistry act as a supplementary guide to the timing of wounds, especially of those inflicted 1–8 hours before death. If a wound had been inflicted eight hours or more before death, it may be timed histologically. The histological study is still an essential part of timing of wounds. In addition to histology and enzyme histochemistry, the biochemical determinations of serotonin and histamine are also applicable to forensic autopsy material.

Q. 18.14. Tabulate the salient distinguishing features of antemortem and postmortem wounds.

Salient distinguishing features of antemortem and postmortem wounds are tabulated in Table 18.1.

Table 18.1: Distinguishing features of antemortem and postmortem wounds

	Antemortem wounds	*Postmortem wounds*
1. Haemorrhage	a. Usually copious, and generally arterial	a. Usually slight, and always venous
	b. Arterial spurting marks may be found	b. No spurting marks but only oozing of venous blood
	c. Blood clotted, the clot being laminated and firmly adherent to the lining endothelium	c. Blood usually not clotted because blood does not coagulate soon after death. The clot, if found, is non-laminated, homogenous, and weakly adherent to the lining endothelium
	d. Clot is rubbery, firm, and variegated in appearance	d. Clot is soft, friable, and yellow ('chicken fat') or red ('currant jelly) in appearance
	e. Deep infiltration staining of edges and cellular tissues which cannot be washed away	e. No infiltration or staining of edges. The cellular tissues are just stained and the staining can be washed away
2. Wound edges	The edges may be gaping, are everted, and somewhat swollen	The edges usually do not gape unless the wound is caused within about two hours after death. They are apposed and not swollen
3. Vital reaction	a. Signs of inflammation and repair are present	a. No signs of any vital reaction whatsoever

(*contd.*)

(*contd.*)

	Antemortem wounds	*Postmortem wounds*
	b. The wounds, if infected, may show the presence of pus and slough	b. –do–
	c. Septic and gaping wounds will show granulation tissue	c. –do–
4. Microscopy	a. Leucocyte and RBC infiltration in between muscle fibres	a. Vessels distended with postmortem clot without infiltration of cells outside the vessel wall
	b. Clot composed of fibrin, RBC, and platelets	b. Clot composed mainly of fibrin and RBC
5. Enzyme histochemistry	Negative and positive vital reactions are seen	Vital reaction absent
6. Serotonin and histamine biochemistry	Distinct increase in wound serotonin and free histamine content	No increase in serotonin or free histamine content

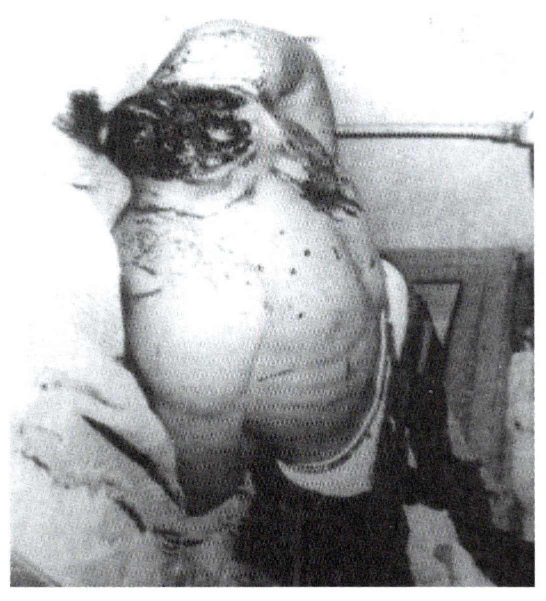

Fig. 18.7: Beheading (decapitation). (*Courtesy*: Dr BV Subrahmanyam)

Q. 18.15. In case of death from wounds, how will you state whether the injuries were suicidal, homicidal, or accidental in nature.

This question arises in every case in which a dead body is found with marks of violence upon it. A reliable opinion is possible from a careful consideration in relation to: (1) scene of crime, (2) details of injury, (3) details of weapon causing the injury, and (4) circumstantial evidence.

Scene of Crime

The suicide finds some secluded place where he is unlikely to be disturbed such as his bedroom or locked bathroom. When a suicide victim cuts his throat, he will do so in front of a mirror and blood splashes will frequently be found on the mirror itself. In cases of suicide, one rarely finds any disorder at the scene beyond a large volume of blood. The presence of wounds in a region ordinarily covered by clothing without any corresponding damage to overlying clothes is suggestive of suicide.

Where a homicidal attack has taken place, a considerable disturbance at the scene is almost inevitable, unless the victim happens to be a child, or very old and frail, or his powers of resistance diminished by drinks or drugs, or where more than one assailant is involved. The body may be found in a position which he could not have assumed, if the wound or injury was accidental or suicidal. Fragments of clothing, hair, or other foreign substances, grasped in the hand of the victim by cadaveric spasm are suggestive of homicide. Presence of scratches, bruises, and defence injuries, strongly suggest a struggle, and corroborative evidence may be afforded by the presence of foot prints of the assailant and blood stains belonging to the assailant's blood group. The cuts and bullet holes on clothes would normally correspond with wounds on the body. In a fatal homicidal attack, the assailant's body, clothing, and shoes are often soiled with the victim's blood.

While the above mentioned features are traditional of a suicidal or homicidal attack, accident is capable of infinite variations. It is only by taking into account all the circumstances that a considered and final opinion can be reached.

A man was put on trial for murdering his wife. Medical evidence showed that the fatal wound had penetrated the left side of the chest to the sternum in the third inercostal space. Close to the sternum, the wound was deep, and had cut the pulmo-nary artery. Further away, the wound became shallower as a mere skin incision. The prisoner alleged that he was cutting his nails with a sharp pen-knife (the admitted weapon), and that, as his wife irritated him, he had pushed her away with the hand holding the knife and brought his hand round in a sweep. The wound precisely corresponded with such an explanation and led to the acquittal of the prisoner. No alternative could be proved.

The Injury

There are certain situations which are selected preferentially by a suicide. These are known as sites of election or preferential sites. A suicide usually selects a site on front of the body over certain vital areas, especially the throat, wrist, elbow, or groin for incised wounds; left side of the chest over the heart, and abdomen, for stab wounds; and right temple, mouth, or pre-cordium for gunshot wounds. Hesitation cuts may be present.

Suicidal wounds take more or less a definite direction, most persons being right-handed. Suicidal incised wounds of the neck are usually directed from left to right and tailing off to a superficial incision on the right. Suicidal stab wounds of thorax are situated almost exclusively over the precordium, and are directed at an angle from above downwards. Suicidal incised wounds on arms may be directed from above downwards and those on lower limbs from below upwards. The suicides rarely inflict contusions, lacerations, or chop wounds.

Incised wounds of a serious nature and stab wounds usually suggest suicide or homicide. Incised wounds on the nose, ears, and genitals, are usually homicidal and are inflicted on account of jealousy or revenge (in cases of adultery). Stab wounds over the abdomen, chest, and limbs, other than over the heart area are suggestive of homicide. Stab wounds on the back are almost always homicidal. Chop wounds of head, face, neck, shoulders, and extremities, are suggestive of homicide or accident. Wounds of the head especially over the vertex, if accidents are excluded, are presumptive of homicide. Gunshot wounds situated on the sides or the front may be homicidal or accidental. Gunshot wounds situated on the back and occipital region are usually homicidal or accidental.

The presence of defence injuries indicate a homicidal attack. However, their absence does not rule out a homicidal attack for it is possible for the victim to be incapable of defence. A child or sleeping person cannot defend himself nor a person who is taken by surprise, who is unconscious, intoxica-ted, or old. In addition, mechanical factors may also contribute to an absence of defence, as for example, the hand being in the trousers, coat pocket, or tied together.

In incised wounds of the neck of homicidal nature, the cut is usually lower than in suicidal wounds. The wound is often more extensive and without any hesitation cuts. Homicidal chop wounds and stab wounds of the chest take almost any direction depending on the relative position of the victim and assailant. Direction is of particular importance in case of firearms, as the direction from which the bullet is fired may indicate the impossibility of its having been self-fired. As a rule, except for incised wounds of the neck where a suicide may inflict many or leave the marks of several attempts before he succeeds in his purpose, a multiplicity of wounds and more so if they are extensive, is presumptive evidence of homicide, if accidents could be excluded, and for which the cause is usually obvious.

Wounds from accident can occur in any part of the body but the mechanism of accident frequently clarifies the situation. They are generally situated on the exposed body parts and mostly on the same side. They merely do not accord with what is known of the features of suicide or homicide. Incised or punctured wounds may be caused accidentally from falls while a person is in the act of running with a pointed instrument in his hand or pocket. Such wounds can also be caused by falling upon sharp pointed objects or broken pieces of glass. Chop wounds on exposed body parts may be caused by machinery. Lacerated wounds of the vertex can occur accidentally, if some weight falls from a height on the head or the victim falls head downwards from a height.

The Weapon

If the weapon is firmly grasped in the hand of the deceased by cadaveric spasm, and there is no evidence of struggle or other injuries, this is confirmatory of suicide. It is occasionally compatible with suicide to find the weapon at some distance or even washed and put away but it is more frequently found lying by the side of the deceased than grasped in the hand.

If the weapon cannot be discovered or is found concealed in a distant place, this is ordinarily presumptive of homicide.

When some broken fragment of the weapon is found in the wound it may serve to identify the weapon or to connect an accused with the crime. Similarly, an accused person may become connected to the crime when some portion of the clothing or hair belonging to him is found in the deceased's hand firmly grasped by cadaveric spasm.

There are some weapons which are not used for inflicting suicidal injuries. If the injuries are caused by such weapons, e.g. lathi (bansdola), iron-bar (fracture of skull, multiple fractures), or an axe (chop wounds), this is suggestive of murder.

Circumstantial Evidence

The actions of the deceased immediately prior to death may clearly indicate the suicidal nature of the act. The mental condition of the victim, his family affairs, and financial condition may be of value as an indication of suicide. Farewell letters, often called 'suicide notes' naturally raise the presumption'of suicide but the possibility of these being forged must always be considered. Blood stains on the body and clothes may give valuable information about the position of the victim at the time of injury and his subsequent movements, in almost all cases, suicidal, homicidal, or accidental.

Note should be taken of the position of the body and distribution of lividity to see if the body has been moved after death. If the victim did not die at the place where his body is found and there is evidence such as mud stains and superficial injuries to suggest that the body has been dragged from elsewhere, it is evidence of murder. In order to convict an accused person on circumstantial evidence, the facts proved in the case must be consistent, with his guilt and utterly inconsistent with his innocence. In judicial language, a certain number of material facts should be incontestably proved which are quite inconsistent with the innocence of the accused.

In accidental injuries including those due to firearms, circumstantial evidence is usually sufficient to show whether they have been accidentally inflicted or not.

A man was put on trial for murdering his wife. Medical evidence showed that the fatal wound had penetrated from the left side of the chest close to the sternum in the third intercostal space. Close to the sternum, the wound was deep and had cut the pulmonary artery. Further away, the wound became shallower as a mere skin incision. The prisoner alleged that he was cutting his nails with a sharp pen-knife (the admitted weapon), and that, as his wife irritated him, he had pushed her away with the hand holding the knife and brought his hand round in a sweep. The wound precisely corresponded with such an explanation and led to the acquittal of the prisoner. No alternative could be proved.

A visit by the forensic pathologist to the crime scene is often valuable to reach the appropriate conclusions.

Dr Subrahmanyam saw a case where a teenager was grazing his cattle near the foundation stone of Banaras Hindu University in Varanasi, India and died. His body presented an atypical firearm injury on the head' with a distorbed bullet lodged inside at the scene. At the scene, there was as 'bullet hit' on the BHU foundation wall as the bullet struck the wall and got deflected and entered the head of the teenager (Recochet Bullet).

19 Trauma, Work Stress, and Disease

Q. 19.1. Discuss in detail the relationship between trauma, work stress, and disease, giving examples.

The relationship between trauma, work stress, and disease assumes importance mainly for two reasons, viz: (1) compensation, and (2) insurance.

Compensation: Under the **Workmen's Compensation Act,** provision is made for disabilities suffered as a result of occupational acquired disease or industrial accidents while at work, provided the worker himself was not negligent or responsible for the injury.

In case of death, especially when there has been no medical attention and the possibility of disease seems remote, a question arises if the ill-effects of work-conditions or previous injury suffered by the worker while at work could be responsible for death.

Insurance: A person may have insured himself for "accident" only. Besides, some life insurance policies include a clause that if death is due to accident then the sum payable is doubled. This is called a double indemnity policy.

When these matters become the subject of investigation, a medical officer is called upon to examine a person: (a) to assess the disability or degree of physical damage, or (b) to perform an autopsy to interpret the relationship of disease or trauma to death.

In case of disability, a very thorough examination is essential, keeping the worker under observation, if necessary, to assess the degree of disablement, either temporary or permanent. An objective and balanced description of damage done by the injury and an opinion on the patient's future prospects at work and recreation is usually sufficient. The most important aspect is evaluation of whether the disabilities, claimed and observed, are consistent with the injury received. The worker may malinger and make false claims or he might have developed a neurosis after the accident. *Malingering* means a deliberate attempt on the part of patient to deceive the doctor.

In case of death, an autopsy should be performed. In a situation where autopsy findings indicate that there is a combination of injury and disease, the medical officer should analyse the data carefully and opine on the relative role of trauma and disease to death. Just because a given episode of stress, exertion, or trauma was antecedent, the assumption of cause and effect relationship is not necessarily warranted.

The following comments are intended to offer some assistance as to the line of approach to be adopted in certain common situations. For convenience, the discussion is grouped into:

1. Trauma and the heart

2. Trauma and the nervous system
3. Trauma and the alimentary system
4. Trauma and malignancy
5. Disease from non-traumatic accident

TRAUMA AND THE HEART

Injury to any part of the body may predispose to myocardial infarction with or without coronary thrombosis, if the injury is sufficiently severe to cause hypovolaemic shock and coronary arteries are previously narrowed by atherosclerosis. In such a case, the injury causes a protracted episode of circulatory failure, and myocardial infarction occurs during the period of shock. Diagnosis should, however, be confirmed by clinical and laboratory tests in the living and appropriate findings at autopsy in the dead.

Thoracic trauma may lead to: (a) cardiac bruising, (b) myocardial infarction with or without coronary thrombosis, (c) subintimal haemorrhage in a coronary artery leading to coronary thrombosis, (d) arteriovenous communication, (e) dissecting aneurysm, and (f) rupture of aneurysm.

If the heart has sustained a significant degree of bruising as a result of thoracic trauma, heart failure should be apparent almost immediately. A cardiac bruise either causes death or disability within a few minutes, or recovery occurs without permanent or progressive damage to the heart.'

Occupational trauma, as defined by effort at work, can precipitate death by giving rise to circulatory overloading, or by aggravating previously existing disease, such as, coronary atherosclerosis, or aortic aneurysm. Narrowing is sufficient to explain death and a clot or acute obstruction is not necessary. It is frequent for death from partial coronary stenosis by atheroma to be precipitated by some exertion resulting in a greater demand of: (1) blood, (2) the pumping action of the heart, and (3) oxygen demand of the muscle of the left ventricle. Climbing stairs, working a hand pump, lifting a weight, etc., may precipitate such deaths, and if the deceased at the time of collapse was engaged in some such work as a part of his employment, then a claim for compensation may succeed. In determining the relationship of stress to death in such cases, the autopsy findings must include evidence of previous damage to the heart muscle (fibrosis), narrowing of the coronary vessels, and evidence of activity of disease in the form of infiltration of vessels' coats by white blood cells (adventitial lymphocytosis). Periodic health check-ups of workers are, therefore, essential, and if the doctor finds any such problematic condition he should inform the authorities and also warn the worker of the danger. Cardiac conditions which predispose to acute heart failure following physical exertion or excitement and which frequently result in sudden death include syphilitic aortitis with or without aortic valvular insufficiency, aortic valvulitis with stenosis, and hypertensive heart disease usually with coronary atherosclerosis.

A worker whose pre-existing aneurysm ruptured while tightening a bolt by a spanner was awarded compensation under the Workmen's Compensation Act, the Court having ruled that such exertion provided stress for the catastrophe to occur (Clover Clayton & Co *vs* Hughes, 1910, AC 242).

TRAUMA AND THE NERVOUS SYSTEM

Instances are on record where it is difficult to refute completely the direct cause and effect relationship between: (a) head injury and meningitis, (b) head injury and epilepsy, (c) head injury and psychosis, and (d) head injury including occupational stress and rupture of a congenital cerebral aneurysm.

It is now an accepted fact that intracerebral haemorrhage can occur due to violence alone without any evidence of disease of blood vessels.

To attribute trauma as a cause for disease or disability, the following criteria should be satisfied:

1. The disease must not have been present before the injury but developed after injury was sustained, e.g. onset of epilepsy following head injury.
2. The disease is such as to be compatible with the nature of trauma ascribed to it, e.g. meningitis following violence to the head with or without physical damage.
3. The length of interval (latent period) that elapsed between injury and development of disease is compatible, e.g. tetanus developing 3–10 days after injury (sometimes 2–3 weeks after injury).
4. The disease does not develop spontaneously, e.g. tetanus.

A 40-year-old man met with a traffic accident. He sustained a laceration of the left foot and died in the hospital 10 days later due to tetanus.

TRAUMA AND THE ALIMENTARY SYSTEM

Whenever a history is obtained of a blow to the abdomen, the patient should be kept under observation until all likelihood of a ruptured abdominal viscus can be dismissed.

A blow to the epigastric region may cause death by inhibition of the heart through reflex action on the solar (coeliac) plexus, without leaving a mark externally or to the viscera.

The result of trauma to the bowel may be very serious. Perforation of a peptic ulcer may cause rapid death and some of these cases give rise to compensation claims when death occurs due to some abdominal injury while at work. The sudden rush of irritating matter, gastric juices, haemorrhage, and bile into peritoneal cavity may cause sudden collapse and death. Perforation of lower small intestine and large intestine are usually not followed by intense shock, similar to the shock of peptic ulcer perforation, and may not cause death, if timely surgical aid is available.

The liver is easily lacerated and ruptured especially if it is fatty, congested, enlarged, or diseased. Death may not occur immediately. Sometimes, bleeding occurs between the liver and its capsule (subcapsular haematoma). Serious symptoms become apparent only when the capsule ruptures. The damage is often fatal due to bleeding from the organ into the peritoneal cavity.

A kick or punch on the upper abdomen may injure the duodenum and pancreas and cause death within a few days from resultant chemical peritonitis. External injury to the abdominal wall may not always be visible in such cases.

TRAUMA AND MALIGNANCY

A number of proved cases indicate that trauma may occasionally cause cancer. The occurrence of osteogenic sarcoma and development malignancy in a scar tissue after injury, have been documented.

Cancer, on rare occasions, develops at the site of long-standing unhealed wound of the skin, in the chronically irritated skin, or in the scarred skin provided the trauma that was responsible for scar formation was definitely something more than a single mechanical injury, e.g. severe burns, X-ray burns, and chronically inflamed lesions, like varicose ulcer, and chronic sinus tracts, e.g. draining of a chronic osteomyelitic sinus, which may cause skin cancer adjacent to the site of continued irritation.

In accepting trauma as a cause of cancer, the following criteria should be satisfied. They are based on **Ewing's postulates.**

1. The tumour site prior to injury was normal.
2. The injury was sufficiently severe to disrupt continuity of tissues at the injury site and so initiate a reparative proliferation of cells.
3. The tumour followed injury within a reasonable length of time.

4. The tumour is of a type that might reasonably develop as a result of regeneration and repair of specific tissues that received the injury.
5. The exact nature of the tumour can be established by clinical, X-ray, and microscopic examinations.

A 42-year-old man was hit on anterior chest wall just above right clavicle with a large pipe and local bruise ensued. Three and a half month's later, a non-tender mass 6 × 8 cm was present at the site of bruise in the subcutaneous tissues. X-rays of shoulder and chest were non-contributory. Death occurred nine months after injury. The diagnosis at autopsy was rhabdomyo-sarcoma of right shoulder region with visceral metastasis.

A 20-year-old man sustained an open comminuted fracture of tibia in a motor vehicle accident. He developed chronic osteomyelitis with a draining sinus that persisted for many years. Ultimately, a squamous cell carcinoma developed in the draining sinus and he died from metastatic squamous cell carcinoma after an interval of approximately 20 years after the original injury.

The more closely a tumour resembles the ordinary processes of repair the greater is the likelihood that it did in fact result from an injury. The assertion that a given tumour was caused by a single mechanical injury is untenable unless it can be shown that the injury was responsible for prolonged chemical or mechanical irritation and definite signs and symptoms of a pathological process continued at the site of trauma until a malignant tumour appeared and was positively diagnosed. There is no evidence to suggest that biopsy of a tumour predisposes either to local acceleration in growth or metastasis. Intermittent pressure or massage may do so.

Mechanical injuries of skin or mucous membranes sometimes result in transplantation and isolation of groups of epithelial cells. Such masses appear as solid masses or small cysts but they are not true tumours in the correct sense of the term as they have no ability to *invade* and destroy adjacent tissue.

DISEASE FROM NON-TRAUMATIC ACCIDENTS

The term 'accident' generally includes any fortuitous or unexpected happening which causes personal disability or death. Thus, heat stroke or food poisoning would constitute an accident within the meaning of the definition.

A number of employees of a certain company drank water from a common water bucket which was filled at a nearby spring by a water boy assigned to the crew. The spring was contaminated and a number of employees developed typhoid fever. The court in its ruling specifically stated that there need not be an external wound or violence to create liability under the law. The accidental nature of the injury is not lost by calling consequential injury a disease or by the fact that a dangerous sub-stance was taken into the body by ingestion rather than by external wounding. (Union Mining Company *vs* Samuel Blank, 28 Atlantic, 568).

A man, travelling by his car, on his way from Bombay to Poona (a distance of about 120 miles), took dinner (along with some alcohol) at a hotel in Lonavala (about half way from Bombay to Poona), and died after 36 hours. The postmortem appearances (ulceration in the small intestine) enter-tained a distinct possibility of death due to 'Salmonella food poisoning'. The relations got the benefit of accident insurance policy of the deceased. (Guru and Oriental Insurance Company, 1973).

20 Regional Injuries

Injuries and death due to trauma are inescapable from the modern way of life. Their correct interpretation is vital to the reconstruction of events in forensic medicine. The subject is so vast that it has been possible to present herein only the salient features of various bodily injuries from a medicolegal standpoint.

HEAD

Q. 20.1. Comment on 'head injury'.

Injuries to the head are very frequent as a result of traffic accidents, assaults, and falls. If the brain is affected, the injury is serious; if the brain is not affected, the injury is likely to be simple. In such a traumatic episode, if the dura remains intact, it is called **closed head injury** irrespective of whether the skull is fractured or not. If the dura is lacerated or torn, it is called an **open intracranial injury** as it is open to possible infection.

In giving an opinion on a case of head injury shortly after its infliction, the following points should be kept in mind:

1. No injury to the head is too trivial to be ignored because of the possibility of septic complications.
2. The skull and/or its contents may be severely injured without any external evidence of injury. Hence, it is imperative that every case of head injury, however, trivial it, may look externally, should be X-rayed and admitted to the hospital for observation. This will obviate a charge of negligence on the part of the doctor. In examining a comatose patient or an intoxicated one, every care should be taken to exclude head injury.
3. Survivors of open head injury have a higher incidence of **post-traumatic epilepsy** as compared to those with closed head injury. It is especially common when infection has occurred, or when a spicule of bone has penetrated the meninges. It ensues in about 10 per cent of cases of blunt head injury especially in the parietotemporal area. It appears usually within a few weeks to about two years.

SCALP

Q. 20.2. Briefly discuss scalp injuries with special reference to their role in causing intracranial infections.

Wounds of the scalp may or may not be associated with fracture of the skull and/or injury to the intracranial contents and vice versa. Most wounds are caused by application of blunt force to the head and take the form of contusions or lacerations. Sometimes, a bruise over the scalp, well covered with hair, can only be detected by palpation. An effusion of blood over the top of the head or forehead may gravitate down to the loose tissues causing **black eyes**

Note. This chapter is edited by Dr G Veera Nagi Reddy, Professor & Principal, Narayana Medical College, Nellore

(supraorbital haematoma). Owing to the free manner in which the scalp moves over the closely subjacent bone, some linear lacerated wounds may simulate incised wounds. Hair round about the injury must be shaved to ensure proper examination, with a magnifying lens, if necessary. Irregular edges of the wound, crushed hair bulbs, and tissue bridging will be seen. The presence of foreign bodies may provide an important clue as to the origin of the wound.

Injuries to the scalp predispose the victim to **intracranial infections** even in absence of skull fracture or external wounds. Meningitis may develop by spread of infection from a septic scalp wound through diploic veins. Diploic veins lie in the spongy tissue between the two tables of the skull and communicate, in the interior of the skull with meningeal veins and sinuses and, on the exterior of skull with veins of the pericranium. Emissary veins which pass through apertures in the skull connect veins of the scalp and face with parasagittal, lateral, and cavernous sinuses. Therefore, infected wounds of the scalp and face may be complicated by thrombophlebitis of cranial sinuses through the emissary veins.

SKULL

The adult skull is a remarkably strong structure. It is not resilient and tends to fracture, if subjected to undue stress. When violence is applied to the skull, certain factors play a part in the determination of the type and character of the resultant effects.

The amount of energy a blow can transmit to an object it strikes can be computed from the following formula:

$$\text{Kinetic energy} = \frac{MV^2}{2G}$$

where M is the (mass) weight in pounds, V the velocity in feet per second, and G the gravitational acceleration (32 feet per second).

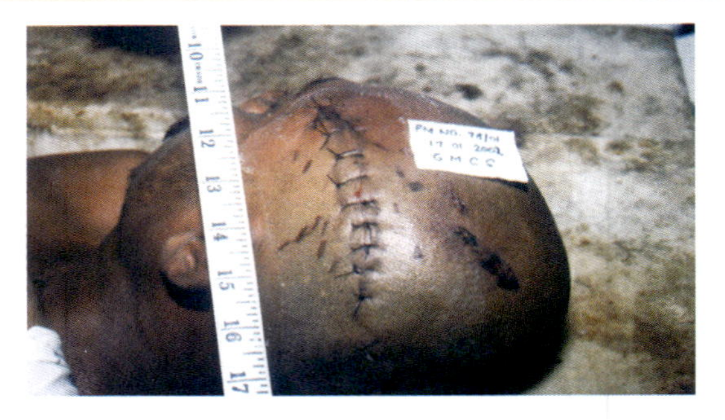

Fig. 20.1: Surgical stitch of sclap injuries

Thus, an iron crow bar is effective on account of its weight (m) while a bullet on account of its velocity (v), the damage of the latter being greater on account of its being squared. The other factors that influence the resultant effects are: (a) the size of the area bearing the weight of impact, (b) the extent to which the tissues can absorb the momentum of the striking object, and (c) the movement as a whole of the part that is struck.

FRACTURES OF THE SKULL

The skull may fracture as a result of direct or indirect violence. Direct violence can result from:

1. Compression of the head by obstetric forceps during delivery
2. When the head is crushed under the wheel of a vehicle
3. When the head is struck by a moving object, e.g. brick, bullet, machinery, hammer, lathi, axe, etc.
4. Head in motion striking an object, e.g. in falls and traffic injuries
5. Repeated blows to the head as in boxing 'punch drunk'. Indirect violence results from: (a) fall from a height on feet or buttocks, (b) pressure transmitted from below, e.g. by an explosion, and (c) a blow on the chin when the force is transmitted from the mandible to the skull.

Separation of sutures occurs only in young persons due to a blow on the head with a blunt weapon or from cerebral oedema. While this may occur alone, it is usually associated with a sutural fracture *(diastatic fracture).*

The varieties of fractures met with are: fissured, stellate or radiating, depressed (signature fracture), elevated, punctured, guttered, crushed or comminuted, and ring fracture. These varieties may be combined in some cases. The fracture may involve the vault or base or both and may be caused by direct or indirect violence. The base of the skull, by virtue of its irregular shape and several foramina passing through it, is relatively weak and is, therefore, the most common site of skull fractures. *In all medico-legal autopsies, the dura should be stripped thoroughly from the vault and the base so that the presence of fractures may be verified or excluded.* Unless this is done, even large fractures are likely to be missed.

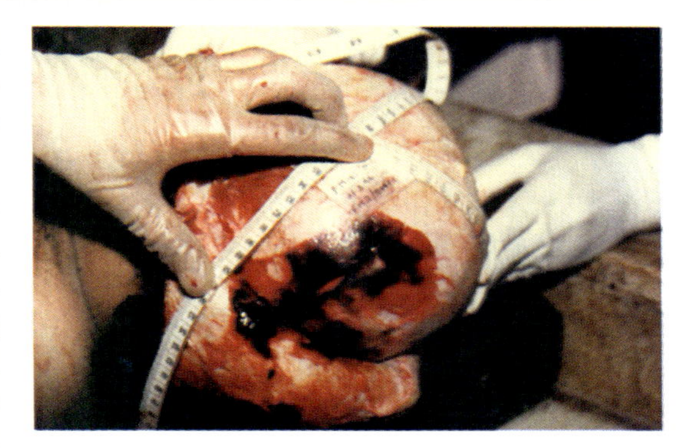

Fig. 20.2: Haematoma—skull

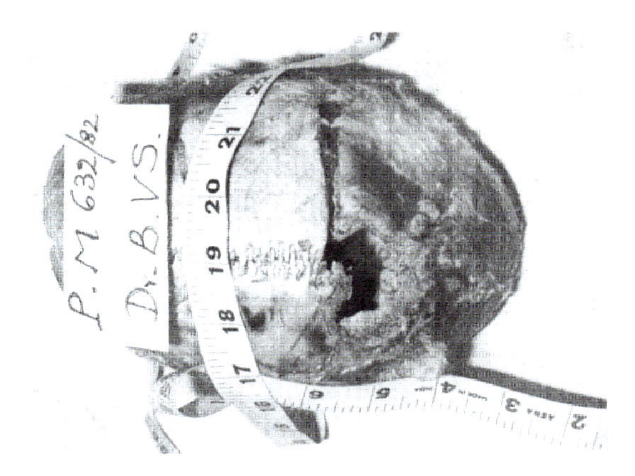

Fig. 20.3: Skull fracture—bone missing

Q. 20.3. Name the varieties of common fractures of the vault of the skull, and give a brief description of each.

The following varieties of fractures of the vault of the skull are commonly encountered: (1) fissured, (2) depressed, (3) comminuted, (4) pond or indented, (5) gutter, (6) penetrating, and (7) elevated.

Fissured fracture: This is a linear fracture or crack involving the outer or inner table or both. The outer table being strong, the fracture may sometime involve the inner table only as it is fragile. Such a fracture cannot be detected by an X-ray. It can only be detected at autopsy. The sharp edges of the fractured inner table may penetrate the dura and lacerate the underlying brain, and consequently be followed by traumatic epilepsy in due course when the original traumatic episode may have been forgotten.

The fracture is caused by direct physical violence to the head due to blows from a stick or indirectly by a fall. The site of impact is indicated by a haematoma on the scalp. In general, an injury sustained by a fall is at the level of the brim of the hat while an injury due to blows is above this level. In the case of a blow resulting in a fall, the fracture lines due to the fall are arrested by those produced by the blow.

When a blow is struck on one side of the head which is stationary, fracture of the vault occurs at the point of impact by direct violence and the fracture line runs parallel to the direction of force. The fracture may occur on the opposite side by contre coup if the head moves and its movement is suddenly arrested by coming in contact with a hard substance on the opposite side, e.g. a fall on the ground. Linear fractures follow the path of least resistance and are deflected from the thicker and more resistant bony portions of the skull, such as the glabella, frontal and parietal eminences, petrous mass, and occipital protuberance, but course down through the thinner and less resistant bones, such as frontal sinuses, orbital roof, and parietal and occipital squama.

Fissured fractures should not be confused on X-ray examination with natural depressions found in the skull and occasionally reported as fissures by the radiologists.

During a quarrel, a retired government secretary was injured on the head. An X-ray of skull was taken and the radiologist reported the presence of a fissure in the skull. The fissure was misinterpreted as a linear fracture and the assailant charged with grievous hurt. When it was pointed out to the court that the fissure on X-ray examination was a natural depression in skull due to middle meningeal artery and not a fracture, the accused was acquitted.

Depressed fracture: This is caused by a heavy weapon with a small striking surface, e.g. hammer. The fractured bone is driven inward and its shape may indicate the type of weapon with which it is produced. It is, therefore, also known as a *signature fracture.* Differences in depth of various portions of the depression may also indicate the relative positions of the assailant and victim when the blow was struck. The deepest part of the depression often marks the most advanced part of the striking surface. As late effect of depressed skull fracture, *post-traumatic epilepy may occur.*

Comminuted fracture: This is caused by vehicular accidents, falls from height, and blows from weapons with a large striking surface, e.g. a heavy iron-bar. The bone is broken into two or more pieces (comminuted) is often a complication of a depressed fracture and has a stellate appearance when there is no displacement of fragments.

Pond or indented fracture: Pond fractures occur in children due to elasticity of their skull bones. The fracture is due to forcible impact against some protruding object. Fissured fractures may be seen round the periphery of the dent.

Gutter fracture: When a part of the thickness of skull bone is removed, e.g. in glancing bullet wounds, the fracture is known as a gutter fracture. It is usually accompanied by irregular depressed fracture of the inner table. In some cases, only a longitudinal depression of outer table of skull may be present without loss of bone.

Penetrating fracture: This is a clean cut opening due to a penetrating weapon, such as, a dagger or a bullet. The characteristics of a skull wound of bullet entry and exit have already been outlined in the Chapter 17 on 'Firearm Injuries'.

Elevated fracture: This is the result of a blow from a moderately heavy sharp-edged weapon, e.g. axe, machete, which elevate one end of bone above the surface of the skull while the other end may dip down in the cranial cavity injuring dura or the brain. It may indicate the relative position of the assailant and victim.

Q. 20.4. Name the common sites of fractures of the base of the skull, and give a brief description of each.

The common sites of fracture of the base of the skull are:

1. Anterior cranial fossa
2. Middle cranial fossa
3. Posterior cranial fossa
4. Around the foramen magnum, known as ring fracture.

Fracture of the anterior cranial fossa: This is usually due to direct impact although fissured fractures in the orbital plate may be due to contre coup injury. A heavy blow on the chin sustained in boxing may transmit the impact through maxilla to the base of skull and may result in contre coup fracture of the cribriform plate of the ethmoid. The fracture manifests itself by escape of blood and cerebrospinal fluid from nose in addition to extravasation of blood in the orbit which reveals itself as a *black eye (spectacle haemorrhage, raccoon eyes).*

Fracture of the middle cranial foss: This is due to direct impact behind the ear or crush injuries of head. It is followed by escape of blood and cerebrospinal fluid from ear, if the petrous part of temporal bone is fractured. Occasionally, it may cause an arteriovenous communication between carotid artery and cavernous sinus. Mastoid haemorrhage from a fracture of middle cranial fossa (Battle's sign) may be confused with retroauricular scalp bruise.

Fracture of the posterior cranial fossa: This is commonly due to direct impact on the back of the head, e.g. striking the back of the head on the ground. It may be followed by escape of blood and cerebrospinal fluid in the tissues of the back or neck.

Ring fracture: This term is commonly used to signify any fracture round the foramen magnum. Technically, it means a fissured fracture about 3.5 cm outside the foramen magnum at the back, involving middle ear sideways, and roof of nose anteriorly. It is rare and usually requires a lot of force to produce. It results from—(a) fall from a height on feet or buttocks, (b) sudden violent turn of the head on the spine, (c) severe blow on vertex which drives the skull downwards on the vertebral column, and (d) a heavy blow directed underneath the occiput or chin.

MECHANISM OF CEREBRAL INJURY

Q. 20.4. Explain the principles and mechanism of cerebral injury.

Certain principles must be remembered for a clear understanding of the mechanism of cerebral injury:

1. The adult skull is a remarkably strong structure. Unless it is fractured, it does not change shape. However, the brain can be easily distorted (displaced by haemorrhage, lacerated, or torn). Therefore, injury to the brain can occur even without injury to the skull.
2. Any impact (blow) on the head produces momentary acceleration. The brain responds by gliding and rotation as the head is eccentrically fixed to the spinal column and neck. The rotational (torsional, tearing, angular, shearing) strains are predominant. *They pull the constituent particles of brain apart (like twisting a pack of cards) and are, therefore, very harmful.* The consequent brain injury is proportional to the rotational strain.
3. The harmful effect is increased when the brain movement (gliding) is prevented by the bony prominences of anterior and middle cranial fossa (the orbital and cribriform plates and lesser wings of sphenoid). Depending on the momentum, the brain injury may result in—(a) haemorrhage due to tearing of blood vessels, (b) selective damage to the cortical tracts (neurons/axons) in the direction of the strain, and (c) actual laceration of the brain.
4. Changes in the rate of movement are thus of great importance in producing brain damage.
5. Since the cerebellum is smaller and lighter than cerebral hemispheres, it is less likely to be damaged by rotational strains.

COUP AND CONTRECOUP INJURY

Q. 20.5. Discuss coup and contrecoup injuries in terms of their medicolegal significance.

These types of injuries are generally seen in the region of the head but may occur elsewhere also.

A **coup injury** (coup = blow) is one which occurs immediately subjacent to the area of impact. The smaller the impact area the greater is the likelihood of a coup injury. The effects are immediate resulting in contusions and haemorrhage. As for example, if the head is fixed (in a case where a person is lying on the ground) and there is violent impact over the occiput, the fracture and underlying brain damage will be located beneath the site of impact. This is known as a coup injury.

A **contrecoup injury** (contre = opposite; coup = blow) is one which is situated on the contralateral side of the area of impact. It is sustained in falls and traffic injuries when a moving head decelerates suddenly by hitting a hard surface. As for example, when a person falls upon the back of his head striking the ground with his occiput, he may sustain brain injury at the site of impact, that is, at the occipital lobes (coup injury), and a more pronounced injury to the frontal lobes. The latter is known as contrecoup injury. *It can occur only when the head is free to move.* It is due to sudden deceleration of the moving head, causing linear and (more harmful) rotational strains to the brain. Such injury occurs most frequently in the temporal poles, frontal poles, and orbital surfaces of frontal lobes. In temporal impact, the contrecoup damage may not be on the contralateral hemisphere but on the opposite side of the ipsilateral hemisphere from impact against the falx cerebri.

In short, with blows, the brain shows much larger contusions underlying the area of impact (coup) than on the site opposite to impact (contrecoup). The reverse is true in cases of head injuries caused by falls in which the contrecoup injuries, usually located in relatively inaccessible portions, are larger than the coup contusions. *Thus, it is possible to conclude, on the basis of localisation of craniocerebral injuries, if they resulted from a fall or from blows.*

Sometimes, the location of injury is neither beneath nor fully opposite the point of impact. It is situated in a position between coup and contrecoup contusions. It is known as **intermediate coup contusion** and is usually sustained when the moving head strikes a hard surface. Such a lesion can mimic spontaneous intracerebral haemorrhage arising in deep cerebral parenchyma. Brainstem contusions can be regarded as an example of this type of injury. Intermediate contusions in the hemispheres or brainstem are commonly produced in injury situations where the moving head impacts at the vertex.

The mechanism of cerebral injury of the contre coup type is of considerable importance to the pathologist at autopsy on a victim of trauma as shown by the following example.

Just before closing time in a certain public house, a slightly inebriated young man suspected another of having insulted his mother. Some time later, the second young man was found dead in the gutter, with a bruise on the chin, two black eyes, and a cut on the back of the head. The rapidly sobered assailant stoutly maintained that he had struck the victim only one blow on the chin, but a charge of at least manslaughter (culpable homicide) hung over him, until the autopsy. This displayed that there was a fracture of the back part of the head and severe 'contre-coup' injury to the front of the brain, resulting in bleeding into eye-sockets, giving the impression of black eyes. This substantiated the story of a single blow on the chin, with subsequent cracking of the back of head on the pavement edge.

INJURIES TO CRANIAL CONTENTS

Q. 20.6. Classify injuries to cranial contents. Give a brief account of: (1) diffuse neuronal injuries, (2) diffuse axonal injuries.

Brain injuries can be **classified** according to the main effect of trauma as:

1. Acceleration/deceleration injuries
2. Impact injuries. The typical acceleration/deceleration injuries are:
   a. Diffuse neuronal injuries
   b. Diffuse axonal injuries
   c. Subdural haematomas. The impact injuries of the brain are—(a) cerebral

concussion, (b) cerebral contusions, (c) cerebral lacerations, and (d) intracranial haemorrhages, e.g. (i) epidural haemorrhage, (ii) subdural haemorrhage, (iii) subarachnoid haemorrhage, and (iv) intracerebral haemorrhage.

Diffuse neuronal injuries (DNI): This is due to sudden acceleration/deceleration movement of the head. The condition is characterised by diffuse neuronal damage involving the brainstem. The damage consists of widespread intracellular disturbances and conduction defects at synaptic junctions. It commonly occurs when the deceleration impact is relatively prolonged, as in case of vehicular accidents (90% cases) in which the head strikes against the padded surfaces, and the rate of deceleration is thereby prolonged. Sagittal head motion produces only mild or moderate DNI while coronal head motion (rotational strain) which commonly occurs in vehicular impacts produces severe DNI. The classical example of such an injury is **concussion.**

Diffuse axonal injuries (DAI): This is encountered in those situations where the rotational strains generated during impact to the head damage the axons and blood vessels. It is the motion of the head that causes injury to the brain resulting in stretching of the axons with consequent disruption and loss of function depending on the impact strain. The cause may be either a severe head injury (not a fall unless it is from more than one's own height) or repeated jolts as in boxing which result in cumulative axonal damage leading to progressive deterioration of brain function known as *punch drunk.* In the latter condition, specific changes are noted clinically in the form of dementia and at autopsy in the form of diffuse axonal injury involving corpus callosum and rostral brainstem (especially superior cerebellar peduncles) and diffuse damage to the white matter of the cerebral hemispheres. There is evidence to suggest that in the case of an intoxicated person dying from sublethal trauma, the death is likeiy to be due to depression of the nervous system as a result of alcohol, aggravated by diffuse axonal injury from trauma, adding up in a fatal outcome.

Microscopic examination of the brain in short survival cases shows widespread white matter damage in the form of ruptured axons and spheroids. *Spheroids* are circular or elongated granular bodies containing cell organelles. They are local dilatations of axons and are seen around the edges of infarcts, in axonal dystrophies, and in other situations of axonal damage. Long survival cases show microglial reaction, myelin degeneration, and sometimes microcavities, in the white matter throughout the cerebral hemispheres, brainstem, and spinal cord. Progressive enlargement of the ventricular system due to loss of bulk of white matter may be misinterpreted at autopsy as traumatic hydrocephalus without arousing any suspicion of DAI.

Q. 20.7. Discuss cerebral concussion from a medicolegal point of view. Include a note on retrograde amnesia and post-traumatic automatism,(mild traumatic brain injury)

Cerebral concussion or stunning is a condition, following head injury, characterised by gross physiological disturbance of brain function due to diffuse neuronal injury (involving the brainstem) but with little or no noticeable anatomical changes. It commonly results from traffic accidents and injuries to head sustained in industry. The condition is more severe when damage is caused to the moving head (deceleration injury) than when it results from blows to the skull. There is sudden loss of consciousness and a tendency to spontaneous recovery. Concussion may be intensified by repeated blows and, depending on the physical stress on the neurons, the neuronal injury may be wholly or partially reversible, or may prove fatal, if it is a complex concussion.

In fatal cases, at autopsy, no naked eye lesions are found in the brain. On histological examination, microscopic haemorrhages may be found in the tissues without any disruption of structure of the tissue itself. There is evidence to suggest that these deaths are due to diffuse neuronal damage consisting of widespread intracellular disturbances and conduction defects at synaptic junctions. In some cases, lesions resulting from the original injury that are distinct from neuronal injury are found, e.g. bruises, lacerations, and intracranial haemorrhages. They can be considered as additional factors which hastened death, the probable true immediate cause of death being DNI.

In less severe cases, the patient regains consciousness after a varying period during which he may show signs of *cerebral irritation*. This condition is characterised by some peculiar symptoms. The patient lies curled up in bed, with his face buried beneath the clothes; he resents all forms of interference and exposure to light. He is not unconscious but pays no regard to his surroundings. He is liable to become violent and abusive, if disturbed. These symptoms disappear after a varying period and recovery may be complete or may be followed by a *postconcussional syndrome*, characterised by headache, dizziness, insomnia, and mental irritability. The syndrome is of medicolegal significance and must be *distinguished from* malingering in those cases where symptoms are prolonged, especially when compensation is involved.

Recovery from concussion is often followed by **retrograde amnesia.** The patient is unable to recollect the exact manner in which he was injured. Such loss of memory generally extends over a period of a fortnight to a month or more. This is important from a medicolegal point of view as the prosecution or defence, in the event of a litigation, may suggest that this selective loss of memory is merely a pretence to escape answering inconvenient questions.

Post-traumatic automatism may sometimes follow. The brain injured person may speak or act in an apparently purposeful manner but has no recollection about it afterwards. The condition is intimately associated with amnesia and its duration usually proportional to the severity of the injury.

As a general rule, a patient with a head injury with a history of concussion should be kept under observation for 24 hours for signs of insidious onset of extradural haemorrhage.

Q. 20.8. Write short notes on: (1) cerebral contusions, (2) cerebral lacerations, (3) cerebral oedema.

Cerebral contusions are caused by extravasation of blood from traumatically ruptured blood vessels and are most often found in those areas of the brain (frontal and temporal lobes) where the cortex is likely to come in contact with irregularities in the internal profile of the skull. They generally involve the crest of the gyri but may extend into the white matter as a wedge-shaped lesion. They are characterized by small punctate or streak-like haemorrhages and associated focal destruction of tissue, with or without oedema. They are more serious when associated with skull fracture and are relatively uncommon in brains with diffuse axonal injury. They enlarge with time, especially in persons with hypertension, liver cirrhosis, or a bleeding disorder. A golden brown area of gliosis, crudely known as blood cyst, results when the contusion is absorbed. **The clinical** manifestations vary with the site and extent of the contused area. **The period** of unconsciousness is longer than that of concussion.

In contrast to blunt trauma injury in adults, brain contusions **in infants** differ morphologically from those of adults. They are found as ischaemic or mild haemorrhagic tears in the subcortical white matter of the frontal lobes and temporal poles. Infant victims of fatal craniocerebral trauma often show very little cortical damage. It is not possible to determine from the location and site of these injuries whether the cause is a blow or a fall.

Cerebral lacerations are caused by the same mechanism as cerebral contusions. Penetrating wounds, such as gunshot injuries or depressed fractures, as well as closed head injuries with a high degree of shearing force (rotational strains) are major causative factors. Unlike cortical contusions which are subpial, however, these are accompanied by **rupture** of pia mater and are usually larger lesions than the contusions. They are generally surrounded by groups of contusions and are prominent in **those** regions where the brain is in contact with jagged areas of the **skull,** especially the temporal poles and orbital surfaces of frontal lobes. Subarachnoid haemorrhage commonly accompanies the lesion because of rupture of pia mater.

When healing occurs, adhesions may form between the brain and dura and such adhesions may result in traumatic epilepsy after months or years when the incidence of original traumatic episode may have been forgotten. Healing of lacerations in cerebral ventricles may result in the formation of large glial cysts, known as *porencephalic cysts,* filled with cerebrospinal fluid. They can be differentiated from blood cysts that formed in the healing of cerebral contusions and lacerations by the presence of blood pigments in the latter.

Cerebral oedema is the most common cause of raised intracranial pressure. It may be related to diffuse neuronal injury and concussion. The amount of fluid in the brain increases and the total weight may increase by at least 100 gm in the extra-cellular compartment of the white matter. At autopsy: (1) the dura is found to be stretched, (2) the brain bulges through the incision, (3) the gyri are pale and flattened, (4) the sulci are widened and obliterated, (5) the cut surface of the brain appears pale, (6) the ventricles are greatly reduced in size, appearing almost slit-like in children, and (7) herniation of the hippocampal gyrus, secondary brainstem haemorrhage, and coning of the cerebellar tonsils are frequently seen in adults, and less commonly in children.

Q. 20.9. What is epidural (extradural) haemorrhage? Give a detailed account of acute and subacute epidural haemorrhage. Add a note on lucid interval.

Epidural or extradural haemorrhage is bleeding between the dura and skull, is almost invariably traumatic. It is commonly seen in falls and traffic accidents. It is associated with skull fracture except in infants and children in whom the dura is strongly adherent to the inner surface of the skull. The condition may be acute or subacute.

Acute epidural haemorrhage is generally due to rupture of the middle meningeal artery as a result of fracture in this area. The dura is lifted locally by the rising pressure of the haemorrhage. It bulges into the cranial cavity and displaces the brain. The patient loses consciousness. This may take few minutes to a few hours or even a day after the injury as the onset of coma may be insidious. Unless the clot is surgically removed, the victim rapidly dies due to displacement of brain with compression of brainstem. *The classical picture* of epidural haemorrhage, viz. an initial loss of consciousness, then a lucid interval, followed by coma due to raised intracranial tension, *is not commonly seen in acute cases.* The most common clinical course is that of severe head injury associated with skull fracture and stupor progressing to deep coma. The usual cause of death is respiratory failure due to compression of the brainstem.

Subacute epidural haemorrhage occurs when the fracture tears dural sinuses, middle meningeal veins, or diploic veins, the last condition being most common. Symptoms are slower in onset, often not appearing for three or more days after the trauma. In about 50 per cent of these cases, lucid interval is encountered, the sequence of symptoms being as follows: unconsciousness due to concussion, consciousness due to recovery unconsciousness due to raised intracranial tension due to bleeding. The **lucid** interval is the state of consciousness between the two states of unconsciousness. In these cases, the apparent recovery and the interval between infliction of injury and onset of symptoms frequently leads to the defence that the blow was not the actual cause of death. Alternatively, this period may cover some further volitional activity which may mislead lay persons as to the actual cause of haemorrhage.

A woman fell from a scooter and except for some bruising of scalp, no other injury was evident. After reaching home, she had a quarrel with her husband on items of dinner resulting in exchange of light blows on the face. She collapsed and died. Autopsy revealed about 100 ml of extradural blood clot beneath a fractured skull at the site of the bruise, clearing the husband from a charge of culpable homicide (manslaughter).

In marked contrast to subdural haematomas, epidural haematomas undergo rapid resolution without anatomic sequelae. Fibroblastic proliferation is rapid on the external surface of the dura. There is practically no expansion of the clot as there is no rebleeding.

Medicolegal significance of epidural haemorrhage:

1. The prognosis is good with proper treatment. It is necessary to emphasise that an epidural haematoma on the contralateral side should be carefully excluded. Instances are recorded in which one epidural haematoma was successfully operated, the other missed, and the patient died.
2. The patient may be discharged from the hospital during lucid interval and die at home; the doctor may be charged with negligence.
3. The condition may resemble drunkenness, and the patient may die in police custody.

Q. 20.10. What is subdural haemorrhage (haematoma)? Give the classification. Discuss each condition in detail. Add a note on the 'age' of a subdural haematoma.

Subdural haematoma is due to a vascular injury where the head rapidly decelerates because of impact to a firm, unyielding surface. It is, therefore, more common in falls and assaults in contrast to diffuse neuronal injury which is commonly encountered in vehicular accidents where the deceleration impact to head is relatively prolonged. It is one of the most common head injuries ending fatally.

Subdural haemorrhage occurs between the under surface of dura and outer surface of the arachnoid mater. It may be due to tearing of cortical veins or injury to dural sinuses but is more commonly due to rupture of the bridging or communicating veins. The bridging veins are small unsupported thin vessels that traverse subarachnoid and subdural spaces and drain the cortical veins into venous sinuses. They are most numerous over the vertex where they drain into superior sagittal sinus. They are commonly ruptured in rotational movements of the brain in relation to skull. Such ruptures are also common from trivial injuries not sufficient to cause unconsciousness or fracture of the skull. Such ruptures occur in persons with atrophic brain, either from disease (alcoholics) or from aging, when the brain can oscillate back and forth within the skull which is now too wide and may thus jeopardize the bridging veins. Since different bridging veins are subjected different degrees of stretching in rotational movements of the head, the resulting subdural haematoma may bear no relationship to the site of application of force. A subdural haematoma may occasionally be secondary to disease processes, e.g. cerebral neoplasms, ruptured cerebral aneurysm or intracerebral haemorrhage ruptured in the subdural space, bleeding disorders, and during anticoagulant therapy. It should be emphasised that subdural haematomas are not necessarily associated with skull fracture and/or brain injuries.

Subdural haematomas are **classified** as acute, subacute, or chronic depending upon the development of clinical signs. Acute subdural haematomas are those in which the signs are evident within 24 hours of injury, subacute when the signs are evident between 24 hours to 7 days, and chronic when the signs develop thereafter.

The **acute subdural haematoma** is due to rupture of a large bridging vein or a cortical artery. The onset of symptoms is usually rapid. The condition becomes life-threatening when approximately 50 ml of blood accumulates. It is an important cause of death in approximately 90% of cases. The high mortality is in part due to the associated brain damage from the acceleration/deceleration injury which caused the haematoma. The brain damage may of neuronal/axonal type and depending on the severity of stress on the neurons/axons, the victim may die irrespective of the haematoma. Even after successful surgical intervention, the cerebral oedema that accompanies the injury makes the prognosis poor.

The **subacute subdural haematoma** is due to bleeding from smaller bridging veins. The signs and symptoms develop gradually. The haematoma is usually associated with minor cerebral contusions or swelling. The mortality from this type of haematoma is less.

Especially in the elderly, with atrophic brains, the torn perforating dural veins may cause chronic subdural haematoma (blood cyst) over the cortex. The haemorrhage is venous, the pressure under which it accumulates is slow, and it may take many weeks before sufficient blood accumulates to exert pressure on the underlying brain. The diagnosis is often difficult. The haematoma is often secondary to a slight, forgotten episode of trauma. As the leakage is extremely slow, there may not be any neurologic effects except slight confusion, forgetfulness, and emotional disorder. These may be mistaken in the young for schizophrenia and in the old for presenile and senile dementia. The haematoma may expand due to recurrent bleeding or renewed trauma to the head and cause compression of the brain several months after the injury. The reparative process within the subdural space gradually changes the haematoma to a network of vascularized membranes. Recurrent bleeding within these membranes and possible osmotic absorption of fluid from adjacent tissues lead to the expansion of haematoma. The haematoma does not resolve, as the subdural space has no mesothelial lining, and such haematomas (blood cysts) are found incidentally at autopsy. *Unsuspected chronic subdural haematoma is a known cause of sudden unexplained death in alcoholics.*

The **chronic subdural haematoma** consists of accumulation of blood encased by an outer membrane underlying the dura and an inner membrane that separates the blood (clot) from the arachnoid. Both membranes are composed of fibrous tissue derived from the dura, from which clot resolution proceeds, as it does elsewhtre in the body. The vascular channels within the membranes have very thin incompletely endothelialised walls making them susceptible to re-bleeding. During the first 4 days, the haematoma undergoes clotting. The first obvious easily detectable change occurs at 10 to 12 days when a fragile membrane envelopes the clot. Under the microscope, the membrane is seen to consist of delicate granulation tissue with thin walled capillaries and actively dividing fibroblasts growing into the clot. Like granulation tissue elsewhere in the body, a mere touch will make it to bleed. This can be demonstrated by a gentle stream of water to run over the dura when the small vessels will be seen to rupture. Thus, it seems likely that a fresh capillary bleeding can occur from the membrane long after the initial bleeding which produced the haematoma. Later, the membrane becomes a tough collagenous structure. The blood within it lyses and proteins breakdown into polypeptides with an increase in osmotic pressure and indrawing of fluid into the haematoma through the semipermeable membrane. This mechanism and recurrent capillary bleeding have both been put forward to explain the expansion of the haematoma.

The age of a subdural haematoma can be of great medicolegal importance in correlating intracranial lesions with events occurring prior to death. Evaluation of microscopic changes in the dura requires several sections from different sites. In the first 24 hours, the changes are slight and consist principally of capillary dilatation with a few perivascular granulocytes. Early proliferation of fibroblasts on the under surface of dura is evident in 2–3 days. At 4–5 days, a thin layer of fibrin is present on the under surface of dura which shows fibroblastic and capillary proliferations. Red cell breakdown, phagocytosis of haemosiderin, and capillary sprouting into the inner pseudomembrane are conspicuous by 5–10 days. A true inner membrane is formed between 2–4 weeks. After 3–4 weeks, connective tissue of the inner membrane begins to have a mature appearance. From 1–3 months, the outer and inner membranes are composed of mature connective tissue with numerous haemosiderin and haematoidin-laden macrophages.

Q. 20.11. Discuss subarachnoid haemorrhage in detail from a medicolegal point of view. Include a brief note on autopsy on cases of traumatic basal subarachnoid haemorrhage.

Subarachnoid haemorrhage may be due to natural causes or trauma. Large collections of blood in the subarachnoid space at the base of the brain are more common in natural diseases than in trauma. Traumatic subarachnoid haemorrhage in this region is due to lacerations of the vital arteries, such as the internal carotid, vertebral, and basilar, and is likely to be immediately fatal. The most frequent natural causes of subarachnoid haemorrhage are:

1. Rupture of a developmental berry aneurysm (usually located at the bifurcation of the vessels of the circle of Willis or one of its major branches), due to a developmental defect in the media of vessels in younger subjects, the most common cause of non-traumatic subarachnoid haemorrhage.
2. Arteriosclerotic changes in the media of blood vessels associated with high blood pressure in older persons.
3. A leaking intracerebral haemorrhage.
4. Disease conditions, like purpuric states, leukaemia, angioma, etc.

The most frequent traumatic causes are: (1) cerebral contusions or lacerations, (2) explosive blast, (3) asphyxia by strangulation, (4) traumatic asphyxia, (5) damage to the vertebral arteries from conditions, like fracture of the upper cervical vertebrae, blows with side of the hand across the neck, etc., and (6) prolonged hyperextension of the head during bronchoscopy. This may result in subarachnoid haemorrhage over the base of the brain, the bleeding originating from rents in basal or vertebral arteries, and may lead to a charge of *malpractice*.

Blows to the face may produce laceration of the internal carotid artery and blows to the neck may produce laceration of vertebral or external carotid artery. Such laceration should be suspected in case of a person who has died almost instantaneously or very soon after a blow on the face or neck. Demonstration of the site of laceration prior to removal of brain is possible by appropriate angiographic study. Such study is essential to arrive at a correct diagnosis without being misled by artifacts encountered during dissection of neck. In the event angiographic (X-ray) facilities are not available, cervical vertebrae should be removed for study of vertebral arteries, if preliminary examination of intracranial arteries at autopsy fails to reveal an obvious source of bleeding.

The following guidelines are offered for **autopsy** on cases of traumatic basal subarachnoid haemorrhage.

Once subarachnoid haemorrhage is identified, the calvarium is replaced and angiographic study of vertebral and carotid arteries (AP and lateral views) undertaken to identify the site of bleeding, either intracranial or extracranial. If there is intracranial arterial damage, the brain is removed after cutting vertebral and carotid arteries flush with dura, the blood gently washed away, and the brain fixed in formalin as usual. The basal cerebral arteries are dissected, and the site of tearing sectioned and photographed. The extra-cranial arterial damage may involve the vertebral or the carotid artery. In such cases also, the brain is removed as in the case of intracranial artery damage. To detect extracranial vertebral artery damage, cervical vertebrae are removed, and vertebral arteries dissected from bony foramina leaving transverse process of C1 intact. The site of tearing is sectioned and photographed and C1 vertebra X-rayed for evidence of fracture of the transverse process. To detect extracranial carotid artery damage, the carotid arteries are dissected out, including the petrous segment, and the site of tearing sectioned and photographed.

In all cases of subarachnoid haemorrhage without apparent trauma, the cerebral vasculature should be scrutinised with great care. The most easily missed cause is the developmental aneurysm. It may not be more than a pinhead swelling. Dissection under a gentle stream of water facilitates the examination. Under no circumstances, one should assume the spontaneous rupture of an intracranial aneurysm that self-destructed and, therefore, could not be identified. The actual anatomic defect must be located. Failure to find such a local cause, e.g. an aneurysm or angioma, should arouse suspicion of foul play or injury.

A boy who wanted to marry a girl against the wishes of his parents collapsed after receiving a slap from his mother. At autopsy, a ruptured developmental aneurysm was found. Its probability of spontaneous rupture on excitement was considered by the court resulting in acquittal of the mother.

Arteriosclerotic vessels with high blood pressure in older persons rupture more easily than normal ones. The condition of blood vessels must, therefore, receive the most careful consideration in all such cases.

It is possible **to testify that** trauma is the cause of rupture of developmental aneurysm when head injury is followed at once by symptoms of bleeding, or by symptoms like more or less continuous headaches in the interval before final rupture.

Q. 20.12. Tabulate the salient features of epidural, subdural, and subarachnoid haemorrhage.

Or

How will you differentiate EDH, SDH, SAH.

Salient features of epidural, subdural and subarachnoid haemorrhage are given in Table 20.1

Table 20.1: Salient features of epidural, subdural and subarachnoid haemorrhage

Epidural (extradural)	*Subdural*	*Subarachnoid*
1. Between skull and dura	Between dura and arachnoid	Between arachnoid and pia
2. Always due to head injury	Mostly due to injury but not always (massive leakage through meninges)	Natural: aneurysm, angioma, high blood pressure. Traumatic: cerebral contusions, damage to internal carotid, vertebral, or basilar artery
3. Present in 2% of head injuries	Found in 5% of all head injuries and in 50% of fatal head injuries	
4. Middle meningeal artery is torn	Chronic/subacute from bridging veins. Acute from cortical contusions	Extremely common in head injuries but also seen in natural disease
5. Often swelling (blood) under the scalp	Often no external manifestation	Due to natural vessel leakage from vessels on brain surface, or vessels from within brain, or from injury
6. Can be confused with heat artefact	Seldom confused with other bleeding	No external manifestation unless other injuries are present
7. Can be space occupying	Often space occupying	Can be artefact from opening the skull. May be space occupying if source arterial
8. Brain surface ironed out by dura	Brain compressed but less ironed out due to dura being external to blood	Brain surface not distorted
9. Usually on one side, and localised	Unilateral or bilateral diffuse	Focal, semi-localised, diffuse, or bilateral
10. Clinical course includes classic lucid interval	Clinical course less well defined	Clinical course depends on cause; also on vessel, amount, rate, and location
11. If fresh, preserve portion for alcohol, and drugs analysis	If fresh, preserve a portion for alcohol and drugs analysis	Seldom sufficient or helpful for analysis
12. At autopsy can be scrapped	Washed by a thin stream of water	Not washable

Q. 20.13. Discuss intracerebral haemorrhage. Tabulate the relevant differences between post-traumatic and spontaneous intracerebral haemorrhage (apoplexy).

Next to non-traumatic subarachnoid haemorrhage from rupture of a berry aneurysm, intracerebral haemorrhage is a common cause of non-traumatic intracranial haemorrhage. It is mainly due to disease of cerebral vessels. When close to the surface, it may be the result of laceration. Deep seated haemorrhages in the cerebrum, cerebellum, and brainstem may occur in association with other brain injuries. However, such haemorrhages are not encountered as a sole and only manifestation of a head injury. A single deep seated haemorrhage is usually due to some disease. Spontaneous haemorrhage in the middle-aged and elderly persons due to rupture of lenticulostriate artery in the region of basal ganglia is common. Isolated haemorrhages in the frontal or occipital lobes are likely to be due to trauma.

Hypertension is usually present in victims of intracerebral haemorrhage. Physical exertion or emotional excitement may precipitate an attack. If such a person were to fall and sustain a scalp injury before death, the haemorrhage may be mistaken to be that of traumatic origin. Only a careful inquiry into the clinical history of the subject can help to arrive at a correct diagnosis. The factors to be considered are: the age of the victim, his race, site and extent of haemorrhage, evidence of vascular disease in cerebral arteries, cardiac hypertrophy, and kidney disease. Sometimes, haemorrhage may not occur at the time of violence but may appear later. In such a case, the delayed haemorrhage can be attributed to the late effects of trauma only if it can be shown that haemorrhage has occurred at or near the site of mechanically injured brain tissue.

In case of gross haemorrhage into the brain after an incidence of trauma, the essential problem at autopsy is to deter-

Table 20.2: Differences between post-traumatic and spontaneous intracerebral haemorrhage (apoplexy)

Post-traumatic haemorrhage	*Apoplexy*
1. Cause: Head injury	Hypertension, arteriosclerosis, aneurysm
2. Age: Usually young healthy persons	Usually adults past middle age
3. Onset: A variable period after injury	Sudden
4. Position: Head in motion	Any position
5. Mechanism: Blunt force injury coup and contre coup	Rupture due to disease
6. Location: White matter of frontal or temporoparietal region	Ganglionic regions
7. Concussion: Concussion and post-concussion syndrome may be present	Absent
8. Coma: Variable. Coma from beginning, or concussion ⇒ consciousness ⇒ coma	No such sequence

mine, if the haemorrhage is post-traumatic or spontaneous (apoplexy) due to leakage from diseased blood vessel. The relevant differences are given in Table 20.2.

Q. 20.14. Comment on alcohol and head injuries.

A person who has consumed alcohol may sustain a head injury. A well-meaning relative or friend may give alcohol to a person who has sustained a head injury. In such situations, it is very difficult to assess the relative importance of each factor to the state of consciousness of the patient. On occasions, after concussion, a person may be confused and disoriented, and the general clinical manifestations may simulate acute alcohol intoxication. Such a person should be watched for 24 hours in a hospital. The principal distinguishing features are tabulated in Table 20.3.

Table 20.3: Distinguishing features between a drunk and a concussed

Drunk	*Concussed*
1. Face: Suffuse, flushed, warm	Pale, clammy
2. Pulse: Fast, bounding	Slow, feeble
3. Pupils: Sluggish reaction to light	Brisk reaction to light
4. Breathing: Sighs, puffs, eructates (belches)	Shallow, irregular, slow
5. Memory: Confused but improving	Retrograde amnesia
6. Behaviour: Unco-operative, and abusive, or loquacious	Quiet, curled up, and photophobia during stage of irritation

VERTEBRAL COLUMN AND SPINAL CORD

Q. 20.15. Name the parts of the vertebral column liable to injury. Briefly describe how such injuries are caused along with their medicolegal significance.

The parts of the vertebral column (spine) most liable to be injured a: (1) the thoracolumbar region, (2) cervicothoracic region, and (3) atlantoaxial region. The thoracolumbar region is susceptible to injury because—(a) this part is near the middle of the column and has, therefore, a greater amount of leverage, (b) it is a junction of comparatively fixed part above and moveable part below, and (c) the vertebrae which form it, though much smaller, bear almost as great a weight as those below. The cervicothoracic region is susceptible to injury because the flexible cervical portion of the spine joins the more fixed thoracic portion. The atlantoaxial region is susceptible to injury because—(a) it enjoys an extensive range of movement, and (b) being near the skull, it is influenced by violence applied to the head.

Fractures of the spine may be due to direct violence, especially if disease is present. They often occur from indirect violence, such as a blow on the chin, hitting the head when diving into shallow water, or may be due to hyperextension (e.g. during bronchoscopy), hyperflexion, or compression (fall of weight on head, fall

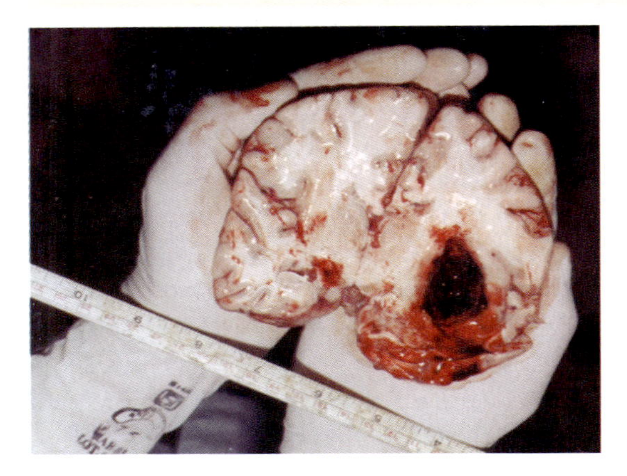

Fig. 20.4: Contusion of brain and intracerebral haemorrhage

from a height on buttocks), and vehicular accidents. Sudden pulling of hair which causes either hyperflexion or hyperextension can cause fracture of the cervical spine. It is not uncommon in India, especially in the villages, for women to hold each other's hair while fighting when such a catastrophe may happen. Hyperflexion and hyperextension injuries may produce rupture of the posterior and anterior longitudinal spinal ligaments respectively and result in instability of the spinal column and possible spinal cord damage. Compression fractures usually do not injure the spinal cord but may cause damage to the spinal nerves.

Fractures are often difficult to detect arid haemorrhage under the prevertebral fascia should be taken as an indication of whiplash injury or fracture of cervical spine which should be looked for with care. When any injury to cervical spine is suspected, an X-ray should be taken before autopsy and the involved segment of spine retained. **To demonstrate injury to the cervical spine at autopsy,** the neck organs should be removed, the anterior longitudinal ligament of the vertebral column exposed and examined, the posterior aspect of the neck incised and dissected down to spinous processes, and the ligaments surrounding the rim of foramen magnum and odontoid process incised, and the cervical spine examined. At this stage, the spinal cord can be removed and examined after fixation, if necessary.

Fractures of the spine need not necessarily damage the spinal cord but the spinal cord is rarely injured without damage to the spine except in whiplash injury.

Q. 20.16. Discuss injuries to the spinal cord. Give their medicolegal implications. Include a note on: (a) railway spine, (b) whiplash injury.

The spinal cord is susceptible to: (1) concussion, (2) compression, (3) pithing, and (4) laceration. The spinal cord is liable to be damaged also when its vascular supply is interfered with.

Concussion of the spinal cord: This may occur without any evidence of external injury. It may follow a severe blow on the back, a fall from a height, or a bullet injury. It is a common form of injury in railway accidents and motor car collisions and is known as **railway spine.** Symptoms may not appear at once but come on after some hours when the patient may develop transient paralysis of the arms, hands, bladder, rectum, lower extremities, with or without loss of sexual function. Complete recovery may occur unless the cord is lacerated.

Sometimes, a momentary dislocation of the cervical spine in the region of C4–C6 may occur, causing contusion of the spinal cord, followed by self-reduction. Such an injury may occur from a blow on the brow or chin or when a motor car comes to a sudden stop. The forward thrust dashes the head against the windscreen of a car **(whiplash injury)** resulting in hyperextension of the head and consequent injury. This injury is likely to be missed and paralysis resulting therefrom regarded as hysterical unless the cord in this region is carefully examined. An autopsy may show an area of haemorrhagic discolouration on

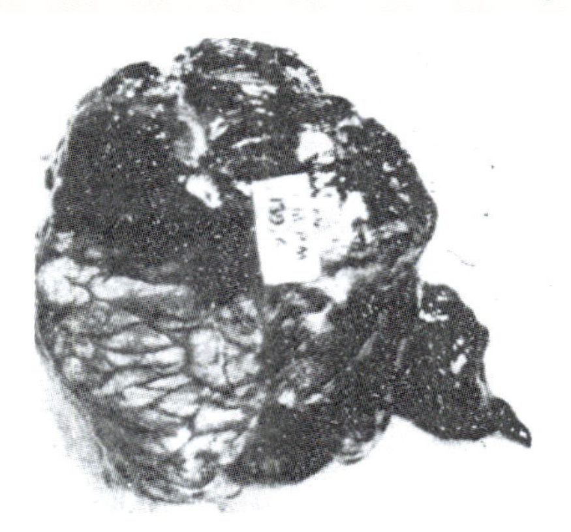

Fig. 20.5: Subarachnoid haemorrhage solely due to trauma. A male aged 50 was alleged to have been beaten with sticks on the head and body on 6-10-1965. He was admitted to the Government General Hospital, Guntur, where he expired in a few hours. He lived for a day after the receipt of injuries. At postmortem, there was contre coup extradural haemorrhage (not shown), subarachnoid haemorrhage as shown in the photograph, and intracerebral haemorrhage also (not shown). There was no disease of the blood vessels showing that such haemorrhages resulted from violence alone

the surface or in substance of the cord, or subthecal effusions of blood. In the case of haemorrhage in the substance of the cord the extent of haemorrhage must be demonstrated by serial sections of the cord (Fig. 20.5).

Examination of living persons for evidence of loss of sexual function (impotency) as a result of assault or accident involving the spine may pose a difficult forensic problem.

Blows on the spine not associated with fracture or dislocation may be followed by oedema, venous thrombosis, and softening of the cord. Therefore, when death is alleged to have been caused by violence and no trace of it is perceptible in other parts of the body, it is necessary to inspect the vertebral column for evidence of some mechanical injury or morbid changes in the spine or cord. **This part of the medicolegal investigation must not be neglected.**

The spine and spinal cord should be **carefully examined** in cases of:(1) local injuries (2) sudden death following trauma without apparent **local** injury (3) death from convulsions (4) battered babies, and (5) when **such** an examination is specifically requested by the investigating officer.

Compression of the spinal cord: This is generally due to fracture or dislocation of the spine. The common sites of fractures, dislocations subluxations, and compression are C4–C6, T3–T6, and T10–L3. If the level of compression is above the fourth cervical segment, death is seldom long delayed on account of asphyxia resulting from paralysis of respiratory muscles. Death usually occurs within 24 hours, if the three lower cervical vertebrae are injured. When upper thoracic vertebrae have been fractured, death may occur after 2 or 3 weeks due to complications of being bed-ridden, viz. bed sores, cystitis, pyelonephritis, etc. Life may be prolonged for years with partial paralysis of the lower limbs, if the lower thoracic or upper lumbar vertebrae have been injured.

Pithing: This is a process of killing brought about by pushing a **small** needle in the nape of the neck between the base of skull and first cervical vertebra or between the second and third cervical vertebrae. A puncture wound in this region proves almost immediately fatal as it injures the medulla and upper cervical cord which contain respiratory and other **vital** centres. The wound may be so small (concealed puncture wound) **that it** may be missed at autopsy. Murder by pithing is not altogether uncommon in India, particularly in cases of female infanticide. So, it should **be kept in** mind and carefully looked for in appropriate circumstances.

Laceration: Laceration of the spinal cord without any external injury is not an uncommon method of causing death, especially in children. The neck is twisted and dislocated, causing laceration of the spinal cord. This can also happen in wrestling. Firearm wounds can also cause laceration of the spinal cord even though the missile has not entered the cord, the damage resulting from near-miss trajectories at higher velocities.

FACE

Q. 20.17. Comment on the forensic importance of injuries to the face.

Injuries to the face by causing permanent disfigurement or loss of sight or teeth often come within the definition of grievous hurt. Such injuries usually involve: (1) the eyes from direct or indirect trauma, (2) the nose, especially in India, due to enmity or sexual jealousy when its tip may be cut off (Fig. 20.6), (3) the nose and ears from forcible pulling out of ornaments, especially during wayside robbery, (4) the teeth from blows over the mouth during an assault, and (5) the face as a whole from boxing or vitriolage. The injuries are not likely to be serious unless the orbit is involved; the injuries indirectly affect the brain, or spine and spinal cord; or the injury or resulting inflammation extends to the brain.

Injuries on the face may indirectly affect the brain or spinal cord from a blow on the chin or brow. The result may be diffuse neuronal/axonal injury, ring fracture of base of the skull, subarachnoid haemorrhage, or fracture/dislocation of upper cervical vertebrae. The so-called *punch drunk syndrome* is a unique example of the cumulative effect of repeated blows on the face.

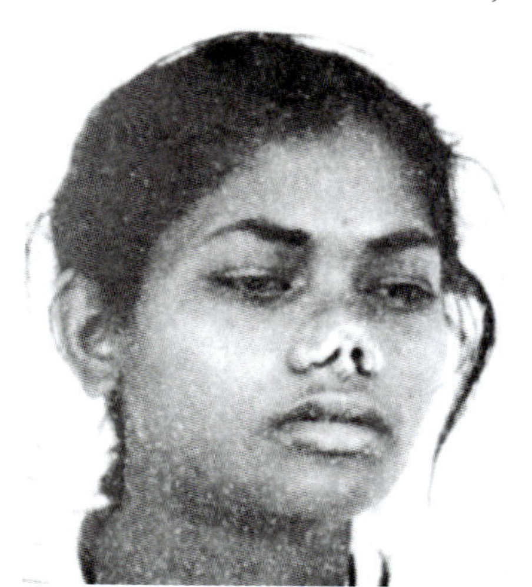

Fig. 20.6: Grievous hurt. Permanent disfiguration of the face. Tip of the nose cut off because the husband suspected his wife's fidelity. She was found talking with a man in a secret place under suspicious circumstances. In India, such punishment is comparatively more common than divorce

NECK

Q. 20.18. Tabulate the differences between suicidal and homicidal cut throat.

Differences between suicidal and homicidal cut thorat are described in Figs 20.7 to 20.9 and Table 20.4.

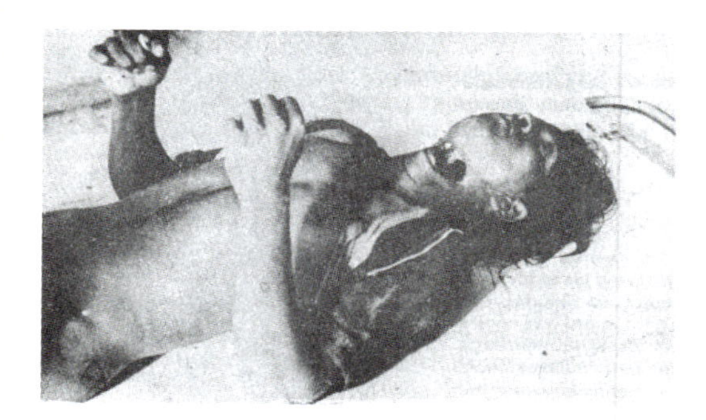

Fig. 20.7: Suicidal cut throat with a hesitation mark in the lower part of the neck (not usual) and clenched hands. Body recovered from a well. On 18th January 1965, at about 5.00 p.m., the deceased R.S. attempted to molest the wife of his master. When the woman raised the alarm, the deceased ran away to the store room, took out a knife, cut his throat, and groaning was heard. After a few minutes, he came out of the room and jumped into the well about 7 metres away from the house (volitional act after the injury). There were blood stains leading from the room to the well. The body was recovered from the well and sent for postmortem examination. It showed fine white froth from the upper respiratory tract and lungs, and cadaveric spasm of hands

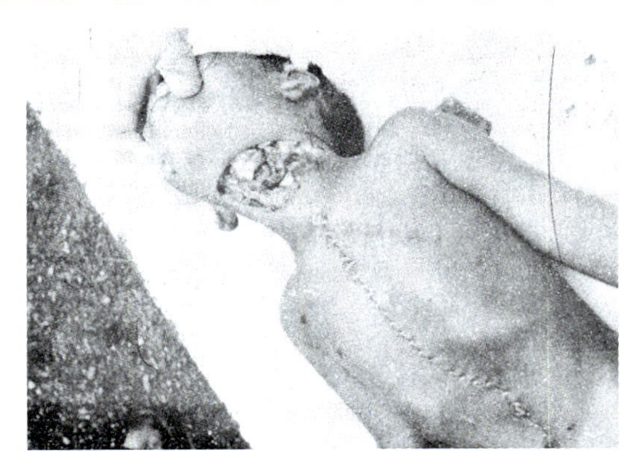

Fig. 20.8: Homicidal cut thorat with a blade. The wound has gone up to the level of the vertebrae. The hyoid is also injured

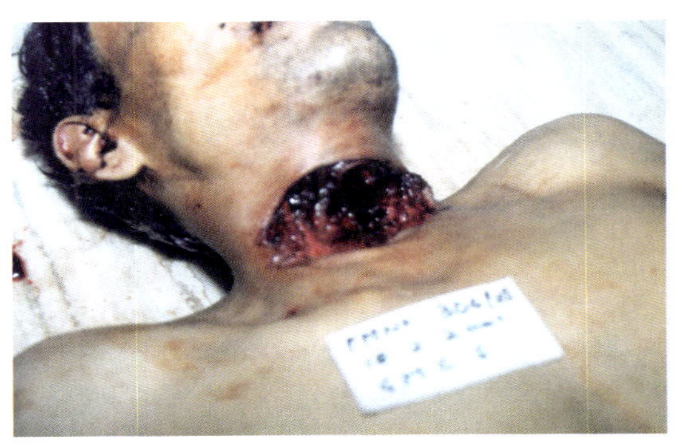

Fig. 20.9: Homicidal slit-throat. (*Courtesy*: Dr BV Subrahmanyam)

Table 20.4: Differences between suicidal and homicidal cut throat

Suicide	*Homicide*
1. Left side of the neck in a right handed person, rarely both sides, commonly above the thyroid cartilage	Usually on the sides, commonly below the thyroid cartilage
2. Marked by hesitation cuts either at the beginning, above, or below the main wound	No such cuts. One or very few deep cuts
3. Gradual deepening and shallowing with tailing on the right in right handed persons	Boldly cut in at commencement. No tailing
4. Main wound may contain many cuts	Main wound usually deep and solitary but sometimes repeated almost parallel wounds
5. Sloped down, when seen	Sloped up, when seen
6. Often accompanied by wounds across wrists or vital parts elsewhere and healed scars	Unaccompanied by wounds to wrists but often associated with other severe injuries
7. No cuts on hands unless from open razor blades between the fingers	Frequent 'protective' cuts, that is, defence wounds in wrinkled skin of grasping surfaces of hands, or on back of forearms
8. As head is thrown back, carotid artery usually escapes injury	Carotid artery and jugular veins are likely to be cut
9. Weapon is usually present, occasionally firmly grasped by cadaveric spasm	Weapon is sometimes present but usually removed by the murderer. Grasping by cadaveric spasm is not reported
10. Secluded, quiet place, usually bedroom or locked bathroom, and in front of a mirror, which may show blood splashes	Considerable disturbance at the scene and even elsewhere is usually found. Scene consistent with homicide

Q. 20.19. Discuss the forensic importance of the hyoid bone.

The hyoid is a U-shaped bone having a body, and a greater and lesser cornu on either side of the body. The lesser cornu is a small conical eminence at the angle of the junction of the body with greater cornu.

The injuries of this bone met within forensic work include mainly fractures and occasionally cuts. Fractures are sometimes encountered in hanging, ligature and manual strangulation, and in direct trauma, such as in run-over injuries of the neck. Cuts are encountered in cut throat injuries only. Fractures require care in diagnosis and pose a significant forensic problem. Cuts are not difficult to diagnose.

In persons, especially over 40 years of age, the bone is ossified and relatively brittle. It is, therefore, likely to fracture easily. In young persons, the bone is resilient and elastic; therefore, it usually does not fracture. However, no age is exempt and the bone may fracture in the young or old when there is sufficient pressure on the neck.

In hanging and ligature strangulation, hyoid fracture is not common, but when it occurs, it is commonly of anteroposterior compression type, involving the greater cornuae at the junction of inner two-thirds and outer one-third, the broken fragments being displaced outward. The periosteum is torn only on the inner side of the bone. Therefore, the broken fragments can be easily moved outward, but inward movement is limited to the normal position only. In throttling (manual strangulation), the fracture is commonly of inward compression type, the broken fragments being displaced inward. The periosteum is torn only on the outer side of the bone. Therefore, the broken fragments can be easily moved inward, but outward movement is limited to the normal position only. A blow from the front of the neck may also result in a similar fracture.

In the living, a careful clinical examination is necessary in addition to an X-ray. In the dead, two types of errors are made by the inexperienced at autopsy. One is to report a fracture when none is present and the other is to miss a fracture when present. Reporting a fracture when it is not present is due to mistaking a normal joint as a fracture and not specifically looking for ecchymosis (infiltration of blood) in suspected area of the fracture. The presence of haemosiderin, on microscopic examination, as evidence of haemorrhage is specially helpful in doubtful cases. Missing a fracture when one is present is due to hasty postmortem examination. It is necessary to feel the bone soon after reflec-tion of the skin over the neck and to look specifically for ecchymosis. An attempt should also be made to determine, if the broken ends of bone are splayed out (as in a blow from the front) or displaced inward towards one another by application of manual pressure to neck as in throttling. It must, however, be remembered that post-mortem decomposition results in separation of joints of this bone and this may give an erroneous impression of a fracture.

CHEST

Q. 20.20. Discuss chest wall injuries in general.

Injuries to the chest wall may or may not be associated with injuries to internal viscera and vice versa. Symptoms and signs of internal chest injury may become evident as much as several hours after the injury.

Blows on the chest wall may produce concussion of the chest (heart—commotio cordis) resulting in death. Sudden violent compression of the chest wall may lead to ventricular fibrillation and death with little or no evidence of injury to the chest wall. In all such cases, it is necessary to take multiple histologic sections of the cardiac conduction system, particularly the cardiac pacemakers. When the force of impact increases, any injury to the chest may result in fractured ribs. In old people, the ribs are easily fractured. Rib fractures may not be apparent on an external examination, and even on X-ray, unless a number of views are taken from varying angles. They occur from direct or indirect violence. In direct violence, such as by blows, stabs, or pressure with knee, the broken ends are likely to be driven inward injuring the underlying structures. In indirect violence, e.g. by muscular contraction during violent coughing or convulsions, fractured ends are generally driven outward. The ribs more vulnerable to fracture are fourth to eighth ribs as they are attached at both ends and are comparatively unprotected. Bilateral symmetrical rib fractures, in the front near the costal cartilages and at the back near the angles, occur in traumatic asphyxia, bansdola, run-over accidents, and the like. *Nobbing fractures* are found in battered babies. *Flail chest* (collapse of the chest) occurs when at least three successive ribs are fractured at two points creating a floating segment of the chest wall. The floating segment is sucked inward during inspiration (paradoxical respiration). Dyspnoea and cyanosis may develop. Extreme degree of flail results in progressive hypoxia and is incompatible with life.

The important complications of rib fractures are:

1. Flail chest
2. Lacerations of lung with pneumothorax or haemothorax
3. Pleurisy, or pneumonia
4. Injury to heart.

Q. 20.21. Discuss lung injuries in general.

The lungs may show numerous injuries depending on the degree of violence. The injuries vary from simple bruising to laceration of the lungs and massive collapse to rupture, with or without fractures of the ribs.

While the elastic rib cage of children and youngsters allow considerable gradual compression of the chest and consequently the lungs without injury, a sudden forcible blow may cause contusion of the lung. In children and youngsters, the effect of such a blow is seen as a subpleural haemorrhage corresponding to the assaulted rib. In some cases, the alveolar air that is compressed may rupture the alveoli and cause intra-alveolar haemorrhage. Sometimes, an impact to the front or side of the chest results in contre coup contusions on the posterior surface of lungs. Such contusions may be mistaken for postmortem lividity and vice versa. Osborn has drawn attention to lung contusions caused by *pincer forces.* These are forces operating in V-shaped areas of chest, especially the costophrenic region. Such an injury may be caused, if an impact is applied to chest during deep inspiration when the lung descends in this region.

Most cases of laceration of lungs are due to traffic accidents, fall of a heavy weight on the chest, compression of chest (traumatic asphyxia), and rarely assault.

Stab wounds involving the lungs are also common. In case of knife wounds, respiratory excursions of the lung sometimes result in extensive lacerations of what might otherwise have been a narrow stab wound. If air enters pulmonary veins, it will be carried to the left side of heart from where it may reach different organs and especially the cerebral and coronary vessels with serious consequences. At autopsy, the blood in the cerebral and coronary arteries will appear segmented.

Except for sudden inhibition and loss of life due to trivial pleural stimuli in highly emotional subjects, as a rule, death is not sudden, unless injuries to lungs are very severe, or there are other associated injuries. The person lives for hours or even days. The injury to the lung is considered serious, if pulmonary emphysema or lordosis is present. In case of injuries to the lungs, subcutaneous emphysema over the chest indicates that the person was alive for some time and death was not immediate. Early death is due to haemorrhage or asphyxia, and at a later period due to lung infection. If a tension pneumothorax develops, death may soon result from circulatory embarrassment. To demonstrate pneumothorax at autopsy, the postmortem opening of thorax should be done under water. Where facilities permit, an X-ray should be taken with the beam in horizontal position.

Generalised trauma to chest, e.g. from blast, may cause multiple tears of the connective tissue of lung substance due to linear and rotational strains. Intrapulmonary bleeding may ensue or the lung may rupture causing pneumothorax or traumatic emphysema of the mediastinum or chest wall.

Severe lung injury following blast, aspiration of gastric contents, near-drowning, paraquat poisoning, irritant gases, and many other causes give rise to *adult respiratory distress syndrome (ARDS),* if the victim lives long enough. The victim suffers from marked dyspnoea and progressive respiratory failure due to fibrosing alveolitis. It is characterised by stiff rigid lungs which though heavy do not appear oedematous. Microscopically, the lungs show swelling and proliferation of the alveolar lining cells, albuminous fluid in the alveoli, thickening of alveolar septa, and formation of hyaline membrane. A condition similar to ARDS, the so-called *respirator lung* develops in a patient on mechanical ventilation for an appreciable period.

Acute pulmonary oedema is a frequent postmortem finding in deaths from violence, particularly head injuries. It develops very rapidly and must not be taken to mean that the individual has survived the accident more than one or two minutes. Such oedema is frequently found in victims reported as having been killed instantly. Subpleural petechial haemorrhages are frequently present in deaths from asphyxia.

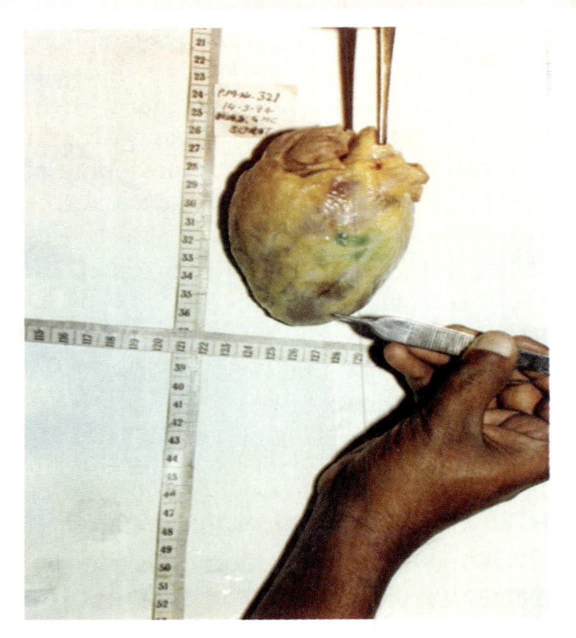

Fig. 20.10: Myocardial contusion. (*Courtesy*: Dr BV Subrahmanyam)

Fig. 20.11: Multiple confluent petechiae on heart surface. (*Courtesy*: Dr BV Subrahmanyam)

Q. 20.22. Discuss heart injuries in general. Differentiate between myocardial contusion and infarction. Add a note on rupture of the heart.

The heart may be injured from non-penetrating or penetrating trauma to the chest. The injury is usually associated with injury to other structures of the chest. It is not commonly realised that cardiac damage, especially contusion, due to non-penetrating trauma occurs frequently and is often missed since signs and symptoms including alterations in the electrical activity as shown by ECG often do not appear until 24 to 48 hours after injury. Sometimes, a posterior cardiac contusion may be mistaken for postmortem lividity and vice versa. A cardiac contusion shows, on microscopic examination, localised interstitial haemorrhage and injured myocardial fibres (Figs 20.10 and 20.11). A mild or moderate non-penetrating cardiac injury may lead to sudden death with or without visible lesion or may cause symptoms of cardiac insufficiency, angina pectoris, auricular fibrillation, or valvular rupture. When there is no visible lesion and death occurs after a sudden blow to the chest, it is due to arrhythmia and even significant microscopic findings are not seen. The condition is sometimes referred to as *commotio cordis*. The diagnosis depends upon good history. If force is applied during the contraction phase of heart, a partial rupture of the papillary muscle may occur.

Pincer lesion of the heart is commonly seen in compression injuries as a contusion of right atrium at the entrance of inferior vena cava and is produced by an impact over the chest in the region of right cardiophrenic angle. With severe violence, e.g. when a driver is forcibly thrown against a steering wheel, the buckled sternum may contuse, crush, rupture, or avulse the heart from the major vessels.

Differentiation between a **myocardial contusion** and **myocardial infarction** is not always easy. Absence of coronary artery disease and a spotty distribution of the heart lesion strongly suggests a diagnosis of trauma. The medical and legal implications of contusion of the myocardium are great. If the physician fails to recognise such a lesion and allows full activity, the patient runs a high risk of dying from: (a) rupture of the injured heart with resulting haemorrhage, (b) heart failure, or (c) disturbance of cardiac rhythm, especially ventricular fibrillation. If intrapericardial bleeding occurs from the site of contusion, circulation may fail due to cardiac tamponade. The bleeding may be rapid or slow, and if rapid, the collection of about 200–300 ml within 24 hours is usually sufficient to cause death by cardiac tamponade. Whether a certain trauma would contuse the heart depends on many factors which include the nature of trauma, age of the victim, and his health. Cardiac contusion may occur after relatively minor trauma to chest wall with very little or no evidence of external injury. In youth, the chest wall is more resilient than in advanced age; hence, a blow is more apt to damage the heart in the young without apparent injury to chest wall than in the aged. Coronary artery disease, in the old, increases vulnerability of the heart to damage and disturbance from traumatic forces. The relationship between chest trauma and coronary arterial spasm or coronary thrombosis is acceptable, only if symptoms follow immediately and there is evidence of injury to the affected vessels. In the event of death, at autopsy, the character of the thrombus and the age of myocardial infarct should correspond with the duration of the interval between injury and death.

Penetrating wounds of the heart are extremely serious and usually fatal. A rupture or penetrating wound of the atria is more dangerous than a wound of the ventricular muscle because auricular wall is thin and less contractile, and therefore, bleeds profusely. Similarly, a penetrating injury of right ventricle is more dangerous than that of the left. Death is not immediate in fatal cases. Death may be delayed in those cases where valvular mechanism exists for the entry and exit of blood into ventricles from the pericardial cavity after penetrating wounds. The potential of volitional acts after stab wounds of the heart must be remembered.

According to Moritz, the common sites of traumatic rupture of heart are: right atrium, left ventricle, right ventricle, left atrium, interventricular septum and valves. Any traumatic rupture of the heart must be differentiated from spontaneous rupture. In **traumatic rupture,** the heart is generally ruptured on the right side and toward its base. The ribs and skin over them are usually damaged. Rarely, the rupture may occur without any external mark of violence. **Spontaneous rupture** of a healthy heart is not possible. An unhealthy heart, especially the left ventricle, weakened by coronary disease or infarction can rupture under increased blood pressure and sudden exertion.

ABDOMEN

In case of violence, whilst abrasions may be found on the abdomen, gross and fatal internal injuries are frequently present without any external sign of injury or abrasion. The abdominal wall may yield allowing the mesentery, gut, stomach, and liver to be pinned and crushed across the spine, with uncontrolled internal haemorrhage. Whenever a history is obtained of a blow over the abdomen, the patient should be kept under observation until all likelihood of a ruptured abdominal viscus can be dismissed. This should be specially remembered in cases of patients who have become unconscious following trauma and in alcohol intoxicated persons in whom intoxication may mask the symptoms of visceral injury.

Q. 20.23. Discuss the forensic importance of injuries to: (1) stomach, (2) intestines, (3) appendix.

Stomach: Rupture of the stomach may occur as a result of crushing injury due to vehicular accident. There may or may not be any mark of external injury on the abdominal wall. In case of rupture of stomach, disease or ulceration of the stomach should be excluded even though history of violence is forthcoming. The stomach is vulnerable to rupture by compression when it is full. Traumatic rupture of the stomach may also be due to over-distension as in cases where an anaesthetic tube lies in the oesophagus by mistake, or in drowning where much air and water may be gulped into the stomach. The defects resulting from increased bursting tension are linear and tend to follow the lesser curvature. The defects produced by direct contusion or crushing may be quite irregular, tend to be linear, and in contrast to rupture, usually lie at right angles to the lesser curvature. They ordinarily involve both anterior and posterior walls and generally cross the lesser curvature. The first and frequently the only layer of the gastric wall to give way is the mucous membrane.

The mechanically produced gastric ulcer differs in several respects from peptic ulcer. In a mechanically produced ulcer, the lesion is linear, there is extensive submucosal bleeding, and the area is undermined to the extent to which the mucosa has been torn away from the submucosa. In a peptic ulcer, the mucosa is always thickened; margins are indurated, regular, and punched out; and adhesions to surrounding structures may be present.

It is possible to consider mechanical injury as producing peptic ulcer: (a) if it can be shown that the patient had no gastric or duodenal lesion prior to injury, (b) if the injury was applied directly over stomach or duodenum, (c) if there was continuity of signs and symptoms between injury and development of chronic peptic ulcer, and (d) there is positive X-ray evidence.

Perforation of peptic ulcer may cause rapid death and some of these cases give rise to compensation claims when death occurs due to some abdominal injury at work. The sudden rush of irritating matter, gastric juices, haemorrhage, and bile into the peritoneal cavity causes sudden collapse and death.

Intestines: Lacerations or ruptures may occur from blows or kicks on the abdominal wall or crushing due to vehicular accident which may or may not leave a visible mark of injury on the abdominal wall. The ruptures are often multiple and occur along the antimesenteric border. Even the mesentery may be torn from its attachment. In case of rupture, disease or ulceration of the intestine should be excluded even though history of violence is forthcoming. The jejunum is the commonest site of rupture, followed by ileum, duodenum, caecum, and large intestine. Perforations of lower small intestine and large intestine are usually not followed by intense shock of peptic perforation and may not cause death, if timely surgical aid is available.

In stab wounds and firearm injuries of the abdomen, the small intestine is injured more frequently than the large intestine, and the stomach usually escapes. The rectum is injured from falling on a pointed object, from perineal injuries, and injuries from foreign bodies thrust through the anus in sexually perverted individuals.

Rupture of the intestine does not necessarily deprive a person of the ability to walk.

Appendix: A diagnosis of traumatic appendicitis in a case in which the appendix has not been examined is untenable. In case of early acute appendicitis, it would be justifiable to conclude that the disease developed after the abdominal trauma was sustained. In case of subacute or chronic appendicitis, the injury in question could have precipitated a clinical attack or caused exacerbation or extension of an already existing disease. A blow on the right iliac fossa is likely to injure an already diseased appendix rather than a normal one. It is more readily injured, if adhesions are present. If it is already inflamed, even so mild a trauma as massage may—(a) cause disruption of protective periappendical fibrinous adhesions, (b) lead to tearing of protective inflammatory barrier of an already existing abscess, (c) cause perforation at site of an ulcer, or (d) lead to rupture. Bissel has stressed the increased vulnerability of an appendix containing a faecalith to mechanical injury.

Q. 20.24. Discuss the forensic importance of injuries to: (1) pancreas, (2) liver, and (3) spleen.

Pancreas: The pancreas weighs about 90 gm. Wounds of the pancreas are rare. They are usually accompanied by injuries to other abdominal organs. When the stomach is empty, pancreas alone may be vertically ruptured by being pressed against the spinal column, by direct violence. Such an injury commonly occurs when a bicycle handlebar impacts in the epigastric zone. A kick or punch in the upper abdomen may injure the pancreas and cause death within a few days from resultant chemical peritonitis. External injury to the abdominal wall may not be visible in such cases. Therefore, **it is necessary to make routine serum amylase determination to exclude pancreatic damage in all cases of violent non-penetrating abdominal injury.** Pinkham states that persistent elevation of serum amylase is suggestive of pseudocyst formation.

Liver: The liver weighs about 1.5 kg. It is susceptible to injury because of its large size, central location, and relative friability. It is commonly ruptured by a fall, blow, or kick on abdomen, or a crushing injury due to a vehicular accident which may or may not leave a mark on the abdominal wall. The rupture usually involves the right lobe, the convex surface, and the inferior border. Death is due to shock and haemorrhage. Death may not occur immediately. Sometimes, the bleeding occurs between the liver and its capsule (subcapsular haematoma). Serious symptoms become apparent only when the capsule ruptures. The haemorrhage is usually slow, as compared to rupture of the spleen, on account of the relatively low pressure in the hepatic sinusoids. The liver is easily lacerated and ruptured even from mild violence, if it is fatty, congested, enlarged, or diseased. The damage is usually fatal as bleeding from the organ is hard to stop and the liver being essential to life cannot be removed in toto.

Spleen: The spleen weighs from 150–200 gm. Its susceptibility to injury is due to (a) weakness of its supporting tissues, (b) thinness of its capsule, and (c) extreme friability of its pulp especially when it is enlarged or congested. It is ruptured by a fall, blow or kick on the abdomen, or a crush injury due to vehicular accident, which may or may not leave a mark on the abdominal wall. The rupture usually involves the concave or inner surface and causes death from haemorrhage, which is often profuse. In some case, symptoms of gross intra-abdominal bleeding may not occur for several hours or days after the rupture due to haematoma collecting under the intact capsule. Serious symptoms become apparent only when the capsule ruptures. Pathological examination in such cases will disclose organizing haematoma in the spleen.

Spontaneous rupture of a diseased spleen has been reported. Of this, the much enlarged malarial spleen is the one that most commonly ruptures from minor trauma. Other causes of splenomegaly in which spontaneous rupture may occur include leukaemia, Banti's disease, typhoid fever, and kala-azar. While the possibility of spontaneous rupture of a much enlarged spleen cannot be denied, what can be positively denied is that a normal or even a moderately enlarged spleen can rupture spontaneously. This is specially *emphasised*, as in the case in which a person is accused of having caused the death of another by assaulting him so that his spleen ruptured, the defence, relying on statements contained in medical books that an enlarged spleen may rupture spontaneously, almost invariably attempts to establish the possibility of this having happened.

A common but by no means a constant postmortem finding in death from acute haemorrhage is a contracted, pale, shrunken spleen, almost devoid of blood. Microscopic examination often discloses collapsed and virtually empty sinusoids.

Q. 20.25. Discuss the forensic importance of injuries to the urogenital system.

Kidneys: Each kidney normally weighs about 140 gm. Its small size, relative toughness and protected location render it relatively immune to mechanical injury. Blows on the loins may cause contusions or lacerations of the kidney. Owing to its deep situation in the abdomen, rupture of the kidney is rare from direct violence, unless consider-able force is applied to the lumbar region. The kidney may be ruptured from slight indirect violence, if it is weakened by disease, e.g. hydronephrosis. Death is due to collapse, haemorrhage, or complications of the injury. Penetrating wounds of the kidney may be produced by bullet injuries or pointed weapons thrust in the loins. Cases of nephrolithiasis in which renal injury and calculus formation are deemed to have cause and effect relationship have been reported.

Urinary bladder: Rupture of the urinary bladder may occur from fracture of the pelvis, or a blow or kick on the abdomen when the bladder is distended. Often, in cases of rupture from violence, no external marks of injury may be found. Death occurs from shock or peritonitis due to extravasation of urine. The violence leading to rupture of the bladder may be accidental, e.g. fall from a height or on a projecting object. Rupture of the bladder may occur from a sharp instrument perforating through the vagina in cases of abortion, or during delivery by pressure of the child's head on the urethra causing overdistension. The latter is specially important as it may result in a **charge of negligence** against the attending doctor. Generally, the site of rupture is intraperitoneal, if the bladder is distended at the time of injury and extraperitoneal, if it is partially full. Spontaneous rupture of the normal bladder is rare.

Traumatic rupture of the bladder occurs more frequently in men than in women. The susceptibility of drunken persons to bladder rupture is due to the fact that they are likely to have distended bladders. Delayed rupture of the bladder is occasionally seen in women after a pelvic operation in which the blood supply of its posterior wall has been interfered with.

Male urethra: The male urethra may be ruptured usually under the pubic arch by a kick on the perineum, a fall astride a projecting object, a fracture of the pubic bone, or by a foreign body, e.g. during forcible catheterisation or cystoscopy. Death may result from extravasation of urine or the rupture may heal, if the tear is slight and prompt surgical aid is forthcoming. However, a stricture may follow as a consequence.

Uterus: Rupture of non-pregnant uterus is rare. The gravid uterus may rupture during obstructed labour, from instrumental criminal abortion, or due to a blow or kick on the abdomen without any external mark of injury. Death may result from shock, haemorrhage, peritonitis, or septicaemia. Injuries due to abortion are discussed in the Chapter 30 on 'Abortion'.

External genitals: *Male*—In certain tribes, the penis is extirpated by razor or knife as punishment for adultery. Removal of the genitals is occasionally practiced by certain tribes to manufacture eunuchs for immoral purposes. Such wounds may be attended by severe or fatal haemorrhage. It must be remembered that external genitalia are among the first structures to be destroyed by animals. The testes may be contused by blows, kicks, or squeezing. Sudden death may follow from shock. Self-inflicted injuries may be seen in insane persons. The most common cause of mechanical injury of the spermatic cord is accidental clamping or incision in the course of surgical repair of a hernia.

In the *female,* contusions or lacerations of the vulva and vagina may result from kicks or falls on a projecting object. A kick on the vulva, like a blow on the head, may look like an incised wound but careful examination will reveal the difference. Owing to the vascularity of the part, such an injury may prove fatal from excessive haemorrhage. In certain tribes, the usual punishment for adultery is branding the vulva with red hot iron, or introduction of powdered chillis in the vagina. Cases of injury by thrusting a stick, foreign body, or a blunt weapon into the vagina either as a form of punishment, rape, sexual assault, or to procure abortion are not uncommon. Death may result from cellulitis, peritonitis, or involvement of the abdominal organs. Injuries due to rape are discussed in the Chapter 27 on 'Rape'.

BONES

Q. 20.26. Discuss fractures from a medico-legal point of view.

Q. 20.27. Comment on: (1) age of fracture, (2) antemortem and postmortem fracture.

A fracture is defined as a break in the continuity of a bone. If the break is due to trauma, it is known as a traumatic fracture. If it is mainly due to a pre-existing disease, and occurs after minimal trauma, it is known as a pathological fracture. Fractures showing a single break are known as simple fractures. Such fractures may be very thin (linear fractures), partial (green stick fractures), or complete (transecting fractures). The transecting fracture may be transverse, oblique, or spiral depending upon the fracture line. Fractures showing multiple breaks are known as comminuted fractures. If the skin above the fracture is intact, the fracture is known as a **closed fracture.** If the skin above it is lacerated, the fracture is known as an **open (compound) fracture** because it communicates with the outside air and is open to infection. Infection of a fracture is an important cause for delayed union, osteomyelitis, and even death from septicaemia.

Certain types of fractures are unique to the type of force applied. It is, therefore, possible to derive, from a systematic analysis of radiographs of fractured bones, especially long bones, a great deal of information about the injury and the type of load involved. Engineers refer to the application of force to an object as **loading.** An object can be loaded in four ways, viz: (a) tension (traction or pulling apart), (b) compression (pressing together), (c) bending (angulation), and (d) torsion (twisting). The clinically important ways in which long bones can be loaded are: combination of compression, bending, and torsion, and from these result the five basic injury patterns of fracture of long bones, viz:

1. Diaphyseal impaction (axial compression)
2. Transverse fracture (bending load)
3. Spiral fracture (torsion load)
4. Oblique transverse or butter-fly fracture (axial compression + bending load)

5. Oblique fracture (axial compression + bending + torsion load). In comminuted fracture, the loading forces are variable.

The **loading principle** has direct application to improperly coordinated weight bearing as an important factor contributing to ill-health and the occurrence of fracture. It is common knowledge that if the alignment of weight bearing bones is not proper, e.g. after spinal fracture or fracture of the bones of the lower extremity, considerable ill-health may result due to consequent arthritis deformans. Lack of proper muscular coordination resulting in disadvantageous weight bearing constitutes a particularly important cause for a further fracture, especially of the neck of the femur, in old persons. It is, therefore, essential for doctors who treat such cases to have a clear understanding of the biomechanics of these injuries so as to avoid a charge of **malpractice.**

While fractures have special characteristics and fall within the domain of surgery and orthopaedics, a certain number of cases require special consideration from a medicolegal point of view. Fractures occurring in the insane or other people under restraint are of great importance owing to the usual assumption that the attendants or guardians have used undue violence. Fractures occurring after convulsive therapy may involve consideration - of informed consent. Postmortem fractures caused by cardiopulmonary resuscitation may be mistaken as those due to violence.

Fractures may result from direct violence, such as blows or indirect violence, such as falls, or the action of muscles. Fractures caused by muscular action are usually simple fractures. Bones weakened by disease may also disintegrate and fracture spontaneously (pathological fracture).

In children, the bones being more flexible than in the adult, partial fractures (green stick) are more common. In young growing persons, slipping of the epiphysis is common, most common in the distal end of the radius, capitulum and internal epicondyle of the humerus, and distal end of the tibia; inhibition of growth may follow and lead to permanent disability. In old persons, indirect violence, e.g. a fall, may fracture the neck of the femur; muscular contraction during violent coughing may fracture the ribs; or convulsions may fracture the olecranon, calcaneum, patella, or femur. In elderly subjects, most spontaneous fractures occur due to disease, e.g. osteoporosis from any cause, such as disuse, drugs (steroids), or disease. Stress fractures have been described and occur in a manner similar to fatigue fractures in metals. Such fractures occur mostly in metatarsals or tibia after prolonged walking in persons unaccustomed to this form of exercise. At autopsy, the presence of a fracture is determined by suitable movements and palpation. *It is necessary to dissect the site carefully to detect the presence of any associated disease that may have caused or contributed to fracture.*

In criminal cases, the defence might rely on the abnormal condition of the bones where the violence causing the fracture was slight. Legally, an assailant, intending hurt, has to take his victim as he finds him; a fracture constitutes grievous hurt.

Sometimes, a plea may be raised that the fracture is due to accident (indirect violence) and not due to direct violence. A fracture caused by a direct violence can be judged from its position and the presence of a bruise or wound of the skin in the region of fracture. In some cases, however, no bruise or wound may be found but such a fracture is usually transverse and sometimes comminuted. When the fracture is due to indirect violence, such as a fall, the fracture occurs at the weakest part of the bone, is usually spiral or oblique, and may not be accompanied by a bruise or a wound.

In order to ascertain the cause of a fracture, it is essential to note the appearance of the injury, the relative position of the fragments, and the presence or absence of contusion of the soft parts. Certain injuries suggest certain forms of violence, e.g. battered baby syndrome. X-ray examination should always be done in all cases of fracture, whether simple or compound. It provides a permanent record and enables the medical officer not only to establish the presence or absence of a fracture which may be disputed later but also to obviate the stigma of negligence. It also helps him to get an idea of the age of the fracture and sometimes information about the method of its infliction (nobbing fracture).

Age of fracture: This is already discussed in the Chapter 18 on 'Injuries—Medicolegal Aspects'.

Antemortem or postmortem fracture: It is not always easy to say whether a fracture has been produced before or after death. A fracture produced shortly before or shortly after death will present similar characters except that in the former case there may be comparatively greater effusion of blood which will infiltrate the adjacent tissues. A fracture caused some hours before death would be indicated by oedema and active cellular infiltration into the surrounding parts and between the fractured edges of the bones as well as by similar changes in the injured muscles. From long periods before death, there will be microscopic or even naked eye signs of commencing organisation. Fractures caused after death are not accompanied by such changes. When long bones are fractured in the living, fatty material from the bone marrow, known as fat emboli, can travel to distant portions of the body, where they produce characteristic lesions which are seen on gross and microscopic examination. Externally, they are seen as punctate haemorrhages in the skin looking like flea bites. They may be seen in the eyelids, conjunctivae, and skin of any part of the body but especially the chest. Internally, they may be visible as punctate haemorrhages in the white matter of the brain. Diagnosis may be confirmed by microscopic examination of the frozen sections of the tissue stained for fat, with Sudan III or osmic acid. These changes do not develop, if the fracture occurs after death.

JOINTS

Q. 20.28. Discuss the forensic importance of joint injuries.

While this subject mainly falls within the domain of surgery and orthopaedics, a brief account pertaining to injuries of joints, sprains, subluxations, and dislocations, from a medicolegal point of view is given below since dislocations and powers of permanent impairment of any joint come within the definition of grievous hurt.

Mechanical injuries of joints are classified as acute and chronic. Acute lesions result from single traumas. Chronic lesions result from repeated traumas.

Acute lesions: Any trauma involving the synovial membrane or articular cartilage results in oedema and haemorrhage. The amount of serous fluid which accumulates is out of proportion to the apparent severity of the local injury. It is usually absorbed in a few days.

Blood ordinarily does not collect in a joint cavity unless the trauma is severe, e.g. sprain or fracture, or the patient has a haemorrhagic diathesis. An intra-articular haematoma is organized from the synovial surface and the ingrowth of connective tissue frequently results in the formation of a fibrous membrane or pannus which covers and separates the articular surfaces. Repeated episodes of haemorrhages, e.g. in patients with a haemorrhagic diathesis, lead to chronic pathological changes, especially in the knee joints, which become enlarged due to organised and organising granulation tissue. Ankylosis may occur and lead to an action for damages against the doctor for alleged faulty treatment.

The fibrocartilaginous menisci, especially the semilunar cartilages of the knee joint, are frequently injured in football players as a result of sudden forceful twisting movement at the knee joint. The torn portion of the meniscus may be detached and form a joint mouse and may permanently remain as a foreign body in the joint, limiting its movements.

The hyaline cartilage covering the articular surfaces of the bone may be lacerated by any twisting impact occasionally in normal persons but commonly in those whose proprioceptive sensibilities have been impaired. In the latter case, the joints are likely to be subjected to stresses which cannot be tolerated by a normal person. The ultimate result would be a joint mouse, if the articular cartilage is torn and detached, and osteochondritis dessicans.

Chronic lesions: These resemble ordinary wear and tear. Weight bearing joints, such as knees, ankles, hips, and spine, are commonly affected. The changes resemble those due to arthritis deformans. Such changes are frequently seen in a joint subjected to abnormal stress due to changes in the axis of weight bearing. The changes appear in a single joint or in the joints of a single extremity and their relationship to unusual mechanical stress is obvious, e.g. shoulder and elbow joints of workers with pneu-matic tools.

Arthritis deformans predisposed to by neuropathic arthropathies may be precipitated and considerably aggravated by trauma of any dimension. This type of chronic mechanical injury of joints is seen occasionally in syringomyelia and other disorders of the nervous system which result in loss of pain and proprioceptive sensations.

Sprain, subluxation, and dislocation: When a joint is forced to move in some direction beyond the limits permitted by the elasticity of its ligaments, a sprain, subluxation, or dislocation is said to have occurred. The different terms represent varying degrees of severity and not different types of injuries. The essential factor is stretching or laceration of the ligaments, capsule, or both. The amount of intra-articular haemorrhage is directly proportional to the damage to the synovial membrane. These injuries are important for two reasons: (1) They produce immediate disability, and (2) even after healing, the joint may remain unstable on account of lengthening and loss of tone of supporting structures with consequent predisposition to recurrent sprain or dislocation.

Dislocations are caused by direct or indirect violence, like blows, falls, and muscular action, or spontaneously when the joints are diseased, e.g. late stages of tuberculosis of the hip. They are not common in old people, in those whose bones are brittle, and in children in whom separation of epiphysis is more common. Normally, they do not pose any danger to life unless they are between the vertebrae or compound when they may cause death due to secondary complications. Diagnosis is not difficult unless the symptoms have completely disappeared after reduction. Even then, paralysis or muscular atrophy due to involvement of a nerve may help, e.g. in dislocation of a shoulder joint.

Punctured, incised, or lacerated wounds of the joints are likely to become infected and give rise to complications.

The points of **differentiation** of a dislocation from a fracture are:

1. The lesion is necessarily in the vicinity of a joint
2. There is restricted mobility instead of abnormal mobility
3. Crepitus is absent
4. If the bone ends can be felt, they are smooth and rounded, not sharp and angular.

Age of dislocation: In recent cases, the colour changes in the bruise accompanying it, and in older cases, the amount of fibrous tissue may give some indication.

21

Transportation Injuries

In order of frequency, the injuries can be described as:

1. *Vehicular injuries (motor vehicle, motorcycle, moped and mini-bike, and bicycle)*
2. *Rilway injuries*
3. *Aircraft injuries.*

MOTOR VEHICLE INJURIES

With an increasing use of vehicles, injuries due to them are so common nowadays that it is necessary for a medical officer to be able to assess the injuries, the mechanisms by which they are caused, the cause of death, and if intoxication by alcohol or drugs played any part. The injuries often assume a definite and distinguishing pattern in the case of a pedestrian, and a driver or a passenger, depending on the type of impact.

PEDESTRIAN INJURIES

Q. 21.1. Comment on motor vehicle injuries to pedestrians with special reference to: (1) primary impact injuries, (2) secondary impact injuries, (3) secondary injuries, (4) run-over injuries.

Three patterns of injuries are often seen, viz:

1. Primary impact injuries by the vehicle striking the victim
2. Secondary injuries due to the victim falling on the ground or other stationary object
3. Run-over injuries due to the vehicle running over some part of the victim.

The primary impact injuries are sometimes subdivided into two groups, viz. (a) those due to initial impact of the vehicle, and (b) those due to a subsequent impact with the same vehicle, as may result from being lifted on to the vehicle after the initial impact (secondary impact injuries).

Primary impact injuries: These are injuries caused by the impact between the vehicle and the pedestrian. The height of the pedestrian often determines the site and nature of injuries. They are usually found on the head in children and on the trunk and legs in adults due to some part of the car, e.g. bumper, fender, lights, radiator, or bonnet, hitting the body.

If a pedestrian is struck from behind, he may sustain a fracture dislocation of the thoracic spine or lumbar spine. An almost simultaneous impact on the buttocks may drive the femoral head through the acetabulum. Striae, like superficial tears of the abdomen or inguinofemoral regions, may be seen due to over-stretching of the skin. Projections of the car may cause specific injuries, e.g. *bumper fractures,* i.e. fracture of the tibia and fibula of one or both legs. Not infrequently, injuries are at different levels on the two legs or absent on one leg suggesting that the victim was walking or running when struck. The fracture is usually spiral or wedge-shaped. In the latter, the base of the triangular fragment of the bone indicates the site of impact and the apex points the direction in which the vehicle was moving. When bumper fractures are present, it is advisable to measure the distance from the heel to the fracture site as this gives information regarding the height of the bumper and if brakes were applied. When brakes are applied before the accident, the distance from the heel to the fracture is less than the height of the bumper. The front bumper tends to rise during acceleration and dip under breaking.

If the pedestrian is hit from the side, there may be a unilateral fracture of the nearest leg or sometimes only bruising in the absence of fracture.

If the pedestrian is facing the vehicle, he may sustain intra-abdominal injuries and/or injuries to the chest wall and thoracic contents. Sometimes, the pelvis may be fractured.

External injuries may be found in any region of the body which has been struck by the vehicle and sometimes the pattern may correspond with some portion of the vehicle. The importance of scaled photography, in such patterned injury in hit and run accident, to preserve such valuable evidence, is obvious.

Secondary impact injuries vary according to the nature of the impact. If the point of impact is at or above the centre of gravity as is the case when children are concerned, the victim is directly thrown to the ground as a result of primary impact and may be run-over by the same car, with consequent undercarriage injuries and stains from grease, oil, etc.; the hot exhaust pipe may cause burns. However, if the victim is an older child or an adult, the point of primary impact will be beneath the centre of gravity and it tends to lift the pedestrian up onto the bonnet or hood, or sometimes even on the road behind the vehicle, depending on the speed of the car. Secondary impact injuries may then occur from contact with the windshield and may result in severe head injuries and lacerations. The body may then fall sideways and be run-over by a passing vehicle.

Secondary injuries: These are found on parts opposite to primary impact and on the head, and are due to the person violently falling on the ground. They are most pronounced over the unclothed areas of the body but may be found also beneath the clothing even if this remains intact. Injuries due to contact with the ground include abrasions (grazes) and bruises over the face, hands, hips, and legs, and lacerations over the bony prominences, and these are usually soiled with traces of dirt. Fractures of ribs are common. Occasionally, the skull or cervical spine may be fractured and in these cases, there is frequently a contre coup brain damage indicating that the injury was due to a moving head striking a stationary object. All kinds of intracranial haemorrhages and brain injuries may occur.

Run-over injuries (Figs 21.1 to 21.4): Children are often involved in accidents of this nature. The severity of injuries will depend upon the part of the body run-over and the weight and speed of the vehicle. When a limb is run-over by the wheel of a light motor vehicle the skin and subcutaneous fat may be dragged away from the deeper muscles with or without any break in the continuity of the skin. This is known as **degloving.** Tyre marks may be present on the unclothed parts or even clothed parts, if the clothes are not thick. The grease and oil stains from the undercarriage will be present on the clothing and the wound. The hot exhaust pipe under the vehicle may cause burns. If the wheel moves over the trunk, rupture of viscera may occur and, if it moves over a fleshy part, an avulsion injury may result with extensive degloving of a wide area, usually the thigh.

Body structure

1. Cross member under windshield
2. Roof frame, front
3. Roof frame, side
4. Roof frame, rear
5. C-pillar
6. Rear-facing panel
7. Rear floor and spare-wheel pan
8. Side member, rear
9. B-pillar
10. Cross member under rear seat
11. A-pillar
12. Cross member under driver's seat
13. Side member
14. Wheel well
15. Engine-support cross member
16. Side member, front
17. Cross member, front
18. Radiator cross member

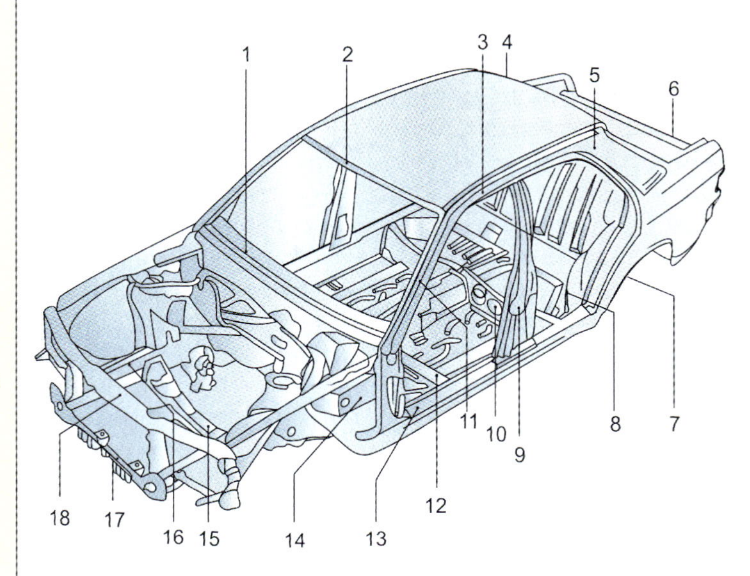

Fig. 21.1: The body structure of a motor vehicle

Fig. 21.2: **Patterned injury** (imprint abrasion) found on the side of a child involved in a traffic accident. The injury is caused by the tread mark of the tyre of the vehicle. (*Courtesy*: Dr NK Mohanty)

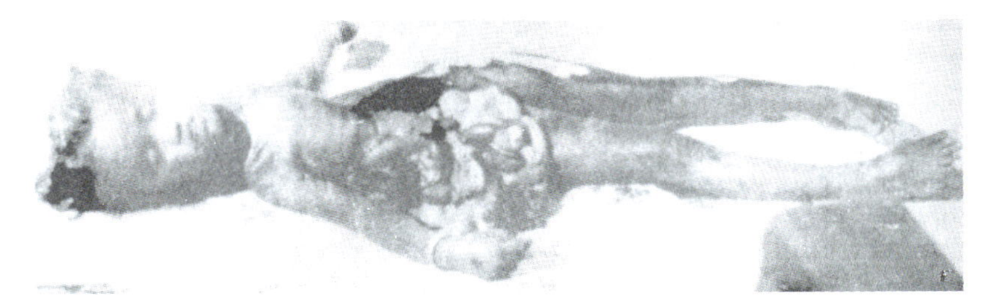

Fig. 21.3: This child was run-over by a bus. Rupture and extensive herniation of the abdominal organs are seen

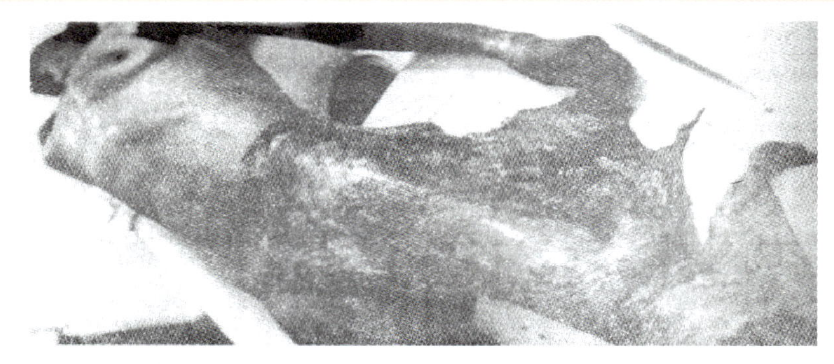

Fig. 21.4: *Extensive degloving of the skin* of the thigh suggestive of a run-over accident. The movement of the wheel has separated the skin and subcutaneous tissues from deeper structures

Mason reports on the frequency of injuries of body areas in pedestrian accidents as follows: Considering the dynamics of pedestrian accidents, legs are involved in 85% and head between 50 to 80%, followed by arms, and then pelvis, followed by chest or abdomen. Injuries to the neck and spine are relatively infrequent in over-all terms.

DRIVER AND PASSENGER INJURIES

Q. 21.2. Discuss the general sequence of events in driver and passenger injuries in motor vehicle accidents.

After the pedestrians, the driver is the most frequent casualty in road traffic accidents as, on most occasions, he is the only occupant of the vehicle. Next in frequency is the front seat passenger followed, far less frequently, by rear seat passengers.

The driver and passenger injuries depend upon the type of impact crash, viz:

1. Front impact crash
2. Side impact crash
3. Rear impact crash
4. Roll-over crash
5. Other type of mishaps.

While the injury patterns are discussed here under five categories, it must be remembered that different types of combinations can occur. As for example, a car after a collision may roll over and be deflected sideways into a tree or another stationary object. The resulting injuries can be better understood from the **sequence** of three collisions that occur.

The first collision has been defined as that between the vehicle and its environment, i.e. when the car strikes another car head-on or a fixed object such as a tree or electric pole, and stops. It produces vehicular damage. The second collision has been defined as that between the occupants and the interior of the car. Although the car stops, the occupants continue to move in the same direction and same velocity as the car was moving. The unrestrained occupants will strike some part of the interior of the vehicle and be injured. The third collision has been defined as that between the internal organs and the cavities which contain them. Although the body as a whole stops moving, the internal organs continue to move in the direction of impact and this may result in serious internal injuries even without evidence of corresponding external injury.

Q. 21.3. Discuss motor vehicle injuries due to: (1) front impact crash, (2) side impact crash, (3) rear impact crash, (4) roll-over crash, and (5) other mishaps, e.g. ejection, fire, and submersion.

Front Impact Crash

This means that one car strikes another car head-on, or it strikes a fixed object, such as a tree. While the vehicle rapidly decelerates and stops, the occupants continue to move forward striking against the interior of the vehicle, unless they are restrained. It is important to know that the windscreen of most cars nowadays is made of a layer of glass followed by a layer of plastic and then a layer of glass so that it bulges when the head impacts against it and the victim does not sustain severe cuts from large fragments of glass which used to happen when windshields were made exclusively of glass.

The driver tends to receive a different pattern of injury as compared to either the front seat or rear seat passenger. The driver may receive a momentary warning of the impending collision and brace himself against the steering wheel. Fractures of the wrists and arms may thus occur as well as fractures of the legs and pelvis from pressure against the foot pedals. If the driver is unaware of such a warning, his knees will impact against the dashboard, his chest against the steering wheel, and his head against the windshield. An impact of the knees against the dashboard commonly causes fractures of the tibia, fibula, femur, hips, and pelvis. *Steering wheel impact injuries* depend on the severity of the impact. The circular rim of the steering wheel may cause fractures of the teeth, jaws, and facial bones, as well as, imprint abrasions, minor bruises and contusions of the chest, or rib fractures. Fractured steering wheel spokes may penetrate the chest and lacerate the heart and lungs. With severe thoracic compression, partial or complete rupture of the aorta may occur, usually at the junction of the aortic arch and the descending aorta, and is supposed to be due to tensile stresses generated at this point. Serious steering wheel injuries are less frequent, if the car is fitted with energy absorbing compressible steering wheel column. Impaction of the head against the windshield may cause abrasions and superficial vertical cuts of the face. Tiny pieces of windshield glass may be found in these injuries or loose on the clothing. Severe impact against the windshield pillar may cause avulsion of the skin of the forehead, basilar skull fractures, closed head injury, and dislocation of the atlanto-axial joint.

The most dangerous place in the car is the front passenger seat. The front seat passenger may not receive the momentary warning of the impending collision. Without a seat belt, he is at risk of severe impaction of his head against the windshield and its consequences. Severe whiplash injury to the cervical and thoracic spine may occur due to rapid acceleration or deceleration. Contact with the dashboard may cause injuries to the knee.

Passengers of the rear seat often escape such injuries because of the absence of impact against the windshield and dashboard and of the cushioning effect of the front seat. However, they may be thrown about violently within the passenger compartment and sustain injuries as a result of contact with projections of the car's interior. Expulsion through bursting doors may give rise to severe secondary injuries due to striking the road and being run-over by other vehicles.

Side Impact Crash

A vehicle that is struck on the side by another vehicle or that skids sideways into a fixed object sustains a side impact. This is a common pattern in an intersection and is, therefore, a frequent occurrence in urban areas.

Injuries are often severe because the side of an automobile has a thin metal wall and no other deformable structural components to absorb the forces of impact. Since the occupants of the vehicle move toward the side of impact the persons sitting on that side run the greatest risk. Dicing injuries may help to locate the position occupied by the victim in the automobile. **Dice injuries** are characteristic right-angled or V-shaped cuts caused by the diced or cubical fragments of tempered glass of a broken side window being struck by or striking the victim.

Cervical spinal fractures are common as well as fractured ribs, contusions, lacerations, and explosive tearing of the lungs, on the side of the impact. The heart and aorta are less frequently injured. In the abdomen, a lateral impact on the left frequently lacerates the spleen, left kidney, and left lobe of the liver. An impact on the right side commonly causes lacerations of the right lobe of the liver and right kidney. The pelvis may be fractured from impact on either side.

Rear Impact Crash

Low velocity rear impacts are relatively common. In a typical case, the occupants move backwards. The head and neck are not supported by the back of the seat and, therefore, are at risk, if the car does not have a head restraint. The head bends backwards over the top of the seat forcing the neck to hyperextend. Then, in a type of recoil, the head moves forwards until the chin strikes the front of the chest and the neck is hyperflexed. This is known as *whiplash* or acceleration-deceleration injury. The result is muscle spasm and possible ligamentous injury in the neck. Neck fractures are rare.

The gas (petrol) tank is at the rear end of most cars. A high velocity rear impact crash can deform and puncture the gas tank, and gasoline may spill on the road. A spark from a metal part or the pavement can ignite the escaped gasoline and result in a rapidly spreading fire.

Seat back failure is a rare occurrence. The occupant loading the back of the seat may cause the hinge mechanism or other support of the seat back to fail. The seat back tilts backwards and the occupant may then slide up the back of the seat striking the head on some part of the back of the passenger compartment and sustain serious head and neck injury.

An intrusion of the striking vehicle into the passenger compartment may result in additional impact injuries.

Roll-over Crash

Although the automobile may suffer severe damage in a roll-over crash, the occupants receive surprisingly moderate impact as the vehicle is not brought to a sudden stop and the impact is spread over a period of time. The crashing of different sides of the vehicle absorbs the forces of impact. If the passenger compartment remains intact, the belted occupants frequently survive the crash.

Non-belted occupants are subject to two types of injury, viz. (a) tumbling around inside the vehicle, and (b) from striking the interior of the vehicle. Fractures and subluxation of cervical spine may occur. The occupant may also be ejected from the car.

If the roof or other part of the car intrudes inside the vehicle, further injuries occur.

Following a roll-over crash, occupants may become mixed and in the event some one dies and others survive this may create a difficult problem for investigators to figure out who the driver was since the survivors always claim that they were the passengers and the dead person was the driver. The identity of the driver can be established by:

1. Finding the fibres of driver's clothing in the broken steering wheel when such is the case.
2. Brake or accelerator pedal marks on the soles of the shoes when present.
3. Location of dicing injuries and other impact trauma, e.g. from door handles, etc., specific to the position of the driver.

4. Physical evidence transfer from motor vehicle to body and body to motor vehicle.

Other Mishaps

The other mishaps that may follow the occupants of the car, are: (a) ejection, (b) fire, and (c) submersion.

Ejection: Ejection depends on the vehicle doors opening during impact. Sometimes, an occupant may be ejected even through the windows. It increases the multiplicity and severity of the injury regardless of the position occupied by the occupant. The head, chest, and abdomen of the ejected occupants bear the brunt of the impact. Rib fractures, injuries of the chest viscera, and contusions and lacerations of the liver are common. Head injury is often the cause of death.

Fire: Fire after a vehicle crash is rare. The majority of vehicular fire burn injuries are associated with vehicles not involved in collisions. In rare cases, burn injuries may be the only cause of death.

Submersion: Drowning is another rare cause of death in accidents when a car is submerged in water.

Dicing injuries: Dicing injuries are injuries caused by glass pieces of side or back windows of a vehicle. They are superficial, linear and angular cuts.

SEAT BELTS

Q. 21.4. Discuss the role of restraint systems (seat belts) in road traffic fatalities.

Of the various types of restraint systems, the full torso restraint consisting of lap belt and double shoulder harness is extremely effective. It is in use in military training. For all practical purposes, the most popular and efficient seat belt is the three point harness which consists of both a diagonal arid transverse strap set in an inertia recoil housing. The recently introduced air bag restraint system has reduced considerably the gravity and incidence of chest and facial trauma.

Seat belts offer greatest benefits in frontal collisions and roll-over crashes. When wearing seat belts: (a) injuries are of lower average severity except perhaps whiplash, (b) probability of severe head injury is lower, (c) probability of being ejected from the vehicle is lower, and (d) there are fewer major or fatal injuries to the head, neck, chest, and abdomen.

If properly worn, the injury produced by the belt itself is rare and when it does occur the injuries are mainly abrasions and bruising to the chest and abdomen.

In some circumstances, failure to wear a seat belt may result in a reduction of damages. Any evidence in respect thereof may be of importance in investigation of such accidents.

AUTOPSY

Q. 21.5. Discuss the special features of autopsy on a case of motor vehicle accident. Mention the points that require special consideration.

An appropriately performed autopsy can reveal the various factors contributing to the accident, e.g.: (1) environmental factors, such as a defect in the road, presence of ice on the road; poor visibility due to fog or obscure traffic signals; and air pollution with carbon monoxide, (2) mechanical factors, such as defective brakes; presence or absence of seat belt, air bag, or collapsible steering column; and (3) antecedent factors in the victim, such as epilepsy, cardiac syncope, intake of alcohol and/or drugs like antihistaminics, hypnotics, and tranquillisers, or psychological conditions—leading to suicide. Alcohol and some drugs have deleterious effects on concen-tration and performance. The automobile meets with many features that the suicide seeks in a weapon. It is familiar, easy to operate, and powerful. It provides a setting in comfort, and it offers an opportunity to account for the death in a socially acceptable manner. Supportive evidence for suicide includes: (1) a history of depression, (2) the imprint of the gas pedal pattern on the sole of the shoe, and (3) absence of skid marks leading to the site of collision. The role of the automobile to commit homicide is also postulated.

In addition to routine precautions, the following points require special consideration: (1) scene of mishap, (2) description of clothing, (3) history, (4) findings regarding injuries both external and internal, and (5) specimens for laboratory analysis. Photographs of the scene, clothing, and injuries should be routinely taken. Since some states limit the damages to be recovered, if the victim was not wearing a seat belt, any injuries consistent with *seat belt injuries* should be carefully recorded.

Scene of Mishap

A concise description of the scene of mishap with appropriate sketches and photographs is essential. It is important that the investigating officer at the scene observes: (a) the path of the vehicle, (b) the vehicle itself, and (c) the position of the victims, when found.

The path leading to and from the scene indicate the direction of travel, speed, and attempt to stop the car by application of brakes. Skid marks and drag marks, when present, are helpful. Absence of skid marks and a high-speed impact may indicate a suicidal attempt. Extensive drag marks (grazes) indicate that the victim is a pedestrian and not an occupant ejected from the car. The amount and direction of blood on the road should be noted.

The vehicle should be inspected from both outside and inside for: (i) sites of impact, (ii) type and magnitude of damage, and (iii) presence of blood, hair, cloth fibres, etc.

Small children with a lower centre of gravity are usually thrown to the ground and may be run over by the same car. Adult pedestrians are thrown up onto the bonnet or hood and then thrown to the ground. In hit and run accidents, if tyre marks are present, a scaled photograph should be taken for subsequent comparison with the tyres of a suspected vehicle.

Clothing

The clothing should be described with special attention to imprint marks, tears, amount of bleeding, and foreign bodies, especially glass particles, metal, grease, and paint, which may indicate the part of the vehicle that struck the victim. In a hit and run accident, such imprint marks and foreign bodies transferred from the vehicle to the pedestrian's clothing provide valuable evidence in respect of the suspected vehicle. Sometimes, fibres of the clothing in the broken steering wheel help to identify who the driver was. Shoes may show brake, clutch, or accelerator pedal marks on tile soles, and such marks help to identify the driver from the passengers. Other helpful sings are: seat belt abrasions, dice injuries, and location of injuries from impact with projecting parts, e.g. door handles.

History

The history should include:

a. The condition of the eyes as regards opacities of the cornea, lens, or blindness.
b. If the victim was suffering from any disease, e.g. heart, epilepsy, haemorrhagic disorder, or diabetes.
c. The drugs that he was using (or abusing).
d. If he was depressed or under unusual stress.

Injuries

These should be systematically described as: (a) external injuries, and (b) internal injuries, with their characteristics.

External injuries: These are recorded in detail as to location, type (abrasion, bruise, laceration, cut, etc.), pattern if any, and degree (size and depth). The external injuries are influenced to some extent by the clothing, age, and physical state of the deceased. Leathery skin and acid stains will be found on the face and clothes of the victim, if the car battery has ruptured during the accident and spilled its contents thereon.

Pedestrian injuries are carefully documented (and photographed with a scale in view) in order to relate them to the part of the vehicle which struck the victim. When bumper fractures are present, the distance from the heel to the fracture site is measured as this gives information about the height of the bumper and if brakes were applied. If the impact is on the buttocks and the legs are hyperextended by the impact, parallel stretch lines may be seen in the inguinal region. The obese may suffer severe fat destruction and degloving with consequent fat embolism and severe blood loss.

In left hand driven cars, dice injuries are found on the left side of the face and arms of the driver and right side of the front seat passenger. The reverse is the case with right hand driven cars. The steering wheel and various parts of the instrument panel are responsible for characteristic patterned injuries. Likewise, seat belt marks often indicate the side on which the front seat occupant was positioned.

Dicing injuries: Dicing injuries are the injuries caused by glass pieces of side or back windows of a vehicle. They are cuts which are superficial, liner or right-angled.

Tailgating: When a speeding motor cyclist undershoots the tail board of a vehicle it is called tailgating or under running or passing underneath the back. This leads to head, neck or shoulder smashing against the tail board leading to respective injuries.

Internal injuries: The distribution of fatal injuries is mostly related to the head and chest. Due to extraordinary resilience of the skin, serious internal injuries may be present without any evidence of corresponding external injury. It is, therefore, necessary to incise suspected areas of impact, especially the buttocks and the thigh, for evidence of subcutaneous damage. In run-over injuries, extensive degloving could have occurred even without any significant damage to the skin. Before opening the chest, pneumothorax should be ruled out and the presence or absence of air and fat emboli determined. Then each major organ system is examined, the sequence depending on the choice of the dissector and the injuries on the victim. The examination of the central nervous system should cover the following:

The scalp is inspected for haemorrhage and the calvarium for fractures. The skull cap is then removed and the primary impact lesions, viz. extracerebral haemorrhages in the epidural, subdural, subarachnoid, and intraventricular spaces, and intracerebral contusions and lacerations are then looked for. It may be possible to determine coup and contre coup contusions. However, it should be remembered that an impact on the frontal area does not normally produce any contre coup injury to the opposite occipital lobes. The brain is then removed, the dura stripped, and the base of the skull inspected for fractures. Fractures of the base of the moving skull are usually linear and generally follow the line of force. From a medicolegal standpoint, the study of fracture lines provides objective evidence about the manner in which head injury has been sustained. The spine and spinal cord are then examined. Posterior approach is more convenient for this purpose. The atlantoaxial region is more susceptible to injury from violence applied to the head. Dislocations, ligament tears, and fracture of the odontoid process are looked for. These injuries are commonly missed, if rigor mortis has set in or posterior aspect of the cervical spine is not explored for evidence of haemorrhage which may not be apparent anteriorly. After removal of the spinal cord, cervical spine is sawed away from the upper thoracic spine, anterior and posterior longitudinal ligaments inspected, and a sagittal cut made through the vertebral bodies to expose disc tears and vertebral fractures. The spinal cord is examined for any haemorrhagic discolouration on the surface or in the substance. Nowadays, in some institutions, the brain and spinal cord are removed as one unit for better appreciation of injuries in the upper cervical region of the cord. If any pathological condition is encountered during examination of the nervous system, e.g. scar, tumour, infection, or aneurysm, it is specifically recorded.

In the neck, asphyxia due to compressive obstruction or aspiration should be ruled out. The tongue is examined for the presence of bite marks and the teeth for hyperplasia of gums as indications of epileptic disorder. Damage to neck vessels is specially looked for.

In the thorax, rib fractures may penetrate the lungs and cause pneumothorax. Compression of the thorax may rupture the alveoli and cause intra-alveolar haemorrhage. Flail chest occurs when at least three successive ribs are fractured at two points. It results in severe dyspnoea.

The chest organs are first examined in situ and then removed en bloc. The amount of blood in the pleural cavities is measured. The most common injury is rupture of the aorta at the junction of the aortic arch and the descending aorta and is supposed to be due to tensile stresses generated at this point. The ruptured ends appear almost as if they are cut. In absence of a ruptured aorta, one should specifically look for the presence of ladder tears at the junction of aortic arch and descending aorta. Cardiac contusion may occur after relatively minor trauma to the chest wall and should not be confused with myocardial infarct. Such a contusion may result in traumatic coronary thrombosis. Traumatic rupture of the heart may occur, commonly on the right side and toward the base. It should not be confused with spontaneous rupture. Raasch Jr describes a transverse tear of the right atrium just medial to coronary sinus in the area of the AV node in a moderate number of chest injury cases and this may explain some of the arrhythmias.

In the abdomen, the peritoneum and abdominal contents as a whole are examined, the amount of blood in the peritoneal cavity measured, and the course of any injury traced. Then, each organ is examined individually. Two types of injury are usually encountered, viz. laceration of a solid organ and rupture of a hollow viscus.

The liver is most commonly injured. It is easily lacerated and ruptured, if it is fatty, enlarged, or diseased except severely scarred or fibrosed. Sometimes, the bleeding occurs between the liver and its capsule (subcapsular haematoma). Serious symptoms become apparent only when the capsule ruptures. The spleen can also be lacerated and rupture similarly, if it is enlarged or diseased. Sometimes, symptoms may become apparent only when the capsule ruptures from the increasing pressure of the enlarging haematoma. On account of its important immunological function, it is desirable to retain a part of the spleen, when possible, in preference to complete splenectomy. Rupture of a hollow viscus is followed by chemical or bacterial peritonitis or both on account of spillage of their contents and haemorrhage.

Injuries to extremities result in fractures of bones, soft tissue damage, and haemorrhage. Crushing of the tissues releases acid metabolites from the damaged muscles similar to those associated with incompatible blood transfusion. An attempt by the kidney at excretion of these metabolites results in acute tubular necrosis and renal failure. Crush injuries may be complicated by fat or other emboli.

Laboratory Specimens

In a hit and run accidents, the victim's clothing and hair should be examined for foreign bodies, e.g. glass, metal, grease, or paint fragments, for comparison with material which may be found on a suspected vehicle. Sometimes, clothing may show imprint marks. A blood sample should be analysed for the presence and amount of alcohol and drugs since the question of *contributory negligence* may subsequently arise. Blood samples must be retained for blood grouping and DNA fingerprinting in case a hit and run vehicle is found with blood or traces of tissues upon it. Sometimes, hair samples may be required for the same purpose. If sufficient blood is not obtainable, vitreous fluid from the eye can be analysed for alcohol. Normally, about 8–10 ml of blood usually remains in the pulmonary trunk even when the aorta has been transected. The urine should be screened for commonly abused drugs. In some circumstances, samples may have to be preserved from liver, lung, kidney, brain, heart and bile.

Microscopic examination is essential in evaluation of underlying disease, such as cirrhosis of the liver, fatty liver, myocardial infarct, etc. Bacteriological studies are important in the study of delayed deaths due to infection. Postmortem radiology, e.g. angiography of the vessels of the head and neck and computerized axial tomography are helpful for the study of subtle problems in relation to the vascular bed. A lacerated vertebral artery demonstrated radiologically will require posterior neck dissection with ample photography.

MOTOR CYCLE INJURIES

Q. 21.6. Discuss motor cycle injuries.

Motor cycles are very unsafe because:

1. They have less stability than four wheeled vehicles.
2. Even small motor cycles can attain high speed.
3. Their size is relatively so small that they are easily overlooked by larger vehicles.
4. Their weight is relatively much less than average four-wheeled vehicles and they are, therefore, at a mechanical disadvantage.
5. The vehicle does not remain upright in an accident and the motor cyclist receives no protection from it, but
6. He is almost always thrown off and, therefore, subject to very severe impact forces. Motor cycle injuries are mainly a problem of rural areas and moderate sized cities and suburbs in the developing countries.

The most common causes of motor cycle accidents are: alcohol and drugs, reckless driving, and environmental factors, e.g. pot holes, oil slicks, poor visibility, etc. Sometimes, loss of control over the motor cycle may result in its crashing against a stationary object, with a fatal outcome. If cables or wires are stretched across the road as supports to poles or towers and the driver is reckless or does not see them or loses control over the vehicle, he may have his head or extremities amputated. Such an event is not very uncommon.

When an accident happens, the injuries are often severe as there is very little crushable material to absorb the impact and the driver and/or passengers are always thrown off.

All types of injuries may be present. In a high-speed impact of a motor cycle, there may be primary injuries as a result of initial impact followed by secondary injuries from striking the ground. Primary injuries are mostly open fractures of the tibia and fibula. Secondary injuries are mostly fractures of the skull and cervical spine as well as contusions of the brain.

A fracture of the skull with associated brain injury is the most common cause of death but multiple injuries constitute a typical feature of fatal motor cycle accidents. Submersion may occur when the motor cyclist tries to cross a frozen lake not realizing that the ice is not thick enough to sustain the weight of the vehicle and its rider.

Head and neck injuries include skull fractures, contusions and lacerations of the brain, intracranial haemorrhages, ocular and orbital open lesions, facial fractures, cervical fractures, and lesions of the spinal cord. Thoracic injuries include fractures of the sternum, clavicle, and ribs; haemopneumothorax; contusions and lacerations of the lungs and heart; and rupture of aorta. Abdominal injuries include lacerations of the liver, spleen, and kidney; rupture of the bowels and urinary bladder; and fracture of the pelvis. In the upper extremity, fractures of the radius, ulna, and metacarpals are common. In the lower extremity, open fractures of the tibia and fibula are most often seen. Fractures of femur and metatarsals are not uncommon. Traumatic amputations both in the upper and lower extremities may be seen. Thermal injuries, when present, are due to hot metal sliding against the street and fire caused by gas tank puncture.

Skid marks (grazes) on the skin due to contact with road gravel are commonly seen and the direction of travel may be easily identified by the presence of skin tags at the rear most (far) end of these scratches.

The use of crash helmets has reduced fatalities at low speeds but afford little or no protection at high speeds. A crash helmet is designed to reduce friction of the head against the ground and make deceleration less drastic by allowing the protected head to skid across the ground rather than to come to an abrupt halt. A full face helmet is better than an open face helmet. It affords greater protection against facial excoriations and fractures as well as against spinal injuries.

MOPED AND BICYCLE INJURIES

Q. 21.7. Write short notes on: (1) moped (mini-bike) injuries, (2) bicycle injuries.

In a **moped (mini-bike),** where the speed is lower, the usual fatal injury is due to another motor vehicle striking the rider. Primary impact injuries of the legs with secondary injuries to the head, shoulder, and trunk are commonly seen.

The injury panorama is basically the same as that in motor cycle accidents but a moped is estimated to be only one-third as dangerous as a motor cycle.

The majority of fatal **bicycle accidents** are collisions between a bicycle and a motor vehicle. The most common cause of death is craniocerebral injury.

When a bicyclist is struck by a motor vehicle he sustains primary impact injuries where he is struck by the vehicle and secondary injuries at points of impact with the pavement and bicycle. Whilst being thrown off the bicycle, he may sustain injuries from the handle bars and other projecting parts.

Head injuries include dental trauma, fractures of facial bones, contusions of the brain, fractures of the skull and cervical spine. Trunk injuries include mainly superficial contusions and excoriations. Fractures of ribs, spine, and pelvis are sometimes seen. Intrathoracic and intra-abdominal lesions are seldom seen but handle bars may cause rupture of the bowels and laceration of the liver, spleen, or kidney. The injuries to the extremities include shoulder contusions, clavicular fractures, metacarpal fractures, knee and ankle distortions, and fractures of the lower part of tibia and fibula but not so often of femur or metatarsals.

An injury peculiar to the bicycle riders, especially children, is the bicycle spoke injury which occurs when a child falls from a bicycle and his foot and leg are wedged between the spokes of the wheel. The result is compression or crushing of soft tissues of the leg. The most common site of skin necrosis is at the level of the lateral or medial malleolus. Other common areas are over the Achilles tendon or the lateral aspect of the foot. Fractures of the ankle or lower part of the tibia or fibula may also be seen.

RAILWAY INJURIES

Q. 21.8. Discuss the medicolegal aspects of railway injuries.

Railway injuries may be suicidal or accidental. A simple decapitation is commonly an indication of suicide and rarely of accident. Traumatic amputation of the limbs or trunk is commonly an indication of accident or rarely of a person throwing himself in front of a moving train. The nature of the injuries will depend upon the position of the victim when struck. On electrified lines, electric burns and charring may be found, the extent of which will depend upon the duration of contact with the live rail, and may include bone.

Suicidal Injuries

If a person jumps in front of a train, the injuries are very severe, and although primary impact may be demonstrated, usually the primary impact injuries are too extensive to afford any helpful interpretation. On occasions, a simple decapitation may occur (Fig. 21.5).

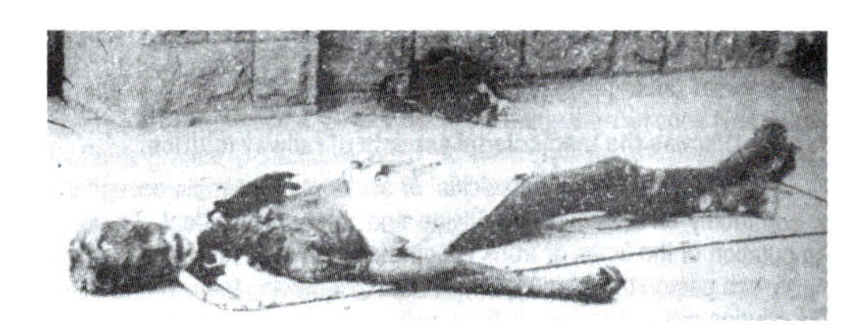

Fig. 21.5: Railway accident. Severed head (decapitation)

Accidental Injuries

These are sustained while trying to board a fast moving train, walking on the rails or crossing them; while leaning out of the window; during a fall from a train; and during collisions.

Boarding a fast moving train: The person may be thrown off with resultant impact injuries and risk of getting crushed between the train and the platform.

Rail walking and crossing: While walking on the rails, the injuries are usually severe and consist of impact injuries caused by contact with parts of the front of the engine and secondary injuries due to being thrown and possibly run-over (Fig. 21.6). While crossing, the primary impact will be on the side and will usually involve the head and shoulders.

Leaning out of a window: This will produce almost exclusively head injuries, the injured person being found either in the carriage or on the side of the line.

Fall from a train: Such injuries are usually in the nature of multiple abrasions with impact injuries due to striking objects. Shock is usually a prominent feature.

Collisions: The victim will frequently show characteristic fractures of the legs similar to those found in motor car accidents. In addition, transmitted force may cause compression fractures of the spine. And, secondary injuries due to falling luggage or parcels usually occur.

Fig. 21.6: The right leg and left upper arm were severed in a run-over train accident

Difficulties in Diagnosis of Railway Accident Deaths

It is not uncommon in India to kill a person and to place his body on a railway track and make it appear like a case of suicide or accident. This aspect needs to be excluded in all cases when a dead body is found on a railway track. While it may be difficult to give any opinion, if the body is decomposed or badly crushed and mutilated, it is possible in a number of cases to come to some definite conclusion by considering the following factors: history, scene of crime, injuries, hypostasis, rigor mortis, and laboratory examination of viscera.

History: A careful inquiry should be made, if the deceased was depressed, had some incurable or chronic disease, if he was associated with drugs of abuse, or if he was a member of some criminal gang.

Scene of crime: Evidence of extensive blood stains covering a large area may indicate that the person was living at the time of accident.

Injuries: The presence of marks of throttling (manual strangulation) or stab injuries definitely points to homicide. The nature of railway injuries, whether antemortem or postmortem, solves much of the problem. The age of the various injuries, as determined by the naked eye, microscopic examination, and enzyme chemistry, is also helpful.

Hypostasis: The incidence, extent, and degree of fixation of postmortem lividity is important. It may provide a valuable clue about the time since death which may be different from the time of the accident.

Rigor mortis: The presence and extent or absence of rigor mortis should be noted. It may offer supplementary evidence about the time since death.

Laboratory examination: Chemical examination of viscera may provide evidence regarding poisoning.

AIRCRAFT INJURIES

Q. 21.9. Discuss the medicolegal aspects of aircraft injuries.

Aircraft injuries result from either crash accidents or flight accidents. The majority of aircraft accidents are crash accidents occurring while landing or taking off. Flight accidents are normally very few.

Crash Accidents

The sudden deceleration on crashing is responsible both for the break-up of the aircraft and for most of the injuries to the occupants. Both while landing or taking off, the passengers are usually secured to their seats by lap-type safety belts. On crashing, the forward momentum of the upper part of the body across the safety belt throws the head on to the back of the seat in front resulting in a fractured skull. The impact may also be sufficiently severe to cause rupture of the liver, spleen, kidney, and abdominal aorta. Fire may occur in a fatal crash and complicate the primary injuries by incineration. The fire contains a high proportion of carbon monoxide fumes. If the occupants survive the impact as well as the fire, they are likely to be overtaken by carbon monoxide from the fumes before they can escape.

A very great problem in the aircraft crash is that of identification, as the bodies are burnt and charred, or are dismembered and body parts often co-mingled and scattered over a wide area, sometimes inaccessible for some days. The methods used for identification include collection and correlation of specific and non-specific relevant data. Specific data collection relates to finger prints, dental identification, and X-ray comparisons. Non-specific data collection relates to personal property, such as documents, jewellery, diary, etc; body features, such as scars, tattoos, operations, vaccinations, hair pattern, implanted devices, etc.; and visual identification and photographs. Specially organized team work is necessary for this purpose. DNA typing, when in routine use, could be most helpful.

Flight Accidents

Most turbine powered and jet aircrafts fly at an altitude between 25,000 and 40,000 feet. Normally, the cabins are pressurized in such a way that the inside pressure is not allowed to fall below that found at an altitude of 8,000 feet, so that the effects of anoxia are minimal. Door or window failure with explosive loss of cabin pressure may occur, resulting in immediate loss of life from hypoxia amongst those with heart or lung disease. If the height is not restored to a reasonably safe altitude between 15,000 to 20,000 feet, in at most quarter of an hour, even the young and fit would also suffer. At the same time, the rush of air out of the cabin is sufficient to blow a standing or even a seated occupant out with it with consequent injuries, which are mostly severe.

The deliberate destruction of commercial aircraft in flight has important medicolegal implications. The main difficulty facing the investigators is to distinguish sabotage from explosive decompression due to structural failure. In the event of sabotage being shown to be the cause of the accident, the responsibility for insurance passes from the "All Risk" insurers to those underwriting "War Risks". In these days of advanced technologies, an unexplained disaster in air should be suspected to be due to sabotage until the contrary is proved. The major parts of the aircraft would be found scattered over a very wide area without any logical pattern in case of midair explosions.

22 Thermal Injuries

A **thermal injury** is defined as tissue injury due to application of heat in any form to the external or internal body surfaces. Such injury may result from: (1) dry heat, as for example, by application of hot substances, and by flames—simple burns, (2) moist heat—scalds, (3) chemicals—corrosive burns, (4) electric contact, electric spark, flashes of lightning—electric burns, and (5) X-rays, ultraviolet rays, radium, laser, microwave oven—radiation burns. While each form has distinctive surface features, indirect results are virtually the same, for they involve capillary damage (followed by fluid exudation), necrosis of injured tissue and shock. Electrical injuries carry the added danger of cardiac arrhythmia and death. Sections 324 and 326 IPC deal with punishments to be awarded in such cases.

Characteristics: Burns produced by radiant heat from **hot substances** cause whitening of skin. On direct contact, such substances produce a blister; if kept in contact for a longer time, they produce roasting and charring of body parts. If any object is to be handled comfortably for any appreciable time, the temperature of skin/object interface should not exceed 42°C. The skin proteins coagulate and full thickness burns result, if the deepest layers of skin reach a temperature of 45°C. Burns produced by a **flame** are characterised by roasted (dry, shrivelled, charred) patches of skin or deeper parts of body, singeing or burning of hair or clothing, and deposits of carbonaceous material on the body. There may be vesicles or blisters, all round the burnt areas.

The characteristics of burns produced by moist heat **(scalds),** electricity, and lightning, are discussed separately.

Burns produced by **corrosives** are characterised by inflammatory redness of skin, ulcerated patches of skin, discolouration and staining of skin and clothing, and presence of the chemical in the stains. Strong alkali burns will cause skin to be white and soggy with a soapy feel to touch. Singeing of hair is absent and vesicles are rarely found when burns are due to corrosive acids or alkalis. When phosphorus dissolved in carbon disulphide has been employed, vesication will probably be found, because phosphorus becomes oxidized by air and is ignited when carbon disulphide evaporates. Chemical burns may be followed by a keloid scar and disfigurement.

Burns produced by **X-rays** vary in intensity depending on the strength of the dose, period of exposure, and the type of tissue irradiated. Skin may become inflamed and red (dermatitis) but after a short period, inflammation subsides leaving a slight bronzing. The skin may blister. Finger nails may be affected by degenerative changes including warty growths. There may be atrophy of superficial tissues and obliteration of superficial blood vessels resulting in shedding of hair, epidermis, and the formation of indolent ulcers (with a tendency to malignancy). The cicatrix (scar) formed from healing of such ulcers is radiate in shape and is associated with pigmentation of the surrounding skin. In rare cases, bluish discolouration resembling a bruise may appear below the skin and this gradually becomes the seat of extensive and deep sloughing. Healing takes place after a long delay with considerable degree of atrophy of skin. Burns caused by **radium** are very similar to X-ray burns. **Sun's light** which contains **ultraviolet rays** may cause burns from sunbathing when there is over-exposure. Such burns may vary from erythema to vesication. Dermatitis has been recorded. The most frightening new findings about sun exposure link it to rapid and unexpected increases in the incidence of skin cancer. And, one sunburn may be enough to bring it on. Recent studies by Arthur Sober of the Harvard Medical School show that people who experience a single blistering sunburn during childhood or adolescence are twice as likely as others to develop malignant melanoma later. Burns caused by **laser** radiation therapy affect skin, eyes, and other tissues. Skin is charred depending on energy of impact of the laser beam. The greatest hazard is to eyes; corneal and retinal burns may cause blindness. Burns caused by **microwave** ovens affect the tissues in direct proportion to their water content. Thus, skin and muscles which contain more water than subcutaneous fat will be heated more than fat. The appearance will be like a sandwich with burnt skin, sparing of subcutaneous fat, and burnt muscle.

Q. 22.1. Give the classification of burns. Describe their effects.

Q. 22.2. Write short notes on: (1) rule of nines, (2) burn index, (3) age of a burn, (4) causes of death from burns.

BURNS

Burns may be classified into three degrees, viz. (1) epidermal, (2) dermoepidermal, and (3) deep. This classification is helpful to assess the degree of damage sustained by the victim. If there is partial loss of skin thickness (first degree burns), it is self-healing. If full thickness of skin is lost (second degree burns), it will require skin grafting. If there is deep burning (third degree burns), it will cause loss of function. Long-term results of survival from severe burning may cause considerable disfigurement and disablement which must be considered in assessing damages.

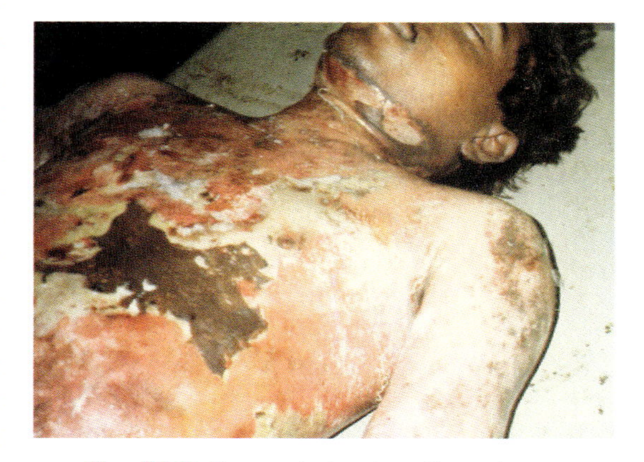

Fig. 22.1: Burns during healing phase

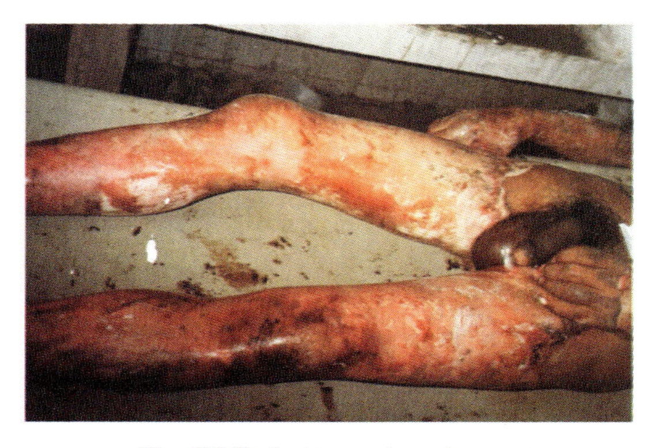

Fig. 22.2: Antemortem burns

Epidermal burns: The affected part is red (erythema). Usually, there is a blister covered by pale avascular epidermis and surrounded by a thin bright red area of inflammation. Singeing of hair is present. These burns are very painful but repair is complete without scar formation. The presence of pin-prick sensation indicates that this skin area is viable. Its absence suggests loss of full thickness of skin although oedema may mislead the inexperienced doctor.

Dermoepidermal burns: The whole thickness of skin is destroyed. There is coagulation necrosis of epidermis and dermis. The lesions have a dry white leathery appearance. The necrosed tissue separates within about a week leaving an ulcer with scar formation. The scar may contract causing disfigurement and impairment of function. These burns are associated with considerable pain and shock.

Deep burns: The affected area is completely charred, there being gross destruction of skin, subcutaneous tissue, muscles, and bones. Nerve endings are also destroyed. The burns are, therefore, relatively painless.

The estimation of burnt surface area **in an adult** is usually worked out by the **rule of nines (Fig. 22.3):** Nine per cent for head and each arm, 18% for front or back of trunk, nine per cent for front or back of each leg, and one per cent for perineum, thus making a total of one 100% for the body. Roughly, one per cent of surface burn is equivalent to the area covered by the palm of the individual. *In children,* the estimation of burnt surface is worked out by the use of *Lund and Browder chart.* If the burnt area is more than 15% in an adult and 10% in a child, the loss of circulating blood volume must be replaced or irreversible shock is likely to set in.

Effects of burns: All three stages may be found together. Scarring is usually less after scaids than from burns. Keloid scarring with destruction of tissues and considerable deformity occurs in corrosive burns. *Curling's ulcer* is an occasional sequel to severe burns. It is seen as a sharply punched out mucosal defect in the stomach and/or duodenum.

The effects of burning mainly depend upon:

1. Temperature and duration of exposure
2. Extent and position of burns
3. Age of victim

Temperature and duration of exposure: The severity of burns, whether of first degree, second degree, or third degree depends on the degree of heat and the duration of exposure. The higher the temperature the more severe are the burns. The lowest temperature that would cause burns is 44°C if sustained long enough (about five hours). This is manifested by law suits concerning unconscious patients burned by forgotten hot water bottles. Only three seconds are needed, if the object is at 60°C. It takes only about a second or less for a partial thickness burn at 63°C and about a second or less for a full thickness burn at 71°C. The relationship between temperature and time is nonlinear and as temperature rises severe burning can occur in fraction of a second.

Extent and position: The surface area burnt is more important than the degree of burn in assessing prognosis of a given case. As for example, a first degree burn over a wide area is more dangerous than a third degree burn over a limited area. Destruction of one-third of skin area is usually fatal though instances are known when victims with 80 per cent burns have survived with skilled treatment when appropriate facilities are available.

The burn index was devised by the Brook Army Medical Center Burn Unit of the US Army. It combines depth and area to gain insight into prognosis and effectiveness of treatment. In this system, half point is used for each per cent area of second degree and 1 point for third degree burns. As per their experience, at about 45 points, the mortality rate is 50 per cent. While this may have changed now in view of the improvement in treatment, it is still a good guide to determine the relative severity of burns and enables relative prognosis to be estimated in conjunction with age.

Burns on the head, neck, trunk, and genitals are said to be more dangerous than on other parts of the body, on account of possible involvement of vital structures.

Age: Infants, young children, and the elderly are particularly vulnerable to initial shock and subsequent complications.

Age of a burn: Redness occurs immediately after a burn, vesication within two to three hours, and purulent inflammation may be found within 3.6 to 72 hours. Superficial sloughs of third degree burns are thrown off in about a week and deeper sloughs in about a fortnight. After this period, granulation tissue begins to cover the burnt surface, and the final result is formation of a scar.

Cause of death: Death may occur from *primary neurogenic shock* instantaneously from fear or pain, or within 24 to 48 hours from severe pain caused by extensive burns, or from injury to a vital organ from burning, or from oligaemic shock. If victim survives, this stage merges rapidly into stage of *secondary shock* due to exudation of serum from burnt area and consequent depletion of blood volume. Apart from actual burning, death may occur from *asphyxia (suffocation)* due to inhalation of smoke containing carbon dioxide, carbon monoxide, and other products of combustion which may be poisonous (in recent years, cyanide intoxication has been recognised as important, especially where plastics and paints are burning), or *accidental injuries horn* falling structures while trying to escape from a burning house, or from *fat embolism.* It has been postulated that death may occur even without the inhalation of smoke due to rapid consumption of oxygen by intense fire. This is not correct. If there is no oxygen, the fire would be extinguished.

Death may be delayed for some days and then it may be due to *acute tubular necrosis* owing to general toxaemia arising from destruction of tissue by burning, or due to *inflammation,* such as meningitis or peritonitis. Thereafter, the chief danger to life is the occurrence of *sepsis* in burned areas, or intercurrent disease, especially of the respiratory system.

Complications and *exhaustion* are responsible for delayed deaths. Curling's ulcer may develop in one or two weeks after severe burning. Tetanus, gangrene, and erysipelas are other complications. Gross hypoproteinaemia producing oedema, ascites, pleural and pericardial effusions is seen in some cases.

If the victim recovers, fibrosis and contraction of scar in burnt area usually lead to pronounced disability and disfigurement.

Fatal period: Death from shock occurs within 1 to 2 days in over 50% cases. Toxaemia persists up to 3 to 4 days and accounts for deaths occurring from 4 to 5 days or longer. Usually, most fatalities occur within the first week. In suppurative cases, death may occur after 5 to 6 weeks or longer.

Q. 22.3. Describe in detail the postmortem appearances in a case of death from burns. How will you proceed with the examination, and what specific peculiarities you are likely to find?

Q. 22.4. Comment on: (1) pugilistic attitude, (2) heat fracture, (3) heat haematoma.

The postmortem appearances vary considerably and depend on the extent of fire, how long the person survived during the fire, and how long the burning went on after death. A complete postmortem

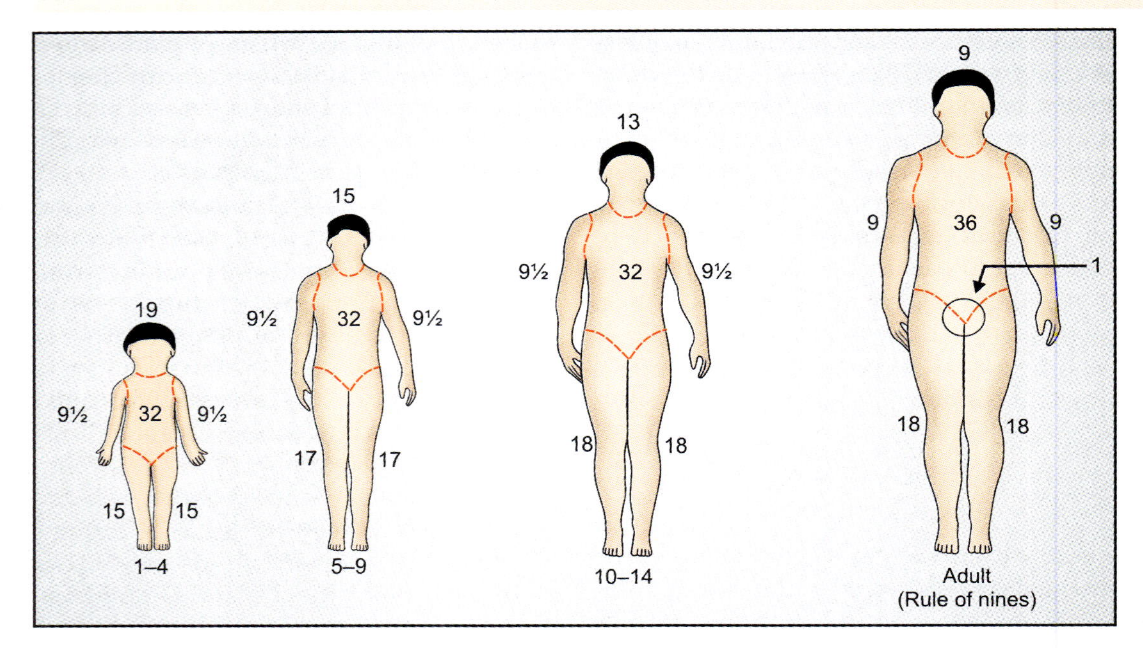

Fig. 22.3: Rule of nines. Estimating body surface area percentage by age. Burns affecting over 33% of the body surface are usually fatal unless very adequately treated

examination should be carried out even when the body appears to be almost completely incinerated. Internal organs may be in a relatively good condition as: (1) the body is composed mainly of water to the extent of 75% of its weight, and (2) body tissues are poor heat conductors. In the electric crematorium at Mumbai, there is an arrangement for automatic cut out when the temperature reaches 600°C. However, when the body burns, the temperature rises up to 1000°C. House fires can very rarely generate such high temperature.

External appearances: Clothes should be removed with care for future examination including the presence of kerosene, petrol, or some other combustible substance. The distribution of burns on clothing may throw light on the manner in which it was ignited, posture of the victim, path taken by the flame, and possibly the presence of inflammable material (Fig. 22.4).

The clothes and body give a strong smell of burning, if burns are antemortem in

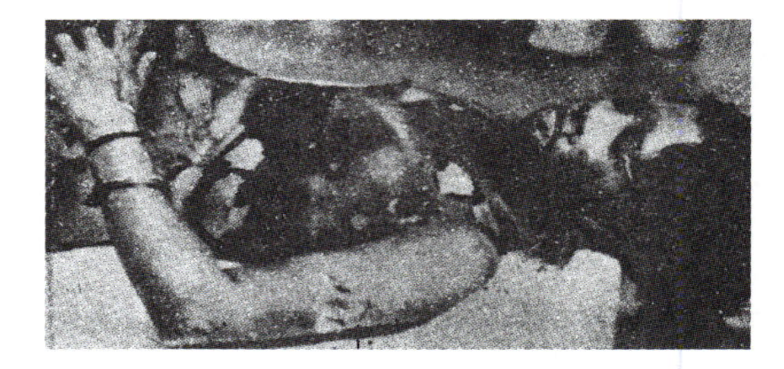

Fig. 22.4: Kerosene burns. This photograph shows patchy destruction of the skin, singeing of hair,and deposition of black soot on the body, especially the face and waist

nature. The burnt areas will be found reddened and blistered, or charred. Blisters may be either ruptured or collapsed. Blisters are due to increased permeability of superficial blood vessels due to heat. They contain serous fluid of a jelly-like consistency, rich in albumin and chlorides. The blister fluid coagulates in vitro on heating (or on treatment with nitric acid). When examined under a microscope, it shows presence of red and white blood corpuscles. When clothes of the victim catch fire, the burns are generally found on areas covered by loose clothes. The parts of body protected by tight clothing, such as belt, shoes, brassieres, or a buttoned collar, are apt to escape burning. Unburnt skin about wrist and ankles may indicate that the victim was tied before the fire started. Similarly, a mark surrounding the neck may indicate that the victim was strangled. Hair may be singed or bulbous at intervals. Deposit of carbonaceous material on body or in the nostrils may be found. Microscopically, in a burn, skin shows petechial haemorrhages in deeper layers; epithelial cells are elongated, flattened, and stain deeply with haematoxylin and eosin; and vacuolisation of epidermal and dermal layers is prominently seen.

The face is swollen and distorted, and the tongue protruded. Froth, often pink-stained, may appear at the mouth and nostrils as a result of heat irritation of the air passages and lungs. Owing to effect of heat on blood, the veins stand out, giving a *marbled appearance.* Postmortem lividity is cherry red in colour from carbon monoxide poisoning.

The body presents the so-called attitude of defence, known as **boxing attitude, pugilistic attitude** (Fig. 22.5), or **fencing posture.** It is due to heat stiffening. The legs are flexed at the hips and knees; the arms are flexed at the elbows and held out in front of the body; and the fingers are hooked like claws. This attitude is present

Fig. 22.5: Typical pugilistic attitude in a case of burns. The body is slightly bent, the limbs are flexed, and the skin tense and shows frequent splits. (*Courtesy*: Dr PP Phatnani)

whether a living or dead body is burnt and has, therefore, no medicolegal significance. The condition is due to coagulation of proteins other than those affected by rigor mortis. It *differs from* rigor mortis in that it is permanent and does not pass off. The skin is tense, leathery, hard, and frequently shows splits owing to tension and these may be mistaken for wounds. This condition can be *distinguished from violence:* (1) by presence of nerves, blood vessels, and connective tissue, running across the split from side to side, (2) there is no clotted blood in these fissures and no extravasation of blood in the surrounding tissues since heat coagulates blood in the vessels, and (3) there is no bruising or other signs of vital reaction in margins of heat rupture split.

One should also note presence or absence of any fractures remembering that fractures may be produced by sudden contraction of muscles as a result of heat (*heat fractures*). It is also necessary to remember that a relatively intense fire may destroy portions of the extremities and it is not unusual to find complete absence of the limbs, or partial absence at lower elbow or forearm level, and somewhere below the knee.

Internal appearances: These will depend upon whether death has resulted from shock or asphyxia, or whether the individual survived the immediate effects of burning and died from subsequent complications, such as, acute tubular necrosis; inflammation of serous surfaces, e.g. peritonitis; and intercurrent disease, e.g. pneumonia.

In **asphyxial cases,** inhaled smoke is seen as black particles of soot mixed with mucous covering the congested lining of the air passages. Soot frequently extends deeply into the lungs. If there is any doubt about its presence, mucus from respiratory passages may be examined under the microscope for presence of carbon particles. Occasionally, soot is swallowed and may

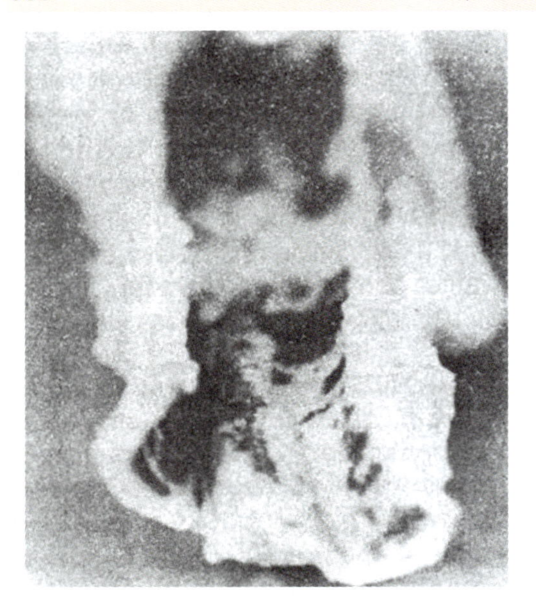

Fig. 22.6: Soot in the trachea in a case of death due to burns. Where death is due to asphyxia, inhaled smoke is seen mixed with mucus covering the lining of the air passages. This is a vital sign and provides sure evidence that the person was alive at the time of burning. (*Courtesy*: Dr AA Qureshi)

be recovered from oesophagus or stomach (Fig. 22.6). These signs do not necessarily prove that any burns were antemortem but that the victim was alive when the fire was in progress, which is not the same conclusion. In addition, the mucosa of the trachea and bronchi may be injected or filled with froth, or if hot air is inhaled, mucosa of larynx and trachea may be necrosed and detached in shreds. Microscopically, epithelial cells lining the respiratory passages appear elongated and flattened. The lungs may be shrunken, congested, or oedematous, and pleural cavities may contain blood-stained serous effusion. Scattered petechial haemorrhages are seen in various organs. Heart chambers are usually full of clotted blood.

Blood is thick due to haemoconcentration, and is cherry red in colour on account of presence of carboxyhaemoglobin. While saturations of 30–50% HbCO are common, a blood level of more than 10% carbon monoxide in a non-smoker may be considered as evidence of smoke inhalation and consequently that the victim was alive after the fire started spectroscopic bands of CO are seen in blood and the presence of carbon monoxide in blood can be detected by *Kunkei's test*. If blood is not available for carbon monoxide determina-tion, skeletal muscle can be utilised. To determine if a person was a smoker or not, urine can be analyzed for the presence of nicotine. When inflammable substances, e.g. kerosene or petrol, are used for self-immolation or homicidal burning, the body burns rapidly but there is hardly any inhalation of smoke. Carbon monoxide level in such cases, therefore, is not elevated. In March 1990, in Mumbai, a girl by name Rita, who was in the examination hall, answering a question paper, had such a misfortune when her so-called boy friend doused her with petrol and set her to fire since she refused to marry him.

Reduced calibre of small blood vessels may result from contraction of soft tissues and this may be *misinterpreted* by the inexperienced. There are a number of cases in which the calibre of coronary arteries has been misinterpreted following the crash of an aircraft with subsequent fire.

When the head has been exposed to intense heat, the scalp may show fissures. After the scalp has burned away, when the skull is heated, **heat fractures** may occur. The heat fracture is a flaked fracture affecting the outer table of the skull. It is usually located on either side of the skull above the temples and consists of several lines which radiate from a common centre and may cross a suture line. Outward bursting of bone flaps and protrusion of brain tissue through the defect may occur as a result of steam pressure within the skull. When fractures are present at the base of skull, one can assume that these are not produced as a result of steaming of brain. Such fractures, of course, could have resulted from falling structures during an attempt to escape from a burning house. The brain may be congested and oedematous, or shrunken, and extradural haemorrhage (heat haematoma) may be found. The **heat haematoma** is due to rupture of vessels caused by heat with subsequent escape and coagulation of blood and has certain characteristics. It is a soft, friable clot, of light chocolate colour, and may be pink, if blood contains carbon monoxide. The clot is not uniformly solid, but is spongy and is not closely related to the site of heat fractures. This is in contrast to traumatic fractures where the intracranial haematoma is closely related to the fracture site. If the haematoma is purely a postmortem phenomenon, it will have the same carbon monoxide concentration as in the blood, whereas if it an antemortem lesion sustained before the fire began, it will be free from carbon monoxide.

The internal organs should be examined carefully for evidence of natural disease or trauma which may have produced death prior to fire. The hyoid bone, thyroid cartilage, and soft tissues of neck should be carefully examined to rule out strangulation. Toxicological screening should include, in addition to carbon monoxide, alcohol, commonly used drugs that affect behaviour and that may explain why the victim did not escape, and other products of combustion, e.g. cyanide, etc.

In delayed death from burning, there may be cloudy swelling of viscera, acute tubular necrosis, and occasionally Curling's ulcer.

Q. 22.5. Discuss the role of a medical officer handling a case of death due to burns.

Q. 22.6. Comment on: (1) antemortem and postmortem burns, (2) burning as a cause of death, (3) dowry deaths, (4) postmortem burning, (5) difficulties in diagnosing death from burns.

The medical officer is normally only concerned with fatalities due to burns or with circumstances in which bodies are recovered from burning buildings. The following questions, therefore, require to be determined: (1) identity of the deceased, (2) whether the burns are antemortem or postmortem, (3) whether burns are the cause of death, and (4) whether they are suicidal, homicidal, or accidental.

Identification: If heat stiffening has produced pugilistic attitude with clenched fists, forced extension of the digits reveals relatively intact finger pads suitable for fingerprinting. Frequently, in severely burned bodies, tissue fluid collects between the layers of skin. In the hands, the skin detaches as a glove including finger nails. Either the detached glove or the remaining hand whichever is less damaged may be used to obtain fingerprints. The skin of the feet may detach in like fashion. A similar process occurs in decomposition and following prolonged immersion in water or fluid medium. The removal of the superficial layers of skin by wiping or rubbing renders a tattoo mark better recognisable. Wiping of areas thought to be tattooed may reveal a tattoo mark previously obscured. For racial identification, patches of intact skin under areas of tight clothing are helpful.

When complete incineration of a body has occurred, every fragment of bone, teeth, metal articles, etc., should be carefully retained for examination and consequent identification. Depending on the bony structure remaining, it is often relatively easy from X-rays to get some idea of race, sex, age, and general build of the individual. The skull and long bones serve as indicators of race. The non-pregnant uterus and prostate may not undergo incineration even in severe burning and help to determine sex. Portions of pelvic bones also help similarly. Teeth and non-united ossific centres of bones aid in determination of age.

Metallic objects, such as buckles, safety pins, hair pins, buttons, zippers, keys, and necklaces, may give a clue to sex and perhaps identity of the person involved. A full description of any pathologic changes in the organs should be given and the absence of any organ as a result of surgical removal should be noted as a valuable aid to identification. DNA typing is yet not in routine use.

Antemortem and postmortem burns: A person may be murdered and heat may be applied to the dead body to conceal the crime. It is, therefore, necessary to know the differentiating features of antemortem from postmortem burns. The differentiation depends on presence of a vital reaction as seen by naked eye or by histological examination.

An antemortem burn shows redness of the parts. If vesication is present, blisters are surrounded by a thin bright red area of inflammation; they contain highly albuminous fluid, chlorides, and blood corpuscles; and when ruptured, the base is found to be injected. When a vesicle contains pus, it means that the person has lived for at least 36 hours after the injury. There is some controversy about the significance of red areas at the margins of blisters. Some claim that this is a sign of vital reaction (inflammation); others, however, point out that when fresh tissue is heated it contracts and the blood within it shifts to the adjacent less heated margins.

A postmortem blister is limited in size, contains air, or if it contains fluid, this is practically non-albuminous, and does not contain chlorides, and blood corpuscles; there is no line of hyperaemia round the blister; and its base is not injected. Blisters may also be seen in putrefaction but these differ from antemortem blisters by the absence of a vital reaction; elevation of entire epidermis from corium to form the covering of the blister; and the presence in the blister mainly of putrefactive gases and of a little reddish-coloured fluid. Such blisters do not contain any albuminous fluid or chlorides. In case of doubt, it is best to excise the vesicle and its related tissues and examine histologically for evidence of a tissue reaction.

Table 22.1: Differentiating features of antemortem and postmortem burns

	Antemortem burns	*Postmortem burns*
1. Line of redness	Present	Absent
2. Vesicles	Contain albuminous fluid and chlorides	Contain air
3. Infection	Pus and sloughing	Nil
4. Healing	Granulation	Nil
5. Soot in upper respiratory tract	Present	Absent
6. Carboxyhaemoglobin in blood	Absent Present	
7. Enzymes	Increase in enzymes	No such increase

The differentiating features of antemortem from postmortem burns are given in Table 22.1.

Burning as a cause of death: The presence of antemortem blisters, finding of particles of soot in air passages, oesophagus, and stomach, and cherry red colour of blood due to presence of carbon monoxide are **certain signs** of death from burning as a result of a conflagration. Their absence suggests some other cause.

The bodies of two badly burned women were recovered following a house fire. The unburned body of a man was found in a part of the house which was not damaged by flames. Subsequent investigation of circumstances revealed that all three had been drinking, when an argument developed during which the man stabbed the women and attempted to dispose off their bodies by setting fire to the premises. To exculpate himself, he went to sleep in another part of the house but succumbed to inhalation of carbon monoxide with blood saturation of 65%. He also had a blood alcohol level of 0.28%. The two women were likewise markedly intoxicated. Autopsy showed that both had died of multiple stab wounds and both were dead before the fire started as evidenced by absence of carbon monoxide in their blood.

Suicide, homicide, or accident: Once the medical officer determines that the cause of death is thermal burns with or without inhalation of toxic products of combustion, the manner of death inevitably will be a matter of careful evaluation of the scene and circumstances of death. If the individual stood in full view in a public place, poured petrol on his clothing, and then lit a match, the manner of death would clearly be suicide. However, if identical remains are recovered from a building which has been deliberately set on fire by another then the manner of death would be homicide. The distribution of burns in most cases is extremely important in relation to the manner of death. Consider for a moment the case of a burnt child. The police may feel that the child has been abused while the parents claim that the child crawled into hot water. If the child has been abused by holding its wrists and ankles and then dipped in hot water, sparing of hands and feet with severe burning of the buttocks will result. If the child crawled into a tub containing hot water, the distribution of burns would be different: burns on the hands, legs, and a small area on the abdomen with sparing of the back and buttocks. In most cases, the water mark of burns can be demonstrated. Careful diagramming of area involved in burns and if possible posturing the child in the position in which the water mark would line up and tell its own story is a very crucial thing to do, if possible, under such circumstances.

Suicidal burning is relatively common among Indian women, mostly on account of domestic worries, cruelty by the husband and in-laws, or because of the problem of dowry or some disease. In suicide, the circumstances are usually evident and perhaps the most frequent method of doing this is to soak the clothes in kerosene and then to set them on fire. It is very difficult to extinguish such flames. Sometimes, suicidal burning is resorted to as a mode of public protest.

Homicidal burning is rare but cases are recorded where fire, kerosene, petrol, hot metals, and corrosive substances have been used with criminal intent. Homicidal cases are fairly common in India mainly due to suspected infidelity of the woman or inadequate dowry. Among adult females, burns are produced usually on the pudenda as a punishment for adultery. The body may then be burnt to conceal the crime. The battering of children in the West may not always be by mechanical violence and a variety of thermal injuries have been reported. Deliberate focal lesions from cigarettes and burning of buttocks and other areas on hot plates and radiator bars are examples of this form of child abuse. If such injuries have occurred at different times suggesting repetitive child abuse, the diagnosis is more certain.

DOWRY DEATHS

Commonly known as *bride burning* cases, these are a bane of the Asian society, mainly in developing countries. Fire accelerants, such as kerosene and petrol are used, the former most frequently, being readily available as domestic fuel. In order to establish evidence for homicidal burning in such cases, it is helpful to collect material from the scene, such as bedding, pillows, carpet, etc., on which kerosene stains may be found; clothing of the offender, if smelling of kerosene; wipings of floor, if kerosene traces are still observed; and soil from the dwelling, if kerosene-stained, etc. These should be sent along with victim's burnt clothing for chemical analysis to the laboratory. The exhibits may be packed in glass jars, if small, or covered in polythene wrappers to prevent loss of kerosene traces, or put in polythene bags, if possible. The smell of kerosene may be masked by odour of burnt clothes in intimate contact with victim's body, or may be too faint on other exhibits which might have been collected after sufficient lapse of time. The detection of kerosene residues on these exhibits is generally not on the basis of free liquid kerosene hydrocarbons, as these have been lost due to burning or subsequent evaporation, but mainly on the basis of solid hydrocarbon residues, such as alkyl naphthalenes present in kerosene. Likewise, leaded petrol, i.e. motor gasoline having anti-knock lead alkyls, would leave a residue of lead, though no petroleum hydrocarbons would be left for analysis. The use of polythene wrappers or containers does not vitiate the chemical-instrumental detection of such solid residues. The general experience is that in most crime cases, involving suicidal or homicidal burning with kerosene, the results of detection of kerosene residues are positive on the victim's clothes in spite of sufficient degree of burning and/or on other articles seized from the scene despite evaporation of the substance. However, in case of negative results in spite of highly sensitive instruments, like gas chromatograph having been used for detection, these should be interpreted with caution. The degree of burning, loss on exposure even of (slowly volatile) solid residues before transmission to the laboratory, improper packing, improper selection of the piece or portion of garment (ordinarily, the whole garment should be sent to the laboratory), etc. may bring in negative results and this should not be misconstrued as fire accelerant like kerosene not having been used. The presence of soot, if any, especially on face and waist, should be given special consideration in such cases.

The *investigation procedure and law* dealing with dowry deaths in India have been made more stringent lately, looking to the gravity of this social menace. The dowry deaths, though mostly involving homicidal burning as described above, may involve homicidal poisoning. It is understood that zinc phosphide (highly toxic, LD50 40 mg/kg) and especially aluminium phosphide (3 gm Celphos tablets containing 56% active ingredient which may be mistaken for a medicinal preparation) are frequently misused in the dowry death cases in rural areas. It is reported that a part of a Celphos tablet may kill a person. Prescribing punishment for dowry deaths (IPC 304B) has been recently enacted. A criminal charge may also be brought under other related sections of the Indian Penal Code, viz. section 498A (causing cruelty to a married woman), and section 34 (more than one person acting with common intent).

Sharada Chikne was cooking food in her home at Irani Chawl, Kurla(West), Mumbai, on the morning of September 26,1998. She was suddenly enveloped in flames, when as alleged, her nylon sari caught fire. Sharada was taken to the Lokmanya Tilak Hospital, Sion, and later during the day was shifted to Masina Hospital, Byculla, where she succumbed to burns on the same day, September 26,1998. There were some disputes between Sharada, her husband Rajesh, and the in-laws. Sharada had even approached a women's welfare organisation (Sakhya) for settlement of those disputes in 1997. The women's organisation suspected foul play because of some previous disputes between Sharada, Rajesh, and his parents. The Kurla police registered a case of dowry death against Rajesh, his father Nivruti Chikne, his mother Suman, and sisters Kamal, Shakuntala, and Aruna, under section 498 A (causing cruelty to a married woman), 304B (causing dowry death) read with section 34 (more than one person acting with common intent) of the Indian Penal Code. (The Times of India, Mumbai, Page 5, November 24,1998).

In view of the increasing number of dowry deaths, the following guidelines have been laid down by the Government of India for investigation of such cases (section 176(1) CrPG), and the law in respect thereof has been suitably amended.

The victim of dowry death is usually a young female in the age group of 18–30 years. She is harassed to an extent as to drive her to commit suicide. Usually, the mode of death is burns but in some instances, mechanical injuries may be inflicted by the husband or his relations; rarely, she may be poisoned (vide supra).

The procedure of examination will depend upon the mode of death, either burns, injuries, or poisoning. In all cases of unnatural death.of a female within seven years of marriage or if she is below the age of 30 years, autopsy has been made compulsory (section 174 (3) CrPC) and in case of death due to burns, it has to be carried out by two medical officers. Section 113A (IEA) deals with presumption as to abetment of suicide by a married woman.

Postmortem burning should be suspected: (a) when autopsy reveals that death has occurred before the fire, (b) there is evidence that death was due to violent means other than fire, and (c) there are unsuspected victims.

Bodies may be burnt after death in order to conceal homicidal injuries or poisoning and for this reason, complete autopsy should always be performed in cases of bodies removed from burning houses. Only where fire charring is extreme, evidence of injury is likely to be obscured. Burns might obscure evidence of strangling with, say a scarf, but not so readily other injuries, fractures or bullets, which may be revealed by radiographic examination. Blood should be preserved for alcohol estimation and chemical analysis where necessary. If it cannot be obtained from heart, bone marrow may be used. Absence of carbon monoxide in blood of a person found dead in a burned house is a strong presumptive evidence that the person was dead when fire began. Presence of unsuspected victim should also arouse suspicion of homicide.

In a charred body of Mr HR, recovered from a burning house, it was possible to infer that he had received several blows about the body and a heavy blow to the skull before he died of burns. As a result of blows, some of the subcutaneous fat cells which had broken loose from the general surface entered the bloodstream in the form of globules. These globules were trapped in pulmonary capillaries and readily identified as such by examining stained lung sections microscopically. It was, therefore, possible to infer that—(1) the deceased suffered violence to some part of his body, and (2) he was alive when the wound was inflicted. When skull was opened, a traumatic clot was found. As a result of violence, the victim had become unconscious. However, he lived long enough after the fire started, to inhale particles of soot in the smoke, and have the circulating blood impregnated with a substantial amount of carbon monoxide enough to cause death before the flames actually reached the body. However, the haematoma caused by violence did not contain any carbon monoxide.

An incident is recorded of an old man known to be smoking in bed resulting in occasional small fires. He was found dead one evening and the cause of death was thought to be fire caused by smoking in bed. However, autopsy revealed a large defect in right parietal bone with extensive fractures of the base of skull, and absence of carbon monoxide in blood sample. The conclusion was that he was dead before fire began and that the fire was set after death to conceal the crime.

Accidents account for a very large proportion of burns. These deaths are seen most frequently in infants, children, the aged, and epileptics. Children are prone to burning by playing with matches or lighted material, interfering with a kitchen fire, or falling into hot water. Accidental deaths occur when persons who are under influence of alcohol or drugs are unable to escape when a fire breaks out. The combination of intoxication and smoking in bed is extremely dangerous, and the latter practice is prohibited in many American hotels. Clothing catching fire is another frequent cause of death from burns, especially in young children, and such accidents are common when fire crackers are exploded in festive season. Females, especially women who put on saris, are at a greater risk of burns during cooking.

Since severe burning destroys the usual evidence of death by strangulation, throttling, violence, etc., strong suspicion of homicidal death should be aroused in extensively burned bodies. In short, the possibility of accidental death from fire generally decreases in direct proportion to the extent of destruction of the body by fire.

Spontaneous combustion of the human body cannot occur. On careful investigation, such situations reveal that an ignition source, e.g. stove, electric heater, or open flame, is present near the body, in a closed environment. The source ignites some material, e.g. clothes or bedding whereby a flame hot enough to melt body fat is produced. The material acts as a wick and those parts of the body where there is ample fat burn and then self-extinguish when most of the fat has been consumed, leaving part of one or more limbs intact. It is certainly human combustion but not spontaneous.

Preternatural combustibility is rare. Inflammable gases, such as hydrogen, methane, and hydrogen sulphide, may be formed in the alimentary tract as a result of digestive processes and bacterial fermentation. They may be belched out or let off from anus, and if a flame is nearby, they may ignite causing a burn at the site. During operations on large bowel, when galvanocautery is used, a mild explosion may occur due to ignition of these gases. After death, such gases are produced in abdomen due to putrefaction and if these gases be ignited, a certain amount of burning in region of trunk may occur but complete combustion of body is impossible.

Difficulties in Diagnosis of Death from Burns

A person may be killed by throttling or poisoning. The dead body may then be burnt to conceal the crime and to make it appear like death from burning. Even under such circumstances, a careful autopsy examination settles the issue. The differentiating features of antemortem and postmortem burning as well as evidence in respiratory tract and blood provide valuable clues. Chemical analysis of viscera also helps. Sometimes, determination of cause of death may present an extremely difficult problem. A chain smoker who was under treatment for an extensive myocardial infarct died of a ruptured heart. The cigarette he was smoking dropped on the bed causing fire and consequent postmortem burns on his body. A doctor who performed the autopsy gave "burning" as a cause of death. Suspicion was aroused due to presence of postmortem burns on the body. At re-examination, ruptured heart was found, and the whole episode could be reconstructed in proper perspective.

Q. 22.7. What is a scald? Give its classification and medicolegal significance.

SCALDS (Fig. 22.7)

A scald is an injury resulting from application of liquid at or near boiling point, or from steam. In such cases, only the superficial layers of the skin are affected. The severity of injury depends primarily on the temperature and duration of contact. Burns result in 20 seconds at 131°F, 3 seconds at 140°F, 2 seconds at 150°F, and in 1 second at 158°F. Almost all scald burns

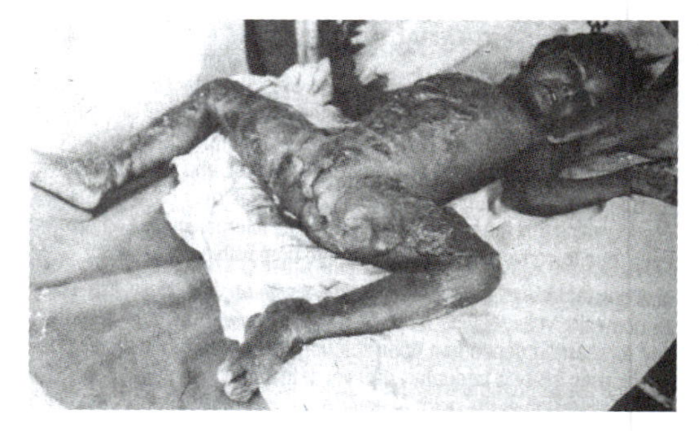

Fig. 22.7: Scalds. This child was accidentally injured by boiling water. The injury is characterised by **extensive area of damaged skin, abundance of blisters, and absence of singeing of hair and charring of the body**

caused by inadvertent turning of hot water tap could be avoided, if the setting of hot water heater does not exceed 120°F.

By its very nature, the injury is likely to be limited to the skin, or mouth and throat when hot liquids are drunk. A greater depth of injury is achieved on contact with liquids, such as hot oil, tar, or molten metals which are many times hotter than boiling water. In these cases, deeper layers of skin are also affected.

The liquid responsible for scalding may be seen on the clothes and body. Sometimes, its smell may be obvious. The skin is soddened and bleached in appearance. Vesication (blistering) is an important feature. Vesicles are abundant along the course of the running liquid. The clothes are usually wet. Burning of clothes, singeing of hair, deposition of carbonaceous material and charring of tissues (common in burns) are not seen. Since the hot fluid or steam is cooled during its passage through the clothing, the distribution of scalds is normally on unclothed parts of the body. Likewise, hot liquid is cooled while being dispersed. Therefore, scalds are severe at places where hot liquid has come into initial contact with skin. As the liquid runs down the body, the degree of scalding also progressively diminishes.

Scars of scalds are much thinner than those of burns and cause much less contraction and disfigurement.

Scalds are *classified* in three degrees:

1. Reddening of skin (erythema)
2. Blister formation (vesication due to increased capillary permeability)
3. Necrosis of the dermis (deeper layer of skin)

Redness appears at once and blistering takes place within a few minutes. The blisters are surrounded by a thin bright red area of inflammation. There is reddening and swelling of the papilla in the floor of the blister. If the blistered skin is removed, it will leave a pink raw surface. If superheated steam is inhaled, the mucosa of larynx and trachea may be necrosed and detached in shreds. Laryngeal oedema may be responsible for death.

The differentiation between antemortem and postmortem blister is already outlined in Table 22.1.

Scalds are usually accidental due to splashing of fluid from cooking utensils or pouring hot water during bath. Children may upset the vessels containing boiling liquids or suck the spouts of kettles containing hot milk or tea resulting in severe scalds of mouth and throat. Boiling water may be thrown with intent to injure or annoy. Deliberate scalding by hot fluid is common in child abuse. A straight horizontal burn pattern across the body or an extremity is always suggestive of forceful immersion.

Q. 22.8. Tabulate the salient distinguishing features of burns from dry heat, moist heat, and chemicals.

OR

Differentiate between burns, scalds and chemical burns.

Table 22.2 describes the salient distinguishing features of burns from dry heat, moist heat/scalds and chemicals.

ELECTRICITY

This subject is dealt with in considerable detail on account of the universal use of electricity and the paucity of awareness of its dangers. It is not unusual to find improperly wired devices in home, a situation which can be easily remedied and danger avoided by having the circuit checked by a circuit tester.

Electric current may be direct or alternating. Alternating current is more dangerous than direct current and the usual frequency of 50–60 cycles (Hertz) per second is extremely dangerous as it can effectively stimulate human muscle and corresponds to the fibrillation frequency of

Table 22.2: Distinguishing features of dry heat, moist heat/scalds and chemical burns

	Dry heat	*Moist heat/scalds*	*Chemicals*
1. Cause	Flame, heated solid substance or radiant heat	Steam or any liquid at or near boiling point	Corrosive acids and alkalis
2. Site	At and above the site of flame	At and below the site of contact	At and below the site of contact
3. Clothing	Burnt and may be adherent to the body	Usually wet but not burnt	Characteristic stains
4. Skin	Dry, shrivelled, charred	Sodden and bleached	Stained, corroded
5. Vesicles	At circumference of burnt area	Most marked over burnt area	Rarely found
6. Red line	Present	Present	Absent
7. Singeing	Present	Absent	Absent
8. Charring	Present	Absent	Present, in case of mineral acids
9. Trickle marks	Absent	Present	Present
10. Discolouration	Skin roasted and charred	Skin bleached	From action of chemical on skin
11. Ulceration	Absent	Absent	Present
12. Scar	Thick and causes disfigurement	Thin and causes less disfigurement	Keloid scar and much disfigurement

the myocardium. Below about 10 hertz, more current flow is needed to stimulate a muscle, and above about 300–400 hertz, there is a similar diminution in muscle stimulation so that by the time a frequency of 10,000 hertz, that is, 10 kilohertz, is reached, far greater current flow is needed to stimulate the muscle.

To understand the effect of passage of electric current through the body, it is possible to draw a very close analogy to the behaviour of water in pipes. Voltage (electromotive force) or the force of electricity to travel from one place to another can be likened to the pressure in pounds per square inch or kilograms per square centimetre. Current flow is usually expressed in amperes which is analogous to gallons or litres per minute. Resistance expressed in ohms is much the same as diameter of the pipe which may be affected by internal corrosion and narrowing by chalky deposits.

Q. 22.9. Briefly describe the effects of the passage of an electric current through the body.

The effect of passage of a current through the body depends upon: (1) strength of the current (amperes), (2) length of exposure, (3) direction of the current, (4) resistance offered, and (5) preparedness for shock.

Current: The degree of damage to tissues is proportional to the quantity of electricity flowing through them per unit time. It should be measured in coulombs, i.e. the product of amperes and seconds. A *coulomb* is the quantity of electricity which flows from a steady current of one ampere in one second. So far, amperes are usually accepted as an index of current flow, and the formula in common use is: amperage = voltage/resistance.

The ordinary domestic supply varies from 110–120 volts (USA) to 220–240 volts (India). The quantity varies from 5 amperes of a lightning circuit to 15 amperes of a power circuit. Death from less than 50 volts is not common. Since voltage is usually constant, the most important factor in electrocution is resistance. Thus, if the resistance is low (e.g. wet skin), the strength of the current is automatically increased, and death may ensue. A current of 1 milliampere (mA) will produce tingling and 5 mA muscular tremors. Between 9 and 16 mA, there is risk that the individual will be unable to release an energised conductor. At about 50 mA, muscular control is lost and there is paralysis. Between 75 and 100 mA, there will be ventricular fibrillation, and at 2 amperes and above, ventricular arrest.

The circuit fuse does not blow until 15,000 to 20,000 mA, that is, 15 to 20 amperes are flowing. It is, therefore, obvious that it will not protect a human being. It is installed to protect the wiring. If, therefore, the fuse is replaced by a nail or a thick piece of copper wire to prevent it from blowing, there is risk of overheating and fire. In highly sophisticated circuits, ground fault circuit interrupters are installed. They monitor the current flowing through the supply wire, compare it with the amount returning through the second wire, and if the disparity exceeds about 5 mA, which is potentially dangerous to a human being, the circuit is automatically disconnected.

Exposure: A low ampere current, if passed through the body for a longer time, may cause a fatal result. A fatality from a domestic supply will ensue, if the passage of a current through the body is not broken, as for example, when an unearthed metal apparatus is grasped and the victim is unable to release the grip.

Direction: A electrical current follows the routes of least resistance which are the blood filled vessels, and may thus reach the heart even though it does not lie in a straight line between entrance and exit. Cardiac disease would, therefore, appear to predispose to death even after a low voltage shock.

Resistance: The skin when dry is a bad conductor of electricity, the normal resistance being about 1000–1500 ohms. When it is wet, the resistance is reduced to about 200–300 ohms, and effective area of contact is also increased. This fact accounts for the greater danger in fitting electrical apparatus near a bath. The better the contact between a person and the 'earth' when an electric shock is sustained, the more dangerous will be its effects. As for example, a person standing with dry shoes on a dry surface may scarcely notice a shock which could prove fatal to some one standing with bare feet on a wet surface. *This fact must be kept in mind in claims that injury or death is impossible as all safety measures are provided for.*

Preparedness for shock: One is quite familiar with the difference in nervous reaction between a tap on the shoulder which is expected and one which is not expected. It is said that a man who frequently used to hold a 240 volts live wire for a bet in a public house was instantly killed when he inadvertently leaned against a defective switch. He was not prepared for the shock.

Q. 22.10. Give a brief description of various kinds of electric burns.

There are three kinds of electric burns, viz: (1) contact burns, (2) spark burns, and (3) flash burns, depending on the nature of contact and strength of the current. All of them have one feature in common. Their depth is greater than the surface appearance would suggest, and severe sloughing of tissues may occur later. In addition, burnt areas may have non-singed hair suggesting that the heat effect was from an internal and not an external source, due to conversion of electricity into heat within the tissues.

A **contact burn** is due to close contact with an electrically 'live' object with domestic voltage. The damage varies from a small and superficial injury to charring depending upon the time the contact is maintained. A characteristic injury is frequently present at the point of entry and exit. The commonest lesion at the point of entry is a raised blister containing either gas or a little fluid. The lesion is often seen on the pads of fingers or thumb. At the point of exit, the tissues are frequently split in the form of punctured or lacerated wounds (Figs 22.8 to 22.11).

A **spark burn** (Fig. 22.11) is due to poor or intermittent contact with electrical equipment and the resistance of dry skin. The damaged area shows a dry pitted lesion (often very tiny) due to arcing of current from the conductor to skin. A

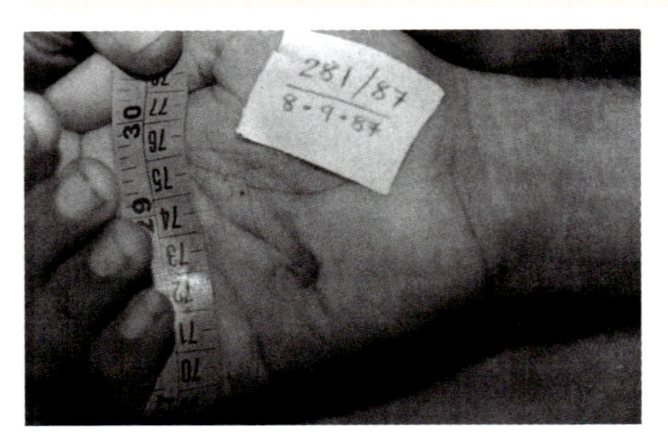

Fig. 22.8: Electrical injury—entry mark

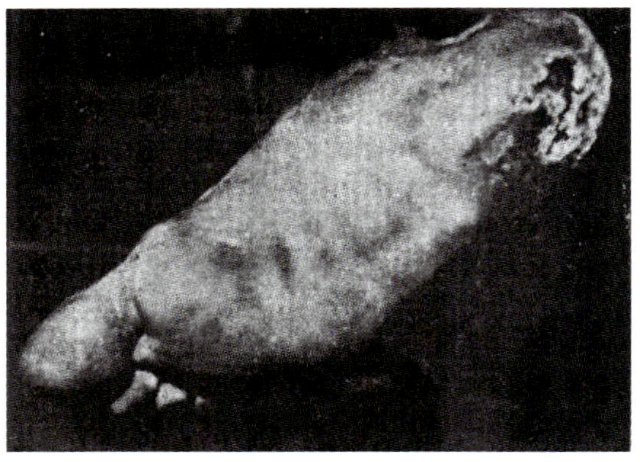

Fig. 22.9: Death due to **electrocution.** This person accidentally touched alive-wire. While there was no injury at the point of entry, an **exit wound** was seen on the right heel as shown in this photograph. (*Courtesy*: Dr J Chandra)

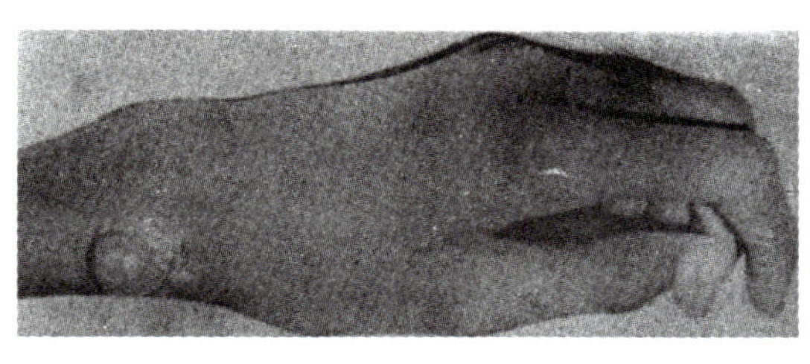

Fig. 22.10: Burn from electric spark on the left wrist of a girl aged 15 years. The burnt area shows a central white zone and surrounding hyperaemia, which in this case, has assumed the form of a vesicle. (*Courtesy*: Dr DR Kothari)

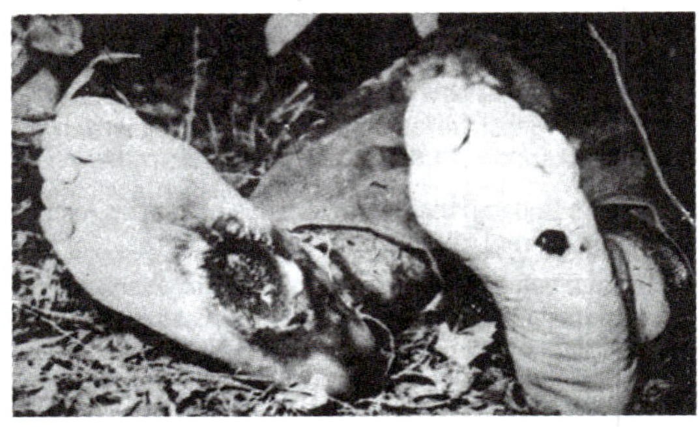

Fig. 22.11: Electrical injury. Wound of entry and exit. This man was wearing rubber shoes. He accidentally placed his foot on live wire carrying a high tension current (voltage 110,000)

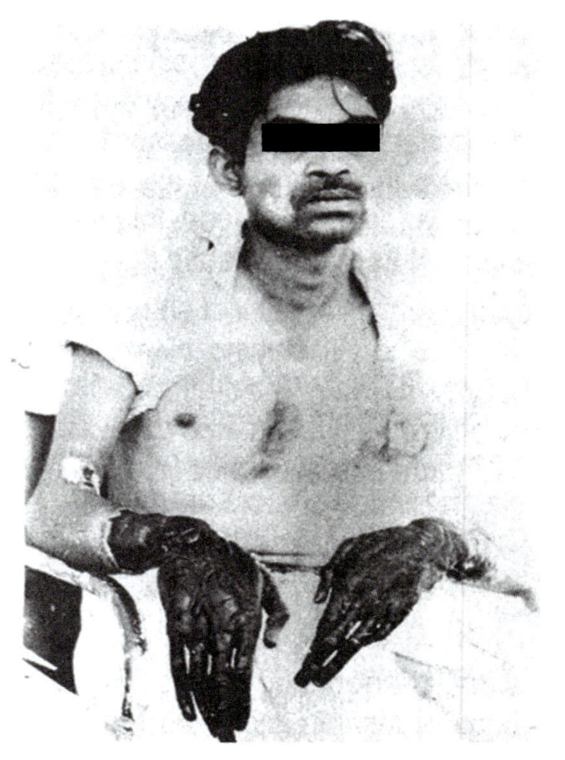

Fig. 22.12: Gangrene of both hands following an electrical shock. Blood vessels are good conductors of electricity. Intense and sustained spasm of the arteries may occasionally occur and lead to gangrene of the affected limb. A small electrical burn is also seen at the flexure of right elbow where the current has jumped across the bend instead of passing round it

yellowish parchment like scab may form with a pale halo round it due to capillary contraction. These lesions may be multiple but still hard to find especially on the calloused hands of a workman and microscopic examination may be necessary to establish their nature. Similar lesions may be found on the soles of feet where metal studs on shoes have arced to the skin.

Flash burns are due to contact with very high voltage lines, that is in excess of 1,000 volts. Since these power lines are not insulated, any direct or indirect contact by a person on the ground (good conductor) results in electrocution. Contact is sometimes accidentally made during kite flying, installing an aerial for radio or television, or while operating some tall equipment, e.g. crane. While the crane is insulated and, therefore, the workmen will not be burnt but a person on the ground who touches the crane will be electrocuted. Flash burns are commonly seen in the lines-men working on the grid system and sometimes in thieves stealing copper wires from high voltage overhead lines.

With very high voltages, there may be actual arcing of current to an approaching person without actual contact occurring. The victim may be hurled from the vicinity by the force of muscular contraction. All types of burns may occur. Actual charring of tissues with carbonisation is common but depending on the degree there may be: (1) brownish discolouration of large areas of skin apart from actual burning, (2) arborescent pattern of lightning burns, or (3) *crocodile skin effect* consisting of *multiple spark burns over large areas of skin*. The temperature generated by an arc current may be in the neighbourhood of 4,000°C.

Q. 22.11. Discuss in detail the characteristics of injuries resulting from: (1) low voltage current, (2) high voltage current.

Low voltage currents are those involving voltages under 1,000 which include a vast majority of electrical circuits encountered in households on a daily basis. High voltage currents are those which involve currents above 1,000 volts. These are confined almost entirely to the transmission of power by way of overhead and underground lines as well as certain industrial situations. However, high voltages may be encountered in the home, e.g. in television receivers and a few other sophisticated modern devices.

Low Voltage Current Injuries

The effect of passage of a low voltage current is different for different pathways, e.g. skin and muscles—convulsions (used as shock treatment in certain psychiatric disorders); lower nerve centres—ejaculation (used for artificial insemination in breeding animals); heart—ventricular fibrillation; and respiratory centre—paralysis.

At the moment of contact, there may be generalized muscular spasm which may cause the victim to grasp the conductor firmly or may throw him some distance away. Sudden death may occur, if the current passes through the heart or respiratory centre. Sometimes, the victim may appear to be dead but may actually be in a state of *suspended animation.* Injuries and after-effects of burns, rather than the current itself, may cause death.

A characteristic burn is frequently present at the point of entry and exit. It may, however, be absent, e.g. when due to an electric blanket or an electrical appliance in use falling into a bath of water. The clothing including headgear, gloves, and shoes, should be carefully examined for evidence of burns on outside as well as inside of garments even though there may be no injury to skin.

The electrical burn is not a true burn but an electrical necrosis. It is called a **Joule burn** or endogenous burn (caused by heat generated by the electric current) in contrast to an exogenous burn which is caused by application of heat. The burnt area is dry, charred, and insensitive. At the site of entry, it is devoid of usual signs of inflammation and red line of demarcation as seen in ordinary burns but instead shows a grayish white ulcer-like opening with everted and corrugated margins and necrosed tissue. It may resemble in shape the object causing electrocution. If the site of entry happens to be the tip of fingers, the skin ridges are flattened and the finger print pattern is lost. Microscopically, there is compression of the stratum corneum and flattening of the papillae of the corium with the occurrence of spaces of varying size giving a lace-like or honey comb appearance. A further differentiating feature between an electrical burn and a thermal burn is that the electrical burn may show a deposit of metallisation, the so-called current pearls, when electrocution results from an electrode. At the site of exit, tissues are frequently split in the form of punctured or lacerated wounds. If exit is at the feet, the shoes may be torn. Microscopically, the exit wound is similar to the entrance burn except for presence of metallisation at the wound of entry. Small lesions may sometimes be found at the flexures of a limb where the current has jumped across the bend instead of passing round it. Gangrene of a part of limb due to intense and sustained spasm of arteries, followed by thrombosis, may occasionally occur. In rare cases, the victim may be completely charred with heat coagulation of muscles (Zenker's degeneration) often with spiralling and fragmentation of muscle fibres.

If recovery occurs, a state of restlessness, irritability, and excitement generally ensues. *The sequelae are important from an insurance point of view.* Angina pectoris may occur immediately or after a few days and may disappear or lead to myocardial necrosis followed by delayed death. Thrombosis of the arteries may lead to oedema and gangrene of limbs. Late effects, such as necrosis and secondary haemorrhage, or disturbance of the central nervous system due to cell degeneration, may arise months after the incident.

High Voltage Current Injuries

High voltage current results in higher flow of current and, therefore, the likelihood of severe burns correspondingly increases. It may also produce injuries resembling bullet, stab, or cut wounds. Small balls of molten metals derived from the metal of contacting electrode, so-called *current pearls,* may be carried deep in the tissues. Analysis of this material for elemental content may identify the offending electrode. If the victim survives high voltage electrocution, conduction of electricity through bloodstream may result in coagulation of blood and blockage of blood vessels leading to gangrene, and consequent amputation. The breakdown of tissues can result in shock and renal failure. If the current should pass through the head, there may be onset of mental changes which may last for several months.

While injuries resulting from high voltage electrocution are usually obvious, the source may sometimes be occult when, for example, an overhead powerline falls on a metal fence which is touched some distance away. A powerline which has fallen into a puddle of water can be extremely dangerous. One falling on top of motor vehicle will affect the occupant when the attempts to leave the vehicle.

Q. 22.12. What is the cause of death in electrocution? How will you investigate a scene of electrocution? Briefly describe the autopsy findings.

Cause of death: Death may result from instant shock due to vagal inhibition. With domestic supply, it usually results from ventricular fibrillation. With high voltage, death is usually due to electrothermal injury or from paralysis of respiratory

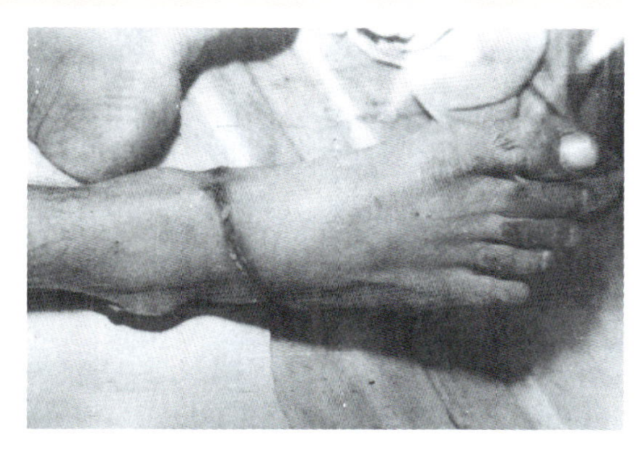

Fig. 22.13: Electrical injury by hightension cable wire. (*Courtesy*: Dr Iliyas Sheikh, Surat)

centre. In extensive burns, the fatal outcome may be due to haemoglobinuric nephrosis.

Investigation: The examination of the scene, the wiring, and position of any electrical apparatus in relation to the deceased are of vital importance. The outlet into which the appliance was plugged should also be checked with a circuit tester. Normally, the current flows from the supply wire into an appliance, causes it to operate, and returns through another wire. The coverings of the appliance and its wires separate the individual from the electric current. However, if the coverings of the apparatus or its wires are defective or if the skin is wet, e.g. when a person is taking bath, and accidentally comes in contact with the defective appliance or touches the wire, or a heater falls in the bath, a pathway is opened up for electricity to pass from the supply wire into the person and thence to the ground, instead of returning by way of another wire in the usual manner. The result is electrocution. Once this concept is understood, the investigation and evaluation of electrical injuries becomes much simple. In as much as no burns are visible in approximately 35 to 45% of persons dying of low voltage electrocution, an enquiry into the circumstances of death and examination (autopsy) of the electrical device in use at the time is essential for proper investigation. Besides, a person sustaining a fatal electrical injury has about 15 seconds of consciousness and activity before collapsing from ventricular fibrillation and during this period, he may shout or unplug the offending equipment. If and when help arrives, there may be no sign that the equipment was operating and the true cause of death may well be overlooked. Transient faults in the equipment can be extremely elusive during the investigation process. It is not commonly realised that in simple appliances, such as an electric lamp, the switch is usually designed to be in the input wire. If through some error the polarity is reversed, the current may be present on many of the lamp components with resulting danger of electrocution. The following examples highlight some of these principles. On a number of occasions, in cases of electrocution, there are no burns; the autopsy is essentially negative; and only the evaluation of circumstances and examination of the appliances in use by Volt-ohm meter (VOM) helps to arrive at the cause of death.

A person dies in a bath tub and an electric device is found therein. Autopsy of the victim alone cannot tell if the device was pushed in deliberately (homicide), or pulled in deliberately (suicide), or fell in when touched (accident). Only an enquiry and investigation into the circumstances may provide an answer. It is not commonly realised that dropping of an electrical appliance, which is turned off, into water can cause electrocution. Though the current flow inside the device has stopped, the terminal of the attached electric cord is still charged.

A number of men were working in automobile repair department in the section dealing with repairs to body work. A coin operated machine was recently installed to provide non-alcoholic cold drinks. A few days later, when one of the workers went near it and inserted the coin he suddenly collapsed. Autopsy was essentially negative. Another worker reported feeling a shock when he touched the machine. When a volt meter was applied to the device it was found that the entire metal casing was energised to 110 volts 60 hertz (cycles). Subsequent examination revealed that the supply wire was touching the inside of the machine and the grounding wire intended to connect the frame of the device to earth as a precautionary basis had been disconnected. It only needed a workman with wet hands and standing on a damp floor to touch the machine for sufficient current to flow to cause death.

Two men were working under a house to remove old flooring which was to be replaced. They were cutting the floor with a reciprocating electrically powered saw with a metal casing. When the first man was tired, the saw was disconnected. After a brief spell when the device was reconnected and cutting resumed by the second man, it was only a few seconds when he shouted for help saying that he got a shock. The co-worker pulled out the plug and attempted to revive his companion but this was unsuccessful. Examination of the body did not reveal any natural disease nor any electric burn though the history was strongly suggestive of death due to electrical injury. When the electric saw was first connected to a test device there was no evidence of any malfunction. Further examination revealed that a piece of adhesive tape was wound round the handle. Removal of this tape revealed that two of the three screws designed to hold the two halves of the handle together were missing and the third one was loose. Removal of half the handle showed that the electric supply wires had become worn and it was only when the handle was squeezed by the operator that the metal frame made contact with the electric wiring and then the current would pass to the worker. The worker was a good conductor as he was sweating because of hot weather and he was standing on damp ground beneath the building. The device should have been operated on three wires but the safety or ground wire had been disconnected and the device was working only on two wires.

A workman was drilling a hole in the ceiling using an older style tool with a metal casing and a number of ventilation holes for cooling. Accidentally, a fragment of the metal from the ceiling fell down, made its way through the ventilation hole, short circuited the internal armature to the casing, was partially melted by the flow of electricity, and then thrown free, leaving little or no evidence of its presence. The workman was thrown away from the tool by muscular contraction and injured. A complete disassembly of the tool by a knowledgeable person was necessary to demonstrate the small burns and contact points, such as a small bead of melted metal, within the tool itself, to investigate the circumstances of the injury.

Postmortem appearances: One of the difficulties encountered in investigating electrocution deaths with currents of low voltage is the absence of any evidence of injury either on clothing or on body. Electrical discharge marks on hands of workmen are commonly missed. Where electrocution is a possibility, the flexor surface of the fingers should be carefully examined, if necessary, by breaking the rigor or cutting the flexor tendons at the wrist. In a number of cases, the injury may be confined solely to clothing. Current marks may be hidden inside oral cavity from accidentally putting live wires in mouth or drinking water from a fountain in contact with electric current. Injuries may be found in urethra as a result of voiding urine on high tension wires. Such injuries are generally missed.

The external signs of electrocution may vary in extreme cases from complete absence of any visible marks to charring of the deceased with heat coagulation of muscles. In a number of cases, external lesions are usually observed at sites of entry and exit of the current. These lesions may be absent when there is extensive contact between the skin and conductor. The special characteristic features of these lesions have already been discussed: The face is usually calm, eyes congested, and pupils dilated. Rigor mortis develops early and postmortem lividity is well developed. Internally, there are no findings which can be considered characteristic. Pulmonary oedema and general appearances of asphyxia may be present. Cerebral oedema and perivascular haemorrhages have been described. Injury to bones sometimes occurs.

Q. 22.13. Discuss in detail the medicolegal significance of death from electrical injuries.

The diagnosis of death from electric shock depends on the history, local lesions of entrance and exit of the current, when present, and absence of any other cause of death. Most deaths are accidental and are caused by contact with broken and non-insulated wires in faulty domestic or industrial appliances.

Iatrogenic **accidents** may lead to a charge of **negligence.** Traumatic injury may be sustained during convulsions and deaths have been reported from electric shock itself from *electroconvulsive therapy* in the treatment of mental disorder. *Invasive* diagnostic or therapeutic *procedures* requiring use of electricity are associated with their own hazards; when skin or mucous membrane is penetrated, the resistance of skin is eliminated; since blood is an excellent conductor of electricity, death may be caused by misapplication of very low intensity currents.

In hospitals, it is important that stringent safety precautions are observed because of the circumstances. From time to time, patients and their relatives may wish to bring electrical appliances, such as radio, tape recorder, or television in the hospital. In the hospital environment, normal protective mechanisms may have been bypassed, for instance, by passing a wire through the skin directly into the heart. In such a case, far lesser current flow can pose a threat to heart rhythm. There are on record instances in which a nurse or attendant has walked to the patient's bedside with an electrical appliance and the patient promptly collapsed just because sufficient current flowed and made its way directly to the heart by way of such device.

Pacemakers to control heart rhythm are increasingly in use and it is possible that some designs may be affected by microwave radiation from domestic and restaurant cooking devices. It is always advisable to remove the pacemaker from a deceased person and to refer it to a testing facility to determine if it was functioning properly, and if not, whether the placement of electrode was correct.

A person found dead and apparently drowned in a swimming pool is a potential victim of electrocution, if the pool has underwater lighting. From time to time, other swimmers report experiencing tingling sensation while in water and this should alert the investigating officer. One can encounter, for example, an instance in which the underwater lighting is working but the earth or ground wire has been disconnected leading to electric discharge through water within the pool if a fault should develop or water leak in the wires.

Particularly unpleasant injuries not necessarily resulting in death can arise from the misuse of starter or booster cables used when the battery in one vehicle is used to start another in which the battery is discharged or worn out. It should be noted that there is a proper sequence and procedure for connecting the cables which depend on the design of vehicle and whether the electrical system is a positive or negative ground "earth". If it is not done properly, it is possible for hydrogen liberated within the battery to explode and spray the persons with sulphuric acid.

In recent years, the search for an ideal weapon, one that will produce incapacitation but negligible risk of death, has led to the development of a number of electrical devices for law enforcement officers and the police. The weapon is designed to generate high voltages at very low current flow, just sufficient to stun or incapacitate but insufficient to injure. Misuse of such a device can cause death, if improperly applied or used with malicious intent. It will paralyse the individual to a degree that breathing is impeded.

In the field of demolition and mining, blasting caps are used to initiate explosion of the main charge through a pair of electric wires exposed at one end. They may act as a receiving aerial and if a radio is operated too close, it may initiate an explosion and cause an accidental mishap. For this reason, radios are not allowed within a certain distance where blasting is in progress. However, such an explosion may sometimes be deliberately set off.

Nowadays, in some places, aluminium wiring is used instead of copper. The problem arises in its use with receptacles and terminals designed for use with copper wiring since aluminium behaves differently from copper in terms of tendency to expand, corrode, and creep, known as tendency to relax under stress. If the installations are made correctly using appropriate terminations, there is no problem but the mixture can result in local generation of heat, flickering of lights, intermittent connections, and fire.

Cases of **suicide** by electric shock have been recorded. A wire is connected to an appropriate portion of the body and the switch turned on. Alternatively, one may climb a transmission pole and touch a high tension wire.

Homicide, though rare, is possible. An electric shock may be given in malice. A handle in a bath may be energised. The execution of judicial sentence of death in certain western countries is carried out by electrocution. The condemned person is strapped to a wooden chair. One cap-like electrode is placed over his shaved scalp, moistened with a conducting paste, and the other on one leg. An alternating current of 7.5 amperes at a pressure of about 2,000 volts is passed through the body for about a minute and repeated once again for a similar period to ensure that life is extinct. In death from such high voltage electrocution, third degree burns are found at the site of contact between the electrodes and skin. The brain is heated to 63°C and vacuolation around the blood vessels has been noted.

Difficulties in Diagnosis

From time to time, it is tempting to calculate the current which might have flowed from a high voltage source through some unfortunate individual. Naturally, under such circumstances, it will be necessary to determine from the electric company the voltage involved. Suppose the company informs that the individual was injured by contact with a 7, 200 volt line and you think that you will be able to make your calculations on your own. This is not possible for a majority of investigators and physicians as they are not familiar with the behaviour of multiphase circuits. The voltage which is quoted is very often between the particular wire and ground or earth, whereas the voltage between wires would be equal to square root of 2, that is, 1.414 times greater on two phase circuits, and square root of 3, that is, 1.732 times greater between individual wires of 3 phase circuits. These factors are sufficient to give a very misleading picture. Therefore, when in doubt, it is advisable to consult a knowledgeable electrical engineer.

A person may be killed by throttling or poisoning. Electric burns may then be caused on his fingers so as to make it appear like death from electric shock. In such a case, even microscopic examination of the lesions is not of much use to differentiate antemortem from postmortem electric burns. Only a careful postmortem examination for evidence of injuries and chemical analysis of viscera for evidence of poisoning always help.

LIGHTNING

Q. 22.14. What is lightning? Describe the injuries caused by lightning.

A natural electric discharge in the atmosphere is called lightning or lightning flash. From time to time, individuals die as a result of being struck by lightning and the possibility of such a death may be overlooked unless certain practical factors are kept in mind. Sound travels about a mile in 5 seconds in a thunder storm at average altitude. Thus, if a flash is seen and then after 10 seconds the thunder sound is heard, it means that the discharge is approximately 2 miles away from the observer. However, when the distance is more, e.g. if the thunder sound is heard after about 30 seconds, it may not be possible to associate a particular flash with a particular sound with the result that the actual cause of death/fire may be misinterpreted, especially in a sparsely populated area. Grass and forest fires caused by lightning strike may thus be misinterpreted and so also death of cattle taking shelter under trees.

For instance, a boy is found lying next to his bicycle at the side of an unpaved road, the bicycle is not particularly bent or damaged, but his clothes are torn and he shows a number of injuries consistent with having fallen from the bicycle. In such circumstances, suspicion may be aroused that he was lightly struck or deflected by the draft of a passing vehicle whereas in fact he could have been struck by lightning. If the person making the initial examination assumes that the death was traffic related, the possibility of lightning could conceivably be overlooked unless he is familiar with the signs and circumstances of lightning strike.

It is important, therefore, that though fatalities from lightning are not common, all those who may be called upon to deal with cases of violence or sudden death understand the bizarre phenomena which accompany it. The appearances closely resemble those produced by criminal violence, as for example, disarranged torn clothing, split skin, fractured bones, and a variety of curious skin markings. Arborescent marks or filigree burns, looking like branches of tree on the chest, green in colour due to copper and haemoglobin reaction and magnetisation of metallic objects (iron) on the body of the victim help in diagnosing leghtening death.

Q. 22.15. Describe the mechanism of injury in lightning strikes. Mention the safety precautions. Briefly give the symptoms, signs, cause of death, postmortem appearances, and medicolegal aspects.

Mechanism of injury: Lightning is an electrical discharge from cloud to earth through an object. It liberates terrific amounts of electrical energy. The electric current is direct, not alternating, of about 20,000 amperes and about 100–1000 million volts. A flash lasts about 1/1000th of a second. Although a flash appears to be a single strike, research has shown that very often multiple strikes occur both from cloud to earth and earth to cloud in such rapid succession that it appears as one. The charge may be conducted by trees or metal objects in contact with living persons. When the path of lightning to earth is impeded by a poor conductor, violent damage at once takes place. The direct effects are as follows:

1. *Burning by heat* due to resistance: Burns may appear as zigzag lines. As moist skin offers less resistance than dry skin, they are often found in moist areas and folds of the skin. If blisters are formed, they are due to electrolytically formed gas than from burns.
2. *Arborescent marks* due to the passage of electric current: These marks are so called because of their appearance like that of a branching tree. They are due to

rupture of the smaller blood vessels at several places giving rise to ecchymoses with an arborescent pattern. These markings fade with time.

3. *Fusing and magnetisation of metallic articles,* such as rings, spectacle frames, pen-knives, keys and watches, due to tremendous heat which is liberated and due to the electrical discharge. Nylon clothings are melted. *These are useful signs eliminating suspicion of foul play.*
4. *Physical damage,* such as violence and torn clothing by being at the centre of the thunder clap (blast effect), if the electrical discharge finds its way through the feet, the skin may be ruptured at the point of exit and the shoes may be torn. The ear drums may be damaged due to sudden over pressure (air expands when heated).
5. *Cardiac failure* due to the passage of a current.
6. In those who survive, *development of intense oedema of skin at point of current entry.* This is probably due to paralysis of local capillary and lymphatic vessels as a result of electrical injury to nerve supply of vessels or to vessels themselves. The resulting dilatation of blood vessels allows fluid to escape and local oedema to form.

Lightning, as opposed to more conventional form of electrical current, passes normally along the outer surfaces of a hollow conductor, and thus persons in the building are relatively safe from electrocution. Occasionally, persons inside a building may be affected when lightning strikes a chimney or television aerial and passes down through a living room. Most deaths have taken place when a tree or other form of shelter beneath which a person is taking refuge is struck.

Safety precautions: Persons who spend a lot of time outdoors should remain indoors when significant storms are nearby. When outside, they should seek shelter within a protective structure, e.g. a building. One should avoid standing in open doors and windows, and near indoor fire places with open chimneys. Electric equipment should be avoided or turned off or else the wires may conduct a part of the lightning to the user. If caught outdoors, shelter should be sought in caves, depressions in the ground, valleys or an area at the foot of a cliff, and if this is also not possible, shelter may be taken beneath short trees adjacent to tall trees since it is the taller trees that will be struck first. Metal articles should be avoided and so also isolated trees. If in flat areas, one should stay away from hill tops, wire fences, and small boats in the middle of flat bodies of water as they accord greater exposure. Surprisingly, a metal bodied car or lorry is not all that bad place for shelter because if the vehicle is struck the charge will travel over the surface of the vehicle rather than come through it and strike the occupant. This of course would not apply to open vehicles.

A local lobster fisherman was found dead in his small boat when the boat was observed travelling in circles. When it was boarded and brought to a halt, it was found that he had gaping lacerations along right side of his lower jaw and in both clavicular areas coming down toward upper sternal area. These lacerations were an inch and half wide, about an inch in depth, and between six to nine inches in length. Initially, it appeared that some crime had been committed; however, examination disclosed that there was evidence of lightning strike: his keys were magnetised and showed evidence of arcing of current; he was wearing a metal neck chain with a yellow metal medallion and vaporised metal was found within the wound. It was, therefore, possible to infer that he had been struck by lightning while in his boat, the moisture on and around his neck had vaporised at the moment of strike and produced lacerations, and the melted portions of the metal found in the tissues came from the neck chain and medallion. The cause of death was, therefore, determined to be lightning strike and the manner of death accident.

Symptoms and signs: Lightning stroke usually causes immediate unconsciousness. Even when an individual is more remote from the flash, concussion may result. All lesions found in high tension current may be present and Pritchard explains them on the basis of development of *electrostatic forces.* These are forces which develop when the body is charged with high voltage current. They exert mechanical repulsion between all similarly charged particles and cause lesions. Even sudden violent displacement of persons from one another is accounted for by such electrostatic forces. The most trivial lesions are streaky surface burns which involve only the epidermal layer of skin causing erythema with pattern like branches of a tree and, therefore, known as **arborescent markings.** The injuries caused by lightning manifest as various type of wounds, fractures of bones, and thermal injuries. Rupture of tympanic membrane is not uncommon. In view of enormous energy involved, the injuries are more diffuse and the most strange phenomena may be observed.

Cause of death: Death is due to electrothermal injuries from high voltage direct current, or involvement of the central nervous system with paralysis of cardiac or respiratory centre.

Postmortem appearances: The lesions already described may be present on the body or rarely absent, and only the inside of clothing may exhibit burns. Rigor mortis appears soon after death and passes off quickly. Internally, pulmonary haemorrhages and oedema, parenchymal necrosis, changes in central nervous system, and fractured bones may be found.

Medicolegal aspects: The diagnosis of death from lightning depends on exclusion of any other cause of death; history of thunderstorm in the vicinity; and possibly other evidence of lightning, such as damaged trees, dead cattle; appearance of various lesions on the body, such as arborescent markings, fractures, wounds, torn clothes, burns on body and underneath metal articles on clothing; and fusing and magnetising of metallic articles, such as pen-knives and watches. Deaths from lightning stroke are invariably accidental.

EXPLOSIONS

An explosion has been defined as a phenomenon resulting from sudden release of energy which is then dissipated by a blast wave, by translocation of objects in space, or by the generation of heat.

Explosions are caused when an explosive device is detonated or an explosive is accidentally ignited. Explosives are substances which have a shattering or brisant effect when they explode. Such effect is utilised particularly for blasting in quarrying, mining, tunnelling, and demolition work, where large masses of solid material have to be broken up quickly and cheaply.

Dynamite is the term used nowadays in a wider sense to comprise various explosives consisting of nitroglycerol, ammonium nitrate, saltpetre, and aromatic nitro compounds. Their shattering power is reduced by adding common salt.

Dynamites are exploded by a detonating device. There are various types of detonating devices depending on the purpose for which the explosive is required. For ordinary blasting as used in quarrying, mining, tunnelling, etc., the main explosive is detonated by striking a blasting cap containing a small amount of highly sensitive ignition powder. The detonator may be designed for electric detonation. Alternatively, a detonator may be ignited by a slow burning fuse, generally called safety fuse. Modern artillery shells are complex and fitted with relatively elaborate fuse. The detonation equipment is designed to ignite the charge by impact and/or after a certain predetermined length of time **(time fuse).**

Q. 22.16. Discuss the medicolegal significance of injuries from explosions (by explosive devices)

The injuries from explosions are mainly due to four factors, viz: (1) blast or shock wave, (2) flame or hot gases, (3) flying missiles, and (4) anoxia.

Blast: When a high explosive is detonated, it produces a *shock* wave which spreads concentrically from the explosion site, at the speed of sound, causing a tremendous blast effect. Anything in the immediate vicinity is completely obliterated. A body thus exposed is so shattered that its study will be limited to identification of remains and of foreign metallic and other matter embedded in fragmentary tissues which provide some clue as to the source of explosion.

If the explosion occurs at a slightly greater distance, it may blow the victim against a wall or toss him through the air causing blunt force injuries.

Depending upon the effect of pressure waves, blast lesions ensue. The parts of the body most readily damaged by blast waves are the hollow organs which contain gas or air, such as lungs, bowels, or ear drums, and others which are most fragile and easily displaced, e.g. brain and abdominal viscera. Intracranial haemorrhages occur with considerable frequency.

Blast effects are easily transmitted in water. The hollow viscera are mainly prone to underwater explosions and since there are no injuries due to secondary impacts, the victim presents very little external but massive internal damage.

Flame or hot gases: Burns or burning of the body may occur due to flame or hot gases of explosion. Burns produced by explosion in mines or from gun powder are usually very extensive and accompanied by blackening and tattooing due to unexploded particles of powder being driven into the skin (Fig. 22.14).

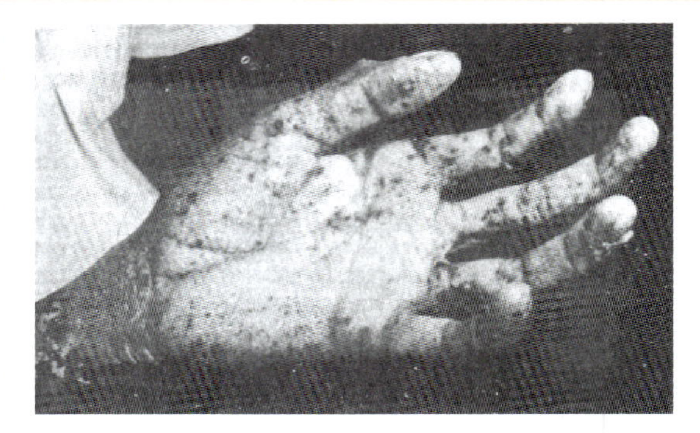

Fig. 22.14: Tattooing effect on hand due to explosion in a mine. The tattooing is due to unburnt particles of powder which have been driven into the skin. (*Courtesy*: Dr PG Paul)

Flying missiles: As a result of explosion, flying pieces of explosive debris may be driven through air against the skin causing abrasions, bruises, lacerations, and ragged perforations of various sizes and shapes. The parts of body most affected by flying fragments may indicate the position of detonation. As for example, explosions at ground level may cause serious damage to feet, legs, and lower parts of the body of nearby victims. Letter bombs for obvious reasons cause most damage to hands, face and front of the body.

Anoxia: Depending on contents of the explosive, various gases may be liberated. Such gases include carbon monoxide, nitrous and nitric gases, hydrogen sulphide, sulphur dioxide, and hydrocyanic acid. Their inhalation may result in poisoning (histotoxic anoxia).

Cause of death: Death may result from a variety of causes. The body may be completely disintegrated as a result of blast effect while in the vicinity of blast. When one is some little distance away from it, death may result from burns, blunt force injuries, and falling debris. In still other cases, death results from asphyxia due to inhalation of products of combustion, and in some cases, from crush syndrome. A victim may be little injured but may die from profound shock. Another possible cause of rapid death after explosion without severe injury is systemic air embolism.

Postmortem appearances: When the body is badly shattered, there will be problems of identification. Apart from injuries due to burns, flying missiles, falling debris, and the effect of poisonous gases liberated by the explosive, the blast wave produces scattered foci of small haemorrhages in brain, lungs, bowel, and mesentery. Passive hyperaemia and/or oedema cause serious secondary brain and lung lesions. Intracranial haemorrhages, contusion of brain and heart, and aortic injuries, ruptured stomach and bowel, and bladder injuries have been described.

In the investigation of injuries or deaths as a result of explosive device, it is necessary to have good photographs and sketches of the scene. Complete body X-raying of victims is imperative before clothing is removed. Fragments of bomb may be trapped within clothing or body tissues. Clothing and foreign material removed from clothes or body should be carefully preserved for laboratory examination. The recovered tiny fragments may reveal the bomb mechanism. Time spent on such search is usually rewarding. Distribution of injuries should be carefully drawn on a diagram to facilitate subsequent assessment of the relationship of explosion to the individual.

Medicolegal Aspects

Injuries from bombs used to be mainly accidental in the past. Their homicidal use is now common with the use of bombs by terrorists to destroy specific targets, such as government buildings, bridges, public transport vehicles, premises occupied by their opponents, etc. The bombs are used by them indiscriminately and without warning to terrorise the community, or as booby traps against law enforcement officers. The composition of the bomb varies. If home made, it may consist of sugar-sodium chlorate mixture and carried in a box or parcel to the premises to be attacked or left in the transport vehicle according to plan. Impact bombs and bombs with timing devices, known as time bombs, are very complex. A time bomb may be left at some place to coincide with someone's arrival at a particular time when it may explode. Alternatively, an impact bomb may be thrown or left at a venue of a meeting or nearby where it may explode as a result of friction when someone walks over it or a car passes over it. While explosives are notorious for their destructive effects, incendiary bombs, like Napalm, primarily cause burns. The *Molotiv Cocktail* is another variety of incendiary bomb. It is designed to be hand thrown. It is used by terrorists and in guerilla warfare. When a material suspected to be an explosive is discovered, the area should be cordoned off at once and examination of material including defusing undertaken by an expert.

The deliberate destruction of commercial aircraft in flight has important medicolegal implications. The main difficulty facing the investigators is to distinguish sabotage from explosive decompression due to structural failure. In the event of sabotage being shown to be the cause of accident, the responsibility for insurance passes from the "All Risk" insurers to those underwriting "War Risks". In these days of advanced technology, any unexplained disaster in air should be suspected to be due to sabotage until the contrary is proved. The major parts of the aircraft would be found scattered over a very wide area without any logical pattern in case of mid-air explosions caused by sabotage.

23 Violence in the Home

In the present society which is gradually becoming over-democratic it is natural that the old values of sanctity of life, respect for elders, and affection for family members should change and personality problems develop due to consequent stresses of life. These ultimately result in violence. The main victims of this changing pattern of life are children, wives, and the elderly. *The common pathological features of all types of non-accidental violence in the family are multiple injuries of varying age and aetiology.* Various terms are attached to the various forms of violence, such as battered babies, battered wives, battered elderly, etc., though battering is not the only feature.

BATTERED BABY (CAFFEY SYNDROME)

Q. 23.1. Give a detailed account of battered baby or Caffey syndrome from a medicolegal point of view.

The battered baby syndrome is a term used to define a clinical condition in young children usually under three years of age, who have received non-accidental violence or injury, on one or more occasions, at the hands of an adult responsible for the child's welfare. Six patterns of child abuse are recognised: (1) physical abuse, (2) nutritional deprivation, (3) sexual abuse, (4) intentional drugging, (5) neglect of medical care or safety, and (6) emotional abuse.

The victim is often an unwanted child, an illegitimate child, or a child whose father's paternity is doubted. The precipitating factor is usually a cry which interferes with either a parent's sleep or the outing, or their television programme. Battering is the result of sudden loss of temper under such and allied circumstances. The type of persons involved in child battering have frequently a low IQ. Some have a history of family discord, long-standing emotional problems, and financial stress, while others have a history of criminal background. Recent reports suggest that such parents had received similar treatment from their parents in their own childhood.

Injuries are commonly multiple, although all are not necessarily severe. They usually follow a pattern with one or more localised bruises on the head quite inconsistent with a simple fall, or bruises on the face, trunk, and extremities consistent with grip marks. Tearing of the frenum of upper lip and of alveolar margin of gums to stifle cries is commonly encountered.

Major injuries which prove fatal include head injuries, e.g. fractured skull and subdural haematoma, or visceral injuries, e.g. ruptured liver and mesenteric haemorrhages. Clinical and radiological evidence may be obtained that injuries have occurred at different times.

The syndrome must be considered in any child: (1) in whom the degree and type of injury is at variance with the history given, (2) when injuries of different ages and in different stages of healing are found, (3) when there is purposeful delay in seeking medical attention despite serious injury, (4) who exhibits evidence of fracture of any bone, subdural haematoma, failure to thrive, soft tissue swelling or skin bruising, or (5) who dies suddenly.

In the Eastern culture, babies are considered as gifts from God and cases of battered baby syndrome are rare. However, instances of ill-treatment of young children **(child abuse)** who work as domestic servants are not uncommon. While child labour is prohibited, instances are on record when employers have beaten such children with sticks or branded with a pair of hot torigs. The crime comes to light only when such children complain to some one who knows their mother tongue.

Autopsy

The history may be completely misleading as to circumstances surrounding death. The external and internal examination should, therefore, be very thorough and supported by sketches, photographs, X-rays, microscopic sections of pertinent lesions, and toxicological analysis. Photographs should include views of the entire body showing distribution of injuries and close-up views showing their details. Colour photographs will show difference in ages between the various bruises.

External examination: Clothing should be examined for the degree of its cleanliness and state of repair. Weight, height, head circumference, and state of nutrition should be noted. The state of nutrition is assessed by subcutaneous fatty depot, and degree of diaper rash and its sequelae, such as infections, scarring, or loss of pigmentation. Special note should be made of any evidence of insect infestation including fresh bites or secondary infection in more recent bites.

The external examination should also record any instance of suspected trauma, either remote or recent, noting in precise detail size, shape, location, colour, and degree of healing. Asymmetry of head or extremities, tearing of frenum of upper lip, burn scars, swelling of joints, and congenital deformities should be specially looked for. Fresh burns from cigarettes ends may be found. Careful examination of eyes may reveal subconjunctival haemorrhages, detached retina, and even displaced lenses. Genitalia should be specifically looked at for evidence of sexual abuse, such as pinching of scrotum and application of ligature to penis in males and concealed puncture wounds in females. Search should be made over the exterior of body for any type of trace evidence that may afford a clue to the actual assailant or the nature of weapon used.

X-raying of whole body is essential to reveal skeletal changes, either due to battering or natural disease, e.g. scurvy or osteogenesis imperfecta. If subtle changes due to battering are noted, another X-ray after evisceration is more revealing. A certain minimum number of photographs is essential: (1) the child in its clothing, (2) all external injuries, and (3) injuries and abnormalities found during examination.

Internal examination: Head: The scalp should be examined for bruising which is more easily felt than seen. Any type of brain injury may be found. Careful differentiation between coup and contre coup lesions will help to determine, if the injury resulted from a moving object striking a fixed head or a moving head striking a fixed object. Cerebral oedema is more common, than in the adult, after head injury. A number of deaths after head injury in a child are caused by raised intracranial tension without skull fracture, meningeal haemorrhage, or visible brain injury. Cerebral oedema at autopsy is diagnosed by a heavy brain, flattened gyri, obliterated sulci, and slit-like ventricles. Direct violence to the head and sometimes shaking can cause bleeding into the vitreous, dislocation of the lens, and retinal detachment. If there is history of impairment of vision, the posterior two-thirds of the eye globe can be removed and inspected by opening the orbits through the anterior cranial fossa.

Neck: The neck should be dissected following a V-shaped incision and the structures examined layer by layer. Any obstruction or lesion of the airway should be noted. Injuries to hyoid, thyroid cartilages, and soft tissues are looked for.

Chest and abdomen: The important lesions to look for are fractures of ribs, vertebral bodies, and ruptured viscera due to blunt injuries. Localised fractures of ribs are due to impact with a blunt object and multiple fractures are generally due to compression. Such fractures may be attributed to resuscitation. In most cases, the different ages of rib fractures help to rule this out. *Nobbing fractures* are specially looked for. They are due to the assailant holding the child with both hands and shaking it violently, thus fracturing ribs on both sides close to the spine, and giving a nobbing appearance when the ribs begin to heal. The viscera that commonly rupture are mainly central and include duodenojejunal junction, pancreas, and liver. Many of these injuries result from compression, e.g. kneeling on the child, which crushes the midline structures against the spine and ruptures hollow viscera due to raised intraluminal pressure. Microscopic study of all fracture sites and organs is essential to assist dating of episodes of trauma.

Extremities: Avulsion and chipping of epiphyses at the knee and elbow and raised periosteum with subperiosteal calcification are particularly suspicious. Any asymmetry of arms or legs indicate fracture or deep haemorrhage. *Deep incisions are necessary for adequate examination* to show damage to soft tissues, extent of haemorrhage, and deep scarring which is evidence of prolonged maltreatment. Incisions on soles of feet may reveal unsuspected haematomas.

After the autopsy is over, it is advisable to have a re-check for injuries when some obscure injuries and imprint of wounds caused by grip marks may be observed.

Autopsy findings likely to be mistaken for child abuse are:

1. Mongolian spots (on buttocks)
2. Swelling of wrists and ankles from too tight clothing
3. Neck creases simulating ligature mark
4. Facial mottling
5. Resuscitation bruises on the chest

Laboratory data: Routine histological examination should be conducted of every organ system (especially the immune system and the gastrointestinal tract) to rule out the possibility of underlying, obscure, constitutional, debilitating disease which might lead to progressive wasting and failure to thrive. DNA testing may become routine in future.

Bacteriological cultures of blood, lung, and cerebrospinal fluid are necessary when infectious disease is suspected as a contributory factor of death.

Adequate specimens should be taken for routine toxicological analysis. Sometimes, the child is chronically given alcohol or anti-histaminics to provide continuous sedation. In addition, role of lead as a primary or contributing factor in the death of these children should be ruled out. Lead poisoning may occur in children from eating paint on cribs, beds, or toys.

Only when all facts concerning the circumstances are available and autopsy is complete, it is possible to give an opinion on the cause and manner of death.

Q. 23.2. Write short notes on: (1) battered wives, (2) battered elderly.

BATTERED WIVES

The use of corrective force against the wife is still rife in all cultures and even socially acceptable in some cultures. Busuttil defines a battered wife as a woman who has suffered demonstrable and repeated physical injuries at the hands of the man with whom she lives or from the father of one of her children. Domestic discord, often in families with numerous children, and drunkenness are mainly responsible. It is not commonly realised that the offence is encountered in all socioeconomic groups, and the possibility of wife battering cannot be dismissed irrespective of the social standing of the batterer in the community. The injuries are multiple bruises on exposed parts, viz. the face and arms, but may also involve breasts and occasionally the vulva, especially when the husband is suspicious of the wife's fidelity. Sometimes, the tip of the nose may be cut off.

Generally, women have accepted, since times immemorial, ill-treatment at the hands of men they live with. They are reluctant to bring to light their personal problems for fear of shame and disgrace. Some prefer just to leave home whilst others indulge in self-hurt, poisoning, or attempted suicide by burning, drowning, etc. The offence comes to light when the victim requires hospital treatment or dies under suspicious circumstances.

In India, battering and torture are common in certain communities where the customs of the society require the bride to bring dowry and the amount of dowry is considered inadequate. The Government of India have enacted special legislation to counter this problem (refer dowry deaths in the Chapter 22 on Thermal Injuries). Under Domestic Violence Act, married women in India are provided protection with deterrance to erring in laws family members including husband.

The chief offender is the man whose moral restraints are thinned by personality disorder, character defects, emotional stress, drinks, gambling, and instigation by family members. Temporary lapse of sanity resulting in homicide is an important factor when the man suspects the fidelity of his wife and kills (over-kills) her.

A visit to a doctor or emergency department for a trivial unexplained injury should arouse the examiner's suspicion of wife battering. When a woman complaining of unendurable behaviour at the hands of her husband seeks help from a medical practitioner, he has an important role to play. He must include in his report an assessment of injury to her health by physical or other means.

Times are now changing. Marriage is now being considered as a partnership of equals, and not a holy life long alliance—come what may. The battered woman syndrome cites instances where a cycle of abuse can eventually lead a woman to kill an abusive husband to escape his continuous threats and beatings (*see* Chapter 33 on Mental Illness—irresistible impulse).

BATTERED ELDERLY

The concept of joint families has almost disappeared now with the result that respect for the elderly is decreasing day by day. They are considered as a source of burden or a hindrance to the independence and privacy of the younger generation. They are, therefore, neglected, often insulted, and occasionally battered. However, in the latter case, it is rather difficult to differentiate between non-accidental and accidental injuries.

The elderly suffer from decreased skin elasticity, loss of flesh, atheromatous changes in their arteries, osteoporosis, and even hypovitaminosis. The most trivial trauma may result in bruising, subdural haematoma, fracture of neck of the femur, and so on.

In due course, the presence of the elderly becomes intolerable and there are instances where financial incentives, such as inheritance of property, insurance claims, etc., have hastened their death. A number of these deaths are likely to be premature. However, they are usually classified as natural, on account of their age. *It would appear that old age home is now becoming a safer place for them as a practical reality of life.*

Elder battering includes forced starvation, physical and psychological naglect, demanding for property and money, assaults, etc.

Battered Husbands

Battered husbands are also not uncommon. Many financially dependent husbands and weaklings are subjected to psychological and physical torture.

Section 5

24. Impotence, Sterility, Sterilisation, and Artificial Insemination
25. Virginity, Pregnancy, and Delivery
26. Legitimacy
27. Natural Sexual Offenses
28. Unnatural Sexual Offenses
29. Sexual Perversions/Deviations
30. Abortion
31. Infanticide
32. "Cot Deaths" or SIDS

24

Impotence, Sterility, Sterilisation, and Artificial Insemination

IMPOTENCE AND STERILITY

Q. 24.1 Define the terms impotence, sterility, fertility, and frigidity. Mention the circumstances in which a person may plead impotence in a court of law.

Impotence means inability of a man to perform or woman to take part in sexual intercourse. **Sterility** means inability on the part of the male to procreate or on the part of the female to conceive children. **Fertility** is the opposite of sterility. It means the ability to procreate or conceive children. **Frigidity** means inability to respond warmly to sex arousal stimulus. In the act of sexual intercourse, the male partner is the active partner while the female partner is generally the passive partner. It is the male who has to develop and maintain penile erection sufficient enough to indulge in the act. If as a result of the act, the ovum is fertilised, the woman bears a child, provided successful embedding of the ovum can occur. Therefore, in general, impotence refers more to the male and sterility to the female. Members of either sex may be either impotent or sterile or both. The difference between the two must be clearly understood. Impotence gives a just cause for nullity of marriage, sterility gives no such cause.

A decree was refused in a case where a woman, before marriage, had undergone an operation, which rendered her sterile though competent to have intercourse.

The question of impotence or sterility in either sex may arise in civil and in criminal cases.

In **civil cases,** this question may arise in the following circumstances, viz: (1) Nullity of marriage and divorce, in those cases where marriage cannot be consummated on account of impotency, and (2) in cases of contested paternity and suits for adoption, when the alleged father pleads impotency and/or sterility as his defence.

In **criminal cases,** this question may arise in the following circumstances, viz: (1) Accusations of adultery, rape, and unnatural sexual offenses, where the alleged condition of impotence is put forward as a defence (2) in claims for damages where loss of sexual function is claimed as a result of an assault or accident, and (3) in cases where a sterile woman puts forward a supposititious child to claim property.

Q. 24.2. Describe the procedure for examining and certifying an alleged case of impotency/sterility.

Examination of a case of impotency: In medicolegal cases, the examination should be undertaken only under instructions from a law enforcement authority. Before examining, care should be taken to obtain informed consent. A general examination should then be made followed by systemic examination. Special attention should be directed to the nervous system and an assessment of the mental condition should be made. The private parts must be examined for sensations, injuries, or malformations, and it should be determined whether there is any impediment to intercourse and whether it is permanent and irremediable. A remediable impediment does not give cause for nullity of marriage. It should also be ascertained, if the impotence existed prior to marriage as impotence occurring subsequent to marriage does not constitute a ground for divorce. Under section 3 of the Bombay Hindu Divorce Act, 1947 (Bombay Act No. XXII of 1947), a husband or wife may sue for divorce on the ground that the defendant was impotent at the time of marriage and continues to be so at the time of the institution of the suit, and is, therefore, incapable of fulfilling the rights of consummation of marriage. The incapacity, however, (1) must have existed prior to marriage, (2) must be permanent, and (3) is incurable by an operation even if the individual is willing to submit to it.

A man may be potent with one particular woman but not with another (impotence quoad hanc). Legally, marriage is a contract between two persons of opposite sex, which presupposes on the part of each the lawful use of the body, or in other words capability of the fulfillment of the act of physical union, by coitus. Therefore, in a divorce suit, the potency must be ascertained in relation to the married partner only.

If the medical officer finds that the person is normal in all respects, i.e. physically well developed, his genitals are normal, his secondary sex characters are also well developed, and any obvious cause of impotence is excluded, he is justified in certifying that there is nothing to suggest that the person is impotent. Accordingly, **an opinion can be given only in a negative form** that there is nothing found on examination which would prevent the consummation of marriage.

Cases of alleged impotency from disease or following trauma, or electric shock requiring medical evidence, often cause difficulty.

A mill worker suffered from avulsion of two-thirds of his penile skin when his dhoti got accidentally caught in the strap of a running machine. He was admitted at the KEM Hospital, Bombay, where skin from his thigh was grafted and he made uneventful recovery. After discharge from the hospital, he complained of impotency. The following opinion was given: Impotency means loss of erection. The centre for erection lies in the spinal cord. In this case, the vertebral column and the spinal cord are not injured in the accident. Erection is due to the blood rushing into the cavernous tissues of the penis. In this case, the cavernous tissues are also not injured. When he lifted his dhoti to allow for examination, his testes automatically went up indicating that the nervous system is normal. In view of these findings, there is nothing to suggest that the person has become impotent as a result of injury. However, he could have developed psychological impotence which generally clears off after some compensation is received. (Extract from expert opinion given by Dr CK Parikh).

Examination of a case of sterility: In the male, the semen is examined. It is desirable for him to abstain from coitus for a week. The sample is obtained by masturbation or prostatic massage and examined within 2 hours for spermatozoa. In the female, attention is directed to the development of uterus, and patency of fallopian tubes. Any defect of vagina is likely to be obvious. An opinion can then be given on the basis of available findings.

Q. 24.3. Discuss the causes of impotence and sterility in the male.

The causes of impotence and sterility in the male may be classified as follows: (1) age, (2) malformations, (3) local and general diseases, (4) injuries and addictions, (5) psychic causes, and (6) operations.

Age: The power of coitus (erection) commences earlier than puberty though spermatozoa are not usually found then. Accordingly, a boy is sterile but not impotent before puberty. In general, one should depend more on the development of the private parts of the individual than on the age, for in cases of precocious development, the sexual organs may be well in advance of the development as a whole; also, poor physical development of the sex organs is a common cause of impotence. There is no upper limit regarding potency or sterility of men. As long as live spermatozoa are present in the seminal fluid, the individual is presumed to be fertile.

Malformations: Absence or non-development of the penis constitutes absolute impotence. Certain malformations of the male external genitals, such as intersexuality may prevent intercourse. Conditions, like hypospadias and epispadias, may prevent proper deposition of semen in vagina and result in sterility. Males in whom the testes have not descended are not necessarily either sterile or impotent, but sterility is not uncommon amongst such individuals.

Local and general diseases: Acute diseases of the penis, such as gonorrhoea, syphilis, etc., may cause temporary impotence. Large hernia, elephantiasis or large hydrocele may impose a mechanical obstacle to coitus and produce temporary impotence. Many debilitating diseases, such as acute fevers, diabetes, and pulmonary tuberculosis cause temporary impotence. Neurological conditions, such as GPI, tabes dorsalis and tumour of the cauda equina may result in permanent impotence. Certain endocrine disorders, such as hypopituitarism, produce sexual infantilism and impotence. Diseases which may result in sterility include mumps, testicular atrophy, and diseases of the testes and epididymis.

Injuries and addictions: Injury to head, spinal cord, or cauda equina may result in impotence. Chronic alcoholism and addiction to narcotics, like opium, cause impotence. Excessive and continued use of certain drugs, such as bromides, cocaine, marihuana, and tobacco, may also produce impotence. Injury to testicles will in time cause sterility. Occupational exposure to lead may lead to sterility. Exposure to X-rays, without proper protection, may also lead to sterility, either temporary or permanent.

Psychic causes: Cases of impotence in the male from psychological causes greatly outnumber all other causes except at the extremes of life. These conditions may be temporary or permanent. Fear of impotence or fear of inability to complete the act may also cause temporary impotence (first night impotence in the bridegroom) but is soon overcome. Emotional disturbances are responsible for weak erection or non-erection and consequent impotence. Sexually perverted people may be impotent. Disgust for the act may result in impotency. Dislike for the partner may preclude an erection and prevent coitus and this is of special significance in cases of nullity of marriage and divorce where potency is to be ascertained in relation to the married partner only.

The Honourable Mr Justice Coyajee at the High Court at Bombay passed a decree of nullity of marriage in the divorce suit of RR Saraiya *vs* Kusum Madgavkar, on the ground that the husband was impotent as regards his wife, although he was generally potent (impotence quoad hanc).

Operations: Partial amputation of the penis as a surgical treatment for certain conditions of the glans penis renders a male impotent. Vasectomy renders a male sterile but not impotent. Lithotomy operations may sometimes cause sterility from injury to the ejaculatory ducts.

Q. 24.4. Discuss the causes of impotence and sterility in the female.

The causes of impotence and sterility in the female are the same as those in the male, viz: (1) age, (2) malformations, (3) local and general diseases, (4) injuries and addictions, (5) psychic causes, and (6) operations.

Age: As the woman is the passive agent in the sexual act, there can be no limit to the oldest age at which she could be potent to allow the act. Commencement of fertility, as a rule, is indicated by the commencement of menstruation. Menstruation is not a sign of bodily maturity but in most cases, it is merely a sign of puberty and ovulation. As a rule, fertility ceases at menopause with the cessation of menstruation though an occasional exception may occur. After menopause, the woman becomes sterile but not impotent. Post-menopaused women may lobe interest in sexual intercourse.

Malformations: Absence of the vagina or one which is rudimentary in character is often found in cases of inter-sexuality and is the cause of permanent impotence in the female. The presence of a very firm or imperforate hymen and adhesions of the labia may be a temporary barrier; none of these conditions render the woman necessarily sterile or impotent. The conical cervix and the absence of the uterus, ovaries or fallopian tubes produce sterility but not impotency.

Local and general diseases: Local diseases of the genital organs in the female do not ordinarily produce impotency provided the vagina is normal. Owing to the painful and spasmodic contraction of the constrictor muscles of the vagina at the time of intercourse, *vaginismus* may lead to temporary impotency. Loss of the ovaries by disease or operation, obliteration of the tubes (chronic salpingitis) and various pathological conditions of the genital organs cause sterility. Further, conditions, like rectovaginal fistula, disorders of menstruation, leucorrhoea and acid discharge, may contribute to it. General diseases which so frequently cause impotence in men have no effect on women, as the function of the female is passive. Thus, a woman suffering from paraplegia can become pregnant.

Injuries and substance abuse: As in the male, occupational exposure to lead, or exposure to X-rays without proper protection may lead to temporary or permanent sterility. Chronic alcoholism and abuse of narcotics, such as opium, may also lead to sterility.

Psychic causes: Whereas in men, the impotence resulting from psychological causes is passive leading to non-erection, in women it is of an active nature leading to spasm of the vagina (vaginismus) precluding intercourse. The condition may be caused by fear, disgust, emotion or excessive irritability of the vaginal mucosa.

Operations: Ligature of both the fallopian tubes or any operation that disrupts the patency of both fallopian tubes results in sterility of the female but not impotence. Hysterectomy also leads to sterility.

Q. 24.5. Comment on: (1) sterilisation, (2) artificial insemination, (3) test-tube baby, (4) surrogate motherhood.

STERILISATION

This is a procedure which renders a person (male or female) sterile without any interference with potency. The purposes for which it is employed are: (1) As a family planning measure, to limit the size of the family, (2) as a therapeutic measure, for the health of the mother—(a) to limit the additional strain of looking after a new-born, especially if the mother is suffering from some chronic disease, such as pulmonary tuberculosis, chronic nephritis, diabetes, or valvular disease of the heart, or (b) if the act of delivery poses a danger to her very existence, as for example, if she has a contracted pelvis and she requires each time a caesarian section for delivery, (3) as a eugenic measure, to prevent children with physical or mental defects being born, as is being done in some countries, and (4) for convenience, when done for any other purpose.

The sterilisation in the male is effected by vasectomy. The operation is simple, and does not involve loss of work-time. After vasectomy, the patient should be advised to refrain from intercourse for two months or longer till such time when two consecutive sperm counts are negative.

The sterilisation in the female is effected by ligature of both fallopian tubes. A simple technique is to visualise the pelvis through a peritoneoscope and cauterise the isthmal end of the fallopian tubes.

Before sterilising an individual: (a) a written consent from both the husband and wife is essential, and (b) if the sterilisation is for contraceptive purposes, that is as a family planning measure, it is desirable to restrict the operation to those who are over 30 years of age and who have at least two children, one of whom is a male. In respect of consent, the sterilising surgeon must inform the spouses that—(1) there is no absolute guarantee of sterility after the operation, and (2) the procedure may prove irreversible. The consent form which is signed by the spouses may contain this information to avoid future controversy.

ARTIFICIAL INSEMINATION

Artificial insemination (AI) may be defined as the deposition of semen in the vagina, the cervical canal, or the uterus by instruments to bring about pregnancy which is not attained or is unattainable by sexual intercourse. The seminal fluid used for this purpose may be either from the woman's husband or from a donor. The procedure is known as AIH (artificial insemination homologous) in the former and AID (artificial insemination donor or heterologous) in the latter. In order to side-step certain psychological and legal issues, the husband's semen may be mixed with that of the donor (AIHD), so that there is a technical possibility that the husband may actually be the father of the child. The usual practice is to deposit one ml of semen just above the internal os by means of a sterile syringe, at or about the time of ovulation, i.e. 14th day after menstruation. The semen should be collected by masturbation, preferably after a week's abstinence, and used within about 2 hours. The method has been resorted to under the following circumstances: (1) when the husband is impotent but fertile, (2) when the husband is sterile, (3) where there is Rh incompatibility between husband and wife, and (4) when the husband is suffering from some hereditary disease so as to prevent mentally or physically handicapped child being born. In the first case, AIH is practiced, while in the next two, AID or AIHD, and the last one AID.

Precautions to be Taken by a Doctor

No special precautions are necessary in cases where AIH is practiced. The following precautions are essential in cases where AID is practiced:

1. The knowledge and full consent of both spouses are essential. The consent must be in writing.
2. The identity of the donor and recipient must not be revealed to each other nor should the donor know the result of insemination.
3. The donor must be below the age of 40, not related to either spouses, and should have children of his own. In race and

characteristics, he must resemble as closely as possible the husband of the woman to be inseminated.

4. The donor must be in robust health both physically and mentally. He should not be suffering from any hereditary or familial disease. The medical examination should exclude such diseases as tuberculosis, diabetes, epilepsy, endocrine dysfunction, and psychosis, and should include Wassermann reaction and Rh grouping.
5. The donor must be screened for AIDS antibody initially at the time of donation and be retested after three months. The semen should be frozen and not used until the result of the second test is known.
6. The wife of the donor must agree for donating semen for the purpose of insemination and the semen should be obtained from an act of masturbation.
7. A female nurse should be present when the insemination procedure is carried out.
8. The doctor who administers AID should avoid delivering the child because he knows who the true father is but cannot give this information in the birth record of the child as it would amount to perjury on his part.

Legal Problems

In cases where the difficulty arises from the impotence of a husband who is nevertheless fertile, it would seem that artificial insemination with the semen of the husband (AIH) can be regarded as a justifiable and unobjectionable procedure. However, the birth of a child in wedlock as a consequence of such insemination does not constitute evidence of proper consummation of marriage.

When for any reason. AIH is not possible and artificial insemination is done with the semen of an unknown donor (AID), the position is radically different from the above. The legal issues arising therefrom are as follows:

a. There is danger of litigation against the doctor following the birth of a defective child.
b. The husband is not the biological father of the child and, therefore, the child is illegitimate. By adoption, legitimate status can be obtained.
c. The illegitimate child is not the rightful successor to the father's property.
d. The maintenance and custody of the child in the event of divorce would raise complex issues.
e. There is risk of incestuous relationship between the offspring and children of the donor.
f. The process of AID can certainly be regarded as an adulterous act not only by the woman concerned but also by the donor, if he himself was a married man. If the husband was unaware of the matter, he will almost certainly be entitled to use his wife for divorce and the practitioner for damages.

Artificial insemination, except in animals, is not yet popular in India. The law in India is, therefore, not clear on the various legal issues arising from AID. However, the consensus of opinion is as follows:

a. For all practical purposes, the husband is accepted as the father of the child. The child is therefore treated as legitimate, and entitled to inherit parent's property.
b. The recipient is not guilty of adultery because there is no physical union in the form of coitus (Section 497 IPC). For the same reason, the donor is not guilty of adultery.
c. Since the 'act' is performed with the consent of both spouses, it cannot be a ground for divorce.

While the practice of artificial insemination by a donor must be strongly discouraged, married couples who want a child under such circumstances should be urged to adopt one. The practice of AID or AIDH may lead to psychiatric problems in both the husband and wife. Even the child may suffer mental trauma when he comes to know about the method of his birth.

TEST-TUBE BABY

The common abnormality leading to sterility in the female is the failure of the ovum to reach the uterus. In some of these cases, the technique of in vitro fertilisation (test-tube baby) may offer a chance of child-bearing. The process consists of removing a mature ovum from the wife fertilising it with the husband's sperm in the laboratory, and implanting the resultant zygote in the uterine cavity.

SURROGATE MOTHERHOOD

Surrogate motherhood is a scientific freak between the process of re-implanting (test-tube baby) and adoption. In this process, the in vitro fertilised ovum is implanted in the hired uterus of another woman or another woman's ovum is fertilised with the sperm of the barren woman's husband. The resultant infant is passed on to its biological father and his wife at birth. The procedure raises many legal, ethical, and social problems. Nonetheless, the procedure in demand with the changing role of women, who now hold important positions in commerce, industry, science, and politics, and would naturally find it inconvenient to bear a child. As of now there is no law controling issues connected to surrogacy in India.

NEW FERTILITY TECHNIQUE

This technique permits any man, no matter how few, misshapen, or immobile his sperms are, to father a child. It involves the direct injection of a single human sperm into an ovum in a petri dish. The transfer is done with a pipette to hold the ovum and special glass needles to inject the washed sperm. The method requires extraordinary skill and costly equipment with the result that it is very expensive at present. However, its astounding success has lead to an entire industry for such in vitro fertilisation labs, which treat couples who had been told that the man was hopelessly infertile, and thus also avoid the complex problems of AID. The technique is developed by Dr Andre C Van Steirteghem of the Brussels Free University in Belgium.

Q. 24.6. What is mitochondrial transfer and three parent baby?

In place of faulty mitochondrial DNA of a would be mother, a healthy mitochondrial DNA by donation from another women is introduced. This is carried out to facilitate prevention of inherited conditions like heart problems, liver failure, brain disorders, blindness and muscular dystrophy. This is the three parent in vitro fertilization where babies are borne from genetically modified embryo, having DNA from a mother and father and a female donor. Britain has legalized the three parent IVF techniques. This is an example of the technology utilization to produce designer babies by genetic engineering.

25

Virginity, Pregnancy, and Delivery

VIRGINITY

A virgin (virgo intacta) is a woman who has never had any **sexual** intercourse. **Defloration** means loss of virginity.

Q. 25.1. Describe the signs of virginity. Include a detailed note on hymen.

The **signs of virginity** in a healthy woman are seen in the genitals.

Genitals: The labia majora are rounded, firm, elastic, and completely close the vaginal orifice; their lower portions fuse in the midline to form the posterior commissure. The labia minora are two thin folds of skin within the labia majora. They are soft, small, pink, and sensitive. Their lower portions fuse in the midline and form a fold called fourchette. The depression between the fourchette and hymen is called fossa naviculars. The clitoris is small. The vestibule (space between the labia minora) is narrow; and the fourchette and posterior commissure are intact. The fourchette and fossa navicularis disappear after rupture of the hymen leaving a more open vulva below and behind. The mucosa of the vagina is rugose, reddish in colour, sensitive to touch, and its walls are approximated. The hymen is intact.

The **hymen** (Fig. 25.1) is a membranous structure about 1 mm thick. It varies in position, con-sistency, structure and shape. In children, the hymen appears as a taut membrane when the thighs are separated. When examined in lithotomy position, the hymen in a small girl appears to be situated deeply because of the rotundity of the labia majora on account of their excessive fat content. Therefore, it may escape injury in attempted rape on them. As the girl approaches puberty, the hymen enlarges and gradually appears as a fold of mucous membrane when the thighs are separated. Shortly after puberty, it reaches the adult form, being situated at the orifice of the vagina and partially closing it. In consistency, the hymen may vary from a thin parchment-like membrane to a firm and fleshy or tough and cartilaginous one well supplied with blood vessels. Its structure may be unyielding or elastic and easily distensible. The normal hymen lies between these extremes in consistency and structure. It is supplied with blood vessels sufficient to cause recognisable though not severe haemorrhage when it is ruptured. It is not sufficiently distensible to admit the male organ without rupture. In the unruptured state, it barely admits the tip of the little finger. The usual shape is annular or semilunar, i.e. crescentic with *the broader part lying posteriorly*. It may be imperforate, leaving no opening; cribriform having a number of small openings; or septate having two openings. The edge may be straight or partly folded, and sometimes fringed or fimbriated (Figs 25.2 and 25.3).

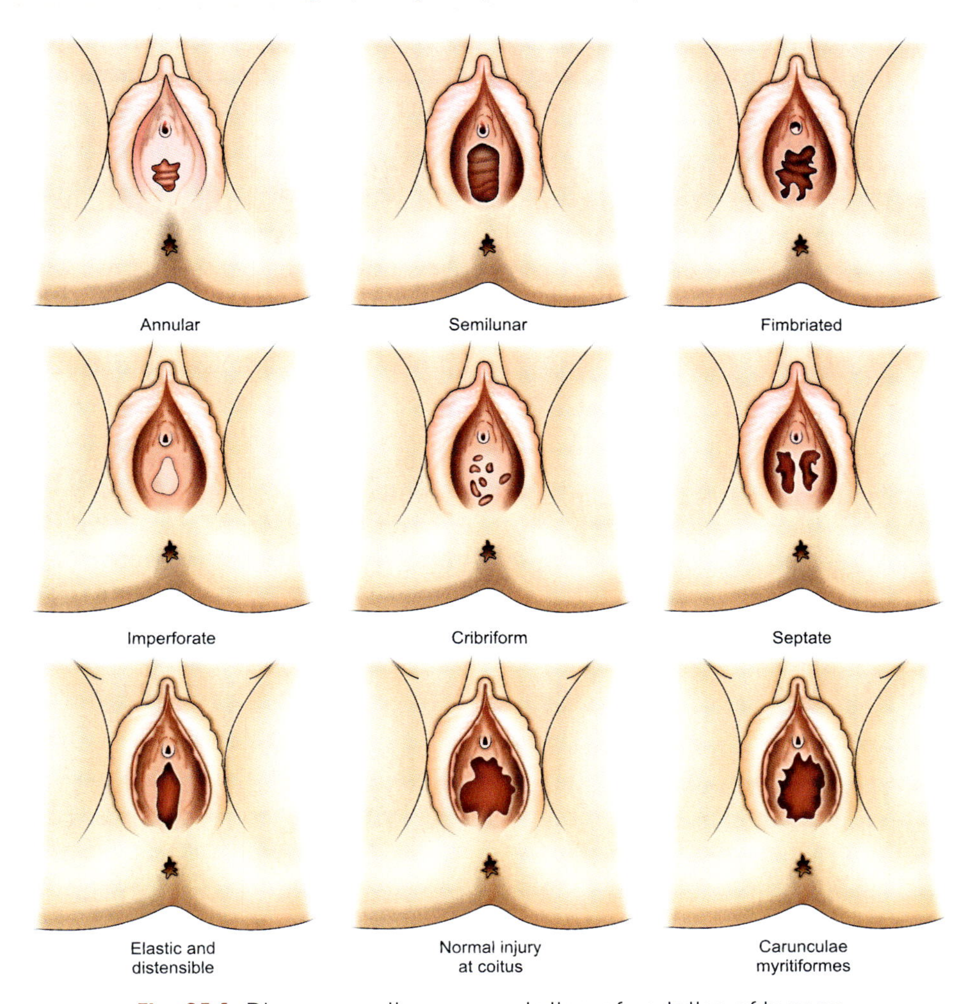

Fig. 25.1: Diagrammatic representation of varieties of hymen

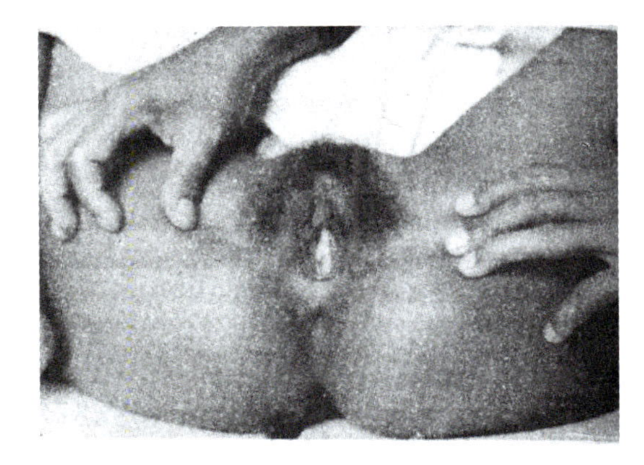

Fig. 25.2: Vaginal examination in lithotomy position. A case of kidnapping. The hymen shows tear at 8 o'clock position

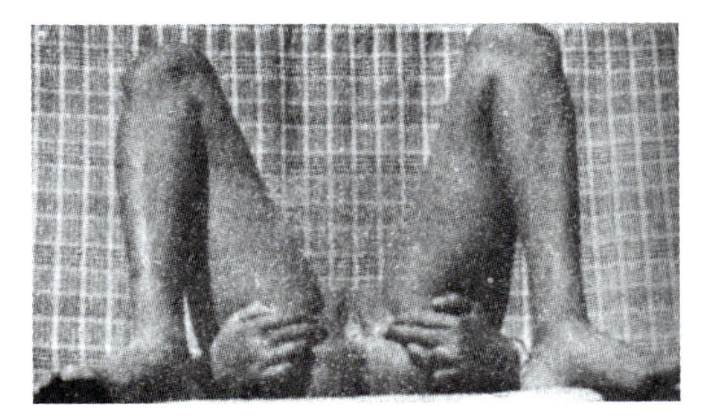

Fig. 25.3: Normal appearance of hymen in a virgin. The hymen barely admitted the tip of the little finger. (*Courtesy*: Dr GB Sahay)

The absence of these characteristics does not necessarily indicate habituation to sexual intercourse, since masturbation, scratching due to irritation, trauma, sanitary tampons, and gynaecological examination may affect the virgin condition.

The hymen is usually ruptured at the first coitus, and at first only presents a torn appearance. With frequent intercourse, the opening of the hymen is enlarged and after the birth of a child, the hymen is completely lost, its presence being represented by several small knobs of tissue known as carunculae hymenales or myrtiformis.

The *principal signs of virginity* may thus be **summarised** as: (1) an intact hymen, (2) a normal condition of the fourchette and posterior commissure, and (3) a narrow vagina with rugose walls.

Q. 25.2. Discuss the circumstances under which the question of virginity would assume importance. Briefly discuss the diagnosis of virginity with special reference to true and false virgins.

The question of virginity assumes importance in the following circumstances, viz: (1) cases of nullity of marriage, (2) cases of divorce, and (3) cases of defamation where the chastity of a woman is involved.

Diagnosis of virginity: Though many conditions are likely to change upon defloration, they are not certain to do so. The diagnosis of virginity is, therefore, difficult in certain cases. In such circumstances, attention should be paid to the following signs.

The hymen is always present in some form or the other in a virgo intacta but rarely it may be congenitally absent.

The hymen may be intact but this does not prove virginity. If the hymen is thick and distensible. In such a case, a sexual intercourse may not rupture the hymen. *Such cases where sexual connection has taken place without rupture of the hymen are known as false virgins* (Fig. 25.4). Thus, with an intact hymen there can be true virgins and false virgins. Their **differentiating features** are as follows:

If (a) a woman has an intact hymen, (b) its edges are distinct and regular, and (c) the hymenal opening when stretched barely admits the tip of the little finger, the findings are in favour of true virginity (Fig. 25.5). On the other hand, if the hymen is intact but its edges are undulated and the hymenal opening admits two fingers to pass through easily, it is difficult to say on the basis of intactness of hymen alone whether the woman is a true virgin or a false virgin. In that case, one should rely on accessory signs of virginity to determine the correct status. If (a) the labia majora are

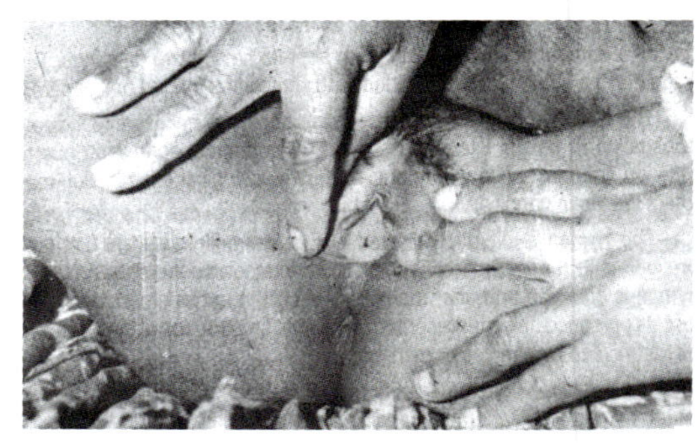

Fig. 25.4: Appearance of the hymen and external genitals of a **false virgin**. The hymen is thick, fleshy and distensible. Signs of virginity are lost. The fleshy labia majora and enlarged clitoris are visible. (*Courtesy*: Dr SS Baxi)

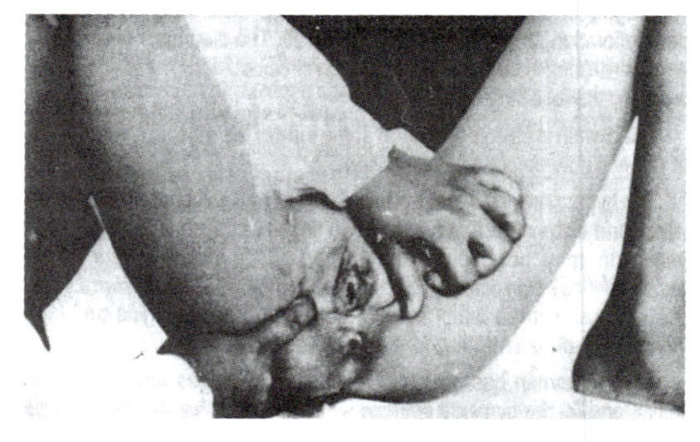

Fig. 25.5: A typical case of a fimbriated hymen. Compare it with fig. 25.2. (*Courtesy*: Dr GB Sahay)

fleshy and do not completely close the vaginal orifice, (b) the labia minora are cutaneous and not covered by the labia majora, (c) the clitoris is enlarged, (d) the vestibule is gaping, (e) the fourchette is torn, and (f) the vagina is roomy, there is no doubt about the case being a false virgin in spite of an intact hymen. But if on the contrary, the accessory signs are in true virgin state, the probabi-lities are much greater in favour of true virginity.

The hymen may be ruptured in a true virgin by digital and sanitary pad insertions, by trauma and by perineal injury. Small ruptures of the hymen may be caused by the passage of blood clots during menstrual periods.

The free margin of the semilunar or crescentic hymen is sometimes *fimbriated* showing numerous notches which *resemble torn hymen* or artificial tears. However, these notches are usually symmetrical, occur anteriorly, do not extend to the vaginal wall, the mucous membrane over the notches is intact, and there are no signs of inflammation. Tears caused by coitus or introduction of foreign body are usually uniform, occur posteriorly, extend to the vaginal walls, are not covered by mucous membrane, and there are signs of inflammation.

Some hypertrophy of the labia and clitoris may result from masturbation.

In girls, who have not had intercourse, the vaginal walls are rugose and firm. A single act of intercourse does not alter the genital parts much, except perhaps the rupture of the hymen but repeated acts cause the vaginal walls and the labia to lose their tone. The rugosity of the vaginal walls is not affected by intercourse but by the birth of the first child. Sometimes, rugosity of vaginal walls may be absent in a virgin. It is therefore not a diagnostic sign of virginity.

It is, therefore, from a joint consideration of the various signs mentioned above that a satisfactory evidence of the virgin state or otherwise can be obtained.

PREGNANCY

Pregnancy is a condition which occurs in the female when she carries a fertilised ovum within the uterus. It is likely to occur during the period between puberty and menopause.

The *signs of pregnancy* in the living can be divided into: (1) presumptive signs, (2) probable signs, and (3) positive or conclusive signs.

Presumptive Signs

These are usually subjective in character and of some value in clinical work; however, *in forensic cases, no reliance can be placed on their presence.* These signs are: (1) suppression of menstruation, (2) morning sickness, (3) sympathetic disturbances, (4) changes in the breasts, (5) pigmentation of the skin (6) quickening, (7) changes in the vagina, and (8) urinary disturbances.

Suppression of menstruation: Menstruation normally ceases after impregnation and does not recur until some months after child birth. However, instances are known of women who have never menstruated becoming pregnant, and menstruation continuing during early months of pregnancy. Again, cessation of menses may result from ill-health, intense desire for pregnancy, or fear of pregnancy after illicit intercourse.

Morning sickness: This often only amounts to nausea and occasionally vomiting which takes place on getting up in the morning. It is usually marked in a primigravida. Though a frequent phenomenon in the early stages of pregnancy yet it is of no great significance, as it is often caused by other conditions, e.g. migraine, ascariasis, gastritis, etc.

Sympathetic disturbances: Salivation, perverted appetite, and irritability of temper may occur and are caused reflexly by pregnancy. Even minor exertion causes fatigue.

Changes in the breasts: The breasts increase in size and become firmer. There is a deposit of pigment round the nipple and Montgomery's tubercles appear clearly by the end of the second month. These tubercles are enlarged sebaceous glands and appear as raised spots in the areola. The physiological activity of the breasts is also increased. By the third month, a clear transparent secretion can be squeezed out of the nipples on pressing the breasts. This is known as **colostrum.** It is a thin yellowish fluid consisting of free fat globules and large phagocytic cells filled with droplets of fat. In contrast, milk is a thick whitish fluid and consists mostly of large fat globules and only a few phagocytic cells. Colostrum is present for about 10 days after delivery when it is replaced by milk. After the sixth month, striae, also known as *silver lines,* similar in appearance to linea albicantes on the abdomen, are seen on the breasts due to stretching of the skin and resultant scar formation in the cutis due to rupture of the deeper layers of the skin. The surface veins of the breasts become prominent and are seen as blue lines. Rarely, pregnancy may occur without any changes in the breasts. These signs are sometimes found in non-pregnant women due to various uterine and ovarian diseases, and in any case are of value only in the first pregnancy.

Pigmentation of the skin: The vulva becomes darker in colour, and a dark line extends from the pubis to beyond the umbilicus, the so-called **linea nigra (dark lines).**

Quickening: This is the mother's subjective sensation of the movements of the foetus and occurs at about four to four and half months. When a woman is quick with child, a conviction is not corried, trial is postponed and women also are allowed pregnancy leaves.

Changes in the vagina: These are due to increased vascularity and venous stasis due to pressure of the gravid uterus after the fourth month. These changes form the basis of *Jackquemier's sign* or *Chadwick's sign.* The mucous membrane of the vagina gradually changes from pink to violet and then deepens to blue.

Urinary disturbances: In the early weeks and in the few weeks before delivery, the pressure of the gravid uterus causes frequency of micturition.

Probable Signs

These are: (1) changes in the abdomen, (2) softening of the lower uterine segment, (3) softening of the os, (4) presence of cervical mucus plug, (5) intermittent uterine contractions and relaxations, (6) ballottement, (7) uterine souffle, and (8) biological tests. *In forensic cases, no reliance can be placed on their presence.*

Changes in the abdomen: Progressive enlargement of the abdomen is a prima facie evidence of pregnancy but may be due to other causes. The upper level of gravid uterus at different periods of pregnancy is as follows:

1. Up to first 3 months—in pelvic cavity.
2. Fourth month—just above the symphysis pubis.
3. Fifth month—midway between the symphysis pubis and the navel (umbilicus).
4. Sixth month—at the level of the navel.
5. Seventh month—midway between the navel and xiphisternum.
6. Eighth month and early part of ninth month—at the level of xiphisternum.
7. Later part of ninth month and thereafter—below the level of xiphisternum.

Because of the stretching of the abdominal skin due to the gravid uterus, striae known as **striae gravidarum** or **linea**

albicantes are seen on the abdominal wall. They result from scar formation in the cutis due to rupture of the deeper layers of the skin. The umbilicus becomes flush with the abdominal skin surface by about the seventh month and by about the ninth month, it may become everted. These changes and the striae indicate progressive enlargement of the abdomen. They are, therefore, found in ascites and other conditions which bring about abdominal distension.

Softening of the lower uterine segment: At about the sixth week, the lower uterine segment becomes so soft and compressible that if one hand is placed on the abdomen just above the symphysis pubis and two fingers of the other hand are introduced in the posterior fornix, they can be felt touching each other as if there is no uterus in between. This is also known as *Hegar's sign.*

Softening of the os: This refers to softening of the cervix from below upwards from the second month onwards due to increased vascularity. This is also known as *Goodell's sign.* The cervix is felt as soft as the lips. In the non-pregnant state, it is felt as hard as the convex surface of the nails.

Presence of cervical mucus plug: During pregnancy, the cervix is blocked by a thick, viscid mucus plug.

Intermittent uterine contractions and relaxations: These are felt by palpation of the abdomen after the fourth month. Each contraction lasts about a minute and relaxation for about 2 to 3 minutes. This is often referred to as *Braxton-Hick's sign.*

Ballottement: This is a test to elicit the presence of the foetus floating in the liquor amnii from the fourth to the seventh months. It is best elicited during the fourth and fifth months when the foetus is small as compared to the amount of liquor amnii. The test fails, if liquor amnii is scanty or when the fetus is large. There are two methods to elicit this, viz. the external and internal ballottement. *External ballottement* is elicited by placing the palms of both hands on the abdomen on either side of the midline and giving a sudden impulse by the fingers of one hand towards the other when the foetus moves in the direction of the push and is felt by the other hand. *Internal ballottement* is carried out by giving a sudden impulse to the foetus by means of two fingers inserted in the anterior fornix. The foetus moves up and can be felt by the other hand placed on the abdomen, or by the fingers of the same hand after a moment when it settles down to its original position.

Uterine souffle: This is a soft blowing murmur heard on either side of the uterus, by auscultation just above the inguinal ligament, from about the fourth month onwards. It is synchronous with the maternal pulse and is due to the passage of blood though the dilated uterine vessels.

Biological tests: Biological tests of value in the early diagnosis of pregnancy are certain biological tests which depend on the presence of gonadotropic hormones in the pregnant woman's blood and their excretion in the urine. These tests are accurate in 98 per cent of cases. These are: the Aschheim-Zondek test, the Friedman test, the Hogben test or female frog test, the rapid rat test, the Ghoul-Mainani test or the male toad (frog) test, and the immunological tests of which agglutination–inhibition test is now in common use.

The **immunological** (agglutination–inhibition) **test** or Latex test is based on the antigenic property of human chorionic gonadotrophin (HCG). A drop of urine of the woman suspected to be pregnant and a drop of antiserum to HCG are mixed on a glass slide for 30 seconds. To this, two drops of sensitised latex particles are mixed and shaken. Absence of agglutination indicates that the test is positive. The advantages of this test are: (1) The test is simple, rapid and less cumbersome, (2) no animal or special equipment is required, (3) the test is sensitive, and (4) the result can be read in two minutes.

The biological tests are available within about 12–15 days of impregnation and remain positive for about seven days after delivery. A negative result may be given when in fact pregnancy is present but the ovum has died and a positive result may be obtained in certain pathological conditions, such as hydatidiform mole and chorionepithelioma as these conditions also produce chorionic gonadotrophin, which forms the basis of the biological tests.

Q. 25.3. Discuss positive or conclusive signs of pregnancy.

Conclusive Signs of Pregnancy

These are: (1) hearing of the foetal heart sounds, (2) feeling the foetal movements and parts, (3) radiograph of the foetus, (4) ultrasonography, (5) presence of foetal cells in the mother's blood, and (6) other technically advanced imaging techniques. *In forensic cases, these are the only signs to be relied upon.*

Hearing of the foetal heart sounds: Between the fourth and **fifth month,** the pulsations of the foetal heart may be recognised and counted. Their rate is usually about 160 at the fifth and 120 at the ninth month. **A foetal heart beat establishes the fact of a pregnancy beyond all dispute and shows that the child is living.** While their presence affords the strongest affirmative evidence, their absence furnishes uncertain negative evidence and in such a case, several examinations should be made before an opinion is formed. Uterine souffle, i.e. a soft blowing murmur heard over the uterus, may be confused with foetal heart sounds. It should be remembered that uterine souffle corresponds to the maternal pulse. Foetal heart sounds are not heard when: (1) examination is made before 18 weeks, (2) the abdominal wall is very fat, (3) there is an excessive quantity of liquor amnii, (4) when the position of the foetus in the uterus is such that transmission of sounds is not possible, or (5) the foetus is dead.

Feeling the foetal movements and parts: Foetal movements may be felt by placing the hands on the abdomen after the fourth month and may be seen by the **fifth month.** These are not always evident but when they occur, they cannot be mistaken for anything else and constitute indisputable evidence of a child living at the time of examination. Foetal parts, such as the head and limbs, can sometimes be identified manually.

Radiograph of the foetus: Under favourable conditions, the presence of a foetus may be diagnosed by X-ray examination as early as the middle of the **fourth month** and each succeeding week renders the diagnosis more certain and easy. In as much as X-ray exposure may damage the foetus, uterine scan, when possible, should be preferred.

Ultrasonography (silent sound waves that safely pass through body tissues): This procedure is used to detect foetal heart beat as early as the 12th week. It can also indicate the size of a baby's head, follow the baby's growth, and detect physical abnormalities like those of the spine. Gestation ring is seen by sweets. If pregnancy does not grow further, a blighted ovum is seen. If the fetus is dead in utero over lapped bones and collagens of spine and rib-cage are seen.

Presence of foetal cells in the mother's blood can be detected as early as the fifth week of pregnancy. Even the sex of the foetus can be determined by looking at the DNA sequences from the Y chromosomes in these cells. The technique is not in common use.

Advanced imaging techniques are also not in common use at the present moment.

Q. 25.4. Comment on 'signs of pregnancy' in the dead.

From the external appearance of the body alone, the chief signs will be those present at the stage of pregnancy at which the woman died, but no special importance can be attached to them. In postmortem examination, the following diagnostic signs should be looked for, viz: (1) the presence of an ovum or foetus, (2) uterine changes, and (3) the corpus luteum.

The presence of an ovum or foetus: The presence of an impregnated ovum, embryo, foetus, placenta, membranes, or any other product of conception, in the uterus after death, is positive proof of pregnancy (Fig. 25.6). In a body which is disinterred, traces of foetal bones may be found among the remains or by means of X-ray examination.

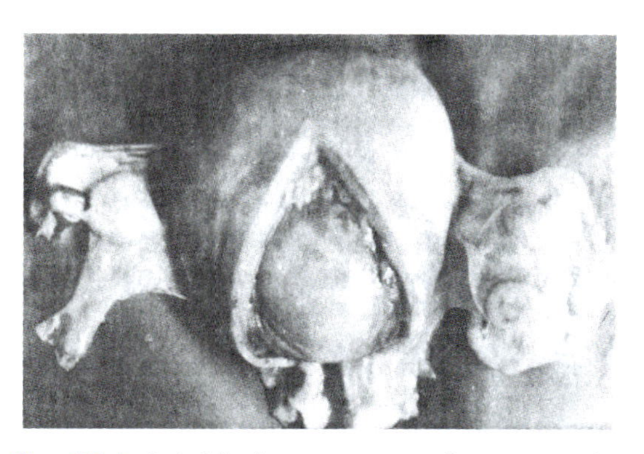

Fig. 25.6: **Suicide by a pregnant woman.** An unmarried woman suspected to be pregnant committed suicide. The presence of **foetus in the uterus affords positive proof of pregnancy and the presence of corpus luteum in the ovary affords corroborative evidence.** (*Courtesy*: Dr NK Patoria)

Uterine changes: As a result of pregnancy, the uterus is thickened and increased in size, both in its length and width. A microscopic examination of the uterus may show the presence of chorionic villi indicating the fact of pregnancy.

Corpus luteum: Presence of corpus luteum in the ovary affords corroborative evidence of pregnancy. Its presence *per se* has no forensic value. Cases have occurred in which there has been absence of a corpus luteum, although the subjects were pregnant; also corpus luteum has been found in the ovaries of women who were neither pregnant nor menstruating.

Q. 25.5. Mention the circumstances under which the question of pregnancy may form the basis of medicolegal investigation.

The examination of a woman for pregnancy should be undertaken only after obtaining her informed consent in writing. The doctor should explain the reasons for the examination and its possible consequences. He should make it clear that she cannot be compelled to submit to the examination, and that her consent must be voluntary. This applies not only to civil but also to criminal cases. *Medical proof of pregnancy must be based absolutely on conclusive evidence* and if there is any doubt, a further examination should be made at a later date, when the evidence will have become more certain.

The following are the principal circumstances wherein pregnancy may be feigned and an opinion on pregnancy may be required.

1. When a woman advances pregnancy as an excuse to avoid attending the court as a witness. Pregnancy in itself is not an excuse except when it is so far advanced that delivery is imminent or she or the child is likely to suffer risk by such attendance.
2. When a convicted woman pleads that she is pregnant, as a bar to hard labour or execution. Under section 416 of the Criminal Procedure Code, if a woman sentenced to death is found to be pregnant, the High Court shall order the execution of the sentence to be postponed, and may, if it thinks fit,

commute the sentence to transportation for life. The main purpose is to spare the child who is innocent. In such a case, a civil surgeon or any government authorised doctaor for that purpose will be required to certify if the woman is quick with a child or not.

3. When a woman after her husband's death feigns to be pregnant so that she might be entitled to the estate left by her deceased husband on behalf of the prospective heir.
4. When a woman who suing for damages for breach of promise of marriage or for seduction, claims to be pregnant.
5. When a woman blackmails a person and accuses him that she is pregnant by him, to compel marriage.
6. When an unmarried woman, a widow, or a wife living apart from her husband is defamed or libelled to be pregnant. She may like to vindicate herself.
7. When a woman alleges pregnancy to claim greater compensation from some person or persons, through whose culpable neglect her husband has died.
8. When a woman claims more alimony, in case of divorce, on account of the responsibility of the prospective child.
9. When the pregnancy is suspected to be the motive for suicide or murder. A woman having illicit sexual intimacy with her paramour may become pregnant. When she discovers this, she may commit suicide, or her husband or paramour may murder her. In such a case, the dead body has to be examined for proof of pregnancy.
10. When a woman is accused of criminal abortion, infanticide, concealment of birth or pregnancy, she may like to vindicate herself.
11. When a woman requests for termination of pregnancy, under the MTP (Medical Termination of Pregnancy) Act, the pregnancy having resulted from rape.

DELIVERY

Delivery means the expulsion or extraction of the child at birth. Sometimes, a doctor is asked to examine a woman for signs of delivery and, if there is evidence of such delivery, to state the probable time since her delivery. While there is no general diagnostic sign, the signs of delivery are better marked, the more recent the delivery and the more mature the child; hence, it is important to make the examination at the earliest possible moment.

Q. 25.6. Write short notes on: (1) signs of recent delivery in the living, (2) signs of recent delivery in the dead, (3) signs of remote delivery in the living, (4) signs of remote delivery in the dead.

Signs of Recent Delivery in the Living

The examination for evidence of recent delivery should include an examination for any sign which would be consistent with a precipitate labour.

If it is the first child, general appearances of indisposition may be present. The woman may look pale, exhausted and ill. The pulse is soft and quick and there is a slight increase in temperature. The intermittent contractions of the uterus, known as after-pains, are usually present for the first four or five days. These signs are not diagnostic of recent delivery as they may be found in any other illness or at the time of the monthly course. The signs of general indisposition may be absent in strong women.

Besides the general appearances, **breasts** are enlarged, tense, and knotty. The surface veins are dilated and there is dark pigmentation round the nipples. Striae are seen on the breasts and Montgomery's tubercles found prominent. On pressure, colostrum can be squeezed out for about 10 days after delivery. It is replaced by milk thereafter.

The **abdomen** is lax and shows striae gravidarum and linea nigra. *The diagnosis does not depend on the external appearances mentioned here but on the local examination.*

The **vulva** is bruised and gaping, the vagina is roomy, the fourchette and posterior commissure are destroyed, and the perineum may be lacerated, the age of the tear being of value to fix the time lapsed ofter delivery. The **uterus** is enlarged. It does not shrink to its original size immediately after delivery. The fundus lies about 2.5 cm below the umbilicus. It diminishes at the rate of about 1.5 cm a day for the first few days. On palpation, it feels like a hard cricket ball in two or three days, in the lower abdomen above the pubis. By the tenth day, it is on level with brim of the pelvis. In two to three weeks, the fundus sinks below the level of the pubis into the pelvic cavity. It reaches its normal size in about six weeks. The cervix is soft and patulous and its edges torn and lacerated transversely. The internal os begins to close within the first 24 hours. The external os is soft and patent admitting **two** fingers for the first few days, and one finger with difficulty at the end of a week. It closes in two weeks. There is a **vaginal discharge,** with a peculiar sour disagreeable odour. This discharge is known as **lochia.** It contains red cells, leucocytes, decidual debris, vaginal epithelium, peptones, and cholesterol crystals. During the first three days, it is blood-stained and, therefore, known as *lochia rubra.* During the next three days, it becomes paler and serous and is known as *lochia serosa.* After the next three days, it becomes yellowish or greenish and then whitish, when it is called as *lochia alba.* It then gradually loses all colour till it finally disappears in about 15 days. Lochia is a discharge which is a part of the healing process of the uterus after delivery. The discharge is, therefore, blood-stained in the beginning and whitish later. All the above signs are more characteristic of a full term delivery than of a premature one. They are likely to disappear within about 10 days or even earlier in a strong and vigorous woman, especially if she happens to be a multipara.

From the extent of stretching and laceration of the parts, an idea may be obtained of the size of the foetus, or if this is known, the rapidity of the birth may be gauged. The sooner a woman is examined after an alleged delivery, the greater are the chances of obtaining useful information. The biological tests may be of value in certain cases. They remain positive for about a week or so after delivery. Usually, after two or three weeks, it is impossible to fix the date of delivery with any degree of certainty.

Signs of Recent Delivery in the Dead

All the local signs mentioned above may be present and these can be easily explored. The breasts may be examined for signs of physiological activity and the uterus can be seen undergoing involution till it reaches its normal size in about six weeks. The size of the uterus will vary with the period of gestation and the time after delivery when death occurred. Soon after full term delivery, the uterus is flabby, about 22–30 cm long, about 5 cm in thickness, contains large clots of blood, weighs about 900 gm, and its inner surface is lined by decidua. After two or three days, the uterus measures about 18 cm in length, about 4 cm in thickness, and weighs about 600 gm. At the end of a week, it is about 12–15 cm in length, about 3 cm in thickness, and weighs about 450 gm. At the end of a fortnight, it is about 10–12 cm in length and weighs about 300 gm. Usually in six weeks, the uterus reaches its normal size, that is about 7–8 cm in length, 5 cm in breadth, about 2 cm in thickness, and weighs a little over 100 gm. The placental site can be identified shortly after full term delivery by its dark colour and coarsely granular appearance. It is about 15 cm in diameter and covered with clotted blood, lymph, and portions of decidua. The site measures 3–4 cm at the end of second week, and about 1–2 cm at the end of six weeks.

The opening of its vessels are well marked and can be identified up to eight or nine weeks after delivery. The ovaries and fallopian tubes are usually congested but may become normal in a few days. When there is any doubt from naked eye appearances histo-logical examination may be resorted to, when endometrium may show the presence of trophoblastic epithelium and chorionic villi, and the sectioned ovaries may show the presence of a large corpus luteum. It must be remembered that after about two months, it is not possible to give the exact period of delivery.

Signs of Remote Delivery in the Living

A previous pregnancy usually leaves permanent marks on a woman, especially if the pregnancy has gone to full term. The extent and character of the signs found will depend upon whether the woman is primiparous or multiparous. The diagnosis of a previous pregnancy may be considered justifiable, if all or a majority of the following signs are present.

The breasts are lax, soft and pendulous. They are frequently wrinkled, if the woman has nursed her baby and occasionally show subcutaneous scars (linea albicantes). The nipples are enlarged with a persistent dark areola around them, and Montgomery's tubercles are usually present. Milk can frequently be squeezed from the nipples. The abdominal walls tend to be lax and show the presence of linea albicantes on the lateral aspects. There is commonly a deeply pigmented line (linea nigra) from the pubis to the umbilicus. There may be a scar due to old laceration of the perineum and the absence of signs of virginity, i.e. the hymen is ruptured, the vagina open and gaping, and a non-rugose condition of the vaginal walls. These signs do not prove that delivery has taken place as they may be simulated by other conditions, and if only one child has been born, these signs may be very slight. The only sign which proves delivery is the appearance of the os uteri. In a parous woman, the internal os is not well defined while the external os is transverse, irregular, fissured, and may admit the tip of the finger. In a nulliparous woman, the internal os is well defined while the external os is rounded with a dimple in the centre and the orifice closed.

Signs of Remote Delivery in the Dead

The uterus is larger, thicker and heavier than the nulliparous uterus. However, it must be remembered that uterus undergoes atrophy in old age. The walls are concave from inside forming a wider and rounded cavity, while the walls of the nulliparous uterus are convex on the inner aspect and form a cavity which is smaller in capacity and triangular in shape. The top of the fundus in a parous woman is convex and on a higher level than that of the broad ligaments; in a nulliparous woman, it is at level with the broad ligaments. The cervix and the body are about the same length in the virgin, while in a parous woman, the body is twice the length of the cervix and in the later, the arbor vitae have disappeared. *Arbor vitae* is the name given to the mucosal folds in the canal of uterine cervix which extends from internal os to external os. The canal is spindle-shaped and has two transverse mucosal folds, one on anterior and another on posterior edge of the canal. Numerous oblique mucosal folds run from these transverse folds, giving the appearance of a tree and hence the name arbor vitae. The edges of the cervix may show cicatrices on account of previous tears and lacerations caused during delivery. The external os is enlarged and the internal os is not so well defined as that in the virgin. The placental site is elevated and tinged with blood pigment for six months, and on cutting sections, endarteritis obliterans can be seen in the blood vessels for years afterwards.

Q. 25.7. Comment on the circumstances under which the question of delivery may come before a court of law.

The examination of a woman for evidence of delivery should be undertaken only after obtaining her informed consent in writing. The establishment of the fact of delivery may become important under the following circumstances, viz: (1) in cases of alleged abortion or infanticide, (2) in cases of feigned delivery, (3) in cases of concealment of birth, (4) in connection with legitimacy, (5) in libel actions of disputed chastity, and (6) blackmail.

Abortion or infanticide: When a woman is alleged to have aborted, or delivered and killed the child.

Feigned delivery: A woman may pretend pregnancy and delivery and subsequently produce a child to claim inheritance to property. Supposititious child is a child who is supposed to be the child of that woman but actually not. She has presented a child as her own though not actually delivered by her.

Concealment of birth: If a child is born to an unmarried woman or a widow, or out of lawful wedlock, the woman might wish to conceal the child out of shame.

Legitimacy: Only a child born during lawful wedlock *within a competent time* is known as a legitimate child and is entitled to inherit the parent's property.

Disputed chastity: When an unmarried woman, a widow or a wife living apart from her husband, is defamed or libelled to have delivered a child, she may like to vindicate herself.

Blackmail: A woman may produce a supposititious child and blackmail someone as the father to extort money.

26 Legitimacy

Q. 26.1. What is meant by legitimacy? In what medicolegal matters does the question of legitimacy usually arise?

Q. 26.2. Comment on: (1) superfecundation, (2) superfoetation.

By legitimacy is meant the legal status of a person born in lawful wedlock. Under section 112 of the Indian Evidence Act, a **legitimate child** has been defined as one born during the continuance of a valid marriage between his mother and any man or within 280 days after its dissolution by divorce, or death of the husband, and the mother remaining unmarried.

An **illegitimate** or **bastard child** is one which is born out of lawful wedlock, or not within a competent time after the dissolution of the marriage by divorce, or death of the husband, or born within lawful wedlock when procreation by the husband was not possible because (a) he was under the age of puberty, (b) he was physically incapable of procreation due to illness, malformations, impotency, or sterility, (c) he did not have sexual access to his wife during the time that the child could have been begotten, or (d) there is incompatibility between the blood group between the child and alleged father. An illegitimate child becomes legitimate by the subsequent marriage of parents, if the child is born out of lawful wedlock.

The question of legitimacy and disputed paternity arises under the following circumstances, viz: (1) nullity of marriage, (2) divorce, (3) inheritance, (4) affiliation (adoption) cases, and (5) suppositious children.

Nullity of marriage: Legally, marriage is a contract and it can be nullified if—(a) either party is under the age of marriage contract, (b) either party was already validly married, (c) both parties are of the same sex, (d) either party was suffering from incurable impotency, insanity, HIV infection, leprosy, or venereal disease in a communicable form prior to marriage, (e) either party was so intoxicated at the time of marriage as not to understand the nature of the marriage contract, (f) there is wilful refusal to consummate marriage, and (g) the respondent wife at the time of marriage was pregnant by any person other than the husband.

Divorce: This means dissolution of a previously valid marriage, if the intrauterine age of the child is proved to be greater than the period of access between the parents, the dissolution of marriage is allowed by the court on the ground of adultery. The other grounds for divorce include: (a) desertion, (b) cruelty, (c) criminal sex practices, e.g. rape, sodomy, or bestiality, and (d) incurable insanity, HIV infection, leprosy, or venereal disease in a communicable form.

Inheritance: Only a legitimate child can inherit property of its parents. Hence, in a case of inheritance, the question of legitimacy of a child may arise and medical evidence may be required concerning the following facts, viz: (1) age in regard to pregnancy, (2) duration of pregnancy, (3) unusual forms of pregnancy, such as superfecundation and superfoetation, and (4) paternity.

Age in regard to pregnancy: While from time to time cases are recorded of young girls delivering children, in India, at present, 18 years is the earliest age at which a female can contract a valid marriage and a legitimate conception can take place. Greater importance is probably associated with the age of certain women at the time of their delivery late in life, since important legal issues may emerge.

Duration of pregnancy: While the normal average duration of pregnancy is accepted as 280 days which is equal to *ten times the normal intermenstrual period* of 28 days, it must be considered possible that the duration of pregnancy could be shorter or longer where the individual menstrual cycle is shorter or longer. The editor knows a lady, wife of a doctor colleague, otherwise healthy, but she says she has periods only once in six months may be quantifiable menstrual blood. A lactating woman may become pregnant again before starting a menstrual cycle also.

Where the duration of gestation is shorter than normal, the question of viability of the child arises. **Viability** means the **stage of maturity** at which a foetus with normal intrauterine development is able to maintain a separate existence after birth. A child is viable after 210 days or seven months of intrauterine life, or rarely 180 days or six months but in most of these cases the foetus is immature. *The stage of maturity is generally reflected by the weight of the child at birth.*

A four pound baby was born after a gestation period of 172 days. On medical evidence that the baby was normal and survived normally without any special care or efforts to keep it alive, the Court accepted the husband's contention that he was not the father of the child and granted divorce. (Bombay High Court First Appeal No. 666 of 1959).

Where the duration of gestation is longer than normal, the child must be larger and heavier than normal, and the ossific centres more fully developed, or else it is unusual and suspicious. Mckeown and Gibson from their investigation on 15,629 births conclude that for medicolegal purposes, a period of 354 days from coitus to birth is not impossible. (BMJ: 1952,1, 938–41)

Unusual forms of pregnancy: *Superfecundation and superfoetation are unusual forms of pregnancy.*

By **superfecundation** is meant the fertilisation of two separate **ova** which have been discharged from the ovary at the same period of ovulation by two separate acts of coitus. This is quite possible. Both infants are equally developed.

A case has been recorded in literature where a woman who had coitus first with a fair-skinned male and subsequently with a dark-skinned male gave birth to twins one of which was fair-skinned and the other dark-skinned, and both equally developed.

Herberer records a case of disputed paternity where on the basis of blood group tests, it was contended that the defendant could not have been the father of one of the twins.

By **superfoetation** is meant the fertilisation of two separate ova discharged from the ovary at different period of ovulation. Since menstruation may take place for two or three months after impregnation has occurred, superfoetation is possible during this period, but it must be regarded as a very unlikely occurrence. It may occur in cases of double uterus or uterus didelphis.

Two infants in different stages of development may be born.

Paternity: The word paternity literally means fatherhood but the term is used here in a broader sense to mean parenthood. The supposed parent may or may not be the real father. In cases of disputed paternity, blood group tests are resorted to. In India, these tests are carried out by the Haffkine Institute in Mumbai, Central Forensic Science Laboratory at Delhi, the Serologist of India at Kolkata, and several other forensic science laboratories all over the country. DNA testing is now common.

Any evidence obtained from parental resemblance in feature, figure, gestures and other personal peculiarities, such as deformities, has limited value in forensic work. Cases of **atavism** occur in which the child does not resemble its parents but its grand parents (atavis = grand father). This kind of evidence also has very limited value in determining cases of disputed paternity.

Affiliation (adoption) cases: These are popularly known as suits for adoption. They are cases which are brought before the court for fixing the paternity of an illegitimate child. Under section 125 CrPC, an individual must adopt his illegitimate child or support him up to a certain age. In the latter case, a magistrate of the first class may make a maximum allowance of rupees 500 hundred per month for the maintenance of such a child, after taking into consideration only the necessities of life, such as food, clothing and lodging, and not luxury.

Supposititious child: A supposititious child means a fictitious child. A woman may pretend pregnancy as well as delivery and later produce a child as if it is her own. She may substitute a living male child for a dead child or for a living female child born of her. The purpose is to extort money by blackmail or divert succession to property. The medical officer must be able to say from the examination of the woman, if she was pregnant and delivered a child, and from the paternity tests, if the child is likely to be hers. Such evidence is useful only in those cases where the age of the supposititious child does not correspond to the date of the pretended pregnancy and subsequent delivery.

MAITRI KARAR (FRIENDSHIP CONTRACT) (LIVING TOGETHER ON CONTRACT)

This is a contract which enables a married man to live with other woman without obtaining a divorce. Such a contract not only enables the men to neglect their wives but also cheat the women with whom they have set up another home. These contracts are encountered mainly in Gujarat, India. The Gujarat High Court has held that the maitri contracts are not enforceable in law. If the man decides to leave the woman, she cannot claim maintenance nor can she ask for a share in the property the man possesses. Only if she has any children by him can she claim maintenance under section 125 CrPC. Such contracts, despite their dubious nature, are likely to gain momentum in the changing values of life unless the divorce laws are suitably liberalised and replaced by new ones that reflect the changing social conventions of our times.

What is Atavism?

When a child resembles grand parents and not the parents such child is atavistic child and the process is called atavism.

27

Natural Sexual Offenses

Sexual offenses are acts of illegal sexual intercourse with a second person or with an animal to obtain sexual gratification. In contrast, *sexual perversions* are acts intended to result in sexual gratification without sexual intercourse.

The laws and customs of society normally permit heterosexual intercourse between a man and his wife as provided by nature with the sex organs intended for reproduction. Accordingly, any intercourse by a man with any other woman who is not his wife would constitute an offence in law unless there is a valid consent. If such intercourse is carried out with the use of sex organs in the natural manner, the alleged act, by convention, is known as natural sexual offence. However, when a man is deprived of the company of a woman for a long time and the natural means of sexual gratification are not available to him (sex-starved), or if his mental condition is abnormal, he is likely to indulge in sex practices against the order of nature. These are known as unnatural sexual offenses. Women may also indulge in such practices under similar circumstances.

Sexual offenses are thus classified as:

1. Natural sexual offenses, viz.—(a) rape, (b) incest, and (c) adultery.
2. Unnatural sexual offenses, viz.—(a) sodomy, (b) buccal coitus, (c) tribadism, and (d) bestiality.

RAPE

The circumstances in which the act of coitus or attempted coitus may render a man liable to the charge of rape vary slightly from state to state but the basic features of various state laws are essentially the same.

Rape is generally defined as unlawful sexual intercourse by a man with a woman against her will, without her consent, or with her consent when it has been obtained by unlawful means, e.g. fraud, putting her in fear of death or hurt, drugging, or impersonation. In most jurisdictions, it is unlawful for a person in position of authority to have sexual intercourse with any female under their care/custody. Such an act is designated as custodial rape. It is defined as rape by persons, such as police officers, jail wardens, hospital staff, etc., who abuse their position to commit the offence when the woman is in their custody/care.

As Wecht has rightly pointed out, much more is known scientifically in the detection and proof of rape than is usually and customarily utilised in most cases. If one keeps in mind the horrendous impact that an actual attack of rape has on the victim, and similarly the tremendous harm that is inflicted upon a falsely accused individual, one cannot deny the importance of applying scientific principles in the handling of a rape case. A trial of rape cannot be based upon emotional reactions of any party.

Law on Rape in India

Under section 375 IPC, rape is defined as unlawful sexual intercourse by a man with his wife under the age of 15 years, with any other woman under the age of 18 years, or above that age, against her will, without her consent, or with her consent when it has been obtained by unlawful means. The unlawful means are: (a) putting her or any other person in whom she is interested in fear of death or hurt, (b) impersonation, that is, when the man knows that he is not her husband and that her consent is given because she believes that he is another man to whom she is or believes herself to be lawfully married, and (c) with her consent when, at the time of giving such consent, by reason of unsoundness of mind or intoxication or the administration by him personally or through another of any stupefying or unwholesome substance, she is unable to understand the nature and consequences of that to which she consents.

Penetration of labia majora, mouth, urethra, or anus is rape. Sexual intercourse by a man with his wife, even against her will, is not rape, if she is above 15 years of age and medial procedure or intervention also not rape.

Section 376 IPC lays down the punishment for the offence of rape which may extend from seven years to life imprisonment and even death and also fine. The sentencing judge has discretionary powers to impose a lesser sentence.

Explanation: **Custodial rape** is defined as rape by persons who are in position of authority, e.g. police officers, jail wardens, hospital staff, etc., and who abuse their position to commit the offence when the woman is under their custody/care.

Gang rape: When a woman is raped by one or more in a group of persons acting in furtherance of their common intention, each is deemed to have committed gang rape.

Section 228 IPC prohibits disclosure of the identity of the victim of rape. Under section 327 CrPC, the inquiry into and trial of rape or an offence under section 376 IPC shall be conducted in camera and it is not lawful for any person to print or publish any matter in relation to such proceedings *except with the permission of the court.*

Section 114IEA lays down that in a prosecution for rape under section 376 IPC where sexual intercourse by the accused is proved and the question is whether it was without the consent of woman alleged to have been raped and she states in her evidence before the court that she did not consent, *the court shall presume that she did not consent.* This applies to cases of custodial rape and gang rape.

Q. 27.1. Discuss the medicolegal aspects of the various points emphasised in the definition of rape. Include a note on: (1) indecent assault, (2) valid consent.

The definition of rape emphasises certain aspects, such as: (1) unlawful, (2) sexual intercourse, (3) by a man, (4) of a woman, (5) against her will, and (6) by force, or (7) by impersonation. Their medicolegal implications are as follows:

Unlawful: This implies that there is such an act as a lawful sexual intercourse of a woman by force or against her will. The only sexual intercourse deemed lawful (as provided in the exception in Section 375 IPC) is the normal one between a legally married man and woman. A husband, therefore, cannot be charged with rape against his wife provided she is of the age specified by law of that particular country (in India, the specified age at present is 16 years and above), even if he has intercourse with her by force and against her will, as she cannot retract the implied consent given at the time of marriage, unless a separation order is in force. However, the husband has no right to enjoy his wife's body without regard to the question of safety to her, nor can he assist another man to commit rape on her.

Sexual intercourse: In law, this term is held to mean the slightest degree of penetration of the labia majora by the penis with or without emission of semen or rupture of hymen. It is, therefore, quite possible to commit legally the offence of rape without producing any injury to the genitals or leaving any seminal stains. Inability to produce penile erection does not preclude the ability to commit rape. In such instances, corroborative evidence will be required to prove the offence. If rape cannot be proved or there is any reasonable doubt as to the intent to rape, the accused may be convicted of the lesser offence of **indecent assault** on a female committed with intent or knowledge to outrage her modesty. (Section 354 IPC lays down punishment for such an offence). However, what constitutes an outrage on female modesty differs according to the country and race to which the woman belongs. To kiss or place the hands on the shoulder of a woman would outrage the modesty of a Hindu or Mohammedan woman but not that of an European. To examine a woman against her will and without her consent also constitutes such an offence, which a doctor must remember, lest he may be charged with it. In most such offenses, the accused has tried to undress her, pressed her breasts under the guise of examination, or inserted a finger in the vagina.

By a man: In India, the law does not presume any limit of age under which a boy is considered physically incapable of committing rape. In a charge of rape brought against a boy, the court decides the question of his potency from evidence of the case and is guided by sections 82 and 83 IPC in awarding punishment. Likewise, there is no upper limit and even old people aged 80 and above are said to have committed rape.

Of a woman: This means that an offence can only be committed against a woman, and a woman, therefore, cannot rape a man although she may be guilty of an indecent assault upon him. Similarly, animals cannot be raped. There is no age limit below or above which rape cannot be committed.

Against her will: This is the substance of the definition and raises a number of important points. The essence of the offence is that it should take place against the wishes of a woman, i.e. without her valid consent. A *valid consent* is one which is free, voluntary, and given when the woman is in full possession of her senses; if obtained by fraud, fear or force, it is not a free consent (Section 90 IPC). In India, a woman of and above the age of 18 years can give such consent.

A girl of 14 years consulted a physician for suppressed menstruation. He had intercourse with her stating that it was a part of treatment. He was convicted of the offence of rape. (R *vs* Carr, 4 Cox D.C. 223).

In 1923, a singing teacher named Williams was charged with rape for persuading a young pupil that a sexual intercourse with him would improve the quality of her voice.

Invalid consent in rape: The consent given by a female is **invalid** when—(a) she is under the age specified by law, (b) she is mentally retarded, (c) she is intoxicated or otherwise stupefied, (d) it is obtained by fraud, force, or putting her or any person in whom she is interested in fear of death or hurt, or (e) it is obtained after the act. The law provides the same protection to a prostitute against sex assaults as it does for chaste women, but when a charge of rape is made by a prostitute, the case must be more closely scrutinised. Something more than medical evidence would be required to establish such a charge. *Medical proof of intercourse is not legal proof of rape.* In short, rape is not a medical diagnosis but a legal definition and inference.

Whether a man can have intercourse with a woman without her knowledge while in a state of natural sleep is largely a matter of common sense. It is impossible for complete sexual intercourse to take place on a nubile virgin during her natural sleep without her knowledge, as the pain caused by the first act of coitus would certainly wake her up; however, partial penetration within the terms of law can occur to constitute the crime. It is possible, though improbable, for sexual intercourse to take place, in the case of a woman used to it. Kerr records an instance where a woman woke up to find her grandson having connection with her. Rape may be committed without the knowledge of a woman under the influence of narcotics or anaesthetics, in a state of coma as after an epileptic attack, and possibly while in an hypnotic trance.

The usual means of showing *lack of consent* include: (1) any evidence of fraud, (2) administration of drinks or drugs, (3) any evidence of threat, (4) use of force, (5) signs of struggle, or (6) physical disproportion between the parties. Below is an excellent example of modus operandi to perpetrate fraud.

Rape in Rome: Miss World, Israel's Linor Abargil, was sexually assaulted when she was in Italy for a fashion show. According to her, the travel agent who was issuing the ticket, offered to drive her to Rome instead. Shortly after starting out, he tied her up and assaulted her. He then apologised and drove back to Milan. The man has been arrested and charged with rape. Good, but why didn't she get off the car? (There was danger of serious bodily injury or loss of life). (Sunday Times of India, Mumbai, December 6,1998).

By force: Under the Indian law, it is essential that the woman should resist the force to her utmost. It would not amount to rape if after half-hearted resistance she gave consent. Shouting, crying, biting, beating suggest force and resistance.

The resistance offered depends upon the type of woman, her age, development, whether she is a virgin or not, and on the class of society to which she belongs. While in most cases, signs of resistance are to be expected, in some they may be slight or even absent. Inability to resist from terror or a feeling of helplessness at her situation, may lead a woman to succumb to the force of a ravisher without offering that degree or even any degree of resistance which is generally expected of a woman so situated.

Impersonation: This may be possible—(1) when the woman is under the effect of drink, drugs, illusion, or hypnotic trance, (2) if she is mentally defective, (3) when she is asleep, and (4) rarely, when she is awake but lying in the dark. If she intentionally or with her knowledge takes drugs or intoxicants, she cannot claim this as lack of consent.

INTRAMARITAL RAPE

Legally, it is assumed that consent to sexual intercourse is implicit in the contract of marriage. It has, therefore, been assumed that a husband cannot rape his wife. This principle has been slowly eroded over the years and it is now accepted that the supposed marital exemption in rape is a thing of the past and cannot form any part of modern law. It was at one time customary to require the victim of rape to offer utmost resistance to guard her chastity, no matter what degree of violence was used. Nowadays, it is asking too much to expect a woman to prefer being throttled or suffer serious bodily harm so as to avoid unwanted sexual intercourse. Successful treatment of venereal disease, easy availability of therapeutic abortion, and widespread use of contraceptive pills demand rethinking on the tradition.

The common law must take prevailing social attitudes into account. They do not recognise any privilege whereby the husband has an absolute right to enjoy his wife's body even against her will and less so by the use of force. Marriage in modern times is regarded as a partnership of equals and no longerone in which the wife is subordinate to the husband. Enlightened jurists regard rape as an aggravated form of assault and hold that it is a criminal offence to assault a wife, irrespective of the position as to sexual intercourse and marriage. This line of reasoning is to be found in the South Australian Legislation, wherein, the Criminal Law Consolidation Act 1930–1980 Section 73(5) states that a husband can be convicted of rape upon his spouse only if, inter alia, the offence consists of or is associated with an assault occasioning actual bodily harm or an act of gross indecency or threats to those ends.

Bobbittism: In 1993–1994, in Virginia, USA, in the case of Bobbitt *vs* Bobbitt, Mrs Bobbitt accused her husband of rape but the jury did not return a verdict of guilty against Mr Bobbitt mainly because—(1) they were not legally separated, (2) Mrs Bobbitt did not scream or shout at the material time, or (3) show any sign such as a bruise on her body as evidence of the act against her will. (Also refer to Bobbitt's case in the chapter on insanity under irresistible impulse).

EXAMINATION OF THE RAPE VICTIM

Q. 27.2. Describe in detail the procedure of examination of a victim of rape. Include a note on Locard's principle of exchange.

Q. 27.3. Describe the possible findings in a virgin, a woman used to sexual intercourse, and a child, alleged to have been raped.

Forensically trained sexual assault nurse examiner (SANE) and the sexual assault response team (SART)—coordinate activities in relation to sexual assault victims to provide various services, viz. medical, legal, social, etc. in USA, (outlined In the Chapter 2 on "Introduction to Forensic Nursing": A New Perspective in Health Care).

Informed consent of the victim should be obtained in writing in the presence of a witness if she is of and over the age of consent (12 years of age in India). If she is under the age of consent or a mentally subnormal person, the written consent of the parent or guardian should be taken (section 90 IPC). The examination should be made in the presence of a third person, either a female nurse or a female relation unless the doctor happens to be a female doctor. Section 53(2) of the Criminal Procedure Code lays down that whenever a female is to be examined, the examination should be made only by, or under the supervision of, a female registered medical practitioner. In India, victim of rape should generally be examined by a lady doctor. Only if lady doctor is not available a male doctor may examine in the presence of a female nurse/attendant. If the victim refuses the examination, she cannot be forced to submit for examination.

A full examination will have as its principal features: (1) the preliminary data, (2) the statement of the victim and others separately, (3) signs of struggle on clothes and body, (4) examination of genitals, urethra, mouth or anus for—(a) local signs of violation, (b) injuries, (c) presence of spermatozoa and other microorganisms, and (d) any evidence of sexually transmitted disease, (5) collection of laboratory specimens, (6) inference, and (7) advice on follow-up.

The Preliminary Data

This includes name in full, address, age, occupation and social status, date, time of arrival, consent for examination, identification marks, by whom examination is requested, and the name of the female nurse present at the time of examination.

The Statement

The statement of the victim in her own words must be written down as much as possible word for word. The amount of violence used, the position of the assailant, and the mode of attack should be elicited. It is necessary to inquire, if vaginal, oral, or rectal contact occurred. Her statement should be noted with reference to pain, haemorrhage, sensation as to penetration and emission, and the appearance of any discharge. It should also be ascertained, if she cried for help, or was too terrified to do so, or she fainted. Enquiry should be made of the events after the alleged assault, e.g. if she has changed her clothing, bathed or passed urine. Any delay in making a complaint to the authorities should have a proper explanation. A record should be made of the statement of others who accompany her. *The degree of agreement of the various statements is important.*

Signs of Struggle

These should be looked for on the clothes and the body. The **clothing,** if they are the same as that worn at the time of the crime should be examined in good light for evidence of a struggle, such as tears in the fabrics, marks of mud or grass, or stains of blood or semen. When clothes are torn, corresponding injuries to the body may be present and should be looked for. Mud and blood stains, when present, are generally seen on the back clothes while seminal stains are seen on the front clothes. Stains may be found on the material, e.g. handkerchief, used for cleaning after the assault. When blood stains are seen, it must be ascertained if they are due to menstruation. On microscopic examination, menstrual blood is found to contain endometrial cells from the uterus, epithelial cells from the vagina, and a large number of micro-organisms which are not found in ordinary blood. *Trichomonas vaginalis* or *Monilia* may be present. Blood should be taken for grouping and DNA characteristics to determine if the stains belong to the victim or assailant. Seminal stains should also be grouped to ascertain subsequently if they match with the assailant's blood group. The clothing should be retained, carefully dried, labelled, and forwarded to the forensic science laboratory for examination of suspicious stains, either blood, semen, or both.

If there is **some other physical evidence,** such as, foreign hairs, pieces of clothing that could not have been derived from the victim, a trouser button identical with those of the assailant who has one missing, it is a valuable corroboration and should be looked for and noted. This is in accordance with **Locard's principle of exchange,** that when two objects come into contact with each other, there is always some transfer of material from one to the other. Such transfer may or may not be visible to the naked eye.

The woman usually scratches the assailant during the struggle and this may result in injury to her nails which should be recorded. The debris under her nails should be removed and examined for the presence of tags of epithelium, blood, fibres, etc. of the assailant.

The **whole body** should then be examined for marks of violence. An attempt at undressing the victim should not be made but she should be requested to do so herself. The apparent development of the victim is important to note in connection with the ability to offer resistance. However, if the throat has been gripped or if the head has received a blow, the victim's capacity for any resistance may have been greatly impaired. Injuries found on the body must be described specially with reference to the possibility of self-infliction or corroboration of her tale. The injuries may be found (1) about the cheeks, lips, and neck to stiffle the victim's cries for help, (2) about the wrists and arms to restrain her, (3) on the back from impact of gravel or hard ground while pinning her, (4) about the inner sides of knees and thighs while separating her legs, and (5) on the breasts from rough handling. The breasts may also show bitten nipples. The injuries may be scratches, bruises, nail marks, and bites in the form of abrasions, contusions, and lacerations, etc. They should be described in full, like any other injuries, with data to assess their age, to see if they tally with the time of the alleged incident. Biting of any description involves transfer of saliva from which blood group substances can be identified in secretors. An outline body diagram showing location, relative size, and nature of injuries is highly desirable. There may be Teeth bite marks imprint when the whole mouth was used to press the breast. (Love-bite)

As a matter of practice, a second examination may be carried out 48 hours later when deep bruises may be easier to see or when the victim is during menstrual cycle after cessation of bleeding.

Examination of Genitals, Urethra, Mouth and Anus

This should take place in good light and, when possible, in the lithotomy position, with the parts fully exposed. The sooner the examination is made the better, and menstruation should not be a cause for delay. Menstruation is not a bar to illegal sexual intercourse.

Local signs of violation: The presence or absence of blood stains about the legs or vagina, urethra, mouth, anus should be observed and if present, it should be ascertained whether such stains could be due to menstruation, or blood from victim or assailant. If dry, they should be scraped with a clean blunt scalpel and preserved for examination. The pubic hair should be examined for matting from seminal fluid or blood, and for foreign hairs. If the hairs are matted together, a portion must be cut off and kept for examination. The pubic hair should also be combed out to collect non-matching male pubic hair and a comparison sample of plucked hair preserved for laboratory examination. Some believe that hair need not be plucked and that cutting would be alright provided all other foreign hairs have been removed by combing, etc.

Genital injuries: The vulva, hymen, vagina and the perineum should be examined for any injuries. To determine the degree of hymenal rupturing and whether this is recent or old, a glass rod with a small spherical head (Glaister Keene Rod), warmed to body temperature, if possible transilluminated, may be introduced into the vagina and partially withdrawn to display the edge of the hymen. Signs of recent rupture are ragged tears in the hymen with lack of epithelial healing, but with oedema and haemorrhage. Women who pay no attention to the cleanliness of their genital region often have superficial areas of erythema, irritation and occasionally abrasions, and, therefore, any superficial injuries found in this area must be carefully assessed in the light of **personal hygiene** of the woman. Redness due to long-standing inflammation or to irritation by a chronic discharge must be distinguished from the effect of recent injury. It must be noted at this stage, if the gait is normal. When genital injury is present, the gait is broad-based and painful.

The **distensibility** of the vagina should be noted in relation to the number of fingers it can admit without causing discomfort. If it can admit two fingers easily, sexual intercourse has probably occurred.

The extent of violence to the private parts **will depend upon the age of the victim and her previous condition with reference to intercourse,** whether virgin, sexually active, or a child, as discussed below. Slaughter states that colposcopic examination, within 72 hours of assault, is an important adjunct to traditional simple macroscopic assessment of genital trauma.

Rape on a virgin: Any bruising, laceration or swelling of the vulva is noted. The labia are then opened by gentle traction in order to examine the hymen for rupture. Laceration of this structure occurs with the first intercourse, and in a virgin this is the principal evidence of the crime.

The *character and extent of injury* will vary in different cases depending upon the nature of the hymen, disproportion between male and female parts, extent of penetration, and amount of force used. With the first intercourse, tearing of hymen usually occurs posteriorly at one or other side or in the middle. The semilunar hymen often ruptures on both sides. The annular hymen which nearly closes up the vaginal orifice may suffer several tears. The fourchette is torn and the fossa naviculars disappears. Even the posterior commissure may be ruptured. The latter injury usually does not occur in consenting sexual intercourse unless there is much disproportion between the male and female parts.

Soon after the act, the torn margins are sharp and red, and bleed on touch. Even when examined after 3 to 4 days of offence, the edges of laceration are congested and swollen. The surrounding tissues are also swollen and tender.

With *violent intercourse,* laceration of vaginal wall invariably occurs posteriorly or slightly posteriorly. The gait is broad based and painful.

In *indecent assault,* due to digital penetration, the laceration is usually single, may be lateral, and is often incomplete.

Rape on sexually active women: In women who have had considerable intercourse, even without childbirth, the hymen is completely destroyed, the vaginal orifice dilated and the mucous membrane wrinkled and thickened. Rape on married

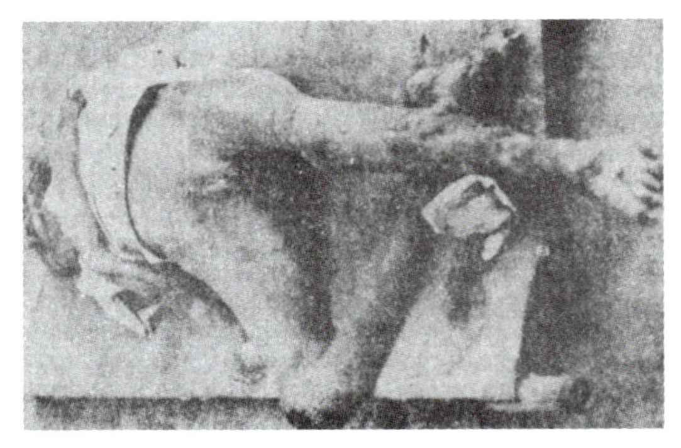

Fig. 27.1: An adult female—a victim of sexual assault and murder. The under clothes are missing. Abrasions and bruises are seen on inner thighs and legs. The vagina is swollen and congested. She was murdered after the act (*Courtesy*: Dr AA Qureshi)

women and females who have had previous intercourse causes little or no damage to the parts unless considerable violence is used. However, marks of genital injury should be looked for since rape is generally associated with greater violence than consensual sexual intercourse. In the absence of genital injury, the presence of signs of violence in other parts of the body, and the presence of spermatozoa in the vagina or on the clothes form the chief evidence of the crime. It must be remembered that in a normal sized adult female, severe genital injuries usually result from insertion of objects other than penis and they are indicative of sadistic or masochistic sexualism rather than coitus (Fig. 27.1).

Rape on children: In young children, as the vagina is very small and hymen deeply situated, the adult penis cannot penetrate it. In rare cases of great violence, the organ may be forcibly introduced, causing rupture of the vaginal vault and associated visceral injuries. Such injuries might result in death. Usually, violence is not used and the penis placed either within the vulva or between the thighs. And as such, only redness and tenderness of the vulva may be caused. The hymen is usually intact. In many charges of rape or attempted rape, since the victim

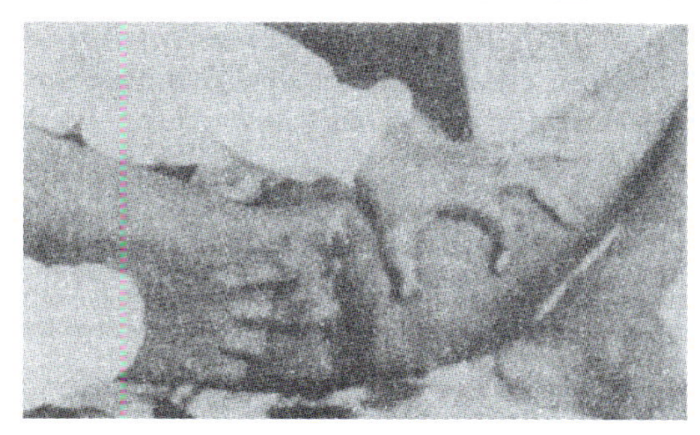

Fig. 27.2: Rape on a girl of nine years. Note the tear in the perineum and the blood flowing out from the tear

is usually a child, the presence of a discharge from the vagina, due to gonorrhoea or inflammation of the parts, is the only cause of suspicion. There may be no signs or very few signs of general violence, since the child has no idea of the act and is also unable to offer resistance (Fig. 27.2).

Presence of spermatozoa and other microorganisms: Normally, sperms remain motile in the vagina for about six to eight hours and occasionally 12 hours. Nonmotile forms are detectable for about 24 hours with occasional reports of 48 to 72 and very rarely 96 hours. Motility persists longer at body temperature. The sperms remain motile in the uterine cavity for 3–5 days. Nonmotile forms may be found in the female genital tract for weeks or months after death. To demonstrate the presence of sperms, the vaginal contents are aspirated by means of a blunt-ended pipette. A wet preparation is then made on a slide and examined under a microscope for motile spermatozoa. If motile sperms are seen, it would mean that intercourse has taken place within about 12 hours. If the sperms are not motile, it is not possible to say exactly when intercourse took place except that it may be over 12 hours and within about 24 to 48 hours and occasionally up to 72 hours. Intact spermatozoa are rarely found in the vagina after 72 hours after coitus. In such a case, sperm heads and tails can be separately demonstrated by using picroindigocarmine which stains sperm heads red and the tails green and red. A smear is also made from the vaginal contents, fixed by gentle heat, and stained by Ziehl-Neelson method, and examined for the presence of spermatozoa and smegma bacilli.

The absence of sperms in the vagina does not mean that sexual intercourse has not taken place. It may be due to non-emission, aspermia, previous vasectomy, very old age, or poor technique by the examining doctor. Detection of seminal fluid from vasectomised males requires the demonstration of prostatic acid phosphatase which should be qualitatively distinguished from vaginal acid phosphatase by electrophoresis. Quantitatively, the normal level of acid phosphatase in the vagina is 340 international units (IU) per litre. It rises to about 3000 IU in about 2 to 3 hours after intercourse and gradually returns to normal in about 12 to 24 hours. Any level higher than 340 IU indicates seminal fluid.

As a result of the discovery of semen specific glycoprotein (P30), acid phosphatase test is used only as a screening test. P30 is present in both normal and aspermic semen. Graves et al found that in some instances P30 test was positive when acid phosphatase test was negative. P30 is detectable in vaginal fluid for a mean period of 27 hours after intercourse as compared to 14 hours for acid phosphatase. If semen is identified, determining of genetic markers, if need be, can be done by enzyme studies and DNA typing.

Swabbing of mouth, vagina, urethra and anus for sperm detection should always be perfor-med on rape victims.

The presence of smegma bacilli is suggestive of coitus. Its absence is without any significance. Smegma bacillus is seen as an acid-fast rod-shaped organism thicker than the tubercle bacillus.

Sexually transmitted diseases (STDs): The diseases for which the victims are at risk appear to be—(a) chlamydial infection, (b) gonorrhoea, (c) syphilis, (d) chancre, (e) genital warts, (f) genital herpes, and (g) trichomoniasis. Hepatitis B and HIV infection may be considered, if the assailant appears to be so infected.

Chlamydial infection is common. Its prophylaxis is the same as that for gonorrhoea. Trichomoniasis, genital warts, and genital herpes are not common. They need to be considered, if symptoms arise. Most authors, therefore suggest a cervical culture for gonorrhoea and Chlamydia (if laboratory facilities are available), and a blood test for syphilis, and other tests as required. The following procedure is recommended.

The presence or absence of any urethral or vaginal discharge should be noted. It may be due to gonorrhoea, vaginitis, worms, or uncleanliness. The presence of sores should also be looked for. They may due to syphilis or chancroid. Blood should be examined for T cells, if there is suspicion of transmission of **HIV.** A substantial drop of T cell count at the end of 3 weeks is a serious warning and needs further investigation.

In gonorrhoea, a purulent discharge is generally seen after three days. A thin film of the discharge is made on two or three glass sides, fixed, and stained by Gram's method, and examined under the high power of a microscope. Gonococci, when present, are seen as intracellular, Gram-negative, bean-shaped diplococci. In case of a negative result, an opinion can be given only after three consecutive examinations have been made at intervals of one week each. A negative smear at the time of examination may be of significance, if a positive smear is obtained within a few days of assault.

If oral or rectal contact has occurred, specimens for gonorrhoea culture need to be taken from the mouth, pharynx, and tonsillar area, or the rectum.

If there is a sore which is suspected to be syphilitic, the discharge is examined under dark ground illumination for the presence of *Treponema pallidum*. Blood for serological examination (VDRL) is also collected. An initial negative result followed by a positive result at six weeks or later is of value. If the sore is suspected to be due to chancroid, the smear made from the discharge or bubo fluid when stained by Gram's method will show the presence of Ducrey's bacillus. It is a Gram-negative *Streptobacillus* with rounded ends.

The STD can be attributed to the accused only when—(1) the accused is also suffering from the same venereal disease, (2) the disease appeared in the victim after its known period of incubation after the alleged sexual assault, and (3) the victim was not suffering from the disease prior to this assault. The incubation period of gonorrhoea is 2–8 days. If may vary from 1–15 days. The incubation period of syphilis is 2–8 weeks, the average being 25 days. The incubation period of chancroid varies from 3 weeks to 3 months.

Collection of Laboratory Specimens

In some jurisdictions, *sexual assault kits* are provided by the law enforcement agency. They contain packaging materials, and instruction for collection and preservation of evidence that conform to standards laid down by the crime laboratory.

In those jurisdictions where no such kits are provided, it is necessary to consult the crime laboratory.

Forensic science laboratory to ensure that the evidence meets with its requirements.

As detailed already in the text, the specimens to be collected from the victim for laboratory examination include:

1. Clothing—stained, torn, foreign matter
2. Scrapings of dried blood stains—grouping, DNA characteristics

3. Scrapings of dried seminal stains—grouping, sperms, P30 glycoprotein, DNA characteristics
4. Hairs—matted pubic hair, combed foreign hair, plucked hair
5. Broken nails and debris from under the nails
6. Blood—grouping, alcohol, drugs, VDRL, T cells
7. Saliva—secretor status
8. Swabs from any soiled area of skin; from bite marks for saliva; and from mouth, pharynx, urethra, vagina, cervix, and anus for spermatozoa, microorganisms, P30 glycoprotein, and sexually transmitted disease. Other specimens, e.g. head hair, body hair, urine (for drugs, pregnancy), etc. are collected at the discretion of the examiner. The examination should be tailored to the requirements of the particular case and collection of all samples may not be necessary.

The Inference

This depends very much upon circumstances. The site of alleged offence may be examined, if it appears desirable. In children, the examiner must not always expect signs of struggle as they are normally not capable of exercising sufficient resistance to provoke injury. The superstitious belief that sexual intercourse with a virgin cures venereal diseases has, on occasions, led to rape. Some girls are too terrified when an attack of rape is made upon them; they do not offer any resistance, with the result that their bodies do not bear evidence of injuries as might be expected from a struggle, while locally there may be all the expected signs of the accomplished act of penetration. In such a case, the acts and the **demeanour of the girl** (distressed, dazed, shocked, tearful, aggressive, etc.) immediately after the alleged commission of crime should be subjected to very critical investigation, as these may provide valuable evidence, corroborative or otherwise, regarding the alleged ravishing. The **mental condition** and any **signs of drunkenness** should be particularly noted. If, on laboratory examination, a drug is found, the doctor should be prepared to state if the amount of drug is consistent with the degree of intoxication that would make valid consent improbable or impossible.

The **opinion** as to commission of the crime of rape is based on a consideration of: (1) scene examination, (2) signs of struggle, (3) presence of blood and/or seminal stains on clothes and body, (4) presence of seminal matter in the vagina, (5) transmission of venereal disease, and (6) laboratory reports and the examining doctor does not offer opinion that rape is committed or not committed. As it is the domain of Judiciary, he only says whether sexual intercourse evidence is there, whether evidence of force is there.

False accusations: The possibility of false accusation must be kept in mind. In reality, if it were not for the fact that rape can take place from fear, the problem might be fairly easy to solve for 'a fully conscious woman of normal physique will resist having her legs separated by one man against her will'. **It has been very aptly said, "Rape is an allegation, easily made, hard to prove and harder to disprove".**

Vulval and vaginal injuries may be maliciously produced in children by instruments or fingers and a false charge of rape brought against an individual with a view to take revenge or extort money from him. Artificial bruises may be produced by using marking nut juice. The vagina may be irritated by using chillis. Sometimes, frog's or fowl's blood may be used for staining the clothes and private parts. Solutions of starch or egg albumin may be used to stain the clothes and such stains simulate seminal stains.

Sometimes, the girl is a consenting party, and it is only after the act that she becomes frightened and brings a charge to save her reputation.

One girl who had connection several times with her fiance became alarmed at some blood on her garments. She, therefore, alleged that after he had left her, she was attacked, and had amnesia till she regained consciousness to find her underclothes blood-stained. As her fiance had left her in the passage outside her house where they had been talking from 1.00 a.m. till 2.00 a.m., it seemed unrealistic to incriminate a third party. Suspicion was strengthened by her repeated statements that her fiance would never do such a thing and she could trust him anywhere. She finally admitted her involvement with him, and then asked what she was to tell her mother!

A girl, a alleged victim of rape, was asked if she struggled to her utmost to which she said she did. She was asked if she shouted to which she said she did not. When asked, why not, she stated that she was afraid of waking up her mother who slept in the next room!

Often, the victim's story gives a strong indication of the falsity of the charge. The girl who tells of a cloth smelling of chloroform being placed over her mouth after which she immediately became unconscious and on recovering her senses found her clothes in disorder, and complains that she has been raped, is likely to be an hysterical one, rather than a victim of rape. The statement of a woman who presents no signs of struggle and who appears to have offered no resistance to her assailant that she was under the influence of a drug must be accepted with great caution. Probably, she is making an attempt to clear herself at the expense of her partner. In such a case, a close inquiry must be made into the history of the case, the manner in which the drug was given, whether in food or in drink, the amount taken, the special taste if any noted, the time elapsing before symptoms arose, and the nature of the symptoms. The complainant must be pressed for details and the story may be so clear that drugging may be ruled out! Blood and urine should be preserved for chemical examination, if deemed necessary. It should be remembered that drugs, like Rohypnol (Roche), and Chloral hydras in alcoholic drink, have been used as stupefying poisons prior to rape.

When a woman's husband is away and she becomes pregnant, she may claim rape to help cover up her activities during his absence.

False charges **can be disproved** in many cases by medical evidence in regard to the (a) statement of the victim which is neither convincing nor consistent in relation to the time of reporting the crime, scene, consent, and circumstances, (b) injuries, the dating of which does not correspond to the time of the alleged incident, (c) doubtful story about administration of drugs, and (d) results from laboratory specimens.

Accusations of indecent assault or rape have been brought in the past against doctors and dentists as a result of dreams or hallucinations, accompanied by erotic sensations, which some women experience under light anaesthesia. If the patient is restless or struggling while under the anaesthetic or emerging from its effects, there may be disarrangement of her clothing upon which she may place the worst interpretation. As on rare occasions, some doctors and dentists have taken advantage of the opportunity afforded by examination or anaesthesia, it is advisable for them to avoid such a charge by having a female nurse, a female relation, or husband, present during examination or narcosis on a woman.

Follow-up

The aim is to aid the victim to recover from the traumatic experience of sex assault and regain dignity and self-respect. Accordingly, follow-up involves:

1. Treatment of injuries
2. Tetanus prophylaxis
3. Prevention and termination of pregnancy

4. Prevention and treatment of any sexually transmitted disease
5. Referral to crisis intervention centres for support by social workers and psychiatrists.

Accidents Following Rape

Death may occur from shock due to fright/ or emotion or from haemorrhage due to injuries to genitals and perineum. Death may occur from suffocation, if mouth and nostrils are closed by the hand or cloth to prevent crying or shouting. The act of rape may inflict violent psychic or mental trauma and may cause personality derangement. Sometimes, the assailant may murder the victim after rape to silence her permanently. This is usually accomplished by throttling with the bare hands of the assailant or by strangulation with a ligature from material readily available at hand, e.g. nylon stocking, pantyhose, or the scarf of the victim. Victims from certain cultures may commit suicide out of shame and stigma to the family.

EXAMINATION OF THE ACCUSED

Q. 27.4. Describe in detail how you would proceed to examine a person accused of rape.

The principal features of the examination are:

1. The preliminary data
2. Physical examination and mental condition
3. Signs of struggle on clothes and body
4. Local examination of the genitals

Preliminary data: This includes the name, age, occupation, address, brought by whom, identification marks, consent for examination, time of examination, and brief history. In most jurisdictions {sec. 53(1) CrPC 1973 in India}, an accused can be examined and necessary evidence, e.g. blood, swabs, etc., collected even without his consent and by use of force if such an examination is desirable to ascertain the accused's part in an alleged sexual offence.

The examination of the accused should always be made as soon as it can be arranged for, and the exact time and date should be mentioned. If the accused is arrested soon after the crime, the police should not allow him to go to the bathroom unsupervised under any pretext, until the medical examination has been finished, lest he may wash off the stains on his body and clothes and destroy valuable evidence. The accused's account of the matter need not concern the doctor in the same way as that of the victim but note should be taken of it especially if he refers to injuries or the use of force. He may allege that the process began on the basis of consent and injuries are the result of postcoital fighting since remuneration was expected and not forthcoming or it was considered inadequate.

Physical examination: The examiner should note the **size** and **physique** of the alleged assailant to determine the ability of the victim to offer resistance and to assess genital injuries sustained by her. The **mental condition** and any **signs of drunkenness** should be specially noted.

Signs of struggle: A search should be made for **injuries** which the victim says she influcted on the assailant during the alleged struggle. The **clothing** should be carefully examined for missing buttons or presence of foreign hairs, foreign fabrics', lip-stick or make-up soiling, mud stains, grass, etc. The blood and seminal stains are usually found on the front of the undergarments. If blood stains are found on the clothes, blood group should be ascertained, and a microscopic examination for vaginal epithelium and bacterial flora made. The demonstration of seminal stains on clothing is always capable of innocent explanation! It merely indicates a recent emission. General marks of violence, such as bites (Fig. 27.3), bruises and scratches, may be

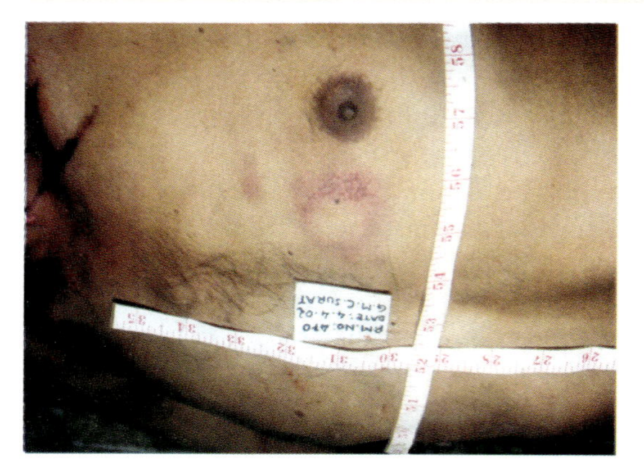

Fig. 27.3: Bite marks on male breast area

found on the face, hands or private parts. They should be described in full like any other injuries with data to assess their age.

Genitals: Seminal stains and blood stains may be found about the pubic hair. The blood stains, if dry, should be scraped with a clean blunt scalpel and preserved for examination. The penis should be examined for presence of smegma under the prepuce. **Smegma** is a thick cheesy secretion with a disagreeable odour. It consists of desquamated epithelial cells and smegma bacilli. The presence of thick uniform coating of smegma under the prepuce or round about corona glandes is inconsistent with a recent intercourse. The smegma is rubbed off during intercourse and it takes about 24 hours to accumulate. The presence of a torn frenum is consistent with a recent intercourse. **Frenum** is a small fold of skin or mucous membrane that checks or curbs the movement of a part or organ. It may be torn due to forcible introduction of the organ into the vagina or due to disproportion between the size of penis and vaginal opening. The presence of venereal discharge or syphilitic chancre should be specifically looked for and the victim examined for the existence of such venereal disease with due regard to its incubation period. In a recent case, the penis should be examined for the presence of vaginal epithelial cells on its surface, unless the assailant has used a condom. The status of the rapist as regards HIV infection should be determined.

The accused should also be examined to determine, if there is anything to suggest that he is impotent. If necessary, his blood can also be taken for grouping. And, this may be of value, if the group of the seminal matter found on the victim can be ascertained. The greatest possibility of grouping the assailant's semen taken from the vagina exists when the female is a non-secretor.

As already detailed in the text, the specimens to be collected from the accused for laboratory examination include:

1. Clothing—stained, torn, missing buttons, foreign matter
2. Scrapings of blood and seminal stains—grouping, DNA characteristics
3. Hair—matted pubic hair, combed foreign hair
4. Debris under the nails
5. Blood—grouping, alcohol, drugs, VDRL, HIV antibodies
6. Saliva—secretor status
7. Swabs from coronal sulcus, prepuce, and urethra for evidence of sexually transmitted disease. Other specimens, such as head hair, body hair, urine (for drugs), etc., are collected at the discretion of the examiner.

INCEST

This is the act of sexual intercourse by a man with a woman within a certain degree of blood relationship. A man may not have sexual intercourse with a woman whom he knows to be his mother, daughter, sister, or granddaughter, nor a woman within the same limits of relationship. In India, incest *per se* is not a cognisable offence and police cannot take any notice of it unless the offence can be brought into any of the penalising sections, such as 376 and 497 IPC. The offence is probably more common than is thought of. The commonest example is the father and daughter and depends upon lust and brutality. Instances of brothers and sisters are less common and may be due to personality disorder or mental subnormality. Medical examination is concerned with demonstrating evidence of habitual intercourse rather than of fresh defloration.

Q. 27.5. Give a detailed proforma for investigation of sexual offenses.

Proforma for Investigation of Sexual Offenses

Requisition from of Police of Division
Vide his letter No dated

1. Name of the individual: 2. Sex:
3. Parent's or guardian's name:
4. Address:
5. Occupation: 6. Caste:
7. Married or single: 8. Age, as stated by:
9. Persons accompanying or brought by:
10. Time and place of examination:
11. Consent of the individual for examination:
12. Signature of the individual consenting or left thumb impression
13. In the case of minors, consent of the guardian and his/her signature or left thumb impression:
14. Name of nurse present at the time of examination:
15. Marks of identification: 1. 2.

Physical Examination—Female

1. Height: 2. Weight:
3. Breadth: Inspiration: Expiration:
4. Chest girth at the level of the nipples:
5. Abdominal girth at the level of the navel:
6. General build and appearance:
7. Voice: 8. Teeth:
9. Hair: Axillary: Pubic:
10. Mammae — development of breasts — milk in:
11. Generative organs — development of genitals:
12. Onset of puberty—date:
13. Ossification report from radiological examination:
14. Age: 15. History:
16. Date and hour when the female first made complaint and the precise words employed by her at the time, i.e. a detailed account of the occurrence as given by the woman:
17. General behaviour:
18. Date and exact time when the rape was said to have been committed:
19. Place where it occurred:
20. The exact circumstances under which the rape was committed, e.g. whether the parties were standing or lying on the ground:
21. Whether or not the female was menstruating at the time:
22. Whether she was sensible during the whole time that the offence was committed or under the influence of alcohol, or other intoxicants:
23. General feeling of those accompanying the female towards herself and towards the accused:
24. Whether she uttered any cries or was too terrified to do so:
25. Clothing—if changed—when:
26. Whether bath was taken—when:
27. Whether urine was passed—when:
28. Whether motion was passed—when:
29. Mental condition and signs of drunkenness, if any:
30. Gait: 31. Intelligence:
32. Demeanour:
33. Examination of clothes including under-linen worn at the time of alleged rape and preserved for examination of:
    (a) Blood, (b) Semen (including grouping, if possible), (c) others discharges, (d) Mud-dirt
34. Is venereal disease present? Is there a possibility of HIV transmission?
35. Genitals—pubic hair—length—matted or not: Vulva: Vagina: Hymen: Fourchette: Perineum: Cervix:
36. Injuries to cheeks, lips, mammae, thighs, and genitals:
37. Smears:
    a. from vagina, for spermatozoa and other micro-organisms
    b. from urethra for gonorrhoea
    c. from sore for evidence of syphilis or chancroid:
38. Blood group examination, if consent available:
39. Other examinations, e.g. for pregnancy, HIV infection:

Opinion

a. There is evidence/no evidence of sexual intercourse
b. There is evidence/no evidence of force

Station Signature of the Medical Officer
Date: and his Designation

Physical Examination—Male

1. Height: 2. Weight:
3. Breadth: Inspiration: Expiration:
4. Chest girth at the level of the nipples:
5. Abdominal girth at the level of the navel:
6. General build and appearance:
7. Voice:
8. Teeth:
9. Hair: Scalp: Beard: Moustache:
   Axillary: Pubic:
10. History:
11. General behaviour:
12. Mental condition and signs of drunkenness, if any:
13. Whether bath was taken — when:

(contd.)

(*contd.*)

14. Whether urine was passed — when:
15. Whether motion was passed — when:
16. Clothing (describe) — if changed — when:
17. Stains on clothing and on body:
18. Injuries on clothing and on body:
19. Injuries on genitals — scars if any:
20. Is venereal disease present?
21. Genitals—pubic hair—length—matted or not:
    a. Penis—normal or abnormal, any abnormality – describe:
       — prepuce circumcised or not:
       — smegma: frenum:
    b. Any evidence of impotence:
23. Blood group examination if necessary:
24. Other examinations, e.g. for HIV infection and his designation:

Opinion

From the foregoing examination, I find nothing to suggest that the said accused is incapable of performing the sexual intercourse.

Station Signature of the Medical Officer
Date:

PROTECTION OF CHILDREN FROM SEXUAL OFFENCES

In India, an act has come in vogue in 2012, for the protection of children from sexual offences.

This act defines 'child' for the purpose, defines penatrative sexual assault, aggressive penatrative sexual assault. Sexual assault, aggravated sexual assault, sexual harassment, and punishments for these acts. Abetments have same punishments. Attempts have half of the punishment, using child for pornographic purposes and its punishment is also prescribed.

Medical examination of a child is to be conducted on the same lines of see. **164 A of CrPC.** Medical examination shall be conducted by a registered medical practitioner employed in a hospital run by the government or a local authority and in the absence of such a practitioner by any other registered medical practitioner with the consent of such woman or of a person competent to give such consent on her behalf within 24 hours from the time of receiving the information of such offence. Registered medical practitioner examine her person prepare a report of his examination giving the following particulars. If the victim is a girl, examination shall be conducted by a woman doctor in the presence of the parent or any person in whom the child has trust or in the presence of a woman nominated by the head of the 'medical institution'.

1. The name and address of the woman and of the person by whom she was brought
2. The age of the woman
3. The description of material taken from the person of the woman for DNA profiling
4. Marks of injury, if any, on the person of the woman
5. General mental condition of the woman
6. Other material particulars in reasonable detail

Report shall state reasons for each conclusion arrived.

The report shall specifically record that the consent of the woman or of the person competent to give such consent on her behalf.

Exact time of commencement and completion of the examination shall also by noted in the report.

Registered medical practitioner shall, without delay forward the report to the investigating officer who shall forward it to the magistrate.

Child under this act is one who is below the age of 18 yrs. Under section 3, penetrative sexual assault **(PSA)** is when the accused penetrates his penis to any extent into the vagina, mouth, urethra or anus of a child or makes the child to do so with him or any other person. Penetrative sexual assault is also said to be done when he inserts to any extent any object or a part of the body other than penis into the vagina, urethra or anus or makes the child to do so with him or any other person, or when he manipulates any part of the child to cause penetration into vagina , urethra or any part of the body of the child or makes the child to do so with him or any other person or he applies his mouth to the penis, vagina, anus urethra of the child or makes the child to do so to such person or any other person. Punishment—not less than 7 years, may extend upto life imprisonment and fine.

Section 5: ***Aggrevated penetrative sexual assault (APSA):*** When PSA is committed by a police officer on duty or out of duty in his PS or any other place, PSA is committed by member of army or security forces, by management or staff of jail, remand or protection home, by staff or management of government or private hospital, gang penetrative sexual assault, or the PSA is with weapons, fire-heated substance, corrosive or PSA caused grievous hurt or bodily harm or sex organ injury or PSA caused temporary or permanent mental illness or PSA caused pregnancy of child, or infects child with HIV or any other life-threatening disease or infection that causes temporary or permanent physical incapica-tation or mental illness to perform regular tasks or PSA on mentally or physically disabled child, PSA more than once or repeatedly, PSA on a child below 12 years, PSA by a blood relative or any other relative or staying in same or shared house premises, PSA by management , owner, staff of institution providing service to child, or PSA on a child knowing she is pregnant, PSA and attempt to murder on a child or PSA in a communal or sectarian violence or PSA by a person convicted earlier under this act or under any other legal provisions or commit PSA and strips the child or parade naked in public.

Punishment: Not less than 10 years or up to life and fine.

Sec. 7: Sexual assault: When a person does any act with sexual intent involving physical contact without penetration of vagina, penis, anus or breast of child or makes the child to do so on him or any other person, it is called sexual assault.

Punishment: Not less than 3 years and up to 5 years and fine.

Sec. 9: Aggravated sexual assault (ASA): When sexual assault is caused by a police officer, a member of armed forces or security force or by a public servant or management or staff of hosptial, jail, educational or religious institution it is called (ASA) aggravated sexual assault.

When more than one person is involved it is called gang sexual assault, ASA causing physical or mental incapicitation or dis-ability or infects child with HIV or any other infection which temporarily or permanently impairs the child physically or mentally incapicitated or ill to perform regular tasks, taking advantage of mental or physical disability commits more than once or repeatedly, chuild below 12 years, relative by blood or otherwise or sharing house or house hold or owner or manage-ment or staff providing services to children, in a position of trust or authority or a child knowing she is pregnant or SA and attempt to murder or during communal or sectarian violence or by a person already convicted for sexual offence under this or any other law or commits SA and strips naked and parades the girl.

Punishment: Not less than 5 years and extendable up to 7 years + fine.

Sec. 11: Sexual harassment: Sexual harass-ment is committed when with sexual intent a person, utters any word, makes sound, or gesture or exhibit any object or part of the body or makes a child exhibit body or any part to be seen by him or by any other person, shows any object for pornographic purposes. Or when a person repeatedly follows or watches or contacts a child directly or through any other means, or when a person threatens to use any form of media, or the involvement of a child in a sexual act or ensices a child for pornographic purpose or gives gratification on that court.

Sec. 12: Punishment: Up to 3 years + fine.

Sec. 13: Pornographic purposes: Using child in any form of media for sexual gratification by representation of sexual organ of a child, or using a child engaged in real or simulated sexual act with or without penetration.

Sec 14: Punishment: 5 years and fine.

Second conviction: 7 years and fine.

As in S.3: If the child is used by directly participating he is punished not less than 10 years.

As in S.5: Life imprisonment and fine, if the person in volved is a police officer or public servant case.

As in S.7: Not less than 6 years + fine or even up to 8 years, if the person touches vagina, penis, breast, etc., by directly participating in pronographic acts.

As in S.9: Not less than and even 8 years up to 10 years + fine, if the person involved is police officer or army person or public servant case.

- Wherever medical examination is requested it must be carried out meticulously, reports prepared without delay and handed over to the police officer or magistrate.
- *Recent ammendements to IPC and CrPC.*

28 Unnatural Sexual Offenses

Section 377 IPC defines unnatural sexual offenses as sexual intercourse against the order of nature with any man, woman, or animal, and lays down punishment for the same. Penetration is sufficient to constitute the offence; proof of emission is immaterial. These offenses include sodomy, buccal coitus, tribadism and bestiality. In all these *deviations*, it is necessary to have the assessment of the mental state of the accused by a skilled *psychiatrist* and Forensic Medicine expert for opinion.

Q.28.1. What is sodomy? Mention the procedure of examination and the signs that you will observe in the participants. Discuss the difficulties in diagnosis.

SODOMY

The practice of sodomy was said to be common in a town, mentioned in the Bible, by the name of Sodom, from which the word sodomy is derived. In modern practice, sodomy means anal intercourse between two males (homosexual sodomy), or between a male and a female (heterosexual sodomy). It is also called buggery. It is termed gerontophilia when the passive agent is an adult, and paederasty, when the passive agent is a young boy, the boy being known as a catamite. The active agent is one who performs the act and the passive agent is one on whom the act is performed. Sodomy may be performed by two men who alternately act as active and passive agent. The question of consent does not arise and it is no defence that the passive party was the accused's wife. Both offenders are punishable under section 377 IPC, but when the offence is done without the consent of the passive agent, the active agent alone is guilty.

In England and Wales, the Sexual Offenses Act 1967 has legalised homo-sexuality in a private place between two consenting males over 21 years of age, provided they are not merchant seamen on a UK merchant ship or members of HM services. In India, the apex count has refused to do so and left it to the Parliament.

There is a class of people in India known as **'eunuchs'** who act as passive agents in sodomy. They are, therefore, known as male prostitutes. They accommodate their clients for intercourse via the mouth, armpits, and intercrural folds also. Among them, there are two groups, the hijrahs, and the zenanas. The **hijrahs** add to their tribes by recruiting boys and *castrating* them, the castration being performed by their barbers. When the wound heals, the scar invaginates. Their external genitals, therefore, resemble those of the female on a cursory examination. Being castrated before puberty, female characteristics, such as feminine voice, feminine distribution of fat and hair, and development of breasts, are common. They clothe like women, dress their hair similarly, wear ornaments and adopt female tastes and habits. The **zenanas** live separately from the hijrahs and *their genitals are intact*. Both the hijrahs and the zenanas maintain a line of separation between themselves and the female prostitutes. The present editor (Dr Subrahmanyam) has seen a number of hijras brought for Medicolegal examination, ages ranging from 12 to 65 yrs. In a sweep the young boy's genitals are cut off and to a waist thread an eyed long needle is tied which he is asked to keep inside stump of urethra except when voiding urine until sphincteric action developed at the stump. Hot oil soaked in cotton is used in dressing the wound.

Homosexual practice is common in all classes of society. The offence is common among prisoners, members of the armed forces, and sailors, who are sex-starved by circumstances. The act is difficult to perform against the will unless the person is drugged or drunk.

For the investigation of the crime, a medical examination of both passive and active agents is necessary. It should be remembered that **false charges** may be made for the purpose of blackmail and men may be tricked into homosexual relationship by men masquerading as women whilst on shore, particularly in the eastern seas. They can be identified by the blue bird tattoo design on the extensor surface of the web of the thumb.

Examination of the Passive Agent

Preliminary particulars include name, age, sex, occupation, address, by whom examination is requested, time of arrival, time of examination, identification marks, and consent for examination. A brief history especially as regards the use of lubricant and degree of penetration as narrated should be recorded. The examination should be carried out in the knee-elbow position, and in the presence of a third person. In most charges of sodomy, the victim is a boy or young man. If he is not accustomed to sodomy, the following signs may be found.

Genital signs: The anal orifice is found dilated, irritable, and tender to touch, and a zone of bruising may be seen around the orifice. There are often slight abrasions between the anus and the tip of the coccyx. If there is gradual but forcible overstretching, a radial fissure of the mucous membrane of the anus will be found. If sudden violence is used, there is often a triangular bruised tear of the posterior part of the anus with its base external.

Anal and perianal swabs must be taken for examination of spermatozoa, evidence of venereal infection (including HIV), and presence of a lubricant. A sample of hair, preferably any matted hair, should also be taken. The anal canal and lower rectum should then be carefully inspected through a proctoscope and any area of injury or abnormality of the mucosal lining must be noted. The person may complain of pain when the anal canal is being examined. Gait and defaecation may also be painful.

Other signs: Additional evidence may be found, e.g. presence of spermatozoa on the clothing, and signs of struggle. The clothing should in all cases be subjected to laboratory examination for the presence of stains either seminal, faecal, blood or mud.

The only **evidence of sodomy** is the presence of semen in the anus. Any opinion as to the cause of dilatation should be guarded, and merely state that it is consistent with the entry of a penis.

Examination of the Habitual Passive Agent

The habitual passive agent of sodomy is usually a young boy (catamite), or eunuch (hijrah) in India. The signs which an examiner should look for are as follows:

Genital signs: The anal skin is smooth and thick, and the anal opening is situated more deeply than usual, due to the absorption of fat, giving the appearance of a funnel-shaped depression. The anal sphincter is lax, the opening patulous, the canal dilated, and there is loss of rugosity of the anal mucosa. The presence of a fissure or fissure scar is not uncommon, and external and internal haemorrhoids may be present.

Other signs: Additional evidence is commonly found from the incriminating stains on the clothes as described above. In addition, anal hair may have been shaved but not necessarily the pubic hair. Signs of implanted venereal disease is a strong corroborative evidence. Homosexuals commonly exhibit feminine traits as regards dress, cosmetics, gait, and manner of speaking.

Examination of the Active Agent

The accused should be examined for abrasions and bruises on the glans or tearing of the frenum of the penis, for the traces of faeces and lubricant about his genitals, and for the peculiar smell transferred by the anal glands. Faecal soiling, blood and foreign hairs are most likely to become trapped in the area of the coronal sulcus particularly in the uncircumcised. His clothes should be examined for the presence of stains either seminal, faecal, blood or mud, and his body for marks of a struggle. In addition, any evidence of venereal disease should be looked for. If there is no great disproportion between the size of the anus and that of the penis, it is highly improbable that any sign will be found. In an habitual active agent, there may be elongation and constriction of the penis with consequent angulation of the urethra, on account of the constricting force of the sphincter ani.

Difficulties in Diagnosis

Examination of alleged sexual offenses between males presents rather more difficulty to the inexperienced doctor. In fact, it is not surprising that many pathologists who have not examined anal orifices in life are misled by the appearances after death when the sphincter is relaxed. An extremely difficult examination is in connection with divorce when the woman alleges abnormal practices against the husband. The anal orifice can be quite lax following childbirth, particularly if there has been a perineal tear, and some healed fissures and old haemorrhoids may be a normal finding, making it extremely difficult to say for certain whether the allegation is true unless it has been a persistent practice. And, such a practice is not uncommon.

Q. 28.2. Write short notes on: (1) buccal coitus, (2) tribadism.

Buccal coitus or intercourse per os also falls under section 377 IPC and is punishable accordingly. Intercourse through the mouth is usually practiced by adult males on children. It is also called sin of Gomorrah because it was prevalent in a Biblical town of that name. Buccal swabs from the victim within about 8 hours of oral-penile contact, provided there has been no cleaning of teeth nor consumption of hot drinks, will frequently reveal seminal traces. Rarely, faint teeth marks and abrasions may be seen on the penis of the assailant. **Fellatio** means the oral stimulation or manipulation of the penis by either the male or female. **Cunnilingus** means the oral stimulation of the female genitals.

Tribadism is a form of mental aberration known as lesbian love or **lesbianism.** According to Greek mythology, the female population of the Isle of Lesbos practiced this perversion and hence the name. It is also known as **female homosexuality.** It means gratification of sexual desire of a woman by another woman. The instrument of passion is usually the clitoris which may be enlarged. Milesian females used an artificial phallus or penis for this purpose.

Tribadism is usually indulged in by women who have repulsion for men or who suffer from nymphomania (perverted uncontrollable sexual desire). The condition is of little medicolegal interest and medical examination is of no value in deciding whether the offence has taken place.

Q. 28.3. What is bestiality? How will you proceed to examine the accused? What signs are you likely to come across in the accused and the beast?

Bestiality (bestio-sexuality) or Zoophilia means sexual intercourse by a human being with a lower animal, either through the anus or the vagina. The offence is punishable under section 377 IPC. Any animal, either domesticated on the farm or kept as house pet, such as donkey, pig, goat, cattle, chicken, dog, or cat that the person feels suitable for the purpose, may be used. Generally, sheep are used by males, and dogs and cats by females, as they are easily available, relatively docile, and convenient in size. On most occasions, the animal manipulates the genitalia by mouth and actual coitus is not quite common.

The accused may be a young person employed to look after the animals, a sex-starved lonely individual, or one suffering from some mental aberration. The superstitious belief that venereal diseases are cured by sexual intercourse with a lower animal may lead to bestiality.

The sure evidence of bestiality is the finding of human spermatozoa in the genital tract of the animal, and animal hair on the inside of the pants or under the prepuce (Locard's principle of exchange). Both the accused as well as the animal should be examined.

Findings on the accused: The penis may be contaminated with faecal matter, vaginal secretion, or hair of the animal. There may be injury to penis, if such intercourse is through the anus. Dung stains, animal hair, and injuries due to kicks, teeth or claws of the animal may be found on the clothes and on the body of the accused. In the event, the animal is injured during the act, and if as a result thereof, there are blood stains on the clothes or on the body of the accused, important evidence may be obtained by establishing species of blood stains by the precipitin test.

Findings on the animal: Human spermatozoa may be present in the vagina or anus of the animal. The spermatozoa of lower animals can be differentiated from those of men microscopically. Sometimes, human hair may be found sticking to the animal. Human hair can be differentiated from animal hair by microscopic examination. Injuries may be found on the orifice of the animal. The presence of gonorrhoeal discharge in the vagina of an animal is a positive sign of bestiality as gonorrhoea does not naturally occur in animals. Examination by a veterinary surgeon is helpful. Prof. MKR Krishnan reported a case of bestiality with a shegoat. One husband was punished for abetting and aiding bestiality by sexually exciting a dog and forcing his wife to have sexual intercourse.

29 Sexual Perversions/Deviations

Q. 29.1. What is meant by a sexual perversion/deviation. Briefly discuss the various sexual deviations that you commonly come across in medicolegal work.

Sexual perversions/deviations are habitual acts aimed to obtain sexual gratification without sexual intercourse. These include: (1) sadism, (2) masochism, (3) fetichism, (4) exhibitionism, (5) transvestism, (6) uranism, (7) voyeurism, and the less common ones, viz, (8) frotteurism, (9) urolagnia, etc. A person who indulges in such acts is known as a sexual pervert or deviate. In all such cases, it is necessary to have the mental state of the accused assessed by a skilled psychiatrist.

Sadism: This is a sexual perversion in which the infliction of pain is a necessary and sometimes the sole factor for sexual gratification. The term is derived from the name of a Frenchman, Marquis de Sade (1740–1814) who wrote books in which the characters enjoyed being cruel. This perversion is more common in the males. The sadist bites, flogs, injures or ill-treats the partner. Injuries may be inflicted on any body area but breasts and external genitalia are commonly selected. The author has come across a case in which a man used to cause cigarette burns on his wife to get an erection. In extreme cases, there is a frenzy to commit a violent act, known as *lust murder* (psychological equivalent of coitus). The sadist may perform sexual intercourse on the dying or dead victim *(necrophilia);* he may tear out the genitals or other organs and drink the blood or eat such flesh to satisfy the sexual desire *(necrophagia).* A repeat murder may be committed when the frenzy returns.

Masochism: This is the reverse of sadism. It is more common among males. Victims of this perversion obtain sexual enjoyment only when they receive a painful stimulus from women. Such painful stimulus may entirely replace the ordinary sex stimulus. The term is derived from the name of an Austrian Novelist Leopold Sacher Masoch (1836–1895) who described such characters suffering from this perversion. Rarely, accidental hanging may occur in a masochist during his masochistic exercises *(autoerotic deaths).* Generally, sadism and masochism are found together with one type dominant over the other. The combination of sadism and masoctism is called as **bondage.**

Fetichism: This is a perversion in which sexual gratification is associated with contact and sight of certain parts of the female body, or even clothing, or other articles known as fetish objects. A fetish object is an object which attracts a person with irrational fascination amounting to magical attraction. Thus, the clothing, kerchief or shoes of a woman act as a sexual stimulus to a fetishist. He would want to have these objects for sexual gratification and may masturbate in them. This may lead the fetishist to steal such objects or follow women having such objects and he may thus come in conflict with the law in connection with charges of theft or offenses against public decency. The variety of fetish objects is almost limitless. A fetishist who is fascinated by female hair may follow females with long hair and resort to cutting them.

Exhibitionism: As the name suggests, the term applies to acts of men whose sexual desire consists principally of the exhibition of the genitals with or without performance of masturbatory acts in the presence of women and young girls. Occasionally, women may expose themselves in public. Exhibitionism is an obscene act punishable under section 294 IPC.

Transvestism: This is a perversion in which the personality is dominated by the desire to be identified with the opposite sex. The fantasy indulged in is clearly 'being a woman' if a male, and 'being a man' if a female. It is also known as **eonism,** after the name of a Frenchman Chevalier d'Eon de Beaumont who practiced this perversion. Transvestite males find sexual pleasure in wearing female garments (trans = across; vest=dress). The clothes worn are usually underclothes, brassier, knickers, etc. of an expensive and alluring type. This perversion is sometimes found in females who dress themselves in male attire. The close association of transvestism with sexual asphyxia is already discussed earlier.

Uranism: This is a general term given to the perversion of sexual instincts, and includes sexual gratification by fingering, fondling, fellatio, cunnilingus, etc. **Fellatio** means oral stimulation of the penis by the male or female, and **cunnilingus** means oral stimulation of the female genitals. This perversion is more common than generally thought of.

Voyeurism: In voyeurism, also known as *scoptophilia,* the desire to observe the genitals of others or to watch sexual intercourse becomes the condition of erotic excitement and gratification. Voyeurs, therefore, frequent parks and nudist camps and peer into lighted bedrooms at night and are commonly known as "Peeping Toms". Such perverts may get themselves into social difficulties and become the object of criminal proceedings.

Frotteurism: This is a compulsion to rub the genitalia against another person, usually in lifts or crowds. It is often accompanied by other perversions.

Urolagnia: Also known as *coprophilia,* this is a perversion, in which sexual excitement is provoked by the sight or odour of urine or faeces. Barker records a case in which one patient afflicted with this perversion was compelled to smear his partner's body with faeces before attempting intercourse.

Pedophilia: This is sexual abuse of a child by an adult. It includes sexual assault, molestation, exploitation, grooming, sexual penetration with an object, nonpenetrative activity, prostituting a child, or trafficking in child pornography, etc. causing depression, post-traumatic stress disorder, anxiety, physical injury or STD transmission in the child.

Q. 29.2. What is voyeurism? What is its punishment?

Voyeurism is the act of watching the victims genital, posteriory or exposed breasts covered only in underwear or the victim is using a lavatory or the victim is doing a sexual act not done in public. The perpetrator or his agent capturing such images is punished for the first offence 1 to 3 years, for subsequent offences 3 years to 7 years and also with fine (IPC 354-C).

30

Abortion

By abortion is meant the expulsion of the products of conception at any period of gestation before full term. The distinctions between abortion, miscarriage, and premature labour are not recognised in law and all are referred to as abortion. These terms are sometimes used to signify expulsion of the embryo or foetus during the first, second, and third trimesters of pregnancy respectively.

Abortions are **classified** in two groups:

1. Those which occur naturally or spontaneously, and are known as natural.
2. Those which occur as a direct result of interference with the pregnancy, and are known as artificial. Artificial abortions may be either — (a) legal or justifiable, and (b) criminal.

Natural Abortion

Natural, spontaneous or **accidental abortion** occurs in about 10 to 15% of all pregnancies. It may result from:

1. Constitutional disease of the mother, such as high fever, infectious diseases, viral diseases, and syphilis.
2. Local diseases of her generative organs, such as inflammations, chronic displacements, fibroid tumours, and congenital malformations of the uterus.
3. Sudden shock, fear, joy, sorrow, and reflex irritations.
4. Predisposition which some women have to abort from trivial causes, such as a fall or an accidental blow on the abdomen.
5. Any cause which brings about the death of the foetus in utero, such as faulty development, syphilis, diseases of the decidua, and degeneration of placenta.

Q. 30.1. What do you understand by artificial abortion? Mention the indications for legal abortion under the Medical Termination of Pregnancy Act, and the procedure laid down for the same.

Artificial or Induced Abortion

An artificial abortion is one which occurs as a direct result of interference with pregnancy. It may be: (1) legal or justifiable when performed in accordance with legal provisions, or (2) criminal, when performed otherwise.

Legal or Justifiable Abortion

The **Medical Termination of Pregnancy (MTP) Act, 1971** (Act No. 34, of 1971), legalises abortion on the following grounds, viz: (1) therapeutic, (2) eugenic, (3) humanitarian, and (4) social.

Therapeutic grounds: These relate to conditions where the continuance of pregnancy would involve risk—(i) to the life of the pregnant woman, or (ii) of grave injury to her physical or mental health. The indications include conditions, such as:

1. Organic heart disease with failure, active tuberculosis, and severe diabetes.
2. Hypertension complicated by cardiac or renal failure.
3. Nephrotic syndrome.
4. Pulmonary hypertension.
5. Hepatocellular failure, acute hepatitis, or acute pancreatitis.
6. Toxaemia of pregnancy.
7. Hydatidiform mole or acute hydramnios.
8. Uterine haemorrhages or infected uterus after attempts at criminal abortion.
9. Malignant neoplasms of breast or female genital tract.
10. Repeated caesareans or irreducible prolapse of the gravid uterus.
11. Threatened insanity.

Eugenic grounds: These include conditions where there is substantial risk that the child, if born, is likely to suffer from such physical or mental abnormalities as to be seriously handicapped. The indications include conditions, such as:

1. German measles, smallpox, chickenpox, viral hepatitis, or other serious viral infections, if contracted within the first trimester of pregnancy.
2. Exposure to X-rays and other radiation. The possibility of foetal abnormality needs to be considered, if the pelvis has received over 30 rads, and is almost certain, if the exposure is over 200 rads.
3. When the pregnant woman has received cytotoxic drugs, thalidomide, LSD, etc.
4. When the parents have some inheritable mental condition or chromosomal abnormalities.

Humanitarian grounds: These include those cases where pregnancy has been caused by rape. According to WHO, health is not merely absence of disease but a positive state of overall physical, mental, and social well being. Thus, where any pregnancy is alleged by the pregnant woman to have been caused by rape, the anguish caused by such pregnancy is presumed to constitute grave injury to her mental health.

Social grounds: These relate to conditions (a) where pregnancy in a married woman is the result of contraceptive failure, or (b) that the environment of the pregnant woman, during the continuance of pregnancy and at the time when the child would be born and thereafter so far as is foreseeable, would involve risk of injury to her health.

No contraceptive is 100% effective. Therefore, where any pregnancy occurs as a result of failure of any device or method used by any married woman or her husband for the purpose of limiting the number of children, the anguish caused by such unwanted pregnancy is presumed to constitute a grave injury to the mental health of the pregnant woman.

Pregnancy can also be terminated on environmental grounds, for example:

1. If the woman has some heart disease, has no one to help in her domestic work, and the strain of rearing a child is likely to be too much for her.
2. If the new arrival is likely to create financial difficulties leading the family to poverty line.
3. If the woman has already two children, she is doing all her work by herself and lives in a single room where she cooks, the family eats, and sleeps.
4. If there is already a subnormal child who requires considerable attention making it impossible to look after the new arrival.

The Medical Termination of Pregnancy Act lays down the following **requirements for termination of pregnancy.**

In an emergency, any registered medical practitioner, irrespective of his experience or training in obstetrics and gynaecology, can terminate pregnancy at any place irrespective of its duration, if he is of the opinion formed in good faith that the termination of such pregnancy is immediately necessary to save the life of the pregnant woman.

Except in an emergency, where the duration of pregnancy does not exceed 12 weeks, a pregnancy can be terminated on the opinion of one registered medical practitioner; and where the duration exceeds 12 weeks but is less than 20 weeks, opinion from two registered medical practitioners is necessary. It is essential that (i) the opinion must be formed in *good faith,* (ii) *the registered medical practitioner* must have *specified experience or training* in gynaecology and obstetrics, (iii) such practitioner must have been *registered with a certifying board* for this purpose, and (iv) the termination must be carried out in a hospital maintained by government or at a *place approved* by the government. The *written consent only of the woman* is essential; consent of the husband is not necessary; and in case where she is a minor or mentally defective, written consent from her guardian is essential.

Q. 30.2. Mention the circumstances under which criminal abortion is resorted to. Briefly state the law in relation to abortion. State the medicolegal points that a doctor must bear in mind while treating a case of criminal abortion.

Criminal Abortion

In India, criminal abortion is resorted to mostly by widows who are prevented from remarriage by social customs, by unmarried girls who have become pregnant from illicit intercourse, or when family honour is at stake. Criminal abortion appears to be practiced even in the married in all classes of society to avoid additions

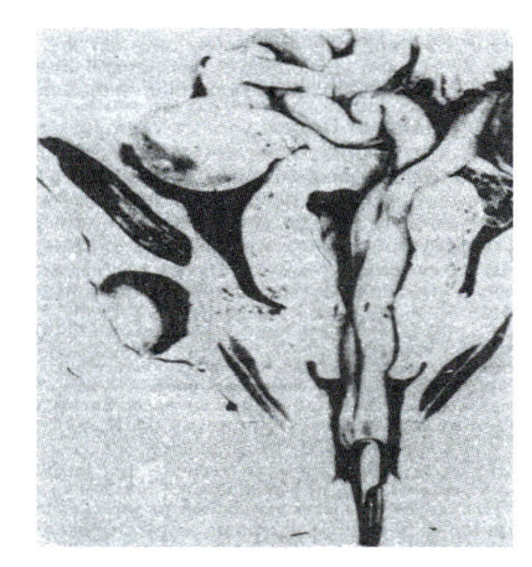

Fig. 30.1: Criminal negligence and criminal abortion. The uterus is perforated. The foetus is lying in the abdomen. The small intestine is pulled out from the perforation by the forceps mistaking it for some product of conception

to their families. Nearly all criminal abortions take place at about the second or third month, when the woman has become certain of cessation of her periods and morning sickness has confirmed pregnancy. This period is specially suitable because the fact of her being pregnant is unknown to others (Fig. 30.1).

The law regards criminal abortion or attempted criminal abortion as a serious antisocial act, and the offenses are dealt with under section 312 to 316 of the Indian Penal Code. The punishment varies from 3 to 10 years of imprisonment.

The following precautions should be taken by a doctor while treating a woman who has undergone criminal abortion:

1. The usual preliminary particulars should be noted.
2. The information regarding a woman having undergone abortion is a professional secret (doctor–patient privilege).
3. He should gather as much information as possible from the woman regarding the manner in which abortion was attempted or performed and the circumstances under which it was done. He should record her general condition and

the signs present in her genital organs, and treat her to the best of his ability.

4. The practitioner should be cautious and not attempt in his surgery any treatment which could lead to criminal charges. If such treatment is possible in the patient's house, it is advisable for him to inform a professional colleague that he has such a case under his care.
5. If the patient is seriously ill, the police should be informed.
6. If death is imminent, he should arrange for a dying declaration, or a dying deposition by informing the nearest magistrate.
7. He should refuse to issue a death certificate, if she dies but should report the matter to the police.

Q. 30.3. Describe in detail the methods in common use to procure abortion.

Q. 30.4. Write short notes on: (1) ecbolics, (2) emmenagogues, (3) abortion stick.

The two methods in common use to procure abortion are: (1) the administration of **drugs,** and (2) the application of mechanical **violence.** A proportion of abortions are a result of combination of these methods.

Use of Drugs

Many drugs used as abortifacients have no effect on the uterus or foetus unless they are given in toxic doses. Death may result from the toxic effects of these drugs, without abortion occurring! The drugs which are commonly used as abortifacients may be classified as: (1) those acting directly on the uterus, and (2) those acting indirectly on the uterus.

Drugs acting directly on the uterus: These are ecbolics and emmenagogues. **Ecbolics** increase the uterine contractions. Commonly used ecbolics are ergot, quinine, cotton root bark, and pituitary extract. It must be remembered that at the end of the third month the foetus is 9 cm long, floating in an ample supply of amniotic fluid, and the os uteri is closed. Contraction of the uterine wall in these circumstances is not likely to cause abortion nor damage the floating foetus or affect the placental circulation to any extent. Therefore, they usually fail in the earlier months of pregnancy. **Emmenagogues** increase the menstrual flow. Commonly used emmenagogues are the synthetic oestrogens, oil of savin, borax and apiol. They do not appear to have an abortifacient effect except perhaps in very large doses, sufficient to produce other effects, unpleasant and even dangerous.

Drugs acting indirectly on the uterus: The drugs commonly used for this purpose are emetics, drastic purgatives, essential oils, and metals. Emetics, drastic purgatives, and essential oils bring about pelvic congestion. Metals have poisonous effects on the system generally.

Emetics and purgatives are taken on the basis that any violent stimulation of the gastrointestinal tract may result in abortion by reflexly promoting uterine contractions but such effect is not constant. Large doses of volatile or essential oils act as irritants to the genitourinary channel but their effect on the uterus is also not constant. Such doses cause extensive damage to the renal glomeruli and tubular epithelium, and even death. Heavy metals or their salts have been employed to procure abortion, often with a fatal result. Lead in the form of diachylon pills has been used extensively for this purpose. It causes tonic contractions of the uterus and also has a direct toxic effect on trophoblastic epithelium. It, therefore, results either in abortion or a dead foetus. Symptoms of lead poisoning frequently appear, and in some of these cases, they have caused death.

In India, the drugs that are used to procure abortion include the seeds and the unripe fruit of *Carica papaya*, the unripe fruit of pineapple, the seed of the Gajar (*Daucus carota*), the milky juice of madar (*Calotropis* *gigantea*), the bark of Lal chitra (*Plumbago rosea*), Karela (*bitter gourd* or *Momordica charantia*), Sanguinaria, etc. They have no specific effect on the uterus.

Mechanical Violence

Mechanical violence may be: (a) general, or (b) local. General violence acts directly on the uterus or indirectly by promoting congestion of the pelvic organs or haemorrhage between the uterus and membranes. Local violence acts by—(i) causing local irritation followed by septic abortion, or (ii) dilatation of the cervix with or without rupture of the membranes. The methods resorted to for this purpose are: (1) self-instrumentation, (2) abortion stick, (3) syringing fluids into uterus under pressure, (4) dilatation of the cervix, (5) rupture of membranes, (6) curettage, and (7) use of electricity.

General violence: Such violence includes severe exercise, cycling, jumping from heights, rail travel, etc. It generally fails except in women predisposed to abort. Massage of the uterus through the abdominal wall may occasionally succeed and so also cupping of the hypogastric region in later months of pregnancy. *Cupping* is carried out as follows: A coin is placed on the hypogastrium. A small piece of camphor is lighted on it. A cup/mug with its mouth downward is placed over the lighted wick. The consumption of oxygen by the wick results in partial vacuum in the inverted cup, which is then pulled. This can result in partial separation of the placenta followed by abortion.

Local violence: The method employed depends largely upon the skill and upon the knowledge of the anatomy of the pelvic parts, and accordingly, the interference may be classified as (a) unskilled, (b) semi-skilled, and (c) skilled.

Unskilled interference: This is commonly restricted to self-instrumentation. A woman who is driven in desperation to do something may use anything at hand that is capable of penetration, such as a pencil, knitting needle, hair pin, nail, etc. With self-induced abortions or those carried out by unskilled abortionists, there may be no attempt whatsoever at asepsis. Thus, there is a great danger of sepsis being introduced.

In India, the so-called midwife/abortionist uses an **abortion stick.** It is either a thin wooden or bamboo stick about 15 to 20 cm long, or a twig of similar length from some irritant plant, such as, madar (*Calotropis gigantea*), chitra (*Plumbago zeylanica*), lal chitra (*Plumbago rosea*), or kaner (*Nerium odorum*). When the stick is used, it is equipped at one end with cotton wool or a piece of rag soaked in an irritant substance, such as marking nut juice or paste prepared from white arsenic, red lead, or asafoetida. The twig may be used by itself. The abortion stick or the twig is introduced in the os of the uterus. While abortion with or without rupture of the membranes may occur, sepsis may also ensue. And, locally, there may be excoriation, bruising, and perforation in the upper part of the vagina or the uterus as a result of irritation from the substances used and the violence perpetrated during the introduction of the stick.

Semi-skilled interference: The abortionist usually tries to achieve some degree of asepsis. He is likely to use a syringe capable of injecting substances into the uterine cavity under pressure. It is not commonly appreciated that the injection of a small quantity of glycerine into the uterus is often employed with success. In most cases, a solution of soap, potassium permanganate, lysol, or mercuric perchloride is used. With such irrigations, death may occur from shock, air or fat embolism, or from absorption of the poison. In few cases, uterine contractions are set up and abortion may follow. A little more calculating abortionist may insert a laminaria (sea tangle) tent into the cervix where it swells and dilates the cervix. A soft rubber catheter is then passed into the uterus without perforating the membranes. It acts as an irritating foreign body and causes uterine contractions which expel the foreign body as well as the foetus. Uterine sounds (dilators) are sometimes employed to dilate the cervix while pointed objects are employed to rupture the membranes. When dilatation of the cervix or perforation of the membranes has occurred, abortion usually follows several hours later.

Skilled interference: During the first three months, pregnancy can be terminated by vacuum aspiration or dilatation of cervix under anaesthesia and evacuation of the uterus with index finger and a flushing curette. The advantages of vacuum aspiration are the simplicity of the procedure, less haemorrhage, and less danger of perforation of the uterus. Prior use of laminaria tent, 12 hours before, acts as an aid to dilatation of cervix. During the next three months, prostaglandins F2D can be used to terminate pregnancy either via amniocentesis or cervix, or the membranes may be ruptured by a sound followed by packing of cervical canal and vaginal fornices. During the last three months, amniotic fluid replacement therapy is generally used. The method consists of removing amniotic fluid and replacing it with an equal volume of 20% saline or 50% glucose. Abortion occurs in about 12 to 24 hours. In some advanced countries, electricity is used to induce abortion. The negative electrode is applied to cervix in the posterior vaginal cul-de-sac and positive electrode over the sacrum or lumbar vertebra. The uterus expels its contents when the current is passed. The crime is difficult to detect unless there is a burn or mechanical injury.

Q. 30.5. State the circumstances under which a case of abortion is brought to the notice of the medical officer. Mention the points he should remember while examining the woman. Describe the possible complications that may occur.

In a case of abortion, medical examination is required when (1) abortion is alleged to have followed a blow, quarrel, vehicular accident, or fright, and compensation is claimed, (2) some one has complained about illegal abortion, (3) the woman is charged with illegal abortion and she denies it, and (4) death has resulted from a criminal abortion. The opinion is formed from a consideration of the history of the woman, and an examination of her body, genitalia, and of the aborted material, if available.

Examination of the Woman

The doctor must be on his guard against fabricated abortions. These are cases where an assaulted woman tries to exaggerate the offence by simulating an abortion. She may produce a menstrual blood clot, human foetus, or even an animal foetus to substantiate the charge.

If there is history of direct trauma to the uterus and if examination of the aborted material fails to reveal any anomaly, then only the cause and effect relationship of trauma and abortion should be regarded as probable.

In criminal abortions, history may not be available. If there is a history of the use of drugs or instruments, all available facts and circumstances should be carefully reviewed.

In the living, the appearances of the genitalia are similar to those in a normal delivery, and the findings will depend upon the period that the gestation has reached, the mode of abortion practiced, and the time that has elapsed since abortion.

When drugs have been used, their toxic side effects are generally evident. If abortion has resulted from an instrumental method, such as dilatation end curettage, the tooth marks produced by the volsellum forceps may be seen on the cervix.

A suspicion of criminal abortion should be aroused when the patient shows signs and symptoms of localised sepsis, generalised septicaemia, extreme pallor, or mechanical injuries. The appearance of external genitals and vagina, the condition of the os, the presence of recent tears, the marks of forceps or other instruments, the size of the uterus, the character and amount of discharge, and the state of abdominal walls and breasts, should be noted. In abortion during the earlier months of gestation, the signs are very ill-defined and return to normal within a few days. Signs persist for a longer time, if sepsis has taken place or abortion has been carried out during the later months of gestation.

In the dead, the possibility of post-mortem delivery as a result of pressure of putrefactive gases generated in the abdomen must be kept in mind. A visit to the crime scene may be undertaken, if deemed necessary. The pointers to criminal abortion are: (1) sudden death of a pregnant woman, (2) disturbed underclothing, (3) presence of abortifacient drugs or instruments, and (4) fluid, soapy, or haemorrhagic discharge from the vagina.

The doctor should note the presence or absence of the signs of pregnancy visible on the exterior of the body and, in a primipara, the expression of fluid from the breast may be of indirect value in the diagnosis of a recent abortion. The genital tract should then be examined for chemical or mechanical injuries. In case of local introduction of drugs, the mucous membrane of the vagina may show signs of laceration, bruising or necrosis from caustic substances. In case of curettage, scrape marks may be seen on the inside of the uterus (Fig. 30.2).

Special attention should be directed to the condition of pelvic contents. An

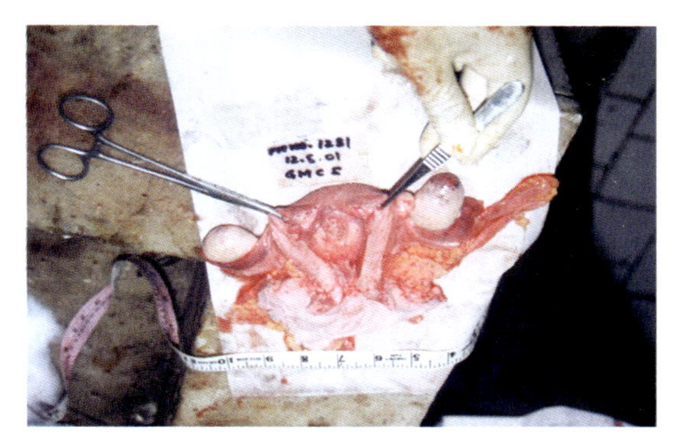

Fig. 30.2: Uterus opened with adnexa. See the fetus in site

examination should be made for evidence of uterine or extrauterine infection, e.g. cellulitis or peritonitis. Thrombophlebitis of pelvic veins may occur. Such complications are common, if the vaginal or uterine wall has been perforated. The extent and spread of the infective process should be noted to get an idea about the time since abortion. The uterus and its appendages with the vagina attached should be carefully dissected to get a better view of these parts. In clostridial infection, the serosal surface of the uterus may be brownish; the skin may also show brownish discolouration.

It is advisable to weigh the uterus and measure its size. The non-pregnant uterus weighs about 40 gm (the parous uterus weighs about 100 gm) and is 7.5 cm long, 5 cm broad, and 2.5 cm thick. The length is approximately 10 cm at the end of the third month, 12.5 cm at the end of the fourth month, 16 cm at the end of the sixth month, 20 cm at the end of the eighth month, and 27 cm at the end of the ninth month.

The cervical canal and the cavity of the uterus should be examined to see if anything has been passed through them; if there is any fluid, and if so, its nature; any foreign substances; and any laceration. If the foetus is still present, the cervix should be examined to see if the mucous plug is present, displaced, fragmented, or absent. The cavity of the uterus should be examined for a placental site or for remains of foetus, placenta, or membranes. Histological sections should be made of all material removed from the uterus, cervix, or vagina. The ovaries should be examined for the presence of a corpus luteum. If the vaginal or uterine wall has been injured, dating of the injury by microscopy or enzyme histochemistry should be attempted. In certain cases of abortion where there is suspicion that a poisonous substance has been locally used, it may be necessary to submit specimens of the vagina or uterus and its appendages for toxicological examination. Where there are no signs of local injury and should there be reason to suspect that drugs have been used, the condition of the urinary tract and gastrointestinal tract should be examined very carefully and appropriate viscera submitted for chemical analysis. Amniotic fluid, if available, may be saved in the quest for lysol, soap, or saline allegedly used in attempted abortion.

Complications from criminal abortion: Death may occur from shock, haemorrhage, air or fat embolism, and sepsis. When poisonous substances have been administered death may supervene from their effects. The injection of soap solution causes widespread local necrosis and death may follow from infection originating in the damaged tissue. Massive intravascular haemolysis not infrequently follows the introduction of solutions of soap, potassium permanganate, lysol, and mercuric perchloride into the gravid uterus. In such cases, death, when it occurs, is due to renal failure. Disseminated intravascular coagulopathy (DIC) and cerebral damage including butterfly haemorrhagic infarction in the basal ganglia may follow when abortion is induced by intrachorionic injection of hypertonic saline or glucose after the 12th week.

Shock may occur immediately from reflex vagal inhibition due to stimulation of the trigger area, namely, the cervix of the uterus by attempts at dilatation without an anaesthetic.

Haemorrhage results from internal injuries or perforation of the vagina or the uterus. It may follow incomplete separation of membranes or the placenta from the uterine wall. The uterus and pelvic organs are pale and anaemic, if death took place as a result of haemorrhage from criminal abortion but they are congested if death took place during menstruation. This *differentiation* is important in dealing with defence pleas that haemorrhage was due to menstruation and not to criminal abortion.

Air and fat emboli result when a liquid or soapy solution is injected under pressure by means of a syringe into the uterus. This causes separation of the membranes and consequent exposure of the uterine raw surface through which air and fat (soap) may enter the maternal circulation, resulting in death in a few minutes or few hours. Marked cyanosis is suggestive of death due to air embolism.

As a preliminary step in the **diagnosis of air embolism,** regional radiological examination (and preferably computerised tomography if available) is of value. At autopsy, the significant findings are: distension of right ventricle under pressure and bright red frothy blood in the right side of the heart, vena cavae, pulmonary arteries, and coronary veins. The heart and blood vessels may be punctured under water when bubbles of air will be seen coming out of them.

Later, death may occur from **sepsis** (*Clostridium welchii*, haemolytic streptococci, and anaerobic streptococci), tetanus, or renal failure. In case of peritonitis, a careful search may be required to identify a small perforation of the uterus. It is often necessary to make serial transverse sections of the uterus after it has been fixed in order to recognise such a wound and follow its tract. When sepsis is suspected as the cause of death, blood sample and swabs from the cervix and uterine cavity should be submitted for bacteriologic culture. *Clostridium perfringens* may cause fulminating septicaemia within 18 to 24 hours. If death does not occur, sub-involution of the uterus may result along with symptoms of displacement, menorrhagia, leucorrhoea, etc.

Q. 30.6. How will you examine the aborted material? If it contains a foetus, how will you estimate foetal age.

During abortion, the whole embryo (in early pregnancy) or portions of it may be expelled from the uterus. Small portions of the ovum may be expelled in blood clots. Any material found within the uterus or expelled from it should be the subject of detailed naked eye and microscopic examination. It is always advisable to remove a piece of tissue from what is thought to be the placental site. Nothing should be accepted as a result of conception, if it does not show some constituent part of an ovum, e.g. chorionic villi or decidual cells. If a foetus is passed during an abortion, its dimensions should be documented, and an attempt made to estimate its approximate age.

An estimate of **foetal age** in medicolegal work is frequently of importance. For this purpose, the following data about the development of the foetus may give some guidance in forming an approximate idea as to the age of a foetus. In the data, the crown-heel length of the embryo or foetus is based on **Hess's rule** which states that the square root of the length of the foetus in centimetres gives the approximate age of the foetus in months in the first five months. For example, the age of the foetus of 9 cm is 3 months, its length will be 9 cm.* After the fifth month, however, the length in centimetres divided by five gives the age in months. For example, the age of a foetus of 30 cm is six months. The average accepted weight of a foetus is about 400 gm at 20 weeks' gestation and this increases by about 400 gm every four weeks, until 36 weeks' gestation, when the foetus should weigh about 2 kg. During the last four weeks of pregnancy the foetus increases in weight by about 200 gm each week. Thus, at full term, the average weight of the foetus is about 3 kg. However, the length gives a more accurate assessment of the period of gestation, being far less variable than the weight.

Q. 30.7. Give an account of foetal development at various stages of its intrauterine life.

By convention, the term **ovum** is used till implantation occurs in about a week or ten days. It is called **embryo** till the end of second month of gestation, and **foetus** thereafter. **Infant** is the term applied from birth till the end of one year. **Neonate** is an infant in the first month of extrauterine life.

At the **end of the first month,** the entire ovum is about the size of a pigeon's egg. The length is about 1 cm. It weighs about 2.5 gm. The eyes are seen as two dark spots and the mouth as a cleft. The limbs appear as bud-like processes.

At the **end of the second month,** the foetus is about 4 cm in length and 15 gm in weight. Eyes and nose are recognisable. The hands and feet are webbed. The anus is seen as a dark spot. The umbilical cord begins to develop. Clavicle, mandible, ribs, and vertebrae show the centre of ossifica-tion. The sex is not distinguishable.

At the **end of the third month,** the length is about 9 cm, and weight about 80 gm. Fingers are well separated. Nails begin to appear in the form of thin membranes on the fingers and toes. The sex is not yet distinguishable. Placenta is formed.

At the **end of the fourth month,** the length is about 16 cm, and weight about 200 gm. Sex is easily recognised. Lanugo is visible on the body. The pupillary membrane is visible. The convolutions of the brain begin to appear. Meconium is seen in the duodenum. The placenta weighs about 90 gm.

At the **end of the fifth month** (Fig. 30.3), the length is about 25 cm, and the weight about 400 gm. Vernix caseosa appears on the body. It is supposed to protect the foetal skin from amniotic fluid. Fine hair on the scalp are visible. Lanugo is quite distinct. Meconium is seen at the beginning of the large intestine. Ossific centre in os calcis appears. The placenta weighs about 180 gm.

At the **end of the sixth month,** the length is about 30 cm, and the weight about 900 gm. Hair appears on the head. The eyebrows and eyelashes are beginning to form, the eyelids are adherent and the pupillary membrane is still present. The skin is red and wrinkled for want of fat. The navel is situated a little above the pubis. The testicles lie close to the kidneys and the scrotum is empty. Meconium is seen in the upper part of the large intestine. The centres of ossification are seen in the four divisions of the sternum. The placenta weighs about 300 gm. The foetus is *viable* in some cases.

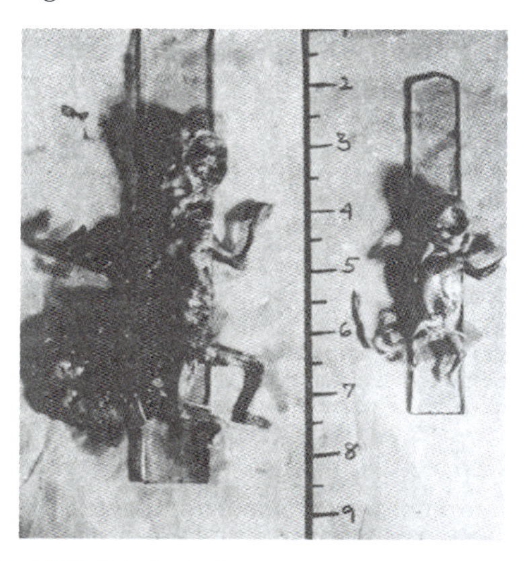

Fig. 30.3: Criminal abortion. (Left) Dead foetus, partly decomposed, 5 months old. (Right) Dead foetus, 2½ months old

At the **end of the seventh month,** the length is about 35 cm, and the weight **about** 1.5 kg. Subcutaneous fat begins to be deposited. The nails are thick but do not extend to the tips of fingers and toes. The eyelids are open. The pupillary membrane has almost disappeared. The testicles may be found in the external inguinal ring. Meconium is seen in the whole of large intestine. Primary centre of ossification of talus has appeared. The foetus has attained viability. The placenta weighs about 350 gm.

At the **end of the eighth month,** the length is about 40 cm, and weight about 2 kg. Scalp hair is thicker. The skin is red, but not wrinkled, and covered with soft hair. Lanugo has disappeared from the face. The nails nearly reach the tips of the fingers and toes. The left testicle, but not the right, has descended to the scrotum. The placenta weighs about 450 gm.

At the **end of the ninth month,** or **just before birth,** the crown-heel length is about 48–52 cm, crown-rump length about 28–32 cm, head circumference about 30–35 cm, and weight about 2.5 to 3.3 kg. The scalp is covered with dark hair 2–3 cm in length. Lanugo is seen only over the shoulders. Vernix caseosa is present over the flexures of joints and neck folds. Nails have grown over the tips of the fingers and toes. The umbilicus is midway between xiphisternum and symphysis pubis. Both the testicles have descended to the scrotum or the labia have closed the vulva. Meconium is seen at the end of large intestine. Ossific centre appears at the lower end of femur, and also perhaps in cuboid, and sometimes in the upper epiphysis of tibia (Fig. 30.4). The ossific centre in the femur is about 0.5 cm in diameter. Signs of maturity are present. The placenta is about 22 cm in diameter, 1.5 cm thick at the centre, and weighs about 500 gm. The umbilical cord is about 50–55 cm long and 1 cm thick. It appears fleshy, with a mild spiral twist, and a glistening surface.

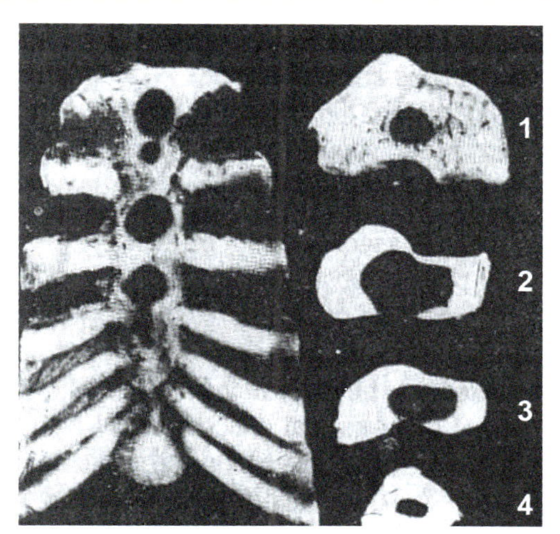

Fig. 30.4: Ossific centres in sternum and other bones **in a mature foetus.** Right-ossification centres in the various divisions of the sternum. Left—1. Lower end of femur (transverse); 2. Calcaneum; 3. Talus; 4. Cuboid. (From: Sydney Smith-Forensic Medicine. By courtesy of Publishers: J. and A. Churchill Ltd., London)

Q. 5.30. Explain clearly the differences between natural and criminal abortions from a medicolegal point of view.

Natural abortion being common, criminal interference should not be alleged without clear proof. In natural abortion in early stages, the ovum is usually expelled intact, and any laceration suggests mechanical interference. In later stages, the site, extent and appearance of injuries together with the physical development of the foetus help to distinguish natural from criminal abortion. Marks of violence on the abdomen or wounds on the membranes or on foetus provide positive evidence of criminal interference. Table 30.1 summarises the salient distinguishing features of natural and criminal abortions.

Table 30.1: Distinguishing features of natural and criminal abortions

	Natural abortion	*Criminal abortion*
1. Cause	Predisposing diseases	Pregnancy in unmarried women and widows
2. Genital injuries	Not usually present	May be present
3. Foreign body in genital tract	Nii	May be present
4. Sepsis	Not usually	Frequent
5. Signs of violence on abdomen	Nil	May be present
6. Toxic drug effects	Nil	May be present
7. Foetal injuries	Nil	May be present

31

Infanticide

The law in respect of infanticide differs somewhat in different countries. In India, infanticide means the unlawful destruction of a newly born child, and is regarded as murder in law. It is punishable under section 302 IPC, by death or transportation for life and also fine. However, it differs from ordinary murder, as it is necessary to prove that the child was born alive. A newly born infant under this Act is defined as one who is in the first year of its life. However, in most cases, the infant is killed soon after birth. Foeticide is the destruction of the foetus at any time prior to birth. Neonaticide is the destruction of the child in the first month.

Infanticide is mostly committed by unmarried women and widows, and sometimes by married women also. In certain communities, where dowry is prevalent, infanticide of female children is common, while infanticide of male children may be resorted to by prostitutes.

Q. 31.1. Outline the procedure for autopsy on an infant/stillborn. Include the technique to demonstrate ossific centres.

Autopsy on Infants and Stillborns

Rokitansky's evisceration technique is specially suited for autopsy on infants. The procedure here is almost the same as that employed in the adult but with a few deviations.

External Examination

This should include: (1) clothes and wrappings, (2) appearance of the body, (3) maturity data, (4) malformations and birth injuries, (5) state of the umbilical cord, and (6) placenta.

Clothes and wrappings: They may be torn old clothes of the mother, newspaper, plastic bag, blanket, etc. They help in identity.

Appearance of the body: Vernix caseosa cannot be easily removed and persists for a day or two after birth. Its absence or presence, therefore, might indicate if the body has been washed or not. Marks of violence may be found in the form of nail marks and contusions round about the mouth, nose, neck and head. Foreign bodies may be found in the mouth and upper respiratory passages. The state of other natural orifices should also be observed at this stage. The presence or absence and the position and character of caput succedaneum should be noted. This should not be mistaken for violence to the head, nor the violence to the head of a battered baby for caput succedaneum. The nape of the neck should be carefully examined for any injuries, including barely visible punctured wounds.

Decomposition changes, if any, are similar to those seen in the adult and help to ascertain the time since death. It must be remembered that the bodies of newborn infants are normally sterile. When they breathe and swallow, microorganisms gain entrance to the body. Therefore, in stillborn infants, putrefaction can only occur by invasion of the body by external organisms, i.e. from outside inwards while in live-born infants, it occurs from within outwards commencing from the abdomen and chest.

Any evidence of maceration or mummification suggests intrauterine death.

Maturity data: This will help to fix the intrauterine age. The crown-heel length of a mature newly born child is about 48–52 cm, crown rump length about 28–32 cm, head circumference about 30–35 cm, and weight about 2.5 to 3.3 kg.

Malformations and birth injuries: The head must be examined for bulging fontanelles (hydrocephalus) and the back for spina bifida. Hands and feet should be inspected for abnormal number of digits, the mouth and palate for cleft palate, and the rectum for patency. Irregularities in consistency of bone must be looked for (osteogenesis imperfecta is associated with many broken bones). If there is any evidence of birth injury, it should be specially noted.

Umbilical cord: This is examined to determine its length, whether unduly short or long, and whether it has been cut, tied (indicates that the delivery has been attended by someone), torn or still attached to the placenta. Normally, the umbilical cord is 50–55 cm long, and 1 cm thick. It appears fleshy, with a normal spiral twist and a glistening surface. The cut end is examined for signs of a vital reaction. The cord is also be examined for abnormal twists, knots, and for any evidence of displacement of Wharton's jelly. Signs of vital reaction in the stump indicate the interval between birth and death. Displacement of the Wharton's jelly indicates that the cord may have been used as a ligature to strangulate the infant. The region of the umbilicus should be examined to determine possible infections and a histological examination of the cord is essential, if infection is suspected.

Placenta: The placenta is about 22 cm in diameter, with a central thickness of 1.5 cm. It weighs about 500 gm. Common histological abnormalities in stillbirths include placental infarcts, haemorrhagic endovasculitis, retroplacental haematomas, acute chorioamnionitis, and hydrops.

Internal Examination

Head: The scalp is opened by the usual incision from ear to ear and the flaps reflected. The skull is opened by cutting with scissors anteroposteriorly and across, and reflected as four flaps. Observation is made regarding injuries to fontanelles (especially punctured wounds through anterior fontanelle), tears of meninges, tentorial tears (common in forceps delivery), haemorrhages and lacerations of brain.

Mouth: A newborn infant is often smothered by stuffing wads of paper or cloth into the mouth. Therefore, the interior of the mouth should always be examined when infanticide is suspected.

Neck: This is examined for internal injuries, and trachea for foreign body, froth, mucus, amniotic fluid, etc. The region of the nape of the **neck** deserves special attention.

Thorax: The shape of the chest, whether dome-shaped or flat is noted. Before opening the thorax, the abdomen is opened and the position of the diaphragm noted by passing a finger up to its concave arch.

The lungs are examined for their volume, colour, consistency, weight, and the presence of petechial haemorrhages.

The four chambers of the heart are opened to see the difference in colour of blood and whether it is normal. Observation is also made regarding the patency of foramen ovale and ductus arteriosus.

Abdomen: Stomach is removed by ligating both ends and tested for floatation. The contents are examined for presence of milk, poison, blood, amniotic fluid, mucus, and squamous epithelium.

The intestines are examined for presence of air, and for presence of meconium and its position which will help to fix the intrauterine age of the foetus. It is in the upper part of the small intestine in early months and is expelled within 24 hours after birth.

Other viscera: These are examined for their development, any malformations, asphyxial signs, and injuries.

Genitals: These are examined for any malformations. The position of the testes, whether descended or where located, is noted.

Limbs and sternum: These are examined for presence of ossific centres to fix the age of the foetus. Centre of ossification for the calcaneum appears by the fifth month, the four divisions of the sternum by the sixth month, talus by the seventh month, and lower end of the femur by the ninth month. At birth, a centre of ossification is usually present in the cuboid and upper end of tibia.

The following **technique** is usually adopted to **demonstrate** the **ossification centres** at autopsy. For the ossific centres in the sternum, the bone is placed on a wooden board and sectioned in its long axis with a cartilage knife. This exposes centres in the various divisions of the sternum. Alternatively, the bone is scraped clean, front and back, and transilluminated by holding it up against light so as to visualise the various ossific centres. For the ossific centre in the lower end of the femur and the upper end of tibia, the leg is flexed against the thigh and a horizontal incision made across and into the knee joint. A number of cross-sections are made through the epiphysis starting from the articular surface and continuing until the largest cross-section of the ossification centre is reached. In the lower end of the femur, this is seen clearly as a brownish-red nucleus which is surrounded by a bluish-white cartilage. This centre appears about the 36th week. Between 37 and 38 weeks, it measures about 1 to 1.5 mm in diameter, and at full term, it generally measures 2 to 5 mm. A centre of ossification in the upper end of tibia is found in some cases, but in others, it appears after birth. To expose the ossific centres in the bones of the foot, the heel of the foot is placed on a sponge and firmly held by one hand, and with the other hand an incision is made through the interspace between the third and fourth toes and carried downwards through the sole of the foot and heel. Centres in calcaneum and talus which usually appear towards the end of the fifth and seventh month respectively of intrauterine life are exposed. The cuboid may show an ossification centre which is present at or shortly after birth. Thus, the ossification centres give information about the viability and maturity of the newborn.

Q. 31.2. The dead body of a newly born child has been picked up from a dustbin. State the medicolegal questions involved.

In all cases where the dead body of an infant is found under suspicious circumstances, the alleged mother should be examined for: (1) signs of recent delivery, (2) any other condition explaining abnormal delivery responsible for injury to the newborn (e.g. contracted pelvis, precipitate delivery), and (3) for her mental condition. As regards the child, the following medicolegal questions have to be answered:

1. Was the child stillborn or dead-born?
2. Was the child born alive?

3. If born alive, how long did the child live?
4. What was the cause of death?

Q. 31.3. What is meant by a stillborn child and a dead-born child? How will you examine and establish that a child was stillborn or dead-born?

Conventionally, a **stillborn child** means a child which is born after the 28 weeks (age of viability) of pregnancy and which did not at any time after being completely expelled from its mother, breathe or show any other sign of life. The fact that the newly born child may be in a state of suspended animation must be borne in mind. The incidence of stillbirths in general is about 6% of all births and in primiparas about 9%. Stillbirths are due to many causes both before and during birth. They often occur among illegitimate and immature children, and where the labour is unassisted, or prolonged. Scalp oedema, cephalhaematoma, or severe moulding of the head are signs of prolonged labour and are indicative of stillbirth or death from natural causes shortly after birth.

A **dead-born child** is one which has died in utero and may show signs of rigor mortis, maceration or mummification.

Rigor mortis: Rigor mortis may occur in a dead foetus before birth. The most common cause is antenatal haemorrhage in the mother.

Maceration: This is a process of aseptic autolysis of a foetus dead in utero. It occurs when the dead foetus remains in the uterus for 3–4 days surrounded by liquor amnii but with the exclusion of air. It does not occur, if the dead foetus is born within about 24 hours. It is characterised by softening and degeneration of tissues. The process is aseptic because the foetus being enclosed in the membranes is in a sterile condition. When death has occurred for more than 3–4 days, depending on the time interval, the body is so softened and flaccid that it flattens out when placed on the table. The cuticle is raised in blisters containing thin fluid or is peeling and the true skin is brownish-red. The cellular tissues and organs are oedematous and body cavities full of reddish serum. The umbilical cord is thickened and soft. The bony junctions both in the skull and in the joints are lax and abnormally mobile. The skull bones override each other, an important radiological sign, known as *Spalding's sign,* which enables the diagnosis of this condition even when the foetus is in the uterus. The smell is somewhat rancid. If the membranes are ruptured after the death of the foetus and air gains admission into liquor amnii, the foetus undergoes putrefaction instead of maceration. *Putrefaction* is characterised by nauseating and unpleasant odour, green colour of the skin, and formation of gases. The latter findings differentiate it from maceration where the colour of skin is brownish red and gases do not form. Rarely, a child which has remained surrounded in amniotic fluid after death may get converted into *adipocere.*

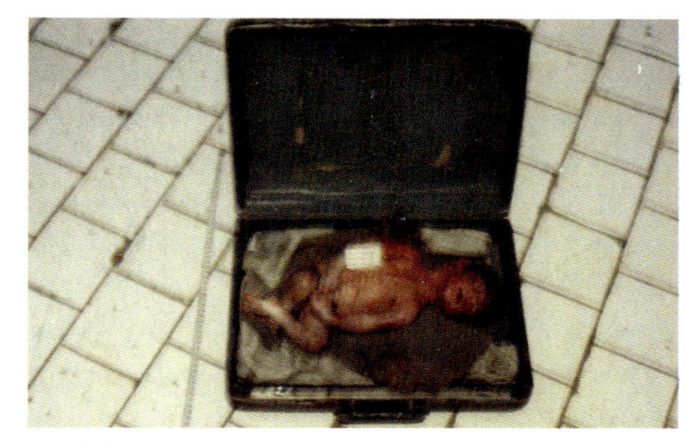

Fig. 31.1: Disposing unwanted fetus in a closed briefcase found on railway platform scare created, if there is any bomb inside. (*Courtesy*: BV Subrahmanyam)

Mummification: Mummification results when death of a foetus occurs from a deficient supply of blood or when liquor amnii is scanty, and when no air has entered the uterus. In this condition, the foetus is dried up and shrivelled.

Q. 31.4. A newly born child has been brought to you for autopsy. What signs will lead you to conclude that the child was born alive.

Q. 31.5. Mention the findings by which a medical officer can establish the viability of the child at postmortem?

Q. 31.6. Comment on: (1) hydrostatic test, (2) stomach-bowel test, (3) forensic criteria for live-birth.

A child is live-born according to English law when, after complete extrusion from the mother, irrespective of the attachment or severance of the cord, it exhibits some signs of life like crying, movements of limbs, twitching of eyelids, respirations and pulsations. In India, if any part of a living child has been born, though the child may not have breathed or been completely born, it constitutes live-birth. The evidence in respect of live-birth can be circumstantial and from postmortem examination.

Circumstantial evidence: In **civil cases,** the evidence of a witness who saw the child cry, move or open its eyes or felt the pulsations of the heart or cord will be accepted as proof of live-birth. However, a mere cry or muscular movement does not constitute such a proof. A child may utter a cry either in the uterus (*vagitus uterinus*) or in the vagina (*vagitus vaginalis*), and it may be heard even outside the delivery room. This occurs when the membranes are ruptured, air has gained access to the uterus, and the infant has been stimulated by some operative manipulation or asphyxia. As cellular life continues after the death of the individual, the muscles may twitch for some time after the body is dead; it is, therefore, quite unsafe to assume that twitching of muscles indicates life.

Evidence on postmortem examination: The law presumes that every newbom child found dead was born dead, until the contrary is proved. Therefore, **in criminal cases,** the only evidence of live birth admissible in court is the opinion of an expert founded on postmortem examination of the body of an infant. In giving such an opinion, the points to be considered are: (a) degree of maturity of the child, (b) signs of establishment of respiration, and (c) other signs, if any.

Degree of Maturity

In law, a foetus which has not attained the completion of the seventh month of intra-uterine life is not viable unless excellent facilities for resuscitation are available. An *immature infant* is one who weighs 2000 gm or less at birth regardless of the time of gestation.

Viability means the stage of maturity at which a foetus with normal intrauterine development is able to maintain a separate existence after birth. A child is viable after 210 days, or seven months of intrauterine life, and in some cases after 180 days or six months but in most of these cases the foetus is immature. The appearance of foetus at various stages of development has been already outlined. The following description represents appearance of a full term mature infant.

Appearance of a full term mature infant: The crown heel length is about 48–52 cm, crown rump length about 28–32 cm, head circumference about 30–35 cm, and the weight about 2500 to 3300 gm, the female infant being usually about 100 gm less in weight. The head is well covered with hair about 2–3 cm in length. The lanugo (fine, soft, downy hair) is seen only over the shoulders. The skin is covered with vernix caseosa which is readily seen in the flexures of the joints and neck folds. **Vernix caseosa** is a white cheesy substance, made up of sebaceous secretion and epithelial cells. Being sticky, it cannot be easily removed. It protects the foetal skin against maceration while in liquor amnii. The limbs and the body are plump and the face has lost its wrinkles. The pupillary membrane is absent. The cartilages have formed in the nose and the ears, and nails project beyond the finger tips and to the end of the toes. The umbilicus is midway between xiphisternum and symphysis pubis. The umbilical cord is fleshy, with a normal spiral twist and a glistening surface. Both the testicles have descended into the scrotum or the labia have closed the vulva. Meconium is present in the large intestine. **Meconium** is a green viscid substance made up of inspissated bile and mucus. It is generally expelled in a day or two after delivery. The lower end of the femur shows a centre of ossification about 1/2 centimetre in diameter. A centre of ossification may be present in the cuboid and upper end of tibia.

Generally, while length is a reliable indication of maturity, it is better to rely upon the presence or absence of centres of ossification as evidence of maturity, since small children as well as large, may be born mature.

Signs of Establishment of Respiration

Prior to independent life, the lungs are functionless and receive only a limited supply of blood necessary for their vitality and growth. Following birth, the process of aeration of lungs becomes operative and the pulmonary circulation becomes established. These two vital functions which occur at birth of a living child produce physical changes in: (1) the chest, (2) lungs, and (3) stomach and bowels. These changes are as follows:

Chest: The chest is flat before respiration. Its circumference is about 1–2 cm less than that of the abdomen at the level of the umbilicus. When full respiration is established, the shape of the chest becomes arched or drum-shaped. The highest point of the diaphragm is found at the level of the fourth or fifth rib, if respiration has not taken place and at the level of sixth or seventh rib, if respiration has taken place. However, these are not reliable signs as full respiration may not have been established at birth, and the shape of the chest and the position of the diaphragm may be affected by pressure of putrefactive gases in the thorax or abdomen.

Lungs: When respiration has not taken place, the lungs are found lying at the back of the thoracic cavity behind the heart and thymus gland, and covered with wrinkled loose pleura. They are small, smooth, of a uniform dark blue-red colour, with sharp edge, and appear liver-like. They are non-crepitant on squeezing, and on section, they appear solid and exude blood but not froth. When placed in water they usually sink. If full respiration has taken place, the distended lungs fill the thoracic cavity overlapping the heart and thymus gland, and the covering pleura becomes taut. They are voluminous with rather uneven surface due to expanded air vesicles, and round edges. As the blood becomes aerated by the expanded vesicles, their colour becomes light red and the surface appears marbled or mottled, due to patches of expansion and aeration alternating with collapsed dark bluish-red areas. They crepitate on pressure and exude frothy blood on section. When placed in water, they usually float. The foetal lungs can assume rosy colour on exposure to air after death but air cells can never be distended. In artificially inflated lungs, mottling is absent.

The **hydrostatic test** for live-birth depends on changes in the specific gravity of lungs due to respiration. The specific gravity of a non-respired lung is about 1050 (heavier than water) and that of a respired one about 950 (lighter than water). Non-respired lungs, therefore, sink in water and respired lungs float.

Briefly, the test procedure involves cutting the lungs into lobes and then into pieces, squeezing them firmly in a towel or by placing some weight on them, and testing them for floatation.

This test is of **no value whatsoever** in forensic work for the following reasons:

1. The slightest degree of decomposition invalidates any interpretation of the floatation test.
2. Resuscitation attempts make the evaluation of the test difficult or even impossible.
3. Instances are recorded when control tests have shown that the lungs of a still-born may float while the lungs of undoubtedly live-born, even those who have lived for days, may sink. Meixner found apparently respired alveoli in lung sections from a dead infant taken from the uterus of a dead mother.
4. It is now accepted that some expansion of air sacs of the lungs in the foetus does occur towards the end of pregnancy as a result of some amniotic fluid moving in and out of the bronchial tree – the so-called trial breathing. Thus, an undoubted stillbirth may sometimes reveal quite extensive alveolar expansion.
5. Shapiro states that it is not possible to distinguish histologically the lungs of stillborn infants from those of live-born.

The best way to seek proof of respiration is, therefore, to look at, feel, and listen to the lungs in the manner discussed above.

Fodere's test or the static test for live-birth depends on the fact that there is an increased flow of blood to the lungs when respiration is established and, therefore, the absolute weight of the lung is increased. The ratio of the weight of the lungs to that of the body is about 1:70 before respiration and little less (not 1:35 as stated in various textbooks) afterwards. This test is of minor importance in medicolegal work.

Stomach and bowels: When respiration has been established, it is probable that air will be swallowed and so may pass into the stomach and small intestine. The test to determine its presence is known as the stomach-bowel test or *Breslau's second life test*. The *drawbacks* of the test are: (1) air may not have been swallowed although the infant may have been born alive, and (2) a positive result may be obtained, if putrefactive gases have developed or when artificial respiration is given; in the latter case, air may be found in the stomach but not in the intestine. The test is of no value in medicolegal work.

The physical changes brought about by the establishment of respiration in a live-born child are contrasted with the appearances as found in a stillborn child in Table 31.1.

Other Signs

If the body of the infant is clothed, if there is obvious washing of vernix caseosa, if there is presence of milk in the stomach, or if there is evidence of separation of the umbilical cord, then these naturally point to live-birth. The absence of meconium from the large intestine is not proof of live-birth, but is suggestive of it, for meconium is not completely expelled, as a general rule, until several hours after birth. In a breech presentation and also in severe anoxia, meconium may be excreted completely before birth. The middle ear at birth is filled with a gelatinous substance, and at a varying interval, this is replaced by air which enters through the eustachian canal. The time at which this takes place is very variable and, therefore, this test is of no value. The test is known as *Wredin's test. When gelatin is not present but its place is taken by air, this is considered as positive Wredin's test. It indicates live birth.*

Forensically, **to diagnose live birth,** certain incontrovertible criteria should, therefore, be present, e.g. (1) viable child, (2) well expanded lungs, (3) vital reaction in the stump of the umbilical cord, and/or (4) presence of milk in the stomach.

Q. 31.7. Mention the factors that you will take into consideration to determine the length of survival of a child after birth.

Some indication of the length of time that a child has lived after birth may be obtained

Table 31.1: Contrast of physical changes between live-born and stillborn child

	Live-born child	*Stillborn child*
Chest	Arched or drum-shaped, its circumference greater than that of abdomen, and intercostal spaces wider	Flat, its circumference less than that of abdomen, and intercostal spaces narrow
Diaphragm	Level of sixth or seventh rib	Level of fourth or fifth rib
Lungs a. Position	Fill the thoracic cavity, overlapping heart and thymus gland, with taut covering pleura	Lying at the back of thoracic cavity behind heart and thymus gland, with covering pleura wrinkled and loose
b. Volume	Voluminous	Small
c. Edges	Rounded	Sharp
d. Colour	Mottled pink	Uniform, dark-blue red
e. Appearance	Marbled due to expanded air vesicles	Smooth and not marbled
f. Consistency	Spongy, elastic, and crepitant	Dense, firm, liver-like, and non-crepitant
g. Air vesicles	Visible, sometimes individually	Expanded air sacs not seen on surface
h. Squeezing under water	Bubbles produced are small and uniform in size	If any gas bubbles escape, they are large and uneven due to decomposition
i. When cut	Exude frothy blood though not decomposed	Exude little blood but no froth unless decomposed
j. Hydrostatic test	Of no value	Of no value
k. Static test	Ratio of weight of lung to body less than 1:70	Ratio of weight of lung to body about 1:70
Stomach-bowel test	Of no value	Of no value

by observing: (1) changes in the skin, (2) caput succedaneum, when present, (3) changes in the umbilical cord, (4) changes in the circulation, and (5) changes in the foetal haemoglobin.

Changes in the skin: The skin of the newly born infant is covered with vernix caseosa chiefly in the flexures of the joints and neck folds. It persists for a day or two unless the body is washed. The colour of the skin is bright red at birth, becomes darker on the second or third day, and physiological jaundice is evident between the third and sixth days. The skin finally assumes its original colour in about a week to 10 days. Fine desquamation of the skin begins about the second day and is complete in about a fortnight.

Caput succedaneum: This is a valuable sign when present. It may not be present in precipitate labour. It is an oedematous swelling of the presenting part of the head during delivery. A haemorrhagic swelling of this region is known as *cephalhaematoma.* Caput succedaneum gradually disappears in about a day to about a week after birth. Cephalhaematoma shows the usual changes common with bruises and disappears in about a fortnight.

Umbilical cord: Changes in the umbilical cord begin to appear from the cut end to its base at the umbilicus soon after birth. The clotting occurs in the cut end after two hours and the umbilical cord begins to dry in about 12–24 hours, drying commencing at the free end. An inflammatory zone of redness appears near the attached end in 36–48 hours. The cord mummifies in about 2–3 days, and drops off in 5–6 days, leaving a raw area. Healing of the ulcer with formation of scar occurs in 10–14 days. No conclusions can be drawn from the mummification of the cord as this also occurs in a dead body; on placing the cord in water it swells up to its normal appearance. Conclusions can be drawn from the other changes, viz. separation of the cord, process of healing of the ulcer, and formation of a cicatrix. All these are vital processes.

Circulation: The umbilical arteries, umbillical vein, ductus venosus, ductus arteriosus, and foramen ovale which were necessary to carry out the foetal circulation are no longer required and, accordingly, undergo obliteration at variable periods. In a few hours after birth, the lumen of the umbilical arteries becomes shrunken and contraction along the whole length is complete in two or three days. The umbilical vein and ductus venosus begin to contract by about the second or third day after birth and close by about the fourth or fifth day. The ductus arteriosus begins to contract from the aortic end in about three or four days and is completely obliterated in about a week to 10 days. The closure of foramen ovale generally occurs by the second or third month. In a few cases, it might be closed at birth; in some, it remains open up to about 2 years; and in very few, it persists throughout life.

Foetal haemoglobin: Foetal haemoglobin differs from adult haemoglobin in its globin component as it is manufactured in the liver in the foetal state. At five months of intrauterine life, about 94 per cent of haemoglobin is of the foetal type. At birth, it is about 80 per cent. As the infant grows, the foetal haemoglobin changes to adult haemoglobin. By about the sixth month, almost all haemoglobin has changed in this manner. Foetal haemoglobin is recognised by its isoelectric point, alkali resistance, spectrogram, and fractional crystallisation methods. The change from foetal haemoglobin to adult haemoglobin constitutes a progressive change in the newborn infant and it is helpful in assessing the period of survival after birth, especially in the first three months.

Q. 31.8. What are the causes of death in the newborn? Describe the common methods employed to commit infanticide.

Q. 31.9. Write short notes on: (1) precipitate delivery, (2) pseudo-precipitate delivery, (3) unconscious delivery, (4) abandoning of children, (5) concealment of birth.

Death may occur from: (1) natural causes, (2) accidental causes, or (3) criminal causes.

Natural Causes

There are many natural causes of death in newly born children such as: (1) immaturity (weight less than 2 kg) or general debility, (2) malformations inconsistent with the maintenance of life, (3) diseases of the mother, such as syphilis and specific fevers, e.g. smallpox, (4) diseases of the child affecting its lungs, heart and brain, and (5) other causes which include spasm of the larynx from mucus or meconium being aspirated in the larynx; haemorrhage from the umbilical cord, stomach, rectum or genitals; placenta praevia or an abnormal gestation; and erythroblastosis foetalis.

Accidental Causes

Accidents causing the death of the child may occur during or after birth.

During birth, the causes of death include: (1) prolonged labour, (2) prolapse of the cord, (3) knots or twists in the cord, (4) premature separation of the placenta, and (5) death of the mother.

Prolonged labour may cause death without leaving any postmortem sign especially if the foetus is of weak constitution; death may result from pressure on the head leading to haemorrhage or to fracture. Prolonged partial asphyxia may so damage the nerve cells that though the child may be born alive, it may not be capable of surviving, and may die shortly after birth. Prolonged labour is comparatively common in a primipara, and in such instances, the caput succedaneum is quite prominent.

In *prolapse of the cord,* death occurs from asphyxia. The cord is firmly pressed upon by the advancing head, especially in breech presentation. In such cases, the lungs will be found free from air, but petechiae or ecchymoses may be found on the surface of the lungs, and foreign substances, such as lanugo, particles of vernix caseosa, meconium and mucus may be found in the respiratory passages. Other signs of asphyxia may be found.

Knots in the cord may lead to death from asphyxia. Twisting of the cord round the neck of the child rarely causes any difficulty when assistance is at hand but may lead to strangulation.

Premature separation of placenta may also lead to death from asphyxia.

When the *mother dies* during the act of delivery, there is very little chance of saving the child if death occurred slowly from haemorrhage, but it may be saved, if it can be extracted soon after sudden death of the mother, if she was previously in good health.

After birth, the causes of death include: (1) suffocation, and (2) precipitate or unconscious labour.

A child may die from *suffocation,* if it is born with membranes over the head (cul-de-sac), thus covering the mouth and nostrils. It may also die from suffocation, if its face is pressed accidentally in the clothes or from drowning, if the face is submerged in the discharges, such as blood, liquor amnii, or meconium.

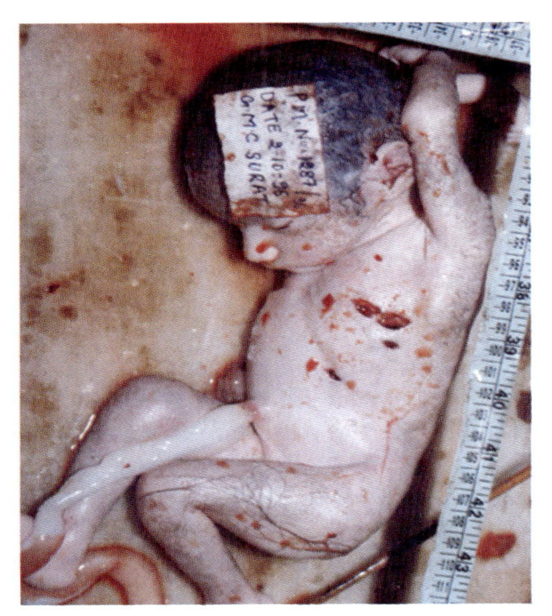

Fig. 31.2: Stabs on fetus in utero seen at autopsy on mother with stab injury

Precipitate labour may lead to the death of the foetus from accidental causes. This is a condition in which the child is born suddenly without the usual labour pains. In such cases, the child may be born while the mother is in an upright position, and by falling to the ground sustain injuries to the head which may lead to death; even the child may fall from the maternal passages into a lavatory pan containing faeces or a pot containing urine and death may ensue.

In such cases, microscopic examination of the lungs will reveal the foreign particles from the drowning fluid. In any case of true precipitate labour, most of the following conditions are present: (1) the woman is usually a multipara, (2) there is a recent or old laceration of the perineum, (3) the pelvis is large and roomy, and the child small relative to the size of the pelvis, (4) head moulding is absent, (5) caput succedaneum is absent or slight, (6) placenta must still be attached to and born with the child, or the umbilical cord must be long enough to reach from the uterus to the ground, or the cord must be torn, (7) foreign matter, such as mud, sand or gravel may be found on the hair or injured scalp of the child, and (8) there is no evidence of other marks of violence. While precipitate delivery sometimes occurs in women who have borne many children, it is hardly possible in a primipara. Medicolegally, the condition is important as a charge of infanticide may be brought about when the death of the foetus is due to injury from precipitate labour. Alternatively, in a case of infanticide, death of a child may be attributed to precipitate labour. In precipitate labour, all the three stages of labour are telescoped into one and the birth of baby and delivery of placenta occur together. Accidental death is common in precipitate labour.

Pseudoprecipitate delivery may occur in a primipara. The woman may have had labour pains but was either unaware of their significance or was not able to distinguish the sense of fullness produced by the descent of a child from the feeling of a bulky evacuation. However, it is inconceivable that birth can take place in a primipara without any warning whatever, though it is possible for a woman, even a multipara, to go to full term, being unaware of the fact that she was pregnant.

Unconscious delivery may occur during epileptic fit, coma, hysteria, hypnosis, and under the influence of narcosis, anaesthetics or deep drunkenness since the contractile power of the uterus is independent of volition. Consciousness may be lost during child birth in cases in which there is a cardiac condition. Apart from such cases, it is highly improbable that any primiparous woman would deliver during ordinary sleep without being aroused.

A 42-year-old multipara suddenly delivered a child while defaecating. At autopsy, the lungs were found completely inflated. The cause of death was suffocation and drowning by faeces and urine. The child was small as compared to the size of the pelvis and the woman had an old laceration of the perineum (true precipitate delivery).

A girl was charged with infanticide. She was in labour pains for some time. Believing that she was about to have a bulky evacuation, she went to the toilet where she delivered a child, which was subsequently removed from the lavatory pan and rescued by means of a warm bath and other means. The appearance of the child was consistent with the girl's statement. There was no mark of violence and nothing to show an attempt at murder. The umbilical cord had ruptured due to a fall. (Pseudoprecipitate delivery).

A servant girl delivered herself a child in a lavatory pan during a period of some 30 minutes between her early morning routine and serving breakfast. She did the normal forenoon's work and walked a distance of eight miles in the afternoon to dispose of the child's body. It was, she said, her first pregnancy (infanticide).

Criminal Causes

These include: (1) acts of commission that is the use of mechanical violence and poisoning, and (2) acts of omission or neglect.

Acts of commission: Deaths from violence may take place in the same way as in adults but certain methods of infanticide are common, namely—(1) suffocation, (2) strangulation, (3) drowning, (4) fracture of the skull, (5) fracture and dislocation of the cervical vertebrae, (6) other injuries, and (7) poisoning.

Suffocation, by pressing the face on the pillow, or by closing the nose and mouth by a cloth or by hands, is common. It may leave no traces but the application of more force than is necessary, the usual event, will leave marks of violence, especially bruising of the inner aspects of the lips. Sometimes, even mucus and squamous respiratory epithelium from the victim may be found in the smothering material. Infants are sometimes suffocated to death by pressure on the chest. The presence of foreign bodies, e.g. rag or cotton wool, in the mouth or air passages when accompanied by internal signs of asphyxia points to homicidal suffocation.

Strangulation, either by hand or by ligature, is common. When manual strangulation is resorted to, bruises from the pressure of the fingers or depression and scratches from the finger nails will be observed, and there is commonly injury to the deeper tissues. In case where a ligature is used, the ligature is frequently left in situ and should be preserved as evidence. It should be remembered that natural folds on the skin of the neck, especially of fat infants, somewhat resemble marks caused by a ligature. Close examination and dissection of such marks will reveal the true condition. Ligature, though suggestive, is not absolute proof of strangulation, unless corroborative evidence is demonstrated. It could be due to assist self-delivery in obstructed labour. Occasionally, umbilical cord is used as a ligature to simulate accident. In such cases, examination of the cord may show that it has been roughly handled, and Wharton's jelly has been displaced. In accidental deaths with the umbilical cord tightly twisted round the neck, there is no excoriation in and around the ligature mark and the lungs are generally found in a foetal condition (Figs 31.3 and 31.4).

Drowning is not a common form of infanticide. The usual practice is first to kill an infant by suffocation or strangulation and then to throw the body into a dustbin, cesspool, well, tank or river with a view to conceal the crime. Sometimes, the child is wrapped in a clothing or newspaper before such disposal and in such cases, the wrapping may give a clue to the identity of the victim. A living body may be similarly thrown.

Fractures of the skull, by dashing the head on the floor or wall, or inflicting blows on the head, usually leave unmistakable marks of violence. The skull of a newborn, being soft and pliable, fractures differently from that of an adult. The fracture in the thin membranous bone of the skull resembles a ragged tear. If precipitate or difficult labour is alleged, the characteristics of precipitate labour and the fracture should be carefully checked. The fracture of the skull in a case of precipitate labour is generally a fissured fracture usually involving the parietal bones. It may radiate to the frontal and squamous portions of the temporal bone. The scalp is lacerated. The fracture of the skull in a case of difficult labour is chara-cterised either by a spoon-shaped depression or a minor fissured fracture of the parietal bones without any laceration of the scalp. However, in such a case, the caput succedaneum is often marked.

Fig. 31.4: Infanticide by strangulation with a ligature. The unknown body of a newly born female child with a ligature around the neck by a torn saree-cloth was found decomposing on the bank of a lake at Thirupparangundram. The body was partially eaten by fishes and crabs. At postmortem, death from asphyxia by strangulation was confirmed. (*Courtesy*: Dr PG Paul)

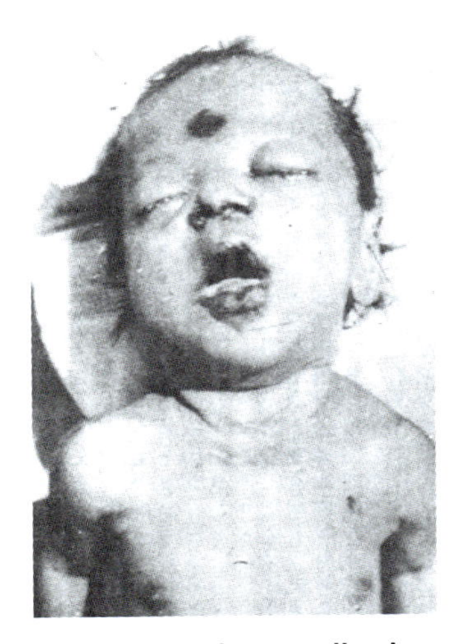

Fig. 31.3: Infanticide by smothering. A three weeks old female child was found in a flush-out latrine at the Jhansi Rani Park, Madurai. At postmortem, there was clear evidence of smothering and strangulation by a soft ligature-like cloth.

Fracture and dislocation of the cervical vertebrae may be produced by twisting the neck. They may be produced accidentally by forcible rotation of the neck while correcting a malposition of the foetus or to extract the head in a breech presentation.

Other injuries, such as stabs and incised wounds are rare. Stab wounds may be caused by needles, pins or scissors and may penetrate the heart, brain, medulla or other internal organs. Punctures through the fontanelles, inner canthus of the eye, up the nostrils, down the throat, nape of the neck, or up the rectum should be kept in mind as they are mostly concealed and thus might be readily missed.

Poison may be used for the purpose of infanticide. Opium, calotropis juice, madar, tobacco and dhatura are employed in some countries, and insulin, antihistaminics, tranquillisres, and hypnotics in others. In suspicious cases, the stomach and other necessary viscera should be preserved for chemical analysis.

***Acts of omission*:** The law presumes that a woman who is about to deliver should take ordinary precautions to save her child after it is born. She is guilty of criminal negligence, if she fails to do so. Deaths from omission at birth more commonly relate to: (1) omission to make the necessary preparation for the birth of the child (e.g. arrangement for medical aid), (2) omission to tie the cord after dividing it, (3) omission to remove the child from the mother's discharges, (4) omission to protect the child from cold and heat, and (5) omission to supply proper food to it.

A woman must make necessary provisions for the birth of her child. As soon as she gets labour pains, she must arrange for medical aid. Evidence to the effect that no provision of any kind has been made suggests that the woman had the intention of doing away with the child unless she was not aware of her pregnancy till the birth of her child or she fainted owing to the sudden onset of violent labour pains and did not know what followed next.

The Abandoning of Children

Section 317 IPC deals with exposure and abandonment of a child under 12 years. Under this section, whoever, being the father or mother of a child under the age of 12 years or having the care of such child, shall expose or leave such child in any place with the intention of wholly abandoning such child is punishable. The offender may be tried for murder or culpable homicide as the case may be if the child dies in consequence of the exposure.

Concealment of Birth

In a case where infanticide is not proved, the mother is usually charged with a lesser offence of concealment of birth. According to section 318 IPC, whoever, by secretly burying or otherwise disposing of the dead body of a child, whether such child dies before or after or during its birth intentionally conceals or endeavours to conceal the birth of such child, is punishable for this offence. Under this section, concealment of birth is a crime. It is not necessary to prove live-birth. It is sufficient that there has been a birth and that the child was dead at the time of concealment. For the purpose of this section, a foetus is considered a child, if it has attained such maturity as to be capable of maintaining a separate existence.

32 "Cot Deaths" or SIDS

Also known as *sudden infant death syndrome* (SIDS), it is defined as the sudden and unexplained death of any infant who was either well or almost well prior to death, and whose death remains unexplained even after a thorough autopsy, including an investigation, and toxicological examination, if necessary.

The death rate is between 2 to 3 per 1000 live births. Death usually occurs between the ages of two weeks to two years with a peak around two to four months, strikes boys somewhat more often than girls, is more common among low birth weight babies and among lower income families, among children whose mothers smoke or are drug addicted, and is commonly associated with seasonal upper respiratory diseases. The incidence is about threefold among twins, most twins being premature and of low birth weight. About half of the victims have some symptoms of a cold during the week prior to death, and a few have a history of bowel upset.

Two clinical features of crib death are nearly universal, viz. the babies die during sleep, and the death is silent. Most cases of so-called overlaying are actually victims of SIDS.

The diagnosis, by definition, is retrospective. The role of virus infection is obscure. Other possible causes, such as milk-allergy, parathyroid inadequacy, and adrenal insufficiency have not been substantiated, and the role of laryngospasm and cardiac arrhythmia has not been fully worked out.

The fact that the baby does not make a sound possibly indicates that laryngospasm may be the terminal event. Gentle nasal obstruction due to respiratory infection leads in some infants but not in others to cessation of respiration (apnoea) with no attempt at breathing through the mouth. This observation leads to the belief that quite trivial respiratory infection may trigger SIDS in an infant aged 2 to 4 months.

At autopsy, the trachea contains a small amount of oedematous fluid, sometimes blood-stained (due to terminal pulmonary oedema and congestion); petechial haemorrhages are found on the visceral surface of pleura, pericardium and thymus (probably due to agonal respiratory efforts); and often there is microscopic evidence of respiratory inflammation. There is usually evidence of a brief burst of spasmodic motor activity; bladder and bowels are empty, and sometimes blanket fibres are found under the finger nails.

Q. 32.1. Describe various sections of IPC dealing with pregnancy-related deaths.

IPC 312 causing miscarriage: Whoever voluntarily causes a woman with child to miscarry, shall, if such miscarriage be not caused in good faith for the purpose of saving the life of the woman, be punished with imprisonment of either description for a term which may extend to three years, or with fine, or with both; and, if the woman be quick with child, shall be punished with imprisonment of either description for a term which may extend to seven years, and shall also be liable to fine.

Explanation: A woman who causes herself to miscarry, is within the meaning of this section.

IPC 313 causing miscarriage without woman's consent: Whoever commits the offence defined in the last preceding section without the consent of the woman, whether the woman is quick with child or not, shall be punished with imprisonment for life, or with imprisonment of either description for a term which may extend to 10 years, and shall also be liable to fine.

IPC 314 death caused by act done with intent to cause miscarriage: If act done without woman's consent, whoever, with intent to cause the miscarriage of a woman with child, does any act which causes the death of such woman, shall be punished with imprisonment of either description for a term which may extend to 10 years, and shall also be liable to fine.

If the act is done without the consent of the woman, shall be punished either with imprisonment for life or with the punishment above mentioned.

Explanation: It is not essential to this offence that the offender should know that the act is likely to cause death.

IPC 315 act done with intent to prevent child being born alive or to cause it to die after birth: Whoever before the birth of any child does any act with the intention of thereby preventing that child from being born alive or causing it to die after its birth, and does by such act prevent that child from being born alive, or causes it to die after its birth, shall, if such act be not caused in good faith for the purpose of saving the life of the mother, be punished with imprisonment of either description for a term which may extend to 10 years, or with fine or with both.

IPC 316 causing death of quick unborn child by act amounting to culpable homicide: Whoever does any act under such circumstances that if he thereby caused death he would be guilty of culpable homicide, and does by such act cause the death of a quick unborn child, shall be punished with imprisonment of either description for a term which may extend to 10 years, and shall also be liable to fine.

Illustration: A, knowing that he is likely to cause the death of a pregnant woman, does an act which, if it caused the death of the woman, would amount to culpable homicide. The woamn is injured, but does not die; but the death of an unborn quick child with which she is pregnant is thereby caused. A is guilry of the offence defined in this section.

IPC 317 exposure and abandonment of child under 12 years, by parent or person having care of it: Whoever being the father or mother of a child under the age of 12 years, or having the care of such child, shall expose or leave such child in any place with the intention of wholly abandoning such child, shall be punished with imprisonment of either description for a term which may extend to seven years, or with fine, or with both.

Explanation: This section is not intended to prevent the trial of the offender for murder or culpuble homicide, as the case may be, if the child die in consequence of the exposure.

IPC 318 concealment of birth by secret disposal of dead body: Whoever, by secretly burying or otherwise disposing of the dead body of a child whether such child die before or after or during its birth, intentionally conceals or endeavours to conceal the birth of such child, shall be punished with imprisonment of either description for a term which may extend to two years, or with fine, or with both.

PART 3: Forensic Psychiatry

Section 6

33 Forensic Psychiatry (Mental Illness/Impairment)

Psychiatry is that branch of medical science which deals with the study, diagnosis, treatment, and prevention of mental illness. Forensic psychiatry deals with the correlation and application of such knowledge to purposes of law for the administration of justice. The basic features of various state laws in respect of mental illness are essentially the same. It is, therefore, possible to apply the concepts outlined here in most jurisdictions with minor modifications.

The term 'mentally ill person' is used to designate any member of the community who is unable on account of mental illness to look after himself and manage his own affairs or is dangerous to himself or to others. This disorder may be so great or of such a kind *(certifiable mental illness/legal unsound mind)* that it becomes advisable in the interest of the patient or the community to segregate such an individual and deprive him of his liberty and his rights as a citizen. Mental illness is, therefore, a social problem and medically it takes the form of various types of mental diseases.

The law assumes that a mentally ill person is not responsible for his actions and, therefore, if such a person commits a crime he is not punished for it. While this is perfectly reasonable, it leads to the plea of mental illness being put forward on totally inadequate grounds even in many trials of murder cases. In as much as the law presumes that every person is mentally sound until the contrary is proved, there is no subject in legal medicine which has given rise to greater controversy than fixing the degree and form of mental illness which shall free a person from a contract which he has entered into or from the consequence of a wrongful act that he has committed.

The legal term **'mentally ill person'** as used in the Mental Health Act, 1987 (of India), means a person who is in need of treatment by reason of any mental disorder other than mental retardation. Such illness covers psychoses (organic and functional), neurotic disorders, and various organic disorders. The term **'insanity'** is obsolete now but is loosely used to refer to any mental impairment severe enough to be apparent and/or to cause problems. It is, however, commonly used in strictly legal context, such as insanity defence. **Legal unsoundness of minds, IPC 84** or **certifiable mental illness,** refers to a serious mental disorder sufficient to warrant legal restraint of the sufferer as provided under the Act.

Q. 33.1. Briefly explain the meaning of the following terms as used in forensic psychiatry: (a) affect, (b) confabulation, (c) delirium, (d) delusion, (e) fugue, (f) hallucination, (g) illusion, (h) intelligent quotient, (i) lucid interval, (j) neurosis (k) psychopath, (l) psychosis, (m) stupor, (n) twilight states.

Affect: This means the outward manifestation of a person's feelings, tone, or mood.

The terms affect and emotion are commonly **used** interchangeably in affective (mood) disorders.

Confabulation: When there is a pathological loss of memory, e.g. in Korsakoff's psychosis, and early stages of dementia, the patient fills the gaps with purely imaginary events. These fabrications are called confabulations. Thus, a patient who might not have even left the room talks of his having visited some places during the period of lapse, or he may describe with a wealth of detail how he went to work while he has been in bed in the hospital for the whole day.

Delirium: This is an acute confusional state. It may occur during high fever, as a result of drug or alcohol intoxication or withdrawal, head injury, metabolic upsets, or mental stress. It is characterised by clouding of consciousness, disorientation, incoordination and abnormal experiences, such as hallucinations, delusions and illusions. The patient is, therefore, often impulsive and may commit suicide or some violent act. Under section 84 IPC, he is not held responsible for such acts, if he lost consciousness to such an extent as would prevent him from knowing the nature of the act or distinguishing between right and wrong. The condition lasts from a few hours to days and weeks and ends with full or varying degree of recovery.

Delusion: Delusion is a false, but firm, belief in something which is not a fact despite proof to the contrary. It indicates a serious disorder, such as schizophrenia or GPI. It is important from a medicolegal point of view as it affects the conduct and actions of the sufferer and may lead him to commit suicide, murder, or some other crime. Such a person is not fully responsible for his acts. The following are some examples of common types of delusions: **Hypochondriacal delusions** are common in depressions of later life. For instance, the patient may say, he has cancer, is unable to swallow, that his bowels are obstructed, etc. **Delusions of poverty** are common in the depressions. The patient states that he is ruined financially and has no money, and concern over relatives may lead to beliefs that they are starving, sick or even dead. **Nihilistic delusions** are common in involutional melancholia and consist in statements by the patient that there is no world, he does not exist, that his body is dead, etc. **Delusions of infidelity** occur in chronic alcoholism and schizophrenia. The patient suspects the fidelity of his wife although she is chaste, and assaults her. **Delusions of grandeur** may occur in GPI, mania, and schizophrenia. The patient believes that he has untold wealth, is related to ministers, has divine powers, etc., though in fact, the position is otherwise. **Delusions of persecution** (paranoid delusions) occur in schizophrenia, paranoid states, affective disorders (disorders of mood, e.g. mania and depression), organic syndromes, and alcoholic and drug psychoses. The patient imagines that attempts are being made by his near relatives to poison him or kill him. He may believe that people, things or events refer **(delusions of reference)** to him in a special way; or his thoughts, feelings and actions are being influenced **(delusions of influence)** via radio, hypnotism, or some other means with a view to harm him. **Paranoid** is the term used to describe all delusions of being affected in some harmful or persecutory way.

Fugue: This is a disturbed state of consciousness in which the affected person performs acts of which he appears to be conscious but of which on recovery he has no recollection. It is encountered in a dissociative disorder (somatisation), and epilepsy.

Hallucination: This means a false perception without a sensory stimulus. Any sensation may be involved. Thus, in simple terms, a hallucination means seeing, hearing, smelling, tasting, or touching some thing that is not actually present. Visual and auditory hallucinations are more common than others. Visual hallucinations occur in states of altered consciousness and epilepsy and are more common than auditory hallucinations in these conditions. They may consist of flashes of light, frightening faces, wild animals, or terrifying scenes. Auditory hallucinations occur in schizophrenia and severe depressive disorders. The patient hears people abusing him and demanding his death. Hallucinations of smell (olfactory) and taste (gustatory) may occur in schizophrenia and temporal lobe epilepsy. They are often associated, the patient stating that his room has an unpleasant smell and his food has a peculiar taste. Such hallucinations often act as basis for persecutory delusions, viz. the patient stating that his room is poisoned with gas or that his food is being tampered with. Hallucinations of touch (tactile) may be found in states of altered consciousness (i.e. organic psychosis) and schizophrenia. They commonly occur in cocaine psychosis. As a result of such hallucinations, the patient may commit some violent act.

Illusion: This means a false interpretation of an external object or stimulus which has a real existence, e.g. mistaking a stick for a snake, a dog for a lion, the stem of a tree on the roadside for a ghost, and so on. The bereaved, the aged at night, and delirious patients are particularly liable.

Intelligence quotient (IQ): This means the intellectual capacity of an individual in relation to his chronological age expressed as a percentage. For this purpose, the maximum adult age is taken as 16 years, and an IQ between 90 and 110 is considered normal or average. It is rare for those with an IQ of below 50 to look after themselves independently.

Lucid interval: This is a period in the course of mental disease during which there is complete cessation of symptoms of insanity. Lucid interval is commonly met with in depression and mania (bipolar disorder). During this period, the insane person can make a valid will, and can give evidence which is valid. He can judge his acts soundly and is legally responsible for his deeds. However, in criminal cases, it is difficult to decide, if some mental aberration was not present at the time of committing the crime and it is advisable to regard the person as insane. Lucid interval is also seen in head injuries, i.e. extradural haemorrhage, when it is necessary to arrange for a dying declaration.

Neurosis: This is a condition in which the patient suffers from emotional or intellectual disorders but does not lose touch with reality.

Psychopath (sociopath): This is a **personality disorder** where the person is neither mentally ill nor mentally defective but does not conform to normal social standards of behaviour. It is characterised by (1) lack of normal conscience, (2) absence of normal feelings, e.g. love, affection, consideration, sympathy, (3) temper outbursts and impulsive behaviour with verbal or physical attacks without sufficient provocation, and (4) failure to learn from experience or punishment. The impulsive outbursts knows as *"short circuit reactions"* or *"psychotic episodes"* indicate that the psychopath feels much better after an outburst though his victim may be devastated.

Psychosis: This is a disorder characterised by withdrawal from reality, as if living in another world, a world of fantasy, as shown by the presence of delusions and hallucinations.

Stupor: In general medicine, this term is used to signify a degree of unconsciousness in which the patient will still respond to a painful stimulus. In psychiatry, it is used to describe a state of complete suppression of speech, movement and action, not accounted for by profound disturbances of consciousness. Stupor is common in schizophrenia, depression, hysteria, epilepsy, metabolic upsets, opium poisoning, and certain diseases of the central nervous system.

Twilight states: These are conditions of diminished awareness of relatively short duration, during which the patient may carry out actions of which he has little or no subsequent memory (amnesia). Twilight states may occur as somatisation or epileptic phenomena (psychomotor automatism).

Q. 33.2. Give a modern classification of mental disorders

Some of the mental disorders that are liable to lead the sufferer into conflict with the law can be conveniently classified and discussed under the following headings:

1. Mental retardation (mental subnormality, mental handicap)
2. Organic psychoses:
   a. Dementia
   b. Drug-induced psychoses
   c. Confusional states and psychoses following epilepsy, pregnancy and child birth, trauma, and general diseases
3. Functional psychoses:
   a. Schizophrenia
   b. Paranoid states
   c. Affective disorders (mania, depression)
4. Neurotic disorders
5. Personality disorders (e.g. sociopathic personality)
6. Sexual deviations

Of the above, the first four groups of disorders are important from a medicolegal point of view in relation to mental illness. Sociopathic personality is briefly described under definitions. Sexual deviations are considered elsewhere in this book.

Q. 33.3. Comment on the term mental retardation as understood in the forensic sense.

The Mental Deficiency Act, 1927 recognises, Earlier three groups of mental development defects, viz. idiocy, imbecility, and feeble mindedness (morons). These are generally grouped under the term **amentia.** This term is now replaced in the new classification of mental disorders by the term 'mental retardation' and includes mental subnormality and mental handicap.

The term mental retardation signifies a condition of retarded, incomplete, or abnormal mental development. It may be present at birth or may become manifest during early childhood. It can be congenital or acquired, and may be associated with stigmata of physical deformity. It is graded according to IQ level as mild IQ 50–55 to 70; moderate IQ 35–40 to 50–55; severe IQ 20–25 to 35–40, and profound IQ below 20 to 25. The severely afflicted have a multiplicity of developmental defects, mental as well as physical, and do not survive long even with expert nursing care.

In **medicolegal practice,** the term mentally retarded is used to signify a person with low intelligence and also impaired social functioning. The impaired social functioning is characterised by abnormally aggressive and seriously irresponsible (impulsive) conduct. Clearly, a person with low intelligence, whose behaviour is dangerous to others (e.g. fire-setting), or to himself (e.g. wandering in front of a car), comes within the meaning of this term. The impairment in social behaviour may require the court to appoint a legal guardian. The inability of such a person to learn (low IQ) means that he will repeat his wrong doings (antisocial acts), e.g. shop-lifting, theft, house breaking, and even more serious crimes, such as arson, sexual offenses and murder. Mental retardation may be advanced as a ground for mitigation, reason to be excused trial, reason for diminished responsibility, or to be excused guilt. Obviously, the severely subnormal and those whose subnormality requires supervision cannot be held responsible for their impulses as they have no critical intellect or judgement.

Q. 33.4. Give a brief account of: (a) dementia, (b) drug-induced psychoses, (c) confusional states.

Dementia

The term dementia denotes cases in which the mind has reached a certain, usually normal or acceptable, stage of development and then shows signs of deterioration. Dementia manifests as decline of intellectual functions of memory, comprehension and reasoning ability, and emotional changes in the life of the patient.

The principal forms of dementia are: (a) organic dementia, (b) senile dementia, and (c) dementia paralytica or GPI. In all these conditions, gross limitation of mental capacity is a late symptom, and the early changes, as a rule, are slight. The first indication of illness may come from his inconsistent behaviour detected by his associates in different spheres of activity.

Organic dementia: This is a condition of impairment of the mental faculties due to some lesion of the brain, localised or diffuse. The early stages may be characterised by restlessness and irritability with delirium, excitement or depression. These usually pass off, and a progressive mental deterioration sets in, with marked loss of memory, confusion as to time and place, mistakes as to identity, and general childishness.

Senile dementia: This is caused by the onset of old age and cerebral arteriosclerosis. Progressive mental deterioration sets in. The patient loses his memory, becomes childish, silly and sometimes perverted in his behaviour. Delusions are not uncommon. Mostly they relate to his security in later life, with the result that he becomes suspicious and even animose towards those members of the family who are responsible for his care and comforts.

Dementia paralytica or GPI: In the early stages, the patient shows loss of interest in his affairs, and becomes negligent and apathetic. There is blunting of moral sense with the result that he may micturate in public or commit a petty theft. Loss of control of sex instinct may lead him to pxpose his genitals in public or to assault young girls. Impulsive outbursts of violence may take place in later stages.

Drug-induced Psychoses

Certain drugs, such as alcohol, heroin/morphine, cannabis indica, and cocaine used habitually may produce a great variety of mental conditions. LSD brings about sharp changes in awareness and perception.

Alcohol: This usually produces (1) delirium tremens in a chronic alcoholic: (a) when he has been deprived of alcohol for a day or two, (b) after a heavy bout of drinking, or (c) due to injuries and infections, (2) acute confusional state, with its usual characteristics, and (3) Korsakoff's psychosis, characterised by loss of memory for recent events, extreme dissociation, and confabulation. Chronic alcoholism leads to alcoholic dementia where the mind loses critical faculties and is subject to delusions and hallucinations which lead to violent behaviour. Commonly, the wife is the victim of such outbursts and when her fidelity is suspected, she may be killed (sexual jealousy crime of a homicidal nature).

Heroin/morphine: In an addict, this produces progressive deterioration with loss of interest in his environment, of intellectual efficiency, and of self-respect. He becomes quite untrustworthy and will commit almost any crime to obtain a supply of his drug, if he is faced by the prospect of deprivation.

Cannabis indica: Continued use of this drug produces insanity known as **hashish psychosis,** characterised by hallucinations of a highly sensuous type. In some cases, delusions of grandeur or persecution develop. The addict is likely to commit sexual jealousy crimes of a homicidal nature. Following the continued use of cannabis or rarely after its consumption for the first time, the person may *run amok.*

Cocaine: Psychosis due to continued use of cocaine is characterised by delusions of persecution and hallucinations, chiefly visual and tactile (insects creeping under the skin). Prolonged use leads to profound physical and mental deterioration, and sexual perversions.

LSD: Lysergic acid diethylamide "Bad trips" occur. Acute anxiety, depersonalisation, and psychotic episodes persist for months or years. The drug may permanently damage brain cells.

Confusional States

Confusional conditions sometimes occur from excess of physical or mental fatigue, acute infectious diseases, childbirth, and other stresses of life. The condition is characterised by restlessness, insomnia, confused ideas, and mistaken identities. The patient is in a very apprehensive state of mind. Visual and auditory hallucinations are common. *Recovery is the rule.* The manifestations are common in acute delirium and stupor.

Acute delirium: This condition occurs as a complication of continuous high fever or severe mental stress. In the early stages, the patient is irritable, restless, and sleep-less. The restlessness then becomes acute and consciousness is clouded. The patient talks wildly. Delusions and hallucinations are common. Restlessness and irritability continue day and night and the patient may die from exhaustion in a week or two.

Stupor: This condition is met with in schizophrenia, manic-depressive illness, and epilepsy. It is characterised by temporary suspension of mental function. The patient is apathetic, his face expressionless, and speech suppressed. He lies in bed in a monotonous posture and does not care for food or even call of nature. In an acute case, there is total absence of emotion, perception, and thought. In less acute cases, some degree of perception may remain. In all cases, the patient's mind is probably dominated by an obsession or delusion.

Q. 33.5. Discuss the role of epileptic psychosis in medicolegal work.

Epileptic Psychosis

The plea of epileptic automatism is frequently used in serious crimes when no other defence is available. It is, therefore, necessary to understand this condition in proper perspective.

While epilepsy may exist without obvious intellectual impairment, it is commonly associated with a certain degree of mental blunting and, in some cases, by definite psychosis.

The characteristic epileptic convulsion is well known. The disturbance and the consequent cortical discharge is confined exclusively to the motor cortex. However, it may implicate or be confined to the higher centres responsible for the mental processes and actions of the individual. Such a psychiatric disturbance may arise before the motor discharge, after it, or may entirely replace it. When it arises before the motor discharge, it is known as pre-epileptic confusional state, and when it arises after the motor discharge, it is known as post-epileptic automatism. When it replaces the motor discharge by some violent act (epileptic equivalent), it is known as masked epilepsy or psychomotor epilepsy.

In **pre-epileptic confusional state,** the patient drifts into a moody irritable state for a few days before the onset of the fit (convulsions). This moody irritability may reach a stage in which consciousness is clouded. The patient may have delusions and hallucinations, under the influence of which he is liable to be dangerous and may perform criminal acts. He usually regains his normal state soon after the cessation of convulsions.

In **post-epileptic automatism,** there is lapse of consciousness. The patient performs acts without volition. He has no recollection of them afterwards when consciousness returns. When such automatic actions take place, the characteristics of such automatism are as follows:

1. Automatism is generally more pronounced after an attack of petit mal than after a typical fit (grand mal).
2. The automatic action tends to occur after each fit in the same person and is of the same type in each attack.
3. The action is either an habitual action or similar thereto. Examples of such actions are:
   a. A person going to some shop, picking up something, and being arrested for theft
   b. A person micturating in a public place and being arrested for indecency
   c. A person accustomed to firearms—shooting some one
   d. A woodcutter or butcher inflicting incised wounds or killing some one.
4. There is usually total amnesia for the act or rarely faint blurred memory of epileptic automatic phase.

In **masked** or **psychomotor epilepsy,** there is no convulsion. The mental disturbance causes the convulsions to be replaced by some outrageous act, such as murder (epileptic equivalent). These cases are characterised by excessive brutal force and by the fact that the ingredients necessary for a premeditated attack are absent. The victim is usually a stranger, there is no motive, there are no accomplices, there is absence of preparedness, and there is no attempt on the part of the patient to hide the crime or to escape.

It is important to point out here that the days of epilepsy as a stock defence to a murder charge are now over with the invention of EEG. The lawyers for the defence have now shifted their dubious cases of insanity to the unchartered territory of amnesia or mental black-out, where the EEG has so far not been able to chase them.

Q. 33.6. Give a brief account of psychosis due to: (a) pregnancy and child birth, (b) trauma (c) general diseases.

Psychosis due to Pregnancy and Child Birth

Psychosis may occur at any time from the beginning of pregnancy to the end of lactation. During pregnancy, delusions and dislike or hatred towards the husband may occur, and the patient may develop tendency to suicide. Postpartum psychosis may result in mania with a tendency to homicide. The woman may kill her infant. Psychosis late in the puerperium may manifest as depression with a tendency to suicide. Lactational psychosis is characterised by mental confusion, hallucinations, delusions, and depression. These may eventually lead to suicide or infanticide.

Post-traumatic Psychosis

A head injury is generally followed by some degree of mental impairment, either temporary or permanent. Damage to the brain at birth or during early childhood may cause mental subnormality or give rise to epilepsy. In adults, mental symptoms following head injury are more common in those abusing alcohol. Sudden mechanical injury to the brain causes concussion, a state of disturbed consciousness. Other symptoms, especially organic headaches may persist for a considerable length of time. Confusional and delirious states may occur. The patient may develop traumatic epilepsy. Even in the absence of clinical evidence, a number of individuals show some form of non-specific brain damage as seen by abnormal EEG. In some claims of permanent brain damage following head injury, while neurologists have found no evidence of damage psychologists have convincingly shown permanent brain damage as revealed by psychological tests. In a case where the evidence regarding brain damage is disputed, it is important to have an opinion from a second psychologist on the reliability of the tests employed and the extent to which they can measure changes in mental activity.

Psychosis due to General Diseases

Acute infectious diseases may bring on a confusional state in the beginning, and sometimes depression with suicidal tendency after recovery. Patients suffering from venereal diseases sometimes become depressive. They are obsessed with the idea of their uncleanliness and feel unfit to associate with others. Mental symptoms are prominent in certain endocrine diseases, especially thyroid deficiency. Deficiency diseases, especially pellagra and beriberi, are responsible for certain cases of psychosis. Porphyria may sometimes produce organic psychotic states.

Q. 33.7. Give the modern concept of schizophrenia.

Schizophrenia

The term schizophrenia is now used to cover a group of conditions that have certain characteristics in common and that may arise in a number of different ways. Four sub-groups are recognised, viz: (1) schizophrenia simplex, (2) hebephrenic schizophrenia, (3) catatonic schizophrenia, and (4) paranoid schizophrenia. The key factors are disorder of thought and disintegration of emotional stability *(split personality)*, that is a split between thought and emotion: a person may be killed and the schizophrenic may describe with interest and pleasure how he had attacked the victim.

Disorder of thought is marked by misinterpretation of reality due to hallucinations, illusions, and delusions with the result that the patient lives in a world of his own. Disintegration of emotional stability is marked by changes in behaviour, e.g. withdrawn, depressive, violent, etc. Either element may predominate at any stage.

The illness begins in early adolescence. As the disease progresses, the person withdraws from the environment (emotional disintegration). He lacks drive and ambition, gives up his hobbies, loses interest in friends, and is indifferent to his surroundings. The patient may react to happenings of great importance as if they are of no concern to him **(schizophrenia simplex).**

On the other hand, his thinking may become so disorganised (thought disintegration) by hallucinations, illusions, and delusions that he may become impulsive and may commit any crime, the impulse arising at any stage of the disease but is more common in early stages **(hebephrenic schizophrenia).** The impulse may not be present in consciousness at the time of actual commission of crime and any confusion of the mind may not be apparent. Sir Sydney Smith records the instance of a man who heard hallucinatory voices telling him to kill his mother with a razor but was afraid at the last moment; next day when his mother entered his room and although he did not then hear any voices, he went downstairs, got a razor, and coming up behind his mother cut her throat.

The most marked form of withdrawal from reality is stupor. It may alternate with rigidity and excitement **(catatonic schizophrenia).** The stage of stupor may lead to suicide. The stage of excitement may lead to a wild and impulsive homicidal attack on those round him, even a stranger, without any provocation. Homicidal impulses usually precede suicidal ones.

Finally, his distortion of thought with persecutory or grandiose delusions and hallucinations, while retaining much of his original personality, may pose a distorted view of the world around him. The patient imagines that people, things, or events refer to him in a special way (delusions of reference) and attempts are being made by his near relations to poison him or kill him (delusions of persecution) because he is a very important person (delusions of grandeur). He may believe that everyone is against him and trying to harm him **(paranoid schizophrenia).** In such a state, he may commit any crime. Since much of the personality is preserved, in some cases with systematised delusions, the crime may not be the result of a sudden impulse but is usually preceded by much complaining and planning, and it would appear that the requirements of the legal test of insanity (certifiable mental illness) cannot be met with in such cases (Raman Raghavan case: case 2 at the end of this chapter). In such cases, the question of responsibility is difficult to judge owing to the split between thought and emotion: a criminal act may be committed and even skillfully covered up though the emotional state may be plainly psychotic.

33.7a. Write short note on othello syndrome.

The patient suffers from delusions of infidelity in the purest form. He believes his wife has illicit relations with somebody based upon insignificant, minimal or no evidence. These people may be associated with stalking, cyber stalking, sabotage and violence. Family history of mental illness including pathological, morbid, delusional jealousy is forth coming. This may be seen also in all kinds of cerebral insult or injury. These men may use hands in contrast to jealous women who use blunt objects or knife. Associated sexual dysfunction may be seen. Suicide or partner murder or both may be the end result. Alcohol and drug abuse, e.g. cocaine or amphetamines may be associated. Diffuse cerebral cortical changes in right frontal lobe are seen on MRI in these cases. The person goads the partner to confess infidelity (though not true). Once she confesses succumbing to pressure, the accuser explodes into violent acts.

This dangerous state of morbid jealousy sometimes referred to as the **Othello syndrome** is in fact an example of paranoid schizophrenia. The person has delusions of infidelity about his wife or mistress and he assaults her. The end result may be murder or attempted murder.

Q. 33.8. Give a brief account of the modern concept of paranoid states (delusional insanities).

Patients who harbour a variety of delusions with or without hallucinations, but who do not show the disturbances of mood and thinking typical of the other groups of schizophrenia, are grouped together under the general heading of paranoid states. These conditions tend to commence in middle age or later and run a chronic course. The personality is well preserved. The term **paranoia** is sometimes applied to those rare patients who gradually develop delusions of persecution of a systematised nature and retaliate by a violent act. The illness may take years to develop although the onset is generally between 25 and 40 years. It is more common in men than in women. Some paranoiacs living in society, dress in odd ways and are regarded as eccentrics, queer inventors, or perhaps exponents of some strange social or religious system, of which they become the leaders. However, in due course, they are admitted to psychiatric hospitals because of some friction with society. The term **paraphrenia** is sometimes applied to those patients who develop more or less systematised delusions, ideas of reference, and vivid hallucinations of which the auditory type is most marked. The illness develops insidiously, usually later in life than the schizophrenic illness, and may occur round about the age of 45 years. The emotional responses remain normal while intellectually the patient may not deteriorate and may be able to carry on effectively within the community. Often however, their morbid beliefs cause trouble with their neighbours whom they suspect of being hostile to them and not uncommonly they call the police for help against their imagined persecutors. Even an attempt may be made to get redress by an ordinary process of court. When he fails to get redress, he considers that judges have been bribed and tries to procure justice by doing some violent act himself against his alleged enemies, or killing some prominent personality to focus the attention of the public to his grievances.

Q. 33.9. Comment on affective disorders with special reference to manic depressive psychosis.

This is a group of disorders characterised by prominent and persistent disturbance of mood (affect). The disorder is usually episodic but may be chronic. Manic-depressive psychosis is a typical example.

Manic-Depressive Psychosis

This form of illness includes both mania and depression. These are different manifestations of the same disorder. At different times throughout life, the mood varies between extreme poles of cheerfulness (mania) and sadness (depression). This is, therefore, known as **bipolar disorder.**

Commonly, an attack of maniacal excitement alternates with an attack of depression with a lucid interval between the two. However, for ease of understanding, the two forms are described separately.

Mania: This state is less common than depression. The patient is excited, restless, and talkative. The excitement is accompanied by euphoria which is not compatible with the circumstances of the patient. In severe cases, he may be violent and dangerous. The most severe degree of mania is known as **delirious mania.** In this condition, there is clouding of consciousness with disorientation and impulsiveness. Auditory and visual hallucinations may be present and are often associated with delusions of grandeur followed by delusions of persecution, and the patient may commit some violent act under the influence of the latter.

Depression: This is more common than mania. Feeling of depression and loss of interest in normal activities are the main features. They are not warranted by the patient's circumstances. Refusal to take food, lack of personal attention, and suicidal tendencies may be present. Hallucinations and delusions are common and the patient constantly feels the presence of imaginary evil or danger. Practically, every patient suffering from depression is potentially suicidal. However, homicidal acts are by no means uncommon. The act may be performed in a confusional state or with complete consciousness. In the latter, it takes the form of an irresistible impulse, as for example, a mother throwing the child out of the window. Homicidal behaviour, particularly, towards emotionally significant persons, like family members, may be observed. The other crime characteristic of the depressive state is shop-lifting. The culprit is usually a respected middle-aged woman with a full purse who shop-lifts in a state of confusion, as a cry for help, and as indication of her depressed state of mind. Such a patient is in need of urgent psychiatric help.

NEUROTIC DISORDERS

This group includes conditions, such as anxiety neuroses, hysteria, phobias, and depressive neuroses. These are characterised by the fact that the patient though suffering from emotional or psychological disorder does not lose touch with reality. Generally, these conditions do not lead to conflict with the law except in compensation cases. Of interest to the forensic expert are the depressive neuroses and the fugue states. In the former, the depressed mood may lead to a suicidal attempt which may be the first sign that a person is ill with a depressive neuroses. In an occasional case, the depressive state may be so severe that the concomitant tension leads to a homicidal outburst even where the previous personality was good. The fugue state, encountered in dissociative disorder (hysteria) and epilepsy, may be advanced as a defence to a criminal charge.

Q. 33.10. Describe in detail how you will proceed to diagnose mental illness?

Diagnosis of Mental Illness

In well-defined cases of mental illness, and severe mental retardation, there is no difficulty in diagnosis, but in early stages of any mental illness, even psychoses, diagnosis is difficult as the behaviour may appear normal. Besides, there is a significant difference between a certifiable mental disorder (legal insanity) and mental illness. The law tends to regard mental illness as a disease of the intellect, whereas it usually affects the emotional sphere of the mind. Therefore, when a medical witness is called to give an expert evidence he should make a critical clinical appreciation of facts at his disposal obtained from a detailed—(1) family history, (2) personal history, (3) physical examination, (4) mental condition, (5) laboratory investigations when required, and (6) such other sources of information that may be possible. If necessary, the person should be kept under close observation during which period his manners and movements should be carefully watched before giving a definite opinion as to whether he is mentally ill to an extent as to warrant legal restraint (certifiable mental disorder).

Family history: Specific inquiries should be made about the incidence of serious illness or nervous breakdown in the family. More intensive investigation need be undertaken in this field, if there is evidence of a strong genetic factor in this illness.

Personal history: This carries the history from infancy up to the present personal, marital, or occupational difficulties, and the development of personality. This must also cover use of any intoxicating drugs and all serious illnesses, both structural and functional, to which the patient has been subject.

Physical examination: This is important whether or not there is any evidence of deformities and malformations or the patient complains of physical symptoms. The main points to note are the following:

1. Head—big, small, normal.
2. Eyes—slanting, proptosis, normal.
3. Pupils—reaction, accommodation.
4. Bridge of the nose—flattened, normal.
5. Lips—thick, normal.
6. Tongue—large, foul, furred, normal.
7. Extremities—long, short, normal.
8. Hands and feet—flat, broad, moist with sweat, normal.
9. Fingers—any extra digit, long, short, normal.
10. Skin—dry, mottled, wrinkled, hairy, normal.

11. Genitals—infantilism, precocious development, normal.
12. Other organs—any defect, normal.
13. Temperature, pulse, respiration—increased, decreased, normal.
14. Other information—habits, sleep, etc.

Mental status: Observations should be assessed and recorded under the following heads:

1. General appearance and behaviour—natural, suspicious, perplexed.
2. Gait—peculiarity, if any.
3. Talk: manner and content—normal, shouting, slurring, slow, logical, disconnected.
4. Subjective state: mood and attitude to consultation—euphoria, depressed, apathetic, anxious.
5. Content of thought—delusions.
6. Perception—illusion, hallucinations.
7. Contact with reality—depersonalisation, derealisation. (These mean loss of that subjective conviction of the actual identity between one's self and one's body, or of the actuality of the rest of the world, normally taken for granted).
8. Sensorium and formal intelligence—orientation, memory, attention.
9. Insight and judgement—does the patient know that he is mentally abnormal?
10. Handwriting—tremor, misspelling, omission of letters.

Laboratory investigations: Examination of blood, urine, and CSF as well as X-rays and electroencephalographic studies may help.

Other sources of information: Teachers, friends, relations, colleagues or employers may be able to say about the habits and behaviour of the patient and if any notable departure has been observed therefrom.

It is safe for a medical practitioner **to diagnose certifiable mental illness** in a case where a person's ability to think, respond emotionally, remember, communicate, interpret reality, and behave appropriately is sufficiently impaired so as to interfere grossly with his capacity to meet the ordinary demands of life. Thus, he is in such a state of mental disorder that either his own health or safety or that of others is at risk.

Q. 33.11. Give the objectives and salient features of the Mental Health Act, 1987.

The objectives of the Act are to:

1. Regulate admission of the mentally ill patient to a psychiatric hospital or psychiatric nursing home and to protect his rights while under detention.
2. Prevent harm to himself and the society by the mentally ill person.
3. Protect citizens from being detained in psychiatric hospitals without sufficient cause.
4. Fix liability for maintenance charges of mentally ill patient admitted to the hospital or nursing home.
5. Provide facilities to establish guardianship or custody of the mentally ill patient and management of his property.
6. Establish central and state authority for mental health services.
7. Provide for licensing and control of psychiatric hospitals by the state government.
8. Ensure legal aid to the mentally ill patient at state expense in certain cases.

Under the Act, the psychiatric hospital or psychiatric nursing home should have facilities for outdoor treatment also. It may be inspected by the authorities to determine, if it is being maintained in accordance with the license conditions, as regards facilities, admission, discharge, leave of absence, and behaviour of the guardians or managers of the mentally ill patient. Various proformas are provided for application to establish a psychiatric hospital, for medical certificates for the reception of the mentally ill, leave of absence, case record, etc.

Q. 33.12. Describe the duties of a registered medical practitioner in the matter of certification under the Mental Health Act.

The certificate in respect of mental health is a legal document and must meet with the following requirements:

1. It must be issued in the prescribed form.
2. Two medical certificates are required of which one must be from a doctor in government service.
3. The patient should have been examined not earlier than 10 days before an application for reception is made.
4. Each doctor must examine the patient separately without consulting each other and form his opinion on the basis of his own observations and from the particulars communicated to him.
5. Each certificate should clearly state that the patient is suffering from mental disorder of such a nature and degree as to warrant his detention in a psychiatric hospital or registered psychiatric nursing home and that such detention is necessary in the interest of his health and personal safety or for the protection of others.
6. If it is not possible to give an opinion on the mental status of the person who is alleged to be mentally ill and is brought before a magistrate under section 23 or 25, the magistrate may permit the observation of such a person under section 28 in an observation ward of a general hospital, general nursing home, or any other suitable place for a period of 10 days at a time, extendable to a maximum of 30 days, to enable the medical officer to determine, if the medical certificate in respect of such a person can properly be given or not.

A doctor who is not in government service is under no compulsion to accept the examination of a mentally ill person but if he does so, he should do it with care. Any doctor who issues a certificate carelessly on inadequate grounds or a false certificate is liable to face serious consequences.

Q. 33.13. Discuss feigned mental illness (insanity). Tabulate the salient features of true and feigned insanity.

Symptoms of mental disorder are occasionally feigned by persons accused of criminal offence in order to prevent a trial, to procure an acquittal, or to escape the consequences of a business transaction or deed executed by them. Personnel in army, navy and other services may do so, to escape the punishment for gross neglect of duty or when they desire to leave the service and which they are not allowed to do.

The detection of such malingering is one of the responsible duties of a medical officer. In some cases, it may require prolonged and careful observation. Such a person may be kept under observation, for 10 days, extendable with the permission of the magistrate by a further periods of 10 days, up to a maximum of 30 days. It is unwise to form hasty conclusions.

Table 33.1 describes salient features of true and feigned insanity.

Table 33.1: Salient features of true and feigned unsoundness of mind

	True unsoundness of mind	*Feigned unsoundness of mind*
1.	Onset is usually gradual or rarely sudden but almost always without any motive	Onset is always sudden and not without some motive
2.	Predisposing or exciting cause may be present, e.g. family history of insanity, grief, sudden loss of money, etc.	No predisposing or exciting cause is usually present
3.	There is usually a peculiar facial expression in well-developed cases of insanity.	Facial expression is generally normal even when the person pretends to be mad outright. Frequent changes of facial expression are not characteristic of insanity
4.	The individual shows signs and symptoms of insanity irrespective of his conduct being observed or not	The individual pretends to be insane only when he is observed and there is total absence of symptoms when he thinks he is alone and unobserved

(contd.)

(*contd.*)

True unsoundness of mind	Feigned unsoundness of mind
5. Signs and symptoms usually point to a particular type of mental illness	Signs and symptoms are not uniform and do not indicate any particular type of mental illness
6. A truly insane person can stand violent exertion for several hours or days without exhaustion, or sleep	Violent exertion necessary to feign maniacal frenzy (which is generally imitated by impostors) leads to exhaustion, and sleep
7. Habits invariably dirty or filthy. An insane may smear his body with stool or urine	Habits usually not dirty or filthy, though a false show may be up to that effect
8. Physical manifestations of true insanity, viz. dry, harsh skin, furred tongue, constipation, anorexia, and insomnia are present	Physical manifestations of true insanity, viz. dry, harsh skin, furred tongue, constipation, anorexia, and insomnia are not present
9. Not worried about being repeatedly examined	Dislike for repeated examination is obvious

Q. 33.14. Describe the various ways by which mentally ill persons may be placed under restraint.

Q. 33.15. Discuss the procedure for admission of a mentally ill person to a psychiatric hospital or a registered psychiatric nursing home.

Restraint of the Mentally Ill

A mentally ill person needs to be restrained for his own safety or for the safety of others. If the lawful guardian of such a patient is unable to keep him under control for any reason, or if there be no guardian at all, the state is legally justified to take charge of such a patient and to put him under restraint. Such restraint may be: (1) immediate, or (2) by admission to a psychiatric hospital or registered psychiatric nursing home after certain conditions have been complied with.

Immediate Restraint

Immediate restraint becomes necessary and, therefore, is permissible in case of an insane person who is dangerous to himself or to others. Such restraint under the personal care of attendants, e.g. by safely locking up in the room, may be imposed either by the consent of a lawful guardian of the mentally ill person, or without his consent, if there is no time to obtain it, in order to prevent danger, but such restraint must last only so long as the danger lasts. Immediate restraint may also be imposed in cases of delirium due to disease, viz. delirium tremens, but the restraint must cease with the subsidence of symptoms and a valid reception order needs to be obtained.

Admission to a Psychiatric Hospital

A mentally ill person may be admitted to a psychiatric hospital or registered psychiatric nursing home: (1) as a voluntary patient, (2) under certain special circumstances on application by a relative or friend, (3) under reception order on application by—(a) medical officer, or (b) husband, wife, or other relation, (4) under reception order on production of the mentally ill person before a magistrate, (5) as a mentally ill prisoner, and (6) as escaped mentally ill person.

Voluntary patient: Any person, not being a minor, who considers himself to be a mentally ill person and desires admission to a psychiatric hospital or nursing home for treatment, may request the medical officer in charge for being admitted as a voluntary patient. In case of a minor, the request must be made by the guardian. The medical officer in charge may make such inquiry as he may deem fit within a period of 24 hours and if satisfied that the applicant or the minor requires treatment as an inpatient he may admit him as a voluntary patient.

Under section 18(1), such a patient may leave the hospital upon giving 24 hours' notice in writing to the medical officer, and in the case of a minor by his guardian doing so, subject to the provisions of section 18(2) and 18(3).

Under section 18(2), when a minor voluntary patient attains majority the medical officer shall intimate this fact to the patient and unless a request for his continuance as an inpatient is made by the patient within a period of one month from such intimation the medical officer shall discharge him subject to the provisions of section 18(3).

Under section 18(3), if the medical officer is satisfied that the discharge of a voluntary patient under section 18(1) and under 18(2) is not in the interest of such voluntary patient he shall constitute a Board of two medical officers and elicit their opinion for continuance of further treatment. If the Board is of the opinion that such voluntary patient needs further treatment the patient shall not be discharged but his treatment shall be continued for a period not exceeding 90 days at a time.

Under special circumstances: A medical officer may admit a mentally ill person to a psychiatric hospital for a period not exceeding 90 days, on an application made on his behalf by a relative or friend, provided that such application is supported by two medical certificates in the prescribed form and manner, or two medical practitioners working in the hospital are satisfied about the condition of the patient for such admission.

Such patient or his relative or his friend may apply to the magistrate for his discharge and the magistrate may after giving notice to the person at whose instance he was admitted and after making such inquiry as he may deem fit either allow or dismiss the application.

Reception order on application: An application for reception may be made—(a) by the medical officer in charge of a psychiatric hospital, or (b) by the husband, wife or other relative of the mentally ill person.

Where the medical officer is satisfied that (1) the mentally ill person undergoing treatment under a temporary treatment order is suffering from mental disorder of such a nature and degree that his treatment requires to be continued for more than six months, or (2) that it is necessary in the interest of his health and personal safety or for the protection of others to do so, he may make an application to the concerned magistrate for detention of such patient.

The husband or wife, or in their absence, a relative who is not a minor and who has seen the alleged mentally ill person within 14 days before the date of application, may make an application, supported by two medical certificates in the prescribed form and manner, to the concerned magistrate for the detention of such person under a reception order in a psychiatric hospital.

The personal attendance of the patient may or may not be necessary according to the discretion of the magistrate. If the magistrate is satisfied that a reception order may properly be made forthwith he may make such an order. If the magistrate is not so satisfied, he fixes a day for the consideration of the application and may also make such inquiries concerning the alleged mentally ill person as he thinks fit.

Reception order on production of mentally ill person before a magistrate: An officer in charge of a police station may take into protection any person found wandering at large within the limits of his station whom he has reason to believe to be so mentally ill as to be incapable of taking care of himself or is dangerous by reason of his mental illness. Such person is produced before the concerned magistrate within 24 hours excluding the time necessary for the journey and if the magistrate thinks it fit to proceed further he may get him examined by a medical officer and pass a reception order for the detention of the said person as an inpatient in a psychiatric hospital.

Such a patient can be sent to any particular licensed psychiatric hospital, if a friend or relative undertakes to pay the maintenance charges and the medical officer in charge of such hospital consents to admit him.

An officer in charge of a police station shall report to the concerned magistrate any mentally ill person within the limits of his station who is **not under proper care and control or is ill-treated or neglected** by any relative or other person in whose charge he is. Any private person can also report such incident to the concerned magistrate. If the magistrate thinks it fit to proceed further in the matter he may entrust the mentally ill person to the care of a relative or other person legally bound to maintain him and if such a person wilfully neglects to comply with this order he will be fined. However, if there is no person legally bound to maintain him or such a person is unable to do so for any reason, the magistrate may issue an order for the reception of such a mentally ill person as an inpatient in a psychiatric hospital.

Mentally ill prisoner: A mentally ill prisoner is one who has committed a crime while being mentally ill or one who has become mentally ill while undergoing a sentence in jail for some offence already committed. He can be admitted as an inpatient in a psychiatric hospital on a reception order from a magistrate after the person's mental illness is medically certified.

Escaped mentally ill person: If any person, not being a mentally ill prisoner, who is admitted to a psychiatric hospital under any order, escapes from such hospital, he may, by virtue of such order, be retaken as an inpatient by any police officer or servant of such hospital or by any other person authorised in that behalf by the medical officer in charge, within a period of one month from the date of his escape. In case of a mentally ill prisoner, he can be retaken at any time.

Q. 33.16. Describe the procedure for the discharge of the mentally ill, under the Mental Health Act.

The discharge of a mentally ill person from a psychiatric hospital or a psychiatric nursing home is governed mainly by sections 18, 40, 41, 42, 43, and 44 of the Mental Health Act. Section 18 provides for the discharge of a voluntary patient. Section 40 relates to discharge by medical officer in charge. Section 41 pertains to discharge on application. Section 42 deals with discharge on the undertaking of relative, friends, etc. Section 43 provides for discharge at request, and Section 44 relates to discharge of a person subsequently found on inquisition to be of sound mind.

1. Under section 18, a voluntary patient is discharged at request on giving 24 hours' notice in writing to the medical officer in charge provided he does not need further treatment and is fit to be at large.
2. Under section 40, a medical officer in charge of a psychiatric hospital may discharge any patient other than a mentally ill prisoner on the recommendation of two medical practitioners, one of whom shall preferably be a psychiatrist. If such a patient is undergoing treatment by order of any authority the medical officer shall forward a copy of the discharge to such authority.
3. Under section 41, where any patient is detained in a psychiatric hospital under an order made in pursuance of an application, he shall be discharged on an application made in that behalf to the medical officer in charge by the person on whose application the order was made provided the patient is not dangerous and is fit to be at large.
4. Under section 42, where any relative or friend of a mentally ill person detained

in a psychiatric hospital or psychiatric nursing home under section 22, 24, or 25 desires that such person shall be delivered over to his care and custody, he shall furnish a bond to the concerned authority in this behalf undertaking to take proper care of such mentally ill person and ensuring that the said mentally ill person shall be prevented from causing injury to himself or to others, whereupon such mentally ill person shall be discharged.

5. Under section 43, any person, other than a mentally ill prisoner, detained in pursuance of an order, who feels that he has recovered from his mental illness, may make an application, supported by a medical certificate from the medical officer in charge, to the magistrate for his discharge. The magistrate may, after making such inquiry as he may deem fit, pass an order discharging him or dismiss the application.
6. Under section 44, if any person detained in a psychiatric hospital in pursuance of a reception order is subsequently found on inquisition to be of sound mind or capable of taking care of himself and managing his own affairs, the medical officer in charge shall forthwith, on the production of a copy of such findings duly certified by the district court, discharge such person from such hospital.

It must be remembered that a mentally ill person has an inherent right to ask for repeated examination of his mental condition in order to secure his release from the hospital, if found reasonably cured though not 100% back to normalcy.

Q. 33.15. Discuss the various aspects of different civil responsibilities of a mentally ill person.

Civil Responsibilities of the Mentally Ill

The subject of civil responsibility of a mentally ill person is generally considered in relation to: (1) management of property, (2) contracts, (3) marriage, (4) competency as a witness, (5) validity of consent, and (6) testamentary capacity.

Management of property: The Mental Health Act, 1987 provides for legal proceedings to be followed in cases concerning protection of the person and of the property of the mentally ill person. The court may appoint a guardian to take care of the person of the mentally ill and may appoint a manager to manage the property, if the mentally ill person is not able to look after himself or manage his property.

Contracts: Under section 12 of the Indian Contract Act (Act IX of 1872), a contract is invalid if one of the parties at the time of making it was, by reason of mental illness, incapable of understanding it, and forming a rational judgement as to its effect upon his interests. However, a mentally ill person is liable for contracts entered into during lucid intervals. The validity of ordinary contracts entered into by persons of unsound mind will depend mainly on the circumstances which accompany the act. Contracts entered into with a mentally ill person may be binding if the other party can show that he was not aware of the person's mental illness, and that the contract is a fair one.

Marriage and divorce: Marriage is regarded as a contract by the Divorce Act, 1869. It can be declared null and void, if one of the parties was at the time of ceremony incapable of understanding the nature of the contract and the duties and responsibilities which it creates. Mental illness occurring subsequent to marriage is not a ground for divorce, save under exceptional circumstances.

Competency as a witness: Under section 118 of the Indian Evidence Act, a mentally ill person is not competent to give evidence, if he is prevented by his illness from understanding the questions put to him and giving rational answers to them. He is competent to give evidence during **lucid interval**.

Validity of consent: Section 90 of the Indian Penal Code lays down that consent to certain acts is not valid, if such consent is given by a person who, from unsoundness of mind or intoxication, is unable to understand the nature and consequence of that to which he gives consent. The question of invalidity of consent may arise in cases of rape, causing death or grievous hurt, and abetment of suicide.

Testamentary capacity: This means the capacity of a person to make a valid will. The law defines it as the possession of a sound disposing mind *(compos mentis)*, which must be certified by a doctor. A will to become valid must fulfil the following conditions:

1. The testator must be a major.
2. He must have a sound disposing mind at the time of making the will.
3. He must understand the nature and consequence of his act.
4. He must know what property he has, to whom he is giving it, and has good reason for his action.
5. He is executing it voluntarily and without any undue influence by any other person.
6. He must sign it in the presence of two witnesses of which one should be a medical man. Both witnesses should also sign in the presence of each other and of the testator.
7. None of the witnesses should be beneficiaries from the will. It should be remembered that a mentally ill person can make a valid will during lucid intervals. A person suffering from delusions can also make a valid will provided the delusions are not related to the property. A person can also make a valid will during fits of drunkenness unless the individual was so drunk as not to know the nature of what he was doing and unless it was repudiated in sober moments. Extreme age, feeble health and mental sluggishness do not prejudice the ability of a person to make a valid will unless the mind has become so impaired as to be unable to understand the nature of the act. An aphasic person may signify by a nod or shake of his head his approval or otherwise of questions put to him, and is not prevented by this disability from making a valid will. A will may be contested but cannot be declared invalid on ground of eccentricity because it does not constitute mental illness in the legal sense of the term.

Q. 33.18. Define criminal responsibility in relation to insanity (mental illness). Describe the legal test to determine the same. Discuss the plea of insanity in relation to murder.

Criminal Responsibility of the Mentally Ill

In law, responsibility means liability to punishment. The law presumes that every person is sane and accountable for his actions until the contrary is proved. The burden of such proof rests upon the person setting up the defence of mental illness. The law assumes that a person who is proved to be insane is not responsible for his actions, as he is devoid of free will, intelligence and knowledge of the act. As the society must be protected against the attacks of such a person and a mentally ill person is ordered to be kept under care in a psychiatric hospital, jail, or other suitable place of safe custody.

The Legal Test

The test for unsoundmind which precludes responsibility for the commission of crime has the following requirements:

1. There should be some evidence of mental disease or defect.
2. This mental disease or defect must exist at the time of the commission of the crime.

3. It should be of such a degree that the person is unable to understand that the act is wrong and/or contrary to law.

Evidence regarding these requirements is offered during the trial as a defence to the criminal charge. Counter-evidence may be offered and the ultimate determination by the court will find the defendant guilty of the criminal charge, or not guilty of the criminal charge by reason of unsound mind.

Unsound Mind (Insanity) and Murder

The plea of unsoundness may be raised by way of defence to any criminal charge, but for most practical purposes, such pleas are confined to charges of murder. The medical witness must rely solely upon his examination of the accused to arrive at an opinion as to sanity or insanity. He must take into account such factors as the mental history of the accused, his physical condition, and present mental condition in relation to the nature of the crime. When persons of unsound mind commit the crime it is—(a) purposeless or motiveless in nature, (b) committed upon persons usually held dear by the culprit, or occasionally upon those who are strangers to him, and (c) its perpetration is without any preparedness, accomplices or secrecy.

Nature of crime: Normally, there is a motive when violence is perpetrated or murder committed by a sane person, though it may not be always possible to elicit such motive. The insane person, by reason of his unsoundness of mind, is unable to understand the nature of his action, and therefore, there is generally no motive when he commits violence or murder.

Victims of crime: A sane person takes revenge only on those who are his enemies or against whom he has some grudge. Normally, he spares his near relations, and does not attack strangers without provocation. In short, he has a definite target to hit. An insane person is not able to distinguish friends, relations or strangers from enemies. He, therefore, attacks any one—friend, relation, stranger, or enemy, even without provocation. His target is not definite. He may, therefore, commit multiple murders. Such murders may include his wife, children, relations, friends, and strangers.

Perpetration of crime: Normally, a sane person makes certain *preparations* before making any attempt to attack any one. He may arrange to have accomplices, and select proper time and place. He will arrange for his safe escape and, as far as possible, all these arrangements are kept secret. The perpetration of crime may also be kept secret by disposal of the victim's body or destroying evidence of crime. Even an appropriate alibi is prepared to meet with an unforeseen eventuality. On the contrary, because of unsoundness of mind, the attack by the person of unsound mind is spontaneous, i.e. without any preparation whatsoever. There are no accomplices. There is no selection of time or place. No attempt is made to run away from the scene of crime or to keep anything secret with the result that the victim's body is neither concealed nor evidence of crime destroyed.

In a charge of murder of the mayor, the defence raised a plea of insanity which was being disputed.

Prosecution: "Why wasn't this killing a simple matter of revenge?".

The doctor answered, "If the accused merely wanted to injure the mayor out of revenge, he would have hardly picked a time when the mayor was accompanied by his body guard in broad day light. And, the fact that the accused kept on shooting at the mayor even after he fell dead convinces me that he was actuated by some force within him that was beyond his control".

Q. 33.19. Discuss the plea of unsound mind (insanity) in relation to criminal charges other than murder.

Unsound Mind and Other Pleas

The law of insanity and criminal responsibility is embodied in section 84 IPC while sections 85 and 86 deal with drunkenness and criminal responsibility. The application of these sections vis-a-vis the various pleas commonly raised is described below:

Delirium: This is a condition characterised by clouding of consciousness, impairment of mental processes, disorientation, and abnormal experiences, such as delusions and hallucinations. The patient is, therefore, impulsive and may commit suicide or some violent act. He is not legally responsible for such an act under section 84 of the Indian Penal Code which lays down that nothing is an offence which is done by a person who, at the time of doing it, is by reason of unsoundness of mind, incapable of knowing the nature of the act, or that he is doing what is either wrong or contrary to law.

Drunkenness: Section 85 of the Indian Penal Code lays down that nothing is an offence which is done by a person who, at the time of doing it, is by reason of intoxication, incapable of knowing the nature of the act, or that he is doing what is either wrong or contrary to law, provided that the thing which intoxicated him was administered to him without his knowledge or against his will. Section 86 lays down that in cases where an act done is not an offence unless done with a particular knowledge or intent, a person who does the act in a state of intoxication shall be liable to be dealt with as if he had the same knowledge as he would have had if he had not been intoxicated, unless the thing which intoxicated him was administered to him without his knowledge or against his will. In short, drunkenness caused by the voluntary use of alcohol or some other intoxicating drug is no excuse for the commission of a crime but produced by drunkenness, voluntary or otherwise, absolves one from criminal responsibility, if it can stand the legal test embodied in section 84 or 85.

Hypnotism: This is a condition brought about by suggestion. In this state, the patient's suggestibility is very much increased. The heightened suggestibility of the hypnotic state may be utilised with advantage in therapy. Accordingly, hypnosis can be used with benefit in certain conditions of ill health including states of depression and mental disorders. It has also been used instead of anaesthesia in manipulative and dental operative procedures and child-birth. In cases of hysterical paralysis and aphonia, the patient can often be brought to full use of the affected parts. Hypnotic suggestion may abolish asthmatic attacks in some subjects. It should, however, be remembered that the bizarre effects which can be produced by suggestion lend themselves to public exhibition and are certainly not without their dangers.

The induction of hypnosis, if in the right hands, is safe and cannot be considered improper. Most authorities believe that a person under hypnosis does nothing that is opposed to his deeply felt ideas of right or wrong, and hence it is presumed that a civilised person will not commit an heinous crime under the hypnotic trance. However, some people after wilfully committing the crime take the plea of hypnotism as a self-defence, but since a person cannot be hypnotised against his will, such plea is not tenable.

Impulse: This generally means the sudden and irresistible force compelling the person to the conscious performance of acts without motive or forethought. In the author's opinion, in most cases, it amounts to a sudden and temporary lapse of sanity during which period a person may commit some horrible act without realising that it is wrong or contrary to law. A case has been recorded in which an abused wife cut off the penis of her husband by a kitchen knife and threw it out of the window when the husband had forcible sex with her.

The clinical types of irresistible impulses are kleptomania (stealing articles of little value), pyromania (setting fire to things), mutilomania (maiming animals), and sexual impulses including sexual perversions and acts of a suicidal or homicidal nature. Such types of impulses are met with in mental subnormality, dementia, schizophrenia, manic-depressive states, obsessive compulsive neurosis, and epileptic psychosis.

It should, however, be remembered that most crimes are the result of temptation or impulses, such as rage, jealousy, etc. that are not resisted and such **unresisted impulses** have no place in law. An **irresistible impulse** would be such as none would be able to resist, as for example, an impulse to get out of a house which is on fire. As long as the patient is able to realise the difference between right and wrong and the nature and consequences of the act, the defence plea of irresistible impulse for committing a crime is not tenable. Exemption from criminal responsibility is not extended to such persons. Mental disorder must be present to claim an exemption.

Somnambulism (sleep walking): This is a state of dissociation occurring in sleep. Literally, it means walking during sleep. It is more common in children than in adults. The patient leaves his bed and makes his way, perhaps to his study room, perhaps downstairs, perhaps out of the house. He rarely injures himself. He is not asleep but in a state of dissociated consciousness in which he may live through a state of vivid hallucinatory experience. Electroencephalographic studies do not indicate the 'awake' pattern. The mental faculties are so concentrated at this stage that he can solve a problem that defied him during waking hours. He may commit a theft or even a murder in this state. The condition forms a good defence plea for criminal offenses.

Somnolentia or semisomnolence: This is a state midway between sleep and waking and in which the mind is in a confused state, as if the person has suddenly woken up from deep sleep. It is similar to the one occurring after an epileptic fit. During this state, a person may commit some horrible or illegal deed, and is not criminally responsible for it. Or not will be decided after through examinations.

Q. 33.20. Comment on McNaghten rules and the criticism in respect of their inadequacy.

McNaghten Rules

The present legal test on the defence plea of insanity is based on McNaghten rules. McNaghten was an accused in a criminal case. He, while labouring under a delusion of persecution, shot Mr Drummond, the private secretary of the Prime Minister Sir Robert Peel, at Charing Cross, London, in mistake for the latter. Evidence of insanity was led and a verdict of "not guilty by reason of insanity" was given. The public reacted adversely to the acquittal and a discussion took place in parliament. The House of Lords put certain questions to all the 14 judges in connection with this case. From the answers given by them, some rules were framed for the criminal responsibility of the insane, and they have been named after McNaghten. According to these rules, to establish defence on the ground of insanity, it must be clearly shown that at the time of committing the act, the accused was labouring under such defect of reason from disease of the mind as not to know the nature and quality of the act he was doing, or if he did know this, that he did not know that what he was doing was wrong or contrary to law. It must be borne in mind that the defence can be founded only on a known and nameable disease of the mind. Lesser conditions which may prevail temporarily at the time of the act do not suffice, and these include rage, jealousy, transient loss of control, and others including unresisted impulse.

The legal test of insanity that is accepted in India is embodied in Section 84 IPC which lays down that nothing is an offence which is done by a person who at the time of doing it is by reason by unsoundness of mind, incapable of knowing the nature of the act, or that he is doing what is either wrong or contrary to law.

With the advances in medicine, insanity is better understood now and many criminologists and psychiatrists are of the opinion that McNaghten rules are now totally outdated and require a complete revision. Some of the states in the West have already formulated certain improvements in these rules.

Criticism of McNaghten Rules

The primary defect of McNaghten rules is that the criterion for deciding that a person is insane is purely an intellectual one. There is no place for emotional factors or the ability of the individual to control his impulses. Medicine has now come to recognise that there is no mental disorder, however partial, that does not have its repercussions throughout the rest of the affected mind. Consequently, it is now accepted that intellectual defect means deficient emotional control. Allowance is, therefore, being made in some states for all such well-known phenomena as the disordered ideation of the schizophrenic, post-hypnotic and epileptic automatisms, and the overwhelming influence of affective disorders which may, for example, cause a depressed person to murder his wife or children whom he loves and whom he knows full well it is normally wrong to kill.

Q. 33.21. Discuss the improvements in McNaghten rules brought about by some countries.

Doctrine of Partial Responsibility

This doctrine is recognised in some of the states in the West. According to it, if a person who has committed a crime is suffering from some aberration or weakness of mind, though not completely insane, he is not fully but only partially responsible for his act. Thus, a charge of murder may be reduced to one of culpable homicide not amounting to murder or manslaughter. This doctrine is applicable in cases of depression, obsessional states, paranoid states, and certain organic states.

Durham Rule

In 1954, the United States Courts of Appeals in the case of Durham vs United States held that an accused is not criminally responsible, if his *unlawful act* was the *product of mental disease* or mental defect. This corresponds very nearly to the strong subjective sense that psychiatrists have of what responsibility should mean. It has an advantage over the irresistible impulse rule in that it covers acts which are the result of slowly rather than suddenly formed resolutions, such as the acts of the melancholic and the paranoiac.

Currens Rule

Currens rule (1961) postulates that an accused is not criminally responsible, if at the time of committing the act he did not have the *capacity to regulate his conduct* to the requirements of the law as a result of mental disease or mental defect. This is similar to the irresistible impulse rule, proposed by Lord Justice Atkin's Committee in 1923 but withdrawn in 1924.

American Law Institute's Test

Under this test (1970), proof that a criminal defendant as a result of mental disease or defect *lacked substantial capacity either to appreciate the wrongfulness of his conduct or to conform his conduct to requirements of law* now constitutes defence to a criminal charge. This test does not cover repeated criminal or otherwise antisocial acts of psychopaths.

Norwegian System

Norwegian law provides that no defendant considered to suffer from mental illness or unconsciousness at the time of committing the offence may be punished. The term insane means whatever doctors at the time classify as mental illness. Thus, there is no difference between medical and legal insanity. The term unconsciousness includes a series of abnormal mental states characterised by peculiar conduct associated, among other things, with a total loss of memory. Many pathologic states, such as hysterical or schizoid reaction, or epileptic seizure, are considered legally as predisposing the offender to a state of unconsciousness during which time he could not be considered responsible for his actions. Once insanity or unconsciousness is established as existing at the time of the crime, this is a complete defence under the Norwegian law. No other element, e.g. a lack of knowledge that what he did was wrong, or a casual link between insanity and crime needs to be established.

ILLUSTRATIVE CASES

The following examples are intended to illustrate the application of the principles of civil and criminal responsibility in respect of some common problems, viz: (1) testamentary capacity, (2) schizophrenia, (3) somnambulism, (4) carbon monoxide automatism, (5, 6 and 7) irresistible impulse, (8) illusion, (9) epilepsy, and (10–13) selfinduced insanity with: (a) drink—alcohol (b) drug—LSD, and (c) insulin.

Case 1. Testamentary capacity: An archi-tect aged 76 was referred to a psychiatrist on 5 February 1959 for examination of his mental condition. It was then found that (1) his memory was impaired for recent events, (2) he could not find appropriate words in his talk, and (3) though his orientation was alright, he did not remember the extent of his property and the income he was deriving therefrom.

In August 1960, the patient was seen again when it was found that his mental condition had progressively deteriorated over the period. He forgot his way back home whenever he went out, and could not tell the month, or the year, nor his age or date of birth. His wife was appointed guardian in August 1961.

The will that he was supposed to have made on 12 February 1959 was being challenged after his death in 1963. The psychiatrist opined that the testator could have made a simple will in February 1959 with a little guidance. By simple will he meant that a particular individual will inherit the property. However, at the material time, he would not have been able to instruct anyone as regards certain complex clauses in the will. The testator was adjudged to be not *compos mentis* and the will declared void.

Case 2. Schizophrenia: One Sindhi Dalwai, *alias* **Raman Raghavan,** was arrested by the Bombay Police on 27 August 1968 under section 302 IPC on charge of murder of two persons namely—(1) Lalchand Jagannath Yadav, and (2) Dular Jaggi Yadav at Chinchawali village, Malad, Greater Bombay, on or about the night between 25 and 26 August 1968. After the preliminary trial in the court of Additional Chief Presidency Magistrate, 19th Court, Esplande, Bombay, when the accused had made a confession, the case was committed to Sessions Court, Bombay. When the trial started in the Court of Additional Sessions Judge, Bombay, on 2 June 1969, the counsel for defence made an application that the accused was incapable of defending himself on account of unsoundness of mind and he also submitted that even at the time of committing the alleged offenses the accused was of unsound mind and incapable of knowing the nature of his acts or that they were contrary to law.

The accused was, therefore, sent to the Police Surgeon, Bombay, who observed him from 28 June 1969 to 23 July 1969 and opined as follows: The accused is neither suffering from psychosis nor mentally retarded. His memory is sound, his intelligence average, and he is aware of the nature and purpose of his acts. He is able to understand the nature and object of the proceedings against him and is not certifiably insane.

With this medical opinion, the trial proceeded. The accused pleaded guilty. During the trial, a psychiatrist of Nair Hospital, Bombay, was cited as a defence witness. He had interviewed the accused in Arthur Road Prison on 5 August 1969 and gave evidence that the accused was suffering from a disease called chronic paranoid schizophrenia (paraphrenia) for a long time and was, therefore, unable to understand that his actions were contrary to law.

In defence, it was said, "The accused did commit the act of killing with which he is charged. He knew the nature of the act, viz. killing human being, but did not know, either it was wrong or contrary to law". The Additional Sessions Judge, Bombay, held the accused guilty of the charge of murder and sentenced him to death. The convict declined to appeal.

Before confirming the sentence, the High Court of Bombay ordered that the Surgeon General, Bombay, should constitute a Special Medical Board of three psychiatrists to determine whether the accused was of unsound mind, and, secondly, whether in consequence of his unsoundness of mind, he was incapable of making his defence.

The members of the Special Medical Board interviewed the convict on five different occasions for about two hours each time. In their final interview when they bade him goodbye and attempted to shake hands with him, he refused to do so saying that he was a representative of *'Kanoon'*(God) who would not touch people belonging to this wicked world. The examination report was as follows:

Details about childhood history are not available. No reliable history about mental illness in his family is obtainable. According to the data available, he had been habitually stealing since his childhood. He hardly had any school education. He had been seclusive and not of a socially mixing type. Since his return from Poona in 1968, he had been living in jungles outside the suburbs of Bombay.

X-rays of skull, routine blood examina-tion, serological test for syphilis, cerebro-spinal fluid (CSF) examination including tests for syphilis, urine and stool examination and EEG examination were non-contributory.

He was of average intelligence (as found by Bhatia's Performance Tests) and there is no organic disease to account for his mental condition.

Throughout the five interviews, he showed ideas of reference and fixed and systematised delusions of persecution and grandeur. The delusions which the accused experienced were as follows:

1. That there are two distinct worlds, the world of 'Kanoon' and this world in which he lived.
2. A fixed and unshakable belief that people are trying to change him into a woman, but that they are not successful, because he was a representative of 'Kanoon' or he himself was 'Kanoon'.
3. A fixed and unshakable belief that he is a power or 'Shakti'.
4. A firm belief that other people are trying to put homosexual temptations in his way so that he may succumb and get converted into a woman.
5. That homosexual intercourse would convert him into a woman.
6. That he was 101 per cent man. He kept on repeating this.
7. A belief that government brought him to Bombay to commit thefts and made him commit criminal acts.
8. An unshakable belief that there are three governments in the country, viz. the Akbar Government, the British Government, and the Congress Government and that these governments are trying to persecute him and to put temptations before him.

Psychological Mechanisms Operating in this Case

His being a representative of 'Kanoon', protection was afforded to him in any assaults on his person or against his persecuting enemies. He could kill anyone who he thought was his enemy because 'Kanoon' wanted it so.

His feelings of sexual inferiority and inadequacy were overcompensated by grandiose delusions like his being a 101 per cent man, and that by pressing a button he could change the sex of other people, a button which was visible to him only and not to ordinary mortals like us.

A rebellious, superior attitude served to bolster up his self-esteem and to prevent a realistic but painful self-evaluation. The war against the three persecutory governments, viz. Akbar, British and Congress (Indian) governments (which also quarrelled among themselves) was waged in self-defence.

His apparent normal behaviour in the prison, his running away from the scene of crime, his normal talk when he was not preoccupied with his delusions, raised the question of malingering or feigning insanity. This was not a case of malingering because:

1. He had confessed having committed the murders.
2. He had not appealed against the sentence.
3. He was not at all worried or concerned about his death sentence.
4. Unlike a malingerer, he had not over-played his part.
5. Multiple murders are generally against malingering.
6. His behaviour did not change whether he was aware or not aware that he was being observed.
7. Symptoms and signs were in conformity with the diagnosis of a recognised psychosis, viz. paranoid schizophrenia, where a part of the personality is pre-served intact, and which is responsible for his normal routine activities.

Conclusions and Opinion

1. Sindhi Dalwai *alias* Raman Raghavan is of unsound mind. He is suffering from a psychosis called chronic paranoid schizophrenia or paraphrenia, the latter being an old term for chronic paranoid schizophrenia with auditory hallucinations. He is dangerous to the society and hence certifiably insane.
2. Sindhi Dalwai knew the nature of the act, i.e. he knew that he was killing human beings.
3. He did know that what he did was wrong and contrary to the law of the land but he firmly believed that what he was doing was right and in tune with the law of 'Kanoon' whose law according to him is obligatory for him to follow.
4. There was such a degree of unsoundness of mind resulting in such a degree of defect of reason that he was incapable of cooperating with and instructing his defence counsel in the conduct of the trial and the court proceedings. The reasons for this incapability were: (a) complete lack of insight into his illness, (b) firm and unshakable delusions that only the law of 'Kanoon' mattered and the law of this world did not apply to him and hence his inability to participate in the Court procee-dings, (c) his complete lack of realisation of the gravity of the crime and the seriousness of his death sentence, and (d) that his judgement was so much influenced by his delusions and hallucinations that he was incapable of rational thinking and behaviour.

Case 3. Somnambulism: A student in a dormitory got up in the middle of night and walked so noisily to the clothes rack that other occupants also woke up. He then put his hands in the pocket of other man's trousers. Several students tried to restrain him and handed him over to the police. He pleaded total amnesia during the period which was accepted as a fact on account of his lack of effort to walk silently, and to avoid suspicion, or arrest.

Case 4. Carbon monoxide automatism: The accused was a well-known scientist with a clean record for driving. After a particu-larly long working day with only snacks for lunch, he was driving home, in the evening, 20 miles. He was tired, and feeling very sleepy about half-way home, opened the car windows. He found it bitterly cold and shut them. He remembered nothing after this except a vague memory of a slight jar. When he got out of the car, his off-side head lamp was smashed, and realising that he had had an accident, he went to the police. He learned to his horror that he had been driving on the wrong side of the road though at a moderate speed, and had killed a man stepping off the right hand curb. An aeronautic expert on testing his car for carbon monoxide found 50 per cent greater concentration than would be tolerated in an aircraft cockpit. His car had a leaking exhaust pipe, and his confusion and amnesia could be accounted for by carbon monoxide poisoning resulting therefrom.

Case 5. Irresistible impulse: After the death of her mother, a woman, AB, who was separated from her husband lived with her wealthy aged aunt, who was virtually helpless, both physically and mentally. At the time of her mother's death, AB had promised her mother that she will not leave the aunt. Over the years, AB suffered from depressive psychosis and committed suicide by a heavy dose of a sedative. But before this, she killed her aunt by a blow on the head. The aunt had left a large sum of money to AB, and a small amount to other relatives. AB's heirs claimed the money because she had died after the aunt. On the principle that a person guilty of slaying cannot claim any benefit under the will of the person whom he or she has killed, the will was contested. A plea was put forward that though AB died later, she cannot inherit aunt's property and hence her heirs had no claim to it.

AB knew exactly what she was doing and also knew that it was legally wrong. The defence had, therefore, to be based on 'irresistible impulse'. She had promised her mother at her death bed that she will not leave the aunt. She, therefore, could not help killing her before committing suicide. The judge recorded that "by no exercise of will could AB, in the mental condition in which she was at the time, have desisted from the act of killing her aunt and subsequently herself, though she knew what she was doing and that it was wrong".

Incidentally, it may be mentioned that this case shows the inadequacy of McNagthen's rules and why they need revision.

Case 6. Irresistible impulse: An ex-servicemen, finding that his wife had had an affair with a local publican, shot the adulterous publican neatly between the eyes, at some convenient time. It was not possible to plead either (1) McNagthen insanity, for obvious reasons, or (2) provocation because the accused took too long a time after the incident to commit murder. The defence was based on the concept of *"mens rea'* in the sense of voluntary action and deliberate intent. Under this concept, it was possible to establish that the accused was unable to resist the impulse to make away with his wife's lover and lacked the necessary element of intent or *mens rea.*

Case 7. Irresistible impulse: Mrs. Lorena Bobbitt, had undergone physical, sexual, and emotional battering at the hands of her husband. She was living in a state of constant fear of being battered. On June 23, 1993, her husband returned late from a night of drinking, and (raped) had forcible sex with her. She cut off his penis. In defense, it was pointed out that repeated physical and sexual abuse had psychologically devastated her and rape pushed her over the edge of temporary insanity. She went to the kitchen to calm herself where she experienced a rush of mental pictures of abuse and terror from her four year marriage. She yielded to an irresistible impulse to strike back as she picked up a 12-inch kitchen knife lying on the kitchen table and dismembered him. The jury (in Virginia, USA) accepted the defense of irresistible impulse. (Also refer to Bobbitt's case in the Chapter 27 on Rape under the topic 'Intramarital Rape).

Case 8. Illusion: A man came home unexpectedly and found his wife in bed with another man. She was not really his wife. They had lived together for five years in a *de facto* relationship. He took out a kitchen knife and, after a short lecture on the advantages of fidelity, stabbed both parties to death. He was charged with murder and pleaded provocation. It was then discovered that there could be no defence of provocation in the absence of legal marriage. Therefore, the defence had to be based on the concept of illusion. "Staying together for five years, the accused believed that the woman was his wife and acted in the heat of passion".

Case 9. Epilepsy: An ideal example of dubious epilepsy defence and how such a defence can boomerang on the unfortunate defendant if it fails may be found in the trial of Jack Ruby. Ruby was allegedly overcome by horror and indignation when he heard of the assassination of President Kennedy by Lee Harvey Oswald. He walked into the police station and just as Oswald was being transferred to a waiting car, he shot Oswald who died on the spot. A defence of epileptic automatism and unconscious act was put up. The facts did not support such a defence. The EEG readings were dead against him, and Ruby was found guilty of first degree murder.

Case 10. Drunkenness: An exceedingly drunken man repeatedly stabbed another man who was also comatose, with drink. For some reason, the assailant had got into his head that the latter was a dummy who had been put into his room for a practical joke by his drunken comrades. He realised the real substance of his act in the morning upon waking. A defence plea was put for-ward that the assailant was so intoxicated that he was not capable of forming the necessary intent to kill the victim. The senselessness of the act, the lack of motive, and the numerous stabs on the body satisfied the court that his story was true.

Case 11. LSD: Mr L committed his crime under the influence of LSD, a drug which appears to have few useful functions besides raising interesting legal problems. On his 'trip', Mr L saw himself as descend-ing to the centre of the earth and fighting an army of snakes. In fact, he fought and killed his wife who was sharing his bed. A defence of diminished responsibility was accepted.

Case 12. LSD: LSD was pleaded as a defence in one of the New York cases but few details are available. The accused was charged with murder. His defence was that he was under the influence of LSD, and he was found not guilty on the grounds of insanity. There appears to have been no suggestion that the defence ceased to be available because his own actions had brought about insanity.

Case 13. Insulin: A male nurse at a mental hospital assaulted one of the patients. His defence was that he did not remember assaulting the patient, that he was a diabetic, and had taken a dose of insulin that morning. Medical evidence called on his behalf was that his action might have been caused by hypoglycaemia, a deficiency of blood sugar after an injection of insulin. The trial judge ruled that a mental condition arising from hypoglycaemia amounted to a disease of the mind: the blow was not a conscious, deliberate or a volitional act.

Q. 33.22. Offer your comments on—is crime a mental illness?

While it is understandable that a mentally ill person may not be able to regulate his conduct to the requirement of law and commit a crime, it must be clearly understood that all crimes are not the result of mental illness. The change in attitude from punishment to treatment towards criminality derives from a time when persons charged with criminal acts showed markedly abnormal mental traits. But the tribe of such abnormal persons is ever increasing by the addition of less abnormal or even normal persons and a new form of so-called illness *"criminosis"* appears to have come into existence as a result of stresses and strains of present day life accentuated by inflation. Under the circumstances, it would be wrong to consider every criminal as a mentally ill person. The various defence pleas of mental illness raised in several crimes would, therefore, require close scrutiny. It has almost become a fashion to commit a crime and then raise the defence plea of insanity, automatisms, amnesia, etc., which ever suits the circumstances of the case. The latest addition to the scene is XYY chromosome constitution.

Physicists speak of a vector force as a ultimate force exerted upon an object by various pressures which try to move it in various directions. What the object ultimately does depends on the resultant vector. Similarly, human beings react in accordance with a vector force resulting from innumerable individual pressures pushing them this way and that. Some are hereditary, others environmental, and many others cannot be usefully classified either way.

Murder is a crime, so is issuing a false certificate, or illegally parking a car, or even tax evasion. It is obvious that we can hardly blame ordinary mental illness or one poor Y chromosome for all these crimes when it suits us. One must, therefore, reasonably conclude that human beings, despite faults, shortcomings and unfortunate circumstances, must assume responsibility for their actions according to the legal standards set up for the particular society.

PART 4: Forensic Biology and Serology

Section 7

34

Forensic Examination of Biological Fluids, Stains, and Other Materials

Forensic Science Laboratory: In India, forensic science laboratories aid the crime investigation by analysing various types of samples transmitted by the investigating agencies. The medical doctor transmits the samples through the police to the FSL. All states of have FSLs in the capitals. CFSLs are located in Kolkota, Delhi (CBI), Hyderabad, etc. The various body fluids, ballistic evidence, semen, hair, poisons, and other trace evidence from scene of crime, accused and victims are **analysed**. Regional and mobile units or clues teams carry out the collection of evidence and analysis. This section deals with the forensic examination.

The topics discussed in this section are intended to give the non-specialist health care provider a sound basic understanding of what can be done. In problem cases, it is highly desirable to contact an expert in the crime investigation laboratory/FSL.

FORENSIC EXAMINATION OF BIOLOGICAL FLUIDS, STAINS AND OTHER MATERIALS

In the investigation of crimes, such as murder, robbery, rape, etc., the examination of biological materials plays an important role in connecting the criminal with the crime. Such biological specimens may be in the form of body fluids, stains, or other material, e.g. blood, semen, saliva, urine, faecal matter, milk, and hair. These are briefly discussed here with special reference to their medicolegal applications.

BLOOD

This topic is discussed under the following headings; (1) general considerations, (2) different blood group systems, (3) DNA profiling, (4) disputed paternity and maternity, and (5) examination of blood stains.

General Considerations

Blood is a complex viscous fluid with a pH of about 7.4. It is mainly composed of two parts, viz: (1) cells (about 45%), and (2) plasma (about 55%). The total volume of blood is about 8 to 8.5% (80–85 ml/kg) of body weight.

Cells: There are three types of cells, viz. (a) red blood cells (RBCs), (b) white blood cells (WBCs), and (c) platelets. The RBCs of men and mammals are circular, biconcave, and non-nucleated, with the exception of camel in whom they are oval and non-nucleated. In birds, fish, reptiles, and amphibians, they are oval and nucleated. This distinction enables a differentiation to be made between mammalian and non-mammalian blood. The RBCs contain water (65%), and solids (35%) of which 33% is haemoglobin and the remaining a mixture of proteins, blood group substances, phospholipids, cholesterol, diphosphoglycerates, aminosugars, etc. WBCs are nucleated cells larger in size than the RBCs. They are classified according to their morphology and staining properties as: (a) granulocytes which include neutrophils, eosinophils, and basophils, (b) lymphocytes, and (c) monocytes. Platelets are non-nucleated, round or oval biconvex discs of varying sizes but smaller than the RBCs.

Plasma: Plasma contains mainly water (91–92%) and solids (8–9%). The solids include—(a) inorganic substances, such as sodium, potassium, calcium, magnesium, phosphorus, iron, copper, etc., (b) organic substances, such as albumin, globulin, fibrinogen, prothrombin, etc., (c) non-protein nitrogenous substances, such as urea, uric acid, xanthine, creatine, etc., (d) fats, such as neutral fats, phospholipids, cholesterol, etc., (e) carbohydrates, and (f) other substances, like antibodies, enzymes, and colouring matter, namely, bilirubin, carotene, and exanthophyllin.

The various components of blood form the basis of the different laboratory methods employed for the examination of blood and blood stains.

Basic Genetic Principles

The characters of the body are controlled by hereditary factors called genes which are present in every cell. They are passed from parent to offspring in the gametes. The genes exist in pairs known as alleles or allelomorphs. Alleles are pairs of contrasting genes, one derived from each parent. If the two genes comprising an allelomorphic pair are identical, the individual is said to be **homozygous**, but if they are different, **heterozygous.**

The type of an organism judged by its characters as a whole is designated as the **phenotype,** while its genetic constitution is designated as its **genotype**. Thus, to say that a person's blood belongs to group A is to give its phenotype; *but two group A blood may be genetically different;* they may be either AO or AA. The blood groups are controlled genetically by a system of multiple allelomorphs. For example, group O is due to the operation of a pair of allelomorphic genes OO. It is not possible to distinguish serologically between the homozygote AA from the heterozygote AO and the same is the position with the genotype BB and BO, the serologically demonstrable blood group (phenotype) being A and B, respectively. However, genotypes can be inferred in case of phenotypes AB and O group. AB individuals are always heterozygous genotype AB, and group O individuals homozygous genotype OO.

Blood Groups as Hereditary Factors

The different blood groups in various systems, such as ABO, MN, Rh, Gm, PGM, EAP, GLO-I, etc., are hereditary factors and their inheritance is governed by the following two principles:

The **first principle** is that the group characteristics are established at an early age; they are specific to the individual; and once established, they are unchanged throughout life.

The **second principle** is that the characteristics of the antigens are inherited as per **Mendel's Laws of Heredity.** Therefore, the individual cannot possess any antigen which both his parents lack.

In the ABO system: (1) agglutinogen A, A1, A2, or B cannot appear in the child unless it is present in one or both parents, (2) an O parent cannot have an AB child and AB parent an O child, (3) if two parents are of the genotype AO and AO, a child OO may be born, (4) parents of AA or AO genotype may have an A child, and (5) the combination of A1B parent with A2 child and vice versa is not possible.

In the MN system: (1) agglutinogen M or N always appears in the blood of a child as it is always present in the blood of the parents, (2) two M parents cannot have an N child and vice versa, (3) in matings where both parents are either type M or N, the child is always of the same type as the parents, (4) in matings where one parent is type M and other type N, all children are type MN, (5) in matings where one parent is homozygous (M or N) and the other heterozygous (MN), all children are of parental types in a 50 to 50 ratio, and (6) in matings where both parents are MN, children of all three types are possible.

In the Rh system: (1) Rh negative parents cannot produce an Rh positive child, and (2) Rh positive homozygous parents cannot produce Rh negative children while Rh positive heterozygous parents can produce Rh positive and Rh negative children.

The secretor factor, haptoglobins, Gc groups and the abnormal haemoglobins are also inherited according to Mendel's laws. Accordingly, two parents who are non-secretors cannot produce a child who is a secretor. Similarly, an HpM mother cannot produce an Hp2-2 child.

DIFFERENT BLOOD GROUP SYSTEMS

Q. 34.1. Write a short essay on different blood group systems.

There are several quite distinct and unrelated types of differences between the blood of different individuals. These are due to: (1) the red cell antigens responsible for ABO, MN, Rh, and other blood groups, (2) blood proteins, such as haptoglobins, Gc, Gm and Inv immunoglobulin types, and various varieties of haemoglobin, (3) polymorphic enzymes mostly present in the red cells, and (4) white cell antigens. The secretor status (vide infra) allows blood group determination in the absence of blood stains or blood. The systems described below are in common use in forensic work.

Grouping Based on Red Cell Antigens

The red cell antigens are identified by simple objective tests. A person's red cells are mixed with the antiserum specific for a given blood group antigen. If the red cells contain the antigen, they are agglutinated (clumped) by the antiserum. For some groups, there are testing sera that will identify the full composition of the person's blood group and his genotype can be determined. Where antisera are available for only one of the pair of genes, the phenotype alone can be identified, i.e. the tests will not distinguish between individuals homozygous for the detectable product of the genes and heterozygous individuals who have inherited the detectable gene from one parent and the non-detectable from the other one.

ABO system: The ABO system divides mankind into four main blood groups, viz. A, B, AB, and O depending on the presence or absence in the red blood cells of two agglutinogens known as A and B. The corpuscles of group A contain agglutinogen A; those of group B, agglutinogen B; those of group AB contain agglutinogens A and B; while those of group O contain neither A nor B (but contains an H substance). It is now known that there are two important subgroups of A, namely A1 and A2. These are also found in group AB giving rise to subgroups A1B and A2B. Antibodies to A and B are normally present in the serum.

An integral part of the ABO system is the **secretory system.** Approximately 80% of the population secrete ABO blood group substances in most of the cells and fluids of the body. These individuals are known as secretors. The rest, approximately 20%, who secrete very little or no blood group substances, are known as non-secretors. All secretors also secrete a substance called 'H' substance. Accordingly, an A blood group person will secrete in his body cells and fluids group A substance and H substance; B blood group person group B substance and H substance; and O blood group person only H substance. The secretor system is determined by two alleles Se and se, the former being dominant over the latter. The resulting genotypes are SeSe, Sese, and sese. ABH group specific substances are found in high concentration in saliva, semen, vaginal secretion and gastric juice, and in low concentration in sweat, tears and urine. It is, therefore, often possible to determine the blood group of an individual from an examination of these secretions, e.g. from saliva on cigarette end or from a seminal stain, and such examination may provide vital clues in the solution of a crime (Fig. 34.1).

MN system: Agglutinogens M and N exist in the red blood cells. Human blood can thus be divided into types, M, N and MN. No blood lacking both agglutinogens has been found. As in ABO system, there are no corresponding antibodies in this system.

Rh system: This is so called because it was first found by means of an antiserum produced by injecting rabbits with the red cells of rhesus monkeys. While performing the test with only one reagent, anti-D or anti-Rho, only two principal types can be defined, viz, Rh-positive and Rh-negative. For routine testing in cases of disputed paternity, five anti-Rh reagents should be used, each defining different Rh specificity, namely anti-D, anti-C, anti-E, and anti-c, and anti-e. Some authors have used different nomenclature to describe these reagents.

The great multiplicity of Rh antigens is useful in cases of disputed paternity, on account of their complexity and good discrimination power (evidential value). The Rh antigens are often responsible for so-called haemolytic disease of the newborn, as well as for unexpected, untoward reactions in cases where transfusion of compatible ABO blood has been given.

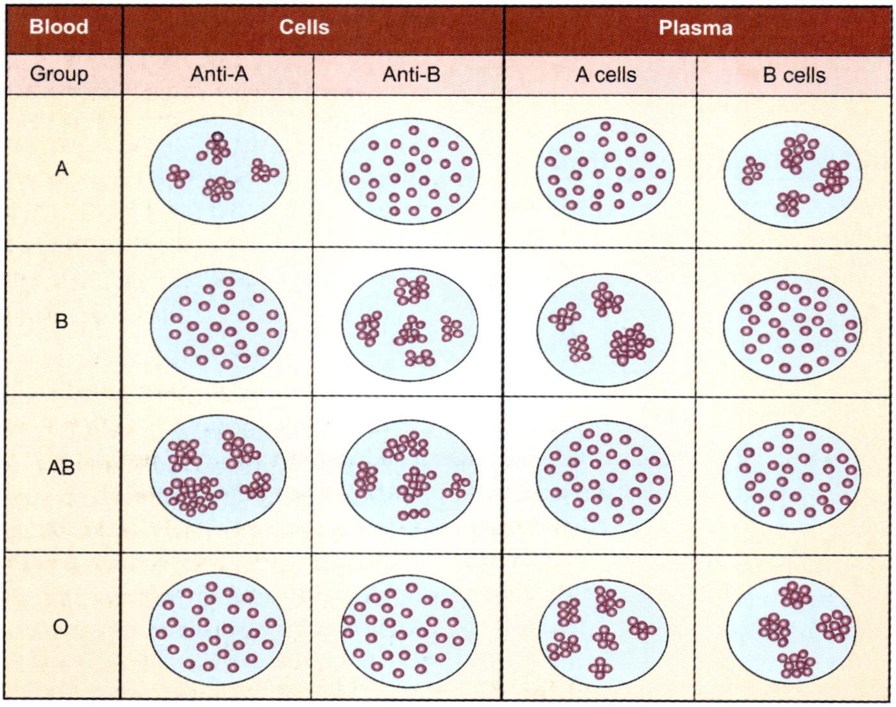

Blood	Cells		Plasma	
Group	Anti-A	Anti-B	A cells	B cells
A				
B				
AB				
O				

Fig. 34.1: ABO grouping reactions. O group cells are clumped by anti-H serum (not shown)

Other groups: Other specific characteristics independent of the above groups have also been recognised. They are named after the subjects in whom they were first detected. Thus, there are the Lutheran, Lewis, Duffy, Kell, Kidd, Diego, and many others yet to be discovered. They may be used for medicolegal work when specific antisera/reagents are available.

Grouping Based on Blood Proteins

The plasma proteins which have proved most useful are: (1) haptoglobin (Hp), (2) group specific component globulin Gc, (3) Gm and Inv immunoglobulins, and (4) haemoglobin types. They are usually demonstrated by electrophoresis.

Haptoglobin is an alpha-2 glycoprotein having the special function of mopping up the residues from aging and degenerate haemoglobin. It occurs in either homogeneous or heterogeneous combination of two forms, so that three types are possible, viz. Hp1-1, Hp2-1, and Hp2-2. They can be identified in liquid blood and dried stains.

The group specific component, globulin Gc, is independent of haptoglobin. It gives the phenotypes Gc1-1, Gc2-1 and Gc2-2. It is not capable of being identified in dried stains.

The inherited antigenic determinants of the **Gm and Inv systems** are located on molecules of the immunoglobulins, a family of serum proteins with antibody activity. There are at least 23 antigens identified within the Gm system, and at least 3 antigens in Inv system. The Gm and Inv serum types are detected by antibody neutralisation method, which is useful for typing fresh blood and blood stains.

Haemoglobin may be of the foetal type, adult type, or abnormal, e.g. S type in Blacks, as determined by electrophoresis.

Grouping Based on Enzymes

The systems which are most likely to be helpful in forensic work are (Figs 34.2 to 34.4): (1) phosphoglucomutase (PGM), (2) erythrocyte acid phosphatase (EAP), (3) glyoxalase-1 (GLO-I), (4) esterase D (EsD), (5) adenylate kinase (AK), and (6) adenosine deaminase (ADA). They are usually demonstrated by electrophoresis.

Grouping Based on White Cell Antigens

Human leucocyte antigen (HLA): In this system numerous antigens are present in four different closely linked loci. These antigens can be identified by histolymphotoxicity tests. By permutation and combination of these antigens, there can be various phenotypes which will help in disputed paternity cases. The test is not routinely used because — (1) a fresh blood sample is required, (2) lymphocytes have a short lifespan, (3) the test equipment and antisera are costly, and (4) wide experience on HLA testing is necessary to ensure accurate results. In tissue grafts, the better the HLA match between the donor and the recipient, the better are the chances for the survival of the graft.

Q. 34.2. Give a brief account of the application of blood groups in forensic work. Add a note on: (a) inheritance claims, (b) Rh hazards, and (c) transfusion errors.

Blood groups can be determined from blood, soft tissues, hair, nail, dental pulp, bone, and body secretions.

The application of blood group determination to medicolegal problems is resorted to for the following purposes:

1. Disputed paternity and maternity (vide infra)
2. To determine the possible source of blood stains in circumstances, such as murder, wounding, rape, and vehicular accidents (vide infra)
3. Inheritance claims
4. Rh hazards
5. Transfusion errors.

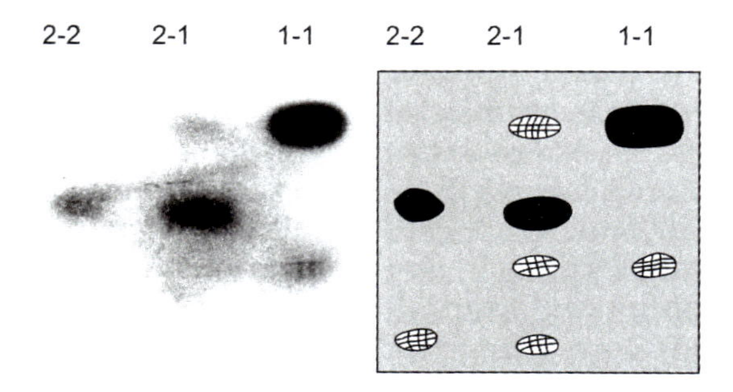

Fig. 34.2: PGM isoenzyme variants (left) and their **diagrammatic representation** (right)

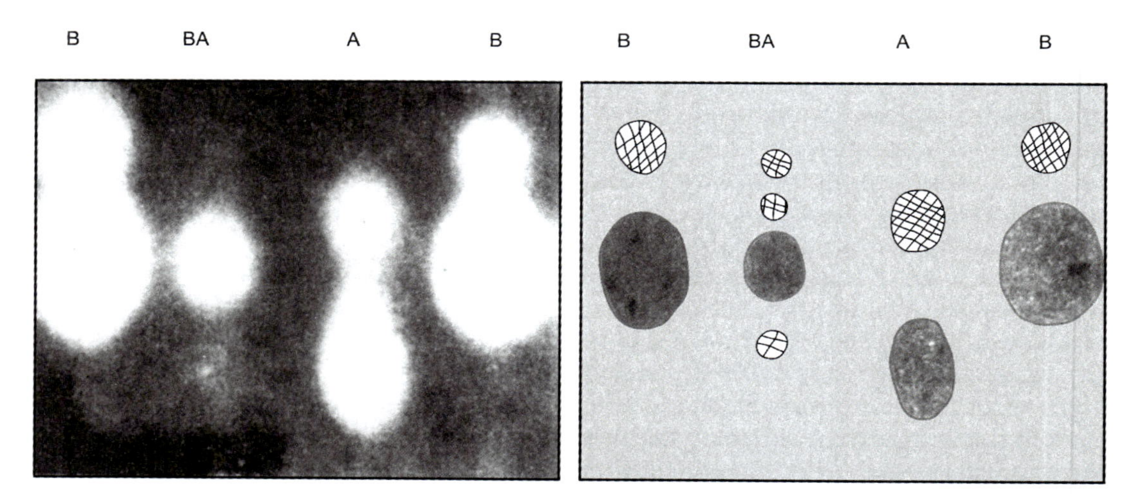

Fig. 34.3: EAP isoenzyme variants (left) and their **diagrammatic representation** (right)

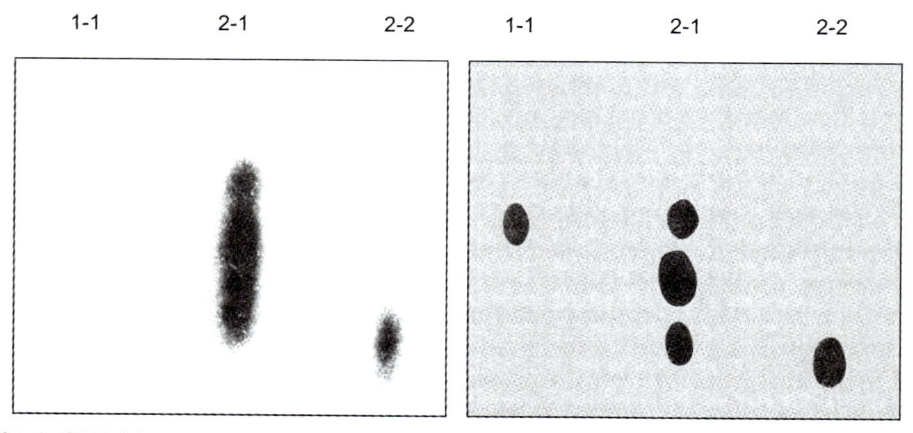

Fig. 34.4: GLO-I isoenzyme variants (left) and their **diagrammatic representation** (right)

In **inheritance claims,** the question of legitimacy arises since **a** legitimate child only can inherit the parent's property. Blood group determination is helpful in such cases.

Rh hazards: The Rh factor has an important practical bearing on the aetiology of haemolytic disease of the newborn and in unexpected reactions in cases where transfusion of compatible ABO blood has been given. An Rh negative mother may receive Rh antigen from the foetus through the placenta when the child is Rh positive, the father having been Rh positive. This Rh antigen produces Rh antibodies in the mother who may thus develop haemolytic reactions, if transfused with Rh positive blood after the birth of the child. This anti-Rh agglutinin may also pass from the mother by way of the placenta into the foetus (which is Rh positive) and the child may develop hydrops, erythro-blastosis foetalis, or haemolytic disease of the newborn. Rh positive blood transfused into an Rh negative individual will also produce anti-Rh agglutinin in the recipient serum. Consequently, when a second trans-fusion from an Rh-positive donor is given at a later date, haemolysis may follow.

The **transfusion errors** and **adverse reactions** relate to (1) compatibility testing in the laboratory, (2) neglect of expiry dates, and (3) presence of pathogenic organisms in the transfused blood.

Q. 34.3. Describe the blood transfusion reactions.

Blood Transfusion Reactions

Complications in the form of blood transfusion reactions associated with blood transfusion can be:

1. **Haemolytic reactions** — Intravascular / Extravascular
2. **Febrile reactions**
3. **Anaphylactoid reaction**
4. **Bacterial reactions**
5. **Mechanical**
6. **Transmission of disease**

Circulatory Overload

Rare complications:

- Transfusion haemosidrosis
- Immunosuppressive effects

Massive Blood Transfusion

Complications:

- Haemostatic failure
- Electrolyte abnormalities
- Hypothermia
- Impairment of O_2 transport

Intravascular haemolytic reactions: These are caused by cytotoxic complement fixing IgM (anti-A, anti-B) or IgG lytic antibodies. Anti-A or anti-B antibodies are usually implicated although occasionally, anti-Lewis anti-Kell antibodies are responsible.

The RBCs agglutinate and lyse in the intravascular compartment with the complement fragment liberating histamine from mast cells. Free Hb is liberated and bound to haptoglobin. Which is then cleared by RES. When all circulating haptoglobin is cleared, the free haemoglobin combines with albumin to form methaemalbumin this may be detected by Schumm's test, which becomes positive 6–12 hours after the haemolytic reaction.

Clinical features: Immediate rigor, pyrexia, headache, urticaria, flushing dyspnoea, cyanosis, hypotension and pain. Within an hour of these symptoms, haemoglobinuria, oliguria and bleeding occur.

Extravascular haemolytic reactions: These are usually due to a non-complement binding of IgG antibody to the Rhesus, Kidd, Duffy and Kell blood group systems and often occur in two stages. A fast stage in which the pre-existing antibodies are taken up by the incompatible cells, which are then destroyed in the liver and spleen and a slow stage in which the antibodies, as they are formed combine with the remaining incompatible cells, which are then removed from circulation.

The clinical signs of jaundice, fever and unexplained anaemia are usually delayed and may follow the transfusion by some days.

Febrile reactions: Most common transfusion reaction. They are often due to all antibodies directed against neutrophils or platelet antigens.

Anaphylactoid reaction: Most of the transfusion reactions manifested as anaphylactoid cases are due to plasma components, with severe reactions occurring when blood with antibodies to IgA deficiency otherwise the clinical signs are usually mild, presenting with urticaria, rash and fever. If the reaction is severe, then donor and recipient immunoglobulins, anti-immunoglobulin antibodies and complement levels of the serum of the recipient should be measured.

Bacterial infection: Catheter site infection—may be due to an infection from the catheter site (commonly staphylococcal or streptococcal) or an infection from contaminated blood.

Mechanical: Air embolism, microembolism, e.g. platelets, fibrin, denatured protein, neutrophil.

Transmission of disease: Hepatitis A, B, C and D

- AIDS
- CMV
- EB virus, etc.

Circulatory overload: Rare complications

- Transfusion haemosiderosis
- Immunosuppressive effects
  - Enhanced metastatic spread of carcinoma
- Improved renal allograft survival

Massive Blood Transfusion

Haemostatic failure: Commonest causes of bleeding due to massive transfusion are surgical bleeding, dilution of coagulation factors and disseminated intravascular coagulation (DIC). The coagulation factor in stored blood is often inactive.

Electrolyte abnormalities:

a. *Potassium disorder:* Hyperkalemia may occur immediately, hypokalemia may also be seen.

b. *Citrate toxicity:* Excessive citrate will chelate calcium and magnesium reducing ionised calcium, which will produce a severe reduction in cardiac output long before any anticoagulant effect occurs), and magnesium levels.

c. *Metabolic acidosis:* Lactic acidosis, occur particularly in presence of shock or hypothermia.

d. *Delayed alkalosis:* The 5.6 mm of sodium citrate per unit of CAPD preserved blood is metabolised to form 16.8 mm of sodium bicarbonate.

Hypothermia

Hypothermia can induce cardiac arrhythmias, shift in oxygen Hb dissociation cause to left and downward potassium ion movement into ICF.

Even in an emergency when blood transfusion is urgently required, delay due to testing offers less risk than an unmatched transfusion or one which is not fully compatible. If expiry dates are not observed, transfusion reaction may arise from leakage of electrolytes from damaged red cells. The blood may also contain pathogenic organisms, such as malaria, syphilis, hepatitis B, and AIDS virus. These must be excluded before use.

DNA PROFILING (DNA FINGERPRINTING)

This test looks directly at a person's genetic make-up. The DNA molecule is composed of sugars, phosphates, and nitrogenous bases which form the functional unit known as a nucleotide. A series of nucleotides joined together produces the twisted ladder pattern of the double-stranded helix which characterises the DNA molecule's appearance. The four types of nitrogenous bases pair among themselves to form the rungs of the ladder, and the sugars and phosphates link together to form the sides of the ladder. With the exception of truly identical twins, the structure of each person's DNA is unique. The essence of DNA profiling in forensic work is comparison between two samples.

Samples for DNA testing must contain nucleated cells, e.g. leucocytes, seminal fluid, brain, bone marrow, muscle, skin, dental pulp, hair with root sheath cells, and dried stains.

Identity of a criminal is determined by comparing the accused man's DNA profile with a biological item, e.g. blood or seminal stain, found at the scene of crime. Identification is absolute, if tests are properly performed.

The technique has many applications and is likely to be widely used in forensic work. The blood or the few hair roots on the crime weapon can be matched with complete confidence with the victim's blood. Seminal fluid in the vagina of a rape-murder victim can be matched against the blood DNA pattern of a suspect. DNA testing surpasses blood group secretor tests in that it can distinguish between mixed semen and vaginal fluids from a swab which can confuse blood group techniques. In paternity testing, an absolute identification can be made, rather than a more probable exclusion. Other applications include linking body parts, baby mix-ups, and identification of persons suffering from loss of memory, and allied situations. Even the sex of a foetus can be determined by looking at DNA sequences from the Y chromosome in the foetal cells present in the mother's blood as early as the fifth week of pregnancy. When advances are made in genome mapping, it is possible that the technique may be useful to identify physical features, such as eye colour, hair colour, and appearance, etc., of a skeleton from DNA.

DISPUTED PATERNITY AND MATERNITY

Q. 34.4. Give a succinct account of disputed paternity and maternity.

Blood groups are inherited according to Mendelian principles, viz: (1) A blood group antigen (substance) cannot appear in a child unless it is present in one of the parents, (2) if one of the parents is homozygous for a particular blood group antigen, that antigen must appear in the child's blood, and (3) if a child is homozygous for a particular blood group antigen, the gene for the same must have been inherited by it from each of the parents.

In cases of disputed paternity or maternity, it is possible to determine the groups of one parent, if the groups of the child and the other parent are known, or if the groups of both parents are known, to determine the blood groups possible for the child. The evidence that is to be found is negative only, i.e. that a particular child is not produced by a particular father or mother. When allegations are made against two different persons, it may be possible to exclude one of them at least. As for example, if the agglutinogen A is present in a child but not in its mother, it must have been present in its father. If two men allege to be the father of one child and if one of them shows the agglutinogen A in his blood and the other does not, the one who does not show the agglutinogen A is not his father, while the other who shows the agglutinogen A may be the father. And, it should be remembered that assessment of probability of paternity, especially as between two possible fathers, is sometimes a matter of great importance to the persons concerned.

If a suspected person can be excluded, it can restore great harmony to the family.

The question of **disputed paternity** arises in the following circumstances, viz:

1. Alleged *adultery* and suits for nullity of marriage: When the child is born in lawful wedlock and the husband denies that he is the father of the child, and seeks divorce on this ground.
2. *Blackmailing:* When a child is born out of lawful wedlock and the mother accuses a certain man as the father of the child but the man denies the accusation and
3. Suits for *maintenance of illegitimate children:* Under section 125 CrPC, an individual must adopt his illegitimate child or support him up to a certain age. In the latter case, a first class magistrate may order an allowance up to Rs. 500 per month for this purpose.

The ABO grouping system can exclude paternity in one-sixth of all cases. Addition of the MN system can exclude paternity in one-third of the cases. Addition of the Rh subgroups will exonerate about 50 per cent of wrongly accused men. The other factors, if determined, will raise the figures to about 60 per cent and examination of saliva adds another 2.5 per cent to the chance. The addition of groupings based" on blood protein and red cell enzyme variants such as phosphoglucomutase can raise 'non-fathers' exclusion rate to about 90 per cent. The human leucocyte antigen (HLA) system alone can demonstrate non-paternity in 90 per cent of cases but in combination with other grouping systems it can raise 'non-fathers' exclusion rate up to 98 per cent. In actual practice, this percentage of exclusion is never achieved as many of the men accused are actually the natural fathers of the children in question. DNA profiling is fool-proof, it provides absolute certainty rather than a probable exclusion as in other systems. *The considerations of non-paternity mentioned above also apply in cases of non-maternity.*

The question of **disputed maternity** arises in the following circumstances, viz. (1) when two women claim the same child, (2) when there has been an allegation of interchange (baby swaping, baby sneaking) of a child with another in the maternity home or hospital, either purposely or accidentally. (3) In case of a kidnapped child, when the woman who has kidnapped the child claims to be the mother, having given birth to the child at home and birth certificate is, therefore, not available. She may name a friend as alleged father; and (4) In case of a suppositious child, when a woman pretends pregnancy and delivery and brings forth a suppositious child to pass it off as her own.

Illustrative Cases of Disputed Paternity and Maternity

Case 1. Alleged father AB, mother O, child O. Paternity is excluded since an AB father must contribute either A or B to the child.

Case 2. Alleged father A, mother O, child AB. Maternity is excluded. The father could contribute the A antigen only. An O group mother cannot contribute B antigen.

Case 3. Father A, MN, CDe; mother A, MN, CDe; child A, N, CDe; kidnapper woman B, MN, cDE. Friend of kidnapper and alleged father O, MN, CDE, Parentage by kidnapper and her friend is excluded because (i) a cDE mother must transmit one of c and E factors to her child, and (ii) a mother of group B and a father of group O cannot produce a child of group A. Incidentally, there is no evidence of exclusion between the true parents and baby.

BLOOD STAINS

The points that are usually required to be determined regarding stains are: (1) the nature of the stain, (2) if due to blood, the species (human or animal) it has come from, and (3) if human, the group to which it belongs. In some cases, it is also necessary to determine the character and causation of stain. To determine these facts, the following examinations are carried out, viz.

physical, chemical, physicochemical, microscopic, spectroscopic, immunological, and enzymological.

Q. 34.5. Give a brief account of physical examination of blood stains.

Physical Examination

Visit to the scene of crime provides valuable clues. The examination should include: (a) clothing, (b) size, shape, and direction of blood spots, (c) character of the stain, (d) age of the stain, (e) condition of the body, and (f) other causes of the stain.

Scene of Crime

In the case of stains, it is the routine practice of the police to take photographs of the scene of crime. Black and white photographs of blood stains are not of much value since walls from which blood stains are scraped give the same appearance as stains. Colour photographs, are, therefore, preferable and may be taken when facilities permit. Special note should be made of the amount of blood at the scene. It would help to evaluate the seriousness of the injuries and give some indication of the length of survival of the victim after the assault.

Clothing: If victim was asleep in supine position when wounded, blood would flow towards the back and stains would be found at the appropriate places on the clothes. As for example, if his throat is cut, his shirt collar and clothing at the back are blood-stained; while, if the victim was standing when wounded blood will fall vertically downwards on the clothes as well as on the body.

If blood stains are found on the underwear or petticoat of the victim, they are suggestive of injuries to the genital organs or a sexual assault.

If the clothes are soaked with blood, it would mean that the victim bled profusely and lived for some time after the injury.

Size, shape and direction of blood spots: The size and shape of the stain indicate the height from which blood has fallen and the direction of the fall of blood. When blood falls directly downwards on to a flat surface, the stains flatten out in the form of a circle, if the height does not exceed a few centimetres. With the increase in height, the circle shows projections round the circumference, the number of projections being directly proportional to height. Spurting (arterial) blood striking the surface obliquely, produces elongated stains resembling exclamation marks, the sharp end of the mark indicating the direction of the spurt. The more oblique the fall, the more elongated is the stain.

A trail of blood stains indicates that the victim received his injuries at some distance from the place at which the body was found. It may suggest attempted running or sometimes attempted suicide. A person may attempt to cut his throat, walk for some distance and then jump into a well. In such circumstances, a trail of blood is usually found.

Character: Sometimes, it is possible to determine if blood came from (a) living or dead body, (b) artery or vein (c) victim or assailant, (d) infant or adult, and (e) male or female.

Living or dead body: Blood which has effused during life can be peeled off in scales on drying due to the presence of fibrin. Blood which has flowed after death tends to break up into powder on drying.

Artery or vein: Blood coming from the arteries of a living person will be scattered in spurts over surfaces upon which it has been projected. Venous blood comes out in the form of oozing or a continuous stream which will produce a pool if the victim is at rest and separate widespread drops, if he is ambulant. It should, however, be remembered that a considerable pool of blood may collect under a dead body and it could be postmortem in nature due to opening of a large blood vessel, e.g. after stab injuries on a dependent part. Generally, in most bleeding wounds, blood is poured out simultaneously from arteries and veins.

Victim or assailant: It is generally difficult to determine whether blood stains belong to the victim or an assailant, unless they are of different group. Stains on the inner side of the garments usually belong to the victim while those on the outer side may have come from the victim or assailant. Stains on dark clothes (Fig. 34.5), if not clearly visible, may be revealed by photographing in ultraviolet or infrared light.

Blood stains may bear marks of finger or foot prints. These may help to connect the accused with the crime. Sometimes there may be some blood disease, e.g. leukaemia, filariasis, either in the victim or the assailant. This provides identifying data. Traces of blood may be found underneath the finger nails of the victim as a result of struggle or of the assailant in case of throttling. Such stains can be typed and grouped. The specimen can be collected either by nail clippings, and if such mutilation is resisted, by nail scrapings with the help of cuticle sticks or the blunt end of a tooth prick.

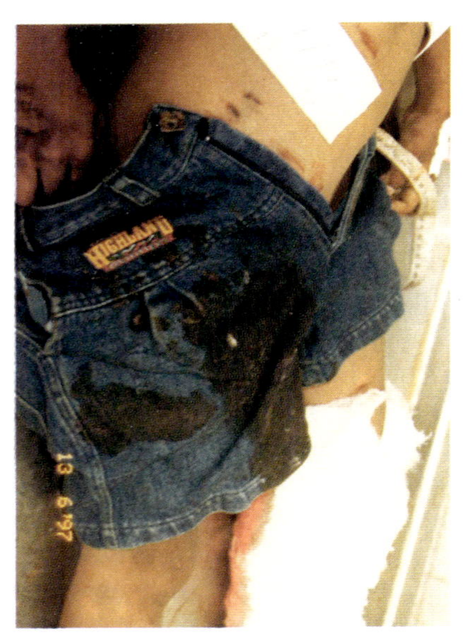

Fig. 34.5: Blood stain on garment

Infant or adult: In general, the red blood cells of infants exhibit more fragility, haemoglobin of foetal type is present up to about six months, and the blood when shed forms a thin and soft coagulum. In the adult, the red blood cells are non-nucleated, their fragility is within certain limits, haemoglobin is of the adult type, and the blood when shed forms a thick and firm coagulum. Foetal haemoglobin differs from adult haemoglobin in its globin component. The adult haemoglobin is denatured by alkali while the foetal haemoglobin is not. Other methods in use to recognise foetal haemoglobin are: (1) electrophoresis, (2) spectroscopy, and (3) fractional crystallisation.

Male or female: In normal females, sex chromosomes are present as a homologous pair (XX). In the interphase, one of the X chromosomes remains condensed and can be stained with orcine reagent. This X chromosome is known as the Barr body, and the sex can be determined from the Barr body count (in WBC) as mentioned earlier. In normal males, sex chromosomes are present as a heterogeneous pair (XY). The Y chromosome is fluorescent to quinacrine when the stained slide is examined under the fluorescence microscope. At least, 50 nuclei in a smear should show the presence of Y bodies to report a positive result.

Age of the stain: One should always note when visiting the crime scene if any effused blood has coagulated, the extent of coagulation, and also whether spots of blood are dry or not. If blood has not clotted or dried, it indicates recent bleeding. It takes half an hour for a drop of blood to dry in ordinary circumstances. The appearance of clotted blood is very typical and if a fabric has been soaked in blood, it becomes stiffened because of proteins.

Recent stains on white cloth are at first red. Due to conversion of haemoglobin into methaemoglobin and haematin, the colour gradually changes to reddish brown within about 24 hours, dark brown or even black within a few days and remains so for several years, depending on the thickness of the stain and the conditions to which it has been exposed. On some dark fabrics, the stains are difficult to locate and may easily escape an examination by the naked eye; washed stains on white fabrics look yellowish and they are also very hard to detect. It is generally helpful to use ultraviolet and infrared light to detect such stains. On many metallic articles, blood stains appear as dark staining spots or smears, and when desiccated, show fissures and cracks. Such stains when recent are more soluble in distilled water or normal saline than old ones in which haemoglobin gradually changes to methaemoglobin and finally to insoluble haematin. Thus, the most that can be said regarding the age of a stain is that it is recent, or not very recent, and even that opinion sometimes is not possible.

Condition of the body: A person may collapse after receiving an injury, e.g. multiple stab wounds. A large pool of blood may be found. It indicates that the victim was alive when wounded and lived for sometime after the injury.

When there are number of wounds on the body but the amount of blood is scant, it would mean that either the blood has been wiped out in which case smears are found or that the body has been moved from elsewhere. Both situations are suggestive of murder.

Other causes of stains: To eliminate baseless defence pleas, it is necessary to know the manner in which stains may be innocently produced, e.g. from menstruation, parturition, abortion, haematemesis, blood vomiting, bug bites, etc. In all such cases, the causation of such stains can be determined from their appearance, distribution, microscopic examination, and other corroborative evidence.

The most common defence in cases of assault on females is that the stain is from menstruation. *Menstrual blood* is found on female garments or clothes that have been used as diapers. It has a disagreeable smell. Being mixed with urine and vaginal mucus, it is more fluid. It is acidic in reaction owing to the presence of vaginal secretion but the ordinary method of testing the reaction is not applicable. On microscopic examination, it is found to contain endometrial cells from the uterus, epithelial cells from the vagina, and a large number of microorganisms which are not found in ordinary blood. *Trichomonas vaginalis* or *Monilia* may be present. Confirmation of menstrual stain is also possible by the following methods, viz: (1) fibrin degradation product (FDP), (2) amino acid pattern, and (3) lactate dehydrogenase isoenzyme.

Parturition and abortion stains are usually associated with staining due to liquor amnii. The colour may be yellowish or greenish from admixture with meconium. The quantity of proteins is less than that in normal blood, and particles of vernix caseosa and lanugo may be seen. On microscopic examination, epidermal cells are seen.

Stains due to *haematemesis* are chocolate-coloured and acidic in reaction due to the action of gastric secretion. However, the ordinary method of testing the reaction is not applicable. On naked eye and microscopic examination, the presence of food particles with sarcinae and other bacteria suggest gastric source of blood.

Stains on garments *due to bugs, fleas and louse bites* are common. This blood is human blood sucked from the wearer of the garment and will give all the reactions for human blood, but the appearance of spots is quite characteristic. They are small and usually found on the inside of the garment. In the larger ones which are due to squashing of bugs or lice, in addition to this appearance, fragments of hair or scales or gut of the insect may be found on microscopic examination.

Some stains especially old ones, due to red paint, fruit juice, banana leaf juice, vegetable dyes, rust, faeces, paan (betel leaf), red lead, kumkum (mercury sulphide), etc., simulate blood stains. To differentiate them, two screening tests may be employed: (1) ammonia turns vegetable stains and fruit stains green, whilst nitric acid turns aniline dyes yellow, blood being unchanged, (2) an alkaline solution of aminophthalic acid hydrazide is mixed with hydrogen peroxide and sprayed on the suspected area with an atomizer. The area is rendered luminescent, if the stain is due to blood. Even when stains are profuse and appear to be certainly due to blood, a scientific confirmation of this fact is advisable.

After physical examination is carried out at the crime scene, the various exhibits, e.g. clothes, stained weapons, etc., should be air-dried if necessary, and forwarded to the forensic science laboratory (FSL), properly preserved, without any delay.

Q. 34.6. Give a brief account of the commonly employed chemical tests to determine the presence of blood in the stains.

Chemical Examination

The most commonly employed chemical tests to determine the presence of blood in the stain are: (1) the benzidine test, and (2) the phenolphthalein or Kastle-Meyer test. Occasionally, leucomalachite green test and toluidine blue test are also used.

Benzidine Test

Two reagents are required, namely a 10% solution of benzidine in glacial acetic acid, and hydrogen peroxide (20 vols). Both should be freshly prepared. When the benzidine solution is added to the suspected solution, a greenish blue colour is obtained on addition of hydrogen peroxide, if blood is present.

The most convenient way of carrying out this test without harming the garment or disturbing the stain is as follows: A piece of (wet) white filter paper is pressed firmly on the suspected stain. The benzidine reagent is dropped on the paper. If blood is present, in however minute a quantity, a greenish blue colour develops at once when the hydrogen peroxide is added. If it appears before adding the peroxide, it indicates the presence of any oxidising agent but not blood. The test is given by blood of almost any age or even blood that has been subjected to heat or cold. The test is positive with dilution of one part of blood in 500,000 parts and is commonly used in medicolegal work.

Owing to the potential carcinogenic nature of benzidine, some laboratories prefer alternative tests.

Phenolphthalein Test (Kastle-Meyer Test)

The principle of this test is as follows: Phenolphthalein is reduced by zinc dust in a strongly alkaline medium. If this reduced phenolphthalein is oxidised by nascent oxygen liberated by the action of peroxidase on hydrogen peroxide, a pink or purple colour is obtained, if blood is present.

The phenolphthalein reagent is prepared by dissolving 1 to 2 grams of phenolphthalein and 20 to 25 grams of potassium hydroxide in 100 ml of distilled water. About 15 grams of powdered zinc is added and the solution heated until the pink colour disappears.

A few drops of the reagent followed by hydrogen peroxide are added to the aqueous extract of the suspected stain. If blood is present, a pink or purple colouration is produced at once. The test is extremely delicate giving reaction with dilution of one part of blood in 5,000,000 parts.

The **principle of both** the above mentioned tests is the same. They detect the presence of haemoglobin, the colouring matter of blood, a peroxidase, which in the presence of hydrogen peroxide, oxidises colourless bases to coloured salts. It is also possible to utilise the same peroxidase reaction but at a much higher sensitivity by using luminal reagent. It gives bright fluorescence in the presence of blood. A negative result excludes the presence of blood. A positive result is given by many other substances in addition to blood, such as pus, saliva, mucus, several plant juices, formalin, and oxidising agents, such as nitric acid, copper sulphate, dichromates, ferric salts, etc. However, an expert can eliminate such substances, as described below, and then these tests can be used as confirmatory tests.

The common interfering substances that give the above reactions are the plant peroxidases from plant juices and oxidising agents mentioned above.

The plant peroxidases are heat labile. They are destroyed by heating the stain at 100°C for 30 minutes. The stain then does not give blue colour with benzidine. If the stain is either of blood or blood contaminated with plant juice, it will, however, give blue colour with benzidine, even after heating. Oxidising agents react directly with benzidine. They do not require hydrogen peroxide to develop a blue colour. The test is, therefore, performed as follows: First add benzidine to the stain, wait for a while, and observe the colour. If no colour develops, it means that oxidising agents are absent. If colour develops, it means that oxidising agents are present. In such cases, interference from oxidising agents can be adequately removed by using other chemical, microchemical, TLC, or spectroscopic methods.

Phenolphthalein test can also be performed in a similar manner with similar results.

Q. 34.7. Describe briefly the commonly employed physicochemical tests to confirm the presence of blood in the stain.

Physicochemical Examination

The most commonly employed physicochemical tests to confirm, if necessary, the presence of blood in the stain are: (1) thin layer chromatography (TLC), and (2) electrophoresis.

Thin layer chromatography (TLC): A thin layer of silica gel (silica gel G) is prepared on a suitable glass plate. An appropriate quantity of sample extract, standard haematin chloride solution, and control sample of blood are placed on the prepared gel. The plate is then placed in a chamber having a convenient solvent system (methanol + acetic acid + water). After the desired run of the solvent to a certain height (front), it is removed from the chamber. When the plate is dried benzidine and hydrogen peroxide are sprayed on it. If the stain contains blood, the sample extract should give a blue spot at the same height as compared to the standard haematin chloride solution and control sample of blood.

Electrophoresis: One per cent agar gel (lonagar no. 2) is prepared on a suitable glass plate. The different test samples (sample extracts) along with the standard controls, e.g. blood, vegetable juices, and other body secretions are placed on the agar plate. Electrophoresis is carried out keeping constant voltage (5 to 6 volts/cm) for 30 minutes. The gel is then stained by pouring a small quantity of benzidine and hydrogen peroxide. If the sample stain extract contains blood, it gives a peculiar pattern that is drop-shaped, the tail of which has moved towards the anode, the main bulk of haemoglobin remaining at the origin.

Q. 34.8. Describe briefly the commonly employed microchemical tests to confirm the presence of blood in the stain.

Microscopic (Microchemical) Examination

By microscopic examination of the stain, we may obtain information about the presence of haemoglobin, the colouring matter of blood. For this purpose, two chemical tests are employed, viz: (1) Takayama's haemochromogen crystal test, and (2) the haemin crystal test (Teichmann's test). These are also known as microcrystal tests. It should be remembered that it is not possible to detect red blood cells in stains unless the stain is very fresh.

Material for the microscopic examination of red blood cells is obtained by soaking the stain in normal saline or preferably Vibert's fluid in a watch glass. Vibert's fluid is prepared by mixing two grams of sodium chloride and one-half gram of'mercuric chloride in 100 ml of distilled water.

Takayama's Haemochromogen Crystal Test

This consists in the production of salmon-pink crystals of haemochromogen and is carried out by using Takayama's reagent solution. The composition of Takayama's solution is as follows: Sodium hydroxide (10%) 3 ml, pyridine 3 ml, saturated solution of glucose 3 ml, and distilled water 7 ml. The first named reagent acts as an alkali and blood solvent, and the glucose as a reducing agent.

The test is performed as follows: The powdered material scraped from the stain or some of the dried stain extract is placed on a glass slide and covered with a cover slip. Two or three drops of Takayama's reagent solution are run in under the cover slip and the slide examined under the microscope after five minutes. If blood is present, haemochromogen crystals resembling haemin (reduced alkaline haematin) crystals are seen. These crystals are acicular in shape, salmon-pink in colour, and dispersed in clusters, sheaves, and several other forms.

If the reagent is freshly prepared, it may take almost up to half an hour before crystals can form. Slight warming of the slide, preferably at 37°C in an incubator especially in cold weather, hastens the reaction.

The test is easy to perform, reliable, delicate, and gives good results even with old stains. It has the additional advantage that typical spectrum of haemochromogen is seen when the crystals are examined with a microspectroscope. This test, therefore, can be employed as a confirmatory test for the presence of haemoglobin.

Haemin Crystal Test (Teichmann's Test)

The principle is to covert the haemoglobin of the stain into haemin, which in the presence of halogen, is converted into salt and forms brown rhombic crystals.

A small portion of the suspected material (a suitable amount is one thread from a garment) is placed on a slide. Glacial acetic acid mixed with a small crystal of sodium chloride is then run in under the cover-slip and heated gently till a few bubbles appear. The slide is then allowed to cool and examined under the low power of the microscope, when the typical brown rhombic crystals of haemin will be seen. Similar crystals may be obtained from indigo dyed fabrics not stained with blood but they do not give off bubbles of gas on addition of a drop of hydrogen peroxide.

To ensure the production of crystals, the stain must be dry, the acid must be anhydrous, and the slide must not be overheated. The crystals are permanent and can be mounted in Canada balm for preservation, if necessary.

This test is of academic rather than practical value. It was popular once but is now superseded by the haemochromogen crystal test on account of the uncertainty of obtaining haemin crystals, even with stains known to be due to blood.

Q. 34.9. Discuss the principle and importance of spectroscopic examination of blood in the stains.

Spectroscopic Examination

This is based on the principle that haemoglobin and its derivatives give characteristic absorption bands when viewed through a spectroscope. When white light passes through a prism, it is broken up into a spectrum, consisting of its constituent colours. When such a spectrum is viewed through blood, certain colours are absorbed. The absorbed colours appear as dark bands known as absorption bands and the full spectrum is known as absorption spectrum. It varies with the type of blood pigment (Fig. 34.6).

The spectroscopic test is one of the confirmatory tests for blood. Its sensitivity is about 1:5,000. This is, therefore, considered one of the best tests for identification of blood in stains. In medicolegal practice, a special type of spectroscope, known as a microspectroscope, is used for this purpose.

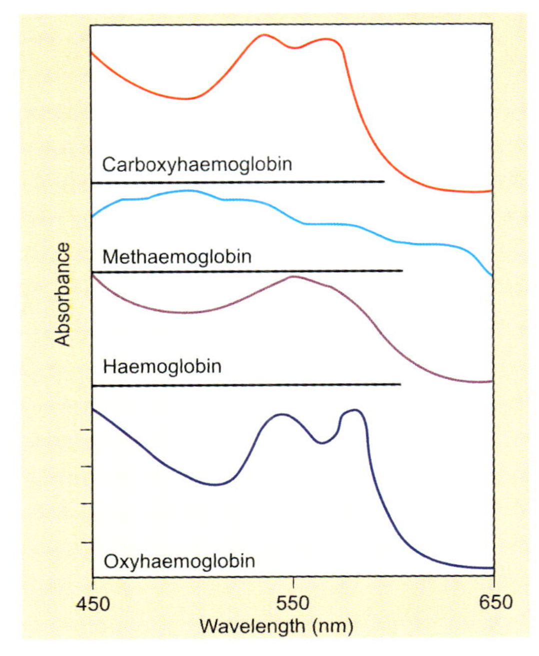

Fig. 34.6: Absorption spectra of haemoglobin and some of its derivatives

If the sample contains fresh oxygenated blood, i.e. **oxyhaemoglobin,** two dark absorption bands will be seen between the D and E lines in the yellow green region of the spectrum, the one nearer the D being about half the breadth of the other and more defined. Addition of a reducing agent like ammonium sulphide will cause these bands to coalesce into one broad band of **reduced haemoglobin** between D and E. An oxidising agent will reverse the change. The addition of an alkali to reduced haemoglobin will form **haemochromogen** and this compound may be crystallised out as already described. Haemochromogen presents two absorption bands, one dark and sharply defined in the yellow almost midway between D and E lines and the other fainter in the green part of the spectrum. If these three spectra are obtained from the same stain, it is conclusive proof of the presence of haemoglobin and so of blood.

If the stain is old or has been exposed to any extent, a certain amount of **methaemoglobin** will have been formed. It is a darker pigment which is formed when blood is decomposing. It may occur in vitro due to many substances and in vivo as a result of poisoning by certain substances, such as nitrites, phenacetin, sulphonal, etc., and in enterogenous cyanosis. The spectrum shows four bands, one in the red, two similar in position to oxyhaemoglobin, and a fourth faint band in the green. A reducing agent will change methaemoglobin back to haemoglobin and thereafter, it will behave as such.

Carboxyhaemoglobin has a spectrum so much like that of oxyhaemoglobin that the scaled spectroscope is necessary to define the degree of shift to the right (towards the violet). It behaves like oxyhaemoglobin except that it is unaffected by reducing agents.

For spectroscopic examination, a sizeable stain, about one sq cm is required. A **recent**

blood stain may be made to yield all the spectra mentioned above but an old blood stain which has become insoluble may yield the spectrum of haemochromogen only.

In addition to a hand spectroscope, a **spectrophotometer** generally available nowadays in most laboratories, is profitably used to identify the haemoglobin and its derivatives through their readily discernible absorption spectra.

Q. 34.10. Comment on the methods most suitable for routine use for detection of blood in the stains.

The benzidine and phenolphthalein tests have a sensitivity of 1:500,000 and 1:5,000,000 respectively and can be accepted as specific provided the interfering substances are eliminated as already described.

If further confirmation is desired, recourse can be had to TLC and electrophoresis which are equally sensitive and quite specific.

The microscopic and spectroscopic methods are also quite specific for confirmation of blood in the stain but they require a certain amount of blood constituents in the stain which sometimes may not be available while examining the actual crime articles.

Q. 34.11. Describe the immunological and enzymological methods to determine the species origin of blood stain.

Detection of Species Origin

Once it is determined that the stain is that of blood, it is necessary to determine if the blood under examination is that of a human being or is derived from any other source (animal) for three reasons: (1) Sometimes, a plea is raised that the blood stain has been derived form animal blood, especially when the accused is a butcher or a hunter, (2) some animals possess blood group antigens (substances) similar to those found in human beings; it is, therefore, necessary to rule out any contamination from such source, and (3) in cases of suspected illegal shooting of prohibited species of animals, such as peacock, sambar, neelgai, tiger, etc., when it is imperative to determine the exact species of animal from which blood has been derived. The following immunological and enzymological methods are used for this purpose.

Immunological Methods

The commonly employed immunological methods are:

1. Precipitin test
2. Haemagglutination-inhibition test
3. Latex test

Precipitin test: This test depends upon the fact that when a foreign protein, like human blood serum, is injected into an animal, certain specific antibodies known as precipitins are formed in that animal's blood which precipitate that specific foreign protein. The specific foreign protein which causes the production of the precipitins is known as precipitinogen. For example, if a rabbit, fowl or any other suitable animal is injected with repeated small doses of human serum, either subcutaneously, intramuscularly, intravenously, or intraperitoneally, its serum after a certain time will be found to contain the antibodies-precipitins. This serum is separated and used for precipitin test of the material suspected to contain human blood.

It will be found to cause a precipitate when mixed with human blood serum even in the most minute amounts; in fact, it will cause a precipitate when mixed with blood or albuminous material from a different species of animal. The test will, therefore, demonstrate the presence of protein substances obtained from any part of human body. The origin of skin, flesh, bone, or even secretions, such as saliva, milk and semen can be established by this test.

The test is performed by using the following three techniques, viz: (a) test tube, (b) gel diffusion (Fig. 34.7), and (c) cross-over electrophoresis (COE). The

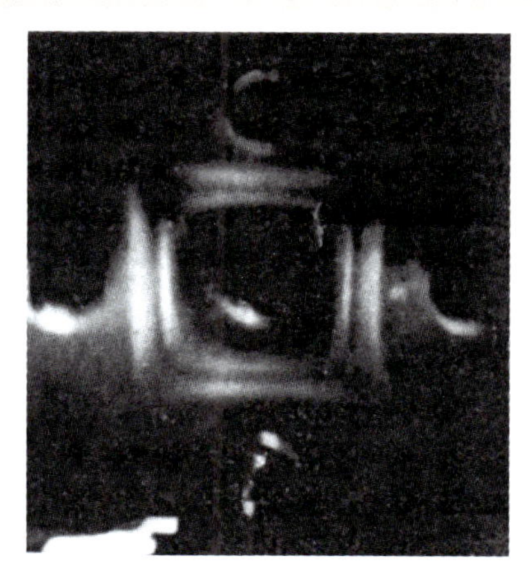

Fig. 34.7: Gel diffusion technique. The central hole contains antihuman serum and peripheral holes contain human blood (control) and extracts from crime articles

procedure for these tests is beyond the scope of this book.

Haemagglutination-inhibition test: It is known that red cells, sensitised by incomplete anti-Rh antibodies and washed free of serum, are agglutinated by serum of a rabbit previously immunised against human globulin. When this rabbit serum is previously mixed with human serum, then agglutination is inhibited. If, therefore, anti-human globulin serum is mixed with an extract of a human blood stain and subsequently tested against sensitised red cells, the agglutination reaction will be inhibited. This inhibition is not produced with the possible exception of the apes, by other than human blood and this forms the basis for this test.

Latex test: A saline extract of the blood stain is mixed with a dilute suspension of latex particles sensitised with antiserum. A positive reaction is shown by agglutination of the particles into clumps. The test requires only a drop of each solution and minimum equipment and the result can be read with the naked eye. This method is as sensitive and as specific for human blood like any other. Though the saline extraction may require up to several hours for old stains, the actual test can be made in five minutes.

Enzymological Methods

Blood as well as blood stains of human and several other animal species give specific isoenzyme electrophoretic patterns which enable the differentiation of human beings as well as different species of animals. The proteins which give similar enzyme reaction are known as isoenzymes. The most common enzymes for this type of reaction are: peroxidase (Px), lactate dehydrogenase (LDH), malate dehydrogenase (MDH), and esterases (Es). These methods are less time consuming when known control samples are available. An additional advantage of these methods is that closely related animals, e.g. man–monkey, bullock–buffalo, sheep–goat, etc., can also be differentiated. The commonly employed methods are: (1) LDH, and (2) Px.

LDH: Eight per cent monomer concentration of acrylamide is used for preparation of gel. Glass tubes (6 mm × 9 cm) are selected to prepare the gel columns. Vertical disc electrophoresis is performed in a refrigerator at 4 mA/tube for 2 hours. Isoenzyme bands separated on electrophoresis are stained for visualisation. For staining purposes, the gels are incubated in dark with the staining reagent at 37°C for 60 minutes (Fig. 34.8).

Px: The same electrophoretic procedure is followed as that for LDH with modification. The electrophoresis is carried out for 80 minutes and a mixture of benzidine and hydrogen peroxide is used to develop isoenzyme bands (Fig. 34.9).

Discussion

As a rapid and sensitive screening method to detect the presence of human blood in a large number of crime articles, COE is the best choice when specific antihuman serum is available. In the experience of the FSL in

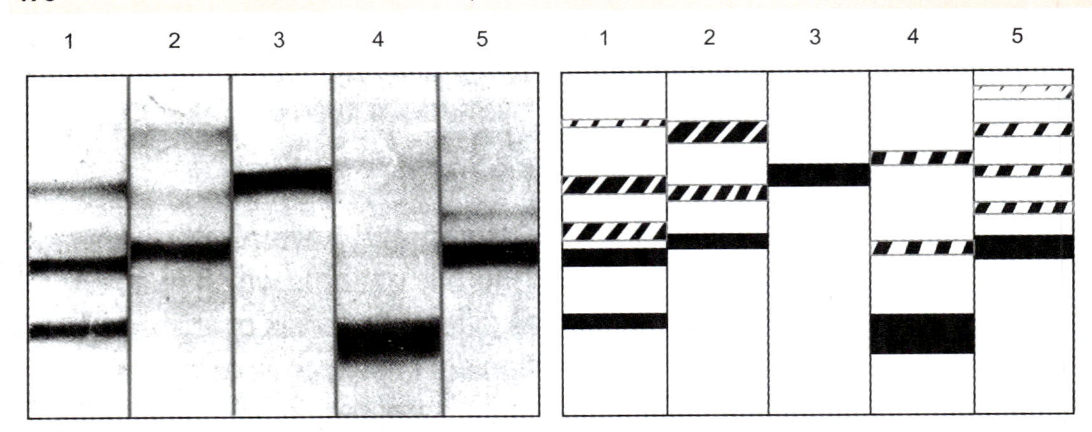

Fig. 34.8: Lactate dehydrogenase (LDH) isoenzyme patterns of different species in acrylamide gel (left) and their diagrammatic representation (right). (1) human, (2) goat, (3) fowl, (4) pig, and (5) buffalo

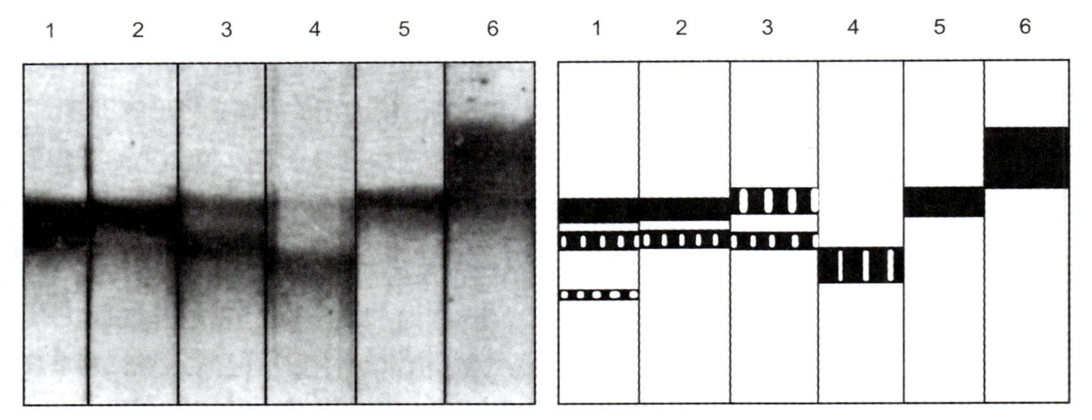

Fig. 34.9: Peroxidase (Px) isoenzyme patterns of different species in acrylamide gel (left) and their diagrammatic representation (right): (1) human, (2) goat, (3) buffalo, (4) bullock, (5) pig, and (6) fowl

Mumbai, to prepare antihuman serum, only one intramuscular injection of species-specific human globulins is quite effective. As the quantity of antigens (species-specific substances or amount of blood) in the crime articles is unknown, it is most convenient to work on R type antibodies. The concentration of antigen or antibodies will have no dissolving effect on the precipitate when R type antisera are used while excess of antigen or antibody will dissolve the precipitate of H (horse) type antisera. Rabbit-like animals (sheep, goat, etc.) which produce R type antibodies are selected for this purpose.

The partial antigens (blood group substances similar to those found in human beings) are also present in animals. These substances interfere with the grouping tests when human blood is contaminated with animal blood. To exclude such interference, other animal antisera should be used along with antihuman serum while performing the precipitin test.

The proteins responsible for precipitin reaction are mainly serum globulins. They are soluble in water. Therefore, they may not be present in sufficient quantity in blood stains found on actual washed crime articles. In such cases, enzyme methods, like LDH and Px, are recommended, as these enzymes are present on cell wall of RBCs and are still available for giving a positive reaction.

Whenever it is necessary, in the context of crime to specify the class or species of animal blood, COE should be used as a screening test. Confirmation of the specific animal species is done by gel diffusion test or enzyme test. In gel diffusion test, the unknown extract results should always be compared with known standards (controls). If lines of unknown extract and known standards exactly meet one another, it is called *complete identity*. If there is extension of one line only showing a spur it is called *partial identity*. If there is extension of both lines showing cross-spurs, it is called *non-identity*. Complete identity of the sample must be established with known standards before a definite opinion can be given. It is, therefore, recommended that COE, gel diffusion, and enzyme tests can be used for routine laboratory examination of species origin (human, animal, and the class of animal).

Q. 34.12. Name the methods for detection of blood groups in stains. Comment on the limitations and problems in such work.

Detection of Blood Groups in Stains

Once the human origin of blood stain is confirmed, their grouping is attempted. The **methods commonly used** for grouping in stains are: (1) immunological, and (2) enzymological. The immunological methods in common use are: (a) absorption-elution (b) mixed agglutination, and (c) absorption-inhibition. The enzymological methods in common use are: (a) vertical disc, (b) vertical or horizontal slab, (c) isoelectric focusing, and (d) cellulose acetate membrane, etc. The details of these methods are beyond scope of this book.

Some of the **limitations** of blood stain grouping are: (1) The amount of blood in the stain which is ordinarily available is small, (2) blood stains are rarely on clean articles and are certainly never sterile; the presence of bacteria can give rise to reactions with the antisera making interpretation difficult, and (3) in contrast to fresh blood where both agglutinogens and agglutinins are available for the determination of blood groups, in tests on blood stains it may be possible to carry out tests only for agglutinogens so that an absolute diagnosis for blood group is not possible.

While using ABO, MN, Rh, Gm, etc., systems, problems in grouping may arise owing to (1) pseudoagglutination, (2) cold agglutinins, (3) low titre or weak agglutinogen, (4) infancy, as the agglutinins develop during the first few months after birth, (5) the difficulty of preparing good M and N sera which incidentally are also unstable, and (6) the presence of an extremely rare suppressor gene (the Bombay gene) that suppresses A or B antigen. In this case, the blood cannot be grouped by routine ABO method but by the use of anti-H antisera when a reaction is obtained.

Discussion

The ABO, Gm, Rh, and MN (immunological) systems are used routinely for stain grouping. ABO and Gm are the most stable systems. They have good discrimination power also. Though Rh also has good discrimination power, the antigens are not stable and hence it can give good results provided the articles for examination are received within four weeks. MN grouping in dried blood is difficult and disappointing for two reasons: (1) High titre antisera are not available, and (2) M antigen is a precursor of N antigen, and, therefore, it is often difficult to confirm the N group. Still, some laboratories are using this system for confirming M^+ or M^-.

To increase the evidential value of stain grouping, the expert should attempt more than one system. Preference should be given to the ABO and Gm systems which are most stable and also have good discrimination power. The other systems, despite their limitations, may be used in the following preferential order, viz. PGM, GLO-I, EAP, EsD, and Rh.

SEMEN

Semen is a fluid secretion containing cellular elements. The fluid portion is formed in the seminal vesicles and prostate and contain a high concentration of choline and lecithin secreted by the seminal vesicles and acid phosphatase and spermine secreted by the prostate. The cellular elements consist of spermatozoa and epithelial cells formed by the testes. Semen is a thick, yellowish white, glairy, opalescent secretion having a characteristic odour known as seminal odour. The normal quantity of semen in one ejaculate varies from 2 to 5 ml. In a healthy adult male, the total number of spermatozoa in one ejaculate is about 200 to 500 millions (one hundred million per ml) of which at least 80% are motile. The secretion is slightly alkaline in reaction. Its liquefaction occurs within a short period due to prostatic fibrinolysin.

The question of detecting seminal stains arises in charges of rape, sodomy, and bestiality. These stains are usually found on the clothing but may be found on the body of either the victim or the accused, on the bed clothes, or where the offence is committed. These are sometimes found mixed with blood, mucus, pus or faeces, especially on the articles of clothing.

Q. 34.13. What examinations will you carry out to test a specimen for seminal stains? How will you collect material for such examination? Give a brief account of physical examination.

The examination of seminal stains may be carried out by four methods, viz. physical, chemical, microscopic, and electrophoretic. The material for examination is **collected** as follows:

1. The portion of the fabric bearing the stain is cut, dried in the shade to prevent putrefaction, and carefully preserved.
2. If pubic hair is matted together, a portion is cut and kept for examination.
3. To demonstrate the presence of semen in vagina, swabs are taken on sterile gauze/cloth and smears prepared on sterile slides.
4. Dried or drying seminal fluid on the thighs and perineum is collected on a piece of moistened cloth and dried.
5. Dry stains on smooth surfaces is gently scraped with a clean, blunt scalpel into a glass container.

Physical Examination

Garments submitted for laboratory examination are often dirty and may contain a variety of stains. Those of reddish colour are commonly composed of blood; of a yellowish colour, from vaginal discharge or urine; of a brownish colour, from faeces; while those of a grayish appearance may be due to semen. A preliminary examination under filtered ultraviolet light can be made, when stains of urine, leucorrhoeal discharge, and seminal fluid will show a bright fluorescence. The fluorescence of seminal stains is of a bluish white colour and such stains are selected for further examination.

Q. 34.14. Give a brief account of the commonly performed chemical tests to determine that the stain is a seminal one.

Chemical Examination

The tests most commonly performed for this purpose are: (1) acid phosphatase test, (2) Florence test, (3) Barberio's test, and (4) creatine phosphokinase test.

Acid phosphatase test: A high concentration of acid phosphatase is found only in the semen of human beings and monkeys. This is a quantitative test. The amount of acid phosphatase is estimated in a measured specimen, e.g. one square centimetre of stained material. It gives a positive reaction in old stains, in the absence of demonstrable sperms, and aspermia inhibition of acid phosphatase activity of semen by l-tartaric acid, though non-specific, is a valuable screening test.

Florence test: A drop of watery solution of the stain is placed on a glass slide and allowed to dry. A coverslip is placed over this and a drop of Florence reagent, which contains potassium iodide and iodine in distilled water, is run under it. If seminal matter is present, dark brown crystals resembling haemin crystals will form in a short time. This is due to the formation of choline periodide. A negative result may be obtained when the choline content is low or the stain decomposed. A positive reaction may be obtained with other body tissues containing choline. Vaginal secretion does not give a positive test.

Barberio's test: The reaction depends upon the presence of spermine in semen. A few drops of Barberio's reagent consisting of a saturated aqueous or alcoholic solution of picric acid when added to spermatic fluid produces crystals of spermine picrate which are needle-shaped, rhombic and of a yellow colour. This test is positive even without the presence of spermatozoa. The disadvantage of this test is the pleomorphic nature of crystals, which sometimes take the form of a deposit without any structure.

Creatine phosphokinase test: Spermatozoa contain a high concentration of creatine phosphokinase which is more than double the amount contained in any other body fluid. Levels of over 400 units/ml is almost diagnostic of seminal stain.

Q. 34.15. Give a brief account of microscopic examination of seminal stains.

Microscopic Examination

This demonstrates the presence of spermatozoa from fresh unstained smears and those which have been fixed and stained. In case of a fabric, where the stain has dried, the stained portion is cut and soaked in a small quantity of acidulated water in a watch glass for ½ to 1 hour, if the stain is recent or 2 to 4 hours, if the stain is old. By means of a pair of clean forceps, the fabric is removed from the solution and dabbed gently several times on a clean slide. The smear is allowed to dry, then fixed, stained, and examined under high power objective. Human spermatozoa are about 50 microns long, and consist of a head measuring 5 microns in length and 3 microns in breadth, a short body, and a long filamentous tail. The head is ovoid and flattened when viewed in front, and about one-third the size of a human red blood corpuscle, and is pear-shaped when viewed in profile. In the stained specimen, the hind part of the head of the sperm acquires a deep blue tint whilst the front and middle of the head and its tail are stained deep red.

Under the microscope, it is not difficult to recognise a spermatozoon when it is intact because of its large and obvious head, its neck, and filamentous tail. If only disconnected heads and tails are found, as is sometimes the case in stains that have been roughly handled, a definite opinion regarding spermatozoa can be given only by an expert. The disconnected head may be confused with numerous microorganisms, like yeast, *Trichomonas vaginalis*, and cellular material of vaginal or other origin. Therefore, as a rule, a complete spermatozoon is necessary before a positive result can be given on routine microscopic examination. However, the presence of a Y chromosome can identify the disconnected head of a spermatozoon under fluorescent microscope (vide infra). The failure to find complete spermatozoa or separate heads and tails in a stain extract does not exclude the possibility of the stain being a seminal one. The fabric may have been washed or the sperms may have been filtered to leave only the fluid fraction on the fabric or the male may be azoospermic, very old, or undergone vasectomy more than six months ago.

Fluorescence microscopy can be used for the detection of spermatozoa. It is based on the principle that the Y chromosome is fluorescent to quinacrine. With this method, it is possible to detect both intact spermatozoa as well as the disconnected heads which often show the presence of fluorescent Y bodies in them.

Q. 34.16. Give a brief account of electrophoretic methods in common use to detect a seminal stain.

Electrophoretic Methods

Two methods are in common use, viz: (1) acid phosphatase, and (2) lactate dehydrogenase.

Acid phosphatase (Fig. 34.10): Acid phosphatase is a common enzyme and is encountered, in addition to semen, in other body fluids, fruits, vegetables, fungi, and bacteria. Polyacrylamide gel electrophoresis followed by staining with methyl umbelliferyl phosphate reagent enables the seminal acid phosphatase to be distinguished from the acid phosphatase present in other substances and even vaginal secretion, on account of differences in mobility. This method is superior to LDH method since semen can be identified even in the absence of sperms, i.e. in azoospermic or vasectomised persons.

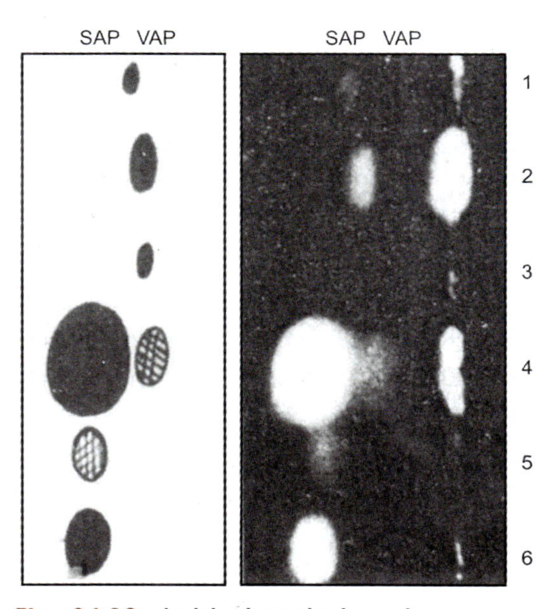

Fig. 34.10: Acid phosphatase isoenzyme patterns in acrylamide (slab) and their diagrammatic representation. SAP = seminal acid phosphatase; VAP = vaginal acid phosphatase. 1, 2 and 3—vaginal fluid; 4—mixture of vaginal fluid and semen; 5 and 6—semen

Lactate dehydrogenase (Fig. 34.11): The sperm specific lactate dehydrogenase (LDHx) isoenzyme can be separated from other LDH iso-enzymes of semen by using polyacrylamide gel electrophoresis. The advantages of this method are:

1. LDHx isoenzyme is stable in stains in tropical conditions for over four weeks.
2. The isoenzyme pattern of human semen is different from that of commonly encountered animals.
3. Positive results are obtained in a much larger number of cases than is possible with microscopic examination.
4. Vaginal fluid also shows a characteristic isoenzyme pattern in which the LDHx specific band for semen is absent but instead a slow moving extra band is present.

Q. 34.17. Discuss the relative importance of the various methods commonly employed to detect seminal stains.

As a quick and sensitive screening method for detecting semen in a large number of samples, l-tartrate inhibitable acid phosphatase test is the best choice. The major drawback of this test is that vaginal secretion also gives a positive reaction. However, the vaginal secretion contains less quantity of acid phosphatase and takes longer time for the reaction, as compared to semen. In sexual offence cases, these two body fluids are commonly mixed with each other. Therefore, this test should be used to establish the absence of semen/vaginal

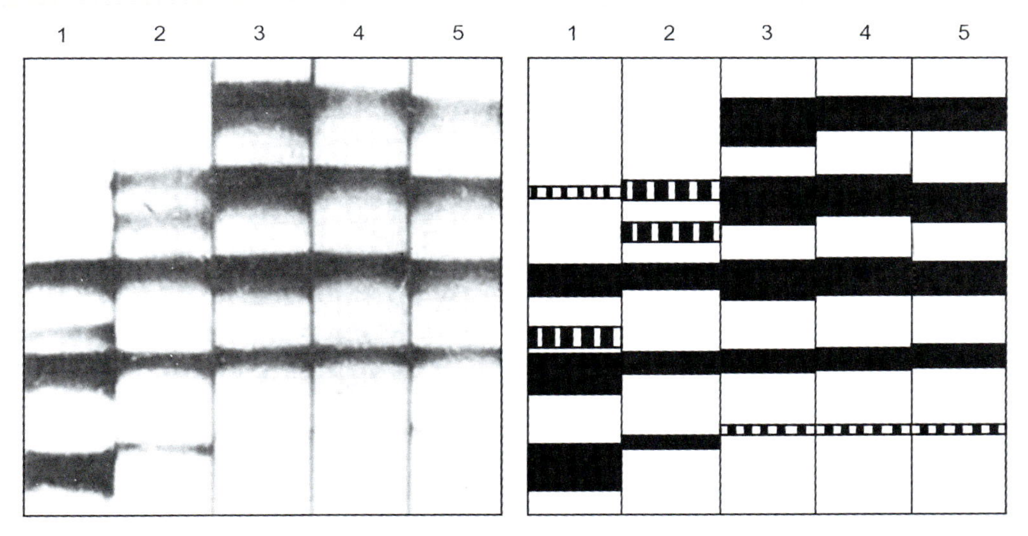

Fig. 34.11: Lactate dehydrogenase isoenzyme patterns of different human body fluids in acrylamide gel and their diagrammatic representation. (1) blood, (2) semen, (3) vaginal fluid, (4) nasal secreation, and (5) saliva

fluid. Whilst the Florence test is not sufficiently sensitive, interference from vaginal secretion can be definitely ruled out. However, many plant and fruit juices possess choline; it is, therefore, not possible to use this test independently.

While microscopic identification of spermatozoa is quite reliable and specific, it is not always successful in old stains on account of the fragility of spermatozoa in dried seminal stains under tropical conditions. Though LDH isoenzyme method is superior to microscopic detection of spermatozoa, it has limitations; it cannot be used, if azoospermic or vasectomised persons are involved in the crime. The alternative choice, therefore, is to use the electrophoretic method for the detection of seminal acid phosphatase. It is thus evident that at least one confirmatory test should be used in conjunction with l-tartrate acid phosphatase screening test. Other confirmatory tests can be used, if necessary.

Q. 34.18. Write short notes on: (a) identification of species origin of seminal stains, (b) blood groups in seminal stains, (c) proof that a stain is seminal in origin.

Identification of Species Origin

To substantiate an opinion based on microscopical observation of morphological differences in human and animal spermatozoa, it is necessary to have the confirmation of the species by the precipitin test. It can be done in a manner similar to that described for blood stains. However, more specific anti-human semen serum can also be used for the confirmation of seminal stains in place of anti-human serum which is commonly used for blood. The LDH isoenzyme pattern of human semen is different from that of animal. Therefore, it can be used for the detection of species origin. When fluorescence microscopy is used for the detection of spermatozoa or heads of spermatozoa the presence of Y bodies will confirm that the semen or seminal stain is of human origin. The Y body is not seen in animal spermatozoa.

Blood Groups in Seminal Stains

The specific agglutinable substances A and B are present in the semen of secretors. Secretor status is confirmed by using anti-Le^a and anti-Le^b for the saliva samples of the individual. If the seminal stains are from a secretor, absorption-elution method can be employed to determine the ABO blood group substances; any interference from microbial growth can be eliminated, if absorption-inhibition method is also used. Gm, PGM and GLO-I systems can be used to individualise semen or seminal stains.

Proof of Semen

A complete spermatozoon is necessary before a positive microscopic result can be given. If only disconnected heads and tails are found, a definite opinion as regards spermatozoa can only be given on the basis of biochemical and other advanced tests, already described.

One must remember that seminal fluid does not contain spermatozoa in cases of azoospermia, vasectomy more than six months ago, or very old persons. This fact assumes importance in a case where the accused has undergone vasectomy as a family planning measure and bases his defence to a charge of sexual assault on the absance of sperms on laboratory examination.

In the absence of sperms, a stain should be opined as seminal: (1) if it gives characteristic fluorescence to ultraviolet light, (2) l-tartrate acid phosphatase screening test is positive, and (3) there is a high level of acid phosphatase and creatine phosphokinase. Alternatively, a positive Florence test and l-tartrate acid phosphatase screening test confirms the diagnosis. An electrophoretic seminal acid phosphatase pattern may be used as an additional confirmatory test, if necessary. Its origin (human or animal) is confirmed by the precipitin test, and the source (from which person) can be identified by using different grouping systems, such as, ABO, Gm, PGM, and GLO-I.

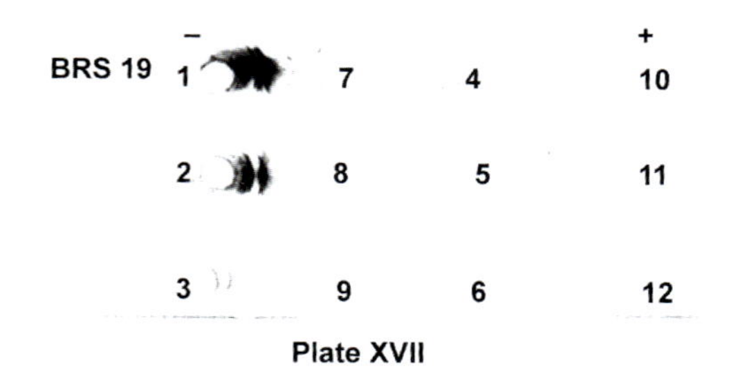

Fig. 34.12: Semen by gel diffusion. (*Courtesy*: Dr BV Subrahmanyam)

Q. 34.19. Write short notes on examination of: (a) saliva stains, (b) urine stains, (c) faecal matter stains, (d) milk stains.

Saliva

The identification of saliva on cigarette or 'bidi' ends and on clothes is important in crime investigation. A sample of saliva may be obtained from both the suspect as well as the victim in crimes, such as sexual offenses to determine the secretor status. To collect a sample of saliva for analysis, the mouth should be thoroughly rinsed with water five minutes before collecting the sample. To stimulate flow of saliva, the subject should chew a small square of paraffin wax (not chewing gum).

Saliva can be detected by measuring the amylase activity by the starch-iodine test and/or Phadebas test. Some individuals produce saliva with little or no amylase activity. These tests, therefore, need to be supplemented by other tests, such as examination of buccal epithelial cells under the microscope.

The precipitin test is used to determine species origin and the absorption-elution method for blood group substances. For ABO grouping, some authors suggest the use of absorption-inhibition and absorption-elution methods together with suitable dilutions in both the methods to eliminate any non-specific reaction.

Urine

Examination of urine and its stains may be necessary in cases of murder and sexual assault.

Urine stains on fabric may appear pale yellow or may have no naked eye appearance of their presence. These give fluorescence when examined under ultraviolet light. A concentrated extract of the stain may give a characteristic smell due to ammonia evolved by bacterial degradation of urea.

The chemical tests to detect urine from the stains depend on the presence of urea and creatinine in urine. Urastrat method or p-dimethylaminocinnamaldehyde is used to detect the former and TLC for the latter. The precipitin test can be attempted to determine the species origin.

Faecal Matter

The examination of faecal matter or its stains may be necessary in cases of sodomy and bestiality. Its presence on penile swabs and other garments may be of evidential value.

Faecal matter is generally brown in colour due to urobilinogen. In infants, it is yellow due to unchanged bilirubin and milk diet. The colour of faecal matter may change to green, black or red depending on diet, drugs, or pathological conditions.

The suspected faecal stains are examined under the microscope for the presence of faecal elements and confirmed by chemical tests. A small portion of the suspected stain is macerated in 2–3 drops of water in a micro-aid test tube. Liquid portion is pipetted out and the residue placed on a glass slide to make a smear, and the smear examined under the microscope for the presence of plant cells, starch, muscle fibres, body cells, bacteria and yeast. The microscopic observation may be confirmed by the chemical tests, viz. the urobilinogen test and the acid phosphatase test. A precipitin test can be used to determine the species origin.

Milk

The detection of colostrum or milk stains on undergarments, like a brassiere or blouse, is sometimes important in crimes involving pregnancy, abortion, and concealment of birth.

By the third month of pregnancy, a clear transparent secretion can be squeezed out of the nipples on pressing the breasts. This is known as colostrum. It is a thin yellowish fluid consisting of free fat globules and large phagocytic cells filled with droplets of fat. In contrast, milk is a thick whitish fluid and consists mostly of large fat globules and only a few phagocytic cells. Colostrum is present for about 10 days after delivery when it is replaced by milk. The identification of milk stains involves the detection of casein and lactose. To determine species origin and grouping, the same methods as those described for blood can be followed.

Colostrum contains many antibodies and trypsin inhibitor. The detection of trypsin inhibitor confirms the presence of colostrum. Trypsin inhibitor is not present in milk.

HAIR

The examination of hair assumes importance in: (1) identification, (2) sexual offenses, especially rape and bestiality, (3) crimes when hair or fibres found at the scene, on weapons, clothes, etc., (4) hit and run accidents when specimens of hair removed from various parts of the motor car are sent by authorities for comparison with victim's hair, and (5) chronic poisoning by metals.

Q. 34.20. Give a succinct account of examination of hair from a medicolegal point of view.

The points to be considered in the examination of hair are: (1) the nature, i.e. if the material is hair or some other fibre, (2) if it is hair, its source, whether human or animal,

(3) if human, the race, age, sex, situation, and special features for identification, (4) evidence in relation to suspected crime, and (5) in case of dead bodies, the time since death, if possible.

Nature: Hair, both human and animal, consist of three zones, viz. (1) cuticle, (2) cortex, and (3) medulla (Figs 34.13 to 34.15).

The cuticle is the outer zone. It consists of non-pigmented scales of keratin and forms a certain pattern. The cortex is the middle zone of varying thickness. It consists of longitudinally arranged elongated cells without nuclei, and a varying amount of pigment, which gives hair its colour. The medulla is the inner zone. It is known as the medullary canal or the central shaft. It contains a considerable amount of pigment in animals and shows a characteristic pattern. Medullary index is the ratio of the diameter of the medulla to the diameter of the shaft. In human hair, only the cortex is pigmented; the medulla is narrow, absent, or fragmented. The root has the appearance similar to that of shaft except that it is enlarged in the form of bulb or knob. The tip of the hair is tapering and generally non-medullated.

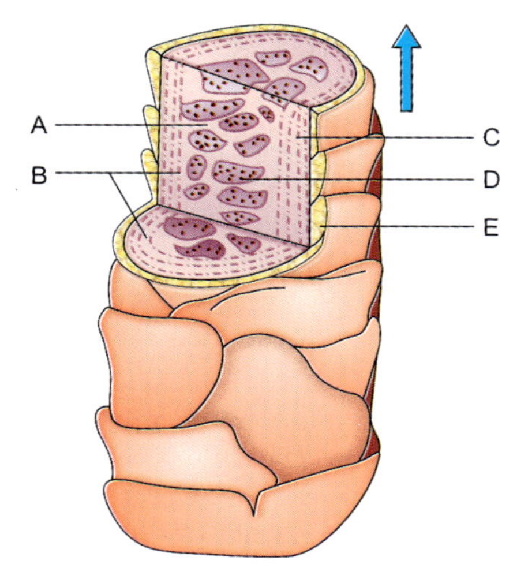

Fig. 34.13: Diagrammatic representation of a typical hair shaft. Arrow points towards the tip. A—medulla, B—pigment granules, C—cortex, D—air sac, and E—cuticle

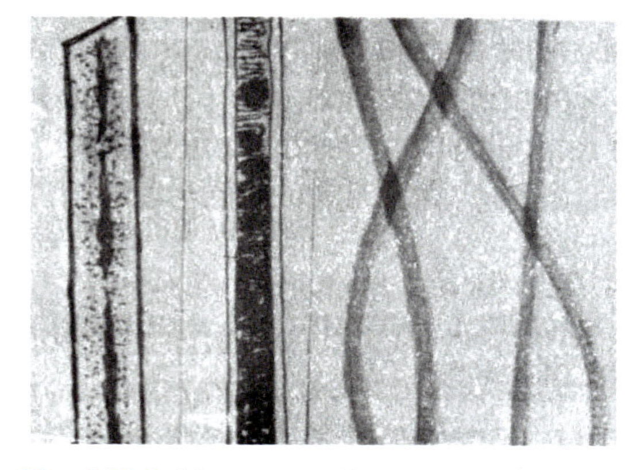

Fig. 34.14: Diagrammatic representation of **hairs and fibres.** From left to right; human hair, cat hair, and wool fibres

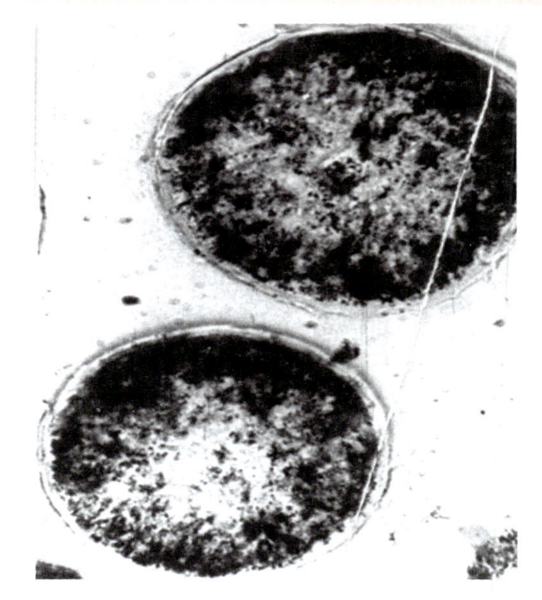

Fig. 34.15: Non-medullated and medullated human hair cut section. The white line is an artefact. (*Courtesy*: Dr BV Subrahmanyam)

Fibres are devoid of cuticle and, many fibres especially the synthetic ones, are quite homogeneous. On microscopic examination of cross-section, the cuticular impression is absent and the fibre has no structure comparable to that of hair.

Source: From the appearance of the cuticle and medulla, the relative size of medulla

Table 34.1: Differentiating features of human and animal hair

	Human hair	*Animal hair*
1. Texture	Fine and thin	Coarse and thick
2. Cuticle	Scales are small, flattened (type VII), serrated, and surround the shaft completely (coronal)	Scales are large, polyhedral (types I to VI), wavy, and do not surround the shaft completely (imbricate)
3. Medulla	Narrow. May be absent, fragmented, or discontinuous	Broad, always present, and continuous
4. Cortex	Thick. 4–10 times as broad as medulla	Thin. Rarely more than twice the breadth of medulla
5. Medullary index	Less than 0.3	More than 0.5
6. Pigment	More towards the periphery of cortex	Uniform, peripheral, or central
7. Precipitin test with intact root	Specific for human	Specific for animal

and cortex, and from the examination of hair in cross-section, an idea may be gained as to the source of hair. Table 34.1 summarises the differentiating features of human and animal hair.

Identification: The data essential for this purpose include (Fig. 34.14): (1) race, (2) age, (3) sex, (4) situation, and (5) special features.

Race: This is already dealt with earlier in the Chapter 3 on Personal Identification.

Age: This can sometimes be determined from examination of hair. The lanugo hair of the newborn is fine, soft, downy, non-pigmented, non-medullated, and with smooth-edged flattened scales. This is replaced by hair which is comparatively less fine, pigmented, medullated, and with a more complex scale pattern. Other data, such as—(1) age sequence of appearance of hair in various parts of the body, (2) changes that pubic and axillary hair undergo in the adolescent stage, and (3) changes in hair due to old age, also helpful for age determination, have already been included in the Chapter 3 on Personal Identification.

Sex: Sexing of human hair is possible by studying the sex chromatin (X and Y bodies) from hair root cells of the scalp. In addition, beard and moustache hairs of the male are the only hair whose sex can be determined. The characteristics and distribution of hair help in determining sex. Male hairs are generally thicker, coarser and darker than female hair. Female scalp hairs are generally fine, long and gently taper to an end. The distribution of pubic hair in the male and female is already outlined. The presence of hair on certain parts of the body in the male and its absence in the female have also been outlined earlier.

Situation: Hairs from different parts of the human body sometimes present differentiating characteristics, e.g. scalp hair, pubic and axillary hairs, beard and moustache hair, eyelashes, etc., as briefly outlined below:

Scalp hairs are long and soft with a tapering end. Constant combing causes the tapering end to fray out into a brush-like form. Periodical cropping shows sharp cut tips which become blunt and round about a week later. On cross-section, scalp hairs appear oval or circular in outline. Pubic and axillary hairs are short, stout, and curly. Beard and moustache hairs are usually coarse. The tips are mostly cut. On cross-section, they are more oval and more flattened than scalp hair. Hairs from eyebrow, eyelid, nose, or ear are short and stubby with a wide medulla. They taper rapidly to a fine tip. Further differentiation is possible with the evaluation of certain morphological indices, like the hair index, medullary index, scale count index, and so on, the details of which are beyond the scope of this book.

Special features: Examination of hair is of importance in a variety of circumstances. Although one cannot say that a hair came from a particular individual, by careful comparison, one can often state that it could have come from him. In the comparison of hair debris, grease, etcetera, adherent to the hair, may be of as much value in determining the ownership of hair as the study of its structure. Determination becomes easy, if there is some known peculiarity of hair, such as patchy white hair, dyed hair, bleached hair, and curly or artificially waved hair. It should, however, be remembered that hair may have been cut or dyed with a view to conceal the identity.

ABO blood groups, and other blood group systems, such as PGM, EsD. and GLO-I can be determined even from a single hair from any part of the body and this may help in identification. In a dead person, since hair resists putrefaction, it forms an important means of identification when the rest of the body is putrefied. The elemental composition of hair may be determined by neutron activation analysis. This method may be helpful in identification when comparison samples are available.

Evidence about crime: A careful examination of hair, and stains on hair may provide valuable clues as regards the nature of offence and cause of death.

Animal hair may be found on the human body and vice versa in bestiality. Similarly, in cases of rape and other sexual offenses, pubic hair of the assailant may be found on the body of the victim and vice versa. (Locard's principle of exchange).

In case of sexual offenses, the matted pubic hair of the victim should be cut and sent for chemical examination. The pubic hair should also be combed out to collect non-matching male pubic hair.

Injuries to hair show characteristic changes. In injury, as for example to the head, scalp hair may be damaged by the blow and indications of this may be found in a ruptured appearance of the cortical layer. Hair may get scorched or singed due to burns or firearm injury. Singed hair are swollen, black, fragile, twisted or curled and have peculiar disagreeable odour due to burning of keratin. Carbon may be found deposited on them. The tip of a singed hair swells out to resemble a bulb in shape. Microscopically, the width of the singed hair is more than that of normal and it shows vacuolation. The end of the hair may tell of the mode of its removal. The hair bulb, if present, is normally rounded but if forcibly extracted, there will be rupture of the hair sheath and irregularity of the bulb. When hairs fall naturally, the root will be atrophied and the root sheath absent. When hair has been cut by a sharp weapon, an examination of the tip of the hair will show if it has been recently cut. A recently cut hair shows a sharply cut edge with a projecting cuticle. It becomes square after about a week, smooth after about two weeks, and rounded after about a month.

Occasionally, in the event of homicide, some hair belonging to the assailant may be found firmly clutched in the deceased's hands. It helps to identify the murderer. The presence of hair on a weapon of assault provides a link between the weapon and the victim. Likewise, presence of hair on vehicles involved in hit and run accidents provides a link between the vehicle and the victim.

Careful examination is required to detect the presence of stains on hair to indicate the nature of assault. One should specially look for mud stains, seminal stains, blood stains, and salivary stains. Mud stains on the hair indicate struggle; seminal stains sexual offenses; blood stains injury or sexual offenses; and salivary stains asphyxial deaths.

In case of poisoning, especially metallic, if the person has not died in the acute stage, the hair retain traces of the position poison for a considerable time. Chemical examination in such cases would reveal the presence of the poison in the living as well as in exhumed bodies. For this purpose, hairs should be plucked with their roots intact, preferably with the help of flat tipped forceps. A minimum of 15 hairs is desirable. The analysis of successive short lengths of hair from the base to the tip gives an approximate indication of arsenic dosage or the intermittent period of such administration. In the last few years, it has been discovered that many drugs, e.g. cocaine, marihuana, etc., are deposited in human hair and they can be detected by sophisticated techniques.

Time since death: Hair ceases to grow after death but due to drying and shrinkage of skin, there is an apparent growth of hair on the face. The rate of growth of hair is about 0.4 mm per day. An approximate idea of the time since death may be obtained from this, if the time of last shave is known. Loosening of hair occur due to shrinkage of skin in 48–72 hours after death. This may also provide some idea about the time since death. In exhumed bodies, if a person has been buried in a shallow grave, scalp hair change colour in about 1–3 months; in a deep grave such a change occurs in about 6–12 months.

35 Collection and Preservation of Biological Materials

While this is dealt with in detail at appropriate places in the text, a few guidelines are provided here for emergency department personnel.

Biological material deteriorates very rapidly as it is susceptible to atmospheric conditions. It should, therefore, be sent to the forensic science laboratory (FSL), properly preserved, as quickly as possible. Relevant information with special reference to the crime should accompany the specimen.

Blood

Blood from injured victims or suspects, whose blood is likely to be present on exhibits being sent by the investigating officers, should be collected and preserved, for grouping, as already outlined in the Chapter 5 on Medicolegal Autopsy. About 2–3 ml of blood is sufficient. Two blood stains with a diameter about 5 cm each should be prepared on sterile cloth. The blood-stained cloth should be properly dried in air (shade), and then forwarded to the FSL along with control piece of cloth, in properly labelled sterile containers.

Postmortem blood, similarly collected and preserved, can also be sent likewise. When blood is not available, bone, bone marrow, muscle, and molar or premolar teeth can be removed, with the usual precautions, and sent in a labelled sterile container, after the specimen is properly dried in air. It is not commonly realised that hair roots can also be grouped (enzymes). Therefore, while sending blood specimen, a few combed or plucked hair with root intact should also be sent.

To collect dried transferred blood from the person of the victim, accused, etc., a clean and sterile cotton cloth piece moistened with physiological saline is taken, and the excess saline removed by squeezing. The dried blood from the stain is then transferred on to this cloth piece by gentle rubbing without causing any injury to the person concerned. This cloth piece is dried in air and forwarded to FSL, in a suitable container.

It is not commonly realised that every emergency case or unexpected death has actual or potential medicolegal aspects that must be recognised. While the best specimen for hospital use is the most recent one, the best for forensic purpose is usually the first or initial one. After hours or days of intensive therapy, it will be impossible to determine what the concentration of alcohol, drug, or carboxyhaemoglobin was at the time of injury. Availability of proper specimens to decipher objective data is necessary for the administration of justice.

Saliva

Saliva should be collected in sterile tubes, heated in a boiling water bath for 10 minutes, cooled, and then transferred to a sterile phial before despatch. Also two stains of unheated saliva, with a diameter about 5 cm each without any preservative, prepared on sterile cotton cloth, properly dried should be sent in a labelled sterile container.

Swabs and Smears

In sexual offenses, vaginal/anal/penile swabs, as required, should be sent along with their smears on slides for microscopic examination. Swabs should be taken on sterile gauze/cloth and their smears prepared on sterile slides. These should be dried in air or preferably a desiccator and the swabs despatched in sterile test tubes and slides in clean wrappers.

Hair

Hair samples are required for species origin, grouping, and identification (comparison). Control samples should be whole hair strands with root intact obtained by plucking and should be representative of the hair on the particular part/s of the body in question.

In sexual offenses, pubic hair may be useful for detection of semen and/or blood, etc. Such hair should be cut, dried preferably in a desiccator, and sent in a sterile test tube. The pubic hair should also be combed out to collect non-matching hair to establish transfer of pubic hair during the offence. Control samples of hair should be obtained from the suspect as well as the victim by plucking with the roots intact. It is not commonly realised that blood (enzyme) grouping and sexing are possible from the hair root.

When samples of scalp hair are required, both cut and pulled hair from at least six different areas of the scalp should be taken and labelled as to their site. In the recent O.J. Simpson double murder case (California, June 1994), the Judge authorised the prosecution to collect a total of 40–100 scalp hairs to match the ones found at crime scene.

Nails

Nails, stained with extraneous blood or likely to show tags of epithelium of the assailant, scratched during the struggle, should be carefully clipped without damaging the underlying tissue of the person concerned, or scraped with the help of tooth prick, and collected in separate envelopes. In case of suspected poisoning in the dead, all the nails (fingers and/or toes) should be removed entire and collected in separate envelopes.

PART 5: Clinical and Forensic Toxicology

Section 8

36. Introduction and Law Relating to Poisons

37. Toxicological Evidence

38. Common Household Poisons

39. Mineral Acids and Caustic Alkalis

40. Organic Acids

41. Vegetable Acid Poisons

36

Introduction and Law Relating to Poisons

INTRODUCTION

Many Western textbooks devote only a small part of their text to clinical and forensic toxicology. In some parts of the world, such as South East Asia, Africa, and the Indian subcontinent, many poisons, such as acids, alkalis, phenols, arsenic, antimony, madar, powdered glass, dhatura, oleander, strychnine, aconite, etc., that produce obvious lesions, are still being used. They are easy to detect, both clinically and at autopsy. In the West, pharmaceutical substances, agrichemical substances, and medicinal preparations, active in low dosage, are now being used as poisons. Most of these substances do not produce any gross or even histological changes in the body, and are, therefore, difficult to detect. This section includes commonly used substances both in the West and in other parts of the world. Accordingly, it would appear long to the reader. However, the use of this book on an international basis has necessitated such indulgence. Study of poisons helps the practitioner to manage poisoning cases brought to him in day-to-day practice . The nature of poisons varies from place to place and depends on availability, accessibility, occupation, etc. Common poisons are of plants, animals or chemical origin. Their actions vary depending on the dose, route and health of the person consuming.

Q. 36.1. Define toxicology. Give the legal definition of poison.

Toxicology deals with the effect of toxic substances on the body when administered by any route. Poisons are substances which are deleterious or injurious to the body leading to disease, deformity or death or illness, infirmity or death.

Toxicology is the science which deals with poisons with reference to their sources, properties, mode of action, symptoms which they produce, lethal dose, nature of the fatal results, treatment, methods of their detection and estimation, and autopsy findings. It is also concerned with law regarding their sale and prescription. Forensic toxicology deals with the medical and legal aspects of the harmful effects of poisonous substances on the human body. Sections 284, 299, 300, 304A, 324, 326, and 328 IPC deal with offenses relating to administration of poisons.

A **poison** is a substance which, when administered, inhaled or ingested, is capable of acting deleteriously on the human body. Thus, almost anything is a poison. There is really no boundary between a medicine and a poison, for a medicine in a toxic dose is a poison and a poison in a small dose may be a medicine. *In law,* the real difference between a medicine and a poison is the intent with which it is given. If the substance is given with the intention to save life, it is a medicine but if it is given with the intention to cause bodily harm, it is a poison.

Toxinology is the science which deals with toxins produced by plants, animals, bacteria, and fungi, which are harmful to man.

Q. 36.2. Briefly discuss the important provisions regulating the control of drugs in your country.

In India, these are: (1) the Drugs and Cosmetics Act, 1940 and the rules made thereunder, and (2) Narcotic Dugs and Psychotropic Substances Act, 1985.

1. Under the **Drugs and Cosmetics Act, 1940,** a cosmetic means any article intended to be rubbed, poured, sprinkled or sprayed on, or introduced into, or otherwise applied to, the human body or any part thereof for cleansing, beautifying, promoting attractiveness or altering the appearance, and includes any article intended for use as a component of cosmetic but does not include soap. The Act has been further amended by Drugs (Amendment) Act, 1964 (13 of 1964) to include Ayurvedic and Unani drugs. The main aim is to control quality, purity, and strength of drugs. The label or container of medicine should display the formula or a list of ingredients contained in the drug. The Act provides stringent punishment in respect of offenses concerned with drug adulteration.

   Under the **Drugs and Cosmetics Rules, 1945,** the drugs are classified in certain **schedules,** and regulations are laid down for their storage, display, sale, dispensing, labelling, prescribing, etc.

   Schedule H and L drugs are required to be labelled with the words "SCHEDULE H DRUG" and "SCHEDULE L DRUG", *Warning* — To be sold by retail on the prescription of a registered medical practitioner only. The prescription shall mention the name and address of the person for whose treatment it is given. Any such prescription must be compounded in the authorised premises (chemist's shop) only by or under the supervision of a qualified pharmacist and must not be dispensed more than once unless specifically asked for. At the time of dispensing, a note should be made of the name and address of the patient, the date on which the prescription is dispensed, the serial number under which it is entered in the register (in case of poisons), the batch number, and the date of expiry of potency. In addition, the poisons are subject to the following regulations:

   a. A person must possess a license to stock, sell or distribute poisons listed in the rules.
   b. The supply of listed poisons must be entered in a register which must be maintained for this purpose.
   c. These poisons must be kept in authorised premises only in a cupboard or drawer reserved solely for this purpose and to which customers are not permitted to have access.
   d. They must be kept in leakproof containers labelled with the word "poison" in red letters.
   e. Certain poisons are not allowed to be kept in more than the given concentration while others have to be coloured.

2. The **Narcotic Drugs and Psychotropic Substances Act, 1985,** prohibits cultivation, manufacture, possession, sale, purchase, transport, import, export, etc., of these drugs and substances except for medical and scientific purposes as provided in the Act.

Narcotic drugs covered under the Act are: (a) cannabis (hemp), (b) coca leaf, (c) opium, and (d) any other narcotic substance or preparation which the Central Government may declare to be a manufactured drug.

A *psychotropic substance*, according to the Act, means any substance, natural or synthetic, or any natural material or any salt or preparation of such substance or material, specified in the scheduled list of 77 psychotropic substances, which include substances, like cannabis, amphetamines, tranquillisers, LSD, etc. The Act views the addict with sympathy, and makes some special provisions in this regard.

Narcotic drugs and psychotropic substances are also subject to stringent national and international control in all countries. The Convention on Narcotic Drugs is applicable to drugs, such as opium, opium alkaloids, coca and coca alkaloids, cannabis and its products, and synthetic drugs, such as pethidine, etc. The convention on Psychotropic Substances is applicable to substances, such as hallucinogens, like LSD; stimulants, like amphetamines; hypnotics, like secobarbital, methaqualone; and tranquillisers, like meprobamate, diazepam, etc.

The **aim** of all these regulations and acts is to: (a) control manufacture, storage, distribution, sale, dispensing, and import–export of drugs, (b) penalise people for possession and use of certain drugs, (c) maintain quality of drugs, (d) compel the manufacturers to list dangerous ingredients in patent medicines, and (e) prevent cases of addiction and poisoning,

Q. 36.3. Write short notes on: (1) human poisoning, (2) cattle poisoning.

Human poisoning: The circumstances may be suicidal, homicidal, stupefying, or accidental.

The poisons used for *suicidal* purposes are: potassium cyanide, hydrocyanic acid, opium, barbiturates, organophosphorus compounds, and oleander, etc., according to availability and use in the particular place. A *suicidal poison of choice* must be cheap, easily available, and capable of being administered in any food or drink. It must have a pleasant taste and no repulsive smell. The lethal dose should be small, and the lethal period short and preferably painless.

The poisons used for *homicidal* purposes are: arsenic, antimony, aconite, thallium, organophosphorus compounds, oleander, madar, strychnine, powdered glass, rarely insulin and other drugs, and very rarely cultures of disease germs. Opium is sometimes used to kill children. An *ideal homicidal poison* should be cheap, easily available, colourless, odourless, and tasteless. It must be capable of being administered in any food, drink, or drug without arousing any suspicion. The symptoms should resemble any natural disease or serious illness. The lethal dose should be small and the lethal period sufficiently long to permit the poisoner to escape safely and not to arouse any suspicion thereafter. There should be no antidote and no possibility of its detection either at autopsy or by laboratory methods. In some countries, death by homicidal poisoning is more common than violence because bloodshed is considered to be a more brutal crime than poisoning.

The poisons used for *stupefying* purposes are: alcohol, dhatura, cannabis indica, and cigarettes containing arsenic, dhatura or cannabis. In the West, and occasionally in India, chloral hydrate mixed with alcoholic beverage is similarly used. The latest addition to this is Rohypnol (Roche).

Accidental poisoning commonly takes place as a result of: (1) carelessness in storing poisonous and non-poisonous materials together, (2) quack remedies, (3) bites by poisonous animals, such as snakes and scorpions, (4) greater use of chemicals in industry and for household purposes, and (5) putting poisonous substances in food containers.

Cattle poisoning: Cattle poisoning is generally resorted to by cobblers for the sake of hides. Rarely, cattle are destroyed by owners when they are useless. The poisons used to destroy cattle are: abrus precatorius, arsenic, yellow oleander, and parathion. Sometimes, aconite, madar, nux vomica seeds and snake venom are also used.

Q. 36.4. Classify poisons according to their mode of action. Add a brief note on each group.

According to their mode of action, poisons are classified in six groups, viz: (1) corrosives, (2) irritants, (3) neurotics, (4) cardiac, (5) asphyxiants, and (6) miscellaneous.

Corrosives: A corrosive poison is simply a highly active irritant and not only produces inflammation but also actual ulceration of the tissues. This group consists of strong acids and strong alkalis. These include *mineral acids,* such as sulphuric acid, nitric acid, hydrochloric acid; *organic acids,* such as oxalic acid, carbolic acid, acetic acid, salicylic acid; *vegetable acid,* as for example, hydrocyanic acid; and *concentrated alkalis,* such as caustic soda, caustic potash, and carbonates of ammonium, sodium and potassium.

Irritants: Irritant poisons produce symptoms of pain in the abdomen, vomiting and purging. The postmortem appearances are usually evident to the naked eye, and show redness or ulceration of the gastrointestinal tract. This group consists of inorganic, organic, and mechanical substances. Corrosives in dilute solutions act as irritants.

Inorganic: The inorganic subgroup consists of non-metallic and metallic poisons. The *non-metallic* poisons include phosphorus, chlorine, bromine, and iodine. The *metallic* poisons include arsenic, antimony, mercury, lead, copper, thallium, zinc, manganese, barium and radioactive substances.

Organic: The organic subgroup consists of vegetable and animal poisons. The *vegetable poisons* include castor seeds, croton seeds, abrus precatorius, colocynth, ergot, capsicum, semicarpus anacardium (marking nut), calotropis (madar), and plumbago rosea (lal chitra) and plumbago zeylanica (chitra). The *animal poisons* include cantharides, snakes, scorpions, spiders, and poisonous insects.

Mechanical: The mechanical subgroup includes coarsely powdered glass, chopped hair, dried sponge, and diamond dust.

Neurotics: Neurotic poisons act chiefly on the nervous system though some neurotics have a local irritant action. All alkaloidal poisons fall into this group. The chief symptoms in general are usually headache, drowsiness, giddiness, delirium, stupor, coma, and sometimes convulsions or paralysis, though individual poisons may have characteristic effects. Postmortem examination usually does not show any marked changes on naked eye examination and the cause of poisoning has to be inferred from the history and symptoms or from the result of analysis of the viscera.

This group consists of poisons which have specific action on the cerebrum, spinal cord, and peripheral nerves, the poisons being known as cerebral, spinal, and peripheral, respectively.

Cerebral: The poisons acting on the cerebrum may have a somniferous, inebriant or deliriant effect. The *somniferous* poisons include opioids; the *inebriant* ones include alcohols, anaesthetics, sedatives and hypnotics, fuels, and agrochemical compounds; while the *deliriant* ones include dhatura, belladonna, hyoscyamus, and cannabis indica.

Spinal: The poisons acting on the spinal cord include nux vomica and its alkaloids, and gelsemium.

*Peripheral:*The poisons acting on the peripheral nerves include curare, and conium.

Cardiac: These are poisons acting on the heart and include digitalis, oleander, aconite and nicotine.

Asphyxiants: These are poisons acting on the lungs and include irrespirable gases, such as carbon monoxide, carbon dioxide, sewer gas, and some war gases.

Miscellaneous: As the name suggests, poisons having widely different pharmacological actions are put together in this group. It includes analgesics and antipyretics; antihistaminics; tranquillisers; antidepressants; stimulants; hallucinogens; street drugs; and designer drugs.

Q. 36.5. Write short notes on: (1) routes of administration of poisons, (2) action of poisons.

Routes of Administration

Poisons may gain entry into the body by *enteral route,* e.g. by mouth or by rectum, to be absorbed across the enteral mucous membrane; *parenteral route,* e.g. by injection either intradermal, subcutaneous, intramuscular, intravenous, intra-arterial, intraperitoneal, intrathecal or into the bone marrow; by *inhalation* through the air passages; by *external application* on wounds, unbroken skin; *introduction into natural orifices,* such as rectum, vagina, urethra, nose, eyes, subsynovial, intracardiac, etc. and by *sublingual route.*

Action of Poisons

The action of poisons may be—(1) local, (2) remote, (3) local and remote combined, and (4) general.

The *local action* results from its direct action on the part and may cause corrosion as in the case of strong mineral acids; or congestion and inflammation as in the case of irritants. Such poisons generally produce gross naked eye changes seen at the postmortem examination.

The *remote action* is due to absorption of the poison into the system. It may be either specific or non-specific. The *specific action* depends on the effect of the poison on certain organs with which it has special affinity, e.g. opioids on the cerebral cortex; strychnine on the spinal cord; and digitalis on the heart muscle. Remote action may be localised to a definite organ, e.g. the liver during detoxication, or kidney during excretion. Certain poisons, such as corrosives, are capable of producing a remote *non-specific action,* such as shock, similar to that which often results from severe mechanical injury.

Certain poisons, e.g. oxalic acid, carbolic acid, produce both *local and remote actions.*

General action results when the absorbed poison evokes response from a wide variety of tissues beyond the limits of one or two systems, e.g. arsenic, mercury, lead, barbiturates, paraquat, etc.

Q. 36.6. Discuss the factors which modify the action of poisons.

These are: (1) dose, (2) form of poison, (3) method of administration, and (4) condition of the body.

Dose

As a general rule, small doses produce therapeutic action; large doses produce toxic effects. However, there are certain *exceptions* to this general rule:

1. Some individuals have an *idiosyncrasy* (inherent intolerance) towards certain drugs and foods resulting in intense symptoms. This is seen with drugs, such as morphine, cocaine, quinine, aspirin, and many others, and certain articles of food, e.g. mushrooms, eggs, milk, and shell-fish.
2. Some individuals are allergic towards certain drugs. *Allergy* means hypersensitivity acquired as a result of previous administration of the toxic agent or induced by the simultaneous presence of another poison. Penicillin is the most important modern example of acquired hypersensitivity. Many protective sera are other examples.
3. *Habit* diminishes the effects of certain poisons, since a *tolerance* toward them is gradually developed. Such tolerance is common in the case of alcohol, opioids, pethidine, and tobacco. It should not be confused with addiction.

4. Two poisons, as for example, alcohol and barbiturates in non-toxic doses, when administered simultaneously may cause toxic symptoms due to *synergism* which means that the final response is greater than the sum of their individual actions. The effect is called additive, if the final response is equal to the sum of their individual actions.
5. If a poison exerts an emetic effect, a large dose may induce violent vomiting and mitigate the evil effects of a poison. Occasionally, a *large dose acts differently* from a small dose of the same poison. As for example, a large dose of arsenic may produce death by shock while a small dose results in gastrointestinal irritation.
6. Some poisons, such as arsenic, mercury, lead, barbiturates, digitalis and carbon monoxide, are eliminated slowly and may accumulate in the body *(cumulative poisons)*. Their repeated administration even in small doses may result in *chronic poisoning*.

Form of Poison

Under this heading, the important factors to be considered are: (1) physical state, (2) chemical combination, and (3) mechanical combination.

1. ***Physical state:*** Gases and vapours act more rapidly than fluid poisons. Fluid poisons act more rapidly than solid ones, of which fine powders act more quickly than coarse ones. Synthetically coated pills soluble in the alkaline contents of the small intestine might have their action delayed for several hours.
2. ***Chemical combination:*** The toxic effects of substances may vary greatly from chemical combination. Some substances become inert, e.g. acids with alkalis; and strychnine with tannic acid. Some substances become poisonous, such as lead carbonate and copper arsenite which are insoluble in water but are rendered sufficiently soluble by the hydrochloric acid in the stomach, to make their poisonous effects felt. Some substances, such as alcohol and barbiturate, in non-toxic doses may prove toxic due to synergism.
3. ***Mechanical combination:*** The action of a poison is considerably altered when combined mechanically with inert substances. Alkaloids when taken with animal charcoal fail to act. Corrosive acids or concentrated alkalis, when sufficiently diluted with water, act as irritants.

Method of Administration

A poison acts most rapidly when inhaled in gaseous or vaporous form or when injected intravenously; next, when injected intramuscularly or subcutaneously; and least rapidly when swallowed. There is further slowing of action, if the substance ingested is partly soluble, or the stomach is full. There is still further slowing of action if the poison is applied to unbroken skin. Certain poisons act differently when they are introduced through different routes. Snake venom is highly toxic when injected but is harmless when ingested. Cocaine acts as a local anaesthetic when injected and as a deliriant and convulsant when ingested.

Condition of the Body

Under this head, the important factors to be considered are: (1) age, (2) state of health, and (3) sleep and intoxication.

1. ***Age:*** Poisons have greater effect at the two extremes of age.
2. ***State of health:*** Persons in poor health are more susceptible to poisons, e.g. a 30% concentration of carbon monoxide in blood may kill a person suffering from coronary heart disease. In certain diseases, the tolerance of the body to certain drugs is increased, e.g. hypnotics and opiates in mania or delirium tremens, and strychnine in paralysis.

3. ***Sleep and intoxication:*** The bodily functions are at low metabolic level during sleep and intoxication. The action of a poison is, therefore, delayed if a person goes to sleep after taking it or if a person is intoxicated when he takes a poison.

FATE OF POISONS IN THE BODY (TOXICOKINETICS)

Unless the poison is given in a small amount and in a liquid state, the greater part of it may be lost by vomiting or diarrhoea. Once it is absorbed, the body may deal with it in one of several ways. It may be excreted unchanged. Commonly, it will be partly or completely metabolised, or converted to another active compound prior to further metabolism *(biotransformation).* When not completely metabolised, it may be detected in the original form or in the form of intermediate products in the tissues (e.g. liver, bile) or the excreta (e.g. urine). Certain tissues, such as the epi-dermis, nails, hair, and bones, may retain inorganic poisons, such as arsenic, after it is eliminated from the rest of the body, and the bony skeleton may hold such poisons as arsenic, lead, and radioactive isotopes for long periods.

Q. 36.7. How will you diagnose a case of poisoning?

To diagnose poisoning, it is essential that one should be familiar with the outstanding symptoms and signs of poisoning in the living persons together with its effects as found in the examination of the dead.

Poisoning in the Living

The evidence of poisoning depends upon whether the poisoning is acute or chronic:

Acute poisoning: Symptoms suddenly appear soon after the suspected food, medicine or fluid has been taken, although in bacterial food poisoning, the symptoms may be delayed. The person, previously known to be in good health, is affected with a group of symptoms which do not conform to ordinary illness. Other persons who have taken similar food, medicine or fluid, are also affected similarly and simultaneously. The symptoms rapidly increase in severity and are followed by death or recovery. Poison can be detected in the ingested food, medicine, and fluid, or vomit, gastric lavage, blood, urine and stool of the victim.

Chronic poisoning: Symptoms develop insidiously and gradually. There is an exacerbation of symptoms after the suspected food, medicine or fluid is administered. There is remission or even complete disappearance of symptoms on the removal of the patient from his usual surroundings. Poison can be detected in the food, medicine or fluid which is being administered or in the vomit, urine or stool of the victim. While the main symptoms in chronic poisoning are usually malaise, and gradual deterioration of health, repeated attacks of undiagnosed gastrointestinal irritation should arouse suspicion of homicidal poisoning.

Poisoning in the Dead

The evidence of poisoning will depend on: (1) postmortem examination, (2) chemical analysis, (3) experiments on suitable animals, and (4) moral and circumstantial evidence. Poisons retard the action of putrefactive organisms to some extent. In a number of cases, therefore, the bodies are comparatively well preserved.

Postmortem examination: This should be carried out in the manner already described in the Chapter 5 on 'Medicolegal Autopsy'. The smell from the clothes and body, froth at nose and mouth, stains about the lips and chin, colour of skin and postmortem lividity, marks of injection, and condition of natural orifices may help to diagnose poisoning. The alimentary system should be examined very carefully since signs of corrosives and irritant poisons are likely to be found therein. These signs may manifest as hyperaemia, softening, ulceration, and perforation.

Chemical analysis: The most important proof of poisoning is the analytical detection of poison in the parenchyma of the organs of the body. The finding of poison in the food, medicine or fluid, alleged to have been taken, is corroborative. However, clinical and postmortem findings form a clinging evidence in cases where CA is negative.

Experiments on suitable animals: The suspected food, medicine or fluid, or the poison extracted from the viscera, can be fed to domestic animals, such as the dog and cat. These animals are affected by the poison in the same way as human beings. Such procedure is not acceptable in some countries. In India, Prevention of Cruelty to Animals Act enunciates the guidelines and punishment.

Moral and circumstantial evidence: Clues regarding the recent purchase of poison by the victim or accused, his behaviour, the conduct of those looking after the victim, suicide note, and history of quarrel or financial problems may also provide valuable information. The body may be disposed of clandestinely or hastily.

Q. 36.8. Mention the duties of a doctor when he examines a case of suspected poisoning.

In all cases of poisoning, the doctor must record the *preliminary particulars,* viz. name in full, age, sex, occupation, address, date and time, brought by whom, history, dying declaration necessary or not.

The doctor's first duty is to *treat* his patient. If the doctor in private practice is certain that his patient is suffering from suicidal or accidental poisoning, he is not bound to supply information of his own accord to the police or magistrate. However, if he is summoned by the investigating police officer or magistrate for such information, he should do so. In accidental poisoning, if there is any indication of danger to the general public, as for example, from food poisoning from a public eating house or contamination of public drinking water, the doctor *must notify* the public health authorities at once.

If the doctor is convinced that homicidal poisoning has occurred, he has a duty to protect society; he *must inform* the nearest police officer or magistrate (Sec. 44 CrPC). He should take every precaution to prevent the possibility of further administration of the poison to the patient.

In *every case* of suspected poisoning, the doctor must keep the records of the case in meticulous detail. He must collect and preserve properly and in separate containers stomach washings, and samples of vomit and urine passed in his presence only, and blood likely to contain poison, for transmission to the forensic science laboratory (FSL). Any suspicious article, such as—(1) utensils used for preparing the poison, (2) bottles or containers of solid or liquid medicine found at the scene, (3) food or drink lying near the patient, or (4) clothes or bed sheet soiled by vomit, urine or faeces, should be preserved for possible future examination. If the patient is serious, arrangement for taking a dying declaration should also be made. In the *event of death,* a death certificate should not be issued but the fact of death must be communicated to the nearest police officer for necessary investigation. Any opinion about the nature of poison can be given only after report from the forensic science laboratory.

The doctor in charge of a government or public hospital must report to police all cases of poisoning, either suicidal, homicidal or accidental, admitted to his institution.

Q. 36.9. Describe in detail the general principles of treatment of acute poisoning.

Q. 36.10. Write short notes on: (1) household emetics, (2) stomach tube, (3) chelating agents.

If the poison is known, specific treatment must be instituted. If not, treatment is given on general lines. The *main aim* of treatment is to help the patient to stay alive by attention to respiration and circulation while he is assisted to get rid of the poison by metabolism or excretion. While to some extent, the details will vary according to the portal of entry of the poison (inhalation, injection, contact or ingestion), the main objects include: (1) removal of unabsorbed poison from the body, (2) use of antidotes, (3) elimination of the absorbed poison, (4) treatment of general symptoms, and (5) maintenance of the patient's general condition.

Removal of Unabsorbed Poison from the Body

Depending upon the route of entry, the following principles should be kept in mind.

Inhaled poisons: If the poison, e.g. carbon monoxide, automobile exhaust or gas from a sewer has been inhaled, the patient should be removed to fresh air and artificial respiration commenced at once. The air passages should be kept free from mucous by postural drainage and aspiration.

Injected poisons: If the poison has been injected, a tight tourniquet should be applied proximal to the point of injection. It must be released every 10 minutes for 1 minute to prevent gangrene. The wound may be excised and poison removed by suction, and/or neutralised chemically. The common examples of injected poisons are hypnotics, insulin, snake bite, insect bite, etc.

Contact poisons: If the poison be spilled or sprayed on skin, eye or wound, or be inserted into vagina, rectum or urinary bladder, the best way to treat it is to wash it out with plain warm water and/or to neutralise it by a suitable antidote.

Ingested poisons: The object is to remove from the stomach as soon and as much of the poison as possible. For this purpose, (1) vomiting (emesis) may be induced, and/or the (2) stomach washed out (gastric lavage).

1. If the patient is conscious and cooperative, and **vomiting** is not contraindicated (corrosives, strychnine, petroleum distillates, coma, severe cardiac or respiratory diseases, and advanced pregnancy), it should be induced either by tickling the fauces or by the use of emetics.

   Household emetics, such as warm water, one tablespoonful of mustard powder (15 gm) or two tablespoonful of common salt in a tumblerful (200 ml) of tepid water, readily available in every household, may be used in an emergency. Ipecac 1–2 gm or ipecac syrup in a dose of 30 ml does act as an emetic in about 20–30 minutes. The dose may be repeated one time.

   Apomorphine, 6 mg by subcutaneous injection, followed by naloxone hydrochloride (Narcan) 5–10 mg i.m. or i.v., to counteract its narcotic effects, may be used: (1) it produces prompt vomiting within three to five minutes, (2) it facilitates gastric lavage by removing gastric contents which may obstruct the stomach tube, and (3) it produces reflux of upper intestinal contents (enteric coated tablets, etc.) into the stomach. When apomorphine is given by mouth, about twice the hypodermic dose is required and vomiting is not produced for half an hour.

2. **Gastric lavage** (stomach washing), if not contraindicated, may be life-saving, if undertaken within four to six hours after the ingestion of poison (Fig. 36.1).

It is *contraindicated* mainly in corrosive poisoning except carbolic acid for fear of rupture of the stomach. In other cases, it can be performed after taking necessary precautions. As for example, (1) in strychnine poisoning, convulsions should be controlled; (2) in kerosene or volatile poisons or in comatose conditions, airway should be sealed by cuffed intubation to avoid the high risk of aspiration into the air passages; and (3) in hypothermia, body temperature would need careful attention.

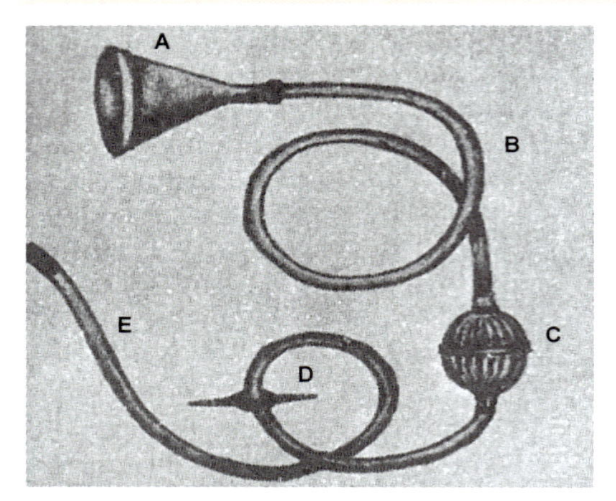

Fig. 36.1: Stomach tube. (A) A filter funnel is attached to the upper end of the rubber tube, (B); (C) Suction bulb; (D) Mouth gag with a central hole. The mouth gag covers the 50 cm mark from the lower end of the rubber tube (E) which is rounded and perforated

Procedure: The patient should be prone or semiprone on his side with hips higher than his head, as this will aid respiratory drainage and also prevent regurgitated material from entering the respiratory tract. The dentures, if any, must be removed. The airway must be clear and a mouth gag with a central hole is necessary especially in unconscious patients to prevent the rubber tube being bitten off by the teeth. In adults, for gastric lavage, the **stomach tube** (Fig. 36.2) is usually satisfactory. It is a flexible rubber tube (not stiff) about 12.7 mm in external diameter and about a metre and a half in length. A filter funnel is provided at the upper end. A suction bulb is also provided to suck out fluids when siphon action fails and to push air into the tube to force out any obstruction. The lower end is blunt and rounded to avoid any injury when it is being passed and is perforated by more than one opening on its sides to allow the administered fluid to enter the stomach easily. The distance between the lips and the cardiac end of the stomach is about 45 cm in the adult. Therefore, the tube is marked at a point about 50 cm from the lower end. In emergency, a soft rubber tube of suitable length to one end of which a funnel is attached forms an efficient stomach tube. The lower end of the tube should be lubricated with liquid paraffin, glycerine, milk or some other substance, and passed through the hole in the middle of the mouth gag, over the tongue (depressing it, if necessary), and down the oesophagus. At about the mark, the tip of the tube should be lying in the stomach in the adult, and one **must make sure of this** by any one of **the following tests:** If little air is forced down the tube, one should be able to hear bubbling sounds through the stethoscope applied over the stomach. If the tube has entered the trachea, a hissing noise is heard at the funnel end; besides, if the patient is not unconscious, reflex coughing takes place and bubbles of air will come out of the funnel-end dipped in water.

Fig. 36.2: Procedure of stomach-wash in a child. The child is wrapped in a blanket to avoid struggling. The stomach contents are removed by means of a French rubber catheter to which a syringe is attached

After testing, about quarter litre of plain warm water (35°C) is run into the funnel, which is held above the level of the patient's mouth. The fluid enters the stomach by gravity. The funnel is then lowered, below the level of the patient's stomach, over a receptacle, to allow the gastric contents to siphon off. Subsequent washings are done with half litre of fluid. Using too much fluid for the first wash is likely to sweep the poison onwards into the duodenum. The first washing, which is usually done with warm water, should be preserved for chemical analysis. The process is then repeated either with warm water or other fluid preferably containing an appropriate antidote until the returning fluid is of the same colour and character as the lavage fluid. Stomach washing is based on Syphon mechanism.

When the poison is thus removed, some of the antidote or other suitable solution may be left in the stomach to deal with the effects and after-effects of whatever small quantities may have escaped lavage or are later excreted in the stomach. The useful solutions for this purpose are: magnesium sulphate or sodium sulphate to ensure purgation of any poison that has passed the intestine; sodium bicarbonate to counteract the irritation of the stomach in aspirin poisoning and to accelerate salicylate excretion; activated charcoal to adsorb alkaloids; and liquid paraffin as a demulcent fluid.

Before the stomach tube is withdrawn, it should be **pinched** to prevent aspiration of material into the lungs.

In children, a Ryle's tube or a number 8 to 12 French rubber catheter is usually satisfactory. About 25 cm length is necessary to reach the stomach. The catheter is passed through the nose or the mouth into the stomach with the usual precautions and the stomach wash done using a 50 ml glass syringe. Many centres do not do stomach wash nowadays as a matter of routine. It is more or less replaced by administration of activated charcoal.

Use of Antidotes

Antidotes are remedies which counteract or neutralise the effect of poisons without causing appreciable harm to the body. They need to be used because: (a) the poison may not have been completely removed by emesis or gastric lavage or these procedures are contraindicated, (b) the poison is already absorbed, or (c) the poison has been administered by route other than ingestion. They can be classified into four groups, in accordance with their mode of action, namely: (1) mechanical or physical, (2) chemical, (3) physiological or pharmacological, and (4) universal.

Mechanical or physical antidotes: These are substances which impede the absorption of poisons by their presence. These are few in number, such as demulcents, bulky food, and activated charcoal. Demulcents are substances, such as fats, oils, milk, egg albumin, etc., which prevent the absorption of the poison by forming a coating on the mucous membrane of the stomach. They act in this manner both in corrosive and irritant poisoning. Fats, oils, and milk, however, should not be used for fat-soluble poisons, e.g. phosphorus, organophosphates, DDT, etc. Bulky food, such as banana, acts as a mechanical antidote to glass by imprisoning its particles and thus preventing its action. Activated charcoal is specially useful in adsorbing alkaloidal poisons, such as strychnine, and to a lesser degree, mineral poisons. It is given in a dose of 30–60 gm in children and 60–100 gm in adults in five times the quantity of water. The correct dose of activated charcoal is about 5 to 10 times the amount of drug ingested.

Chemical antidotes: These are substances which act either by direct chemical action or by oxidising the poison to form a non-toxic or an insoluble compound. Some of the examples are as follows:

Dilute acetic acid or vinegar neutralises alkalis by direct chemical action. Canned fruit juice is an useful alternative for this purpose. Dilute alkalis, e.g. milk of magnesia, will neutralise acids; however, bicarbonates should not be used owing to the risk of rupture of stomach from the liberated carbon dioxide. Tannin (strong tea) produces insoluble compounds with most alkaloids, glucosides and metals.

Potassium permanganate is an oxidising agent effective against all oxidisable poisons, such as most of the alkaloids, amidopyrin, antipyrine, barbiturates, phosphorus, cyanides, etc. The usual strength of the solution is 1:1,000 approximately (1 gm in a litre) and even 100–150 ml of this solution can be left in the stomach without any harm. A weak solution of iodine, 15 drops of the tincture to a tumblerful (200 ml) of water, may be helpful in the absence of permanganate.

Physiological or pharmacological antidotes: These agents produce effects which are opposite to that of the poison. Examples of physiological antagonists are: atropine for pilocarpine, diazepam for strychnine, naloxone for morphine, atropine and oximes for organophosphorus compounds, N-acetyl cysteine for acetaminophen, and mazicon for benzodiazepins. However, the *antagonism* is usually not complete and the remedy may itself produce most undesirable side effects.

Certain **chelating agents** are widely used as specific antidotes against some heavy metals. These are substances which produce a firm non-ionized cyclic complex (chelate) with cations. Such compounds can form stable, soluble, non-toxic complexes with calcium and certain heavy metals. The important amongst them are BAL, (British anti-Lewisite or 2,3-Dimercapto propanol) EDTA (ethylenediaminetetraacetate) and versenate (calciumdiethyltetraacetate) for arsenic; EDTA and versenate for mercury and lead; N-penicillamine for mercury, lead and copper; and desferrioxamine-B (DFM) for iron.

BAL (British anti-Lewisite), also called dimercaprol is used in the treatment of certain types of heavy metal poisoning. It is given deep intramuscularly as a 10 per cent solution in arachis oil with benzyl benzoate. In severe poisoning, a dose of 3 mg/kg is administered at 4 hourly intervals for the first 2 days, at 6 hourly intervals during the third day, and at 12 hourly intervals thereafter for about 10 days. BAL is contraindicated, if the liver is extensively damaged.

EDTA is a chelating agent and is effective in lead, mercury, and copper poisoning. The usual adult dose is 1 gram twice daily for periods up to 5 days given by slow intravenous infusion in isotonic glucose saline. After an interval of 2 days, this course of treatment may be repeated. EDTA has been shown to be superior to BAL in some respects for the treatment of poisoning by arsenic and mercury. It is contraindicated in renal damage.

Penicillamine (cuprimine) is a degradation product of penicillin and has the advantage that it can be given orally, continually, and that it is much less toxic than EDTA. It is the treatment of choice in copper, lead and mercury poisoning. A dose of 30 mg/kg body weight up to a total of 2 grams per day in four divided doses given orally is satisfactory. It is specially useful in hepatolenticular degeneration (Wilson's disease) which is caused by a disorder of copper metabolism.

Desferrioxamine chelates iron. It is chiefly valuable in the treatment of acute iron poisoning. In certain chronic diseases, such as haemochromatosis characterised by excessive retention of iron in the tissues, desferrioxamine is useful in accelerating the removal of iron from the body.

Universal antidote: It is an antidote that is used in those cases where the nature of the ingested poisons is unknown or where it is suspected that a combination of two or more poisons has been taken. It consists of a mixture of readily available substances, as follows:

Constituents	*Quantity*	*Purpose*
1. Powdered charcoal (burnt toast)	2 parts	Adsorbs alkaloids
2. Magnesium oxide (milk of magnesia)	1 part	Neutralises acids
3. Tannic acid (strong tea)	1 pari	Precipitates alkaloids, certain glucosides and many metals

The mixture is administered in a dose of a tablespoonful stirred up in a tumblerful (200 ml) of water, and may be repeated once or twice. Even when given soon after the ingestion of poison, *it is not very effective.* Though it is called universal antidote, it is not a Panacea in all cases. Infact, in many institutions, this is replaced by activated charcoal administration. However, its immediate household or hospital use can not be written off.

Elimination of the Absorbed Poison

This may be achieved by accelerating its *excretion* especially in the urine. Ample amounts of fluid should be administered to maintain adequate diuresis. Salicylates and phenobarbitone can be easily excreted in alkaline urine; amphetamines and quinine can be easily excreted in acid urine. Elimination by *catharsis* (magnesium citrate or sulphate, sorbitol) when not contra-indicated may be encouraged.

Peritoneal dialysis has been used for salicylate poisoning in children and may have a place in those centres not yet possessing artificial kidney. *Haemodialysis* has been employed for removing barbiturates, boric acid, glutethimide, methyl alcohol, salicylates and thiocyanates from the blood. *Haemperfusion* is superior to haemodialysis for removal of lipid-soluble drugs. *Exchange transfusion* is only feasible with small children and has been applied to poisonings by salicylates, barbiturates, iron salts, carbon monoxide, etc. All toxic substances, including non-dialysable ones, are removed by this technique.

A new alternative to lavage, dialysis, and haemoperfusion is **whole bowel irrigation.** The technique is promising; however, the patient needs to be carefully monitored throughout the procedure.

Treatment of General Symptoms

The treatment of symptoms should be applied as indications arise. Morphine should be given for pain, oxygen or artificial respiration for respiratory failure, cardiac stimulants for failing circulation, and an anaesthetic, barbiturates, or diazepam for convulsions. Saline infusion may be useful to counteract dehydration as well as to enhance diuresis to excrete toxic substances. The addition of sodium bicarbonate to the infusion may be of value when the alkali reserve is diminished. Administration of glucose will combat depletion of liver glycogen, and the restoration of potassium or sodium balance may be necessary.

Maintenance of the Patient's General Condition

The patient should be kept warm and comfortable. Once the struggle to preserve life has been won, one of the main dangers to the patient is the subsequent development of upper respiratory tract infection. This is a special hazard in elderly people, in those who were unconscious for an hour or more, in those who had had a respiratory infection before poisoning, and in those who inhaled a very small amount of vomitus. To avoid this risk, prophylactic administration of antibiotics to all cases is desirable. The importance of good nursing care (especially for the unconscious patient) and physiotherapy cannot be overemphasised.

Any patient known to have or suspected of having attempted suicide should not be allowed to leave the hospital without being interviewed by a psychiatrist who can institute further necessary supportive psychotherapy.

Q. 36.11. Describe the salient features of the Scandinavian method for treatment of poisoning cases.

This is a method of intensive supportive therapy. The regimen consists of: (1) assessment of the patient, (2) emergency measures, and (3) general care.

Assessment of the Patient

Clinical examination is made to assess the disturbance in vital functions, e.g. central nervous system, respiratory system, cardiovascular system, and body temperature, and also to detect any coincident disease which may influence the treatmeni given.

Central nervous system: Impairment of the level of consciousness is the most constant feature of hypnotic, sedative and psychotropic drug poisoning. Depending on the response of the stimulus, the patient's state of consciousness is classified into four grades:

Grade 1: Drowsy but responding to vocal commands.

Grade 2: Unconscious but responding to minimally painful stimuli.

Grade 3: Unconscious but responding only to maximum painful stimuli, e.g. rubbing the patient's sternum with the knuckles of the clenched fist.

Grade 4: Unconscious and not responding to painful stimuli.

Respiratory system: Once a clear airway is established, the adequacy of ventilation is determined by arterial puncture and measurement of blood pH, pCO_2, pO_2 and standard bicarbonate or by Wright's spirometer which signifies the presence of respiratory impairment, if the minute volume is less than four litres. If arterial blood gas analysis is not possible at short notice, the pCO_2 is measured by the rebreathing method.

Cardiovascular system: Cardiovascular function is responsible for maintaining blood pressure and peripheral circulation/tissue perfusion. A systolic blood pressure less than 90 mm Hg in persons above 50 years and less than 80 mm Hg in young persons is indicative of shock. Tissue perfusion is best assessed by measuring the urinary output.

Body temperature: Body temperature is monitored by using a low reading rectal thermometer graduated from 0°–50°C. A rectal temperature below 36°C is indicative of significant hypothermia, and it would contribute to shock, acidaemia and hypoxia.

Emergency measures: This includes management of respiratory failure, cardiac failure and prevention of further absorption of poison, on usual lines.

General care: This includes management of hypothermia, correction of water and electrolyte imbalance, treatment of infection and general nursing care, on usual lines.

It is claimed that the intensive supportive therapy described here reduces the mortality rate to 2%. However, the techniques involved in the therapy require facilities which are generally difficult to be obtained in a majority of places where poisoned patients are initially admitted for treatment.

Q. 36.12. Describe Glasgow Coma Scale: (a) The toxicity rating, (b) minimum lethal dose, (c) usual fatal dose, (d) toxicokineties, (e) poison information centre.

Toxicity rating of a poison is decided based upon the quantity of the dose required to cause fatality. If the dose is less the toxicity is more. The grading in order of severity to least severity is:

a. Super toxic = 6 → usual fatal dose is below 5 mg/kg body weight
b. Extremely toxic = 5 → usual fatal dose range is 5 mg to 50 mg/kg body weight
c. Very toxic = 4 → 51 to 500 mg/kg body weight
d. Moderately toxic = 3 → 501 mg/kg to 5 g/kg
e. Slightly toxic: 2 → 5.1 – 15 g/kg
f. Practically non-toxic – 1 → more than 15 g/kg.

Minimum lethal dose is the minimum dose level which is fatal to 50% of animal that are administered that dose (LD 50).

Usual fatal dose is derived from animal experimental data and statistics of human poisoning. The higher the toxicity rating, the greater is its (toxicity) potency.

Toxicokinetics means the various changes the poison undergoes upon entering the

system before it courses in its process of metabolism/catabolism, we shall be hurveldy.
Poison information centre—Poison.

GLASGOW COMA SCALE

Introduction

- A neurological *scale* which aims to give a reliable, objective way of recording the conscious state of a person for initial as well as continuing assessment.
- A patient is assessed against the criteria of the scale.
- The resulting points give the **Glasgow Coma Score (GCS)**.
- Initially used to assess level of consciousness after head injury.
- The scale was published in 1974 by Graham Teasdale and Bryan J. Jennett, professors of neurosurgery at the University of Glasgow.
- The scale comprises three tests: eye, verbal and motor responses.
- The three values separately as well as their sum are considered.
- The lowest possible GCS (the sum) is 3 (deep coma or death).
- The highest is 15 (fully awake person).

Best Eye Response

There are 4 grades starting with the most severe:

1. No eye opening.
2. Eye opening in response to pain. (Patient responds to pressure on the patient's fingernail bed; if this does not elicit a response, supraorbital and sternal pressure or rub may be used).
3. Eye opening to speech. (Not to be confused with an awaking of a sleeping person; such patients receive a score of 4, not 3.)
4. Eyes opening spontaneously.

Best Verbal Response (V)

There are 5 grades starting with the most severe:

1. No verbal response.
2. Incomprehensible sounds. (Moaning but no words).
3. Inappropriate words. (Random or exclamatory articulated speech, but no conversational exchange).
4. Confused. (The patient responds to questions coherently but there is some disorientation and confusion).
5. Oriented. (Patient responds coherently and appropriately to questions such as the patient's name and age, where they are and why, the year, month, etc.)

Best Motor Response (M)

There are 6 grades starting with the most severe:

1. No motor response.
2. Extension to pain (decerebrate response: adduction, internal rotation of shoulder, pronation of forearm).
3. Flexion in response to pain (decorticate response).
4. Withdraws from pain (pulls part of body away when pinched; normal flexion).
5. Localizes to pain. (Purposeful movements towards changing painful stimuli; e.g. hand crosses midline and gets above clavicle when supraorbital pressure applied).
6. Obeys commands. (The patient does simple things as asked).

Interpretation

- Generally, comas are classified as:
- Severe, with GCS ≤8
- Moderate, GCS 9–12
- Minor, GCS e ≥13

The GCS has limited applicability to children, especially below the age of 36 months.

The verbal performance of even a healthy child would be expected to be poor consequently the paediatric Glasgow Coma Scale, a separate yet closely related scale, was developed for assessing younger children.

It is claimed that the intensive supportive therapy described here reduces the mortality rate to 2 per cent. However, the techniques involved in the therapy require facilities which are generally difficult to be obtained in a majority of places where poisoned patients are initially admitted for treatment.

37 Toxicological Evidence

Q. 37.1. Write an essay on 'toxicological evidence'.

In the present era, the advances of synthetic chemistry and the fast changing conditions of living have placed an ever increasing number of highly poisonous substances within the reach of modern man. More people take (toxic) chemicals and medications now than ever before. Such substances play a primary or secondary, direct or indirect, role in bringing about unnatural death. Under such circumstances, a medical practitioner is more likely to miss a case of poisoning, especially of a homicidal nature, unless he is constantly aware of its possibility. In addition, chemical analysis has become so complex that it needs to be handled only by competent analysts having proper facilities, working with all possible assistance from the medical practitioner and pathologists as regards clinical symptomatology and autopsy findings.

To appreciate the role and responsibilities of the various concerned agencies in proper perspective, this topic is discussed under the following headings: (1) toxicological evidence—forensic aspects, (2) toxicological evidence—analytical aspects, and (3) toxicological evidence—interpretation.

FORENSIC ASPECTS

A poison is commonly defined as a substance which, when administered, is capable of acting deleteriously on the body. There is really no delineation between a medicine and a poison because a medicine in a toxic dose is a poison and a poison in a small dose may be a medicine. In law, the real difference between a medicine and a poison is the intent with which it is given and its intrinsic capacity to do the bodily harm. If the substance is given with the intention to provide relief from some symptoms or to save life, it is a medicine but if it is given with the intention to cause bodily/mental harm, it is a poison. As for example, chloral hydrate, in a dose of 300 mg when used as a hypnotic, is a medicine but when used in a higher dose, say 3 gm, as knock out drops to render a victim of robbery or rape helpless, it is a poison. Similarly when a barbiturate is given in a therapeutic dose for the relief of insomnia, it is a medicine; even if it is given in a higher dose for the control of convulsions, it is still a medicine. However, such a high dose if given to a normal healthy person would cause coma and possibly death and then it is a poison.

Though generally, the dose determines the toxicity, it must be remembered that certain factors modify the action of a substance introduced in the body. An individual may be adversely affected by a nontoxic dose of a given substance. For example, individuals having idiosyncrasy, allergy, or suffering from some cardiac or debilitating disease are more adversely affected by a nontoxic dose than a person in good health. Conversely, a person habituated or addicted to a certain drug can tolerate much larger doses of that drug without apparent harm as compared to a normal healthy person.

Proof that poisoning has occurred is based mainly on the following factors, viz: (1) signs and symptoms suggesting exposure to a toxic substance, (2) autopsy findings, (3) evidence of pathologic lesions associated with a particular toxic substance, and (4) conclusive evidence of absorption of a toxic substance in the tissues and body fluids of the deceased as determined by chemical analysis.

Symptoms and Signs

While it is not possible to catalogue all the possible toxic substances within the reach of modern man, an attempt has been made in the ensuing pages to cover the main diagnostic signs, symptoms, and other relevant details of a number of common poisons. For this purpose, the material has been organized in the following manner:

A table of common household poisons is given. A glance at the data will show what poison the product probably contains. This is followed by a detailed discussion of a number of common poisons, the less common ones being discussed in small types. Thereafter, an alphabetical poison table has been provided, containing almost all common poisons encountered anywhere. The table shows at a glance the toxicological characteristics of the various poisons and provides a convenient summary and an integrated picture of their differing aspects.

Autopsy Findings

At autopsy, the medical officer suspects the presence of poison: (1) when he notes any peculiar smell on opening the body (substances which may be detectable by their smell, unless masked by putrefactive odour, are: alcohol, camphor, carbolic acid, conium, cyanide, kerosene, nicotine, opium, organophosphorus compounds, paraldehyde, petroleum products, phosphorus, and oil of wintergreen, etc.), (2) when there is some other evidence, such as (a) presence of foreign material in the form of powder, capsules, tablets, or leaves in the stomach, (b) irritation, ulceration or discolouration of the mucous membrane of the stomach, (c) laryngeal oedema—common in deaths from alcohol and barbiturates, (d) acute lung congestion and oedema provided heart disease and intracranial lesions could be excluded, (e) acute swelling of the brain with or without a pressure cone, (f) markedly distended urinary bladder, and (g) intravascular sickling, (3) from negative evidence, such as no trauma or no signs of disease in any organ to account for the cause of death, or (4) when the body is decomposed.

Evidence of Pathological Lesion

Sometimes, in a case of fatal poisoning, no poison may be found on chemical analysis especially when a large time interval between time of ingestion and death is involved. However, in many of these cases, during the period of survival, pathological changes in the organs would have occurred which are demonstrable by gross and/or microscopic examination. Although such changes may not be specific for that particular poison it is still possible to attribute death to such a substance on circumstantial evidence, e.g. carbon tetrachloride poisoning resulting in death after about a week or 10 days after exposure. After such interval, carbon tetrachloride would not be detected by chemical analysis. However, it is a hepatotoxic and nephrotoxic agent. When such changes are observed and there is a history of exposure, it is possible to implicate carbon tetrachloride as a cause of death, although these changes are not specific for this poison. Similarly, in thallium poisoning, diagnostic changes may be found in hair roots.

ANALYTICAL ASPECTS

Analytical toxicology, an important branch of forensic science, deals with the detection and estimation of a variety of poisons in biological and other materials in low concentration.

The most important proof that poisoning has occurred depends on evidence of absorption of a toxic substance in the body. The most direct evidence of such absorption is the detection of a toxic substance followed by its quantitative estimation in tissues obtained at autopsy or occasionally in blood, urine, and gastric material obtained from a living patient.

The exception to the general rule requiring evidence of absorption of a toxic agent relates to cases involving ingestion of corrosive mineral acids and alkalis, e.g. concentrated sulphuric acid and sodium hydroxide which are generally identifiable in the gastrointestinal contents.

The common poisons met with in India are insecticides, pesticides and the poisonous plants, such as dhatura, aconite, strychnos nux vomica, opium, oleander, etc., which grow wild and may be collected without suspicion on account of their medicinal use. Sedatives, tranquillisers and other synthetic drugs are commonly misused in the West. In India, such misuse is confined to bigger cities only.

Poisoning as a possible cause of death is usually indicated by scene investigation (prescriptions, medications, containers, etc.), history of the case, autopsy findings, by gross or microscopic pathologic findings or absence thereof. Analysis is greatly facilitated when such information is forthcoming.

Where a specific substance is suspected as the causative agent, direct analysis for this substance may initially be made. This will either confirm the suspicion or rule out the substance as a factor concerned with death. As a rule, general systematic toxicological analysis is undertaken, even when a particular poison is suspected.

It is beyond the scope of this chapter to present details of the various analytical procedures. A reference may be made to standard textbooks on analytical toxicology for this purpose.

Other Examinations

In addition to chemical analysis, other examinations, such as histopathological, indirect biochemical, biological/pharmacological, serological, etc., become occasionally necessary in forensic toxicology. Blood is useful for all these examinations except histopathological.

Embalming and Toxicological Analysis

In dealing with cases of suspected poisoning, autopsy should be performed prior to embalming. The embalming process (though not prevalent in India) interferes with both the qualitative identification of the poison and its quantitation, as shown by the following examples:

1. Cyanide reacts chemically with formalin in the embalming fluid so that it is no longer identifiable as such.
2. Most embalming fluids contain methyl or ethyl alcohol or both so that analyses for these substances are rendered meaningless. So, it is extremely difficult, if not impossible, to detect and identify most volatile poisons in an embalmed body.
3. Fixation of the tissues by formalin makes them more resistant to the action of organic solvents used for extraction of non-volatile organic compounds, e.g. most drugs. Therefore, no or low recoveries of such substances will result.

In the case of already embalmed disinterred bodies, it is desirable to furnish the toxicologist a sample of embalming fluid, used for burial, as control, should any positive chemical findings be obtained. Likewise, tissues from those parts of the body least affected (e.g. buttock muscle, centre of liver, vitreous) by embalming fluid should be retained for analysis. In India also bodies are sometimes not embalmed and consequently such problems are not commonly encountered.

Putrefaction and Toxicological Analysis

Putrefaction complicates the problems of toxicological analysis and leads to difficulties in interpretation of results, as shown by the following examples:

1. Some substances that might be present in the tissues may undergo chemical changes and may no longer be identifiable, e.g. nitrite. In the case of hydrolytic chemical changes, the breakdown product instead of/in addition to the original poison may be detected, as in the case of aconite, parathion, carbaryl, etc.
2. Putrefaction of normal tissue components may produce substances which yield chemical reactions similar to those obtained from basic toxic compounds, such as, neurine, beta-phenylethyl amine, tyramine and other amines. Though these can create considerable interference problems, methods to overcome the same are available.
3. Volatile substances may be lost as a result of putrefaction.
4. Ethyl alcohol may be produced from normal tissue components in *advanced putrefaction.*

Despite these limitations, most toxic substances are still identifiable, and these include amongst others: carbon monoxide, cyanide, fluoride, barbiturates, organophosphorus compounds, endrine, hyoscine, strychnine, yellow oleander, nicotine, etc., and inorganic poisons, such as arsenic, antimony, mercury, lead, thallium, etc.

INTERPRETATION

The report of the chemical analyst usually includes detection of the poison. In the case of some poisons, like methyl alcohol, ethyl alcohol, cyanide and drugs, the report also includes their concentration/tissue level. The poison levels in the tissue, in general, vary a lot from one fatal case to another. The report, therefore, also includes a toxicological interpretation of the quantitative data obtained from the poison case in question, i.e. whether or not the observed tissue level of the poison detected is of the same order as that found in other fatal cases involving that poison. For this purpose, the data bank at the institution or that from the literature is utilised. This is a proper modern approach than that of working out *the ingested fatal dose.* The latter *cannot be evaluated with any certainty* and, therefore, has been given up in modern toxicological practice. However, the analyst should maintain a detailed record of his work on quantitation, etc., including the substances for which negative results were obtained. The record should also include all weights and volumes of samples taken up for analysis, the dates of work, when started and when completed, and the test results.

Proper interpretation of an analytical result also requires that the analyst is knowledgeable about the pharmacokinetics of the poison called as toxicokinetics and the technique of reporting, as shown below:

1. In the absence of history or any other clue of poisoning, such as due to insulin, the general scheme of chemical analysis would give negative results.
2. Despite history of exposure to a toxic substance, no positive analytical finding may be obtained. There are several reasons for this apparently contradictory result: (a) The poison may have been vomited out, excreted, neutralised, metabolised, detoxified, or the poison is so obscure or present in such small quantity that it cannot be detected in the

general scheme of analysis and by the available methods of chemical analysis: A case has been recorded where succinylcholine was used as an injection with homicidal intent. It is metabolised to succinic acid and choline, which are normal constituent of the body tissues. Thus, chemical detection of the drug in the body tissues is difficult save in exceptional circumstances. (b) Less and less amount of poison would remain with higher time gap between ingestion and death, and in some instances, a long survival period may leave the poison residues beyond the detection limit. (c) The absorbed poison is not evenly distributed in various organs and this relative distribution varies substantially with different poisons. (d) The distribution of poison may also vary with its mode of administration. As for example, blood levels may be higher than liver levels when the poison is administered by the intravenous route. The reverse generally applies when the poison is administered orally. (e) The analyst has to look for all possible types of poisons in whatever little amount of specimen he has received. There are chances of missing the detection of poison, when too little of the specimen is submitted for analysis. Sometimes, the relevant tissues and/or the controls may not have been submitted. As for example, in snake bite poisoning, in the absence of tissue round the site of bite for immunological examination, the general scheme of chemical analysis would fail to provide any proof of poisoning. Any unusual delay in submission and analysis especially in cases of in vitro labile compounds may also fail to provide proof of poisoning. (f) Detection of highly potent toxic substance (very low LD) is quite difficult. (g) The sample may not have been properly preserved. (h) Problems posed by putrefaction are already outlined. (i) If the victim has been treated, the medication itself may alter the poisonous substance and make its detection difficult or even impossible. (j) For reasons not clear, in deaths due to intravenous narcotism, sometimes even when the victim was found with the needle with syringe attached still in the vein, no narcotic is detected. Considering such diverse limiting factors, non-detection of poison in postmortem tissues need not necessarily be interpreted as "no poison" having been involved.

3. The isolated material may not be identical due to alteration by biochemical processes. Common examples are the findings of phenobarbitone when primidone has been taken and the finding of oxazepam when diazepam has been taken, or morphine when heroin is involved. There could be many instances when the original poison and the metabolite or even the latter alone would be detectable.

The most commonly used narcotic among the addict population is heroin which is diacetyl morphine. The metabolic processes degrade the compound to morphine which is detected from the liver, bile and urine. If at autopsy, a fresh needle puncture mark is found and the presence of heroin can be demonstrated at this site, it would be justifiable to say that morphine in the tissue was derived from the usage of heroin.

Codeine is methyl morphine. The metabolic processes degrade only a small part of the absorbed codeine to morphine. Therefore, finding of high concentration of codeine with small amounts of morphine would suggest that the origin of the latter was probably codeine. The finding of high concentration of morphine and only small amount of codeine, on the other hand, would indicate that the former was due to the use of either morphine or heroin along with codeine, usually also with other prominent opium alkaloids, as in street samples of (crude) heroin.

A finding of quinine, caffeine, or methaqualone which are commonly used as active adulterants in street samples of heroin, in suspected narcotic deaths of persons having relatively fresh as also old needle marks may suggest the possibility of heroin addiction even though no narcotic may be demonstrable in the postmortem tissue or fluids.

4. The reaction to a therapeutic dose of a substance may range from slight effect to signs of over-dosage. Therefore, the so-called lethal dose cannot be fixed in any rigid sense. As such, the giving of an ordinarily fatal dose may result in a significant survival rate whereas high, yet ordinarily non-lethal doses sometimes result in death. Such results are due to personal variation in response of each individual. Age, weight, sex, state of health, route of administration, and the association of other synergic substances (all these) play an important part. The lethal dose is the dose that kills in the case in question. It may be remarkably small in those who are seriously ill or who show idiosyncrasy or allergy to the poison. Such a dose may hardly have any effect on those who are habituated or addicted to the particular substance. What is usually implied by the term "minimum lethal dose" is the smallest dose that has been recorded as fatal to a healthy person of that age group. It is roughly around ten times the maximum pharmaceutical dose, in the case of drugs. In the interpretation of toxicological data, the pharmacologically evaluated LD^{50} is a good guide to go by.
5. From the analytical report of the poison concentration in a given body tissue/fluid, it is possible to arrive at a proper interpretation by comparing the observed concentration(s) with those recorded in fatal poisoning cases involving the poison in question. The earlier toxicological practice to arrive at the conclusion about the lethal dose on the basis of the poison level in postmortem tissue/fluid such as liver or blood not being rational or precise is no longer held strictly valid in modern toxicological practice. Looking to the complexities involved, such an exercise has to be done with utmost caution.
6. Every quantitative measurement has a certain degree of uncertainty and as a result the figure quoted without a probable error can be misleading. The reasonable range of probable error would be around 2 standard deviations. It is, however, important that the recipient of the result understands as near as possible what the result signifies.
7. Normal concentrations (values) are averages of many observations. Therefore, when a substance that is normally not present in the body is isolated, it indicates exposure to this substance. However, when a substance that is normally present is isolated it becomes necessary to consider the order of magnitude before interpreting the result as exposure to the toxic levels of this substance. Generally, the normal levels would be orders of magnitude (1 order of magnitude lower means $10^{-1} = 1/10$ times or one-tenth) lower than observed fatal levels, say, in the case of insecticidal poisoning, vis-a-vis the environmental pollution levels in normal samples. The normal levels are ordinarily, i.e. under similar analytical conditions and using the usual analytical methodology, not detectable, i.e. below the detection limits under the ordinary course of analysis. Determination of normal levels requires much higher sensitive methodology.

Likewise, the average arsenic content of hair is about 1/2 ppm (part per million) but the range of normal values may be up to 4 ppm. Therefore, while an analytical result of 3 ppm may look like over-exposure when compared with the normal average, such a conclusion should not be hastily arrived at without considering the statistical significance of the normal data, the extreme observed values and the co-efficient of variation (CV = 100 × standard deviation divided by the mean or average value, expressed as a percentage). It should also be remembered that arsenic is concentrated in hair and nails. A course of ordinary dose of arsenic over an extended period could lead to a concentration in hair of over 70 ppm, as reported by the Royal Commission on Arsenical Poisoning, in therapy of dermatological cases, while the concentration in other tissues would be comparatively low.

It is the responsibility of the medical officer to determine the cause of death and time since death. The toxicologist as a result of his analysis provides the evidence that a potentially toxic substance was taken and also indicates its residual level in the post-mortem tissue/fluid, and may in certain cases be able to give a good guess of the dosage taken. If the observed poison level is in the range of a toxic or lethal level and if all other clinical and pathologic findings fit then it can be said that poisoning is the cause of death. It is generally possible to give a rough estimate of the likely survival time after exposure to fatal amounts of various materials.

38

Common Household Poisons

Q. 38.1. Give a brief outline of common household poisons.

The poisons in daily use may be conveniently dealt with in three groups, viz. domestic household poisons, medicinal household poisons, and garden poisons, as per the following table:

DOMESTIC HOUSEHOLD POISONS	
Preparation	*Toxic components*
1. **Babies and children:**	
a. Baby powder	Boric acid
b. Crayons (chalk)	Coloured with copper, arsenic, lead compounds
c. Crayon (wax)	Para-nitroaniline, azo dyes
d. Fireworks	Arsenic, antimony, lead, thiocyanate, phosphorus
e. Toys (paints)	Lead, chromium, copper, etc.
2. **Cosmetics:**	
a. Cuticle remover	Potassium hydroxide, trisodium phosphate
b. Depilatories arsenic	Barium sulphide, thallium
c. Hair wave	Thioglycolate salts, bromates
d. Nail polish removers	Acetone, ethylacetate
e. Sun tan lotions	Denatured alcohol, methyl salicylate
3. **Kitchen:**	
a. Baking powder	Tartaric acid (mild irritant)
b. Baking soda	Sodium bicarbonate (causes alkalosis in doses over 5 gm/kg)
c. Dish washing compounds (machine)	Sodium polyphosphates, sodium carbonate
d. Domestic fuel	Kerosene
e. Domestic gas	LPG (Accumulated gas explodes with air when flame/spark is provided)
f. Fire extinguishing fluids	Carbon tetrachloride, methyl bromide
g. Matches	Antimony, phosphorus sesquisulphide, potassium chlorate
4. **Rat poisons:**	
a. Rat paste	Potassium/zinc/aluminium phosphide, barium carbonate, thallium acetate
b. Rodine (brown bran paste)	Yellow phosphorus
c. Warfarin	It is a 4-hydroxy coumarin
5. **Sanitary:**	
a. Deodorants	Formaldehyde, naphthalene
b. Drain cleaners	Sodium hydroxide
c. Lysol	Phenol
6. **Miscellaneous:**	
a. Anti-rust products	Ammonium sulphide, naphtha, oxalic acid
b. Cleaning solvents (inflammable)	Petroleum hydrocarbons
c. Cleaning solvents (non-inflammable)	Carbon tetrachloride, trichlor-ethylene
d. Dentifrices, mouth-washes	Hydrogen peroxide
e. Fluorescent lamps	Beryllium
f. Furniture polish	Turpentine, denatured spirit
g. Ink remover	Sodium hypochlorite (5%), oxalic acid
h. Insecticide (spray)	Organochloro, organophosphorus and carbamate insecticides
i. Lavatory cleaners	Mineral acids
j. Marking ink	Aniline
k. Moth balls	Naphthalene
l. Paint removers	Sodium hydroxide, acetone, methylene chloride (carbon monoxide)
m. Shoe polish	Aniline, nitrobenzene
n. Straw hat cleaner	Oxalic acid

(*contd.*)

MEDICINAL HOUSEHOLD POISONS	
1. Antiseptics	Iodine
2. Cough remedies	Codeine
3. Headache remedies	Aspirin, phenacetin, analgin
4. Pep tablets	Benzedrine
5. Sleeping preparations	Barbiturates
6. Throat tablets	Potassium chlorate
7. Tonic syrup	Easton's syrup (strychnine)
8. Others	Antidepressants, tranquilisers, antibiotics, etc.
9. Hair dye (Vasmol)	Paraphenylene diamine' resorcinol, etc.

GARDEN POISONS	
1. Fungicides	Lead arsenate, copper compounds, organic mercurials, lime, sulphur
2. Insecticides, pesticides	Nicotine, tar oils, organochloro and organophosphorus compounds, carbamates, cyanides etc.
3. Weed killers (herbicides)	Sodium chlorate, arsenious oxide and arsenites, dinitrocresol, paraquat

Corrosives

By corrosion is meant dissolution or gradual wearing away by chemical action. The corrosive poisons are classified as follows:

1. Mineral acids	a. Sulphuric acid
	b. Nitric acid
	c. Hydrochloric acid
2. Organic acids	a. Oxalic acid
	b. Carbolic acid
	c. Acetic acid
	d. Salicylic acid
3. Vegetable acid	a. Hydrocyanic acid
4. Alkalis	a. Caustic potash and soda
	b. Ammonium hydroxide

39

Mineral Acids and Caustic Alkalis

Q. 39.1. Give the general characteristics, symptoms and signs, treatment, post-mortem appearances, and medicolegal aspects of poisoning by mineral acids and strong alkalis. Add a note on vitriolage.

Mineral Acids and Caustic Alkalis

Mineral acids and strong alkalis are corrosive poisons. In dilute solutions, they act as irritants. The symptoms and signs of the group as a whole are very similar. Their action is mainly a local one on the tissues of the alimentary tract and to some extent on the respiratory tract. As a rule, there is no remote systemic action with the exception of shock. Their action is characterised by: (1) extraction of water from the tissues, (2) coagulation of cellular proteins, and (3) conversion of haemoglobin into haematin.

General symptoms and signs: The onset of symptoms is immediate. Soon after swallowing the poison, there is burning sensation in the mouth, throat, oesophagus, stomach, and abdomen, followed by intense thirst, difficulty in swallowing, continuous retching, and vomiting of shreddy blood-stained material. The vomit may be acidic or alkaline in reaction depending upon the substance taken. There are signs of corrosion of mouth, lips, or both. The tongue is swollen or shrivelled according to the nature of the corroding agent. With the ingestion of corrosive acids, the bowels tend to be constipated and the urine scanty, but with alkalis, there may be tenesmus and frequency of stools with blood and mucus. Traces of poison may also find their way into the trachea and be followed by respiratory tract symptoms'. Dyspnoea is often present from oedema of the glottis and is more marked in the volatile or strong fuming fluids. Collapse from shock sets in, with cold clammy skin, pale anxious face, sunken eyes, dilated pupils, rapid feeble pulse, and sighing respirations. Consciousness is usually retained until near the end, and death may result from primary shock, suffocation due to oedema of the glottis, or perforation of the stomach. If the quantity of poison swallowed is small, death may be delayed until hypostatic pneumonia develops. The patient may recover and death may ensue later from complications, such as stricture of the oesophagus with resulting emaciation and malnutrition. The sites likely to be affected by local contact and the early, late, and delayed effects of corrosives are shown diagrammatically in Fig. 39.1.

Treatment: Stomach wash and emetics are contraindicated. However, a soft stomach tube or Levine tube can be passed with care within about an hour of the ingestion of poison to prevent serious caustic burns of the stomach wall followed by ulceration, contraction, and even stricture. If an acid has been taken, alkaline carbonates are

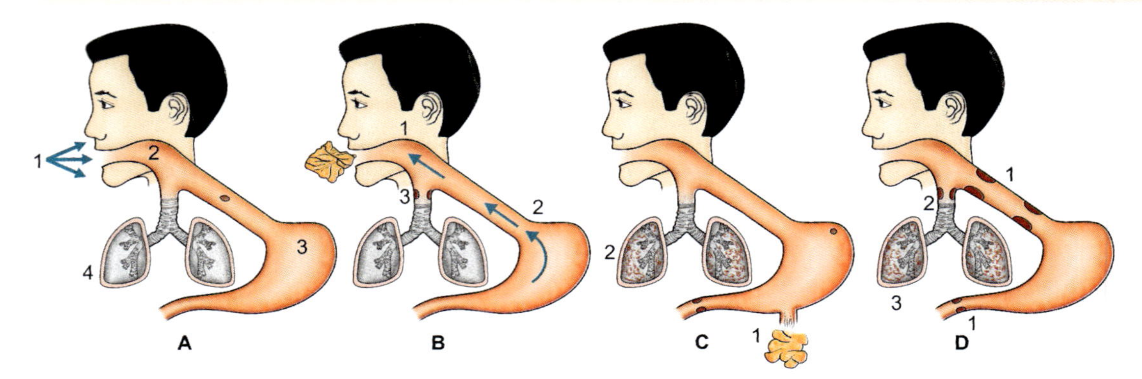

Fig. 39.1: Diagrammatic representation of **the site of action and the effects of corrosives:**
A. Sites likely to be affected by local contact: (1) Skin—face or elsewhere, (2) mouth and thorat, (3) upper alimentary tract, (4) respiratory tract
B. Early effects: (1) Pain and shock, (2) vomiting, (3) dyspnoea due to respiratory obstruction from laryngeal oedema
C. Late effects: (1) Perforation of stomach, (2) pulmonary oedema or bronchopneumonia
D. Delayed effects: (1) Oesophageal or pyloric stricture, (2) laryngeal stricture, (3) pulmonary fibrosis

contraindicated. Weak alkalis and plenty of water or neutralising agents, such as milk and egg albumin, should be given. In the case of an alkali, a weak acid, such as vinegar, will neutralise its effects. Morphine by injection is necessary to relieve pain, ice to suck to relieve thirst, intravenous fluids to combat fluid loss, and corticosteroids for shock and to prevent oesophageal stricture. Tracheostomy may be necessary, if there is acute oedema of the glottis. The other treatment is along the lines indicated for general treatment of poisoning.

Postmortem appearances: These may be expressed generally as signs of corrosion and partial destruction of the parts with which the poison has been in contact. Externally, the lips may be burnt and trickle marks may be found running from the mouth to the chin, neck, and chest. Internally, they vary in extent from localised patches to extensive areas, particularly in stomach. Perforation of the stomach is common with sulphuric acid. Irritation of the respiratory tract is found in case of volatile poisons, e.g. nitric acid, hydrochloric acid (Fig. 39.2).

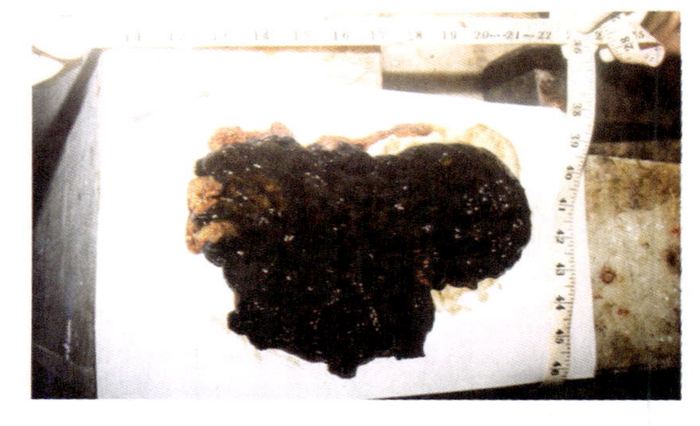

Fig. 39.2: Corrosive substance in stomach

Medicolegal aspects: Attempted suicide with corrosives is **not seen now** owing largely to the use of other less painful substances, like barbiturates, synthetic narcotics, and organophosphorus compounds. Corrosives are rarely used for homicide owing to their painful action. They are sometimes thrown on the face out of jealousy or in fits of rage. This is known as vitriolage. They cause severe injury or even death from accidental spilling.

Vitriolage (Fig. 39.3): This means throwing of any corrosive; not necessarily sulphuric acid, on a person with malicious intent out of jealousy, hatred or vengence to seek

Fig. 39.3: Vitriolage. The facial disfigurement of this person is due to throwing of sulphuric acid by some one out of malice. The injury is characterised by corrosive stains on the skin and trickled marks. In this case, eyes are spared. The permanent disfigurement of face results in grievous hurt

revenge. These fluids are usually thrown on the face with the object of destroying vision or causing facial disfigurement and this results in grievous hurt. Sulphuric acid (oil of vitriol) is most commonly employed for this purpose and hence it is called vitriolage. Nitric and carbolic acids are sometimes used. The use of caustic soda, caustic potash, iodine and marking nut juice has also been recorded. Sulphuric acid produces severe chemical burns. They are characterised by discolouration and staining of skin and clothing (brown or black in sulphuric acid and yellow in nitric acid), trickle marks, absence of vesication and red line of demarcation, and the presence of the chemical substance in the stains. Immediate treatment consists of washing away the corrosive acid with large amount of water and soap or dilute solution of sodium or potassium bicarbonate. Later, a thick paste of magnesium oxide is applied. The raw surface may afterwards be covered with antibiotic ointment; when the eyes are involved, they should be washed at once with a large amount of water followed by irrigation with 1% solution of sodium bicarbonate. A few drops of olive oil are then instilled into the eyes. Eyedrops containing antibiotics and steroids are helpful. Acid attacks have been on the increase. Consequently, in a separate section in the law for punishment in these cases, rigorous punishment up to seven years is recommended acid attack.

Q. 39.2. What is acid attack? What is its punishment?

Acid attack is throwing or attempting to throw acid or any acid substance or with corrosive or burning nature and which can cause bodily injury leading to scars or disfigurement or temporary or permanent disability or grievous hurt to that person. The punishment ranges from 5 to 7 or 10 years to life imprisonment and fine depending on gravity of the case which is paid to victim as compensation. (IPC Section 326A and Section 326B)

40 Organic Acids

The important poisons amongst this group are oxalic, carbolic, acetic, and salicylic acids. They have a powerful and rapid action. They act as strong irritants locally and also possess a powerful remote action after absorption.

Q. 40.1. Give the general characteristics, symptoms and signs, treatment, post-mortem appearances, and medicolegal aspects of oxalic acid poisoning.

OXALIC ACID

Oxalic acid is a corrosive acid. It is a crystalline substance, sparingly soluble in water, and resembling in appearance magnesium sulphate and zinc sulphate. It can be **differentiated** from them by the following features:

	Oxalic acid	*Magnesium sulphate*	*Zinc sulphate*
1. Taste	Sour and acidic	Bitter and nauseating	Bitter and metallic
2. Reaction	Strongly acidic	Neutral	Slightly acid
3. Heat	Sublimes	Not so	Not so
4. Sodium carbonate	Effervescence but no precipitate	No effervescence but a white precipitate	No effervescence but a white precipitate
5. Ink or iron stains	Bleaches	Not so	Not so

Symptoms and signs: The character and severity of the symptoms depend upon the amount and the concentration of the acid swallowed.

It has two distinct effects, local and remote, e.g. shock, hypocalcaemia, and renal damage. Even dilute solutions cause serious systemic effects. Oxalic acid combines with serum calcium to form insoluble calcium oxalate (hypocalcaemia).

Local action: It readily corrodes the mucous membrane of the alimentary tract but rarely the skin.

Remote action: Large doses cause rapid death from *shock* (narcotic effect). There is a sour taste in the mouth and burning in the throat and stomach. This is followed by persistent vomiting. The vomit is black in colour 'coffee ground' due to altered blood. If the case is of short duration, the intestinal tract is not affected, but when life is prolonged, there is pain and tenderness over the abdomen and purging and tenesmus may appear. After absorption, signs of collapse soon appear.

Numbness and tingling indicate the effects of *hypocalcaemia* on the nervous system. Spasmodic twitching of muscles of the face and extremities and even convulsions may follow.

Where death is not rapid, evidence of irritation of the kidneys may be found as oxalic acid has a *nephrotoxic action.* There may be oliguria, and the urine contains albumin, blood, and calcium oxalate crystals. The presence of calcium oxalate crystals in the urine is termed *oxaluria.* These crystals have the shape of an envelope when seen under a microscope.

Fatal dose: The average fatal dose of the poison is about 15 to 20 gm. The smallest recorded fatal dose is 5 gm.

Fatal period or survival time: Death usually occurs within an hour. The longest recorded period is five days.

Treatment: Since the degree of corrosion is not as severe as in mineral acids, a soft stomach tube can be passed with care and the stomach washed out using lime water. *Warm water should not be used for stomach wash as it may dissolve more acid.* The antidote for oxalate poisoning is any calcium preparation which converts the poison into insoluble calcium oxalate, the most readily available preparation being chalk. A suspension of 30 gm of chalk in water or milk will neutralise about 20 gm of oxalic acid. Alkalis, such as soda, potash or ammonia, should not be given as their oxalates, are soluble. Calcium gluconate may be given by mouth or 10 ml of a 10% solution intravenously. In severe cases, parathyroid extract should be given. Urinary output should be checked to detect the possibility of renal damage and fluid intake controlled as found necessary. The rest of the treatment is symptomatic.

A woman aged 50 swallowed about 30 gm of oxalic acid in beer. In half an hour she complained of burning pain in the stomach and was found rolling about. Chalk and water were freely given and she recovered.

Postmortem appearances: If the poison is taken in a concentrated form, the appearances are similar to those in poisoning by mineral acids, except that the lips and chin do not show staining. The mucous membrane of the tongue, mouth, throat and gullet is commonly white as if bleached but is sometimes reddened by irritation.

The stomach contains a dark brown gelatinous liquid due to the formation of acid haematin. The mucous membrane is corroded and detached in varying degrees depending on the concentration of the acid. Perforation, however, is rare. The blood vessels in the submucous layer may be seen distinctly as *dark lines* due to acid haematin. The outer coat of the stomach may be inflamed.

If the effects are only narcotic, there will be congestion of lungs, liver, kidneys and brain, without any local changes. Where death has been delayed, inflammation will be found in the upper portion of the small intestine and the kidneys.

Medicolegal aspects: Oxalic acid and its salts are used in industry as bleaching agents, and in calico printing. Its household use for bleaching has made it a dangerous substance. Accidental poisoning is due to its being mistaken for magnesium sulphate or sodium bicarbonate. Oxalates occur in the leaves of rhubarb and have caused poisoning when the leaves are used as safe vegetables. Oxalic acid is sometimes taken with suicidal intention but rarely used for homicide on account of its sour taste and rapid action. Solutions containing oxalic acid cause falling off of hair when poured on the head. Oxalic acid is sometimes used to erase writing in attempts at forgery.

Q. 40.2. Give the general characteristics, symptoms and signs, treatment, postmortem appearances, and medicolegal aspects of carbolic acid (phenol) poisoning.

CARBOLIC ACID (PHENOL)

When pure, carbolic acid (phenol) consists of colourless, prismatic needle-like crystals having a sweetish burning taste and characteristic phenolic smell. Though it does not turn blue litmus red and has no acid reaction, it is called an acid because it forms carbolates (salts) when acted upon by strong bases. It is slightly soluble in water and readily soluble in glycerine and alcohol. It liquefies and becomes pink on exposure to light and air. The commercial acid is mixed with impurities, like cresol and may be dark brown in colour. Carbolic acid enters into the composition of most disinfecting agents, such as Dettol and lysol.

Symptoms and signs: Poisoning by carbolic acid is known as carbolism. It has two actions, viz. a local action on the skin, and alimentary tract, and a remote action after absorption. It is rapidly absorbed from the alimentary tract, rectum, vagina, serous cavities, wounds, and even intact skin.

Local action: *Skin*—It is a coagulant of protein but does not enter into any firm combination with it, and thus it has remarkable penetrating qualities. It, therefore, causes necrosis and sloughing of the tissues. Carbolic acid acts as a mild corrosive and anaesthetic upon the skin and mucous membranes. It causes eschar formation.

Alimentary tract: Hot burning pain extends from the mouth to the stomach, followed by tingling and anaesthesia. Swallowing and speech become painful and difficult. Vomiting may not take place owing to the anaesthetic action on the stomach. The lips, mouth and tongue are corroded. The chin and cheeks may be burnt. These burns appear white, bleached and hardened. They later become brown, the dead tissue sloughing rapidly.

Remote action: *Shock* ensues, both local (corrosive) and the more remote (central nervous depressant) action of phenol being rapidly established. The victim feels giddy. The skin is cold and clammy, pulse weak and thready, pupils contracted and pinpoint, temperature subnormal, and breathing stertorous and laboured. The ***breath smells*** strongly of carbolic acid. On account of contracted pupils and cold and clammy skin, it is likely to be mistaken for opium poisoning.

When death is not rapid, evidence of irritation of kidneys may be found as carbolic acid has a ***nephrotoxic action.*** There may be suppression of urine or oliguria. The urine contains albumin, blood casts and metabolic products of carbolic acid, viz. hydroquinone and pyrocatechol. On standing or when exposed to air, the metabolic products are oxidised resulting in dark smoky green colour of the urine. This is known as *carboluria* and served as a warning of the toxic action of carbolic acid when it was used as an antiseptic dressing in the past. Coma usually follows rapidly and death results from paralysis of the respiratory or cardiac centre.

The presence of carbolic acid in the urine is indicated by addition of a little ferric chloride when the urine turns blue or little bromine water when urine forms a white precipitate of tribrom phenol. The urine containing carbolic acid also reduces Benedict's and Fehling's solution.

Fatal dose: Twenty drops of pure phenol have caused death and probably twice that quantity of most carbolic disinfectants would be dangerous.

Fatal period: Death from carbolic acid usually occurs in three to four hours. It has, however, followed in three minutes and has been delayed for as many as 60 hours.

Treatment: Since the degree of corrosion is not as severe as mineral acids and the tissues are also hardened by carbolic acid, a soft stomach tube can be passed with care. Thorough gastric lavage using a 10% solution of glycerine in water or plain water to which some magnesium sulphate is added should be carried out and continued until the washings no longer emit phenolic odour. Then, about one ounce of magnesium sulphate or two ounces of medicinal liquid paraffin may be left in the stomach. Magnesium sulphate forms an insoluble sulphocarbolate. Alcohol which tends to prevent the cauterising action of phenol may be given in 10% solution but as it does not combine in any way, it should be removed shortly afterwards. Demulcents, such as white of an egg or milk may be helpful. Intravenous saline with sodium bicarbonate should be administered to render the urine alkaline. Other treatment should be along general lines. The surface (skin or mucous membrane) burns should be washed with water, followed by a local application of castor oil. If this is not available, burns may be mopped with soap and water or swabbed with alcohol.

Postmortem appearances: The grayish-white stains produced by the poison may be present at the angles of the mouth and on the chin, and its odour is usually perceptible. The mucous membranes of the mouth and oesophagus are swollen, hardened and discoloured and the tongue is usually white and swollen.

The mucous membrane of the stomach forms projecting folds and prominent rugae. It is thickened, more or less brownish in colour, and looks leathery. The contents appear dark brown mucoid with characteristic phenolic smell. The peritoneal surface of the stomach is injected. The duodenum and upper part of the small intestine may show evidence of corrosion and injection of vessels. The liver and spleen frequently show a whitish hardened patch where the stomach has been in contact with them, due to the transudation of phenol. The glottis may show some swelling and congestion. The lungs and brain are frequently congested. The kidneys may show parenchymal degenerative changes.

The viscera to be sent to the chemical examiner should be preserved in saturated solution of sodium chloride and not in rectified spirit, which is used to preserve viscera in poisoning with other corrosives.

Medicolegal aspects: Carbolic acid and its derivatives are used as antiseptics, disinfectants, and surface anaesthetics. Some of these substances were used in the past to commit suicide. They are now displaced by soporifics. Phenol is rarely used for homicide because of its smell and taste. It is sometimes used to procure abortion. Accidental poisoning may occur from indiscriminate medicinal use of this substance.

A healthy woman, aged 30, swallowed nearly 15 ml of an alcoholic solution of carbolic acid containing 35.8 per cent of the poison. About half the poison was removed by the use of stomach pump, the remaining half having been absorbed. The most prominent symptoms were insensibility within 10 minutes and dizziness speedily passing into profound coma, irregular breathing and pulse, contracted pupils, cyanosis, fall in body temperature to 94°F, and haemoglobinuria which appeared one hour after the poison was taken and lasted for seven and half hours. The urine gave reaction for carbolic acid for two days. The woman recovered with energetic treatment.

SN on Carboluria: Urinary findings of carbolic acid go by the name of carboluria. In this, patient's urine is clear in start but latter becomes smoky in colour. This is due to hydroquinone and pyrocatechol, which are the products of carbolic, acid in urine.

SN Ochronosis or phenol marasmus: In chronic expesure to phenol, amount surgeous, nurses, etc., who used it as disinfectoment, a group of manifestations known as ochronosis or Phenol and skin pigmentation, vertigo, headache anorexia and loss of weight.

41

Vegetable Acid Poisons

Under this heading, the following poisons are discussed, viz. hydrocyanic acid and its salts, the cyanides.

Hydrocyanic acid is a general protoplasmic poison. It inhibits the cytochrome oxidase system for oxygen utilisation in cells. Death is due to cytotoxic or histotoxic anoxia, although the blood may contain a normal oxygen content. Other enzyme systems are also inhibited but to a lesser degree. Cyanides show, in addition, a corrosive effect on the mucous membrane.

Q. 41.1. Give the general characters, symptoms and signs, treatment, postmortem appearances, and medicolegal aspects of poisoning by hydrocyanic acid and cyanides.

HYDROCYANIC ACID AND CYANIDES

Hydrocyanic acid, also known as cyanogen or prussic acid, is a colourless gas with a penetrating odour resembling that of bitter almonds. Liquid hydrocyanic acid is a highly volatile colourless fluid. Hydrocyanic acid combines with bases of several metals and strong alkalis to from cyanides (salts). The cyanides are white powders and are used in photography, electroplating, metallurgy, tanning, fumigation of ships, and in agriculture to prevent plant decay. The pharmacopoeial preparation of hydrocyanic acid contains about 2% of the anhydrous acid while Scheele's acid, which is commonly used in veterinary practice, contains 4 per cent.

Hydrocyanic acid is a vegetable acid naturally found in many fruits, e.g. peach, plum, and bitter almonds, and leaves of cherry-royal, a preparation which is used medicinally. It exists in the form of glycoside amygdalin, which is harmless. The enzyme emulsin hydrolyses it and liberates the harmful hydrocyanic acid. It is also liberated from cyanides by reaction with acids.

Hydrocyanic acid is readily absorbed from mucous membrane and is very toxic when inhaled. The rapidity with which the (salts) cyanides, upon ingestion, cause death will depend on the amount of hydrochloric acid present when the salt was swallowed and the subsequent liberation of hydrogen cyanide which is absorbed by the gastric mucosa. Cyanides tend to change into carbonates, if kept too long but the mixture is still poisonous.

Symptoms and signs: Inhalation of the gas results in instantaneous death. When a large dose of liquid hydrocyanic acid is swallowed, symptoms usually occur at once but in some cases there is an interval of about one minute. This may allow the victim to perform certain voluntary acts, such as corking or throwing away the bottle or walking some distance. If death is delayed for a few minutes, agonising dyspnoea, convulsions and dilated pupils may be noted.

With a small dose, the individual first experiences headache, confusion, giddiness, nausea and some loss of muscular power. The characteristic smell of bitter almonds may be noticed at the mouth and in the breath. There may be violent convulsions before the patient loses consciousness and dies. A small quantity of fine froth may appear at the mouth. In gaseous form, it has bitter almond odour, but 20 to 40% of population may not be able to appreciate the odour as this depends on a sex-linked recessive trait inheritance.

Following ingestion of the salts, e.g. potassium cyanide, the symptoms appear after about 10–20 minutes as it has to be acted upon by hydrochloric acid of the gastric juice to liberate hydrocyanic acid. Principal symptoms include giddiness, dyspnoea, dilated and fixed pupils, convulsive seizures, and loss of muscle power. There may be a corrosive effect on the mouth, throat and stomach, and epigastric pain and vomiting. The face is cyanosed, the jaw may be tightly clenched, and froth may be seen at the mouth. The respirations are spasmodic, and the pulse almost imperceptible. Death occurs from respiratory paralysis.

Chronic poisoning occurs from repeated exposure to non-lethal doses of hydrocyanic acid or cyanides among photographers, gilders and others who handle these preparations. Such persons suffer from headache, vomiting, diarrhoea, chronic cachexia, and mental disturbances.

Fatal dose: 50 to 60 mg of the pure acid, 30 drops of the pharmacopoeial preparation, 60 drops of crude oil of bitter almonds, and 200 mg of potassium cyanide have proved fatal.

Fatal period: Death in some cases is immediate but the average period may be taken as about two to ten minutes for hydrocyanic acid and 30 minutes for sodium or potassium cyanide.

Treatment: Only immediate treatment may be of value. The aim is to reverse the cyanide-cytochrome combination. This is achieved by converting haemoglobin to methaemoglobin so that the cyanide will combine with methaemoglobin to form cyanmethaemoglobin, which is non-toxic. Also, cyanide can be converted to relative non-toxic thiocyanate. Treatment should, therefore, be as follows. Survival for four hours is usually followed by recovery.

Two 20 ml ampoules of 1.5% Dicobalt *tetracemate* (Kelocyanor) are injected intravenously followed by 20 ml of 50% glucose. Intravenous administration of 50 ml of 1% sterile aqueous solution of methylene blue (methylthionine chloride, USP) may also be used as an antidote. It converts haemoglobin into methaemoglobin which combines with free cyanide thereby removing it from the reaction. Hydroxocobalamin: 50 mg/kg in commercial solution (1000 μg/ml) as an IV infusion works by combining with cyanide and forming cyanocobalamin which is excreted in urine.

In the case of potassium cyanide or dilute hydrocyanic acid poisoning, the stomach should be lavaged with a 5 to 10% solution of sodium thiosulphate, 'or a mixture of sulphates (ferrous and ferric) of iron followed by a solution of potassium carbonate to form Prussian blue which is inert. Emetics may be used, if a stomach tube is not readily available.

In poisoning by inhalation with hydrocyanic acid gas (cyanogen), the patient should be removed from the source of contamination. The use of artificial respiration and 100% oxygen is of the highest value. Intravenous administration of sodium nitrite and sodium thiosulphate will be necessary and should be repeated if symptoms reappear. In case of mercury cyanide poisoning, injection of BAL may be necessary.

Postmortem appearances: These are those of asphyxia. The appearances are external and internal.

Externally, there is smell of bitter almonds from the body. The face, lips, and body surface frequently show irregular pink patches. Sometimes, the skin is livid or cyanosed and the nails blue. There may be fine froth at the mouth. The eyes may be bright, glistening and prominent with dilated pupils. The postmortem staining is pink often incorrectly referred to as cherry red. Rigor mortis sets in early, if there have been convulsive seizures.

Internally, the characteristic smell of bitter almonds is usually present in the stomach, serous cavities and brain. The mucous membrane of the stomach may be pink, and the other organs together with blood, are usually of the same shade owing to the impeded oxygenation of the tissues by the cyanide and the postmortem formation of cyanmethaemoglobin. Blood stained froth may be found in the trachea and bronchi. The brain and meninges are hyperaemic and petechial haemorrhages appear in the pleura and pericardium, brain, meninges and lungs.

When potassium cyanide has been taken, there may be slight corrosion of the mouth and reddening of gastric mucous membrane which may be of a brick red to brown colour due to the formation of alkaline haematin. The stomach may contain frank or altered blood from the erosions and haemorrhages in its walls.

The brain, lungs, blood, stomach contents, urine, and vomit should be preserved for chemical analysis taking care that the samples present no hazard to those packing, transporting, or unpacking them.

It is necessary that the dissector takes precautions to prevent ill-effects from inhalation of cyanide from stomach contents during autopsy and the rubber gloves worn are in perfect condition.

Medicolegal aspects: Hydrocyanic acid and cyanides are used principally as suicidal agents, the cyanides being about three times as common as the acid owing to their more common usage in the garden and in photography. Since cyanides satisfy most conditions of a suicidal poison of choice, they are usually resorted to by those who have firmly made up their mind to commit suicide. Some suicide bombers use cyanide to die before they are cought or after their task is over. Hitler appears to have killed himself by cyanide.

Accidental poisoning occasionally occurs when it is used for fumigation or disinfection. Chemists and laboratory assistants are sometimes overcome by the sudden evolution of hydrocyanic acid following the pouring away of cyanide solutions into sinks already containing strong acid residue.

Homicidal poisoning is rare because of the peculiar smell and taste of the acid. Hydrocyanic acid is also used as a cattle poison. The double cyanides, viz. potassium ferrocyanide and potassium ferricyanide are non-toxic but may produce poisonous symptoms and cause death when taken with acids.

In some countries, hydrocyanic acid is used for **judicial execution.** The condemned person is strapped to a chair. Cyanogen is evolved by dropping cyanide 'eggs' into a pan containing strong acid. The inhalation of fumes of cyanogen causes instantaneous death.Cult suicide by about 900 people taking by mouth cyanide solution prepared by Dr Schat, a doctor of the group happened with the doctor ending himself by shooting himself with a gun. Near Baroda in India in a field cyanide contaminated water caused death of three people. Industrical effluents should be properly disposed, otherwise such incidents are liable to be repeated.

Illustrative Cases

A woman swallowed 50 ml of a solution of potassium cyanide, used for photographic purposes. The quantity taken amounted to 300 mg. In 2 minutes, she became unconscious, the whole of the body was slightly convulsed, and the pupils were dilated. She foamed at the mouth, the pulse was small and feeble, and she died within 20 minutes.

A man bought a 7 lb tin of Cymag to fumigate a small greenhouse. He sprinkled one-third over the staging, shut the door and returned to the house. Finding he had left his keys in the greenhouse he went back and opened the door. He was found lying with his feet on the threshold and his head in the house. His keys were still on the staging. Analysis showed traces of cyanide in the lungs but no perceptible cyanide in the stomach or other viscera.

Section 9

42

Non-Metallic Poisons

IRRITANT POISONS

The irritant poisons are classified as: (1) inorganic poisons (non-metals and metals), (2) organic poisons (vegetables and animals), and (3) mechanical poisons. Corrosives in very dilute solutions act as irritants.

Irritant poisons cause symptoms of gastroenteritis and also exert a marked depressant action after absorption. Chronic metallic poisoning leads to such a lingering death that chronic arsenic poisoning has been known as a **'slow-poison'.**

General symptoms and signs: The onset of symptoms and signs which is variable is usually within half an hour to an hour. There is burning sensation in the mouth, throat, oesophagus, stomach and abdomen, followed by intense thirst, difficulty in swallowing, continuous retching, painful vomiting and diarrhoea. The vomited matter at first consists of normal stomach contents, but later becomes bilious in character and may be of dark brown appearance due to altered blood. The diarrhoea is severe, accompanied by tenesmus and consists at first of loose stools and later of stools mixed with mucus and blood. Collapse from shock sets in with cold clammy skin, pale anxious face, rapid feeble pulse, and sighing respirations. Cramps may affect the muscles of the limbs. Consciousness is usually retained during this period. Convulsions and/or coma may follow. Death occurs within 24 hours from shock, or in a few days from exhaustion. The patient may recover and death may ensue later from stricture of the oesophagus or other sequelae.

Postmortem appearances show changes chiefly in the stomach, and frequently in the duodenal and rectal portions of the intestinal tract.

NON-METALLIC POISONS

The important poisons in this group are: (1) phosphorus, and (2) iodine.

PHOSPHORUS

Q. 42.1. Give the general characters, symptoms, signs, treatment, postmortem appearances, and medicolegal aspects of phosphorus poisoning. Add a note on necrobiosis of liver.

Phosphorus exists in two forms, viz. white as crystalline and red as amorphous. The white one becomes yellow on exposure to the air. It is, therefore, also called yellow phosphorus. It exists in the form of translucent, waxy, luminous cylinders. It is slightly soluble in alcohol, freely soluble in carbon disulphide, and insoluble in water. Being easily oxidisable, it is kept submerged in water to prevent ignition. When exposed to atmosphere, it gives off dense white fumes of phosphoric and phosphorus acids with a strong odour of garlic and are luminous in the dark. The fumes glow with pale yellow colour *(phosphorescence).* Red phosphorus is inert unless contaminated with yellow phosphorus. It is non-luminous, amorphous, odourless, insoluble in carbon disulphide, and does not give off fumes when exposed to air. Mixed with powdered glass, it is used on the side (striking surface) of the match box. The tip of the match stick contains a mixture of potassium chlorate and antimony sulphide.

Phosphorus is a protoplasmic poison. It affects cellular oxidation. Its effect on cellular metabolism is comparable to ischaemia. Under such anoxic condition, the metabolism of the cells diminishes considerably. This is known as necrobiosis, which is classically manifested in the liver. Deposition of glycogen in liver is inhibited while deposition of fat is increased.

Acute Poisoning

Symptoms and signs: There are two phases in the symptoms, primary, due to the local irritant action on the gastrointestinal tract, and secondary, due to the action of the absorbed poison, and there is usually a considerable interval between them.

The primary symptoms usually occur within two to six hours. There is burning pain in the throat, oesophagus and stomach with intense thirst, frequent gaseous eructations, nausea, vomiting, and diarrhoea. The patient may complain of a garlic taste in the mouth and a garlic odour may be perceived in the breath. The vomited matter is darkened by blood, smells of garlic, and is luminous in the dark. The faeces may be dark, luminous and offensive. The luminosity of vomit and faeces is diagnostic. This primary irritative stage lasts one to two days and may be so severe that the victim dies from collapse and cardiac failure. However, this is *not the usual course* and remissions are common after the usual bouts of vomiting and diarrhoea. Contact of phosphorus with skin produces slow healing burns.

In the **usual clinical course,** there is a remission lasting for about two to three days. Then, secondary symptoms occur due to the absorbed poison damaging mainly the liver and kidneys. The original symptoms return, and in addition, there is jaundice and distension of the abdomen due to enlargement and necrosis of the liver. In the early stages, the liver is enlarged due to fatty degeneration (necrobiosis) and in late stages, it is shrunken due to necrosis (acute yellow atrophy). Purpura and epistaxis may follow due to hypoprothombinaemia. The faeces are pale. The urine is scanty and concentrated, strongly acid in reaction, and contains blood, albumin, bile, and sometimes sugar and crystals of tyrosine, leucine and cystine due to disturbed metabolism. Pregnant women abort with alarming flooding. Nervous system involvement manifests as frontal pains, insomnia, ringing in the ears, impaired vision, formication, cramps, and paralysis. Priapism is frequent. Death results from hepatic and renal insufficiency. The clinical picture is suggestive of acute yellow atrophy of the liver.

Fatal dose: A dose of 60–120 mg is usually considered a fatal dose, though as with all gastric irritants, vomiting may permit recovery from much larger doses.

Fatal period: Death may occur from collapse within 24 hours. In the normal course, it may occur in six to seven days or longer.

Treatment: Demulcents (oily and fatty substances including milk) are contraindicated as they dissolve and promote absorption of phosphorus. The stomach should be lavaged with 0.5% solution of potassium permanganate repeatedly, till no more smell of garlic is perceptible, and the bowel evacuated by a brisk purgative. Potassium permanganate acts as a chemical antidote. It oxidises phosphorus to harmless compounds, viz. phosphoric acid and phosphates. A dilute solution of copper sulphate (0.1%) may be used *as an antidote* instead of permanganate. 200 mg of copper sulphate may be given every five minutes until vomiting occurs. Copper sulphate is reduced by phosphorus and is precipitated as metallic copper on the particles of phosphorus, thus rendering them inert. Liquid paraffin may retard absorption and may be given. Intravenous saline is useful to combat shock, calcium gluconate, if blood calcium is diminished, and sodium bicarbonate to maintain alkali reserve. Intravenous dextrose may be needed to protect the liver. Peritoneal or haemodialysis may be necessary to combat renal failure. Skin burns should be thoroughly washed with 1% copper sulphate solution.

Postmortem Appearances

If death takes place within the first 24 hours, the appearances generally are those of a highly irritant poison, consisting of inflammation or erosion of the mucous membrane of the pharynx, oesophagus, stomach and intestines, with cloudy swelling of the liver and kidneys. The contents of both stomach and bowel may be luminous in the dark, and the body may smell of garlic.

Where the **usual course** has been followed and death takes place after an interval of a few days, characteristic external and internal appearances are found.

External: The body may be emaciated and may smell of garlic. Jaundice and haemorrhages both under the skin and from various natural orifices of the body are the special features of external examination.

Internal: Fatty degeneration and haemorrhages are the special features of the internal examination. The toxic effects are well marked in the stomach and intestines, liver, heart, kidneys, and blood.

The mucous membrane of the **stomach and intestine** is yellowish or grayish white in colour, softened, inflamed, or even corroded. Patchy areas of erosion with haemorrhages and perforation are common. The contents of the stomach and intestines may have a garlicky odour and may be luminous in the dark.

The liver undergoes **necrobiosis.** Its characteristics and differentiating features from acute yellow atrophy are as follows:

Fatty degeneration of the heart muscle, kidneys and voluntary muscle fibres is present. Subendocardial haemorrhages in the left ventricle are common. The blood may appear tarry and its coagulability is diminished.

	Necrobiosis	*Acute yellow atrophy*
1. Size	Enlarged at first but shrunken later	Smaller with a wrinkled capsule
2. Colour	Uniformly yellow	Dirty yellow
3. Consistency	Soft and greasy	Hard and brittle
4. Structure	Fatty degeneration with necrosis of some cells and purpuric spots	Necrosis of most cells without damage to supporting connective tissue
5. Stage of poisoning	Early	Late

In a case of suspected phosphorus poisoning, the **viscera** for chemical analysis should be **preserved** in saturated solution of common salt and not in spirit as the luminosity is lost. Sometimes, the chemical examiner reports the presence of phosphates in the viscera. This has no significance. Finding of phosphorus in free form only is of significance.

Medicolegal Aspects

Yellow phosphorus is an ingredient of fireworks and certain rodent and insect poisons. Accidental deaths in children who have eaten fire crackers or rat pastes are known. Occasionally, rat pastes and vermin killers which contain yellow phosphorus (zinc phosphide, aluminium phosphide) are taken to commit suicide. The smell and taste of phosphorus in the form of rat poison can be disguised when mixed in strong sweet tea or coffee; it can then be used as a homicidal poison because (a) symptoms appear after some delay and resemble acute liver disease, and (b) death occurs after a few days. However, it must be remembered that phosphorus can be detected even in putrefied bodies. Phosphorus, concealed in moist paper, wet cloth, or dung, is occasionally used to set fire to postal letter boxes and huts. Phosphorus is certainly not responsible for the so-called spontaneous combustion in cotton bales. It is due to heat generation from bacterial fermentation or drying oils.

Chronic Poisoning

It results from frequent inhalation of phosphorus fumes over a period of years. The gas commonly attacks the lower jaw in the region of a decayed tooth where the suppurative microorganisms are already present. The first symptom is toothache, followed by swelling of the jaw, loosening of the teeth, necrosis of gums, and then sequestration of bone in the mandible. This is known as the **phossy jaw.** It is an osteomyelitis of the jaw bone with multiple sinuses discharging foul smelling pus. Constitutional symptoms, such as weakness, weight loss, anaemia, jaundice, and pain in the joints are common.

Illustrative Cases

A 43-year-old man was admitted to hospital three days after ingesting 1.2 gm of yellow phosphorus in the form of rat poison. Within a few hours of taking the poison his skin felt hot and flushed. He said he had such flatulence as if he had eaten many onions. The next day there were no symp-toms. On the third day, he became mildly jaundiced and vomited black syrup-like material which contained altered blood and mucus. In hospital next day, vomiting continued in spite of gastric lavage with permanganate. He became oliguric and had persistent diarrhoea. On the day after admission, he suffered from a series of convulsions, followed by spastic, then flaccid quadriplegia, and died.

In 1952 at the County of London Sessions, Ekpeyong Eyo was sentenced to 12 months' imprisonment for administering rat poison to a number of students. The rat poison had been added to tea, coffee and soup.

An airman was shot whilst navigating a plane over enemy territory, the bullet entering the left thigh and passing into the abdomen. The wound emitted a visible vapour with the characteristic smell of phosphorus. The missile fragments were removed by operation but most of the phosphorus estimated at 200 mg was not recovered. For 2 days, the patient made good progress, then became semi-comatose. The skin became yellow, anuria developed and death occurred on the sixth day after the injury. The autopsy showed fatty degeneration and necrosis of the liver and fatty degeneration of the kidney.

Hunter records the case of a match dipper of 30, who after 12 years' employment with yellow phosphorus developed pain in the upper jaw. Three teeth were extracted but the socket broke down and the jaw sloughed. Sequestra were removed from both sides, and eventually, 5 years later, the whole lower jaw had to be removed.

IODINE

Iodine occurs as brown, scaly crystals with a metallic lustre and unpleasant taste. At all temperatures, it gives off a violet-coloured vapour possessing a characteristic odour.

Iodine has a direct action on the cells by precipitating proteins. The effects are thus similar to those produced by acid corrosives and the principal manifestations of poisoning are vomiting, collapse, and coma. The vapours of iodine are strongly irritant to the respiratory passages.

Q. 42.2. Give symptoms, signs, treatment, postmortem appearances, and medicolegal aspects of iodine poisoning. Add a note on iodism.

Symptoms and signs: When iodine is swallowed, the symptoms are those of a corrosive and irritant poison. There is burning pain extending from the mouth to the stomach. The taste is unpleasant and thirst intense. The lips and oral mucosa are stained yellow or brown. Its irritant action on stomach and bowels is characterised by severe pain in the abdomen with vomiting and diarrhoea, the vomit and stool being dark, yellow, brown, or blue, and with a peculiar smell of iodine. The micturition is painful and the urine may be suppressed or scanty. When voided, it is dark brown, contains albumin, and has a strong smell of iodine. In addition to the irritative symptoms, it causes marked depression, weak pulse, delirium and collapse.

Injection of iodine compounds may cause sudden fatal collapse as a result of hypersensitivity. Inhalation of iodine vapours is responsible for oedema of the glottis and death from asphyxia.

Prolonged ingestion of iodine or iodine compounds leads to chronic poisoning called *iodism*. This term is also used for idiosyncratic reactions to iodides or to iodine. The classical features are headache, acute coryza, bronchial catarrh, conjunctivitis, and oedema of the face and eyelids which clear up when the drug is withheld. Severe cases may be accompanied by collapse.

Fatal dose: The fatal dose of iodine in the solid form is about 2 gm. 8–10 ml of tincture iodine may cause death. Iodides have been given in large doses over long periods without any ill-effect though alarming symptoms have been recorded from a single dose of less than 1 gram.

Fatal period: The average fatal period is 24 hours. Rapid death may occur from anaphylaxis.

Treatment: The stomach should be washed out with 1% starch solution or 5% solution of sodium thiosulphate. Demulcents, such as starchy foods, eggs, milk, oils, etc., are helpful. In cases of intolerance, the administration of the drug should be stopped forthwith and antihistamines and/or steroids administered. In chronic poisoning, the use of iodine or iodides should be discontinued. High sodium chloride intake speeds up the recovery.

Postmortem appearances: Skin rashes and oedema of the eyes and face may be observed. The mucous membranes and lips may be stained yellow or brown. There may be excoriation and corrosion of mucous membranes of the mouth, oesophagus and stomach. There may be oedema of the glottis, and sometimes acute oedema of the lungs and effusion of fluid into the pleural and pericardial sacs. The kidneys show glomerular and tubular necrosis. The heart and liver may show fatty degeneration.

Medicolegal aspects: Tincture of iodine is occasionally taken to commit suicide. Iodine preparations cannot be used for homicidal purposes as they colour farinaceous foods blue. Iodine in strong solution has been employed for vitriolage. Injection of iodine compounds may cause sudden fatal collapse. Children may be attracted by its rich colour and may ingest it. A weak solution of iodine, 15 drops of the tincture to a tumblerful (200 ml) of water,' may be helpful in the absence of potassium permanganate, as a chemical antidote against all oxidisable poisons. During travel, water can be made potable by addition of 5 drops of 2% tincture of iodine per quart or litre of suspect drinking water and waiting for 20 minutes. If water is cloudy, double or four times the quantity of tincture of iodine drops will be required.

43 Metallic Poisons

The important poisons in this group are: arsenic, mercury, lead, copper, thallium, and zinc. They cause symptoms of gastroenteritis and also exert a marked depressant action after absorption.

ARSENIC

Arsenic is a grey substance which is said to be non-poisonous as it is insoluble in water and, therefore, cannot be absorbed from the alimentary canal. However, it is continuously changing into arsenious oxide or white arsenic which is tasteless and very poisonous. Arsenic causes toxicity by combining with sulphydryl enzymes, and thus interfering with cell metabolism. Locally, it causes irritation of the mucous membranes and remotely depression of the nervous system.

Sources of Arsenic

In therapeutics, arsenic is only of **historical interest,** being very rarely used now. The element or its derivatives are met with in industry and agriculture.

Arsenious oxide (As_2O_3): The term arsenic or white arsenic refers to arsenious oxide, also known as arsenious acid and arsenic trioxide, or *Sankhya* and *Somalkhar* in the local language. It occurs in two forms, either as a white crystalline powder or as opaque, brittle mass, resembling enamel. It has no smell or taste, and is sparingly soluble in water. Arsenic powder, in spite of its heavy weight, floats on the surface of water and adheres to the side of the vessel. Therefore, it is commonly given mixed with milk, tea, or coffee in homicidal poisoning.

Sulphides of arsenic: These are the yellow orpiment (hartal) or arsenic trisulphide (As_2S_3) and the red realgar (manseel) or arsenic disulphide (As_2S_2).

Copper compounds of arsenic: These compounds include Scheel's green (copper arsenite), Paris green or emerald green (copper acetoarsenite), etc., and go by the name *Hirwa* in the local language.

Others: The other compounds include arsenate of lead and arsenites of sodium and potassium and organic compounds.

Q. 43.1. Describe the symptoms, signs, treatment, and postmortem appearances of a case of acute arsenic poisoning.

The principal manifestations of acute arsenic poisoning are acute gastrointestinal disturbances. Subacute and narcotic manifestations also occur under certain circumstances.

Symptoms and signs: Symptoms in *acute poisoning* usually manifest within 15 to 30 minutes after the dose, but may be delayed, if arsenic is taken with food. There is nausea and burning pain in the oesophagus, stomach and epigastrium. Severe, continuous and persistent vomiting follows.

Vomit initially contains stomach contents, later bile, and finally, mucus mixed with altered blood. The main effect, however, is diarrhoea accompanied by tenesmus and anal irritation. The stools are tinged with blood, watery like the rice water stools of cholera, and contain shreds of mucous membrane and fragments of the poison in three or four hours. Intense thirst is a constant feature but drinking water accentuates the vomiting. Painful cramps in the legs may develop due to dehydration, and the urine may be suppressed. Skin eruptions may appear in late stages. In many cases, remissions occur during which the patient is moderately comfortable. The symptoms then recur. Collapse sets in, with cold clammy skin, pale anxious face, sunken eyes, dilated pupils, rapid feeble pulse, and sighing respirations. Convulsions or coma may precede death.

In some cases where the patient survives the initial acute attack, the poisoning becomes *subacute,* the symptoms persisting in lesser degree for some time. The patient becomes progressively weak and may die of heart failure and weakness in 7 to 10 days.

When a large dose of arsenic is taken and the poison is quickly absorbed, the symptoms of gastroenteritis may be absent, and symptoms of *narcotic poisoning,* such as vertigo, headache, spasms, followed by stupor and vascular collapse may be present. Death occurs in 2–3 hours.

Fatal dose: The fatal dose of arsenic in an adult is usually stated as 120–200 mg.

Fatal period: In the narcotic form, the average fatal period is about 2 to 3 hours. In the gastrointestinal form, it is about 12 to 48 hours. A patient who survives the acute attack may die 7–10 days later from subacute poisoning and heart failure, or some weeks later from chronic poisoning with its attendant damage to liver and kidney.

Treatment: Though vomiting has occurred, the **stomach** should be repeatedly **washed out** with warm water and milk to remove arsenic particles adherent to mucous membrane of the stomach. Then **freshly precipitated hydrated ferric oxide** (which is rather slow to prepare) is administered as an antidote with the object of forming ferric arsenite, a harmless salt. The precipitate is given suspended in water, in tablespoonful dosage, at short intervals, for two or three days. If ferric oxide cannot be quickly prepared, calcined magnesia or charcoal may be substituted. Treatment must be immediate. Butter and greasy substances are useful to prevent absorption. No alkalis should be given by mouth since they increase the solubility of white arsenic. A saline purgative, such as sodium sulphate, left in the stomach, is beneficial.

The systemic effects should be treated by intramuscular injection of **dimercaprol** (BAL) in oily solution. By virtue of its two 'SH' radicals, it combines with free arsenic and also dislodges arsenic from combination with tissue SH groups. It thus reverses the inhibition of tissue oxidation through sulphydryl enzymes by arsenic, and forms a non-toxic BAL-As complex which is excreted by the kidneys.

Parenteral fluids should be administered to counteract dehydration, glucose to combat liver damage, sodium bicarbonate to regulate acid–base balance, **morphine** to control pain and **ice** to control thirst. Blood or plasma transfusion may be needed. Particular attention should be given **to** supporting the heart. Anuria may require dialysis by **artificial kidney** treatment. Additional symptoms should be treated along general lines.

Postmortem appearances: The character of the appearances depends very largely upon the quantity taken and the period which has elapsed before death.

Externally, in acute poisoning, the body presents a dehydrated and cyanosed appearance with sunken eyeballs. The skin is wrinkled and may be jaundiced. Rigor mortis lasts longer than usual.

Internally, the stomach appearance is classically described as **red velvet.** The mucosa appears red, oedematous, and swollen in patches corresponding to deposit of arsenic particles. It is covered with a considerable amount of tenacious mucus tinged with blood. Small acute ulceration or large erosions may be found at the pyloric end. Submucous petechial haemorrhages are common. The mucous membrane of the small intestine is inflamed usually in its upper part, and of the large intestine, the rectum is most prone to inflammation.

Petechial haemorrhages under the endocardium of the left ventricle are comparatively common and may be found even when the stomach presents little sign of irritation. Haemorrhages may be found in the abdominal organs, and occasionally, there may be widespread haemorrhages in larynx, trachea and lungs.

The liver may show patchy fatty degenerative changes and, less frequently, necrosis with jaundice. The heart and kidneys may show fatty degeneration. Decomposition is not significantly retarded by the presence of arsenic in acute poisoning.

Q. 43.2. Describe the symptoms and signs of various stages of chronic arsenic poisoning. Add a note on treatment and postmortem appearances.

Chronic arsenic poisoning may result from: (1) the after effects of an acute attack, (2) accidental ingestion of repeated small doses by those working with the poison, (3) taking food or drink in which there are traces of the poison, and (4) when the excretory function is interfered with or if the intake exceeds the excretory capacity of the body.

Symptoms and signs: In chronic poisoning, irrespective of the mode of administration, a classical state of ill-health results as represented by the following **four stages:** (1) the first stage of nutritional and gastro-intestinal disturbances, (2) the second stage of catarrhal changes, (3) the third stage of skin rashes, and (4) the fourth stage of nervous disturbances.

First stage of nutritional and gastrointestinal disturbances: The earliest sign is gradual emaciation. Loss of appetite, nausea, and intermittent attacks of vomiting and diarrhoea are common. These alimentary disturbances may be misdiagnosed.

Second stage of catarrhal changes: A little later, the patient may feel as if he has a common cold. The mucous membranes are inflamed, resulting in conjunctivitis, running of the eyes and nose, coughing, hoarseness of voice, and bronchial catarrh.

Third stage of skin rashes: At this stage, there is irritation of the skin, often accompanied by a vesicular eruption and sometimes this assumes the form of a nettle rash for which arsenical poisoning may be mistaken. After long exposure, there may be a patchy brown pigmentation of the skin called 'rain drop' type pigmentation, and this may give rise to a mistaken diagnosis of Addison's disease. Hyperkeratosis of the palms and soles follow. At this stage, there may be falling out of the hair and brittleness of nails. White bands known as **Mee's lines** crossing the nails of the fingers and toes may be noticed; they indicate periods of arrested growth due to interference with normal metabolism.

Fourth stage of nervous disturbances: At this stage, there is tingling and numbness of the hands and feet and tenderness of the muscles, sometimes with paresis. Arsenical **neuritis** closely resembles that *associated with chronic alcoholism.* Other symptoms include headache, drowsiness, and impairment of vision and mental activity.

There may be evidence of liver damage, kidney damage, and bone marrow depression at some stage. Involvement of the heart is a common feature of chronic poisoning, and may prove fatal. The diagnosis of chronic arsenical poisoning rests entirely on a balanced assessment of the whole symptomatology including the circumstances. No one symptom or sign is diagnostic. In West Bengal, many patients with skin rashes started going to doctor. Attention was drawn to this sudden splurge of cases. On further investigation, it became clear that people in that area are consuming water containing non-acceptable doses of arsenic contaminated water due to arsenic containing effluents.

Treatment: The treatment of chronic poisoning consists in removal of the patient from further exposure. Dimercaprol (BAL) has greatly improved the prognosis. Vitamin B complex and intravenous sodium thiosulphate are useful. The other treatment is symptomatic. Complete recovery may require six months to one year.

Postmortem appearances: In chronic poisoning, retardation of decomposition is evident. The effects of long-standing absorption of the poison are seen in progressive emaciation; anaemia; fatty degenerative changes in the heart muscle, liver and kidneys; in addition to congestion of the gastrointestinal tract. Microscopy may disclose peripheral neuropathy. The skin changes have been described under symptomatology.

Samples of hair and nail should be taken for analysis. For this purpose, hair must be complete with their bulbs, and nails should be whole. Arsenic is also deposited at the end of long bones which may be examined for the presence of poison. A few centimetres of the shaft of lower end of femur is suitable for this purpose.

POISONING BY ORGANIC ARSENICAL COMPOUNDS

These are commonly known as the arsphenamines. They were used in the past for treatment of syphilis, parasitic blood diseases, and *Trichomonas vaginalis*. Their chief toxic manifestation from intravenous use is an immediate anaphylactic reaction, known as the *nitritoid crisis,* which may end fatally. Administered repeatedly even in medicinal doses, toxic manifestations include exfoliative dermatitis (arsenical dermatitis), toxic jaundice, nephritis, agranulocytosis, optic atrophy and *arsenical encephalopathy*. Death may ensue from convulsions and coma with cyanosis and anuria.

Q. 43.3. State the points in favour of and against arsenic as an ideal homicidal agent.

In the past, arsenic was a **popular homicidal agent** because:

1. It is cheap, easily available, and the lethal dose is small (120 mg for an adult).
2. It is practically tasteless, odourless, and can, therefore, be given in food, drink, or 'paan' (betel leaf) without arousing suspicion.
3. The symptoms in acute poisoning come on within quarter to half an hour, thus providing opportunity to the poisoner to make good his escape.
4. Acute poisoning may be confused with cholera or bacterial food poisoning.
5. Chronic poisoning by small doses produces delayed death from progressive debility resembling certain diseases.

The **disadvantages** in the use of arsenic as a homicidal poison are:

1. It retards putrefaction. The body is, therefore, well preserved.
2. It does not deteriorate. Therefore, chemical analysis of viscera reveals its presence even after several years.
3. Heat does not destroy it. Therefore, it can be detected even from charred remains, if the body is burnt.

4. In chronic poisoning, as it is excreted in hair, nails, bones, skin, etc., its detection is possible when any of these structures is available.

Q. 43.4. Write short notes on: (1) tolerance, (2) absorption, (3) distribution, (4) elimination, (5) uses, and (6) postmortem imbibition of arsenic.

Tolerance: Certain individuals develop the habit of arsenic eating (arsenophagia), either as a tonic or as an aphrodisiac. They develop a certain amount of tolerance to bear it up to 250 mg or perhaps more in one dose. Chronic poisoning may occur in due course. Those who eat arsenic are called as arsenophagists.

Absorption: Arsenicals are rapidly absorbed from the alimentary tract and skin. Irritation, corrosion and systemic absorption occur when pastes containing arsenicals are applied to the skin.

Distribution: After absorption, arsenic is found in the greatest quantity in the liver. The kidneys contain proportionately less, and the other organs contain traces according to their blood content. In cases in which life is prolonged, it may be found in the muscles for a matter of days, in the bones for a matter of weeks, and in keratin tissues, hair, nail, and skin for months.

Elimination: Arsenic is eliminated mainly by the urine, but also in faeces bile, sweat, and other secretions. After a single dose, it may be found in the urine within half an hour and continues to be excreted for about 10 to 14 days or even longer. In chronic intermittent poisoning, arsenic is excreted in keratin tissues and bones. Hair and nails will show successive deposits of arsenic. Arsenic will probably not be found in the hair until about a week after ingestion but is present in the hair for long periods even, after all traces have left the viscera.

Uses: The various compounds of arsenic are in use in the arts, industry and agriculture. Arsenious oxide is a constituent of rat poisons, sheep dip, printer's ink, etc. It is also used for the preservation of timber and leather against white ants. Sulphides of arsenic are used as depilatories. Copper compounds of arsenic have been in use for colouring artificial flowers, children's toys, and wallpapers. Arsenate of lead is used as a fungicide and insecticide. Arsenites of sodium and potassium are used in weed killers, sprays for fruit trees, sheep dip, and insect poisons. Various cosmetic preparations contain arsenic in one form or the other. Arsenic is used by the quacks for the cure of various diseases ranging from common cold to cancer.

Suicide, homicide, accident, or other purposes: Arsenic used to be a popular agent for homicidal purposes in the past. It was then generally administered in 'paan' (betel leaf), tobacco, tea, coffee, or with some article of food. Fly papers and weed killers have been soaked in tea or wine and used with homicidal intent. Mass homicidal poisoning has sometimes occurred when arsenic is mixed in some article of food or in drinking water from a well or tank. Arsenic is sometimes applied locally in the form of a paste or ointment to abortion sticks to procure abortion.

Accidental cases of poisoning by arsenic sometimes occur. Poisoning in children may occur, if they chew paint or eat vermin or bait or ant syrup containing arsenic. Accidental poisoning may also occur from its injudicious medicinal use as an aphrodisiac, or in the treatment of various diseases by quacks.

Arsenic has also been used as a cattle poison, with success, it is fed to the animal mixed with fodder.

In 1952 in France, a chemist Jacques Cazenive, 59, was held responsible for the death of 73 children and injury to 270. The cause of death was "Baumol", a talcum powder made by the chemist which contained arsenic which had replaced zinc dioxide as an ingredient. An epidemic of sores and burns had arisen in the locality from the use of this powder.

On the evening of 16 January 1923, one Azimullah, aged 70, was served by a woman with two loaves of bread and potato curry mixed with arsenic. Shortly after eating one loaf with the vegetable, he started getting burning pain in the throat, to relieve which some 'ghee' (butter) was administered. Vomiting, followed by purging, commenced and he died next morning. The chemical examiner, UP, detected arsenic in the viscera as well as in the bread. *(Allahabad High Court Criminal Application No. 449, 1923).*

A daughter-in-law who failed to bring an additional doftry of ten thousand rupees for a car was sought to be done away with by the son of a landlord of Badal and his mother who conspired with a doctor to administer arsenic to her in small doses. At the end of three months, she was taken to Delhi almost dying, for treatment. The chemical examiner of Uttar Pradesh found sufficient arsenic in her hair, nails and the scales from the soles of her feet to establish the crime. *(Annual Report of FSL, UP, lor 1958).*

A person who was living with the deceased had illegal connection with his daughter-in-law. He poisoned her with arsenic to get rid of her. The police who received the report of this suspicious death went to the spot and found the body burning on the pyre. They collected the ashes and bones in which arsenic was discovered. *(FSL, UP, Report for 1948).*

Postmortem imbibition of arsenic: Certain samples of earth contain small traces of arsenic probably derived from the use of arsenical weed killers in the burial ground, or on account of drainage of water contaminated by arsenic. It is known that when a dead body is buried in such earth, small quantities of arsenic may enter the dead body. Where the soil contains arsenic, and arsenic poisoning is suspected, samples of earth from around the dead body should be collected for chemical analysis at the time of exhumation. In arsenical poisoning, the concentration of arsenic in various organs should be *more* than that in the earth.

Baden records the case of one London husband whose numerous rich wives died one after other of suspected poisoning. Scotland Yard exhumed their bodies and found arsenic. The man went to the gallows proclaiming his innocence, and years later, a curious student of toxicology tested the soil where the wives were buried and found that it was full of natural arsenic. The poison could well have seeped into the coffins. The student wondered if the wives were really poisoned. However, it was too late.

MERCURY (PARA)

Metallic mercury, also known as quicksilver, is a liquid metal with a bright silvery lustre. It exists in nature as the metal itself and as the sulphide (cinnabar or *ras sindoor).* Metallic mercury is not poisonous, if swallowed because it is not absorbed. It vaporises at room temperature and causes poisoning, if vaporised mercury is inhaled, swallowed, or rubbed into the skin. Mercury depresses cellular enzymatic mechanisms by combining with sulphydryl groups. Mercuric compounds being soluble are more poisonous than mercurous compounds which are less soluble.

Sources of Mercury

Mercuric chloride or corrosive sublimate: Also known as perchloride of mercury, it is in the form of white crystalline powder or tablets or use as a germicide. It has an acrid metallic taste, no smell, and is commonly the cause of acute poisoning.

Mercurous chloride or calomel: Also known as subchloride of mercury, it is a heavy, amorphous, white tasteless powder, insoluble in water.

Others: Other poisonous mercurial salts are mercuric oxide or red precipitate *(sipichand),* mercuric ammonium chloride or white precipitate, mercuric potassium iodide, mercuric nitrate, and mercuric cyanide.

Organic compounds of mercury: These were used principally as diuretics in the past, and as fungicides in seed commerce.

Q. 43.5. Describe the symptoms, signs, treatment, and postmortem appearances of acute mercury poisoning.

Symptoms and signs: The symptoms commence soon after the poison is swallowed. The taste is metallic, with a feeling of constriction in the throat, a burning sensation from mouth to stomach, and pain radiating over the abdomen. The mouth, tongue, and fauces become corroded and the mucous membrane appears grayish white. There is nausea, with frequent vomiting of long stringy masses of white mucus, mixed with blood, followed by profuse purging, often bloody, with painful tenesmus. Collapse sets in, with cold clammy skin, pale anxious face, sunken eyes, dilated pupils, rapid feeble pulse, and sighing respirations. Syncope, convulsions and general insensibility usually precede death which may take place in a few hours.

If death is not rapid, on the second or third day, salivation may develop, the gums may become swollen and inflamed, and the breath foul. Some loosening of teeth and ulcerative glossitis may follow. A renal lesion soon appears due to *nephrotoxicity* of mercury. The urine contains albumin and blood and death ensues from urasmia. Caecum and large intestine show areas of erosion, corrosion, and necrosis, due to re-excretion of mercury.

Fatal dose: The fatal dose of corrosive sublimate is about 1 to 2 gm.

Fatal period: Death may occur within a few hours but is usually delayed for 3 to 5 days. Delayed deaths are usually due to uraemia.

Treatment: The stomach should be washed out with 250 ml of a 5% solution of sodium formaldehyde sulphoxylate and about 100 ml of this solution left in the stomach. This substance reduces the per-chloride to a less soluble (less toxic) mercurous compound. Egg albumin which forms an insoluble albuminate of mercury may be administered. It is soluble in excess of albumin and must, therefore, be removed without delay by emetics or gastric lavage. Activated charcoal is also effective in the usual dosage; addition of magnesium sulphate increases its adsorptive power and hastens the removal of ingested poison. BAL and penicillamine derivatives (cuprimine) are effective antidotes. Where the kidneys show signs of damage, administration of alkaline fluids, peritoneal dialysis or haemodialysis may be necessary. The general treatment of shock and collapse will also be required, and symptomatic treatment should be given as indications arise.

Postmortem appearances: The appearances of corrosive poisoning will be present, if the poison is taken in a concentrated form. Otherwise, the signs of irritant poisoning will be observed.

The tongue is white and sodden in appearance and the mouth generally has a diffuse grayish white escharotic appearance. *Eschar* means a hard crust over a raw surface, e.g. material covering a deep burn. The mucous membrane of the alimentary tract is inflamed and corroded. The muscular coats are so softened that it is difficult to remove the organ without rupture. Mercury has a selective action on the caecum and large intestine which show intense inflammation, ulceration, and even gangrene. The kidneys show a toxic nephritis. The liver and heart may show fatty degeneration, and heart subendocardial haemorrhages also.

Q. 43.6. Give a brief account of chronic poisoning by mercury.

This may be the result of: (1) the after effects of an acute attack, (2) injudicious medical administration, and (3) continuous accidental absorption in those working with the metal or its salts as in the manufacture of thermometers, barometers, fur felt, mirrors, and ultraviolet apparatus, or in police officers engaged in finger print detection work where finger print powder contains mercury.

The **symptoms and signs** of chronic mercury poisoning are: excessive salivation with metallic taste in the mouth, loosening of teeth with painful inflamed gums, and occasionally a *blue-black line on the gums* as with lead poisoning. Irritation of the skin may occur. Nephritis is a serious complication. Abortion is common. *Mercuria lentis,* i.e. discolouration of the capsule of the lens of the eye due to deposition of mercury, as observed through a slit-lamp, is one of the early symptoms of chronic mercury poisoning. It has no effect on visual acuity. Nervous symptoms, such as tremors, and mental symptoms known as erethism, are seen in chronic mercury poisoning. The **tremor** is known as the **hatter's shake,** because it is common in workers of that industry. It is coarse, intentional, and affects the hands, arms, tongue, and later the legs. **Erethism** is a peculiar disturbance of the personality characterised by shyness, irritability, tremors, loss of memory and insomnia. It is common in workers in mirror industry.

Treatment consists of removal of the patient from exposure to mercury and promoting elimination of the mercury by bowels and kidneys. The rest of the treatment is symptomatic.

At **postmortem,** the changes in the large intestine, due partly to re-excretion, are often very striking, with necrosis which spreads, and may involve practically the whole of the lower bowel. Kidney damage consisting of tubular nephritis, and fatty degeneration of the liver and cardiac muscle are observed.

In death from mercury poisoning, in addition to routine viscera, bones, teeth, hair and nails should also be preserved for chemical analysis.

Q. 43.7. Comment on medicolegal aspects of poisoning by mercury.

Accidental poisoning may occur from: (1) accidental ingestion of antiseptic solutions containing the perchloride or cyanide, or of antiseptic tablets of the perchloride or iodide, (2) soluble salts employed as vaginal douches, (3) absorption of mercurial preparations applied to the skin, and (4) intravenous administration of organic mercurials as diuretics.

In children, accidental poisoning may occur from: (1) the use of ammoniated mercury in some bleaching creams, and (2) swallowing the sulphocyanide of mercury stick or tablet, the chief constituent of *Pharoah's serpents,* which when ignited, give out pungent smell and ash in the form of a long tortuous figure resembling a snake, and hence the name.

Suicidal and homicidal poisoning is rare. After absorption, mercury passes rapidly to the foetus in utero through the placental circulation and causes abortion.

Chronic mercury poisoning occurs in industrial workers from continued inhalation of volatalised mercury. The effect of chronic poisoning may be delayed for many years. *Much responsibility, therefore, rests on the medicolegal expert to establish a cause and effect relationship.*

LEAD (SHISHA)

As with other metals, the soluble compounds of lead are more poisonous than lead itself, except when lead is in the volatile state. Lead may obtain access to the body by inhalation, by ingestion, or by absorption from the skin or mucous surfaces. The primary effect of lead is to cause spasm of the capillaries and arterioles. The toxic effects result from fixation of lead in certain tissues, such as the brain and peripheral nervous system.

Sources of lead: The principal salts of lead which produce toxic effects are the acetate (sugar of lead or salt of saturn), the oxide (litharge, *mudrasang)* converted into the oleate in the form of diachylon, the carbonate or white lead *(safeda),* the tetroxide or the red lead (vermillion, *sindur*), the yellow chrome or the chromate of lead, and tetraethyl lead.

Q. 43.8. Describe the symptoms, signs, treatment and postmortem appearances of acute lead poisoning.

Acute lead poisoning is rare. Symptoms are similar to those of acute arsenical, or mercurial poisoning, except that diarrhoea is replaced by constipation and the stool is blackened and offensive. The principal manifestations are gastrointestinal or central nervous system disturbances.

Symptoms and signs: The symptoms consist of metallic astringent taste, dry throat, thirst, nausea, and vomiting with colic-like pains in abdomen, relieved by pressure. There may be purging but more usually constipation. The faeces are offensive and black owing to the formation of lead sulphide and the urine is suppressed. When the case is protracted, the patient may suffer from cramps in the legs and arthralgia. Headache, drowsiness and paralysis of the limbs may be observed. Finally, collapse precedes death. Acute cases may survive and develop the symptoms of chronic poisoning.

In poisoning by tetraethyl lead, gastric symptoms are absent or slight. Cerebral symptoms, the so-called **lead encephalopathy,** predominate. It is characterised by headache, sleeplessness, tremors of the eyes, mouth and fingers, sometimes paralysis, or loss of vision, hallucinations, excitement, and delirium or apathy; and convulsions (Fig. 43.1). The patient may suffer from permanent mental changes or insanity.

Fatal dose: The fatal dose of absorbed lead has been estimated to be 0.5 gram. Fatal dose of lead acetate is about 20 grams, and lead carbonate about 4 grams. A drop or two of pure tetraethyl lead may cause serious symptoms.

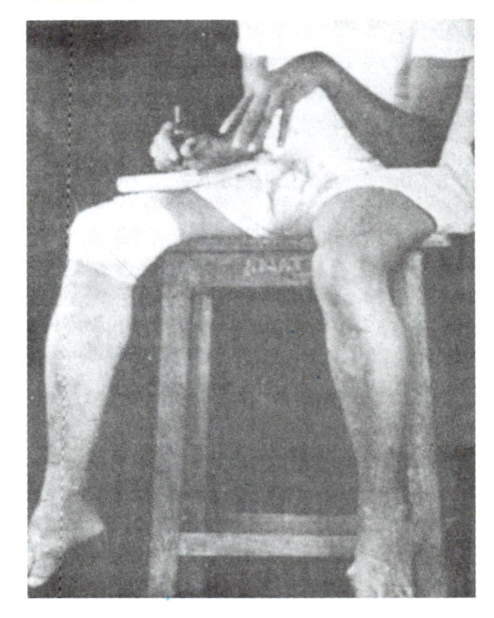

Fig. 43.1: Paralysis due to chronic lead poisoning. Big joints are generally affected while small joints escape. In this case, there is wrist drop and foot drop. The right wrist joint is also getting affected. Note the manner in which he writes. The knee is inflamed and hence bandaged. (*Courtesy*: Dr GB Sahay)

Fatal period: Death may occur on the second or third day. Acute poisoning is rare, and may be followed by chronic poisoning.

Treatment: The stomach should be washed out with a 1% solution of magnesium or sodium sulphate followed by ample washings with plain water to remove the lead sulphate formed. Morphine and atropine help to relieve painful colic. The bowel should be cleared at regular intervals to get rid of excreted lead. Calcium favours the deposition of lead in the skeleton. A diet rich in milk, and administration of calcium salts and vitamin D are helpful. Calcium versenate (EDTA) and penicillamine are useful antidotes. Peritoneal or haemodialysis may be necessary. The rest of the treatment is symptomatic.

If commercial tetraethyl lead is spilled on the skin, washing the area with kerosene within 15 minutes after contact, will remove the poison quantitatively. When gasoline containing tetraethyl lead is swallowed, the treatment is the same as that for gasoline.

Postmortem appearances: These are chiefly of gastroenteritis. The gastric mucosa is congested. There may be eroded patches. The large intestine may contain black-coloured faeces.

Q. 43.9. Give a detailed account of chronic lead poisoning (plumbism, saturnism, or saturnine poisoning).

Lead poisoning is nearly always of the chronic type. It is encountered in various industries, e.g. through ingestion in type-setting, plumbing, battery work, and glazing pottery; through inhalation in the manufacture of white lead, smelting, from paint in oxyacetylene ship breaking, diamond cutting, file making, turning, car welding and polishing; and through ingestion and inhalation in painting, coach building, lacquering, tinning, vitreous enamelling, and colour and dye manufacture and use. In home, chronic lead poisoning may occur from use of 'ghee' (butter) stored in tins or taking food cooked in tinned vessels. Formerly, it used to occur from drinking water supplied through lead pipes.

Chronic poisoning may also result from the mobilisation of lead already stored in the body tissues, especially the bones, e.g. in acidosis, and symptoms of acute or chronic poisoning may develop, even years after the original absorption of lead.

Symptoms and signs: Although chronic poisoning correctly describes prolonged exposures, *manifestations often are acute.* The main symptoms and signs are: facial pallor; anaemia with punctate basophilia; lead line; colic and constipation; paralysis; encephalopathy; renovascular manifestations; reproductive system manifestations; and general symptoms.

Facial pallor: The facial pallor particularly about the mouth is one of the earliest and most consistent sign. It is supposed to be due to vasospasm.

Anaemia with punctate basophilia: The blood shows hypochromic anaemia, associated with polychromasia, punctate basophilia, reticulocytosis, poikilocytosis, an increase in mononuclear cells and decrease in polymorphonuclear cells. **Punctate basophilia** means the presence of many dark-blue-coloured pinhead like spots in the cytoplasm of red blood cells. These are stained with basic dyes and hence the name. The condition is due to toxic action of lead on porphyrin metabolism, porphyrins are excreted in the urine, the amount being as much as 500 μg/day.

Lead line: This is a stippled *bluish-black line* due to subepithelial deposition of lead sulphide granules on the gums at the junction with the teeth (not on the teeth). It is seen on the gums of carious teeth, especially noticeable on the upper jaw. Its colour is due to the action of hydrogen sulphide liberated by microorganisms from decomposing protein food around carious teeth in the presence of circulating lead. A somewhat similar line may be seen in cases of mercury, copper, bismuth, iron and silver poisoning.

Colic and constipation: The colic generally affects intestines, ureters, uterus and blood vessels. It is relieved by pressure on the abdomen. It is a late manifestation but constitutes an acute symptom of chronic plumbism. Obstinate constipation (also known as dry belly ache) is associated with it.

Paralysis: This is usually a late manifestation, seen in less than 10 per cent of cases. Onset may be gradual or sudden. There is commonly paralysis of extensor muscles of wrist (wrist drop) but peroneal muscles (foot drop) or other muscle groups may also be affected. The paralysis is associated with degeneration of nerve and atrophy of muscle, and is said to be due to interference with the resynthesis of phosphocreatinine.

Encephalopathy: Lead encephalopathy, in some form or the other, is said to be present in every case of plumbism but is more common in poisoning by tetraethyl lead. It is common in children and is characterised by recurrent convulsions and progressive mental deterioration. Optic atrophy may occur.

Renovascular manifestations: Vascular constriction results in hypertension and arteriolar degeneration. Arteriosclerotic nephritis may occur.

Reproductive system manifestations: Menstrual disorders, such as dysmenorrhoea, amenorrhoea, and menorrhagia, are common. Toxic action on the trophoblastic epithelium and tonic contractions of the uterus result either in a dead foetus or abortion. It is also responsible for sterility in both sexes.

General symptoms: These consist of general weakness, anorexia, dyspepsia, metallic taste in the mouth, foul breath, headache, vertigo, irritability, drowsiness and arthralgia.

Diagnosis: Clinically, this may be suspected from colic, punctate basophilia, and a bluish-black line on the gums. Palsy or encephalopathy may be contributory. More than 200 punctate basophilia cells per cmm is diagnostic and so also the presence of 0.25 mg of lead per litre of urine. Lead interferes with the enzyme system concerned with the synthesis of haem resulting in excretion of porphyrins in the urine. X-ray evidence of transverse opaque bands at the end of long bones is present in children. In poisoning by tetraethyl lead, liver may appear abnormally opaque on X-ray.

Treatment: The aim is to remove the source of exposure and then excretion of the stored lead. EDTA combines with lead, promotes its mobilisation and urinary excretion in an inactive form, and affords rapid control of the signs and symptoms of poisoning including those of lead encephalopathy. The combination of EDTA and BAL is more effective than EDTA alone. During convalescence, long-term control of plumbism will be achieved by oral administration of penicillamine daily. Other symptoms are treated on general lines. If lead paralysis has developed, massage to the affected muscles is helpful.

Postmortem appearances: In chronic forms, the findings confirm the clinical features already described. Bone marrow shows hyperplasia of erythroblasts and leucoblasts with decrease in fat cells. A long bone, teeth, hair and nails should be preserved in case analysis becomes desirable.

Q. 43.10. Comment on medicolegal aspects of lead poisoning.

Acute poisoning is rare. Lead is rarely used for homicidal purposes. Lead poisoning is usually accidental. It may occur in children from eating paint on cribs, or beds, or toys. Subacute or chronic lead poisoning may be caused by the contamination of food or drink. Apart from industrial poisoning, accidental chronic poisoning has occurred from the use of lead monoxide (litharge) as a remedy for syphilis by quacks, rarely from the continued use of vermillion by married Hindu women to the scalp, and from the use of Diachylon paste to procure abortion. Sometimes, lead poisoning may occur from lead missiles embedded in the tissues due to gunshot injury. Red lead is occasionally used as a cattle poison either alone or mixed with white arsenic.

COPPER (TAMBA)

Metallic copper is not poisonous but some of its salts are poisonous, e.g. the sulphate or the **blue vitriol** (Nila tutia), which occurs in large blue crystals, and the subacetate or verdigris (Zangal), which occurs in bluish green mass or powder. Two other copper compounds, viz. the arsenite and the acetoarsenite, have already been considered along with arsenic. Copper is a powerful inhibitor of enzymes.

Q. 43.11. Describe the symptoms, signs, treatment, and postmortem appearances of acute poisoning by copper.

Symptoms and signs: These commence within 15–30 minutes with a metallic taste in the mouth, salivation, thirst, burning in the stomach, colicky abdominal pain, vomiting, diarrhoea, and collapse, the usual effects of any irritant poison. The vomited matter is green or blue and must be distinguished from bile or bilious vomit. Addition of ammonium hydroxide turns the copper vomit deep blue while bile remains unchanged. The stools are liquid and brown but not bloody. The urine is inky in appearance, diminished in amount and contains albumin and casts. Uraemia may occur. There may be severe headache and breathing may be difficult. In severe cases, jaundice and muscle cramps occur. Cold perspiration indicates circulatory collapse. Convulsions and coma precede death.

A woman was admitted to the hospital with severe vomiting of bluish green colour and it was suspected as a case of copper sulphate poisoning. Addition of ammonium hydroxide confirmed the bilious nature of the vomit. On enquiry, it was revealed that she was pregnant, and it was a case of unusually severe pregnancy vomiting.

Fatal dose: About 30 gm of copper sulphate or verdigris is fatal.

Fatal period: This varies from 12–24 hours. It may be delayed for 3–5 days or even a week.

Treatment: The stomach should be washed with 1% solution of potassium, ferrocyanide which forms an insoluble compound, cupric ferrocyanide. Albumins form an insoluble albuminate of copper and are very valuable. Demulcent fluids are also necessary. Penicillamine, BAL and EDTA are helpful and may be given in the usual dosage.

Postmortem appearances: The skin may be yellow owing to jaundice. Greenish blue froth may be present at the mouth and nostrils. Bluish or greenish colouration of the gastric mucosa and stomach contents is diagnostic. The mucous membrane is congested, inflamed, and occasionally eroded in patches. The intestinal mucous membrane may show the same appearances. The liver may be soft and fatty.

Q. 43.12. Give a brief account of chronic copper poisoning. Add a note on medicolegal aspects of copper poisoning.

In **chronic poisoning,** the main symptoms and signs are allied to poisoning with lead. The usual symptoms consist of a metallic taste in the mouth; a green line on the gums at the base of the teeth; gastrointestinal symptoms, such as nausea, vomiting, colic, diarrhoea or constipation; and general signs of progressive emaciation, viz. anaemia, malaise and debility. The evidences of implication of nervous system are also very similar, viz. peripheral neuritis, with wrist drop or foot drop in some cases. Wilson's disease may possibly occur. Bronzed diabetes may be present. The treatment is similar to that of chronic poisoning by mercury.

The chief postmortem appearances consist of parenchymatous injury to the heart, liver, and kidneys. Mallory has described haemochromatosis (bronzed diabetes) from chronic copper absorption.

Medicolegal aspects: Copper occurs in some fungicides and in small medicinal doses in tablets with the sulphate of iron and manganese. Copper sulphate is used as an *antidote* in phosphorus poisoning.

Copper sulphate is sometimes used to commit suicide. It is not used for homicide owing to its colour and metallic taste. It is sometimes swallowed by children attracted by its colour. Accidental poisoning occurs when copper has been added to keep the green colour of vegetables. Copper sulphate is rarely been used as a cattle poison. Copper subacetate is formed by the action of vegetable acids on improperly tinned copper vessels. It may cause poisoning from contamination of food stored in such vessels.

THALLIUM

Thallium is a soft white heavy metal with a lustrous colour which tarnishes on exposure to air and forms thallus oxide. The metal and its compounds are highly toxic, the important ones being thallium acetate and thallium sulphate. These salts being soluble, colourless and nearly tasteless can be easily administered by mouth in food or drink. They are readily absorbed from the skin also. Toxic symptoms from thallium poisoning resemble those of lead.

Q. 43.13. Give a succinct account of thallium poisoning. Add a note on its medicolegal aspects.

Symptoms of acute thallium poisoning appear about 12–36 hours after a toxic dose. They include abdominal pain, vomiting and diarrhoea. Neurological symptoms may predominate and these include peripheral neuritis, impaired vision, ataxia and convulsions. Loss of hair occurs two weeks after ingestion.

Chronic poisoning may occur in workers engaged in the manufacture of rat and vermin poisons, depilatory pastes, luminous paints and in the glass and dye industries. Besides falling of the hair, inhibition of growth and sexual development, nephritis, peripheral neuritis and mental disturbances have been described. Transverse lines on the finger nails, known as *Mee's lines,* are also seen. This is called as Thalotoxicosis. The triad of thallium: 1. alopecia with skin rash, 2. Painful peripheral neuropathy, 3. Mental confusion with lethargy.

Thallium poisoning should normally be suspected when there are gastrointestinal symptoms, polyneuritis, and loss of hair from head, lateral two-thirds of the eyebrows, and axilla. An X-ray of the abdomen showing a high density hepatic opacity is diagnostic.

In R *vs* Fletcher (1953), Mrs Fletcher was accused of murdering her husband with "Thalrat" rat poison. Mr. Fletcher suffered from depilation, polyneuritis and pain in the extremities. He was nervous and crying. He died after 11 days, his condition not being diagnosed. At postmortem, arsenic and lead were sought with negative results. 100 mg of thallium was found in his body.

Hausman and Wilson report the case of a woman who was given an unknown quantity of thallus sulphate. Initially, a burning sensation in the feet radiating to the knees was recorded. By the fifth day, she had severe leg pains and could not walk. Thereafter, her condition deterio-rated and she became lethargic and un-responsive until the eleventh day, when she died.

The fatal dose is about one gram of a soluble salt. Death follows a fatal dose in two days to two weeks depending upon the amount ingested.

Treatment must follow the general procedure for heavy metal poisoning.

At autopsy, if death has occurred soon after ingestion, there is gastroenteritis with liver and kidney damage. In the central nervous system, chromatolysis and swelling as well as degeneration of ganglion cells may be found. In 7 days, the hair follicles begin to show oedema of epithelial cells with dissolution of rete layers and brittle proximal end of hair. Thallium may be recovered from blood, urine, liver and kidney. Diagnostic changes may be found in the hair roots. Thallium resists putrefaction and heat. It can, therefore, be detected in decomposed bodies and even in the ashes of cremated bodies.

Medicolegal aspects: Thallium is used as an ideal homicidal poison in some European countries and Australia where it is also used as a rodenticide. Accidental intoxication may result from its therapeutic use as a depilatory or from its accidental ingestion when used as a rodenticide. Chronic poisoning occurs from industrial exposure.

ZINC

Zinc is a bluish white, lustrous metal. The toxic effects are confined mainly to three salts of the metal, namely, the sulphate **(white vitriol),** the action of which is irritant; the chloride, which is corrosive; and the phosphide which is used as a rodenticide.

Q. 43.14. Give a succinct account of poisoning by zinc. Add a note on zinc phosphide.

Symptoms and signs: The symptoms from zinc sulphate are chiefly those of gastrointestinal irritation, and consist of metallic taste in mouth, pain in gullet, stomach and abdomen, vomiting and diarrhoea. Collapse may follow. The chloride has a stronger corrosive action, destroying the mucous membrane of the mouth, throat, oesophagus and stomach. Vomiting is severe, there is purging with tenesmus and blood, and symptoms of shock. There may be remission of symptoms followed by recurrences.

The symptoms and signs of **chronic poisoning** are closely allied to those of lead and copper.

Fatal dose: The smallest fatal dose of zinc sulphate is about 15 gm. The chloride is more toxic, 400 mg having proved fatal.

Fatal period: Death from zinc sulphate poisoning, though rare, has occurred in 2 hours after taking 90 gm and on the fifth day after taking 15 gm. In poisoning by zinc chloride, death occurs within a few hours from shock or after several weeks from after-effects of the poison.

Treatment: The stomach should be washed out unless marked vomiting has removed the poison. There is no specific antidote. Sodium bicarbonate in tepid water should be given freely. Demulcents should also be given and the case treated on general lines.

Postmortem appearances: These are similar to those of other irritants in the case of the sulphate, and corrosives in the case of the chloride.

Medicolegal aspects: Cases are recorded in which the soluble salts have been administered occasionally to commit suicide, homicide, or abortion. Zinc sulphate has been taken in mistake for Epsom salt. Accidental poisoning may occur through eating food cooked or stored in galvanised iron vessels.

Zinc phosphide is a steel-grey-coloured crystalline powder with garlicky odour. It is an effective and economic rodenticide. In human beings, its action starts immediately after it comes in contact with gastric acid, when highly toxic phosphine gas is released.

Following ingestion, there is metallic taste in the mouth, and burning in the throat, oesophagus and stomach, followed by nausea, vomiting, diarrhoea, and abdominal pain. The patient may complain of garlic taste in the mouth and garlic odour may be perceived in the breath. Sometimes, there may be a symptom-free period followed by gastrointestinal disturbances, evidence of liver damage, and haemorrhages in the skin. The liberated phosphine gas causes dyspnoea, pulmonary oedema, and bradycardia, followed by circulatory collapse or neurological symptoms, coma, and death. Shock, oliguria, acidosis, tetany, and convulsions are other features.

The fatal dose of zinc phosphide is 5 grams. The fatal period varies from a few hours to 24 hours.

As for treatment, if skin or clothes are contaminated, the clothing should be removed and the affected parts washed thoroughly with soap and water. If the poison is ingested, vomiting may be induced by giving a tablespoon of salt in a glass of warm water and the treatment continued till the vomiting fluid is clear. Gastric lavage may be undertaken with 3–5% solution of sodium bicarbonate which minimises the conversion of zinc phosphide to phosphine. Zinc phosphide adheres firmly to the crypts in the mucous membrane of the stomach and even if a small quantity remains in the stomach after vomiting or gastric lavage, it is sufficient to cause death by slow absorption. It is, therefore, particularly important to keep the patient under observation for delayed symptoms after initial recovery. General supportive measures include administration of vitamin K, corticosteroids, and sedatives. Other symptomatic measures may be taken as need arises.

Pathological findings from ingestion of zinc phosphide include petechial haemorrhages in the skin, garlic odour on opening the stomach, grayish black residues of the poison sticking to the mucous membrane of the stomach, and congestion of liver, spleen, kidney, brain, and lungs. Even necrobiosis of the liver and other findings similar to phosphorus poisoning may be seen.

Zinc phosphide is an effective rodenticide and pesticide. It is easily available and cheap. It may, therefore, be used for suicidal purposes. It has been used with homicidal intent in cases of **dowry deaths.** Accidental poisoning amongst children and farmers is known.

Q. 43.15. Write short note on 'metal fume fever'.

Metal fume fever due to expoture to zinc fumes shows chills, fever, muscle pains, fatigue, cough, dysproce, salivation, sweating, tachycardia, cyanosis fever resolve 36 hours after exposur to fumes ceases. The worker is free at week end and fever reappears on Monday hence called as Monday fever. This is seen also on exposure to fumes of chromium, cadmium, cobalt, manganese, mercury, magnesium, etc. Treatment is symptomatic and chelating agents.

44 Vegetable Poisons

The important poisons in this group are: ricinus communis, croton tiglium, abrus precatorius, colocynth, ergot, capsicum, semecarpus anacardium, calotropis gigantea and procera, and plumbago rosea and zeylanica. They act as irritants due to an active principle contained in them. Externally, they produce inflammation, vesication, pustulation, and callous sores. Internally, they produce mainly symptoms of gastrointestinal irritation. Death results from exhaustion leading to collapse.

Fig. 44.1: Castor seeds

RICINUS COMMUNIS (CASTOR OIL PLANT, ARANDI)

Q. 44.1. Give a brief account of poisoning from ricinus communis. Add a note on toxalbumin (phytotoxin).

This plant grows all over India. Its seeds are oval, of a glossy brown colour, and mottled. They are of two sizes, the big and small. The small seeds resemble croton seeds and are about 1.25 cm long and 0.85 cm broad (Fig. 44.1). The entire plant is poisonous. It contains an active principle called ricin which is a toxalbumin. A **toxalbumin** or **phytotoxin** is a toxic protein. It acts like a bacterial toxin. It causes agglutination and lysis of red cells and has antigenic properties. Castor seeds are poisonous when eaten in the raw state but harmless when swallowed entire or after cooking. The residue (press cake) left after extraction of oil from the seeds contains ricin and is poisonous. The extracted oil (castor oil) does not contain ricin and is, therefore, not poisonous. Ricin is a supertoxicpoison.

Symptoms and signs: The raw seeds, when eaten, cause burning in the throat, salivation, nausea, copious and painful vomiting, colicky abdominal pain, bloody purging, followed by collapse. Dehydration and cramps are common. Coma and convulsions may precede death. The dust from the residue may cause dermatitis, conjunctivitis, rhinitis, and occasionally asthma and allergy.

Fatal dose and fatal period: The fatal dose is 6 mg of ricin, which is equivalent to about ten seeds. Several days elapse before death takes place.

Treatment: There is no specific antidote for ricin poisoning. Treatment must, therefore, be based on general principles.

Postmortem appearances: Fragments of seeds may be found in the stomach. The bowel is inflamed and there are occasional erosions and submucous haemorrhages. There may be haemorrhages in internal organs.

Medicolegal aspects: Accidental cases occur among children from eating the seeds. The seeds have been administered in food with homicidal intent. The powder of the seeds causes local irritation of the skin, and mucous membrane of the nose and eyes. In the George Markov political assassination in London, a tiny sphere drilled out to carry ricin was injected from an air weapon concealed in an umbrella.

CROTON TIGLIUM (JAMALGOTA, NEPALA)

Q. 44.2. Give a brief account of poisoning from croton tiglium.

This plant grows all over India. The seeds and the oil (croton oil) extracted from the seeds are poisonous. The seeds resemble small castor seeds in size and shape (oval) but differ in their appearance (Fig. 44.2). They are blackish-brown in colour with a white oily kernel and have longitudinal lines on them. The oil is brownish in colour, viscid in appearance, unpleasant in smell, and bitter in taste. The active principle is crotin, a toxalbumin, which is an irritant and vesicant. A less poisonous glycoside, crotonoside, is also present.

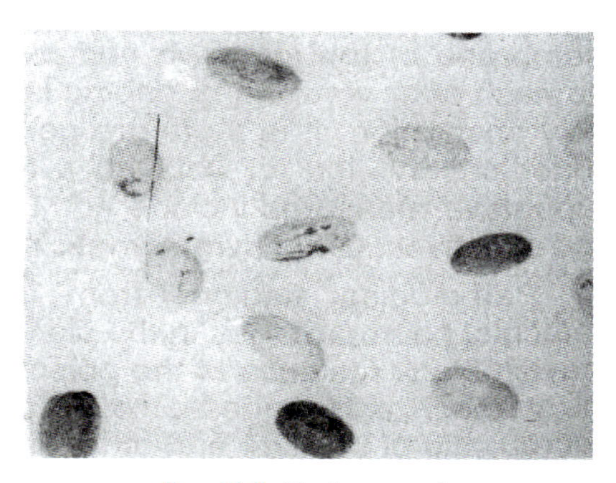

Fig. 44.2: Croton seeds
(Note the difference in appearance)

Symptoms and signs: These are similar to poisoning by ricin. The oil causes blistering externally, and on ingestion causes severe gastrointestinal irritation with burning pain in the abdomen, vomiting, powerful purging, and frequently a burning pain at the anus. In substantial dosage, collapse precedes death.

Fatal dose and fatal period: The fatal dose is 20 drops of the oil or four seeds. Death may occur in about four to six hours or may be delayed for three to six days.

Treatment: The treatment is based on general principles.

Postmortem appearances: These are similar to those described under ricinus communis.

Medicolegal aspects: Croton oil has been administered in food with homicidal intent. Poisonous symptoms have been produced by eating the seeds or inhaling their dust. Accidental poisoning has resulted from the use of croton oil as a purgative. It has been used as an abortifacient. Wild tribes have used the oil as an arrow poison.

ABRUS PRECATORIUS (JEQUIRITY BEAN)

Q. 44.3. Give a brief account of poisoning from abrus precatorius. Add a note on sui.

This is also known as Indian liquorice, Rosary pea, crab's eye, gunchi or rati. The plant is found all over India and though all its parts are poisonous, the seeds are commonly used as poison. They are of the size of a small pea, about 0.85 cm long and 0.65 cm broad, and have an average weight of 120 mg (Fig. 44.3). They are tasteless, odourless, oval, and red in colour, with a black spot on one pole. The active principle is abrin, a toxalbumin, and its actions resemble those of viperine snake bite.

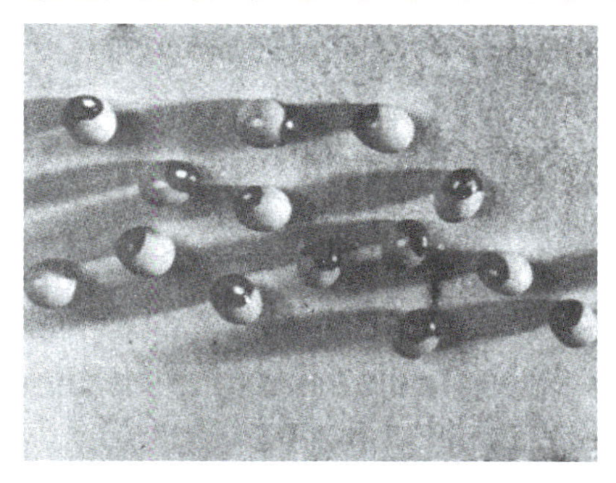

Fig. 44.3: The seeds of **abrus precatorius**

Symptoms and signs: When the seeds are swallowed raw or after cooking, they are not poisonous. Poisonous symptoms resembling viper bite follow if an extract is injected under the skin or into a wound. Such a method is used to poison cattle by means of sui.

Suis are fine needles prepared by decorticating the seeds and powdering them, followed by mixing the powder with opium, onion, dhatura and spirit or water to make into a paste, and the paste shaped into small sharp needles, which are allowed to harden by drying in the sun. The needles are 15 mm long and weigh about 90–120 mg. Two or three of them are fitted to the holes made in a small wooden stick, with which a blow is struck to the animal. This results in a local lesion, characterised by oedema, necrosis and oozing of haemorrhagic fluid from the puncture site. The animal becomes apathetic and drowsy. It is disinclined to take food. In three or four days, it is unable to move, drops down, becomes comatose and dies. Convulsions may precede death. The symptoms resemble those of viper snake bite, for which they may be mistaken.

Human poisoning is characterised by a local painful swelling and ecchymosis, followed by necrosis. The patient suffers from vertigo, cardiac arrhythmia, convulsions and death. When ingested, there is nausea, vomiting, abdominal pain, diarrhoea, and collapse.

Fatal dose and fatal period: The fatal dose is 1–2 seeds by mouth or 90–120 mg abrin by injection. The fatal period is 3–5 days.

Treatment: This consists of dissecting out the sui and injection of anti-abrin. The rest of the treatment is symptomatic.

Postmortem appearances: The injured site is swollen, inflamed and necrosed. Fragments of sui are usually found in the wound. Haemorrhagic patches are seen under mucous membranes. Internal organs are congested and haemorrhagic.

Medicolegal aspects: Suis are used to kill cattle either to produce cheap hides or for revenge. Human poisoning by keeping a sui-spike between fingers and giving a slap or contaminating wounds thereby, is recorded. Malingerers use the powdered seeds to produce conjunctivitis. The use of abrus as an arrow poison is known.

COLOCYNTH (BITTER APPLE, INDRAYANI)

Q. 44.4. Give a brief account of poisoning from colocynth. Add a note on glycosides.

Colocynth is obtained from the dried pulp of the fruit of *Citrullus colocynthis* or bitter apple. The plant grows widely throughout India. The pulp freed from the seeds is called colocynth, and occurs as white, spongy, light fragments having an intensely bitter taste. The active principle is a resinous glycoside, colocynthin, which is a proved irritant of the gastrointestinal tract (Fig. 44.4). **Glycosides** are substances found in plants and are composed of a sugar and a non-sugar compounds, the latter having a toxic action.

Symptoms and signs: In overdose, colocynth produces severe abdominal pain, yellow vomiting, yellow-coloured watery stools often blood-stained, collapse, and occasionally death.

Fig. 44.4: Fruit of colocynth, (above) and the plant (citrullus colocynthis or bitter apple) below

Fatal dose and fatal period: The fatal dose is about 1 to 2 gm. The fatal period varies from 24 hours to a few days.

Treatment: General management and symptomatic, dopamine.

Postmortem appearances: There is irritation of the alimentary tract and occasionally inflammation of kidneys and the urinary bladder.

Medicolegal aspects: Colocynth is occasionally taken to commit suicide. As it causes congestion of the pelvic viscera, it has been used to procure abortion.

ERGOT

Q. 44.5. Give a brief account of ergot poisoning. Add a note on ergotism.

Ergot is the sclerotium (compact mycelium or spawn) of the parasitic fungus *Claviceps purpurea*, which grows on cereals, like rye, barley, wheat, etc. It gradually replaces the grain by forming a curved dark purple mass, larger than the original grain. Such mass, when dried and powdered, forms the ergot of the market. It has a peculiar colour and disagreeable taste. It contains several active principles of which the important ones are ergotoxin, ergotamine, and ergometrine. They stimulate smooth muscles of the arterioles, intestines and uterus. Ergot is used especially for its stimulant action on the uterus and in the treatment of migraine. It is in common use in veterinary practice also.

Symptoms and signs: Acute poisoning is rare. The main symptoms are irritation of the throat, dryness and intense thirst, nausea, vomiting, diarrhoea, pain in the abdomen, tingling in the hands and feet, muscle cramps, dizziness and a feeling of coldness, all resulting from contractions of the smooth muscle. Abortion and haemorrhages in the uterus may occur. Bleeding from nose and other mucous membranes is common after large doses.

Chronic poisoning (ergotism) is not common now. It used to be caused by the ingestion of ergot-contaminated flour. The symptoms are those of gastrointestinal catarrh, followed by a convulsive or gangrenous form. *Convulsive ergotism* is due to changes in the central nervous system which cause very painful tonic contractions of voluntary muscles, drowsiness, headache, and giddiness, and lead eventually to madness. The patient complains of itching, a feeling of numbness, and formication, that is, cutaneous sensation as if ants are creeping under the skin. Severe psychiatric disturbances are common. *Gangrenous ergotism* may resemble Raynaud's disease. It is characterised by vasomotor disturbances, e.g. pain and numbness leading to gangrene of the fingers, toes, nose, and ears. Gangrene also occurs in the intestine and forms ulcers. Complete recovery usually occurs, if the use of ergot derivatives is discontinued prior to the appearance of gangrene.

Fatal dose and fatal period: The fatal dose of ergot may be as low as 1 gm. Death may occur in 24 hours or may be delayed for several days.

Treatment: In acute poisoning, the stomach and bowel should be emptied of the poison. In chronic poisoning, the use of ergot preparations should be discontinued. The rest of the treatment is purely symptomatic. Vasodilators are helpful.

Postmortem appearances: They are not characteristic. The internal organs are congested. Particles of the sclerotia may be detected in the stomach. Gangrene of the fingers and toes may be present.

Medicolegal aspects: Acute poisoning may occur when ergot is taken in a large dose to procure abortion. Chronic poisoning results from ingestion of ergot contaminated bread for a long time.

CAPSICUM (CHILLIS)

Q. 44.6. Give a brief account of capsicum from a medicolegal point of view. Differentiate chilli seeds from dhatura seeds.

Capsicum fruits are powdered and universally employed as a condiment, the condiment being known as red pepper or *lalmirch.* It has a pungent smell and taste which lasts for a long time. The active principles are capsaicin and capsicin, exceedingly acrid, volatile, non-alkaloidal, non-fatal substances (Figs 44.5 and 44.6).

Symptoms and signs: Applied to the skin, it causes irritation and vesication. When thrown in the eyes, it causes burning, lachrymation, and redness. When ingested in sufficient quantity, it acts as an irritant poison, and causes burning sensation in the mouth, throat, oesophagus, and stomach.

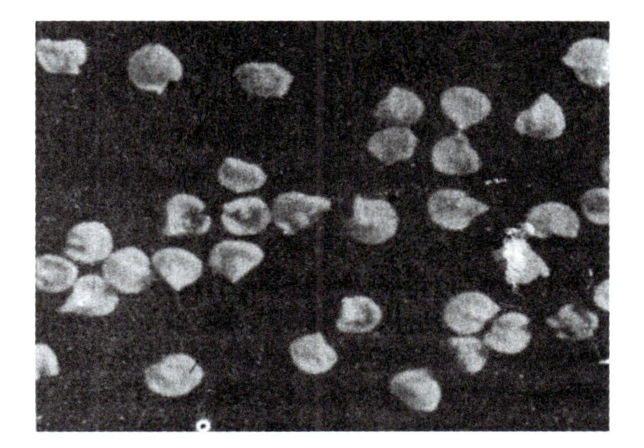

Fig. 44.5: Chilli seeds

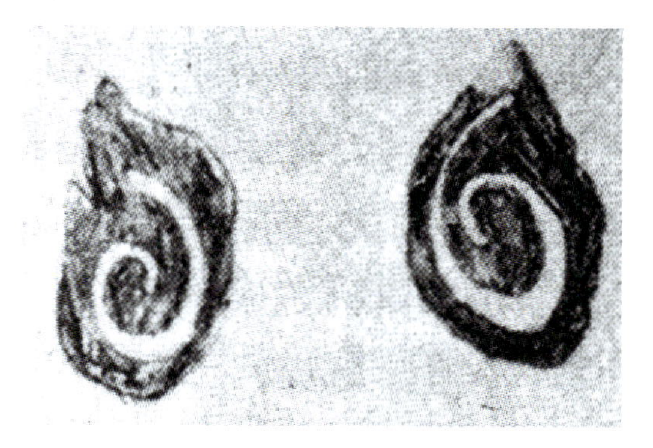

Fig. 44.6: Section of capsicum seeds. Embryo is curved inwards

Treatment: When applied to the skin, it should be washed out with water and irritation treated symptomatically. When ingested, the tongue should be scraped by a blunt edged instrument and ice given to suck. When thrown in the eyes, they should be washed in saline, and antibiotics applied. Cortisone drops may be helpful.

Medicolegal aspects: The powder is used as a means of torture to extort money or a confession of some guilt by introducing it into the nostrils, eyes, urethra, vagina, or rectum; burning it under the nose; and rubbing it on the breasts of the females. It may be thrown into the eyes to facilitate robbery. The fumes from burning chillis irritate the eyes and upper respiratory passages. Superstitious people use them to scare away devils and ghosts. Recently, Indian police want to resort to chilli bomb to facilitate clearing the mobs in agitations.

The seeds, about 0.30 cm long and wide, resemble dhatura seeds (Figs 44.7 and 44.8) and may be differentiated from them as follows:

	Chilli seeds	*Dhatura seeds*
1. Size	Small and thin	Large and thick
2. Colour	Pale yellow	Brown or black
3. Appearance	Smooth and round	Kidney-shaped, finely pitted and reticulated
4. Smell	Pungent	Odourless
5. Taste	Pungent	Bitter
6. Convex border	Single edge	Double edge
7. On section	Embryo curved inward like figure 44.4	Embryo curved outward

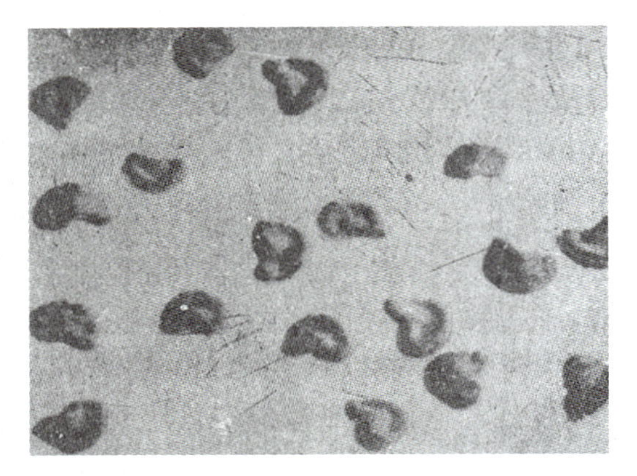

Fig. 44.7: Dhatura seeds

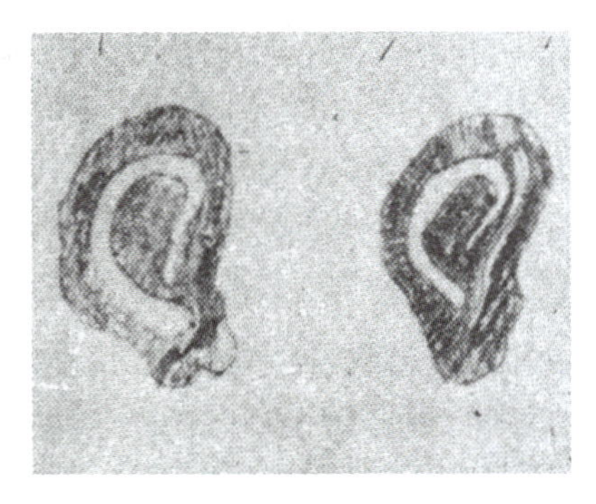

Fig. 44.8: Section of dhatura seeds. Embryo is curved outwards

SEMECARPUS ANACARDIUM (MARKING NUT)

Q. 44.7. Give a brief account of poisoning from semecarpus anacardium. Differentiate artificial bruise from true bruise.

The fruit of this plant is known as Bhilawan or the marking nut because its juice is used by dhobis (washermen) as marking ink on clothes. The nut is black, roughly cone-shaped, and has a thick pericarp. The contained juice is brown, oily, and acrid. Its active principles are semecarpol and bhilawanol (Fig. 44.9).

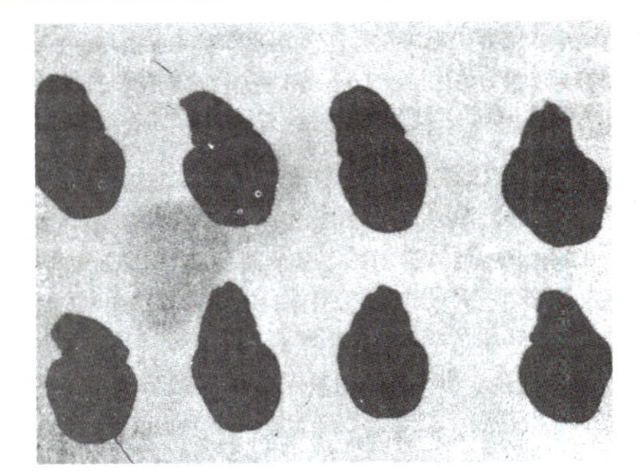

Fig. 44.9: Marking nuts. (*Courtesy*: Dr NK Mohanty)

Symptoms and signs: When the juice is applied to skin, it causes irritation and painful blisters containing acrid serum which causes an eczematous eruption on any part of the skin with which it comes into contact. The lesion resembles a bruise which may later ulcerate and slough. Internally administered, the juice is much less irritant. Taken in larger doses, it causes blisters in the mouth and throat and severe gastroenteritis, followed in some cases by dyspnoea, cyanosis, tachycardia, coma, and death.

Fatal dose and fatal period: The fatal dose is about 5 to 10 gm and death may result within 12 to 24 hours.

Treatment: This is symptomatic. When applied externally, the parts should be washed with warm water and bland liniments applied.

Postmortem appearances: The findings confirm the clinical features. The blister fluid should be preserved in rectified spirit and sent to a forensic science laboratory for analysis, if necessary.

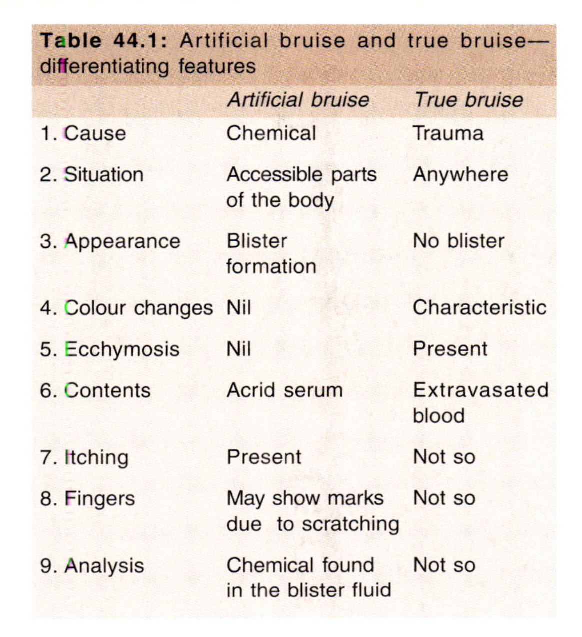

Table 44.1: Artificial bruise and true bruise—differentiating features

	Artificial bruise	*True bruise*
1. Cause	Chemical	Trauma
2. Situation	Accessible parts of the body	Anywhere
3. Appearance	Blister formation	No blister
4. Colour changes	Nil	Characteristic
5. Ecchymosis	Nil	Present
6. Contents	Acrid serum	Extravasated blood
7. Itching	Present	Not so
8. Fingers	May show marks due to scratching	Not so
9. Analysis	Chemical found in the blister fluid	Not so

Medicolegal aspects: The juice is used as an abortifacient by application to the os uteri by means of an abortion stick. It is applied to the genitals as a punishment for adultery. It is used by malingerers to produce an artificial bruise to support a false charge; its presence, however, can be detected by chemical analysis of the blister fluid. The juice may be instilled into the eyes to produce an irritant conjunctivitis. This is resorted to by personnel in army, navy or air force when they wish to leave the job or by inmates of jail to avoid work. Accidental poisoning may occur from internal administration by quacks. The juice, like vitriol, has been thrown on the face with evil intentions.

Table 44.1 summarises the differentiating features of an artificial bruise and true bruise.

CALOTROPIS (MADAR, AKDO)

Q. 44.8. Give a brief account of poisoning from calotropis.

This plant (Fig. 44.10) grows wild almost everywhere in India. There are two varieties, viz. *Calo-tropis gigantea* which has

Fig. 44.10: Calotropis (madar) plant with flowers and buds. (*Courtesy*: Dr NK Mohanty)

purple flowers and *Calotropis procera* which has white flowers. They yield four active principles, viz. uscharin, calotoxin, calactin, and calotropin. The leaves and the stem, when cut or crushed, yield an acrid milky juice, which is acidic in reaction and bitter in taste; when heated or allowed to stand, it forms a white clot leaving a clear straw-coloured serum. The serum contains an active principle, gigantin, which is highly toxic, while the clot contains a less poisonous resin.

All the parts of the plant are used in Indian medicine, the flowers as digestive stimulants; the leaves as external poultice; the powdered root as an emetic; and the milky juice as a vesicant, depilatory, and for treatment of chronic skin conditions. The juice is used by tanners for removing hair from the hides and for deodourising them.

Symptoms: When the juice is applied externally, the skin becomes red and vesicates. When instilled into the eyes, it produces fulminating conjunctivitis which may result in permanent impairment of vision. When taken internally, it acts as a gastrointestinal and cerebrospinal poison. There is an acrid bitter taste, burning pain in the throat and stomach, and nausea, vomiting and diarrhoea, followed by dilated pupils, tetanic convulsions, collapse and death. When powdered madar root is used as snuff, death ensues immediately.

Fatal dose and fatal period: The fatal dose is uncertain. The fatal period is about 12 hours.

Treatment: This is on general lines, viz. gastric lavage with warm water, and administration of demulcents, stimulants and other drugs as indicated by the symptoms.

Postmortem appearances: These include dilated pupils, froth at the nostrils, stomatitis, and acute inflammation of the alimentary tract. The stomach may show an acute ulcer or perforation. The viscera including the brain and its meninges are congested.

Medicolegal aspects: Madar juice has been used—(1) sometimes for infanticide by mixing it with milk or water, (2) by ingestion and by local application on an abortion stick to procure abortion, (3) as a cattle poison by introducing a smeared cloth in the rectum of an animal or mixing it with fodder, (4) to produce artificial bruises, and (5) rarely for suicide or homicide. The root of calotropis procera is highly poisonous to cobras and other poisonous snakes. Snake charmers use it to control the newly caught snakes which cannot even stand its smell. The use of calotropis as an arrow poison is known.

PLUMBAGO ROSEA (LAL CHITRA) AND PLUMBAGO ZEYLANICA (CHITRA)

Q. 44.9. Give a brief account of poisoning from plumbago rosea and plumbago zeylanica.

The roots of these plants contain an active principle, plumbagin, a highly acrid crystalline glycoside. When the bruised root or twigs are applied externally, the skin becomes red and vesicates. Taken internally in small doses, the plant acts as a sudorific and stimulates the contraction of the muscular tissue of the heart, intestine and uterus. Taken internally in large doses, the plant acts as an irritant poison and produces the same symptoms as those of calotropis poisoning. The treatment and postmortem appearances are also similar.

The fatal dose is not certain. The fatal period is also uncertain.

Medicolegal aspects: The root is ingested as an abortifacient or applied to the cervix directly or as a paste via the abortion stick. Malingerers use it to produce artificial bruise. It is rarely used as a homicidal poison.

Illustrative Cases

A woman was given a quack medicine containing plumbago root by her paramour to cause miscarriage. She suffered from severe gastrointestinal irritation with vomiting and diarrhoea and died after 10 days. At postmortem, the foetus was found to have separated from the gravid uterus.

Jitan Ali Mir of Murshidabad was sentenced to four years of imprisonment for bringing a false charge of dacoity (robbery) and torture. He had produced artificial bruises on his skin by application of plumbago rosea to fabricate the complaint and bring about such a charge.

A woman mixed a small quantity of the powdered root of Lal Chitra with milk and gave it to her husband who started vomiting and purging within 2 hours and died the same day.

45 Animal Poisons

The important topics in this group are: cantharides, snakes and scorpions. The symptoms produced by cantharides are those of local irritation, and irritation of the gastrointestinal and genitourinary tracts. The symptoms produced by snakes and scorpions are mainly local, neurotoxic, haemotoxic, and myotoxic.

CANTHARIDES (SPANISH FLY)

Q. 45.1. Give a brief account of symptoms, signs, treatment, postmortem appearances, and medicolegal aspects of poisoning by the Spanish fly.

The spanish fly is about 2 cm long and 0.75 cm broad. The colour of its head, legs and wing sheaths is shiny emerald green. The powder of the dried body is grayish brown and contains shining green particles. The active principle is cantharidin which causes a blister or vesicle on the skin. Therefore, the spanish fly is also known as *blister beetle or* cantharis vesicatoria. Cantharis may be administered in the form of powdered beetles, the tincture, or the active principle.

Symptoms and signs: When applied to skin, an inflammatory response results in 2–3 hours, and vesicles form later. When swallowed, symptoms appear in about an hour. There is burning sensation in the mouth, throat, oesophagus, stomach, and abdomen, followed by intense thirst, difficulty in swallowing and speech, nausea, vomiting of blood-stained material, and diarrhoea with blood and mucus. As time ensues, nephrotoxic effects manifest by a dull pain in the loins and a constant desire to micturate but only small amount of blood-stained urine is passed *(strangury)*. The inflammation extends to the urinary bladder and urethra. In the male, persistent and painful erection of the penis *(priapism)* may occur with frequent seminal emissions. In the female, engorgement of the vulva, and abortion may occur. Convulsions and coma precede death. Blister formation may take place in the mouth and other parts of the alimentary tract in contact with the poison.

Fatal dose: 1.5 gm of the powder, one ounce of the tincture, and 10 mg of the active principle, cantharidin, is regarded as a fatal dose.

Fatal period: This varies from 24 hours to a week.

Treatment: The stomach is washed out with warm water. Fatty substances and alcohol must be avoided but demulcents and albumin may be given. The rest of the treatment is symptomatic.

Postmortem appearances: The whole alimentary tract from the mouth downwards shows intense inflammation. The stomach contents are bloody, and parts of the powdered beetle may be found as shining elytra or wing cases of the insect. The shining wings of the beetle resist putrefaction and provide a clue to the identity of the poison. The kidneys and the genitourinary tract show severe inflammation. Pelvic viscera are congested. Pericardial and endocardial haemorrhages are common. The lungs may be oedematous and air passages may show blood-stained mucus.

Medicolegal aspects: Cantharis is used as (1) an aphrodisiac, (2) an abortifacient, (3) a counter-irritant to the skin in the blistering plaster, and (3a) in hair oils to promote hair growth.

Accidental poisoning may occur: (1) from eating fowls which have ingested cantharides, (2) from use of blistering plaster, and (3) when it is used as an aphrodisiac or abortifacient.

SNAKES (OPHIDIA)

Q. 45.2. Give a medicolegal classification of snakes. Tabulate the differentiating features of poisonous and non-poisonous snakes.

For medicolegal purposes, snakes are classified into two groups, viz, **poisonous** and **non-poisonous.** This classification is not quite correct as some of the non-poisonous snakes can kill small animals by their poison. The differentiating features of the poisonous and non-poisonous snakes are given in Table 45.1.

The **poisonous snakes** are further **classified** on the basis of poison secreted by them into three main types, viz. (1) elapids (secreting neurotoxic venom), (2) vipers (vasculotoxic), and (3) sea snakes (myotoxic).

Elapids: This group consists of cobra, king cobra, common krait, banded krait, and the coral snake. The head is nearly of the same width as that of the neck and the pupils are round. The fangs are situated anteriorly but being covered with a fold of mucous membrane, they may be difficult to see. They are short, fixed, and grooved. Generally, therefore, the snake cannot bite through the clothing or inject a complete dose. The tail is usually round.

Vipers: This group consists of pit vipers and pitless vipers. The pit is situated between the eye and the nostril and helps to detect

Table 45.1: Differentiating features of poisonous and non-poisonous snakes

	Poisonous	*Non-poisonous*
1. Belly scales as seen by turning the snake with belly upwards	Large, and cover the entire breadth of the belly. Some harmless snakes also have such belly scales (Fig. 45.1A)	Small like those on the back or moderately large but do not cover the entire breadth of the belly (Fig. 45.1B,C)
2. Head scales	Small (vipers) (Fig. 45.2) (a) Large with conspicuous pit between the eye and nostril (pit vipers) (Fig. 45.4) (b) Third labial touches the eye and nasal shields (cobra, king cobra, or coral) (Fig. 45.5) (c) Central row of scales on back enlarged, and under surface of the mouth with only four infralabials, the fourth being the largest kraits, and perhaps bands or half rings across the back (Figs 45.6 and 45.7)	Large (Fig. 45.3) with the exceptions as outlined under the poisonous snakes, viz. pit vipers, cobra, king cobra, coral, and kraits
3. Fangs	Long and canalised like hypodermic needle (Figs 45.8 and 45.9)	Short and solid
4. Tail	Compressed	Not markedly compressed
5. Habits	Generally nocturnal	Not so
6. Bite	Two fang marks with or without small marks of other teeth	A number of small teeth marks in a row

warm blooded prey in the dark. The head is triangular and wider than the neck and the pupil is vertical. The fangs are long, movable and canalised like hypodermic needle. This snake can, therefore, bite through clothes and give a complete dose. The fangs are easy to see when erected but, being too big, lie tucked up by the side of the upper jaw. While the bites of pit vipers are seldom fatal to human beings, those of pitless vipers are dangerous. The tail is usually tapering. The bamboo snakes belong to the category of pit vipers while the Russell's viper and the saw-scaled viper belong to the category of pitless vipers.

Sea snakes: They are found in the vicinity of sea coasts. They have small heads, and flat rudder-like tail to help in swimming. The nostrils are situated on the top of the snout and are valved to enable free breathing. Their belly plates are not broad and they have dull and tuberculated scales on their back. Their venom apparatus is delicate with very short fixed fangs which are situated posteriorly. Therefore, generally, they do not bite.

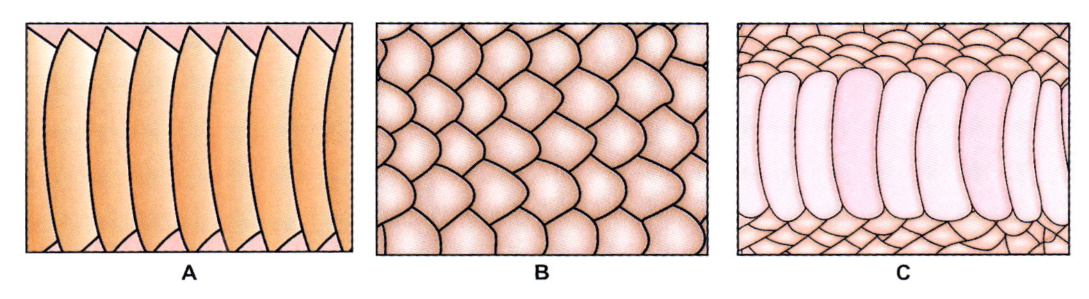

Fig. 45.1: Large belly scales covering the entire breadth of the belly as in (A) Belly scales small like those on the back as in (B) or moderately large but not covering the entire breadth of the belly as in (C)

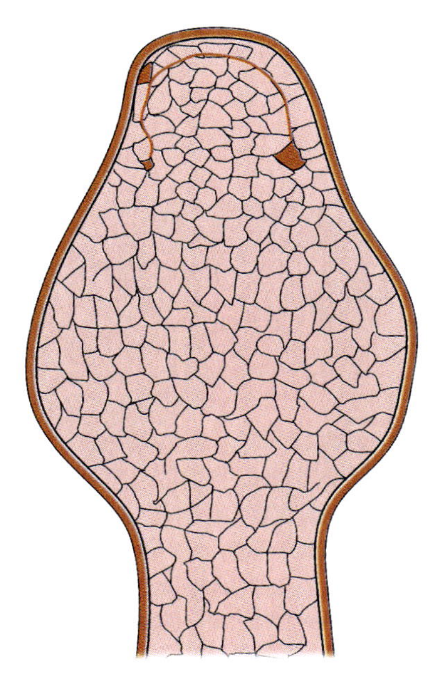

Fig. 45.2: Small head scales of poisonous snakes, e.g. Russel viper

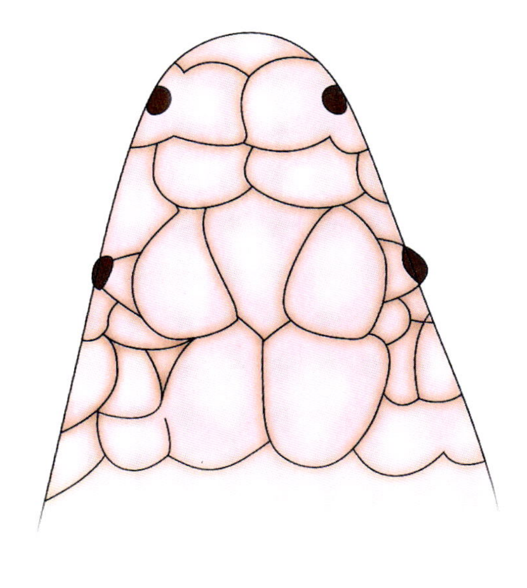

Fig. 45.3: Large head scales of non-poisonous snakes. Some poisonous snakes have large head scales

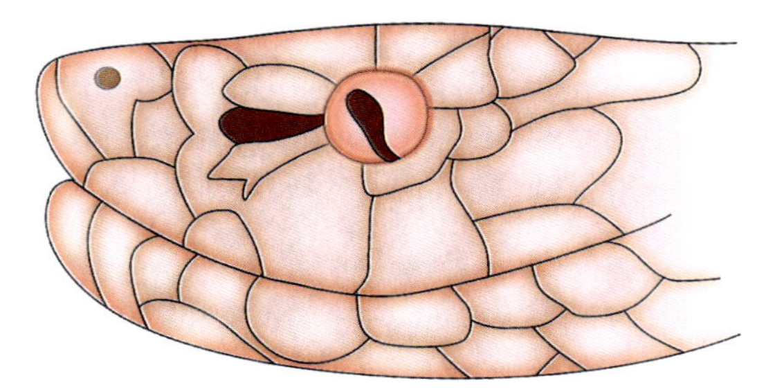

Fig. 45.4: Pit vipers. Head scales large and with a conspicuous pit P between the eye and nostril. The pupil is vertical

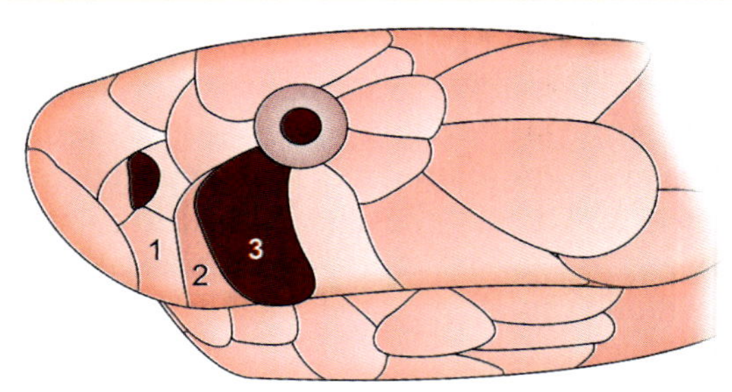

Fig. 45.5: Cobra, king cobra or coral. Head scales large and third labial touching the eye and nasal shields. The pupil is round

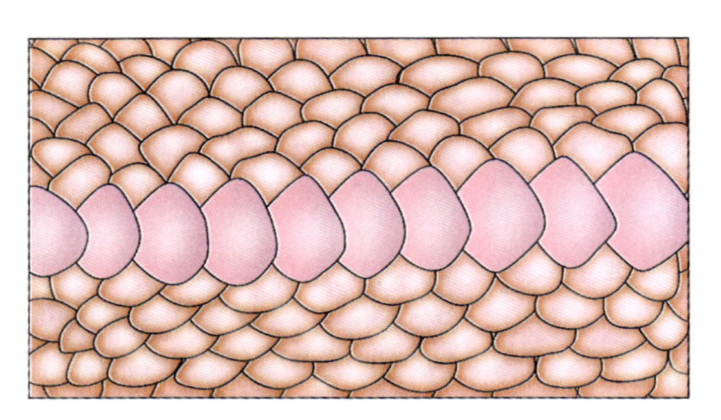

Fig. 45.6: Kraits. Central row of scales on back enlarged along with characters of Fig. 45.5

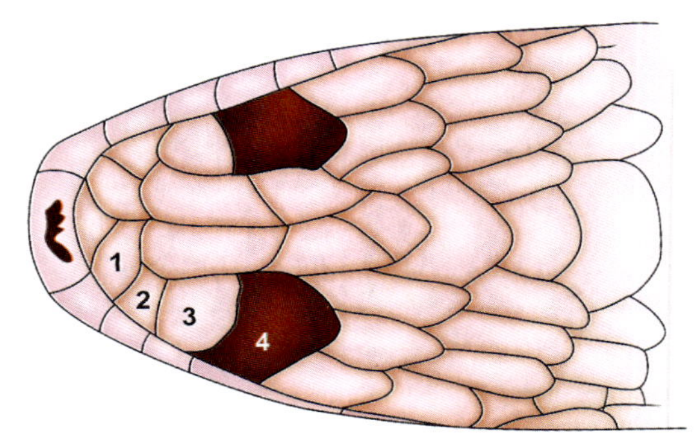

Fig. 45.7: Krait. Under surface of the mouth with only four infralabials, the fourth being the largest (the central mental scale is not to be counted) along with characters of Fig. 45.5

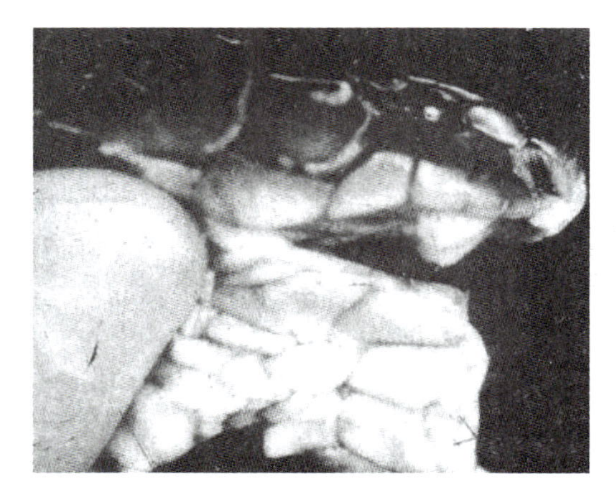

Fig. 45.8: Elapid fangs (cobra in this case) being converted by mucous membrane are difficult to see. (*Courtesy*: Dr HA Reid)

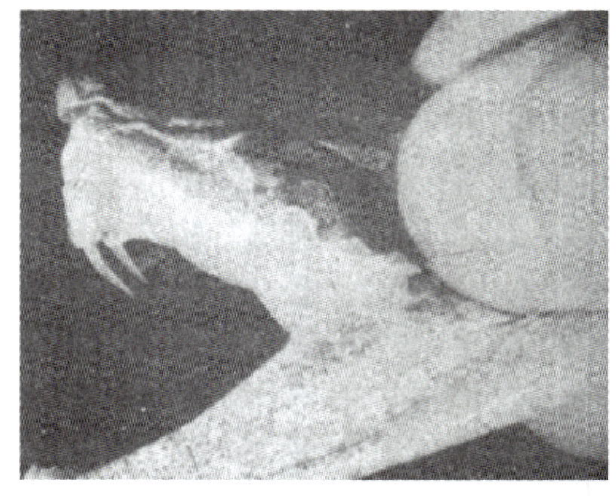

Fig. 45.9: Viper fangs are easy to see in the erected position as in this case. (*Courtesy*: Dr HA Reid)

Q. 45.3. Name the poisonous snakes of India and tabulate the differentiating features of the different groups.

The most **poisonous snakes in India** according to their severity are the krait and cobra among the elapids and the Russell's viper and the saw-scaled viper among the vipers. The differentiating features between the elapids and the vipers are given in Table 45.2.

Q. 45.4. Give the main characteristics of the important poisonous snakes of India.

The important poisonous snakes of India are the cobra, king cobra, common krait, banded krait, common green pit viper, Russell's viper, and saw scaled viper. Their characteristics are given below:

Cobra (naja tripudians, naag, or kala samp): This snake (Fig. 45.10) grows to a length of about 1.5 to 2 metres. Its colour is usually black but may be variable. The head is nearly of the same width as that of the neck which is generally provided with a hood bearing a spectacle mark. It expands its neck to form a hood only when enraged. In the absence of a hood, the cobra is identified by 2 or 3 series of very dark or black belly scales under and below the neck or by the divided tail shields. The cobra prefers populated areas and its distribution in India is widespread.

Fig. 45.10: Cobra. (*Courtesy*: Dr NK Mohanty)

Table 45.2: Differentiating features between the elapids and the vipers

	Elapids (cobra)	*Vipers*
1. Body	Long and cylindrical	Short with narrow neck
2. Head	Nearly of the same width as that of the neck, covered by large scales or shields special in form or number	Triangular and wider than the neck and usually covered by numerous small scales
3. Pupils	Round	Vertical
4. Maxillary bone	Carries other teeth also besides the poison fang	Carries only the poison fang
5. Fangs	Short, fixed and grooved, and so, usually cannot bite through clothing or may give only a sub-lethal dose	Long, movable, and canalised, and so, can bite through clothing and may also inject a fatal dose
6. Tail	Round	Tapering
7. Venom	Neurotoxic	Vasculotoxic
8. Other characteristics	Ovo-viviparous	Oviparous

King cobra (naja bungarus, humadryad, raj naag, or raj samp): This snake is bigger than the common cobra. It grows to a length of about 2.5 to 4.5 metres. The young king cobra is jet black in colour while the adult king cobra may be yellow, green, brown or black. There are usually white or yellow cross-bars or chevrons on the body. It has a hood but no spectacle mark on it. The tail scales are entire proximally but divided distally. The king cobra prefers jungles or forests and is found in their vicinity.

Common krait (bungarus caerulus, manyar, kalotaro, chitti, or kawriya): This snake grows to a length of 1 to 1.25 or even 1.50 metres. Its colour is usually glistening black and has single or double white arches across the back beginning some distance from the head. It has a central row of hexagonal scales on the back and a creamy white belly. The head is covered with large shields and the tail scales are entire. The common krait prefers to live in or near the house, is widespread in India, and is responsible for a number of cases of snake bite in India.

Banded krait (bungarus fasciatus or koelea krait): This snake (Fig. 45.11) is bigger and stouter than the common krait and grows to a length of about 2 metres. In addition to the distinguishing features of the common krait, the banded krait as the name suggests, has alternate black and yellow bands across its back. It is commonly found in Assam, Bengal and parts of South India.

Common green pit viper (lachesis gramineus, bamboo snake, or hara phisi): This snake grows to a length of 30 to 100 cm. Its colour is usually vivid green, rarely yellow or brown. The body is flat and broad and the head is triangular with a pit between the eye and the nostrils. The flanks have a yellowish white line. The tail is long with divided scales. This variety usually occurs in the hills and is widely distributed in India.

Russell's viper (daboia, charn viper, ghonus, or khadchitro): This snake (Fig. 45.12) grows to a length of about 1.5 metres. Its colour is brown or buff and has three rows of black diamond-shaped spots or chains on the back. It is stouter than any other poisonous snake in India. It can be identified by (1) a flat triangular head with a distinct V mark, with its apex pointing forward, (2) small head scales, (3) broad undivided belly plates, and (4) a narrow short tail with shields divided in two rows. Its nostrils are bigger than those of other Indian snakes. It makes a terrific hissing sound when about to bite. It prefers plains. It is found throughout India but not in dense jungles.

Fig. 45.12: Russell's viper

Saw-scaled viper (echis carinata, phoorsa, echis, or afai): This snake (Fig. 45.13) grows to a length of 50 to 75 cm. Its colour is brown or brownish grey or greenish. It can be identified by (1) a triangular head with a white mark on it resembling an arrow, (2) a wavy line on each flank with diamond-shaped areas between the upper curves of the two wavy lines, (3) small head scales, (4) broad belly plates, (5) undivided tail shields, and (6) body scales serrated like a saw, and hence the name. The reptile makes a peculiar rustling sound when it moves on account of the rough scales of the back. This snake is found throughout India.

Fig. 45.11: Banded krait

Fig. 45.13: Saw-scaled viper

Q. 45.5. Discuss the characteristics of snake venom.

In the fresh state, it is a clear transparent, amber tinted fluid and dries into a yellow granular mass which retains its activity for many years. It contains toxalbumins and several toxic principles, such as the following:

1. Fibrinolyses
2. Proteolysins
3. Neurotoxins (predominant in elapid venom)
4. Cholinesterase (predominant in elapid venom)
5. Haemolysins (predominant in viper venom)
6. Thromboplastin (predominant in viper venom)
7. Agglutinins
8. Cardiotoxins
9. Coagulase, hyaluronidase, lecithinase, etc.

Elapid venom is mainly neurotoxic, viper venom mainly vasculotoxic, and sea snake venom myotoxic.

A **neurotoxic venom** causes muscular weakness of the legs and paralysis of the muscles of the face, throat and respiration. The neurotoxins of cobra venom produce both convulsions and paralysis, whereas krait venom causes only muscular paralysis. Local symptoms at the site of the bite are minimum as compared to those caused by vasculotoxic venom.

A **vasculotoxic venom** produces enzymatic destruction of cell walls and coagulation disorders. As a result, the endothelium of blood vessels is destroyed, red cells are lysed, and other tissue cells are destroyed. Locally, there is oozing of haemolytic blood, and a spreading cellulitis. Haemorrhages from external orifices of the body are common. Other functional disturbances are related to the involved organ, e.g. convulsions from haemorrhage in the brain.

A **myotoxic venom** produces generalised muscular pain, followed by myoglobinuria, three to five hours later, ending in respiratory failure in fatal cases.

Q. 45.6. Discuss in detail the hallmarks of a venomous snake bite.

The hallmark of attack by a venomous snake is the presence of fang marks; these are usually two but only one may be evident, if the bite is sideways on. In contrast, bites by non-poisonous snakes produce a characteristic U-shaped set of teeth marks. One can get an idea about the size of the snake from the distance between the fang marks.

Symptoms and signs: It is important to realise that poisonous snake bite is not necessarily the same as snake bite poisoning.

Poisoning may occur from bite (injection) or absorption of venom through cuts or scratches. In some cases, instantaneous death occurs from shock due to fright, even before any symptoms commence.

The degree of toxicity depends upon the size of the person bitten, the potency of the venom, the main toxic principles it contains, and the amount injected, which in turn depends upon the age, size, sex and species of the snake, whether it had recently taken a prey, whether the bite is on bare skin or through clothing, the type of fang whether canalised or grooved, and the season and the time of bite. In the case of vipers where the channel is complete and the fangs movable, the snake gives a complete dose. In the case of elapids, e.g. a cobra, the groove is variously formed and the fangs being rigid, the transfer of venom is rarely substantial. The season is also important because snakes which have recently emerged from hibernation have a particularly potent venom. Nocturnal bites may be more serious than those which occur during the day.

A **bite from an elapid snake** is attended by **mild local symptoms** as compared to bite by viper, but by **marked neurotoxic effects.** There is slight burning at the site of the bite which shows a triple response. This is followed about 15 minutes to two hours by marked neurotoxic effects such as giddiness, lethargy, muscular weakness and spreading paralysis. There is salivation and even vomiting. Weakness in the legs is manifested by staggering. This is followed by difficulty in speaking and swallowing. Ptosis and paralysis of the extraocular muscles may occur. Breathing becomes slow and laboured. The patient is conscious but unable to speak. After a couple of hours, respirations cease with or without convulsions and the heart stops. In the event of recovery, the skin and cellular tissues surrounding the bite mark undergo necrosis (Figs 45.14 to 45.16).

A **bite from a viper** is attended by **severe local symptoms** and **marked vasculotoxic effects.** There is intense local pain, swelling,

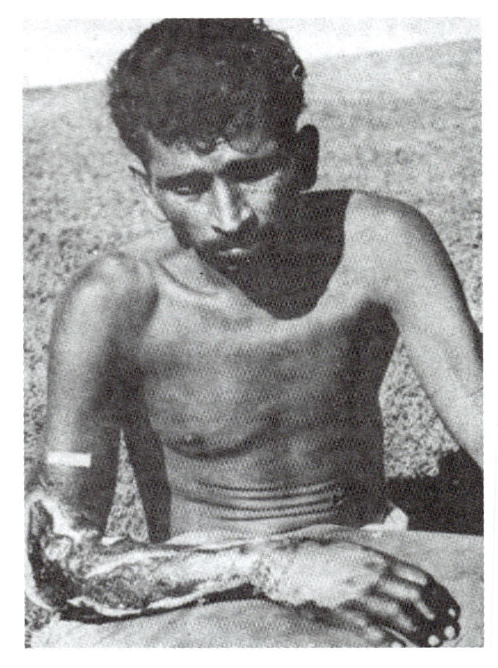

Fig. 45.15: Same patient as in Fig. 45.14 showing extensive but superficial necrosis after cobra bite. (*Courtesy*: Dr HA Reid)

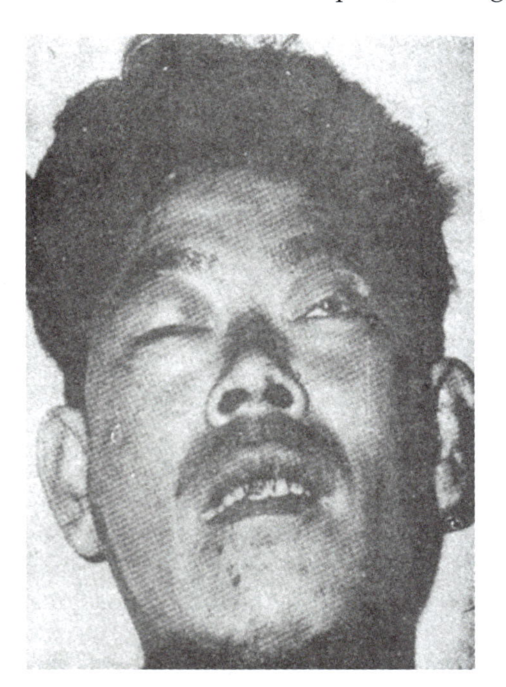

Fig. 45.14: This person was **bitten** on the hand by a **elapid snake** (cobra). Ptosis indicates systemic elapid poisoning. (*Courtesy*: Dr HA Reid)

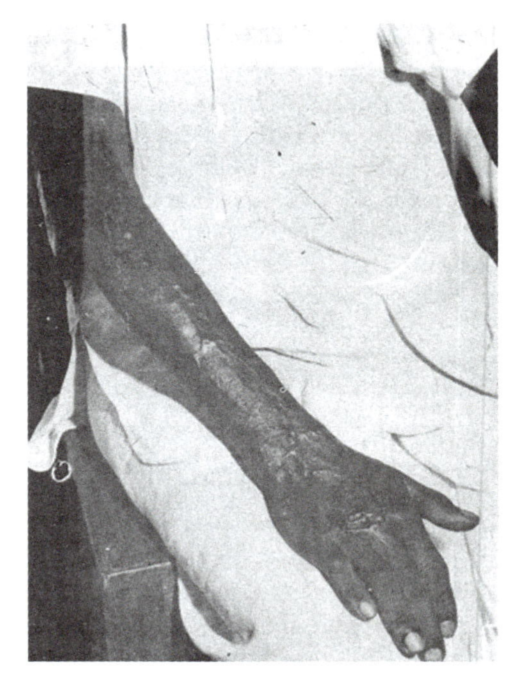

Fig. 45.16: Same patient as in Fig. 45.14 showing healing after necrosis from a cobra bite six months later. (*Courtesy*: Dr HA Reid)

ecchymosis and severe oozing of haemolytic blood. Serous and serosanguinous blisters sometimes appear. Nausea and vomiting occur. Intravascular haemolysis may lead to haemoglobinuric nephritis. Petechial haemorrhages, **bleeding** from the gums, haemoptysis and bleeding from the mucous membrane of the rectum and other orifices of the body are common. Collapse sets in with cold clammy skin, rapid feeble pulse, and dilated pupils insensitive to light, followed by coma and death. In the event of recovery, the local lesion suppurates and undergoes superficial necrosis (Figs 45.17 to 45.20).

Fig. 45.17: This patient was bitten on the left leg by a viper. Swelling of the bitten part and spreading cellulitis of the leg are seen. The skin of the right leg has been opened in similar area for comparison. (*Courtesy*: Dr NK Patoria)

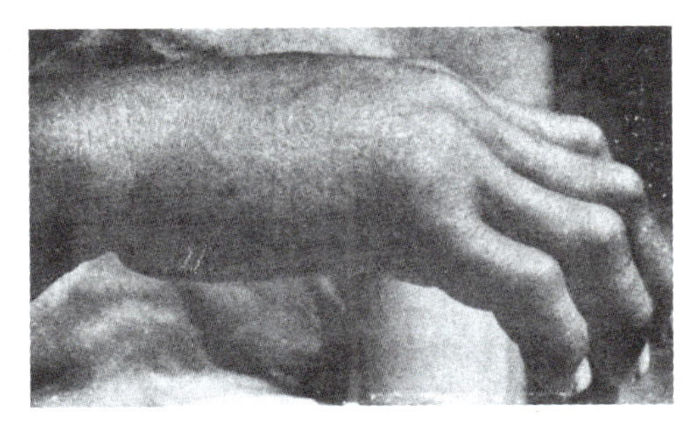

Fig. 45.18: This patient was **bitten by a viper** on the hand. Swelling of the hand is seen. (*Courtesy*: Dr HA Reid)

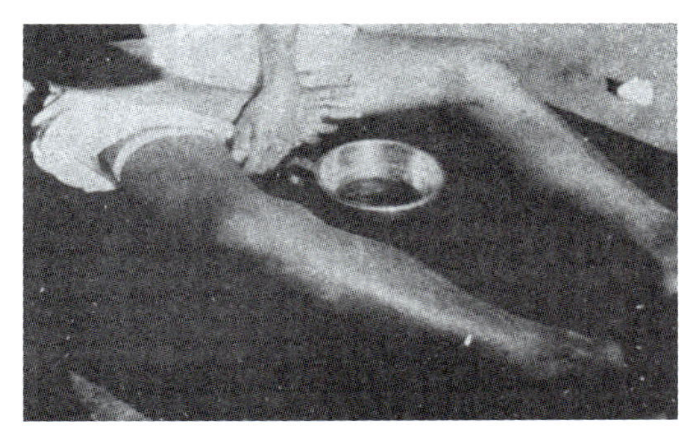

Fig. 45.19: Same patient as in Fig. 45.18. This figure shows blood-stained spit after viper bite. (*Courtesy*: Dr HA Reid)

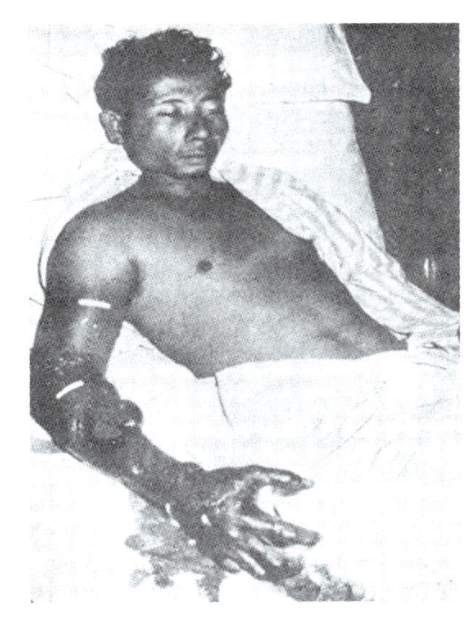

Fig. 45.20: Same patient as in Fig. 45.18. The patient is in a state of shock from systemic poisoning after viper bite. Serous and serosanguinous blisters are seen on the hand. (*Courtesy*: Dr HA Reid)

A **bite from a sea snake** is felt as a **sharp initial prick** becoming painless later. After one or two hours, **generalised muscular pain** and stiffness develop, starting in the neck and limb girdle. Myoglobinuria causes a characteristic brown discolouration of the urine and serum transaminase becomes elevated. Hyperkalaemia resulting from leakage of cellular potassium following extensive muscle damage may become a problem. Respiratory failure may ensue (Fig. 45.21).

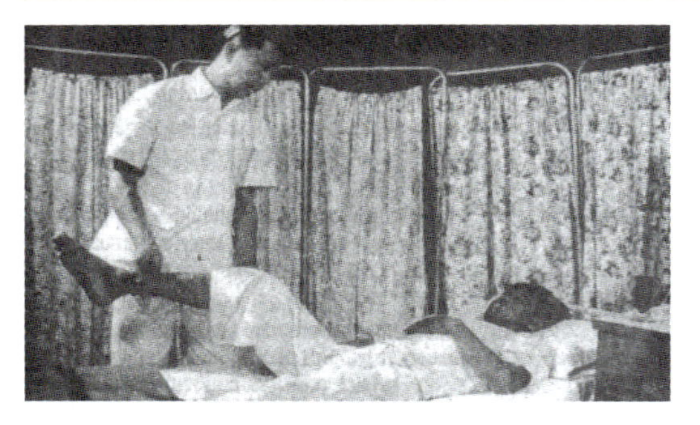

Fig. 45.21: This patient was bitten by a sea snake. There were no local symptoms. Movement of neck, trunk and limbs—leg straightening as shown here—became very painful. A few hours later, urine was brown from myo-globinuria. Electrocardiogram showed typical pattern of hyperkalaemia. (*Courtesy*: Dr HA Reid)

Fatal dose: 15 mg of the dried cobra venom, 20 mg of the viper venom, 6 mg of the krait venom, and 8 mg of the saw-scaled viper venom are fatal. The amount of dried cobra venom yielded in one bite is about 200–350 mg. The viper bite yields about 150–200 mg, the krait about 20 mg, and the saw-scaled viper about 25 mg.

Fatal period: Death may occur instantaneously from shock due to fright. Generally, death from cobra venom occurs within a few minutes to few hours while that from viper venom in a few days. Sea snake bite is mostly not fatal.

Q. 45.7. Give the main principles of treatment of venomous snake bite.

The main principles of treatment include: (1) allaying anxiety and fright, (2) prevention of the spread of venom, (3) use of antivenin and other antitoxic therapy, and (4) general measures.

Allaying anxiety and fright: The patient should be reassured by pointing out that (1) all snakes are not poisonous, (2) even poisonous snakes are not fully charged with poison, and (3) even a snake fully charged with poison cannot always inject a lethal dose.

Prevention of spread of venom: Spread of snake venom through the body is mostly by diffusion and lymph circulation. Therefore, efforts to reduce lymph circulation are helpful and this can be achieved by (1) immobilisation, (2) application of tourniquet, (3) cleansing the wound, and (4) incision and suction.

Immobilisation: Activity increases the spread of venom. The bitten part should, therefore, be immobilised. Besides reducing the spread of venom, immobilisation eases the pain of snake bite.

Tourniquet: Application of a tourniquet is possible only when the bite is on a limb. If the bite is on face, neck or trunk, firm pressure over the bitten area may be applied. Material, such as a rubber tube, handkerchief or grass, that is available on the spot can serve as a tourniquet. It should be applied approximately 5 cm proximal to the bite and tight enough to occlude the superficial venous and lymphatic circulation without impeding the arterial or deep venous blood flow. Normally, an additional tourniquet at a distance of 5 cm proximal to the first one is desirable. It should be released for a minute every half an hour or for 30 seconds every quarter hour to allow the escape of small quantity of toxin to enter the general circulation where it is destroyed. It should probably be applied up to two hours. Longer use could lead to aggravation of the tissue damage. Nowadays, It is felt that torniquet application is not necessary. However, it may be applied lightly to prevent lymphatic flow.

Cleansing the wound: The wound should be cleaned with plain water or saline.

Incision and suction: It is said that free incisions of the wound through the fang marks (avoiding blood vessels, nerves and periosteum), and thorough sucking either with a breast pump or mouth (only if there is no injury in the mouth, tongue or lips) can remove up to 20% of the injected venom, if done within the first 30 minutes. For parts of the body where a tourniquet cannot be applied, suction is specially to be relied upon. When the poison is sucked by mouth, the sucker should spit out the saliva and bloody fluid quickly and rinse the mouth well. It is not advised nowadays. Cryotherapy (application ice) is also not allowed.

This method appears to have some place only in those few cases of poisonous snake bites where there is likely to be considerable delay, say more than 4 hours, in reaching the hospital, and in those areas where antivenin is not available.

Antivenin: It is of two kinds, either specific or polyvalent. Specific antivenin is prepared by hyperimmunising horses against the venom of a particular snake while polyvalent antivenin is prepared by hyperimmunising horses against the venoms of four common poisonous snakes, viz. (1) cobra, (2) common krait, (3) Russell's viper, and (4) saw-scaled viper. The strength of the polyvalent antivenin is such that 1 ml will neutralise 0.6 mg of dried cobra venom, 0.45 mg of dried krait venom, 0.6 mg of dried Russell's viper venom, and 0.45 mg of dried saw-scaled viper venom.

The mortality from poisonous snake bite is nearly 40%. Antivenin treatment reduces it to less than 10%. It should be given as per instructions accompanying the phial.

While antivenin is very effective even when given after a delay, it is important to establish the necessity for its use. Delayed serum sickness type of response is quite common and fatal anaphylactic reaction may occur. It should, therefore, be given only if signs of systemic poisoning, e.g. ptosis or haemorrhagic signs develop after snake bite. Its use may also be considered in all patients with extensive local tissue damage because the risk of systemic poisoning in such cases is high. Injection of antivenin, if done at the site of the bite within a few minutes, can help to ameliorate local necrosis.

A test dose prior to therapeutic dose is necessary to test for serum sensitivity. Serum is available in the form of lyophilised powder in an ampoule. It retains its potency for 10 years. It is dissolved in distilled water or normal saline before injection. The initial dose of the serum is determined by the concentration of the serum, the size of the patient, the size of the snake, and the nature of the venom. It should preferably be large enough to combine with all the venom present in the body. The concentration of the serum and dosage data for adults and children accompany the package. Generally, for an adult, 60 ml of polyvalent serum is injected initially, one-third being given subcutaneously or locally around the bite, the other third intramuscularly, and the remaining third intravenously. The intravenous dose can be repeated any time, if collapse appears or every six hours till the symptoms disappear.

If a person is sensitive to serum, desensitisation is achieved by injecting multiple small doses under cover of adrenaline, antihistamines, and corticosteroids.

In as much as antivenin can neutralise circulating toxin only and not the toxin fixed in the tissues, the toxin's action at tissue level may be antagonised by neostigmine-atropine therapy in case of elapid bite and heparin along with supportive fibrinogen transfusion in case of viper bite.

While symptoms of systemic poisoning generally do not ensue in bites from sea snakes, the principles already outlined here hold good in management of sea snake bite poisoning also. Sea snake antivenin can be effective even when started several hours after the onset of poisoning symptoms.

When antivenin is not available local infiltration of carbolic soap around the site of the bite in case of elapid snakes and heparin in case of vipers is recommended.

General measures: Stimulants are helpful in paralytic cases and artificial respiration is often required. Transfusion of whole blood may be helpful in haemorrhagic cases. Steroids are effective in combating the allergic manifestations of antivenin therapy. Aspirin, short-acting barbiturates, and antibiotic prophylaxis to combat secondary infection together with general supportive measures are beneficial. A patient bitten by an elapid snake, if not dead in two hours will probably recover rapidly and completely. A patient bitten by a viper is in danger for a much longer time, and convalescence is very protracted.

Q. 45.8. Give a succinct account of postmortem appearances and medicolegal aspects of venomous snake bite.

Postmortem appearances: One or two bite marks about 1 cm deep in case of elapid and 2.5 cm deep in case of viper may be found. There is some swelling and cellulitis about the bitten part.

If the venom is predominantly neurotoxic, there are no definite appearances indicating the cause of death except the signs of asphyxia.

In case of viper bite, the local appearances are more striking due to severe oozing of blood from the puncture site. The blood is generally fluid and haemolysed causing early staining of the blood vessels. There are haemorrhages in the lungs and in the serous membranes. Endocardial haemorrhages are seen especially in the left ventricle. Petechiae are also found within the kidney pelvis, and mucosa of the urinary bladder, stomach, and intestines. Blood fails to clot normally even after addition of thrombin because of the extremely low level of fibrinogen. Arterioles and capillaries are characterised by blurred walls and swollen endothelial cells. Other findings include necrosis of the renal tubules, and cloudy swelling and granular changes in the cells of other organs.

Medicolegal aspects: Snake bite is generally accidental, rarely homicidal and still rarely suicidal (Cleopatra). Cattle are sometimes poisoned by chamars (cobblers) for the sake of hides by a peculiar method. A cobra is placed in an earthen vessel with a banana. The cobra is irritated by applying heat to the vessel. It bites the fruit, the pulp of which is then smeared on a rag, and the rag thrust in the animal's rectum with the help of a bamboo stick. Sui (abrus precatorius) poisoning of cattle resembles viperine snake bite.

SCORPIONS

Q. 45.9. Briefly discuss scorpion bite from a medicolegal point of view.

Scorpions have a crab-like appearance with a long, fleshy, five segmented, tail-like postabdomen, ending in a broad sac and a prominent hollow sting which communicates by means of a duct with the venom secreting glands. The venom contains toxalbumins having neurotoxic and haemotoxic actions. Its toxicity is greater than that of snakes but only a small quantity is injected. Red scorpion venom contains a potent cardiotoxin (Fig. 45.22).

Fig. 45.22: Scorpion. (*Courtesy*: Dr NK Mohanty)

Symptoms and signs: The local irritation is characterised by redness and burning pain radiating from the site. There may be headache, giddiness, nausea, profuse perspiration, priapism, excessive salivation, ventricular premature contractions dilated pupils, urticaria and muscular cramps followed in some cases by coma. Although the duration of symptoms is ordinarily 24 to 48 hours, neurologic manifestations may persist for up to one week. While the mortality in adults is negligible, children may succumb to pulmonary oedema. Pathologic findings in cases of death are widespread haemorrhages. Myocardial damage is found in deaths from red scorpion stings.

Treatment: A ligature should be tied proximal to the site of the sting, provided the bite is on a limb, the site incised, if necessary, and the wound washed with plain water, ammonia or potassium permanganate. A local infiltration of an anaesthetic lessens pain and immobilisation of the bitten part diminishes absorption of venom. A specific antivenin is available for most species and should be tried. Injection of calcium gluconate, 10 ml of 10% solution slowly intravenously relieves muscular cramps and injection of atropine helps to prevent pulmonary oedema. The rest of the treatment is symptomatic.

Medicolegal aspects: Scorpion poisoning is accidental.

46 Mechanical Poisons

Mechanical poisons are actually not poisons because they are not absorbed but produce symptoms of irritant poisoning solely in consequence of their mechanical action, on the part with which they come in contact. Such substances, as explained in the definition of poison, are included in section 328 IPC within the meaning of poison, and include powdered glass, pins, needles, chopped hair, etc., the most common being powdered glass.

POWDERED GLASS

Q. 46.1. Give a brief account of poisoning by powdered glass.

Powdered glass merits special attention, as this substance and similar products such as powdered diamonds are mentioned in the literature as poisons.

Symptoms and signs: When taken internally, coarse particles of powdered glass produce a sharp burning pain in the throat, stomach and abdomen. There is nausea and vomiting, the vomit being blood-stained. There is generally constipation but sometimes diarrhoea with tenesmus and blood. Death may occur from shock, if stomach or intestine has been perforated. Due to presence of silica which is radio-opaque, glass pieces may cast a faint shadow on X-ray and this helps in diagnosis.

Treatment: This consists of giving bulky food, such as large quantity or rice or banana, to envelop the fragments of glass within it, and then emetics and laxatives but no violent purgatives. The rest of the treatment is symptomatic.

Postmortem appearances: There is inflammation of the stomach and intestines. Erosions and ulcerations may also be found. Occasionally, there may be a perforation. Fragments of powdered glass may be found adherent to tenacious mucus secretion of the stomach.

In a fatal case of suspected homicide, viscera should not be preserved in glass vessels. The glass recovered from viscera and its relationship to glass seized from an accused person can be decided by spectroscopic examination for unusual elements.

Medicolegal aspects: Mixed with food, coarse particles of powdered glass have been administered with homicidal intent. Finely powdered glass is less destructive in its effects; well-powdered glass bangles administered in food by women with a view to kill their husbands have resulted in failure of their mission! Accidental contamination of food with glass may occur from the glass container itself. It is sometimes used to destroy cattle.

47

Food Poisoning and Poisonous Foods

The term 'food poisoning' may be used in a general or special sense. When the term is used in its general or wider sense, it includes all illnesses resulting from ingestion of foods containing non-bacterial or bacterial products. When the term is used in its special or restricted sense, it means that the poisoning is due to bacterial products only. The bacterial products include bacteria and their toxins. The poisoning resulting therefrom is, by convention, known as **bacterial food poisoning**. The non-bacterial products include poisons derived from plants and animals, and inorganic chemicals. Foods containing such products are, by convention, known as **poisonous foods**.

The illness is **characterised by:** (1) simultaneous attack of many persons at the same time, (2) history of ingestion of common food by all sufferers, and (3) similarity of signs and symptoms in a majority of cases.

Generally, diagnosis poses no problem except when only one or two persons may be affected, when it may be missed and a suspicion of poisoning from other sources may be aroused. Further, in case of attempted poisoning, it may be alleged that the symptoms are due to some article of food or drink. A medical practitioner coming across a case of food poisoning from a public eating house must report it to public health authorities.

BACTERIAL FOOD POISONING

This is of three types, viz. (1) infection type, (2) toxin type, and (3) botulism.

Infection type: This results from ingestion of viable microorganisms that multiply in the gastrointestinal tract and produce a true infection, e.g. Salmonella group of organisms.

Toxin type: This results from toxins produced by multiplying organisms that have gained access to the prepared food, e.g. enterotoxin produced by the Staphylococcus.

Botulism: This results from ingestion of preformed botulinum toxin in the preserved food. The toxin is produced by *Clostridium botulinum*.

Q. 47.1. Give a brief account of infection type of food poisoning.

In this type of food poisoning, the organisms multiply in the gut and cause gastroenteritis. The common organisms responsible for the attack are the Salmonella group of organisms, and occasionally, the Shigella group.

The natural reservoir of Salmonella organisms is in certain birds, mammals and reptiles. Food may be contaminated with infected excreta of mice or rats, or infection may be transferred by flies or by human carriers employed in the handling of food. Shigella infection is the result of contamination of food or water supplies with the faeces of the individuals who either have the disease or, less often, are asymptomatic carriers of the organism.

The outbreak of Salmonella food poisoning is likely to occur whenever large amounts of food are prepared and the unconsumed food kept for future meals. Accordingly, such food poisoning is reported far more frequently from canteens, restaurants, hospitals and other institutions than from private houses.

Symptoms and signs: Depending on the susceptibility of individuals to Salmonella food poisoning, while some participants may remain free from symptoms, others may be severely affected.

The incubation period is longer than staphylococcal food poisoning. A delay of 12 hours or more is usual. The onset is sudden. A chill may be the initial symptom, followed by headache, nausea and vomiting, severe abdominal cramps, and marked prostration. Three characteristics that differentiate it from staphylococcal food poisoning are: (1) muscular weakness, (2) fever, and (3) persistent, very foul smelling diarrhoea. The diagnosis rests on the isolation of the causative organism from the patient and suspected articles of food.

Treatment: The stomach should be washed and the bowel emptied by a cathartic, if diarrhoea is not present. For infection with the Salmonella group of organisms, the antibiotic of choice is chloramphenicol. Ampicillin or septran can also be used. For infection with the Shigella group of organisms, ampicillin and tetracyclines are used. Cotrimoxazole is as good as ampicillin and preferred by some. The rest of the treatment is symptomatic.

Postmortem appearances: These are those of gastroenteritis and general toxaemia. The mucosa of alimentary tract is inflamed or even ulcerated. Internal organs are congested.

Q. 47.2. Give a brief account of toxin type of food poisoning.

For this type of poisoning to occur, (1) the food must be contaminated by a strain of organism that produces enterotoxin, (2) it must be suitable for growth of this organism, and (3) the infected food must be kept at a temperature suitable for bacterial growth and for a sufficiently long time so that an appreciable quantity of enterotoxin is formed. Food such as milk, custard, and previously prepared meat dishes are the chief sources.

Most cases are due to some strains of staphylococci which produce a heat stable enterotoxin. Other toxin producing organisms which may give rise to such food poisoning are *Proteus vulgaris*, *Streptococcus viridans* (milk streptococci), *B. coli*, and *Clostridium welchii* when present in large numbers.

Symptoms and signs: The toxin being already present in food, the symptoms develop rapidly within one to four hours. The first symptom is salivation, followed by acute gastroenteritis, and recovery in about 24 hours.

Unlike Salmonella food poisoning, this condition is not an infection. But like botulism, it is the result of ingesting preformed toxins contained in the food. The characteristics that differentiate it from botulism are: (1) symptoms appear rapidly and are mainly gastrointestinal, (2) they are of short duration, and (3) recovery is usually prompt and complete.

Treatment: This is largely symptomatic and on the same lines as in Salmonella food poisoning.

Postmortem appearances: These are the same as those found in Salmonella food poisoning.

Q. 47.3. Give a succinct account of botulism.

The term botulism is derived from 'botulismus' meaning a sausage, since large outbreaks of the disease were first observed following ingestion of improperly cooked sausage. The causative agent is an anaerobic spore forming bacillus, *Clostridium botulinum*, which produces an exotoxin. It is commonly found in the soil. The toxin is, therefore, likely to be present in such soil contaminated undercooked or canned foods. The foods that are most often responsible are meat, fish and vegetables. **The toxin is destroyed by heat at 80°C for 30 minutes and, therefore, adequate cooking gives protection against it.** The toxin paralyses the muscles by blocking nerve impulses at the myoneural junction. It blocks the action of acetylcholine.

Symptoms and signs: The symptoms commence within 12–36 hours. The initial symptom is usually diplopia from ocular muscle palsy, followed by difficulty in swallowing and speech. The picture is thus one of bulbar palsy. Respiratory paralysis with extension to the breathing centre closes the scene. Gastrointestinal symptoms are rare. The temperature is normal or subnormal throughout. The victim is usually conscious to the end. The fatal dose of contaminated food may be less than 5 grams. Death may occur within 24–48 hours or may be delayed for a week. The diagnosis rests on the isolation of the bacillus from food, or patient's vomit, faeces, or viscera.

Treatment: The stomach should be washed out and the bowels emptied by saline purges, if necessary. The administration of anti-botulinum serum is an urgency. Management of bulbar and respiratory failure is as for poliomyelitis. Mortality is 60 to 70%.

Postmortem appearances: The pathological changes consist of congestion and haemorrhages in all the organs and especially in the central nervous system. Degenerative changes occur in the liver and the kidneys.

Q. 47.4. Give a brief account of poisonous foods.

By usual implication, this term excludes conventional food poisoning by bacteria and their toxins and is restricted to poisoning by articles of food due to: (1) contained toxic principles, (2) metallic contamination, and (3) food allergy.

Containing toxic principles: The articles of food containing toxic principles are poisonous food grains, infected rye, adulterated oil, and poisonous mushrooms. The most common food grain so affected is *Lathyrus sativus* (kesari dal), which gives rise to lathyrism, a spastic paralysis of the lower limbs. The other food grains which may be so affected are *Lolium temulentum* (darnel), *Stigmata maides* (maize), and *Paspalam scrobiculatum* (kodra). The manifestations are usually neurological, viz. spastic paraplegia and polyneuritis. The contaminated rye (*Claviceps purpurea*) produces convulsive or gangrenous type of ergotism. The mustard oil contaminated with argemone oil (katkar oil) produces dropsy. The poisonous mushrooms produce symptoms of irritant poisoning, neurotic poisoning, or both.

Metallic contamination: This is probably more common than dangerous. Various metallic poisons formerly occurred in food stuffs as dyes, preservatives or colouring matter. Such severe poisoning is not common nowadays.

Food allergy: This is due to sensitivity to certain articles of diet, usually proteinaceous in nature. It is followed by an illness characterised by nausea, vomiting, diarrhoea, fleeting joint pains, and urticaria. Oedema of the glottis and asthmatic seizures may follow. Many articles of food are implicated, viz. shell fish, eggs, tomatoes, strawberries, mussels, etc. In this, the individual factor plays a very important part. The abnormality is not in the food but in the allergic individual. Diagnosis is generally not difficult. Antihistaminics and steroids are of value.

1. Smallpox presents with a characteristic rash in a centrifugal in distribution (i.e. more abundant in the face and extremities).
2. Potentially delayed recognition of the disease by health personnel because of its rarity and presumed eradication of the disease.
3. Increased mobility and crowding of the population.
4. Virtually nonexistent immunity to smallpox among the population at risk because of the absence of naturally occurring disease and the discontinuation of routine vaccination in the early 1970s.

The syndrome generally presents with the classic triad of—(1) symmetric, descending, and progressive flaccid paralysis that always begins in bulbar musculature in (2) an afebrile patient with, (3) a clear sensorium. The bulbar palsies are prominent and can be summarized in part as the 4 Ds: diplopia, dysarthria, dysphonia, and dysphagia. Anticholinergic signs and symptoms, such as dry mouth, ileus constipation, and urinary retention, are often present. Sensory changes, however, are not observed. Because the toxins do not cross the blood–brain barrier, central nervous system symptoms are absent.

Anthrax: The initial phase fallows an incubation period of 1–10 days and begins with the insidious onset of mild fever, myalgia, malaise, nonproductive cough, some chest or abdominal pain, and in some cases, nausea and vomiting. The second phase develops within 1–3 days and begins abruptly with acute dyspnea, diaphoresis, further fever, and cyanosis. Stridor may result from tracheal compression by enlarged mediastinal lymph nodes. In up to 50% of cases, obtundation, seizures, and nuchal rigidity may develop as a result of complicating anthrax meningitis. This stage is of rapidly progressive shock, associated hypothermia, and death occurs within 24–36 hours.

BIOTERRORISM

Q. 47.5. What biologic agents have the potential to be used as weapons of mass destruction?

Bacterial agents: Anthrax, tularemia, plague, Q fever, glanders and melioidosis.

Viral agents: Smallpox, viral hemorrhagic fevers, Venezuelan equine encephalitis.

Biologic toxins: Botulinum, ricin, staphylococcal enterotoxin B and T–2 mycotoxins.

Q. 47.6. What epidemiologic clues should raise suspicion that a disease outbreak is due to bioterrorism?

- Large epidemic with a similar disease or syndrome, especially in a discrete population.
- Unusually numerous cases of unexplained diseases or deaths.
- Disease that is unusual to the geographic area or transmission season.
- Multiple simultaneous or serial epidemics of different diseases in the same population.
- Disease outbreaks of the same illness in noncontiguous areas.
- Disease known to be transmitted by a vector that is not present in the local area.
- Single case of a disease due to an uncommon agent (e.g. smallpox).
- Unusual age distribution for common diseases.
- Unusual strains or variants of organisms or antimicrobial resistance patterns different from those circulating in the local area.
- More severe disease than expected for known pathogen or failure to respond to standard therapy.

- Similar genetic type of agents isolated from distinct sources at different times or locations.
- Unusual routes of exposure for a pathogen (e.g. inhalational route for a disease that normally develops through other exposure).

Smallpox: The disease usually begins after a 12- to 14-day incubation period (range: 7–17 days) and consists of high fever, malaise, and prostration with headache and backache. These symptoms are followed by the appearance of a maculopapular rash that progresses to papules (1–2 days after appearance of rash), vesicles(4th–5th day), pustules (7th day), and finally scab lesions (14th day). Other organs are seldom involved. Death, which commonly occurs during the second week of illness, most likely results from the toxemia associated with circulating immune complexes and soluble variola antigens.

Q. 47.7. What clinical features distinguish smallpox from other viral diseases, such as measles and chickenpox?

Q.47.8. What factors make smallpox an extremely potent bioterrorism agent?

These factors give smallpox the potential for rapid spread and the ability to cause illness that can certainly overwhelm existing medical and public health system. A single suspected case of smallpox should be treated as a national health emergency, and the proper authorities should be promptly notified.

Q. 47.9. What is botulism?

Botulism is a clinical syndrome brought about by ingestion or inhalation of the toxins produced by the spore-forming bacillus *Clostridium botulinum*. These toxins, which exist in seven distinct antigenic types, exert their cytotoxic effect by preventing acetylcholine release at the neuromuscular junction, resulting in blockade of neuromuscular transmission and flaccid muscle paralysis.

Q. 47.10. How is the diagnosis of botulism established?

Laboratory testing is generally not critical to the diagnosis of botulism. The standard test is the mouse bioassay, in which type-specific antitoxin protects mice against any botulinum toxin in the sample. Sample specimens include serum, gastric aspirates, stool, and respiratory secretions. Polymerase chain reaction may be used to detect *C. botulinum* genes in environmental sample.

Q. 47.11. Describe the classic appearance of the cutaneous form of anthrax.

Cutaneous anthrax is initiated when spores of *B. anthracis* are introduced into the skin through cuts or abrasions or by biting flies. The primary lesion—a painless, pruritic papule appears 1–7 days.

Section 10

48

Somniferous Poisons (Opioids)

The poisons in this group are known as somniferous or narcotic poisons because they are used to lessen pain and induce sleep (somniferous or narcotic effect). The important poison in this group is opium. Its action is characterised by two sets of symptoms, viz. excitement and narcosis, of which the latter, as the group indicates, predominates. **Heroin** (Brown sugar) is a synthetic derivative of opium. It is also a potent narcotic analgesic but with a very high addiction potential. **Pethidine** (meperidine, demerol) is a synthetic analgesic having a morphine-like action. It causes a greater degree of euphoria as compared to morphine. However, its potential for addiction is also high. Such addiction is difficult to treat, and carries considerable mortality.

OPIUM AND MORPHINE

Opium (*Afim*) is the dried juice obtained by incision of the unripe capsules of the white poppy, *Papaver somniferum*, a plant which grows in India, its activity is due to the phenanthrene and isoquinoline group of alkaloids. The phenanthrene group comprises morphine (about 10%), codeine (about 0.5%), thebaine (about 0.3%), and their synthetic derivatives, such as dionin, **heroin**, etc., and the narcotic properties are due to them. The isoquinoline group comprises papaverine (about 1%) and narcotine (about 6%) which have mild analgesic but no narcotic properties. The ripe and dry poppy capsules (Fig. 48.1) contain only a trace of opium and are used for their sedative and narcotic effect. The poppy seeds (*khas khas*), creamish in colour, are harmless as they do not contain opium. They are used as food. They yield a bland oil which is used for cooking and lighting purposes.

Fresh crude opium is dark brown but becomes black on standing. It occurs in rounded, irregular, flattened masses, with a characteristic smell and a bitter taste. The principal alkaloids of opium used in medicine are morphine and codeine. These act as narcotics or sedatives. Apomorphine, prepared from morphine, is chiefly used as an emetic. Poisoning may occur from any of the preparations containing opium, its alkaloids or their derivatives.

Fig. 48.1: Poppy capsules with scarification. (*Courtesy*: Dr NK Mohanty)

Q. 48.1. Give a brief account of symptoms, signs, fatal dose, and fatal period in a case of opium poisoning.

Symptoms and signs: These are practically those of morphine poisoning on account of the high morphine content of opium. They usually appear within half an hour to an hour after ingestion and within about 3–5 minutes after injection. The poison acts on the central nervous system causing first a stimulation and later a depression followed by narcosis. Accordingly, the effects can be described in three stages, viz (1) excitement, (2) stupor, and (3) narcosis.

Stage of excitement: This stage is absent if the dose taken is large. In adults, there is a sense of wellbeing of brief duration. Laughter, hallucinations, and rapid heart rate occur. In children, convulsions may occur.

Stage of stupor: The stage of excitement is soon followed by weariness, headache, giddiness, a sense of weight in the limbs, diminished sensibility, and a strong tendency to sleep from which the patient can be roused by painful stimuli. The pupils are contracted, face and lips cyanosed, and an itching sensation felt all over the skin. The pulse and respiration are almost normal.

Stage of narcosis: The patient passes into deep coma from which he cannot be aroused. The muscles are relaxed and reflexes are abolished. The pupils are contracted to pin point and do not react to light. The blood pressure falls. The pulse is rapid and feeble. The breathing is slow, gradually diminishing in rate. The skin is cold, with profuse perspiration, and the temperature is subnormal (hypothermia—body temperature less than 35°C).

In fatal termination, there is marked cyanosis. Froth escapes from the mouth. Breathing is sighing and irregular (Cheyne-Stokes type), the rate being 2 to 4 per minute. Pulse is imperceptible. Pupils dilate terminally when asphyxia ensues but still do not react to light. Coma deepens and death results from asphyxia due to respiratory paralysis. The breath may smell of opium throughout the illness.

Fatal dose: In a person not addicted to opium, 200 mg of morphine and its equivalent of opium (2 gm) is fatal. 10 ml of tincture of opium is regarded as a dangerous dose. The fatal dose of tincture of opium recorded in children varies from 1–3 drops.

Fatal period: The usual fatal period is about 9 to 12 hours.

Q.48.2. Discuss the diagnosis and differential diagnosis of a case of opium poisoning.

Diagnosis: If the crude drug or one of its preparations is used, the breath smells of opium (raw flesh-like). The pin point immobile pupils, Cheyne-Stokes respirations, slow pulse, cyanosis, froth at the nose and mouth, and moist perspiring skin are the outstanding features. Opium suspends all body secretions except sweat so that even during the comatose state, the skin, although cold, is often bathed in profuse perspiration resulting in subnormal temperature and hypothermia (temperature less than 35°C).

Differential diagnosis: Opium or morphine poisoning clearly resembles (1) intracranial lesions, such as cerebrovascular accidents especially pontine haemorrhage, (2) metabolic conditions, such as uraemic coma and diabetic coma, (3) alcohol poisoning, (4) carbolic acid poisoning (5) organophosphorus poisoning, and (6) other comatose conditions, such as epileptic coma, hysterical coma and barbiturate poisoning, from which it must be distinguished.

Cerebrovascular accidents: These generally occur in elderly hypertensive persons. The onset is abrupt and there is hemiplegia. The pupils are unequal and breathing stertorous (noisy). In pontine haemorrhage, though the pupils are contracted to pin point, there is hyperpyrexia due to stimulation of the heat regulating centre in the third ventricle.

Metabolic conditions: In uraemic coma, the breath has ammoniacal smell, urinary findings are characteristic, there is history of kidney disease, and there are cardiac manifestations. In diabetic coma, the breath smells of acetone, breathing is of the Kussmaul type, popularly known as air-hunger, blood sugar is raised, and urinary findings are characteristic.

Alcohol poisoning: The breath smells of alcohol. The pupils may be contracted but dilate on pinching the face or neck and slowly return to their original size (MacEwan's sign), and there is no paralysis.

Carbolic acid poisoning: The smell of breath, the stained patches on the lips and the mouth, and the green colour of the urine are characteristic.

Organophosphorus poisoning: There is froth at the mouth and nostrils and the breath may have kerosene-like or garlic-like smell. The pupils are constricted and there are other features of muscarinic and nicotinic effects of the poison.

Other comatose conditions: In epileptic coma, there is history of previous attacks. In the majority of cases, there is a fit, with or without a preliminary aura. The patient loses consciousness, and the muscles are convulsed for a few seconds or minutes during which he may bite his tongue or otherwise damage himself. The coma usually clears up in about an hour. In hysterical coma, there is also a previous history of attacks. The patient is usually a female. The fit usually occurs in the presence of bystanders. While the muscles are convulsed, the tongue is usually not bitten and the patient rarely injures herself. Recovery is also rapid. In barbiturate poisoning, the pupils are not pin point, but frequently show alternate contraction and dilatation, the respiration is shallow but the rate is greater, and there is suppression of urine.

Q.48.3. Discuss briefly the treatment, post-mortem appearances, and medicolegal aspects of a case of opium poisoning.

Treatment: Emetics usually fail due to depression of the vomiting centre. The stomach should be washed out first with tepid water (only if the patient is seen in early stages), the return being retained for analysis, and then with a solution of potassium permanganate, 1:5000 strength, till the washed water returns with its original pink colour. Some solution should be left in the stomach to oxidise the alkaloid that might be excreted in the stomach after absorption. In the absence of potassium permanganate, the stomach should be washed out with an infusion of tea or tannic acid or a mixture of finely powdered animal charcoal and water. Gastric lavage should be carried out even after hypodermic injection of the drug as the alkaloid is re-excreted into the stomach after absorption. The intestines should be cleared out by enemata, or by purgatives, such as magnesium sulphate 15 gm orally.

Nalorphine (lethidrone) is a specific antidote to morphine and related opium alkaloids. It is given intravenously in a dose of 5 to 10 mg every 15 minutes till the pupils begin to dilate, respirations become normal, the patient is aroused, or a maximum of 40 mg is administered. However, the drug of choice nowadays is naloxone, which is a pure antagonist. It is given in a dose of 0.4 to 0.8 mg intravenously or intramuscularly and can be repeated every 10 or 15 minutes, up to a maximum of 10 mg with similar criteria.

If the patient is seen in the early stages, he should be kept awake by making him walk in the open air, supporting him during the procedure, and taking care not to exhaust him. Depending on his condition, artificial respiration and oxygen may be necessary. Antibiotics are necessary in cases of prolonged coma. Body warmth must be maintained. The rest of the treatment is symptomatic. The treatment must be continued till the patient is conscious, and even then, care must be taken that a relapse does not occur.

Postmortem appearances: These are those of comatoasphyxia. The appearances are external and internal.

Externally, the smell of opium is present. The face is deeply cyanosed, almost black; the finger nails blue; and the neck veins engorged and distended. The postmortem lividity is almost black, and is better seen in a fair-skinned body. There is froth at the nose and mouth, but neither so fine nor so copious as in drowning.

Internally, the stomach may show the presence of small, soft, brownish lumps of opium. The trachea, bronchi, lungs and brain exhibit a marked degree of venous congestion. In addition, the trachea and bronchi are covered with froth and the lungs are oedematous. The blood is usually dark and fluid.

In cases of suspected opium poisoning, blood, bile and brain should be preserved in addition to routine viscera.

Medicolegal aspects: Opium is so easily obtained everywhere in India, and death from its use is so painless that it is the poison of choice for suicidal purposes.

On account of its black colour, characteristic odour and bitter taste, it is rarely used for homicidal purposes. It is sometimes used for infanticide. Death has resulted from the breastfeeding of an infant by a woman who had smeared her nipple with tincture of opium with evil intention.

Accidental poisoning may occur from drugging of infants and children to keep them quiet or from overdose of a medicinal preparation.

Sometimes, opium is used to steady the nerves before doing some bold act, e.g. homicide. It is rarely used for doping race horses and as a cattle poison.

Opium and its preparations cause addiction, of which, heroin (diacetyl morphine), an artificial alkaloid derived from morphine, is the most dangerous. Brown sugar is crude heroin.

Q. 48.4. Give a brief account of opium addiction (chronic poisoning).

Opium addiction (morphinomania or morphinism), is the result of regular use of opium or its preparations either medically for relief of pain or otherwise as an aphrodisiac, or just to get 'high' (euphoric feeling of well-being). Because of the user's rapid development of tolerance and the high physical dependence induced, larger and larger doses are required to get the same effect, and later, just to remain normal (prevent withdrawal symptoms). The result is chronic poisoning characterised by physical, mental, and moral degeneration. Physical degeneration manifests as emaciation, infection especially skin ulceration, anorexia, constipation, impotence, sterility, etc. Mental degeneration manifests as loss of memory, irritability, depression, and gradual dementia. Moral degeneration manifests itself as crimes which the addict commits to get the supply of the drug. Death from loss of tolerance to the drug and infection is common and suicide far more common than in the general population.

HEROIN (BROWN SUGAR)

This is a synthetic derivative of opium, available in the form of white to dark brown powder. It is a potent narcotic analgesic with a strong euphoric effect. It is sold illegally on the street under the name smack, brown sugar, junk, and dope. It can be smoked, inhaled as a snuff, or injected.

Amongst all the addictive drugs, it is the most dangerous.

The place where heroin activities are conducted is generally known as a *shooting gallery*. A small amount of heroin, dissolved in water, heated and filtered through a small piece of cotton or the filter of a cigarette is injected intravenously as a test dose. This process of injecting a small amount, withdrawing some blood to ensure that the needle is in the vein and to keep the lumen open, is known as 'booting' or 'fooling'. It helps to assess the potency of the drug and to keep high by intermittent injection.

Tolerance occurs very rapidly. If the drug is then withheld, the patient experiences withdrawal symptoms, such as sweating, malaise, anxiety, depression, a general feeling of heaviness, and cramp-like pains in the limbs. Further and larger doses are then required to allay these symptoms. With larger doses, a confusional state with hallucinations, illusions, and personality changes rapidly develops. The withdrawal symptoms are severe and include twitching and convulsions. The addiction is quite severe, difficult to treat, and carries considerable mortality.

Sometimes, the user collapses suddenly and dies. He is found in an obscure place (shooting gallery) which he has chosen to ensure privacy. These factors and the lifestyle which commonly involves the abuse of alcohol and other drugs result in bruises or injuries that may simulate an assault and lead to a suspicion of homicide. The body may be dumped to a different location with consequent inappropriate postmortem rigidity and lividity.

Heroin is so rapidly metabolised that no detectable drug may be found in the blood after 30 to 60 minutes of injection. However, morphine alkaloids may be detected in the urine for hours or days after a single exposure. At autopsy blood, urine, bile, and liver should be collected. Lungs and brain may also be preserved as heroin's concentration in these organs in acute deaths is higher.

Q. 48.5. Short note on meperidine or pethidine.

Pethidine causes muscle twiching, tremors convulsions. It causes dilated pupils and tachycardia. Poisoning is treated with naloxone, diazepam and carbamazapine. The abuse used to be common among medical and paramedical people. The present editor (Dr Subrahmanyam) saw a case of positive pethidine detected on chemical analysis in a case of a person found hanged to a tree on the out skirts of a village near the Andhra Border of Tamil Nadu, India. It was later found that he was sedated with pethidine and then hanged.

Q. 48.6. Write short note on fentanyl.

Fentanyl is synthetic substance related to pethidine.

It is an anaesthetic. Its abuse is seen in west. Its duration of action is small. It enters brain repidly. Produces peak analgesia in 5 minutes after IV injection.

It abolishes reflex effects of painful stimuli. Heart rate decreases because of vagal stimulation. It causes marked respiratory depression. Naloxone is given to counteract mental clouding and respiratory depression. Muscle relaxant may be required to combat increased tone of chest muscles. Famous pop singer Michael Jackson died after fentanyl and other drug use.

Q. 48.7. Write short note on propofol.

Propofol is a powerful anaesthetic. It is called as milk of amnesia. It is commonly used to render patients unconscious for surgery. Popking Michael Jackson was found to have been administered propofol causing his death. Other substances found are midazolam, diazepam, lidocaine and ephidrine. His death was attributed to propofol.

49

Drug Dependence

Below is a glossary intended to supplement the main text by providing an explanation as well as a definition of certain important terms commonly used in the description of drug dependence.

Addictive drugs: Drugs which when taken result in compulsive use, usually in increasing amounts, on account of tolerance. However, tolerence should not be confused with addiction.

Drug: Any chemical that changes the way the body works or the way one thinks, feels, or acts. It is normally given to relieve pain or cure disease.

Drug abuse: This term now covers (1) use of drugs to affect the mind and body for non-medical reasons, (2) using substances which are illegal, (3) using chemicals that were never intended to be put into the body, e.g. glue sniffing, and (4) excessive use of therapeutic drugs.

Habituation: The condition arrived at from repeated consumption of a drug. Usually, it involves a desire (not a compulsion) to continue taking the drug, but with little or no need to increase the dosage.

Hypnotics: These are drugs which produce sleep, as for example, barbiturates.

Narcotics: These are drugs that relieve pain and produce sleep or stupor, e.g. opium, morphine, pethidine, etc.

Physical dependence: This means that the body needs the drug (even in the absence of psychological dependence) to feel normal and function properly. The physiology of the body is altered to such an extent that the cells can function satisfactorily only when such drugs with their increasing dosage are continued. The presence of withdrawal symptoms (especially physical pain) is a proof of physical dependence.

Psychological dependence: This means that the mind needs the drug. There is a craving for the repeated or compulsive use of a drug to satisfy emotional or personality needs. When the drug is discontinued, pleasure or absence of discomfort are involved, but not physical pain.

Psychotropic drugs: These are drugs that alter mental functions by their action and include stimulants, depressants, narcotics, and hallucinogens.

Sedatives: Drugs which produce a calming effect on the central nervous system.

Stimulants: Drugs which produce wakefulness, exhilaration, alertness, and such other effects, by acting on the central nervous system, e.g. amphetamines.

Tolerance: Development of body or tissue resistance to the effects of a drug so that larger doses are required to produce the original effect.

Q. 49.1. Write short notes on: (1) drug addiction, (2) drug habit, (3) drug dependence, (4) physical dependence, (5) psychological dependence, (6) pregnancy and addiction.

Drug addiction is defined as a state of periodic or chronic intoxication, harmful to the individual and to society. It is produced by repeated consumption of a drug, either natural or synthetic. It is characterised by (1) craving or actual need to continue taking the drug and to obtain it by any means, (2) a tendency to increase the dose, (3) a psychological and sometimes physical dependence upon the effects of the drug, and (4) withdrawal symptoms when the drug is withdrawn.

Drug habit is defined as a condition which results from the continued use of a drug, which does not cause much harm to the individual or society. The common habit forming drug is caffeine (coffee). The habit is characterised by (1) a tendency (but not craving) to take the drug and repeat it, as and when convenient, (2) harmful effects mainly to the individual, and (3) psychological but not physical dependence upon the effects of the drug.

WHO has coined the term **drug dependence** to replace the terms "drug addiction and drug habit". It has been defined as a state, psychological or physical, in which a person has the compulsion to take a drug on a continuous or periodic basis, either to experience its pleasurable effects or to avoid the discomfort of its absence. The number of drugs which are being used for addiction is increasing day by day. The common drugs of addiction are: (1) volatile anaesthetic solvents commonly toluene, known as glue sniffing, (2) alcohol, (3) hypnotics, such as barbiturates, (4) tranquillisers, (5) narcotic analgesics, such as opium, morphine, heroin and pethidine, (6) stimulants, such as amphetamine and methylphenidate (Ritalin), (7) cocaine, and (8) drugs causing dependence distortion of the senses, such as marihuana, LSD, and phencyclidine (PCP, angel dust).

These drugs are taken either singly, or in combination, and administered either by the oral route, by subcutaneous injection (skin popping), intravenous injection (main lining), or as, snuff. A recent fashion, probably to avoid detection by the authorities, is to inject the drug subcutaneously under a tattoo mark or intravenously into the venous plexus under the tongue, or by injection in the rectum or vagina. LSD is usually taken on a sugar cube or by putting a drop on a blotter paper and licking it when the drug effect is desired.

Drugs should normally be used for sound medical reasons only. With the increasing stresses of life and the varieties of drugs available, they are now being used for recreation, in an attempt to enhance performance, to produce a change to some desired state, to control anger or distress, to promote well-being, or as important tool for some unique experience in awareness, relationships and spiritual growth (more being, as with hallucinogens).

The terms hard drugs and soft drugs are sometimes used in the discussion on addiction. The term **hard drugs** refers to narcotics, such as opium, morphine, heroin, pethidine, etc. The term **soft drugs** refers to non-narcotics which are frequently abused, and these include: hypnotics, e.g. barbiturates; stimulants, e.g. amphetamines; non-narcotic analgesics, e.g. pentazocine; tranquillisers, e.g. diazepam, and chlordiazepoxide; and hallucinogens, e.g. LSD, phencyclidine, glue, etc.

Those who use the drugs for sound medical reasons are not likely to become addicts. A majority of addicts are neurotic individuals with personality problems. They use the drugs just for 'kick' or to escape from the realities of life. Repeated use of the drug leads to tolerance and the addict must have it under any circumstances, and by any means, including crime, sexual perversions, and prostitution. When under the influence of the drug, the addict appears calm and composed; when the effect wears off, he is restless, irritable, or depressed—generally but not always the reverse of the drug action itself.

Addiction is harmful to the individual because it leads to mental and physical degeneration. It is also harmful to the society as it leads to moral degeneration. Mental degeneration manifests itself in careless behaviour. The addict disregards conventions, customs, and feelings of others. Physical degeneration manifests itself in careless habits. The addict is constipated, emaciated due to loss of appetite, and his personal hygiene is very poor. He is likely to suffer from skin diseases and infections. Impotence and sterility are common. Moral degeneration manifests itself in crimes, which the addict commits to get the supply of his drug. He may tell lies, cheat, steal, or resort to any other means. Death from accidental overdosage and infection is common and suicide is several times more common than in the general population. Addiction in pregnant women can lead to premature, stillborn, or addicted infants.

Addiction is difficult to break. The treatment must preferably be carried out in an institution to ensure adequate supervision so that the addict does not obtain secret supplies from anywhere. The cardinal principles of treatment include detoxification by appropriate drugs, cheerful company, plenty of exercise in open air, good appetising food, attention to bowels, and psychotherapy. Those who originally used the drug for some disease and have thus acquired addiction are likely to be cured with lesser difficulty than those who used the drug mainly for its kick or other effect.

Pregnancy and addiction: The negative effects of drug abuse on the developing foetus have now been identified. Women who smoke during pregnancy deliver infants with significantly lower birth weight than non-smoking women. Babies born of alcoholic mothers often present **foetal alcohol syndrome (FAS)** characterised by prenatal growth deficiencies in length and weight, short palpebral fissures, microcephaly, and CNS anomalies. Maternal cocaine abuse can result in premature delivery of an infant with serious cardiovascular and CNS complications, low birth weight, poor feeding patterns, irritability, tremors, and involuntary movements.

In some states in the US, criminal charges have been brought against pregnant and postpartum drug addicts. Some of these charges are: foetal endangerment, involuntary manslaughter, child endangerment, assault with a deadly weapon, child abuse, criminal neglect, and possession and distribution of a harmful (controlled) substance to a minor.

DRUG ABUSE DEATHS

Drug deaths may occur in epidemics, e.g. heroin and methyl alcohol. Epidemics of 'khopri' deaths in India due to consumption of adulterated alcohol are common in areas where alcohol is prohibited. Falciparum epidemic in New York in 1933 was due to sharing the common equipment contaminated by malarial blood. Sudden death known as overdose or acute reaction is not uncommon. It is probably due to some unexpected sensitivity causing cardiac arrest following arrhythmia. In such a case, the addict may be found with the needle and syringe still in the vein. Drug administration may trigger intravascular sickling in certain heamoglobinopathies resulting in sudden death. Other complications include sepsis, bacterial endocarditis, viral hepatitis, and AIDS.

Q. 49.2. Outline the procedure to investigate a death due to narcotism (drug abuse death).

The diagnosis of death due to narcotism is based on (1) examination of the scene where the body is found, (2) investigation of the circumstances, (3) history obtained from friends and relations, (4) autopsy examination, and (5) toxicological evidence.

It should be remembered that (1) drug abuse victims are commonly found in obscure or unusual piaces where they have sought privacy to inject the drugs, (2) they are often moved from the scene and dumped to a different location a few hours after death so that the case may at first sight appear to be a homicide, and (3) the pattern of rigor mortis or lividity may not be consistent with the position of the body when seen by the doctor. All such factors and the lifestyle which frequently involves abuse of alcohol and other drugs may result in bruises that may simulate assault and mislead the investigator as to the real cause of death.

In a skin popper, a skin incision at the injection site may reveal (1) black debris in the dermis from carbonaceous material of the sterilised needle, (2) acute or chronic abscesses or diffuse subcutaneous scarring, and (3) foreign body granulomatas (skin popping).

In main liners, hyperpigmented linear needle track scars (tracers) overlying sclerosed, thrombosed, subcutaneous veins of the antecubital fossa, forearms, and dorsal aspects of hands are common.

In addicts, using the inhalation method irritation, congestion, and atrophy of the nasal mucosa is common. Perforation of the nasal septum may be seen.

The most conspicuous feature of a fatal narcotic injection is severe congestion and oedema of the lungs which manifest as **shaving cream froth at the nose and mouth filling the trachea and bronchi**. This gives rise to the suspicion of drowning, if the victim is found in the bathroom, a common place for drug administration. Foreign body granulomatas in lungs are found, if drugs, such as barbiturates and methadone, meant for oral use, are injected intravenously. Hepatic lymph adenopathy is common. Subacute bacterial endocarditis may be seen. The urinary bladder is frequently distended and often this is the *only clue* to death from drugs.

If any drug packets or injection equipment are recovered at the scene of death or from the deceased's clothing or personal effects, like shoes, wallet, etc., they should be properly preserved for laboratory examination, if incision through the skin reveals a needle track or fresh subcutaneous perivenous extravasation, the entire area should be excised and a corresponding control sample taken from the other side. The toxicologist may be able to detect either the narcotic or the adulterant (quinine). Stomach contents may show intact tablets or capsules and suggest the type of drug ingested. Liver, bile and kidneys should be preserved as in any other case of poisoning. Urine may show the presence of either the drug or the metabolic products. A majority of abused drugs can be routinely detected in the urine. Blood is required for determination of the narcotic and gamma globulin levels. In inhalation or solvent abuse cases, the whole lung should be taken with the trachea tied for analysis of bronchial air.

SOLVENT ABUSE/GLUE SNIFFING

Q. 49.3. Give a brief account of solvent abuse commonly known as glue sniffing.

The phenomenon of solvent abuse, now widespread in many parts of the world, involves deliberate inhalation of a variety of substances, especially organic solvents, to achieve pleasurable distortion of the senses. The inhalation results in a state of intoxication characterised by euphoria, sometimes of an erotic nature, and distortion of perception leading to actual hallucinations. As the most common substance inhaled initially was a toluene-based adhesive (the glue), the habit came to be known as glue sniffing. Many other non-adhesive solvent substances are now used for this purpose. Therefore, this habit is now appropriately known as 'solvent abuse'. Apart from toluene, the other substances commonly inhaled include gasoline, xylene, benzene, butane, propane, fluorocarbons, carbon tetrachloride, organic bromine derivatives, aerosol products, finger nail polish, and thinners for adhesives and paints.

When the substance to be inhaled is not a viscous glue, it is placed/sprayed on a rag/handkerchief and inhaled direct as a pad over the nose and mouth. If the substance is viscous, it is placed in a plastic bag which covers the face or head, and then inhaled. In most cases, death is due to cardiac arrest following an arrhythmia triggered by sensitisation of the myocardium to the action of catecholamines, such as adrenaline. When a large plastic bag is used to cover the head and re-breathe the contents, the abuser runs the risk of rapid death from hypoxia. When concentrated solvent vapour is used to breathe from an overhead plastic bag, the erotic hypoxia and the enhanced hallucinogenic effect of the solvent combine to give heightened sexual pleasure and correspondingly heightened risk of death.

A visit to the scene is worth undertaking when possible. Aerosol cans, plastic bags, and balloons may be found. The sniffing equipment, when available, should be preserved for laboratory examination. Clothing may have been soiled by the solvent; they should be packed as soon as possible in a suitable, solvent resisting bag to retain any vapour, and also preserved for forensic examination. The face may show skin lesions due to chronic or recent solvent abuse. Froth is seen at the nose and mouth. Pathological changes may be observed in the myocardium and central nervous system in acute intoxication, and also in the liver and kidneys in chronic intoxication, it is, therefore, essential to determine the state of the myocardium, brain, liver and kidneys by histological examination in all cases suspected of having died from solvent abuse. The other samples for laboratory examination include blood, urine, and lung.

Q. 49.4. Write short note on body packer syndrome.

A body packer is a person who transports illicit drugs from one country to other by swallowing condoms filled with the substance or balloons containing heroin or cocaine. Upon reaching the destined place, these are defecated using cathartics. Some people keep in rectum or vagina. An X-ray or ultrasound examination helps in diagnosis. These people when caught are dealt with as per the law. Drug trafficking is a serious crime and the guilty have to face even up to death sentence in some countries.

50 Inebriant Poisons

This group of poisons are characterised by two sets of symptoms, viz. excitement and narcosis, the stage of excitement being well marked in some and that of narcosis in others. The classical inebriant is alcohol. The discussion in this chapter is restricted to ethyl alcohol, Arrack (country liquor), methyl alcohol, isopropyl alcohol, and ethylene glycol.

ALCOHOL (ETHYL ALCOHOL)

The term alcohol in popular use refers to ethyl alcohol (ethanol) which is present in various fermented and distilled beverages. It is a transparent, colourless, volatile liquid having a spirit-like odour and burning taste. It is the active ingredient of many social beverages, such as wines, beers, whiskeys, and brandies, its approximate percentage in such beverages being as follows, as per ISI (Indian Standards Institution, now Bureau of Indian Standards) specifications:

Beverages	*Alcohol % by volume*	*Proof (degrees)*
Rum	42.8	75
Whiskey, brandy	42.8	75
Gin	42.8/40.0/37.2	75/70/65
Wines	8–15.5	14–27
Beers	2–10.0	3.5–17.5
Country liquor	11.4–45.7	20–80

Proof spirit indicates a mixture containing 57.10% by volume or 49.28% by weight of absolute alcohol. The proof strength of a liquid is obtained by dividing the alcohol per cent (volume strength) by 0.571. The percentage of alcohol in a liquid is obtained by multiplying the proof strength by 0.571. *Rectified spirit* contains 95% by volume of alcohol. In *absolute alcohol,* the remaining water content is removed by special technique, bringing it down to not more than 0.2% water. (*In the United States, the term proof refers to twice the percentage of alcohol by volume.* Thus the common 80-proof whiskey sold in USA contains 40% alcohol by volume). One drink is generally defined as a 12 oz beer, a 4 oz glass of wine, or a 1 1/4 shot of 80-proof alcoholic beverage).

Arrack is an eastern name for any **country liquor,** distilled from coco-palm, rice, sugar, or jaggery. Its strength may be as high as that of whisky. It is commonly fortified with potassium bromide, chloral hydrate, dhatura or bhang for a greater kick. Different provinces in India have different names for such liquors. {In Andhra Pradesh, it is known as Gudamba (derived from gud = jaggery); in Maharashtra, Khopri; and in Gujarat, Lattha}. Such inferior or adulterated country liquor should not be confused with country liquor/country spirit manufactured according to IS specifications.

Country liquor, *per se,* while more intoxicating than either imported or Indian-made foreign liquor, e.g. whisky, will have the same clinical effects as ethyl alcohol. Serious toxic effects are common when (1) the liquor is adulterated by denatured spirit which contains methyl alcohol, or (2) the so called country liquor is prepared from toxic preparations, like varnish and french polish containing methyl alcohol. Death has followed from consumption of the so-called country liquor 'Khopri' in Maharashtra and 'Lattha' in Gujarat.

Q. 50.1. Give a brief account of the metabolism of ethyl alcohol.

Ethyl alcohol is rapidly absorbed from the gastrointestinal tract. The rate of absorption depends upon (1) concentration of alcohol in the fluid imbibed, (2) presence or absence of food in the stomach, (3) condition of the stomach wall (gastrectomy, chronic gastritis, etc.), (4) rate of drinking, (5) quantity of alcohol ingested, (6) weight of the person, and (7) development of tolerance. The first two factors are most important. Alcohol is absorbed more rapidly from concentrated than from dilute solutions; the presence of food in the stomach, especially fats and proteins, will retard absorption, milk being very effective for this purpose.

Following absorption, *the concentration of alcohol in blood reaches a maximum in about 45 to 90 minutes after ingestion.* The concentration of alcohol in various tissues after equilibrium is established is as follows: With blood as 1.00, the average for brain is 1.17, plasma 1.16, urine 1.33, vitreous and bile 1.12, liver 0.91, and blood clot 0.77. These ratios vary a little.

Approximately, 90% of absorbed alcohol is oxidised in the liver, the remaining 10% is excreted mainly by the kidneys and lungs. Normally, the body can metabolise about 1/2 fluid ounce of absolute alcohol, roughly equivalent to one drink (one fluid ounce of whisky or 12 ounces of beer) every hour. If the intake exceeds this measure, the subject manifests signs and symptoms of drunkenness unless he has developed tolerance. The average fall is around 15–18 mg ethanol per 100 ml of blood per hour. It is, therefore, possible to calculate how long after a given dose the body will be alcohol-free and to estimate with reasonable accuracy what the blood-alcohol concentration was a few hours before a blood analysis was made.

It is important to know that the concentration of alcohol in blood varies continuously, first increasing during the period of absorption, and then decreasing on account of metabolism. Since the glomerular filtrate has a concentration similar to that in the plasma, a given sample of urine will reflect the average blood alcohol concentration during the time the urine has accumulated in the urinary bladder. As the bladder may have contained urine before taking alcohol, it is necessary to empty the bladder and use a second sample collected within 30–60 minutes for any such test.

Q. 50.2. Give a succinct account of acute ethyl alcohol poisoning.

Ethyl alcohol *depresses* the central nervous system irregularly in descending order from cortex to medulla. It first depresses the higher centres which control judgement and behaviour (stage of excitement—blood alcohol 30–100 mg%), then the motor centres (stage of incoordination—blood alcohol 100–300 mg%), and finally the vital centres in the medulla (stage of narcosis—blood alcohol over 300 mg%). The breath smells of alcohol throughout.

The effects appear early in those who are mentally or physically fatigued, in epileptics, in persons with head injury, and in those who have taken barbiturates or other CNS depressants.

The statutory limit for a charge of drunken driving in most states in USA is 0.08–0.10%; in Canada and Britain 0.08%; in Scandinavian countries 0.05%; in Austria 0.04%; and in Czechoslovakia, Poland, other East European countries 0.03%, and India 0.15%.

Stage of excitement: This is a feeling of well-being and pleasure resulting from inhibition of the higher centres. The drinker converses well, laughs and smiles readily, or becomes angry easily. He may disclose secrets. He may behave in an obscene manner or talk in vulgar language. Sexual desire may be aroused.

Stage of incoordination: There is incoordination of thought, speech, and action, which manifest as impaired judgement, confusion, slurred speech, and staggering gait. The drinker may suffer from hiccups and is untidy in his appearance. He may become morose, euphoric, or irritable—depending on his inherent emotions. Nausea and vomiting are common. The pupils are dilated. Most offenses are committed in this stage. Impaired judgement may lead to accidents, sexual excesses, violence, and crime.

Stage of narcosis: The patient passes into deep sleep and responds only to strong stimuli. The pulse is rapid, temperature subnormal, breathing stertorous, and the pupils may be contracted. However, on pinching the neck or face, they dilate initially and slowly return to their original size. This is known as *MacEwan's sign* and is helpful to differentiate alcoholic coma from other comatose conditions. If this stage lasts for more than 12 hours, death ensues from paralysis of the cardiac or respiratory centre or later from the effects of pulmonary oedema. However, a recent opinion states that this test is not found positive.

Death from acute alcoholism is not common. Recovery occurs with acute depression and gastrointestinal irritation which continue for 24 hours or longer. Headache is also present as an hangover effect and is due to cerebral oedema. A *hangover* means a temporary state of indisposition usually following recovery from drunkenness.

The approximate relationship between the alcoholic content of blood and clinical manifestations is tabulated in Table 50.1.

The table is intended to provide a general guideline of clinical manifestations in relation to blood levels in those persons who are not regular and excessive drinkers, recovery has been recorded after blood alcohol levels of 780 mg% and above.

Fatal dose: This will depend on the age and habits of the patient and the strength of the liquor taken. Death usually occurs from large quantity taken in a short time. A concentration of 0.35% (350 mg%) and above of alcohol in blood is generally sufficient to cause death.

Fatal period: The usual fatal period is 12 to 24 hours though death may be delayed for 5 to 6 days.

Table 50.1: Blood alcohol level and clinical manifestations

%	Mg%	Effect
Less than 0.03%	Less than 30	Not Noticeable
0.03–0.05	30–50	Selective impairment
0.05–0.10	50–100	Slight impairment
0.10–0.15	100–150	Under the influence
0.15–0.20	150–200	Drunk
0.20–0.30	200–300	Very drunk
0.03–0.35	300–350	Stupor to coma
Over 0.35	Over 350	Comatose to death

1. *Selective impairment:* Increase in reaction time; impairment of complex skills, such as flying an aircraft or driving a motor vehicle. Detectable only on detailed examination.
2. *Slight impairment:* Flushed face; dilated pupils; euphoria; loss of restraint.
3. *Under the influence:* Flushed face; dilated sluggish pupils; euphoria; loss of restraint; test errors; stagger on sudden turning.
4. *Drunk:* Flushed face; dilated sluggish/inactive pupils; clouding of intellect; incoordination of thought, speech, and action; staggering gait with reeling and lurching while making sudden turns.
5. *Very drunk:* Flushed or pale face; pupils inactive, contracted or dilated; mental confusion; marked incoordination of thought, speech, and action; staggering, reeling gait with tendency to lurch and fall; vomiting; amnesia.

Cause of death: Death is due to depression of the respiratory centre. Alcohol may be lethal at relatively lower blood levels when combined with other central nervous system depressants, such as barbiturates, carbon monoxide, or morphine, and/or in the presence of some natural disease of heart or lungs.

Q. 50.3. Explain selective impairment from alcohol intoxication with special reference to driving a motor vehicle.

A motor vehicle is a complicated piece of machinery, the handling of which requires skill, dexterity, and mental acuity, all of which are selectively reduced, even eliminated, by alcohol. Thus, an individual may be intoxicated to the point of being unable to operate an automobile safely while appearing sober.

Research shows that a driver's ability is adversely affected with a blood alcohol content of .03–.05% (or sometimes even less), which means consumption of just two beers in about an hour. Alcohol causes faulty depth perception, poor peripheral vision, distorted colour vision, and reduced night vision. For example, after an impaired driver's pupil is exposed to the glare of oncoming headlights, it can take from two to eight seconds to adapt to the dark conditions as compared to one second required by a non-impaired eye. In addition, an alcohol impaired driver's ability to judge distance may also be reduced, making it difficult to change lanes or determine whether a car is approaching, moving away, or standing still.

Driving ability is generally impaired even in the hangover phase due to the after-effects of alcohol on judgement, perception, reaction time, and coordination. An increase of one-tenth of a second in reaction time means that a car travelling at 80 km an hour needs an additional 2.2 metres of road to pull up.

Q. 50.4. Describe briefly the treatment and postmortem appearances in a case of death from ethanol poisoning. Add a note on medicolegal aspects.

Treatment: The stomach should be lavaged with care with 5% solution of sodium bicarbonate in warm water. The patient should be kept warm. Isotonic saline with 5% glucose (preferably fructose) may be required to deal with symptoms of hypoglycaemia, if present.

The increase in intracranial pressure which often occurs can be treated with saline purges and intravenous hypertonic glucose solution. When there is respiratory depression, artificial respiration may be necessary along with oxygen inhalation. Very serious cases will require haemodialysis or peritoneal dialysis.

Postmortem appearances: The clothes are generally in a disorderly/torn condition. Stains due to vomit or blood may be present. The tongue may be furred. Rigor mortis lasts longer than usual. Bruises are generally found on various parts of the body. Other injuries may be present.

An odour of alcoholic beverages is often evident on opening the body. The blood is fluid and dark. The brain is slightly oedematous. Shrinkage of cerebral cortex (grey matter) is common in chronic alcoholics. In individuals who sustain head injury with subdural or epidural haemorrhage and survive for hours to days, the analysis of the brain blood clot may reveal initial blood alcohol level at the time of injury. Vitreous analysis is very helpful in all cases. Oedema of the larynx, a bolus of food obstructing the larynx (cafe coronary), fatty liver, or acute haemorrhagic pancreatitis are commonly found when death has been sudden or unexpected. The stomach usually shows signs of alcoholic gastritis to a varying degree. The mucous membrane of the small intestine is oedematous but not ulcerated. This finding is important from an insurance point of view when death occurs after consumption of alcohol and food.

A traveller left Mumbai for Poona (a distance of about 200 km) in his car commencing his journey at about 10.00 p.m. At about 12.00 midnight, he halted at a wayside restaurant where he consumed alcohol and ate food. At about 2.00 a.m., he resumed his journey reaching Poona at about 6.00 a.m. About 10.00 a.m., he started vomiting and died at about 11.00 a.m. next day. At postmortem, extensive ulcerations were found in the small intestine. Laboratory examination confirmed that this was a case of Salmonella food poisoning—a suspicion already aroused at autopsy from the finding of ulcerations of the small intestine.

In addition to the usual viscera, vitreous fluid/CSF may be preserved for chemical analysis. Blood should be collected from a peripheral vein, and precautions for its preservation as mentioned under collection of samples should be followed.

Medicolegal aspects: Poisoning by alcohol is comparatively common, although death directly due to its ingestion occurs in a far smaller number of cases. However, there is a liability to fatal complications, such as head injuries, serious bleeding from trivial injuries, suffocation (cafe coronary), drowning, and exposure. A strong relationship exists between alcohol, crime, and violence. Chronic alcoholism is a common cause of *sexual jealousy crimes*, especially those of a homicidal nature. A passenger who accepts a lift from the driver of a motor vehicle whom he knows to be drunk accepts the risk of contributory negligence in the event of an accident.

CHRONIC POISONING (ALCOHOLIC ADDICTION)

This results form continued use of alcohol. It is characterised by a gradual physical, moral and mental deterioration (alcoholic dementia). Physical degeneration manifests as lack of personal hygiene, loss of appetite, chronic gastroenteritis, wasting, peripheral neuropathies, impotence and sterility, and fatty changes in the liver and heart. Alcohol is a hepatotoxic poison. Cirrhosis of liver is common. A useful index of liver damage is the level of enzyme gamma-glutamyl transpeptidase in the serum, the normal level being less than 36 units. Moral degeneration manifests as crimes which the addict commits to get his drink. He becomes suspicious of his wife's fidelity and may assault her or the suspected paramour. Mental degeneration results in dementia. Three common clinical syndromes which result from chronic alcoholism are: (1) delirium tremens, (2) Korsakoff's psychosis, and (3) acute hallucinosis.

Delirium tremens is a state of excitement with hallucinosis which usually lasts 3 to 4 days, it results from (1) an unusual bout of drinking, (2) sudden withdrawal of alcohol, (3) acute infection, e.g. pneumonia or influenza, (4) shock from injury, e.g. fracture of a bone, and (5) exposure to cold. It is characterised by an attack of acute insanity in which the main symptoms are sleeplessness, marked tremors, excitement, fear and hallucinations chiefly visual and occasionally auditory. He may seek escape from his terrifying new world by suicide. He is often violent with a tendency to homicide. He is for the time being insane and not responsible for his actions.

Treatment involves sedatives, such as chlorpromazine 100 mg four times a day orally, intravenous hypertonic glucose to relieve cerebral oedema, and withdrawal of some CSF to reduce intracranial tension. Infection, if present, must be treated energetically.

Korsakoff's psychosis is a syndrome characterised by hallucinations, disorientation and multiple neuritis. The patient's memory for recent events is lost and he fills the gap by confabulation. This state lasts about from one month to a year.

Acute hallucinosis is a state of hallucination chiefly auditory with systematised delusions of persecution lasting from weeks to months. It is a psychiatric emergency; the patient may become homicidal or suicidal in response to his hallucinations. These patients must be hospitalised, sedated, observed closely, and treated as for delirium tremens.

The drug antabuse (disulfiram) acts by sensitising the patient to even a small dose of alcohol, and is the most suitable treatment for almost all cases. It is administered in a single daily dose of 0.5 gm and can be continued for a long time. It can be given in tea or any other non-alcoholic beverage even without the patient's knowledge (in some countries). Temposil (calcium carbamide citrated), 50 mg tablet once a day also sensitises the individual to alcohol and can be used in place of antabuse with lesser side effects. Hypnosis and psychotherapy are helpful.

Postmortem appearances in patients dying after chronic ingestion of large amounts of alcohol include degenerative changes in the liver, kidneys and brain, atrophic gastritis, cirrhosis of the liver, and cardiomyopathy.

DRUNKENNESS

Q. 50.5. Define drunkenness.

Or

Describe insobriety. Give a brief account of the clinical tests and the laboratory specimens required to diagnose it.

Drunkenness is a condition which results from excessive intake of alcohol and the person is so much under its influence that (1) he loses control over his mental faculties, (2) he is unable to perform the duties on which he is engaged at a particular time, and (3) he may be a source of danger to himself or to others.

In places where there is **no prohibition,** drunkenness in itself is not a crime unless it is accompanied by some act of commission or omission which causes danger to the life or property of the individual or to some other persons. Thus, a person may be charged with being drunk and disorderly, or being drunk and in charge of a vehicle. A doctor may be charged for operating or delivering a baby negligently when intoxicated.

Diagnosis

Under section 53 (1) of the CrPC, an examination of the accused can be carried out by a medical officer at the request of the police even without his consent and by use of force, if necessary. Such examination may include taking of fluids in cases of suspected intoxication.

Clinical Examination

Clinically, in the absence of head injury and other pathological conditions, a person is definitely under the influence of alcohol, if there is **smell** of alcoholic beverage in his breath and/or in the vomited matter (if any), **provided** there is a combination of all or most of the following groups of symptoms or signs, viz:

1. *General demeanour:* Excited, hilarious, talkative, abusive.
2. *Clothes:* Disarranged, disorderly.
3. *Eyes:* Suffusion of the conjunctivae. *Pupils* may vary from extreme dilatation to extreme contraction and may be equal or unequal. *Fine lateral nystagmus* is indicative of alcoholic intoxication.
4. *Tongue:* Dry, furred, or excessive salivation.
5. *Speech:* Slurred and incoherent. Certain test phrases, e.g. British Constitution may be asked.
6. *Memory:* Loss or confusion particularly as regards recent events and appreciation of time. Simple sums of addition or substraction may be asked.

7. *Coordination:* Impaired. Unable to thread a needle, button his clothes, stand with his heels together with eyes closed, or pick up coins dropped on the floor. Gait uncertain, reeling or falling. Stagger on sudden turning. Tremors of the hand make writing difficult. The signature can be compared with that on the driving license. Finger-nose test is impaired.
8. *Reflexes:* Delayed and sluggish.
9. *Unusual actions:* Hiccups, belching, vomiting, fighting.

Thus, the important clinical signs of drunkenness are: (1) smell of alcoholic beverage in breath, (2) loss of self-control and disordered clothing, (3) sluggish dilated pupils and fine lateral nystagmus, (4) slurred or incoherent speech, (5) unsteady gait, and (6) confused mental state or impaired memory for recent events.

The common laboratory tests include estimation of alcohol from (1) blood, (2) urine, (3) breath, and at autopsy, and (4) vitreous fluid, bile, and other tissues.

Collection of Samples

Blood: The skin is cleaned with soap and water or a solution of 1:1000 mercuric chloride. A syringe free from the slightest trace of alcohol and other chemicals (preferably a fresh disposable syringe) should be used. 5 mg of sodium fluoride and 15 mg of potassium oxalate can be used as preservative for 5 ml of blood. Blood container should be tightly stoppered to prevent loss of alcohol by evaporation and labelled with name, date, time of taking the specimen and signature of the medical officer. It is kept in a refrigerator and sent as soon as possible to the laboratory.

Vitreous fluid can be taken in place of blood tor postmortem alcohol estimation in drunken individuals from whom a blood sample is not obtainable due to extensive trauma. Only crystal clear colourless fluid should be used. It can be collected slowly with a syringe and 20 gauge needle. CSF, vitreous, or bile can also be used when it is difficult to obtain blood due to decomposition.

Urine: The urine sample is collected in the usual manner in a large, chemically clean, sterilised, screw capped bottle. It is desirable to ask the patient to empty the bladder and use a second sample collected within 30 to 60 minutes. 30 mg of phenyl mercuric nitrate is used as a preservative for every 10 ml of urine. The bottle is screwed, sealed, and labelled with appropriate particulars.

Breath: The person is asked to blow into a special container or directly into a breath analyser (drunkometer, intoximeter, alcometer). This is a preliminary screening test based on the principle that alcohol reacts with an oxidising agent and produces change in its colour, proportional to the amount of alcohol. The amount of alcohol in approximately 2,100 ml of alveolar air is taken to be the same as that in 1 ml of blood. Electronic breathalysers not necessarily working on the principle of chemical reaction of alcohol with an oxidising agent are also available. These give quantitative results. Some of these devices with print-out of results of analysis have been accepted for court work abroad. Even so, the uncertainty arises out of the important assumption that the absorption was already complete in the given case; if not, overestimates of blood-alcohol concentration are likely.

Q. 50.6. Comment on the value of laboratory tests in the diagnosis of drunkenness.

While dealing with analytical findings on specimens containing alcohol, the following facts must be borne in mind:

1. The site of blood collection is important. Blood for alcohol estimation should be collected from a peripheral vein.
2. Alcohol concentration may fall slightly on storage.

3. Alcohol can be produced in the body after death or during storage due to fermentation. It is, therefore, essential that: (a) blood sample is not contaminated during collection, (b) a proper preservative is added, (c) the sample is preserved in a refrigerator, and (d) analysis is done as quickly as circumstances permit.
4. In dealing with embalmed bodies, the possibility of alcohol in the embalming fluid must be considered.

Blood tests: The blood alcohol tests prove with reasonable accuracy the concentration of alcohol which was present at the time of taking the sample. The amount of alcohol eliminated by the body over a given period of time may also be estimated with a fair degree of accuracy. These tests also prove what the probable effect of alcohol was on the person concerned. Volatile substances, like acetone, ether, paraldehyde, may be estimated as alcohol unless sensitive methods are used.

Urine tests: A sample of urine collected within 30–60 minutes after the person has completely emptied his bladder will indicate with reasonable accuracy the average blood-alcohol level over the time the sample was collected, the ratio of urinary alcohol to blood-alcohol being approximately 4:3. Examination of urine may be of great value in indicating if the person is a diabetic, is suffering from ketosis, or has recently taken barbiturates or other drug.

Breath tests: The breath alcohol test needs special apparatus, specially trained operator, and active cooperation of the person. The limitations of the test have already been outlined.

DIFFICULTIES IN DIAGNOSIS

Conditions which simulate drunkenness must be ruled out before diagnosing insobriety. There are other difficulties as well.

1. The chief conditions most likely to be mistaken for drunkenness are: mental disease, shock, head injury, hypoglycaemia, and poisoning from carbon monoxide, opium, atropine, dhatura, barbiturates, amphetamines, antihistaminics, insulin, and the like. Less likely to be mistaken for drunkenness are uraemia, disseminated sclerosis, ataxia, Meniere or Parkinson's disease, and cerebellar tumour.
2. Head injury and alcoholism may be associated.
3. The combination of drugs of the barbiturate group and alcohol can enhance the symptoms of intoxication due to synergistic action. Other drugs that are dangerous in combination with alcohol include narcotics, tranquillisers, antihistaminics, and hypnotics. Therefore, persons who are taking these preparations for medicinal reasons may be unfit to drive after a very small dose of alcohol. The doctor, while prescribing such drugs, should warn the patient accordingly.
4. Mentally unstable subjects, epileptics, and those who have suffered from cerebral trauma at some earlier date may show an excessive reaction to small amounts of alcohol.
5. There is no single clinical test which by itself would justify a medical practitioner in coming to the conclusion of drunkenness in a person.
6. Laboratory tests, being objective, certainly enhance the value of clinical tests.
7. Alcohol acts differently on different individuals and so also on the same individual at different times. Intoxication in females is approximately 25% more than in males.

Therefore, in giving evidence, the expert witness should explain to the court the limitations of the tests and the inferences to be drawn from them and base his expert testimony on a combination of test results and observations of the accused by the police and/or doctor.

ALCOHOL AND PROHIBITION

Alcohol is a drug of addiction and is responsible for many socioeconomic problems, crimes, morbidity and mortality. It is a contributory factor in many deaths. Therefore, some states in India and elsewhere have imposed prohibition laws in an effort to reduce the magnitude of the problem, but this has brought about its own complications.

In places where **prohibition** is **in force,** drinking by itself without a permit is a crime, and so also possession of liquor without a license. Sale of liquor is subject to strict control. Therefore, illicit distillation is being done on a large scale. Misuse of toxic preparations, such as varnish and French polish is responsible for considerable ill health and even death among such illicit drinkers.

For the charge of drunkenness, the defence plea is usually that the accused had consumed non-prohibited liquor (tonics), like Asavas or Aristhas (ayurvedic preparations—14% alcohol) or Wincamis (20% alcohol) but these in their permitted/prescribed or practical dosage cannot result in incriminating blood-alcohol levels, say, 50 mg% and above.

The Bombay Prohibition Act (BPA)

The relevant sections of the Act (BPA) operative at present in Maharashtra and Gujarat states in relation to drinking, drunkenness, pleas in relation to drinking of non-prohibited preparations and possession of intoxicants provide as follows:

Section 84 provides penalty for being found drunk or drinking in a common drinking house or being present for the purpose of drinking. Section 85 provides punishment for being drunk and disorderly in any street, thoroughfare, or public place. Subsection 2 of section 66 provides that if the concentration of alcohol in the blood of the accused is not less than 0.05% (50 mg%), then the burden of proving that the liquor consumed was a medicinal or toilet preparation, or an antiseptic preparation or solution, or a flavouring extract or essence of syrup containing alcohol, the consumption of which is not in contravention of the Act, shall be upon the accused person and in the absence of such proof, the court shall, presume the contrary.

Under section 129A, a prohibition officer or any police officer, who has reasonable grounds for believing that a person has consumed an intoxicant, is authorised to get such a person medically examined and his blood tested for the quantitative estimation of alcohol. If the person is a female, such examination shall be carried out and blood collected by or under the supervision of a female registered medical practitioner, with strict regard to decency. It is ruled by the Bombay High Court that the sample of blood thus taken and examined does not violate Article 20(3) of the Constitution. Rule 3 of the BP (Medical Examination and Blood Test) Rules deals with the clinical examination and certification of a person by a registered medical practitioner in alleged consumption cases. Rule 4 provides for the manner of collection of blood and forwarding of blood specimen to the chemical examiner. Rule 5 deals with certificate of test in relation to blood sample examined by the chemical examiner.

Sections 65 and 66(1) provide penalty for illegal import, export, manufacture, sale, purchase, or transport of an intoxicant without proper license, permit, or authorisation.

Under the BPA, the problems which generally arise pertain to (1) consumption of liquor, and (2) possession of liquor.

1. Consumption Cases

The common questions raised at criminal trials in consumption cases are: (1) Has the person consumed liquor, and (2) if so, what is his blood alcohol level.

Under the BPA and rules made thereunder, the prohibition officer or police officer produces the concerned person for medical examination and/or collection of his blood. The medical officer examines the person and issues a certificate in the prescribed Form "A" containing the result of his clinical examination as to whether the person has or has not consumed alcohol and is or is not under its influence. The medical officer collects and forwards in the *manner prescribed* the blood of such person to the chemical examiner vide Form "B" who issues a certificate in the prescribed Form "C" as regards the percentage of alcohol and such other particulars as may be necessary or relevant.

The medical officer should make a thorough clinical examination as outlined under **"diagnosis of drunkenness"** and observe all precautions as mentioned under "collection of blood sample" to comply with the rules under the BPA. The collected sealed sample should be sent to the chemical examiner by registered post or through a special messenger with a forwarding letter bearing his (medical officer's) seal to avoid any possibility of tampering.

Determination of Blood/Urine Alcohol

The chemical examiner, after checking the sample in forensic context, may determine the alcohol content of blood by a suitable method including the modified versions of **Kozelka and Hine/Cavett method.** The latter involves aeration/distillation or diffusion under low pressure. It utilises the principle that alcohol is easily oxidised to acetic acid by oxidising agents, such as potassium dichromate and sulphuric acid. Each ml of N/20 dichromate solution that is reduced in the process is equivalent to 0.575 mg of alcohol. Other modern available methods may also be used.

The advantages of this method are: (1) Distillation/diffusion and oxidation are carried out separately but simultaneously, (2) volatile decomposition products, like aldehydes, sulphides, and ketone bodies do not interfere with the analysis, and (3) the apparatus is inexpensive, its assembly simple, and its use easy and rapid.

The specific requirements of the method are: (1) All reagents must be of recognised analytical quality, and (2) the apparatus must be cleaned carefully before use.

Depending upon the type of sample, resources available, need for accuracy, and need for specificity, other methods for estimation of blood alcohol may be used. These include: (1) gas chromatography, (2) alcohol dehydrogenase (ADH) method, and (3) breathalysers. The principle of the various methods is briefly outlined below.

Gas chromatography: A measured microlitre quantity of sample containing alcohol is put into a previously heated chamber. The vaporised alcohol is carried by an inert carrier gas, usually nitrogen, through a column packed with a suitable adsorbent material. The various constituents of the sample are separated due to differences in adsorption, etc./and detected by a sensitive detector. A record on a moving chart (chromatogram) provides the qualitative and quantitative analysis.

The advantages of this method are: (1) The procedure is simple, sensitive, and reasonably specific, (2) only small quantity of a sample is required, and (3) the analysis is not interfered with by other ingredients, e.g. other alcohols, aldehydes, ketones, etc. These elute at different intervals and the chromatogram records separate peaks for these substances, if present.

This technique is very useful when deaths are due to consumption of poisonous liquor. Alcohol and other denaturants, especially methyl alcohol are simultaneously recorded, identified, and quantified.

ADH method: This biochemical method is based on the principle that the enzyme ADH (alcohol dehydrogenase) converts alcohol into acetaldehyde with co-enzyme NAD (nicotinamide adenine dinucleotide, previously called DPN, diphosphopyridine nucleotide or co-enzyme-1). The reaction is driven to completion by maintaining a high pH and removing acetaldehyde with semicarbazide. The increase in absorbance at 340 nm (NADH) is monitored on a spectrophotometer.

Breathalysers: The principle of the test and its admissibility in court work are already described under collection of breath sample in the diagnosis of drunkenness.

Interpretation of Results

The degree of intoxication has great bearing in cases of sudden deaths, assaults, accidents, and when diminished responsibility is claimed as a defence. Under the BPA, a person having a blood alcohol level of 0.05% (50 mg%) and above has legally committed the offence of consumption. As per recent amendment of Section 117 of the Motor Vehicles Act, it is an offence to drive or attempt to drive a motor vehicle with any quantity of alcohol in blood (no threshold limit specified).

The amount of alcohol consumed can be estimated from the blood alcohol level. When the blood alcohol level is 0.1%, that is 100 mg%, the amount ingested is approximately 0.85 ml of absolute alcohol per kg of body weight. In a person with 70 kg body weight, this would amount to approximately 60 ml (70 × 0.85) of absolute alcohol or approximately 140 ml of hard liquor, such as whisky, brandy, etc., of 75° proof strength. Therefore, when the blood alcohol level in such a person is 0.05% or 50 mg%, the legal limit, the amount ingested would be 30 ml of absolute alcohol, or about 150 ml (five and a quarter fluid ounces) of 20% alcohol, the maximum percentage that can be.found in a medicinal preparation, like Wincarnis. This means that a medicinal preparation, when taken in a prescribed dose [the prescribed dose being about 30 ml (a fluid ounce = 28.4 ml) or less], cannot produce blood alcohol level above or anywhere near the prescribed legal limit of 0.05% or 50 mg%. (These numbers are different in other countries.)

In the interpretation of analytical findings, it is essential to make sure that necessary precautions in collection, preservation, and storage of the sample have been followed, the analytical method correctly applied, and results interpreted in proper perspective keeping in mind the limitations already outlined under 'value of laboratory tests' in the diagnosis of drunkenness.

The defence attorney has a right to make certain on cross examination that the samples were properly collected, preserved, transported, and analysed; there was no possibility of mix-up or tampering with the sample; and the chain of evidence has been maintained.

Formulae for alcohol level in blood/tissue

Concentration of alcohol in blood is expressed as mg% (w/v), or as percentage as follows:

50 mg% (w/v) = 0.05% (w/v), i.e. 50 mg alcohol per 100 ml blood.

It is also expressed as mg% (w/w) in solid tissues, like viscera sent for chemical analysis, i.e. so many mg alcohol per 100 grams tissue.

Widmark's formulae to estimate alcohol: $a=cpr$, where a is the total amount of alcohol in gm absorbed in the body; c is the concentration of alcohol in blood (in gm/kg); p is the weight of the person (in kg); and r is a constant namely 0.68 in men and 0.5 in women. For urine analysis, the formula is $a=3/4\ qpr$, q being concentration of alcohol in urine (in gm/litre).

Example: 70 kg male has consumed 120 ml (around 4 fluid ounces) of 75% proof liquor. His blood alcohol (peak) level will be

$$\frac{120 \times 0.428 \times 0.8 \times 1000}{70 \times 10 \times 0.68} \text{ mg\% w/v} = 86 \text{ mg\%}.$$

(75% proof strength = 42.8% by volume; density of alcohol has been rounded up as 0.8).

2. Possession Cases

The common questions raised in possession cases are: (1) Whether the sample contains ethyl alcohol, (2) Whether the sample is altered spirit, denatured spirit, medicinal preparation, toilet preparation, antiseptic preparation, flavouring syrup, etc., (3) Whether the sample is fermented wash (from brewing), and (4) Whether the sample conforms to the specifications on the label, if any.

Under section 117, any prohibition officer or police officer is authorised to search in the presence of panchas (public persons) any person, article or premises, believed to provide evidence of possession of an intoxicant, and take charge of such articles in the prescribed manner.

Under section 121(1), he may open any package and examine any goods and may stop and search any vehicle or other means of conveyance for evidence of intoxicant.

Under section 123(1), he may seize and detain any article likely to contain an intoxicant and forward the article under section 123(2) to the nearest police station. The article so seized is forwarded to the chemical examiner for examination of contents and opinion thereon.

A selection of tests is carried out on the article to detect the various constituents, and the results reported by the chemical examiner in the prescribed proforma.

METHYL ALCOHOL

Methyl alcohol (wood alcohol, wood spirit, wood naphtha, carbinol, or methanol) is a colourless liquid with a faint spirit-like odour and a burning nauseous taste. It is used in industry for denaturing rectified spirit so as to render it non-drinkable. Rectified spirit mixed with five per cent methyl alcohol is known as methylated spirit, and is used in arts and manufacture under the name of denatured spirit or denatured alcohol. It is found as an antifreeze in gas lines and is also used as a solvent in paint removers, varnish, etc.

Q. 50.7. Describe the mode of action, symptoms and signs, treatment, and post-mortem appearances in a case of methyl alcohol poisoning.

Mode of action: Methyl alcohol is more toxic than ethyl alcohol. Since it is slowly excreted from the body, it acts as a cumulative poison. During metabolism, it is converted into formaldehyde and formic acid. These metabolites are responsible for its toxic action. The symptoms correlate with the degree of acidosis.

Symptoms and signs: The symptoms may appear within an hour after ingestion but are commonly delayed. Poisoning is manifested by headache, dizziness, nausea, vomiting, and pain in the abdomen. There is marked muscular weakness and depressed cardiac action. Spirit-like odour is usually present in the breath. Dyspnoea and cyanosis are common. Acidosis results from accumulation of acid metabolites. The poisonous effects are most marked in the eyes, causing either temporary blindness or, in severe cases, atrophy of the optic nerves resulting in permanent blindness. Other toxic effects relate to liver and kidney. Convulsions are common as a terminal event in fatal cases, and death occurs from respiratory failure.

Finding of intestinal contraction is diagnostic of methanol poisoning. Contraction affects either the small bowel or the large bowel or both, being described as resembling a thick pipe of very narrow lumen.

Dr Subrahmanyam has seen a serious case of 25 persons admitted in Suryapet Civil hospital where people who consumed illicit liquor presented with varying stages of loss of vision including total blindness.

Fatal dose: About 60 to 240 ml would kill most adults. 15 ml is known to cause blindness. Serious symptoms have been produced in children by intake of 1 ml/kg of denatured alcohol containing methyl alcohol.

Fatal period: Death may occur within 24 to 36 hours or may be delayed for 3 to 4 days.

Treatment consists of (1) preventing absorption by gastric lavage (2) use of bicarbonate to combat acidosis, and (3) administration of ethanol as a competitive antagonist. Whole bowel irrigation is excellent, if facilities permit.

The stomach should be lavaged with 5% solution of sodium bicarbonate in warm water. Acidosis will require oral administration of sodium bicarbonate in a dose of 2 gm (1/2 teaspoonful) in 250 ml of water every two hours to maintain neutral or slightly alkaline urine. If oral therapy is not possible, 50 gm of sodium bicarbonate dissolved in one litre of 5% dextrose solution can be given intravenously along with 10–15 units of insulin. The plasma bicarbonate level should be maintained at around 20 mEq per litre. Intravenous administration of molar sodium lactate is helpful. Oral administration of 50% ethyl alcohol in a dose of 0.75 to 1 ml/kg body weight for three to four days is beneficial. It prevents methanol oxidation to formaldehyde and formic acid and aids meanwhile its excretion in urine and breath.

Indications for haemodialysis include any ocular findings, metabolic acidosis, renal failure and a blood methanol level over 50 mg%.

Antidote 4-methylpyrazole is a specific alcohol dehydrogenase inhibitor. It blocks the formation of formaldehyde and formic acid. Excretion of methanol can then occur by renal or pulmonary routes. It has few side effects. It should be used, if available.

Folinic acid speeds up metabolism of formic acid and may be used. The rest of the treatment is symptomatic. Eyes should be kept covered to protect from strong light.

Postmortem appearances: Cyanosis is marked. The blood is generally fluid and dark. Cerebral and pulmonary oedema are seen. The gastrointestinal mucosa is inflamed. The liver shows necrobiosis and kidneys show tubular degeneration. Viscera and postmortem blood should be preserved as outlined under ethyl alcohol poisoning.

Medicolegal aspects: Accidental poisoning may occur. Poisoning is generally due to consumption of liquor containing methyl alcohol by drinkers of cheap illicit liquor, methanol having got into the liquor by accident or design, the latter for economic gain by the most unscrupulous bootleggers.

ISOPROPYL ALCOHOL

Isopropyl alcohol is found in rubbing alcohol. It is a colourless liquid with a faint alcoholic odour. It is twice as potent as ethanol on a weight to weight basis and is also slowly metabolised with the result that the patient is more drunk and for a longer time as compared to ethanol. It is consumed by alcoholics as a cheap substitute for ethanol or to get a greater kick. One of the metabolic products is acetone which is a CNS depressant.

Symptoms and signs: Poisoning is manifested by headache, dizziness, nausea, vomiting (haematemesis), and acute pain in the abdomen, followed by marked muscular weakness, depressed cardiac action, and collapse. There is a characteristic fruity odour of acetone in the breath giving the impression of diabetic ketoacidosis. In children, hypoglycaemia may occur. In severe cases, coma persists for more than 24 hours and death ensues from respiratory arrest. Isopropyl alcohol is excreted unchanged by the kidneys and lungs. Its half-life is about 8–12 hours.

Fatal dose and fatal period: Infants have been poisoned by isopropyl alcohol baths. More than a single swallow is a toxic dose for children. The lethal dose for an adult (70 kg) is about 2.5 ounces of 70% isopropyl alcohol. The average fatal period is 24 hours.

Treatment: Supportive treatment is all that is necessary. In severe intoxication, dialysis is essential. Hypoglycaemia will need intravenous glucose.

Postmortem appearances: Cyanosis is marked. The blood is generally fluid and dark. The gastrointestinal mucosa is inflamed and haemorrhagic. The stomach contents may emit fruity smell of acetone. Cerebral and pulmonary oedema are seen. The kidneys show tubular degeneration.

Medicolegal aspects: Poisoning is mainly accidental from isopropyl baths in infants and ingestion by children less than six years old. Drunkards may use it in place of ethanol and get poisoned thereby.

ETHYLENE GLYCOL

The glycols are easily available, being widely used as antifreeze agents in cooling systems of radiators of motor engines and solvents in industry. Their action is characterised by the intoxicating features of alcohol and irritant features of oxalate poisoning. The toxic compounds are ethylene, diethylene, and hexyl glycols, of which ethylene glycol is most commonly encountered in medicolegal work as a source of intoxication and suicidal or accidental poisoning.

Symptoms and signs: When ingested, the intoxicating effects resemble drunkenness, soon progressing to coma and death within 24 hours unless specific treatment can be given on an emergency basis. Glycol is metabolised in the body but a small amount is converted to glyoxal, glycolic acid, formic acid, glyoxylic acid, and oxalic acid. The metabolites cause metabolic acidosis and may damage the kidneys. Hypoglycaemia may occur. The patient may suffer from focal or generalised seizures. If the intoxication is acute, the patient develops pulmonary oedema and congestive heart failure in 12–36 hours, and kidney failure in 48–72 hours.

Fatal dose and fatal period: The fatal dose is about 100 ml and the fatal period about 24–72 hours.

Treatment: If the patient is promptly seen after ingestion, lavage may be helpful. Pyridoxine and thiamine help conversion of glyoxalate to non-toxic byproducts. 4-methyl pyrazole is useful as an antidote. Serious cases require emergency treatment, such as dialysis, whole bowel irrigation, or competing ethanol. The indications for emergency treatment include: (a) history of ethylene glycol ingestion, (b) metabolic acidosis, and (c) an ethylene glycol level greater than 20 mg/dl.

Postmortem appearances: Autopsy appearances include cerebral oedema, chemical meningoencephalitis, acute tubular necrosis, and oxalate crystals in the tissues.

Medicolegal aspects: Ethylene glycol poisoning is mostly accidental or suicidal. Drunkards may consume it in place of ethanol.

51

Sedatives and Hypnotics

Sedatives are drugs which produce a calming effect on the central nervous system while hypnotics are drugs which produce sleep. The important substances which are considered from this group are: (1) chloral hydrate, and (2) barbiturates.

CHLORAL HYDRATE

This is a colourless crystalline substance having a peculiar bitter-sweet but nauseous taste and aromatic smell. It is a powerful and reliable hypnotic. In small doses, it produces natural sleep but in larger doses (5 to 6 gm), it is a depressant of the central nervous system and paralyses the vital centres. The pharmacopoeial dose is 0.3 to 1.2 gm.

Q. 51.1. Discuss the medicolegal aspects of chloral hydrate poisoning.

Symptoms and signs: It is absorbed rapidly from the stomach, small intestine, and rectum. When ingested, there is retrosternal burning sensation followed by nausea and vomiting in early stages. Later, there is drowsiness merging into coma. The blood pressure falls, respiration becomes slow and shallow, and death results from paralysis of the respiratory and cardiac centres. Sometimes, a rash may be seen on the skin due to idiosyncrasy.

Prolonged use of chloral hydrate produces tolerance and may lead to addiction (physical dependence). The symptoms are mainly digestive, nervous, cardiac, and cutaneous. Pain, nausea, vomiting and gastritis due to irritant action of the drug are very striking. In addition, erythematous and urticarial rashes may occur along with tremors, convulsions, and depression. Delirium tremens may supervene when the drug is withdrawn.

Fatal dose: The lethal dose for an adult is about 5 gm but varies greatly.

Fatal period: Death usually takes place in about 8 to 12 hours but may be delayed for two to three days.

Treatment: The stomach should be washed out with warm water containing an alkali which will decompose the unabsorbed chloral hydrate. Haemodialysis may be necessary. The rest of the treatment is symptomatic.

Postmortem appearances: These are those of asphyxia. The peculiar odour of chloral hydrate may be perceived in the stomach contents.

There is irritation of the gastric mucosa. In chronic poisoning, fatty degeneration of liver, kidney, heart, and other internal organs may be seen.

Chloral hydrate rapidly deteriorates after death. Chemical analysis of the viscera should, therefore, be done as a matter of urgency.

Medicolegal aspects: Accidental poisoning may result from a large dose used as a hypnotic. It is rarely used for suicide. It is often added to liquor for a greater kick. It is covertly added to beer with homicidal intent. Chloral hydrate (sometimes known as dry wine) is used in alcohol to produce sleep in, say, a watchman. Its action is so rapid that it has been given the name "knock out drops"; it renders a victim of robbery or rape suddenly helpless. Long continued use leads to addiction.

BARBITURATES

These compounds are used as sedatives, hypnotics and, when given intravenously, as anaesthetics. They are also useful in psychiatric disorders, epilepsy, and strychnine poisoning.

Barbiturates are classified into four groups as follows, depending on whether their action is long, intermediate, short, or ultrashort.

Long action — Effect from 1 to 8–12 hours or — up to 1–2 days — Fatal dose 3–4 gm

a. Barbitone (veronal—white tablets)
b. Barbitone sodium (medinal—white tablets)
c. Phenobarbitone (gardenal, luminal—small white tablets)
d. Methyl phenobarbitone (prominal—small white tablets)

Intermediate action — Effect from 1/2 to 4–8 hours — Fatal dose 2–3 gm

a. Allobarbitone (dial—white tablets)
b. Amylobarbitone (amytal—blue capsules)
c. Aprobarbitone (allonal/somnifaine—white tablets)
d. Butobarbitone (soneryl—pink tablets)
e. Pentobarbitone (nembutal—yellow capsules)

Short action — Effect from 1/4 to 2–4 hours — Fatal dose 1–2 gm

a. Cyclobarbitone (phanoderm—white tablets)
b. Hexobarbitone (evipan—white tablets)
c. Quinal barbitone (seconal—red capsules)
d. Quinal with amylobarbitone (tuinal—red/blue capsules)

Ultrashort action 15–20 minutes — For duration of anaesthesia — Fatal dose 1 gm

a. Thiopentone sodium (pentothal—white powder or solution)
b. Methohexobarbitone (brevital—white powder or solution)

Barbiturates depress the central nervous system and the effect varies from mere tranquillity to deep coma depending on the dose. They are cumulative, being partly destroyed in the liver and slowly excreted in the urine.

Q. 51.2. Discuss barbiturate poisoning. Give its medicolegal aspects. Add a note on chronic poisoning (addiction).

Symptoms and signs: Poisoning is manifested by giddiness, ataxia and slurred speech, a short period of confusion (incorrectly called *automatism*), excitement, and delirium, followed by stupor and later coma. The limbs are flaccid, reflexes are lost, and the pupil reacts to light by alternate contraction and dilatation.

As poisoning advances, the face becomes cyanotic; blood pressure falls; temperature is subnormal; respirations are slow, sighing and periodic (Cheyne-Stokes), or rapid and shallow; and bowel sounds are absent. Oliguria may be present, the urine containing albumin and sugar. *Barbiturate blisters* are found on sites of friction or pressure, such as interdigital clefts, axilla, and inner aspects of the knees and calves. Death is due to respiratory or cardiac failure in early stages or due to bronchopneumonia or oedema of the lungs in late stages. Sometimes, the patient may make gradual recovery.

Fatal dose: The fatal dose of a long-acting barbiturate is 3–4 gm, medium acting 2–3 gm, and short acting 1–2 gm. In general, the sedative (therapeutic) dose when doubled becomes a hypnotic dose (induces sleep) and the minimum lethal dose is about ten times the therapeutic dose. The lethal blood levels are as follows:

- Long acting barbiturates ... 10 mg/100 ml
- Intermediate acting barbiturates ... 7 mg/100 ml
- Short acting barbiturates ... 3 mg/100 ml

Alcohol potentiates the action of barbiturates so that sublethal doses of either may cause death jointly with the other.

Fatal period: Commonly, the patient remains in coma for 24–48 hours before death takes place. Occasionally, coma may last for several days and the patient may die subsequently.

Treatment: Gastric lavage should be carried out with warm water using potassium permanganate solution and suspension of animal charcoal. A concentrated solution of magnesium sulphate should be left in the stomach to ensure purgation and minimise intestinal absorption. Body warmth must be maintained.

To maintain a clear airway, the foot-end of the bed should be raised and respiratory mucus aspirated as and when necessary. Oxygen should be given continuously to counter cyanosis. Artificial respiration may be necessary.

For circulatory depression and shock, intravenous doses of 2.5 mg of metaraminol (Aramine) at 20 minutes intervals should be given till the systolic blood pressure reaches 100 mm Hg. If two or possibly three consecutive injections of metaraminol fail, this treatment should be abandoned.

If the coma is prolonged, amphetamine sulphate in a dose of 10 mg every half an hour may be given till obvious improvement occurs. Prophylactic administration of antibiotics is necessary to prevent pulmonary complications. Dialysis and exchange transfusion, or whole bowel irrigation, where facilities permit, are valuable.

The urinary bladder will require catheterisation. Forced osmotic diuresis using intravenous chlorothiazide and/or mannitol (500 ml of a 20% solution) results in considerable increase in the elimination rate of barbiturates. The rest of the treatment is symptomatic.

Postmortem appearances: These are mainly those of asphyxia. Fine froth is seen emerging from the nose and mouth. Residual capsules or powder of the drug in the stomach may be found. There may be evidence of bronchopneumonia or of oedema of the lungs. The kidneys may show degeneration of the convoluted tubules. Other organs may be congested. The brain should be preserved for chemical analysis in addition to stomach, liver, spleen, kidneys, blood, and urine. Barbiturates are chiefly excreted in the urine and this affords a ready means of detecting both acute and chronic poisoning even during life. As ultrashort-acting barbiturates are quickly redistributed in the body and usually administered intravenously, it is more practical to detect them in body fat, after death by chemical analysis. The present editor (Dr Subrahmanyam) saw a case wherein barbiturate lumps were found in the stomach in a case brought for autopsy examination. Even the dead pet dogs contained the barbiturate in stomach, when autopsied. Barbiturate blebs are seen on the back of the person who consumed barbiturates.

Medicolegal aspects: Most deaths from barbiturates are either suicidal or accidental. The popularity of barbiturates as soothers for the harrying pace and anxieties of modern life has resulted in a number of addicts who might poison themselves from an overdose taken accidentally or through mental confusion from barbiturate automatism or simultaneous ingestion of alcohol. In some states in the US, judicial execution is carried out by a lethal intravenous injection of which sodium pentothal is the chief ingredient, the other ingredients being saline, Pavulon (muscle relaxant), and potassium chloride.

Chronic poisoning (addiction) may occur from prolonged use of barbiturates in epilepsy or psychotherapy. It is characterised by apathy, loss of power of concentration and somnolence, sometimes accompanied by other signs, such as vertigo, tremors, ataxia, thick speech, delirium, hallucinations which are usually visual, emotional instability, and general mental deterioration. The urine may show albumin, sugar and casts. The dependence is both physical and psychological. The treatment is the same as that for other drugs of addiction. Withdrawal convulsions have been reported after about 4 to 5 days after withdrawal of the drug.

Barbiturate automatism: Barbiturate automatism is a condition that can cause death of a person, when the consumer forgets to have taken the early dose and continues to take automatically till coma supervenes and even death may ensue.

52

Fuels

The important fuels discussed under this heading are all derived from petroleum, chief amongst which are kerosene, petrol and naphtha.

PETROLEUM (ROCK OIL)

Petroleum contains gas and liquid constituents. It is an oily liquid found under the ground in several parts of the earth. The refined oil is known as kerosene. The other products which are separated during the process of purification are classified into 2 groups according to their boiling point in relation to kerosene. Those which are lighter and boil at a lower temperature than kerosene are known as gasoline, and include ether, pentane, hexane, octane, petrol, naphtha, benzine, etc. Those which are heavier and boil at higher temperatures than kerosene include the lubricating oils, vaseline and paraffin. In general, among the petroleum distillates, the toxicity is inversely proportional to the boiling point. Therefore, while liquid paraffin and vaseline are in common use in medicine as harmless products, ether, petrol, naphtha, benzine, etc. are highly poisonous when swallowed or inhaled.

Petroleum distillates are irritants because they dissolve fats. They also depress the cells of the central nervous system. The effect on liver, kidneys and bone marrow may be from contaminants, such as benzene.

Q. 52.1. Give a brief account of kerosene poisoning.

Symptoms and signs: After ingestion of lighter distillates, there is a kerosene taste, a sensation of burning in the throat, nausea, vomiting, colicky pain and diarrhoea. The breath, vomit and urine smell of kerosene. The respirations become slow and shallow. Cyanosis develops. Lung complications, such as bronchopneumonia, and pulmonary oedema, are common. The central nervous system depression results in giddiness, weakness and drowsiness followed by coma and death from respiratory failure.

Inhalation of fumes causes headache, vertigo, nausea, vomiting, and lung complications followed by intense excitement, hallucinations and convulsions. In fatal cases, cyanosis, unconsciousness and coma precede death.

Chronic poisoning is known to occur from inhalation in persons who handle petroleum products. The principal symptoms are dizziness, weakness, weight loss, anaemia, nervousness, pain in limbs, peripheral numbness, and paraesthesias. Treatment requires isolation of the patient from exposure and symptomatic management.

Fatal dose and fatal period: Ingestion of more than 10 ml of kerosene may be fatal. Petroleum products spread over a large surface area, such as the lung, and cause intense pulmonary irritation. Fatal period is, therefore, a few hours.

Treatment: If ingested, the stomach should be washed out with warm water containing 5% sodium bicarbonate. Its absorption can be slowed by giving 250 ml of liquid paraffin orally, followed by a saline cathartic. If the poison has been inhaled, the patient must be removed to the open air and artificial respiration persisted in. The rest of the treatment is symptomatic.

Postmortem appearances: There may be acute gastroenteritis and kerosene odour may be observed in the contents of the stomach and lungs. Pulmonary oedema and bronchopneumonia are found. Degenerative changes in the liver and kidneys and hypoplasia of the bone marrow occur after prolonged period of inhalation. Other signs of asphyxia may be seen. In case of death from petroleum, the lungs and the brain together with other viscera should be preserved for chemical analysis in saturated saline (Fig. 52.1).

Fig. 52.1: Kerosene poisoning. This woman took an unknown dose of kerosene and died inspite of treatment. In addition to cyanosis (asphyxial death), froth is seen emerging from the mouth and nose. However, it is neither so fine nor so copious as in drowning

Medicolegal aspects: Kerosene is occasionally used for self-immolation. Homicidal attempts by pouring kerosene on clothes and igniting them are common in case of dowry deaths in India. However, most fatalities are accidental. The majority of cases have been young children who have taken kerosene in mistake for water. Isolated cases of petroleum poisoning and death occur among persons attempting to suck petrol from car tanks through rubber tubing.

Dr Subrahmanyam saw a case of kerosene poisoning in Dachur. A toddler drank water from a broken drinking glass, that turned out to be kerosene and was brought to the primary health care centre, with respiratory manifestation. Administration of crystalline penicillin and constant monitoring lead to recovery and discharge.

53

Agrichemical Poisons

The potent chemicals used in agriculture may harm persons by accidental exposure, either during their application to crops or due to careless storage. In Sri Lanka, many thousands of hospital admissions each year are for agrichemical poisoning with over a thousand deaths annually. Of these, about three-quarters are self-administered, the remainder being accidental and occupational.

The commonly used agricultural chemicals are the organophosphorus compounds, viz. alkyl and aryl phosphates; the chlorinated compounds, such as DDT and Endrin; the carbamates, such as aprocarb (Baygon) and Carbaryl (Sevin); the coal-tar product, naphthalene; herbicides, such as paraquat; and the metallic compounds, such as zinc phosphide and aluminium phosphide. The discussion here is restricted to: (1) organophosphorus compounds, (2) chlorinated compound—endrin, (3) coal-tar product—naphthalene, (4) herbicide—paraquat, and (5) the metallic compound—aluminium phosphide. Zinc phosphide is discussed under zinc.

ORGANOPHOSPHORUS COMPOUNDS

The development of a number of organophosphorus compounds for use as pesticides, vermicides, and rodenticides, has introduced several dangerous new poisons. Chemically, these organic compounds are the alkyl and aryl phosphates. The commonly used alkyl phosphates include hexaethyl tetraphosphate (HETP), tetraethyl pyrophosphate (TEPP), octamethyl pyrophosphoramide (OMPA), and malathion. The commonly used aryl phosphates include parathion (Folidol), and Diazinon (Tik-20). Poisoning can occur from inhalation, ingestion and absorption through unbroken skin. The poisonous effects may be cumulative. These compounds are powerful inhibitors of cholinesterase at the myoneural junctions and synapses of the ganglions; acetylcholine, therefore, accumulates and results in hyperexcitation of the voluntary and involuntary muscles. A drop in the activity of cholinesterase to 30 per cent of normal or lower is associated with toxic symptoms.

Q. 53.1. Describe the action of organophosphorus compounds on the human body. Give a brief account of poisoning by any one of them.

The main toxic effects are: (a) muscarine-like, (b) nicotine-like, and (c) on the central nervous system.

As a result of the muscarine-like effects, the following symptoms and signs are observed:

1. ***Bronchial tree:*** Tightness in the chest with prolonged wheezing expiration is suggestive of bronchospasm and increased secretion. Therefore, there is

discomfort or pain in the chest, dyspnoea, cough, pulmonary oedema, froth at the mouth and nose, and cyanosis. The effects simulate bronchial asthma.

2. *Gastrointestinal:* Anorexia, nausea, vomiting, abdominal cramps, epigastric and substernal tightness (? cardiospasm) with heartburn and eructations, diarrhoea, tenesmus, and involuntary defaecation.
3. *Sweat glands:* Increased sweating.
4. *Salivary glands:* Increased salivation.
5. *Lacrimal glands:* Increased lacrimation. Tears may be red due to porphyrin in lacrimal glands.
6. *Heart:* Slight bradycardia.
7. *Pupils:* Slight miosis, occasionally unequal, and later more marked miosis.
8. *Ciliary body:* Blurring or dimness of vision.
9. *Urinary bladder:* Frequency of micturition and involuntary micturition.

As a result of **nicotine-like** effects, the following symptoms and signs are observed:

1. *Striated muscle:* Easy fatigue, mild weakness, muscular fasciculations, cramps, generalised weakness of muscles of respiration with dyspnoea and cyanosis.
2. *Sympathetic ganglia:* Pallor, occasional elevation of blood pressure.

As a result of action on the central nervous system, the following effects may appear approximately in the following order:

1. Irritability, apprehension, restlessness.
2. Fine fibrillary tremors of hands, eye lids, face or tongue.
3. Mental confusion progressing to stupor and muscular weakness with tremors and convulsions.
4. Coma with absence of reflexes and depression of respiratory and circulatory centres.

Symptoms and signs: Illness first affects involuntary muscles and secretory glands, then voluntary muscles, and finally vital brain centres. According to the route of entry, the respiratory or gastrointestinal symptoms are more marked. The respiratory symptoms may mimic an attack of bronchial asthma. The initial complaint is headache, malaise and a sense of tightness in the chest, and dimness of vision due to pin-point pupils. In the next two to eight hours, there may appear, approximately in this order, nausea, abdominal cramps, vomiting, diarrhoea, profuse sweating and salivation, frequent urination, and muscular twitching. This symptom complex is sometimes called SLUD, the prominent symptoms being salivation, lacrimation, urination, and defaecation. In some cases, chromogenic tears (red tears) may be shed due to accumulation of porphyrin in the lacrimal glands. If poisoning is severe, pulmonary oedema, coma, convulsions and possibly death may ensue. Death is generally caused by paralysis of musculature but may result from respiratory failure, circulatory arrest, oedema of lungs or brain.

The author has come across a case where a doctor was charged with administering organophosphorus compound by injection to his wife. Her illness resembled bronchial asthma for which she was treated with injection of adrenaline but died. On a complaint of suspicious death, an autopsy was performed. Organophosphorus compound was detected from the injection site and viscera.

Fatal dose: The average fatal dose of HETP is 160 mg by intravenous (i.v.) or intramuscular (i.m.) route and 350 mg orally; OMPA 80 mg by i.v. or i.m. route and 175 mg orally; TEPP 45–50 mg i.m. or i.v. and 100 mg orally; malathion 1 gm orally;

parathion (Folidol) 80 mg by i.v. or i.m. route and 175 mg orally; and Diazinon (Tik-20) 1 gm orally.

Fatal period: In fatal doses, death may ensue within half to three hours or may sometimes be delayed for few more hours. The acute effects in non-fatal cases last for 6–30 hours, fading during the next 48–72 hours or sometimes persist for as long as 3 weeks.

Treatment: It should aim at (1) decontamination, (2) care of the airway, (3) administration of an antidote, (4) administration of cholinesterase reactivators, and (5) other measures including general measures.

1. *Decontamination:* The physician and those who are in charge of nursing these cases should wear rubber gloves. The patient must be removed from the source of exposure and stripped of all clothes. The exposed areas are decontaminated by washing with tap water and soap or some alkaline solution. If the poison is ingested, the stomach should be washed with tap water with or without potassium permanganate.
2. *Care of the airway:* The foot-end of the bed is raised to ensure drainage of respiratory mucus. Secretions may need to be aspirated, and tracheostomy may be necessary. Artificial respiration may be required, and positive pressure oxygen should be given, if pulmonary oedema ensues.
3. *Antidote:* Atropine blocks the peripheral (muscarinic) actions of the excessive acetylcholine levels built up by the cholinesterase inhibitors, but the central and neuromuscular reactions are unaffected. It is administered in a dose of 2 mg every 15 to 30 minutes i.m. or i.v., till signs of atropinisation appear (flushed face, dry mouth, dilated pupils, fast pulse and warm skin). As much as 12 mg of atropine has been given safely in the first two hours!
4. *Cholinesterase reactivators:* The oxime compounds, Protopam (pralidoxime chloride), pralidoxime iodide and PAM (pyridine aldoxy methiodate) are rapid cholinesterase reactivators and act by dephosphorylating the inactivated cholinesterase. They act as specific antidotes and should be used to supplement atropine therapy. The dose is 1 to 2 gm i.v. for adults and 25 to 50 mg/kg for children, given as a 5% solution in isotonic saline, and repeated every 12 hours, if symptoms persist or recur.
5. *Other measures:* A diuretic and a brisk saline purgative may be useful. Restlessness may be combated by quick acting barbiturates or diazepam. The rest of the treatment is symptomatic. In serious cases, an exchange transfusion may be necessary.

The first four to six hours are most critical in acute poisoning. In delayed paralysis resulting from demyelination, damage is permanent.

Postmortem appearances: The changes are suggestive of asphyxia. Externally, the face is cyanosed. There is froth, usually blood-stained, at the nose and mouth. A kerosene-like smell may be perceived. Internally, the stomach contains greenish oily substances used as diluents, and their kerosene-like or garlic smell is easily perceived. The contents of the stomach are blood-stained, the mucosa is congested, and submucous petechial haemorrhages are seen. The other postmortem findings are: pulmonary oedema, capillary dilatation, petechial haemorrhages, and hyperaemia of lungs, brain and other organs. In delayed paralysis of the extremities induced by parathion, malathion, and other compounds, the findings are demyelination of ascending and descending spinal tracts with degeneration of motor horn cells. Organophosphorus compounds resist putrefaction and poisoning can be detected in exhumed bodies. The viscera for chemical examination should be preserved in saturated saline in suspected cases of poisoning.

Medicolegal aspects: Organic phosphorus compounds are in common use agriculturally and domestically as pesticides, vermicides, and rodenticides. Being easily available, they are used for suicide. They are mixed with alcohol to mask the smell and have been used for homicide. A number of non-fatal cases have been recorded in persons handling fruits sprayed with an organic phosphorus insecticide. A number of accidental deaths through contamination and leakage of these compounds to edible commodities have also been recorded (Kerala food poisoning cases in India). Some of the compounds in concentrated form are intensely poisonous to human beings. Workers engaged in the manufacture, packing, or spraying them are at special risk of accidental poisoning.

CHLORINATED COMPOUNDS

Many chloro compounds have been synthesised as insecticides from dicholoropropene (DD) to the very complex modern synthetics in common use as pesticides. Of this group, the agents which are commonly employed are: DDT, Endrin, Gammexane, Dieldrin, etc. Their effects on mammals are essentially the same from the clinical standpoint and the compounds can, therefore, be described as a group. The chemical prototype for the group is chlorophenothane, which is commonly known as DDT, and its description applies to all the members of the group. However, since endrin poisoning is common in certain parts of India, it is described here.

Endrin

Of all the chlorinated insecticides, endrin is the most toxic. It is a synthetic, fat-soluble but water-insoluble, chemical having an unpleasant taste. It is stable for months to a year or even more. It is sold in the market as Endrin-We 16, Endox-DB-50, Endtox EC-20, Endrex, Tafdrin, and a variety of other trade names. These preparations contain endrin in 20–50% concentration mixed with 50–80% of a solvent such as aromax, a petroleum hydrocarbon smelling like kerosene.

Endrin is chiefiy used against insect pests of cotton, 'paddy', sugarcane and tobacco. It is a popular insecticide with action against a wide variety of plant pests and, therefore, also known as plant penicillin. It is extensively used in India in Andhra Pradesh where poisoning is occurring at an alarming rate since 1959 both in urban and rural populations.

Symptoms and signs: Toxic effects rapidly follow ingestion, inhalation or skin contamination. The main symptoms are salivation, vomiting, abdominal pain, tremors, convulsions, oozing of fine white froth occasionally blood-stained from both mouth and nostrils and severe dyspnoea. Gradually, the convulsions become severe and continuous followed by coma which may terminate in respiratory failure and death. Diarrhoea is not a constant feature. In some cases, convulsions herald the onset of symptoms.

Fatal dose: Toxic symptoms appear with a dose of 1 gm. The lethal dose is about 6 gm.

Fatal period: The fatal period ranges from half an hour to several hours, the majority dying within an hour or two.

Treatment: This is largely symptomatic. Decontamination of the body should be carried out and the airway cared for as outlined under poisoning by organophosphorus insecticides. Barbiturates and diazepam are useful to control convulsions. Calcium decreases the toxicity of endrin. It should be given in a dose of 10 ml of 10% solution intravenously every four to six hours. Atropine does not appear to have any substantial effect but may be tried in desperate cases. Recovery is likely, if onset of convulsions is delayed by more than one hour or if convulsions can be controlled readily.

Postmortem appearances: These are suggestive of asphyxia. Externally, a kerosene-like smell may be noticed emanating from the mouth and nostrils, even in decomposed bodies. Fine white froth, occasionally blood-stained, is common (Figs 53.1 and 53.2). The face and finger nails are cyanosed, the conjunctivae injected, and the pupils dilated. Internally, the respiratory passages contain frothy mucus, and the mucous membrane is congested. Petechial haemorrhages over the lungs and heart are common. The lungs appear large and bulky, and pulmonary oedema is a constant feature. The blood is dark and fluid. The mucous membrane of the oesophagus, stomach, and intestine is congested and emits a kerosene-like smell. The liver, kidneys and brain are also congested. Endrin resists putrefaction and can be detected in exhumed bodies. Since alcohol is generally used to mask the smell of endrin, the viscera for chemical examination should be preserved in saturated saline in suspected cases of poisoning.

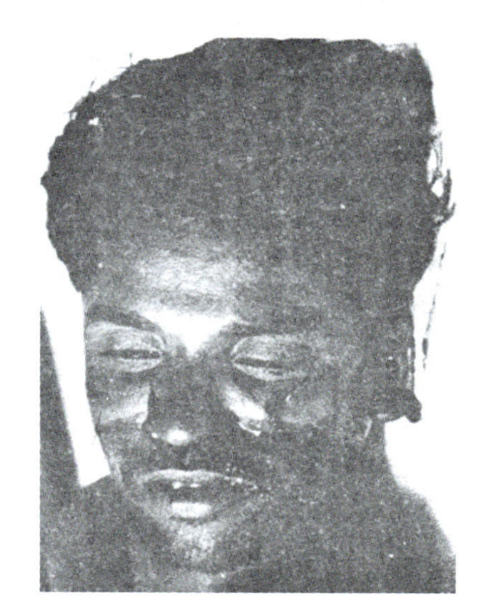

Fig. 53.2: Endrin poisoning. Bloody discharge from the nose. At postmortem, there was no abnormal smell in the stomach. Endrin was detected on chemical analysis even though the body was decomposed. The viscera were preserved in denatured spirit for a long time before chemical analysis. (*Courtesy:* Dr V David Edward)

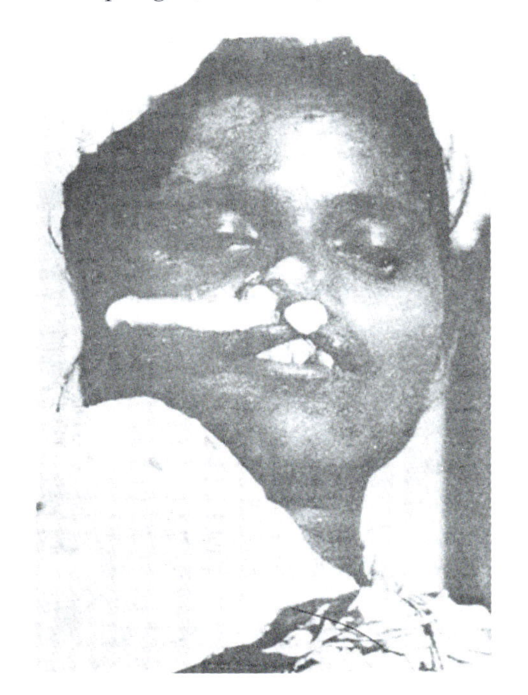

Fig. 53.1: Endrin poisoning. Fine froth is seen emerging from the nostrils. At postmortem, **kerosene-like smell** was detected from the stomach. (*Courtesy:* Dr V David Edward)

Medicolegal aspects: Endrin is freely available and rather cheap. It is, therefore, mostly used for suicidal purposes despite its unpleasant taste and painful death. It has been used for homicidal purposes by mixing it with alcohol especially toddy which masks its smell. It may also be mixed with sweets or other food. The toxic dose is small, so even if the victim recognises the smell while eating, a toxic amount has already been swallowed, and toxic symptoms are bound to ensue. Accidental deaths occur from the use of endrin as an insecticide.

Q. 53.2. Write short notes on: (a) naphthalene (b) paraquat (c) aluminium phosphide.

Naphthalene

This is a solid volatile substance obtained from the middle fraction of coal-tar distillation and has chemical properties similar to benzene. It occurs in large, lustrous, crystalline plates with a characteristic odour. It is used as a deodorant in lavatories, as a pesticide in moth balls, and in the dye industry for the manufacture of indigo and certain azo dyes. Toxic effects follow from its absorption from the skin, and from the respiratory and gastrointestinal tracts. Naphthalene causes haemolysis with subsequent blocking of renal tubules and hepatic necrosis. Haemolysis occurs only in those with hereditary deficiency of glucose-6-phosphate dehydrogenase in the red cells.

When naphthalene is chlorinated, a waxy substance is produced. Such chlorinated naphthalene is used in industry as an insulating coat on electric wires and other electric equipment.

Symptoms and signs: The serious effects of poisoning are acute nephritis, jaundice, haemolytic anaemia, and optic neuritis. When ingested, there is gastric irritation with nausea, vomiting and abdominal pain. Other symptoms include burning sensation in the urethra, pain in the bladder and loins, and occasional strangury. The urine may be dark-brown or black containing albumin and haemoglobin. Severe poisoning may damage the liver and kidneys, and result in convulsions, cyanosis, profuse perspiration, coma and death. When inhaled, naphthalene chiefly causes headache, malaise, nausea, vomiting, conjunctivitis, mental confusion and visual disturbances. Contact with naphthalene dust on bedding has given rise to dermatitis, conjunctivitis, vomiting, headache, jaundice, and haematuria.

Chlorinated naphthalene produces varying degrees of skin irritation and acne, and appears to have a toxic effect on the liver, and various systemic effects similar to those of naphthalene.

Fatal dose and fatal period: The fatal dose of ingested naphthalene is approximately 2 gm. Death may take place in a few hours or be delayed up to two to three days.

Treatment: The patient should be kept warm. The stomach should be washed out with warm water or saline. Bowels should be cleared by magnesium sulphate. Sodium bicarbonate should be administered to maintain an alkaline urine to prevent the precipitation of acid haematin crystals and blocking of the renal tubules. Blood transfusion may be necessary. Hydrocortisone is helpful in limiting naphthalene haemolysis. Chronic poisoning occurs in those who repeatedly handle the drug. The local effects disappear in one to six months after discontinuing exposure.

A case of naphthalene (moth balls) poisoning was brought to new Civil Hospital Surat. Dr Subrahmanyam had seen this case of attempted suicide by an 18 yrs old student. When her mouth was opened, the smell was clear and diagnosis was suggested, she recovered well with treatment.

Postmortem appearances: The skin may be yellow. The gastric mucosa may be yellow, congested or inflamed. Liver and kidneys may show severe damage. The other organs may be congested. The respiratory tract may show signs of irritation.

Medicolegal aspects: Suicide by ingestion of naphthalene has been reported. However, most cases are accidental, the poison having been inhaled from bed clothes heavily dusted with the powder or from ingestion of moth balls by children. Naphthalene is not soluble in water and may remain in a garment after washing. As it is soluble in oil, baby oils may act as a solvent promoting absorption through skin and this may result in accidental poisoning.

Paraquat

Paraquat is a herbicide that is sprayed on unwanted weeds and other vegetation before planting crops. It is absorbed by the foliage and rapidly kills the plant but is inactivated when in contact with the soil. It is produced commercially as a brownish concentrated liquid of the dichloride salt in 10–30% strength under the trade name 'Gramoxone' and for horticultural use, as brown granules called 'Weedol' at about 5% concentration.

Toxicity occurs mainly through ingestion and occasionally through inhalation while spraying. Accidental deaths are generally due to decanting of the concentrate from the original containers.

Symptoms and signs: Concentrated paraquat is irritant to all epithelial tissues. The lips, mouth, pharynx, and oesophagus are superficially eroded. This is followed by blood-stained vomiting and bloody stools. The lungs are affected by direct aspiration, either during swallowing or vomiting. The liver is mainly affected. It undergoes a centrilobular necrosis, with giant mitochondria and crystalline inclusion bodies seen on electron microscopy. Renal failure may develop within two or three days from diffuse tubular damage. Myofibril fragmentation may occur.

Fatal dose and fatal period: 5 ml of swallowed Gramoxone or 1–2 gm of Weedol are usually fatal. Death occurs rapidly from acute hepatorenal failure. Delayed deaths within about two weeks are due to progressive lung damage, where it causes fibrosing alveolitis and rigid stiff lungs [Adult Respiratory Distress Syndrome (ARDS) – *see* Injuries to Lungs].

Treatment: The stomach is washed with tap water; a brisk saline purgative may be useful. Artificial respiration and oxygen may be required. In serious cases, an exchange transfusion may be necessary. The rest of the treatment is symptomatic.

Postmortem appearances: There may be ulceration around the lips and chin due to dribbled paraquat. The mucosa of the mouth and oesophagus may be reddened or desquamated. The stomach may show erosion and patchy haemorrhages. The liver may show fatty change and necrobiosis. The kidneys may reveal cortical pallor, if there is renal failure. In delayed deaths, the lungs are large and stiff, keeping their shape when removed from the chest. There may be fibrinous pleurisy and sometimes slight bloody pleural effusions. The main appearances are microscopic and unless the history is known, the condition may be misdiagnosed as bronchopneumonia.

In addition to histological samples, the viscera to be preserved include the usual blood samples, urine, stomach contents, lungs and liver. Paraquat is excreted over along period and can be detected in the urine at autopsy many days after ingestion.

Medicolegal aspects: Poisoning is mainly accidental and suicidal. Rarely, homicide is possible and the poisoning may be mistaken for viral pneumonia.

Aluminium Phosphide

This is an effective pesticide and rodenticide. It is sold under various trade names, e.g. Celphos, Alphos, Fumigran, Phostoxin, etc. A 3 gm tablet, which resembles a medicinal preparation, contains 56 per cent of the active ingredient. It is easily available and cheap. Therefore, it is frequently misused with homicidal intent in cases of **dowry deaths** in rural India; only a part of the tablet is usually sufficient for this purpose. The toxic effects are due to liberation of phosphine gas when the tablet comes in contact with gastric juice. Symptoms, signs, and other details are similar to poisoning by zinc phosphide, discussed under zinc.

Hair Dye Poisoning

In southern India, Kadapa and Nellore presented cases of attempting to commit suicide with a hair dye popularly called as Vasmol-33, among young women. Rhabdomyolysis evidenced by chocolate-colored urine angioneurotic oedema with stridor and acute renal failure constitute an early triad of manifestations. When patient arrives, a gastric lavage is done. Early tracheostomy, aggressive forced diuresis, and symptomatic management help in recovery. This hair dye is a common, inexpensive and emulsion based. It consists of paraphenylenediamine, resorcinol, propylene glycol, EDTA (ethylenediamine tetra-acitic acid sodium), liquid paraffin, cetostearyl alcohol, sodium lauryl sulphate, herbal extracts preservative and perfumes. It is emerging as a popular suicidal agent more so in women. Average ingested amount was 150 ml. Prompt treatment, early arrival and correct diagnosis show recovery.

54

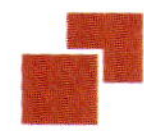

Deliriant Poisons

The poisons in this group are characterised by a well-marked deliriant stage. The important poisons are: dhatura, *Atropa belladonna, Hyoscyamus niger*, and *Cannabis indica*.

DHATURA

The plant commonly grows in waste places all over India. There are two varieties, viz. dhatura alba, a white-flowered plant (safed dhatura), and dhatura niger, a black or purple-flowered one (kala dhatura). The flowers are bell-shaped. The fruits are spherical and have sharp spines, giving the name thorn apple to the plant. They contain yellowish brown seeds resembling chilli seeds (Figs 54.1 to 54.3). Their differentiating

Fig. 54.2: Diagrammatic representation of **dhatura plant, fruit,** and **flower**. (Drawn by Miss AC Parikh)

Fig. 54.1: Dhatura fruit (*Courtesy:* Dr SV Phanindra)

Fig. 54.3: Atrops belladonna plant with leaves, fruit and flowers

features have already been outlined under the topic "Capsicum".An average-sized fruit contains 450 to 500 seeds, and weighs about 8 grams. One hundred seeds weigh about 1 gram. All parts of the plant are poisonous but the seeds and fruits more so. The active principle contains the alkaloids, laevohyoscyamine, hyoscine or scopolamine, and traces of atropine.

An alkaloid is a complex chemical substance found in various plants. It is so called because it behaves like an alkali and combines with acids to form salts. The distribution of alkaloids in the plant is not uniform; some are concentrated in the roots, others in the seeds, still others in the bark, and so on. They act mainly on some portion of the central nervous system, each having its own individual action.

Q. 54.1. Give a brief account of dhatura poisoning.

The alkaloids of dhatura stimulate the higher centres of the brain, and then the motor centres. They inhibit secretion of sweat and saliva, dilate the cutaneous blood vessels, dilate the pupil and stimulate the heat regulating centre situated in the floor of the third ventricle. The initial stimulation is followed by depression and paralysis of the vital centres in the medulla.

Symptoms and signs: The symptoms are described as "dry as a bone, red as a beet, blind as a bat, hot as a hare, and mad as a wet hen". They appear within half an hour, if seeds are taken, or earlier, if a decoction (concentrated water extract) of seeds is used, and almost immediately, if the alkaloids are taken. In most cases, powdered seeds are administered in food.

The earliest symptom is a bitter taste in the mouth. Due to inhibition of salivation, there is dryness of the mouth and throat (dry as a bone) resulting in difficulty in talking, dysphagia and unquenchable thirst. The face is flushed due to dilatation of cutaneous blood vessels (red as a beet). The pupils are dilated, insensitive to light, and the power of accommodation for near vision is paralysed (blind as a bat). The body temperature is raised. The skin is dry and hot (hot as a hare) due to inhibition of sweat secretion and stimulation of heat regulating centre. There is vomiting. These symptoms are soon followed by giddiness and unsteady gait, the person staggering like a drunken individual. The mind is affected early, the patient being at first restless and confused, and later becoming delirious, and mutters indistinct words (mad as a wet hen). He is subject to visual and auditory hallucinations. He appears to grasp at imaginary objects, picks at his clothings, and tries to pull imaginary threads from the tips of his fingers. The delirium passes off in an hour or so and the patient becomes drowsy (Figs 54.4 and 54.5). There may be a scarlatiniform rash. The drowsiness may progress to stupor or coma and rarely death from respiratory paralysis. Secondary delirium may appear when the patient recovers.

The important symptoms and signs can be summarized under 9 Ds, viz: (1) dryness of the mouth and throat, (2) difficulty in

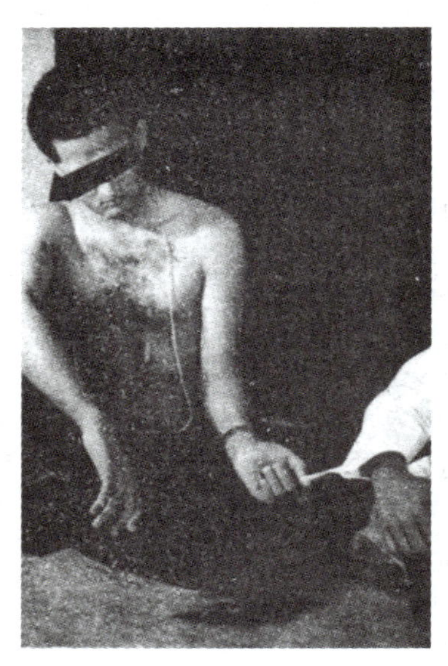

Fig. 54.4: Acute dhatura poisoning. The victim picks at the clothings. (*Courtesy:* Dr GB Sahay)

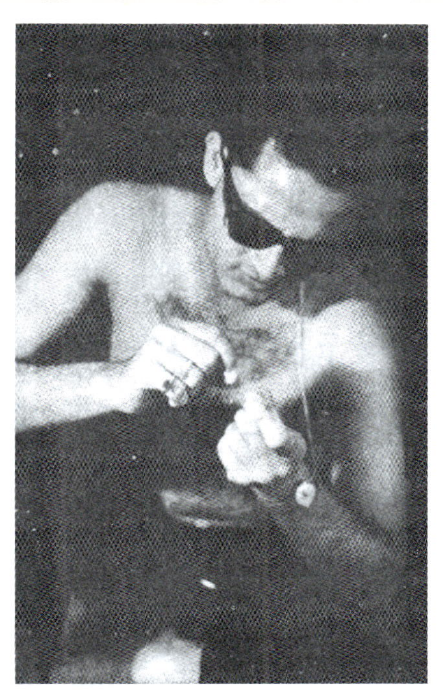

Fig. 54.5: Visual hallucination in acute dhatura poisoning. The victim is seen, pulling out imaginary threads from the nail bed. His pupils are dilated. He is, therefore, wearing goggles to avoid flash of light. (*Courtesy:* Dr GB Sahay)

talking, (3) dysphagia, (4) dilatation of cutaneous blood vessels, (5) dilatation of pupils, (6) dry hot skin, (7) drunken gait, (8) delirium, and (9) drowsiness. And, these may be mistaken for drunkenness, or heat stroke.

Fatal dose and fatal period: This is about 100 to 125 seeds. The lethal dose for the alkaloids is about 60 mg for adult and 4 mg for children. Death usually occurs within 24 hours.

Treatment: The stomach should be evacuated to remove the remnants of the crushed seeds by a stomach wash with either a weak solution of potassium permanganate or 4 to 5% tannic acid. Physostigmine in a dose of 1–4 mg (repeated, if necessary, at intervals of 1 to 2 hours) or Neostigmine (2.5 mg i.v. every 3 hours) act as physiological antidotes. Purgatives are beneficial and the rest of the treatment is symptomatic. Moistening of the tongue and change in the size of the pupils towards the normal are valuable guides in treatment. In non-fatal cases, recovery takes a day or two, the effect on the pupils being the last to disappear.

Postmortem appearances: These are those of asphyxia. Dhatura seeds may be found in the stomach. There is congestion of the gastrointestinal tract. Dhatura seeds resist putrefaction and are found even when the body is decomposed.

Medicolegal aspects: In India, dhatura is employed mainly as a stupefying poison prior to robbery, kidnapping, and rape. It is sometimes known as a *road poison* as it is commonly encountered during a journey. The powdered seeds are mixed with food, tea, drink, or in 'paan' (betel leaf) and given to an unwary traveller by an apparently obliging person. On ingestion of such material, the traveller becomes very drowsy. When he wakes up, he finds that his pockets are picked, removable belongings lost, and the apparently obliging person vanished. If he goes to the police station to lodge a complaint, he is taken to be a drunkard on account of his drunken gait and difficulty in talking. Generally, the railways and pilgrim places put warning boards asking the travellers not to accept any food or 'prasad' from strangers to obviate such mishaps.

A small dose either due to inhalation of smoke, smoking, or from ingestion deprives the person of his reasoning ability. At times, he appears to be in the right state of mind but actually does not know with whom he is talking, nor remembers what has happened when the alienation (intoxication episode effect) is over. Such an effect is achieved when the victim is exposed to fumes from burning the seeds mixed with resin, or by mixing dhatura with tobacco in cigarettes. The smoker, during the temporary twilight phase, will allow his pockets to be picked without any resistance or would even give away any valuable article, e.g. a wrist watch if asked for! Children can be easily kidnapped by giving them candy or sweets mixed with dhatura. They comply with the instructions of the poisoner to follow him! Likewise, women have been abducted, robbed and raped.

Accidental cases occur (1) when children and adults eat the raw fruit or seeds mistaking them for edible fruits or capsicum seeds respectively, (2) from the use of dhatura as an aphrodisiac, and (3) when the decoction of seeds is added to country liquor or toddy for a greater kick.

HYOSCYAMUS NIGER

Also known as scopolamine or henbane and khorasani ajwayan in the local language, this plant grows in the Himalayan ranges at high altitudes. All parts of the plant are poisonous. They contain the alkaloids atropine, hyoscine and hyoscyamine. The symptoms and signs closely resemble those of poisoning by dhatura. 125 mg of hyoscyamine or 15–30 mg of hyoscine hydrobromide would lead to a fatal outcome in 24 hours in most cases. The treatment is similar to that for poisoning by dhatura. Postmortem appearances are also similar to those for dhatura. Hyoscyamus seeds may be found in the stomach. Hyoscine resists putrefaction.

Hyoscyamus has varied uses. In small doses, it is used as medicine. Its calming effect is used in controlling tremors in Parkinson's disease, in delirium, and psychotic conditions. It is also used to control the spasms of asthma and whooping cough. It has proved useful in cases of depression. In good old days, it was used in combination with morphine to produce twilight sleep to facilitate painless childbirth. In war, it is used to control shell-shock. Poisoning is generally accidental through an overdose or rarely homicidal as in the Crippen case. In forensic work, it can be used as a ***truth serum*** or *lie detector*. It is said that a criminal under its influence is half awake and half asleep. His mental condition becomes such that he is not able to fabricate lies or withhold truth during interrogation, which he could do during his normal waking state.

CANNABIS INDICA

Q. 54.2. What is cannabis? Describe its preparations. Give the symptoms of acute poisoning. Discuss the medicolegal significance.

Also known as cannabis sativa or Indian hemp (Fig. 54.6) in India, Dagga in South and Central Africa, and Hashish in Egypt, this plant grows all over India, and all its parts are poisonous. Its cultivation is restricted by law. The active principle is not an alkaloid but a fat-soluble oleoresin, cannabinol (tetrahydrocannabinol – THC). The poison is absorbed both from the digestive and respiratory tract. It is a stimulant of the central nervous system and is used in the following four forms.

1. ***Bhang:*** Also known as *siddhi, patti*, or *sabji*, it is prepared from the dried leaves and fruit shoots which are used as an infusion in the form of a beverage. It contains the active principle in a concentration of 15% and is the least potent.

Fig. 54.6: **Cannabis sativa** or **Indian hemp**, (Draw by Miss AC Parik)

2. *Majun:* This is a sweetmeat made with bhang. It produces grandiose delusions, in addition to all the effects of bhang.

3. *Ganja:* This consists of the flowering tops of the female plant, specially grown so that there is a large amount of resinous exudate. It contains the active principle in a concentration of about 25%. The resin has a rusty green colour and characteristic odour. It is mixed with tobacco and smoked in a pipe. In India, it is largely indulged in by *sadhus* and *fakirs*, a class of people who dress in scarlet-coloured loose clothes and claim to have renowned the worldly bonds (Fig. 54.7).

4. *Charas:* Also known as hashish, it is the resinous exudate from the leaves and stems of the plant. It is of dark green or brown colour. It is smoked with tobacco in a pipe or '*hookah*' and is the most potent of all cannabis preparations, containing the active principle in a concentration varying between 25 and 40%.

The drug is commonly used for its supposed aphrodisiac, hypnotic and analgesic actions. It leads to psychological dependence and intense craving in children. The active principle being fatsoluble, is stored in fat cells of the body where it acts like a time release capsule, the effect of a single dose lasting for over 7 days.

Fig. 54.7: A **ganja addict.** A temple priest smoking ganja in a pipe to get the religious fervour. (*Courtesy:* Dr MN Ganapathy)

The term marihuana or marijuana (pot, grass, tea, Mary Jane) is used in America to refer to cannabis. It is a Mexican term meaning 'pleasurable feeling'. The form in which it is generally used is similar to *ganja*. It is eaten alone or as part of confection, or drunk in beer or some other beverage, or smoked in cigarettes (Reefers). These cigarettes contain about 500 mg of Indian hemp and are known as reefers or weed. Their use appears to lead to heroin addiction, especially in teen-agers.

Symptoms and signs: In a small dose, the effects are somewhat similar to those of alcohol causing euphoria at first followed by narcosis. The patient is pleased with himself, has a feeling of cheerfulness and well-being, and tends to become talkative. His appetite is increased and he eats his food with great relish, and may seek sexual enjoyment. In a susceptible person or with a larger dose, there is loss of perception of time and space. He is the subject of visual hallucinations. He sees nude beautiful women dancing before him, playing music, and singing amorous songs. This stage is followed by one of narcosis characterised by giddiness, confusion, and ataxia. Commonly, there is tingling and numbness of the extremities or in severe cases generalised anaesthesia. The victim may pass into deep sleep for about six hours and wake up fully recovered. Rarely, drowsiness may be followed by coma and collapse, and death may occur from respiratory paralysis.

Insanity in India is often attributed to the chronic use (addiction) of this drug in any form, and is known as *hashish insanity*. In some cases, delusions of grandeur or persecution develop. The addict is likely to commit sexual jealousy crimes of a homicidal nature. Following the continued use of cannabis or rarely after its consumption for the first time, he may *run amok*.

Fatal dose and fatal period: The minimum lethal dose of charas is about 2.0 gm, of ganja about 8.0 gm, and of bhang about 10.0 gm per kilo body weight. Death may occur in about 12 hours in acute poisoning.

Treatment: This is on the same lines as other narcotics. Broadly, it consists in washing out the stomach with warm water; hypodermic injection of strychnine; strong tea or coffee by mouth or per rectum; and artificial respiration, if necessary. Saline purgatives may be helpful.

Postmortem appearances: There are no characteristic findings. The usual appearances of asphyxia are found.

Medicolegal aspects: Most cases of poisoning are accidental or due to overindulgence. Its use in chocolates causes intense craving among children for its euphoric effects. The 'Bhola Manucca' chocolates sold near a school in Bombay, India, which caused a mishap were found to contain THC. Majun and charas are sometimes used as stupefying poisons prior to robbery, kidnapping, and rape.

Impaired judgement trom marihuana use may lead to accidents, sexual excesses, violence, and crime. Rarely, the victims **run amok**. This is a condition resulting from the continued use of cannabis or even its use for the first time. It is characterised by a frenzied desire on the part of the person to commit murders. A number of individuals are killed, the first ones being those against whom the assailant has some real or imaginary enmity, followed by others who are in the way, until the homicidal tendency lasts. The person may then commit suicide or surrender himself to the police.

Ganja is taken to steady the nerves before performing some bold act, e.g. homicide. Charas and ganja are sometimes used to dope cigarettes. Smoking such cigarettes is stated to improve memory recall. Sadhus and temple poojaris (priests) use them to get into a religious mood. Majun and charas are used by road poisoners to stupefy persons to facilitate robbery.

55

Spinal Poisons

This group of poisons act mainly on the spinal cord. The action may be a stimulant one resulting in the production of spasms or a depressant one resulting in paralysis and loss of sensation. Strychnine is an example of the former variety of poison and gelsemium of the latter.

STRYCHNOS NUX-VOMICA (KUCHILA)

Strychnine is a powerful alkaloid obtained from the seeds of strychnos nux-vomica (Fig. 55.1) and other species of strychnos plants which grow in India. The ripe fruits of the plant contain seeds which are poisonous. The seeds are hard and flat, about 2 cm in diameter and ½ cm in thickness, and slightly convex on one side and concave on the other. They are yellowish-brown in colour and have a shining hard pericarp (outer coat) covered with fine silky hair. They are intensely bitter in taste and contain the active principles strychnine, brucine and loganin. The bark, wood and leaves of the plant contain brucine but no strychnine. Brucine has the same physiological actions as strychnine but of a much milder degree (5–10%). The amount of loganin that is present in the seeds is in too small a quantity to exert any substantial toxic effects.

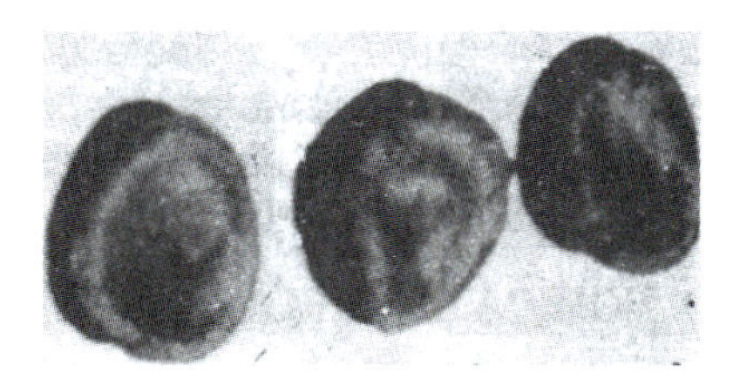

Fig. 55.1: Seeds of strychnos nux-vomica. (*Courtesy:* Dr NK Mohanty)

Strychnine stimulates all parts of the central nervous system and particularly the anterior horn cells of the spinal cord causing greatly increased reflex excitability. Normal inhibition of spread of motor cell stimulation is lost so that any slight stimulus, such as noise, light, or air breeze, causes violent reflex generalised muscle spasms.

Q. 55.1. Describe the signs, symptoms, differential diagnosis, treatment, and autopsy appearances of a typical case of strychnine poisoning.

Symptoms and signs: If unbroken nux-vomica seeds are ingested, they are not poisonous as the hard pericarp is not soluble in the digestive juices. If broken seeds are taken or the seeds chewed, there is an intensely bitter taste in the mouth. Within 15 minutes to an hour, symptoms of poisoning appear. The patient is anxious and restless. He may complain of stiffness of muscles before typical convulsions occur. These convulsions are at first clonic (intermittent) and then tonic (sustained) in nature. They affect simultaneously both the flexors and extensors. During this stage, the muscles become so stiff and rigid that the body is arched, with only the back of the head and heels touching the ground. This state is known as opisthotonos. Sometimes, the body is curved forward (emprosthotonos) or sideways (pleurothotonos). The chest is more or less fixed so that breathing is difficult and cyanosis ensues. Blood-stained froth may be seen at the mouth. The facial muscles contract into a fixed grin, the so-called risus sardonicus and eyes appear prominent and staring. After about a minute, the convulsion passes off and the muscles are completely relaxed. The patient looks comparatively normal, though somewhat exhausted, and breathing is resumed. This remission is only temporary. As poisoning progresses, spasms increase in severity, duration, and frequency. Any sound or movement will elicit a spasm. Death usually supervenes either during a spasm and is due to asphyxia from spasm of respiratory muscles, viz. diaphragm, thoracic, and abdominal muscles or from exhaustion due to repetition of spasms. The mind remains clear till the end, the patient experiencing extreme pain during convulsions. Death is incredibly painful.

Diagnosis: Strychnine poisoning may in some respects resemble tetanus, epilepsy and hysteria. Epilepsy is to be distinguished by the loss of consciousness and clonus, and hysteria by the character of the convulsions. The chief differentiating points between strychnine poisoning and tetanus are given in Table 55.1.

Table 55.1: Differentiating points between strychnine poisoning and tetanus

Strychnine	*Tetanus*
1. History of poisoning	History of injury
2. Onset is sudden	Onset is gradual
3. Generalised convulsions	Lock jaw
4. Chest fixed during convulsions	Not so
5. Complete relaxation in between seizures	Relaxation between the spasms is never complete
6. Ends fatally in a few hours	Death rare within a few few hours
7. Chemical analysis reveals the poison	Not so

Fatal dose and fatal period: Ingestion of one crushed seed or about 15–30 mg of strychnine, that is, the alkaloid content of one seed of nux-vomica is fatal. The usual fatal period is 1–2 hours.

Treatment: The patient should be kept in bed in a dark, quiet room. Quick anaesthesia with chloroform, or an intravenous barbiturate, if spasms permit, should be effected. The stomach is then washed out with a dilute solution of potassium permanganate. A suspension of animal charcoal should be introduced to adsorb any free strychnine and afterwards removed. Tannic acid may be used, if charcoal is not obtainable. Barbiturates, like phenobarbitone sodium, sodium amytal, etc., act as antidotes and should be given intravenously in doses of 500–750 mg, and repeated in similar or lesser dosage as often as required. The quantity should be sufficient to put the patient to sleep or if convulsions are present, enough to stop them. A mild convulsion should be awaited before repeating the dose. Avertin anaesthesia per rectum in a dose of 250 mg, repeated as required, is very helpful. Other useful drugs include mephenesin (mynesin), a muscle relaxant by slow intravenous drip in a dose of 3 mg/kg body weight, and intravenous diazepam in a dose of 2.5 mg. The former acts by paralysing the voluntary muscles while the latter acts as an anticonvulsant by inhibiting the polysynaptic reflexes in the spinal cord and is preferable to barbiturates as it causes less respiratory depression. Artificial respiration, oxygen and supportive therapy may be necessary.

Postmortem appearances: These are those of asphyxia. Rigor mortis sets in almost immediately after death and passes off early. The remains of the seeds may be found in the stomach. Strychnine resists putrefaction and can be detected from viscera in exhumed putrefied bodies. In deaths from suspected strychnine poisoning, brain and spinal cord should be preserved for analysis in addition to usual viscera.

Medicolegal aspects: Poisoning from strychnine is mostly accidental from its use as an aphrodisiac, from an overdose of a medicinal preparation, or when children eat the seeds out of curiosity. Homicide is rare on account of the intensely bitter taste and the convulsions that follow rapidly after ingestion, but has been recorded. Suicide with strychnine is rare because death is incredibly painful. Nux vomica seeds are used to destroy cattle. Strychnine is used to kill stray dogs, as a rodenticide, and sometimes as an arrow poison.

56 Peripheral Nerve Poisons

These act especially on the end-plates of the motor nerve terminals. Poisoning from them is very rare. The important poisons in this group are curare and conium.

CURARE

Curare (urare, woorara), a black resinoid mass, almost wholly soluble in water, is obtained from the bark and wood of the plant strychnos curare. The active principles are the alkaloids curarine or curarina and curine. Curare is used in therapeutics as a muscle relaxant and to prevent violent convulsions. It paralyses motor nerve endings in voluntary muscles by interfering with the production of acetylcholine. Like snake venom, it causes symptoms when injected or absorbed through an injured surface but not when swallowed.

Symptoms and signs: The voluntary muscles become paralysed and the affected person is unable to move. The muscles of respiration become involved and death follows from asphyxia. The mind remains clear till the end.

Fatal dose and fatal period: 30–60 mg of curare is fatal in about an hour or two.

Treatment: If the drug is applied to a wound or introduced by an arrow, a ligature should be applied at the proximal end and the poison washed out with a solution of potassium permanganate or sucked out with impunity provided there is no injury to the lips, tongue or gums. Prostigmine is a physiological antidote and its intravenous administration in a dose of 2 ml of 1 in 2,000 solution has been recommended. Artificial respiration with oxygen may be necessary.

Postmortem appearances: These are those of asphyxia.

Medicolegal aspects: Poisoning from curare is mainly accidental. Curare is used as an adjunct in anaesthesia to bring about muscle relaxation, and to prevent injury in shock therapy in certain mental diseases, and fatalities from such use are rare. Curare may be used in strychnine poisoning. The use of arrows poisoned by curare is well-known.

CONIUM (HEMLOCK)

Also known as spotted hemlock or conium maculatum, this is an umbelliferous plant and is so-called from the purple spots on its stem. It grows in waste places. The whole plant has a mousy odour which is intensified by crushing the leaves or stems. All parts of the plant are poisonous. The toxic properties are due to the alkaloids coniine and methyl. Coniine which causes paralysis of the motor nerve terminals in the muscles, gradually spreading to the motor cells of the cord and brain. A tincture, extract and succus are made from the plant.

Symptoms and signs: There may be some gastric irritation which causes pain and vomiting. This is followed by muscular weakness and gradually increasing paralysis due to depression of the motor nerves. The lower limbs are first affected and the paralysis ascends till the muscles of respiration are affected. Delirium, convulsions or coma may supervene and the patient dies of asphyxia due to respiratory paralysis. The breath may have a mousy odour. The mind remains clear almost till the end.

Fatal dose and fatal period: A piece of plant about 1 cm in diameter may produce fatal poisoning within a few hours.

Treatment: This is on general lines and consists of lavage of the stomach with a dilute solution of tannic acid, artificial respiration, oxygen inhalations, and stimulants.

Postmortem appearances: These are those of asphyxia. The remains of the roots or leaves should be looked for in the stomach contents and preserved for laboratory analysis.

Medicolegal aspects: Symptoms may be caused by ingestion, injection, or even inhalation as coniine is a volatile alkaloid. Poisoning by it is mostly accidental, chiefly from the plant being mistaken for parsley or some other harmless herb. One case is recorded of a child who died of poisoning from blowing whistles made of conium twigs. This plant is of great historic interest. The ancient Greeks used the juice of the fruit or the infusion of the leaves as a state-poison. Socrates was killed by the use of hemlock.

57 Cardiac Poisons

These are poisons having an action mainly on the heart, either directly or through the nerves. Digitalis, oleander, aconite and nicotine are important in this group.

DIGITALIS PURPUREA (DIGITALIS OR FOXGLOVE)

This is a poisonous plant. Its roots, leaves, and seeds contain several glycosides of which digitoxin, digitalin, digitalein, and digitonin are the most poisonous and have a cumulative action. The glycosides act directly on the heart muscle and improve the function of a failing heart. The normal heart is affected very little unless toxic doses are administered. Its main toxic effects are: irritation of the stomach, slowing of heart rate leading to heart block, extrasystoles, and ventricular fibrillation.

Symptoms and signs: Toxic symptoms by overdose or more insidious cumulative action are indicated by nausea, vomiting, abdominal pain, diarrhoea, depression, headache and giddiness. Toxic effects on the heart include bradycardia (the rate may fall to 20 per minute), heart block, extrasystoles, and fibrillation. There is a feeling of faintness and precordial oppression. The respirations become slow and sighing. The patient becomes drowsy, and the condition may deepen into coma. Convulsions may precede death.

Fatal dose and fatal period: The usual fatal dose is 15–30 mg of digitalin or 4 mg of digitoxin. The fatal period varies from half an hour to 24 hours.

Treatment: The stomach should be washed with a solution of tannic acid. If parts of the plant have been taken, the bowels should be evacuated. Atropine in a dose of 0.6 mg should be given hypodermically to combat bradycardia. Potassium salts may be given to reduce extrasystoles provided the kidney function is normal. Specific antidotes, such as novocaine or propranolol for digitalis-induced arrhythmias, are helpful. Trisodium EDTA may help to lower serum calcium. The rest of the treatment is symptomatic. ECG monitoring is necessary as a guide to treatment.

Postmortem appearances: These are not characteristic. There may be irritation of the gastric mucosa and digitalis leaves or seeds may be found in the stomach. The seeds are reddish brown, remarkably small, and somewhat angular in shape, with peculiar markings. These characteristics make it easy to distinguish them from seeds of other poisonous plants, such as hyoscyamus, dhatura, belladonna, etc.

Medicolegal aspects: Poisoning is mainly accidental from an overdose of a medicinal preparation or from eating leaves by mistake. Digitalis is a cumulative poison and persons taking it for a long time may suddenly develop symptoms of poisoning. Homicidal poisoning is recorded and it is interesting to note that *no suspicion of poisoning may arise in such cases.* Rarely, it may be used to simulate heart disease, and result in death.

An old lady ingested about 50 tablets of digoxin for heart disease, on one afternoon, and died the same evening.

A young man swallowed a decoction (concentrated water extract) of foxglove by mistake for a purgative medicine. He was seized with vomiting, pain in the abdomen and purging. He became drowsy, his pulse became irregular, and pupils were dilated. Convulsions preceded his death, which occurred after 22 hours.

A nurse, employed to look after a patient, forged certain wills, and poisoned her patient with toxic doses of digitalis, to benefit financially from these wills.

Mr KA, a 23-year-old student of Kanpur (India) feigned heart disease by ingestion of a toxic dose of digitalis to frighten his fiancee. He was admitted to the hospital for treatment of heart disease. Diagnostic ECG changes were found.

OLEANDER (KANER)

The oleander plant grows wild in India. Its graceful flowers are used as offerings in the temples. There are two varieties, viz. the white (*Nerium odorum*), and yellow (*Cerbera thevetia*). The white one bears white or pink flowers and is known as *Nerium odorum* or true oleander in contradistinction to the yellow oleander, which bears yellow bell-shaped flowers (Figs 57.1 to 57.3). In addition, the yellow oleander bears globular fruits about 5 cm in diameter, containing a single nut, triangular in shape and light brown in colour. The nut contains pale yellow seeds (Fig. 57.4). A plant closely allied to *Cerbera thevetia* is *Cerbera odollam* (*Dabur, Dhakur*). It also grows wild all over India.

Nerium Odorum (White Oleander, Kaner)

All the parts of the plant are poisonous. The active principle is nerin consisting of three

Fig. 57.1: Nerium odorum (white oleander) with flowers (*Courtesy:* Dr NK Mohanty)

Fig. 57.2: Nerium odorum (*Courtesy:* Dr R Sivakumar)

Fig. 57.3: Cerebra thevetia. (*Courtesy:* Dr SV Phanindra)

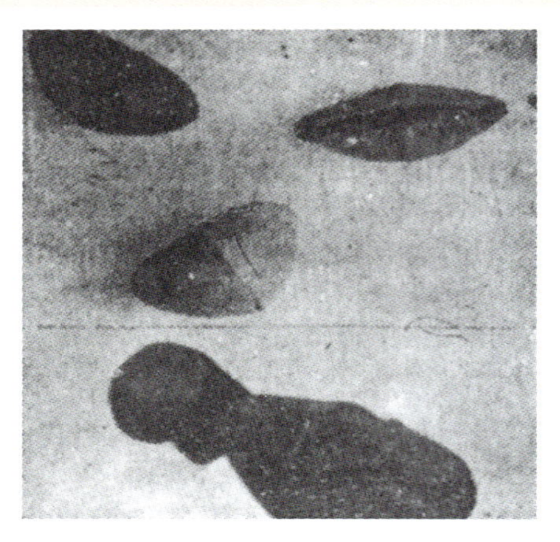

Fig. 57.4: The triangular **nuts of yellow oleander** having two cells, each containing a pale yellow seed

glycosides, viz. neriodorin, neriodorein and karabin, the last one being so-called after the vernacular name of the plant. The principal action of neriodorin is similar to that of digitalis causing death from cardiac failure. Neriodorein causes muscular twitchings and tetanic spasms more powerful than those of strychnine. Karabin acts on the heart like digitalis and on the spinal cord like strychnine.

Symptoms and signs: Vomiting, pain in the abdomen, and frothy salivation usually occur, followed by restlessness. The pulse is slow and weak, and respirations hurried. There is difficulty in swallowing and often lock jaw. Muscular twitchings of the extremities deepen into tetanic spasms, frequently affecting one side more than the other. This is followed by exhaustion, drowsiness, coma and death from heart failure.

Fatal dose and fatal period: About 15 grams of the root can kill an adult in about 24 hours.

Treatment: This consists in washing out the stomach and treating the symptoms. Administration of an anaesthetic is usually necessary. Morphine injection seems to be beneficial.

Postmortem appearances: These are not specific. Petechial haemorrhages on the heart are a characteristic feature. *Nerium odorum* resists heat and can, therefore, be detected even from the burnt remains of the dead body.

Medicolegal aspects: Suicide with decoction (concentrated water extract) from root, leaves, or fruit of *Nerium odorum* is common among village girls, in certain parts of India on account of dowry problems or matrimonial mishaps. The root is commonly used both locally and internally for procuring abortion. Accidental poisoning is sometimes met with when (1) any part of the plant is used as a lovephilter (increases attraction between the giver and taker), (2) the decoction of the leaves is applied externally to reduce swellings, (3) the root is used internally as a remedy for venereal diseases, or (4) the root in the form of a paste is used in treatment of cancerous conditions and other growths. The use of *Nerium odorum* as a cattle poison has been recorded. For this purpose, it is mixed with the fodder or a rag smeared with the juice of the root is thrust in the animal's rectum.

Yellow Oleander (Cerbera Thevetia, Pila Kaner)

This plant (Fig. 57.3) also is highly poisonous. The active principles are the three glycosides, viz. thevetin, thevotoxin and cerberin. Glycosides are substances found in plants and are composed of a sugar and a non-sugar compound, the latter having a toxicological action. Thevetin and thevotoxin are isolated from the kernels of the seeds. Thevetin and cerberin reside in the milky juice which exudes from all the parts of the plant. Thevetin is a powerful cardiac poison. Thevotoxin is less toxic than thevetin and resembles the glycosides of digitalis in action. Cerberin has an action like strychnine.

Symptoms and signs: These consist of a burning sensation in the mouth with tingling of the tongue, dryness of the throat, vomiting, diarrhoea, headache, dizziness, dilated pupils, irregular action of the heart somewhat resembling that due to digitalis, drowsiness, collapse, coma, and death. Tetanic convulsions are occasionally observed.

Fatal dose and fatal period: 8 to 10 seeds or 15 to 20 gm of the root prove fatal to an adult, death ensuing within 24 hours.

Treatment: This is the same as that of poisoning by *Nerium odorum*. Good results have been achieved by intravenous administration of molar solution of sodium lactate to combat acidosis and 5 per cent glucose solution with 1.2 mg of atropine, 2 ml of adrenaline 1:1000 and 2 mg of noradrenaline (if blood pressure is low) to counteract heart block.

Postmortem appearances: These consist of signs of gastrointestinal irritation, congestion of the various organs, generalised engorgement of veins and subendocardial ecchymoses. Yellow oleander resists putrefaction and can be detected even years after death in exhumed putrefied bodies.

Medicolegal aspects: The root and seeds of yellow oleander are used for suicide by women in certain parts of India, on account of dowry problems or matrimonial mishaps. They are also used for abortion. Cattle poisoning occurs when the seeds are crushed, mixed with fodder, and fed to the animal.

CERBERA ODOLLAM (DABUR, DHAKUR, PILIKIRBIR)

This plant grows wild all over India. The fruits resemble unripe mangoes. A toxic milky juice comes out of all the parts of the plant. The active principles are a glycoside cerberin and a weak alkaloid cerebroside having a digitalis like action. The symptoms include gastrointestinal irritation and cardiac toxicity. There is bitter taste in the mouth with nausea, vomiting, abdominal pain and diarrhoea. These are generally followed by irregular respiration, general weakness, bradycardia, collapse, and death from heart failure.The fatal dose is kernel of one fruit and the fatal period 1 to 2 days. Treatment is similar to poisoning by *Cerbera thevetia*. Poisoning is common in Tamil Nadu and Kerala in India where the kernel of the fruit is eaten by women to commit suicide, mostly on account of dowry problems or matrimonial mishaps. Accidental poisoning occurs in children who eat the fruit in mistake for an edible one. The powdered kernel may be added to alcohol with homicidal intent.

ACONITE (MITHAZAHAR, MITHA BISH)

This plant is known as *Aconitum napellus* or monkshood. In India, it grows in the Himalayan ranges. All parts of the plant are poisonous, the root being most potent. The dry root (Fig. 57.5) is tapering, slightly arched, usually shrivelled, and with longitudinal wrinkles. It is 5–10 cm long, 1–2 cm thick at the upper extremity, and dark brown externally. It is white internally, when freshly cut, but becomes pink on exposure to air. It has an acrid, sweetish taste, which gives it the name Mitha Bish (Mitha = sweet; Bish = poison). It is sparingly soluble in water. The chief active principle is the alkaloid aconitine, a very potent poison; the other active principles are picraconitine, pseudoaconitine and aconine. It stimulates and then depresses the myocardium, smooth muscles, skeletal muscles, central nervous system, and peripheral nerves.

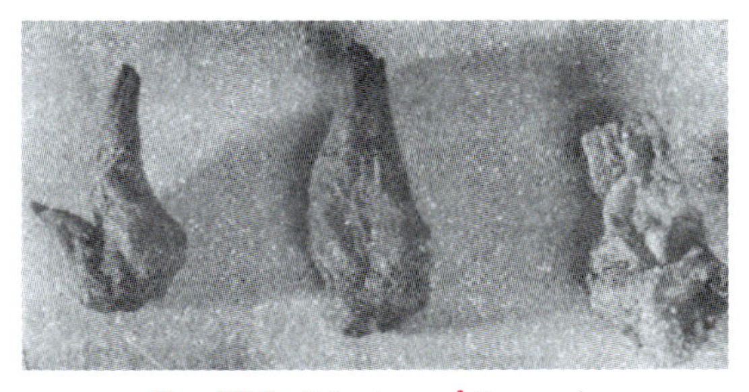

Fig. 57.5: Dried aconite roots

Q. 57.1. Describe the symptoms, signs, treatment, postmortem appearances, and medicolegal aspects of aconite poisoning.

Symptoms and signs: Contact with any of the preparations of aconite produces immediate tingling and numbness which extend over the whole body. There is tingling and numbness in the lips, mouth, tongue and pharynx, followed by salivation, nausea, vomiting, and diarrhoea. The patient feels giddy, his vision and speech are impaired, the limbs become weak, and he is unable to stand or walk. Twitching of the muscles and convulsions may occur. The pulse is slow and irregular (vagal stimulation) when collapse takes place. The breathing is rapid at first but soon becomes slow, laboured and shallow. The pupils alternately contract and dilate but remain fully dilated in the later stages. Mind remains clear till the end. Death ensues from cardiac arrhythmia or respiratory paralysis.

Fatal dose and fatal period: One gram of the root, 250 mg of the extract, 25 drops of the tincture, or 4 mg of the alkaloid prove fatal. The average fatal period is about six hours.

Treatment: Gastric lavage should be affected with a solution of tannic acid (10 gm in 2 litres of water) or strong tea or potassium permanganate (1:1000) to precipitate any remaining alkaloid. The heart may be supported by hypodermic injections of atropine 1 mg, or digitalin 0.25 mg. Cardiac arrhythmias may require 50 ml of 0.1% novocaine given slowly intravenously. Artificial respiration and oxygen inhalation may be necessary. The rest of the treatment is symptomatic.

Postmortem appearances: The findings are not characteristic. Remnants of the plant or root may be found in the contents of the stomach. The odour of chloroform may be perceived when the liniment is swallowed. Aconite is largely destroyed in the body and also by alkalis. It is, therefore, difficult to detect it after death. The alkali present in wood ash meant to preserve the vomit may destroy aconite. Therefore, acetic acid is added to rectified spirit in the ratio of 1:2 and such acidified spirit is added to preserve the vomit.

Medicolegal aspects: Aconite is one of the most potent poisons known to mankind. Accidental poisoning occurs from (1) eating the root in mistake for horse-radish root, (2) quack remedies, (3) therapeutic application of liniment containing aconite or drinking it, and (4) when added to liquor for a greater kick.

Homicidal cases are not uncommon. It is sometimes administered to the victim with betel leaf to disguise its tingling taste. Aconite is said to be useful to hunters to destroy tigers and elephants (*arrow poison*), to the rich to destroy troublesome relatives, and to jealous husbands to destroy unfaithful wives. It offers the following advantages as a homicidal poison:

1. It is cheap and easily available.
2. The lethal dose is small, and the fatal period is also short.
3. Its colour can be disguised by mixing it with pink-coloured drinks.
4. Its taste can be masked by mixing it with sweets or by giving it with betel leaves.
5. It is largely destroyed in the body and, therefore, cannot be detected by chemical analysis.

The root of aconite is extensively used by tribals as an arrow poison. The use of aconite root as a cattle poison has been recorded. Sometimes the root is used as an abortifacient.

NICOTINE (TOBACCO)

Q. 57.2. Discuss nicotine (tobacco) poisoning.

Tobacco is the leaf of the tobacco plant, *Nicotiana tabacum*. The dried leaves (tambaku) are chewed or used in the form smoke or snuff. All parts of the plant except the ripe seeds contain the alkaloid nicotine, a pyridine derivative, as the active principle. Nicotine is used extensively in agricultural and horticultural work as fertilisers, fumigants, and insecticide sprays. Poisoning is caused by absorption either through intact or broken skin, by inhalation, or ingestion. Nicotine first stimulates, then depresses, and later paralyses autonomic ganglia.

Symptoms and signs: Mild poisoning occurs when tobacco is chewed or smoked for the first time or when insecticide spray has been inhaled. Dizziness, nausea, vomiting, headache, perspiration, general weakness, and mild rise in blood pressure with increased pulse rate may occur. These symptoms subside in a few hours.

Acute poisoning occurs when nicotine is absorbed in poisonous amounts. There is burning in the mouth, throat, and stomach, followed by rapid progression of symptoms of mild poisoning, passing into prostration, convulsions, respiratory slowing, cardiac irregularity and coma. Death may occur from cardiac arrhythmia, exhaustion, or respiratory failure.

Chronic poisoning results from the continued use of tobacco by chewing, smoking or from exposure to nicotine during processing, storage or insecticide spray. Those who chew tobacco suffer from chronic cough, laryngitis, pharyngitis, and bronchitis; and those who handle it suffer from dermatitis. In all, tobacco stains on teeth, bad odour in breath, angiospasms and muscular tremors may be found. In addition, there may be amblyopia, blindness, cardiac arrhythmia with extrasystole and chest pain suggesting angina pectoris. Occlusive thromboangiitis obliterans is common and an increase in the incidence of cancer of the mouth, tongue, throat, larynx, and lungs is common. Non-thrombocytopenic purpura has been reported after smoking mentholated cigarettes.

Fatal dose: The fatal dose is about 60 mg of nicotine or about 2 gm of tobacco. One cigarette contains one gram of tobacco, about half the lethal dose! A teaspoonful of insecticide is fatal.

Fatal periods: Death may occur rapidly in a few minutes when nicotine is swallowed. In some, it may be delayed for a few hours.

Treatment: If nicotine has contaminated the skin, it should be removed by flooding the skin with water and scrubbing it vigorously with soap. If it is ingested, the stomach should be washed with warm water containing activated charcoal, tannin (strong tea), or potassium permanganate. A purgative, such as sodium sulphate, 15 gms in 100 ml of water is useful. The function of the heart will need careful attention; artificial respiration and oxygen may be necessary. The rest of the treatment is symptomatic. Those with chronic nicotine poisoning should be removed from the risk of further exposure. Patients with leukoplakia, hyperacidity, peptic ulcer, respiratory problems, high blood pressure, angina, thromboangiitis obliterans, and tobacco amblyopia should stop smoking permanently.

Postmortem appearances: These are those of asphyxia. There may be characteristic smell in the stomach with brown discolouration of its wall, if nicotine has been swallowed or of the skin, if it has been spilled. Depending on the strength of the poison, there may be gastric irritation and pulmonary oedema. Nicotine resists putrefaction.

Medicolegal aspects: Nicotine is a drug of addiction and leads to psychological dependence. Its use leads to serious, oral, dental, respiratory, and cardiac problems resulting in chronic disability and decreased life expectancy. In many cases, the poisoning is mainly accidental and occurs from (1) chewing a large dose, (2) ingestion of the decoction (concentrated water extract), (3) absorption through skin when applied as a poultice, (4) excessive smoking, or (5) exposure to'fertilisers, insecticides, and fumigants. Malingerers soak tobacco leaves in water and bandage them in the arm pits to become sick with fever in the next 6–8 hours and avoid duty. Tobacco has been used for infanticide in certain parts of India.

58

Asphyxiants (Irrespirable Gases)

Asphyxiants mainly produce respiratory embarrassment. The important asphyxiants amongst others include carbon monoxide, carbon dioxide, hydrogen sulphide and some war gases. Carbon monoxide reduces the oxygen carrying capacity of the blood; carbon dioxide produces oxygen lack in the tissues; hydrogen sulphide paralyses the respiratory centre.

CARBON MONOXIDE

Q. 58.1. Mention the sources, clinical features, treatment, and postmortem appearances of carbon monoxide poisoning. Add a note on medicolegal aspects.

This is a colourless, odourless, non-irritant gas which cannot be perceived by the senses. It is formed by incomplete combustion of carbon and organic matter. The principal sources are: water gas, and illuminating gas; gases resulting from explosion in mines, from dynamite and other high explosives; from improperly regulated oil heaters, large oil lamps, and gas heaters without efficient fiues; and from gases formed in crank cases, exhaust of vehicular engines, cycle engines, and in burning houses.

The affinity of carbon monoxide for haemoglobin is about 200–300 times greater than that of oxygen. It displaces oxygen and combines with haemoglobin to form carboxyhaemoglobin which is a relatively stable compound. This results in tissue anoxia. It was formerly thought that the toxicity of the gas is due to its anoxic action but recently Lo Menzo and Pentelez have shown that dissolved CO interferes with some vital cellular enzymes.

Symptoms and signs: These depend upon the degree of saturation of carbon monoxide in the blood. The approximate relationship between carboxyhaemoglobin level and clinical manifestations is summarised in Table 58.1.

Table 58.1: Symptoms of saturation of carbon monoxide in blood

Saturation of haemoglobin with CO	*Symptoms*
0–10%	No appreciable symptoms
10–20%	Shortness of breath on exertion, mild headache, lassitude and flushed skin
20–30%	Throbbing headache, buzzing in the ears. Breathlessness, muscular weakness and in coordination, dulling of senses
30–40%	Severe headache, dizziness, nausea, vomiting, collapse on slight exertion. Breathlessness. Mental confusion, impaired judgement, muscular weakness and incoordination. Dim vision
40–50%	All symptoms intensified. May be mistaken with drunkenness. Incoordination, staggering, mental confusion, loss of memory, palpitation and dyspnoea
50–70%	Intermittent asphyxial convulsions, coma, Cheyne-Stokes respiration, respiratory para-lysis and death
Above 70%	Rapidly fatal due to respiratory arrest

The gas being odourless and non-irritant, the onset of symptoms is insidious. A feeling of lassitude merges into a state of drowsiness with a dulling of the senses which is followed by stupor and coma. The rapidity with which these symptoms develop depends on the concentration of the gas and the length of exposure. If a person breathes carbon monoxide in a low concentration for a considerable length of time, especially during sleep, he will be poisoned just as effectively as though he were exposed to a high concentration for a shorter period. When a low concentration of gas is inhaled, coma may not supervene immediately but the victim may not be able to escape from the dangerous atmosphere and save himself as his senses are dulled, judgement impaired, and he does not appreciate the danger he is exposed to. In the event, he is able to appreciate the danger, he cannot escape on account of muscular weakness and incoordination. He does not call for help due to lethargy and mental confusion. When a high concentration of gas is inhaled, there is sudden muscular weakness, followed by rapid coma and death. The patient may show reddish patches on the skin and occasionally blisters. If recovery follows after coma, its completeness varies with the depth of anoxia and the length of time during which the brain suffered. Confusional states are common and disorientation or amnesia sometimes occurs. Symmetrical softening of the basal nuclei due to prolonged anoxia may cause Parkinsonism. The patient may also show symptoms referable to the respiratory or cardiac systems.

Fatal dose and fatal period: When a person is at rest, 0.1% of carbon monoxide in the atmosphere will result in stupor and coma in two and a half to three hours, but with exercise an hour would suffice. A1% concentration will result in stupor and coma in 15–20 minutes. The debilitated, diseased or drunk may succumb to lower saturations.

Treatment: The patient must be removed at once to fresh air and body warmth maintained. No further treatment may be necessary, if the patient is conscious and breathing. Giving oxygen speeds elimination of CO. Artificial respiration is necessary, if breathing is even slightly irregular. Whole blood transfusion is useful in grave cases. Prophylactic antibiotics against lung infection are helpful. Even after normal respiration has returned, the patient should be kept at absolute rest till all acute symptoms disappear.

Postmortem appearances: Externally, fine froth may be seen at the mouth and nose. The colour of the skin, especially in areas of postmortem staining, and in fair-skinned persons, is bright cherry red, if saturation of CO in biood exceeds about 30%. Below 20%, such colouration is not visible. Skin blisters may be seen on those areas of the body in contact with the ground or where skin is in apposition, such as axillae and the inner side of the thighs. The lesions are due to hypoxia. *Internally,* blood, tissues and viscera are of a bright cherry red colour, if there is more than 5 gm COHb/100 ml of blood. Serous effusions are common. The brain may be oedematous and petechial haemorrhages may be seen on the meninges. Necrosis and cavitation of the basal ganglia, notably the putamen and globus pallidus, may be found in cases of prolonged hypoxia. The lungs may be oedematous or show bronchopneumonia. Myocardial degeneration, and necrotic patches in the cardiac muscle are not uncommon. Carboxyhaemoglobin is stable and can be detected even in highly putrefied bodies.

In cases of suspected carbon monoxide poisoning, a layer of 1–2 cm of liquid paraffin should be added immediately over the collected blood sample to avoid exposure to air.

If carbon monoxide poisoning is suspected, the following two simple tests are helpful: (1) A sample of suspected blood is diluted with four times its volume of water and a few drops of 3% aqueous tannic acid solution are added to it. It is then shaken well. If more than 10% carbon monoxide is present, it forms a pinkish white precipitate. (2) A sample of suspected blood is diluted with about 20 times its volume of water and 10 drops of 10% caustic soda is added to it. Normal blood becomes greenish brown but blood containing more than 10% carbon monoxide retains its bright red colour as no methaemoglobin is formed.

Medicolegal aspects: A determined suicide may sit in his car and connect a tube from the exhaust to his nostril, or remain near the exhaust pipe in his garage with doors closed. Due to the weakness that soon sets in, he cannot get up and turn off the gas, even if he wishes to do so. Accidental exposure to the gas occurs due to leakage from sources of domestic supply, lime burning, burning buildings, and explosions in confined spaces, such as in mines. Persons with a history of epilepsy, convulsions, etc. may lose consciousness in the CO environment. A few cases have been reported in which the driver and passengers in a closed car have been affected by the exhaust gases finding their way into the car. And, especially when the driver is so affected, automatic acts of medicolegal significance may occur (see illustrative cases in the Chapter 33 on Forensic Psychiatry)

CARBON DIOXIDE

This is a heavy, colourless, odourless, poisonous gas which results from complete combustion of carbon containing compounds. It is formed during fermentation and decomposition of organic matter. Other sources of exposure are refrigerating plants, manholes, wells, cellars, and hold of ships, and re-breathing in closed spaces, e.g. children hiding in discarded refrigerators.

Symptoms: The symptoms vary with the concentration of the gas. Inhalation of pure CO_2 may cause a vagal inhibitory response with spasm of the glottis and instant death. Air containing 20–30% CO_2 can be breathed without noticeable effects for a little while. As concentration further increases, there is diminished respiration, fall of blood pressure, throbbing headache, drowsiness, coma, and gradual death from pulmonary oedema and haemorrhage. At 40% concentration, the interference with oxygen supply causes dyspnoea, discomfort, drowsiness, and muscular weakness. At 50% concentration, there may be immediate unconsciousness with or without convulsions and death from deficiency of oxygen supply to the brain and tissues.

Fatal dose and fatal period: The minimum fatal concentration is 25 to 30% and high concentration of 50% and above cause instant collapse and death.

Treatment: The patient must be removed at once to fresh air and body warmth maintained. Artificial respiration and oxygen should be given freely. Then, an amine buffer intravenously; is useful. Cardiac stimulants are required.

Postmortem appearances: These are those of oxygen lack, viz. marked cyanosis, deep congestion of viscera, dilatation of the pupils, and petechial haemorrhages. Sometimes, there is froth at the mouth and nostrils.

Medicolegal aspects: Poisoning by carbon dioxide is usually accidental. The gas being heavier settles at the bottom and may affect workmen associated with well sinking, well cleaning and descending in pits or hold of ships. Unloading ships which have carried a cargo of grain which may have become wet and fermented may cause poisoning. A medical source of excess carbon dioxide is a depleted oxygen cylinder and a new carbon dioxide supply working through a common union. Failure to recognise serious respiratory depression and cyanosis may provide cause for unexpected deaths from carbon dioxide under anaesthesia.

HYDROGEN SULPHIDE

Hydrogen sulphide or sulphurated hydrogen is a colourless gas with a smell of rotten eggs. It is found where sulphur containing organic material is undergoing decay, as in sewers, cesspools, privies, and tannery vats. It is produced in the manufacture of artificial silk and other industries where sulphur is used. It is formed in human intestine during life and in the body after death when putrefaction sets in.

The toxicity and rapidity of action are comparable to hydrocyanic acid. It converts oxyhaemoglobin of the blood to methaemoglobin. In life, this action does not proceed further and there is no formation of sulphmethaemoglobin. This occurs principally after death.

Symptoms and signs: If pure hydrogen sulphide is inhaled, death occurs at once from paralysis of the respiratory centre. If the concentration is less intense, it produces giddiness, nausea, pain in the abdomen, laboured breathing and irregular heart action. There may be delirium, convulsions or coma preceding death which occurs from asphyxia. Pulmonary oedema and bronchopneumonia may occur. In lesser concentrations, there is conjunctivitis, irritation of the air passages, a feeling of languor and sleepiness, and death may occur during sleep without the patient regaining consciousness. A 0.2% concentration in air would be fatal in a few minutes.

Treatment: The patient should be removed at once to fresh air and body warmth maintained. Artificial respiration with oxygen may lead to recovery unless the respiratory centre is very depressed. Supportive treatment with stimulants is necessary.

Postmortem appearances: The general signs of asphyxia are present. The offensive smell of the gas is noted on opening the body. Postmortem staining is bluish green in colour and there is a tendency to rapid putrefaction. In some cases, the colour of organs is darker brown than usual due to the postmortem combination of hydrogen sulphide and methaemoglobin.

Medicolegal aspects: Poisoning from hydrogen sulphide is always accidental, causing a number of deaths in sewer workers.

WAR GASES

Q.58.2. Explain the term war gases. Classify them. Briefly describe their actions.

The term war gases is inappropriate as all the substances used are not gases nor used in times of war only. The term is meant to signify an agent suitable for destruction or damage, according to need, e.g. in war, or to disperse unruly mobs. These substances may be either true gases, smokes, vaporised liquids, or fine powders. An ideal war gas must have the following qualities:

1. It must be capable of being manufactured cheaply in enormous quantities, preferably as a by-product of some industry.
2. It must be definitely toxic in low concentration, so that it is effective against troops distributed over a wide area.
3. The substance must be heavier than air so that it will not be easily dispersed.
4. It must be capable of enough volatilisation to pervade the terrain which is assailed.
5. Its chemical composition must be stable and not of a type to corrode the containers in which it is stored.

The substances employed as war gases are **classified** according to their primary physiological actions as follows:

1. Lacrimators or tear gases	a. Chloracetophenone (CAP) b. Bromobenzyl cyanide (BBC) c. Ethyl iodoacetate (KSK)
2. Lung irritants or asphyxiants or choking gases	a. Chlorine (Cl_2) b. Phosgene ($COCl_2$) c. Chloropicrin d. Diphosgene
3. Vesicants or blister gases	a. Mustard gas b. Lewisite
4. Sternutators or nasal irritants or vomiting gases	a. Diphenyl-chloro-arsine (DA) b. Diphenylamine chloroarsine (DM) c. Diphenyl cyanoarsine (DC)
5. Nerve and blood poisons or paralysants	a. Carbon monoxide b. Hydrocyanic acid c. Hydrogen sulphide
6. Nerve gases	a. Toxic chemicals with action like acetylcholine
7. Miscellaneous	a. Yellow/red rain b. MIC (Methyl isocyanate)

Lacrimators: Also known as tear gases, the chemicals in common use are: chloraceto-phenone (CAP), a finely divided powder with an odour like locust flowers; bromo-benzyl cyanide (BBC), a heavy oily, dark brown liquid with an odour like sour fruit; and ethyl iodoacetate (KSK), also a similar liquid with an odour like that of pear drops. They are fired in artillery shells and cause intense irritation of the eyes with severe lacrimation, spasm of the eyelids, and temporary blindness.

The regular gas mask protects against these substances. The treatment after exposure is to irrigate the eyes with normal saline and to apply sodium bicarbonate solution to any irritation which might develop in the nose or face.

Lung irritants: Also known as asphyxiants or choking gases, these are lethal chemicals used to kill the enemy. Chlorine (Cl_2) and phosgene ($COCl_2$) are gases (liquids under pressure) which can be released from tanks, canisters and gas shells. Chloropicrin and diphosgene are liquids which are used in gas shells. Phosgene and diphosgene are sometimes known as green cross. When these substances are inhaled, they cause dyspnoea, tightness of the chest, coughing, and irritation of the eyes, followed by rest-lessness, rapid and stertorous breathing, cyanosis, collapse, and death within a day or two from acute pulmonary oedema or bronchopneumonia.

The regulation gas mask, if put on in time affords sufficient protection against any of the lung irritants. Treatment consists of removing the victim to fresh air and administration of oxygen, cardiac stimulants or venesection as the symptoms indicate. Codeine may be necessary for irritating cough and antibiotics for infection. If the eyes are inflamed, they may be irrigated with normal saline.

At autopsy, there is moderate irritation and inflammation of the conjunctivae and lids. There may be irritation and desquama-tion of epithelium in the upper respiratory tract. There is foam in the air passages. The lungs are markedly oedematous, and cyanotic. The viscera are congested. There are petechial haemorrhages on the pleura and serous effusions in the pleural cavity. In addition, the most bizarre injuries due to bursting of shells may be found.

Vesicants: Also known as blister gases, these are discharged in artillery shells so as to impregnate the area of attack. The chemicals used as vesicants are mustard gas (dichlorethyl sulphide, *yellow cross*, yperite) and lewisite (chlorvinyl dichloroarsine). Both are volatile irritant liquids, mustard having the smell of garlic and lewisite the smell of geraniums. Mustard gas causes severe irritation of the eyes, nose, throat and respiratory passages. It penetrates the clothes, and causes intense itching blisters, and ulcers in the moist areas of the skin, in rare instances, the stomach is inflamed as a result of swallowing the chemical and this results in nausea, vomiting and gastric pain. The lewisite repidly blisters the skin and inflames the mucous membranes. After absorption, it causes haemolysis of the red cells and may produce signs of arsenic poisoning.

The regulation gas mask protects the wearer from inhaling the vapour but does not protect the skin from burns, unless special clothes are wom. The treatment is symptomatic—removal of contaminated clothes, washing the body with soap and water, and attention to eyes, respiratory irritation, and burns. BAL is a good antidote for lewisite poisoning.

Sternutators: Also known as *nasal irritants* or *vomiting gases*, these are organic compounds of arsenic. They are fired in artillery shells and after explosion permeate the air and cover the landscape. The commonly used compounds are diphenylchloroarsine (DA) diphenylamine chloroarsine (DM), and diphenylcyanoarsine (DC). A person inhaling the air or swallowing food or water contaminated by these chemicals suffers from intense irritation of the nose and sinuses with excessive sneezing, malaise, headache, salivation nausea, vomiting, pain in the chest and prostration.

The regulation gas mask will protect against the sternutators. The treatment is symptomatic. Sodium bicarbonate is useful as a mouth wash.

Nerve and blood poisons: Also known as paralysants, the substances tried have been carbon monoxide, hydrocyanic acid, and hydrogen sulphide. Carbon monoxide may be formed by the combustion of the explosive when a large shell bursts in a dugout and causes poisoning of soldiers trapped in such cavities. Hydrocyanic acid and hydrogen sulphide, despite their toxicity, are not suitable as war gases and have not been employed in that role to any extent.

Nerve gases: These are chemicals related to phosphate esters in toxicity. They are colourless and odourless volatile liquids. Toxic effects follow inhalation, ingestion, or absorption through skin. The chemical causes inactivation of cholinesterase and consequent acetycholine poisoning, similar to organophosphorus poisoning.

Miscellaneous: Very little is known about this group, except that gruesome tragedies followed from "yellow/red rain" which struck Laotian tribesmen, and MIC (methyl isocyanate) which struck inhabitants near Union Carbide Factory in Bhopal (India).

Yellow/red rain: Laotian tribesmen were struck by two gases; one coloured yellow and the other red. They experienced the combined effects of mustard gas, phosgene, chlorine, and nerve poison. Both the gases made their victims feel as if their body was going to blow up. Coughing yielded blood. There was burning in the throat and swallowing was painful. These symptoms were followed by eyes turning yellow as if the victims had jaundice, the vision becoming blurred, and the nose tingling as if hot pepper had been inhaled. Breathing caused sharp pain, teeth felt loose, and the gums smelled rotten. Any one whose bare skin was touched by a droplet suffered severe necrosis of the affected area and high fever with the skin red and turning bluish black. It took about 2 weeks to die, the victims being in severe agony throughout.

Methyl isocyanate (MIC): This is a fairly stable liquid below 27°C. It is highly volatile and reacts vigorously with moisture, alkaloids, and many common solvents. It, therefore, must be stored under strictly inert conditions. It is used in the manufacture of pesticides, adhesives, and plastics. Even if a very small dose is ingested, inhaled, or absorbed through the skin, it usually proves fatal. In Bhopal, India, victims dying within 48 hours of exposure complained of severe burning in the throat, unbearable eye irritation, chest pain, and laboured breathing. Death was due to pulmonary oedema. Those who survived for 5 to 6 days experienced the original symptoms.and neurological effects, such as motor weakness, paralysis in some cases, convulsions, coma and cerebral oedema leading to death. Those who survived over a week developed delayed symptoms, such as shivering, dyspnoea, jaundice, weakness of limbs, and died due to exhaustion. Those who survived longer suffered from fibrosing alveolitis. In pregnant women who survived the exposure, abortion, premature delivery, and stillbirths have been common. Like many other agrochemicals, as long-term effect, MIC may turn out to be a cancer causing and mutagenic substance. Chemical analysis of the blood reveals the presence of MIC, cyanide ions, and monomethylamine in the body.

The treatment is symptomatic. It consists of administration of hydrocortisone against inflammation, antibiotics (tetracycline and ampicillin) against lung infection, eyedrops against eye irritation, and oxygen to combat respiratory failure. Sodium thiosulphate may be tried as an antidote.

PART 6: Forensic Pharmacology

Section 11

59

Analgesics and Antipyretics

The discussion under this heading is restricted to four selected topics, viz. (1) drugs in common therapeutic use, (2) commonly abused drugs, (3) drugs having no medicinal value, and (4) street drugs or designer drugs.

The drugs in common therapeutic use are: (a) analgesics and antipyretics, e.g. aspirin and paracetamol (acetaminophen), (b) antihistaminics, e.g. antazoline, chlorpheniramine, diphenhydramine, and promethazine, (c) tranquillisers, e.g. chlorpromazine, meprobamate, and reserpine, and (d) tricyclic antidepressants, e.g. amitriptyline and imipramine.

The commonly *abused drugs* are: (a) the stimulants, e.g. amphetamines (speed), methyl phenidate (Ritalin), and cocaine (crack). The others, such as drugs of addiction, substance abuse, marihuana, etc., are already discussed.

The drugs which have *no medicinal value* in the present state of knowledge mainly include hallucinogens, e.g. LSD, peyote, mescaline, and phencyclidine.

Street drugs or *designer drugs* are those drugs which are not obtained from legally manufactured sources but from surreptitious ones.

ANALGESICS AND ANTIPYRETICS

An analgesic is a drug which relieves pain without inducing sleep. An antipyretic is a drug which lowers the temperature in cases of pyrexia. The commonly used preparations in this group are: aspirin and paracetamol.

ASPIRIN

Aspirin (acetylsalicylic acid) is a white crystalline powder with an acid taste. It is one of the most common household remedies for pains, aches, and pyrexias.

Symptoms and signs: Poisoning results from idiosyncrasy or overdose. The symptoms include giddiness, buzzing in the ears, oedema of the face and eyelids, skin rash, cyanosis, dyspnoea, and later flushed skin and pyrexia. Aspirin irritates the mucous membrane of the stomach. Therefore, nausea and vomiting are common, and there may be haematemesis and melaena due to erosion of gastric mucosa. Fatal haemorrhage may occur due to hypoprothrombinaemia. Hyperpnoea is an important indication of aspirin poisoning and is due to stimulation of the respiratory centre. This leads to hyperventilation which in turn produces a respiratory alkalosis. Complex acid–base disturbances may follow. Aspirin causes severe acidosis due to reduction of alkali reserve. Ketosis, albuminuria and glycosuria are not uncommon. Hyperpyrexia and encephalopathy are seen. The mental changes are called salicylate gags restlessness, hallucinations and convulsions. The breath smells of acetone and a mistaken diagnosis of diabetic coma may be made. Dr Subrahmanyam saw an young woman taking a single Aspirin tablet and presenting with hemarthrosis and multiple petechial haemorrhages scattered over the body. Death may occur due to cardiac failure, respiratory failure and hypoprothrombinaemia.

Aspirin in urine can be **detected** by addition of a few drops of ferric chloride when it develops a violet colour.

Fatal dose and fatal period: Even a small dose may prove fatal due to idiosyncrasy. The minimum fatal dose is 5–10 gm. The fatal period varies from a few minutes to several hours.

Treatment: Gastric lavage is carried out with warm water and some quantity of 5% solution of sodium bicarbonate left in the stomach to combat the acidosis. Forced alkaline diuresis, peritoneal dialysis, and haemodialysis are useful. Exchange transfusion may be necessary in severe cases. Special attention should be directed to restoration of electrolyte balance and the possibility of potassium loss. Intravenous fluids are required to counter the effect of dehydration from vomiting and sweating. Vitamin K should be given, if there is abnormal bleeding. Blood or platelet transfusions are very helpful.

Postmortem appearances: There may be rashes on the skin. Particles of aspirin may be seen in the stomach. The gastric mucosa is congested and eroded. Petechial haemorrhages may be seen at other sites in the body due to hypoprothrombinaemia. Pulmonary oedema is common.

Medicolegal aspects: Poisoning is generally accidental from idiosyncrasy or overdosage.

Reye's syndrome: Reye's syndrome presents acute hepatic failure and encephalopathy. This is precipitated in children below 15 years of age, if they are patients of influenza or chickenpox. To start with, the patient is lathargic (stage I) then he becomes stuporous and shows conjugate deviation of eyes and sluggish pupillary reaction (stage II). Then he enters coma and progressive stages of coma. First he presents a decorticate posture, later decerebrate rigidity and inconsistant oculocephalic reflex. Finally pupillary reaction stops, no response is shown to painful stimuli, oculocephalic reflex becomes negative and assumes a flaccid posture and the end comes soon. In cases of recovery, permanent neurological deficits may hamper the life.

PARACETAMOL (ACETAMINOPHEN)

Paracetamol, a metabolite of phenacetin, is now becoming a more common cause of overdosage because of its widespread use in place of aspirin. However, in India, this is not common.

Symptoms and signs: In acute poisoning, paracetamol does not behave like aspirin. It does not affect acid–base balance. It does not stimulate respiration. It does not increase cellular metabolism. It has no cardiovascular system effects. Bleeding from mucosal at erosion may rarely occur. The symptoms can be described under three stages, viz. gastrointestinal, latent, and hepatic failure. In the first stage, the symptoms are deceptively mild. Vomiting is seldom severe or accompanied by other symptoms and the patient remains fully conscious. This may lead to a false sense of security. In the second stage, after a lapse of about 24 hours, though the liver undergoes damage, the patient is relatively pain-free. He may complain of anorexia, epigastric pain, and malaise, due to hepatic damage. In untreated victims, the third stage of hepatic failure is seen after about three to five days. It is characterised by liver failure, gastrointestinal haemorrhage, cerebral oedema, renal tubular necrosis, and cardiomyopathy. In cases where patient survives the III stage, complete resolution of the liver injury occurs.

Fatal dose and fatal period: Ingestion of 20 tablets each of 500 mg of paracetamol is usually fatal within three to five days.

Treatment: The important considerations in management are as follows:

1. All patients who have taken an overdose or suspected of having done so should be admitted to the hospital since the history and the clinical state of the patient may be misleading. A patient apparently well 12 hours after taking an overdose may die of acute hepatic failure up to 5 days later.
2. Gastric lavage should be carried out, if the patient is admitted within four hours of taking an overdose.
3. While protracted vomiting needs adequate hydration, it is important to remember that paracetamol can cause fluid retention. More than 2.5 litres of intravenous fluids daily would be risky.
4. Complications of severe hepatic necrosis, such as hypoglycaemia, metabolic acidosis and generalised bleeding should be treated with dextrose infusion, bicarbonate infusion, vitamin K_1 and whole blood or plasma respectively. Oral methionine 10 grams over 12 hours in 4 doses prevents hepatic damage, if given within 10 hours.
5. Haemodialysis may be necessary for acute renal failure. Its value, however, is uncertain.
6. In cases of moderate or severe poisoning, N-acetylcysteine (Mucomix) should be given orally. It is most effective when given within 16–24 hours of overdosage. It prevents hepatic damage. The initial dose is 140 mg/kg followed by 70 mg/kg every four hours for a total of 17 doses. While it may cause skin rash, nausea, vomiting and drowsiness which may last for 48 hours, these side effects are acceptable in view of the serious dangers of paracetamol poisoning.
7. In patients with evidence or suspicion of cerebral oedema, intravenous administration of hypertonic glucose is useful.

Postmortem appearances: Remains of paracetamol tablets may be found in the stomach. The typical findings are skin rashes, jaundice, petechial haemorrhages, gastrointestinal bleeding, hepatic necrosis, renal tubular necrosis and cerebral oedema.

Medicolegal aspects: Poisoning is generally accidental due to overdosage and indiscriminate use as an analgesic and antipyretic. Patients who attempted suicide have regretted the choice of this drug on account of the painful interval between ingestion and death. More common in children. Long-term use of paracetamol for pain relief may develop toxic hepatitis, more commonly among patients also taking isoniazid, rifampicin, barbiturates, and in AIDS victims. In children, low body temperature, oliguria and hepatomegaly are seen. Intentional over dosage as on at most at suicide has been in vogue in USA and UK. In India, these are not very common.

60 Antihistaminics

Antihistaminics are drugs which antagonise the action of histamine. They are used in allergic disorders and other conditions, such as colds, motion sickness, and Parkinson's disease. The common preparations include: antazoline (Antistine), chlorcyclizine (Histantin), chlorpheniramine maleate (Piriton), diphenhydramine (Benadryl), halopyramine hydrochloride (Synopen), mepyramine maleate (Anthisan), and promethazine hydrochloride (Phenergan). Many antihistaminics have other effects, such as anticholinergic, antiadrenaline, and anti-serotonin effects. They are classified as non-sedating, like cetirizine; mildly sedating, like chlorpheniramine and cyclizine; moderately sedating, like antazoline, doxylamine; and highly sedating, like diphenhydramine, hydroxyzine.

Symptoms and signs: Overdosage produces complex clinical signs resulting from initial depression followed by excitation of the central nervous system. In young children, the excitatory effects are more prominent and hyperpyrexia may occur.

There is dryness of the mouth, nausea and vomiting. Drowsiness, headache, blurred vision, urinary retention and nervousness are common. In a large overdosage, fixed dilated pupils, disorientation, ataxia, hallucinations, stupor and coma occur. Sometimes, an excitatory effect predominates resulting in hyperreflexia, tremors, excitement, nystagmus, and convulsions. Death results from respiratory failure and cardiovascular failure.

Over dose causes excitation, muscular incoordination, hypotension.

Fatal dose: The fatal dose is about one gram.

Treatment: The stomach should be washed out with warm water and a small amount of sodium bicarbonate solution left in the stomach. 10 mg Diazepam intravenously will control the convulsions; short-acting barbiturates are not quite effective. The rest of the treatment is symptomatic.

Postmortem appearances: These are those of asphyxia.

Medicolegal aspects: Poisoning is usually accidental from overdosage or indiscriminate use.

61 Tranquillisers

Tranquillisers are drugs which relieve anxiety and mental tension without producing sedation (drowsiness) or sleep. They are used in various neurotic conditions, anxiety states, and for the relief of tension, so common nowadays due to the complexities of life. They are also used in anaesthesia for their muscle-relaxant properties. A large number of tranquillisers are available in the market under different trade names. The common ones include diazepam, chlorodiazepoxide, oxazepam, lorazepam, alprazolam.

Symptoms and signs: Common; symptoms of poisoning are restlessness, tremors, diplopia, nightmares, hallucinations, drowsiness, weakness, incoordination, followed by cyanosis, respiratory depression, coma, and collapse. The individual tranquillisers may produce some characteristic signs, such as jaundice due to chlorpromazine, aplastic anaemia due to meprobamate, and reactivation of peptic ulcer due to reserpine.

Treatment: The absorption should be delayed by the use of activated charcoal or milk. The stomach should then be washed out or emetics given. The rest of the treatment is symptomatic. Flumazenil orally or IV injection of 0–3 to 1.0 mg.

Postmortem appearances: These are non-specific.

Medicolegal aspects: Poisoning is generally accidental from overdosage or indiscriminate use, or rarely suicidal.

62 Antidepressants

Antidepressants are drugs used generally in psychiatric practice to treat endogenous depression. These drugs have an initial sedative effect followed by an anti-depressant effect after a week or more. Amitriptyline and imipramine are the tricyclic antidepressant (TCA) drugs in common use. Prozac and Zoloft are recent additions.

Symptoms and signs: Dryness of the mouth, blurred vision, sweating, dizziness, and urinary retention are prominent initial features. Hypotension, tachycardia, tremors, confusion and abdominal pain are common. Allergic jaundice sometimes occurs. Acute overdosage may result in convulsions, cyanosis, coma, respiratory depression, and cardiac arrhythmias ending in death. These features appear one to two hours after taking the dose and seldom last longer than 18–24 hours but sudden death from cardiac arrhythmias may occur up to six days.

Fatal dose: The fatal dose varies from 1–2 gm.

Treatment: Treatment is mainly supportive and involves gastric lavage, management of arrhythmias; maintenance of blood pressure; control of convulsions; and artificial respiration, if necessary. ECG monitoring is advisable. It is important to avoid quinidine and procainamide to control arrhythmias as they have action on the heart similar to TCA. Physostigmine, though very efficacious in reversing CNS effects and counteracting some cardiac effects, may precipitate a cholinergic crisis and should not be tried till other therapy has been used. The rest of the treatment is symptomatic.

Postmortem appearances: The findings are non-specific. Liver damage may be present.

Medicolegal aspects: Poisoning is accidental or suicidal.

63

Stimulants

These are drugs which stimulate the central nervous system and produce a false sense of euphoria which is followed by depression. The commonly abused preparations are amphetamines and cocaine.

AMPHETAMINES

Amphetamines (pep pills, ups, speed) have varied uses. The alpha and beta adrenergic effects from their use appear to be due to release of neurotransmitters in a fashion similar to cocaine. The commonly used preparations are Benzedrine, dexamphetamine sulphate (Dexedrine), and methylphenidate (Ritalin). They are used as appetite suppressants, mood elevators, for the relief of fatigue, and in the treatment of narcolepsy. These drugs can be taken orally, by inhalation, and even intravenously for 'kicks' or as sex stimulants. Tolerance is common and leads to addiction.

Symptoms and signs: Toxic effects manifest as euphoria, talkativeness, restlessness, insomnia, tremors, dry mouth, nausea, vomiting, diarrhoea, abdominal cramps, palpitations and tachycardia. Mania and delirium with hallucinations, mainly auditory, result from larger doses. Convulsions and coma are characteristic features of severe poisoning.

Chronic poisoning, also known as addiction occurs from the continued use of these drugs over a long period of time for the relief of fatigue and elevation of mood. Profound behavioural changes may occur including a characteristic amphetamine psychosis clinically resembling acute paranoid schizophrenia. The symptoms usually disappear when drug use ceases.

Fatal dose and fatal period: The fatal dose is 120–200 mg. Death has followed five days after ingestion of 140 mg.

Treatment: The patient should be kept in a darkened room. Gastric lavage with tap water and activated charcoal is recommended. Sedation will be necessary. The rest of the treatment is symptomatic.

Postmortem appearances: Particles of unabsorbed drug may be found in the stomach. Reddish blotches on the skin, generalised oedema of the lungs and pulmonary petechial haemorrhages are common. The adrenals may show haemorrhagic reaction.

Medicolegal aspects: Overdose is a common cause of poisoning. Amphetamines are drugs of addiction. Suicide is sometimes triggered by the prolonged depression and errors of judgement which follow intense stimulation from continued high dosage.

COCAINE

Cocaine is an alkaloid derived from coca, the dried leaves of the plant *Erythroxylum coca*. It is a colourless crystalline substance having a bitter taste. It is a recreational drug of choice for the modern affluent class of persons. Coke, crack, crystal, freebase are different names given to the same preparation with slight modification and in different stages of purity. The common routes of administration are chewing, application to nasal mucous membrane (snorting), smoking, and intravenous injection.

Cocaine is said to reduce appetite and feeling of fatigue. It is commonly used as an aphrodisiac or pleasing intoxicant. Drug addicts use it as snuff, either pure or mixed with boric acid.

Symptoms and signs: Cocaine first acts as a stimulant and then a depressant of the nervous system. The psychoactive effects are due to its action on the neurotransmitter sites by production of dopamine which goes to the pleasure centre of the brain. The stimulant stage is characterised by dryness of the mouth, bitter taste, euphoria, increased physical and mental energy, and stimulation of libido. Restlessness, excitement and delirium may appear. The patient may become maniacal and may have hallucinations. Other physical effects include flushed face, dilated pupils, blurred vision, tachycardia, hyperthermia, and an increased respiratory rate. Toxic dosage will produce incoordination, muscular twitches and convulsions. This is followed by a stage of depression which is characterised by feeble respiration and collapse, ending in death from respiratory or cardiac failure. Myocardial ischemia and infarction due to coronary artery constriction is seen in some cases.

In fact, cocaine is so hard on the body that it is often mixed with heroin to dampen its harsh effects. This combination is called a speedball and can be deadly. A *crack house* is a euphemism for a place where crack cocaine is sold or smoked. Like the *shooting gallery* of heroin, it is a place where people meet to enjoy cocaine and transact illegal activities in relation thereto.

Fatal dose: The ordinary fatal dose is 1 gm orally. The fatal dose after application to mucous membrane may be as low as 30 mg, the drug being rapidly absorbed by this route.

Fatal period: Death usually occurs in about two hours.

Treatment: If the drug is injected, absorption should be limited from the injection site by tourniquet. If applied locally to the nose or throat, it should be removed by washing with warm water or normal saline. If swallowed, the stomach should be washed with a dilute solution of potassium permanganate or tannic acid. Medicinal charcoal may also be employed. Excitement should be controlled by barbiturates or diazepam. Cardiorespiratory stimulants and artificial respiration may be required. Further treatment is symptomatic.

Postmortem appearances: Death being due to asphyxia or cardiac failure, the signs of such form of death are likely to be found. Cocaine is largely destroyed in the human system and it is difficult to detect it by chemical analysis.

Chronic Cocaine Poisoning

The sense of well-being experienced on administration of cocaine causes a number of persons to drift into addiction, also known as cocainism, cocainophagia or cocainomania. The tongue and teeth of habitual cocaine eater are black. When cocaine is used as a snuff, there is generally ulceration of the nasal septum. The symptoms of chronic cocaine poisoning are characterised by anorexia, loss of weight, weakness, tremors, impotence, moral deterioration and insanity. The effects of cocaine lead to increased erotic tension in women and nymphomania. In men, the condition leads to many sexual perversions, mainly homosexuality, and libidinous outrages. Insanity is characterised by many delusions of persecution and hallucinations, chiefly tactile, and visual. *Magnan's symptom*, the feeling as if grains of sand are lying under the skin or small insects (cocaine bugs) are creeping on the skin (formication), is the most characteristic tactile hallucination (Figs 63.1 to 63.3). The principles of treatment for abuse are the same as that for any other similar drug. Bromocriptine by mouth 0.625 mg 6 hourly reduces craving for cocaine and counters withdrawal symptoms also.

Medicolegal Aspects

Cocaine is a drug of abuse and produces physical and psychological dependence. Poisoning is due to its use either as a recreational drug, an anaesthetic or an aphrodisiac. It has been used as a local application to the glans to increase the duration of the sexual act. Urethral injections are specially dangerous. Prostitutes inject a solution of cocaine into the vagina. This gives the individual a sense of local constriction and systemic exhilaration. Injecting cocaine with unsterile equipment can transmit AIDS, hepatitis, and other infections. Body packers who smuggle cocaine by intracorporeal route wrap cocaine in plastic bags and swallow or insert the drug in body orifices. The packages may break and large amount of cocaine may be spilled with fatal result. The Spanish police caught a woman smuggling more than a kilogramme of cocaine hidden inside implants in her breasts. The woman had two breast implants containing cocaine implanted in her. She had two open cuts under each of her breasts, (Deccan Chronicle 13.12.2012).

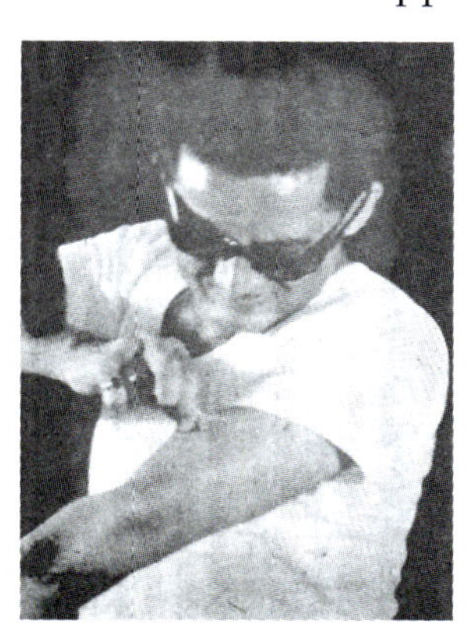

Fig. 63.1: Magnan's symptom. The cocaine addict is trying to squeeze out sand particles from under the skin. (*Courtesy*: Dr GB Sahay)

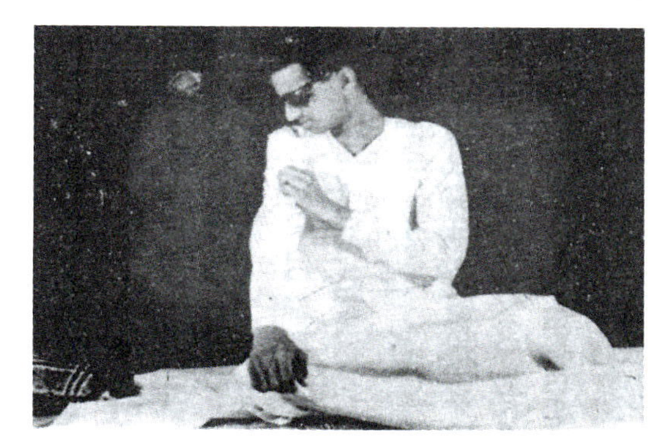

Fig. 63.2: Magnan's symptom. The cocaine addict is disturbed by feeling of insects (cocaine bugs) creeping on the skin. (*Courtesy*: Dr GB Sahay)

Fig. 63.3: Magnan's symptom. The cocaine addict is looking for cocaine bugs under the pillow. (*Courtesy*: Dr GB Sahay)

64

Hallucinogens

Hallucinogens (psychedelics) are drugs which produce bizarre effects on the mind, such as distortion of time, space, sound, colour, and other sensations (synaesthesia). The important hallucinogens are LSD, peyote, mescaline, and phencyclidine. The psychotropic effect resulting from their use is known as 'atrip'. When the effect is a panic reaction, it is known as 'abadtrip'. When the trip experience recurs in a drug-free state, it is known as a 'flash back'.

LSD, PEYOTE, MESCALINE, PHENCYCLIDINE (PCP)

LSD, chemically known as lysergic acid diethylamide, is synthesised from rye ergot. It is tasteless, odourless, and the most potent, widely used hallucinogenic drug, having a powerful effect in minute closes. It is available in the form of clear liquid, thin squares of gelatin window panes, and pills of varying size and colours. It is usually taken on a sugar cube or by putting a drop on a blotter paper and licking it when the drug effect is desired (microdots.) Thin squares of gelatin and clear liquid can be put in the eyes, and the pills can be eaten. 25–50 µg produce all the effects. It causes central sympathetic stimulation. The person experiences a dream-like state or out of the body fealing. Loss of contact with reality, swaying field of vision objects distorted like images in a curved mirror and on closing the eyes unending series of colorful images even nudes appear. Mydriasis, hippus vertigo, altered time sense, and impaired ability to concentrate, Many of these persons get supreme relaxation, and happy feeling. Uncontrolled laughter or sometimes weeping is seen.

Peyote is obtained from a variety of cactus (peyotol) plants. It is available in the form of hard brown discs, tablets, and capsules. It can be chewed, swallowed, taken in tea, or smoked. It is not as potent as LSD. It is used by tribal Indians of the arid regions for their religious ceremonies.

Mescaline is another hallucinogen derived from the peyotol plant. Its availability, use, and effects are similar to those of peyote.

Phencyclidine (PCP, angeldust, killer weed) is available in the form of liquid, white crystalline powder, capsules, and pills. It can be taken orally, smoked, and injected.

Hallucinogens do not have any valid medicinal use at the present moment. They are taken by youngsters in a spirit of adventure, just for kicks. A more profound reason is a desire to escape from the realities of life, or to enter a world of fantasy where they can expand their mind, feel more creative or super-human, and can have communion with nature, divine spirits, or God.

Hallucinogens act primarily on the central nervous system and interfere with the filtering mechanisms of the mind causing alterations in perception, thinking, and mood. Sensory perception is uniquely altered (synaesthesia) — sounds being seen, colours heard, and sense of time, space and distance bordering on eternity. Thinking is altered to a dream state and the awareness of body boundaries is lost (out of body experience). The user experiences phantasies and hallucinations, mainly visual in character. Mood changes rapidly to ambivalent emotions, such as depression and elation, happiness and sadness, simultaneously. Such experiences commonly thrill the user and are known as normal trips. Some users experience a bad trip. It consists of an acute panic reaction instead of the expected psychedelic (thrilling) experience, and usually lasts for about eight hours, during which period paranoid delusions, violent behaviour, automatism, or depression may occur. Dangerous actions, like trying to fly or running into a traffic, have been reported. The effects are best described by the following example of a person who accidentally ingested a dose of LSD as small as 15 μg.

"My soul left my body and flew in space, sometimes at speed greater than a rocket and other times at snail's speed. The medium through which it passed was dark on some occasions and had dazzling lights on other. Sounds were seen and colours were heard with great brilliance and intensity. Objects in the environment had changed in form and colour. Flat things appeared to have three dimensions. Complex patterns of faces and eyes were in evidence. I was in a land familiar but unknown. Things began to talk to me and I saw meaning in objects and events which seemed only trivial in routine life. I felt very strange and got into a panic. Everything looked incredibly beautiful or horrible. I laughed and wept and was elated and depressed. Although the experience ceased after some time, I had unpredictable flash backs of such a fantasy for many months".

Symptoms and signs of use: The potential hazards from the use of hallucinogens are primarily psychological and include: intense anxiety, panic, depressive and paranoid reactions, mood changes, confusion and inability to distinguish between reality and fantasy. Particularly striking are the sudden recurrences (flash backs) of the adverse effects, especially bad trips, of LSD, some up to 18 months after the last dose of the drug. The drug may permanently damage brain cells.

Fatal dose: The drug being effective in minute doses, no human deaths have been reported from overdosage. LSD can be estimated from blood apart from other organs by microanalytic methods, the quantity being very small.

Treatment: The aim should be to limit stimulation and abort the experience by use of tranquillisers. Psychotherapy may help.

Medicolegal aspects: Hallucinogens produce psychological dependence. They pose hazards from 'bad trips' and flashbacks even months after the last dose. Panic attacks, depression, and paranoid reactions are common. Suicide attempts, suicide, homicide and deaths by misadventure have been reported. The feeling of being able to fly may lead the user to jump out of the window. Since hallucinogens can affect time and space perception, their use may result in serious errors of judgement, when driving a vehicle or operating machinery.

65

Street Drugs and Designer Drugs

Street Drugs

As the name suggests, these are drugs to be obtained, not from pharmacies but, from surreptitious sources (on the street) as they are sold in contravention of the drug rules. This group of drugs includes stimulants, depressants, narcotics, hallucinogens, inhalants, and designer drugs.

It is natural that quality control of street drugs is non-existent and many such drugs are likely to be adulterated with substances that look, taste, or even feel like the original drug. Frequently, even the user himself does not know what he has actually taken. In the event of poisoning, the treatment poses a major problem; forensic problems arise in the event of death.

On account of the fear of AIDS and other infectious diseases, **addicts have now turned to smoking, snorting, and ingestion of drugs and the true addict may not have any needle mark**—a cardinal sign of the addict a little while ago. The complications from the use of such drugs mainly pertain to the nervous, cardiac, and respiratory systems, with few specific symptoms that will help the clinician to arrive at a diagnosis and administer appropriate treatment. Therefore, any patient, who has agitation, delirium, confusion, coma, hyperthermia, and cardiac or respiratory symptoms that seem out of place should be suspected as a possible user of street drugs and treated accordingly.

If the patient is agitated, it is often appropriate to treat as if the intoxicant is cocaine. This treatment is appropriate for amphetamines, phencyclidine and anticholinergic intoxicants. Hyperthermia is the worst prognostic indicator in these patients, unless the temperature can be effectively controlled by rapid cooling. Patients with cardiac problems will need continuous monitoring and attention to rate and rhythm of the heart and maintenance of blood pressure at the appropriate level. Patients with respiratory depression should receive naloxone until the possibility of narcotic poisoning has been ruled out. Mezicon should be used to treat benzodiazepine overdosage. The rest of the treatment is symptomatic.

Designer Drugs

The term 'designer' is used to indicate an analog, i.e. a compound similar in its action to another compound but different in its structure. To circumvent legal problems in the storage, distribution, and sale of street drugs, clandestine laboratories manufacture new drugs by altering the chemical structure of a known drug, either legal or illegal. Since substitution of the base leads to many products, a large number of compounds are possible. These drugs are incredibly cheap to produce and some of them are more toxic than the original drug. The compounds so produced are called designer drugs (analogs) and are not illegal even though the parent compound is officially restricted. These synthetic chemicals can be safely sold till they are brought within the purview of drug control regulations.

Designer drugs are classified in four main groups, viz. (1) stimulants (amphetamine group), (2) depressants (methaqualone group), (3) narcotics (opioid group), and (4) hallucinogens (phencyclidine group).

Drugs based on the amphetamine chemical structure include MDMA, MDA, DOM and others. At moderate doses, these drugs produce hallucinations similar to LSD. Known on the street as ecstasy, MDMA has been associated with sudden death through cardiac arrhythmia. An acute choreoathetoid disorder may be seen. Hyperthermia with seizures or muscular hyperactivity leading to rhabdomyolysis and potential acute renal failure are relatively common. Hypertension with complaints of chest pain are common but, unlike cocaine, rarely lead to ECG changes. Other complications include cerebral haemorrhage and death. There are not many analogs of drugs of the methaqualone group. Complications from their use include slurred speech, staggering gait, altered perception, respiratory depression, coma, and death. The narcotic analogs of the opioid group include Fentanyl and Meperidine or Pathedine: Over dose of pethidine causes mydriasis, tremors, hyper-reflexia, delerium, myoclonus, convulsions. After intramuscular injection, its action is for 2–3 hours. It is redasive and emphoriant. Tachycardia is seen. After IM injection, also corneal anaesthesia may be seen. Dry mouth and beterred vision are also encountered. They produce analgesia, euphoria, drowsiness, respiratory depression, convulsion, coma, and death. The analogs of the phencyclidine group cause illusions, hallucinations, impaired perception, and bad trips with their consequences.

Alphabetical Poison Table

(Revised by Dr SK Singhal, Professor of Forensic Medicine and Toxicology, ACPM Medical College, Dhule 424 005, India; Dr CK Parikh, Medicolegal Consultant, Mumbai 400 005, India; and Dr Patrick Besant-Matthews, Forensic Pathologist, Dallas, Texas, USA).

Name and action	*Main symptoms and signs*	*Average fatal dose and fatal period*	*Treatment*	*Medicolegal points and poison sources*
Abrus precatorius Contains toxalbumin, abrin, Locally irritant	When injected, swelling, ecchymosis, necrosis. Vertigo, cardiac arrhythmia, convulsions. When ingested, nausea, vomiting, abdominal pain, diarrhoea, and collapse	1–2 seeds 3–5 days	Removal of sui. Antiabrin if available. Hydrochloric acid pepsin mixture. $NaHCO_3$ to alkalinize urine.	Accidental from overdosage. Suicidal. Treatment of endogenous depression. Cattle poison. Homicidal use. Arrow poison. Malingerer's conjunctivitis
Acetaminophen (Tylenol)	See paracetamol.			
Acetic acid Irritant. Corrosive if concentrated	Intense pain, mucous membranes softened and yellowish white, suffocation, irritable cough, hemoglobinuria	60 ml Up to 48 hours	Stomach wash with milk or lime water. Egg white or milk of magnesia orally. 10 mg morphine i.m. for pain. Eye wash	Accidental Suicidal. Vinegar is antidote for caustic alkalis
Aconite First stimulates and then depresses myocardium, smooth muscles, skeletal muscles, CNS and peripheral nerves	Sweetish taste. Tingling followed by numbness in mouth and pharynx spreading to whole body. Nausea, vomiting, diarrhoea. Alternate contraction and dilatation of pupils and impaired vision. Vertigo, muscle spasm, ataxia. Irregular pulse, fall of blood pressure, labored breathing, cardiorespiratory failure.	1 gm of root, 250 mg of extract, 1.5 ml of tincture, 4 mg of toxoid	Stomach wash with tannic acid (10 gm in 2 liters of water) or 0.2% KI solution. Stimulants. Atropine 2 mg i.m. Novocaine 50 ml 0.1% i.v. Oxygen, artificial respiration. Digoxin 0.5 mg tablet, tds.	Homicidal. Accidental from use as medicine by quacks or mistaking it for edible food. Arrow poison. Cattle poison

(contd.)

(contd.)

Name and action	Main symptoms and signs	Average fatal dose and fatal period	Treatment	Medicolegal points and poison sources
Alcohol (ethyl) Cerebral depressant Hepatotoxic	30–50 mg% concentration in blood causes selective impairment of complex skills. 50–100 mg% alcoholic-smell, dilated pupils, euphoria, loss of restraint. 100–150 mg% test errors. 150–200 mg% clouding of intellect; incoordination of thought, speech, and action; staggers on sudden turning. 200–300 mg% reeling gait with tendency to lurch and fall, vomiting, amnesia. Above 300 mg% stupor, convulsions, coma, hypothermia. *Chronic poisoning* leads to physical, moral, and mental deterioration	Above 0.35 mg% concentration in blood 150–180 ml of absolute alcohol 12–24 hours	Serious cases, hemodialysis or peritoneal dialysis. Gastric lavage with 5% $NaHCO_3$ in warm water. Maintain body temperature. 2 gm $NaHCO_3$ orally 2 hourly to prevent acidosis. Saline purge. Isotonic saline with 5% glucose i.v. Oxygen, artificial respiration. Treat addiction by Antabuse 0.5 gm or Temposil 50 mg daily. Hypnosis and psychotherapy are helpful	Accidental from overdrinking. Increased incidence of head injury, suffocation, drowning, vehicular accidents, murder, rape. Addiction problems
Aluminum phosphide	See zinc phosphide			
Ammonia Irritant. Corrosive if concentrated	Acrid soapy taste. Pain, vomiting, purging. Sneezing, coughing, choking. Gelatinous necrotic areas. Pulmonary irritation. Perforation of stomach.	30 ml of 25% concentration 24 hours	Neutralism by vinegar. Give milk, white of egg, plenty of water. 10 mg morphine i.m. Ice sucking. Cortisone 1 mg per kg body weight tds. Antibiotics. Eye wash	Accidental Suicidal Vitriolage
Amphetamines (Speed) CNS stimulant	Flushed face, sweating, excitement, restlessness, insomnia, tremors, ventricular tachycardia, hypertension, delirium, hallucinations, convulsions, coma. In *chronic poisoning*, psychosis resembling acute paranoid schizophrenia	120–200 mg Up to five days	Gastric lavage, sedation with chlorpromazine. Cardiorespiratory resuscitation, and general measures. Haloperidol 5–10 mg i.v. slowly to combat CNS effects. Forced diuresis in severe poisoning	Accidental, overdosage. Addiction problems. Appetite suppression, mood elevation, treatment of narcolepsy. Misuse by students and athletes
Antidepressants CNS antidepressant and sedation	Dry mouth, blurred vision, sweating, dizziness, tremors, hypotension, cardiac arrhythmias, confusion, urinary retention, convulsions, cyanosis, respiratory depression, collapse	1–2 gm Up to six days	Gastric lavage, treat arrhythmias, maintain blood pressure, ECG monitoring. Artificial respiration. Physostigmine 2–4 mg i.v. over two minutes to reverse CNS effects and to counter some cardiac effects to be used cautiously	Accidental from overdosage. Suicidal. Treatment of endogenous depression

(contd.)

(contd.)

Name and action	*Main symptoms and signs*	*Average fatal dose and fatal period*	*Treatment*	*Medicolegal points and poison sources*
Antihistaminics Antiallergic Anticholinergic Antiadrenaline Antiserotonin Sedative	Dry mouth, nausea, vomiting, drowsiness, lethargy, ataxia, aplastic anaemia, agranulocytosis, fixed dilated pupils, coma. Sometimes only excitation with tremors, delirium, convulsions, hyperreflexia	Up to 1 gm Uncertain	Gastric lavage, leave dilute $NaHCO_3$ in stomach. Diazepam 10–20 mg i.v. to control convulsions. Prostigmine 1 mg i.m. Oxygen. Artificial respiration	Accidental. Treatment of allergic conditions, colds, motion sickness, and Parkinson's disease
Antimony Irritant. Inhibits sulphydryl enzymes	Metallic taste, burning in throat, vomiting, dysphagia, profuse bloody diarrhoea, muscle cramps, oliguria, skin eruptions. In chronic cases, irritability, bleeding gums, emaciation, nephritis, hepatitis	750 mg of tartar emetic. 100–200 mg of butter of antimony chloride 24 hours	Same as that of arsenic poisoning for tartar emetic, and hydrochloric acid poisoning for butter of antimony. Large quantity of water render antimony chloride as insoluble chloride	Accidental. Homicidal, use in alloys type metal foil, batteries, matches, and medicine
Arrack	See alcohol (ethyl)			
Arsenic Irritant. Inhibits sulphydryl enzymes	Burning pain in throat and abdomen, severe vomiting, tenesmus, bloody liquid purging, with shreds of mucus. Muscle cramps. Mind remains clear. Acute poisoning resembles cholera. Chronic poisoning resembles certain diseases	120–200 mg 24 hours	Stomach wash. Demulcents. Freshly prepared hydrated ferric oxide. 10% solution of BAL i.m. 3 mg per kg body weight 4 times on first day, then twice daily for 10 days. 10 mg morphine i.m. Ice sucking. Intravenous fluids. Dialysis	Homicidal. Accidental Abortifacient. Aphrodisiac. Cattle poison. Used in weed killers and rat pastes
Aspirin Gastric irritant. Non-narcotic analgesic and antipyretic	Flushed face, oedema of face, skin rash, tinnitus, deafness, hyperpnoea, nausea, vomiting, hematemesis, melena, hypoprothrombinemia, acute renal failure, pulmonary oedema, respiratory arrest	5–10 gm Few minutes to few hours	Gastric lavage. Leave some dilute $NaHCO_3$ in stomach. Restoration of electrolyte normality and acid base balance. Vit K_1. Blood or platelet transfusion. Forced alkaline diuresis. Peritoneal dialysis, hemodialysis. General measures	Accidental Idiosyncrasy
Atropa belladonna	See datura	125 mg 24–48 hours	See datura	Accidental stupefying

(contd.)

(contd.)

Name and action	*Main symptoms and signs*	*Average fatal dose and fatal period*	*Treatment*	*Medicolegal points and poison sources*
Barbiturates Cerebral depressant Hypnotic	Nausea, confusion, drowsiness, ataxic gait, deep sleep, shallow breathing, fall of blood pressure. Skin rash, blisters, cyanosis, absent bowel sounds, alternate contraction and dilatation of pupils. Areflexia. Cardiorespiratory failure	Long acting barbiturates 3 grams 24–48 hours	Stomach wash, enema, maintain body warmth. 2.5 mg metaraminol i.v. for 2–3 doses to raise BP to 100 mm Hg. Coramine i.v. 5 ml 25% followed by 10 ml in 15 minutes, then 20 ml every 30 minutes till reflexes return. Forced diuresis. Hemodialysis. Exchange transfusion. Stimulants. Artificial respiration	Suicidal. Accidental overdose from sleeping tablets or treatment of epilepsy. Automatism. Addiction problems. Ingredient of lethal i.v. injection for judicial execution
Barium Locally irritant Cardiac depressant	Abdominal pain, vomiting, purging. Cardiac arrhythmia (missed beats), rise in blood pressure, areflexia and paralysis	1 gram 12 hours	Give magnesium sulphate 15 gm. After some time, stomach wash with magnesium sulphate 60 gm in 10 liters. 10 ml 10% i.v. sodium sulphate. 10 mg morphine i.m. Enema	Accidental during use of barium sulphate in X-rays. Suicidal occasionally
Benzene (Benzol) CNS depressant Asphyxiant	When inhaled, dizziness, eye irritation, ringing in the ears, nausea, vomiting, cyanosis, muscular prostration, delirium, convulsions, coma. When ingested, pain in the stomach, nausea, vomiting, giddiness, excitement followed by depression, collapse, coma, respiratory failure	10–15 ml Few minutes to three days	If inhaled, remove the patient from source, oxygen, artificial respiration, supportive treatment. If ingested, gastric lavage (avoid aspiration). Artificial respiration, blood transfusion	Accidental Suicidal
Bromides Cerebral depressant Somniferous	Nausea, vomiting, abdominal pain. Loss of memory, confusion, coma, paralysis. In *chronic cases,* skin rash, headache, coryza, anorexia, emaciation, delusions, ataxia, psychosis	Above 50 mg% in blood Average 6–12 hours	Sodium chloride 1 gram orally hourly. In unconscious patients, 1 liter normal saline i.v. daily for 4 days. Oxygen, diuretics, analeptics as required	Accidental Idiosyncrasy

(contd.)

(contd.)

Name and action	*Main symptoms and signs*	*Average fatal dose and fatal period*	*Treatment*	*Medicolegal points and poison sources*
Calotropis Local gastrointestinal and cerebrospinal irritant	If applied to skin, vesication. If applied to eyes, conjunctivitis, impaired vision. If ingested, bitter taste, burning pain in throat, salivation, stomatitis, nausea, vomiting, diarrhoea. Dilated pupils, delirium, tetanic convulsions	Uncertain 12 hours	Gastric lavage with warm water or $KMnO_4$ 1:5,000. Demulcents. 10 mg morphine i.m. Stimulants and other drugs as indicated by symptoms	Accidental from use in medicine and as depilatory. Abortifacient. Infanticide. Cattle poison. Artificial bruise. Arrow poison
Cannabis Cerebral deliriant Hallucinogen	(Toxic preparations are: bhang, majun, ganja, and charas). Euphoria, visual hallucinations, drowsiness, deep sleep, coma. In *chronic poisoning,* weakness, moral and mental deterioration, loss of sexual power, insanity	10 gm of bhang, 8 gm, of ganja, and 2 gm of charas per kg body weight 12 hours	Gastric lavage. Saline purgatives. Intravenous fluids. Oxygen and artificial respiration. Tranquillisers. General measures	Accidental. Stupefying for roadside robbery, kidnapping, and rape. Running amok. Addiction problems, refers
Cantharides Vesicant. Irritant	Burning in throat and stomach, vomiting, diarrhoea. Strangury, hematuria, priapism, seminal emissions. Delibrium. Necrosis of gastric mucosa	1.5 gm of powder. 1 oz of tincture. 10 mg of active principle 24 hours	Stomach wash. White of egg. Liquid paraffin. Alkaline diuretics. 10 mg morphine i.m. for pain	Aphrodisiac Abortifacient Accidental
Capsicum Irritant	If applied to skin, irritation and vesication. If ingested, Burning pain, salivation and local inflammation. If applied to eyes, burning pain and lacrimation	Not fixed Not known	Wash the skin. Wash the eyes with saline, applied antibiotics and cortisone drops. If ingested, blunt scraping of the tongue and ice sucking help	Accidental. Robbery. Torture. Seeds resemble datura seeds
Carbolic acid Corrosive Neurotoxic Nephrotoxic	Burning pain, hardening and whitening of mucous membranes, phenolic smell in breath, contracted pupils, carboluria (urine turns green or black on standing), giddiness, sweating, convulsions, coma	20 drops of pure phenol 3–4 hours	Stomach, wash with 10% glycerine. 60 ml liquid paraffin orally. White of egg. Alkaline saline i.v. 60 ml of castor oil orally followed by 30 gm sodium sulphate purgative	Accidental Abortifacient Homicidal
Carbon dioxide Respiratory depressant	Throbbing headache, dyspnoea, mental confusion, cyanosis, drowsiness, muscular weakness, fainting attacks, unconsciousness	Above 30% concentration in blood Not fixed	Remove the patient from source. Artificial respiration. Oxygen. Tham, if available. Stimulants. Maintain body warmth	Accidental

(contd.)

(contd.)

Name and action	*Main symptoms and signs*	*Average fatal dose and fatal period*	*Treatment*	*Medicolegal points and poison sources*
Carbon monoxide Chemical asphyxiant	Dizziness, throbbing headache, nausea, muscular weakness, mental confusion, incoordination, cherry red discoloration of mucous membranes, rash blisters, dilated pupils, convulsions, coma	50–70% saturation of blood Not fixed	Remove the patient from source. If necessary, artificial respiration, oxygen. Maintain body warmth. Blood transfusion. Stimulants. cytochrome C intravenously. Corticosteroids i.v. or 50 ml of 20% mannitol for cerebral oedema	Accidental Suicidal Automatism
Carbon tetrachloride Hepatotoxic Nephrotoxic	When inhaled, irritation of eyes and throat, headache, nausea, vomiting, mental confusion, loss of consciousness, arrhythmia, slow respirations, convulsions. When ingested, dizziness, nausea, vomiting, colic, jaundice, uraemia, convulsions, coma	2–4 ml in adults 1 ml in children 1–2 days	In inhalation, remove patient from source. Oxygen, artificial respiration, supportive treatment. In ingestion, gastric lavage, saline purgative. Treat for hepatic and renal damage. N-acetylcysteine in severe cases. Dialysis	Accidental Anthelmintic overdosage
Caustic potash and soda Corrosive. Irritant when diluted	Acrid soapy taste, burning pain, vomiting and purging with tenesmus, blood and mucus	5 grams 24 hours	Neutralism by vinegar. Demulcents. Ice sucking. 10 mg morphine for pain. Intravenous fluids	Accidental. Vitriolage. Suicidal. Applied to neck of ox or buffalo for revenge
Chloral hydrate Cerebral (respiratory)	Retrosternal pain, nausea, vomiting. Drowsiness, unconsciousness, anaesthesia, loss of reflexes, contracted pupils, coma. Gastric irritation especially in chronic cases	5 grams 12 hours	Stomach wash with $NaHCO_3$. Maintain body warmth. Artificial respiration, oxygen, stimulants, hemodialysis	Accidental. Suicidal. Knock out drops (dry wine) for robbery or rape. Addiction
Chlorine Irritant. Asphyxiant	Dyspnoea, tightness of chest, laryngeal spasm, coughing, pulmonary oedema, cyanosis, collapse. Varying degree of conjunctival irritation	Uncertain 48 hours	Oxygen. Artificial respiration. Venesection. Stimulants. Antibiotics. Wash eyes with boric and solution. Bronchodilators, corticosteroids	Accidental. War gas. Dispersing unruly mobs (Tear gas)

(contd.)

(contd.)

Name and action	*Main symptoms and signs*	*Average fatal dose and fatal period*	*Treatment*	*Medicolegal points and poison sources*
Chloroform Anaesthetic. Cerebral inebriant. Respiratory depressant	When inhaled (paralytic stage), loss of all reflexes, dilated pupils, relaxed muscles, subnormal temperature, chloroform smell. When swallowed, symptoms similar to alcohol	30 ml by mouth. Above 0.04% blood 1/2 hour	When inhaled, give artificial respiration, oxygen, and cardiac stimulants. Maintain body warmth. When swallowed, wash stomach, give demulcents, and stimulants	Accidental. Delayed chloroform poisoning
Cocaine (Crack) Stimulant Hallucinogen. Local anaesthetic	When ingested, euphoria, dysphagia, dry mouth, tingling and numbness, dilated pupils, rapid pulse, hyperthermia, hallucinations, Magnan's symptom cyanosis, black tongue, nasal perforation, nymphomania, homosexuality, psychosis	1 gram 2 hours	If applied locally, wash with water. If injected, ligate proximal to injection site. If ingested, stomach wash with $KMnO_4$ or 5% tannic acid. Oxygen. Artificial respiration, cardiac stimulants, amyl nitrite inhalation	Accidental from anaesthesia or use as an aphrodisiac. Addiction problems
Colocynth Vegetable irritant	Severe abdominal pain, yellow watery stools, irregular pulse, collapse	1–2 grams 24 hours	Stomach wash, demulcents, stimulants, intravenous fluids	Suicidal Abortifacient
Conium Paralysis of motor nerve terminals	Burning, nausea, headache, ascending paralysis of limb muscles, drowsiness, ataxic gait, dilated pupils, ptosis, corna, mousy odor in breath	1 cm of plant Few hours	Stomach wash with 5% tannic acid. Artificial respiration, oxygen inhalations, stimulants	Accidental
Copper sulphate Irritant	Metallic taste, burning pain, nausea, blue vomiting, straining at stools, inky urine or hematuria, jaundice, muscle cramps, collapse (vomit to be differentiated from bilious pregnancy vomit)	30 grams of copper sulphate or subacetate Up to 72 hours	Stomach wash with 1% potassium ferrocyanide. Egg white and milk. 10 mg morphine i.m. BAL. Cuprimine. Magnesium sulphate. Dialysis	Suicidal. Antidote in phosphorus poisoning. Emetic. Accidental
Croton tiglium Contains toxalbumin, crotin. Locally irritant	Externally, vesication, burning, and redness of skin. On ingestion, burning pain, nausea, vomiting, powerful purging and burning at anus, dehydration, cramps, feeble pulse, collapse	4 seeds or 20 drops of the oil 6 hours	Stomach wash, demulcents, intravenous fluids, stimulants	Accidental Abortifacient Homicidal Arrow poison

(contd.)

(*contd.*)

Name and action	*Main symptoms and signs*	*Average fatal dose and fatal period*	*Treatment*	*Medicolegal points and poison sources*
Curare Paralysis of respiratory muscles	Drowsiness, weakness of muscles, shallow respirations, coma	30–60 mg 1–2 hours	Ligate proximally and wash with $KMnO_4$. Artificial respiration, oxygen. Inject prostigmine	Accidental in anaesthesia or shock therapy. Arrow poison
Cyanides (potassium and sodium)	See hydrocyanic acid	200 mg 1/2 hour	See hydrocyanic acid	Suicidal. Accidental. Used for judicial execution sometimes
DDT CNS stimulant	Nausea, vomiting, muscular tremors, convulsions, paralysis of limb muscles, pulmonary oedema, coma. *Chronic poisoning:* anxiety, weakness, anaemia, convulsions, coma	20 grams Up to 6 hours	Gastric lavage. Saline cathartics. Atropine. 10 ml 10% calcium gluconate i.v. Diazepam 10 mg i.v. Oxygen	Accidental Suicidal
Datura Cerebral deliriant	Bitter taste, dryness of mouth, dysphagia and burning pain in abdomen. Hot dry skin, skin rash, dilated pupils, diplopia, pyrexia, giddiness, staggering, vomiting, delirium (symptoms rather like drunkenness or heat stroke). Visual hallucinations, tendency to grasp imaginary objects	100–125 seeds. 60 mg alkaloid for adults and 4 mg for children 24 hours	Stomach wash with 5% tannic acid. Neostigmine (2.5 mg i.v. every 3 hours) or physostigmine 1–4 mg repeated if necessary at 1–2 hours. Tepid sponging for raised temperature. Diazepam 10 mg i.v. to allay excitement. Warm enema	Stupefying. Road side robbery, kidnapping and rape. Accidental. Seeds resemble chilli seeds
Digitalis Cardiotoxic	Nausea, vomiting, abdominal pain, depression, headache, giddiness. Bradycardia, heart block, extrasystoles, ventricular fibrillation. Slow and sighing respiration, convulsions, coma	Digitalin. 15–30 mg. Digitoxin 4 mg. Digitalis 2–3 gm Up to 24 hours	Gastric lavage with 5% tannic acid, atropine 0.6 mg, evacuate bowels. Trisodium EDTA. Potassium chloride 1–2 gm, tds. 100 ml lignocaine i.v. Sedatives or stimulants as required. ECG monitoring. Symptomatic	Accidental. Rarely suicidal. Used by malingerers to simulate sickness
Dinitro weed killers CNS depressant, inhibits cholinesterase	Excessive sweating. Skin stained yellow. Thirst, vomiting, fatigue. Collapse. See Paraquat.	5 ml gramoxone. 1–2 gm Weedol 4 days to 2 weeks	Remove clothes. Decontaminate body by washing. Cold sponging, general measures, sedatives, absolute rest. See Paraquat	Accidental Suicidal

(*contd.*)

(*contd.*)

Name and action	*Main symptoms and signs*	*Average fatal dose and fatal period*	*Treatment*	*Medicolegal points and poison sources*
Endrin Neurotoxic Cholinergic	Salivation, vomiting, abdominal pain, tremors, dyspnoea, white fine froth from mouth and nostrils, convulsions, coma	6 grams 2 hours	Decontaminate body. Gastric lavage, saline cathartics. Atropine. 10 ml 10% calcium gluconate i.v. Paraldehyde. Oxygen. Blood transfusion	Suicidal. Homicidal. Accidental. Plant penicillin
Ergot Vasoconstrictor. Smooth (uterine) muscle contractor	Irritation of throat, thirst, nausea, vomiting, diarrhoea, colicky pain, giddiness, tingling in small muscles, hypoglycemia, anuria. In *chronic cases,* convulsive and gangrenous ergotism	Uncertain Uncertain	Stomach wash with 5% tannic acid. Magnesium sulphate. Intravenous fluids. Amyl nitrite inhalations. Sodium nicotinate 140 mg i.v.	Abortifacient. Accidental from contaminated food
Ether Anaesthetic	If ingested, burning pain, vomiting, dilated pupils, absent corneal reflex, intoxication. When inhaled, it produces features similar to chloroform. Sometimes epileptiform convulsions	30 ml orally More than 0.15% in blood Uncertain	Gastric lavage, demulcents, stimulants. Oxygen, artificial respiration. Anticonvulsants. Maintain blood pressure	Accidental Suicidal Addiction
Ethylene glycol CNS depressant Nephrotoxic	When ingested, effects resemble drunkenness, progressing to nephrotoxicity, hypoglycemia, coma, seizures, collapse	100 ml 24–72 hours	Gastric lavage. Pyridoxine and thiamine help conversion of glyoxalate to non-toxic byproducts. Antidote 4 methyl pyrazole. Dialysis, whole bowel irrigation, or competing ethanol	Accidental Suicidal Use in place of ethyl alcohol
Hallucinogens Mechanism of action on CNS not known	Unusual hilarity, emotional swings, hallucinations, suspiciousness, bizare behaviour, synaesthesia, nausea, vomiting, widely dilated pupils, insomnia, tremors, vertigo, headache, psychotic reactions, bad trips, flashbacks	Uncertain Not known	Limt stimulation, tranquillisers, symptomatic measures, psychotherapy	Accidental Suicidal Homicidal Habit forming
Hemlock	See conium			

(*contd.*)

(contd.)

Name and action	*Main symptoms and signs*	*Average fatal dose and fatal period*	*Treatment*	*Medicolegal points and poison sources*
Heroin (Brown sugar) Narcotic analgesic	Tolerance occurs rapidly. Withdrawal symptoms include sweating, malaise, anxiety, depression, general feeling of heaviness, confusion, hallucinations, personality changes	Uncertain Uncertain	To be treated like any other addiction. Heroin addiction is quite severe and carried considerable mortality	Severe addiction Sudden death
Hydrochloric acid Corrosive. Irritant, if diluted	Intense burning pain, vomiting with blood, thirst; excoriation of lips and shreds of mucous membranes, delirium	20–30 ml 24 hours	Stomach wash (with soft rubber tube, if possible). Give milk, lime water, egg white. 10 mg morphine for pain, ice sucking. Cortisone	Accidental. Vitriolage. Suicidal. To erase ink writing for forgery
Hydrocyanic acid Cellular asphyxia (histotoxic). Inhibits respiratory enzyme, cytochrome oxidase	Headache, confusion, giddiness, nausea, loss of muscular power, smell of bitter almonds, dyspnoea, convulsions, dilated pupils, froth at mouth, subnormal temperature, purple nails. Commonly fatal	60 mg of anhydrous acid. 200 mg cyanides 10 minutes for HCN and 30 minutes for cyanides	Speed is essential. Inject two 20 ml ampoules of 1.5% dicobalt tetracemate (Kelocyanor) i.v. followed by 20 ml 50% glucose. Methylene blue 50 ml 1% i.v. PAPP. Artificial respiration with 100% oxygen. Coramine i.v. slowly	Suicidal. Accidental. Used for judicial execution in some countries
Hydrogen sulphide Local irritant CNS depressant	Irritation of air passages, dizziness, nausea, cyanosis, dilated pupils, tetanic convulsions, stupor, coma	0.2% in air Within few minutes	Oxygen. Artificial respiration. Coramine 2 ml 25% i.v. Supportive treatment	Accidental Exposure in sewers Sewer gas
Hyoscyamus Cerebral deliriant	Bitter taste, dryness of mouth, dysphagia, burning pain in abdomen. Hot dry skin, dilated pupils, diplopia, pyrexia. Giddiness, staggering, vomiting, delirium (symptoms rather like drunkenness or heat stroke)	125 mg of hyoscyamine 15–30 mg of hyoscine 24 hours	Stomach wash with 5% tannic acid. Prostigmine 0.5 mg or pilocarpine nitrate 15 mg subcutaneously. Tepid sponging for raised temperature. 10 mg Diazepam i.v. to allay excitement. Warm enema	Stupefying. Homicidal. Truth serum. Twilight sleep. Sedative in medicine
Iodine Irritant. Corrosive if concentrated	Burning pain, thirst, vomiting, blue stool with blood and smell of iodine. Brown staining of mucus membrane of mouth, Urine smells of iodine. Skin rash. In *chronic poisoning,* pain in frontal region, running nose, bronchial catarrh, parotitis, myxedema, wasting of breasts, testes, etc., ulcers on skin	2 grams of iodine. 10 ml of tincture 24 hours	Stomach wash with 1% starch solution. 100 ml 5% sodium thiosulfate orally. Demulcents. Symptomatic.	Accidental. Idiosyncrasy. Suicidal. Vitriolage

(contd.)

(contd.)

Name and action	*Main symptoms and signs*	*Average fatal dose and fatal period*	*Treatment*	*Medicolegal points and poison sources*
Iron salts Irritant	Gastritis, hematemesis, diarrhoea, encephalopathy	Uncertain Uncertain	Gastric lavage. Leave dilute $NaHCO_3$ in stomach. Electrolyte correction. Desferrioxamine-B	Accidental through over-dosage
Isopropyl alcohol CNS depressant	Fruity odour in breath, headache, dizziness, nausea, hematemesis. Pain in abdomen, muscular weakness, cardiac depression, hypoglycaemia, collapse, respiratory failure	2.5 ounces of 75% 24 hours	Supportive treatment. Glucose i.v. Dialysis	Accidental from baths in infants or use in place of ethyl alcohol
Kerosene Irritant CNS depressant	Burning pain, nausea, colicky pain, diarrhoea, giddiness, cyanosis, dyspnoea, stupor. Smell of kerosene in breath, vomit, and urine. Pneumonia, pulmonary oedema	15 ml Uncertain	Stomach wash with care with warm water containing 5% $NaHCO_3$. Steroids. Antibiotics. Glucose i.v. Liquid paraffin 250 ml orally followed by saline cathartic	Accidental Suicidal
Lead Irritant	Metallic taste, intense thirst, bloody vomiting, paroxysmal colicky pain relieved by pressure, tender abdominal wall, constipation, feeble pulse, drowsiness, muscle cramps, convulsions, peripheral neuropathy, blue-black line on gums in subacute cases. *Chronic poisoning*: Facial pallor, foul breath, anaemia with punctate basophilia, lead line, colic and constipation, paralysis (wrist drop, foot drop), encephalopathy, cardiorenal manifestations, and reproductive system manifestations	Absorbed lead 0.5 gm. Lead acetate 20 gm. Lead carbonate 4 gm. Tetra-ethyl lead few drops Uncertain	Stomach wash with 1% magnesium or sodium sulphate. Give egg white, milk. Calcium gluconate 1 gram i.v. Morphine and atropine. EDTA 1 gram twice daily for 5 days in 5% glucose saline by drip. Penicillamine 1 gram daily for 4 or 5 days by mouth or slow i.v. drip. Vitamin D 100 mg daily. Diazepam i.v. 10 mg or barbiturates i.m. 100–200 mg for convulsions. Wash skin with kerosene if tetraethyl lead is spilled on skin	Abortifacient Accidental Cattle poison
LSD	See hallucinogens			
Manganese Locally corrosive Neurotoxic	Burning pain in entire gastrointestinal tract, thirst, dysphagia, conti-nuous vomiting, corrosion of mucous membrane of mouth. Bronchitis, pneu-monia, liver damage. Chronic poisoning resembles Parkinsonism	10 grams as potassium permanganate 1/2 hour	Stomach wash with powdered charcoal. Milk and egg white. 10 ml 10% calcium gluconate i.v. In chronic poisoning, BAL and EDTA. Parpanit 25 mg i.m.	Accidental

(contd.)

(contd.)

Name and action	*Main symptoms and signs*	*Average fatal dose and fatal period*	*Treatment*	*Medicolegal points and poison sources*
Marihuana	See cannabis			
Marking nut	See Semecarpus anacardium			
Mercury Corrosive and irritant. Nephrotoxic	Metallic taste, salivation, choking, dysphagia, corrosion of mucous membrane of mouth and grayish white patches, vomiting, bloody stools, albuminuria, hematuria, oliguria, uraemia, convulsions, coma. *Chronic poisoning*, 72 hours blue-black line on gums, penetrating ulcers, uraemia, mercuria lentis, tremors (hatter's shake), erethism	Metallic mercury not poisonous. Corrosive sublimate 1–2 gm	Emetics, or stomach wash with magnesium carbonate or sodium formaldehyde sulphoxylate 250 ml 5%, and 100 ml to be left in stomach. Egg white. Activated charcoal orally. Magnesium sulphate. BAL 200 mg twice daily i.m. Sodium thiosulfate i.v. Penicillamine orally, alkaline fluids, dialysis	Accidental Abortifacient Suicidal
Methyl alcohol Neurotoxic, Respiratory depressant	Alcoholic smell, headache, dizziness, nausea, vomiting, pain in abdomen, intestinal contraction – bowel like thick rubber pipe of narrow lumen, muscular weakness, cyanosis, optic neuritis, acidosis, stupor, respiratory failure	15 ml causes blindness 60–240 ml Up to 4 days	Gastric lavage with 5% $NaHCO_3$. Ethyl alcohol 80° proof (brandy) 1 ml/kg body weight 4–6 hourly for 1–3 days. Combat acidosis with $NaHCO_3$ orally or 5% i.v. solution. Protect eyes. Hemodialysis. Antidote 4-methylpyrazole. Folinic acid. Whole bowel irrigation, if possible	Accidental from use in place of ethyl alcohol
Methyl salicylate	See aspirin	30 ml		
Methylene chloride Narcotic, Respiratory depressant	Depending on concentration and exposure, symptoms range from light headedness, nausea, headache, and impairment of concentration and coordination to stupor, irritability, and gait disturbances. Inhalation elevates blood carboxyhemoglobin levels without inhalation of carbon monoxide. Its use as a paint remover in a poorly ventilated setting may stress patients or workers with underlying cardiopulmonary disease or concomitant carbon monoxide exposure	More than 250 ppm Uncertain	Same as inhalation or ingestion of other hydrocarbons. Removal of the patient from exposure, decontamination, support of respiration, monitoring of dysrhythmias, and general measures	Accidental

(contd.)

(contd.)

Name and action	*Main symptoms and signs*	*Average fatal dose and fatal period*	*Treatment*	*Medicolegal points and poison sources*
Morphine Cerebral somniferous (respiratory depressant). Narcotic analgesic	Starts with euphoria and excitement, later nausea with vomiting, drowsiness, deep sleep passing on to deep coma, areflexia. Relaxation of sphincters. Cold, clammy skin (hypothermia), pin point pupils, fall of blood pressure, low respiratory rate (2–4 per minute) and Cheyne-Stokes respiration. Cyanosis, froth at nose and mouth. Pupils dilate before death	200 mg as morphine. 2 grams as opium 12 hours	Stomach wash with potassium permanganate. Maintain body warmth, Naloxone 0.4–0.8 mg i.v. Glucose drip i.v. Oxygen and artificial respiration. Stimulants, such as adrenaline, coramine, or strychnine may be given, if necessary	Suicidal infanticidal. Accidental. Doping race horses. Cattle poison. Morphinism
Mushrooms Parasympathomimetic	Nausea, vomiting, diarrhoea, bloody vomitus and stools, enlarged tender liver and jaundice, oliguria, pulmonary oedema, mental confusion, convulsions, coma	1/2 to 1 mushroom 3–6 days	Gastric lavage, supportive treatment, atropine, exchange transfusion in children, charcoal hemoperfusion in adults	Accidental
Naphtha	See kerosene			
Naphthalene Irritant. Nephrotoxic Hepatotoxic. Hemolytic	Nausea, vomiting, abdominal pain. Strangury, hemoglobinuria. Nephritis. Jaundice. Hemolytic anaemia. Optic neuritis, profuse perspiration, cyanosis, convulsions, coma	2 grams Uncertain	Stomach wash. Magnesium sulphate. $NaHCO_3$ orally to alkalinize urine. Blood transfusion. 25 mg hydrocortisone hemisuccinate i.v. Glucose	Accidental Suicidal. Moth balls
Nicotine Cardiac depressant Carcinogenic potential	Burning pain, bitter taste, nausea, fainting, muscular weakness, tremors, semi-consciousness, irregular pupillary reaction. Cardiac arrhythmia, raised blood pressure, paralysis of respiratory muscles, CNS depression, amblyopia. Chronic poisoning: Increased incidence of heart disease, emphysema, and carcinoma of lungs, lips, and buccal mucosa	Nicotine 1 mg/kg body weight 15–30 gm of crude tobacco Uncertain	Decontaminate the skin. If ingested, stomach wash with warm water and activated charcoal. 15 gm sodium sulphate in 100 ml of water is useful. Atropine, nitrites. Cardiorespiratory stimulants. Oxygen and artificial respiration. Antihypertensive. Symptomatic. Those with chronic poisoning should stop smoking permanently	Accidental. Malingering. Suicidal. Homicidal. Infanticidal. Abortifacient

(contd.)

(contd.)

Name and action	*Main symptoms and signs*	*Average fatal dose and fatal period*	*Treatment*	*Medicolegal points and poison sources*
Nitric acid Corrosive. Irritant if diluted	Burning pain, thirst, yellow coloration of mucous membrane and teeth, yellow brown vomitus, tender and distended abdomen, oliguria, shock. Choking, lacrimation, dyspnoea, and cough are due to inhalation	15–20 ml 18 hours	Stomach wash (with soft rubber tube, if possible). Give milk, magnesium oxide, egg white or melted butter. 10 mg morphine. Intravenous fluids. Ice sucking. Cortisone	Accidental Suicidal Abortifacient Vitriolage
Nitrous oxide Anaesthetic	Hysterical excitement, laughter, light anaesthesia.	Uncertain Uncertain	Inhalation of oxygen and carbon dioxide, artificial respiration, stimulants	Accidental Laughing gas
Nux vomica stychnos Spinal irritant acting mainly on anterior horn cells	Bitter taste, twitching of muscles of face, risus sardonicus, convulsions, opisthotonos, cyanosis, dilated pupils, frothy salivation, epigastric pain. Mind remains clear till the end. Death is incredibly painful	Undamaged seed not fatal. Powdered nux vomica 2 grams. Strychnine 15–30 mg 1–2 hours	Keep patient in dark quiet room. 600 mg pentobarbital or 10 mg diazepam i.v. Mephenesin i.v. 3 mg/kg body weight. Stomach wash with 5% tannic acid. Tubocurarine. Oxygen and artificial respiration	Accidental from prescription errors or eating fruit. Suicidal. Homicidal. Love-philter, Aphrodisiac
Oleander Cardiac depressant	Dysphagia, vomiting, pain, salivation, diarrhoea, lock-jaw, feeble pulse, fall of blood pressure, muscular spasms, drowsiness, coma	Nerium odorum 15 grams. Yellow oleander 8–10 seeds 24 hours	Stomach wash with 5% tannic acid. Molar sodium lactate solution i.v. 5% glucose with 1.2 mg atropine, 2 ml 1:1000 adrenaline, and 2 mg noradrenaline i.v.	Accidental (drug). Suicidal. Abortifacient. Love-philter. Cattle poison
Opium Contains alkaloids	See morphine	2 grams 6–12 hours	See morphine. Methadone may be used in chronic poisoning as temporary substitute	Near ideal suicidal poison. See morphine
Organophosphorus compounds CNS depressant Inhibits cholinesterase	Respiratory symptoms mimic bronchial asthma. Headache, malaise, choking, contracted pupils. Nausea, abdominal cramps, vomiting. Sweating, salivation, lacrimation (sometimes red tears), urination and defecation, mental confusion, stupor, convulsions, areflexia, coma	1 gram of Tik-20 (variable for other compounds) 6 hours	Remove clothing. Decontaminate body. Stomach wash, care of airway. 2 mg atropine i.v. half hourly till pupils dilate. Oxime compound PAM 1 gram 12 hourly. Oxygen. Intravenous fluids. Exchange transfusion. Charcoal hemoperfusion. Diuretic, brisk purgative. Diazepam, if necessary	Accidental Suicidal Homicidal

(contd.)

(contd.)

Name and action	Main symptoms and signs	Average fatal dose and fatal period	Treatment	Medicolegal points and poison sources
Oxalic acid Corrosive, Neurotoxic, Nephrotoxic	Sour taste, burning in throat and stomach, vomiting of bloody mucus, albuminuria and oxaluria, great prostration, shock, muscle cramps, convulsions, coma.	15–20 grams 1–2 hours	Gastric lavage with lime water. Warm water should not be used. Give chalk, calcined magnesia. 10 ml 10% calcium gluconate i.v. Ice sucking. Oxygen	Accidental. Suicidal. To erase ink writing for forgery
Paracetamol (Acetaminophen) (Tylenol) Non-narcotic analgesic and antipyretic	Anorexia, nausea, vomiting, epigastric pain, jaundice, gastro-intestinal hemorrhage, cerebral oedema, renal tubular necrosis	10 grams Up to five days	Oral methionine 10 grams in 12 hours over 4 doses or i.v. cysteamine prevents hepatic damage if given within 10 hours. Gastric lavage, general measures. Cysteamine 2 gm i.v. in 10 minutes and 400 mg in 5% dextrose over 4, 6, and 8 hours. Vit K_1. Charcoal hemoperfusion. Hypertonic glucose i.v. for cerebral oedema. Dialysis	Accidental Suicidal
Paraldehyde Cerebral depressant	Nausea, vomiting, head-ache, giddiness, paral-dehyde odour, drowsi-ness, cyanosis, pulmo-nary oedema, coma	60–90 ml 12 hours	Gastric lavage. 20% acetyl-cysteme (mucocyst) 140 mg/kg orally followed by 70 mg/kg 4 hourly for 3 days. General measures, respiratory stimulants. Maintain body warmth. Oxygen	Accidental Suicidal Addiction
Paraquat Di-nitro weed killer CNS depressant	If splashed, skin and con-junctival irritation. When ingested, blood-stained vomiting, bloody stools, anuria, cyanosis, pulmonary oedema	5 ml Gram-oxone. 1–2 grams of Weedol 4 days to 2 weeks	Remove clothing. De-contaminate body. Gastric lavage. Leave 50 ml 30% suspension of Fuller's earth and a 5% suspension of magnesium sulphate in stomach. Oxygen. General measures. See Di-nitro weed killers	Accidental. Suicidal. Herbicidal. Proprietary preparation Weedol
Pethidine Narcotic analgesic	Flushed face, dilated pupils, dry mouth, tachy-cardia, hyperthermia, drowsiness, coma	2 grams 24 hours	Gastric lavage. Coramine i.v. General measures	Accidental Addiction
Petrol and Petroleum	See kerosene			
Phenacetin Analgesic Antipyretic	Sweating, nausea, vomit-ing, chills, ringing in ears, hypotension, marked cyanosis due to methemo-globinemia, convulsions, coma, skin rash	5 grams Few hours to some days	Gastric lavage, 1% methylene blue 1 mg/kg body weight i.v. Vit C i.v. General measures. Maintain body warmth	Accidental Idiosyncrasy Suicidal

(contd.)

(contd.)

Name and action	Main symptoms and signs	Average fatal dose and fatal period	Treatment	Medicolegal points and poison sources
Phosphorus (elemental) Protoplasmic poison	Burning pain, garlic taste in mouth and garlic odor in breath. Luminous vomit, dark offensive stools, hematuria, convulsions, coma. *Subacute cases*: Jaundice, hemorrhages, formication, cramps, priapism. *Chronic cases:* Marked jaundice, phossy jaw, fractures, abortion in females	120 mg 24 hours	Demulcents not to be used. Stomach wash with 0.5% $KMnO_4$ or 0.1% copper sulphate. Liquid paraffin. Intravenous saline with calcium gluconate and glucose. Oxygen. Vit K_1 200 mg i.v. Corticosteroids 100 mg i.v. for hepatic coma. Peritoneal or hemodialysis	Accidental Suicidal. Abortifacient Accidental from fire works. Homicidal
Plumbago Irritant	When applied to skin, irritation and blister formation. When swallowed, pain in stomach, vomiting, diarrhoea, coma	Uncertain Uncertain	Wash the part with cold water and apply bland liniments. Wash the stomach with 1% tannic acid. Stimulants. Symptomatic	Abortifacient Malingerer's bruise Homicidal
Potassium permanganate Corrosive	Burning pain, nausea, dark colored 10 grams vomiting, dysphagia, pain in stomach. Locally, tissue necrosis	10 grams 1/2 hour	Stomach wash with 10% sodium thiosulfate solution in warm water. Give milk. Intravenous glucose	Accidental Suicidal Abortifacient. Antidote for oxidizable poisons
Powdered glass Irritant	Burning in stomach, nausea, vomiting mixed with blood, sense of apprehension, tender abdomen	Not known Not known	Bulky food like rice, ripe banana and custard. Plenty of water. Give laxatives but no violent purgatives	Accidental. Homicidal. Infanticidal. Suicidal
Rati	See abrus precatorius			
Ricinus communis Contains toxalbumin, Locally irritant	Burning pain, nausea, vomiting, colicky pain, purging, dehydration, cramps, feeble pulse, collapse	6 mg of ricin 10 seeds Uncertain	Stomach wash with warm water. Demulcents. Cold porridge or custard. Intravenous fluids. Stimulants	Accidental Homicidal
Salicylates	See aspirin	30 grams		
Scorpion stinging Neurotoxic Hemolysins	Severe burning pain, giddiness, profuse perspiration, fainting, muscular weakness, drowsiness	Uncertain Uncertain	The ligature proximally. Incise the part, if necessary. Wash with dilute ammonia. Inject 1% novocaine or 0.5% xylocaine locally and 10 ml 10% calcium gluconate i.v. Give hot coffee. Cortisone. Scorpion antivenin, if available	Accidental

(contd.)

(contd.)

Name and action	*Main symptoms and signs*	*Average fatal dose and fatal period*	*Treatment*	*Medicolegal points and poison sources*
Semecarpus anacardium (marking nut) Irritant	External application causes blister formation. Taken orally, severe gastro-intestinal irritation, dyspnoea, cyanosis, tachycardia, coma	10 grams 24 hours	Wash the part with warm water. Apply bland liniments. If taken orally, wash the stomach with warm water. Give milk, ice to suck, and 10 mg morphine i.m. for pain	Accidental. Torture. Abortifacient. Vitriolage. Malingerer's conjunctivitis and artificial bruise
Sewer gas	See hydrogen sulphide			
Snake bite Neurotoxins in elapids, vasculotoxins in vipers, and myotoxins in snakes	Locally, burning at the site, teeth marks, and oozing. *Elapid:* Giddiness, lethargy, muscular weakness, ptosis, paralysis of leg muscles, dimness of vision, dysphagia, cyanosis, convulsions. *Viper.* Nausea, vomiting, hemolysis, hemorrhages, dilatation of pupils, necrosis of renal tubules, collapse. *Sea snake*: Locally sharp initial prick becoming painless. Generalized muscular pain, myoglobinuria, hyperkalemia	15 mg of cobra venom. 40 mg of viper venom. 6 mg of krait venom Few hours in bite from cobra and few days in viper. Sea snake bite not fatal	Apply ligature proximally. Wash the part and incise. Suck the blood by suction pump. Give specific antivenin when available or polyvalent antivenin 20 ml subcutaneously around the bite, 20 ml intramuscularly, and 20 ml intravenously. Repeat i.v. dose if collapse occurs or 6 hourly. Inject atropine 0.6 mg and neostigmine 0.5 mg i.v. to combat fixed toxins of elapids. Inject heparin and fibrinogen in viper bite cases. General measures	Accidental Cattle poison
Sodium nitrite Cardiac depressant	Headache, giddiness, nausea, vomiting, marked cyanosis due to methemoglobinemia, hypotension, hemoglobinuria, collapse, unconsciousness	2 grams Few hours to some days	Gastric lavage. 1% methylene blue 1 mg/kg body weight. Vit C. General measures. Maintain body warmth	Accidental. Used as a mordant by weavers
Spanish fly	See cantharides			
Strychnine	See nux vomica			
Sulfuric acid Corrosive. Irritant, if diluted	Burning pain, thirst, black vomit, detachment of corroded mucous membrane, dysphagia, chalky white teeth. Black trickle marks on lips, cheeks, and chin. Abdominal pain, collapse, coma, death	10–15 ml 12 hours	Stomach wash (with soft rubber tube, if possible). Give milk, magnesium oxide, egg white, melted butter. 10 mg morphine i.m. for pain. Intravenous fluids, oxygen, cortisone	Accidental Vitriolage Abortifacient Suicidal
Tear gas Irritant	Irritation of eyes with flow of tears, spasm of eyelids, photophobia. Cough, bronchial spasm, pain in chest, and frontal headache	— Not fatal	Remove the patient to fresh air. Wash eyes with cold water. Put liquid paraffin drops in eyes and use dark glasses. In severe cases, instill cortisone eyedrops. Atropine and oxygen in threatened pulmonary oedema. Antihistamines are helpful	Accidental. War gas to disperse unruly mobs

(contd.)

(contd.)

Name and action	*Main symptoms and signs*	*Average fatal dose and fatal period*	*Treatment*	*Medicolegal points and poison sources*
Thallium Metallic irritant	Abdominal pain, vomiting, diarrhoea, peripheral neuritis, ptosis, impaired vision, ataxia, convulsions, coma. Loss of hair in delayed or *chronic poisoning*	1 grams 2 days to 2 weeks	Follow treatment of heavy metal poisoning. Gastric lavage. Activated charcoal, saline cathartic, demulcents, BAL. Prussian blue. Maintain blood pressure	Homicidal. Accidental. Rodenticide. Depilatory
Tik-20	See organophosphorus compounds			
Tobacco	See nicotine			
Tranquillisers Anxiolytic and muscle relaxant	Restlessness, tremors, diplopia, drowsiness, weakness, incoordination, cyanosis, pulmonary oedema, collapse, coma, skin blisters	10 grams Uncertain	Gastric lavage, activated charcoal, general measures. Blood transfusion. Antidote is Flumazenil	Accidental. Suicidal. Addiction problems
Turpentine Irritant. Nephrotoxic	Burning in abdomen, vomiting, diarrhoea, strangury, albuminuria, hematuria, cyanosis, collapse, coma	200 ml 48 hours	Gastric lavage with 3–5% bicarbonate solution, demulcents, alkaline diuretics, general measures	Suicidal Abortifacient Counterirritant
Wood alcohol	See methyl alcohol			
Zinc Irritant	Metallic taste, nausea; pain in oesophagus, stomach, abdomen; blood tinged vomiting, diarrhoea, muscle spasms, collapse. Fumes of zinc oxide cause metal fume fever	15 grams of zinc sulphate 400 mg of zinc chloride 24 hours	No emetics. Stomach wash with warm water. Give milk, egg white, black tea, EDTA. 10 mg morphine i.m. for pain	Accidental from food or application to wounds. Abortifacient. Suicidal
Zinc phosphide Irritant	Garlic taste in mouth, garlic odour in breath, nausea, pain in oesophagus, stomach, abdomen, vomiting, diarrhoea, dyspnoea, CNS symptoms, coma	5 grams Up to 24 hours	Remove clothing and decontaminate body (wash with water). Emetics, gastric lavage with 3–5% $NaHCO_3$. Vitamin K, corticosteroids, sedatives treatment	Suicidai. Homicidal, Dowry death, Accidental, Supportive Rodenticide Pesticide

PART 7: Appendix

Section 12

67 Some Important Information

This book, both as regards text and illustrations, is self-sufficient to cater to the varying requirements of the different groups of users. However, to encourage a **professional** *outlook,* this appendix has been prepared. It also includes material which involves methods or leads to results which are of considerable practical importance, although it has not been found possible to include it in the text. Special attention should, therefore, be given to this part.

HEIGHTS AND WEIGHTS

The standards for males and females fixed by the Life Insurance Corporation of India in respect of average height and weight are as follows:

Height	*Standard weight*			
	Men		*Women*	
	kg	*Lbs*	*kg*	*Lbs*
M 1.523 (5′–0″)	—	—	50.8–54.4	112–120
M 1.5484 (5′–1″)	—	—	51.7–55.3	114–122
M 1.5738 (5′–2″)	56.3–60.3	124–133	53.1–56.7	117–125
M 1.5992 (5′–3″)	57.6–61.7	127–136	54.4–58.1	120–128
M 1.6246 (5′–4″)	58.9–63.5	130–140	56.3–59.9	124–132
M 1.65 (5′–5″)	60.8–65.3	134–144	57.6–61.2	127–135
M 1.6754 (5′–6″)	62.2–66.7	137–147	58.9–63.5	130–140
M 1.7008 (5′–7″)	64.0–68.5	141–151	60.8–65.3	134–144
M 1.7262 (5′–8″)	65.8–70.8	145–156	62.2–66.7	137–147
M 1.7516 (5′–9″)	67.6–72.6	149–160	64.0–68.5	141–151
M 1.7770 (5′–10″)	69.4–74.4	153–164	65.8–70.3	145–155
M 1.8204 (5′–11″)	71.2–76.2	157–168	67.1–71.1	148–158
M 1.8278 (6′–0″)	73.0–78.5	161–173	68.5–73.9	151–163
M 1.8532 (6′–1′)	75.3–80.7	166–178	—	—
M 1.8766 (6′–2″)	77.6–83.5	171–184	—	—
M 1.9040 (6′–3″)	79.8–85.7	176–189	—	—

FORMULAE FOR ESTIMATION OF STATURE

The reconstruction formulae of Trotter and Glesser, and Dupertius and Hadden are in general use. Multiplication factors (MF) are devised by some Indian scientists for estimation of stature of Indians of certain states, viz. Bengal, Bihar, and Orissa (Pan); Uttar Pradesh (Nat); and Punjab (Singh and Sohal), and these formulae are in use in India. These factors are based on the results obtained by dividing the average height of the body by the average length of the long bone in question.

MULTIPLICATION FACTORS

Length of	*Bengal, Bihar and Orissa*		*Uttar Pradesh*	*Punjab*
	Male	*Female*	*Male*	*Female*
Humerus	5.31	5.31	5.30	4.97
Radius	6.78	6.70	6.90	6.43
Ulna	6.00	6.00	6.30	5.93
Femur	3.82	3.80	3.70	3.57
Tibia	4.49	4.46	4.48	4.18
Fibula	4.46	4.43	4.48	4.35

USEFUL MEASURES

Normal body temperature = 98.4 – 98.6°F = 37°C approx. Rectal temperature 1½° more than mouth temperature. Temperature lowest in morning and may rise by about 1°F towards evening. To convert Fahrenheit to Centigrade, subtract 32 and multiply by 5/9. To convert Centigrade to Fahrenheit multiply by 9/5 and add 32.

CERTIFICATES

Sickness Certificate

This is to certify that Mr/Ms .... aged about .... bearing the following identification marks has been examined by me this day and I find that he is suffering from .... He is advised to take rest for a period of ....

Identification marks: 1. 2.

Place — Signature and registration number of the doctor

Date

Death Certificate

The following is the specimen of the certificate of the cause of death prescribed by the Bombay Municipal Corporation, Bombay.

To: The Municipal Commissioner, Mumbai.

I do hereby certify that I attended the deceased (full name) .... aged about .... residing at .... during his last illness and that to the best of my belief, the cause of death at (time) .... on (date) .... was as stated below:

Cause of death		*Approximate interval between onset and death*	
1. Disease or condition directly leading to death	(a) .... (due to or as consequence of)	years/days	months/hours
Antecedent cause: Morbid conditions, if any, giving rise to the above cause, stating the underlying condition last	(b) .... (dub to or as consequence of)	years/days	months/hours
2. Other significant conditions contributing to the death but not related to the disease or condition causing it	(c)	years/days	months/hours
Address or rubber stamp of the institution		Signature, designation, degree and registration number of the Medical Officer	

MEDICOLEGAL DOCUMENTS, PROFORMAS, AND LABELS

Below are specimens of summons to witness; letter to chemical examiner for examination of viscera and for report thereon; letter to judicial first class magistrate for police escort to take the viscera to chemical examiner and authorisation of chemical examiner to examine the viscera; form to be used when forwarding substances other than viscera to the chemical examiner; form to report postmortem examination data when forwarding viscera to chemical examiner; form to furnish final opinion on the cause of death after receipt of chemical examiner's report; and labels for postmortem specimens to be forwarded to chemical examiner.

Summons to Witness

IN THE COURT OF SESSIONS ....

Sessions Case No.
Complainant
Accused

To: ....

Whereas complaint has been made before me that accused .... has committed the offence of .... under section .... IPC, and it appears to me that you are likely to give material evidence for the court as an expert, you are hereby summoned to appear before this court on .... at .... to give evidence and not to depart thence without leave of the court and you are hereby warned that if you shall, without just excuse, refuse to appear on the said date, warrant of arrest will be issued to compel your attendance.

Given under my hand and the seal of the court.

Signed ....

Letter to Chemical Examiner/FSL

P.M. No.

Government Hospital/Department of Forensic Medicine
....
Dated

To: The Chemical Examiner, Government of ....
Sir

Sub: Chemical Examination and Report - Request for forward herewith the viscera of .... P.M. No .... dated .... for favour of chemical examination and report.

The case has been referred by S.I. of police of .... vide his letter no .... dated ....

The wooden box containing the viscera has been sent through Police Constable No. .... Name .... of .... Police Station.

A specimen of the seal used is enclosed herewith.

Yours faithfully

Signature of the Medical Officer
and his designation

*Letter for Police Escort and Authorisation of Chemical Examiner/FSL

VERY URGENT

P.M. No.

Government Hospital/Department of Forensic Medicine
....
Dated

To: The Chief/First/Second/Additional/Class Judicial Magistrate
Sir,

Sub: Deputation of Police Constable and Authorisation of Chemical Examiner-regarding

Kindly depute a police constable to take the viscera of the deceased with the following particulars, to the Chemical Examiner, Government of .... at a very early date.

Postmortem No. Date:
Letter No. of Dated
Name of the Deceased:

Kindly also address the Chemical Examiner, Government of .... authorising him to examine the viscera of the above said deceased.

Yours faithfully

Signature of the Medical Officer
and his designation

Copy to: The Sub-Inspector of Police,
.... to take early and necessary action.

*In some States, the Police Officer writes to the Magistrate and obtains the requisition for sending the viscera. He sends the requisition to the Medical Officer. On its receipt,

the Medical Officer sends viscera by post. When escort is required, the Medical Officer writes directly to S.P. who arranges for the same. In some states, the concerned Police Officer does the needful without any such formality.

Form to be used when forwarding Substances other than Viscera to the Chemical Examiner/FSL

From: The ....

To: The Chemical Examiner, Government of

Forwarding the articles mentioned below for examination for .... in connection with the case of ....

Description of articles:

Mode of packing and weight of the parcel: If standard boxes and bottles are used: a. Box No. b. Bottle No.		Copy of Label Impression of seal
Mode of despatch:	Date of despatch:	Date of receipt in Chemical Examiner's Office:

Facts of medicolegal importance in connection with the case:

Signature of the Medical Officer
and his designation

Form to report Postmortem Examination findings to be used when forwarding viscera to the Chemical Examiner/FSL

From: The ....

To: The Chemical Examiner, Government of ....

Dated ....

Description of viscera forwarded for examination:

Mode of packing: Box No. Weight of Parcel:	Bottle No.	Copy of label attached to each article: Impression of seal:
Mode of despatch:	Date of despatch:	Date of receipt in Chemical Examiner's Office:

Information furnished by Police or precis of the case:

Name:	Age:	Sex:	Caste:
Thana or village			

History of the case:

Date and time of despatch of the body: Date and time of receipt:	Date, place, and time of autopsy:	Name of the Medical Officer by whom examination was actually made:	
Appearance of body:	Muscularity:	Stout	Emaciated
Special marks:	Scars	Tattooing	Amount of hair, etc.
Temperature: a. Rectal	b. Environmental		
Rigor mortis: Present – extent	Absent		

Postmortem lividity: Incidence, extent, colour, fixation
Decomposition: If present, character, and extent

State of natural orifices:
- a. Eyes
- b. Ears
- c. Nostrils
- d. Mouth
- e. Vagina
- f. Anus
- g. Urethra

Other particulars:
- a. Features, e.g. relaxed
- b. State of limbs, e.g. contents of hands, if clenched
- c. Position of tongue
- d. State of teeth

Details of injuries:
- a. Position
- b. Character
- c. Size
- d. Age

Thorax:
Ribs and cartilages – injury, disease.

Heart:
- a. Shape, size,
- b. Pericardium
- c. Muscular structure and cavities; clots—ante- or postmortem
- d. State of coronary arteries and other vessels: clots, atheroma, aneurysm.

Respiratory system.
- a. Pleura — condition, contents
- b. Lungs — appearance, colour, consistency, adhesions
- c. Larynx, trachea, and bronchi for foreign bodies or disease.

Abdomen:
- a. Thickness of abdominal wall
- b. Peritoneum and contents of peritoneal cavity
- c. Liver — size, injury, disease
- d. Gallbladder and bile ducts — contents, calculi, stricture
- e. Pancreas, spleen, kidneys — injury, disease

f. Stomach — size, general appearance of stomach wall and mucous membrane; contents — appearance, odour, quantity, state of digestion, presence of foreign body or suspicious matter, if any
g. Intestines — general appearance of intestinal wall, contents.

Generative organs:
a. Urinary bladder — contents, injury
b. Uterus — appearance, size, contents, foreign body, injury
c. Vagina — contents, injury, foreign body, if any.

Head:
a. Scalp — injury, disease
b. Skull — disease, injury, fracture
c. Membranes — appearance, injury, disease, volume and weight of haemorrhage, if any
d. Brain — swelling, shrinkage, flattening, herniation
e. Circle of Willis — aneurysm, embolism.

Spinal canal and cord need not be examined unless any indication of injury or disease exists.

Fractures and dislocations:

More detailed description of any injury or disease, if necessary:

Opinion as to the Cause of Death:

Station:
Date:

Signature of the Medical Officer
and his designation

Furnishing Final Opinion on the Cause of Death after receipt of Chemical Examiner's/FSL Report

Government Hospital/Department of Forensic Medicine
....
Dated ....

To: The Chief/First/Second/Additional/Class Judicial Magistrate
Sir

Sub: Final Opinion on the Cause of Death of the Deceased
.... Furnished

Ref: Chemical Examiner's Report No. Dated
Postmortem Certificate No. Dated
Cr. No. of Dated

On reviewing the case in the light of Chemical Examiner's Report and Postmortem findings, I am of the opinion that the deceased by name .... aged about .... years, appears to have died of ....

Signature of the Medical Officer

Copy to: The sub-Inspector of Police .... for information.

LABELS

Label to be pasted on viscera/preservative bottle

Government Hospital/Department of Forensic Medicine

....

P.M. No.....................
Date: ....

Case No. ....
Police Station ....

Name of the deceased .... Age .... Sex ....
Father's name and address ....
Village .... Police Station .... Post Office .... Dist. ....

Viscera preserved in *Rectified spirit/saturated solution of sodium chloride (*strike out whatever is not required).

a. One bottle for stomach and intestine
b. One bottle for liver and kidneys
c. One bottle for urine, and
d. Separate bottles for additional material.

DATA OF ORGANS

The data of organs should be interpreted in relation to the size of the subject. Generally, the weight of the organs of Indians is somewhat less than that of Westerners. The following table represents the average weight of organs as found in Indians.

Organs			*Weight in gm or capacity in ml*		*Size in cm*
Brain	male		1350–1400 gm		
	female		1250–1300 gm		
Heart	male		275–300 gm		
	female		225–250 gm		
Lungs	male	(rt)	450 gm	(360–540 g)	
		(lt)	375 gm	(325–425 g)	
	female	(rt)	400 gm	(350–450 g)	
		(lt)	350 gm	(300–400 g)	
Liver	male		1400–1500 gm		
	female		1300–1400 gm		26×18×9
Kidney	male	(rt)	140–160 gm		
		(lt)	130–150 gm		12×6×4.5
	female	(rt)	130–150 gm		
		(lt)	120–140 gm		
Spleen	male		150–200 gm		
	female		130–170 gm		12×7.5×3
Pancreas	male		90–120 gm		
	female		70–100 gm		
Pituitary			0.5–0.6 gm		

(*contd.*)

(*contd.*)

Suprarenal: male		10–11 gm		
	female	9–10 gm		
Thyroid:		20–30 gm		
Testis:		20–25 gm		4.5×2.5×3
Ovary:		6–7 gm		3×1.5×1
Uterus:	nulliparous30–40 gm			
	multiparous100–130 gm		7.5×5×2.5	
				increased by 1 cm or more
Stomach:		1100–1200 ml		
Urinary bladder:	250–300 mls			

PROFORMA FOR EXAMINATION OF A CASE OF IMPOTENCY

1 Name of the individual:
2. Age (chronological):
3. Sex:
4. Address:
5. Occupation:
6. Brought by:
7. Time and place of examination:
8. Consent of the individual for examination

(Signature or left thumb impression)

9. Marks of identification: 1. 2.
10. History of the case:

Physical Examination

1. Physical development:
2. Secondary sex characters:
3. Development of genitals:
4. Illness: a. acute b. chronic c. local
   d. injuries e. addictions f. operations
5. Psychic causes:
6. Blood pressure:

Laboratory Examination

1. Urine—routine and microscopic:
2. Blood—VDRL:

Opinion

If everything is normal, the opinion is given in a negative form as follows: From the examination of .... bearing the identification marks ...., there is nothing to suggest that the person is impotent.

Date: Signature of the Doctor
Place: Designation ....

COMMON COURT QUESTIONS

Before attending the Court, the medical witness should master the facts of the case and should refresh his memory from his notes actually written at the time of examination and which may be taken with him in the Court for reference. Such notes may be inspected by the opposing counsel who may cross-examine the witness on the same. He should make, if necessary, a careful study of the recent literature on the subject about which he is to give evidence and prepare himself for the questions that he is likely to be asked. The list below gives common questions on selected topics. A careful perusal thereof, and adequate preparation in relation thereto, would enable members of the medical profession to emerge creditably even from the most exacting cross-examination.

I. Deaths from Hanging or Strangulation

1. Did you examine the body of ...., a late resident of ...., and if so, what did you observe?
2. What do you consider to have been the cause of death? State reasons for your opinion.
3. Did you observe any external marks of violence upon the body? If so, describe them.
4. Did you observe any unnatural appearance on internal examination of the body?
5. Was there any rope or other such article round the neck when you saw the body?
6. Can you state whether the mark or marks you observed were caused before or after death?
7. By what sort of articles do you consider the deceased to have been hanged (or strangled)?
8. Could the marks you observed have been caused by the rope or other article now before you (exhibit no .... of the police charge sheet)?
9. Do you think that this rope could have supported the weight of the body?
10. If strangulation, would great violence be necessary to produce the injuries you describe?
11. What, as far as you can ascertain, were the general characteristics of his previous disposition?
12. Does he appear to have had any previous attacks of insanity?

II. Death from Drowning

1. Did you examine the body of ...., a late resident of ...., and if so, what did you observe?
2. What do you consider to have been the cause of death? State your reasons.
3. Were there any external marks of violence upon the body? If so, describe them.
4. Describe any unnatural appearances which you observed on further examination of the body.
5. Did you find any foreign matter, such as weeds, straw, etc., in the hair or clenched in the hands of the deceased or in the air passages or attached to any other part of the body?
6. Did you find any water in the stomach?
7. What was the condition of the body? Was the body decomposed?
8. Can you estimate the length of time the body was in water?

III. Death from Wounds or Blows

1. Did you examine the body of ...., a late resident of ...., and if so, what did you observe?
2. What do you consider to have been the cause of death? State your reasons.
3. Did you find any external marks of violence on the body? If, so, describe them.
4. Are you of the opinion that these injuries were inflicted before or after death? Give your reasons.
5. Did you examine the body internally? Describe any unnatural appearance which you observed.
6. You say that in your opinion, ... was the cause of death: in what immediate way did it prove fatal?
7. Did you find any appearance of disease in the body?
8. If so, do you consider that, if the deceased had been free from this disease, the injuries would still have proved fatal?
9. Do you believe that the fact of his suffering from this disease lessened his chance of recovery from the injuries sustained?
10. Are these injuries taken collectively or any one of them ordinarily and directly, dangerous to life?
11. Were they caused by manual force or with a weapon?
12. Did you find any foreign matter in the wound?
13. By what sort of weapon was the wound inflicted?
14. Could the injuries be inflicted by the weapon now before you (exhibit no. .... in the police charge sheet)?
15. Could the deceased have walked (so far) or spoken, etc. after receipt of such an injury?
16. Have you chemically or otherwise examined the stains (on the weapon, clothes, etc.) now before you (exhibit no .... in the police charge sheet)?
17. Do you believe the stains to be those of blood?
18. What time do you think elapsed between the receipt of the injuries and death?
19. What was the direction of the wound, and can you form an opinion as to the position of the person inflicting such a wound with respect to person receiving it?
20. Is it possible for such a wound to have been inflicted by anyone on his own person? Give your reasons.
21. Of the several injuries on the body
    a. Which one was specifically responsible for death?
    b. Could you say that all were inflicted on the body at the same time?
    c. Were all injuries produced by the same weapon?

IV. Death from Firearm Injuries

1. Did you examine the body of ...., a late resident of ...., and if so, what did you observe?
2. Are you of the opinion that the injuries are caused by the discharge of a firearm?
3. Were there any other injuries?
4. What kind of weapon fired the shot?
5. Could the injuries have been inflicted by the weapon now before you (exhibit no. ...... in the police charge sheet)? Are the fired bullets consistent with this weapon?

6. Were the injuries inflicted before or after death? Give your reasons.
7. How many bullets hit the victim?
8. What was the cause of death? State your reasons.
9. From what distance and direction were the shots fired?
10. What was the position of the body when struck and the course of the projectile through the body?
11. In case of multiple wounds of entrance and exit, could they have been produced by a single bullet?
12. In case of multiple wounds, were they produced by the same or different weapons?
13. Did you find any slug, bullet, wadding, etc. in the wound or the same had made its exit?
14. Do you think it possible that you could have mistaken the wound of entrance for that of exit?
15. How long did the victim survive?
16. Could the deceased have walked (so far) or spoken, etc. after the receipt of such injury?
17. Is it possible for such injuries to have been inflicted by anyone on his person? Give your reasons.
18. Could these injuries be inflicted accidentally due to the discharge of a gun during a struggle or due to faulty trigger mechanism?

V. Death from Burns

1. Did you examine the body of ...., a late resident of ...., and if so, what did you observe?
2. What do you consider to have been the cause of death? State reasons for your opinion.
3. Describe the extent and character of the injuries on the outside of the body.
4. Describe any unnatural appearances on examination of the body internally.
5. Were there any other injuries, apart from those due to burning? If so, describe them fully.
6. Can you state whether the injuries you observed were caused before or after death? Give reasons for your opinion.
7. How were the burns on the deceased caused? Give reasons for your opinion.
8. What was the distribution of burns on the body of the victim? Did you prepare a diagram or sketch?
9. Could these burns have been inflicted by anyone on his own body? Give reasons for your opinion.
9. Could these burns have been inflicted accidentally? Give reasons for your opinion.
10. How long did the deceased survive the burns?

VI. Abortion Deaths

1. Did you examine the person of Ms ...., a late resident of ...., and if so what did you observe?
2. Are you of the opinion that the deceased was pregnant? If so, give reasons for your opinion.
3. Can you definitely say that abortion has occurred? State reasons for your opinion.

4. Did you see the foetus? If so, what was its intrauterine age?
5. What are the causes of natural abortion?
6. What are the signs of a recent abortion?
7. What circumstances lead you to believe that this is a criminal abortion?
8. In what way do you consider the abortion to have been done in this case?
9. It is alleged that a drug called ...., was used. State the symptoms and effects which the administration internally of this drug would produce. Do you consider that it could produce abortion?
10. Can a woman by herself unaided induce abortion by mechanical means? How do you rule out such a possibility in this case? Give reasons.
11. What do you consider to have been the cause of death? Give reasons for your opinion.
12. (In death due to haemorrhage) is it possible that the deceased died during menstruation rather than due to criminal abortion? If not, state your reasons.
13. (In death due to air embolism) what precautions did you exercise while carrying out the autopsy to determine that the cause of death is air embolism? Did you take any X-rays?
14. What was the approximate time of death? At what time was the autopsy done? Do you think that the interval between time since death and carrying out an autopsy could have brought about decomposition which could have vitiated your findings?

VII. Infanticide

1. Did you examine the body of a (male or female) child sent to you by the police on the ...... of ..... 19? And, if so, what did you observe?
2. Can you state whether the child was completely born alive, or born dead? State reasons for your opinion.
3. What do you consider to have been the cause of death? Give your reasons.
4. What do you believe to have been the intrauterine age of the child? State your reasons.
5. What do you believe to have been the extrauterine age of the child? Give reasons.
6. Did you find any marks of violence or other unusual appearances externally? If so, describe them accurately.
7. Did you find any morbid or unusual appearances on examination of the body internally? If so, describe them accurately.
8. Do you believe the injuries you observed to have been inflicted before or after death? Give your reasons.
9. Can you state how they were inflicted? Give your reasons.
10. Do you consider that they were accidental or not? Give your reasons.
11. Had the infant respired fully, partially, or not at all? Give your reasons.
12. Did you examine the person of the alleged mother of the infant? If so, have you reason to suppose that she was recently delivered of a child? Can you state approximately the date of ,her delivery? Give your reasons.

VIII. Death due to Poisoning

1. Did you examine the body of ...., a late resident of ...., and if so, what did you observe?
2. What do you consider to have been the cause of death? State your reasons.

3. Did you find any external marks of violence on the body? If so, describe them.
4. Did you observe any unusual appearances on further examination of the body? If so, describe them.
5. To what do you attribute these appearances: to disease, poison, or other cause?
6. If to poison, then to what class of poison?
7. Have you formed an opinion as to what particular poison was used?
8. Did you find any morbid appearances in the body besides those which are usually found in cases of poisoning by ....? If so, describe them.
9. Do you know of any disease, in which the postmortem appearances resemble those which you observed in this case?
10. In what respect do the postmortem appearances of that disease differ from those which you observed in the present case?
11. What are the symptoms of that disease in the living?
12. Are there any postmortem appearances usual in case of poisoning by .... but which you did not discover in this instance?
13. Whether not the appearances you mention have been the result of spontaneous changes in the stomach after death?
14. Was the state of the stomach and bowels compatible or incompatible with vomiting and purging?
15. What are the usual symptoms of poisoning by ....?
16. What is the usual interval between the time of taking the poison and the commencement of the symptoms?
17. In what time does .... generally prove fatal?
18. Did you send the contents of the stomach and bowel (or other matters) to the Chemical Examiner?
19. Were the contents of the stomach (or other matters) sealed up in your presence immediately on removal from the body?
20. Describe the vessel in which they were sealed up, and what impression did the seal bear?
21. Have you received a report from the Chemical Examiner? If so, is the report now produced that which you received?
22. What is the estimated quantity of administered poison?
23. In your opinion, was the poison deliberately administered? Or, from the estimated quantity, could it be accidental?
24. (If a female adult) what was the state of the uterus and adnexae?

Questions that may be put to a Chemical Examiner/FSL Scientist

1. Was the poison isolated by you in a pure form or mixed?
2. What was the strength, the absolute quantity, or percentage of poison found by you? Was the strength of the poison sufficient to kill a person?

3. From what organs and from what material, i.e. vomit, urine, articles of food, etc. did you find the poison and in what quantity and percentage?
4. What in your opinion is the fatal dose of this poison?
5. Could this poison be naturally found in the body or present as a result of decomposition?
6. Could this poison have come from the reagents used by you in your analysis? (for lead and arsenic).
7. Was a chemical preservative used in the samples sent to you? Can it affect the estimation of poison?
8. Has the sample been checked in forensic context to ensure that no mix-up has taken place?
9. Has a part of the sample been preserved?

Questions that may be put to a Non-professional Witness in a Case of Suspected Poisoning

1. Did you know .... a late resident of ....? If so, did you see him during his last illness and previously?
2. What are the symptoms from which he suffered?
3. Was he in good health previous to the attack?
4. Did the symptoms appear suddenly?
5. What was the interval between the last time of eating or drinking and the commencement of the symptoms?
6. What was the interval between the commencement of the symptoms and death?
7. What did the last meal consist of?
8. Did any one partake of this meal with?
9. Were any of them affected in the same way?
10. Had he ever suffered from a similar attack before?

    If any of the following symptoms have been omitted in answer to question 2, special questions (11–14) may be asked regarding them as follows:

11. Did vomiting occur?
12. Was there any purging?
13. Was there any pain in the stomach?
14. Was he very thirsty?
15. Did he faint?
16. Did he complain of headache or giddiness?
17. Did he appear to have lost the use of his limbs?
18. Did he sleep heavily?
19. Had he any delirium?
20. Did convulsions occur?
21. Did he complain of any peculiar taste in his food or water?

22. Did he notice any peculiar taste in his food or water?
23. Was he sensible in the intervals between the convulsions? (This is with reference to Nux Vomica).
24. Did he complain of burning or tingling in the mouth and throat, or of numbness and tingling in the limbs? (Aconite).
25. Did he complain of any hallucinations?
26. Did he complain of any visual disturbances?

THE CONSUMER PROTECTION ACT (CPA)

The rights conferred on the consumers by the CPA are: (1) right to safety, (2) right to information, (3) right to choice, (4) right to be heard, (5) right to redressal of their grievances, and (6) right to consumer education. In relation to medical services, the CPA covers problems pertaining mainly to—(a) informed consent, (b) medical malpractice, and (c) product (drugs, medical equipment) liability.

THE CRIMINAL LAW (AMENDMENT) BILL, 2013

New Offences

This new Act has expressly recognised certain acts as offences which were dealt under related laws. These new offences, acid attack, like, sexual harassment, voyeurism, stalking, have been incorporated into the Indian Penal Code:

Section	*Offence*	*Punishment*	*Notes*
326A	Acid attack	Imprisonment not less than ten years but which may extend to imprisonment for life and with fine which shall be just and reasonable to meet the medial expenses and it shall be paid to the victim	Gender neutral
326B	Attempt to acid attack	Imprisonment not less than five years but which may extend to seven years, and shall also be liable to fine	Gender neutral
354A	Sexual harassment	Rigorous imprisonment up to five years, or 'with fine, or with both in case of offence described in clauses (i) and (ii) Imprisonment up to one year, or with fine, or with both in other cases	Gender neutral i. Physical contact and advances involving unwelcome and explicit sexual overtures; or ii. A demand or request for sexual favours; or iii. Making sexually coloured remarks; or iv. Forcibly showing pornography; or v. Any other unwelcome physical, verbal or non-verbal conduct of sexual nature
343B	Public disrobing of woman	Imprisonment not less than three years but which may extend to seven years and with fine	Assaults or uses criminal force to any woman or abets such act with the intention of disrobing or compelling her to be naked in any public place

(*contd.*)

(*contd.*)

Section	Offence	Punishment	Notes
354C	Voyeurism	In case of first conviction, imprisonment not less than one year, but which may extend to three years, and shall also be liable to fine, and be punished on a second or subsequent conviction, with imprisonment of either description for a term which shall not be less than three years, but which may extend to seven years, and shall also be liable to fine	Watching or capturing a woman in "private act", which includes an act of watching carried out in a place which, in the circumstances, would reasonably be expected to provide privacy, and where the victim's genitals, buttocks or breasts are exposed or covered only in underwear; or the victim is using a lavatory; or the person is doing a sexual act that is not of a kind ordinarily done in public
354D	Stalking	Imprisonment not less than one year but which may extend to three years, and shall also be liable to fine	Only for women. TO follow a woman and contact, or attempt to contact such woman to foster personal interaction repeatedly despite a clear indication of disinterest by such woman; or monitor the use by a woman of the internet, email or any other form of electronic communication. There are exceptions to this section which include such act being in course of preventing or detecting a crime authorised by State or in compliance of certain law or was reasonable and justified

Changes in Law

Section 370 of Indian Penal Code (IPC) has been substituted with new sections, 370 and 370A which deal with *trafficking of person* for exploitation. If a person (a) recruits, (b) transports, (c) harbours, (d) transfers, or (e) receives, a person or persons, by using threats, or force, or *coercion*, or *abduction*, or *fraud*, or *deception*, or by abuse of power, or inducement for exploitation including prostitution, slavery, forced organ removal, etc. will be punished with imprisonment ranging from at least 7 years to imprisonment for the remainder of that person's natural life depending on the number or category of persons trafficked. Employment of a trafficked person will attract penal provision as well.

The most important change that has been made is the change in definition of *rape* under IPC. The word rape has been replaced with sexual assault in **Section 375,** and has added penetrations other than penile penetration an offence. The definition is broadly worded and gender neutral in some aspect, with acts like penetration of penis, or any object or any part of body to any extent, into the *vagina, mouth, urethra* or anus of another person or making another person do so, apply of mouth or *touching private parts* constitute the offence of sexual assault. The section has also clarified that penetration means "penetration to any extent", and lack of physical resistance is immaterial for constituting an offence. Except in certain aggravated situations, the punishment will be imprisonment not less than seven years but which may extend to imprisonment for life, and shall also be liable to fine. In aggravated situations, punishment will be rigorous imprisonment for a term which shall not be less than ten years but which may extend to imprisonment for life, and shall also be liable to fine. A new **Section, 376A,** has been added which states that if a person committing the offence of sexual assault, "inflicts an injury which causes the death of the person or causes the person to be in a *persistent vegetative state*, shall be punished with rigorous imprisonment for a term which shall not be less than twenty years, but which may extend to imprisonment for life, which shall mean the remainder of that person's natural life, or with death. In case of "gang rape", persons involved regardless of their gender shall be punished with rigorous imprisonment for a term which shall not be less than twenty years, but which may extend to life and shall pay compensation to the victim which shall be reasonable to meet the medical expenses and rehabilitation of the victim. The *age of consent* in India has been increased to 18 years, which means any sexual activity irrespective of presence of consent with a woman below the age of 18 will constitute *statutory rape*.

Certain changes has been introduced in the CrPC and Evidence Act, like the recording of statement of the victim, more friendly and easy, character of the victim is irrelevant, presumption of no consent where sexual intercourse is proved and the victim states in the court that there has been no consent, etc.

The Criminal Law (Amendment) Act, 2013

Offence	*Changes in ordinance*
Acid attack	Fine shall be just and reasonable to meet medical expenses for treatment of victim, while in the ordinance it was fine up to Rupees 10 lakhs.
Sexual harassment	"Clause (v) any other unwelcome physical, verbal or non-verbal conduct of sexual nature" has been removed. Punishment for offence under clause (i) and (ii) has been reduced from five years of imprisonment to three years. The offence is no longer gender-neutral, only a man can commit the offence on a woman.
Voyeurism	The offence is no longer gender-neutral, only a man can commit the offence on a woman.
Stalking	The offence is no longer gender-neutral, only a man can commit the offence on a woman. The definition has been reworded and broken down into clauses. The exclusion clause and the following sentence have been removed "or watches or spies on a person in a manner that results in a fear of violence or serious alarm or distress in the mind of such person, or interferes with the mental peace of such person, commits the offence of stalking". Punishment for the offence has been changed; A man committing the offence of stalking would be liable for imprisonment up to three years for the first offence, and shall also be liable to fine and for any subsequent conviction would be liable for imprisonment up to five years and with fine.
Trafficking of person	"Prostitution" has been removed from the explanation clause.
Rape	The word sexual assault has been replaced back to rape. The offence is no longer gender-neutral, only a man can commit the offence on a woman. The clause related to touching of private parts has been removed.

a. After the entries relating to section 166, the following entries shall be inserted, namely:

1	*2*	*3*	*4*	*5*	*6*
"166A	Public servant disobeying direction underlaw	Imprisonment for one year or fine or with both	Noncognizable	Bailable	Magistrate of the first class";

b. After the entries relating to section 326, the following entries shall be inserted, namely:

1	2	3	4	5	6
“326A	Voluntarily causing grievous hurt by use of acid, etc.	Imprisonment for not less than ten years but which may extend to imprisonment for life and fine of 10 lakh rupees	Cognizable	Nonbailable	Court of session
326B	Voluntarily throwing or attempting to throw acid	Imprisonment for five years but which may extend to seven years and fine	Cognizable	Nonbailable	Court of session”

c. After the entries relating to section 354, the following entries shall be substituted, namely:

1	2	3	4	5	6
“354	Assault or use of criminal force to woman with intent to outrange her modesty	Impisonment of 1 year which may extend to 5 years, and with fine	Cognizable	Nonbailable	Any magistrate
354A	(1) Sexual harassment of the nature of unwelcome physical contact and advances or a demand or request for sexual favours	Imprisonment which may extend to 5 years or with fine or with both	Cognizable	Nonbailable	Any magistrate
	(2) Sexual harassment of the nature of making sexually coloured remark or showing pornography or any other unwelcome physical, verbal or non-verbal conduct of sexual nature	Imprisonment which may extend to 1 year or with fine or with both	Noncognizable	Bailable	Any magistrate
354B	Assault or use of criminal force to woman with intent to disrobe	Imprisonment of not less than 3 years but which may extent to 7 years and with fine	Cognizable	Nonbailable	Any magistrate

(*contd.*)

(*contd.*)

1	2	3	4	5	6
354C	Voyeurism	Imprisonment of not less than 1 year but which may extend to 3 years and with fine for first conviction.	Noncognizable	Bailable	Any magistrate
		Imprisonment of not less than 3 years but which may extend to 7 years and with fine for second or subsequent conviction	Cognizable	Nonbailable	Any magistrate
354D	Stalking	Imprisonment of not less than 1 year but which may extend to 3 years and with fine	Cognizable	Nonbailable	Any magistrate"

d. For the entries relating to section 370, the following entries shall be substituted, namely:

1	2	3	4	5	6
"370	(1) Trafficking of person	Imprisonment of not less than 7 years but which may extend to 10 years and with fine	Cognizable	Nonbailable	Court of session
	(2) Trafficking of more than one person	Imprisonment of not less than 10 years but which may extend to imprisonment for life and with fine	Cognizable	Nonbailable	Court of session
	(3) Trafficking of a minor	Imprisonment of not less than 10 years but which may extend to imprisonment for life	Cognizable	Nonbailable	Court of session
	(4) Trafficking of more than one minor	Imprisonment of not less than 14 years but which may extend to imprisonment for life	Cognizable	Nonbailable	Court of session
	(5) Public servant or a police officer involved in trafficking of minor	Imprisonment for life which shall mean the remainder of that person's natural life	Cognizable	Nonbailable	Court of session
	(6) Person convicted of offence of trafficking of minor on more than one occasion	Imprisonment for life which shall mean the remainder of that person's natural life	Cognizable	Nonbailable	Court of session

(*contd.*)

(*contd.*)

1	2	3	4	5	6
370A	(1) Employing of a trafficked child	Imprisonment of not less than 5 years but which may extend to 7 years and with fine	Cognizable	Nonbailable	Court of session
	(2) Employing of a trafficked adult person	Imprisonment of not less than 3 years but which may extend to 7 years and with fine	Cognizable	Nonbailable	Court of session”

e. For the entries relating to section 376, 376A, 376B, 376C and 376D, the following entries shall be substituted, namely:

1	2	3	4	5	6
376	(1) Sexual assault	Rigorous imprisonment of not less than 7 years but which may extend to imprisonment for life and with fine	Cognizable	Nonbailable	Court of session
	(2) Sexual assault by a police officer or a public servant or member of armed forces or a person being on the management or on the staff of a jail, remand home or other place of custody or women's or children's institution or by a person on the management or on the satff of a hospital, and sexual assault committed by a person in a position of trust or authority towards the person assaulted or by a near realtive of the person assaulted	Rigorous imprisonmment of not less than 10 years but which may extend to imprisonment for life and with fine	Cognizable	Nonbailable	Court of session

(*contd.*)

(*contd.*)

1	2	3	4	5	6
376A	Person committing an offence of sexual assault and inflicting injury which causes death or causes the person to be in a persistent vegetative state	Rigorous imprisonment of not less than 20 years but which may extend to imprisonment for life which shall mean the remainder of that person's natural life or with death	Cognizable	Nonbailable	Court of session
376B	Sexual assault by the husband upon his wife during separation	Imprisonment for not less than 2 years but which may extend to 7 years and with fine	Cognizable (but only on the complaint of the victim)	Nonbailable	Court of session
376C	Sexual assault intercourse by a person in authority	Rigorous imprisonment for not less than 5 years but which may extend to 10 years and with fine	Cognizable	Nonbailable	Court of session
376D	Sexual assault by gang	Rigorous imprisonment for not less than 20 years but which may extend to imprisonment for life which shall mean the remainder of that person's natural life and compensation to the victim	Cognizable	Nonbailable	Court of session
376E	Repeat offenders	Imprisonment for life which shall mean the remainder of that person's natural life or with death	Cognizable	Nonbailable	Court of session"

f. Entry relating to section 509, in column 3, for the words "Simple imprisonment for one year, or fine, or both,", the words "Simple imprisonment for 3 years and with fine" shall be substituted.

Index

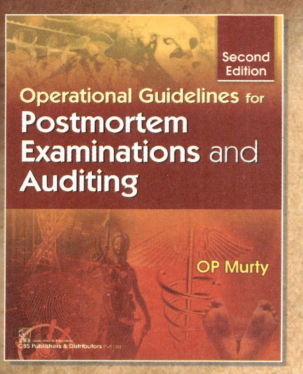

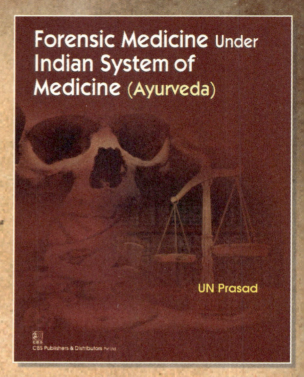

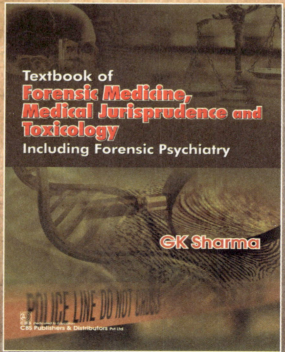